Cognitive Psychology

KU-249-934

Rigorously researched and accessibly written, *Cognitive Psychology: A Student's Handbook* is widely regarded as the leading undergraduate textbook in the field. The book is clearly organised, and offers comprehensive coverage of all the key areas of cognitive psychology. With a strong focus on considering human cognition in context, the book has been designed to help students develop a thorough understanding of the fundamentals of cognitive psychology, providing them with detailed knowledge of the very latest advances in the field.

The seventh edition has been thoroughly updated throughout, and includes:

- extended coverage of cognitive neuroscience
- additional content on computational cognitive science
- new and updated case studies demonstrating real life applications of cognitive psychology
- a fully updated companion website.

Cognitive Psychology: A Student's Handbook will be essential reading for all undergraduate students of psychology. Those taking courses in computer science, education, linguistics, physiology and medicine will also find it an invaluable resource.

Michael W. Eysenck is Professor Emeritus in Psychology at Royal Holloway, University of London. He is also a Professorial Fellow at Roehampton University. He is the best-selling author of a number of textbooks including *Fundamentals of Cognition* (2006), *Memory* (with Alan Baddeley and Michael Anderson, 2014) and *Fundamentals of Psychology* (2009).

Mark T. Keane is Chair of Computer Science at University College Dublin.

COGNITIVE PSYCHOLOGY

A Student's Handbook

Seventh Edition

MICHAEL W. EYSENCK
AND MARK T. KEANE

LONDON AND NEW YORK

Seventh edition published 2015
by Psychology Press
27 Church Road, Hove, East Sussex BN3 2FA

and by Psychology Press
711 Third Avenue, New York, NY 10017

Psychology Press is an imprint of the Taylor & Francis Group, an informa business

© 2015 Taylor & Francis

The right of Michael W. Eysenck and Mark T. Keane to be identified as authors of this work has been asserted by them in accordance with sections 77 and 78 of the Copyright, Designs and Patents Act 1988.

All rights reserved. No part of this book may be reprinted or reproduced or utilised in any form or by any electronic, mechanical, or other means, now known or hereafter invented, including photocopying and recording, or in any information storage or retrieval system, without permission in writing from the publishers.

Trademark notice: Product or corporate names may be trademarks or registered trademarks, and are used only for identification and explanation without intent to infringe.

First edition published by Lawrence Erlbaum Associates 1984
Sixth edition published by Psychology Press 2009

British Library Cataloguing in Publication Data
A catalogue record for this book is available from the British Library

Library of Congress Cataloging in Publication Data
Eysenck, Michael W.
Cognitive psychology: a student's handbook/by
Michael W. Eysenck and Mark T. Keane.
pages cm
Revised edition of the authors' Cognitive psychology:
a student's handbook, 6th ed., published in 2010.
1. Cognition. 2. Cognitive psychology. I. Keane,
Mark T., 1961– II. Title.
BF311.E935 2015
153 – dc23
2014028200

ISBN: 978-1-84872-415-0 (hbk)
ISBN: 978-1-84872-416-7 (pbk)
ISBN: 978-1-315-77800-6 (ebk)

Typeset in Times New Roman and Franklin Gothic
by Florence Production Ltd, Stoodleigh, Devon, UK
Printed by Bell & Bain Ltd, Glasgow

To Clementine with love.
(M.W.E.)

If you can't explain it simply,
you don't understand it well enough.
(Albert Einstein)

Contents

Preface

The Chinese have a saying, "May you live in interesting times." That saying is highly appropriate with respect to cognitive psychology, which has become more and more interesting as time goes by. There have been numerous exciting developments in our understanding of human cognition since the publication of the sixth edition of this textbook. The most striking change in recent years has been the ever-increasing emphasis on studying the *brain* as well as *behaviour*. We continue to use the term "cognitive psychology" to refer to this approach, which forms the basis for much of our coverage of human cognition. Note, however, that the term "cognitive neuroscience" is increasingly used to describe this approach. Research using this approach has become markedly more successful at shedding light on important (and controversial!) theoretical issues.

The approaches to human cognition discussed in detail in this book are more varied than implied so far. For example, cognitive neuropsychology is an important and influential approach that involves focusing on the effects of brain damage as a way of understanding cognition in healthy individuals. Another important approach is computational cognitive science, which involves developing computational models of human cognition. Cognitive neuropsychology and computational cognitive science are both discussed at length in the pages of this book.

An important development has been an increase in cognitive research of direct relevance to real life (e.g., fingerprinting, multitasking, emotion regulation, using mobile phones while driving). As a result, our coverage of real-world research has increased considerably since the previous edition.

As was the case with previous editions of this textbook, the authors have had to work hard to keep pace with developments in theory and research. For example, the first author wrote parts of the book in many far-flung places, including Thailand, Australia, Peru and Hong Kong. Sadly, there have been many occasions on which book writing has had to take precedence over sightseeing!

I (Michael Eysenck) became the proud grandfather of a granddaughter, Clementine, in April 2014 and have dedicated this book to her. We (Michael Eysenck and Mark Keane) would both like to thank the very friendly and efficient staff at Psychology Press, including Ceri Griffiths, Michael Fenton, Mike Travers and Katharine Atherton.

We would also like to thank Hervé Abdi, Anthony Atkinson, Linden Ball, Julie Boland, Bruce Bridgeman, Adele Diederich, Andrew Dunn, Jim Grange, Ken Paller, Amanda Ludlow, Ken Manktelow, Nick Perham, Durk Talsma, and Gill Waters, who commented on various chapters. Their comments proved extremely useful when it came to the demanding business of revising the first draft of the manuscript.

Michael Eysenck and Mark Keane

Visual tour (how to use this book)

TEXTBOOK FEATURES

Listed below are the various pedagogical features that can be found both in the margins and within the main text, with visual examples of the boxes to look out for, and descriptions of what you can expect them to contain.

Key terms

Throughout the book, key terms are highlighted in the text and defined in boxes in the margins, helping you to get to grips with the vocabulary fundamental to the subject being covered.

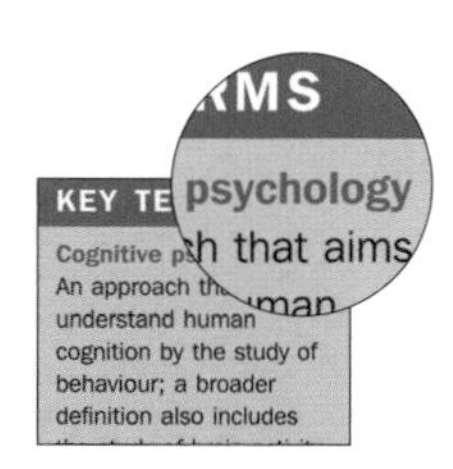

In the real world

Each chapter contains boxes within the main text that explore "real world" examples, providing context and demonstrating how some of the theories and concepts covered in the chapter work in practice.

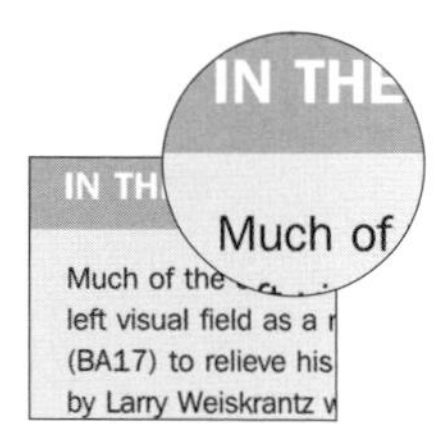

Chapter summary

Each chapter concludes with a brief summary of each section of the chapter, helping you to consolidate your learning by making sure you have taken in all of the concepts covered.

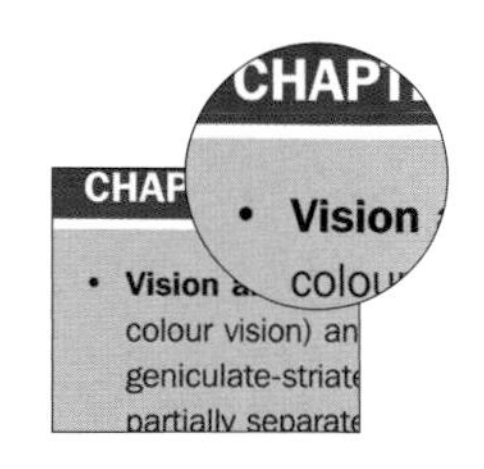

Further reading

Also at the end of each chapter is an annotated list of key scholarly books and journal articles that it is recommended you explore through independent study to expand upon the knowledge you have gained from the chapter and plan for your assignments.

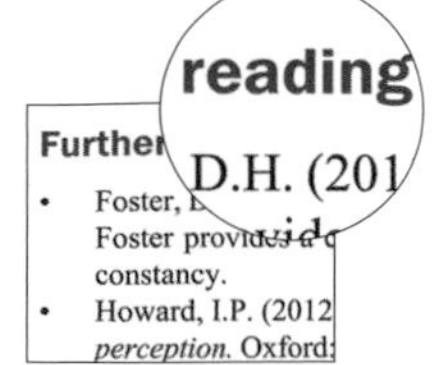

Links to companion website features

Whenever you see this symbol (see left), look for the related supplementary material of the same name amongst the resources for that chapter on the companion website at **www.psypress.com/cw/eysenck**.

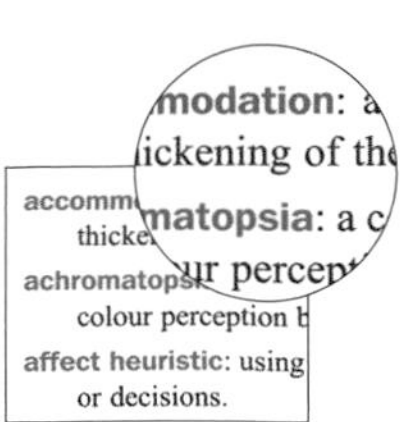

Glossary

An extensive glossary appears at the end of the book, offering a comprehensive list that includes definitions not covered by the key terms boxes in the main text.

CHAPTER

1

Approaches to human cognition

INTRODUCTION

We are now well into the third millennium and there is more interest than ever in unravelling the mysteries of the human brain and mind. This interest is reflected in the substantial upsurge of scientific research within cognitive psychology and cognitive neuroscience. It is striking that the cognitive approach has become increasingly important within clinical psychology. In that area, it is recognised that cognitive processes (especially cognitive biases) play an important role in the development and successful treatment of mental disorders. In similar fashion, social psychologists increasingly assume that cognitive processes help to explain much of social communication.

What is cognitive psychology? It is concerned with the internal processes involved in making sense of the environment and deciding what action might be appropriate. These processes include attention, perception, learning, memory, language, problem solving, reasoning and thinking. We can define **cognitive psychology** as aiming to understand human cognition by observing the behaviour of people performing various cognitive tasks. Note, however, that the term "cognitive psychology" can be used more broadly to include brain activity and structure as relevant information for understanding human cognition. It is in this broader sense that it is used in the title of this book.

The aims of cognitive neuroscientists overlap with those of cognitive psychologists. However, there is one important difference between cognitive neuroscience and cognitive psychology in the narrow sense. Cognitive neuroscientists argue convincingly we need to study the *brain* as well as behaviour while people engage in cognitive tasks. After all, the internal processes involved in human cognition occur in the brain. We can define **cognitive neuroscience** as using information about behaviour and the brain to understand human cognition. Thus, the distinction between cognitive neuroscience and cognitive psychology in the broader sense is blurred.

Cognitive neuroscientists explore human cognition in several ways. First, there are brain-imaging techniques of which functional magnetic resonance imaging (fMRI) (discussed later) is probably the best known. Second, there are electrophysiological techniques involving the recording of electrical signals generated by the brain (also discussed later). Third, many cognitive neuroscientists study the effects of brain damage on human cognition. It is assumed the patterns of cognitive impairment shown by brain-damaged patients can inform us about normal cognitive functioning and the brain areas responsible for various cognitive processes.

The huge increase in scientific interest in the workings of the brain is mirrored in the popular media – numerous books, films and television programmes have communicated the more accessible and dramatic aspects of cognitive neuroscience. Increasingly, media coverage includes coloured pictures of the brain indicating the areas most activated when people perform various tasks.

KEY TERMS

Cognitive psychology
An approach that aims to understand human cognition by the study of behaviour; a broader definition also includes the study of brain activity and structure.

Cognitive neuroscience
An approach that aims to understand human cognition by combining information from behaviour and the brain.

Four main approaches

There are four main approaches to human cognition (see below). Bear in mind, however, that researchers increasingly combine two or even more of these approaches. We will shortly discuss each approach in turn, and you will probably find it useful to refer back to this chapter when reading other chapters. You may find Table 1.1 (towards the end of this chapter) especially useful because it provides a brief summary of the strengths and limitations of all four approaches, which are:

Weblink:
Cognitive Science

1. *Cognitive psychology*: this approach involves trying to understand human cognition by using behavioural evidence. Since behavioural data are also of great importance within cognitive neuroscience and cognitive neuropsychology, cognitive psychology's influence is enormous.
2. *Cognitive neuropsychology*: this approach involves studying brain-damaged patients to understand normal human cognition. It was originally closely linked to cognitive psychology but has recently also become linked to cognitive neuroscience.
3. *Cognitive neuroscience*: this approach involves using evidence from behaviour and the brain to understand human cognition.
4. *Computational cognitive science*: this approach involves developing computational models to further our understanding of human cognition; such models increasingly take account of our knowledge of behaviour and the brain.

COGNITIVE PSYCHOLOGY

It is almost as pointless to ask, "When did cognitive psychology start?", as to enquire, "How long is a piece of string?" However, the year 1956 was of crucial importance. At a meeting at the Massachusetts Institute of Technology (MIT), Noam Chomsky gave a paper on his theory of language, George Miller discussed the magic number seven in short-term memory (Miller, 1956) and Newell and Simon discussed their extremely influential model called the General Problem Solver (see Newell et al., 1958). In addition, there was the first systematic attempt to study concept formation from a cognitive perspective (Bruner et al., 1956).

At one time, most cognitive psychologists subscribed to the information-processing approach based loosely on an analogy between the mind and the computer. A version of this approach popular in the 1970s is shown in Figure 1.1. A stimulus (an environmental event such as a problem or a task) is presented. This causes certain internal cognitive processes to occur, and these processes finally produce the desired response or answer. Processing directly affected by the stimulus input is often described as **bottom-up processing**. It was typically assumed that only one process occurs at any moment in time. This is **serial processing**, meaning the current process is completed before the next one starts.

The above approach is drastically oversimplified. Task processing typically also involves **top-down processing**. Top-down processing is processing influenced by the individual's expectations and knowledge rather than simply by the stimulus itself. Read what it says in the triangle shown in Figure 1.2. Unless you know the trick, you probably read it as, "Paris in the spring". If so, look again and you will find the word "the" is repeated. Your expectation that it was a well-known phrase (i.e., top-down processing) dominated the information available from the stimulus (i.e., bottom-up processing).

The traditional approach was also oversimplified in assuming processing is typically serial. In fact, more than one process typically occurs at the same time – this is **parallel processing**. We are much more likely to use parallel processing when performing a highly practised task than a new one (see Chapter 5). For example, someone taking their first driving lesson finds it almost impossible to change gear, steer accurately and pay attention to other road users at the same time. In contrast, an experienced driver finds it easy.

For many years, nearly all research on human cognition consisted of experiments on healthy individuals under laboratory conditions. Such experiments are tightly controlled and "scientific". Researchers have shown great ingenuity in designing experiments to reveal the processes involved in attention, perception, learning, memory, reasoning and so on. This research has had a major (and ongoing) influence on the studies conducted by cognitive neuroscientists. Indeed, nearly all the research discussed in this book owes much to the cognitive psychological approach.

KEY TERMS

Bottom-up processing
Processing that is directly influenced by environmental stimuli.

Serial processing
Processing in which one process is completed before the next one starts; *see also* **parallel processing**.

Top-down processing
Stimulus processing that is influenced by factors such as the individual's past experience and expectations.

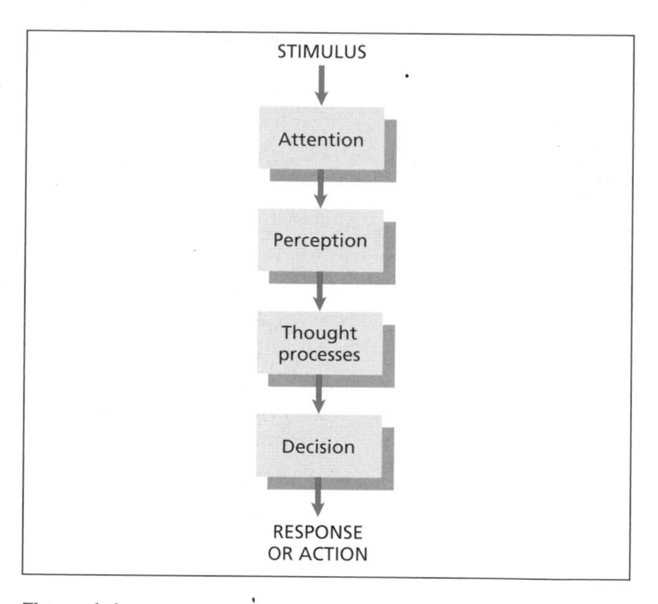

Figure 1.1
An early version of the information processing approach.

Task processes

An important issue for cognitive psychologists is the task impurity problem – most cognitive tasks require a complex mixture of processes, thus making it hard to interpret the findings. This issue has been addressed in various ways. For example, suppose we are interested in the processes involved when a task requires deliberately inhibiting a dominant response. Miyake et al. (2000) studied three such tasks: the Stroop task; the anti-saccade task; and the stop-signal task. On the Stroop task, participants name the colour in which colour words are presented (e.g., RED printed in green) and avoid saying the colour word (which is hard to inhibit) (see Macleod (2015, in press) for a discussion of this task). On the anti-saccade task,

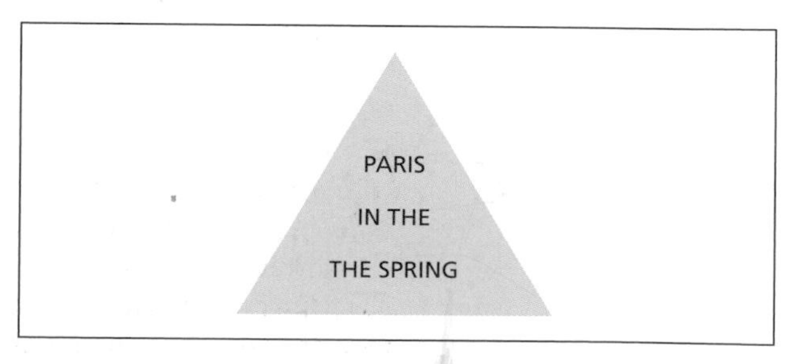

Figure 1.2
Diagram to demonstrate top-down processing.

KEY TERM

Parallel processing
Processing in which two or more cognitive processes occur at the same time.

a visual cue is presented. The task involves *not* looking at the cue but rather inhibiting that response and looking in the opposite direction. On the stop-signal task, participants categorise words as rapidly as possible, but must inhibit their response when a tone sounds.

Miyake et al. (2000) found all three tasks involved similar processes. They used complex statistical techniques to extract what was common to the three tasks. This was assumed to represent a relatively pure measure of the inhibitory process.

Cognitive psychologists have developed several ways of understanding the processes involved in complex tasks. Here we will briefly consider one example. Participants are presented with five words visually and repeat them back. Performance is worse when the words are long than when they are short (Baddeley et al., 1975; see Chapter 6). This probably occurs because participants engage in verbal rehearsal (saying the words to themselves) during word presentation and this takes longer with long words than with short ones. However, see Chapter 6 for an alternative account.

How could we show verbal rehearsal is a process used on this task? Baddeley et al. (1975) used articulatory suppression – participants repeated the digits 1 to 8 in order during presentation of the word list to prevent them rehearsing. As predicted, performance was worse when articulatory suppression was used. In addition, the effect of word length disappeared, thus suggesting its existence depended on verbal rehearsal.

Much of this book is devoted to the ingenious strategies cognitive psychologists have used to uncover the processes involved in numerous tasks. Therefore, there is no need to itemise these strategies here.

Strengths

Cognitive psychology was for many years the engine room of progress in understanding human cognition, and all the other approaches listed above have derived substantial benefit from it. For example, cognitive neuropsychology became important 25 years after cognitive psychology. It was only when cognitive psychologists had developed reasonable accounts of healthy human cognition that the performance of brain-damaged patients could be understood fully. Before that, it was hard to decide which patterns of cognitive impairment were of theoretical importance.

In similar fashion, the computational modelling activities of computational cognitive scientists are typically heavily influenced by pre-computational psychological theories. Finally, the great majority of theories driving research in cognitive neuroscience had their origins within cognitive psychology. Indeed, Coltheart (2011) claimed (controversially!) that cognitive neuroscience has so far made no difference to cognitive theorising.

Cognitive psychology has not only had a massive influence on theorising across all four major approaches to human cognition. It has also had a predominant influence on the development of cognitive tasks and on task analysis (working out how a task is accomplished).

However, we must not de-emphasise the substantial contributions of the three other major approaches discussed in detail later.

Limitations

In spite of cognitive psychology's enormous contributions, it has various limitations. First, people's behaviour in the laboratory may differ from that in everyday life. The concern is that laboratory research lacks **ecological validity** – the extent to which laboratory findings are applicable to everyday life. In most laboratory research, the sequence of stimuli presented to participants is based on the experimenter's predetermined plan and is uninfluenced by their behaviour. Wachtel (1973) called this the **implacable experimenter**. In everyday life, in contrast, our cognitive processing often involves deciding how to change the current situation to suit ourselves.

Second, cognitive psychologists typically obtain measures of the speed and accuracy of task performance. These measures provide only *indirect* evidence about internal cognitive processes. For example, it is hard on the basis of such measures to decide whether the processes used on a complex task occur serially or in parallel.

Third, cognitive psychologists have often put forward theories expressed only in verbal terms (although this is becoming less common). Such theories tend to be vague, making it hard to know precisely what predictions follow from them. Thankfully, this limitation can largely be overcome by computational cognitive scientists developing cognitive models specifying precisely any given theory's assumptions.

Fourth, the findings obtained from any given experimental task or paradigm are sometimes *specific* to that paradigm and do not generalise to other (apparently similar) tasks. This is **paradigm specificity**. It means some findings in cognitive psychology are narrow in scope and applicability (Meiser, 2011). More generally, "Once an experimental paradigm has been introduced, it . . . turns from a tool of research to a target of research" (Meiser, 2011, p. 185). The way to minimise the problems of paradigm specificity is by developing theories accounting for performance across several similar tasks or paradigms.

Fifth, what has been lacking within cognitive psychology is a comprehensive theoretical architecture or framework that would clarify the interrelationships among components of the cognitive system. However, some progress has been made here. The Adaptive Control of Thought-Rational [ACT-R] model (e.g., J.R. Anderson et al., 2004; discussed later in the chapter) is an example of a cognitive architecture.

KEY TERMS

Ecological validity
The applicability (or otherwise) of the findings of laboratory studies to everyday settings.

Implacable experimenter
The situation in experimental research in which the experimenter's behaviour is uninfluenced by the participant's behaviour.

Paradigm specificity
This occurs when the findings with a given experimental task or paradigm are not obtained even when apparently very similar tasks or paradigms are used.

COGNITIVE NEUROPSYCHOLOGY

Cognitive neuropsychology is concerned with the patterns of cognitive performance (intact and impaired) shown by brain-damaged patients. These patients have suffered lesions – structural damage to the brain caused by injury or disease. According to cognitive neuropsychologists, the study of brain-damaged patients can tell us much about normal human cognition.

The above idea does not sound very promising, does it? In fact, however, cognitive neuropsychology has contributed a substantial amount to our understanding of normal human cognition. For example, in the 1960s nearly all memory researchers thought the storage of information in long-term memory depended on previous processing in short-term memory (see Chapter 6). However, Shallice and Warrington (1970) reported the case of a brain-damaged man, KF. His short-term

Weblink:
Cognitive neuropsychology

Max Coltheart.
Courtesy of Max Coltheart.

memory was severely impaired but his long-term memory was intact. These findings played an important role in changing theories of normal human memory.

Since cognitive neuropsychologists study brain-damaged patients, it would be easy to imagine they are interested in the workings of the brain. In fact, the leading cognitive neuropsychologist Max Coltheart (see photo) and many other cognitive neuropsychologists pay little attention to the brain itself. In the words of Coltheart (2010, p. 3), "The principal aim of cognitive neuropsychology is not to learn about the brain. Its principal aim is instead to learn about the mind, that is, to elucidate the functional architecture of cognition."

Other cognitive neuropsychologists disagree with Coltheart (2010). An increasing number take account of the brain, using techniques such as magnetic resonance imaging to identify the brain areas damaged in any given patient. In addition, there is an increasing willingness to consider neuroimaging findings.

Theoretical assumptions

The main assumptions of cognitive neuropsychology have been discussed often over the years (e.g., Davies, 2010). Here we will focus on Coltheart's (2001) very clear account. One key assumption is **modularity**, meaning the cognitive system consists of numerous modules or processors operating fairly independently or separately of each other. It is assumed these modules exhibit **domain specificity** (they respond to only one given class of stimuli). For example, there may be a face-recognition module that responds only when a face is presented.

Is the modularity assumption correct? This issue is very controversial. Probably the majority position is that the human cognitive system exhibits some modularity, but cognitive neuropsychologists often exaggerate its importance. This complex issue is discussed in more detail below.

The second major assumption of cognitive neuropsychology is that of *anatomical modularity*. According to this assumption, each module is located in a specific brain area. Why is this assumption important? Cognitive neuropsychologists are most likely to make progress when studying patients with brain damage limited to a single module. Such patients may not exist if there is no anatomical modularity. Suppose all modules were distributed across large areas of the brain. If so, the great majority of brain-damaged patients would suffer damage to most modules. As a result, it would be impossible to work out the number and nature of modules they possessed.

There is evidence of some anatomical modularity in the visual processing system (see Chapter 2). However, there is much less support for anatomical modularity with most complex tasks. For example, Duncan and Owen (2000)

KEY TERMS

Modularity
The assumption that the cognitive system consists of many fairly independent or separate modules or processors, each specialised for a given type of processing.

Domain specificity
The notion that a given module responds selectively to certain types of stimuli (e.g., faces) but not others.

found the same areas within the frontal lobes were activated when very different complex tasks were performed. The findings of Yarkoni et al. (2011) are also relevant. Across more than 3,000 studies, brain areas such as the dorsolateral prefrontal cortex and anterior cingulate cortex were activated in 20% of them in spite of the huge diversity of tasks involved.

The third major assumption is what Coltheart (2001, p. 10) called "uniformity of functional architecture across people". This assumption is important as can be seen if we consider the consequences if it is false. In that case, we would not be able to use the findings from individual patients to draw conclusions about other people's functional architecture.

Related ideas are also common within cognitive neuroscience. For example, it has often been claimed that face processing in virtually everyone depends heavily on the fusiform face area (Weiner & Grill-Spector, 2012). If there are large individual differences in functional architecture and the brain areas involved in any given cognitive process, this greatly complicates the task of understanding human cognition.

The fourth assumption is *subtractivity*. The basic idea is that brain damage impairs one or more processing modules but does not change or add anything. Why is this assumption important? Suppose it is incorrect and patients develop new modules to compensate for cognitive impairments caused by brain damage. That would greatly complicate the task of learning much about intact cognitive systems by studying brain-damaged patients.

The subtractivity assumption is sometimes incorrect. There is often partial recovery of the cognitive processes impaired by brain damage (Cus et al., 2011). This recovery of cognitive processes can involve recovery of function within the damaged area or the recruitment of different brain regions.

KEY TERM

Dissociation
As applied to brain-damaged patients, intact performance on one task but severely impaired performance on a different task.

Modularity assumption

Modular systems typically involve mostly serial processing in which processing within one module is completed before processing in the next module starts. As a result, there is very limited *interaction* among modules. There is some support for modularity from the evolutionary approach. Species with larger brains tend to have more specialised brain regions that could be involved in modular processing.

The notion that human cognition is heavily modular is rather difficult to reconcile with neuroimaging and other evidence based on brain activity. The human brain possesses a moderately high level of connectivity (Bullmore & Sporns, 2012; see below). This suggests there is more parallel processing than assumed by most cognitive neuropsychologists.

Research in cognitive neuropsychology

How do cognitive neuropsychologists set about understanding the cognitive system? Of major importance is the search for **dissociations**, which occur when a patient performs normally on one task (task X) but is impaired on a second one (task Y). For example, amnesic patients perform almost normally on short-term memory tasks but are greatly impaired on many long-term memory tasks (see Chapter 6). It is tempting (but dangerous!) to use such findings to argue that the

KEY TERMS

Double dissociation
The finding that some brain-damaged individuals have intact performance on one task but poor performance on another task, whereas other individuals exhibit the opposite pattern.

Association
The finding that certain symptoms or performance impairments are consistently found together in numerous brain-damaged patients.

Syndrome
The notion that symptoms that often co-occur have a common origin.

two tasks involve different processing modules and that the module or modules needed on long-term memory tasks have been damaged by brain injury.

Why do we need to avoid drawing sweeping conclusions from dissociations? A patient may perform well on one task but poorly on a second one simply because the second task is more complex. Thus, dissociations may reflect task differences in complexity rather than the use of different modules.

Cognitive neuropsychologists argue that the solution to the above problem is to find double dissociations. A **double dissociation** between two tasks (X and Y) is shown when one patient performs normally on task X and at an impaired level on task Y, whereas another patient shows the opposite pattern. If a double dissociation is found, we cannot explain the findings away as occurring because one task is harder. For example, we have just seen that amnesic patients have impaired long-term memory but intact short-term memory. Earlier we saw that other brain-damaged patients (e.g., KF studied by Shallice and Warrington (1970)) have impaired short-term memory but intact long-term memory. The double dissociation involved here strongly suggests that there is an important distinction between short-term and long-term memory and that they involve different brain regions.

The approach based on double dissociations has limitations. First, it is based on the assumption that separate modules exist (which may be misguided). Second, double dissociations can generally be explained in various ways and so provide *indirect* evidence for separate modules underlying each task (Davies, 2010). Third, it is hard to decide which of the numerous double dissociations in the literature are theoretically important.

Finally, we consider associations. An **association** occurs when a patient is impaired on tasks X and Y. Associations are sometimes taken as evidence for a **syndrome** (sets of symptoms or impairments often found together). However, there is a serious flaw with the syndrome-based approach. An association may be found between tasks X and Y because the mechanisms on which they depend are adjacent in the brain rather than because they depend on the same underlying mechanism. Gerstmann's syndrome is an example. It is defined by four very different symptoms: problems of finger identification; problems in calculation; impaired spelling; and left–right disorientation. It is improbable that the same mechanisms or modules are involved in all four tasks. What is much more likely is that these four symptoms depend on different mechanisms that happen to be anatomically adjacent in the brain.

Single-case studies vs. case series

For much of the history of cognitive neuropsychology, there was a strong emphasis on single-case studies. There were two main reasons. First, researchers can often gain access to only one patient having a given pattern of cognitive impairment. Second, it is often assumed every patient is *unique* because no two patients have precisely the same pattern of brain damage. It was concluded it would be misleading and uninformative to average the performance of several patients even though they allegedly had the same disorder.

You may be surprised to discover that so much research in cognitive neuropsychology has involved individuals. After all, the general recommendation in most psychological research is to use reasonably large samples so we can have confidence in the findings. Within cognitive neuropsychology, there is a movement towards the **case-series study**. Several patients thought to have similar cognitive impairments are tested and then the data of individual patients are compared and variation across patients assessed.

There are several reasons why the case-series approach is generally preferable to the single-case approach (Lambon Ralph et al., 2011). First, it provides much richer data. Using the case-series approach we can actually *assess* the extent of variation among patients rather than simply being concerned about it (as in the single-case approach).

Second, we can develop theories based on most patients within a case series, de-emphasising patients who are "outliers". In contrast, with the single-case approach we do not know whether the one and only patient is representative of patients with that condition or is an outlier.

KEY TERM

Case-series study
A study in which several patients with similar cognitive impairments are tested; this allows consideration of individual data and of variation across individuals.

Strengths

Cognitive neuropsychology has made numerous major contributions to our understanding of human cognition. Here we will briefly consider its strengths. First, it has played a major role in informing theories of language. For example, consider patients reading visually presented regular words (words whose pronunciation is predictable from the pattern of letters), irregular words (words whose pronunciation is not predictable from the pattern of letters) and non-words aloud. We might imagine that patients with damage to language areas would have problems in reading *all* words and non-words. In fact, that is not the case (see Chapter 9). Some patients perform reasonably well when reading regular words or non-words but poorly when reading irregular words. Other patients can read regular words but have problems with unfamiliar words and non-words. These fascinating patterns of impairment have transformed theories of reading (Coltheart, 2015, in press).

Second, findings from brain-damaged patients have often had a substantial impact on memory theories. Perhaps the clearest example is HM, now known to be Henry Molaison. He was an amnesic patient whose long-term memory was severely impaired, except his ability to learn motor skills, whereas his short-term memory was intact (see Chapter 7). These findings provided striking support for three hypotheses. First, there is a major distinction between short-term and long-term memory. Second, long-term memory is divided into at least two different systems. Third, HM had suffered severe damage to the hippocampus, and so the research identified this area as of crucial importance in long-term memory. Eichenbaum (2015, in press) discusses the enormous impact of research on HM in detail.

Limitations

What are the limitations of the cognitive neuropsychological approach? First, the crucial assumption that the cognitive system is fundamentally modular is reasonable but seems too strong. Modular systems tend to be relatively inflexible and based on serial processing. In contrast, human cognitive processing is noted for its *flexibility* and extensive interactions throughout the brain. If the modularity assumption is mistaken, this has implications for the whole enterprise of cognitive neuropsychology (Patterson & Plaut, 2009).

Weblink:
Michael Gazzinga in conversation

Second, other major theoretical assumptions also seem too extreme. For example, neuroimaging research provides only modest support for the assumption of anatomical modularity. In addition, there is little or no convincing evidence supporting the assumption of uniformity of functional architecture.

Third, it is assumed the cognitive performance of patients provides fairly direct evidence concerning the impact of brain damage on previously intact cognitive systems. However, some of the impact of brain damage may be camouflaged because patients develop *compensatory strategies* as they recover. For example, patients with pure alexia (a condition involving severe reading problems) read words by the compensatory strategy of identifying each letter separately. There are also complications resulting from changes in brain functioning during the recovery process (Cus et al., 2011). In other words, many patients exhibit considerable neural plasticity following brain damage (Overgaard & Mogensen, 2011).

Fourth, cognitive neuropsychologists have historically shown relatively little interest in the details of brain functioning and cognitive neuroscience. This seems paradoxical since their focus is on brain-damaged patients. However, findings from cognitive neuroscience are increasingly being combined fruitfully with those from cognitive neuropsychology. For example, this has been done with respect to recognition memory (discussed later).

Fifth, there has been too much emphasis on single-case studies. Some single-case studies (e.g., the famous amnesic patient, HM) have deservedly had a huge impact. However, there are real limitations with single-case studies and the case-study approach provides a richer source of data.

KEY TERMS

Sulcus
A groove or furrow in the surface of the brain.

Gyri
Prominent elevated areas or ridges on the brain's surface ("gyrus" is the singular).

Dorsal
Superior, or towards the top of the brain.

Ventral
Inferior, or towards the bottom of the brain.

Rostral
Anterior, or towards the front of the brain.

Posterior
Towards the back of the brain.

Lateral
Situated at the side of the brain.

Medial
Situated in the middle of the brain.

COGNITIVE NEUROSCIENCE: THE BRAIN IN ACTION

Cognitive neuroscience involves intensive study of the brain as well as behaviour. Alas, the brain is complicated (to put it mildly!). It consists of 100 billion neurons and these neurons are connected in very complex ways. To understand research involving functional neuroimaging, we must consider how the brain is organised and how the different areas are described. Various ways of describing specific brain areas are used. Below we will discuss the three main ones.

Weblink:
Cognitive neuroscience society

First, the cerebral cortex is divided into four main divisions or lobes (see Figure 1.3). There are four lobes in each brain hemisphere: frontal, parietal, temporal and occipital. The frontal lobes are divided from the parietal lobes by the central sulcus (**sulcus** means furrow or groove), and the lateral fissure separates the temporal lobes from the parietal and frontal lobes. In addition, the parieto-occipital sulcus and pre-occipital notch divide the occipital lobes from the parietal and temporal lobes. The main **gyri** (or ridges; gyrus is the singular) within the cerebral cortex are shown in Figure 1.3.

Researchers use various terms to describe more precisely the area(s) of the brain activated during the performance of a given task:

Weblink:
Atlas of the brain

- **dorsal** (or superior): towards the top;
- **ventral** (or inferior): towards the bottom;
- **rostral** (or anterior): towards the front;
- **posterior**: towards the back;
- **lateral**: situated at the side;
- **medial**: situated in the middle.

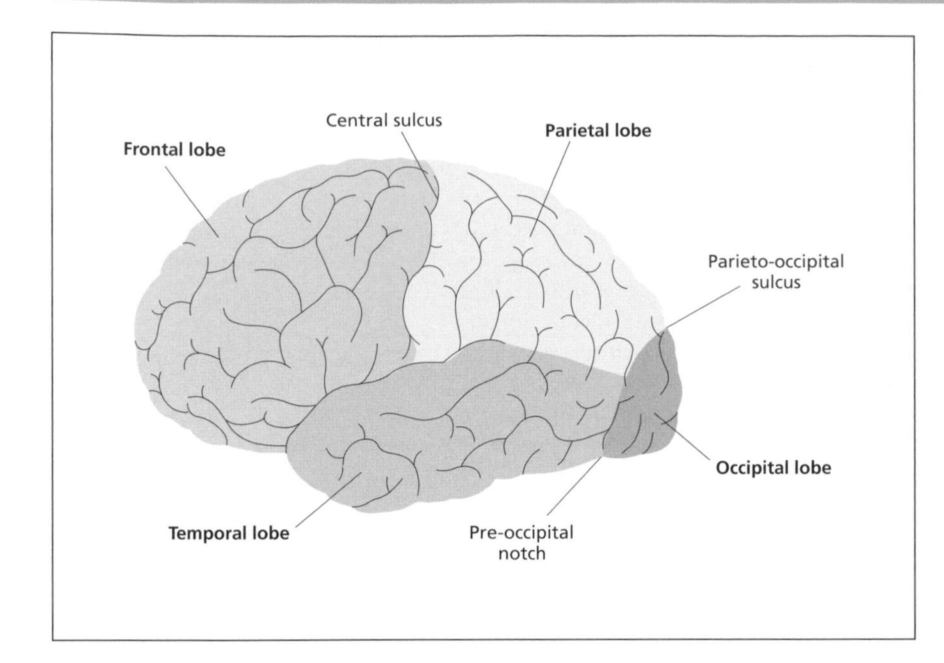

Figure 1.3
The four lobes, or divisions, of the cerebral cortex in the left hemisphere.

Second, the German neurologist Korbinian Brodmann (1868–1918) produced a map of the brain based on differences in the distributions of cell types across cortical layers (see Figure 1.4). Brodmann identified 52 different areas, and we will often refer to areas such as BA17, which simply means Brodmann Area 17.

Third, we can focus on the functions of different brain areas. For example, consider Brodmann Area 17 (BA17). This is often referred to as primary visual cortex because it is an area strongly associated with the early processing of visual stimuli.

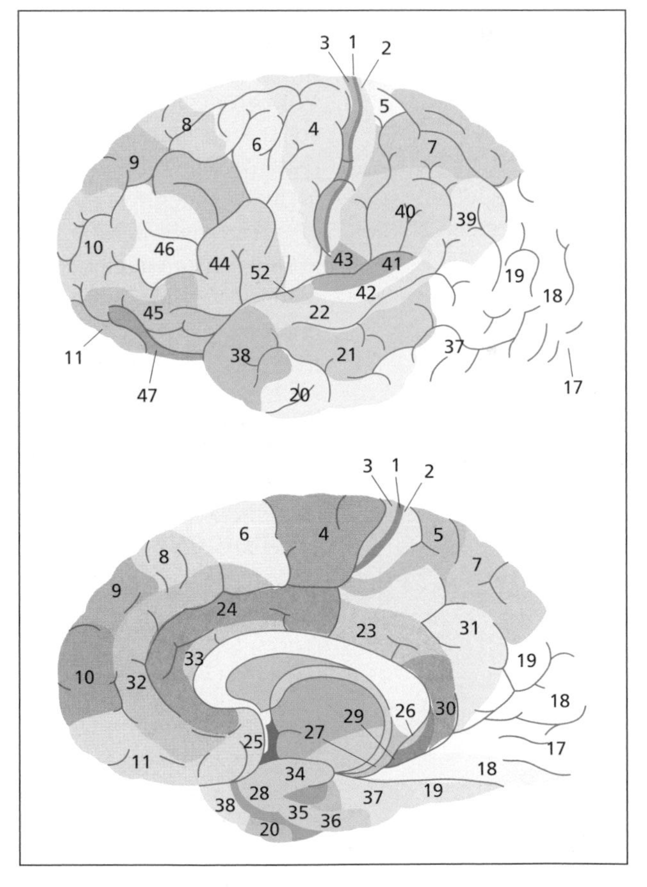

Figure 1.4
Brodmann brain areas on the lateral (top figure) and medial (bottom figure) surfaces.

Brain network organisation

Bullmore and Sporns (2012) argued that two major principles might determine brain organisation. First, there is the *principle of cost control*: costs (e.g., in terms of energy and space) would be minimised if the brain consisted of limited, short-distance connections (see Figure 1.5). Second, there is the *principle of efficiency*: efficiency in terms of the ability to integrate information across the brain. This can be achieved by having very numerous connections, many of which are long-distance (see Figure 1.5). The problem is that these two principles are in conflict – you cannot have high efficiency at low cost.

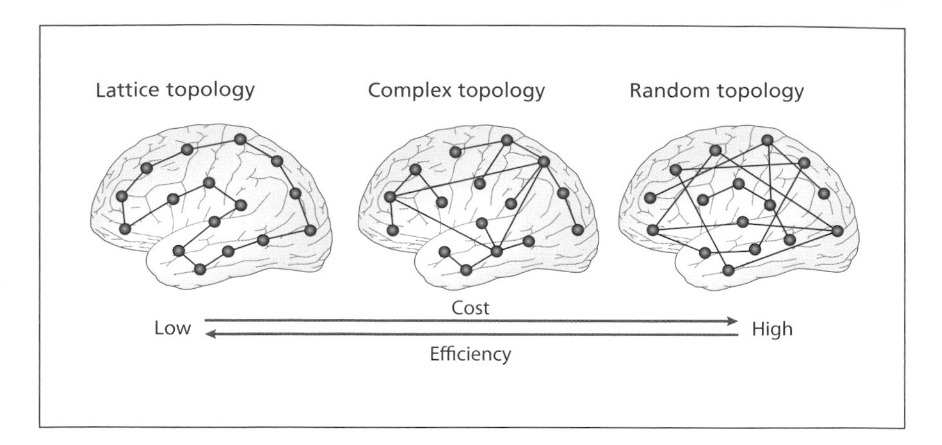

Figure 1.5
The left panel shows a brain network low in cost and efficiency; the right panel shows a brain network high in cost and efficiency; the middle panel shows the actual human brain in which there is moderate efficiency at moderate cost. Nodes are shown as orange circles.
From Bullmore and Sporns (2012). Reprinted with permission of Nature Reviews.

You might think it would be best if our brains were organised purely on the basis of efficiency. However, this would be hugely costly. If all 100 billion neurons in the brain were interconnected, the brain would need to be 12½ miles wide (Ward, 2010)! In fact, neurons mostly connect with nearby neurons and no neuron is connected to more than about 10,000 neurons. As a result, the human brain has achieved a near-optimal trade-off between cost and efficiency (see Figure 1.5). Our brains are reasonably efficient and this has been achieved at manageable cost. Within our brain network, there are *modules* (small areas of tightly clustered connections) and *hubs* (regions that have large numbers of connections to other regions). These hubs include areas (e.g., the anterior cingulate) associated with high-level cognitive processes and consciousness (see Chapter 16).

What light does a focus on brain network organisation shed on individual differences in cognitive ability? Van den Heuvel et al. (2009) found IQ did not correlate with the total number of brain network connections. However, there were impressive associations between IQ and the global efficiency of functional brain networks. The correlation was +0.75 in medial prefrontal cortex (BA9/10) and +0.72 in inferior parietal regions (BA39/40). Thus, how the brain is wired has important implications for the efficiency of cognition.

Techniques for studying the brain: introduction

Technological advances mean we have numerous exciting ways of obtaining detailed information about the brain's functioning and structure. In principle, we can work out *where* and *when* specific cognitive processes occur in the brain. This allows us to determine the order in which different brain areas become active when someone performs a task. It also allows us to find out whether two tasks involve the same brain areas in the same way or whether there are important differences.

Major techniques used to study the brain are:

Weblink:
A visual overview of imaging techniques

- **Single-unit recording**: This technique (also known as single-cell recording) involves inserting a micro-electrode one 10,000th of a millimetre in diameter into the brain to study activity in single neurons. It is very sensitive, since electrical charges of as little as one-millionth of a volt can be detected.

- **Event-related potentials (ERPs)**: The same stimulus (or very similar ones) is presented repeatedly, and the pattern of electrical brain activity recorded by several scalp electrodes is averaged to produce a single waveform. This technique allows us to work out the timing of various cognitive processes very precisely but its spatial resolution is poor.
- **Positron emission tomography (PET)**: This technique involves the detection of positrons (atomic particles emitted from some radioactive substances). PET has reasonable spatial resolution but poor temporal resolution, and measures neural activity only indirectly.
- **Functional magnetic resonance imaging (fMRI)**: This technique involves imaging blood oxygenation using an MRI machine (described later). Functional MRI has superior spatial and temporal resolution to PET, but also provides an indirect measure of neural activity.
- **Event-related functional magnetic resonance imaging (efMRI)**: This "involves separating the elements of an experiment into discrete points in time, so that the cognitive processes (and associated brain responses) associated with each element can be analysed independently" (Huettel, 2012, p. 1152). Event-related fMRI is generally very informative and has become markedly more popular recently.
- **Magneto-encephalography (MEG)**: This technique involves measuring the magnetic fields produced by electrical brain activity. It provides fairly detailed information at the millisecond level about the time course of cognitive processes, and its spatial resolution is reasonably good.
- **Transcranial magnetic stimulation (TMS)**: This is a technique in which a coil is placed close to the participant's head and a very brief pulse of current is run through it. This produces a short-lived magnetic field that generally (but not always) inhibits processing in the brain area affected. When the pulse is repeated several times in rapid succession, we have **repetitive transcranial magnetic stimulation (rTMS)**. Repetitive TMS is used very widely.

  It has often been argued that TMS or rTMS causes a very brief "**lesion**", a lesion being a structural alteration caused by brain damage. This technique has (jokingly!) been compared to hitting someone's brain with a hammer. The effects of TMS are often more complex than suggested so far. In fact, there is often *interference* because the brain area to which TMS is applied is involved in task processing as well as the activity resulting from the TMS stimulation.

Which technique is the best? There is no single (or simple) answer. Each technique has its own strengths and limitations, and so experimenters match the technique to the research question. At the most basic level, the various techniques vary in the precision with which they identify the brain areas active when a task is performed (*spatial resolution*), and the time course of such activation (*temporal resolution*). Thus, the techniques differ in their ability to provide precise information concerning where and when brain activity occurs.

The spatial and temporal resolutions of various techniques are shown in Figure 1.6. High spatial and temporal resolutions are advantageous if a very detailed account of brain functioning is required. In contrast, low temporal resolution can be more useful if a general overview of brain activity during an entire task is needed.

KEY TERMS

Single-unit recording
An invasive technique for studying brain function, permitting the study of activity in single neurons.

Event-related potentials (ERPs)
The pattern of electroencephalograph (EEG) activity obtained by averaging the brain responses to the same stimulus (or very similar stimuli) presented repeatedly.

Positron emission tomography (PET)
A brain-scanning technique based on the detection of positrons; it has reasonable spatial resolution but poor temporal resolution.

Functional magnetic resonance imaging (fMRI)
A technique based on imaging blood oxygenation using an MRI machine; it provides information about the location and time course of brain processes.

Event-related functional magnetic resonance imaging (efMRI)
This is a form of functional magnetic resonance imaging in which patterns of brain activity associated with specific events (e.g., correct vs. incorrect responses on a memory test) are compared.

Magneto-encephalography (MEG)
A non-invasive brain-scanning technique based on recording the magnetic fields generated by brain activity.

KEY TERMS

Transcranial magnetic stimulation (TMS)
A technique in which magnetic pulses briefly disrupt the functioning of a given brain area. It is often claimed that it creates a short-lived "lesion". More accurately, TMS causes interference when the brain area to which it is applied is involved in task processing as well as activity produced by the applied stimulation.

Repetitive transcranial magnetic stimulation (rTMS)
The administration of **transcranial magnetic stimulation** several times in rapid succession.

Lesions
Structural alterations within the brain caused by disease or injury.

Electroencephalography (EEG)
Recording the brain's electrical potentials through a series of scalp electrodes.

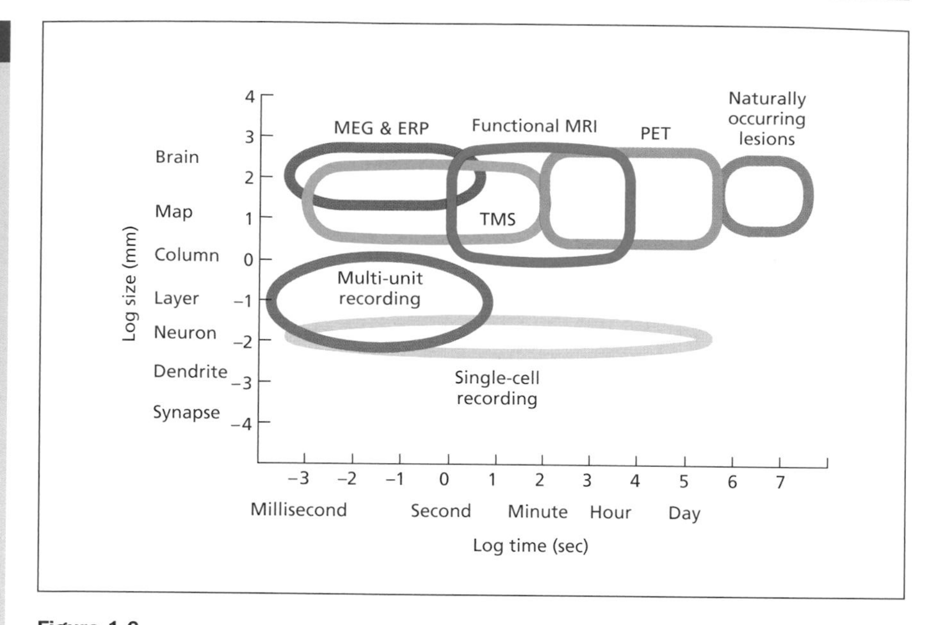

Figure 1.6
The spatial and temporal resolution of major techniques and methods used to study brain functioning.
From Ward (2006), adapted from Churchland and Sejnowski (1991).

Techniques for studying the brain: detailed analysis

We have introduced the main techniques for studying the brain. In what follows, we consider each one in more detail.

Single-unit recording

The single-unit (or cell) recording technique is more fine-grained than any other technique (see Chapter 2). However, it is invasive and so rarely used with humans. An interesting exception is a study by Quiroga et al. (2005) on epileptic patients implanted with electrodes to identify the focus of seizure onset (see Chapter 3). A neuron in the medial temporal lobe responded strongly to pictures of Jennifer Aniston (the actress from *Friends*) but not to pictures of other famous people. This finding needs to be interpreted carefully. It is highly improbable that only a single neuron responds to Jennifer Aniston – only a tiny fraction of the neurons in the medial temporal lobe were studied.

Weblink:
Hubel and Wiesel

Event-related potentials

Electroencephalography (EEG) is based on recordings of electrical brain activity measured at the surface of the scalp. Very small changes in electrical activity within the brain are picked up by scalp electrodes and can be seen on a computer screen. However, spontaneous or background brain activity can obscure the impact of stimulus processing on the EEG recording.

The answer to the above problem is to present the same stimulus (or very similar stimuli) several times. After that, the segment of EEG following each

Weblink:
EEG and MEG

stimulus is extracted and lined up with respect to the time of stimulus onset. These EEG segments are then averaged together to produce a single waveform. This method produces event-related potentials (ERPs) from EEG recordings and allows us to distinguish genuine effects of stimulation from background brain activity.

ERPs have excellent temporal resolution. Indeed, they can often indicate when a given process occurred to within a few milliseconds (ms). The ERP waveform consists of a series of positive (P) and negative (N) peaks, each described with reference to the time in milliseconds after stimulus presentation. Thus, for example, N400 is a negative wave peaking at about 400 ms. ERPs provide very detailed information about the time course of brain activity. A behavioural measure (e.g., reaction time) typically provides only a *single* measure of time on each trial, whereas ERPs provide a *continuous* measure. However, ERPs do not indicate with precision *which* brain regions are most involved in processing, in part because skull and brain tissues distort the brain's electrical fields. In addition, ERPs are mainly of value when stimuli are simple and the task involves basic processes (e.g., target detection) triggered by task stimuli. Finally, we cannot study most complex forms of cognition (e.g., problem solving) with ERPs.

KEY TERM

BOLD
blood oxygen level-dependent contrast; this is the signal measured by **functional magnetic resonance imaging (fMRI)**.

Positron emission tomography (PET)

Positron emission tomography (PET) is based on the detection of positrons – atomic particles emitted by some radioactive substances. Radioactively labelled water (the tracer) is injected into the body and rapidly gathers in the brain's blood vessels. When part of the cortex becomes active, the labelled water moves there rapidly. A scanning device measures the positrons emitted from the radioactive water, which leads to pictures of the activity levels in different brain regions. Note that tiny amounts of radioactivity are involved.

Weblink:
PET

PET has reasonable spatial resolution in that any active brain area can be located to within 5–10 mm. However, it has very poor temporal resolution – PET scans indicate the amount of activity in any given brain region over 30–60 seconds.

Magnetic resonance imaging (MRI and fMRI)

Magnetic resonance imaging (MRI) involves the use of an MRI scanner (see photo) containing a very large magnet (weighing up to 11 tons). A strong magnetic field causes an alignment of protons (subatomic particles) in the brain. A brief radio-frequency pulse is applied, which causes the aligned protons to spin and then regain their original orientations, giving up a small amount of energy as they do so. The brightest regions in the MRI scan are those emitting the greatest energy. MRI scans can be obtained from numerous angles but tell us only about brain *structure* rather than its *functions*.

Weblink:
fMRI

Happily enough, the same principles used to produce MRI can also be used to provide functional information in the form of functional magnetic resonance imaging (fMRI). Oxyhaemoglobin is converted into deoxyhaemoglobin when neurons consume oxygen, and deoxyhaemoglobin produces distortions in the local magnetic field. This distortion is assessed by fMRI, and provides a measure of the concentration of deoxyhaemoglobin in the blood.

Technically, what is measured in fMRI is known as **BOLD** (blood oxygen level-dependent contrast). Changes in the BOLD signal produced by increased

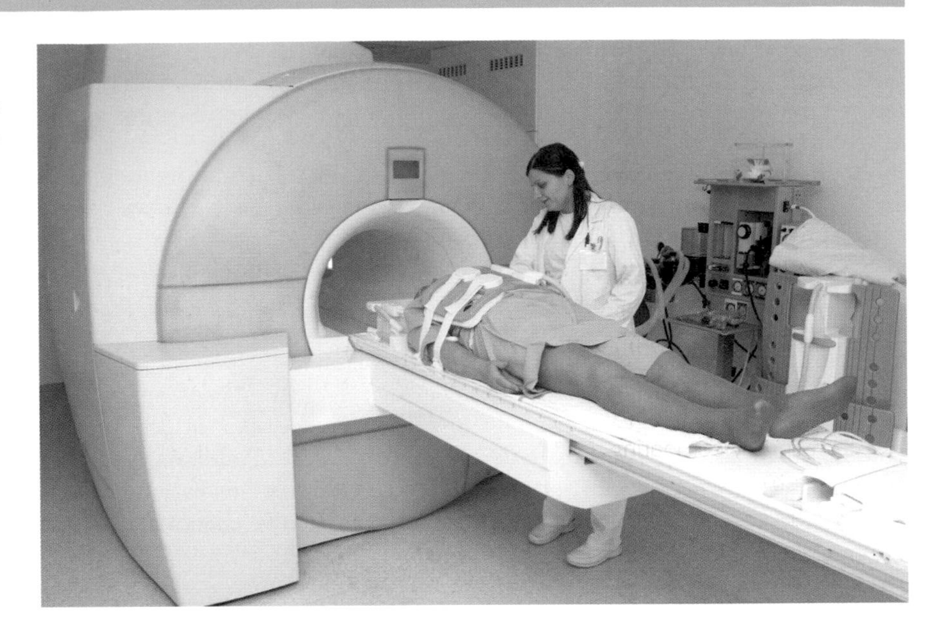

The magnetic resonance imaging (MRI) scanner has proved an extremely valuable source of data in psychology. © Shutterstock.

neural activity take some time to occur, so the temporal resolution of fMRI is about two or three seconds. However, its spatial resolution is very good (approximately 1 mm). Since fMRI has superior temporal and spatial resolution to PET, it has largely replaced it in neuroimaging research.

Suppose we want to understand why our participants remember some items but not others. We can use event-related fMRI (efMRI), in which we consider each participant's patterns of brain activation for remembered and forgotten items. Wagner et al. (1998) recorded fMRI while participants learned a list of words. There was more brain activity during learning for words subsequently recognised than those subsequently forgotten. These findings suggest forgotten words were processed less thoroughly than remembered words at the time of learning.

What are fMRI's limitations? First, it provides an indirect measure of underlying neural activity. Second, there are distortions in the BOLD signal in some brain regions (e.g., close to sinuses, close to the oral cavity). Third, the scanner is noisy, which can cause problems for studies involving auditory stimuli. Fourth, some people (especially those with claustrophobia) find it uncomfortable to be encased in the scanner. Cooke et al. (2007) found 43% of participants in an fMRI study were at least a bit upset by the experience and 33% reported side effects (e.g., headaches).

Fifth, there are constraints on the kinds of stimuli that can be presented to participants lying in a scanner. There are also constraints on the responses they can be asked to produce because even small movements can distort the BOLD signal.

Magneto-encephalography (MEG)

Magneto-encephalography (MEG) involves using a superconducting quantum interference device (SQUID) to measure the magnetic fields produced by electrical brain activity. The technology is complex because the size of the magnetic field created by the brain is extremely small relative to the earth's magnetic field.

IN THE REAL WORLD: CAN COGNITIVE NEUROSCIENTISTS READ OUR BRAINS/MINDS?

There is increasing evidence that cognitive neuroscientists can work out what we are looking at just by studying our brain activity (Tong & Pratte, 2012). For example, Haxby et al. (2001) asked participants to view pictures from eight different categories (e.g., cats, faces, houses) while patterns of brain activity were assessed by fMRI. Computer-based analysis of patterns of brain activity allowed the researchers to predict accurately the category of object being viewed on 96% of trials!

Kay et al. (2008) argued that most previous research on "brain reading" or "mind reading" was limited in two ways. First, the visual stimuli were much less complex than those encountered in everyday life. Second, the experimenters' task of predicting what participants had viewed was simplified by comparing their patterns of brain activity on test trials to those obtained when the same objects or categories had been presented previously.

Kay et al. (2008) overcame the above limitations by presenting two participants with 120 previously unseen natural images of moderate complexity. The fMRI data permitted correct identification of the image being viewed on 92% of the trials for one participant and 72% for the other. This is remarkable given that chance performance was 0.8%! Findings such as these have exciting implications for understanding the brain's precise role in visual perception.

Studies such as that of Kay et al. (2008) indicate that much more information can be extracted from patterns of brain activity than was previously believed. However, these studies are not *directly* involved in mind reading. Many aspects of the brain activity in response to visual stimuli are very relevant to the participant's perceptual representation, whereas other aspects are probably irrelevant (Vilarroya, 2013). Support for this viewpoint was reported by Hung et al. (2005). Computer analysis of brain activity in macaques successfully classified various stimuli presented to them that the macaques themselves were unable to distinguish.

However, MEG provides very accurate measurement of brain activity in part because the skull is virtually transparent to magnetic fields.

MEG has excellent temporal resolution (at the millisecond level) and often has very good spatial resolution as well. However, it is extremely expensive. In addition, some people find it uncomfortable to take part in MEG studies. Cooke et al. (2007) discovered that 35% of participants found the experience "a bit upsetting", and the same percentage reported side effects such as muscle aches or headaches.

Transcranial magnetic stimulation (TMS)

Transcranial magnetic stimulation (TMS) is a technique in which a coil (often in the shape of a figure of eight) is placed close to the participant's head (see photo). A very brief (less than 1 ms) but large magnetic pulse of current is run through it. This causes a short-lived magnetic field that generally (but not always) leads to inhibited processing in the affected area (generally about 1 cubic centimetre in extent). More specifically, the magnetic field created leads to electrical stimulation in the brain. In practice, several magnetic pulses are typically given in a short period of time – this is repetitive transcranial magnetic stimulation (rTMS). Most research has used rTMS but we will often simply use the more general term TMS.

Weblink:
TMS

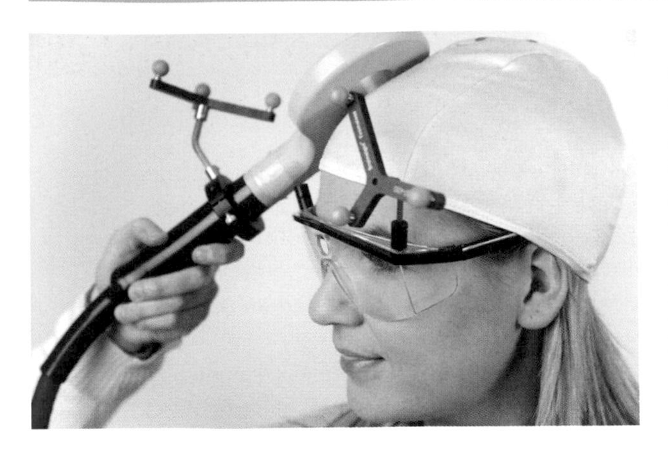

Transcranial magnetic stimulation coil.

University of Durham/Simon Fraser/Science Photo Library.

What is an appropriate control condition against which to compare the effects of TMS or rTMS? One possibility is to compare task performance with and without it. However, TMS creates a loud noise and muscle twitching at the side of the forehead, and these effects might lead to impaired performance. Applying TMS to a non-critical brain area (irrelevant to task performance) is often a satisfactory control condition. The prediction is that task performance will be worse when TMS is applied to a critical area than a non-critical one.

Why are TMS and rTMS useful? As mentioned earlier, they often create a "temporary lesion" so the role of any given brain area in task performance can be assessed. If TMS applied to a particular brain area impairs task performance, we can conclude that brain area is necessary for task performance. Conversely, if TMS has no effects on task performance, then the brain area affected by it is not necessary. Thus, we can often make stronger causal statements about the brain area's underlying performance with TMS than with most other techniques.

TMS can also indicate *when* any given brain area is most involved in task performance. For example, Cracco et al. (1999) asked participants to detect letters. Performance was maximally impaired when TMS was applied to occipital cortex 80–100 ms after letter presentation rather than at shorter or longer delays.

Evaluation

In principle, the greatest advantage of TMS (and rTMS) over neuroimaging techniques is that they increase our confidence that a given brain area is necessary for task performance. TMS allows us to manipulate the availability of a brain region for involvement in the performance of some cognitive task. In contrast, we only establish associations or correlations between activation in various brain areas and task performance with functional neuroimaging.

TMS can be regarded as producing a brief "lesion". However, it has various advantages over research on brain-damaged patients having genuine lesions. For example, we can compare any given individual's performance with and without a lesion with TMS but this is rarely possible with brain-damaged patients. In addition, the experimenter controls the brain area(s) affected by TMS but such control is impossible with brain-damaged patients.

What are TMS's limitations? First, its effects are complex and not fully understood. For example, Allen et al. (2007) found rTMS applied to the early visual cortex of cats not engaged in any task caused an *increase* of spontaneous brain activity lasting up to one minute. However, activity in the visual cortex produced by viewing gratings was reduced by up to 60% by rTMS. The effects of TMS on performance are generally negative but sometimes positive.

Why does TMS sometimes enhance performance? Consider an area x that typically inhibits the functioning of area y. TMS applied to area x will reduce this inhibition and so might enhance the functioning of area y. More generally, brain functioning is remarkably complex and so we would expect TMS to have somewhat variable effects.

Second, it has proved difficult to establish the precise brain areas affected by TMS, some of which can be distant from the stimulation point. However, progress can be made by combining TMS with neuroimaging techniques to clarify the effects of TMS on brain activity (Ziemann, 2011).

Third, TMS can only be applied to brain areas lying beneath the skull but not to areas with overlying muscle. That limits its overall usefulness.

Fourth, there are safety issues with TMS. For example, it has very occasionally caused seizures in participants in spite of stringent rules designed to ensure their safety.

KEY TERM

Meta-analysis
A form of statistical analysis based on combining the findings from numerous studies on a given issue.

Overall strengths

Do the various techniques for studying the brain answer all our prayers? That would be an overstatement. However, cognitive neuroscientists have made substantial contributions to our understanding of human cognition. The major strengths of cognitive neuroscience will be discussed here.

First, cognitive neuroscience has increasingly helped to resolve theoretical controversies that had remained intractable with purely behavioural studies (White & Poldrack, 2013). We will briefly consider two examples. The first concerns speech perception (see Chapter 9). Listeners presented with degraded speech find it much more intelligible when the words are predictable. The crucial issue is *when* knowledge of what is being presented influences speech perception. It might occur *early* and thus directly affect basic auditory processes. Alternatively, it might occur *late* and only after basic auditory processing has finished. Theorists differ in their favoured explanation (Mattys et al., 2012).

Wild et al. (2012) addressed this issue. Listeners heard degraded speech accompanied by visual stimuli that matched or did not match the auditory input. There was more activity in primary auditory cortex (involved in early auditory processing) when the visual input matched the auditory input than when it did not. This strongly suggests knowledge of what was being presented *directly* affected basic auditory processes.

The second example concerns visual imagery (see Chapter 3). There has been much controversy as to whether visual imagery resembles visual perception. Most behavioural evidence is inconclusive. However, brain-imaging research has shown two-thirds of the brain areas activated during visual perception are also activated during visual imagery (Kosslyn, 2005). Kosslyn and Thompson (2003) found in a **meta-analysis** that even brain areas involved in the early stages of visual perception are often activated during visual imagery.

The above findings strongly suggest the processes in visual imagery resemble those in visual perception. However, R.J. Lee et al. (2012) identified important differences using neuroimaging. Participants viewed or imagined common objects and attempts were then made to decide *which* objects were involved based on patterns of brain activation. Identification of perceived objects was much better based on activation in early visual processing areas than subsequent ones, whereas the opposite was the case for imagined objects. Thus, there is more involvement of low-level visual processes in perception than imagery.

Second, it is a major challenge to understand the complexities of the cognitive system and its underlying brain organisation. As we saw earlier, Bullmore and Sporns (2012) argued that the brain is organised into many tight clusters or modules plus long-distance connections among them. The incredible richness of

KEY TERM

Functional specialisation
The assumption that each brain area or region is specialised for a specific function (e.g., colour processing, face processing).

the data obtained from neuroimaging studies means cognitive neuroscientists can (at least in principle) construct theoretical models accurately mimicking the complexities of brain functioning. In contrast, cognitive neuropsychology seems less flexible and more committed to the notion of a modular brain organisation.

Third, another advantage arises from the remarkable richness of neuroimaging data. If it becomes clear that one approach to analysing such data is limited, it is easy to reanalyse them within a different theoretical framework. For example, it used to be assumed that most face processing occurs in the fusiform face area, but this was a substantial oversimplification (Weiner & Grill-Spector, 2012; see Chapter 3). An approach based on the assumption that face processing involves a *network* of brain regions provides a more accurate account (Atkinson & Adolphs, 2011). Thus, cognitive neuroscience can be self-correcting.

More generally, cognitive neuroscientists attach less importance than they used to the assumption of **functional specialisation** – the notion that each brain region is specialised for a different function. Instead, they accept there is substantial *integration* and coordination across the brain. Such functional integration can be studied by correlating activity across different brain regions – if a network of brain areas is involved in a given process, activity in all of them should be positively correlated when that process occurs. There is strong evidence for such functional integration with conscious perception, which seems to depend on coordinated activity across several brain regions (see Chapter 16).

Cognitive neuroscientists have identified an increasing number of major brain networks. For example, Corbetta and Shulman (2002; see Chapter 5) used findings from cognitive neuroscience to identify two attention networks, one concerned with goal-directed attention and the other with stimulus-driven attention. Other brain networks are discussed by Anderson et al. (2013).

Fourth, cognitive neuroscience is often especially useful when combined with other approaches. Here is an example based on the notion that recognition memory depends on two different processes: recollection and familiarity (see Chapter 6 for the full story). These processes differ in that only recollection involves the conscious retrieval of contextual information. It has been argued theoretically that recollection involves the hippocampal system whereas familiarity involves the nearby perirhinal system.

Research within cognitive neuropsychology has produced a double dissociation supporting the above theory. Patients with damage to the hippocampus have impaired recollection but intact familiarity, whereas those with damage to the perirhinal system have impaired familiarity but intact recollection. Neuroimaging research has strengthened the support for the theory. Recollection is associated with more activation in the hippocampus than the perirhinal cortex, whereas the opposite is the case for familiarity (Diana et al., 2007).

General limitations

We turn now to various issues raised by cognitive neuroscience. First, cognitive neuroscientists often *over-interpret* their findings by assuming there are one-to-one links between cognitive processes and brain areas (Brown, 2012). Thus, for example, activation in a small brain region (a "blob") is interpreted as being the "love area" or the "religion area". This approach has been referred to unflatteringly as "blobology".

Blobology is in decline. However, there is still undue reliance on **reverse inference** – a researcher infers the involvement of a given cognitive process based on activation within a given brain region. Here is an example. Individuals exposed to threat-related information typically show activation of the amygdala (part of the limbic system; Sander, 2009). This led many researchers to conclude the amygdala is central to a fear system.

> **KEY TERM**
>
> **Reverse inference**
> As applied to functional neuroimaging, it involves arguing backwards from a pattern of brain activation to the presence of a given cognitive process.

What is wrong with the above conclusion? Other research has shown the processing of most emotions is associated with amygdala activation (Lindquist et al., 2012; see Figure 1.7). This illustrates a key problem with reverse inference – most brain regions are involved in several different cognitive processes and so activation of any given brain area is not very informative (Brown, 2012). This was shown clearly by Yarkoni et al. (2011), who considered areas of brain activation across 3,489 studies. Some brain areas (e.g., dorsolateral prefrontal cortex, anterior cingulate cortex and anterior insula) were activated in 20% of the studies. Such areas are involved in several different cognitive processes.

Second, it is very difficult to bridge the divide between psychological processes and concepts on the one hand and patterns of brain activation on the other. As Harley (2012) pointed out, we may never find brain patterns corresponding closely to psychological processes such as "attention" or "planning".

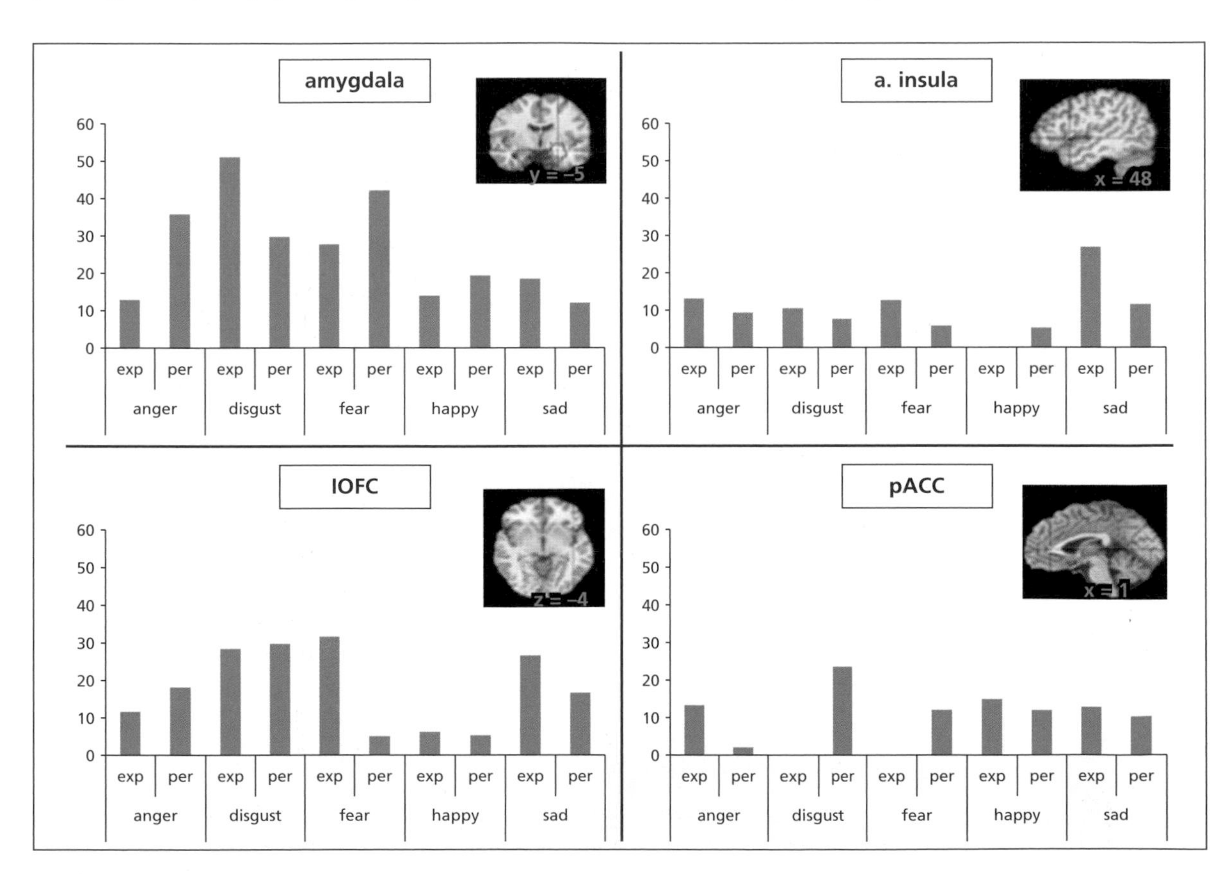

Figure 1.7
Proportion of studies on the experience (exp) and perception (per) of various emotional states (anger, disgust, fear, happiness and sadness) showing amygdala activity. lOFC = lateral orbitofrontal cortex; pACC = pregenual anterior cingulate cortex.
From Lindquist et al. (2012). Reprinted with permission of Cambridge University Press.

Harley (2012, p. 1372) concluded as follows: "Our language and thought may not divide up in the way in which the brain implements these processes."

Third, most neuroimaging studies are *underpowered*, typically using 20 participants or fewer. This produces the problem that "most fMRI analyses will detect only a fraction of the true effects, producing a deceptive illusion of 'selective' activation" (Yarkoni et al., 2010, p. 489). One solution to this problem is to combine findings across studies. As already mentioned, Yarkoni et al. (2011) considered 3,489 studies from which 100,953 activation points were identified. This greatly increased the chances of identifying most true effects while reducing the percentage of false positives. It also made it much easier to identify precisely which cognitive processes were associated with activation in any given area.

Fourth, false positive results (i.e., mistakenly concluding that random activity in a given brain area is task-relevant activation) are common and may occur as often as 15% of the time (Yarkoni et al., 2010). False positives arise because most neuroimaging studies produce huge amounts of data and some researchers fail to correct their statistical thresholds (*p* values required for significance) to take full account of it.

Bennett et al. (2009) provided an amusing example of a false positive finding. They asked their participant to determine the emotions shown in pictures of people in social situations. When they did not correct their statistical thresholds, there was significant evidence of brain activation (see Figure 1.8). The interesting feature of this study was that the participant was a dead salmon! Thus, we know for certain the "finding" was a false positive.

Fifth, most brain-imaging techniques reveal only *associations* between patterns of brain activation and behaviour. For example, performance on a reasoning task is associated with activation of the prefrontal cortex. Such associations are purely correlational and do not show that the brain regions activated are essential for task performance. Brain activation might also be caused by participants engaging in unnecessary monitoring of their performance or attending to non-task stimuli.

Transcranial magnetic stimulation (TMS) offers a partial solution to this causality issue. We can show a given brain area is necessary for the performance of a task by finding that TMS disrupts that performance. However, the complexities of TMS's effects on the brain sometimes mean that caution in interpretation is needed.

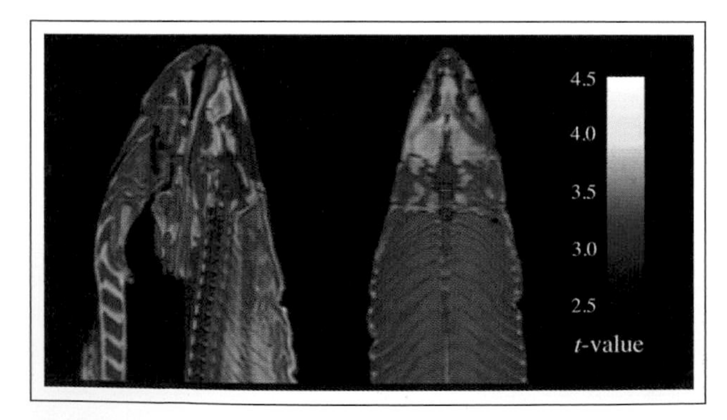

Figure 1.8
Areas showing greater activation in a dead salmon when presented with photographs of people than when at rest.
From Bennett et al. (2009). With kind permission of the authors.

Sixth, many cognitive neuroscientists assume that most brain activity is driven by environmental or task demands. If that assumption is correct, we might expect most brain activity in response to such demands. Surprisingly, that is *not* the case. In fact, the increased brain activity occurring when someone performs a cognitive task typically adds less than 5% to resting brain activity. This is probably much less than the brain energy consumption devoted to *intrinsic* activity within the brain that occurs in unstimulating environments.

Why is the brain so active even when the environment is unstimulating? Part of the answer is that people often devote cognitive resources to predicting future environmental changes (Raichle, 2010). However, the finding that patterns of brain activity are similar in different states of consciousness, including coma, anaesthesia and slow-wave sleep, suggests most intrinsic brain activity reflects basic brain functioning. As a result of intrinsic brain activity, task performance is often associated with *decreased* brain activity in some brain regions rather than the expected *increase*.

Seventh, cognitive neuroscience shares with cognitive psychology problems of ecological validity (applicability to everyday life) and paradigm specificity (findings do not generalise across paradigms). Indeed, the problem of ecological validity may be greater in cognitive neuroscience. Participants in fMRI studies (the most used technique) lie on their backs in somewhat claustrophobic and noisy conditions and have very restricted movement – not much like everyday life!

Gutchess and Park (2006) compared the effects of being in an MRI scanner or simply in the laboratory on long-term recognition memory. Memory was significantly worse in the scanner, presumably because it provided a more distracting or anxiety-creating environment.

Eighth, we must avoid "the neuroimaging illusion", which involves overvaluing the contribution pictures of brain activity make to our understanding of human cognition (see Chapter 14). Keehner et al. (2011) presented neuroscience articles accompanied by brain images. The more three-dimensional the images appeared to be, the more positively the articles were evaluated. Here is a concrete example of the neuroimaging illusion. On 28 August 2007, *The Guardian* had the following headline: "Brain scans pinpoint how chocoholics are hooked." In essence, the researchers involved (Rolls & McCabe, 2007) had found that the sight of chocolate produced more activation in reward centres of the brain in chocolate cravers than in non-cravers. Thus, the findings that so impressed *The Guardian* tell us little more than that chocolate cravers find chocolate rewarding (Beck, 2010)!

KEY TERMS

Computational modelling
This involves constructing computer programs that simulate or mimic human cognitive processes.

Artificial intelligence
This involves developing computer programs that produce intelligent outcomes.

COMPUTATIONAL COGNITIVE SCIENCE

We will start by distinguishing between computational modelling and artificial intelligence. **Computational modelling** involves programming computers to model or mimic aspects of human cognitive functioning. In contrast, **artificial intelligence** involves constructing computer systems that produce intelligent outcomes but may do so in ways bearing little resemblance to those used by humans. Consider Deep Blue, the chess program that defeated the World Champion Garry Kasparov on 11 May 1997. Deep Blue considered up to 200 million positions per second, which is vastly more than any human chess players (see Chapter 12).

Weblink:
AI on the web

Computational cognitive scientists develop computational models to understand human cognition. A good computational model shows us how a given theory can be specified and allows us to predict behaviour in new situations. Early mathematical models made predictions but often lacked an explanatory component. For example, having three traffic violations predicts well whether someone is a bad risk for car insurance but it is not clear why. A major benefit of the computational models developed in computational cognitive science is that they often provide an exploratory and predictive basis for a phenomenon (Costello & Keane, 2000).

KEY TERMS

Cognitive architecture: A comprehensive framework for understanding human cognition in the form of a computer programs.

Connectionist models Models in computational cognitive science consisting of interconnected networks of simple units; the networks exhibit learning through experience and specific items of knowledge are distributed across numerous units.

In the past (and even nowadays), many experimental cognitive psychologists expressed their theories in vague verbal statements, which made it hard to decide whether the evidence fitted the theory. As Murphy (2011) pointed out, verbal theories provide theorists with undesirable "wiggle room". In contrast, a computational model "requires the researcher to be explicit about a theory in a way that a verbal theory does not" (Murphy, 2011, p. 300). Implementing a theory as a program is a good way to check it contains no hidden assumptions or imprecise terms. This often reveals that the theory makes predictions the theorist concerned had not realised!

There are issues concerning the relationship between the performance of a computer program and human performance (Costello & Keane, 2000). It is rarely meaningful to relate a program's speed doing a simulated task to the reaction times of human participants, because its processing times are affected by psychologically irrelevant features. For example, programs run faster on more powerful computers. However, the various materials presented to the program should result in differences in program operation time correlating closely with differences in participants' reaction times when processing the same materials.

Types of models

Most computational models focus on relatively specific aspects of human cognition. For example, some of the most successful computational models provide accounts of reading words and non-words aloud (Plaut et al., 1996; Coltheart et al., 2001; Perry et al., 2007) (see Chapter 9). However, some computational models are more ambitious. This is especially the case with **cognitive architectures**, which are "cognitive models that are domain-genetic [cover many domains or areas] and encompass a wide range of cognitive applicabilities" (Sun, 2007, p. 160). Byrne (2012) evaluated some of the major cognitive architectures including J.R. Anderson et al.'s (2004) Adaptive Control of Thought-Rational [ACT-R], which is discussed later.

There are more computational models than you can shake a stick at. However, numerous otherwise diverse models can be categorised as connectionist models, and so we will focus on them. Many other models are based on production systems, and will be discussed briefly. Our emphasis will be on *what* various computational approaches achieve rather than the details of *how* this happens.

Connectionism

Weblink:
Connectionism

Connectionist models typically consist of interconnected networks of simple units exhibiting learning. Within such networks, each item of knowledge is represented by a pattern of activation spread over numerous units rather than by a single location. Connectionist networks often (but not always) have the following characteristics (see Figure 1.9):

- The network consists of elementary or neuron-like *units* or *nodes* connected together, with a single unit having many links to other units.
- Units influence other units by exciting or inhibiting them.
- The unit usually takes the weighted sum of all the input links, and produces a single output to another unit if the weighted sum exceeds some threshold value.

- The network as a whole is characterised by the properties of the units that make it up, by the way they are connected together, and by the rules used to change the strength of connections among units.
- Networks can have different structures or layers; they can have a layer of input links, intermediate layers ("hidden units") and a layer of output units (see Figure 1.9).
- A representation of a concept can be stored in a *distributed* way by an activation pattern throughout the network.
- The same network can store several patterns without disruption if they are sufficiently distinct.
- An important learning rule used in networks is called *backward propagation of errors* (*BackProp*) (see below).

KEY TERM

Back-propagation
A learning mechanism in connectionist models based on comparing actual responses to correct ones.

Connectionist networks model cognitive performance without using any explicit rules. They do this by storing patterns of activation within the network in which various inputs are associated with various outputs. Connectionist models typically consist of several layers. One layer consists of input units that encode a stimulus as a pattern of activation. Another layer is an output layer producing some response as a pattern of activation. When the network has learned to produce a given response at the output layer following the presentation of a given stimulus at the input layer, it exhibits behaviour that looks rule-based.

"Backward propagation of errors", or BackProp, is an extremely important learning rule. **Back-propagation** is a mechanism allowing a network to learn to associate a given input pattern with a given output pattern by comparing actual responses against correct ones. The network is initially set up with random weights on the links among the units. During the early stages of learning, the output units often produce an incorrect pattern or response following presentation of the input pattern. BackProp compares the imperfect pattern with the known required response, noting the errors. It then back-propagates activation through the network so the weights between the units are adjusted to produce the required pattern. This process is repeated until the network produces the required pattern. Thus, the model learns the appropriate behaviour without being explicitly programmed to do so. Sadly, research in cognitive neuroscience has found little or no evidence of back-propagation in the human brain (Mayor et al., 2014).

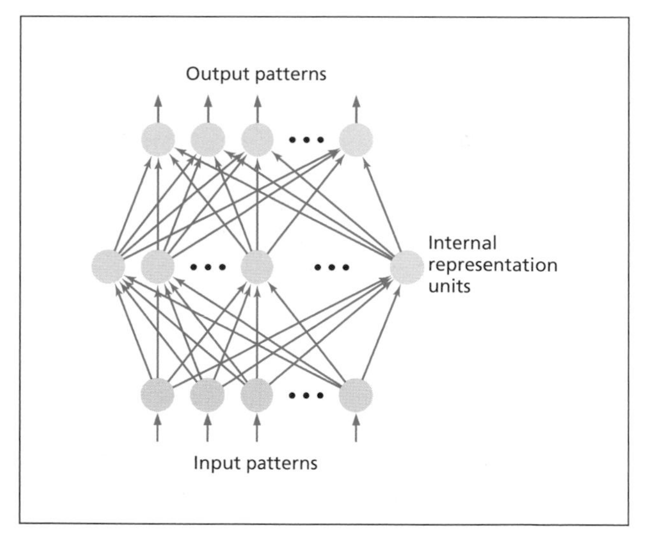

Figure 1.9
A multi-layered connectionist network with a layer of input units, a layer of internal representation units, or hidden units, and a layer of output units, in a form that allows the appropriate output pattern to be generated from a given input pattern.

Reproduced with permission from Rumelhart and McClelland (1986). Copyright © 1986 Massachusetts Institute of Technology, by permission of The MIT Press.

Several connectionist models (e.g., the parallel distributed processing approach of Rumelhart et al., 1986) assume representations are stored in a *distributed* fashion across the brain. There are potential problems with this assumption. Suppose we encode two words at the same time. That would cause numerous units or nodes to become activated, making it hard (or even impossible) to decide which units or nodes belonged to which word (Bowers, 2002). There is also evidence that much information is stored in a given brain location rather than in a distributed fashion (see Bowers (2009) for a review). For example, as mentioned earlier, Quiroga et al. (2005) discovered a neuron in the medial temporal lobe that responded strongly when pictures of the actress Jennifer Aniston were presented but not other famous people (see Chapter 3).

Some connectionist models assume there is *local* representation of knowledge. Localist connectionist models include the reading model of Coltheart et al. (2001; see Chapter 9); the TRACE model of word recognition (McClelland & Elman, 1986; see Chapter 9); and the models of speech production put forward by Dell (1986) and by Levelt et al. (1999; see Chapter 11). It is likely some knowledge is represented locally and some is distributed (see Chapter 7).

KEY TERMS

Production systems
These consist of very large numbers of "if . . . then" **production rules** and a working memory containing information.

Production rules
"If . . . then" or condition-action rules in which the action is carried out whenever the appropriate condition is present.

Working memory
A system holding information currently being processed.

Production systems

Production systems consist of numerous "If . . . then" production rules. **Production rules** can take many forms. However, an everyday example is, "If the green man is lit up, then cross the road." There is also a **working memory** (i.e., a system holding information currently being processed). If information from the environment that "the green man is lit up" reaches working memory, it will match the IF-part of the rule in long-term memory and trigger the THEN-part of the rule (i.e., cross the road).

Production systems come in various shapes and sizes but generally have the following characteristics:

- numerous "If . . . then" rules;
- a working memory containing information;
- a production system that operates by matching the contents of working memory against the IF-parts of the rules and executing the THEN-parts;
- if information in working memory matches the IF-parts of two rules, a conflict-resolution strategy selects one.

Many aspects of cognition can be specified as sets of "If . . . then" rules. For example, chess knowledge can readily be represented as a set of productions based on rules such as, "If the Queen is threatened, then move the Queen to a safe square." In this way, people's basic knowledge can be regarded as a collection of productions.

Newell and Simon (1972) first established the usefulness of production system models in their General Problem Solver, which identified cognitive processes involved in problem solving (see Chapter 12). However, these models have a wider applicability. For example, there is J.R. Anderson et al.'s (2004) ACT-R. This is a cognitive architecture and is discussed next.

ACT-R

John Anderson has produced several versions of Adaptive Control of Thought-Rational [ACT-R]. The version described by J.R. Anderson et al. (2004) is based on the assumption that the cognitive system consists of several modules (relatively independent subsystems). ACT-R combines computational cognitive science with cognitive neuroscience by identifying the brain regions associated with each module (see Figure 1.10). Four modules are of particular importance to human cognition:

Weblink:
Act-R website

1 *Retrieval module*: it maintains the retrieval cues needed to access information; its proposed location is the inferior ventrolateral prefrontal cortex.
2 *Imaginal module*: it transforms problem representations to assist in problem solving; it is located in the posterior parietal cortex.
3 *Goal module*: it keeps tracks of an individual's intentions and controls information processing; it is located in the anterior cingulate cortex.
4 *Procedural module*: it uses production (if . . . then) rules to determine what action will be taken next; it is located at the head of the caudate nucleus within the basal ganglia.

Each module has a buffer associated with it containing a limited amount of important information. How is information from these buffers integrated? According to J.R. Anderson et al. (2004, p. 1058), "A central production system can detect patterns in these buffers and take co-ordinated action." If several productions could be triggered by the information contained in the buffers, one is selected based on the value or gain associated with each outcome plus the amount of time or cost incurred in achieving that outcome.

ACT-R represents an impressive attempt to provide a theoretical framework for understanding information processing and performance on numerous cognitive tasks. It is an ambitious attempt to integrate computational cognitive science with cognitive neuroscience.

What are the limitations of ACT-R? First, it is very hard to provide adequate tests of such a wide-ranging theory. Second, it can be argued that areas of prefrontal cortex (e.g., dorsolateral prefrontal cortex) generally assumed to be of major importance in cognition are de-emphasised. Third, as discussed earlier, research within cognitive neuroscience increasingly reveals the importance to cognitive processing of brain networks rather than specific regions.

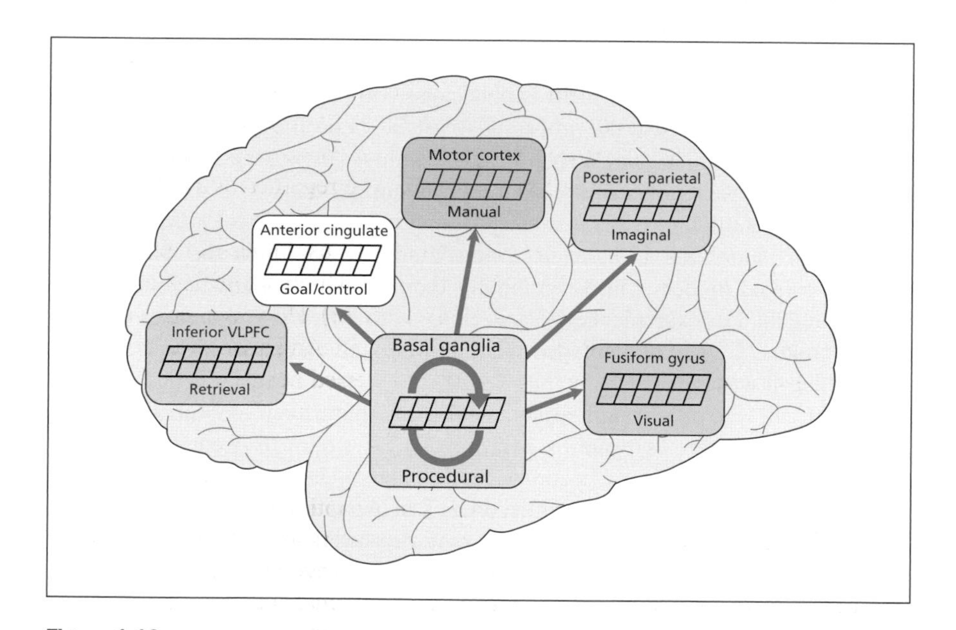

Figure 1.10
The main modules of the ACT-R (Adaptive Control of Thought-Rational) cognitive architecture with their locations within the brain.

Reprinted from Anderson et al. (2008). Reprinted with permission of Elsevier.

Links with other approaches

The great majority of computational models until fairly recently were designed to predict and understand behavioural data from experiments in cognitive psychology. Recently, however, there has been a substantial increase in computational models of direct relevance to cognitive neuropsychology and cognitive neuroscience (e.g., ACT-R).

How are computational models applied to cognitive neuropsychological data from brain-damaged patients? Typically, the starting point is to develop a computational model that accounts for the performance of healthy individuals on some task. After that, aspects of the computational model or program are altered to simulate "lesions", and the effects on task performance are assessed. Finally, the lesioned model's performance can be compared against that of brain-damaged patients (Dell & Caramazza, 2008).

Overall evaluation

Computational cognitive science has several strengths. First, the development of cognitive architectures offers the prospect of providing an overarching framework within which to understand the cognitive system. Such a framework could be very valuable. This is especially so given that much empirical research in cognitive psychology is limited in scope and suffers from paradigm specificity (see Glossary). However, there is controversy concerning the extent to which this goal has been achieved.

Second, the scope of computational cognitive science has increased over time. Initially, it was applied mainly to behavioural data. More recently, computational modelling has been applied to functional neuroimaging data. In addition, many computational cognitive scientists "lesion" their models to see the effects of damage to various parts of the model and to compare their findings against behavioural data from brain-damaged patients.

Third, the development of computational models requires theorists to think carefully and rigorously. This is the case because computer programs must contain detailed information about the processes involved in performing any given task. In contrast, many theories in verbal form are vaguely expressed and it is unclear precisely what predictions follow from their assumptions.

Fourth, it is often possible to make progress by using what is known as *nested incremental modelling*. In essence, a new model builds upon the strengths of previous related models while eliminating their weaknesses and accounting for additional data. For example, Perry et al. (2007) put forward a connectionist dual-process model (CDP+) of reading aloud that improved on the dual-process model from which it was derived.

What are the main limitations of the computational cognitive science approach? First, there is Bonini's paradox: "As a model of a complex system becomes more complete, it becomes less understandable. Alternatively, as a model grows more realistic, it also becomes just as difficult to understand as the real-world processes it represents" (Dutton & Starbuck, 1971, p. 4).

The relation between a map and a territory provides a simple example of Bonini's paradox. A map the same size as the territory it represents would be maximally precise but also completely unusable. In practice, however, the increased complexity of computational models has been accompanied by a substantial increase in their power.

Second, it is sometimes difficult to falsify computational models although typically easier than with theories expressed only in verbal terms. Why is this? The ingenuity of computational modellers means that many models can account for numerous behavioural findings. Of promise for the future is the prospect of computational models being applied more systematically to neuroimaging findings as well as behavioural ones.

Third, there are various ways in which computational modellers increase the apparent success of their model. One example is overfitting (Ziegler et al., 2010). This happens when a model accounts extremely well for a given data set but fails to generalise to other data sets. This can occur when a model accounts for noise in the data as well as genuine effects.

Fourth, human cognition is influenced by several potentially conflicting motivational and emotional factors. Most computational models ignore these factors, although ACT-R (Anderson et al., 2008) has a motivational component in its goal module. We can distinguish between a cognitive system (the Pure Cognitive System) and a biological system (the Regulatory System) (Norman, 1980). Much activity of the Pure Cognitive System is determined by the Regulatory System's needs (e.g., survival, food and water). Computational cognitive science (like most of cognitive psychology) typically de-emphasises the Regulatory System's key role.

Fifth, it is difficult to assess most computational models in detail. As Addyman and French (2012, p.332) pointed out, there are several reasons for this:

> Everyone still programs in his or her own favourite programming language, source code is rarely made available, accessibility of models to non-programming researchers is essentially non-existent, and even for other modellers, the profusion of source code in a multitude of programming languages, writing without programming guidelines, makes it almost impossible to access, check, explore, re-use or continue to develop.

KEY TERM

Converging operations
An approach in which several methods with different strengths and limitations are used to address a given issue.

Weblink:
Comparison between production systems and connectionist models

COMPARISONS OF MAJOR APPROACHES

We have discussed the major approaches to human cognition at length, and you may be wondering which one is the most useful and informative. In fact, that is *not* the best way of thinking about the issues for various reasons. First, an increasing amount of research involves two or more of the approaches.

Second, each approach makes its own distinctive contribution, and so all are needed. In terms of an analogy, it is pointless asking whether a driver is more or less useful than a putter to a golfer – both are essential.

Third, as well as its own strengths, each approach also has its own limitations. This can be seen clearly in Table 1.1. What is optimal in such circumstances is to use **converging operations** – several different research methods are used to address a given theoretical issue with the strength of one method balancing out the limitations of the other methods. If two or more methods produce the same answer, that provides stronger evidence than could be obtained using a single method. If different methods produce different answers, then further research is needed to clarify the situation.

The major goal of research is to enhance our understanding of human cognition. In writing this book, our central aim with each topic discussed has been to focus on research that best achieves that goal. As a result, any given approach

TABLE 1.1 STRENGTHS AND LIMITATIONS OF MAJOR APPROACHES TO HUMAN COGNITION

Strengths	*Limitations*
Experimental cognitive psychology	
1. The first systematic approach to understanding human cognition.	1. Most cognitive tasks are complex and involve many different processes.
2. The source of most of the theories and tasks used by the other approaches.	2. Behavioural evidence provides only indirect evidence concerning internal processes.
3. It is enormously flexible and can be applied to any aspect of cognition.	3. Theories are sometimes vague and hard to test empirically.
4. It has produced numerous important replicated findings.	4. Findings sometimes do not generalise because of paradigm specificity.
5. It has strongly influenced social, clinical, and developmental psychology.	5. There is a lack of an overarching theoretical framework.
Cognitive neuropsychology	
1. Double dissociations have provided strong evidence for various major processing modules.	1. Patients may develop compensatory strategies not found in healthy individuals.
2. Causal links can be shown between brain damage and cognitive performance.	2. Most of the theoretical assumptions (e.g., that the mind is modular) seem too extreme.
3. It has revealed unexpected complexities in cognition (e.g., language).	3. It minimises the interconnectedness of cognitive processes.
4. It transformed memory research.	4. There has been excessive reliance on single-case studies.
5. It straddles the divide between cognitive psychology and cognitive neuroscience.	5. There is insufficient focus on the brain and its functioning.
Cognitive neuroscience: Functional neuroimaging + ERPs + TMS	
1. Great variety of techniques offering excellent temporal or spatial resolution.	1. Functional neuroimaging techniques provide essentially correlational data.
2. Functional specialisation and brain integration can be studied.	2. Much over-interpretation of data involving reverse inferences.
3. TMS is flexible and permits causal inferences.	3. Most studies are underpowered and there are many false positives.
4. Rich data permit assessment of integrated brain processing as well as specialised functioning.	4. Brain functioning is dauntingly complex.
5. Resolution of complex theoretical issues.	5. Difficulty in relating brain activity to psychological processes.
Computational cognitive science	
1. Theoretical assumptions are spelled out in precise detail.	1. Many computational models do not make new predictions.
2. Comprehensive cognitive architectures have been developed.	2. There is some overfitting, which restricts generalisation to other data sets.
3. Computational models are increasingly used to model effects of brain damage.	3. It is sometimes hard to falsify computational models.
4. Computational cognitive neuroscience is increasingly used to model patterns of brain activity.	4. Computational models generally de-emphasise motivational factors.
5. The emphasis on parallel processing fits well with functional neuroimaging data.	5. Computational models tend to ignore emotional factors.

(e.g., cognitive neuroscience, cognitive neuropsychology) is strongly represented when we cover certain topics but is much less represented with other topics.

OUTLINE OF THIS BOOK

One problem with writing a textbook of cognitive psychology is that virtually all the processes and systems in the cognitive system are interdependent. Consider, for example, a student *reading* a book to prepare for an examination. The student is *learning*, but several other processes are going on as well. *Visual perception* is involved in the intake of information from the printed page, and there is *attention* to the content of the book.

In order for the student to benefit from the book, he/she must possess considerable *language skills*, and must have extensive relevant knowledge stored in *long-term memory*. There may be an element of *problem solving* in the student's attempts to relate the book's content to the possibly conflicting information he/she has learned elsewhere. *Decision making* may also be involved when the student decides how much time to devote to each chapter.

In addition, what the student learns depends on his/her *emotional state*. Finally, the acid test of whether the student's learning has been effective comes during the examination itself, when the material from the book must be *retrieved* and *consciously* evaluated to decide its relevance to the examination question.

The words italicised in the previous paragraphs indicate major ingredients of human cognition and form the basis of our coverage. In view of the *interdependence* of all aspects of the cognitive system, there is an emphasis in this book on how each process (e.g., perception) depends on other processes and structures (e.g., attention, long-term memory). This should aid the task of understanding the complexities of human cognition.

CHAPTER SUMMARY

- **Introduction**. Cognitive psychology used to be unified by an approach based on an analogy between the mind and the computer. This information-processing approach viewed the mind as a general-purpose, symbol-processing system of limited capacity. Today there are four main approaches to human cognition: experimental cognitive psychology; cognitive neuroscience; cognitive neuropsychology; and computational cognitive science. However, the four approaches are increasingly combined with information from behaviour and brain activity being integrated.

- **Cognitive psychology**. Cognitive psychologists assume that top-down and bottom-up processes are both involved in the performance of cognitive tasks. These processes can be serial or parallel. Various methods (e.g., latent-variable analysis) have been used to address the task impurity problem and to identify the processes within cognitive tasks. In spite of the enormous contribution made by cognitive psychology, it sometimes lacks ecological validity, suffers from paradigm specificity and possesses theoretical vagueness.

- **Cognitive neuropsychology**. Cognitive neuropsychology is based on various assumptions including modularity, anatomical modularity, uniformity of functional architecture and subtractivity. Double dissociations provide reasonable (but not definitive) evidence for separate modules or systems. The case-study approach is generally (but not always) more informative than the single-case approach. Cognitive neuropsychology is limited because patients can develop compensatory strategies, because it de-emphasises findings in cognitive neuroscience, because it underestimates integrated brain functioning and because the brain damage is often so extensive it is hard to interpret the findings.

- **Cognitive neuroscience: the brain in action**. Cognitive neuroscientists study the brain as well as behaviour using techniques varying in spatial and temporal resolution. Functional neuroimaging techniques provide basically correlational evidence, but TMS can indicate that a given brain area is necessarily involved in a particular cognitive function. The richness of the data obtained from neuroimaging studies is so great that functional specialisation and brain integration can both be assessed. Cognitive neuroscience is a flexible and potentially self-correcting approach. However, findings are sometimes over-interpreted. More research is needed into possible problems with ecological validity in fMRI studies.

- **Computational cognitive science**. Computational cognitive scientists develop computational models to understand human cognition. Connectionist networks make use of elementary units or nodes connected together. They can learn using rules such as back-propagation. Production systems consist of production or "If . . . then" rules. ACT-R is one of the most developed theories based on production systems. Computational models have increased in scope to provide detailed theoretical accounts of findings from cognitive neuroscience and cognitive neuropsychology. They have shown progress via the use of nested incremental modelling. Computational models are often hard to falsify and they generally de-emphasise motivational and emotional factors.

- **Comparisons of different approaches**. The major approaches are increasingly used in combination. Each approach has its own strengths and limitations, which makes it useful to use converging operations. When two approaches produce the same findings, this is stronger evidence than can be obtained from a single approach on its own. If two approaches produce different findings, this indicates additional research is needed to understand what is happening.

Further reading

- Byrne, M.D. (2012). Unified theories of cognition. *Wiley Interdisciplinary Reviews – Cognitive Science*, 3: 431–8. Several major cognitive architectures are discussed and evaluated.
- Moran, J.M. & Zaki, J. (2013). Functional neuroimaging and psychology: What have you done for me lately? *Journal of Cognitive Neuroscience*, 25: 834–42. Joseph Moran and Jamil Zaki discuss how cognitive neuroscience is enhancing our theoretical understanding of human cognition.
- Patterson, K. & Plaut, D.C. (2009). "Shallow draughts intoxicate the brain": Lessons from cognitive science for cognitive neuropsychology. *Topics in Cognitive Science*, 1: 39–58. This article identifies several key issues with respect to cognitive neuropsychology.
- Shallice, T. & Cooper, R.P. (2011). *The organisation of mind*. Oxford: Oxford University Press. This is an authoritative account of the contributions made by cognitive neuroscience.
- Ward, J. (2010). *The student's guide to cognitive neuroscience* (2nd edn). Hove: Psychology Press. The first five chapters of this textbook provide detailed information about the main techniques used by cognitive neuroscientists.
- White, C.N. & Poldrack, R.A. (2013). Using fMRI to constrain theories of cognition. *Perspectives on Psychological Science*, 8(1): 79–83. Corey White and Russell Poldrack indicate ways in which functional neuroimaging can help to resolve theoretical controversies.
- Wilshire, C. (2014). *Cognitive neuropsychology: Exploring the mind through brain dysfunction*. Hove: Psychology Press. Carolyn Wilshire discusses the ways in which cognitive neuropsychology has enhanced our understanding of human cognition.

PART I

Visual perception and attention

Visual perception is of enormous importance in our everyday lives. It allows us to move around freely, to see people with whom we are interacting, to read magazines and books, to admire the wonders of nature and to watch movies and television. Visual perception is also extremely important in helping to ensure our survival. For example, if we misperceive how close cars are to us as we cross the road, the consequences could be fatal. Thus, it is unsurprising that far more of the cortex (especially the occipital lobes at the back of the brain) is devoted to vision than to any other sensory modality.

We will start by considering what is meant by *perception*: "The acquisition and processing of sensory information in order to see, hear, taste, or feel objects in the world; also guides an organism's actions with respect to those objects" (Sekuler & Blake, 2002, p. 621).

Visual perception seems so simple and effortless we typically take it for granted. In fact, it is very complex and numerous processes transform and interpret sensory information. Some of the complexities of visual perception became clear when researchers in artificial intelligence tried to programme computers to "perceive" the environment. Even when the environment was artificially simplified (e.g., consisting only of white solids) and the task was apparently easy (e.g., deciding how many objects were present), computers required very complicated programming to succeed. It remains the case that no computer can match more than a fraction of the skills of visual perception possessed by nearly every human adult.

There is a rapidly growing literature on visual perception (especially from the cognitive neuroscience perspective). The next three chapters provide reasonably detailed coverage of the main issues. In Chapter 2, our coverage focuses on basic processes involved in visual perception. There is an emphasis on the enormous advances that have been made in understanding the various brain systems involved. It seems commonsensical to assume that the processes leading to object recognition also guide vision-for-action. However, we will see that that assumption is oversimplified. Finally, Chapter 2 contains a detailed consideration of important aspects of visual perception such as colour perception, perception without awareness and depth perception.

A major achievement of perceptual processing is object recognition, which involves identifying objects in the world around us. The central focus of Chapter 3 is on the processes underlying this achievement. Initially, we discuss perceptual organisation, and how we decide which parts of the visual input belong together and so form an object. We then move on to theories of object recognition, including a discussion of the relevant behavioural and neuroscience evidence.

Are the same recognition processes used regardless of the type of object? This issue remains controversial. However, most (but by no means all) experts agree that face recognition differs in important ways from ordinary object recognition. Accordingly, face recognition is discussed separately from the recognition of other objects.

The final part of Chapter 3 is devoted to another major controversial issue, namely, whether the main processes involved in visual imagery are the same as those involved in visual perception. As we will see, there are good grounds for arguing that this controversy has largely been resolved (turn to Chapter 3 to find out how!).

The central focus of Chapter 4 is on how we process a constantly changing environment and manage to respond appropriately to those changes. Of major importance here is our ability to predict the speed and direction of objects and to move in the direction we want whether walking or driving. The ability to reach for and grasp objects is also important. Humans are also skilled at the more complex task of making sense of the movements of other people, and this is another topic discussed in Chapter 4.

There are clearly important links between visual perception and attention. The final topic discussed in Chapter 4 is concerned with the notion that we may need to *attend* to an object to perceive it consciously. Failures of attention can prevent us from noticing changes in objects or the presence of an unexpected object.

Issues relating directly to attention are considered in detail in Chapter 5. In that chapter, we start with the processes involved in focused attention in the visual and auditory modalities. After that, we consider how we use visual processes when engaged in the everyday task of searching for some object (e.g., a pair of socks in a drawer). There has been a large increase in the amount of research concerned with disorders of visual attention, and this research has greatly increased our understanding of visual attention in healthy individuals. Finally, as we all know to our cost, it can be very hard to do two things at once. We conclude Chapter 5 by considering the factors determining the extent to which we do this successfully.

In sum, the area spanning visual perception and attention is among the most exciting and important within cognitive psychology and cognitive neuroscience. There has been tremendous progress in unravelling the complexities of perception and attention over the past decade. Some of the choicest fruits of that endeavour are set before you in the four chapters forming this section of the book.

CHAPTER

2

Basic processes in visual perception

INTRODUCTION

Much progress has been made in understanding visual perception in recent years. Much of this is due to the efforts of cognitive neuroscientists, thanks to whom we now have a good knowledge of the brain systems involved in visual perception. We start by considering the main brain areas involved in vision and the functions served by each area. This is followed by a discussion of theories of brain systems in vision. After that, there is a detailed analysis of basic aspects of visual perception (e.g., colour perception, depth perception). Finally, we consider the issue of whether perception can occur in the absence of conscious awareness.

Chapter 3 focuses mostly on the various processes involved in object and face recognition. In the interests of clarity, we generally deal with a single aspect of visual perception in any given section. In fact, however, all the processes involved in visual perception interact with each other.

The specific visual processes we use depend very much on what we are looking at and our perceptual goals (Hegdé, 2008). For example, we can sometimes perceive the gist of a natural scene extremely rapidly (Thorpe et al., 1996). Observers saw photographs, some of which contained an animal, for only 20 ms. EEG recordings (see Glossary) indicated the presence of an animal was detected within about 150 ms.

In contrast, look at the photograph shown in Figure 2.1 and decide how many animals are present. It probably took you several seconds to perform this task. Bear in mind the diversity of visual perception as you read this and the two following chapters.

VISION AND THE BRAIN

In this section, we consider the brain systems involved in visual perception. Much of the posterior (back) half of the cortex is devoted to vision, and visual processing occurs in approximately 25 distinct brain areas (Felleman & Van Essen, 1991). More specifically, the visual cortex consists of the whole of the occipital cortex at the back of the brain and also extends well into the temporal and parietal lobes. However, to understand fully visual processing in the brain, we need first to

Figure 2.1
Complex scene that requires prolonged perceptual processing to understand fully. Study the picture and identify the animals within it.

Reprinted from Hegdé (2008). Reprinted with permission of Elsevier.

consider briefly what happens between the eye and the cortex. Accordingly, we start with that before moving on to visual processing in the cortex.

From eye to cortex

Weblink:
Structure of the eye

There are two types of visual receptor cells in the retina of the eye: cones and rods. Cones are used for colour vision and sharpness of vision (see later section on colour vision). There are 125 million rods concentrated in the outer regions of the retina. Rods are specialised for vision in dim light. Many differences between cones and rods stem from the fact that a **retinal ganglion cell** receives input from only a few cones but from hundreds of rods. Thus, only rods produce much activity in retinal ganglion cells in poor lighting conditions.

The main pathway between the eye and the cortex is the retina-geniculate-striate pathway. It transmits information from the retina to V1 and then V2 (both discussed shortly) via the lateral geniculate nuclei of the thalamus. The entire retina-geniculate-striate system is organised similarly to the retinal system. For example, two stimuli adjacent to each other in the retinal image will also be adjacent at higher levels within that system. The technical term is **retinopy**: retinal receptor cells are mapped to points on the surface of the visual cortex.

KEY TERMS

Retinal ganglion cells
Retinal cells providing the output signal from the retina.

Retinopy
The notion that there is mapping between receptor cells in the retina and points on the surface of the visual cortex.

Each eye has its own optic nerve, and the two optic nerves meet at the optic chiasma. At this point, the axons from the outer halves of each retina proceed to the hemisphere on the same side, whereas those from the inner halves cross over and go to the other hemisphere. As a result, each side of visual space is represented within the opposite brain hemisphere. Signals then proceed along two optic tracts within the brain. One tract contains signals from the left half of each eye, and the other signals from the right half (see Figure 2.2).

After the optic chiasma, the optic tract proceeds to the lateral geniculate nucleus (LGN), which is part of the thalamus. Nerve impulses finally reach V1 in primary visual cortex within the occipital lobe at the back of the head before spreading out to nearby visual cortical areas such as V2.

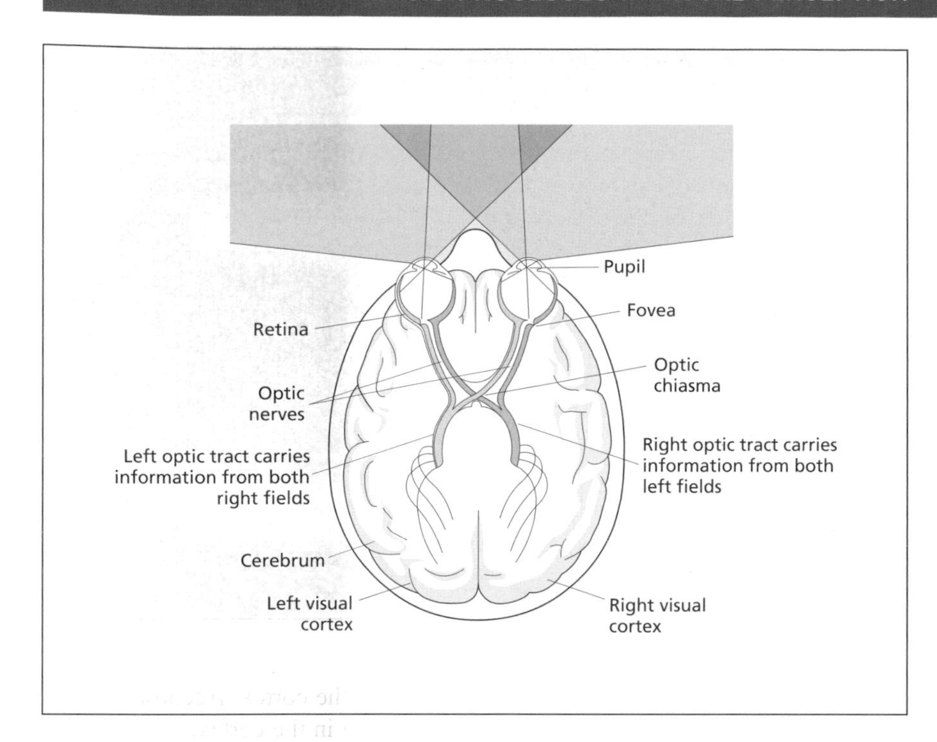

Figure 2.2
Route of visual signals. Note that signals reaching the left visual cortex come from the left sides of the two retinas, and signals reaching the right visual cortex come from the right sides of the two retinas.

There are two relatively independent channels or pathways within the retina-geniculate-striate system:

1 The parvocellular (or P) pathway: it is most sensitive to colour and to fine detail; most of its input comes from cones.
2 The magnocellular (or M) pathway: it is most sensitive information about movement; most of its input comes from rods.

As stated above, these two pathways are only *relatively* independent. In fact, there are numerous interconnections between them, and it is becoming increasingly apparent that the visual system is extremely complex (Wade & Swanston, 2013). For example, there is clear intermingling of the two pathways in V1 (Nassi & Callaway, 2009; Leopold, 2012). Finally, it should be mentioned there is also a Koniocellular pathway, but its functions are still not well understood.

Brain systems

As we have just seen, neurons from the P and M pathways mainly project to V1 in the primary visual cortex. What happens after V1? The answer is given in Figure 2.3. In order to understand this Figure, note that V3 is generally assumed to be involved in form processing, V4 in colour processing and V5/MT in motion processing (all discussed in more detail shortly). The P pathway associates with the ventral or "what" pathway that proceeds to the inferotemporal cortex. In contrast, the M pathway associates with the dorsal or "how" pathway (previously described as the "where" pathway) that proceeds to the posterior parietal cortex. The assertions in the last two sentences are very approximate reflections of a complex reality. For example, some parvocellular neurons project into dorsal visual areas (Parker, 2007).

KEY TERMS

Receptive field
The region of the retina in which light influences the activity of a particular neuron.

Lateral inhibition
Reduction of activity in one neuron caused by activity in a neighbouring neuron.

We will consider the P and M pathways in more detail later. For now, bear three points in mind:

1. The ventral or "what" pathway culminating in the inferotemporal cortex is mainly concerned with form and colour processing and with object recognition (see Chapter 3). In contrast, the dorsal or "how" pathway culminating in the parietal cortex is more concerned with movement processing.
2. There is no rigid distinction between the types of information processed by the two streams. For example, Gilaie-Dotan et al. (2013b) studied patients with brain damage limited to the ventral or "what" pathway. These patients had widespread impairments in motion perception even though visual motion perception is primarily associated with the dorsal or "how" pathway.
3. The two pathways are *not* totally segregated. There are numerous interconnections between the ventral and dorsal pathways or streams (Felleman & Van Essen, 1991; Pisella et al., 2009). For example, both streams project to the primary motor cortex (Rossetti & Pisella, 2002).

As already indicated, Figure 2.3 provides only a rough sketchmap of visual processing in the brain. A more complex picture is presented in Figure 2.4, which reveals three important points. First, the interconnections among the various visual cortical areas are complicated. Second, the brain areas within the ventral pathway or stream are more than twice as large as those within the dorsal pathway. Third, cells in the lateral geniculate nucleus respond fastest when a visual stimulus is presented followed by activation of cells in V1. However, cells are activated in several other areas (V3/V3A, MT, MST) very shortly thereafter.

Finally, note that Figure 2.3 is limited in other important ways. Kravitz et al. (2013) proposed a contemporary account of the ventral pathway (Figure 2.5). The traditional view was that the ventral pathway involved a serial hierarchy proceeding from simple to complex. In contrast, Kravitz argued that the ventral pathway actually consists of several overlapping recurrent networks. Of key importance, there are connections in both directions between the components of the networks.

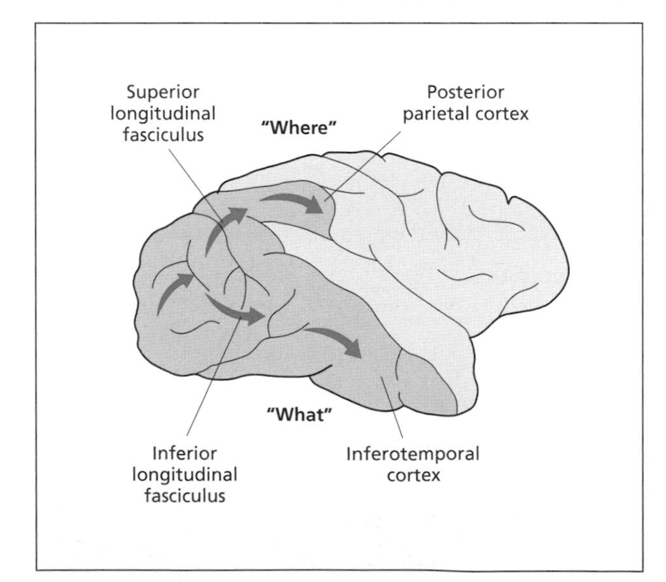

Figure 2.3
The ventral (what) and dorsal (where or how) pathways involved in vision have their origins in primary visual cortex (V1).
From Gazzaniga et al. (2008). Copyright © 2009, 2002, 1998. Used by permission of W.W. Norton & Company, Inc.

V1 and V2

We start with three general points. First, to understand visual processing in primary visual cortex (V1; also described as BA17) and secondary visual cortex (V2; also described as BA18), we must consider the notion of **receptive field**. The receptive field for any given neuron is that region of the retina in which light affects its activity. Receptive field can also refer to visual space because it is mapped in a one-to-one manner on to the retinal surface.

Second, neurons often influence each other. For example, there is **lateral inhibition**, in which a reduction of activity in one neuron is caused by

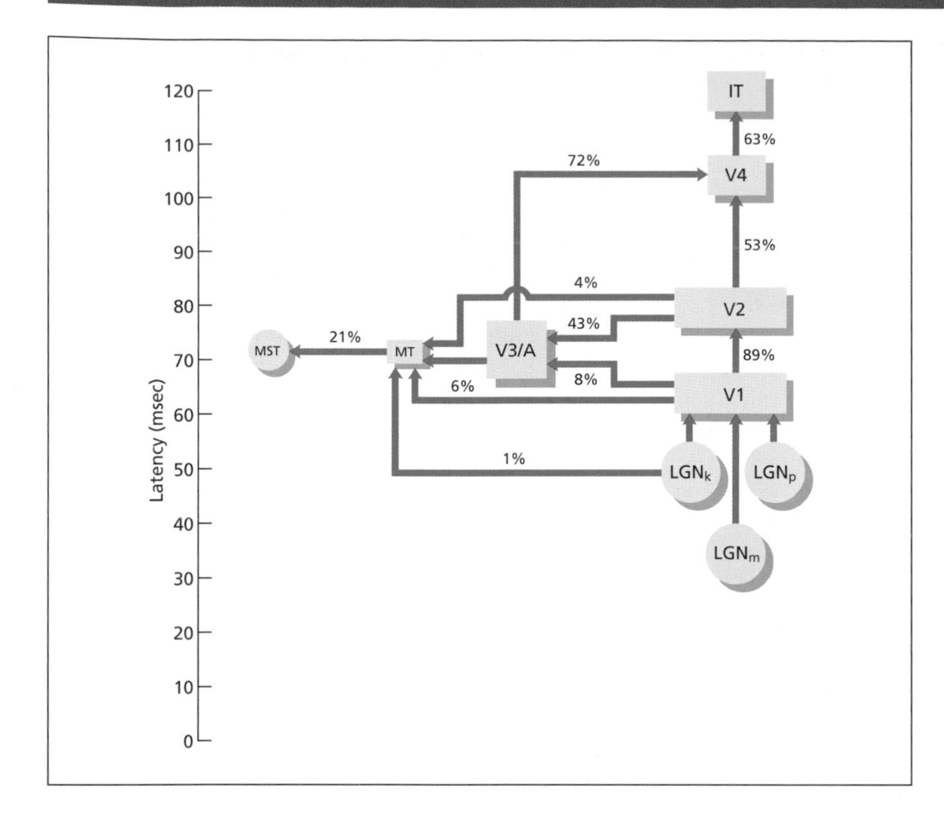

Weblink:
The visual cortex

Figure 2.4
Some distinctive features of the largest visual cortical areas. The relative size of the boxes reflects the relative area of different regions. The arrows labelled with percentages show the proportion of fibres in each projection pathway. The vertical position of each box represents the response latency of cells in each area, as measured in single-unit recording studies. IT = inferotemporal cortex; MT = medial or middle temporal cortex; MST = medial superior temporal cortex. All areas are discussed in detail in the text.
From Mather (2009). Copyright © 2009 George Mather. Reproduced with permission.

activity in a neighbouring neuron. Lateral inhibition is useful because it increases the contrast at the edges of objects, making it easier to identify the dividing line between objects. The phenomenon of simultaneous contrast depends on lateral inhibition (see Figure 2.6). The two central squares are physically identical but the one on the left appears lighter than the one on the right. This difference is due to simultaneous contrast produced because the left surround is much darker than the right surround.

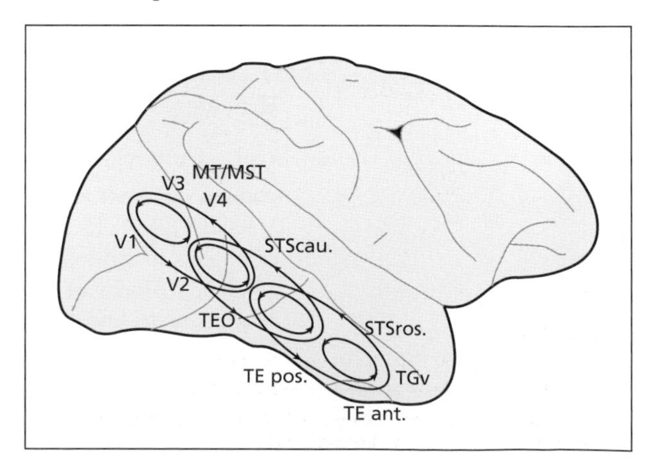

Figure 2.5
Connectivity within the ventral pathway on the lateral surface of the macaque brain. Brain areas involved include V1, V2, V3, V4, the middle temporal (MT)/medial superior temporal (MST) complex, the superior temporal sulcus (STS) and the inferior temporal cortex (TE).
From Kravitz et al. (2013). Reprinted with permission of Elsevier.

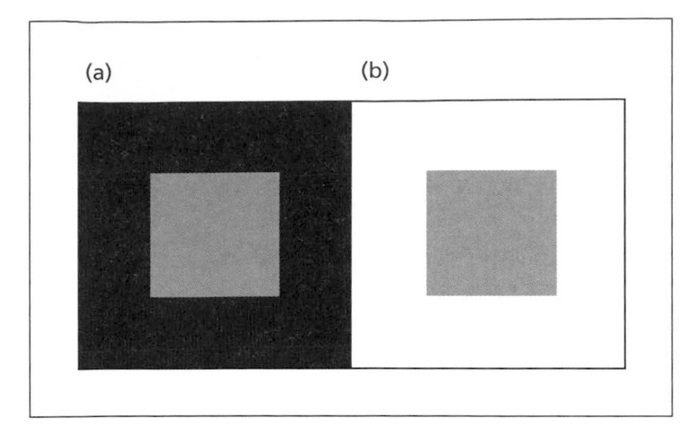

Figure 2.6
The square on the right looks darker than the identical square on the left because of simultaneous contrast involving lateral inhibition.
From Lehar (2008). Reproduced with permission of the author.

Third, the primary visual cortex (V1) and secondary visual cortex (V2) occupy relatively large areas (see Figure 2.4). Early visual processing in these areas is fairly extensive. Hegdé and Van Essen (2000) found in macaques that one-third of V2 cells responded to complex shapes and to differences in orientation and size.

V1 and V2 are both involved in the early stages of visual processing. However, that is not the complete story. There is an initial "feedforward sweep" proceeding through the visual areas starting with V1 and then V2. In addition, there is a second phase of processing (recurrent processing) in which processing proceeds in the opposite direction (Lamme, 2006). Some recurrent processing can occur in V1 within 120 ms of stimulus onset. Boehler et al. (2008) found greater visual awareness of the stimulus when recurrent processing was strongly present (see Chapter 16).

Functional specialisation

Zeki (1993, 2001) put forward a functional specialisation theory. According to this theory, different cortical areas are specialised for different visual functions. The visual system resembles a team of workers, each working on his/her own to solve part of a complex problem. The results of their labours are then combined to produce the solution (i.e., coherent visual perception).

Why might there be functional specialisation in the visual brain? Zeki (2005) suggested two reasons. First, object attributes occur in unpredictable combinations. For example, a green object may be a car, a sheet of paper or a leaf, and a car may be red, black or green. Thus, we must often process *all* an object's attributes to perceive it accurately.

Second, the required processing differs considerably across attributes. For example, motion processing involves integrating information from two or more points in *time*. In contrast, form or shape processing involves considering the *spatial* relationship of elements to each other at one point in time.

The organisation of the main visual areas in the macaque monkey is shown in Figure 2.7. The organisation of the human visual system closely resembles that of the macaque and so reference is often made to human V1, V2 and so on.

Here are the main functions Zeki (1993, 2005) ascribed to these areas:

- V1 and V2: They are involved at an early stage of visual processing; they contain different groups of cells responsive to colour and form.
- V3 and V3A: Cells in these areas are responsive to form (especially the shapes of objects in motion) but not colour.
- V4: The majority of cells in this area are responsive to colour; many are also responsive to line orientation.
- V5: This area is specialised for visual motion. In studies with macaque monkeys, Zeki found all the cells in this area were responsive to motion but not colour. In humans, the areas specialised for visual motion are referred to as MT and MST.

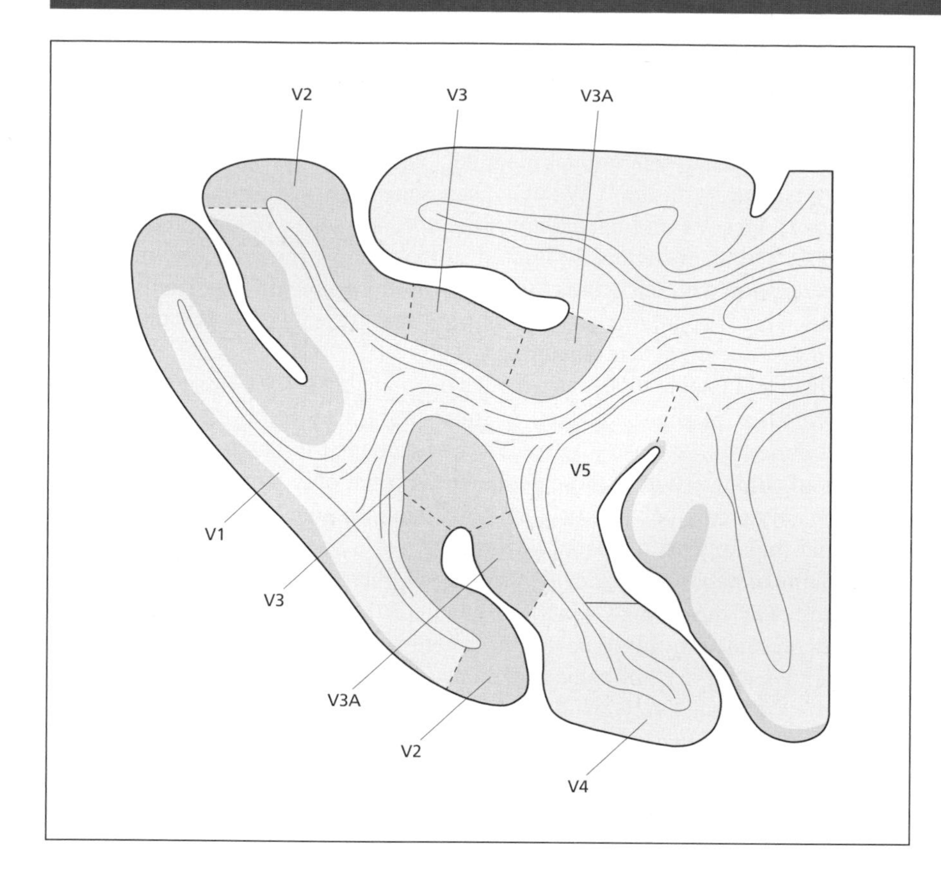

Figure 2.7
A cross-section of the visual cortex of the macaque monkey.

From Zeki (1992). Reproduced with permission from Carol Donner.

Zeki assumed that colour, form and motion are processed in anatomically separate parts of the visual cortex. Much of the original evidence came from studies on monkeys. Relevant human evidence is considered below.

Form processing

Several areas are involved in form processing in humans, including areas V1, V2, V3 and V4 and culminating in inferotemporal cortex (Kourtzi & Connor, 2011). There is evidence that neurons in inferotemporal cortex respond to specific semantic categories (e.g., animals, body parts; see Chapter 3). There is also strong evidence that neurons in inferotemporal cortex are involved in form processing. In one study (Yamane et al., 2008), neurons within inferotemporal cortex responded to three-dimensional object shape. Baldassi et al. (2013) measured neuronal activity within anterior inferotemporal cortex in two monkeys. Many neurons responded on the basis of aspects of form or shape (round, star-like, horizontal thin, pointy, vertical thin) rather than object category.

If form processing occurs in different brain areas from colour and motion processing, we might anticipate some patients would have severely impaired form processing but intact colour and motion processing. That does *not* seem to be the case. According to Zeki (1991), a lesion large enough to destroy areas V3, V4 and inferotemporal cortex would probably destroy area V1 as well. As a result, the patient would suffer from total blindness rather than simply loss of form perception.

KEY TERMS

Achromatopsia
A condition involving brain damage in which there is little or no colour perception but form and motion perception are relatively intact.

Akinetopsia
A brain-damaged condition in which motion perception is severely impaired even though stationary objects are perceived reasonably well.

Colour processing

The assumption that V4 is specialised for colour processing has been tested in several ways. These include studying brain-damaged patients; using brain-imaging techniques; and using transcranial magnetic stimulation (TMS; see Glossary) to produce a temporary "lesion". We will discuss these three kinds of studies in turn.

Suppose area V4 and related areas are specialised for colour processing. If so, patients with damage mostly limited to those areas should show little or no colour perception with fairly intact form and motion perception and ability to see fine detail. This is approximately the case in some patients with **achromatopsia** (also known as cerebral achromatopsia).

Bouvier and Engel (2006) carried out a meta-analysis (see Glossary) involving all known cases of achromatopsia. A small brain area within ventral (bottom) occipital cortex in (or close to) area V4 was damaged in nearly all these cases. The loss of colour vision in these patients was often only partial, suggesting V4 is not the only area involved in colour processing. In addition, most patients had significant impairments of spatial vision.

Functional neuroimaging evidence that V4 plays an important role in colour processing was reported by Goddard et al. (2011). Observers viewed movie segments presented in full or no colour. There was substantially more activation in ventral V4 with the full-colour segments. Wade et al. (2002) had previously found area V4 was actively involved in colour processing but other areas (V1 and V2) were also activated.

Banissy et al. (2012) found that performing a task on a stimulus (diamond shape) was faster when preceded by a prime in the same colour. However, this priming effect was no longer present when transcranial magnetic stimulation (TMS) was administered to V4. This finding occurred because TMS reduced colour processing in V4.

In sum, area V4 and adjacent areas are undoubtedly involved in colour processing. However, V4 is *not* a "colour centre". First, V4 is a relatively large area involved in spatial processing, shape processing and depth perception, as well as colour processing (Roe et al., 2012). Second, some ability to process colour is present in most individuals with achromatopsia and monkeys with lesions to V4 (Heywood & Cowey, 1999). Third, several areas outside V4 (including V1 and V2) are also involved in colour processing.

Motion processing

Area V5 (also known as motion processing area MT) is heavily involved in motion processing. Functional neuroimaging studies indicate motion processing is *associated* with activity in V5 (or MT) but do not show that V5 (or MT) is *necessary* for motion perception. This issue was addressed by McKeefry et al. (2008), who used transcranial magnetic stimulation (TMS; see Glossary) to disrupt motion perception. When TMS was applied to V5/MT, it produced a subjective slowing of stimulus speed and impaired observers' ability to discriminate between different speeds.

Additional evidence that area V5/MT is important in motion processing comes from research on patients with **akinetopsia**. Akinetopsia is a condition in which stationary objects are perceived fairly normally but motion perception is grossly deficient. Zihl et al. (1983) studied LM, a woman with akinetopsia who had suffered bilateral damage to the motion area (V5/MT). She could locate stationary objects by sight, had good colour discrimination and her binocular vision was normal. However, her motion perception was grossly deficient:

> She had difficulty . . . in pouring tea or coffee into a cup because the fluid appeared to be frozen, like a glacier. In addition, she could not stop pouring at the right time since she was unable to perceive the movement in the cup (or a pot) when the fluid rose . . . In a room where more than two people were walking, . . . "people were suddenly here or there but I have not seen them moving".
>
> (p. 315)

S.A. Cooper et al. (2012) reported the case of a 61-year-old with akinetopsia. She perceived static objects normally, but smooth movements of people were seen as "freeze frames". People close to the opening of a train door appeared to "move in slow motion".

V5 (MT) is not the only area involved in motion processing. There is also area MST (medial superior temporal), which is adjacent to and just above V5/MT. Vaina (1998) studied two patients with damage to MST. Both patients performed normally on some tests of motion perception, but had various problems relating to motion perception. One patient, RR, "frequently bumped into people, corners and things in his way, particularly into moving targets (e.g., people walking)" (Vaina, 1998, p. 498). These findings suggest MST is involved in the visual guidance of walking.

There is an important distinction between first-order and second-order motion. With first-order displays, the moving shape differs in luminance (intensity of reflected light) from its background. For example, the shape might be dark whereas the background is light. With second-order displays, there is no difference in luminance between the moving shape and the background. In everyday life, we encounter second-order displays infrequently (e.g., movement of grass in a field caused by the wind).

There is an ongoing controversy as to whether different mechanisms underlie the perception of first-order and second-order motion. Evidence that different mechanisms are involved was reported by Ashida et al. (2007). Repeated presentation of first-order displays led to a substantial reduction in activation in motion areas MT and MST. This adaptation occurred because many of the same neurons were activated by each display. Very similar reductions in activation in the motion areas occurred with repeated presentations of second-order displays. However, there was *no* evidence of adaptation in MT and MST when first-order displays were followed by second-order displays or vice versa. The implication is the two display types activated *different* sets of neurons and thus probably involved different processes.

Support for the notion of different mechanisms for perception of first-order and second-order motion was also reported by Rizzo et al. (2008). They identified 22 patients with a deficit in perception of first-order but not second-order motion, and one patient with a deficit only in perception of second-order motion. This double dissociation suggests different processes are involved in perception of the two types of motion.

However, some evidence suggests first-order and second-order motion perception depend on the same mechanisms. Hong et al. (2012) found direction-

KEY TERM

Binding problem
The issue of integrating different types of information to produce coherent visual perception.

selective responses to both types of motion in several brain areas (V1, V2, V3, V3A, V4 and MT+). These findings suggest none of these areas is specialised for processing only one type of motion. More importantly, the patterns of activation associated with the perception of first- and second-order motion were similar.

Further support for the same-mechanism assumption was reported by Cowey et al. (2006). They disrupted activity in V2/V3 or V5/MT+ via transcranial magnetic stimulation (TMS; see Glossary) and found this led to impairments in the perception of first-order and second-order motion.

How can we reconcile the various findings? First- and second-order motion perception probably depend on similar (but not identical) underlying mechanisms. That assumption provides a potential explanation for the apparently inconsistent findings in this area.

Binding problem

Zeki's functional specialisation approach poses the obvious problem of how information about an object's motion, colour and form is combined and integrated to produce coherent perception. This is the famous **binding problem**, which concerns "how items that are encoded by distinct brain circuits can be combined for perception, decision, and action" (Feldman, 2013, p. 1).

One approach to the binding problem is to argue there is less functional specialisation than Zeki claimed, which would reduce the complexity of the problem. For example, Seymour et al. (2009) presented observers with red or green dots that rotated clockwise or counterclockwise. Assessment of brain activity indicated colour-motion conjunctions were processed in several brain areas including V1, V2, V3, V3A/B, V4 and V5/MT+. Thus, there is extensive binding of colour and motion information even early in processing.

Feldman (2013) argued that there are actually several binding problems. There is the problem of how visual features are bound together. Another problem is how we bind together information over successive eye movements to achieve the subjective perception of a stable visual world. Within the above broader context, it is clear that many different lines of research are relevant. For example, observers need to work out which parts of the visual information available at any given time belong to the same object. The Gestaltists put forward several laws to account for how observers do this (see Chapter 3). Research on selective attention, especially research on visual search (detecting target stimuli among distractors), is also relevant (see Chapter 5). This research shows the important role of selective attention in combining features close together in time and space.

One approach to solving the binding problem is the binding-by-synchrony hypothesis (e.g., Singer & Gray, 1995). According to this hypothesis, detectors responding to features of a single object fire in *synchrony* whereas detectors responding to features of separate objects do not. Of relevance, widespread synchronisation of neural activity is associated with conscious visual awareness (e.g., Melloni et al., 2007; Gaillard et al., 2009).

The synchrony hypothesis is oversimplified. Visual processing of an object occurs in widely distributed areas of the brain and proceeds through several stages. This makes it implausible precise synchrony could be achieved. Another problem is that two or more objects are often presented at the same time. On the synchrony hypothesis, it would seem hard to keep the processing of these objects separate.

Guttman et al. (2007) suggested an alternative hypothesis based on the notion that perception depends on *patterns* of neural activity over time rather than on precise synchrony.

In sum, there are several binding problems, most of which are hard to solve (Feldman, 2013). However, progress has been made. Selective attention undoubtedly plays an important role. Feature binding is typically associated with synchronised activity in different brain areas, but the association is often imprecise. There is also the issue of explaining *why* and *how* synchronised activity occurs.

Evaluation

Zeki's functional specialisation theory has deservedly been influential. It is an ambitious attempt to provide a simple theoretical framework within which to understand a remarkably complex reality. As is discussed later, Zeki's assumption that motion processing typically proceeds somewhat independently of other types of visual processing has received reasonable support.

There are three main limitations with Zeki's theoretical approach. First, the brain areas involved in visual processing are less specialised than implied by the theory. Heywood and Cowey (1999) considered the percentage of cells in each visual cortical area responding selectively to various stimulus characteristics (see Figure 2.8). Cells in several areas respond to orientation, disparity and colour. Specialisation was found only with respect to responsiveness to direction of stimulus motion in MT.

Second, early visual processing in areas V1 and V2 is more extensive than suggested by Zeki. As we saw earlier, Hegdé and Van Essen (2000) found many V2 cells responded to complex shapes.

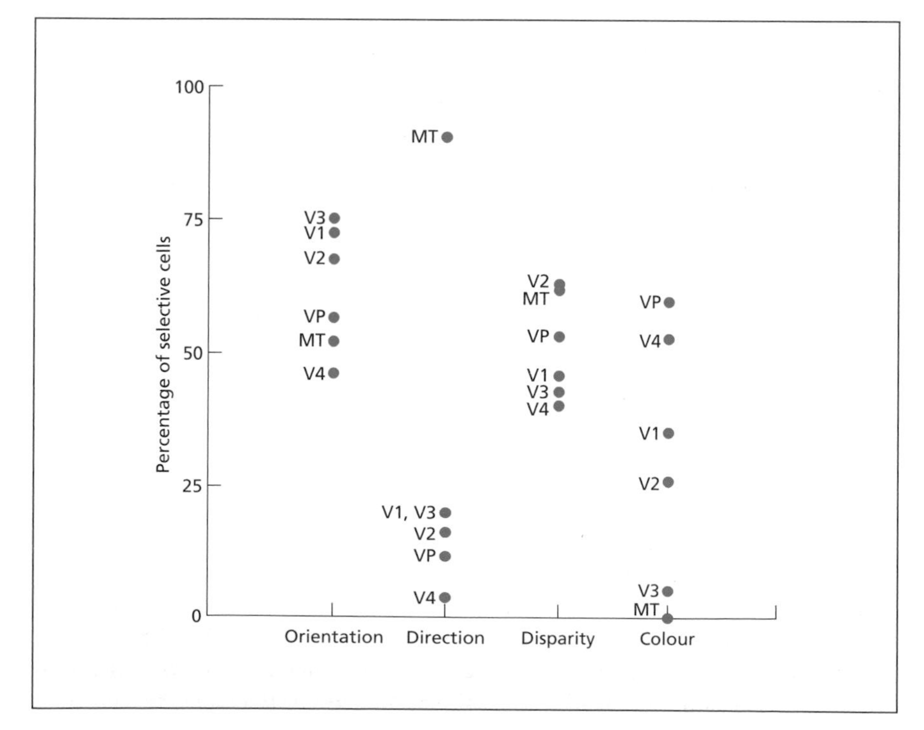

Figure 2.8
The percentage of cells in six different visual cortical areas responding selectively to orientation, direction of motion, disparity and colour.
From Heywood and Cowey (1999).

Third, Zeki and his colleagues have not as yet solved the binding problem. In fairness, there are probably several binding problems and no one has solved them. However, it appears that selective attention is of major importance (Feldman, 2013).

TWO VISUAL SYSTEMS: PERCEPTION AND ACTION

Here is a fundamental question in vision research: what are the major functions of the visual system? Historically, the most popular answer was that the visual system provides us with an internal (and typically conscious) representation of the world outside.

Milner and Goodale (e.g., 1995, 2008) argued that there are two visual systems, each fulfilling a different function or purpose. Their theoretical views represent the development of previous accounts (e.g., Bridgeman et al., 1979). First, there is the vision-for-perception (or "what") system based on the **ventral stream** or pathway (see Figures 2.3 and 2.5). This is the one we immediately think of when considering visual perception. It is the system we use when deciding whether the object in front of us is a cat or a buffalo or when admiring a magnificent landscape. Thus, it is used to identify objects.

Second, there is the vision-for-action (or "how") system based on the **dorsal stream** or pathway (see Figure 2.3), which is used for visually guided action. It is used when running to return a ball at tennis. It is also the system used when grasping an object. When we grasp an object, it is important we calculate its orientation and position with respect to ourselves. Since observers and objects often move relative to each other, orientation and position need to be worked out immediately prior to initiating a movement.

The key differences between these two systems were summarised by Milner (2012, p. 2289):

> The dorsal stream's principal role is to provide real-time "bottom-up" visual guidance of our movements online. In contrast, the ventral steam, in conjunction with top-down information from visual and semantic memory provides perceptual representations that can serve recognition, visual thought, planning and memory.

Schenk and McIntosh (2010) identified *four* core characteristics of the above two processing streams:

1 The ventral stream underlies vision-for-perception whereas the dorsal stream underlines vision-for-action.
2 Coding in the ventral stream is **allocentric** (object-centred; independent of the observer's perspective), whereas dorsal coding is **egocentric** (body-centred; dependent on the observer's perspective).
3 Representations in the ventral stream are sustained over time whereas those in the dorsal stream are short-lasting.
4 Processing in the ventral stream typically (but by no means always) leads to conscious awareness, whereas processing in the dorsal stream does not.

KEY TERMS

Ventral stream
The part of the visual processing system involved in object perception and recognition and the formation of perceptual representations.

Dorsal stream
The part of the visual processing system most involved in visually guided action.

Allocentric coding
Visual coding that is independent of the observer's perspective.

Egocentric coding
Visual coding that is dependent on the observer's perspective.

Finally, there are two other differences assumed theoretically between the two visual systems. First, processing in the dorsal stream is *faster* than in the ventral stream. Second, processing in the ventral stream depends more on input from the fovea (the central part of the retina used for detecting detail) than does dorsal processing.

KEY TERM

Optic ataxia
A condition in which there are problems with making visually guided movements in spite of reasonably intact visual perception.

Findings: brain-damaged patients

Milner and Goodale's theory can be tested by studying brain-damaged patients. Patients with damage to the dorsal pathway should have reasonably intact vision-for-perception but severely impaired vision-for-action. The opposite pattern of intact vision-for-action but very poor vision-for-perception should be found in patients with damage to the ventral pathway. Thus, there should be a double dissociation (see Glossary).

Of relevance to the theory are patients with **optic ataxia**, who have damage to the posterior parietal cortex (see Figure 2.9). Patients with optic ataxia are poor at making precise visually guided movements in spite of the fact that their vision and ability to move their arms are essentially intact. Perenin and Vighetto (1988) found patients with optic ataxia had great difficulty in rotating their hands appropriately when reaching towards (and into) a large oriented slot in front of them. These findings fit with the theory, because damage to the dorsal stream should impair visually guided action.

Patients with optic ataxia do not all conform to the simple picture described in the previous paragraph. First, somewhat different regions of posterior parietal cortex are associated with reaching and grasping movements (Vesia & Crawford, 2012) and some patients have greater problems with one type of movement than the other.

Second, some optic ataxia patients do not have severe problems with all aspects of visually guided actions. For example, Jakobson et al. (1991) studied a female patient, VK, who had difficulty in grasping objects even though her *initial* action planning was essentially intact.

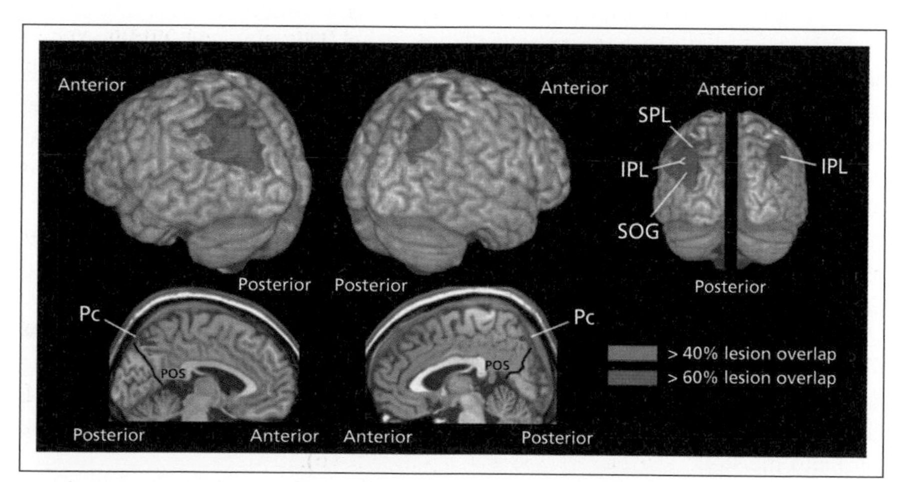

Figure 2.9
Lesion overlap (purple = > 40% overlap; orange = > 60% overlap) in patients with optic ataxia. SPL = superior parietal lobule; IPL = inferior parietal lobule; SOG = superior occipital gyrus; Pc = precuneus.

From Vesia and Crawford (2012). Reprinted with permission of Springer.

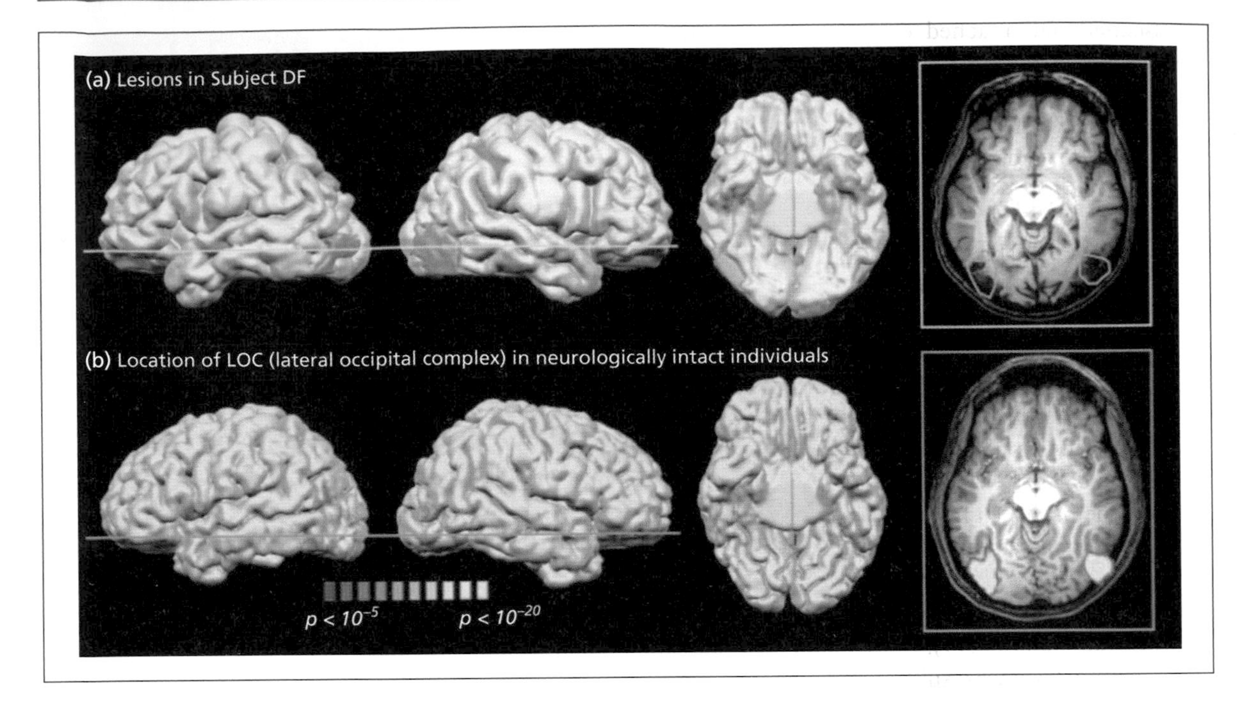

Figure 2.10
(a) damage to DF's lateral occipital complex within the ventral stream is shown in pale blue; (b) location of the lateral occipital complex in healthy individuals.

From James et al. (2003). Reprinted with permission of Oxford University Press.

Third, Pisella et al. (2009) argued that the notion that patients with optic ataxia have intact visual perception but impaired visually guided actions is oversimplified. When patients had access to visual feedback from their own hand, they only had severe problems with visually guided action in *peripheral* vision. There was much less evidence for impaired visually guided action in *central* vision, which is consistent with evidence indicating that many optic ataxics can drive effectively.

What about patients with damage to the ventral stream only? Of relevance here are some patients with **visual form agnosia**, a condition involving severe problems with object recognition even though visual information reaches the visual cortex (see Chapter 3). Probably the most-studied visual form agnosic is DF. James et al. (2003) found her brain damage was in the ventral pathway or stream (see Figure 2.10). DF showed no greater activation in the ventral stream when presented with drawings of objects than with scrambled line drawings. However, she showed high levels of activation in the dorsal stream when grasping for objects.

In spite of having reasonable visual acuity, DF could not identify any drawings of common objects. However, DF "could accurately reach out and grasp a pencil orientated at different angles" (Milner et al., 1991, p. 424).

In another study (Goodale & Milner, 1992), DF held a card in her hand and looked at a circular block into which a slot had been cut. She could not orient the card so it would fit into the slot, suggesting she had very poor perceptual skills. However, DF performed well when moving her hand forward and inserting the card into the slot.

Dijkerman et al. (1998) assessed DF's performance on various tasks when presented with several differently coloured objects. There were two main findings. First, DF could not distinguish accurately between the coloured objects, suggesting problems with object recognition due to damage to the ventral stream.

KEY TERM

Visual form agnosia
A condition in which there are severe problems in shape perception (what an object is) but reasonable ability to produce accurate visually guided actions.

Second, DF reached out and touched the objects as accurately as healthy individuals using information about their positions relative to her own body. This suggests her ability to use visual information to guide action using the dorsal stream was largely intact.

Goodale et al. (1994) gave DF two tasks. One involved distinguishing between two shapes with irregular contours and the other involved grasping these shapes firmly between thumb and index finger. DF performed very poorly on the former task that involved visual perception. However, Goodale et al. concluded that DF "had no difficulty in placing her fingers on appropriate opposition points during grasping" (p. 604).

Himmelbach et al. (2012) argued that this conclusion is unwarranted. They reanalysed DF's performance based on the data in Goodale et al. (1994) and compared it against that of 20 healthy controls (see Figure 2.11). DF's performance on the grasping task was substantially inferior to that of the controls. Similar findings were obtained when DF's performance on other grasping and reaching tasks was compared against that of controls. Thus, DF has greater difficulties in visually guided action than was previously thought.

Figure 2.11
Percentage of errors made when discriminating and grasping irregular shapes by DF (open circles) and by healthy controls (filled diamonds).

From Himmelbach et al. (2012). Reprinted with permission of Elsevier.

In sum, there are fascinating (and theoretically important) differences in visual perception and visually guided action between patients with visual form agnosia and those with optic ataxia. However, the picture is not neat and tidy. Both types of patients have problems with visual perception *and* with visually guided action. That complicates the task of making coherent sense of the findings.

Interactive exercise:
Müller-Lyer

Visual illusions

There have been hundreds of studies of visual illusions. The Müller–Lyer illusion (see Figure 2.12) is one of the most famous. The vertical line on the left looks longer than the one on the right. In fact, however, they are the same length as can be confirmed by using a ruler!

Another well-known illusion is the Ebbinghaus illusion (see Figure 2.13). In this illusion, the central circle surrounded by smaller circles looks smaller than a central circle of the same size surrounded by larger circles. In fact, the two central circles are the *same* size.

There are numerous other visual illusions. Their existence provides us with an intriguing paradox. How has the human species been so successful given that our visual perceptual processes are apparently very prone to error?

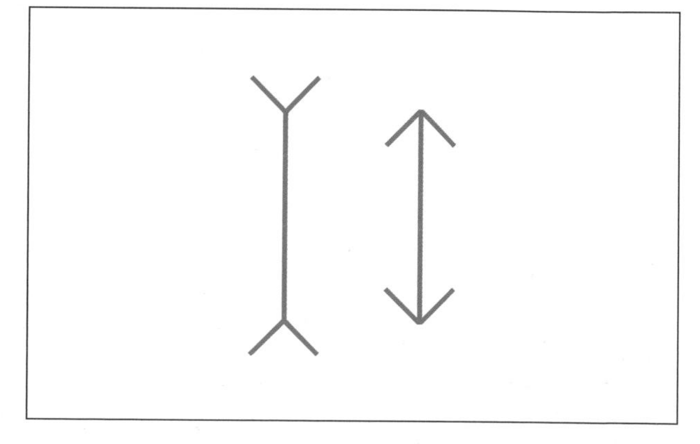

Figure 2.12
The Müller–Lyer illusion.

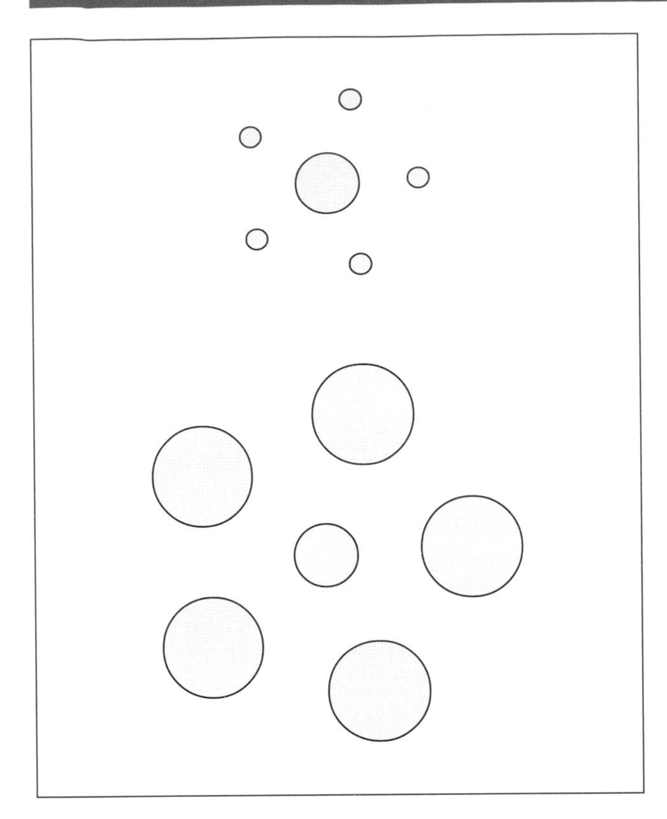

Figure 2.13
The Ebbinghaus illusion.

Milner and Goodale (1995) offered a neat explanation. They argued that most studies on visual illusions have involved the vision-for-perception system. However, we mostly use the vision-for-action system when walking close to a precipice or dodging cars. Milner and Goodale argued that the vision-for-action system provides accurate information about our position relative to objects. These ideas produce a dramatic prediction: actions (e.g., pointing, grasping) using the vision-for-action system should be unaffected by the Müller–Lyer, Ebbinghaus and many other visual illusions.

Findings

Bruno et al. (2008) carried out a meta-analysis (see Glossary) of 33 studies involving the Müller–Lyer illusion in which observers *pointed* rapidly at one of the figures. These studies were designed to involve the vision-for-action system and the mean illusion effect was 5.5%.

For comparison purposes, Bruno et al. (2008) considered 11 studies using standard procedures (e.g., verbal estimations of length) and involving the vision-for-perception system. Here the mean illusion effect was 22.4%. The finding that the mean illusion effect was *four* times greater in the former studies clearly supports the perception–action model. However, the model seems to predict *no* illusion effect with rapid pointing.

Weblink:
Hollow face illusion

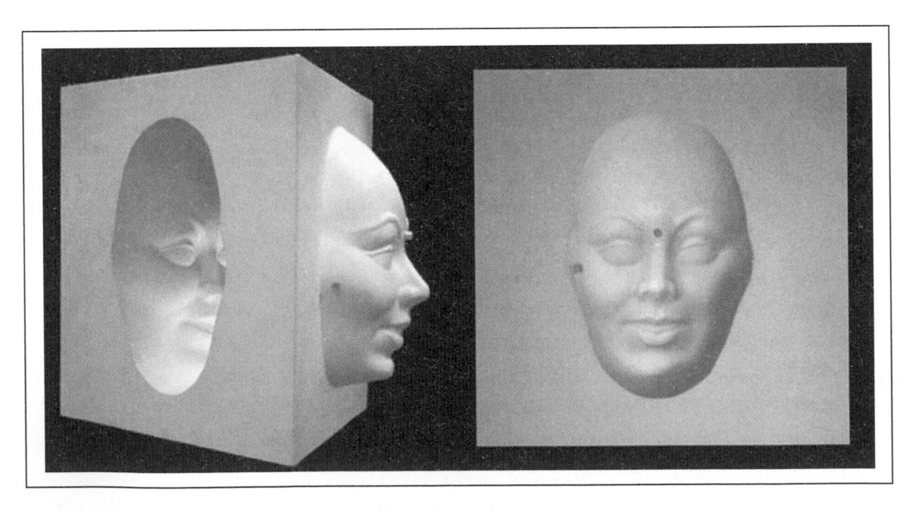

Figure 2.14
Left: normal and hollow faces with small target magnets on the forehead and cheek of the normal face; right: front view of the hollow mask that appears as an illusory face projecting forwards.

Króliczak et al. (2006). Reprinted with permission of Elsevier.

Support for the two-systems approach has also been reported with the hollow-face illusion. In this illusion, a realistic hollow mask looks like a normal face (see Figure 2.14; visit the website: www.richardgregory.org/experiments). Króliczak et al. (2006) placed a target (a small magnet) on the face mask or on a normal face. Here are two of the tasks:

1 Draw the target position (using the vision-for-perception system).
2 Make a fast flicking finger movement to the target (using the vision-for-action system).

Króliczak et al. (2006) found there was a strong illusion effect when observers drew the target position. In contrast, observers' performance was very accurate (i.e., illusion-free) when they made a flicking movement. Both findings were as predicted theoretically.

In the above study, there was a third condition in which observers made a *slow* pointing finger movement to the target. Performance might have been expected to be accurate in this condition because it involved use of the vision-for-action system. However, the illusory effect was fairly strong. Why was this? According to Króliczak et al. (2006), actions may involve the vision-for-perception system as well as the vision-for-action system when preceded by conscious cognitive processes.

More serious problems for the original two-systems approach have accumulated in recent years. With three-dimensional versions of the visual illusions, actions made by observers include grasping as well as pointing. Evidence discussed earlier (Bruno et al., 2008) showed that *pointing* at the Müller–Lyer figure was associated with a greatly reduced illusory effect.

However, the situation is more complex with *grasping*. Franz and Gegenfurtner (2008) reviewed the evidence from studies focusing on the Müller–Lyer illusion. The mean illusory effect was 11.2% with perceptual tasks compared to 4.4% with full visual guidance of the hand movement. In contrast, grasping occurring without the observer being able to monitor his/her hand movement was associated with an illusory effect of 9.4%. These findings probably arose because the action programming involved in grasping requires the ventral stream.

Action: planning + motor responses

We have seen it is not entirely accurate to claim that vision-for-action depends almost entirely on the dorsal stream. Milner and Goodale (2008) argued that most tasks in which observers grasp an object involve some processing in the ventral stream as well as the dorsal stream. Involvement of the ventral stream is especially likely in the following circumstances:

- Memory is required (e.g., there is a time lag between the offset of the stimulus and the start of the grasping movement).
- Time is available to plan the forthcoming movement (e.g., Króliczak et al., 2006).
- Planning which movement to make is necessary.
- The action is unpractised or awkward.

Evidence that the involvement of memory can increase the involvement of the ventral stream in visually guided action was reported by Milner et al. (2003). Two patients with optic ataxia (involving damage to the dorsal stream) made reaching and grasping movements immediately (or a few seconds) after the offset of the target object. Surprisingly, the patients' performance was *better* when reliant on memory. According to Milner et al., the patients did better in the memory condition because they used their intact ventral stream.

As a rule of thumb, actions are most likely to involve the ventral stream when they involve conscious cognitive processes. This can be tested if we distinguish between *effective* and *appropriate* grasping (Creem & Proffitt, (2001). For example, we can grasp a toothbrush effectively by its bristles but appropriate grasping involves picking it up by the handle. Creem and Proffitt argued that appropriate grasping involves accessing stored knowledge about the object and so requires the ventral stream. As predicted, appropriate grasping was much more adversely affected than effective grasping by disrupting participants' ability to retrieve object knowledge.

Van Doorn et al. (2007) provided evidence that the ventral stream is involved in action planning. Participants were presented with a rod of various lengths forming part of a Müller–Lyer figure (see Figure 2.12). They decided whether to pick the rod up end-to-end using a one-handed or a two-handed grip (a decision involving planning). Participants chose a two-handed grip at shorter rod lengths more often when the fins pointed outwards than when they pointed inwards and so this aspect of their behaviour was influenced by the illusion. However, their maximal grip size was unaffected by the illusion. The visual processes guiding action selection (planning) seemed to involve the ventral stream, whereas those guiding motor programming did not.

Canal-Bruland et al. (2013) obtained evidence that some of the effects with visual illusions depend on apparently minor task changes. Participants in two experiments using a one-tailed version of the Müller–Lyer illusion estimated the distance to the endpoint of the shaft or threw a beanbag to that point. When participants stood at the base of the illusion, the usual effects were observed: there was an illusion effect on verbal estimates (perception) but not on throwing (action). However, there were comparable illusion effects on both measures when participants stood 1.5 metres behind the base of the illusion. The precise reasons for this difference in findings are unclear.

Dorsal stream: conscious awareness?

Remember the two systems approach includes the assumption that dorsal-stream processing is not accessible to consciousness. It is hard to test this assumption because of the difficulties in disentangling the relative contributions of the dorsal and ventral streams on most tasks involving visually guided action. Suppose, however, we used a very simple task such as reaching out for a target while avoiding obstacles (e.g., two rods). Milner (2012) reviewed research indicating this task can be performed by the dorsal stream alone and in the absence of conscious awareness. We will briefly discuss relevant evidence.

McIntosh et al. (2004) used an obstacle-avoidance task (see Figure 2.15). They tested a male patient, VE, who had suffered a stroke in the right hemisphere. As a result, he had extinction (see Glossary) involving greatly impaired conscious awareness of a stimulus presented to his left visual field in the presence of another stimulus presented to his right visual field. VE took full account of a rod presented as an obstacle in his left visual field even when he claimed not to have seen it. Thus, his reaching behaviour was influenced by visual information of which he was not conscious.

Evidence that the dorsal stream is crucially important in reaching behaviour is supported by other research (reviewed by Milner, 2012). For example, Schindler et al. (2004) found two patients with optic ataxia (involving extensive dorsal stream damage) showed no ability to vary their reaching behaviour to avoid obstacles.

Roseboom and Arnold (2011) presented visual stimuli to healthy individuals followed by masking to prevent them from being seen. In spite of their total lack of conscious awareness of the orientation of the stimuli presented, they nevertheless learned to orient their grasp reasonably appropriately. Thus, visually guided action can occur in the absence of conscious awareness and with the probable use of the dorsal stream.

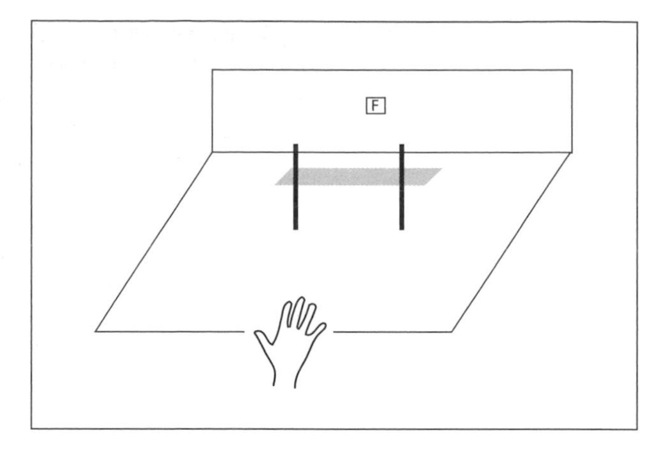

Figure 2.15
The obstacle-avoidance task, which required the participant to move his hand to reach the target zone (strip of grey tape). One or two rods were placed between the hand start position and the target zone to act as obstacles.

From McIntosh et al. (2004). © 2004 The Royal Society. Reprinted with permission.

You may be feeling somewhat bewildered by now. After all, when you reach out to pick up an object, you typically have full conscious awareness of the object, of any obstacles and of the position of your hand. However, such conscious awareness is apparently not *essential* for visually guided action. Nevertheless, it may well be useful. For example, even though Roseboom and Arnold's (2011) participants performed well above chance, their performance was still markedly inferior to what it would have been if the stimuli had been visible.

Overall evaluation

Milner and Goodale's theoretical approach has been very influential. Their central assumption that there are two visual ("what" and "how") systems is probably broadly correct. This assumption has received support from two types of research. First, studies on patients with optic ataxia (damage to the dorsal stream) and visual agnosia (damage to the ventral stream) have produced the predicted double dissociation. Second, studies involving the visual illusions have often produced the surprising (but theoretically predicted) finding that action-based performance (e.g., pointing, sometimes grasping) is almost immune to illusory effects. Third, the assumption that processing in the dorsal stream is not accessible to consciousness has received reasonable support.

What are the limitations of the two systems approach? First, there is too much emphasis on the independence of the two systems rather than their interactions. Cloutman (2013, p. 251) reviewed the evidence and concluded that, "Information is transferred directly between the two pathways at multiple stages and locations along their trajectories".

Second, and related to the first point, there is the thorny issue of *how* these interactions occur given the very different nature of visual processing in the two streams. A possible explanation is provided by the "frame and fill" approach –

rapid, coarse processing in the dorsal stream provides the "frame" for slower and more precise ventral stream processing (the "fill") (Chen et al., 2007).

Third, the original notion (since abandoned by Milner and Goodale (2008)) that visually guided action depends almost entirely on the dorsal stream is incorrect. The dorsal stream is probably used on its own or with minimal ventral stream involvement only when someone performs rudimentary actions to simple targets (Schenk & McIntosh, 2010). The ventral stream seems to be involved whenever action planning and programming are required.

Fourth, the claimed double dissociation between optic ataxia and visual form agnosia is not clear-cut. Some patients with visual form agnosia have severe problems with visually guided action as well as vision for perception (Himmelbach et al., 2012). In addition, some patients with optic ataxia have impaired visual perception for stimuli presented to peripheral vision as well as impaired visually guided action (Pisella et al., 2009).

Fifth, it is often difficult to make firm predictions from the theory. This is because most visual tasks require the use of both processing streams, and subtle changes in the nature of the task can influence their relative use (e.g., Canal-Bruland et al., 2013).

COLOUR VISION

Why has colour vision developed? After all, if you see an old black-and-white movie on television, you can easily make sense of the moving images. One reason is that colour often makes an object stand out from its background, making it easier to distinguish figure from ground. Chameleons very sensibly can change colour to blend in with their immediate surroundings, thus reducing their chances of being detected by predators.

Another reason is that colour perception helps us to recognise and categorise objects. For example, it is useful when deciding whether a piece of fruit is under-ripe, ripe or over-ripe. Predictive coding (which involves processing the unpredicted components of sensory input) is also relevant (Huang & Rao, 2011). It allows us to focus rapidly on any aspects of the incoming visual signal (e.g., discolouring) discrepant with predictions based on ripe fruit.

Before proceeding, we must consider the meaning of the word "colour". There are three main qualities associated with colour:

Weblink:
Colour perception

1 *Hue*: the colour itself and what distinguishes red from yellow or blue.
2 *Brightness*: the perceived intensity of light.
3 *Saturation*: this allows us to determine whether a colour is vivid or pale; it is influenced by the amount of white present.

Trichromacy theory

The cones in the retina are specialised for colour vision. Cone receptors contain light-sensitive photopigment allowing them to respond to light. According to trichromatic (three-coloured) theory, there are three different kinds of cone receptors. One type is especially sensitive to short-wavelength light and generally responds most to stimuli perceived as blue. A second type of cone receptor is most sensitive to medium-wavelength light and responds greatly to stimuli generally seen as yellow-green. The third type of cone receptor responds most to long-wavelength light such as that coming from stimuli perceived as orange-red.

How do we see other colours? According to the theory, most stimuli activate two or all three cone types. The colour we perceive is determined by the *relative* levels of stimulation of each cone type.

Many forms of colour deficiency are consistent with trichromacy theory. Most individuals with colour deficiency have **dichromacy**, in which one cone class is missing. In deuteranopia, medium wavelength (green) cones are missing. In protanopia, long wavelength (red) cones are missing, and in tritanopia, short wavelength (blue) wavelength cones are missing.

Why has evolution equipped us with three types of cones? It is a very efficient system – we can discriminate millions of colours even with so few cone types. Note, however, that many animal species have more than three types of cones, so effective colour vision can be achieved in various ways.

KEY TERMS

Dichromacy
A deficiency in colour vision in which one of the three cone classes is missing.

Negative afterimage
The illusory perception of the complementary colour to the one that has just been fixated; green is the complementary colour to red and blue is complementary to yellow.

Opponent processes

Trichromacy theory does not explain what happens *after* activation of the cone receptors. It also does not account for **negative afterimages**. If you stare at a square in a given colour for several seconds and then shift your gaze to a white surface, you will see a negative afterimage in the complementary colour (complementary colours produce white when combined). For example, a green square produces a red afterimage, whereas a blue square produces a yellow afterimage.

Weblink:
Colour blindness test

Weblink:
Colour afterimages

Weblink:
Opponent processes

Hering (1878) explained negative afterimages. He argued that there are three types of opponent processes in the visual system. One opponent process (red–green channel) produces perception of green when responding one way and of red when responding the opposite way. A second opponent process (blue–yellow channel) produces perception of blue or yellow in the same way. The third opponent process (achromatic channel) produces the perception of white at one extreme and of black at the other.

What is the value of having these three opponent processes? There is evidence (e.g., Tailor et al., 2000; Lee et al., 2002) that the three dimensions associated with opponent processes provide maximally *independent* representations of colour information. As a result, the opponent processes provide very efficient encoding of chromatic stimuli.

Several lines of research support the notion of opponent processes. First, opponent cells have been identified in monkeys (DeValois & DeValois, 1975). Second, the theory accounts for negative afterimages. Prolonged viewing of a given colour (e.g., red) produces one extreme of activity in the relevant opponent process. When attention is then directed to a white surface, the opponent process moves to its other extreme, thus producing the negative afterimage.

The existence of opponent processes also explains some types of colour deficiency. Red–green deficiency occurs when the high- or medium-wavelength cones are damaged or missing, and so the red–green channel cannot be used. Blue–yellow deficiency occurs when individuals lacking the short-wavelength cones cannot make effective use of the blue–yellow channel.

Dual-process theory

Hurvich and Jameson (1957) proposed a dual-process theory combining the ideas discussed so far. Signals from the three cone types identified by trichromacy theory are sent to the opponent cells (see Figure 2.16). There are three channels.

KEY TERMS

Colour constancy
The tendency for an object to be perceived as having the same colour under widely varying viewing conditions.

Illuminant
A source of light illuminating a surface or object.

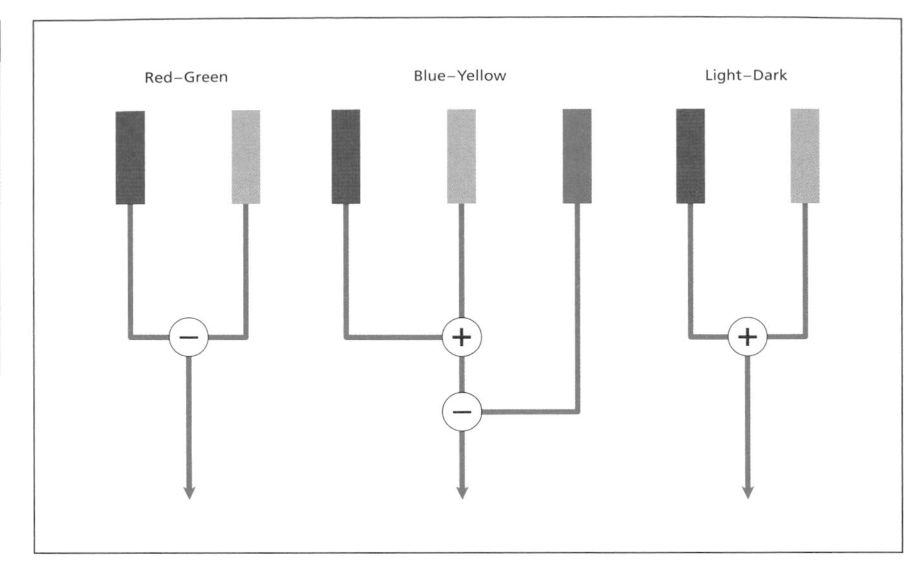

Figure 2.16
Schematic diagram of the early stages of neural colour processing. Three cone classes (red = long; green = medium; blue = short) supply three "channels". The achromatic (light–dark) channel receives non-spectrally opponent input from long and medium cone classes. The two chromatic channels receive spectrally opponent inputs to create the red–green and blue–yellow channels.

From Mather (2009). Copyright © 2009 George Mather. Reproduced with permission.

The achromatic (non-colour) channel combines the activity of the medium- and long-wavelength cones. The blue–yellow channel represents the difference between the sum of the medium- and long-wavelength cones on the one hand and the short-wavelength cones on the other. The direction of difference determines whether blue or yellow is seen. Finally, the red–green channel represents the difference between activity levels in the medium- and long-wavelength cones. The direction of this difference determines whether red or green is perceived.

Evaluation

There is much experimental support for opponent-process theory. However, it is greatly oversimplified (Solomon & Lennie, 2007; Conway et al., 2010). For example, the proportions of different cone types vary considerably across individuals, but this has surprisingly little effect on colour perception. Second, the arrangement of cone types in the eye is fairly *random*. This seems odd because it presumably makes it hard for colour-opponent processes to work effectively. In sum, the processes involved in colour vision are much more complicated than previously believed.

Colour constancy

Colour constancy is the tendency for a surface or object to be perceived as having the same colour when the wavelengths contained in the **illuminant** (the light source illuminating the surface or object) change. The phenomenon of colour constancy indicates that colour vision does *not* depend solely on the wavelengths of the light reflected from objects. Learn more about colour constancy on YouTube: This Is Only Red by Vsauce.

Why is colour constancy important? Suppose we lacked colour constancy. The apparent colour of familiar objects would change dramatically with changes in the lighting conditions. This would make it very hard to recognise objects rapidly and accurately.

It typically does not seem hard to achieve reasonable levels of colour constancy in our everyday lives. In fact, however, it is actually a very impressive achievement. Have a look at the object in Figure 2.17. You probably immediately recognised it as a blue mug. If you look more closely, however, several other colours can also be identified in the mug. The wavelengths of light depend on the mug itself, the illuminant and reflections from other objects on to the mug's surface.

Figure 2.17
Photograph of a mug showing enormous variation in the properties of the reflected light across the mug's surface. The patches at the top of the figure show image values from the locations indicated by the arrows.

From Brainard and Maloney (2011). Reprinted with permission of the Association for Research in Vision and Ophthalmology.

How good is colour constancy?

Granzier et al. (2009a) assessed colour constancy under natural conditions. Observers were initially presented with six uniformly coloured papers similar in colour and learned to name them. After that, they tried to identify individual papers presented at various indoor and outdoor locations differing substantially in terms of lighting conditions.

Granzier et al.'s (2009a) key finding was that 55% of the papers were identified correctly. This may sound unimpressive. However, it represents good performance given the similarities among the papers and the large differences in lighting conditions.

Weblink:
Colour constancy

Reeves et al. (2008) argued that it is important to distinguish between our subjective experience and our judgements about the world. For example, as you walk towards a fire, it feels increasingly hot *subjectively*. However, how hot you *judge* the fire to be is unlikely to change. Reeves et al. found high levels of colour constancy when observers made judgements of the *objective* similarity of two stimuli seen under different illuminants. However, much lower levels of colour constancy were obtained when observers rated the *subjective* similarity of the hue and saturation of two stimuli. Thus, we can use our visual system *flexibly*.

It is often assumed colour constancy should be better when observers are presented with naturalistic three-dimensional stimuli rather than simple two-dimensional scenes. The former stimuli provide much richer information, which should enhance colour constancy. In practice, that is not the case (Foster, 2011). For example, de Almeida et al. (2010) found comparably high levels of colour constancy with two- and three-dimensional stimuli. This non-significant difference may have occurred because observers attended to only a small fraction of the information potentially available in three-dimensional stimuli.

Estimating scene illumination

The wavelengths of light reflected from an object are greatly influenced by the nature of the illuminant (light source). If observers can make accurate illuminant estimates, this could lead to high levels of colour constancy. Observers do sometimes make effective use of information about the illuminant. However, they are typically very insensitive to changes in the illumination (Foster, 2011).

Evidence that observers often make limited use of illumination estimates was reported by Granzier et al. (2009b). Observers estimated a lamp's colour based on the light reflected from the scene it illuminated. They also judged the colour of a surface within the scene (to assess colour constancy). There were two main findings. First, observers' surface colour estimates were much more accurate than their estimates of the colour of the illuminant (i.e., the lamp). Second, there was no correlation between the accuracy of observers' estimates of the lamp's colour and that of the surface. These findings suggest colour constancy does *not* depend on illuminant estimates.

Local colour contrast

Land (e.g., 1986) put forward his retinex theory, according to which we perceive the colour of a surface by comparing its ability to reflect short, medium and long wavelengths of light against that of adjacent surfaces. In other words, we make use of local colour contrast.

Kraft and Brainard (1999) placed various objects (e.g., a tube wrapped in tin foil, a pyramid, a cube) in a box. Under full viewing conditions, colour constancy was 83% even with large changes in illumination. The most important factor was local contrast. When local contrast could not be used, colour constancy dropped to 53%.

Another important factor was global contrast, in which cone responses from the target surface are compared with those across the entire visual scene. When observers could not use global or local contrast, colour constancy dropped to 39%. When observers were also denied information in the form of reflected highlights from glossy surfaces, colour constancy dropped to 11%.

Foster and Nascimento (1994) developed Land's ideas into an influential theory based on local contrast and involving cone-excitation ratios. We can see the nature of their big discovery by considering a simple example. Suppose there were two illuminants and two surfaces. If surface 1 led to the long-wavelength or red cones responding *three* times as much with illuminant 1 as illuminant 2, then the same *threefold* difference was also found with surface 2. Thus, the *ratio* of cone responses was essentially invariant with different illuminants. As a result, we can use information about cone-excitation ratios to eliminate the illuminant's effects and so increase colour constancy.

There is much support for the notion that cone-excitation ratios are important (Foster, 2011). For example, Nascimento et al. (2004) obtained evidence suggesting the level of colour constancy shown in different conditions could be predicted on the basis of cone-excitation ratios.

Foster and Nascimento's (1994) theory provides an elegant account of how illumination-independent colour constancy works in relatively simple visual environments. However, it is of limited value when the visual environment is more complex (Brainard & Maloney, 2011). For example, colour constancy for a given object can be made harder because of reflections from other objects (see Figure 2.17) or because there are multiple sources of illumination present at the same time. The theory does not provide a thorough account of how observers deal with such conditions.

KEY TERM

Chromatic adaptation
Changes in visual sensitivity to colour stimuli when the illumination alters.

Effects of familiarity

Colour constancy is influenced by our knowledge of the familiar colours of objects (e.g., bananas are yellow). In a study by Hansen et al. (2006), observers viewed photographs of fruits and adjusted their colour until they appeared grey. There was over-adjustment. For example, a banana still looked yellowish to observers when it was actually grey, leading them to adjust its colour to a slightly bluish hue. Thus, objects tend to be perceived in their typical colour even when the actual colour differs from the typical one.

Chromatic adaptation

One reason why we show reasonable colour constancy is because of **chromatic adaptation**, in which an observer's visual sensitivity to a given illuminant decreases over time. If you stand outside after dark, you may be struck by the yellowness of the artificial light in people's houses. However, if you spend some time in a room illuminated by artificial light, the light does not seem yellow.

R.J. Lee et al. (2012) exposed observers to sudden changes of illumination between sunlight and skylight conditions. The findings were complex, but some aspects of chromatic adaptation occurred in approximately six seconds. This fairly rapid decrease in the impact of a change in illumination increases colour constancy.

Invariant cell responses

Zeki (1983) found in monkeys that cells in area V4 (centrally involved in colour processing) responded strongly to a red patch illuminated by red light. However, these cells did not respond when the red patch was replaced by a green, blue or white patch even though the dominant reflected wavelength would generally be perceived as red. Thus, these cells responded to the *actual* colour of a surface rather than simply to the wavelengths reflected from it.

Kusunoki et al. (2006) reported similar findings to those of Zeki (1983). They measured the effects of changes in background illumination on neurons in monkey V4. They concluded these neurons "exhibit the property of colour constancy and their response properties are thus able to reflect colour perception" (Kusunoki et al., 2006, p. 3047).

Evaluation

Colour constancy is a complex achievement, and observers often fall well short of complete constancy. In view of its complexity, it is unsurprising the visual system adopts an "all hands on deck" approach in which several factors contribute to colour constancy. Of special importance are cone-excitation ratios that remain almost invariant across changes in illumination. In addition, top-down factors such as our memory of the familiar colours of common objects also play a role. Our understanding of the brain mechanisms underlying colour constancy has been enhanced by the discovery of cells in V4 responsive to colour constancy.

What are the limitations of theory and research on colour constancy? First, we lack a comprehensive theory of how the various factors *combine* to produce colour constancy. Second, most research has focused on relatively simple visual environments and so the processes involved in trying to achieve colour constancy in more complex environments are poorly understood. Third, more research is needed to understand why the extent of colour constancy depends greatly on the precise instructions given to observers.

DEPTH PERCEPTION

A major accomplishment of visual perception is the transformation of the two-dimensional retinal image into perception of a three-dimensional (3-D) world seen in depth. It is crucially important to us to construct 3-D representations of the world around us if we are to pick up objects, decide whether it is safe to cross the road, avoid cliff edges and so on.

Depth perception depends heavily on numerous visual and other cues. We can define a cue as "any sensory information that gives rise to a sensory estimate" (Ernst & Bülthoff, 2004, p. 163).

All cues provide *ambiguous* information, and so it would be unwise to place total reliance on any single cue. In addition, different cues often provide conflicting information. When you watch a movie at the cinema or on television, some cues (e.g., stereo ones) indicate everything you see is at the same distance. In contrast, other cues (e.g., perspective, shading) indicate some objects are closer than others.

In real life, cues to depth are often provided by movement of the observer or objects in the visual environment. Some cues are not visual (e.g., based on touch or hearing). However, the major focus here will be on visual depth cues available even if the observer and environmental objects are static. Such cues can conveniently be divided into monocular, binocular and oculomotor cues. **Monocular cues** are those requiring only one eye, although they can also be used readily when someone has both eyes open. Such cues clearly exist, because the world still retains a sense of depth with one eye closed. **Binocular cues** are those involving both eyes being used together. Finally, **oculomotor cues** depend on sensations of muscular contraction of the muscles around the eye. Use of these cues involves kinaesthesia (the muscle sense).

KEY TERMS

Monocular cues
Cues to depth that can be used by one eye, but can also be used by both eyes together.

Binocular cues
Cues to depth that require both eyes to be used together.

Oculomotor cues
Cues to depth produced by muscular contractions of the muscles around the eye; use of such cues involves kinaesthesia (also known as the muscle sense).

Monocular cues

Monocular cues to depth are sometimes called *pictorial cues* because they are used by artists trying to create the impression of three-dimensional scenes when painting on two-dimensional canvases. One such cue is *linear perspective*. Parallel lines pointing directly away from us seem increasingly close to each other as they recede into the distance (e.g., the edges of a motorway). This convergence of lines creates a powerful impression of depth in a two-dimensional drawing.

The effectiveness of linear perspective in drawings varies as a function of viewing distance. We can see this clearly in a drawing by the Dutch artist Jan Vredeman de Vries (see Figure 2.18). As Todorović (2009) pointed out, this drawing looks distinctly odd when viewed from some distance but creates an effective 3-D effect when viewed from very close.

Weblink:
Cues to depth perception

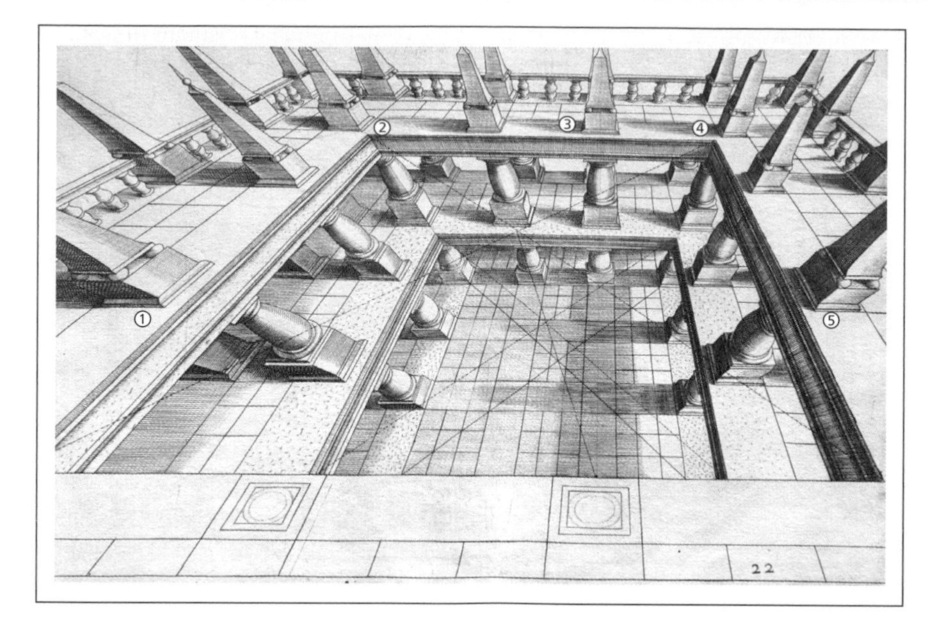

Figure 2.18
An engraving by de Vries (1604/1970) in which linear perspective creates an effective three-dimensional effect when viewed from very close but not from further away.
From Todorović (2009). Copyright © 1968 by Dover Publications. Reprinted with permission from Springer.

KEY TERM

Texture gradient
The rate of change of texture density from the front to the back of a slanting object.

Another monocular cue is *texture*. Most objects (e.g., carpets, cobble-stoned roads) possess texture and textured objects slanting away from us have a **texture gradient** (Gibson, 1979; see Figure 2.19). This is a gradient (rate of change) of texture density as you look from the front to the back of a slanting object. Sinai et al. (1998) found observers were good at judging the distance of objects within seven metres when the ground in between was uniformly textured. However, distances were systematically overestimated when there was a gap (e.g., a ditch) in the texture pattern.

Shading provides another monocular cue to depth. Flat two-dimensional surfaces do *not* cast shadows and so shading indicates the presence of a 3-D object. Ramachandran (1988) presented observers with a visual display consisting of numerous very similar circular patches. Some were illuminated by one light source and the others by a different light source. Observers incorrectly assumed the visual display was lit by a single light source. This led them to assign different depths to different parts of the display (i.e., some "dents" were misperceived as "bumps").

A further cue is *interposition*, in which a nearer object hides part of a more distant one. The strength of this cue can be seen in Kanizsa's (1976) illusory square (see Figure 2.20). There is

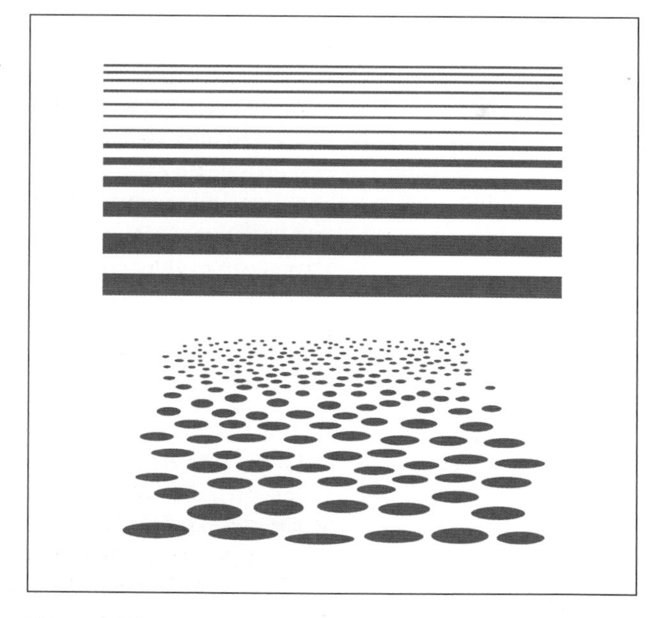

Figure 2.19
Examples of texture gradients that can be perceived as surfaces receding into the distance.
From Bruce et al. (2003).

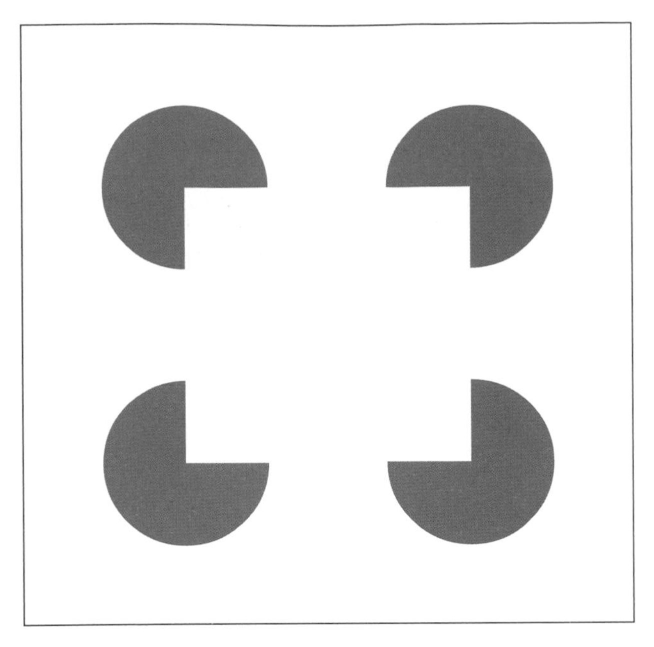

Figure 2.20
Kanizsa's (1976) illusory square.

a strong impression of a yellow square in front of four purple circles even though many of the white square's contours are missing.

Another useful cue is *familiar size*. If we know the size of an object, we can use its retinal image size to provide an accurate estimate of its distance. However, we can be misled if an object is not in its familiar size. Ittelson (1951) had observers look at playing cards through a peephole restricting them to monocular vision. Playing cards of various sizes were presented at a distance of 2.28 metres. The perceived distances were determined almost entirely by familiar size – a half-size card was seen as 1.38 metres away and a double-size card as 4.56 metres away.

We turn now to a cue whose importance has been curiously underestimated: *blur*. There is no blur at the point of fixation, and it increases more rapidly at closer distances than at further ones. The role played by blur was clarified by Held et al. (2012). They argued that **binocular disparity** (the slight difference in the two retinal images; discussed fully later) is a more useful depth cue close to the point of fixation. However, blur is more useful than binocular disparity further away from the fixation point. Held et al.'s findings were consistent with their assumptions (see Figure 2.21).

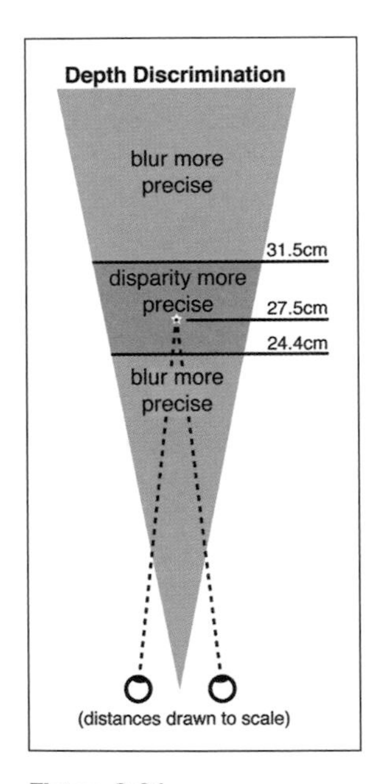

Figure 2.21
Effectiveness of blur and binocular disparity as cues to depth at different viewing distances.

From Held et al. (2012). Reprinted with permission of Elsevier.

Finally, there is **motion parallax**, in which there is movement in one part of the retinal image relative to another. For example, consider what happens when an observer's head moves. This produces large apparent movement of nearby objects in the opposite direction but small apparent movement of distant objects in the same direction. Rogers and Graham (1979) found motion parallax can produce accurate depth judgements in the absence of all other cues.

Cues such as linear perspective, texture and interposition allow observers to perceive depth even in two-dimensional displays. However, much research with computer-generated two-dimensional displays has found depth is often underestimated (Domini et al., 2011). Two-dimensional displays provide cues to flatness (e.g., binocular disparity, accommodation and vergence, all discussed shortly). These flatness cues may reduce the impact of cues suggesting depth.

Oculomotor and binocular cues

The pictorial cues discussed so far can all be used as well by one-eyed individuals as by those with normal vision. Depth perception also depends on oculomotor cues based on perceiving muscle contractions around the eyes. One such cue is **vergence**. It is a depth cue that is based on the fact that the eyes turn inwards more to focus on a very close object than one further away.

Another oculomotor cue is **accommodation**. It refers to the variation in optical power produced by the thickening of the lens of the eye when someone focuses on a close object.

Vergence and accommodation are both very limited. First, they both provide only a single value in any situation. As a result, they can only provide information about the distance of a *single* object at any one time. Second, they are both of value only when judging the distance of close objects, and even then the information they provide is not very accurate.

We turn now to a binocular cue that is dramatically more useful than accommodation or convergence. Binocular disparity is the slight difference or disparity in the images projected on the retinas of the two eyes when you view a scene. This produces **stereopsis**, which is the depth perception produced by binocular disparity.

Stereopsis is very powerful at short distances. However, the disparity or discrepancy in the retinal images of an object decreases by a factor of 100 as its distance from the observer increases from 2 to 20 metres. Thus, stereopsis rapidly becomes less effective at greater distances.

It has sometimes been assumed that stereoscopic information is available early in visual perception and is used in object recognition. However, contrary evidence was reported by Bülthoff et al. (1998). Observers' recognition of familiar objects was *not* adversely affected when stereoscopic information was scrambled. Indeed, the observers seemed unaware the depth information was scrambled! Observers' expectations about the structure of familiar objects were more important than the misleading stereoscopic information.

A key process in stereopsis is to *match* features in the input presented to the two eyes. Sometimes we make mistakes in doing this, which can produce various illusions and other effects. Consider, for example, the **autostereograms** found in the Magic Eye books. An autostereogram is a two-dimensional image containing depth information so it appears to be three-dimensional when viewed appropriately. You can see an autostereogram of a shark if you access the *Wikipedia* entry for autostereogram.

What happens with autostereograms is that the same repeating 2-D pattern is presented to each eye. If there is a dissociation of vergence and accommodation, two adjacent patterns will form an object that appears to be at a different depth from the background.

If you only glance at an autostereogram, you see a two-dimensional pattern. However, if you stare at it and strive *not* to bring it into focus, you can see a three-dimensional image. It often helps if you hold the autostereogram very close to your face and then move it very slowly away while preventing it from coming into focus.

Gómez et al. (2012) wondered why some individuals are much better than others at perceiving three-dimensional objects in autostereograms. They found individual differences in binocular disparity, vergence and accommodation all predicted success (or failure) with autostereograms.

Parker (2007) reviewed research on the brain areas associated with the processing of information relevant to binocular disparity. In general terms, processing of disparity information was more detailed and sophisticated in the ventral stream (see Glossary) than the dorsal stream (see Glossary).

Cue integration

So far we have considered depth cues one by one. However, we typically have access to several depth cues at once. This raises the question of how we *combine* these different sources of information to judge depth or distance. Two possibilities are *additivity* (adding together information from all cues) and *selection* (only using

KEY TERMS

Binocular disparity
A depth cue based on the slight disparity in the two retinal images when an observer views a scene; it is the basis for **stereopsis**.

Motion parallax
A depth cue based on movement in one part of the retinal image relative to another.

Vergence
A cue to depth based on the inward focus of the eyes with close objects.

Accommodation
A depth cue based on changes in optical power produced by thickening of the eye's lens when an observer focuses on close objects.

Stereopsis
Depth perception based on the small discrepancy in the two retinal images when a visual scene is observed (**binocular disparity**).

Autostereogram
A complex two-dimensional image perceived as three-dimensional when not focused on for a period of time.

Weblink:
Depth perception test

KEY TERM

Haptic
Relating to the sense of touch.

information from a single cue) (Bruno & Cutting, 1988). Cues may also be combined in more complex ways.

How should we integrate cue information to maximise the accuracy of our depth perception? Jacobs (2002) argued that we should assign more weight to reliable than to unreliable cues. Since cues reliable in one context may be less so in another context, we should be *flexible* in our assessments of cue reliability.

The above notions led Jacobs (2002) to put forward two hypotheses:

Weblink:
Ambiguous depth cues

1 Less ambiguous cues (e.g., those providing consistent information) are regarded as more reliable than more ambiguous ones.
2 A cue is regarded as reliable if inferences based on it are consistent with those based on other available cues.

Experimentation in this area has benefited from advances in virtual reality technologies. These advances permit researchers to control visual cues very precisely and to provide observers with virtual environments permitting clear-cut tests of hypotheses.

Findings

Evidence supporting Jacobs' (2002) first hypothesis was reported by Triesch et al. (2002). They used a virtual reality situation in which observers tracked an object defined by colour, shape and size. On each trial, two attributes were unreliable or inconsistent (their values changed frequently). Observers attached increasing weight to the reliable or consistent cue and less to the unreliable cues during the course of each trial.

Evidence consistent with Jacobs' (2002) second hypothesis was reported by Atkins et al. (2001). They used a virtual reality environment in which observers viewed and grasped elliptical cylinders. There were three cues to cylinder depth: texture, motion and **haptic** (relating to the sense of touch).

When the haptic and texture cues indicated the same cylinder depth but the motion cue indicated a different depth, observers made increasing use of the texture cue and decreasing use of the motion cue. When the haptic and motion cues indicated the same cylinder depth but the texture cue did not, observers increasingly relied on the motion cue rather than the texture cue. Thus, whichever visual cue correlated with the haptic cue was preferred, and this preference increased with practice.

Most research suggests observers integrate cue information according to the additivity notion in that they take account of most or all cues (Landy et al., 2011). However, they attach additional weight to more reliable ones. These conclusions certainly apply to the numerous studies in which there were only small conflicts between the information provided by each cue.

What happens when two or more cues are in strong conflict? As we will see, observers typically rely heavily (or even exclusively) on only one cue. Thus, observers' depth perception is based on the selection strategy as defined by Bruno and Cutting (1988). This makes sense. Suppose one cue suggests an object is 10 metres away but another cue suggests it is 90 metres away. It is probably not sensible to split the difference and decide it is 50 metres away! We use the selection strategy at the movies – perspective and texture cues are used to produce a 3-D effect, whereas we ignore cues (e.g., binocular disparity) indicating everything on the screen is the same distance from us.

Relevant evidence was reported by Girshick and Banks (2009) in a study on the effects of two cues (binocular disparity and texture gradients) on slant perception. When there was a small conflict between the information provided by the cues, observers used information from both. When there was a large conflict, however, perceived slant was determined exclusively by one cue (binocular disparity or texture gradient). Interestingly, the observers were not consciously aware of the large conflict between the cues.

We have discussed the ways in which observers combine information from different cues. To what extent does such cue combination produce *optimal* performance (i.e., accurate depth perception)? Lovell et al. (2012) addressed this issue. In their study, they explored the effects of binocular disparity and shading on depth perception. Overall, binocular disparity was the more informative cue to depth, but Lovell et al. tested the effects of making it less reliable over trials. Information from the cues was combined optimally, with observers consistently attaching more weight to reliable than unreliable cues.

Knill and Saunders (2003) studied the use of texture and stereo cues on judgements of surface slant. Texture information becomes increasingly useful as slant increases, and Knill and Saunders predicted that observers would make more use of texture cues at greater slants. Their prediction was confirmed. Knill and Saunders also found interesting individual differences in the weight attached to texture and stereo cues. Texture cues were heavily weighted by individuals best able to use such cues and the same was true with stereo cues. Overall, observers combined stereo and texture information in a fashion that was close to optimal.

Evaluation

Much has been learned about the numerous cues observers use to estimate depth or distance. Information from different depth cues is typically combined to produce accurate depth perception. This often happens in an additive fashion with information from all cues being combined. However, there are several situations (e.g., when different cues conflict strongly) in which one cue dominates the others.

As Jacobs (2002) argued, we attach more weight to cues that provide reliable information and are consistent with that provided by other cues. In addition, the weight we attach to any given cue is flexible – we sometimes learn a cue that was reliable in the past is no longer so. Overall, cues are generally weighted to produce accurate depth perception.

What are the limitations of research in this area? First, we spend most of our time estimating distance in settings in which numerous cues are present and there are no large conflicts between them. In contrast, laboratory settings often provide only a few cues, and those cues provide very discrepant information. The unfamiliarity of laboratory settings may sometimes cause suboptimal performance by observers and reduce generalisation to everyday life (Landy et al., 2011).

Second, it is generally assumed the information observers obtain from single cues is accurate. However, that assumption is rarely tested. Third, observers learn reasonably rapidly which cues are more and less reliable. Assessing cue reliability involves comparing the effectiveness of different cues and the complex processes involved are not well understood.

Size constancy

Size constancy is the tendency for any given object to appear the same size whether its size in the retinal image is large or small. For example, if someone walks towards you, their retinal image increases progressively, but their size seems to remain the same.

Why do we show size constancy? Many factors are involved. However, an object's apparent distance is especially important when judging its size. For example, an object may be judged to be large even though its retinal image is very small if it is a long way away. Thus, there are close connections between size and distance judgements. Many other factors influence the extent to which size constancy is observed. Below we briefly consider some of these factors before considering the relationship between size constancy and depth perception.

KEY TERMS

Size constancy
Objects are perceived to have a given size regardless of the size of the retinal image.

Body size effect
An illusion in which misperception of one's own bodily size causes the perceived size of objects to be misjudged.

Findings

Weblink:
Size constancy

Haber and Levin (2001) argued that size perception of objects typically depends on *memory* of their familiar size rather than solely on perceptual information concerning their distance away. They found participants estimated the sizes of common objects with great accuracy using only memory. Then they presented observers with various objects at close (0–50 metres) or distant viewing range (50–100 metres) and asked them to make size judgements. The objects belonged to three categories: (1) those almost invariant in size or height (e.g., tennis racquet, bicycle); (2) those varying in size (e.g., television set, Christmas tree); and (3) unfamiliar stimuli (e.g., ovals, triangles).

What findings would we expect? If familiar size is of major importance, size judgements should be better for objects of invariant size than those of variable size, with size judgements worst for unfamiliar objects. What if distance perception is all-important? Distances are estimated more accurately for nearby objects than more distant ones, so size judgements should be better for all categories of objects at close viewing range.

Haber and Levin's (2001) findings indicated the importance of familiar size to accuracy of size judgements (see Figure 2.22). However, we cannot explain the fairly high accuracy of size judgements with unfamiliar objects in terms of familiar size. Note that the viewing distance had practically no effect on size judgements.

Witt et al. (2008) found good golfers perceived the hole to be larger than not-so-good golfers when putting. They also found golfers facing a short putt perceived the hole's size to be larger than those facing a long putt. They concluded objects look larger when we can act effectively with respect to them, which could explain why the hole always looks remarkably small to the first author when playing golf! Note, however, that A.D. Cooper et al. (2012) obtained evidence suggesting these effects involve memory rather than perception.

Van der Hoort et al. (2011) found evidence for the **body size effect**, in which the size of a body mistakenly perceived to be one's own influences the perceived sizes of objects in the environment. Participants equipped with head-mounted displays connected to CCTV cameras saw the environment from the perspective of a doll (see Figure 2.23). The doll was small or large.

Van der Hoort et al. (2011) found other objects were perceived as larger and further away when the doll was small than when it was large. These effects were

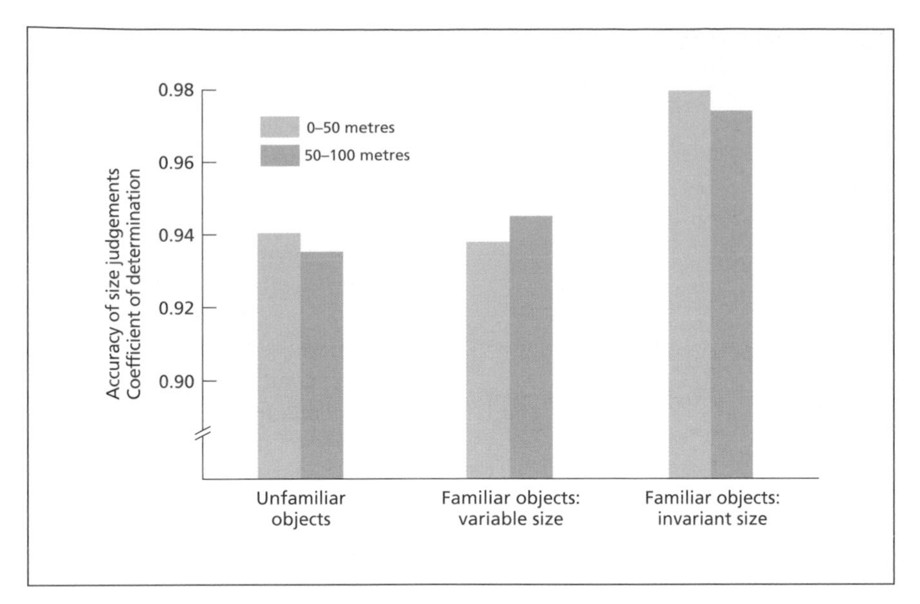

Figure 2.22
Accuracy of size judgements as a function of object type (unfamiliar; familiar variable size; familiar invariant size) and viewing distance (0–50 metres vs. 50–100 metres).
Based on data in Haber and Levin (2001).

greater when participants misperceived the body as their own – this was achieved by touching the participant's and the doll's body at the same time. Thus, size and distance perception both depend in part on our lifelong experience of seeing everything from the perspective of our own body.

We turn now to research considering the relationship between size estimation and perceived distance. If size judgements depend on perceived distance, size constancy should not be found when the *perceived* distance of an object differs considerably from its *actual* distance. The Ames room provides a good example (Ames, 1952; see Figure 2.24). It has a peculiar shape: the floor slopes and the rear wall is not at right angles to the adjoining walls. In spite of this, the Ames room creates the same retinal image as a normal rectangular room when viewed through a peephole. The fact that one end of the rear wall is much farther from the viewer is disguised by making it much higher.

Weblink:
Ramachandran explains the Ames room

What happens when observers look into the Ames room? The cues suggesting the rear wall is at right angles to the viewer are so strong observers mistakenly assume two adults standing in the corners by the rear wall are at the same distance from them. This leads them to estimate the size of the nearer adult as much greater than that of the adult who is farther away. (See the Ames room on YouTube: Ramachandran – Ames room illusion explained).

Figure 2.23
This shows what participants in the doll experiment could see. From the viewpoint of a small doll, objects such as a hand look much larger than when seen from the viewpoint of a large doll. This exemplifies the body size effect.
From Van der Hoort et al. (2011). Public Library of Science. With kind permission from the author.

The illusion effect with the Ames room is so great that an individual walking backwards and forwards in front of the rear wall seems to grow and shrink as he/she moves! Thus, perceived distance seems to drive perceived size. However, observers are more likely to realise what is going on if the individual is someone they know very well. On one occasion, a researcher's wife arrived at the laboratory to find him inside the Ames room. She immediately said, "Gee, honey, that room's distorted!" (Ian Gordon, personal communication).

Similar (but more dramatic) findings were reported by Glennerster et al. (2006). Participants walked through a virtual reality room as it expanded or contracted considerably. Even though they had considerable information from motion parallax and motion to indicate the room's size was changing, no participants noticed the changes! There were large errors in participants' judgements of

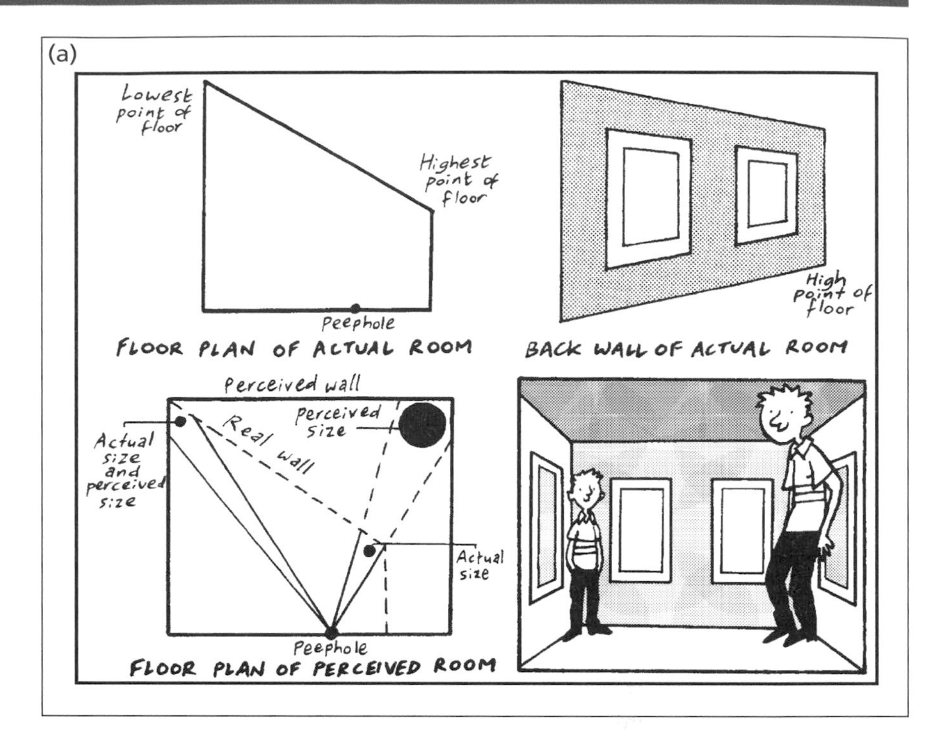

Figure 2.24
(a) A representation of the Ames room. (b) An actual Ames room showing the effect achieved with two adults.
Photo © Peter Endig/dpa/Corbis.

the sizes of objects at longer distances. The powerful expectation that the size of the room would not alter caused the perceived distance of the objects to be very inaccurate.

Nguyen et al. (2011) also showed the close relationship between size and distance perception. They used a virtual environment in which two poles were presented in a tunnel. There were initial training trials in which the size of the poles remained constant and observers judged their distance away. After that, the poles changed in size. When the poles became smaller, observers overestimated the distance away, whereas observers underestimated the distance away when the poles became larger. Thus, the familiar size of the poles established during initial training strongly influenced perceived distance.

Evaluation

Size perception and size constancy depend mainly on perceived distance. Some of the strongest evidence for this comes from studies in which misperceptions of distance (e.g., in the Ames room or in virtual environments) produce systematic distortions in perceived size. In addition, perceived distance can be strongly influenced by perceived or familiar size. Numerous other factors influence size perception and we have mentioned only a few.

What is lacking so far are comprehensive theories of size judgements. Little is known about the relative importance of the factors influencing size judgements or the circumstances in which any given factor is more or less influential. In addition, we do not know how the various factors combine to produce size judgements.

KEY TERMS

Subliminal perception
Perceptual processing occurring below the level of conscious awareness that can nevertheless influence behaviour.

Blindsight
The ability to respond appropriately to visual stimuli in the absence of conscious visual experience in patients with damage to the primary visual cortex.

PERCEPTION WITHOUT AWARENESS

Can we perceive aspects of the visual world without any conscious awareness we are doing so? In other words, is there such a thing as unconscious perception or **subliminal perception** (perception occurring even though the stimulus is below the threshold of conscious awareness?). Common sense suggests the answer is "No". However, there is strong evidence that the correct answer is "Yes". However, we need to be careful in the terms we use. A thermostat responds appropriately to temperature changes and so could be said to exhibit unconscious perception!

Weblink:
Visual illusions

Some of the most important evidence suggesting visual perception does not require conscious awareness comes from research on **blindsight** patients with damage to early visual cortex (V1). Blindsight "refers to the rare ability of V1-damaged patients to perform visual tasks . . . even though these patients claim not to consciously see the relevant stimuli" (Ko & Lau, 2012, p. 1401).

In what follows, we will start by considering blindsight patients. After that, we will discuss evidence of subliminal perception in healthy individuals.

Blindsight

Many British soldiers in the First World War blinded by gunshot wounds that destroyed their primary visual cortex (V1 or BA17) were treated by a captain in the Royal Army Medical Corps called George Riddoch. These soldiers responded to motion in those parts of the visual field in which they claimed to be blind (Riddoch, 1917). Such patients are said to suffer from blindsight, which neatly captures the apparently paradoxical nature of their condition.

What perceptual abilities do blindsight patients possess? According to Farah (2001, p. 162), "Detection and localisation of light, and detection of motion are invariably preserved to some degree. In addition, many patients can discriminate orientation, shape, direction of movement, and flicker. Colour vision mechanisms also appear to be preserved in some cases."

IN THE REAL WORLD: BLINDSIGHT PATIENT DB

Much of the early research on blindsight involved a patient DB. He was blind in the lower part of his left visual field as a result of surgery involving removal of part of his right primary visual cortex (BA17) to relieve his frequent severe migraine. DB was studied in much detail at Oxford University by Larry Weiskrantz who invented the term "blindsight".

DB is a very important patient in research on blindsight (see Weiskrantz, 2010, for an overview). In essence, DB could detect the presence of various objects and he was also able to indicate their approximate location by pointing. He was also able to discriminate between objects that were moving and those that were stationary and could distinguish vertical from horizontal lines. However, DB's abilities were limited – he could not distinguish between different-sized rectangles or between triangles having straight and curved sides. Such findings suggest that DB processed only low-level features of visual stimuli and was unable to discriminate form.

We have seen that DB showed some abilities to perform various visual tasks. In spite of that, he reported no conscious experience in his blind field. According to Weiskrantz et al. (1974, p. 721), "When he was shown a video film of his reaching and judging orientation of lines [by presenting it to his intact visual field], he was openly astonished."

Campion et al. (1983) pointed out that DB and other blindsight patients are only partially blind. They argued in favour of the stray-light hypothesis, according to which patients respond to light reflected from the environment on to areas of the visual field that are still functioning. However, it follows from this hypothesis that DB should have shown reasonable visual performance when objects were presented to his blindspot (the area where the optic nerve passes through the retina). In fact, however, DB was totally unable to detect objects presented to his blindspot.

How is blindsight assessed? There are generally two measures. First, there is a forced-choice test in which patients guess (e.g., stimulus present or absent?) or point at stimuli they cannot see. Second, there are patients' subjective reports that they cannot see stimuli presented to their blind region. Blindsight is defined by an absence of self-reported visual perception accompanied by above-chance performance on the forced-choice test.

We must not exaggerate the preserved perceptual abilities of blindsight patients. As Cowey (2004, p. 588) pointed out, "The impression is sometimes given . . . that blindsight . . . [is] like normal vision stripped of conscious visual experience. Nothing could be further from the truth, for blindsight is characterised by severely impoverished discrimination of visual stimuli."

Blindsight patients typically have extensive damage to primary visual cortex. However, primary visual cortex probably does not contribute *directly* to visual awareness. ffytche and Zeki (2011) studied two patients (FB and GN) with lesions of primary visual cortex. Their visual experience in the blind field was degraded compared to that in the sighted field. However, the key finding was that FB and GN both had visual awareness of stimuli presented to the blind field, especially when the stimuli were moving.

What role does primary visual cortex play in visual perception? Its main function seems to be to process (and then transmit) information on to higher perceptual centres. As a result, damage to V1 has knock-on effects throughout the visual system, leading to greatly reduced activation of subsequent visual processing areas (Silvanto, 2008).

Which brain areas are of major importance in blindsight? Tamietto et al. (2010) provided an important part of the answer in research on GY, a male blindsight patient. Grey stimuli presented to his blind field influenced his behavioural responses to a consciously perceived stimulus presented to his intact field. This effect was associated with activation in the superior colliculus, which lies within the midbrain. This effect disappeared when purple stimuli (which produce very little activation in the superior colliculus) were presented. Thus, the superior colliculus forms part of a route between sensory and motor processes lying outside conscious visual experience.

Schmid et al. (2010) discovered in research on monkeys that blindsight depends in part on the lateral geniculate nucleus, which receives information from the retina early in visual processing. There are direct projections from the lateral geniculate nucleus to areas of visual cortex (BA18 and BA19; see Figure 1.4) that bypass primary visual cortex.

Findings

It would be useful to study the perceptual abilities of blindsight patients *without* relying on their subjective (and possibly inaccurate) reports of what they can see in the blind field. This was done by van der Stigchel et al. (2010). Two patients with blindsight were instructed to make an eye movement towards a target presented in their sighted field. The target was either presented on its own or at the same time as a distractor in the blind field. The direction of the eye movement was influenced by the distractor's presence even though the patients were not consciously aware of it.

GY (discussed earlier) is a much-studied blindsight patient. He has extensive damage to the primary visual cortex in the left hemisphere and a smaller area of damage in the right parietal area caused by a car accident in childhood. In a study by Persaud and Cowey (2008), GY was presented with a stimulus in the upper or lower part of his visual field. On some trials (inclusion trials), he was instructed to report the part of the visual field to which the stimulus had been presented. On other trials (exclusion trials), GY was told to report the *opposite* of its actual location (e.g., "Up" when it was in the lower part).

What did Persaud and Cowey (2008) find? GY tended to respond with the *real* rather than the *opposite* location on exclusion and inclusion trials, suggesting he had access to location information but lacked any conscious awareness of it (see Figure 2.25). In contrast, healthy individuals showed a large difference in performance on inclusion and exclusion trials, indicating they had conscious access to location information. These findings suggest the involvement of conscious processes was much greater in healthy individuals than in GY.

Evidence that visual processing is very different in the intact and blind visual fields was reported by Persaud et al. (2011) in a study on GY. They manipulated the stimuli presented to his intact and "blind" visual field so his performance when judging the location of a vertical grating was comparable in both fields. In spite of this, GY indicated conscious awareness of far more stimuli in the intact field

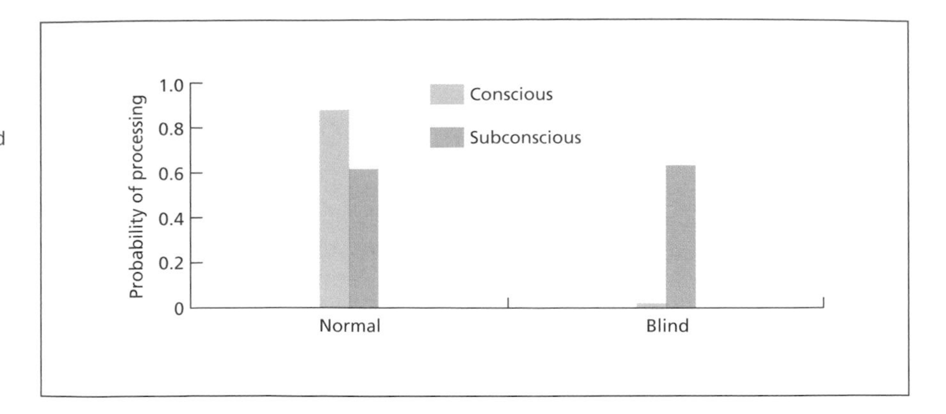

Figure 2.25
Estimated contributions of conscious and subconscious processing to GY's performance in exclusion and inclusion conditions in his normal and blind fields.

Reprinted from Persaud and Cowey (2008). Reprinted with permission from Elsevier.

than the blind one (43% of trials vs. 3%, respectively). Of most importance, there was substantially more activation in the prefrontal cortex and parietal areas to targets presented to the intact field.

Overgaard et al. (2008) gave their blindsight patient, GR, a visual discrimination task. She decided whether a triangle, circle or square had been presented to her blind field. In one experiment, Overgaard et al. used a four-point scale of perceptual awareness: "clear image"; "almost clear image"; "weak glimpse"; and "not seen". In another experiment, GR indicated on a yes/no basis whether she had seen the stimulus.

Consider the findings when the four-point scale was used. There was a strong association between the level of perceptual awareness and the accuracy of her performance when stimuli were presented to her blind field. She was correct 100% of the time when she had a clear image, 72% of the time when her image was almost clear, 25% of the time when she had a weak glimpse and 0% when the stimulus was not seen. Thus, GR used the four-point scale appropriately. If the data for "clear image" and "almost clear image" are combined, GR claimed to have awareness of the stimulus on 54% of trials. On 83% of these trials she was correct.

When Overgaard et al. (2008) used the yes/no measure, GR seemed to have a much lower level of conscious awareness of blind-field stimuli. She indicated she had seen the stimulus on only 21% of the trials and she was right on 86% of those trials. Thus, the use of a sensitive method (i.e., four-point scale) to assess conscious awareness suggests degraded conscious vision sometimes underlies blindsight patients' ability to perform at above-chance levels on visual tasks. Thus, the notion that blindsight patients lack all conscious visual experience in their blind field may sometimes be incorrect.

What do blindsight patients experience?

It is harder than you might imagine to decide exactly what blindsight patients experience when presented with visual stimuli to their blind field. For example, the blindsight patient GY described his experiences as "similar to that of a normally sighted man who, with his eyes shut against sunlight, can perceive the direction of motion of a hand waved in front of him" (Beckers & Zeki, 1995, p. 56).

On another occasion GY was asked about his qualia (sensory experiences). He said, "That [experience of qualia] only happens on very easy trials, when the stimulus is very bright. Actually, I'm not sure I *really* have qualia then" (Persaud & Lau, 2008, p. 1048).

Blindsight patients vary in their residual visual abilities, and so it makes sense to assign them to different categories. Danckert and Rossetti (2005) identified three sub-types of blindsight:

1 *Action-blindsight*: These patients have some ability to grasp or point at objects in the blind field because they have some use of the dorsal ("where") stream of processing (see Figure 2.3). Baseler et al. (1999) found that GY showed activation in the dorsal stream (but not the ventral or "what" stream) to visual stimuli presented in the blind field. This is the most studied sub-type.
2 *Attention-blindsight*: These patients can detect objects and motion and have a vague conscious feeling of objects in spite of reporting they cannot see them. They can make some use of the dorsal stream and motor areas.
3 *Agnosopsia*: These patients deny any conscious awareness of visual stimuli. However, they exhibit some ability to discriminate form and wavelength and to use the ventral stream.

Weblink:
A demonstration of blindsight

Weiskrantz (e.g., 2004) distinguished between Type 1 blindsight and Type 2 blindsight. Type 1 (similar to agnosopsia) includes blindsight patients with no conscious awareness of visual stimuli presented to the blind field. In contrast, Type 2 (similar to attention-blindsight) includes patients with some awareness of such stimuli.

An example of Type 2 blindsight was found in patient EY, who "sensed a definite pinpoint of light", although "it does not actually look like a light. It looks like nothing at all" (Weiskrantz, 1980). Type 2 blindsight sounds suspiciously like residual conscious vision. However, patients tested many times may start to rely on indirect evidence. For example, patients' partial ability to guess whether a stimulus is moving to the left or the right may depend on some vague awareness of their own eye movements.

Ko and Lau (2012) argued that blindsight patients may have more conscious visual experience than is usually believed. Their key assumption was as follows: "Blindsight patients may use an unusually conservative criterion for detection, which results in them saying 'no' nearly all the time to the question of 'do you see something?'" (Ko & Lau, 2012, p. 1402). This excessive caution may occur because damage to the prefrontal cortex impairs the ability to set the criterion for visual detection appropriately. Their excessive conservatism or caution may explain why blindsight patients' reported visual experience is so discrepant from their forced-choice perceptual performance.

Support for Ko and Lau's (2012) position comes from Overgaard et al.'s (2008) finding (discussed earlier) that blindsight patients were excessively reluctant to admit having seen stimuli presented to their blind field. Ko and Lau cite further support for their position in research showing blindsight patients often have damage to the prefrontal cortex in addition to primary visual cortex.

Evaluation

There are various reasons for accepting blindsight as a genuine phenomenon. First, blindsight has been reported in studies in which potential problems with the use of subjective (and possibly distorted) verbal reports have apparently been overcome (e.g., Persaud & Cowey, 2008). Second, there are studies in which evidence for blindsight did not depend on subjective verbal reports (e.g., van der Stigchel et al., 2010). Third, there are functional neuroimaging studies showing many blindsight patients have activation predominantly or exclusively in the dorsal stream (Danckert & Rossetti, 2005). The relevance of this is that the dorsal stream is strongly associated with non-conscious processing (Milner, 2012). Fourth, there is evidence for subliminal processing of emotional information (known as affective blindsight; see Chapter 15).

What are the limitations of research in this area? First, there are considerable differences among blindsight patients with several apparently possessing some conscious visual awareness in their allegedly blind field.

Second, many blindsight patients probably have more conscious visual experience in their "blind" field than appears from yes/no judgements about the presence of a stimulus. This happens because they are excessively cautious about claiming to have seen a stimulus (Ko & Lau, 2012; Overgaard, 2012).

Third, one of the most studied blindsight patients, GY, has nerve fibre connections within the visual system not present in healthy individuals (Bridge et al., 2008). This suggests some visual processes in blindsight patients may be *specific* to them. This would limit our ability to generalise from such patients to healthy individuals.

Subliminal perception

In 1957, a struggling market researcher called James Vicary reported powerful evidence for unconscious perception. He claimed to have flashed EAT POPCORN and DRINK COCA-COLA for 1/300th of a second (well below the threshold of conscious awareness) numerous times during showings of a movie called *Picnic*. This allegedly caused a large increase in the sales of Coca-Cola and popcorn. Alas, Vicary later admitted the study was fabricated.

How can we decide whether an observer has consciously perceived a given visual stimulus? According to Merikle et al. (2001), there are two main thresholds or criteria:

1 *Subjective threshold*: This is defined by an individual's failure to report conscious awareness of a stimulus.
2 *Objective threshold*: This is defined by an individual's inability to make accurate forced-choice decisions about a stimulus (e.g., guess at above-chance level whether it is a word).

Weblink:
Subliminal perception

Weblink:
Kazdin

Two issues arise with these threshold measures. First, as Reingold (2004, p. 882) pointed out, "A valid measure must index *all* of the perceptual information available for consciousness . . . and only conscious, but not unconscious information." That is a tall order. Second, it is hard (or even impossible!) to prove either measure validly indicates zero conscious awareness. For example, Lamme (2010) argued with respect to the subjective threshold that limitations of attention and memory often cause observers' reports to omit some of their conscious experience.

Findings

Naccache et al. (2002) asked participants to decide rapidly whether a clearly visible target digit was smaller or larger than 5. Unknown to them, an invisible masked digit was presented for 29 ms immediately before the target. The masked digit was *congruent* with the target (both digits on the same side of 5) or *incongruent*. In one experiment, a cue signalling the imminent presentation of the target digit was present or absent.

Naccache et al. (2002) reported two main findings. First, there was no evidence of conscious perception of the masked digits: no participants reported seeing any of them (subjective measure) and their performance when guessing whether the masked digit was below or above 5 was at chance level (objective measure). Second, performance with the target digits was faster on congruent than on incongruent trials when cueing was present. This indicates some unconscious perceptual processing of the masked digits had occurred.

Persaud and McLeod (2008) argued that only information perceived with awareness can be used to control our actions. They carried out a study to test this notion. They presented the letter "b" or "h" for 10 ms (short interval) or 15 ms (long interval). In the key condition, participants were instructed to respond with the letter *not* presented. Thus, for example, if they were aware "b" had been presented, they would deliberately *not* say "b" but instead would say "h". The rationale was that participants consciously aware of the letter would inhibit saying the letter actually presented. In contrast, those not consciously aware of it would be unable to inhibit saying it.

What did Persaud and McLeod (2008) find? With the longer presentation interval, participants responded correctly with the non-presented letter on 83% of trials. This suggests there was reasonable conscious awareness of the stimulus. With the shorter presentation interval, participants responded correctly on only 43% of trials (significantly below chance). This finding indicates some processing of the stimulus but in the absence of conscious awareness.

There have been very few attempts to compare different measures of conscious awareness of visual stimuli. Sandberg et al. (2010) addressed this issue. One of four shapes was presented very briefly followed by masking. Observers initially made a behavioural response (deciding which shape had been presented) followed by one of three subjective measures: (1) clarity of perceptual experience (the Perceptual Awareness Scale); (2) confidence in their decision; or (3) wagering variable amounts of money on having made the correct decision.

What did Sandberg et al. (2010) find? First, all three measures indicated above-chance task performance could occur without awareness. Second, the Perceptual Awareness Scale predicted performance accuracy better than the other measures. Third, the Perceptual Awareness Scale indicated the presence of more conscious experience than the other measures (suggesting it was the most sensitive measure). Thus, the optimal method for assessing conscious experience is one (the Perceptual Awareness Scale) that asks observers *directly* to indicate the content of their experience.

The research by Sandberg et al. (2010) suggested that perceptual awareness is graded (i.e., there are variations in its extent). Is that always the case? Windey et al. (2014) argued that it is not. On each trial, they presented participants very briefly with a coloured digit. The task was to decide either whether the digit was red or blue (low-level condition) or whether it was smaller or larger than 5 (high-level task).

Windey et al. (2014) found that perceptual awareness was graded with the low-level task. However, it was all-or-none with the high-level task. They explained the latter finding as follows. According to global workspace theory (Baars, 1988), early non-conscious visual processing involves numerous independent processors carrying out specialised functions (e.g., colour processing, motion processing). Subsequent conscious perceptual awareness is typically associated with synchronised activity across several brain areas (see Chapter 16). This dramatic transformation in brain activity (which is mostly associated with high-level perceptual processing) provides the basis for all-or-none conscious awareness.

There has been much research using neuroimaging and event-related potentials (ERPs; see Glossary). This research is discussed in detail in Chapter 16 and includes studies by Gaillard et al. (2009), Lamy et al. (2009) and Melloni et al. (2007). In essence, it has been found consistently that stimuli of which observers are unaware nevertheless produce activation in several brain areas as predicted by global workspace theory. In one study (Rees, 2007), activation was assessed in brain areas associated with face processing and with object processing while pictures of invisible faces or houses were presented. The identity of the picture (face vs. house) could be predicted with almost 90% accuracy from patterns of brain activation. Thus, even stimuli that are not perceived consciously can be processed reasonably thoroughly by the visual system.

Evaluation

The issue of unconscious or subliminal perception was very controversial. However, there is now convincing evidence for its existence. Some of this evidence is behavioural (e.g., Naccache et al., 2002; Persaud & McLeod, 2008), and some is based on patterns of brain activity (e.g., Melloni et al., 2007; Lamy et al., 2009). It appears there can be substantial processing of visual stimuli up to and including the semantic level in the absence of conscious visual awareness.

What are the limitations of research in this area? First, apart from the study by Sandberg et al. (2010), there has been surprisingly little interest in comparing the validity of different subjective measures of conscious awareness. Second, there is a need for more research in which behavioural and neuroimaging measures are obtained. This would permit greater understanding of the relative advantages and disadvantages of each type of measure as an index of conscious awareness. Third, we need more research investigating the issue of when conscious visual experience is graded and when it is all-or-none.

CHAPTER SUMMARY

- **Vision and the brain**. In the retina, there are cones (specialised for colour vision) and rods (specialised for motion detection). The retina-geniculate-striate pathway between the eye and cortex is divided into partially separate P and M pathways. The dorsal stream (associated with the M pathway) terminates in the parietal cortex and the ventral stream (associated with the P pathway) terminates in the inferotemporal cortex. According to Zeki's functional specialisation theory, different parts of the cortex are specialised for different visual functions. This is supported by findings from patients with selective visual deficits (e.g., achromatopsia; akinetopsia), but there is much less specialisation than claimed by Zeki. There are several binding problems (integrating distributed information about an object to produce coherent perception). Selective attention and synchronised activity in different brain areas both contribute to resolution of binding problems.

- **Two visual systems: perception and action**. Milner and Goodale identified a vision-for-perception system based on the ventral stream and a vision-for-action system based on the dorsal stream. Predicted double dissociations have been found between patients with optic ataxia (damage to the dorsal stream) and visual form agnosia (damage to the ventral stream). Illusory effects found when perceptual judgements are made (ventral stream) are often much reduced when grasping or pointing responses are used. Visually guided action relies much more on the ventral stream than was acknowledged in the original version of the theory. In addition, the two visual systems interact and combine with each other much more than implied by Milner and Goodale.
- **Colour vision**. Colour vision helps us to detect objects and make fine discriminations among them. According to dual-process theory, there are three types of cone receptors and also three types of opponent processes (green–red, blue–yellow, white–black). This theory explains negative afterimages and several kinds of colour deficiency. Colour constancy occurs when a surface seems to have the same colour when there is a change in the illuminant. Several factors are involved in producing the reasonable levels of colour constancy typically found; they include local and global colour contrast; familiarity of object colour; chromatic adaptation; and cone-excitation ratios. Cells demonstrating colour constancy have been found in area V4.
- **Depth perception**. There are numerous monocular cues to depth (e.g., linear perspective, texture, familiar size) as well as oculomotor and binocular cues. Cues are sometimes combined in a simple additive fashion in depth perception. However, they are often weighted, with more weight being attached to reliable cues than unreliable ones. These weightings change if any given cue becomes more or less reliable. If there is a large conflict between two cues, depth perception is determined almost exclusively by one cue. There are close connections between size and distance judgements. However, size perception also depends on other factors, including familiar size, body size and effective interactions.

- *Perception without awareness.* Patients with extensive damage to V1 sometimes suffer from blindsight, a condition in which there is some ability to respond to visual stimuli in the absence of conscious visual awareness. There are several sub-types of blindsight, with some patients reporting limited visual experience in their "blind" field. There are suggestions that blindsight patients may be excessively cautious when reporting on their conscious experience. Subliminal perception can be assessed using a subjective or a more stringent objective threshold. There is reasonable evidence for subliminal perception using both types of threshold. Neuroimaging and ERP studies indicate that extensive visual processing in the absence of conscious awareness is possible.

Further reading

- Foster, D.H. (2011). Colour constancy. *Vision Research*, 51: 674–700. David Foster provides a comprehensive account of theory and research on colour constancy.
- Howard, I.P. (2012). *Perceiving in depth, vol. 3: Other mechanisms of depth perception.* Oxford: Oxford University Press. Ian Howard discusses numerous factors producing depth perception in a comprehensive fashion.
- Landy, M.S., Banks, M.S. & Knill, D.C. (2011). Ideal-observer models of cue utilisation. In J. Trommershäuser, J. Kording & M.S. Landy (eds), *Sensory cue integration* (pp. 5–29). Oxford: Oxford University Press. This chapter is concerned with ways in which observers combine and integrate cues to achieve accurate depth perception.
- Milner, A.D. (2012). Is visual processing in the dorsal stream accessible to consciousness? *Proceedings of the Royal Society B*, 279: 2289–98. David Milner discusses research relevant to the two-systems theory of visual perception he developed with Melvyn Goodale.
- Overgaard, M. (2012). Blindsight: Recent and historical controversies on the blindness of blindsight. *Wiley Interdisciplinary Reviews – Cognitive Science*, 3: 607–14. Morten Overgaard discusses key issues relating to blindsight.
- Wade, N.J. & Swanston, M.T. (2013). *Visual perception: An introduction* (3rd edn). Hove: Psychology Press. This textbook discusses most of the topics considered in this chapter.

CHAPTER

3

Object and face recognition

INTRODUCTION

Tens of thousands of times every day we identify or recognise objects in the world around us. At this precise moment, you are aware of looking at this book. If you raise your eyes, perhaps you can see a wall, windows and so on in front of you. Object recognition typically occurs so effortlessly it is hard to believe it is actually a complex achievement. Evidence of its complexity comes from attempts to programme computers to "perceive" the environment. As yet, no computer can match more than a fraction of the perceptual skills possessed by nearly every sighted human adult.

What makes visual perception complex? First, many objects in the environment overlap, and so we must decide where one object ends and the next one starts. Second, numerous objects (e.g., chairs, trees) vary enormously in their visual properties (e.g., colour, size, shape) and so it is not immediately obvious how we assign such diverse stimuli to the same category. Third, we recognise objects over numerous orientations. For example, most plates are round. However, we can easily identify a plate when it appears elliptical.

We can go beyond simply identifying objects. For example, we can generally describe what an object would look like from different angles, and we also know its uses and functions. All in all, there is much more to object recognition than might initially be supposed (than meets the eye?).

What is discussed in this chapter? The overarching theme is to unravel the mysteries associated with the recognition of *three-dimensional* objects. However, we start with a discussion of how *two-dimensional* patterns are recognised.

After that, we consider how we decide which parts of the visual world belong together and thus form separate objects. This is a crucial early stage in object recognition. After that, general theories of object recognition are evaluated in the light of neuroimaging studies and behavioural experiments on healthy individuals and brain-damaged patients.

Face recognition (which is vitally important in our everyday lives) differs in important ways from object recognition. Accordingly, we discuss face recognition in a separate section. Finally, we consider whether the processes involved in visual imagery of objects resemble those involved in visual perception of objects.

KEY TERMS

Pattern recognition
The ability to identify or categorise two-dimensional patterns (e.g., letters, fingerprints).

Note that other issues relating to object recognition (e.g., depth perception, size constancy) were discussed in Chapter 2.

PATTERN RECOGNITION

We spend much of our time (e.g., when reading) engaged in **pattern recognition** – the identification or categorisation of two-dimensional patterns. Much research on pattern recognition has addressed the issue of how alphanumeric patterns (alphabetical and numerical symbols) are recognised. A key issue is the *flexibility* of the human perceptual system. For example, we can recognise the letter "A" rapidly and accurately across large variations in orientation, typeface, size and writing style.

Patterns can be regarded as consisting of a set of specific features or attributes (Jain & Duin, 2004). For example, the key features of the letter "A" are two straight lines and a connected cross-bar. This feature-based approach has the advantage that visual stimuli varying greatly in size, orientation and minor details can be identified as instances of the same pattern.

It is assumed in several feature theories that pattern recognition involves processing of specific features followed by more global or general processing to integrate information from the features. However, global processing often *precedes* more specific processing. Navon (1977) presented observers with stimuli such as the one shown in Figure 3.1. In one experiment, observers decided whether the large letter was an "H" or an "S"; on other trials, they decided whether the small letters were Hs or Ss.

What did Navon (1977) find? Performance speed with the small letters was greatly slowed when the large letter differed from the small letters. In contrast, decision speed with the large letter was *not* influenced by the nature of the small letters. Thus, we often see the forest (global structure) before the trees (features) rather than the other way around. There is accumulating evidence that the visual system is designed so global or general processing typically precedes local or detailed processing (see later section entitled "spatial frequency").

```
S           S
S           S
S           S
S           S
S           S
SSSSSSSSSSSSS
S           S
S           S
S           S
S           S
S           S
```

Figure 3.1
The kind of stimulus used by Navon (1977) to demonstrate the importance of global features in perception.

Dalrymple et al. (2009) replicated the above finding when the small letters were very small and close together. However, processing was faster at the level of the small letters than the large letter when the small letters were larger and spread out. In this condition, it was harder to identify the large letter. Attention allocation (i.e., which part of the visual stimulus is fixated) is another factor influencing whether global processing precedes local processing (Wagemans et al., 2012b).

Feature detectors

If the presentation of a visual stimulus leads to detailed processing of its basic features, we may be able to identify cortical cells involved in such processing. Hubel and Wiesel (1962) studied cells in parts of the occipital cortex (at the back of the brain) involved with the early stages of visual processing. Some cells responded in two different ways to a spot of light depending on which part of the cell was affected:

1 An "on" response with an increased rate of firing when the light was on.
2 An "off" response with the light causing a decreased rate of firing.

Hubel and Wiesel (e.g., 1979) discovered two types of neuron in primary visual cortex: simple cells and complex cells. Simple cells have "on" and "off" regions with each region being rectangular. These cells respond most to dark bars in a light field, light bars in a dark field, or straight edges between areas of light and dark. Any given cell responds strongly only to stimuli of a particular orientation. Thus, the responses of these cells could be relevant to feature detection.

Weblink:
Hubel and Wiesel (1962)

Complex cells resemble simple cells in responding maximally to straight-line stimuli in a particular orientation. However, complex cells have large receptive fields and respond more to moving contours. Each complex cell is driven by several simple cells having the same orientation preference and closely overlapping receptive fields (Alonso & Martinez, 1998). There are also end-stopped cells. Their responsiveness depends on stimulus length and on orientation.

IN THE REAL WORLD: FINGERPRINTING

An important form of pattern recognition in the real world involves experts matching a criminal's fingerprints (the latent print) against stored fingerprint records. An automatic fingerprint identification system (AFIS) scans through huge databases (e.g., the FBI has the fingerprints of over 60 million individuals). This produces a small number of possible matches to the fingerprint obtained from the scene of the crime ranked in terms of similarity to the criminal's fingerprint. Experts then decide which fingerprint (if any) in the database matches the criminal's.

AFIS focuses on features at two levels. There are three general fingerprint patterns: loop, arch and whorl (circle). Fingerprints also contain more specific features. We have patterns of ridges and valleys known as friction ridges on our hands. Of particular importance are minutiae points – locations where a friction ridge ends abruptly or a ridge divides into two or more ridges. Experts are provided with information about feature or minutiae similarity from AFIS but also make use of microfeatures (e.g., the width of particular ridges).

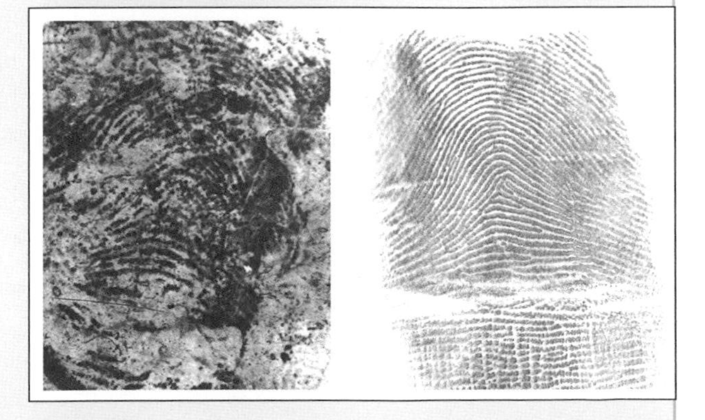

Figure 3.2
The FBI's mistaken identification of the Madrid bomber. The fingerprint from the crime scene is on the left. The fingerprint of the innocent suspect (positively identified by various fingerprint experts) is on the right.
From Dror et al. (2006). Reprinted with permission from Elsevier.

You can see some of the complexities in fingerprint identification by deciding whether the two fingerprints shown in Figure 3.2 come from the same person. Four fingerprinting experts decided they came from the same person, namely, the bomber involved in the terrorist attack in Madrid on 11 March 2004. In fact, the fingerprints are from two different individuals. The one on the left is from the Madrid bomber (Ouhane Daoud), but the one on the right comes from Brandon Mayfield, an American lawyer who was falsely arrested.

Findings

It is commonly believed that fingerprint identification is typically very accurate, with the case of the Madrid bomber a rare exception. In fact, that is not entirely the case. Cole (2005) reviewed 22 real-life cases involving fingerprint misidentification by experts. In over half the cases, the original expert misidentification was confirmed by one or more additional experts. Dror et al. (2012) had experts list all the minutiae on ten fingerprints and then repeat the exercise a few months later. There was total agreement between their two assessments of the same fingerprint only 16% of the time.

Many mistakes are made because of the intrinsic complexity and incompleteness of latent fingerprints. However, top-down processes also contribute towards identification errors. Many such errors involve forensic confirmation bias, which Kassin et al. (2013, p. 45) defined as "the class of effects through which an individual's pre-existing beliefs, expectations, motives, and situational context influence the collection, perception, and interpretation of evidence".

Dror et al. (2006) reported evidence of forensic confirmation bias. Experts judged whether two fingerprints matched having been told incorrectly that the prints were the ones mistakenly matched by the FBI as the Madrid bomber. Unknown to these experts, they had judged these fingerprints to be a clear and definite match several years earlier. The misleading information provided led 60% of the experts to judge the prints to be definite non-matches! Thus, top-down processes triggered by contextual information can distort fingerprint identification.

Further evidence of forensic confirmation bias was reported by Langenburg et al. (2009). They studied the effects of context (e.g., alleged conclusions of an internationally respected expert) on fingerprint identification. Experts and non-experts were both influenced by contextual information but non-experts were influenced more.

Why are experts better than non-experts at deciding accurately that two fingerprints match? According to signal-detection theory (e.g., Phillips et al., 2001), there are two possibilities. First, experts may have an excellent ability to *discriminate* between prints that match and those that do not match. Second, they have a lenient *response bias*, meaning that they have a strong tendency to respond "match" to every pair of prints regardless of whether there is actually a match. The acid test of which explanation is more applicable is the false-alarm rate – the tendency to respond "match" incorrectly to similar but non-matching pairs of prints. Good discrimination is associated with a low false-alarm rate whereas a lenient response bias is associated with a high false-alarm rate.

Thompson et al. (2014) carried out a study on experts and novices using genuine crime scene prints. Both groups responded "match" accurately on approximately 70% of trials on which there was a genuine match. However, there was a substantial difference in the false-alarm rate. Novices incorrectly responded "match" when the two prints were similar but did not match on 57% of trials compared to only 1.65% for experts. These findings indicate that experts have much better discrimination than novices. They also have a much more conservative response bias than novices, meaning they are more reluctant to respond "match".

All these types of cells are involved in feature detection. However, we must not exaggerate their usefulness. These cells provide *ambiguous* information because they respond in the same way to different stimuli. For example, a cell may respond equally to a horizontal line moving rapidly and a nearly horizontal line moving slowly. We must *combine* information from many neurons to remove ambiguities.

Hubel and Wiesel's theoretical account needs to be expanded to take account of the finding that neurons differ in their responsiveness to different spatial frequencies (see later section entitled "spatial frequency"). As we will see, several phenomena in visual perception depend on this differential responsiveness.

KEY TERM

Law of Prägnanz
The notion that the simplest possible organisation of the visual environment is perceived; proposed by the Gestaltists.

PERCEPTUAL ORGANISATION

It would probably be fairly easy to work out which parts of the visual information available to us belong together and thus form objects if those objects were spread out in space. Instead, the visual environment is often complex and confusing, with many objects overlapping others and so hiding parts of them from view. As a result, it can be hard to achieve perceptual segregation of visual objects.

The first systematic attempt to study these issues was made by the Gestaltists. They were German psychologists (including Koffka, Köhler and Wertheimer) who emigrated to the United States between the two World Wars. The Gestaltists' fundamental principle was the **law of Prägnanz**, according to which we typically perceive the simplest possible organisation of the visual field.

Most of the Gestaltists' other laws can be subsumed under the law of Prägnanz. Figure 3.3(a) illustrates the law of proximity, according to which visual elements close in space tend to be grouped together. Figure 3.3(b) shows the law of similarity, according to which similar elements tend to be grouped together.

We see two crossing lines in Figure 3.3(c) because, according to the law of good continuation, we group together those elements requiring the fewest changes or interruptions in straight or smoothly curving lines. Finally, Figure 3.3(d)

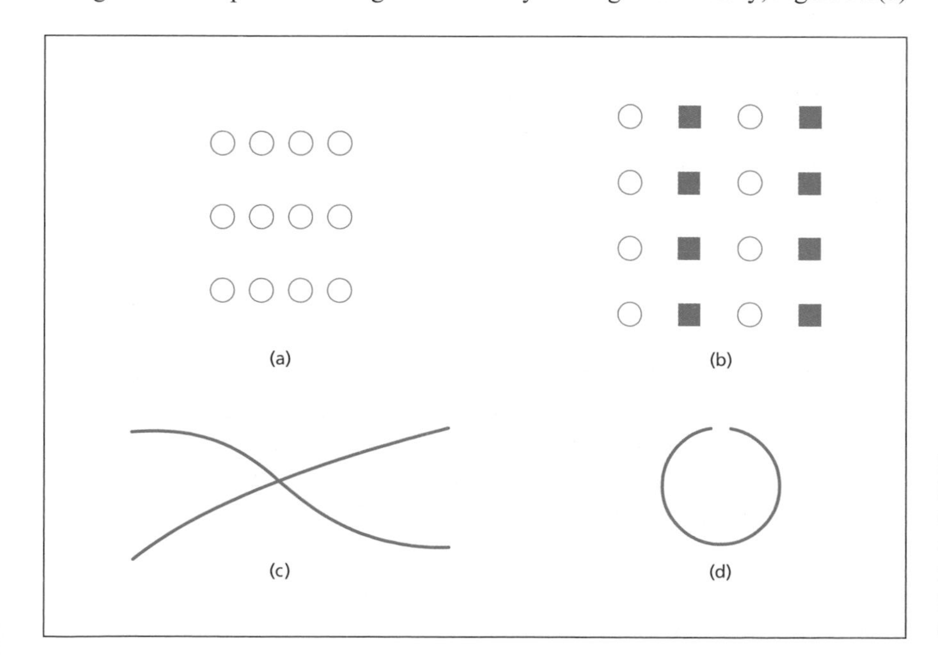

Weblink:
Gestalt laws of perceptual organisation

Weblink:
Article by Max Wertheimer

Figure 3.3
Examples of the Gestalt laws of perceptual organisation: (a) the law of proximity; (b) the law of similarity; (c) the law of good continuation; and (d) the law of closure.

Figure 3.4
An ambiguous drawing that, can be seen as either two faces or as a goblet.

illustrates the law of closure: the missing parts of a figure are filled in to complete the figure (here a circle).

As Wagemans et al. (2012a) pointed out, it is easy to dismiss these grouping principles as "mere textbook curiosities". In fact, however, the various grouping principles "pervade virtually all perceptual experiences because they determine the objects and parts that people perceive in their environment" (Wagemans et al., 2012a, p. 1180).

The Gestaltists emphasised the importance of **figure–ground segregation** in perception. One part of the visual field is identified as the figure, and the remainder is treated as less important and so forms the ground.

According to the Gestaltists, the figure is perceived as having a distinct form or shape whereas the ground lacks form. In addition, the figure is perceived as being in front of the ground and the contour separating the figure from the ground is seen as belonging to the figure. You can check the validity of these claims by looking at the faces–goblet illusion (see Figure 3.4). When the goblet is perceived as the figure, it seems to be in front of a dark background. Faces are in front of a light background when forming the figure.

Various factors determine which region is identified as the figure and which as the ground. Regions that are convex (curving outwards), small, surrounded and symmetrical are more likely to be perceived as the figure than regions lacking these characteristics (Wagemans et al., 2012a). For example, Fowlkes et al. (2007) studied numerous natural images for which observers made figure–ground decisions. Figure regions tended to be smaller and more convex than ground regions. Overall, the findings indicate that cues emphasised by the Gestaltists are, indeed, important in figure–ground assignment.

Weblink:
Figure–ground segregation

Findings

The Gestaltists' approach was limited in that they mostly studied artificial figures, making it important to see whether their findings apply to more realistic stimuli. Geisler et al. (2001) used pictures to study in detail the contours of flowers, a river, trees and so on. The contours of objects could be worked out very well using two principles different from those emphasised by the Gestaltists:

1 Adjacent segments of any contour typically have very similar orientations.
2 Segments of any contour that are further apart generally have somewhat different orientations.

Geisler et al. (2001) presented observers with two complex patterns at the same time and they decided which pattern contained a winding contour. Task performance was predicted very well from the two key principles described above. These findings suggest we use our extensive knowledge of real objects when making decisions about contours.

KEY TERMS

Figure–ground segregation
The perceptual organisation of the visual field into a figure (object of central interest) and a ground (less important background).

Elder and Goldberg (2002) analysed the statistics of natural contours and obtained findings largely consistent with Gestalt laws. Proximity was a very powerful cue when deciding which contours belonged to which objects. In addition, there was a small contribution from similarity and from good continuation.

According to the Gestaltists, perceptual grouping is innate or intrinsic to the brain and so learning based on past experience is de-emphasised. Bhatt and Quinn (2011) reviewed the literature on perceptual grouping in infants. The finding that infants as young as three or four months show grouping by good continuation, proximity and connectedness seems consistent with the Gestalt position. However, other grouping principles (e.g., closure) were only used later in infancy. In addition, infants often made *increased* use of grouping principles over a period of months. Overall, these findings indicate that learning plays an important role in perceptual grouping.

Palmer and Rock (1994) proposed a new principle termed **uniform connectedness** not discovered by the Gestaltists. According to this principle, any connected region having uniform visual properties (e.g., colour, texture, lightness) tends to be organised as a single perceptual unit. Palmer and Rock found grouping by uniform connectedness dominated proximity and similarity when these grouping principles were in conflict. Han and Humphreys (2003) found grouping by uniform connectedness was faster than grouping by proximity only when several objects were present, suggesting it is especially important when observers are presented with multiple objects.

According to the Gestaltists, figure–ground segregation occurs rapidly and so should be uninfluenced by attentional processes. Contrary evidence was reported by Vecera et al. (2004). Observers were presented with two adjacent regions and a visual cue (a small rectangle was presented to one region to manipulate attention). The key finding was that whichever region was attended to tended to be perceived as the figure. Thus, attention can influence the process of figure–ground segmentation. However, Kimchi and Peterson (2008) found figure–ground processing could occur in the absence of attention when the stimuli were relatively simple.

The Gestaltists assumed figure–ground segregation is innate and does not depend on past experience or learning. Contrary evidence was reported by Barense et al. (2012). Participants suffering from amnesia (see Glossary) and healthy controls were presented with various stimuli, some of which contained parts of well-known objects (see Figure 3.5). In other stimuli, the object parts were rearranged. The task was to indicate which region of each stimulus was the figure.

The healthy controls identified the regions containing familiar objects as figure more often than those containing rearranged parts. In contrast, the amnesic patients (who experienced difficulty

KEY TERMS

Uniform connectedness
The notion that adjacent regions in the visual environment having uniform visual properties (e.g., colour) are perceived as a single perceptual unit.

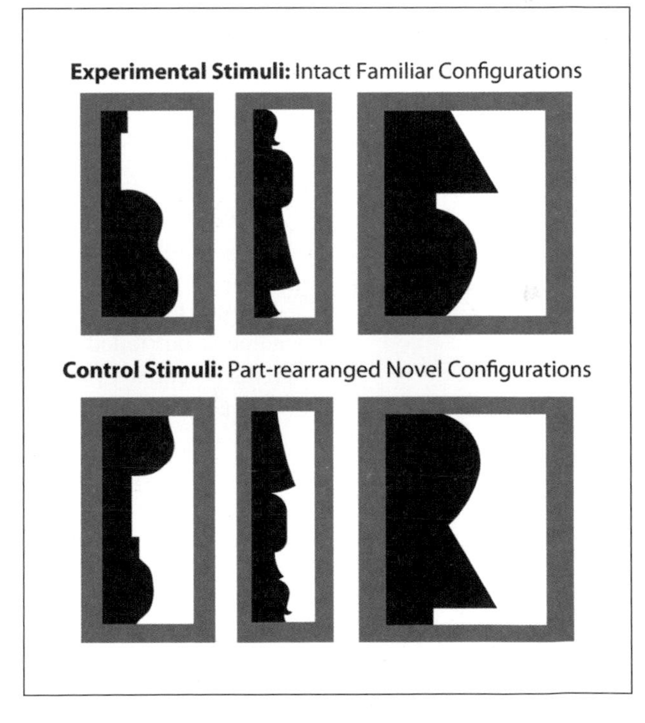

Figure 3.5
The top row shows intact familiar shapes (from left to right: a guitar, a standing woman, a table lamp). The bottom row shows the same objects but with the parts rearranged. The task was to decide which region in each stimulus was the figure.

From Barense et al. (2012). Reprinted with permission of Oxford University Press.

in identifying the objects presented) showed no difference between the two types of stimuli. Thus, figure–ground segregation does not depend solely on basic features such as convexity, symmetry and surroundedness, but also depends on past experience in terms of object familiarity, and thus is not totally innate.

The Gestaltists emphasised the importance of border "ownership" in determining what is figure and what is ground. Relatively recent neurophysiological research has revealed direct links between figure–ground segregation and the responses of numerous neurons in early visual cortex (Layton et al., 2012). These border-ownership neurons are important because they seem to provide high-level information about figure and ground.

Evaluation

What are the strengths of the Gestalt approach? First, the Gestaltists focused on key issues – it is of fundamental importance to understand the processes underlying perceptual organisation. Second, nearly all the laws of grouping they proposed (as well as the notion of figure–ground segregation) have stood the test of time. Most are applicable to complex three-dimensional real-world scenes as well as two-dimensional drawings. Third, the notion that observers perceive the simplest possible organisation of the visual environment (enshrined in the law of Prägnanz) has proved very fruitful. Recent theoretical developments suggest that striving for simplicity may be of central importance in accurate perception (Wagemans et al., 2012b).

What are the limitations of the Gestalt approach? First, the Gestaltists greatly de-emphasised the importance of past experience and learning in determining perceptual grouping and figure–ground segregation. They virtually ignored the extent to which perceptual organisation depends on observers' knowledge of environmental regularities. As Wagemans et al. (2012b, p. 1229) pointed out, the Gestaltists "focused almost exclusively on processes intrinsic to the perceiving organism . . . The environment itself did not interest [them]."

Second, the Gestaltists mostly produced *descriptions* of important perceptual phenomena but failed to provide adequate *explanations*. The law of Prägnanz offered a potentially powerful explanation but the Gestaltists failed to develop it. Several major theoretical explanations of Gestalt phenomena have been proposed by more recent theorists (Wagemans et al., 2012b). For example, there is the Bayesian approach (Kersten et al., 2004). This approach "entails a rational estimate of the structure of the scene that combines fit to the available image data with the mental set of the perceiver (background knowledge, context, etc.)" (Wagemans et al., 2012b, p. 1233).

A key aspect of the Bayesian approach is that observers are responsive to statistical regularities in the world. Thus, for example, we learn the extent to which visual elements that are close together and/or similar belong to the same object. In addition, the Bayesian approach assumes that we use our knowledge of patterns and objects when working out figure–ground segregation.

Third, nearly all the evidence the Gestaltists provided for their principles of perceptual organisation was based on two-dimensional drawings. While most of these principles also apply to real-world scenes, the latter are often very cluttered with important parts of objects hidden or occluded. Thus, perceiving real-world scenes is often far more complex than perceiving two-dimensional drawings.

Fourth, the Gestaltists did not discover all the principles of perceptual organisation. We have seen that uniform connectedness is one example but there are several others (Wagemans et al., 2012a). One is generalised common fate (e.g., when elements of a visual scene become brighter or darker together, they tend to be grouped together).

Fifth, the Gestaltists' approach was too *inflexible*. They did not realise perceptual grouping and figure–ground segregation depend on complex interactions between basic (and possibly innate) processes and past experience. They also did not realise perceptual grouping and figure–ground segregation can occur early in processing or later dependent on the nature of the stimuli and the task.

APPROACHES TO OBJECT RECOGNITION

Object recognition (identifying objects in the visual field) is of enormous importance if we are to interact effectively with the world around us. Our coverage of this important topic will start by considering some basic aspects of the human visual system. After that, we will discuss major theories of object recognition.

Spatial frequency

Hegdé (2008) emphasised that visual perception develops over time even though it may seem instantaneous. The visual processing involved in object recognition typically proceeds in a coarse-to-fine way, with initial coarse or general processing being followed by fine or detailed processing. The advantage of having such a visual system is that we can perceive visual scenes at a very general level and/or at a fine-grained level.

How does coarse-to-fine processing occur? Of major importance, numerous cells in primary visual cortex respond to high spatial frequencies and capture fine detail in the visual image. In contrast, numerous others respond to low spatial frequencies and capture coarse information in the visual image. The details are complex. However, we can see the effects of varying spatial frequency by comparing images consisting only of high or low spatial frequency (see Figure 3.6). Low spatial frequencies in visual input are conveyed rapidly to higher-order brain areas by the fast magnocellular pathway (discussed in Chapter 2), whereas high spatial frequencies are conveyed more slowly by the parvocellular pathway. This speed difference explains why coarse processing typically precedes fine processing.

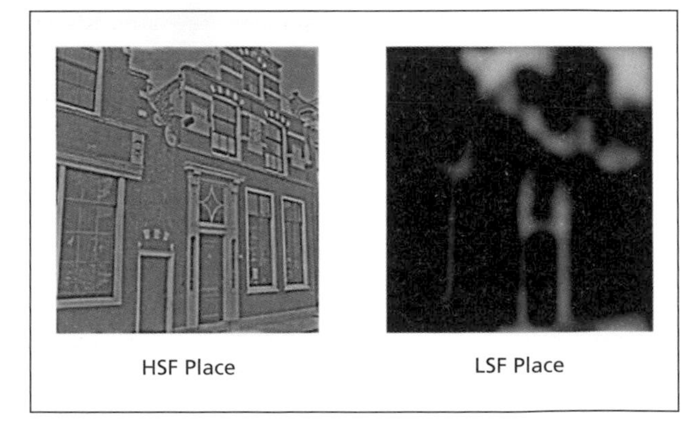

Figure 3.6
High and low spatial frequency versions of a place (a building).
From Awasthi et al. (2013).

Findings

Musel et al. (2012) tested the notion that visual processing typically involves coarse processing followed by fine processing. Young adults were presented with very brief (150 ms) indoor and outdoor scenes proceeding from coarse (low spatial frequency) to fine (high spatial frequency) or vice versa (sample videos can be viewed at

DOI.10.1371/journal.pone.0038493). They decided rapidly whether each scene was an indoor or outdoor one. Performance was faster with the coarse-to-fine sequence, suggesting the visual processing of natural scenes is predominantly coarse-to-fine.

We may have implied that visual processing of scenes proceeds in the same invariant coarse-to-fine fashion regardless of task. In fact, visual processing often exhibits considerable *flexibility*. We can illustrate this by returning to Navon's (1977) discovery that global processing often precedes local processing (discussed earlier). Flevaris et al. (2014) used the Navon task (see Figure 3.1) in which the participants' task involved focusing on the global or local level. It seems likely that global processing is facilitated more by low than by high spatial frequencies, whereas the opposite is the case for local processing.

Flevaris et al. (2014) reported two main findings. First, there was more activation of neurons responsive to low spatial frequencies with the global task than the local one. Second, there was more activation of neurons responsive to high spatial frequencies with the local task. Overall, the findings indicate that visual processing is flexible and responsive to task demands.

Livingstone (2000) argued that a focus on spatial frequencies can help us to explain why the *Mona Lisa* painted by Leonardo da Vinci has a notoriously elusive smile. She produced very low, low and high spatial frequency images of the *Mona Lisa* (see Figure 3.7). As you can see, *Mona Lisa*'s smile is much more obvious in the two low spatial frequency images. Livingstone pointed out that our central or foveal vision is dominated by higher spatial frequencies than our peripheral vision. It follows that, "You can't catch her smile by looking at her mouth. She smiles *until* you look at her mouth" (p. 1299).

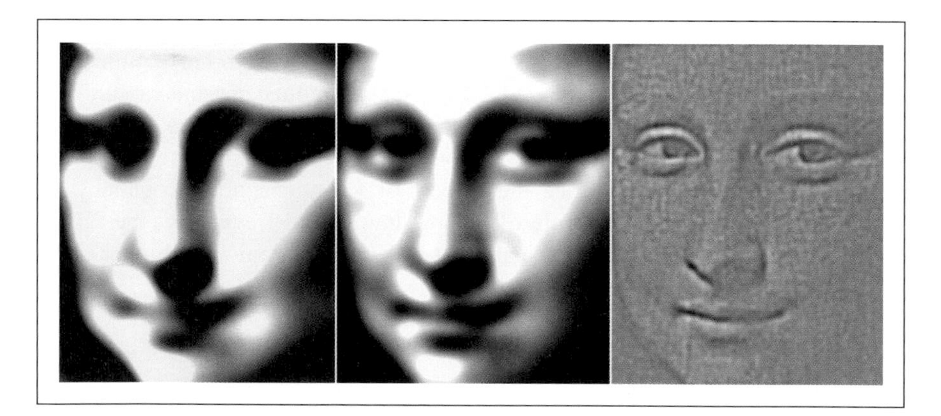

Figure 3.7
Image of *Mona Lisa* revealing very low spatial frequencies (left), low spatial frequencies (centre) or high spatial frequencies (right).
From Livingstone (2000). By kind permission of Margaret Livingstone.

Conclusions

The fact that neurons in visual cortex differ in their responsiveness to high vs. low spatial frequencies is of great importance in understanding visual perception. Here we have emphasised the relevance of this differential responsiveness in accounting for coarse-to-fine visual processing. We have also emphasised that visual processing is flexible and influenced by task demands. As a result, the coarse-to-fine sequence is not invariant. Note that spatial frequencies play a major role in understanding numerous phenomena in visual perception over and above those we have discussed here.

Theories of object recognition

There are numerous theories of object recognition. Before discussing these theories, we will discuss object recognition with respect to Milner and Goodale's (1995, 2008) two-systems model (discussed in Chapter 2). They argued that object recognition and perception depend primarily on the ventral visual stream. This stream is hierarchically organised (see Figure 2.4). Visual processing basically proceeds from the retina through several areas including the lateral geniculate nucleus, V1, V2 and V4, culminating in the inferotemporal cortex. The stimuli causing the greatest neuronal activation become progressively more complex as processing moves along the ventral stream. At the same time, cells' receptive fields increase progressively in size.

In spite of the importance of the ventral stream for object recognition, the dorsal stream is also involved. More specifically, the ventral stream is involved in analytic or detailed visual processing requiring attention, whereas the dorsal stream is involved in holistic or global processing not dependent on attention (Thoma & Henson, 2011). Farivar (2009) reviewed research indicating many three-dimensional shape cues are processed exclusively within the dorsal stream.

The most influential theorist has probably been David Marr (1982). In his computational model, he argued that object recognition involves a series of processing stages and is much more complex than had previously been thought. An assessment of the long-term influence of Marr's theorising is provided by Mather (2015, in press).

Marr (1982) claimed observers construct a series of representations (descriptions) providing increasingly detailed information about the visual environment:

- *Primal sketch*: This provides a two-dimensional description of the main light-intensity changes in the visual input, including information about edges, contours and blobs.
- *2½-D sketch*: This incorporates a description of the depth and orientation of visible surfaces, making use of information from shading, texture, motion, binocular disparity and so on. It is like the primal sketch in being observer-centred or viewpoint-dependent.
- *3-D model representation*: This describes three-dimensionally objects' shapes and their relative positions independent of the observer's viewpoint (it is thus viewpoint-invariant).

Weblink:
Outline of Marr's theory

Marr's theoretical approach has been hugely influential for various reasons. First, he realised object recognition is considerably more complex than had been thought previously. Second, Marr developed a comprehensive computational model of the processes involved in object recognition. That inspired many subsequent theorists to construct their own computational models. Third, Marr's distinction between viewpoint-dependent and viewpoint-invariant representations has served as the focus of a substantial body of research (discussed later).

Irving Biederman. University of Southern California.

One limitation of Marr's approach is that there is an excessive emphasis on bottom-up processes. Marr (1982, p. 101) did admit that, "Top-down processing is sometimes used and necessary." In practice, however, he typically ignored the role played by expectations and knowledge in visual perception. Another limitation is that, "The computations required to produce view-independent 3-D object models are now thought by many researchers to be too complex" (Mather, 2015, in press). That argument is supported by the fact that no one so far has been able to generate 3-D models in the way stipulated by Marr.

Biederman's recognition-by-components theory

Irving Biederman (1987) (see photo) developed and extended Marr's theoretical approach in his recognition-by-components theory. His central assumption was that objects consist of basic shapes or components known as "geons" (geometric ions). Examples of geons are blocks, cylinders, spheres, arcs and wedges. Biederman claimed there are approximately 36 different geons. That may seem suspiciously few to provide descriptions of every object we can recognise and identify. However, we can identify enormous numbers of spoken English words even though there are only approximately 44 phonemes (basic sounds) in the English language. This is because these phonemes can be arranged in almost endless combinations. The same is true of geons. For example, a *cup* can be described by an arc connected to the side of a cylinder. A *pail* can be described by the same two geons but with the arc connected to the top of the cylinder.

The key features of the recognition-by-components theory are shown in Figure 3.8. The stage we have discussed involves determining the components or geons of a visual object and their relationships. When this information is available, it is matched with stored object representations or structural models containing information about the nature of the relevant geons, their orientations, their sizes and so on. The identification of any given visual object is determined by whichever stored representation fits best with the component- or geon-based information obtained from the visual object.

Weblink:
Biederman's theory

As indicated in Figure 3.8, the first step in object recognition is edge extraction. Biederman (1987, p. 117) described this as follows: "[There is] an early edge extraction stage, responsive to differences in surface characteristics, namely, luminance, texture, or colour, providing a line drawing description of the object."

The next step is to decide how a visual object should be segmented to establish its parts or components. Biederman (1987) argued that the *concave* parts of an object's contour are of particular value in accomplishing this task. Leek et al. (2012) assessed eye movements during performance of an object recognition task. As predicted, eye movements were directed most towards internal concave regions.

The other major element is to decide which edge information from an object remains *invariant* across different viewing angles. According to Biederman (1987), there are five such invariant properties of edges:

- *Curvature*: points on a curve.
- *Parallel*: sets of points in parallel.
- *Cotermination*: edges terminating at a common point.
- *Symmetry*: vs. asymmetry.
- *Collinearity*: points sharing a common line.

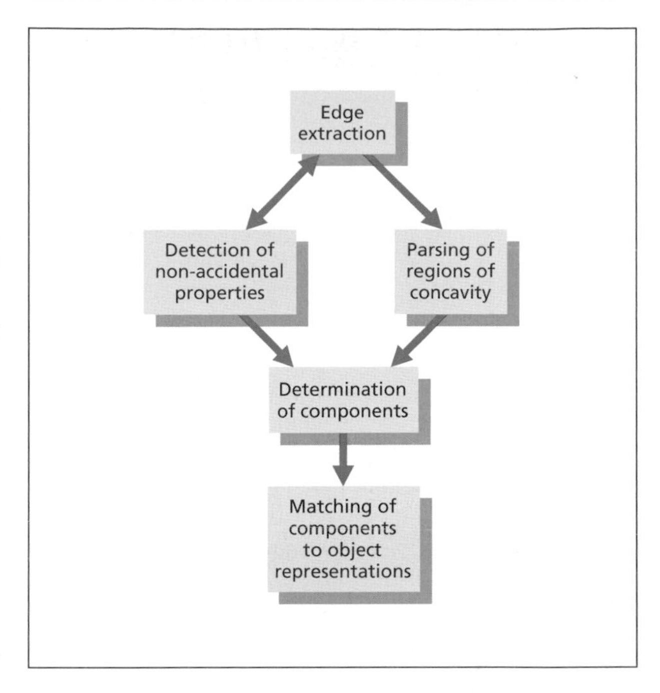

Figure 3.8
An outline of Biederman's recognition-by-components theory.
Adapted from Biederman (1987).

According to the theory, the components or geons of a visual object are constructed from these invariant properties. For example, a cylinder has curved edges and two parallel edges connecting the curved edges. Biederman (1987, p. 116) argued that the five properties:

> have the desirable properties that they are invariant over changes in orientation and can be determined from just a few points on each edge. Consequently, they allow a primitive [component or geon] to be extracted with great tolerance for variations of viewpoint, occlusions [obstructions], and noise.

This part of the theory leads to the key prediction that object recognition is typically viewpoint-invariant, meaning an object can be recognised equally easily from nearly all viewing angles. (Note that Marr (1982) assumed that the 3-D model representation was viewpoint-invariant.) Why is this prediction made? Object recognition depends crucially on the identification of geons, which can be identified from numerous viewpoints. Thus, object recognition from a given viewing angle is difficult only when one or more geons are hidden from view.

An important part of Biederman's (1987) theory with respect to the invariant properties is the "non-accidental" principle. According to this principle, regularities in the visual image reflect actual (or non-accidental) regularities in the world rather than accidental characteristics of a given viewpoint. Thus, for example, a two-dimensional symmetry in the visual image is assumed to indicate symmetry in the three-dimensional object. Use of the non-accidental principle occasionally leads to error. For example, a straight line in a visual image usually reflects a straight edge in the world but might not (e.g., a bicycle viewed end on).

How do we recognise objects when conditions are suboptimal (e.g., an intervening object obscures part of the target object)? Biederman (1987) argued that the following factors are important in such conditions:

- The invariant properties (e.g., curvature, parallel lines) of an object can still be detected even when only parts of edges are visible.
- Provided the concavities of a contour are visible, there are mechanisms allowing the missing parts of the contour to be restored.
- There is generally much redundant information available for recognising complex objects, and so they can still be recognised when some geons or components are missing. For example, a giraffe could be identified from its neck alone.

Findings

Vogels et al. (2001) assessed the response of individual neurons in inferior temporal cortex to changes in a geon compared to changes in the size of an object with no change in the geon. Some neurons responded more to geon changes than changes in object size, thus providing some support for the reality of geons.

A key prediction of recognition-by-components theory is that object recognition is typically viewpoint-invariant. Biederman and Gerhardstein (1993) tested this prediction in a study in which a to-be-named object was preceded by an object prime. Object naming was primed as well when there was an angular change of 135 degrees between the two views of the object as when the two views were identical, thus supporting the prediction.

Biederman and Gerhardstein (1993) used familiar objects. Such objects have typically been encountered from multiple viewpoints, which facilitates the task of dealing with different viewpoints. Unsurprisingly, Tarr and Bülthoff (1995) obtained different findings when they used *novel* objects and gave observers extensive practice at recognising these objects from certain specified viewpoints. Object recognition was viewpoint-dependent, with performance being better when familiar viewpoints were used.

According to the theory, object recognition depends on edge rather than surface information (e.g., colour). However, Sanocki et al. (1998) pointed out that edge-extraction processes are less likely to produce accurate object recognition when objects are presented in the context of other objects rather than on their own. This is because it can be difficult to decide which edges belong to which object when several objects are presented together.

Sanocki et al. (1998) presented observers briefly with objects in the form of line drawings or full-colour photographs, and these objects were presented in isolation or in context. Object recognition was much worse with the edge drawings than the colour photographs, especially when objects were presented in context. Thus, Biederman (1987) exaggerated the role of edge-based extraction processes in object recognition.

As can be seen in Figure 3.8, the theory strongly emphasises bottom-up processes in object recognition. However, top-down processes depending on factors such as expectation and knowledge are often important, especially when object recognition is difficult (Viggiano et al., 2008: this study is discussed shortly).

Evaluation

Biederman's (1987) recognition-by-components theory has been very influential. It provides an answer to the puzzle of how we identify objects in spite of substantial differences among the members of any category in shape, size and orientation. The assumption that geons or geon-like components are involved in visual object recognition is plausible. In addition, concavities and edges are of major importance in object recognition.

What are the limitations of this theoretical approach? First, it focuses primarily on bottom-up processes triggered directly by the stimulus input. By so doing, it de-emphasises the importance of top-down processes based on expectation and knowledge (discussed shortly).

Second, the theory accounts only for fairly unsubtle perceptual discriminations. It explains in part how we decide whether the animal in front of us is a dog or a cat, but not how we decide whether it is a particular breed of dog or cat. This issue is discussed below.

Third, the theory assumes object recognition generally involves matching a stimulus representation independent of the observer's viewpoint with object information stored in long-term memory. As is discussed below, there are numerous exceptions to this prediction.

Fourth, the notion that objects consist of invariant geons is too inflexible. As Hayward and Tarr (2005, p. 67) pointed out, "You can take almost any object, put a working light-bulb on the top, and call it a lamp . . . almost anything in the image might constitute a feature in appropriate conditions."

Does viewpoint influence object recognition?

Form a visual image of a bicycle. Your image probably involved a side view in which both wheels can be seen clearly. We can use this example to discuss a controversy in object recognition. Consider an experiment in which some participants are shown a photograph of a bicycle in the typical (or canonical) view as in your visual image, whereas others received a photograph of the same bicycle viewed end-on or from above. Would those given the typical view identify the object as a bicycle faster than the others?

We will address the above question shortly. Before that, we need to focus on two key terms mentioned earlier. If object recognition is equally rapid and easy regardless of the viewing angle, it is *viewpoint-invariant*. In contrast, if it is generally faster and easier when objects are seen from certain angles, then object recognition is *viewer-centred* or *viewpoint-dependent*. We also need to distinguish between categorisation (e.g., is the object a dog?) and identification (e.g., is the object a poodle?), which requires within-category discriminations.

Findings

Milivojevic (2012) reviewed behavioural research in this area. Object recognition is typically not influenced by the object's orientation when *categorisation* is required. Thus, it appears to be largely viewpoint-invariant with categorisation. In contrast, object recognition is significantly slower when an object's orientation differs from its canonical or typical viewpoint when *identification* is required. Thus, it is viewer-centred with identification.

Research supporting the above conclusions was reported by Hamm and McMullen (1998). Changes in viewpoint had no effect on object recognition when categorisation was required (e.g., deciding an object was a car). However, there were clear effects of changing viewpoint when identification was required (e.g., deciding whether an object was a taxi).

Most research (e.g., Biederman & Gerhardstein, 1993; Tarr & Bülthoff, 1995; Hamm & McMullen, 1998) designed to test whether object recognition is viewer- or object-centred has used behavioural measures (especially reaction times). However, small or non-existent effects of object orientation on reaction times do *not* prove orientation has had no effect on internal processing. Milivojevic et al. (2011) investigated this issue. Participants were presented with a letter or digit in several orientations and instructed to categorise each stimulus as a letter or a digit.

What did Milivojevic et al. (2011) find? First, there were only small effects of object orientation on speed and accuracy of categorisation. Second, there were relatively large effects of orientation on event-related potentials (ERPs; see Glossary). More specifically, early ERP components were larger when the stimulus was not presented upright. These components seemed to reflect processing of low-level features and object classification. Thus, object orientation had very little effect on task performance even though it clearly affected several cognitive processes. Thus, viewer-centred processes were involved even though speed of categorisation did *not* depend on the object's orientation.

Neuroimaging research has contributed to our understanding of object recognition (Milivojevic, 2012). With categorisation tasks, brain activation is mostly very similar regardless of object orientation. However, orientation influences brain activity *early* in processing, indicating that initial processing is viewpoint-dependent.

With identification tasks, there is typically greater activation of areas within the inferior temporal cortex when objects are not in their typical or canonical orientation (Milivojevic, 2012). This finding is unsurprising given that the inferior temporal cortex is heavily involved in object recognition (Peissig & Tarr, 2007). It appears identification requires additional processing when an object is in an unusual orientation; this may involve more detailed processing of object features.

With identification tasks, *learning* is often an important factor. For example, recognising familiar faces is less influenced by view changes than is recognising unfamiliar faces. Zimmermann and Eimer (2013) presented unfamiliar faces on 640 trials. Face recognition was view-dependent during the first half of the trials. Thereafter, as the faces became increasingly familiar through learning, face recognition became more viewpoint-invariant. More information about each face was stored in long-term memory as a function of learning and this facilitated rapid access to visual face memory regardless of facial orientation.

Hayward (2012) discussed much of the relevant research. He concluded that, "the evidence strongly suggests that the ventral visual pathway, which is thought to be the basis for visual object understanding, forms viewer-centred representations of objects" (p. 1159). Why is this so? The most likely reason is that the processing costs incurred in creating viewpoint-invariant representations are too great.

Inferotemporal cortex

Inferotemporal cortex (especially its anterior portion) is of crucial importance in visual object recognition (Peissig & Tarr, 2007). Evidence that inferotemporal cortex is especially important in object recognition was provided by Leopold and Logothetis (1999) and Blake and Logothetis (2002). Macaque monkeys were presented with a different visual stimulus to each eye and indicated which stimulus they perceived. This is known as binocular rivalry (see Glossary). The key finding was that the correlation between neural activity and the monkey's perception was greater at later stages of visual processing. The activation of only 20% of neurons in V1 (primary visual cortex) was associated with perception. In contrast, it was 90% in higher visual areas such as inferotemporal cortex and superior temporal sulcus.

The above findings reveal an *association* between neuronal activation in inferotemporal cortex and perception, but this falls short of demonstrating a *causal* relationship. This gap was filled by Afraz et al. (2006). They trained two macaque monkeys to decide whether degraded visual stimuli were faces or non-faces. On some trials, microstimulation was applied to face-selective neurons within the inferotemporal cortex. This greatly increased the number of face decisions made by the monkeys. Thus, this study shows a causal relationship between activity of face-selective neurons in inferotemporal cortex and face perception.

Suppose we assess neuronal activity in inferotemporal cortex while observers are presented with several different objects presented at various angles, sizes and so on. There are two key dimensions of neuronal responses in such a situation: *selectivity* and *invariance* or tolerance (Ison & Quiroga, 2008). Neurons responding strongly to one visual object but weakly (or not at all) to other objects possess high selectivity. Neurons responding almost equally strongly to a given object regardless of its orientation, size and so on possess high invariance or tolerance.

In general terms, inferotemporal (IT) neurons having high invariance or tolerance seem consistent with theories claiming object recognition is viewpoint-invariant. In similar fashion, inferotemporal neurons having low invariance appear to fit with theories claiming object recognition is viewpoint-dependent. However, we must be careful. As Hayward (2012, p. 1158) pointed out, "View-invariant neurons could reflect a truly object-centred frame of frame, but could also simply have excitatory connections with many different view-specific neurons (therefore functioning as part of a view-based network)."

Do neurons in the temporal cortex have high or low invariance? Logothetis et al. (1995) carried out a classic study in which monkeys were presented repeatedly with unfamiliar objects. The responsiveness of many IT neurons was viewpoint-dependent, that is, it was greater when an object was presented in a familiar viewpoint rather than an unfamiliar one.

Booth and Rolls (1998) found some IT neurons have high invariance and others low invariance. Monkeys initially spent time playing with novel objects in their cages. After that, Booth and Rolls presented photographs of these objects taken from different viewpoints while recording neuronal activity in the superior temporal sulcus. They found 49% of neurons responded mostly to specific views and only 14% produced viewpoint-invariant responses. However, the viewpoint-invariant neurons may be more important to object perception than their limited numbers might suggest. Booth and Rolls showed there was potentially enough information in the patterns of activation of these neurons to discriminate accurately among the objects presented.

What is the relationship between selectivity and invariance or tolerance in inferotemporal neurons? The first systematic attempt to provide an answer was by Zoccolan et al. (2007). There was a moderate *negative* correlation between object selectivity and tolerance. Thus, some neurons respond to many objects in several different sizes and orientations, whereas others respond mainly to a single object in a limited range of views. Why are selectivity and invariance negatively correlated? Perhaps our ability to perform visual tasks, ranging from very precise object identification to very broad categorisation of objects, is facilitated by having neurons with very different patterns of responsiveness to changing stimuli.

Some neurons exhibit what appears to be amazing selectivity. In a study on humans, Quiroga et al. (2005) found a neuron in the medial temporal lobe that responded strongly to pictures of Jennifer Aniston (the actress from *Friends*), but hardly responded to pictures of other famous faces or other objects. Surprisingly, this neuron did *not* respond to Jennifer Aniston with Brad Pitt! Other neurons responded specifically to a different famous person (e.g., Julia Roberts) or a famous building (e.g., Sydney Opera House).

One possible interpretation of the above findings is that your knowledge of a given person (e.g., Jennifer Aniston, your grandmother) is stored in a single neuron. That is incredibly unlikely. Quiroga et al. (2005) studied an extremely small number of neurons out of the approximately one million neurons activated by any given visual stimulus. It is utterly improbable that only a single neuron in the medial temporal lobe responds to Jennifer Aniston. If that were the case, then damage to that one neuron would eliminate all our knowledge of Jennifer Aniston. It is much more likely that our knowledge of, say, Jennifer Aniston is stored in "a relatively few neurons, numbering in the thousands or perhaps even less" (Quiroga et al., 2013, p. 34).

The great majority of the studies discussed in this section have used monkeys. This has been done because the invasive techniques involved can only be used on non-human species. It is generally (but perhaps incorrectly) assumed that basic visual processes are similar in humans and monkeys.

Top-down processes

Until relatively recently, most theorists (e.g., Biederman, 1987) studying object recognition emphasised bottom-up processes. Apparent support for this emphasis can be found in the hierarchical nature of visual processing – during the course of visual processing, neurons higher up the hierarchy respond to increasingly complex stimuli. As Yardley et al. (2012, p. 4) pointed out:

> Traditionally, visual object recognition has been taken as mediated by a hierarchical, bottom-up stream that processes an image by systematically analysing its individual elements, and relaying this information to the next areas until the overall form and identity are determined.

The traditional account focuses on a feedforward hierarchy of processing stages progressing from early visual cortex through to inferotemporal cortex. However, anatomical evidence suggests this is a considerable oversimplification. There are approximately equal numbers of forward and backward projecting neurons throughout most of the visual system (Wyatte et al., 2012; Gilbert & Li, 2013). In essence, backward projecting neurons are associated with top-down processing.

There is an important issue concerning *when* top-down processes have their effects. Top-down processes may occur only *after* object recognition and may relate to semantic processing of already recognised objects. Alternatively (and of more theoretical interest), top-down processes (perhaps involving the prefrontal cortex) may occur *prior* to object recognition and may be necessary for recognition to occur. Before we discuss the relevant research findings, note that top-down processes are more likely to have a major impact on object recognition when bottom-up processes are relatively uninformative (e.g., degraded stimuli, briefly presented stimuli).

Findings

Evidence for the involvement of top-down processes in visual perception has been obtained from research on ambiguous figures having at least two different interpretations. Goolkasian and Woodberry (2010) presented participants with ambiguous figures immediately preceded by primes relevant to one interpretation (see Figure 3.9). The key finding was that the primes systematically biased the interpretation of the ambiguous figures via top-down processes.

Bar et al. (2006) presented participants briefly with drawings of objects that were then masked to make them hard to recognise. Activation in orbitofrontal cortex (part of the prefrontal cortex) occurred 50 ms *before* activation in recognition-related regions of the temporal cortex. This orbitofrontal activation

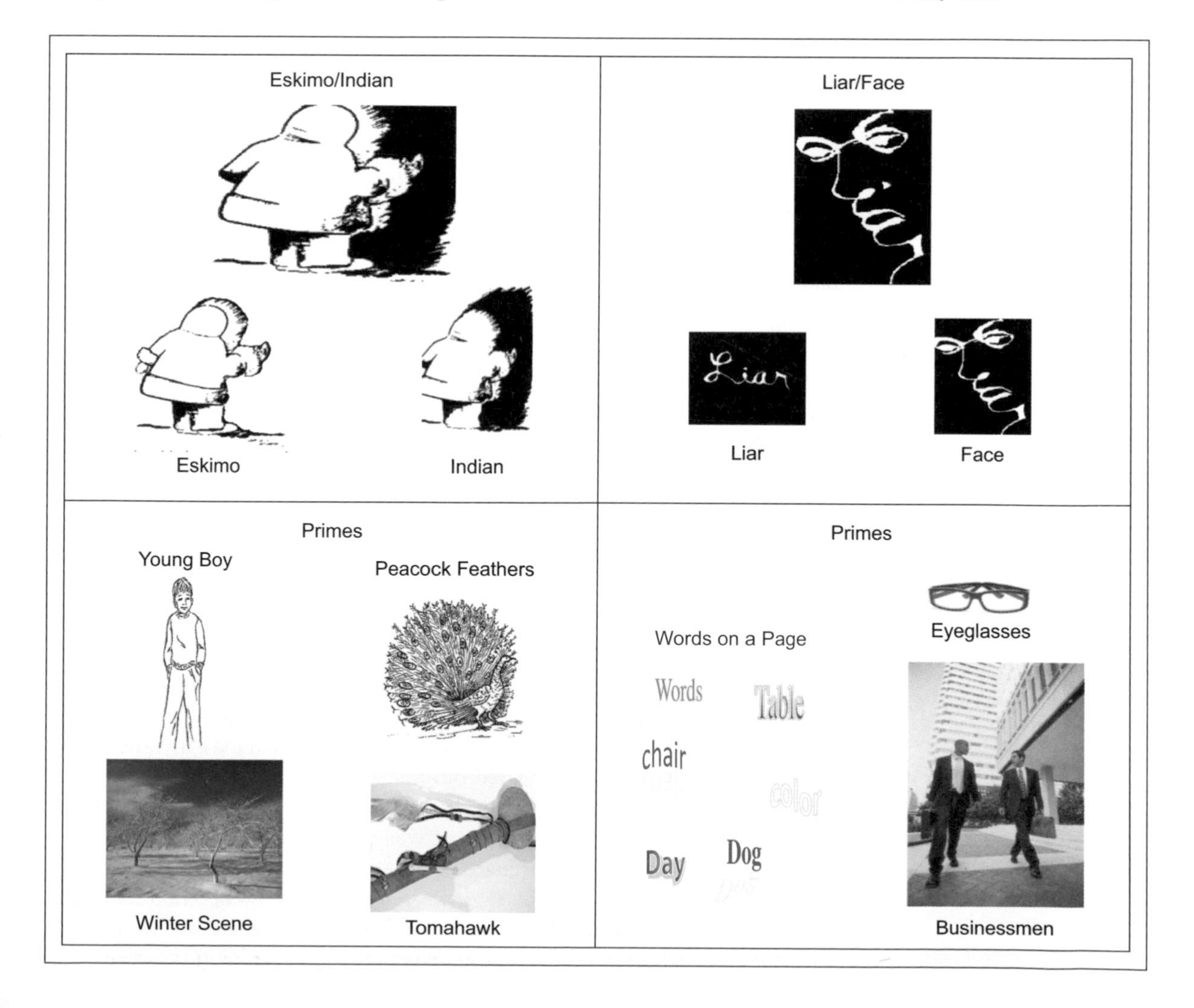

Figure 3.9
Ambiguous figures (e.g., Eskimo/Indian, Liar/Face) were preceded by primes (e.g., Winter Scene, Tomahawk) relevant to one interpretation of the following figure.

From Goolkasian and Woodberry (2010). Reprinted with permission from the Psychonomic Society 2010.

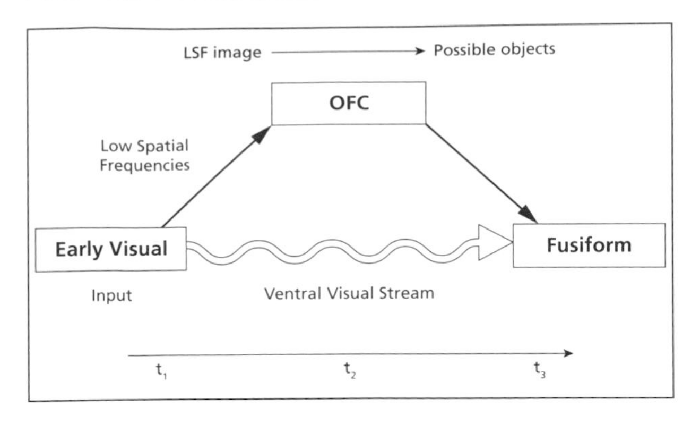

Figure 3.10
In this modified version of Bar et al.'s (2006) theory, it is assumed that object recognition involves two different routes: (1) a top-down route in which information proceeds rapidly to the orbitofrontal cortex, which is involved in generating predictions about the object's identity; (2) a bottom-up route using the slower ventral visual stream.

From Yardley et al. (2012). Reprinted with permission from Springer.

predicted successful object recognition and so seemed important for object recognition to occur. There was less involvement of orbitofrontal cortex in object recognition when recognition was easy (longer, unmasked presentation).

Bar et al. (2006) concluded that top-down processes in orbitofrontal cortex are more important when recognition is difficult than when it is easy. They put forward a model in which object recognition depends on top-down processes involving the orbitofrontal cortex and bottom-up processes involving the ventral visual stream (see Figure 3.10).

Stronger evidence that top-down processes in the prefrontal cortex play a direct role in object recognition was reported by Viggiano et al. (2008). Participants viewed blurred or non-blurred photographs of living and non-living objects under four conditions: (1) repetitive transcranial magnetic stimulation (rTMS; see Glossary) applied to the left dorsolateral prefrontal cortex; (2) rTMS applied to the right dorsolateral prefrontal cortex; (3) sham rTMS (there was no magnetic field); and (4) baseline (no rTMS at all).

What did Viggiano et al. (2008) find? First, rTMS applied to the left or right dorsolateral prefrontal cortex slowed down object-recognition time. Second, rTMS had no effect on object-recognition time with non-blurred photographs. These findings suggest top-down processes are directly involved in object recognition when the sensory information available to bottom-up processes is limited.

Suppose we presented photographs of objects (e.g., mailbox, tractor) to one eye while at the same time presenting high-contrast noise patterns to the other eye to suppress visual awareness of the object. Suppose also that each photograph was preceded by a valid verbal cue (i.e., indicating which object was to be presented), an invalid verbal cue (i.e., indicating an incorrect object was to be presented) or no cue. We might not be very impressed if observers were best at judging which object had been presented when valid cues were used – the valid cues might simply have influenced their judgements about their visual experience rather than perception itself.

An alternative approach could in principle provide more striking evidence that top-down processes influence basic perceptual processes. In essence, a suppressed stimulus is presented on some trials but there is no stimulus on others. Observers decide whether or not a stimulus was presented. The key prediction is that valid cues should lead to superior stimulus-detection performance than invalid cues.

Lupyan and Ward (2013) carried out a study based on the ideas discussed above. Observers were told the suppressed stimulus would be a circle or square or there was no cue. What was presented was a circle, a square, a shape intermediate between a circle and a square or no stimulus. Observers' performance was significantly better when valid (rather than invalid) cues were used (see Figure 3.11). Thus, top-down processes triggered by the verbal labels activated shape information and influenced basic visual detection.

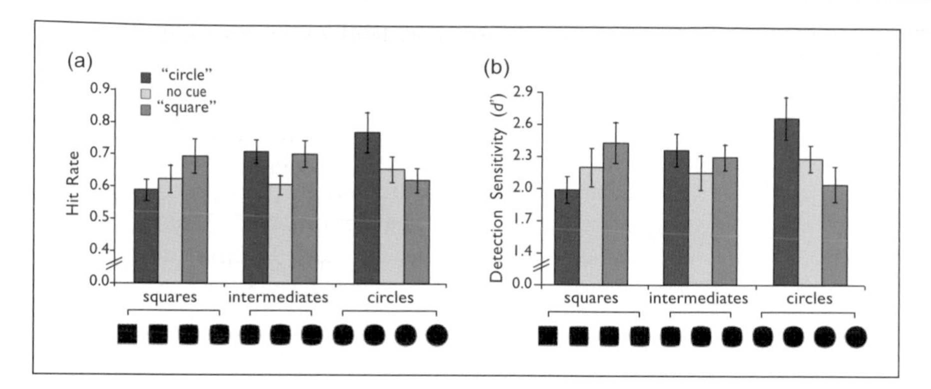

Figure 3.11
(a) hit rates and (b) detection sensitivity for detecting geometric shapes as a function of shape (square, intermediate, circle) and cue (circle, no cue, square). Performance was best when the cue was valid (matched the subsequent shape).

From Lupyan and Ward (2013). © National Academy of Sciences. Reproduced with permission.

Evaluation

Top-down processes often influence visual perception and object recognition and not simply post-perceptual judgements. As Yardley et al. (2012, p. 1) pointed out, "During our attempts to interpret the world around us, perception relies on existing knowledge as much as it does on incoming information." Note, however, that the influence of top-down processes is generally greater when visual stimuli are degraded.

So far as the future is concerned, it is of central importance to understand more fully how bottom-up and top-down processes interact with each other. These interactions probably occur at several levels within the visual system. However, the factors determining whether and where they occur are largely unknown.

FACE RECOGNITION

There are several reasons for devoting a separate section to face recognition. First, recognising faces is of enormous importance to us. We generally identify people from their faces. Form a visual image of someone important in your life. Your image probably contains fairly detailed information about their faces and its special features rather than their physique.

Second, face recognition seems to differ in important ways from other forms of object recognition. As a result, theories of object recognition are of only limited value in explaining face recognition and theoretical approaches specifically devoted to face recognition are needed.

Third, we now have a good understanding of the processes involved in face recognition. One reason for this is the diversity of research – it includes behavioural studies, studies on brain-damaged patients and neuroimaging studies.

Face vs. object recognition

How does face recognition differ from the recognition of other objects? Of importance, face recognition involves more **holistic processing**. Holistic processing involves strong integration of information from an entire object focusing on the relationships among features as well as the features themselves. Holistic processing of faces is more efficient and more reliable than feature processing. It is more *rapid* because facial features are processed in parallel rather

KEY TERM

Holistic processing
Processing that involves *integrating* information from an entire object (especially faces).

KEY TERMS

Face inversion effect
The finding that faces are much harder to recognise when presented upside down; the effect of inversion is less marked (or absent) with other objects.

Part–whole effect
The finding that a face part is recognised more easily when presented in the context of a whole face rather than on its own.

than one by one. Indeed, it is so rapid that familiar faces can generally be recognised in under half a second (Bruce & Young, 1986). It is more *reliable* because individual facial features (e.g., skin shade, mouth shape) are subject to change.

Evidence that holistic processing is used more with faces than other objects comes from studies on the **face inversion effect** (McKone et al., 2007; Bruyer, 2011). The face inversion effect is the finding that faces are much harder to identify when presented inverted or upside-down rather than upright. In contrast, adverse effects of inversion are often much smaller with non-face objects and generally disappear rapidly with practice (McKone et al., 2007). However, the evidence is mixed. Diamond and Carey (1986) found dog experts showed an inversion effect of comparable size for photographs of dog breeds as for faces. In similar research, Rossion and Curran (2010) found car experts had a much smaller inversion effect for cars than for faces. However, those with the greatest expertise showed a greater inversion effect for cars than did those with less expertise.

More evidence in support of the notion that faces are special comes from the **part–whole effect**, which is the finding that it is easier to recognise a face part when it is presented within a whole face rather than in isolation. Farah (1994) studied this effect. Participants were presented with drawings of faces or houses, and associated a name with each face and each house. Then they were presented with whole faces and houses or only a single feature (e.g., mouth, front door). Recognition performance for face parts was much better when the whole face was presented rather than only a single feature. This is the part–whole effect. In contrast, recognition performance for house features was very similar in whole and single-feature conditions.

Weblink:
Thatcher illusion

More evidence suggesting faces are processed holistically was reported by Richler et al. (2011) using composite faces. Composite faces consist of a top half and a bottom half which may or may not be of the same face. The participants decided whether the top halves of two successive composite faces were the same or different. Performance was worse when the bottom halves of the two composite faces were different. This composite face effect suggests that people are unable to ignore the bottom halves and thus that processing of the composite faces is holistic.

If face recognition depends heavily on holistic processing, we might expect individuals who are especially good at such processing to have superior face-recognition ability. That is exactly what Richler et al. (2011) found.

In sum, there is evidence supporting the notion that face and object recognition involve different processes. However, the issues are complex and much additional relevant research is discussed below. Of particular importance is whether the processing differences between faces and other objects occur because there is something special about faces or because we have dramatically more expertise with faces than any object category.

Prosopagnosia

Consider brain-damaged patients with severely impaired face processing. If such patients invariably had great impairments in object processing as well, that would suggest that the two types of processing are similar. However, if face processing differs substantially from object processing, we would expect to find some brain-damaged individuals with severely impaired face processing but not object processing. Such individuals exist. They suffer from **prosopagnosia** (pros-uh-pag-NO-see-uh), coming from the Greek words for "face" and "without knowledge".

Prosopagnosia is a heterogeneous or diverse condition with the precise problems of face and object recognition varying across patients. One reason is that the condition can be caused by brain damage (acquired prosopagnosia) or may occur in the absence of any obvious brain damage (developmental prosopagnosia). Note that there appear to be few (or no) cases of pure prosopagnosia.

In spite of their poor conscious recognition of faces, prosopagnosics often show evidence of covert recognition (face processing without conscious awareness). For example, Simon et al. (2011) presented familiar and unfamiliar faces to a prosopagnosic, PS, who showed an absence of conscious recognition

KEY TERM

Prosopagnosia
A condition mostly caused by brain damage in which there is a severe impairment in face recognition but much less impairment of object recognition; also known as face blindness.

IN THE REAL WORLD: HEATHER SELLERS

Up to 2% of the population suffer from prosopagnosia or face blindness. We can understand the profound problems they experience in everyday life by considering the case of Heather Sellers (see photo) (you can see her on YouTube: You don't look like anyone I know). She is an American woman suffering from prosopagnosia who wrote about her experiences in a 2010 book entitled, *You Don't Look Like Anyone I Know*. When she was a child, she became separated from her mother at a grocery store. When staff at the store reunited mother and child, Heather did not initially recognise her mother. Note, however, that Heather Sellers does not have major problems with all forms of visual recognition: her ability to recognise objects is essentially normal.

Heather Sellers even has difficulty in recognising her own face. As a child, she found it very hard to pick out her own face in school photographs. As an adult, Heather Sellers admits, "A few times I have been in a crowded elevator with mirrors all round and a woman will move, and I will go to get out the way and then realise 'oh that woman is me'." Such experiences made her a very anxious person.

Surprisingly, Heather Sellers was in her mid-thirties before she realised she suffered from prosopagnosia. Why did it take so long? In essence, she identifies other people by relying on their hairstyle, body type, clothing, voice and gait. However, that has not prevented her from being severely embarrassed by her frequent failures to recognise people she knows well. She has also made friends angry by walking straight past them. Most surprisingly, she even failed on occasion to recognise her own husband! According to Heather Sellers, "Not being able to reliably know who people are – it feels terrible like failing all the time."

Heather Sellers. © Patricia Roehling.

of the familiar faces. In spite of that, PS showed more activation in a brain area associated with face processing (the fusiform face area discussed later) when presented with familiar, but not unfamiliar, faces. Thus, familiar faces were processed below the level of conscious awareness.

Why do prosopagnosics have very poor face recognition but reasonable object recognition? One explanation is that they have a face-specific recognition disorder involving damage to a brain area specialised for face processing. Another explanation is that face recognition is much harder than object recognition. Face recognition involves distinguishing among members of the same category (i.e., faces). In contrast, object recognition often only involves identifying the relevant category (e.g., cat, car). According to this viewpoint, prosopagnosics would perform poorly if required to make fine-grained perceptual judgements with objects.

Findings

Weblink:
Prosopagnosia

Weblink:
Video of a prosopagnostic

Busigny et al. (2010b) tested the two above explanations. The visual recognition performance of a male prosopagnosic patient, GG, was compared with that of healthy controls for several object categories: birds, boats, cars, chairs and faces. On each trial, participants were presented with a target stimulus belonging to one of these categories followed by two stimuli from the same category (target + distractor). The participants indicated the one seen previously.

The findings from this study are shown in Figure 3.12. GG was as accurate as the controls with each non-face category. However, he was substantially less accurate than controls with faces (67% vs. 94%, respectively). Thus, GG seems to have a face-specific impairment rather than a general inability to recognise complex stimuli.

Busigny et al. (2010a) found evidence from previous research suggesting at least 13 prosopagnosics had essentially normal levels of object recognition in spite of very poor face recognition. However, they identified two limitations with this research. First, the difficulty of the recognition decisions patients had to make was not manipulated systematically and is hard to assess. Second, the most informative approach is to measure the speed of recognition decisions as well as their accuracy. This had not been done in these earlier studies.

Busigny et al. (2010a) eliminated these limitations in their study of PS, a female prosopagnosic. They manipulated the similarity between target items and distractors on an object-recognition task and recorded reaction times as well as error rates. Increasing the degree of similarity between targets and distractors

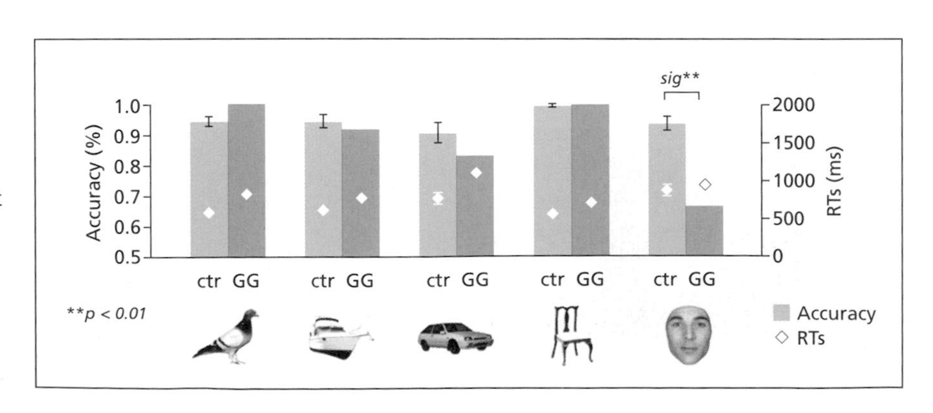

Figure 3.12
Accuracy and speed of object recognition for birds, boats, cars, chairs and faces by patient GG and healthy controls.

From Busigny et al. (2012b). Reprinted with permission from Elsevier.

increased error rates to the same extent in PS and healthy controls. In contrast, PS performed very poorly on a face-recognition task even when it was very easy for healthy controls.

KEY TERM

Fusiform face area
An area that is associated with face processing; the term is somewhat misleading given that the area is also associated with processing other categories of objects.

Suppose face recognition and object recognition involve somewhat different brain areas. If so, we might expect to find patients with severely impaired object recognition but intact face recognition. There is some support for this expectation. Moscovitch et al. (1997) studied CK, a man with object agnosia (impaired object recognition). He performed as well as healthy controls on face recognition regardless of whether the face was a photograph, a caricature or a cartoon, provided it was upright and the internal features were in the correct places.

Why is face recognition so poor in prosopagnosics? A popular explanation is that they have great difficulty with holistic processing. Busigny et al. (2010b) tested this explanation in experiments on the prosopagnosic GG in a study referred to earlier. GG did not show the face inversion or composite face effects. Thus, GG does not perceive individual faces holistically, an ability necessary for accurate perception of individual faces. In contrast, recognition of individual non-face objects does not require holistic processing, and so GG's performance was intact with those objects.

Further evidence of deficient holistic processing of faces in prospopagnosics was reported by Van Belle et al. (2011). In one condition, observers could only see one part of a face at a time (e.g., eye, mouth) – this was done to restrict holistic processing. In this condition, the face-recognition performance of a prosopagnosic, GG, was comparable to that of healthy controls. As expected, GG performed much worse than healthy controls when the whole face was accessible and so holistic processing was possible.

Fusiform face area

If faces are processed differently from other objects, we might expect to find brain regions specialised for face processing. The **fusiform face area** in the ventral temporal cortex (see Figure 3.13) has (as its name strongly implies!) been identified as such a brain region. Two main lines of research support the involvement of this area in face processing. First, this area is often damaged in patients with prosopagnosia (Kanwisher & Yovel, 2006).

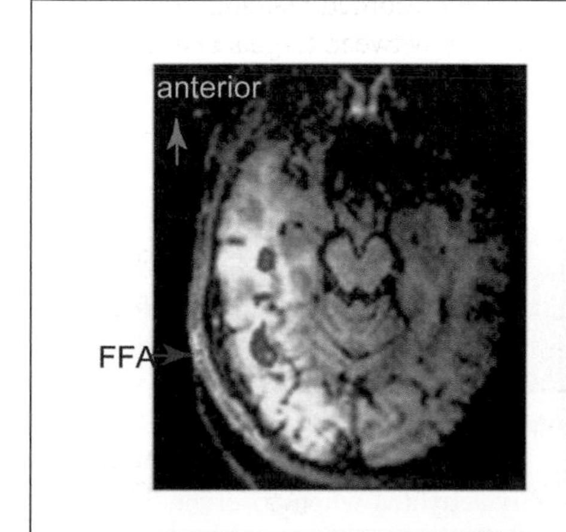

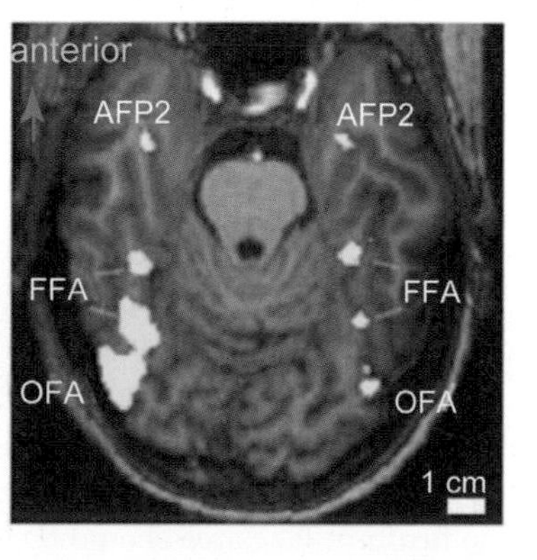

Figure 3.13
Face-selective regions including the anterior face patch (AFP2), the fusiform face area (FFA) and the occipital face area (OFA).

From Weiner and Grill-Spector (2012). Reprinted with permission from Elsevier.

Second, neuroimaging studies indicate that activation in the fusiform face area is typically greater to faces than to other objects. For example, Downing et al. (2006) presented participants with faces, scenes and 18 object categories (e.g., tools, fruits, vegetables). The fusiform face area responded significantly more strongly to faces than any other stimulus category.

Reality is more complex than has been suggested so far. Patients with prosopagnosia often have damage to the occipital face area (see Figure 3.13) as well as (or instead of) the fusiform face area. Such findings led Gainotti and Marra (2011) to argue that face processing involves a *network* including those two areas rather than being localised to the fusiform face area.

Complexity is also found in neuroimaging studies of face recognition. Research has suggested the existence of several brain areas responding selectively to faces (see Figure 3.13). Kanwisher et al. (1997) found only 80% of their participants showed greater activation within the fusiform face area to faces than other objects. Why, then, have so many experts claimed the fusiform face area is of central importance in face processing? One reason is the use of lenient criteria when deciding whether activation in response to faces occurs in the fusiform face area (Weiner & Grill-Spector, 2012). For example, individual data may indicate the involvement of several different areas but combining the data often exaggerates the role of the fusiform face area.

In sum, the fusiform face area is definitely involved in face processing and face recognition for most (but not all) individuals. However, the notion that face processing is *localised* in this area is incorrect. What is much more likely is that face processing involves a brain network including the fusiform face area as well as the occipital face area (Atkinson & Adolphs, 2011). It is also important to note that the fusiform face area is activated when individuals are processing numerous types of objects other than faces.

Expertise hypothesis

Gauthier and Tarr (2002) argued that many findings pointing to major differences between face and object processing should not be taken at face value (sorry!). They pointed out that we have much more expertise in recognising faces than individual members of other categories. This led them to put forward the expertise hypothesis. According to this hypothesis, the brain and processing mechanisms allegedly specific to faces are also involved in processing and recognising the members of any object category for which we possess expertise. Thus, the fusiform face area might more appropriately be called the "fusiform expertise area".

Why is expertise so important in determining how we process faces and objects? A plausible answer is that expertise leads to greater holistic processing. For example, chess experts can very rapidly make coherent sense (engage in holistic processing) when viewing a chess position because they can use their relevant stored knowledge (see Chapter 12). Four main predictions follow from the expertise hypothesis:

1. Holistic or configural processing is not unique to faces but should be found for any objects of expertise.
2. The fusiform face area should be highly activated when observers recognise the members of any category for which they possess expertise.

3 Young children should show less evidence of holistic processing of faces than older children and adults.
4 If the processing of faces and of objects of expertise involves similar processes, then objects of expertise should interfere with face processing.

Findings

The first hypothesis is plausible. Wallis (2013) took a model of object recognition and considered what effects on perception it would predict given prolonged exposure to a given stimulus category. In essence, the model predicted that many phenomena associated with face processing (e.g., holistic processing, the inversion effect) would be found with *any* stimulus category for which an individual had expertise. Repeated simultaneous presentation of the same features (e.g., nose, mouth, eyes) gradually increases holistic processing. Wallis concluded that a single model of object recognition can account for both object and face recognition.

Kundel et al. (2007) presented mammograms showing (or not showing) breast cancer to doctors. The most expert doctors typically fixated almost immediately on the cancer suggesting they were using very fast, holistic processes. However, McKone et al. (2007) reviewed studies on the influence of expertise for non-face objects on the inversion and composite effects discussed earlier. Remember that both of these effects are assumed to involve holistic or configural processing. Expertise generally failed to lead to either effect. However, other studies (including those by Rossion and Curran (2010) and Diamond and Carey (1986)) have reported evidence that expertise with non-face objects is associated with holistic processing.

McKone et al. (2007) reviewed evidence relating to the second hypothesis. There was a modest tendency for the fusiform face area to be more activated by objects of expertise than other objects. However, larger activation effects of objects of expertise were found *outside* the fusiform face area than *inside* it.

Stronger support for the second hypothesis was reported by Bilalić et al. (2010). Chess experts and novices performed various tasks involving chess pieces. The key finding was that chess experts had greater activation than novices in the fusiform face area in all conditions. However, faces elicited greater activation in the fusiform face area than did chess displays for either group (experts or novices). McGugin et al. (2012) found that activation to car stimuli within the fusiform face area was greater in participants with more car expertise.

If the fusiform face area is linked to expertise, we might expect its size to increase during childhood and early adulthood. This expectation has been confirmed: the size of the fusiform face area increases substantially during development (Wallis, 2013).

Evidence relating to the third hypothesis was discussed by Crookes and McKone (2009). Most research suggests young children show some evidence of holistic processing of faces, but that such processing increases during the course of development. However, Crookes and McKone pointed out that it is hard to interpret most findings because there has been a general failure to match task difficulty across age groups. When they took steps to overcome this problem, adult levels of holistic processing were shown by children aged 7 or less.

Evidence supporting the fourth hypothesis was reported by McKeeff et al. (2010). Car experts and novices searched for face targets among distractors. The distractors consisted of cars and faces or watches and faces. Car experts were slower than novices when searching for faces among cars, but the two groups did not differ when searching for faces among watches. Car and face expertise probably interfered with each other because they use the same (or similar) processes.

Evaluation

Interactive exercise:
Bruce and Young

There is support for the expertise hypothesis with respect to all four hypotheses. However, the extent to which each hypothesis is supported remains controversial. A major reason for this is that it is almost impossible to assess expertise level accurately or to control it. Many theorists have adopted extreme positions, arguing that all processing differences between faces and other objects are due to expertise differences or that none is. It is entirely possible that many (but not all) the processing differences between faces and other objects are due to greater expertise with faces. That would imply that faces are special, but less so than has often been assumed.

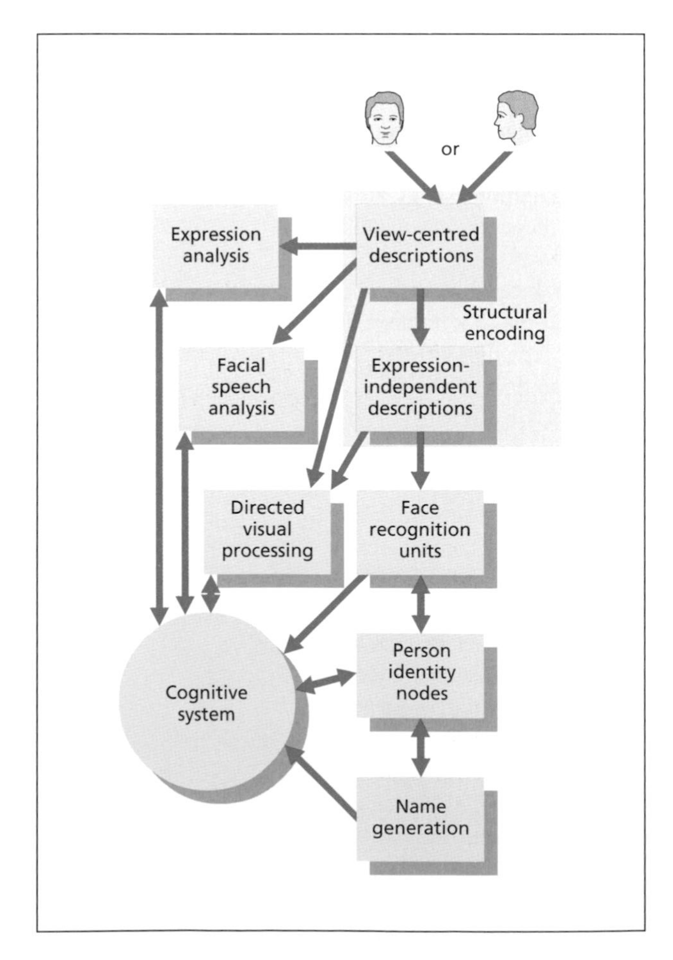

Figure 3.14
The model of face recognition put forward by Bruce and Young (1986).

Theoretical approaches

Several theories and models of face processing and recognition have been proposed. We will focus on Bruce and Young's (1986) model, because it has been easily the most influential theoretical approach to face recognition.

Bruce and Young's model consists of eight components (see Figure 3.14):

1. *Structural encoding*: This produces various descriptions or representations of faces.
2. *Expression analysis*: People's emotional states are inferred from their facial expression.
3. *Facial speech analysis*: Speech perception is assisted by observing a speaker's lip movements (lip-reading; see Chapter 9).
4. *Direct visual processing*: Specific facial information is processed selectively.
5. *Face recognition units*: These contain structural information about known faces; this structural information emphasises the less changeable aspects of the face and is at a fairly abstract level.
6. *Person identity nodes*: These provide information about individuals (e.g., occupation, interests).
7. *Name generation*: A person's name is stored separately.
8. *Cognitive system*: This contains additional information (e.g., most actors have attractive faces); it influences which other components receive attention.

What predictions follow from this model? First, there should be major differences in the processing of familiar and unfamiliar faces. More specifically, various components (face recognition units, person identity nodes, name generation) are only involved in processing familiar faces. As a result, it is much easier to recognise familiar than unfamiliar faces. This is especially the case when, for example, a face is seen from an unusual angle or under unusual lighting conditions.

Second, consider the processing of facial identity (who is the person?) and facial expression (what is he/she feeling?). *Separate* processing routes are involved with the crucial component for processing facial expression being expression analysis. The key idea is that one processing route (perception of facial identity) is concerned with the relatively unchanging aspects of faces, whereas the other route (facial expression) deals with the more changeable aspects.

Third, when we look at a familiar face, familiarity information from the face recognition unit should be accessed first. This is followed by information about that person (e.g., occupation) from the person identity node and then that person's name from the name generation component. As a result, it is possible to find a face familiar without being able to recall anything else about the person, or to recall personal information about the person without being able to recall their name. However, a face should never lead to recall of the person's name in the absence of other information.

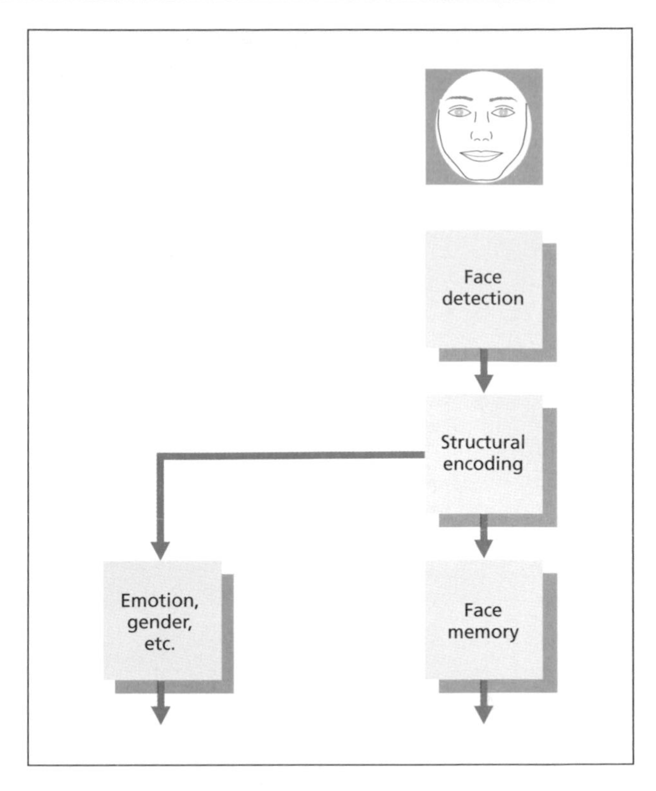

Figure 3.15
Simplified version of the Bruce and Young (1986) model of face recognition. Face detection is followed by processing of the face's structure, which is then matched to a memory representation (face memory). The perceptual representation of the face can also be used for recognition of facial expression and gender discrimination.

Reprinted from Duchaine and Nakayama (2006). Reprinted with permission from Elsevier.

If you struggled with the complexities of the Bruce and Young (1986) model, help is at hand. Duchaine and Nakayama (2006) produced a simplified version including an additional face detection stage (see Figure 3.15). At this initial stage, observers decide whether the stimulus is a face. The importance of this stage can be seen with reference to a prosopagnosic called Edward with extremely poor face recognition. In spite of his problems with later stages of face recognition, he detected faces as rapidly as healthy individuals (Duchaine & Nakayama, 2006).

Findings

According to the model, there are various reasons why it is easier to recognise familiar faces than unfamiliar ones. However, what is especially important is that we possess much more structural information about familiar faces. This structural information (associated with face recognition units) relates to relatively unchanging aspects of faces and gradually accumulates with increasing familiarity

IN THE REAL WORLD: RECOGNISING UNFAMILIAR FACES

Have a look at the 40 faces displayed in Figure 3.16. How many *different* individuals do you think are shown? Produce your answer before reading on.

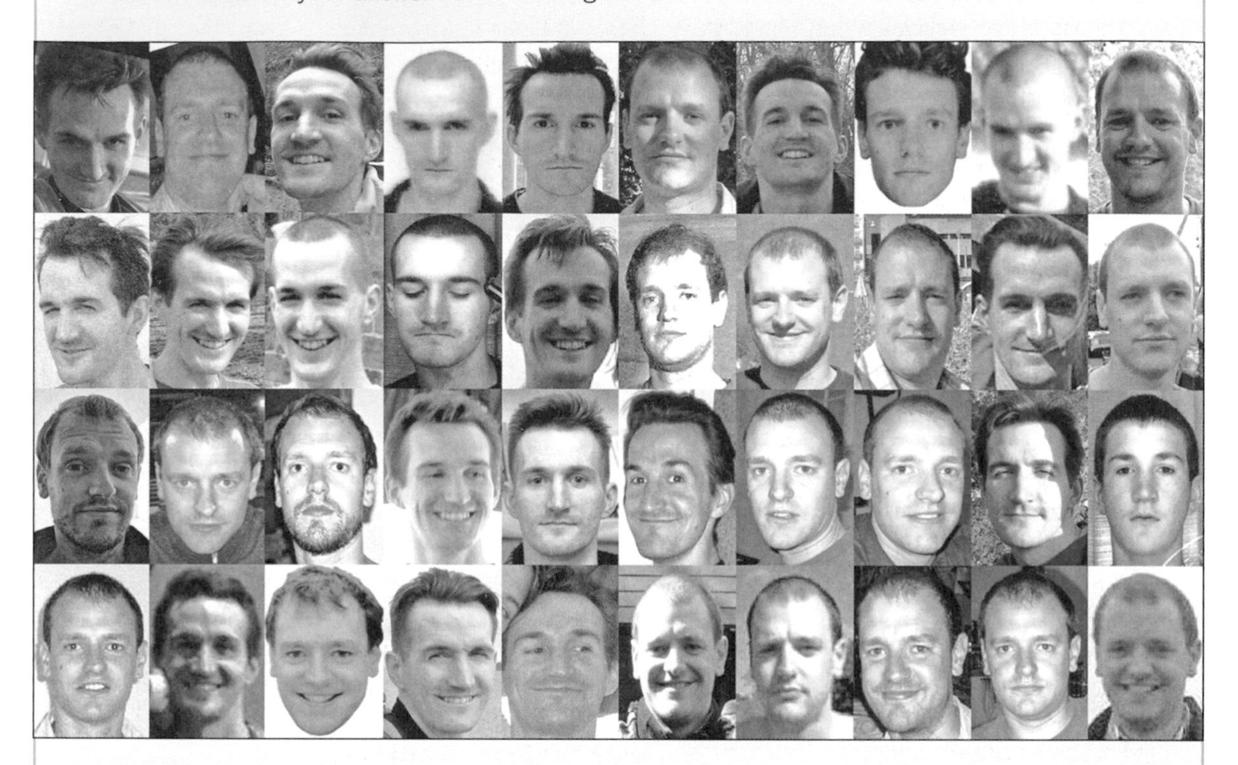

Figure 3.16
Forty face photographs to be sorted into piles for each of the individuals shown in the photographs.
From Jenkins et al. (2011). Reproduced with permission from Elsevier.

In a study by Jenkins et al. (2011; discussed shortly) using a similar stimulus array, participants on average thought 7.5 different individuals were shown. The actual number for the array used by Jenkins et al. and for the one shown in Figure 3.16 is actually only two.

The two individuals (A and B) are arranged as shown below in the array:

A B A A A B A B A B

A A A A A B B B A B

B B B A A A B B A A

B A B A A B B B B B

In the study by Jenkins et al. (2011) referred to above, British participants were presented with 40 face photographs. They sorted the photographs with a separate pile for each person shown in the photographs. The photographs consisted of 20 photographs each of two Dutch celebrities virtually unknown in Britain. On average, participants thought the number of different individuals represented was almost *four* times the actual number.

In another experiment, Jenkins et al. (2011) asked Dutch participants to carry out exactly the same task. For these participants, the faces were familiar. The findings were dramatically different from those of the previous experiment. Nearly all the participants performed perfectly: they sorted the photographs into two piles with 20 photographs of one celebrity in each pile.

In a third experiment, Jenkins et al. (2011) presented 400 photographs consisting of 20 photographs each of 20 unfamiliar individuals. Participants rated the attractiveness of each face. There was more variability in attractiveness ratings *within* than *between* individuals. In other words, there were often large differences in rated attractiveness of two photographs of the same person. As you may have noticed, beautiful celebrities often look surprisingly unattractive when photographed unexpectedly in everyday life.

What do the above findings mean? First, there is considerable within-person *variability* in facial images, which explains why different photographs of the same unfamiliar individual look as if they come from different individuals. Second, the findings also mean passport photographs have limited value. Third, the findings help to explain the difficulties that eyewitnesses have in identifying the person responsible for a crime (see Chapter 8). Fourth, we are much better at recognising that different photographs of a familiar individual are of the same person because we possess much relevant information about that individual.

with any given face. As we see, the differences between familiar and unfamiliar face recognition are perhaps even greater than assumed by Bruce and Young (1986).

What can be done to improve identification of unfamiliar faces? We can use image averaging across several photographs of the same individual (Jenkins & Burton, 2011). This reduces the impact of those aspects of the image varying across photographs of a given individual. As predicted, Jenkins and Burton found identification based on average images became increasingly accurate as the number of photographs contributing to those images increased.

The second prediction is that different routes are involved in the processing of facial identity and facial expression. Haxby et al. (2000) agreed. They argued that the processing of changeable aspects of faces (especially expressions) occurs mainly in the superior temporal sulcus. There is some support for this prediction. Fox et al. (2011) found patients with damage to the face-recognition network had impaired identity perception but not expression perception. In contrast, a patient with damage to the superior temporal sulcus had impaired expression perception but reasonably intact identity perception.

However, the two routes are not entirely independent. Judgements of facial expression are strongly influenced by irrelevant identity information, which indicates a measure of *interdependence* of the two routes (Schweinberger & Soukup, 1998). In contrast, however, judgements of facial identity were not influenced by the emotion expressed. Fitousi and Wenger (2013) found that whether the two routes were independent depended on the precise task. There were two tasks: (A) respond positively if the face has a given identity *and* emotion (e.g., happy face belonging to Keira Knightley); (B) respond positively if the face has a given identity or a given emotion (e.g., happy face or Keira Knightley or both). There was evidence of independent processing of identity and expression with task (B) but not task (A).

The facial-expression route is more complex than envisaged by Bruce and Young (1986). Damage to certain brain regions can affect recognition of some emotions more than others. For example, damage to the amygdala produces greater deficits in recognising fear and anger than other emotions (Calder & Young, 2005). Similar emotion-specific patterns were obtained when brain-damaged patients tried to recognise the same emotions from voices (Calder & Young, 2005). Young and Bruce (2011) admitted they had not expected deficits in emotion recognition to be specific to certain emotions.

The third prediction is that we always retrieve personal information (e.g., occupation) about a person *before* recalling their name. Young et al. (1985) asked people to record the problems they experienced in face recognition. There were 1,008 such incidents, but people *never* reported putting a name to a face while knowing nothing else about that person. In contrast, there were 190 occasions on which someone remembered a reasonable amount of information about a person but not their name, which is also as predicted by the model. Finally, also as predicted, there were 233 occasions on which a face triggered a feeling of familiarity but an inability to think of any other relevant information about the person.

In spite of the above findings, the notion that names are *always* recalled after personal information is probably too rigid. Calderwood and Burton (2006) asked fans of the television series *Friends* to recall the name or occupation of the main characters when shown their faces. Names were recalled faster than occupations, suggesting names can sometimes be recalled before personal information. However, it is possible that other personal information (e.g., character in *Friends*) might have been recalled faster than name information.

Evaluation

Young and Bruce (2011) provided a very useful evaluation of their own model. On the positive side, the model adopted a broad perspective emphasising the wide range of information that can be extracted from faces. In addition, it was ahead of its time in identifying the major processes and structures involved in face processing and recognition. Finally, Bruce and Young (1986) made an excellent attempt to indicate the main differences in the processing of familiar and unfamiliar faces.

The model has various limitations. First, the notion that facial expression is processed separately from facial identity is oversimplified and often incorrect. Second, expression analysis is much more complex than assumed in the model. Third, as Young and Bruce (2011) admitted, they were wrong to exclude gaze perception from their model. Gaze signals are very valuable to us in various ways, including providing useful information about what the other person is attended to. Fourth, the assumption that name information is always accessed after personal information about faces may be too rigid.

Individual differences

Bruce and Young (1986) focused on general factors involved in face recognition. However, much can be learned about face recognition by focusing on individual differences, as we have already seen in our discussion of prosopagnosics. Russell et al. (2009) focused on four "super-recognisers" who had exceptionally good face-recognition ability. They performed at a very high level on several tasks involving face recognition (e.g., identifying famous people from photographs taken many years before they became famous).

Russell et al. (2012) pointed out that face recognition depends more than object recognition on surface reflectance information (the way an object's surface reflects and transmits light) but less on shape information. This suggests that super-recognisers might be especially proficient at using surface reflectance information. In fact, however, they were simply better than other people at using surface reflectance *and* shape information.

Genetic factors probably help to explain the existence of super-recognisers. Wilmer et al. (2010) studied face recognition in monozygotic or identical twins (sharing 100% of their genes) and dizygotic twins (sharing only 50%). The face-recognition performance of identical twins was much more similar than that of fraternal twins, indicating face-recognition ability is influenced in part by genetic factors.

VISUAL IMAGERY

Close your eyes and imagine the face of someone very important in your life. What did you experience? Many people claim forming visual images is like "seeing with the mind's eye", suggesting there are important similarities between imagery and perception. Mental imagery is typically thought of as a form of experience, implying that it has strong links to consciousness. However, it also possible to regard imagery as a form of mental representation (an internal cognitive symbol representing some aspects of external reality) (e.g., Pylyshyn, 2002). We would not necessarily be consciously aware of images in the form of mental representations. In spite of its importance, the issue of whether imagery necessarily involves consciousness has attracted relatively little direct research interest (Thomas, 2009).

If (as is often assumed), visual imagery and perception are similar, why don't we confuse them? In fact, some people suffer from hallucinations with what they believe to be visual perception occurring in the absence of the appropriate environmental stimulus. In **Anton's syndrome** ("blindness denial"), blind people are unaware they are blind and may confuse imagery for actual perception. Goldenberg et al. (1995) described a patient nearly all of whose primary visual cortex had been destroyed. In spite of that, the patient generated visual images so vivid they were mistaken for genuine visual perception. Bridge et al. (2012) studied a young man, SBR, who also had virtually no primary visual cortex but was not suffering from Anton's syndrome. He had vivid visual imagery and his pattern of cortical activation when engaged in visual imagery was very similar to that of healthy controls.

Some other patients have **Charles Bonnet syndrome**, defined as "consistent or periodic complex visual hallucinations that occur in visually impaired individuals with intact cognitive ability" (Yacoub & Ferrucci, 2011, p. 421). One sufferer reported the following hallucination: "There's heads of 17th century men and women, with nice heads of hair. Wigs, I should think. Very disapproving, all of them" (Santhouse et al., 2000, p. 2057). Note, however, that patients are generally (but not always) aware the hallucinations are not real so they are actually pseudo-hallucinations.

Patients with Charles Bonnet syndrome have increased activity in brain areas specialised for visual processing when hallucinating (ffytche et al., 1998).

KEY TERMS

Anton's syndrome
A condition found in some blind people in which they misinterpret their visual imagery as visual perception.

Charles Bonnet syndrome
A condition in which individuals with eye disease form vivid and detailed visual hallucinations sometimes mistaken for visual perception.

In addition, hallucinations in colour were associated with increased activity in areas specialised for colour processing.

In visual perception, bottom-up processes *inhibit* activation in parts of the visual cortex (e.g., BA37). The impoverished bottom-up processes in Charles Bonnet syndrome permit spontaneous activation in areas associated with the production of hallucinations (Kazui et al., 2009).

Anyone (other than those with eye disease) suffering from visual hallucinations is unlikely to remain at liberty for long. How do we avoid confusing images and perceptions? One reason is that we generally know we are *deliberately* constructing images, which is not the case with perception. Another reason is that images contain much less detail than perception. Harvey (1986) found people rated their visual images of faces as similar to photographs from which the sharpness of the edges and borders had been removed.

KEY TERMS

Depictive representations
Representations (e.g., visual images) resembling pictures in that objects within them are organised spatially.

Visual buffer
Within Kosslyn's theory, a short-term visual memory store.

Why is visual imagery useful?

What function is served by visual imagery? According to Moulton and Kosslyn (2009, p. 1274), imagery "allows us to answer 'what if' questions by making explicit and accessible the likely consequences of being in a specific situation or performing a specific action". For example, car drivers may use imagery to *predict* what will happen if they make a given manoeuvre. Top golfers use mental imagery to *predict* what would happen if they hit a certain shot.

Imagery theories

Kosslyn (e.g., 1994, 2005) put forward a very influential theory based on the assumption that visual imagery resembles visual perception. It is known as perceptual anticipation theory because the mechanisms used to generate images involve processes used to anticipate perceiving stimuli.

Weblink:
Kosslyn's lab

According to the theory, visual images are **depictive representations** – they are like pictures of drawings in that the objects and parts of objects are arranged in space. More specifically, information within an image is organised spatially, like information within a percept. Thus, for example, a visual image of a desk with a computer on top and a cat sleeping underneath it would be arranged so the computer was at the top of the image and the cat at the bottom.

Where in the brain are depictive representations formed? Kosslyn argued that they are created in early visual cortex (primary visual cortex (BA17)) and secondary visual cortex (BA18) in a visual buffer. The **visual buffer** is a short-term store for visual information only. This visual buffer is of major importance in visual perception as well as visual imagery. There is also an "attention window" that selects part of the visual buffer and sends information to other brain areas for further processing.

In perception, processing in the visual buffer depends primarily on *external* stimulation. In contrast, visual images in the visual buffer depend on non-pictorial information stored in long-term memory. Information about shapes is stored in the inferior temporal lobe, whereas spatial representations are stored in posterior parietal cortex (see Figure 3.17). In general terms, visual perception mostly involves bottom-up processing, whereas visual imagery depends on top-down processing.

Pylyshyn (e.g., 2002) argued that visual imagery is much less like visual perception than assumed by Kosslyn. According to his propositional theory, performance on mental imagery tasks does *not* involve depictive or pictorial representations. Instead, what is involved is tacit knowledge (knowledge inaccessible to conscious awareness). Tacit knowledge is "knowledge of *what things would look like* to subjects in situations like the ones in which they are to imagine themselves" (Pylyshyn, 2002, p. 161). Thus, participants given an imagery task rely on relevant stored knowledge rather than visual images.

The exact nature of the tacit knowledge allegedly involved in visual imagery is unclear because Pylyshyn has not provided a very explicit account. However, there is no apparent reason within his theory why early visual cortex would be involved during image formation.

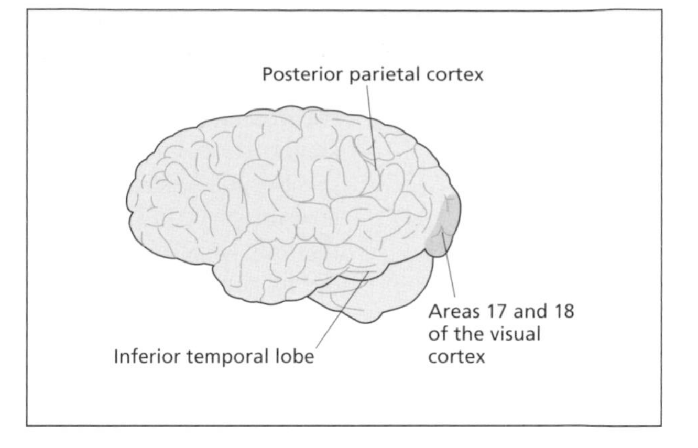

Figure 3.17
The approximate locations of the visual buffer in BA17 and BA18 of long-term memories of shapes in the inferior temporal lobe, and of spatial representations in posterior parietal cortex, according to Kosslyn and Thompson's (2003) anticipation theory.

Imagery resembles perception

If visual perception and visual imagery involve similar processes, they should influence each other. There should be *facilitative* effects if the contents of perception and imagery are the same but *interference* effects if they differ.

Pearson et al. (2008) found evidence of facilitation. They studied **binocular rivalry** – when two different stimuli are presented one to each eye, only one is consciously perceived at any given moment. If one of the two stimuli is presented shortly before the other, that increases the chances it will be perceived in the binocular rivalry situation. Pearson et al. found this when observers initially perceived a green vertical grating or a red horizontal grating. This facilitation effect was greatest when the orientation of the grating under binocular rivalry conditions was the same as the initial orientation and least when there was a large difference in orientation.

Pearson et al. (2008) also considered what happened when the initial single grating was *imagined* rather than *perceived*. The pattern of facilitation in binocular rivalry was remarkably similar to that observed when the initial single grating was perceived.

So far as interference is concerned, we will consider a study by Baddeley and Andrade (2000). Participants rated the vividness of visual or auditory images under control conditions (no additional task) or while performing a second task. This second task involved visual/spatial processes or verbal processes (counting aloud repeatedly from 1 to 10). The visual/spatial task reduced the vividness of visual imagery more than that of auditory imagery because the same mechanisms were involved on the visual/spatial task and visual imagery tasks.

According to Kosslyn (1994, 2005), much processing associated with visual imagery occurs in early visual cortex (BA17 and BA18), although several other areas are also involved. Kosslyn and Thompson (2003) considered numerous neuroimaging studies. Tasks involving visual imagery were associated with activation of early visual cortex in half of them. The findings were most often significant when the task involved inspecting the fine details of images, when the task focused on an object's shape rather than an object in motion, and when sensitive brain-imaging techniques were used.

Interactive exercise:
Kosslyn – mental imagery

Research activity:
Kosslyn

KEY TERM

Binocular rivalry
When two different visual stimuli are presented one to each eye, only one stimulus is seen; the seen stimulus alternates over time.

Ganis et al. (2004) compared patterns of brain activation in visual perception and imagery. There were two main findings. First, there was extensive overlap in the brain areas associated with perception and imagery. This was especially so in the frontal and parietal areas, perhaps because perception and imagery involve similar control processes.

Second, visual imagery was associated with activation in only some brain areas involved in visual perception. Kosslyn (2005) estimated that visual imagery tasks are associated with activation in about two-thirds of the brain areas activated during perception.

Imagery does *not* resemble perception

Have a look at Figure 3.18, which consists of the outlines of three objects. Start with the object on the left and form a clear image. Then close your eyes, mentally rotate the image by 90 degrees clockwise and decide what you see. Then repeat the exercise with the other objects. Finally, rotate the book through 90 degrees. You found it easy to identify the objects when perceiving them even though you probably could not when you only imagined rotating them.

Slezak (1991, 1995) carried out research using stimuli very similar to those shown in Figure 3.18. No observers reported seeing the objects. This was not a deficiency in memory – participants who sketched the image from memory and then rotated it saw the new object. Thus, the information contained in images cannot be used as *flexibly* as visual information.

S.-H. Lee et al. (2012) found evidence for important differences between imagery and perception. Participants viewed or imagined various common objects (e.g., car, umbrella) and activity in early visual cortex and areas associated with later visual processing (object-selective regions) was assessed. Attempts were made to work out which objects were being imagined or perceived on the basis of activation in these areas.

What did Lee et al. (2012) find? First, activation in all brain areas assessed was considerably greater when participants perceived rather than imagined objects. Second, objects being perceived or imagined could be identified with above-chance accuracy on the basis of patterns of brain activation except for imagined objects in primary visual cortex (V1; see Figure 3.19).

Third, the success rate in identifying *perceived* objects was greater based on brain

Figure 3.18
Slezak (1991, 1995) asked participants to memorise one of the above images. They then imagined rotating the image 90 degrees clockwise and reported what they saw. None of them reported seeing the figures that can be seen clearly if you rotate the page by 90 degrees clockwise.

Left image from Slezak (1995), centre image from Slezak (1991), right image reprinted from Pylyshyn (2003), with permission from Elsevier and the author.

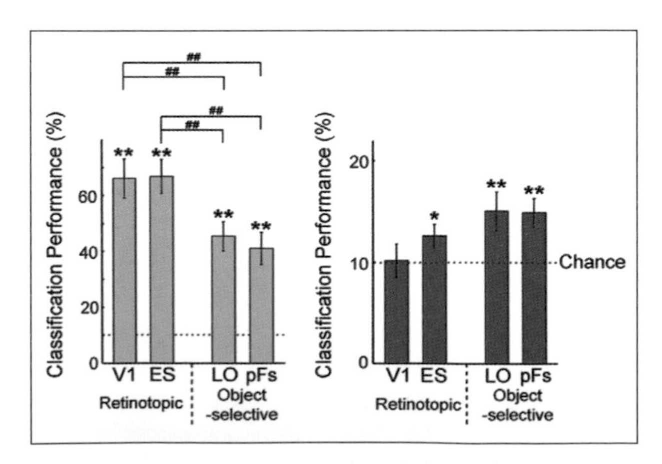

Figure 3.19
The extent to which perceived (left side of figure) or imagined (right side of figure) objects could be classified accurately on the basis of brain activity in early visual cortex and object-selective cortex. (ES = extrastriate retinotopic cortex; LO = lateral occipital cortex; pFs = posterior fusiform sulcus.)

From S.H. Lee et al. (2012). Reproduced with permission from Elsevier.

activation in areas associated with early visual processing than those associated with later processing. However, the opposite was the case with respect to identifying *imagined* objects (see Figure 3.19). These findings point to an important difference between imagery and perception: processing in early visual cortex is very limited during imagery for objects but is extremely important during perception. Imagery for objects depends mostly on top-down processes based on object knowledge rather than on processing in early visual cortex.

Brain damage

If perception and imagery involve the same mechanisms, we might expect brain damage to have similar effects on perception and on imagery. That is often the case but there are many exceptions (Bartolomeo, 2002, 2008). For example, Moro et al. (2008) studied two brain-damaged patients with intact visual perception but impaired visual imagery. They were both very poor at drawing objects from memory but could copy the same objects when shown a drawing.

These patients (and others with impaired visual imagery but intact visual perception) have damage to the left temporal lobe. Visual images are probably generated from information about concepts (including objects) stored in the temporal lobes (Patterson et al., 2007). However, this generation process is not needed (or is less important) for visual perception.

Other patients have intact visual imagery but impaired visual perception. These patients typically have severe damage to primary visual cortex, as in the case of SBR discussed earlier (Bridge et al., 2012). Another patient suffering from Anton's syndrome (blindness denial) was also discussed earlier (Goldenberg et al., 1995). Zago et al. (2010) reported similar findings in another patient with Anton's syndrome having total damage to primary visual cortex.

How can we interpret the findings from brain-damaged patients? In essence, visual perception mostly involves bottom-up processes triggered by the stimulus, whereas visual imagery primarily involves top-down processes based on object knowledge. Thus, it is not surprising that brain areas involved in early visual processing are more important for perception than imagery. It is also unsurprising that brain areas associated with storage of information about visual objects are more important for imagery.

Evaluation

Much progress has been made in understanding the relationship between visual imagery and visual perception. There is strong empirical support for the notion that similar processes are involved in imagery and perception. For example, imagery and perception are both associated with somewhat similar patterns of brain activity. In addition, the predicted facilitatory and interfering effects between imagery and perception tasks have been reported. These findings are more consistent with Kosslyn's theory than that of Pylyshyn.

On the negative side, visual perception and visual imagery are less similar than assumed by Kosslyn. For example, there is the neuroimaging evidence reported by S.-H. Lee et al. (2012) and the frequent dissociations between perception and imagery found in brain-damaged patients. What is required in future is a theory explaining the *differences* between imagery and perception as well as the *similarities*. We already know that there is differential involvement of bottom-up and top-down processes in perception and imagery.

CHAPTER SUMMARY

- **Pattern recognition**. Pattern recognition involves processing of specific features and global processing. Feature processing typically precedes global processing but there are exceptions. Several types of cells (e.g., simple cells, complex cells, end-stopped cells) involved in feature processing have been identified. Other cells responsive to different spatial frequencies are also important in pattern and object recognition. It is often assumed fingerprint identification is typically very accurate. In fact, there is substantial evidence for forensic confirmation bias, which involves contextual information distorting fingerprint identification via top-down processes. Fingerprint experts have a greater ability than novices to discriminate between matches and non-matches and also adopt a more conservative response bias.

- **Perceptual organisation**. The Gestaltists put forward several principles of perceptual grouping and emphasised the importance of figure–ground segregation. They argued that perceptual grouping and figure–ground segregation depend on innate factors. They also argued that we perceive the simplest possible organisation of the visual field, an important notion they failed to develop fully. The Gestaltists provided descriptions rather than explanations. Their approach was inflexible and they underestimated the complex interactions of factors underlying perceptual organisation. The Gestaltists de-emphasised the role of experience and learning in perceptual organisation, but this neglect has been rectified subsequently (e.g., the Bayesian approach).

- **Approaches to object recognition**. Visual processing typically involves a coarse-to-fine processing sequence. This sequence occurs in part because low spatial frequencies in visual input (associated with coarse processing) are conveyed to higher visual areas more rapidly than high spatial frequencies (associated with fine processing).

  Biederman assumed in his recognition-by-components theory that objects consist of basic shapes known as geons. An object's geons are determined by edge-extraction processes focusing on invariant properties of edges and the resultant geon-based description is viewpoint-invariant. Biederman's theory applies primarily to easy categorical discriminations, whereas object recognition is typically viewer-centred when identification is required. The theory is also too inflexible.

  Object recognition is often viewpoint-invariant when categorisation is required. However, it is typically viewer-centred when complex identification (within-category discrimination) is required. Inferotemporal cortex is of crucial importance in visual object recognition. Some inferotemporal neurons seem to be viewpoint-dependent, whereas others are viewpoint-invariant.

Research with ambiguous figures indicates that object recognition often depends on top-down processes. Top-down processes are frequently necessary for object recognition to occur, especially when recognition is hard.

- **Face recognition**. Face recognition involves more holistic processing than object recognition. Deficient holistic processing partly explains why prosopagnosic patients have much greater problems with face recognition than object recognition. The brain areas involved in face recognition (e.g., fusiform face area) may differ somewhat from those involved in object recognition. This may be due in part to the fact that they have special expertise with faces – there is some evidence the brain and processing mechanisms involved in face recognition are also used when recognising objects for which we have expertise.

  Bruce and Young's model assumes there are major differences in the processing of familiar and unfamiliar faces and that processing of facial identity is separate from processing of facial expression. There is good support for the former assumption but not the latter. Super-recognisers have outstanding face-recognition ability, which is due in part to genetic factors specific to faces.

- **Visual imagery**. Visual imagery is useful because it allows us to predict the visual consequences of performing certain actions. According to Kosslyn's perceptual anticipation theory, visual imagery closely resembles visual perception. In contrast, Pylyshyn in his propositional theory argued that visual imagery involves making use of tacit knowledge and does not resemble visual perception.

  Visual imagery and visual perception influence each other in ways predictable from Kosslyn's theory. Neuroimaging studies and studies on brain-damaged patients indicate that similar areas are involved in imagery and perception. However, areas involved in top-down processing (e.g., left temporal lobe) are more important in imagery than perception, and areas involved in bottom-up processing (e.g., early visual cortex) are more important in perception. Thus, there are major similarities and differences between imagery and perception.

Further reading

- Bruce, V. & Young, A. (2012). *Face perception*. Hove: Psychology Press. Vicki Bruce and Andy Young provide a thorough and authoritative account of our current knowledge of face perception.
- Dror, I.E., Champod, C., Langenburg, G., Charlton, D., Hunt, H. & Rosenthal, R. (2011). Cognitive issues in fingerprint analysis: Inter- and intra-expert consistency and the effect of a "target" comparison. *Forensic Science International*, 208: 10–17. Some of the major problems that arise in fingerprint analysis are discussed by Itiel Dror (a leading expert in this field) and his colleagues.
- Ganis, G. & Schendan, H.E. (2011). Visual imagery. *Wiley Interdisciplinary Reviews – Cognitive Science*, 2: 239–52. In this article, the authors provide a comprehensive account of our current knowledge and understanding of visual imagery.
- Hayward, W.G. (2012). Whatever happened to object-centred representations? *Perception*, 41: 1153–62. William Hayward discusses important theoretical issues relating to how observers identify objects presented from different viewpoints.
- Hummel, J.E. (2013). Object recognition. In D. Reisberg (ed.), *The Oxford handbook of cognitive psychology*. Oxford: Oxford University Press. This chapter by John Hummel provides a comprehensive overview of theory and research on object recognition.
- Reisberg, D. (2013). Mental images. In D. Reisberg (ed.), *The Oxford handbook of cognitive psychology*. Oxford: Oxford University Press. Major issues concerning visual imagery are discussed at length by Daniel Reisberg.
- Wade, N.J. & Swanston, M.T. (2013). *Visual perception: An introduction* (3rd edn). Hove: Psychology Press. This textbook provides a good overview of visual perception including object recognition.
- Wagemans, J., Feldman, J., Gepshtein, S., Kimchi, R., Poemerantz, J.R. & van der Helm, P.A. (2012). A century of Gestalt psychology in visual perception: II. Conceptual and theoretical foundations. *Psychological Bulletin*, 138: 1218–52. The Gestaltists' theoretical approach is compared with more contemporary theories of perceptual grouping and figure–ground segregation.
- Wallis, G. (2013). Toward a unified model of face and object recognition in the human visual system. *Frontiers in Psychology*, 4 (Article 497). Guy Wallis argues persuasively that the influential notion that face and object recognition involves different processes may be incorrect.

CHAPTER

4

Perception, motion and action

INTRODUCTION

Most of the research on perception discussed so far in this book has involved presenting a visual stimulus and assessing aspects of its processing. What has been missing (but is an overarching theme in this chapter) is the *time* dimension. In the real world, we move around and/or people or objects in the environment move. The resulting changes in the visual information available to us are very useful in ensuring we perceive the environment accurately. The emphasis on change and movement necessarily leads to a consideration of the relationship between perception and action. In sum, the focus in this chapter is on how we process (and respond to) a constantly changing visual environment.

The first theme addressed in this chapter is concerned with the perception of movement. This includes our ability to move successfully within the visual environment and to predict accurately when moving objects will reach us.

The second theme is concerned with more complex issues – how do we act appropriately on the environment and the objects within it? Of relevance are theories (e.g., the perception-action theory, the dual-process approach) distinguishing between processes and systems involved in vision-for-perception and those involved in vision-for-action. Those theories were discussed in Chapter 2. Here we consider theories providing more detailed accounts of vision-for-action and/or the workings of the dorsal pathways allegedly underlying vision-for-action.

The third theme focuses on the processes involved in *making sense* of moving objects (especially other people). It thus differs from the first theme in which moving stimuli are considered mostly in terms of predicting when they will reach us. There is an emphasis on perception of biological movement when the available visual information is impoverished. We also consider the role of the mirror neuron system in interpreting human movement.

Finally, we consider the extent to which we manage to *detect* changes in the visual environment over time. We will see there is convincing evidence attention plays an important role in determining which aspects of the environment are consciously detected. This issue is discussed at the end of the chapter because it provides a useful bridge between the areas of visual perception and attention (the subject of the next chapter).

KEY TERMS

Optic array
The structural pattern of light falling on the retina.

Optic flow
The changes in the pattern of light reaching an observer when there is movement of the observer and/or aspects of the environment.

Focus of expansion
The point towards which someone in motion is moving; it does not appear to move but the surrounding visual environment apparently moves away from it.

DIRECT PERCEPTION

James Gibson (1950, 1966, 1979) put forward a radical approach to perception that was largely ignored at the time. The dominant approach until 30 years ago was that the central function of visual perception is to allow us to identify or recognise objects in the world around us. This often involves extensive cognitive processing, including relating information extracted from the visual environment to our stored knowledge of objects (see Chapter 3). Gibson argued that this approach is of limited relevance to visual perception in the real world. Vision developed during evolution to allow our ancestors to respond rapidly to the environment (e.g., killing animals, avoiding precipices).

Gibson argued that perception involves "keeping in touch with the environment" (1979, p. 239). This is sufficient for most purposes because the information available from environmental stimuli is much richer than previously believed. We can relate Gibson's views to Milner and Goodale's (1995, 2008) vision-for-action system (see Chapter 2). According to both theoretical accounts, there is an intimate relationship between perception and action.

Gibson regarded his theoretical approach as *ecological*. He emphasised that perception facilitates interactions between the individual and his/her environment. More specifically, he put forward a direct theory of perception:

> When I assert that perception of the environment is direct, I mean that it is not mediated by *retinal* pictures, *neural* pictures, or *mental* pictures. *Direct perception* is the activity of getting information from the ambient array of light. I call this a process of *information pickup* that involves . . . looking around, getting around, and looking at things.
>
> (Gibson, 1979, p. 147)

We will briefly consider Gibson's theoretical assumptions:

- The pattern of light reaching the eye is an **optic array**; it contains all the visual information from the environment striking the eye.
- The optic array provides unambiguous or invariant information about the layout of objects. This information comes in many forms, including texture gradients, optic-flow patterns and affordances (all described below).

Gibson prepared training films in the Second World War describing the problems experienced by pilots taking off and landing. What information do pilots have available while performing these manoeuvres? There is **optic flow** (Gibson, 1950) – the changes in the pattern of light reaching an observer created when he/she moves or parts of the visual environment move. Consider a pilot approaching a landing strip. The point towards which the pilot is moving (the **focus of expansion**) appears motionless, with the rest of the visual environment apparently moving away from that point (see Figure 4.1). The further away any part of the landing strip is from that point, the greater is its apparent speed of movement.

More will be said about optic flow and the focus of expansion. For now, we will consider a study by Wang et al. (2012). They simulated the pattern of optic flow that would be experienced if the participants moved forwards in a stationary environment. Attention was attracted towards the focus of expansion, thus showing its psychological importance.

Weblink:
Gibson's theory

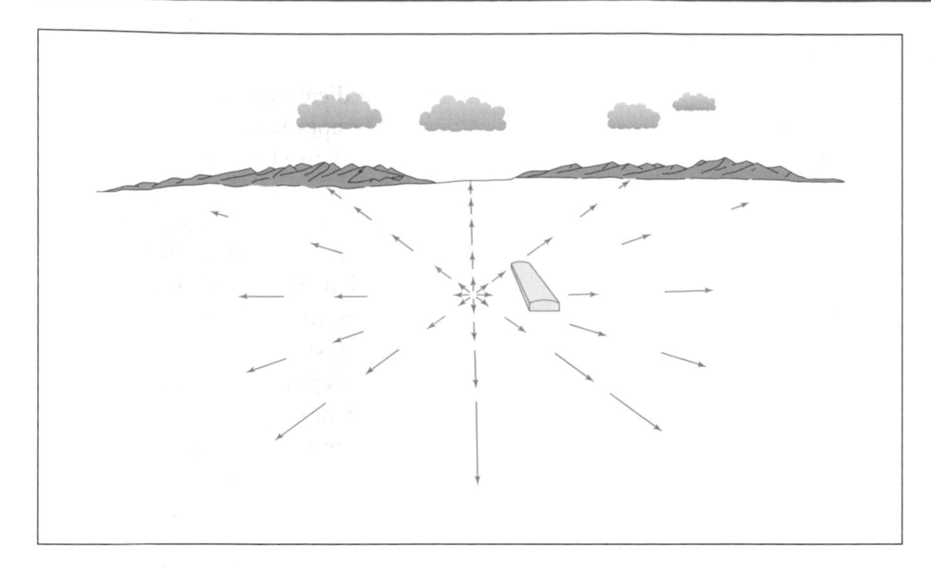

Figure 4.1
The optic-flow field as a pilot comes in to land, with the focus of expansion in the middle.

From Gibson (1950). Wadsworth, a part of Cengage Learning, Inc. © 2014 American Psychological Association. Reproduced with permission.

Weblink:
Optic flow

Gibson (1966, 1979) argued that certain higher-order characteristics of the visual array (**invariants**) remain unaltered as observers move around their environment. The fact they remain the same over different viewing angles makes invariants of particular importance. The focus of expansion (discussed earlier) is an invariant feature of the optic array.

Affordances

How did Gibson account for the role of meaning in perception? Gibson (1979) claimed that potential uses of objects (their **affordances**) are directly perceivable. For example, a ladder "affords" ascent or descent, and a chair "affords" sitting. What Gibson had in mind was that, "affordances are opportunities for action that exist in the environment and do not depend on the animal's mind . . . they do not cause behaviour but simply make it possible" (Withagen et al., 2012, p. 251).

Most objects give rise to more than one affordance, with the particular affordance influencing behaviour depending on the perceiver's current psychological state. Thus, an orange can have the affordance of edibility to a hungry person but a projectile to an angry one.

Gibson had little to say about the processes involved in learning which affordances will satisfy particular goals. However, Gibson (1966, p. 51) assumed that, "The perceptual systems are clearly amenable to learning. It would be expected that an individual, after practice, could orient more exactly, listen more carefully . . . and look more perceptively than he could before practice."

Gibson's notion of affordances has received some support. Di Stasi and Guardini (2007) asked observers to judge the affordance of "climbability" of steps varying in height. The step height judged the most "climbable" was the one that would have involved the minimum expenditure of energy.

Gibson argued that an object's affordances are perceived directly. Pappas and Mack (2008) presented images of objects so briefly they were not consciously perceived. However, each object's main affordance produced motor priming. Thus, for example, the presentation of a hammer caused activation in brain areas involved in preparing to use a hammer.

KEY TERMS

Invariants
Properties of the optic array that remain constant even though other aspects vary; part of Gibson's theory.

Affordances
The potential uses of an object, which Gibson claimed are perceived directly.

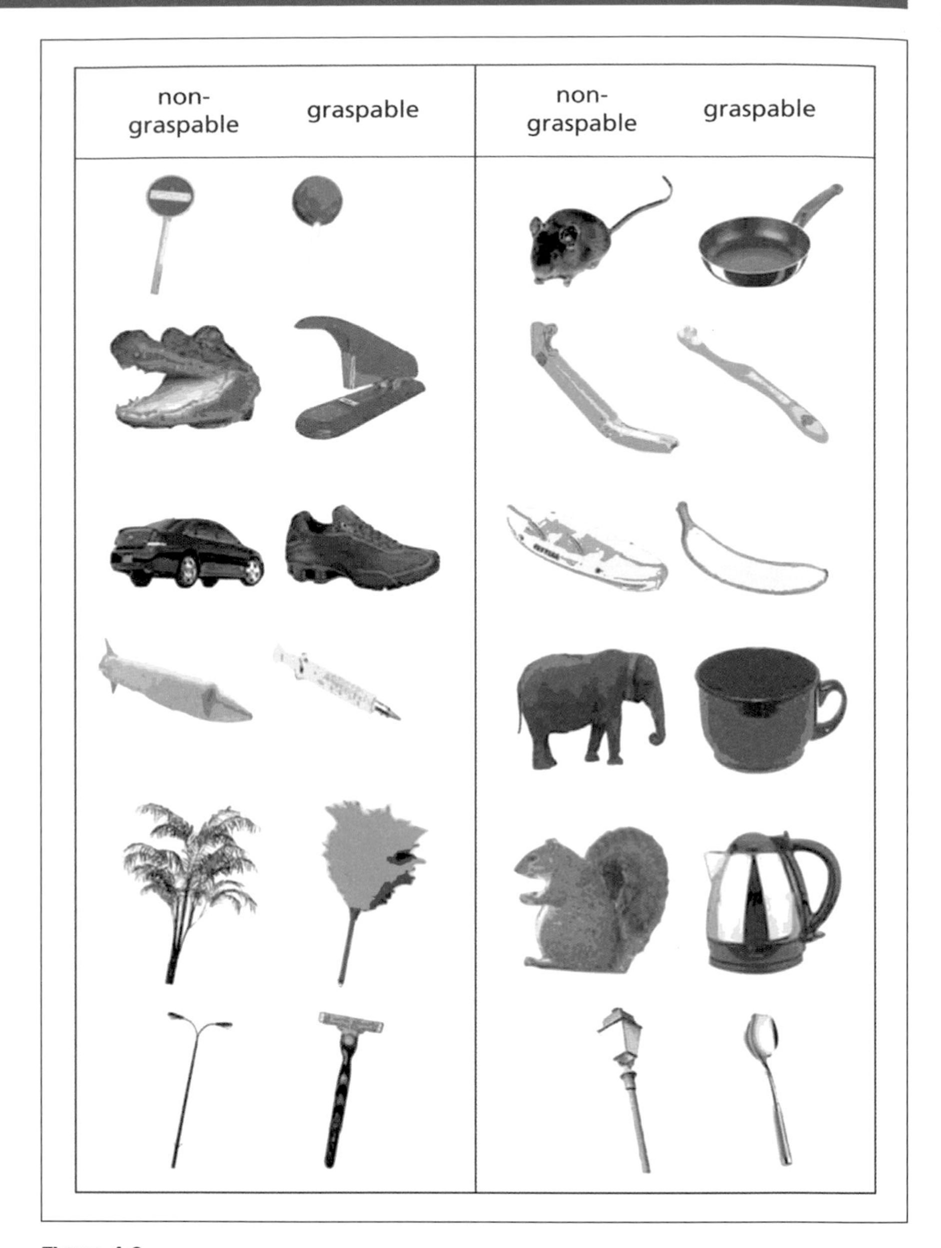

Figure 4.2
Graspable and non-graspable objects having similar asymmetrical features.
From Wilf et al. (2013). Reprinted with permission.

Wilf et al. (2013) focused on the affordance of graspability. They presented participants on each trial with a colour picture of a graspable or a non-graspable object (see Figure 4.2). The participants performed a simple reaction-time task by lifting their arm to perform a reach-like movement. The key finding was that there was faster onset of muscle activity for graspable than non-graspable objects. Thus, the affordance of graspability triggers rapid activity in the motor system.

Other theorists have put forward ideas resembling those of Gibson's notion of affordances. Consider, for example, Barsalou's (e.g., 2009, 2012) situated simulation theory (see Chapter 7). According to this theory, the motor system is typically involved when we understand the meaning of a concept. This extends Gibson's account because Barsalou argues that motor processes can be activated simply by the presentation of a word (e.g., *hammer*) without the object itself being present.

Evaluation

The ecological approach to perception has proved successful in various ways. First, as Bruce and Tadmor (2015, in press) pointed out, "Gibson's realisation that *natural scenes* are the ecologically valid stimulus that should be used for the study of vision was of fundamental importance."

Second, and related to the first point, Gibson disagreed with the previous emphasis of traditional laboratory research on static observers looking at impoverished visual displays. Instead, he argued that the moment-by-moment changes in the optic array provide much useful information.

Third, Gibson was far ahead of his time. It is now often accepted (e.g., Milner & Goodale, 1995, 2008) there are two visual systems, a vision-for-perception system and a vision-for-action system. Gibson argued that our perceptual system allows us to respond rapidly and accurately to environmental stimuli without using memory, and these are all features of the vision-for-action system.

What are the limitations of Gibson's approach? First, the processes involved in perception are much more complicated than implied by Gibson. Many of these complexities were discussed in Chapters 2 and 3.

Second, Gibson's argument that we do not need to assume the existence of internal representations (e.g., object memories) to understand perception is flawed. The logic of Gibson's position is that, "There are invariants specifying a friend's face, a performance of Hamlet, or the sinking of the Titanic, and no knowledge of the friend, of the play, or of maritime history is required to perceive these things" (Bruce et al., 2003, p. 410).

Third, and related to the second point, Gibson greatly minimised the importance of top-down processes (based on our knowledge and expectations) in visual perception. As is discussed in Chapter 3, top-down processes are especially important when the visual input is impoverished or when we are viewing ambiguous figures.

Fourth, Gibson's views are oversimplified with respect to the effects of motion on perception. For example, when moving towards a goal we use many more sources of information than Gibson assumed (see discussion below).

VISUALLY GUIDED ACTION

From an ecological perspective, it is very important to understand how we move around the environment. For example, what information do we use when walking towards a target? If we are to avoid premature death, we must ensure we are not hit by cars when crossing the road, and when driving we must avoid hitting cars coming the other way. If we want to play tennis well, we have to become skilful at predicting exactly when and where the ball is going to strike our racquet. Visual perception plays a crucial role in facilitating human locomotion and ensuring our safety. The main processes are discussed below.

KEY TERMS

Retinal flow field
The changing patterns of light on the retina produced by movement of the observer relative to the environment as well as by eye and head movements.

Efference copy
An internal copy of a motor command (e.g., to the eyes); it can be used to compare actual with desired movement.

Heading and steering

When we want to reach some goal (e.g., a gate at the end of a field), we use visual information to move directly towards it. Gibson (1950) emphasised the importance of optic flow (discussed earlier). When someone is moving forwards in a straight line, the point towards which he/she is moving (the point of expansion) appears motionless. In contrast, the area around that point seems to be expanding.

Gibson (1950) proposed a global radial outflow hypothesis, according to which the overall or global outflow pattern specifies an observer's heading. If we are not moving directly towards our goal, we use the focus of expansion and optic flow to bring our heading (point of expansion) into alignment with our goal.

What we have discussed so far works well in principle when applied to an individual moving *straight* from point A to point B. However, as you can imagine, matters become more complex when we *cannot* move directly to our goal (e.g., going around a bend in the road, avoiding obstacles). There are also additional complexities because observers often make head and eye movements, both of which alter optic flow. The **retinal flow field** (changes in the pattern of light on the retina) is determined by two factors:

1 linear flow containing a focus of expansion;
2 rotary flow (rotation in the retinal image) produced by following a curved path and by eye and head movements.

Weblink:
Optic flow demonstrations

As a result of these complexities, it is often hard for us to use information from retinal flow to determine our direction of heading. Of particular importance is **efference copy**, which is "an internal brain signal informing the visual system of commands to move the eye" (Bridgeman, 2007, p. 924). The information in this signal is used to compensate for the effects of eye movements on the retinal image (Chagnaud et al., 2012).

Findings: heading

Gibson emphasised the role of optic flow in allowing people to move directly towards their goal. Much evidence indicates that the medial superior temporal area is strongly responsive to optic flow (e.g., Smith et al., 2006). Stronger evidence that this area is *causally* involved in heading was provided by Britten and van Wezel (1998). They produced biases in heading perception in monkeys by stimulating parts of the medial superior temporal area.

As indicated above, eye and/or head movements make it harder to use optic flow effectively for heading. Bremmer et al. (2010) considered this issue in macaque monkeys presented with distorted visual flow fields simulating the combined effects of self-motion and an eye movement. Their key finding was that numerous cells in the medial superior temporal area successfully compensated for this distortion.

According to Gibson, a walker tries to make the focus of expansion coincide with straight-ahead of the body. Suppose a walker wore prisms producing a 9 degree error into their perceived visual direction as they walked towards a target. What would happen? Retinal motion would indicate the focus of expansion was *misaligned* compared to the walker's expectation, and so there would be a correction process. Herlihey and Rushton (2012) obtained experimental support for this prediction. Also as predicted, walkers denied access to information about retinal motion failed to show any correction.

We often use factors over and above optic-flow information when making heading judgements. This is unsurprising given the typical richness of the available environmental information. Van den Berg and Brenner (1994) pointed out that we only need one eye to use optic-flow information. However, they found heading judgements were more accurate when observers used both eyes. Binocular disparity (see Glossary) in the two-eye condition provided useful additional information about the relative depths of objects in the display.

Gibson assumed that optic-flow patterns generated by motion are of fundamental importance when we head towards a goal. However, Hahn et al. (2003) found motion is *not* essential for accurate perception of heading. Observers viewed two photographs of a real-world scene in fairly rapid succession. Judgements of heading direction were reasonably accurate in the absence of apparent motion (and thus of optic-flow information).

What information did the observers in Hahn et al.'s (2003) study use to estimate heading direction? Snyder and Bischof (2010) argued that the retinal *displacement* of objects is important – objects closer to the direction of heading show less retinal displacement as we move closer to the target. Snyder and Bischof obtained support for their position, and discovered that objects nearer to the observer were more useful than those further away.

In spite of the above findings, Snyder and Bischof (2010) found displacement information had limited value because it often did *not* permit accurate judgements of heading direction. When the heading direction was complex (e.g., following a curved path), displacement-based information was of little or no use.

What can we conclude from the above findings? Snyder and Bischof (2010) argued that information about the direction of heading is provided by two systems. One system uses movement information rapidly and fairly automatically (as proposed by Gibson). The other system uses displacement information more slowly and with more use of processing resources.

How can we test the above theoretical account? Suppose participants performed a second task at the same time as making judgements about direction of heading. This additional task should have little or no effect on judgements when movement information is available and so the first system can be used. Royden and Hildreth (1999) obtained findings supporting that prediction. In contrast, an additional task should impair judgements about direction of heading when only displacement information is available. Hahn et al. (2003) found this was the case.

Heading: future path

Wilkie and Wann (2006) argued that judgements of heading (the direction in which someone is moving) are of little relevance if he/she is moving along a curved path. According to them, path judgements (identifying future points along one's path) are more important. With curved paths, path judgements were much more accurate than heading judgements (mean errors 5 and 13 degrees, respectively).

According to the above analysis, we might expect people (e.g., drivers) to fixate some point along their future path when it is curved. This is the future-path strategy (see Figure 4.3). An alternative strategy for drivers was proposed

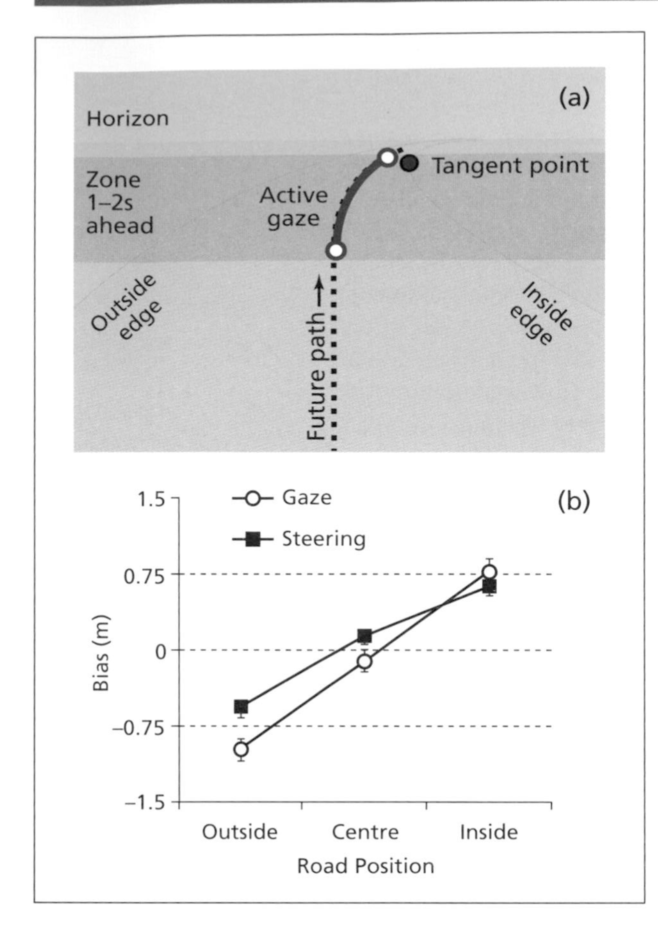

Figure 4.3
The visual features of a road viewed in perspective. The tangent point is marked by the filled circle on the inside edge of the road, and the desired future path is shown by the dotted line. According to the future-path theory, drivers should gaze along the line marked "active gaze".

From Wilkie et al. (2010). Reprinted with permission from Springer-Verlag.

by Land and Lee (1994). They claimed (with supportive evidence) that drivers approaching a bend focus on the **tangent point** – the point on the inside edge of the road at which its direction appears to reverse (see Figure 4.3).

What are the potential advantages of using the tangent point? First, it is easy to identify and to track. Second, road curvature can readily be worked out by considering the angle between the direction of heading and that of the tangent point.

Kandil et al. (2009) studied drivers negotiating 270 degree bends at a motorway junction. When the drivers could use any strategy, they looked at the tangent point far more of the time than the future path (75% vs. 14%, respectively). After that, the drivers were instructed to use *only* the future-path or tangent-point strategy. Driving performance was better (e.g., in terms of lane position) when using the tangent-point strategy.

Other research indicates the tangent point is often *not* very important. Wilkie et al. (2010) instructed drivers to drive in the centre of the road, towards the outside of the road or towards the inside of the road. Drivers' direction of gaze was strongly influenced by these instructions. Instead of looking at the tangent point, drivers fixated where they wanted to be on the road approximately 1.36 seconds later (the future-path strategy) (see Figure 4.3). Only participants told to take the racing line (i.e., to cut the corner) focused frequently on the tangent point.

Mars and Navarro (2012) also argued against the importance of the tangent point. Participants in their study generally gazed at a point approximately 48 cm away from the tangent point in the direction of the centre of the road. This corresponded fairly closely to the point the car's inner wheel would pass over.

Kountouriotis et al. (2012) reported additional findings against the tangent-point hypothesis. According to that hypothesis, it should be very hard to use tangent-point information when the *inside* road edge is degraded or removed. In fact, however, steering was still effective under those conditions. According to the hypothesis, degrading or removing the *outside* road edge should not impair steering because drivers do not need to fixate that edge to use tangent-point information. However, steering was impaired under those conditions. In general, drivers fixated points on the road they intended to pass over.

How can we make sense of the apparently inconsistent findings? Lappi et al. (2013) argued that drivers fixate the tangent point when approaching and entering a bend but fixate the future path further into the bend. A detailed examination of the data from the study by Land and Lee (1994) revealed precisely this changing pattern of fixations as drivers proceeded through bends. Lappi et al. (2013) studied

KEY TERM

Tangent point
From a driver's perspective, the point on a road at which the direction of its inside edge appears to reverse.

drivers' eye movements as they drove along a lengthy curve of constant radius formed by the slip road to a motorway. Drivers' fixations were predominantly on the path ahead rather than the tangent point after the first few seconds (short clips of drivers' eye movements performing this task can be found under supporting information for the article at 10.1371/journal.pone.0068326).

Why do drivers tend to switch from fixating the tangent point to fixating the path ahead as they negotiate curves? The tangent point provides relatively precise information. As a result, drivers may use it when uncertainty about the precise nature of the curve or bend is maximal (i.e., when approaching and entering it). Thereafter, drivers may revert to focusing on the future path.

Evaluation

Gibson's views concerning the importance of optic-flow information have deservedly been very influential. Such information is especially useful when individuals can move *directly* towards their goal rather than following a curved or other indirect path. Indeed, the evidence suggests that optic flow is generally the dominant source of information determining judgements of heading direction. The notion that individuals following a curved path make use of the tangent point is very much in the spirit of Gibson's approach and has received some support.

What are the limitations of Gibson's approach? First, individuals moving directly towards a target often make use of kinds of information ignored by Gibson. Examples include binocular disparity and the retinal displacement of objects. Second, the tangent point is used relatively infrequently when individuals move along a curved path. They typically fixate on points lying along the future path. Third, in general terms, Gibson's approach provides an oversimplified account of heading.

Time to contact

In everyday life we often want to predict the moment there is going to be contact between us and some object. These situations include ones in which we are moving towards some object (e.g., a wall) and those in which an object (e.g., a ball) is approaching us. We might work out the time to contact by dividing our estimate of the object's distance by our estimate of its speed. However, this would be fairly complex and prone to error because information about speed and distance is not *directly* available.

Lee (1976, 2009) argued that we do *not* need to work out the distance or speed of an approaching object to work out the time to contact. Provided we are approaching it (or it is approaching us) at constant velocity, we can make use of tau. Tau is defined as the size of an object's retinal image divided by its rate of expansion. Tau specifies the time to contact with an approaching object – the faster the rate of expansion, the less time there is to contact.

When driving, the rate of decline of tau over time (tau-dot) indicates whether there is sufficient braking time to stop at the target. More specifically, Lee (1976) argued that drivers brake to hold constant the rate of change of tau. Lee's tau-dot hypothesis is consistent with Gibson's approach because it assumes information about time to contact is available from optic flow. In other words, observers can work out time to contact from variables measurable *directly* by the eye.

Lee's (1976, 2009) theoretical approach has been highly influential. However, tau has somewhat limited applicability in several ways in the real world (Tresilian, 1999):

- Tau ignores acceleration in object velocity.
- Tau only provides information about the time to contact with the eyes. However, what is important to drivers when braking to avoid an obstacle is the time to contact with their car. If they use tau, they may find the front of their car smashed in!
- Tau is accurate only when applied to spherically symmetrical objects: do not use it when catching a rugby ball!

Findings

Suppose you try to catch an approaching ball. Lee (1976) assumed your judgement of the time to contact would depend crucially on the rate of expansion of the ball's retinal image. Savelsbergh et al. (1993) tested this hypothesis. They manipulated the rate of expansion by using a deflating ball – its rate of expansion is less than a non-deflating ball. As predicted, the peak grasp closure occurred later to the deflating ball. However, the average difference was only 30 ms, whereas Lee's hypothesis predicts a difference of 230 ms. Thus, participants used additional sources of information (e.g., depth cues) that minimised the distorting effects of manipulating the rate of expansion.

Hosking and Crassini (2010) showed convincingly that tau is *not* the only factor determining time-to-contact judgements. Participants judged time to contact for familiar objects (tennis ball and football) presented in their standard size or with their sizes reversed (e.g., tennis ball the size of a football). Hosking and Crassini also used unfamiliar black spheres.

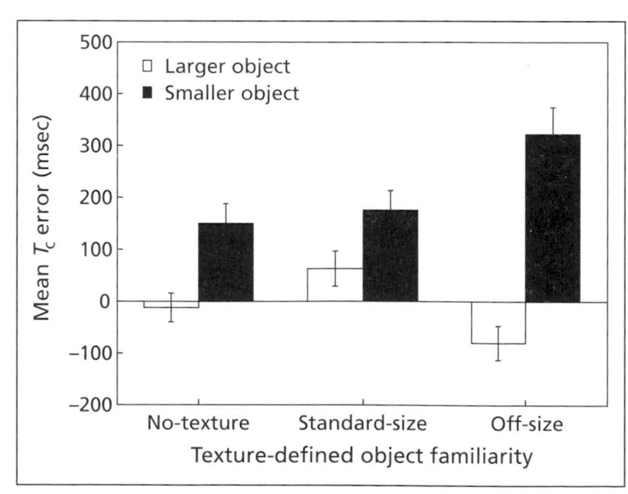

Figure 4.4

Errors in time-to-contact judgements for the smaller and the larger object as a function of whether they were presented in their standard size, the reverse size (off-size) or lacking texture (no-texture). Positive values indicate that responses were made too late and negative values that they were made too early.

From Hosking and Crassini (2010). With kind permission from Springer Science + Business Media.

Hosking and Crassini's (2010) findings are shown in Figure 4.4. Time-to-contact judgements were influenced by familiar size. This was especially the case when the object was a very small tennis ball, which led participants to overestimate time to contact.

Another factor influencing time-to-contact judgements is binocular disparity. Rushton and Wann (1999) used a virtual reality situation involving catching balls, and manipulated tau and binocular disparity independently. When tau indicated contact with the ball 100 ms *before* binocular disparity, observers responded 75 ms earlier. When tau indicated contact 100 ms *after* disparity, the response was delayed by 35 ms. Thus, information about tau is combined with information about binocular disparity, with the source of information specifying the shortest time to contact being given the greatest weight.

Evidence that observers make *flexible* use of information when predicting time to contact was discussed by DeLucia (2013). She focused on the size-arrival effect: observers mistakenly predict that a large approaching object far away will hit them sooner than a closer small approaching object. This effect occurs because observers attach more importance to relative size than tau. However, when both objects move closer, observers switch to using tau rather than relative size to judge which object will hit them first. Thus, the nature of the information used to judge time to contact changes as objects approach an observer.

We turn now to research on drivers' braking decisions. Lee's (1976) notion that drivers brake to hold constant the rate of change of tau was tested by Yilmaz and Warren (1995). They told participants to stop at a stop sign in a simulated driving task. As predicted, there was generally a linear reduction in tau during braking. However, some participants showed large rather than gradual changes in tau shortly before stopping.

Tijtgat et al. (2008) discovered that stereo vision influences drivers' braking behaviour to avoid a collision. Drivers with weak stereo vision started breaking earlier than those with normal stereo vision and their peak deceleration also occurred earlier. Those with weak stereo vision found it harder to calculate distances, which caused them to underestimate the time to contact. Thus, deciding when to brake does not depend only on tau.

Evaluation

The notion that tau is used to make time-to-contact judgements is simple and elegant. There is much evidence that such judgements are often strongly influenced by tau. Even when competing factors affect time-to-contact judgements, tau often has the greatest influence on those judgements. Tau is also often used when drivers make decisions about when to brake.

What are the limitations of research in this area? First, judgements of time to contact are typically more influenced by tau or tau-dot with relatively uncluttered visual environments in the laboratory than under more naturalistic conditions (Land, 2009).

Second, tau is not the only factor determining judgement of time to contact. As Land (2009, p. 853) pointed out, "The brain will accept all valid cues in the performance of an action, and weight them according to their current reliability." As we have seen, these cues can include object familiarity, binocular disparity and relative size. It clearly makes sense to use all the available information in this way.

Third, the tau hypothesis takes no account of the *emotional* value of the approaching object. However, Brendel et al. (2012) found time-to-contact judgements were shorter for threatening pictures than neutral ones. This makes evolutionary sense – it could be fatal to overestimate how long a very threatening object (e.g., a lion) will take to reach you!

Fourth, the tau and tau-dot hypotheses are too limited in scope. We lack a comprehensive theory indicating how the various factors influencing time-to-contact judgements are combined and integrated.

PLANNING–CONTROL MODEL

How do we use visual information when we want to perform an action with respect to some object (e.g., reaching for a cup of coffee)? This issue was addressed by Glover (2004) in his planning–control model. According to this model, people

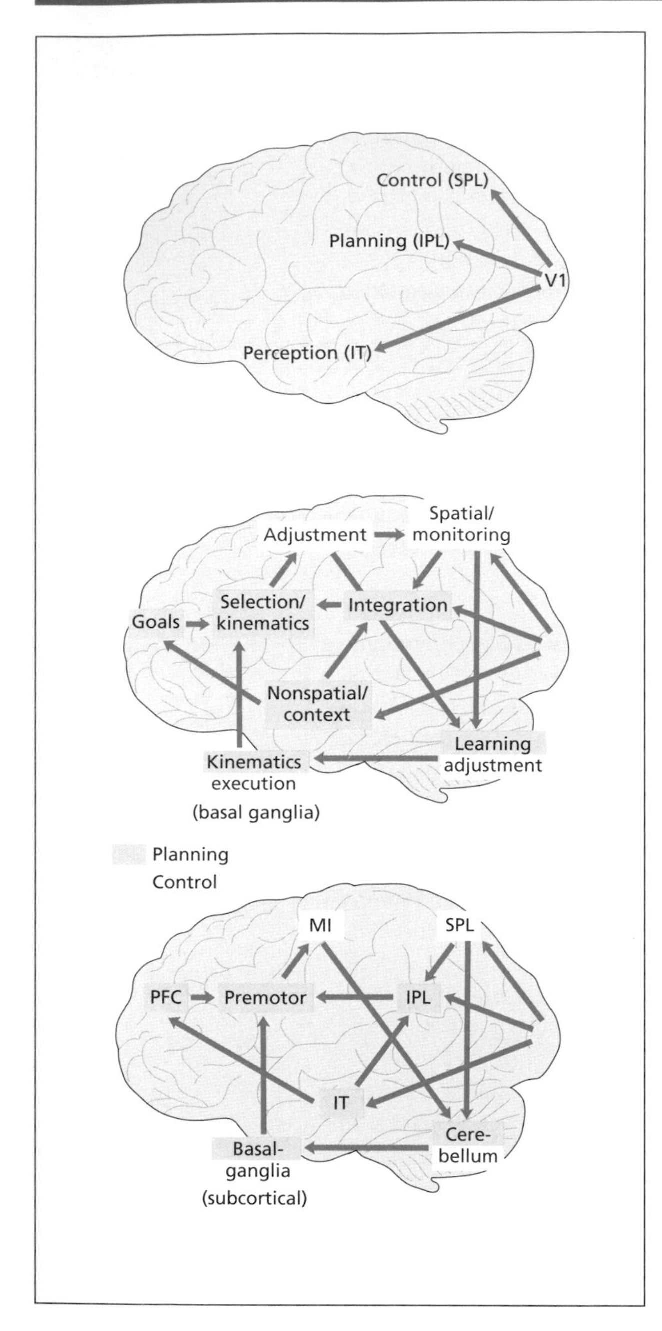

Figure 4.5
Brain areas involved in the planning and control systems within Glover's theory. IPL = inferior parietal lobe; IT = inferotemporal lobe; M1 = primary motor; PFC = prefrontal cortex; SPL = superior parietal lobe.

From Glover (2004). Copyright © Cambridge University Press. Reproduced with permission.

initially use a planning system followed by a control system, although the two systems often overlap in time. Here are the main features of the two systems:

1 *Planning system*

- It is used mostly *before* the initiation of movement.
- It selects an appropriate target (e.g., cup of coffee), decides how it should be grasped and works out the timing of the movement.
- It is influenced by factors such as the individual's goals, the nature of the target object, the visual context and various cognitive processes.
- It is relatively slow because it makes use of much information and is influenced by conscious processes.
- Planning depends on a visual representation located in the inferior parietal lobule together with motor processes in the frontal lobes and basal ganglia (see Figure 4.5). The inferior parietal lobe is involved in integrating information about object identification and context with motor planning to permit tool and object use.

2 *Control system*

- It is used during the carrying out of a movement.
- It ensures movements are accurate, making adjustments if necessary based on visual feedback. Efference copy (see Glossary) is used to compared actual with desired movement. **Proprioception** (sensation relating to the position of one's body) is also involved.
- It is influenced by the target object's spatial characteristics (e.g., size, shape, orientation) but not by the surrounding context.
- It is fairly fast because it makes use of little information and is not susceptible to conscious influence.
- Control depends on a visual representation located in the superior parietal lobe combined with motor processes in the cerebellum (see Figure 4.5).

According to the planning–control model, most errors in human action stem from the planning system. In contrast, the control system typically ensures actions are accurate and achieve their goal. Many visual illusions occur because of the influence of *visual context*. According to the model, information about visual context is used only by the planning system. Accordingly, responses to visual illusions should typically be inaccurate if they depend on the planning system but accurate if they depend on the control system.

In sum, Glover (2004) argued that *independent* planning and control systems are involved in producing actions to objects. A crucial assumption is that these two systems are located in different brain regions within the parietal lobe.

There are similarities between the planning–control model and Milner and Goodale's two-systems model (see Chapter 2). In essence, their vision-for-action system resembles Glover's control system and their vision-for-perception system overlaps with Glover's planning system. However, Glover (2004) focused more on the processing *changes* occurring during the performance of an action. In addition, there are differences between the models in the key brain areas involved.

KEY TERMS

Proprioception
A form of sensation making the individual aware of the position and orientation of parts of his/her body.

Ideomotor apraxia
A condition caused by brain damage in which patients have difficulty in planning and carrying out learned movements.

Findings: brain areas

The model's assumptions that different brain areas are involved in planning and control have been tested in several neuroimaging studies. Glover et al. (2012) used a planning condition (prepare to reach and grasp an object but remain still) and a control condition (reach out immediately for the object). Planning involved a brain network including the middle intraparietal sulcus and posterior medial parietal area. Control involved an independent brain network including the superior parietal lobe, the cerebellum and the supramarginale gyrus (see Figure 4.6). Of most importance, there was practically no overlap in the brain areas activated during the planning and control processes. These findings broadly support Glover's (2004) model.

Neuroimaging studies do not allow us to show task performance *necessarily* involves any given brain area. This issue can be addressed by using transcranial magnetic stimulation (TMS; see Glossary) to produce temporary "lesions" in a limited brain area. Glover et al. (2005) applied TMS to the superior parietal lobe as participants grasped an object that changed in size. According to the model, the superior parietal lobe is involved in the control process, and so that process should have been disrupted by TMS. That is precisely what Glover et al. (2005) found.

Striemer et al. (2011) applied TMS to participants' inferior or superior parietal lobe while they were planning to reach out and touch a target. According to the model, the disruptive influence of TMS on task performance should have been greater when applied to the inferior parietal lobe than the superior parietal lobe. In fact, there was a much larger disruptive effect with TMS applied to the superior parietal lobe.

How can we explain the above findings? Striemer et al. (2011) accepted the inferior parietal lobe may be required for some functions of the planning process (e.g., selecting the goal of the action, selecting the target for the action). However, their findings suggested it is *not* involved in detailed action programming.

According to the model, patients with damage to the inferior parietal lobe should have great problems with action planning. Patients with **ideomotor apraxia** often have damage to the inferior parietal lobe, although other brain areas are also

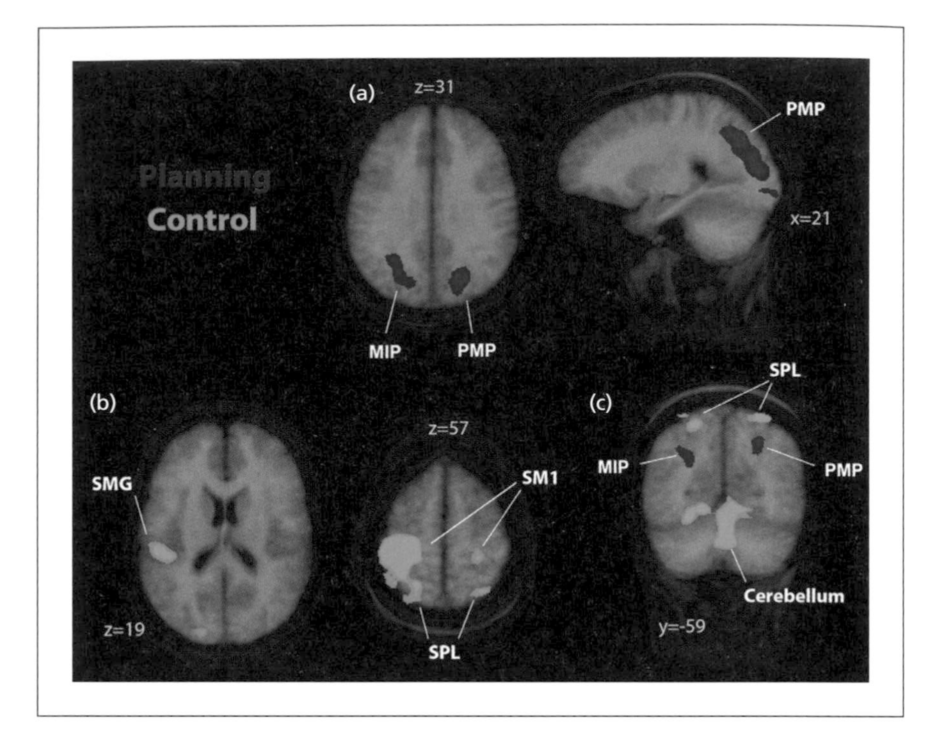

Figure 4.6
(a) Brain areas associated with planning (MIP = middle intraparietal sulcus; PMP = posterior medial parietal area); (b) brain areas associated with control (SMG = supramarginale gyrus; SM1 = primary sensorimotor area; SPL = superior parietal lobe); (c) separation of planning and control regions in the posterior parietal lobes.
From Glover et al. (2012). Reprinted with permission of Wiley.

typically involved. Mutha et al. (2010) found patients with ideomotor apraxia were poor at initiating movements in the direction of the target. However, they were nevertheless able to reach the target accurately. These findings suggest their problems centred more on planning than action control.

According to the model, patients with damage to the superior parietal lobe should have particular problems with the control of action. Damage to the superior and posterior parietal cortex often produces optic ataxia (see Glossary), in which there are severe impairments in the ability to make accurate movements in spite of intact visual perception (see Chapter 2).

Gréa et al. (2002) studied IG, a patient with optic ataxia. She performed as well as healthy controls when reaching out and grasping a stationary object. However, she had much poorer performance when the target suddenly jumped to a new location. These findings suggest IG had damage to the control system. Blangero et al. (2008) found that CF, a patient with optic ataxia, was very slow to correct his movement towards a target that suddenly moved location. This finding suggests his control system was damagd. In addition, however, CF had slowed performance when pointing towards stationary targets in peripheral vision. Blangero et al. concluded that CF was deficient in processing hand location and in detecting target location for peripheral targets.

Interactive exercise:
Planning control

Findings: processes

According to the model, cognitive processes are used more by the planning system than the control system. Supporting evidence was reported by Glover and Dixon (2002). Participants reached for an object with LARGE or SMALL written on it. It was assumed the impact of these words on grasping behaviour would reflect the involvement of the cognitive system. Early in the reach (under the influence of the planning system), participants' grip aperture was greater for objects with the word LARGE on them. Later in the reach (under the influence of the control system) this effect was smaller. Thus, the findings were consistent with the model.

According to Glover (2004), action planning involves conscious processing followed by rapid non-conscious processing during action control. These theoretical assumptions can be tested by requiring participants to carry out a second task while performing an action towards an object. According to the model, this second task should disrupt planning but not control. However, Hesse et al. (2012) found a second task disrupted planning *and* control when participants made grasping movements towards objects. Thus, planning and control can both require attentional resources.

According to the planning–control model, our initial actions towards an object (determined by the planning system) are generally less accurate than our subsequent ones (influenced by the control system). Findings relevant to this prediction are mixed, with some studies reporting contrary evidence. Danckert et al. (2002) discussed findings from a study on grasping in the Ebbinghaus illusion (see Figure 2.13). There was no evidence of any illusory effect (based on maximum grip aperture) even at the onset of movement.

A central assumption of the planning–control model is that visual context influences only the planning system. Mendoza et al. (2006) tested this assumption using the Müller–Lyer illusion (see Figure 2.12). Participants pointed at the end of a horizontal line presented on its own, with arrowheads pointing inwards or with arrowheads pointing outwards. Of crucial importance, this visual stimulus generally *changed* between participants' initial planning and their movements towards it. The arrowheads led to movement errors regardless of whether they were present during planning or online movement control. These findings suggest the processes involved in planning and control are less different than assumed within the planning–control model.

Roberts et al. (2013) required participants to make rapid reaching movements to a Müller–Lyer figure. Vision was available only during the first 200 ms of movement or the last 200 ms. According to Glover's model, performance should have been more accurate with late vision than with early vision. In fact, the findings were the other way around. Thus, visual context had a large effect on late control processes.

Evaluation

Glover's (2004) planning–control model has proved successful in several ways. First, the model develops the common assumption that motor movements towards objects involve successive planning and control processes. Second, much research involving neuroimaging and transcranial magnetic stimulation supports the assumption that areas within the inferior and superior parietal cortex are important for planning and control, respectively. Third, the assumption within the model that *cognitive* processes are involved in action planning appears correct. Brain areas such as dorsolateral prefrontal cortex, the anterior cingulate and the pre-supplementary motor area are involved in action planning and many cognitive tasks (Serrien et al., 2007).

What are the model's limitations? First, the planning and control systems interact in complex ways when an individual performs an action. Thus, the proposed sequence of planning followed by control is too neat and tidy. In practice, it is often hard to know when planning stops and control starts (Ramenzoni & Riley, 2004).

Second, the planning system involves several very different processes: "goal determination; target identification and selection; analysis of object affordances [potential object uses]; timing; and computation of the metrical properties of the target such as its size, shape, orientation and position relative to the body" (Glover et al., 2012, p. 909). This diversity sheds doubt on the assumption that there is a *single* planning system.

Third, the notion that actions based on planning are typically less accurate than those based on control is sometimes incorrect. Various complex factors determine which process is associated with more accurate actions (Roberts et al., 2013).

Fourth, the model is concerned primarily with body movements rather than eye movements. However, coordination of eye and body movements is very important for precise and accurate movements.

Fifth, the model's assumptions concerning the brain areas primarily associated with planning and control are dubious (Striemer et al., 2011).

PERCEPTION OF HUMAN MOTION

We are very good at interpreting other people's movements. We can decide very rapidly whether someone is walking, running or limping. Our focus here is on two key issues. First, how successful are we at interpreting human motion with very limited visual information? Second, do the processes involved in perception of human motion differ from those involved in perception of motion in general? Third, if the answer to the second question is positive, we need to consider *why* the perception of human motion is special.

In what follows, our focus is mostly on the perception of human motion. However, there are many similarities between the perception of human motion and animal motion. The term "biological motion" is used when referring to the perception of animal motion in general.

Perceiving human motion

Weblink:
Biological motion sites

Weblink:
Johansson: Motion Perception part 1

It is unsurprising we can interpret the movements of other people. Suppose, however, you were presented with point-light displays, as was done initially by Johansson (1973). Actors were dressed entirely in black with lights attached to their joints (e.g., wrists, knees, ankles). They were filmed moving around a darkened room so only the lights were visible to observers watching the film (see Figure 4.7 and Johansson: Motion Perception part 1 on YouTube). Do you think you would perceive accurately a moving person in those circumstances? Johansson found observers perceived the moving person accurately with only six lights and a short segment of film.

Subsequent research produced even more impressive evidence of our ability to perceive human motion with very limited information. In one study (Johansson et al., 1980), observers viewing a point-light display for only one-fifth of a second perceived human motion with no apparent difficulty. In another study using point-light displays, Runeson and Frykholm (1983) asked actors to carry out actions naturally or like a member of the opposite sex. Observers guessed the actor's gender correctly 85% of time when he/she acted naturally and 75% in the deception condition.

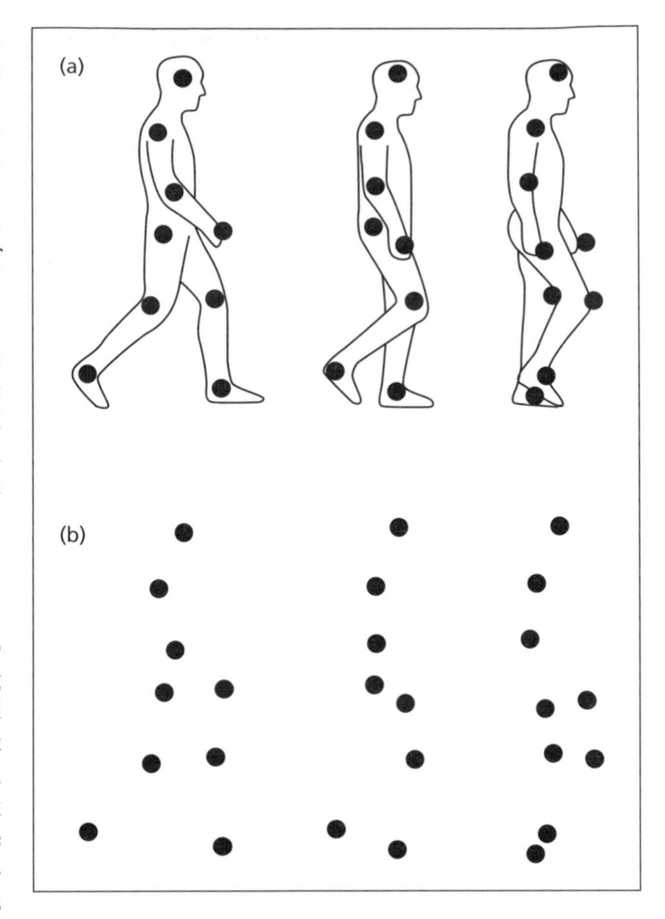

Figure 4.7
Point-light sequences (a) with the walker visible and (b) with the walker not visible.
From Shiffrar and Thomas (2013). With permission of the authors.

Bottom-up or top-down processes?

Johansson (1975) argued that the ability to perceive biological motion is *innate*, describing the processes involved as "spontaneous" and "automatic". Support was reported by Simion et al. (2008) in a study on newborns aged between one and three days. These babies preferred to look at a display showing biological motion than one that did not. Remarkably, Simion et al. used point-light displays of chickens of which the newborns had no previous experience. These findings suggest the perception of biological motion involves relatively basic bottom-up processes.

However, there are changes in biological motion perception during infancy. Pinto (2006) found 3-month-olds were equally sensitive to motion in point-light humans, cats and spiders. By five months, however, infants were more sensitive to displays of human motion. Thus, the infant visual system becomes increasingly specialised for perceiving human motion.

Thornton et al. (2002) showed the perception of human motion can require *attention*. Observers detected the direction of movement of a point-light walker figure embedded in masking elements. There were two mask conditions: (1) scrambled mask (each dot mimicked the motion of a dot from the walker figure; (2) random mask (each dot moved at random). The scrambled mask condition was more difficult because it was harder to distinguish between the point-light walker and the mask. This task was performed on its own or with an attentionally demanding task (dual-task condition).

What did Thornton et al. (2002) find? In the dual-task condition, observers' ability to identify correctly the walker's direction of movement was greatly impaired only when scrambled masks were used (see Figure 4.8). Thus, top-down processes (e.g., attention) can be of major importance in detection of human motion when the visual information available is degraded (i.e., with the scrambled mask).

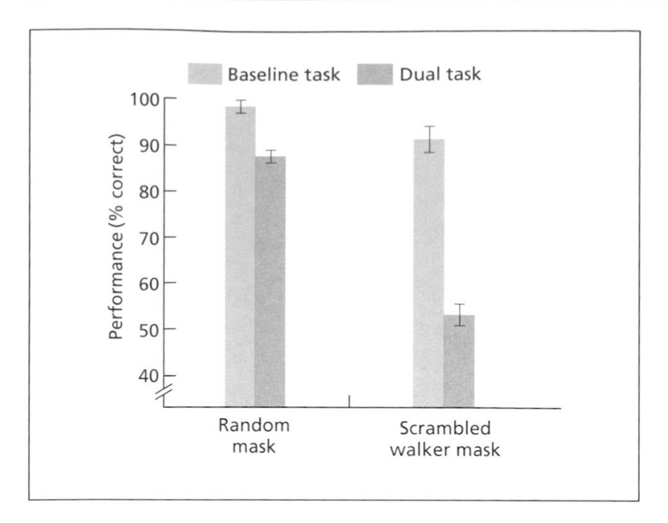

Figure 4.8
Percentage correct detections of a walker's direction of movement (left or right) as a function of the presence of a random mask or a scrambled walker mask and the presence (dual-task condition) or absence (baseline task) of a demanding secondary task. Performance was worst with a scrambled walker mask in the dual-task condition.

From Thornton et al. (2002). Reprinted with permission of Pion Limited, London, www.pion.co.uk.

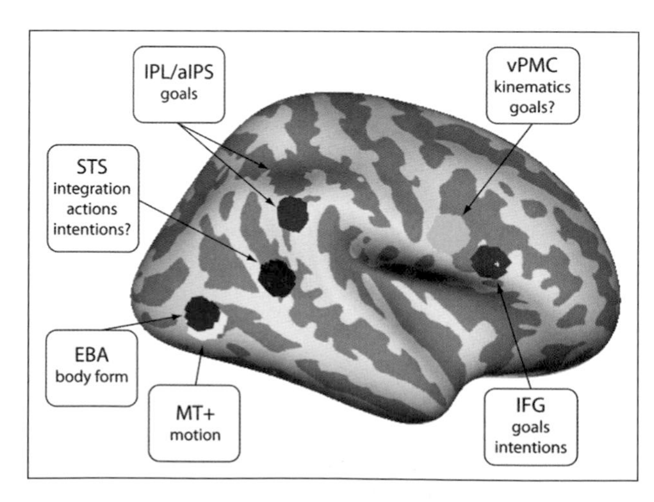

Figure 4.9
Brain regions involved in action observation (IPL = inferior parietal lobule; aIPS = anterior intraparietal sulcus; vPMC = ventral premotor cortex; STS = superior temporal sulcus; EBA = extrastriate temporal sulcus; IFG = inferior frontal gyrus; MT+ = motion-sensitive area.

From Thompson & Parasuraman (2012). Reprinted with permission of Elsevier.

Thompson and Parasuraman (2012) reviewed research on the role of attention in the perception of biological motion. Attention was especially likely to be required when the available visual information was ambiguous or competing information was present. In sum, basic aspects of human and biological motion perception may be innate. However, such perception improves during infant development. In addition, attentional and other top-down processes are needed when the task is relatively complex and/or viewing conditions are poor.

Is human motion perception special?

Much behavioural evidence suggests we are better at detecting human motion than motion in other species (Shiffrar and Thomas, 2013). Cohen (2002) used point-light displays to assess participants' sensitivity to human, dog and seal motion using point-light displays. Performance was best with human motion and worst with seal motion. The same pattern of performance was observed using seal trainers and dog trainers as participants. Thus, the key factor is probably not simply the level of visual experience. Instead, we are more sensitive to observed motions resembling our own repertoire of actions.

We can also approach the issue of the specialness of human motion perception by considering the brain. Major brain areas associated with human motion perception are shown in Figure 4.9. The superior temporal sulcus is of particular importance in the recognition of human actions. Another key area is the inferior frontal gyrus, which is involved in processing to work out the goals of observed actions.

Much evidence points to the key role of the superior temporal sulcus in biological motion perception. Grossman et al. (2005) applied repetitive transcranial magnetic stimulation (rTMS; see Glossary) to the superior temporal sulcus to produce a "temporary lesion". This caused a substantial reduction in observers' sensitivity to biological motion.

Is the superior temporal sulcus more important in biological and human motion detection than other kinds of motion? Much evidence suggests it is. Gilaie-Dotan et al. (2013a) considered the effects of grey matter volume in the superior temporal sulcus on motion detection. This volume correlated positively with the detection of biological motion but not non-biological motion.

Virji-Babul et al. (2008) compared brain activity when observers watched point-light displays of human and object motion. Brain activity was very similar in both cases for the first 200 ms. After that, however, watching human motion was associated with more activity in the temporal lobe (including the superior temporal sulcus) than watching object motion.

Evidence that the processes involved in perceiving biological motion differ from those in perceiving object motion generally comes from studying brain-damaged patients. Vaina et al. (1990) studied a patient, AF. He performed poorly on basic motion tasks but was reasonably good at detecting biological motion from point-light displays. In contrast, Saygin (2007) found in stroke patients with lesions in the superior temporal and premotor frontal areas that their perception of biological motion was more impaired than that of non-biological motion.

Why is biological motion perception special?

There are three main ways to explain the special nature of the perception of biological motion (Shiffrar & Thomas, 2013). First, biological motion is the only type of visual motion humans can *produce* as well as perceive. Second, most people spend more time perceiving and trying to make sense of other people's motion than any other form of visual motion. Third, other people's movements are a very rich source of social and emotional information.

We will start with the first reason (which is discussed further in the next section). The relevance of motor skills to the perception of biological motion was shown by Price et al. (2012). They studied individuals with Asperger's syndrome, a condition that involves severe problems in social communication and often impaired movement. Asperger's individuals performed much worse than healthy controls on biological motion perception and on tests of motor skills. Of most importance, poor motor skills were strongly associated with poor biological motion perception.

Serino et al. (2010) studied patients with hemiplegia (paralysis) of one arm. They were presented with point-light animations of a left or right arm and named the action being performed. Their ability to identify arm movements was much worse when the animated arm corresponded to their paralysed arm than when it did not. Thus, damage to relevant parts of the motor cortex can decrease an individual's sensitivity to the subtleties of human movement.

It is important not to exaggerate the importance of motor involvement in understanding the actions of others. For example, an individual, DC, born without upper limbs, identified manual actions showed in videos and photographs as well as healthy controls (Vannuscorps et al., 2013). However, he was impaired at recognising point-light animations of manual actions when important visual information (i.e., the body part involved) was missing.

We turn now to the second reason listed above. Jacobs et al. (2004) studied the ability of observers to identify walkers from point-light displays. Their performance was much better when the walker was someone observed previously for 20 hours a week or more rather than someone observed for five hours a week or less. Thus, visual experience had a substantial effect on sensitivity to biological motion.

KEY TERM

Mirror neuron system
Neurons that respond to actions whether performed by oneself or someone else; it is claimed these neurons assist in imitating and understanding others' actions.

As for the third reason listed above, Charlie Chaplin showed convincingly that bodily movements can convey social and emotional information. Atkinson et al. (2004) studied observers' ability to identify several emotions shown in point-light displays. Performance was especially high (around 80%) for fear, sadness and happiness. Our ability to identify emotion from point-light displays is partly determined by speed of movement (Barliya et al., 2013). Angry individuals walk especially fast, whereas fearful or sad individuals walk very slowly.

We can show the role of social factors in human motion detection by studying individuals with severely impaired social interaction skills. Adults with autistic spectrum disorders (see Glossary) are significantly inferior to healthy individuals in detecting human motion from point-light displays but do not differ on control tasks (Shiffrar & Thomas, 2013).

Mirror neuron system

Research on monkeys in the 1990s led to a new theoretical approach to understanding biological motion. For example, Gallese et al. (1996) assessed brain activity in monkeys in two situations: (1) the monkeys *performed* a given action (e.g., grasping); and (2) the monkeys *observed* another monkey perform the same action. Their key finding was that 17% of the neurons in area F5 of the premotor cortex were activated in both situations. They called them "mirror neurons".

Weblink:
Mirror neuron system

Findings such as those of Gallese et al. (1996) led theorists to propose a **mirror neuron system**. This mirror neuron system consists of neurons activated when an animal performs an action *and* when another animal performs the same action. This system allegedly facilitates imitation and understanding of the actions of others. The notion of a mirror neuron system has been used to explain aspects of human understanding of speech (see Chapter 9).

The identification of a mirror neuron system in monkeys led to huge interest in finding a similar system in humans. Molenberghs et al. (2012a) reported a meta-analysis (see Glossary) based on 125 human studies. The most important findings were based on "classical" studies in which participants viewed visual images or human actions and/or executed motor actions. The brain regions most associated with the mirror neuron system included the inferior frontal gyrus and inferior parietal lobule (see Figure 4.10). Reassuringly, these brain areas are the human equivalents of the areas most associated with the mirror neuron system in monkeys.

Figure 4.10
Brain areas associated with the mirror neuron system in a meta-analysis of classical studies (defined in text). The brain areas involved included the inferior parietal lobule, the posterior inferior frontal gyrus, the ventral premotor cortex, the dorsal premotor cortex, the superior parietal lobule, the middle temporal gyrus and the cerebellum.
From Molenberghs et al. (2012a). Reprinted with permission of Elsevier.

The studies reviewed by Molenberghs et al. (2012a) show the same brain *areas* are involved in motion perception and action production. However, we need to show the same *neurons* are activated whether observing a movement or performing it. This has occasionally been done. Mukamel et al. (2010) identified neurons in various brain areas (e.g., the supplementary motor area) responding to the perception and execution of hand-grasping actions.

Before proceeding, note the term "mirror neuron system" is somewhat misleading. It is typically assumed mirror neurons play a role in working out *why* someone else is performing certain actions as well as deciding *what* those actions are. However, mirror neurons do *not* provide us with an exact motoric coding of observed actions. As Williams (2013, p. 2962) wittily observed, "If only this was the case! I could become an Olympic ice-skater or a concert pianist!"

Findings

Areas within the mirror neuron system are typically activated when someone observes the actions of another person (Cook et al., 2014). However, this is only *correlational* evidence – it does not show the mirror neuron system is *necessary* for imitation. Mengotti et al. (2013) considered this issue. They applied transcranial magnetic stimulation (TMS; see Glossary) to areas within the mirror neuron system to disrupt its functioning. As predicted, this impaired participants' ability to imitate another person's actions.

Research shows mirror neurons are involved in working out *why* someone else is performing certain actions. For example, consider a study by Umiltà et al. (2001). They used two main conditions. In one condition, the experimenter's action directed towards an object was fully visible to the monkey participants. In the other condition, the monkeys saw the same action but the most important part was hidden behind a screen. Before each trial, the monkeys saw the experimenter place some food behind the screen so they knew what the experimenter was reaching for.

What did Umiltà et al. (2001) find? First, over half the mirror neurons tested discharged in the hidden condition. Second, about half of the mirror neurons that discharged in the hidden condition did so as strongly as in the fully visible condition. Third, Umiltà et al. used a third condition that was the same as the hidden condition except the monkeys knew no food had been placed behind the screen. In terms of the experimenter's actions, this condition was identical to the hidden condition. However, mirror neurons that discharged in the hidden condition did *not* discharge in this condition. Thus, the *meaning* of the observed actions determined activity within the mirror neuron system.

Iacoboni et al. (2005) claimed our understanding of the intentions behind someone else's actions is often helped by taking account of *context*. For example, someone may shout loudly at another person because they are angry or because they are acting in a play. Iacoboni et al. investigated whether the mirror neuron system in humans was sensitive to context using these two conditions:

1. *Intention condition*: There were films clips of two scenes involving a teapot, mug, biscuits, a jar and so on – one scene showed the objects before being used (drinking context) and the other showed the object after being used (cleaning context). A hand was shown grasping a cup in a different way in each scene.
2. *Action condition*: The same grasping actions were shown as in the intention condition. However, the context was not shown, so it was impossible to understand the intention of the person grasping the cup.

There was more activity within the mirror neuron system in the intention than the action condition. This suggests the mirror neuron system is involved in understanding the intentions behind observed actions – it was only in the intention condition that participants could work out *why* the person was grasping the cup.

Lingnau and Petris (2013) argued that understanding the actions of another person often involves relatively complex *cognitive* processes as well as simpler processes occurring within the mirror neuron system. They presented two groups of participants with the same point-light displays showing human actions and asked one group to identify the goal of each action. Areas within prefrontal cortex (which is associated with high-level cognitive processes) were more activated when goal identification was required. Understanding another person's goals from their actions seems to involve more complex cognitive processes than those occurring directly within the mirror neuron system.

Evaluation

Several important findings have emerged from research. First, our ability to perceive human or biological motion with very limited visual information is impressive. Second, the brain areas involved in human motion perception differ somewhat from those involved in perceiving motion in general. Third, perception of human motion is special because it is the only type of motion we can perceive *and* produce. Fourth, there is some support for the notion of a mirror neuron system allowing us to imitate and understand other people's movements.

What are the limitations of research in this area? First, much remains to be discovered about the ways bottom-up and top-down processes interact when we perceive biological motion.

Second, some claims for the mirror neuron system are clearly exaggerated. For example, Eagle et al. (2007, p. 131) claimed the mirror neuron system suggests "the automatic, unconscious, and non-inferential simulation in the observer of the actions, emotions, and sensations carried out and expressed by the observed". In fact, understanding another person's goals from their actions involves *more* than these mirror neuron system processes (Lingnau & Petris, 2013). As Csibra (2008, p. 443) argued, it is more likely that "[mirror neurons] *reflect* action understanding rather than contribute to it".

Third, it is improbable that the mirror neuron system accounts for all aspects of action understanding. As Gallese and Sinigaglia (2014, p. 200) pointed out, action understanding "involves representing to which . . . goals the action is directed; identifying which beliefs, desires, and intentions specify reasons explaining why the action happened; and realising how those reasons are linked to the agent and to her action".

Fourth, the definition of "mirror neurons" is variable. Such neurons respond to the observation and execution of actions. However, there are disagreements as to whether the actions involved must be the same or only broadly similar (Cook et al., 2014).

CHANGE BLINDNESS

Weblink:
Demonstration of change blindness

We have seen in the chapter so far that a changing visual environment provides valuable information. For example, it allows us to move in the appropriate direction and to make coherent sense of the world around us. In this section, however, we will discover that our perceptual system does not always respond appropriately to changes within the visual environment.

Have a look around you (go on!). We imagine you have a strong impression of seeing a vivid and detailed picture of the visual scene. As a result, you are probably confident you could immediately detect any reasonably large change in the visual environment. In fact, our ability to detect such changes is often far less impressive than that.

Change blindness, which is "the surprising failure to detect a substantial visual change" (Jensen et al., 2011, p. 529), is the main phenomenon we will discuss. We will also consider the related phenomenon of **inattentional blindness**, which is "the failure to notice an unexpected, but fully-visible item when attention is diverted to other aspects of a display" (Jensen et al., 2011, p. 529).

KEY TERMS

Change blindness
Failure to detect various changes (e.g., in objects) in the visual environment.

Inattentional blindness
Failure to detect an unexpected object appearing in the visual environment.

Suppose you watch a video in which students dressed in white pass a ball to each other. At some point, a woman in a black gorilla suit walks into camera shot, looks at the camera, thumps her chest and then walks off (see Figure 4.11). Altogether she is on the screen for nine seconds. You probably feel absolutely certain you would spot the gorilla figure almost immediately. Simons and Chabris (1999) carried out an experiment along the lines just described (see the video at www.simonslab.com/videos.html). Very surprisingly, 50% of the observers totally failed to notice the gorilla! This is a striking example of inattentional blindness.

Weblink:
Demonstration of inattentional blindness

Weblink:
Gorillas in the midst

The original research on inattentional blindness was carried out by Mack and Rock (1998). In their early experiments, observers fixated the intersection point of the two arms of a cross presented for 200 ms and decided which arm was longer. On the third or fourth trial, a critical stimulus (e.g., a coloured spot) was presented unexpectedly in a quadrant of the cross within 2.3 degrees of fixation. On average, 25% of observers failed to detect the critical stimulus, thus providing evidence of inattentional blindness.

In subsequent research, Mack and Rock (1998) presented the critical stimulus at the fixation point and centred the cross about 2 degrees from fixation. They expected that presenting the task in this way would eliminate inattentional blindness. In fact, however, detection rates for the critical stimulus dropped to between 40% and 60%! How did Mack and Rock interpret this finding? They argued that objects at fixation are typically the focus of attention. However, when the task (i.e., comparing the arms of a cross) requires focusing attention away from fixation, attention to objects at fixation is actively inhibited.

There has been more research on change blindness than inattentional blindness. Why is change blindness an important phenomenon?

- Findings on change blindness are striking and counterintuitive and so require new theoretical thinking.
- Research on change blindness has greatly clarified the role of attention in scene perception. That explains why change blindness is discussed at the end of the final chapter on perception and immediately before the chapter on attention.

Figure 4.11
Frame showing a woman in a gorilla suit in the middle of a game of passing the ball.

From Simons and Chabris (1999). Figure provided by Daniel Simons, www.theinvisiblegorilla.com.

KEY TERM

Change blindness blindness
The tendency of observers to overestimate greatly the extent to which they can detect visual changes and so avoid **change blindness**.

- Experiments on change blindness have shed light on the processes underlying our conscious awareness of the visual world.
- Whereas most studies on perception consider visual processes applied to single stimuli, those on change blindness focus on dynamic processes over time.

Change blindness in everyday life

You have undoubtedly experienced change blindness at the movies caused by unintended continuity mistakes when a scene has been shot more than once. For example, consider the Bond film *Skyfall*. In one scene, Bond is in a car being followed by a white car. Mysteriously, this car becomes black in the next shot, and then returns to being white! In *Avatar*, there is a scene in which Princess Neytiri's pigtail is at her back and then in the next shot it is over her right shoulder.

Change blindness blindness

We often grossly exaggerate our ability to detect visual changes. In one study by Levin et al. (2002), observers saw various videos involving two people having a conversation in a restaurant. In one video, the plates changed from red to white, and in another a scarf worn by one of them disappeared. These videos had previously been used by Levin and Simons (1997), who found none of their participants detected any changes.

Levin et al. (2002) asked their participants whether they thought they would have noticed the changes without being forewarned. A total of 46% claimed they would have noticed the change in the colour of the plates, and 78% the disappearing scarf. Levin et al. used the term **change blindness blindness** to describe our wildly optimistic beliefs about our ability to detect visual changes.

What causes change blindness blindness? Basic visual processes provide us with clear and detailed information only close to the point of fixation. However, we use top-down processes to "fill in the gaps". This creates the illusion we can see the entire visual scene clearly and in detail (Freeman & Simoncelli, 2011; see Chapter 5 and Figure 5.10).

Other reasons for change blindness blindness were identified by Loussouarn et al. (2011). Change blindness blindness was most common when observers were led to believe the time they took to detect changes was short and their perceived success at detecting changes was high. Thus, change blindness blindness depends in part on overconfidence.

Change blindness vs. inattentional blindness

Change blindness and inattentional blindness are similar in that both involve a failure to detect some visual event that appears in plain sight. There are also some important similarities between the processes underlying change blindness and inattentional blindness. For example, failures of attention often (but *not* always) play an important role in causing both forms of blindness.

In spite of these similarities, there are major differences between the two phenomena (Jensen et al., 2011). First, consider the effects of instructing observers to look for unexpected objects or visual changes. Target detection in change blindness paradigms can still be hard even with such instructions. In contrast, target detection in inattentional blindness paradigms becomes trivially easy. Second, change blindness involves *memory* so that pre-change and post-change stimuli can be compared, whereas inattentional blindness does not. Third, inattentional blindness occurs when the observer's attention is engaged in a demanding task (e.g., counting passes between players), which is not the case with change blindness.

In sum, more complex processing is typically required for successful performance in change blindness tasks than inattentional blindness ones. More specifically, observers must engage successfully in *five* separate processes for change detection to occur (Jensen et al., 2011):

1 Attention must be paid to the change location.
2 The pre-change visual stimulus at the change location must be encoded into memory.
3 The post-change visual stimulus at the change location must be encoded into memory.
4 The pre- and post-change representations must be compared.
5 The discrepancy between the pre- and post-change representations must be recognised at the conscious level.

In the real world, we are often aware of changes in the visual environment because we detect motion signals accompanying the change. Ways of preventing observers from detecting motion signals include making the change during a saccade (rapid movement of the eyes), making the change during a short temporal gap between the original and altered stimuli, or making the change during an eyeblink.

What causes change blindness?

There is no single (or simple) answer to the question, "What causes change blindness?" The main reason is that (as we have just seen) change detection requires the successful completion of five different processes.

Change blindness often depends on attentional processes. We typically attend to regions of a visual scene most likely to contain interesting or important information. Spot the difference between the pictures in Figure 4.12. Observers took an average of 10.4 seconds to do so with the first pair of pictures but only 2.6 with the second pair (Rensink et al., 1997). The height of the railing is of marginal interest whereas the position of the helicopter is of central interest.

Hollingworth and Henderson (2002) studied the role of attention in change blindness. They recorded eye movements while observers looked at a visual scene (e.g., kitchen, living room) for several seconds. It was assumed the object fixated at any given moment was being attended. Two kinds of changes could occur to each visual scene:

1 *Type change*, in which an object was replaced by an object from a different category (e.g., a plate was replaced by a bowl).
2 *Token change*, in which an object was replaced by an object from the same category (e.g., a plate was replaced by a different plate).

Figure 4.12
(a) the object that is changed (the railing) undergoes a shift in location comparable to that of the object that is changed (the helicopter) in (b). However, the change is much easier to see in (b) because the changed object is more important.

From Rensink et al. (1997). Copyright © 1997 by SAGE. Reprinted by permission of SAGE Publications.

What did Hollingworth and Henderson (2002) find? First, change detection was much greater when the changed object had been fixated *prior* to the change (see Figure 4.13a). There was very little evidence observers could accurately detect change in objects not fixated prior to change.

Second, there was change blindness for 60% of objects fixated before they were changed. Thus, attention to the to-be-changed object was necessary (but not sufficient) for change detection.

Third, Hollingworth and Henderson (2002) studied the fate of objects fixated some time prior to being changed. The number of fixations on other objects occurring after the last fixation on the to-be-changed object had no systematic effect on change detection (see Figure 4.13b). Thus, the visual representations of objects last for some time after receiving attention.

Fourth, change detection was much better when there was a change in the *type* of object rather than merely swapping one member of a category for another (*token* change) (see Figure 4.13b). This makes sense given that type changes are more dramatic and obvious.

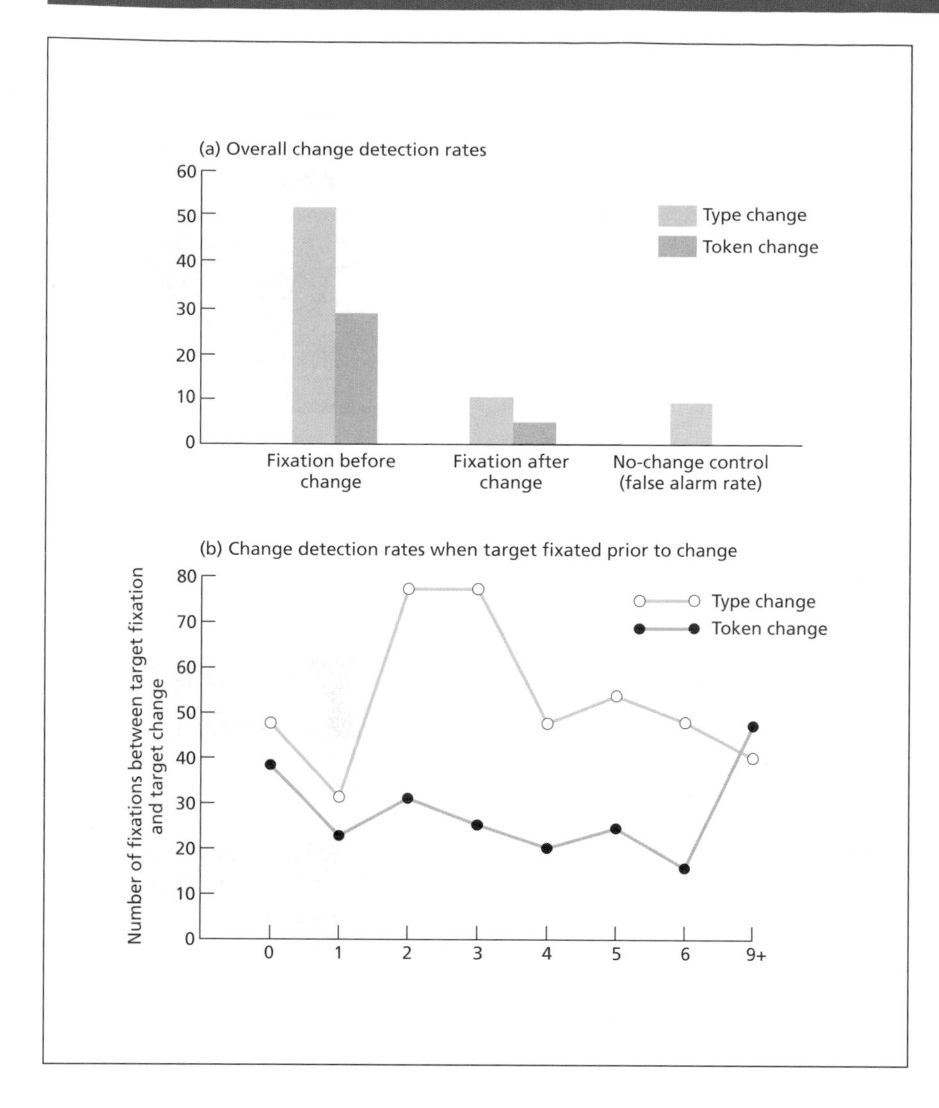

Figure 4.13
(a) Percentage of correct change detection as a function of form of change (type vs. token) and time of fixation (before vs. after change); also false alarm rate when there was no change. (b) Mean percentage correct change detection as a function of the number of fixations between target fixation and change of target and form of change (type vs. token).

Both from Hollingworth and Henderson (2002). Copyright © 2002 American Psychological Association. Reproduced with permission.

Do observers showing change blindness remember the changed object? Busch (2013) gave a recognition-memory test to participants showing change blindness or change detection. Even those showing change blindness manifested some memory for the pre-change and post-change objects. That means the changed object was processed to some extent even in the absence of change detection.

Change blindness may occur because observers fail to *compare* the pre- and post-change representations of the visual display. Evidence that useful information about the pre-change representation can still be available even when there is change blindness was reported by Angelone et al. (2003). In one experiment, observers watched a video clip in which the identity of the central actor changed. This was followed by photographs of four individuals, one of whom was the pre-change actor.

Angelone et al. (2003) compared performance on the line-up task of observers who did or did not detect that the actor's identity had changed. Those who showed change blindness performed as well as those who showed change detection (53% vs. 46%, respectively).

Varakin et al. (2007) extended the above research in a real-world study in which a coloured binder was switched for one of a different colour while participants' eyes were closed. Some participants showing change blindness nevertheless remembered the colour of the pre- and post-change binders and so had failed to compare the two colours. Other participants showing change blindness had poor memory for the pre- and post-change colours and so failed to represent these two pieces of information in memory.

Landman et al. (2003) argued that we initially form detailed representations of visual scenes. However, these representations decay rapidly or are overwritten by subsequent stimuli. Observers were presented with an array of eight rectangles (some horizontal and some vertical) followed 1,600 ms later by a second array of eight rectangles. The task was to decide whether any of the rectangles had changed orientation.

There was very little change blindness provided observers' attention was directed to the rectangle that might change within 900 ms of the offset of the first array. Landman et al. (2003) concluded we can have access to fairly detailed information about the current visual scene for almost 1 second. However, it is important that what we currently perceive is not disrupted by what we perceive next. Such disruption occurs when there is *overwriting* of the previous scene with the current one. A consequence of such overwriting is that we often exhibit change blindness.

Busch et al. (2009) argued that we should distinguish two types of change detection: (1) *sensing* there has been a change without conscious awareness of which object has changed; and (2) *seeing* the object that has changed. Busch et al. used event-related potentials (ERPs; see Glossary). ERP components associated with selective attention and conscious processing of visual changes were associated with seeing but not sensing. Much research is problematical due to a failure to distinguish clearly between sensing and seeing.

Howe and Webb (2014) argued that sensing often occurs when observers detect a *global* change in a visual scene. Observers were presented with an array of 30 discs (15 red, 15 green). On some trials, three discs all the same colour changed from red to green or vice versa. On 24% of trials, observers detected the array had changed without being able to identify any of the discs that had changed. Thus, there was frequently sensing of global change without seeing which objects had changed.

Finally, Fischer and Whitney (2014) proposed a new theoretical approach that may well enhance understanding of change blindness. They argued that perceptual accuracy is sacrificed to some extent so that we can have continuous, stable perception of our visual environment. Observers reported the perceived orientation of black-and-white gratings presented several seconds apart. The key finding was that the perceived orientation of a grating was biased in the direction of the previous grating even when it had been presented ten seconds earlier. The visual system's emphasis on perceptual stability may inhibit our ability to detect changes within the visual scene.

What causes inattentional blindness?

As Jensen et al. (2011) pointed out, detection of an unexpected object in studies on inattentional blindness generally depends heavily on the probability it will attract attention. Two factors are of special importance:

IN THE REAL WORLD: IT'S MAGIC!

Magicians have benefited over the years from the phenomena of change blindness and inattentional blindness (Kuhn & Martinez, 2012). Many people believe magicians baffle us because the hand is quicker than the eye. That is typically *not* the main reason. Most magic tricks involve *misdirection*, the purpose of which "is to disguise the method and thus prevent the audience from detecting it whilst still experiencing the effect" (Kuhn & Martinez, 2012, p. 2).

Many people believe misdirection involves the magician manipulating the audience's attention away from some action crucial to the trick's success. That is often the case but reality is sometimes more complex. Kuhn and Findlay (2010) studied inattentional blindness using a trick involving the disappearance of a lighter, shown on a video recording (see Figure 4.14). The magician picks up a lighter with his left hand and lights it. He then pretends to take the flame with his right hand while looking at that hand. As he reveals his right hand is empty, he drops the lighter from his left hand into his lap in full view.

Kuhn and Findlay (2010) obtained three main findings. First, of the participants who detected the drop, 31% were fixating close to the left hand when the lighter was dropped. However, 69% were fixating some distance away and so detected the drop in peripheral vision (see Figure 4.15). The average distance between fixation and the drop was the same in those who detected the drop in peripheral vision and those who did not detect it. Third, the time taken *after* the drop to fixate the left hand was much less in participants using peripheral vision to detect the drop than those failing to detect it (650 ms. vs. 1,712 ms).

What do the above findings mean? The lighter drop can be detected by *overt* attention (attention directed to the fixation point) or by *covert* attention (attention directed away from the

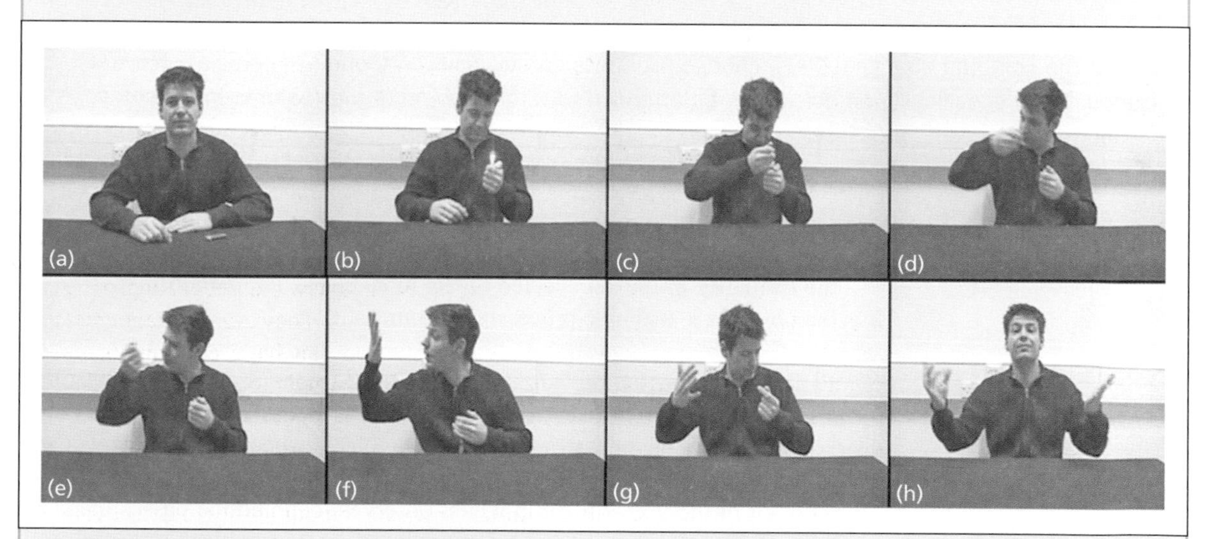

Figure 4.14
The sequence of events in the disappearing lighter trick: (a) the magician picks up a lighter with his left hand and (b) lights it; (c) and (d) he pretends to take the flame with his right hand and (e) gradually moves it away from the hand holding the lighter; (f) he reveals his right hand is empty while the lighter is dropped into his lap; (g) the magician directs his gaze to his left hand and (h) reveals that his left hand is also empty and the lighter has disappeared.
From Kuhn and Findlay (2010). Reprinted with permission of Taylor & Francis.

fixation point). Covert attention was surprisingly effective because the human visual system can readily detect movement in peripheral vision (see Chapter 2).

Many studies (including Kuhn & Findlay, 2010) show the role of inattentional blindness caused by misdirection in magic tricks (Kuhn & Martinez, 2012). However, there is an important difference between misdirection and inattentional blindness as typically studied (Kuhn & Tatler, 2011). Most studies on inattentional blindness (e.g., Simons & Chabris, 1999) require a distractor task to reduce the probability observers will detect the novel object. Misdirection research is more impressive and realistic in that no explicit distractor is needed to produce inattentional blindness.

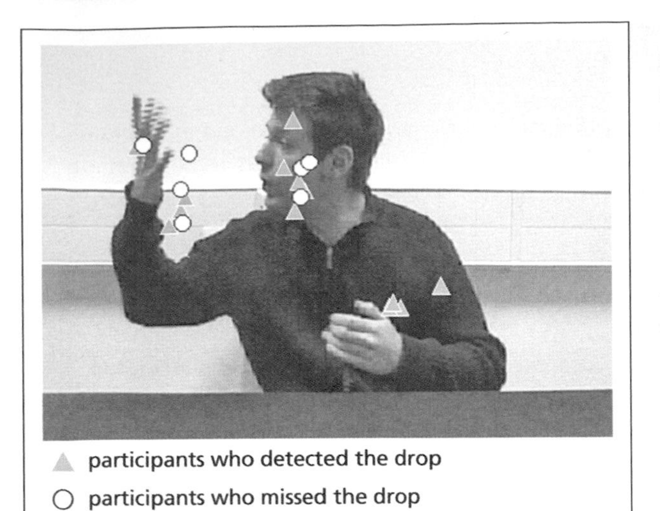

Figure 4.15
Participants' fixation points at the time of dropping the lighter for those detecting the drop (triangles) and those missing the drop (circles).

From Kuhn and Findlay (2010). Reprinted with permission of Taylor & Francis.

Smith et al. (2012) studied change blindness using a magic trick in which a coin was passed from one hand to another and then dropped on the table. The participants' task was to guess whether the coin would land with heads or tails facing up (see online at http://dx.doi.org/10.1068/p7092). The coin was switched during a critical trial from a UK 1p to 2p, 50p to old 10p or US quarter to Kennedy half dollar. All participants fixated the coin throughout the entire time it was visible, but 88% or more failed to detect the coin had changed! Thus, change blindness can occur even though the crucial object is fixated. More specifically, an object can be attended to without some of the features irrelevant to the current task being processed thoroughly.

Weblink:
Magical videos

1 the similarity of the unexpected object to task-relevant stimuli;
2 the observer's available processing resources.

Earlier we discussed the surprising finding (Simons & Chabris, 1999) that 50% of observers failed to detect a woman dressed as a gorilla. Similarity (or rather dissimilarity) was a factor in that the gorilla was black, whereas the team members whose passes the observers counted were dressed in white. Simons and Chabris carried out a further experiment in which observers counted the passes made by members of the team dressed in white or the one dressed in black.

What did Simons and Chabris (1999) find? The gorilla's presence was detected by only 42% of observers when the attended team was the one dressed in white, thus replicating the previous findings. However, the gorilla's presence was detected by 83% of observers when the attended team was the one dressed in black. This shows the importance of similarity between the unexpected stimulus (gorilla) and task-relevant stimuli (members of attended team).

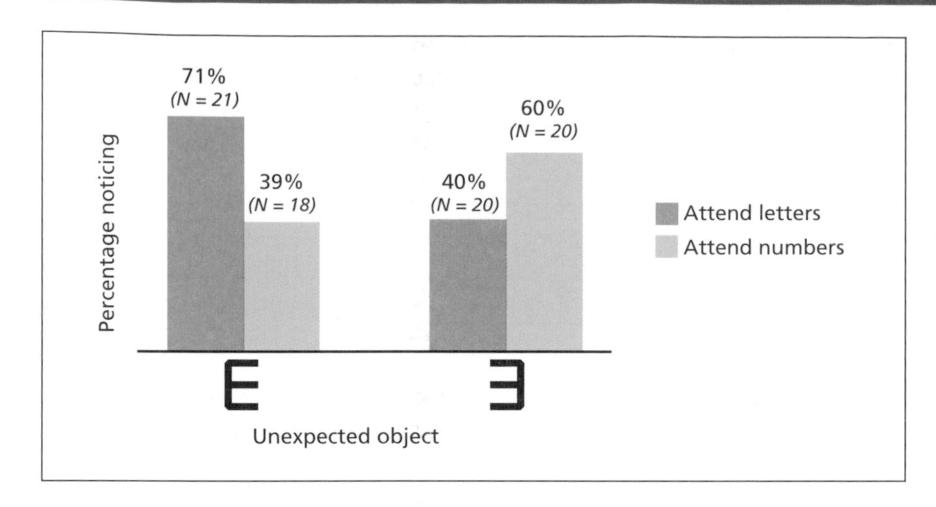

Figure 4.16
Percentage of participants detecting an unexpected object. When it was an E, more participants detected when they were attending to letters than when attending to numbers. The opposite was the case when the unexpected object resembled block-like 3.

From Most (2013). © 2011 Springer-Verlag. Reprinted with permission of the publisher.

Simons and Chabris's (1999) findings indicate the importance of similarity in stimulus *features* (e.g., colour) between task stimuli and the unexpected object. Most (2013) argued that similarity in terms of *semantic category* was also important. Participants tracked numbers (2, 4, 7, 9) or letters (A, H, L, U). On the critical trial, an unexpected stimulus (the letter E or number 3) was visible for seven seconds. Of key importance, the letter and number were visually identical except that they were mirror images of each other. What was of interest was the percentage of observers who noticed the unexpected object.

What did Most (2013) find? There was much less inattentional blindness when the unexpected object belonged to the same category as the tracked objects (see Figure 4.16). Thus, inattentional blindness can depend on attentional sets based on semantic categories (e.g., letters, numbers).

Richards et al. (2012) studied the effects of working memory capacity (related to availability of processing resources and attentional control; see Glossary) on inattentional blindness. Individuals high in working memory capacity were less likely than low scorers to exhibit inattentional blindness.

The findings of Richards et al. (2012) suggest inattentional blindness occurs due to insufficient attentional resources. However, that is not the whole story. Eitam et al. (2013) presented observers with very simple stimuli: a coloured circle surrounded by a differently coloured ring. Performance was close to perfect when the observers tried to identify both colours, indicating they had the processing resources to attend to both stimuli. However, the findings were very different when they were instructed to focus on only the circle or ring. In this condition, there was clear evidence of inattentional blindness with 20% of observers failing to identify the task-irrelevant colour. Thus, inattentional blindness can depend more on attentional set than availability of processing resources.

Evaluation

Change blindness and inattentional blindness are important phenomena occurring in everyday life (e.g., the movies, magic tricks). Most research indicates attentional processes are important, but finer distinctions (e.g., between overt and covert attention) are also needed. Research has increasingly identified various ways change blindness can occur, including a failure to compare the pre- and post-change object representations. Inattentional blindness is mainly due to attentional sets reducing processing of task-irrelevant stimuli not included within the set.

What are the limitations of research in this area? First, there has been a general failure to distinguish between change detection that involves *seeing* the change and change detection that involves only *sensing* a change.

Second, five processes are required for change detection involving seeing to occur and so failure of any of these processes should lead to change blindness. As yet, however, only a few studies (e.g., Varakin et al., 2007) have attempted to distinguish clearly among these potential reasons for change blindness.

CHAPTER SUMMARY

- **Introduction**. The time dimension is of crucial importance in visual perception. The changes in visual information produced as we move around the environment and/or environmental objects move promote accurate perception and facilitate appropriate actions.

- **Direct perception**. Gibson argued that perception and action are closely intertwined. According to his direct theory, movement of an observer creates optic flow, which provides useful information about the direction of heading. Invariants, which remain the same as people move around their environment, are of particular importance. The uses of objects (their affordances) were claimed to be perceived directly. Gibson underestimated the complexity of visual processing and object recognition, and he oversimplified the effects of motion on perception.

- **Visually guided action**. Perception of heading depends in part on optic-flow information. However, there are complexities because the retinal flow field is determined by eye and head movements as well as by optic flow. Heading judgements are also influenced by binocular disparity and the retinal displacement of objects as we approach them.

  Accurate steering on curved paths (e.g., driving around a bend) sometimes involves focusing on the tangent point (e.g., point on the inside edge of the road at which its direction seems to reverse). However, it often involves fixating a point along the future path.

  Calculating time to contact with an object sometimes seems to depend on tau (the size of the retinal image divided by the object's rate of expansion). However, tau only provides accurate information when moving objects have constant velocity. Observers often make use of additional sources of information (e.g., binocular disparity, familiar size, relative size) when working out time to contact.

- **Planning–control model**. The planning–control model distinguishes between a slow planning system used mostly before the initiation of movement and a fast control system used during movement execution. According to the model, planning is associated with the inferior parietal lobe, whereas control depends on the superior parietal lobe. The definition of "planning" is very broad, and the notion that planning always precedes control is oversimplified. There are several exceptions to the theoretical expectation that actions based on control will be more accurate than those based on planning.

- **Perception of human motion**. Human motion is perceived even when only impoverished visual information is available. Perception of human and biological motion involves bottom-up and top-down processes, with the latter most likely to be used with degraded visual input. The perception of human motion is special because we can produce as well as perceive human actions and because we devote considerable time to making sense of it. It has often been assumed that our ability to imitate and understand human motion depends on a mirror neuron system, including brain areas such as inferior frontal regions, the dorsal and ventral premotor cortex, and the inferior and superior parietal lobule. The mirror neuron system is important. However, exaggerated claims have been made concerning its role in human motion perception.
- **Change blindness**. There is convincing evidence for the phenomena of inattentional blindness and change blindness. Attention (covert and overt) is the single most important factor determining whether inattentional and change blindness occur. Inattentional blindness is especially likely to be found when the unexpected object is dissimilar to task stimuli. Five different processes are required for change detection and failure of any of these processes can cause change blindness. There is an important distinction between seeing a changed object and sensing that some change has occurred. The visual system's emphasis on continuous, stable perception probably plays a part in making us susceptible to change blindness.

Further reading

- Bruce, V. & Tadmor, Y. (2015, in press). Direct perception: Beyond Gibson's (1950) direct perception. In M.W. Eysenck & D. Groome (eds), *Cognitive psychology: Revisiting the classic studies*. London: SAGE. Gibson's approach to visual perception and action is evaluated in detail by Vicki Bruce and Yoav Tadmor.
- Cook, R., Bird, G., Catmur, C., Press, C. & Heyes, C. (2014). Mirror neurons: From origin to function. *Behavioral and Brain Sciences*, 37: 177–241. Richard Cook and his colleagues discuss the probable function or functions of the mirror neuron system.

- Glover, S., Wall, M.B. & Smith, A.T. (2012). Distinct cortical networks support the planning and online control of reaching-to-grasp in humans. *European Journal of Neuroscience*, 35: 909–15. Scott Glover and his colleagues provide an update on his planning–control model.
- Jensen, M.S., Yao, R., Street, W.N. & Simons, D.J. (2011). Change blindness and inattentional blindness. *Wiley Interdisciplinary Reviews: Cognitive Science*, 2: 529–46. The similarities and differences between change blindness and inattentional blindness are discussed thoroughly in this article.
- Lee, D.N. (2009). General tau theory: Evolution to date. *Perception*, 38: 837–50. David Lee discusses his theoretical approach to perception of motion that developed from Gibson's theorising.
- Rensink, R.A. (2013). Perception and attention. In D. Reisberg (ed.), *The Oxford handbook of cognitive psychology*. Oxford: Oxford University Press. The relationship between perception and attention (including change blindness and inattentional blindness) is discussed at length by Ronald Rensink.
- Shiffrar, M. & Thomas, J.P. (2013). Beyond the scientific objectification of the human body: Differentiated analyses of human motion and object motion. In M. Rutherford and V. Kuhlmeier (eds), *Social perception: Detection and interpretation of animacy, agency, and intention*. Cambridge, MA: MIT Press/Bradford Books. This chapter provides an overview of what is known about the perception of biological motion.

CHAPTER

5

Attention and performance

INTRODUCTION

Attention is absolutely invaluable in everyday life. We use attention to avoid being hit by cars as we cross the road, to search for missing objects and to perform two tasks at the same time. The word "attention" has various meanings. However, it typically refers to *selectivity* of processing, as was emphasised by William James (1890, pp. 403–4):

> Attention is . . . the taking possession by the mind, in clear and vivid form, of one out of what seem several simultaneously possible objects or trains of thought. Focalisation, concentration, of consciousness are of its essence.

William James (1890) distinguished between "active" and "passive" modes of attention. Attention is active when controlled in a top-down way by the individual's goals or expectations. In contrast, attention is passive when controlled in a bottom-up way by external stimuli (e.g., a loud noise). This distinction is still important in recent theorising (e.g., Corbetta & Shulman, 2002; Corbetta et al., 2008) and is discussed later.

There is also an important distinction between focused and divided attention. **Focused attention** (or selective attention) is studied by presenting individuals with two or more stimulus inputs at the same time and instructing them to respond to only one. An example of focused attention is a predator who keeps track of one animal in a flock. Work on focused or selective attention tells us how effectively we can select certain inputs and avoid being distracted by non-task inputs. It also allows us to study the nature of the selection process and the fate of unattended stimuli.

Divided attention is also studied by presenting at least two stimulus inputs at the same time. However, it differs from focused attention in that individuals are instructed they must attend (and respond) to all stimulus inputs. Divided attention is also known as multitasking, a skill increasingly important in today's 24/7 world! Studies of divided attention provide useful information about our processing limitations and the capacity of attentional mechanisms.

There is another important distinction (the last one, we promise you!), this time between *external* and *internal* attention. External attention refers to "the selection and modulation of sensory information", while internal attention refers to "the selection, modulation, and maintenance of internally generated information, such as task rules, responses, long-term memory, or working memory" (Chun et al., 2011, p. 73). The connection to Baddeley's (e.g., 2007; see Chapter 6) working memory model is perhaps especially important. The central executive component of working memory is involved in attentional control and plays a major role in internal and external attention.

Much attentional research suffers from two limitations. First, the emphasis has been on external rather than internal attention. Second, what participants attend to in most laboratory studies is determined by the experimenter's instructions. In contrast, what we attend to in the real world is mostly determined by our current goals and emotional states.

Two important topics related to attention are discussed in other chapters. Change blindness, which shows the close links between attention and perception, is considered in Chapter 4. Consciousness (including its relationship to attention) is discussed in Chapter 16.

KEY TERMS

Focused attention
A situation in which individuals try to attend to only one source of information while ignoring other stimuli; also known as selective attention.

Divided attention
A situation in which two tasks are performed at the same time; also known as multitasking.

Cocktail party problem
The difficulties involved in attending to one voice when two or more people are speaking at the same time.

FOCUSED AUDITORY ATTENTION

Many years ago, British scientist Colin Cherry (1953) became fascinated by the **cocktail party problem** – how can we follow just one conversation when several people are talking at once? As we will see, there is no simple answer to that question.

Weblink:
A review of the cocktail party effect

Weblink:
Cocktail party study

Listeners face two separate problems when trying to attend to one voice among many (McDermott, 2009). First, there is the problem of *sound segregation*: from the mixture of sounds reaching his/her ear, the listener has to decide which sounds belong together and which do not. Second, after segregation has been achieved, the listener must direct attention to the *sound source of interest* and ignore the others.

Some indication of the complexities of sound segregation is provided by attempts to develop machine-based speech recognition programmes. Such programmes perform almost perfectly when there is a single speaker in a quiet environment. However, they often perform very poorly when several sound sources are all present at the same time (Shen et al., 2008).

McDermott (2009) pointed out that auditory segmentation is often much harder than visual segmentation (i.e., deciding which visual features belong to which objects; see Chapter 9). First, there is considerable overlap of signals from different sound sources in the cochlea, whereas visual objects tend to occupy different regions of the retina.

Second, each sound source adds to the signal reaching the ears. In contrast, nearer objects tend to block out further ones with visual signals reaching the retina. Think how much harder it would be to focus on a single visual object if all objects were transparent!

There is another issue related to focused auditory attention. When listeners manage to attend to one auditory input, how much processing is there of the unattended input(s)? As we will see, various different answers have been proposed to that question.

Cherry (1953) carried out very influential research to address the issues discussed so far (see Eysenck (2015, in press) for a detailed evaluation of his research). He used a **dichotic listening task**, in which a different auditory message is presented to each ear and the listener typically attends to only one. Since it can be hard to ensure listeners are consistently attending to the target message, Cherry made use of **shadowing**, in which the attended message was repeated aloud as it was presented.

Cherry (1953) discovered that listeners solved the cocktail party problem by making use of differences between the auditory inputs in physical characteristics (e.g., sex of speaker, voice intensity, speaker location). When Cherry presented two messages in the same voice to both ears at once (thus eliminating these physical differences), listeners found it very hard to separate out the two messages on the basis of meaning differences alone.

Cherry (1953) found very little information seemed to be extracted from the unattended message. Listeners seldom noticed when that message was spoken in a foreign language or reversed (backwards) speech. In contrast, physical changes (e.g., a pure tone) were nearly always detected. The conclusion that unattended information receives practically no processing was supported by Moray (1959). He found there was very little memory for unattended words presented 35 times each.

KEY TERMS

Dichotic listening task
A different auditory message is presented to each ear and attention has to be directed to one message.

Shadowing
Repeating one auditory message word for word as it is presented while a second auditory message is also presented; it is a version of the **dichotic listening task**.

Where is the bottleneck? Early vs. late selection

How can we explain what happens when we are presented with two or more auditory inputs at the same time? Many psychologists argued that we have a processing bottleneck. Just as a bottleneck in the road (e.g., where it is especially narrow) can cause traffic congestion, so a bottleneck in the processing system can seriously limit our ability to process two or more simultaneous inputs. However, a processing bottleneck could be very useful when solving the cocktail party problem in that it might permit listeners to process only the desired voice.

Where is the bottleneck located? According to Broadbent (1958), a filter (bottleneck) early in processing allows information from one input or message through it on the basis of its physical characteristics. The other input remains briefly in a sensory buffer and is rejected unless attended to rapidly (see Figure 5.1). In sum, Broadbent argued that there is early selection.

Treisman (1964) argued that the bottleneck's location is more *flexible* than Broadbent had suggested (see Figure 5.1). She proposed that listeners start with processing based on physical cues, syllable pattern and specific words and move on to processes based on grammatical structure and meaning. If there is insufficient processing capacity to permit full stimulus analysis, later processes are omitted.

Treisman (1964) also argued that top-down processes (e.g., expectations) are important. Listeners performing the shadowing task sometimes say a word presented on the unattended input. Such breakthroughs mostly occur when the word on the unattended channel is highly probable in the context of the attended message.

Interactive activity:
Triesman

Deutsch and Deutsch (1963) were at the other extreme from Broadbent (1958). They argued that *all* stimuli are fully analysed, with the most important or relevant stimulus determining the response. This theory places the processing bottleneck much nearer the response end of the processing system than does Broadbent's theory (see Figure 5.1). In sum, they argued in favour of late selection.

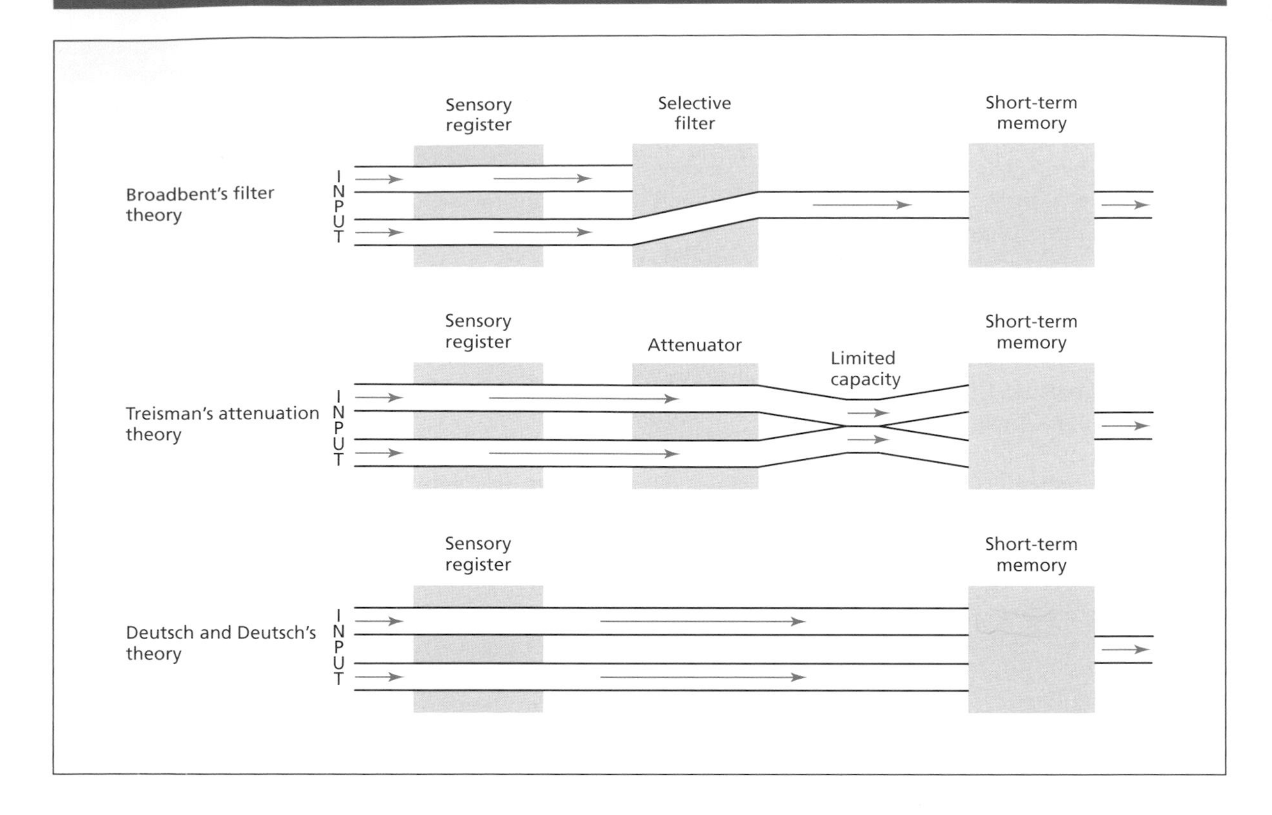

Figure 5.1
A comparison of Broadbent's theory (*top*); Treisman's theory (*middle*); and Deutsch and Deutsch's theory (*bottom*).

Findings: unattended input

Broadbent's approach suggests there should be little or no processing of unattended auditory messages. In contrast, Treisman's approach suggests the amount of processing of unattended auditory messages is flexible, and Deutsch and Deutsch's approach implies reasonably thorough processing of such messages. As we will see, the evidence suggests there is some processing of unattended messages but less than with attended ones.

Treisman and Riley (1969) asked listeners to shadow one of two auditory messages. They stopped shadowing and tapped when they detected a target in either message. Many more target words were detected on the shadowed message.

Bentin et al. (1995) presented different words to each ear and instructed listeners to attend only to words on the left or right ear. There were two main findings. First, there was evidence that the unattended words had received some semantic processing. Second, the extent of semantic processing was less for unattended than for attended words.

Processing of words on the unattended message is often enhanced if they have special significance for the listener. Li et al. (2011) asked listeners to shadow one message while distractor words were presented to the unattended ear. Women dissatisfied with their weight made more shadowing errors than those not dissatisfied when weight-related words (e.g., *fat*, *chunky*, *slim*) were presented to the unattended ear. This increase in shadowing errors reflects the greater processing of weight-related words by women dissatisfied with their weight.

Our own name has very special significance for us. Unsurprisingly, listeners often detect their own name when it is presented on the unattended message

(Moray, 1959). Conway et al. (2001) found the probability of detecting one's own name on the unattended message depends on working memory capacity (Chapter 6; see Glossary). Participants with low capacity were more likely than high-capacity individuals to detect their own name (65% vs. 20%, respectively) because they had less attentional control.

Coch et al. (2005) asked listeners to attend to one of two auditory inputs and to detect targets presented on either input. Event-related potentials (ERPs; see Glossary) were recorded to provide a measure of processing activity. ERPs 100 ms after target presentation were greater when the probe was presented on the attended message than on the unattended one. This suggests there was more processing of the attended than the unattended targets. Similar findings had been reported in several earlier studies (see Talsma and Kok (2002) for details).

It is often hard to interpret greater brain activation for attended than unattended auditory stimuli. It may reflect enhanced processing for attended stimuli and/or suppressed or inhibited processing for unattended stimuli. Horton et al. (2013) investigated this issue. Listeners heard separate speech messages presented to each ear with instructions to attend to the left or right ear. There was greater brain activity associated with the attended message in several brain areas (especially the case around 90 ms after stimulus presentation). Of most importance, this difference occurred because there was *enhancement* of the attended message combined with *suppression* of the unattended message.

Findings: cocktail party problem

It has proved very difficult to devise automatic speech recognition systems that can accurately separate out one voice from several speaking at the same time (Shen et al., 2008). How do humans manage to do this and so solve the cocktail party problem? In general terms, there are bottom-up factors and top-down factors. As we have seen, Cherry (1953) found physical differences (e.g., sex of speaker, voice intensity) were used very efficiently to attend to one voice out of two. However, when there are several voices speaking at the same time, the listener's task becomes much more difficult.

Shamma et al. (2011) pointed out that the sound features of a given source will typically all be present when it is active and absent when it is silent. They refer to this tendency as *temporal coherence*. If listeners can identify at least one distinctive feature of the target voice, they can then distinguish its other sound features via temporal coherence.

There are many cases in which temporal coherence and other bottom-up cues are insufficient to produce sound segregation. In such cases, top-down processes can be used. The likely importance of top-down processes is indicated by the existence of extensive descending pathways from the auditory cortex to brain areas involved in early auditory processing (Robinson & McAlpine, 2009). Various top-down factors dependent on listeners' knowledge and/or expectations can facilitate segregating two speech messages. For example, it is easier to perceive a target message accurately if its words form sentences rather than consisting of random sequences of words (McDermott, 2009).

Familiarity with the target voice is also important. Accuracy of perceiving what one speaker is saying in the context of several other voices is much higher if listeners have previously listened to the speaker's voice in isolation (McDermott, 2009).

Marozeau et al. (2010) considered the effects of top-down factors on the ability to follow a melody in the presence of irrelevant notes. Musicians performed better than non-musicians, showing the influence of expertise and knowledge on sound segregation. Marozeau et al. increased or decreased the amount of sound overlap between the target melody and the other sounds over time. It was easier to follow the melody in the increasing overlap condition, because this condition allowed the listeners to identify the melody early on.

Mesgarani and Chang (2012) studied participants with implanted multi-electrode arrays permitting direct recording of activity within auditory cortex. The participants listened to two different messages (one in a male voice, one in a female voice) presented to the same ear with instructions to attend to only one. The responses within auditory cortex revealed, "the salient spectral [based on sound frequencies] and temporal features of the attended speaker, as if subjects were listening to that speaker alone" (Mesgarani & Chang, 2012, p. 233).

Golumbic et al. (2013) pointed out that people at actual cocktail parties can potentially use *visual* information to follow what a given speaker is saying. Participants heard two simultaneous messages (one in a male voice and the other in a female voice) having been instructed which voice to attend to. Processing of the attended message was enhanced when participants could see a movie of the speaker talking while listening to the message. This probably occurred because the visual input made it easier to attend to the speaker's message.

In sum, human listeners generally manage to achieve the complex task of selecting one speech message from among several such messages. Various bottom-up and top-down processes are involved. Much of what happens within the auditory system is a "winner-takes-all" situation in which the processing of one auditory input (the winner) suppresses the brain activity of all other inputs (the losers) (Kurt et al., 2008).

FOCUSED VISUAL ATTENTION

There has been considerably more research on visual attention than auditory attention. Why is this? The main reason is that vision is our most important sense modality with more cortex devoted to it than any other sensory modality. In addition, it used to be easier to control precisely the presentation times of visual than auditory stimuli. However, as a result of technological advances that is no longer the case.

In this section, we consider four key issues. First, what is focused visual attention like? Second, what is selected in focused visual attention? Third, what happens to unattended visual stimuli? Fourth, what are the major systems involved in visual attention? In the next section, we discuss what the study of visual disorders has taught us about visual attention.

Spotlight, zoom lens or multiple spotlights?

Weblink:
PEBL

Have a look around the room you are in and attend to any interesting objects. Now answer the following question: is your visual attention like a spotlight? A spotlight illuminates a fairly small area, little can be seen outside its beam and it can be redirected to focus on any given object. It has been argued that the same is true of visual attention (e.g., Posner, 1980).

Other psychologists (e.g., Eriksen & St James, 1986) have argued that visual attention is more *flexible* than suggested by the spotlight analogy. According to them, visual attention resembles a zoom lens. We can deliberately increase or decrease the area of focal attention just as a zoom lens can be adjusted to alter the visual area it covers. This makes sense. For example, when driving a car it is generally desirable to attend to as much of the visual field as possible to anticipate danger. However, when we spot a potential hazard, we focus on it to avoid a crash.

A third theoretical approach is even more flexible. According to the multiple spotlights theory (e.g., Awh & Pashler, 2000), we can show **split attention**, in which attention is directed to two or more regions of space not adjacent to each other. Split attention could save processing resources because we would avoid attending to irrelevant regions of visual space lying between two relevant areas.

The notion of split attention has proved controversial. Jans et al. (2010) argued that attention is often very influential in determining motor action. If we could attend simultaneously to two objects separated from each other in space, that would probably interfere with effective action. However, there is no strong evidence that attending to two separated objects at the same time would necessarily disrupt action. Cave et al. (2010) disagreed with Jans et al. They argued that the *flexibility* offered by split attention may often be advantageous rather than problematical.

KEY TERMS

Split attention
Allocation of attention to two (or more) non-adjacent regions of visual space.

Findings

LaBerge (1983) obtained findings supporting the zoom-lens model. Five-letter words were presenting and a probe requiring a rapid response was presented immediately after the word. This probe could appear in the spatial position of any of the letters. In the narrow-beam condition, participants categorised the middle letter. In the broad-beam condition, they categorised the entire word.

Laberge (1983) assumed the probe would be responded to faster when it fell within the central attentional beam than when it did not. As predicted, the zoom lens was narrowly focused on the third letter in the narrow-beam condition but not the broad-beam condition (see Figure 5.2).

Müller et al. (2003) also supported the zoom-lens theory. On each trial, observers saw four squares in a semi-circle and were cued to attend to one, two

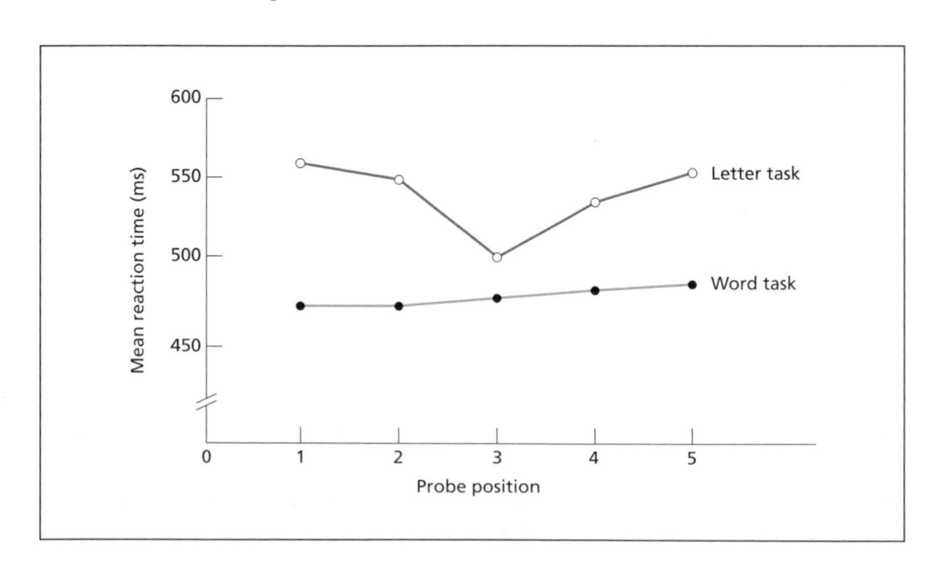

Figure 5.2
Mean reaction time to the probe as a function of probe position. The probe was presented at the time that a letter string would have been presented.
Data from LaBerge (1983).

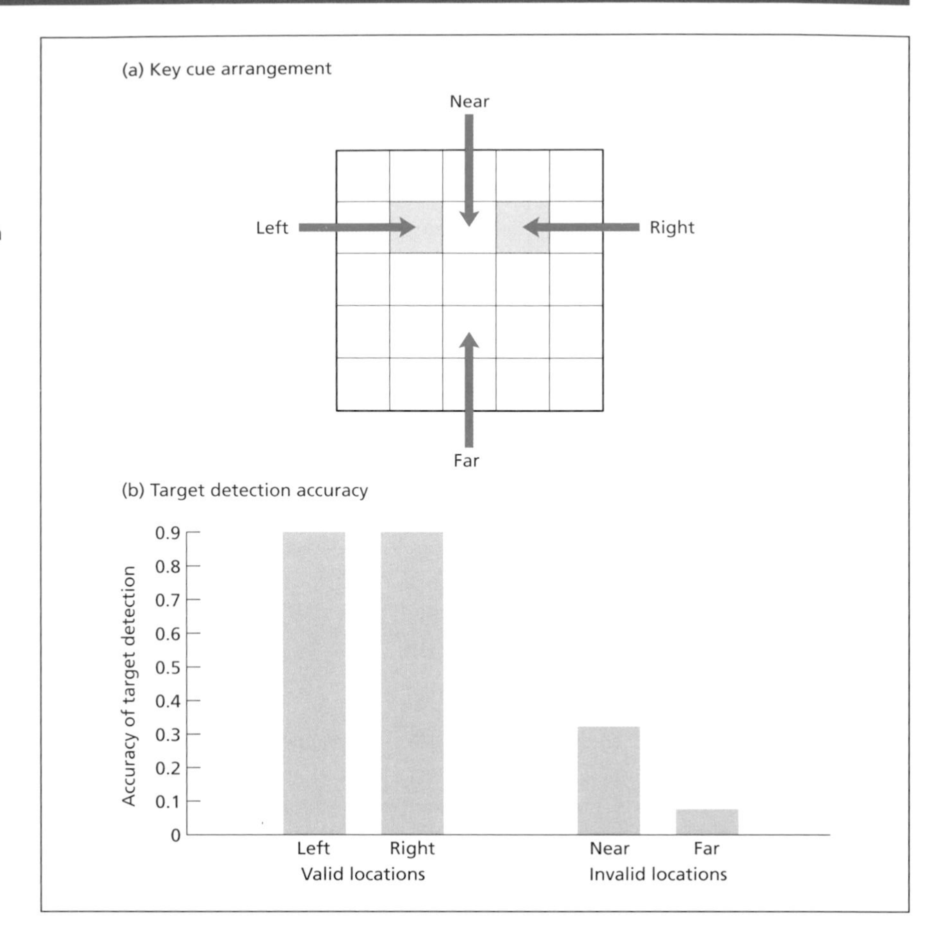

Figure 5.3
(a) Shaded areas indicate the cued locations and the near and far locations are not cued. (b) Probability of target detection at valid (left or right) and invalid (near or far) locations. Both based on information in Awh and Pashler (2000).

or all four. Four objects were then presented (one in each square) and participants decided whether a target (e.g., white circle) was among them. Brain activation in early visual areas was most widespread when the attended region was large (i.e., attend to all four squares) and most limited when it was small (i.e., attend to one square).

We turn now to research on split attention. Suppose you had to identify two digits that would probably be presented to two cued locations a little way apart (see Figure 5.3a). Suppose also that on some trials a digit was presented in the space between the two cued locations. According to zoom-lens theory, the area of maximal attention should include the two cued locations *and* the space in between. As a result, detection of digits presented in the middle should have been very good. In fact, Awh and Pashler (2000) found it was poor (see Figure 5.3b). Thus, attention can resemble multiple spotlights as predicted by the split-attention approach.

Morawetz et al. (2007) presented letters and digits at five locations simultaneously: one in each quadrant of the visual field and one in the centre. In one condition, participants attended to the visual stimuli at the upper left and bottom right locations and ignored the other stimuli. There were two peaks of brain activation indicating enhancement of cortical areas representing the attended areas. However, there was less activation corresponding to the region in between. This pattern of activation strongly suggests split attention.

Further evidence for split attention was reported by Niebergall et al. (2011). They recorded the neuronal responses of monkeys attending to two moving stimuli (random-dot patterns) while ignoring a distractor. The most important condition was one in which there was a distractor between (and close to) the two attended stimuli. In this condition, neuronal responses to the distractor *decreased*. Overall, the findings are most easily explained in terms of split attention with some mechanism reducing attention to (and processing of) distractors located between attended stimuli.

In sum, we can use visual attention very flexibly. Visual focused attention can resemble a spotlight, a zoom lens or multiple spotlights depending on the current situation and the observer's goals.

What is selected?

Theoretical models based upon notions such as a spotlight or zoom lens imply we selectively attend to an area or region of space. This is space-based attention. Alternatively, we may attend to a given object or objects; this is object-based attention. Object-based attention seems likely since visual perception is mainly concerned with objects of interest to us (see Chapters 2 and 3). Support for that viewpoint was discussed by Henderson and Hollingworth (1999). They reviewed research showing that eye movements as observers viewed natural scenes were directed almost exclusively to objects.

Even though we typically focus on objects of potential importance, that does *not* mean we are unable to attend to areas of space. It is likely our processing system is so *flexible* we can attend to an area of space *or* a given object. That would be consistent with the findings discussed previously showing visual attention can resemble a spotlight, a zoom lens or multiple spotlights.

Findings

Visual attention is often object-based. For example, O'Craven et al. (1999) presented participants with two stimuli (a face and a house) transparently overlapping at the same location with instructions to attend to one of them. Brain areas associated with face processing were more activated when the face was attended to than when the house was. In similar fashion, brain areas associated with house processing were more activated when the house was attended to. Thus, attention was object-based rather than being solely space-based.

Hou and Liu (2012) also asked observers to attend to one of two superimposed objects. Various brain areas were involved in top-down attention selection of a given object. However, dorsal fronto-parietal areas seemed of particular importance.

Egly et al. (1994) devised a very popular method for comparing object-based and space-based attention (see Figure 5.4). The task was to detect a target stimulus as rapidly as possible. A cue presented before the target was valid (same location as the target) or invalid (different location from the target). Of key importance, invalid cues were in the *same* object as the target (within-object cues) or in a *different* object (between-object cues). Target detection was slower on invalid trials than valid ones. However, target detection was faster on invalid trials when the cue was in the same object rather than a different one. This suggests attention is at least partially object-based.

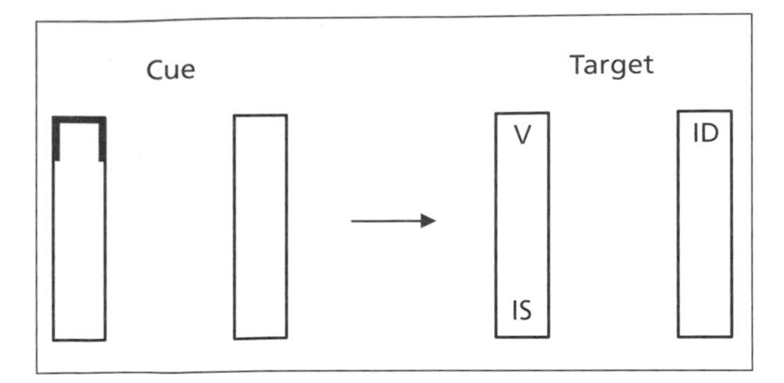

Figure 5.4
Stimuli adapted from Egly et al. (1994). Participants saw two rectangles and a cue indicated the most likely location of a subsequent target. The target appeared at the cued location (V), at the uncued end of the cued rectangle (IS) or at the uncued, equidistant end of the uncued rectangle (ID).

From Chen (2012). © Psychonomic Society, Inc. Reprinted with permission from Springer.

Does object-based attention in the Egly et al. (1994) task occur automatically or does it involve strategic processes? Object-based attention should *always* be found if it is automatic, but should occur only under some circumstances if it involves strategic processes. The evidence indicates object-based attention depends on strategic processes (Shomstein, 2012). For example, Drummond and Shomstein (2010) found no evidence for object-based attention when the cue indicated with 100% certainty where the target would appear. Thus, any tendency towards object-based attention can be overridden when performance would be impaired by using it.

Lee et al. (2012) argued that visual attention is influenced by recent experience. They obtained support using Egly et al.'s (1994) task. Response times overall were faster to targets at an uncued location on the cued rectangle rather than targets on the uncued rectangle: this is the usual finding based on the use of object-based attention. However, this effect (and object-based attention) were not found when the uncued object contained the target on the previous trial. Lee et al. (2012, p. 314) concluded as follows: "Attention closely tracks the short time scale of the environment and automatically adapts to optimise performance to this structure."

The fact that object-based attention has often been found with Egly et al.'s (1994) task does *not* necessarily mean space-based attention is not also present. Hollingworth et al. (2012) addressed this issue using a task resembling that of Egly et al. There were three types of within-object cues varying in the distance between the cue and subsequent target.

Hollingworth et al. (2012) obtained two main findings (see Figure 5.5). First, there was evidence for object-based attention: when the target was far from the cue, performance was worse when the cue was in a different object rather than in the same one. Second, there was evidence for space-based attention: when the target was in the same object as the cue, performance declined the greater the distance between target and cue. Thus, object-based and space-based attention are not necessarily mutually exclusive.

Pilz et al. (2012) also compared object-based and space-based attention using a range of standard tasks (e.g., the one introduced by Egly et al. (1994)). Overall, they obtained much more evidence of space-based attention than object-based attention. They also found convincing evidence of individual differences – only a small fraction of participants showed object-based attention.

When we search the visual environment, it would be inefficient if we repeatedly attended to any given location. In fact, we exhibit **inhibition of return**, which is a reduced probability of returning to a region recently the focus of attention. Of theoretical importance is whether inhibition of return applies to locations or to objects.

KEY TERM

Inhibition of return
A reduced probability of visual attention returning to a recently attended location or object.

The evidence is mixed. Several studies have reported inhibition of return to a given object (see Chen, 2012). List and Robertson (2007) used Egly et al.'s (1994) task shown in Figure 5.4. Object-based effects were "slow to emerge, small in magnitude, and susceptible to minor changes in procedure" (List & Robertson,

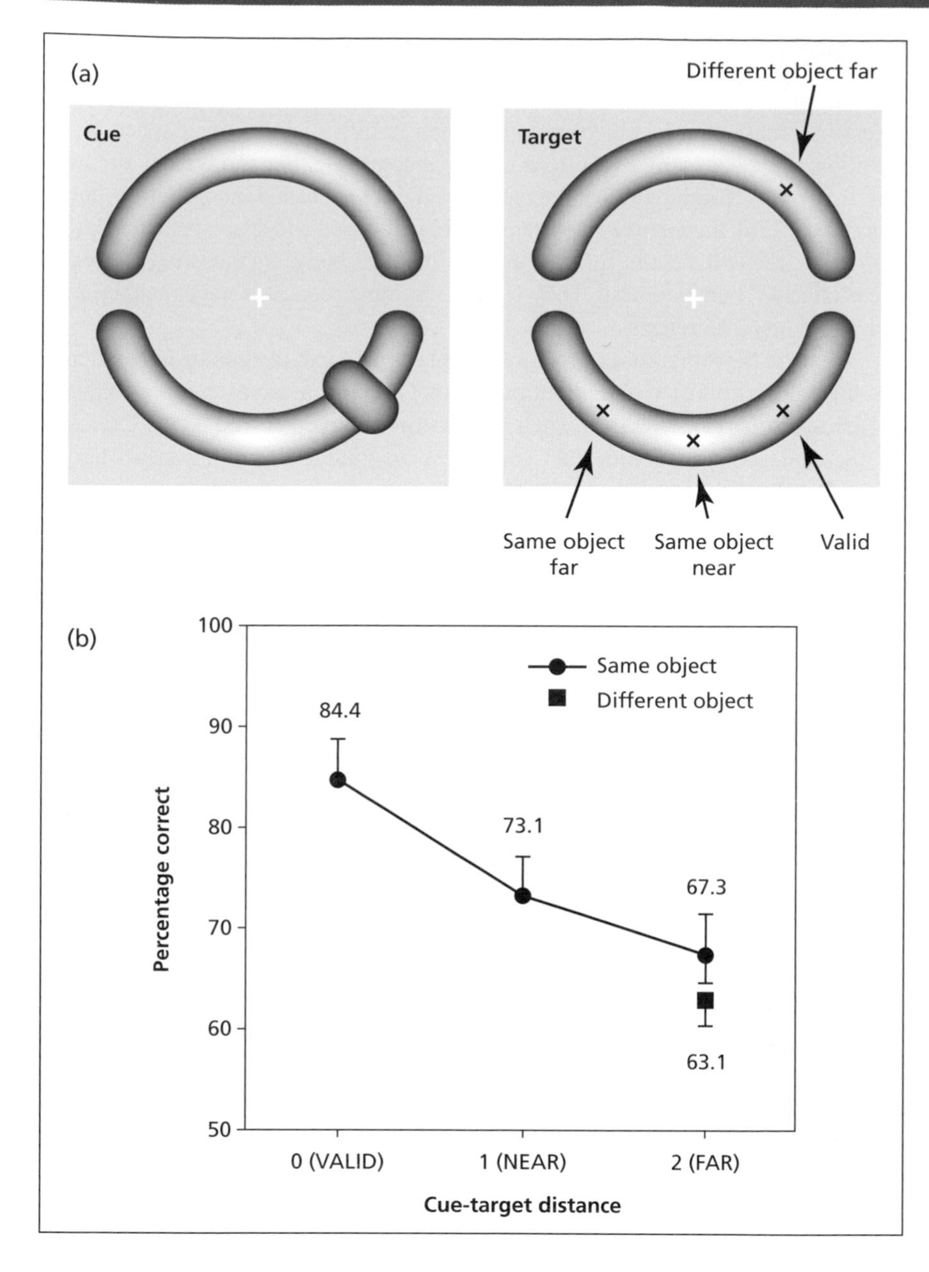

Figure 5.5
(a) Possible target locations (same object far, same object near, valid, different object far) for a given cue. (b) Performance accuracy at the various target locations.
From Hollingworth et al. (2012). © 2011 American Psychological Association.

2007, p. 1332). In contrast, location- or space-based inhibition of return occurred rapidly, was of much greater magnitude and was found consistently. Overall, it is probable that object-based and location-based inhibition of return both exist.

Most research has focused on the distinction between object-based and space-based attention. However, there is also evidence for feature-based attention. For example, suppose you are looking for a friend in a crowd. Since you know she nearly always wears red clothes, you might attend to the feature of colour rather than to specific objects or locations. Kravitz and Behrmann (2011) found that space-, object- and feature-based forms of attention *interacted* with each other to enhance object processing.

Evaluation

Several important findings have emerged from research in this area. First, while object-based attention is much more common in everyday life than space-based attention, there are many exceptions to this general rule. Second, visual attention can involve a combination of space-based, object-based and feature-based processes. Third, the relative importance of object-based and space-based attention is *flexible*. Several factors influencing the balance between these two types of attention have been identified. They include strategic processes, recent experience and individual differences.

What are the limitations of research in this area? First, there is strong evidence that different forms of visual attention interact and influence each other (Kravitz & Behrmann, 2011). However, such interactions have been studied only rarely.

Second, it can be harder than you might imagine to decide exactly what an "object" is. In Chapter 3, we considered the Gestalt laws of perceptual organisation (see Figure 3.3). These laws indicate some of the complexities involved in predicting which visual elements will be attended to (and perceived) as coherent objects.

Third, we need more research focused on understanding why object-based attention is more dominant in everyday life than under laboratory conditions. One possibility is that we have an incentive to attend to objects in everyday life but this is often missing in the laboratory.

What happens to unattended visual stimuli?

Unsurprisingly, unattended visual stimuli receive less processing than attended ones. Martinez et al. (1999) compared event-related potentials (ERPs; see Glossary) to attended and unattended visual stimuli. The ERPs to attended visual stimuli were comparable to those to unattended visual stimuli 50–55 ms after stimulus onset. After that, however, the ERPs to attended stimuli were greater than those to unattended stimuli. Thus, selective attention influences all but the very early stages of processing.

As we have all discovered to our cost, it is often difficult or impossible to ignore task-irrelevant stimuli. Below we consider factors determining whether task performance is adversely affected by distracting stimuli.

Load theory

Lavie's (2005, 2010) load theory is a very influential approach to understanding the effects of distraction. She argued that the extent to which we are distracted by task-irrelevant stimuli depends on the perceptual demands of our current task. High-load tasks require nearly all our perceptual capacity whereas low-load tasks do not. With low-load tasks there are spare attentional resources, and so task-irrelevant stimuli are more likely to be processed than with high-load tasks.

So far we have discussed *perceptual* load. However, Lavie (2005) argued that *cognitive* load (e.g., demands on working memory) is also important. Distraction effects are greater when cognitive load is high than when it is low. Why is this? High cognitive load reduces people's ability to use cognitive control to discriminate between target and distractor stimuli.

In sum, the effects of perceptual load on attentional processes are relatively automatic. In contrast, those of cognitive load involve non-automatic, controlled processes. Thus, perceptual and cognitive load involve different processes and it is assumed their effects on attention are *independent* of each other.

Findings

There is much support for the hypothesis that high perceptual load reduces distraction effects. Forster and Lavie (2008) presented six letters in a circle and participants decided which target letter (X or N) was present. The five non-target letters resembled the target letter more closely in shape in the high-load condition. On some trials, a picture of a cartoon character (e.g., SpongeBob SquarePants) was presented as a distractor. Distractors interfered with task performance only under low-load conditions.

Neuroimaging research supports the importance of perceptual load. Schwartz et al. (2005) assessed brain activation to distractor flickering draughtboards while participants performed a task involving low or high perceptual load. The distractors produced less activation in several brain areas related to visual processing when there was high perceptual load.

Most research testing the hypothesis that high perceptual load reduces distractor processing has involved the visual modality. In contrast, Murphy et al. (2013) tested the hypothesis using the auditory modality. The findings were very different from those in vision – the extent of distractor processing was unrelated to perceptual load. Murphy et al. argued that this difference between the two sense modalities probably occurs because the auditory system does not permit the specific focusing of attentional capacity possible within the visual system.

So far we have focused on distraction by *external* stimuli. However, we can also be distracted by *internal* stimuli (e.g., task-irrelevant thoughts). Participants had significantly fewer task-irrelevant thoughts when performing a task involving high perceptual load than one involving low load (Forster & Lavie, 2009).

The prediction that the effects of distractors should be more disruptive when working-memory load is high rather than low was tested by de Fockert et al. (2001). Participants classified famous written names as pop stars or politicians under low or high working-memory load (involving remembering strings of digits). Distraction was provided by famous faces. These faces impaired task performance more with high working-memory load. In addition, there was more face-related activity in the visual cortex in the high-load condition.

Lavie (2005) assumed cognitive load reduces cognitive or attentional control. If so, we would expect individuals with poor attentional control to resist distraction worse than those with good attentional control. Eysenck et al. (2007) put forward attentional control theory based on the assumption that individuals with anxious personalities have poor attentional control. As predicted by that theory (and by load theory), Moser et al. (2012a) found anxious individuals were much more susceptible to distraction than non-anxious ones.

Various findings indicate load theory is oversimplified. First, Hains and Baillargeon (2011) used human faces as distractors, and found they could not be ignored even when perceptual load was high. This probably happened because of the importance of attending to human faces in our everyday lives.

Second, as mentioned earlier, load theory assumes the effects of perceptual and cognitive load are entirely *independent*. Linnell and Caparos (2011) tested

KEY TERM

Covert attention
Attention to an object in the absence of an eye movement towards it.

this assumption. They discovered perceptual and cognitive processes *interacted* with each other and so were not independent. More specifically, perceptual load only influenced attention as predicted by load theory when cognitive load was low. Thus, the effects of perceptual load are not automatic as assumed by load theory but instead depend on cognitive resources being available.

Evaluation

Load theory has established itself as a major theory of attention. The distinction between perceptual and cognitive load has proved very useful. There is much support for the predictions that high perceptual load will reduce distraction from external and internal stimuli provided visual tasks are used. There is also support for the prediction that high cognitive load produces increased susceptibility to distraction.

What are the limitations of load theory? First, high perceptual load does *not* reduce distraction effects in the auditory modality. Second, some task-irrelevant stimuli (faces) cause distraction even where perceptual load is high. Third, the notion that perceptual and cognitive load have entirely separate effects on attention is incorrect (Linnell & Caparos, 2011). Fourth, the theory is oversimplified because it ignores several factors influencing selective visual attention. These factors include the salience or conspicuousness of distracting stimuli and the distance in space between distracting and task stimuli (Khetrapal, 2010).

Major attention networks

Several theorists (e.g., Posner, 1980; Corbetta & Shulman, 2002) have argued that there are two major attention networks. One attention network is goal-directed or endogenous, whereas the other is stimulus-driven or exogenous.

Posner (1980) studied **covert attention**, in which attention shifts to a given spatial location without an eye movement. In his research, participants responded rapidly to a light. The light was preceded by a central cue (arrow pointing to the left or right) or a peripheral cue (brief illumination of a box outline). Most cues were valid (indicating where the target light would appear), but some were invalid (providing inaccurate information about the light's location).

Responses to the light were fastest to valid cues, intermediate to neutral cues (a central cross) and slowest to invalid cues. The findings were comparable for central and peripheral cues. When the cues were valid on only a small fraction of trials, they were ignored when they were central cues but influenced performance when they were peripheral cues.

The above findings led Posner (1980) to distinguish between two systems:

1 An *endogenous* system: it is controlled by the individual's intentions and is used when central cues are presented.
2 An *exogenous* system: it automatically shifts attention and is involved when uninformative peripheral cues are presented. Stimuli that are salient or different from other stimuli (e.g., in colour) are most likely to be attended to using this system.

Corbetta and Shulman (2002) identified two attention systems. First, there is a goal-directed or top-down attention system resembling Posner's endogenous system. It consists of a fronto-parietal network including the intraparietal sulcus and is the dorsal attention network. This system is influenced by expectations, knowledge and current goals. It is used if observers receive a cue predicting the location or other feature of a forthcoming visual stimulus.

Research activity:
Attention-grabbing adverts

Second, Corbetta and Shulman (2002) also identified a stimulus-driven or bottom-up attention system resembling Posner's exogenous system. It is often described as the ventral attention network. This system is used when an unexpected and potentially important stimulus (e.g., flames appearing under the door) is presented. This system (consisting of a right-hemisphere ventral fronto-parietal network) has a "circuit-breaking" function, meaning visual attention is redirected from its current focus.

What stimuli trigger this circuit-breaking? We might imagine salient or distinctive stimuli would be most likely to attract attention. However, Corbetta et al. (2008) argued that distractors closely resembling task stimuli are more likely than salient stimuli to attract attention from the ventral attention network.

The two attention systems or networks often influence and *interact* with each other. As we will see, the intraparietal sulcus is involved in such interactions. Corbetta et al. (2008) spelled out some of the interactions involved. First, signals from the top-down system suppress distractor information in the stimulus-driven system so goal-directed processing can proceed unimpeded. Second, when the stimulus-driven system detects stimuli irrelevant to the current goal, it sends signals to disrupt processing occurring within the goal-directed system.

The existence of two attention systems makes much sense. The goal-directed system (dorsal attention network) allows us to focus attention on stimuli directly relevant to our current goals. However, if we *only* had this system, our attentional processes would be dangerously inflexible. It is also important to have a stimulus-driven attentional system (ventral attention network) leading us to switch attention away from goal-relevant stimuli in the presence of an unexpected threatening stimulus (e.g., a ferocious animal).

Findings

Corbetta and Shulman (2002) provided evidence for their two-network model by carrying out meta-analyses of brain-imaging studies. In essence, they argued that brain areas most often activated when participants expect a stimulus that has not yet been presented form the dorsal attention network. In contrast, brain areas most often activated when individuals detect low-frequency targets form the ventral attention network.

Subsequent research has clarified which brain areas are associated with each network (Corbetta & Shulman, 2011; see Figure 5.6). Key areas within the goal-directed or dorsal attention network are as follows: superior parietal lobule (SPL), intraparietal sulcus (IPS), inferior frontal junction (IFJ), frontal eye field (FEF), middle temporal area (MT) and V3A. Key areas within the stimulus-driven or ventral attention network are as follows: inferior frontal junction (IFJ), inferior frontal gyrus (IFG), supramarginal gyrus (SMG), superior temporal gyrus (STG) and insula (Ins) (see Figure 5.6). There is much evidence that the temporo-parietal junction is also involved in bottom-up attentional processes (e.g., Shomstein et al., 2010).

Hahn et al. (2006) tested Corbetta and Shulman's (2002) theory by comparing patterns of brain activation when top-down and bottom-up processes were required.

Figure 5.6
The brain areas associated with the dorsal or goal-directed attention network and the ventral or stimulus-driven network. The full names of the areas involved are indicated in the text.
From Corbetta and Shulman (2011). © Annual Reviews. With permission of Annual Reviews.

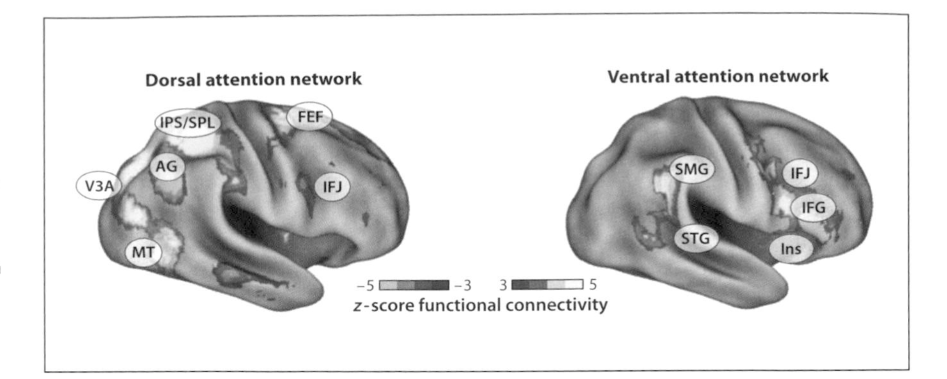

As predicted by the theory, there was practically no overlap between the brain areas associated with top-down and bottom-up processing. In addition, the brain areas involved in each type of processing corresponded reasonably well to those identified by Corbetta and Shulman.

Talsma et al. (2010) confirmed previous research showing that different brain areas are associated with top-down and bottom-up processing. In addition, however, they found top-down and bottom-up processes both made use of a common network of parietal areas.

Neuroimaging studies cannot establish that any given brain area is necessarily involved in stimulus-driven or goal-directed attention processes. Relevant evidence on this issue can be obtained by the use of transcranial magnetic stimulation (TMS; see Glossary) to create a temporary "lesion". Chica et al. (2011) did this. TMS applied to the right temporo-parietal junction impaired the functioning of the stimulus-driven but not top-down attentional system. TMS applied to the right intraparietal sulcus impaired functioning of both attention systems.

Evidence from brain-damaged patients (discussed more fully later) is also relevant to establishing which brain areas are necessarily involved in goal-directed or stimulus-driven attentional processes. Shomstein et al. (2010) had brain-damaged patients complete two tasks. One task required stimulus-driven attentional processes while the other required top-down processes. Patients having greater problems with top-down than with stimulus-driven attentional processing typically had brain damage to the superior parietal lobule (part of the dorsal attention network). In contrast, patients having greater problems with stimulus-driven attentional processing typically had brain damage to the temporo-parietal junction (often regarded as forming part of the ventral attention network).

Chica et al. (2013) reviewed research on the two attention systems and identified 15 differences between them. For example, stimulus-driven attention is faster than top-down attention and is more object-based. In addition, it is more resistant to interference from other peripheral cues once activated. The existence of so many differences strengthens the argument that the two attentional systems are separate.

Indovina and Macaluso (2007) tested Corbetta et al.'s (2008) assumption that the bottom-up attentional system is affected more by task-relevant than salient distractors. Participants reported the orientation of a coloured letter T in the presence of a letter T in a different colour (task-relevant distractor) or a flickering draughtboard (salient distractor). As predicted, the bottom-up system was activated more by task-relevant distractors than salient ones.

Wen et al. (2012) argued that it is important to study interactions between the two visual attention systems. They assessed brain activation while participants responded to target stimuli in one visual field while ignoring all stimuli in the unattended visual field. There were two main findings. First, stronger causal influences of the top-down system on the stimulus-driven system led to *superior* performance on the task. This finding suggests the appearance of an object at the attended location caused the top-down attention system to suppress activity within the stimulus-driven system.

Second, stronger causal influences of the stimulus-driven system on the top-down system were associated with *impaired* task performance. This finding suggests activation within the stimulus-driven system produced by stimuli not in attentional focus led to a breaking of the attentional set maintained by the top-down system.

Evaluation

The theoretical approach proposed by Corbetta and Shulman (2002) has several successes to its credit. First, there appear to be somewhat separate stimulus-driven and top-down attention systems. Second, each attention system involves its own brain network. Third, research using transcranial magnetic stimulation has shown that major brain areas within each attention system play a causal role in attentional processes. Fourth, some ways in which the two networks interact have been identified. Fifth, as we will see in the next section, research on brain-damaged patients has provided good support for dorsal and ventral attention networks.

What are the limitations with this theoretical approach? First, it has proved hard to identify the precise brain areas associated with each attention system. There are various possible reasons for this. However, one likely reason is that the brain areas involved depend on the detailed requirements of a current task (Talsma et al., 2010). Second, the model is oversimplified. Attentional processes are involved in the performance of numerous tasks and it is unlikely all these processes can be neatly assigned to one or other of the model's attention systems. Third, there is more commonality (especially within the parietal lobe) in the brain areas associated with the two attention networks than was assumed theoretically by Corbetta and Shulman (2002). Fourth, much remains to be discovered about how the two visual attention systems interact.

DISORDERS OF VISUAL ATTENTION

We can learn much about attentional processes by studying brain-damaged individuals. Here we consider two important attentional disorders: neglect and extinction. **Neglect** (or spatial neglect) is a condition in which there is a lack of awareness of stimuli presented to the side of space on the opposite side to the brain damage (the contralesional side).

The brain damage is typically in the *right* hemisphere and there is often little awareness of stimuli on the left side of the visual field. This is known as *subject-centred* or *egocentric neglect*. It occurs because of the nature of the visual system – information from the left side of the visual field proceeds to the right brain hemisphere. When patients cancel targets presented to their left or right side (cancellation task), they generally cross out more of those presented to the right.

KEY TERM

Neglect
A disorder involving right-hemisphere damage (typically) in which the left side of objects and/or objects presented to the left visual field are undetected; the condition resembles **extinction** but is more severe.

When patients try to put a mark through a horizontal line at its centre (line bisection task), they typically put it to the right of the centre.

There is also *object-centred* or *allocentric neglect*. This involves a lack of awareness of the left side of objects rather than simply the left side of the visual field (see Figure 5.7). Object-centred neglect is often more important than subject-centred neglect. Gainotti and Ciaraffa (2013) reviewed research on several patients with right-hemisphere damage who drew the right side of all figures in a multi-object scene but neglected the left side of most of them regardless of whether they were presented to the left or right visual field.

There has been much controversy as to whether object-centred or allocentric neglect and subject-centred or egocentric neglect reflect similar or different underlying disturbance to the attentional system. Rorden et al. (2012) obtained two findings strongly supporting the notion that the two forms of neglect are similar. First, the correlation between the extent of each form of neglect across 33 patients was +0.80. Second, there was a large overlap in the brain regions associated with each type of neglect.

KEY TERMS

Extinction
A disorder of visual attention in which a stimulus presented to the side opposite the brain damage is not detected when another stimulus is presented at the same time to the side of the brain damage.

Extinction is often found in patients with neglect. Extinction involves a failure to detect a stimulus presented to the side opposite the brain damage when a second stimulus is presented to the same side as the brain damage. It is a serious condition because multiple stimuli are typically present at the same time in everyday life. Extinction and neglect are closely related. However, most of the evidence suggests they are separate deficits (de Haan et al., 2012). We will discuss neglect in more detail than extinction because it has attracted more research.

Which brain areas are damaged in neglect patients? Neglect is a heterogeneous condition in which the brain areas involved vary considerably across patients. Molenberghs et al. (2012b) found nine brain areas sometimes damaged in neglect patients in a meta-analysis (see Glossary). The main areas damaged are typically in the right hemisphere and include the superior temporal gyrus, the inferior frontal gyrus, the insula, the supramarginal gyrus and the angular gyrus (Corbetta & Shulman, 2011). Nearly all these areas are located within the stimulus-driven or

Weblink:
Patients with stroke

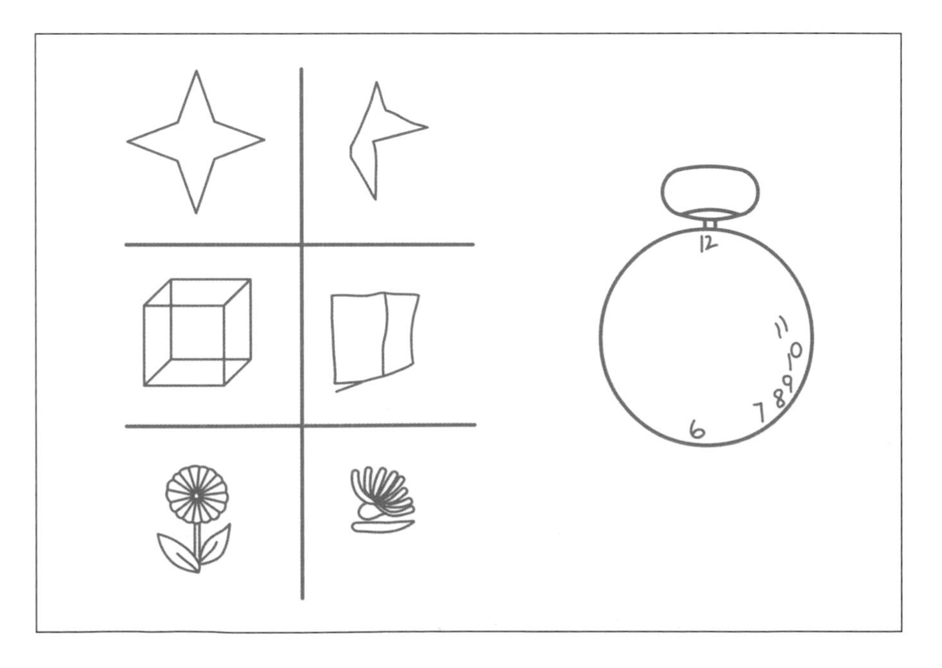

Figure 5.7
Left is a copying task in which a patient with unilateral neglect distorted or ignored the left side of the figures to be copied (shown on the left). Right is a clock-drawing task in which the patient was given a clock face and told to insert the numbers into it.

Reprinted from Danckert and Ferber (2006). Reprinted with permission from Elsevier.

ventral attention network (see Figure 5.6). This suggests the attentional problems of neglect patients depend on brain *networks* rather than simply on specific brain *areas* (Corbetta & Shulman, 2011; Bartolomeo et al., 2012).

Several brain areas can also be damaged in extinction patients. Brain damage is generally centred on the right hemisphere. The temporo-parietal junction and the intraparietal sulcus are especially likely to be damaged (de Haan et al., 2012). When transcranial magnetic stimulation (TMS; see Glossary) is applied to these areas to produce a temporary "lesion", extinction-like behaviour is produced (de Haan et al., 2012).

Conscious awareness and processing

The finding that neglect patients typically report no conscious awareness of stimuli presented to the left visual field does not mean these stimuli are not processed. McGlinchey-Berroth et al. (1993) asked neglect patients to decide whether letter strings formed words. Decision times were faster on "yes" trials when the letter string was preceded by a semantically related object. This effect was the same size regardless of whether the related object was presented to the left or right visual field. Thus, there was some processing of left-field stimuli by neglect patients.

Viggiano et al. (2012) presented pictures of animals and artefacts (e.g., alarm clock, camera) to the left visual field of neglect patients. The patients showed evidence of processing the artefacts but not the animals, perhaps because artefacts trigger information about how to interact with them.

Di Russo et al. (2008) shed additional light on the processing of left-field stimuli by neglect patients using event-related potentials (ERPs; see Glossary). Early processing over the first 130 ms or so after stimulus onset was comparable to that of healthy controls. Only later processing was disrupted by neglect.

Extinction patients also process left-field stimuli presented even though they lack conscious awareness of them. Vuilleumier et al. (2002) presented extinction patients with two pictures at the same time, one to each visual field. The patients showed very little memory for left-field stimuli. After that, the patients identified degraded pictures. There was a facilitation effect for left-field pictures indicating they had been processed.

Sarri et al. (2010) also presented two stimuli together, one to each visual field. Extinction patients had no awareness of stimuli presented to the left visual field. However, these stimuli were associated with activation in early visual processing areas, indicating they were processed to some extent.

Theoretical considerations

Corbetta and Shulman (2011) discussed neglect in the context of their two-system account of visual attention (see earlier discussion). In essence, the bottom-up ventral attention network is typically damaged. However, this damage also impairs the functioning of the goal-directed dorsal attention network even though it is not itself damaged. The assumptions that the ventral network is damaged but the dorsal network is not are supported by the meta-analysis of Molenberghs et al. (2012b), discussed earlier.

How does the damaged ventral attention system impair the functioning of the dorsal attention network? The two attention networks *interact* and so damage to the ventral network inevitably has consequences for the dorsal network. More specifically, damage to the ventral attention network "impairs nonspatial [across the entire visual field] functions, hypoactivates [reduces activation in] the right hemisphere, and unbalances the activity of the dorsal attention network" (Corbetta & Shulman, 2011, p. 592).

De Haan et al. (2012) put forward a theory of extinction based on two major assumptions:

1 "Extinction is a consequence of biased competition for attention between the ipsilesional [right-field] and contralesional [left-field] target stimuli" (p. 1048).
2 Extinction patients have much reduced attentional capacity so it is often the case that only one target [the right-field one] can be detected.

Findings

According to Corbetta and Shulman (2011), the dorsal attention network in neglect patients is typically undamaged but functions poorly because of reduced activation in the right hemisphere and associated reduced alertness and attentional resources. It follows that neglect patients might show enhanced ability to detect visual targets presented to the left visual field if attempts were made to increase their general alertness. Robertson et al. (1998) tested this prediction. Neglect patients became aware of stimuli presented to the left visual field half a second later than stimuli presented to the right visual field. However, this evidence of neglect was no longer present when warning sounds were presented to increase alertness.

Related evidence indicates neglect patients have reduced attentional resources (Bonato, 2012). For example, consider a study by Bonato et al. (2010). They considered the ability of neglect patients to detect targets in the left visual field. Sometimes this was done while performing another, attentionally demanding task at the same time. Healthy participants performed this task almost perfectly with or without the additional task. In contrast, neglect patients' ability to detect targets was markedly worse in the presence of the additional task. This is as predicted on the assumption that neglect patients have limited attentional resources.

It is assumed by Corbetta and Shulman (2011) that neglect patients have an essentially intact dorsal attention network but reduced attentional resources. It follows that such patients might use that network reasonably effectively provided steps were taken to facilitate its use. Duncan et al. (1999) presented arrays of letters briefly, and asked neglect patients to recall all the letters or only those in a pre-specified colour. The dorsal attention network can be used only in the latter condition. As expected, recall of letters presented to the left side of the visual field was much worse than that of right-side letters when all had to be reported. However, neglect patients resembled healthy controls in showing equal recall of letters presented to each side of visual space when they were defined by colour.

The two attention networks typically work closely together. This issue was addressed by Bays et al. (2010), who studied neglect patients having damage to the posterior parietal cortex. They used eye movements during visual search to assess patients' problems with top-down and stimulus-driven attentional processes. Both types of attentional processes were equally impaired (as predicted by Corbetta and Shulman (2011)). Of most importance, there was a remarkably high correlation of +0.98 between these two types of attentional deficit.

We turn now to research on extinction patients. According to de Haan et al. (2012), a major factor producing extinction is biased competition between stimuli. If two stimuli can be *integrated*, that might minimise competition and so reduce extinction. Riddoch et al. (2006) tested this prediction by presenting objects used together often (e.g., wine bottle and wine glass) or never (e.g., wine bottle and ball). Extinction patients identified both objects more often in the former condition than the latter (65% vs. 40%, respectively). Thus, extinction patients can reduce extinction when two stimuli can be combined rather than competing with each other.

There are other ways of testing the biased competition hypothesis. For example, we could impair attentional processes in the intact left hemisphere by applying transcranial magnetic stimulation (TMS; see Glossary) to it. This should reduce competition from the left hemisphere and thus produce lower rates of extinction. The findings are somewhat mixed, but some are consistent with this prediction (Oliveri & Caltagirone, 2006).

De Haan et al. (2012) also identified reduced attentional capacity as a factor causing extinction. In a study discussed earlier, Bonato et al. (2010) studied extinction with or without the addition of a second, attentionally demanding task in extinction patients. As predicted, there was a substantial increase in the extinction rate (from 18% to over 80%) with this additional task.

Reducing neglect

How can we reduce neglect? Remember that Corbetta and Shulman (2011) argued that neglect occurs in part because of reduced alertness. Thus, training to enhance alertness should reduce the symptoms of neglect. Thimm et al. (2009) obtained support for this prediction. At the end of an alertness training course, neglect patients showed improved alertness and reduced neglect.

When neglect patients in the dark try to point straight ahead, they typically point several degrees off to the right. Rossetti et al. (1998) wondered whether this bias could be corrected by having neglect patients wear prisms shifting the visual field 10 degrees to the right. After adaptation, the patients in the dark pointed almost directly ahead and showed reduced bias on several tasks. Newport and Schenk (2012) reviewed research on prism adaptation and concluded it has generally (but not always) proved effective.

Why does prism adaptation have such beneficial effects? Nijboer et al. (2008) found prism-adaptation training made it easier for neglect patients to use goal-directed processes to shift attention leftwards voluntarily. This voluntary attentional shift compensated for their habitual rightward bias. In contrast, prism-adaptation training had no effect on the stimulus-driven attention system.

Overall evaluation

Research on neglect and extinction patients has produced several important findings. First, such patients can process unattended visual stimuli in the absence of conscious awareness of those stimuli. Second, most findings with neglect patients suggest they have damage to the ventral attention network leading to impaired functioning of the undamaged intact dorsal attention network. Third, extinction seems to occur because of biased competition for attention and reduced attentional capacity. Fourth, training programmes designed to reduce the symptoms of neglect have shed light on its underlying processes.

KEY TERM

Visual search
A task involving the rapid detection of a specified target stimulus within a visual display.

What are the limitations of research in this area? First, the precise symptoms and regions of brain damage vary considerably across patients. This makes it hard to produce theoretical accounts applicable to all neglect or extinction patients. Second, the relationship between neglect and extinction remains unclear. However, it is generally assumed they are separate conditions with similar underlying processes. Third, the dorsal and ventral attention networks in neglect patients may interact more than is generally assumed (Bays et al., 2010).

VISUAL SEARCH

We spend much of our time searching for various objects. For example, we try to spot a friend in a large group. The processes involved in such activities have been examined in research on **visual search** in which a specified target is detected

IN THE REAL WORLD: SECURITY CHECKS

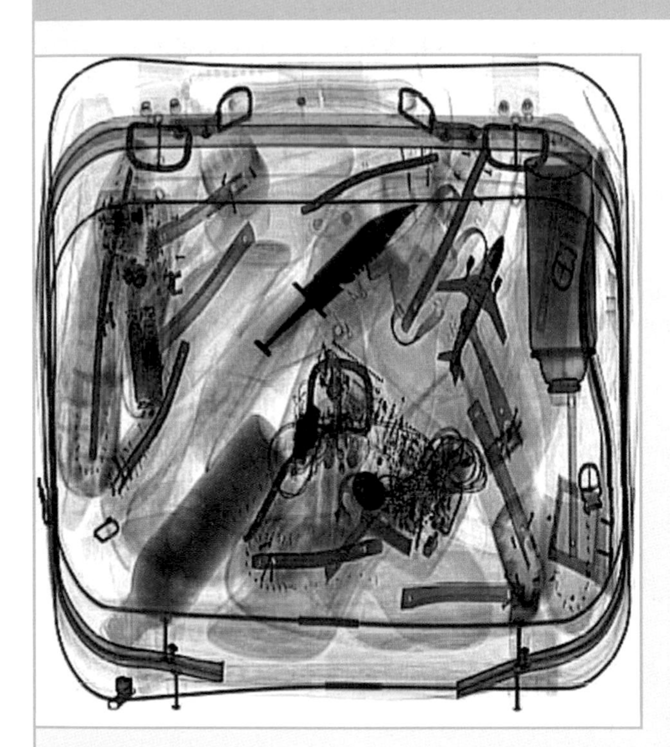

Figure 5.8
See if you can spot the dangerous weapon. It is located a little above the centre of the picture. Its blade and shaft are dark blue and the handle is orange.
From McCarley et al. (2004). Reprinted with permission of the Association for Psychological Science.

Airport security checks have become more thorough since 9/11. When your luggage is X-rayed, an airport security screener sits by the X-ray machine searching for illegal and dangerous items (see Figure 5.8). Training ensures this type of visual search is effective. However, mistakes do occur. For example, on 17 November 2002, a man slipped through security at Ben Gurion airport in Tel Aviv with a pocketknife. He then tried to storm the cockpit of El Al flight 581 en route to Istanbul.

There are two major reasons why it is hard for airport security screeners to detect dangerous items. First, security screeners are looking for a wide range of different objects including knives, guns and improvised explosive devices. This poses special problems. In one study (Menneer et al., 2009), observers detected two categories of objects (metal threats and improvised explosive devices). Some observers looked for both categories on each trial (dual-target search), whereas others looked for only a single category (single-target search). Target detection was worse with dual-target than single-target search.

In the experiment above, the two target categories did not share any obvious features (e.g., colour, shape). When the two categories shared a feature (colour), target detection was comparable in the dual-target and single-target conditions (Menneer et al., 2009). Observers form a search template based on target representations to enable them to detect targets (Bravo & Farid, 2012). When the targets share a colour, this reduces the complexity of observers' search templates.

Second, illegal and dangerous items are (thankfully!) present in only a minute fraction of passengers' luggage. The rarity of targets makes it hard for airport security screeners to detect them. Wolfe et al. (2007) addressed this issue. Observers looked at X-ray images of packed bags and the targets were weapons (knives or guns). When targets appeared on 50% of trials, 80% were detected. When targets appeared on 2% of trials, only 54% were detected.

Why was performance so poor with rare targets? The main reason was excessive caution about reporting a target because each target was so unexpected. There are various ways in which performance on rare targets can be improved. Schwark et al. (2012) gave false feedback to observers indicating they had missed rare targets. This reduced their cautiousness about reporting targets and improved performance. In similar fashion, airport security screeners are often presented with fictional threat items incorporated into the X-ray images of passenger bags. Artificially increasing the number of threat targets improves detection performance (von Bastian et al., 2010).

Finally, there are important individual differences in ability to detect targets. Rusconi et al. (2012) assessed threat-detection performance using security X-ray images. Individuals rating themselves high in attention to detail had superior target-detection performance to those low in attention to detail.

as rapidly as possible. We start by considering an important real-world situation in which visual search can be literally a matter of life-or-death: airport security checks. After that, we consider a very influential theory of visual search before moving on to more recent theoretical and empirical developments.

Feature integration theory

Feature integration theory was put forward by Treisman and Gelade (1980) and subsequently updated and modified (e.g., Treisman, 1998). Within the theory, there is an important distinction between object features (e.g., colour, size, line orientation) and the objects themselves.

There are two processing stages. First, basic visual features are processed rapidly and preattentively in parallel across the visual scene. Second, there is a slower serial process with focused attention providing the "glue" to form objects from the available features. For example, an object of a particular shape and yellow in colour is interpreted as a banana. In the absence of focused attention, features from different objects may be combined randomly producing an **illusory conjunction**.

It follows from the above assumptions that targets defined by a single feature (e.g., a blue letter or an S) should be detected rapidly and in parallel. In contrast, targets defined by a conjunction or combination of features (e.g., a green letter T) should be slower to detect and should require attention.

KEY TERM

Illusory conjunction
Mistakenly combining features from two different stimuli to perceive an object that is not present.

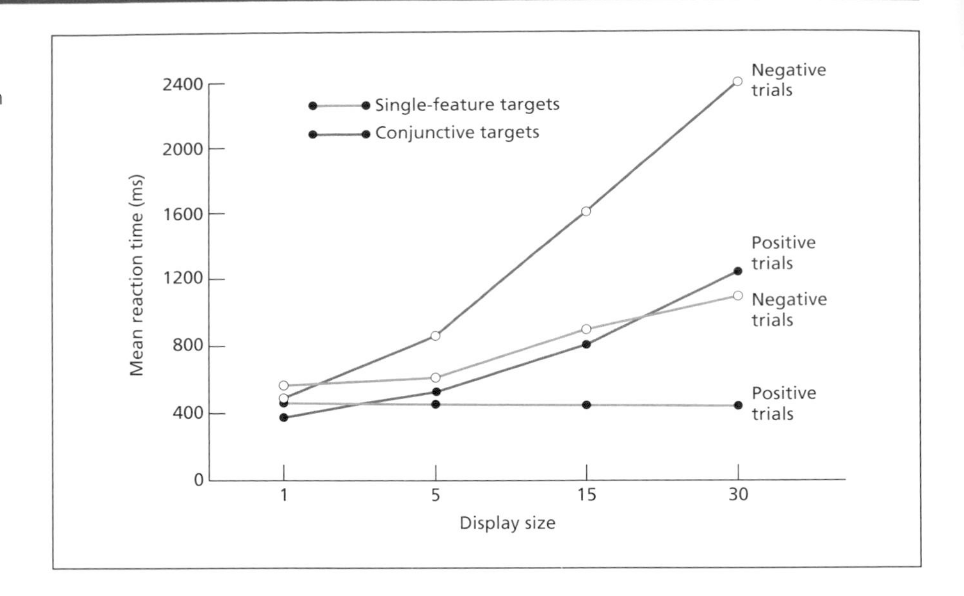

Figure 5.9
Performance speed on a detection task as a function of target definition (conjunctive vs. single feature) and display size.
Adapted from Treisman and Gelade (1980).

Weblink:
Download software

Findings

Treisman and Gelade (1980) tested the above predictions in a study in which the participants searched for targets defined by a single feature or by a conjunction of features. The set or display size varied between 1 and 30 items and a target was present or absent.

Treisman and Gelade's (1980) findings were as predicted (see Figure 5.9). Responding was rapid and there was very little effect of display size when the target was defined by a single feature – these findings suggest there was parallel processing of the items. In contrast, responding was slower and there was a large effect of display size when the target was defined by a conjunction of features – these findings suggest there was serial processing.

According to feature integration theory, lack of focused attention can produce illusory conjunctions involving random combinations of features. Friedman-Hill et al. (1995) studied a brain-damaged patient having problems with the accurate location of visual stimuli. He produced many illusory conjunctions combining the shape of one stimulus with the colour of another.

Limitations

Speed of visual search does *not* depend only on the target characteristics emphasised by Treisman and Gelade (1980). Duncan and Humphreys (1989, 1992) identified two additional factors. First, search is faster when the distractors are very similar to each other because it is easier to identify them as distractors.

Second, there is similarity between the target and distractors. The number of distractors has a large effect on time to detect even targets defined by a single feature when targets resemble distractors (Duncan & Humphreys, 1989). Visual search for targets defined by more than one feature is typically limited to those distractors sharing at least one of the target's features. For example, if looking for a blue circle in a display containing blue triangles, red circles and red triangles, you would ignore red triangles.

According to the original version of feature integration theory, feature processing is necessarily parallel, and subsequent, attention-driven processing is serial. This is an oversimplification. As Wolfe (1998, p. 20) pointed out:

> Results of visual search experiments run from flat to steep RT [reaction time] × set size functions. The continuum [continuous distribution] of search slopes does make it implausible to think that the search tasks, themselves, can be neatly classified as serial or parallel.

How do we know whether visual search is parallel or serial? We can address this issue by using multiple targets. Suppose all the stimuli are targets. If processing is serial (one item at a time), the first item analysed will *always* be a target, and so target-detection times should not depend on the number of items in the display. If processing is parallel, however, observers could take in information from *all* the targets simultaneously. The more targets there are, the more information is available. Thus, target-detection time should decrease as target numbers increase.

Thornton and Gilden (2007) used single-target and multiple-target trials with 29 different visual tasks. The pattern suggestive of parallel processing was found with search tasks when targets and distractors differed only along a single feature dimension (e.g., colour, size). This pattern is consistent with feature integration theory. The pattern suggestive of serial processing was found with complex visual tasks involving the detection of specific direction of rotation (e.g., pinwheels rotating clockwise).

What conclusions can we draw? First, some visual search tasks involve parallel search whereas others involve serial search. Second, Thornton and Gilden (2007) found 72% of the tasks seemed to involve parallel processing and only 28% serial processing. Thus, parallel processing in visual search is more common than assumed by Treisman and Gelade (1980). Third, serial processing is limited to tasks that are especially complex and have the longest target-detection times.

Texture tiling model

According to Treisman's feature integration theory, the greatest problem in visual search is *attention*. Rosenholtz et al. (2012a) argued that the theory attaches too much importance to attention in the context of visual search. Attention may be necessary when the task is to detect a rotated "T" among rotated "L"s. In the real world, however, the major problem in visual search, according to Rosenholtz et al., lies in *perception*. If we fixate a scene, the central area can be seen clearly but there is an increasing loss of information in more peripheral areas. According to Rosenholtz et al., we can represent this information in terms of varying textures at different differences from central fixation: the texture tiling model.

Freeman and Simoncelli (2011) estimated the information available in a single fixation. They presented observers briefly with two different (but related) stimuli viewed at a central fixation point. These stimuli were followed by a third stimulus identical to one of the first two. The observers decided which of the first two stimuli matched the third. Examples of the stimuli used are shown in Figure 5.10. The key finding was that observers could not distinguish between original photographs and those with gross peripheral distortions. Why isn't our conscious perception of the world blurred? We use top-down processes to construct a clear image.

Figure 5.10
Undistorted photograph of the Brunnen der Lebensfreude in Rostock, Germany (left-hand picture) and distorted versions of it (middle and right-hand pictures). With rapid presentation and fixation at the centre (red dot), the two distorted versions appeared nearly identical to each other and to the undistorted photograph.
From Freeman and Simoncelli (2011). Reproduced with permission from Nature Publishing Group.

What is the relevance of this to visual search? Rosenholtz et al. (2012b) argued that performance on visual search tasks is determined mainly by the information contained in (or omitted from) perceptual representations of the visual field. More specifically, visual search is relatively easy when the information in peripheral vision is sufficient to direct attention to the target but hard when such information is insufficient.

Rosenholtz et al. (2012b) tested the above hypothesis using five visual search tasks. They recorded speed of target detection on each task. They also presented participants with blurred images of target + distractor and distractor-only displays having the same limited peripheral information as found in perception. Participants had to *discriminate* between the two display types. Performance speed on the visual search tasks was predicted almost perfectly by the informativeness (or otherwise) of peripheral vision as revealed by discrimination accuracy.

Evaluation

The texture tiling model has contributed much to our understanding of visual search. It appears the information in peripheral vision is much more important in visual search than had been assumed. Conversely, the role of selective attention is probably less important. We saw earlier (Thornton & Gilden, 2007) that most visual search tasks depend on parallel rather than serial processing. This makes perfect sense given that several different kinds of information are typically processed in peripheral vision.

What are the limitations of the model? First, more remains to be discovered about the extent to which observers can use information in peripheral vision to detect targets on visual search tasks. Second, Rosenholtz et al. (2012b) accepted that selective attention often plays a role in visual search, but did not identify *when* it is used. Third, there may be complexities about peripheral vision not explicit in the model. For example, Young and Hulleman (2013) found that observers' visual field was smaller with hard visual search tasks than with easy ones.

Dual-path model

In most of the research discussed so far, the target was equally likely to appear anywhere within the visual display and so search was essentially *random*. This is very different from the real world. Suppose you are outside in the garden looking for your cat. Your visual search would be highly *selective* – you would ignore the sky and focus mostly on the ground (and perhaps the trees). Thus, your search would involve top-down processes based on your knowledge of where cats are most likely to be found.

Ehinger et al. (2009) studied top-down processes in visual search. They recorded eye fixations of observers searching for a person in numerous real-world outdoor scenes. Observers typically fixated the regions of each scene most likely to be relevant (e.g., pavements or sidewalks) and ignored irrelevant regions (e.g., sky, trees) (see Figure 5.11). Observers also fixated locations that differed considerably from neighbouring regions and areas containing visual features characteristic of a human figure.

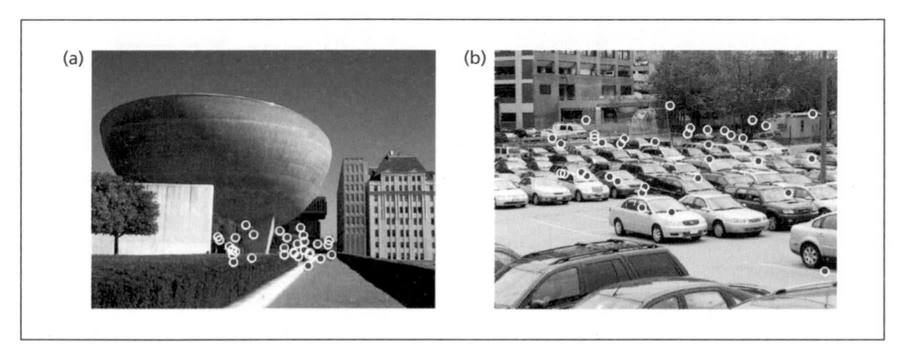

Figure 5.11
The first three eye fixations made by observers searching for pedestrians. As can be seen, the great majority of their fixations were on regions in which pedestrians would most likely be found. Observers' fixations were much more similar in the left-hand photo than in the right-hand one, because there are fewer likely regions in the left-hand one.
From Ehinger et al. (2009). Reprinted with permission from Taylor & Francis.

How can we account for these findings as well as those discussed earlier? Wolfe et al. (2011b) put forward a dual-path model (see Figure 5.12). There is a *selective* pathway of limited capacity (indicated by the bottleneck) in which objects are individually selected for recognition. This pathway has been the subject of most research until recent times.

There is also a *non-selective* pathway in which the "gist" or essence of a scene is processed. Such processing can then help to direct or guide processing within the selective pathway (represented by the arrow labelled "Guidance"). This pathway is of far more use in the real world than traditional laboratory research. It allows us to take advantage of our stored knowledge of the environment (e.g., the typical layout of a kitchen).

Findings

Wolfe et al. (2011a) compared visual search for objects presented within a scene setting or at random locations against a white background. As predicted, the rate

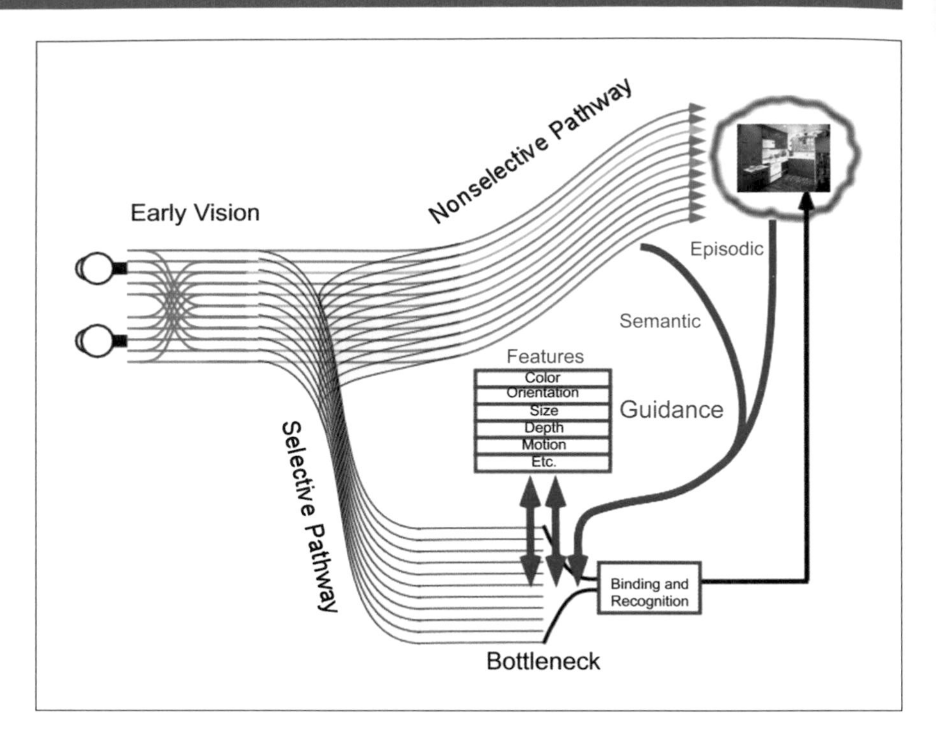

Figure 5.12
A two-pathway model of visual search. The selective pathway is capacity limited and can bind stimulus features and recognise objects. The non-selective pathway processes the gist of scenes. Selective and non-selective processing occur in parallel to produce effective visual search.
From Wolfe et al. (2011b). Reprinted with permission from Elsevier.

of search was much faster in the scene setting (10 ms per item vs. 40 ms per item, respectively). They explained this difference in terms of what they called "functional set size" – visual search in scenes is efficient because observers can eliminate most regions because they are very unlikely to contain the object.

Strong support for the notion of functional set size was reported by Võ and Wolfe (2012) in a study in which observers detected objects in scenes (e.g., a jam jar in a kitchen). The key finding was that 80% of each scene was rarely fixated by observers. For example, they did not look at the sink or cupboard doors when searching for a jam jar.

The findings of Võ and Wolfe (2012) show we can use our *general* knowledge of scenes to facilitate visual search. Hollingworth (2012) wondered whether *specific* knowledge of scenes would also enhance visual search. Their participants performed a visual search task for objects in scenes. Some had previously viewed the scenes with instructions to decide which object was least likely to appear in a scene of that type. Visual search was significantly faster when the specific scenes used had been seen previously, indicating the usefulness of specific scene knowledge.

More evidence that *learning* where targets are likely to be found often plays a major role in visual search was reported by Chukoskie et al. (2013). An invisible target was presented at random locations within a relatively small area on a blank screen. Observers were rewarded by hearing a tone when they fixated the target.

There was a strong learning effect – fixations were initially distributed across the entire screen but rapidly became increasingly focused on the area within which the target might be present (see Figure 5.13).

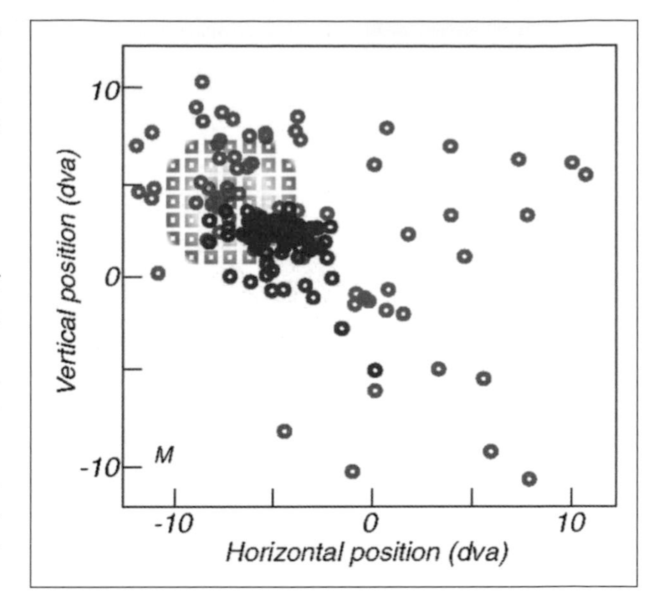

Figure 5.13
The region of the screen fixated on early trials (blue circles) and on later trials (red circles).
From Chukoskie et al. (2013). © National Academy of Sciences. Reproduced with permission.

Evaluation

Our knowledge of likely and unlikely locations of any given object in a scene is the most important determinant of visual search in the real world. The dual-path model is an advance on most previous theories of visual search in that it fully recognises the importance of scene knowledge. The notion that scene knowledge facilitates visual search by reducing functional set size is an important theoretical contribution that has received much support.

What are the limitations of the dual-path model? First, the processes involved in using gist knowledge of a scene extremely rapidly to reduce the search area remain unclear. Second, there is insufficient focus on the learning processes that often greatly facilitate visual search. For example, experts in several domains detect target information faster and more accurately than non-experts (see Gegenfurtner et al., 2011; see also Chapter 12). The model would need to be developed further to account for such effects.

CROSS-MODAL EFFECTS

Nearly all the research discussed so far is limited in that the visual (or auditory) modality was studied on its own. This approach has been justified on the grounds that attentional processes in each sensory modality (e.g., vision, hearing) operate *independently* from those in other modalities. That assumption is incorrect. In the real world, we often coordinate information from two or more sense modalities at the same time (**cross-modal attention**). An example is lip reading, in which we use visual information about a speaker's lip movements to facilitate our understanding of what they are saying (see Chapter 9).

Suppose we present participants with two streams of lights (as was done by Eimer and Schröger (1998)), with one stream of lights being presented to the left and the other to the right. At the same time, we also present participants with two streams of sounds (one to each side). In one condition, participants detect deviant *visual* events (e.g., longer than usual stimuli) presented to one side only. In the other condition, participants detect deviant *auditory* events in only one stream.

Event-related potentials (ERPs; see Glossary) were recorded to obtain information about the allocation of attention. Unsurprisingly, Eimer and Schröger (1998) found ERPs to deviant stimuli in the *relevant* modality were greater to stimuli presented on the to-be-attended side than the to-be-ignored side. Thus, participants allocated attention as instructed. Of more interest is what happened

KEY TERM

Cross-modal attention
The coordination of attention across two or more modalities (e.g., vision and audition).

KEY TERM

Ventriloquism effect
The mistaken perception that sounds are coming from their apparent source (as in ventriloquism).

to the allocation of attention in the *irrelevant* modality. Suppose participants detected *visual* targets on the left side. In that case, ERPs to deviant *auditory* stimuli were greater on the left side than the right. This is a cross-modal effect in which the voluntary or endogenous allocation of visual attention also affected the allocation of auditory attention. In similar fashion, when participants detected *auditory* targets on one side, ERPs to deviant *visual* stimuli on the same side were greater than ERPs to those on the opposite side. Thus, the allocation of auditory attention influenced the allocation of visual attention as well.

Ventriloquism effect

What happens when there is a *conflict* between simultaneous visual and auditory stimuli? We will focus on the **ventriloquism effect** in which sounds are misperceived as coming from their apparent visual source. Ventriloquists speak without moving their lips while manipulating the mouth movements of a dummy. It seems as if the dummy rather than the ventriloquist is speaking. Something similar happens at the movies. We look at the actors on the screen and see their lips moving. The sounds of their voices are actually coming from loudspeakers to the side of the screen, but we hear those voices coming from their mouths.

Certain conditions need to be satisfied for the ventriloquist illusion to occur (Recanzone & Sutter, 2008). First, the visual and auditory stimuli must occur close together in time. Second, the sound must match *expectations* raised by the visual stimulus (e.g., high-pitched sound apparently coming from a small object). Third, the sources of the visual and auditory stimuli should be close together in space.

The ventriloquism effect is an example of visual dominance (visual information dominating perception). Further evidence of visual dominance is available in the Colavita effect (Colavita, 1974). Participants are presented with a random sequence of stimuli and press one key for visual stimuli and another for auditory stimuli. Occasionally, auditory and visual stimuli are presented simultaneously and participants press both keys. On these trials, participants nearly always respond to the visual stimulus but sometimes fail to respond to the simultaneous auditory one (Spence et al., 2011).

It has often been assumed the ventriloquism effect occurs automatically. Supportive evidence is that the effect is still present even when participants are aware of the spatial discrepancy between the visual and auditory input. However, Maiworm et al. (2012) found the ventriloquism effect was smaller when participants had previously heard syllables spoken in a fearful voice. This suggests the effect is *not* entirely automatic and can be reduced when the relevance of the auditory channel is increased.

Why does vision capture sound in the ventriloquism effect? The visual modality typically provides more precise information about spatial location. However, when visual stimuli are severely blurred and poorly localised, sound captures vision (Alais & Burr, 2004). Thus, we combine visual and auditory information effectively by attaching more weight to the more informative sense modality.

Temporal ventriloquism

The above explanation for the ventriloquist illusion is a development of the modality appropriateness and precision hypothesis (Welch & Warren, 1980). According to this hypothesis, when conflicting information is presented in two or more modalities, the modality having the best acuity generally dominates. That hypothesis predicts the existence of another illusion. The auditory modality is typically more precise than the visual modality at discriminating temporal relations. As a result, judgements about the temporal onset of visual stimuli might be biased by asynchronous auditory stimuli presented very shortly beforehand or afterwards. Chen and Vroomen (2013) called this predicted effect temporal ventriloquism.

Chen and Vroomen (2013) review several studies providing evidence of temporal ventriloquism. A simple example is when the apparent onset of a flash is shifted towards an abrupt sound presented slightly asynchronously (see Figure 5.14). Other research has found that the apparent duration of visual stimuli can be distorted by asynchronous auditory stimuli.

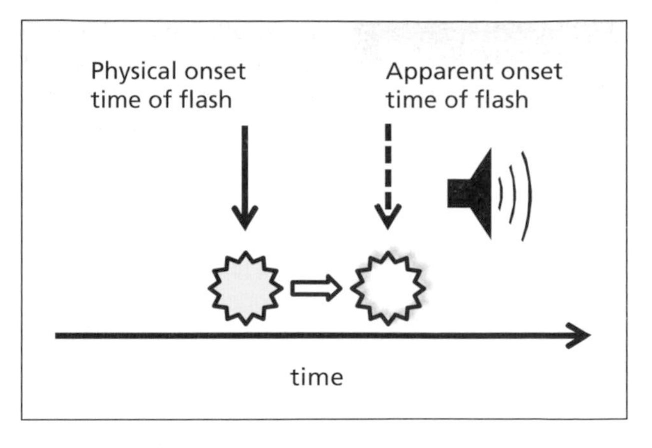

Figure 5.14
An example of temporal ventriloquism in which the apparent time of onset of a flash is shifted towards that of a sound presented at a slightly different timing than the flash.
From Chen and Vroomen (2013). Reprinted with permission from Springer.

IN THE REAL WORLD: USING WARNING SIGNALS TO PROMOTE SAFE DRIVING

Front-to-rear-end collisions cause 25% of road accidents, and driver inattention is the most common cause of such collisions (Spence, 2012). Thus, it is important to devise effective warning signals to enhance driver attention and reduce collisions. Warning signals (e.g., car horn) might be useful in *alerting* the driver to potential danger. Warning signals might be especially useful if they were *informative* because there was a relationship between the signal and the nature of the danger. However, it would probably be counterproductive if informative warning signals required time-consuming cognitive processing.

Ho and Spence (2005) studied the effects of an auditory warning signal (car horn) on drivers' reaction times when braking to avoid a car in front or accelerating to avoid a speeding car behind. The auditory signals were presented to the front or rear of the driver. In one experiment, the sound came from the same direction as the critical visual event on 80% of trials. In another experiment, the direction of the sound did not predict the direction of the critical visual event (i.e., it was from the same direction on only 50% of trials).

What did Ho and Spence (2005) find? First, reaction times were faster in both experiments when the sound and critical visual event were from the same direction (i.e., the sound cues were valid). Second, these beneficial effects were greater when sound and visual event came from the same direction on 80% rather than 50% of trials.

KEY TERMS

Exogenous spatial attention
Attention to a given spatial location determined by "automatic" processes.

Endogenous spatial attention
Attention to a stimulus controlled by intentions or goal-directed mechanisms.

What do the above findings mean? First, auditory stimuli influence visual attention. Second, the finding that the auditory signal influenced visual attention even when non-predictive probably depended on **exogenous spatial attention** ("automatic" allocation of attention). Third, the finding that the beneficial effects of auditory signals were greater when they were predictive than when they were non-predictive suggests the additional involvement of **endogenous spatial attention** (controlled by the individual's intentions). Thus, the informativeness of the warning signal is important.

Subtle effects of warning informativeness were studied by Gray (2011). Drivers had to brake to avoid a collision with the car in front. Auditory warning signals increased in intensity as the time to collision reduced and the rate of increase varied across conditions. In another condition, a car horn sounded. All the auditory signals speeded up brake reaction time compared to a no-warning control condition. The most effective condition was the one in which the rate of increase in the auditory signal was the fastest because this was the condition implying that the time to collision was the least.

Vibrotactile signals produce the perception of vibration through touch. Gray et al. (2014) studied the effects of such signals on speed of braking to avoid a collision. Signals were presented at three different sites on the abdomen arranged vertically. In the most effective condition, successive signals moved towards the driver's head at an increasing rate that reflected the speed he/she was approaching the car in front. Braking time was 250 ms less in this condition than in a no-warning control condition. This condition was effective because it was highly informative.

In sum, research in cross-modal attention shows great promise for reducing road accidents. One limitation is that warning signals occur much more frequently in the laboratory than in real driving. Another limitation is that it is sometimes unclear why some warning signals are more effective than others. For example, Gray et al. (2014) found that upwards moving vibrotactile stimulation was more effective than the same stimulation moving downwards.

Overall evaluation

What are the limitations of research on cross-modal effects? First, our theoretical understanding has lagged behind the accumulation of empirical findings as we saw in the discussion of the effects of warning signals on driver performance. Second, much of the research has involved complex, artificial tasks and it would be useful to investigate cross-modal effects in more naturalistic conditions. Third, individual differences have been ignored in most research. However, there is accumulating evidence that individual differences (e.g., in preference for auditory or visual stimuli) influences cross-modal effects (see van Atteveldt et al. (2014) for a review).

DIVIDED ATTENTION: DUAL-TASK PERFORMANCE

Your life is probably becoming busier and busier. In our hectic 24/7 lives, people increasingly try to do two things at once (multitasking). For example, you may send text messages to friends while watching television or walking down the street. Ophir et al. (2009) used a questionnaire (the Media Multitasking Index) to identify individuals who engage in high and low levels of multitasking. They argued that there are disadvantages associated with being a high multitasker. More specifically, they found high multitaskers were more susceptible to distraction than low multitaskers.

Ophir et al. (2009) concluded that those attending to several media simultaneously develop "breadth-based cognitive control", meaning they are not selective or discriminating in their allocation of attention. In contrast, low multitaskers are more likely to have top-down attentional control. These conclusions were supported by Cain and Mitroff (2011). Only low multitaskers made effective use of top-down instructions to reduce distraction and enhance performance.

In some ways, Ophir et al.'s (2009) findings are surprising. We might expect that prolonged practice at multitasking would have various beneficial effects on attentional processes. For example, we might expect that high multitaskers would be better able than low multitaskers to split attention between two non-adjacent visual locations (split attention is discussed earlier in the chapter) at the same time. Evidence supporting that expectation was reported by Yap and Lim (2013).

Alzahabi and Becker (2013) investigated task switching. A digit and a letter were presented on each trial and a task (digit odd or even?, letter vowel or consonant?) had to be performed on one of the stimuli. On 50% of trials, the type of stimulus to be classified switched from the previous trial, whereas it remained the same on the other (repeat) trials. The key finding was that the high multitaskers showed more efficient task switching than low multitaskers (see Figure 5.15). Thus, high multitasking is associated with beneficial effects on some aspects of attentional control.

Care needs to be taken in interpreting the above findings because all that has been found is an *association* between multitasking and measures of attention. That means we do not know whether high levels of multitasking influence attentional processing or whether individuals with certain patterns of attention choose to engage in extensive multitasking.

What determines how well we can perform two tasks at the same time? The degree of similarity of the two tasks is one important factor. Two tasks can be similar in stimulus modality. Treisman and Davies (1973) found two monitoring tasks interfered with each other much more when the stimuli on both tasks were in the same modality (visual or auditory).

Two tasks can also be similar in response modality. McLeod (1977) showed the importance of this factor. His participants performed a continuous tracking task with manual responding together with a tone-identification task. Some participants responded vocally to the tones whereas others responded with the hand not involved in tracking. Tracking performance was worse with high response similarity (manual responses on both tasks) than with low response similarity.

Probably the most important factor in determining how well two tasks can be performed together is practice. We all know the saying, "Practice makes perfect", and evidence apparently supporting it was reported by Spelke et al. (1976). Two students (Diane and John) received five hours' training a week for

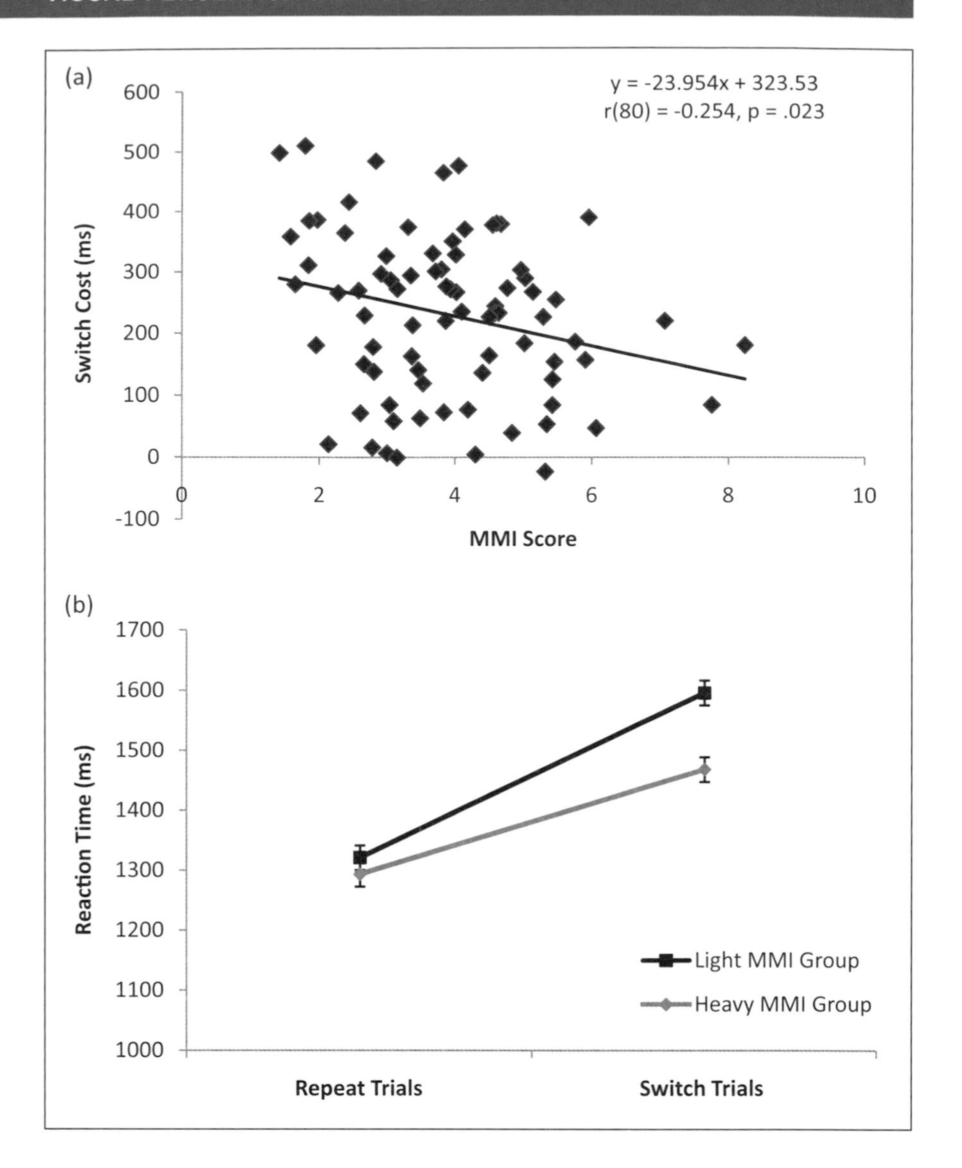

Figure 5.15
(a) Relationship between amount of multitasking (measured by the Media Multitasking Index) and switch cost in ms (switch reaction time – repeat reaction time). (b) Mean reaction times for low and high multitaskers on repeat and switch trials.
From Alazahabi and Becker (2013). © American Psychological Association.

IN THE REAL WORLD: CAN WE THINK AND DRIVE?

Driving a car is the riskiest activity engaged in by tens of millions of adults. More than 40 countries have passed laws restricting the use of handheld mobile or cell phones by drivers to increase car safety. Are such restrictions really necessary? Strayer et al. (2011) reviewed the evidence. The likelihood of drivers being involved in a car accident is *four* times greater when using a mobile phone (whether handheld or hands-free). Overall, 28% of car crashes in the United States are caused by drivers using mobile phones.

Numerous studies have considered the effects of using mobile phones on simulated driving tasks. Caird et al. (2008) reviewed the findings from 33 studies. Reaction times to events (e.g., onset of brake lights on the car in front) increased by 250 ms compared to no-phone control conditions. The figure was similar whether drivers used handheld or hands-free phones and was larger when they were talking rather than listening. Caird et al. found drivers had very limited awareness of the negative impact of using mobile phones – they did not slow down or keep a greater distance behind the car in front.

The 250 ms slowing reported by Caird et al. (2008) may sound trivial. However, it translates into travelling an extra 18 feet (5.5 m) before stopping for a motorist doing 50 mph (80 kph). This could be the difference between stopping just short of a child in the road or killing that child.

It could be argued that laboratory findings do not apply to real-life driving situations. However, Strayer et al. (2011) discussed a study in which drivers in naturalistic conditions were observed to see whether they obeyed a law requiring them to stop at a road junction. Of drivers not using a mobile phone, 21% failed to stop completely compared to 75% of mobile-phone users.

Theoretical considerations

Why does using a mobile phone impair driving ability? One possibility is that the two activities both require some of the same *specific* processes. Bergen et al. (2013) asked drivers performing a simulated driving task to decide whether statements were true or false. Some statements had motor (e.g., "To use scissors, you have to use both hands") or visual (e.g., "A camel has fur on the top of his humps") content, whereas others were more abstract (e.g., "There are 12 wonders of the ancient world"). Only motor and visual statements interfered with driving performance as assessed by the distance from the vehicle in front. These findings suggest that language involving specific processes (e.g., visual or motor) in common with driving can have a disruptive effect.

In spite of the above findings, most theorists have emphasised that the adverse effects of mobile-phone use on driving depend primarily on rather *general* attentional and other cognitive processes. Strayer et al. (2011) identified two relevant attentional processes.

First, driving can cause inattentional blindness, in which an unexpected object is not perceived (see Chapter 4). In a study by Strayer and Drews (2007), 30 objects (e.g., pedestrians, advertising hoardings) were clearly in view as participants performed a simulated driving task. This was followed by an unexpected test of recognition memory for the objects. Those who had used a mobile phone on the driving task recognised far fewer of the objects they had fixated than did those who had not used a phone (under 25% vs. 50%, respectively).

Strayer and Drews (2007) obtained stronger evidence that using mobile phones impairs attentional processes in another experiment. Participants responded as rapidly as possible to the onset of the brake lights on the car in front and event-related potentials (ERPs; see Glossary) were recorded. The magnitude of the P300 (a positive wave associated with attention) was reduced by 50% in mobile-phone users.

Second, Strayer et al. (2011) discussed an unpublished study in which drivers' eye movements on a simulated driving task were recorded. Drivers using hands-free phones were more likely than non-phone users to focus almost exclusively on the road ahead and so were less likely to see peripheral objects. This reduced attentional flexibility of phone users can be very dangerous if, for example, a young child is by the side of the road.

four months on various tasks. Their first task was to read short stories for comprehension while writing down words to dictation, which they initially found very hard. After six weeks of training, however, they could read as rapidly and with as much comprehension when taking dictation as when only reading. After further training, Diane and John learned to write down the names of the categories to which the dictated words belonged while maintaining normal reading speed and comprehension.

Spelke et al. (1976) found practice can dramatically improve people's ability to perform two tasks together. However, their findings are hard to interpret for various reasons. First, they focused on accuracy measures, which can be less sensitive to dual-task interference than speed measures. Second, the reading task gave Diane and John flexibility in terms of *when* they attended to the reading matter, and so they may have alternated attention between tasks. More controlled research on the effects of practice on dual-task performance is discussed later.

When people perform two tasks during the same time period, they might do so by using serial or parallel processing. *Serial* processing involves switching attention backwards and forwards between the two tasks with only one task being attended to and processed at any given moment. In contrast, *parallel* processing involves attending to (and processing) both tasks at the same time.

There has been much theoretical controversy on the issue of serial vs. parallel processing. What has been insufficiently emphasised is that processing is often relatively *flexible*. Lehle et al. (2009) trained people to engage in serial or parallel processing when performing two tasks together. Those using serial processing performed better but found the tasks more effortful. Serial processing was effortful because it required inhibiting processing of one task while the other task is performed.

Lehle and Hübner (2009) also instructed people to perform two tasks together in a serial or parallel fashion, and found they obeyed instructions. Those instructed to use parallel processing performed much worse than those using serial processing. However, most participants receiving no specific instructions tended to favour parallel processing.

Lehle and Hübner used simple tasks (both involved deciding whether digits were odd or even). Han and Marois (2013) used two tasks, one of which (pressing different keys to each of eight different sounds) was much harder than Lehle and Hübner's tasks. The findings were very different. Even when parallel processing was more efficient and was encouraged by financial rewards, participants engaged in serial processing. The difference in findings between the two studies probably reflects the problems in using parallel processing with difficult tasks. There is a more detailed discussion of the role of parallel and serial processing in dual-task performance later in the chapter.

Multiple-resource theory

Wickens, (e.g., 1984, 2008) argued in his multiple-resource theory that the processing system consists of several independent processing mechanisms or resources. The theory includes four major dimensions (see Figure 5.16):

1 *Processing stages*: There are successive stages of perception, cognition (e.g., working memory) and responding.

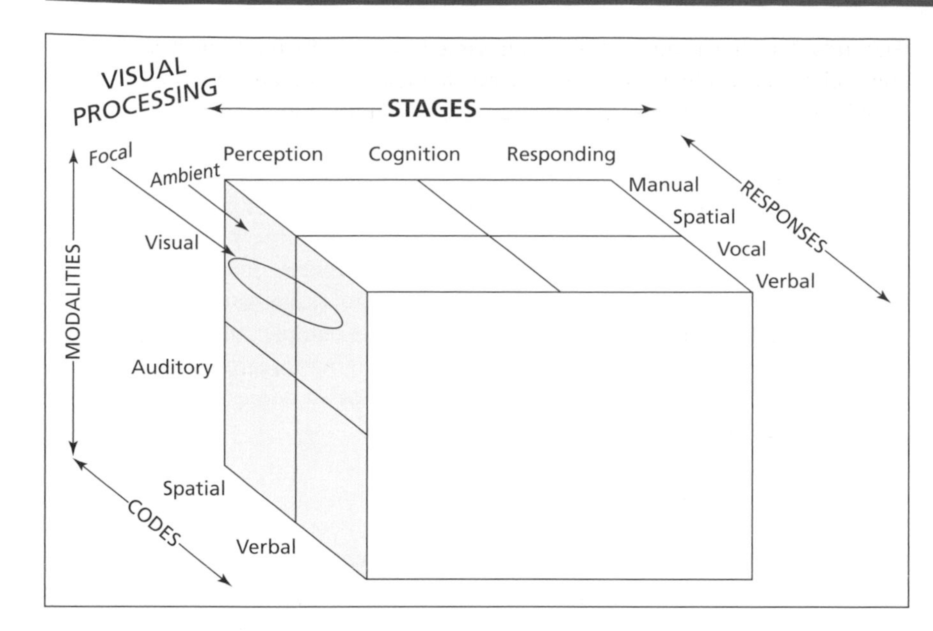

Figure 5.16
Wickens' four-dimensional multiple-resource model. The details are described in the text.

From Wickens (2008). © 2008. Reprinted by permission of SAGE Publications.

2 *Processing codes*: Perception, cognition and responding can all use spatial and/or verbal codes.
3 *Modalities*: Perception can involve visual and/or auditory resources.
4 *Response type*: Responding may be manual or vocal.

Finally, you may notice in Figure 5.16 a distinction between focal and ambient visual processing. Focal vision is used for object recognition, whereas ambient vision is involved in perception of orientation and movement.

What predictions follow from multiple-resource theory? Here is the crucial one: "*To the extent that two tasks use different levels along each of the three dimensions, time-sharing* [dual-task performance] *will be better*" (Wickens, 2008, p. 450; italics in original). Thus, tasks requiring different resources can be performed together more successfully than those requiring the same resources.

Wickens' theoretical approach bears some resemblance to Baddeley's (1986, 2001) working memory model (discussed thoroughly in Chapter 6). Baddeley's working memory model consists of several components or processing resources such as the phonological loop (used to process speech-based information) and the visuo-spatial sketchpad (used to process visual and spatial information). A key prediction of this model is that two tasks can be performed together successfully provided they use *different* components or processing resources.

There is much support for the general approach adopted by multiple-resource theory (Wickens, 2008). For example, findings discussed earlier (Treisman & Davies, 1973; McLeod, 1977) showing the negative effects of stimulus and response similarity are entirely consistent with the theory. Lu et al. (2013) carried out meta-analyses to test aspects of the theory. For example, suppose someone performing an ongoing visual-motor task (e.g., driving a car) is periodically presented with an interrupting task in the visual, auditory or tactile modality. As predicted by the theory, non-visual interrupting tasks (especially in the tactile modality) were processed more effectively than visual ones. It might be expected that the ongoing visual task would be performed better when the interrupting task was auditory rather than visual. In fact, there was no difference. According to Lu et al., the benefits due to the auditory task requiring separate resources from the ongoing task were offset by the more conspicuous and disruptive nature of auditory rather than visual stimuli.

The theory is much oversimplified in several ways. First, successful dual-task performance often requires higher-level processes of coordinating and organising the demands of the two tasks. However, these processes are de-emphasised by the theory. Second, the theory provides little or no detailed information about the numerous forms of cognitive processing intervening between perception and responding. Third, people often use complex strategies in dual-task situations (see the later discussion of neuroimaging research). However, the theory contributes little to our understanding of these strategies.

Threaded cognition

Salvucci and Taatgen (2008, 2011) put forward a theory of threaded cognition, according to which streams of thought can be represented as threads of processing. Thus, for example, processing two tasks might involve two separate threads. The central theoretical assumptions are as follows:

> Multiple threads or goals can be active at the same time, and as long as there is no overlap in the cognitive resources needed by these threads, there is no multitasking interference. When threads require the same resource at the same time, one thread must wait and its performance will be adversely affected.
>
> (Salvucci & Taatgen, 2011, p. 228)

This is because all resources have limited capacity.

Taatgen (2011) discussed some features of threaded cognition theory (see Figure 5.17). Several cognitive resources can be the source of competition between two tasks. These include vision, long-term memory (declarative and procedural), manual control and working memory (called "problem state" in the theory).

The theory differs from Baddeley's (1986, 2007) working memory model in that there is no central executive deciding on the allocation of processing resources. Instead, each thread or task controls resources in a greedy, polite way – threads claim resources greedily when required but release them politely when no longer needed. These aspects of the theory lead to one of its most original assumptions – *several* goals can be active at the same time, each associated with a given thread.

Threaded cognition theory resembles Wickens' multiple-resource theory. For example, both theories assume there are several independent processing resources and no overarching central

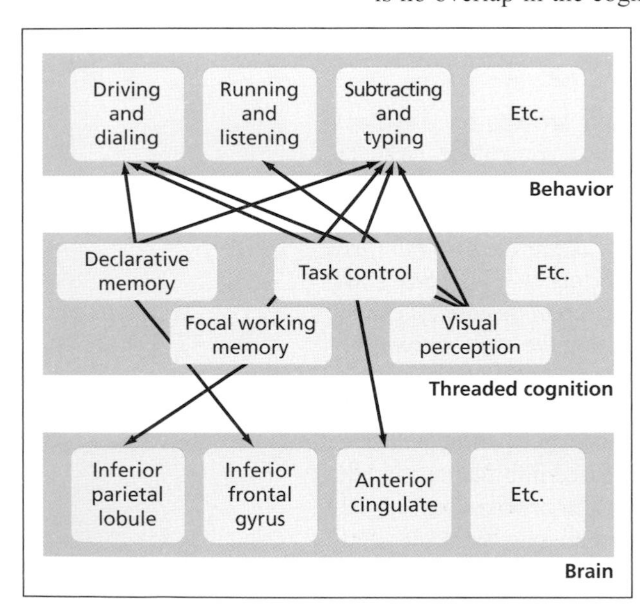

Figure 5.17
Threaded cognition theory. We possess several cognitive resources (e.g., declarative memory, task control, visual perception). These resources can be used in parallel but each resource can only work on one task at a time. Our ability to perform two tasks at the same time (e.g., driving and dialling, subtraction and typing) depends on the precise ways in which cognitive resources need to be used. The theory also identifies some of the brain areas associated with cognitive resources.
From Taatgen (2011). With permission of the author.

executive. However, threaded cognition theory has the advantage that it has led to the construction of a computational model. This computational model makes specific predictions and lends itself to detailed testing in a way that cannot be done with Wickens' theory.

Findings

According to threaded cognition theory, all cognitive resources (e.g., visual perception, working memory, motor control) can be used by only one process at any given time. Nijboer et al. (2013) tested this assumption in a study in which multicolumn subtraction was the primary task with participants responding by using a keypad. There were easy and hard conditions depending on whether digits needed to be carried over (or "borrowed") from one column to the next:

(1: easy)	(2: hard)
336789495	3649772514
–224578381	–1852983463

According to the theory, working memory (focus of attention) is required in the hard condition but not the easy one. Subtraction was combined with a secondary task, which was a tracking task involving visual and manual resources or a tone-counting task involving working memory.

What findings would we expect theoretically? Performance on the easy subtraction task should be worse when combined with the tracking task because both tasks compete for visual and manual resources. In contrast, performance on the hard subtraction task should be worse when combined with the tone-counting task because there are large disruptive effects when two tasks compete for working-memory resources. Nijboer et al.'s (2013) findings were as predicted.

Borst et al. (2013) also found that subtraction performance when carrying was required was more impaired than easy subtraction performance by a secondary task requiring working memory. This is as predicted theoretically. According to the theory, dual-task performance can be enhanced by appropriate environmental support. They tested this prediction with hard subtraction problems by using an explicit visual indicator that "borrowing" was needed. This improved overall performance considerably when both tasks needed working memory.

It is assumed within threaded cognition theory that people often manage the demands of combining two tasks better than is often assumed. For example, consider research on task switching, in which participants switch tasks when instructed by the experimenter. There are typically significant time costs associated with task switching (see Chapter 6). However, task switching may be easier in real life for two reasons. First, people typically *choose* when to switch tasks in everyday life. Second, environmental support is often available to facilitate the performance of one or both tasks. We have just seen the beneficial effects of environmental support in the study by Borst et al. (2013).

According to Salvucci and Taatgen (2008), people switch *flexibly* between tasks to maximise performance. Janssen and Brumby (2010) tested this prediction. Participants drove a simulated vehicle while manually dialling a practised 11-digit telephone number. The participants were instructed to prioritise the driving or dialling task. Flexibility was indicated by the finding that both tasks were

KEY TERM

Underadditivity
The finding that brain activation when tasks A and B are performed at the same time is less than the sum of the brain activation when tasks A and B are performed separately.

performed better when prioritised than non-prioritised. When the driving task was prioritised, participants switched their attention to it earlier in the dialling task than when the dialling task was prioritised. Participants had previously learned to dial the 11-digit telephone number as two chunks: the first five digits followed by the remaining six digits. However, when the driving task was prioritised, they switched attention to it after dialling only three digits.

People do not always adapt optimally to task interference. In the study by Nijboer et al. (2013) discussed earlier, participants chose before each trial which of the two secondary tasks they would perform. One-third of participants showed no evidence of adaptation or learning over trials. The remaining participants took many trials before making the optimal choice consistently. Thus, people often find it hard to use the optimal strategies in dual-task situations.

Evaluation

Threaded cognition theory has proved successful in several ways. First, headway has been made in identifying the most important cognitive resources. Second, computational modelling has permitted detailed testing of the theory's predictions. Third, the theory avoids assuming the existence of a central executive or other high-level executive process that is often vaguely conceived. Fourth, there is evidence supporting the notion that people approach dual-task situations in flexible ways. Fifth, and related to the fourth point, people often have fewer problems with performing two tasks at the same time than generally assumed.

What are the limitations with threaded cognition theory? First, the theory predicts that, "Practising two tasks concurrently [together] results in the same performance as practising the two tasks independently" (Salvucci & Taatgen, 2008, p. 127). This de-emphasises the importance of processes designed to coordinate and manage two tasks performed together (see next section). Second, it may prove inadvisable to exclude anything resembling Baddeley's central executive from the theory. Third, the theory has mostly been tested in situations in which participants perform two relatively simple tasks at the same time. It remains unclear whether the theory is as applicable to dual-task situations involving complex tasks. Fourth, it is unclear why some people find it much easier than others to select optimal task combinations that minimise interference.

Cognitive neuroscience

Suppose we assume the resource demands of two tasks performed together equal the sums of the demands of the two tasks performed separately. We can relate that assumption to brain-imaging research in which participants perform tasks x and y on their own or together. If the assumption is correct, we might expect brain activation in the dual-task condition to be the same as the sum of the activations in the two single-task conditions. This is the *additivity* assumption. You will probably not be surprised to discover this simple prediction is rarely confirmed.

Findings

Several neuroimaging studies have found evidence for **underadditivity** – brain activation in dual-task conditions was less than the sum of the activations in the two tasks singly. For example, consider a study by Just et al. (2001). They

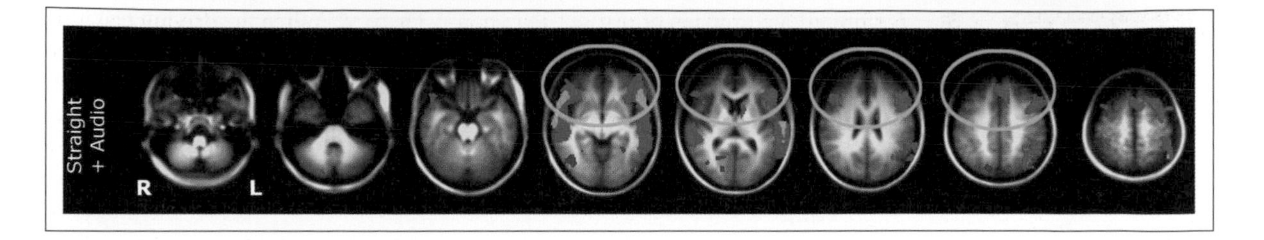

Figure 5.18
Effects of an audio distraction task on brain activity associated with a straight driving task. There were significant increases in activation within the ventrolateral prefrontal cortex and the auditory cortex (in orange). There was decreased activation in occipital-visual areas (in blue).
From Schweizer et al. (2013).

deliberately selected two tasks apparently involving very different processing resources: auditory sentence comprehension and mental rotation of 3-D figures. These tasks were performed together or singly.

What did Just et al. (2001) find? First, performance on both tasks was impaired under dual-task conditions compared to single-task conditions. Second, brain activation in regions associated with language processing decreased by 53% under dual-task conditions compared to single-task ones. Third, there was a 29% reduction of brain activation in regions associated with mental rotation under dual-task conditions.

The above strong underadditivity effects are striking in view of the different processing demands of the two tasks. They suggest limited general resources were available when both tasks needed to be performed at the same time.

More evidence of underadditivity was reported by Schweizer et al. (2013). Participants performed a straight driving task on its own or with a distracting secondary task (answering auditorily presented general knowledge questions). Driving performance was unaffected by the secondary task. However, there were large differences between the two conditions in brain activation. More specifically, driving with distraction reduced activation in posterior brain areas concerned with spatial and visual processing (underadditivity). However, it produced increased activation in the prefrontal cortex (see Figure 5.18), probably because driving with distraction requires extra attentional processes within the prefrontal cortex.

It seems reasonable to assume dual-task conditions often require executive processes absent or less important with single tasks. These executive processes include coordination of task demands, attentional control and dual-task management generally. We would expect such executive processes to be associated with activation in prefrontal cortex.

There is some support for that assumption in the study by Schweizer et al. (2013) discussed above. Stronger support was reported by Johnson and Zatorre (2006). Participants performed visual and auditory tasks singly or together. Their key finding was that the dorsolateral prefrontal cortex (associated with various executive attentional processes) was activated only in the dual-task condition.

The above findings do not show the dorsolateral prefrontal cortex is *required* for dual-task performance. More direct evidence was reported by Johnson et al. (2007) using the same auditory and visual tasks as Johnson and Zatorre (2006). They used transcranial magnetic stimulation (TMS; see Glossary) to disrupt the functioning of the dorsolateral prefrontal cortex. As predicted, this impaired the ability of participants to divide their attention between the two tasks. Johnson et al. (2007) speculated that the dorsolateral prefrontal cortex is needed to manipulate information in working memory in dual-task situations.

T. Wu et al. (2013) reported much greater effects of dual-task conditions on brain activity. Participants carried out simple tapping and visual counting tasks (counting occurrences of a specified letter). There was greater activation within the cerebellum (a structure at the back of the brain involved in coordinating movements and balance) under dual-task conditions. This increased activation was important because it permitted *integration* of the separate brain networks underlying performance on the two tasks.

Evaluation

Brain activity in dual-task conditions differs in several ways from the sum of brain activity of the same two tasks performed singly. Dual-task brain activity often exhibits underadditivity; it sometimes involves the recruitment of additional brain regions; and it can also involve integrated functioning of different brain networks. These findings have much theoretical importance. They indicate clearly that the performance of dual tasks can involve executive and other processes hardly required with single tasks. They also reveal that dual-task conditions can lead to complex reconfigurations of brain processing missing from most existing theories.

What are the limitations of the cognitive neuroscience approach? First, it remains somewhat unclear why the performance of two very different tasks is associated with underadditivity of brain activation. Second, it is often unclear whether patterns of brain activation are *directly* relevant to task processing rather than reflecting non-task processes. Third, there are very mixed findings with respect to the additional involvement of the prefrontal cortex in dual-task conditions, which has not been found at all in several studies. No current theory provides an adequate account of what task characteristics determine whether there is such involvement.

AUTOMATIC PROCESSING

A key finding in studies of divided attention is the dramatic improvement *practice* often has on performance. This improvement has been explained by assuming some processes become *automatic* through prolonged practice. Below we consider major theoretical approaches put forward to explain the development of automatic processing.

Traditional approach: Shiffrin and Schneider (1977)

Shiffrin and Schneider (1977) and Schneider and Shiffrin (1977) made a major contribution to understanding the effects of practice. They distinguished between controlled and automatic processes:

- Controlled processes are of limited capacity, require attention and can be used flexibly in changing circumstances.
- Automatic processes suffer no capacity limitations, do not require attention and are very hard to modify once learned.

In Shiffrin and Schneider's (1977) research, participants memorised up to four letters (the memory set) followed by a visual display containing up to four letters. Finally, participants decided rapidly whether any item in the visual display was the same as any item in the memory set. The crucial manipulation was the type of mapping. With *consistent* mapping, only consonants were used as members of

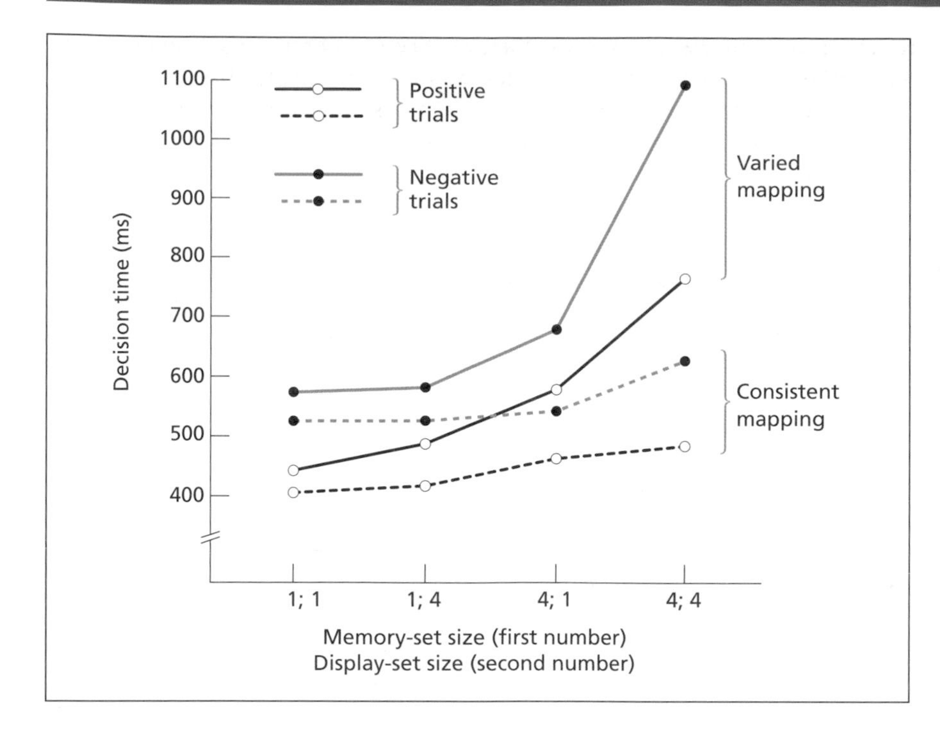

Figure 5.19
Response times on a decision task as a function of memory-set size, display-set size and consistent vs. varied mapping. Data from Shiffrin and Schneider (1977).

© American Psychological Association.

the memory set and only numbers were used as distractors in the visual display (or vice versa). Thus, a participant given only consonants to memorise would know any consonant detected in the visual display *must* be in the memory set. With *varied* mapping, numbers and consonants were both used to form the memory set and to provide distractors in the visual display.

The mapping manipulation had dramatic effects (see Figure 5.19). The numbers of items in the memory set and visual display greatly affected decision speed *only* in the varied mapping conditions. According to Schneider and Shiffrin (1977), a controlled process was used with varied mapping. This involves *serial* comparisons between each item in the memory set and each item in the visual display until a match is achieved or every comparison has been made. In contrast, performance with consistent mapping involved automatic processes operating independently and in *parallel*. According to Schneider and Shiffrin (1977), these automatic processes evolve through years of practice in distinguishing between letters and numbers.

Shiffrin and Schneider (1977) tested the notion that automatic processes develop through practice. They used consistent mapping with the consonants B to L forming one set and Q to Z forming the other set. As before, items from only one set were always used to form the memory set, and the distractors in the visual display were all selected from the other set. Performance improved greatly over 2,100 trials, reflecting the growth of automatic processes.

The greatest limitation with automatic processes is their *inflexibility*, which disrupts performance when conditions change. This was confirmed in the second part of the study. The initial 2,100 trials with one consistent mapping were followed by a further 2,100 trials with the *reverse* consistent mapping. With this reversal, it took nearly 1,000 trials before performance recovered to its level at the start of the experiment!

In sum, automatic processes function rapidly and in parallel but suffer from inflexibility. Controlled processes are flexible and versatile but operate relatively slowly and in a serial fashion.

Evaluation

Shiffrin and Schneider's (1977) theoretical approach has had a massive impact. Their criteria for automaticity are still influential (Ashby & Crossley, 2012), and their findings indicated very large differences between automatic and controlled processes.

What are the limitations with Shiffrin and Schneider's (1977) approach? First, the neat-and-tidy distinction between automatic and controlled processes is oversimplified (discussed further shortly). Second, Shiffrin and Schneider (1977) argued that automatic processes operate in parallel and place no demands on attentional capacity. Thus, when automatic processes are used, the function relating decision speed to the number of items in the memory set and/or the visual display should be a horizontal line. In fact, decision speed was slower when the memory set and visual display both contained several items (see Figure 5.19). Third, the theory is descriptive rather than explanatory – *how* does the serial processing associated with controlled processing turn into the parallel processing associated with automatic processing?

Definitions of automaticity

Moors and de Houwer (2006) rejected Shiffrin and Schneider's (1977) assumption there is a clear-cut distinction between automatic and controlled processes. Instead, they identified four key factors associated with automaticity:

1. *Unconscious*: lack of conscious awareness of the process.
2. *Efficient*: using very little attentional capacity.
3. *Fast*.
4. *Goal-unrelated*: uninfluenced by the individual's current goals.

Moors and de Houwer (2006) argued that the four features above are not always found together: "It is dangerous to draw inferences about the presence or absence of one feature on the basis of the presence or absence of another" (p. 320). They also argued that there is no firm dividing line between automaticity and non-automaticity. The features are continuous rather than all-or-none (e.g., a process can be fairly fast or slow; it can be partially conscious). As a result, most processes involve a *blend* of automaticity and non-automaticity. This entire approach is rather imprecise because few processes are 100% automatic or non-automatic. However, as Moors and de Houwer pointed out, we can make *relative* statements (e.g., process *x* is more/less automatic than process *y*).

Why might the four features of automaticity identified by Moors and de Houwer (2006) often be found together? Instance theory (Logan, 1988; Logan et al., 1999) provides a very influential answer. The theory assumes that task practice leads to storage of information in long-term memory, facilitating subsequent performance on that task. In essence, "Automaticity is memory retrieval: performance is automatic when it is based on a single-step direct-access retrieval of past solutions from memory" (Logan, 1988, p. 493).

This theoretical approach makes coherent sense of several characteristics of automaticity. Automatic processes are fast because they require only the retrieval of past solutions from long-term memory. They make few demands on attentional resources because the retrieval of heavily over-learned information is relatively effortless. Finally, there is no conscious awareness of automatic processes because no significant processes intervene between the presentation of a stimulus and retrieval of the appropriate response.

Instance theory does not distinguish between types of long-term memory. However, there is much evidence for a distinction between declarative memory (involving conscious recollection) and procedural memory (not involving conscious recollection; see Chapter 7).

A limitation of instance theory is that it does not distinguish between different types of long-term memory (see Chapter 7). Ashby and Crossley (2012) argued that we should identify three main memory types: declarative, procedural and automatic. Declarative and procedural memories differ substantially early in practice. With prolonged practice, however, very similar automatic memories are formed regardless of whether the task promotes declarative or procedural learning.

Findings

Shiffrin and Schneider's (1977) research (discussed above) supports the notion that allegedly automatic processes tend to be fast, require little attention and are goal-unrelated (shown by inflexibility when the task goal changed). Evidence there may also be limited or no conscious awareness in the consistent mapping condition used by Shiffrin and Schneider was reported by Jansma et al. (2001). Increasing automaticity as indexed by performance measures was accompanied by a significant reduction in activation in areas associated with conscious awareness (e.g., dorsolateral prefrontal cortex, superior frontal cortex).

Moors and de Houwer (2006) argued that the four features of automaticity are often not found together. There has been a rapid increase in the number of studies supporting that argument. Surprisingly, and in apparent conflict with Shiffrin and Schneider's (1977) theoretical approach, several studies have shown that unconscious processes can influence cognitive control (van Gaal et al., 2012). We will discuss two such studies here. First, van Gaal et al. (2010) examined the executive process of inhibitory control (i.e., preventing execution of a planned response). A subliminal stimulus (one below the level of conscious awareness) produced evidence of inhibitory control involving higher-level processes within the prefrontal cortex (this study is also discussed in Chapter 16).

Second, Capa et al. (2013) varied the reward for successful performance (50 cents or 1 cent) on a task requiring executive processes. Information concerning the size of the reward was presented supraliminally (above the threshold of conscious awareness) or subliminally. There were two main findings. First, performance even in the subliminal condition was better under the higher-reward condition (see Figure 5.20). Second, event-related potentials (ERPs; see Glossary) indicated that participants in the subliminal condition engaged in greater preparatory effort on the task when the reward was higher.

As mentioned earlier, Ashby and Crossley (2012) argued that we should distinguish among declarative, procedural and automatic memories. Much of their research in this area has involved rule-based and information-integration category learning (see Figure 5.21). It is assumed that rule-based learning involves

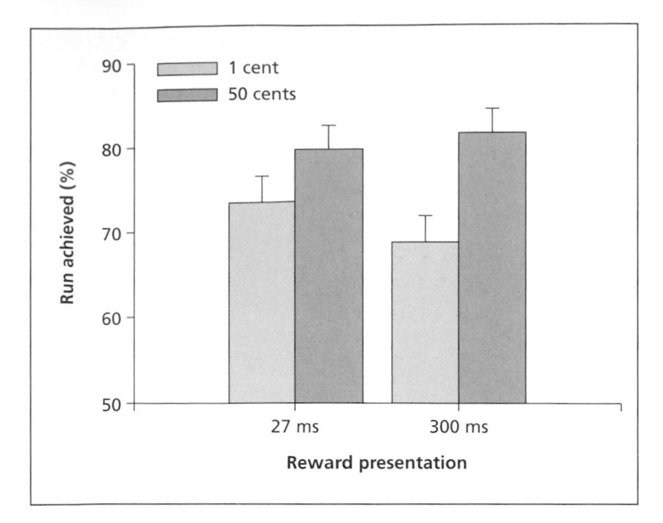

Figure 5.20
Performance on a task-switching task in which information about reward size (1 or 50 cents) was presented subliminally (27 ms) or supraliminally (300 ms).

From Capa et al. (2013). Reprinted with permission of Elsevier.

declarative memory because the rule can be easily described verbally. In contrast, information-integration learning involves procedural memory because the differences between the categories are hard or impossible to describe verbally.

Neuroimaging research (reviewed by Ashby and Crossley, 2012; see Soto et al., 2013) supports the notion there are three types of memory. Early in learning, rule-based performance correlates with activation in prefrontal cortex and the hippocampus (areas associated with declarative memory). In contrast, information-integration performance early on is associated with activation in the putamen (part of the striatum – see Glossary), which is involved in procedural memory. After extensive training (up to about 12,000 trials), none of the above areas correlates with performance. Instead, performance on both tasks correlates only with certain aspects of cortical activation (e.g., in premotor cortex).

Further evidence that tasks initially producing declarative and procedural memories eventually produce very similar automatic memories with sufficient practice was reported by Hélie et al. (2010). Training involving thousands of trials produced two findings that were very similar regardless of whether the task was rule-based (declarative) or information-integration based (procedural). First, switching the locations of the response keys caused severe interference. Second, a second task performed at the same time as the categorisation task did not interfere with categorisation performance.

Conclusions

The assumption there is a clear-cut distinction between automatic and non-automatic or controlled processes is oversimplified. It is preferable to think in terms of *degrees* of automaticity. The infrequency with which "pure" cases of automaticity are found suggests the concept of "automaticity" has limited applicability although degree of automaticity can be identified. In spite of these problems, memory-based accounts provide useful explanations of the development of automaticity. The notion that different types of learning converge on very similar automatic memories with prolonged practice is valuable.

Cognitive bottleneck

Earlier we discussed research (e.g., Spelke et al., 1976) suggesting two complex tasks can be performed very well together with minimal disruption. However, the participants had much flexibility in terms of *when* and *how* they processed the tasks. Thus, it is possible there were interference effects that went unnoticed because of lack of experimental control and/or insensitivity of measurement.

We turn now to perhaps the most sensitive type of experiment for detecting dual-task interference. There are two stimuli (e.g., two lights) and two responses (e.g., button presses), one associated with each stimulus. Participants respond to each stimulus as rapidly as possible. When the two stimuli are presented at the same time (dual-task condition), performance is typically worse on both tasks than when each task is presented on its own (single-task condition).

When the second stimulus is presented very shortly after the first one, there is typically a marked slowing of the response to the *second* stimulus. This is the **psychological refractory period (PRP) effect**. It is a robust effect – Ruthruff et al. (2009) found there was still a large PRP effect even when participants were given strong incentives to eliminate it. Note that when the time interval between the two stimuli is increased, there is much less slowing of response to the second stimulus.

KEY TERM

Psychological refractory period (PRP) effect
The slowing of the response to the second of two stimuli when presented close together in time.

The PRP effect has direct relevance to the real world. Hibberd et al. (2013) studied the effects of a simple in-vehicle task on braking performance when the vehicle in front braked and slowed down. They obtained a classic PDP effect – braking time was slowed down most when the in-vehicle task was presented very shortly before the vehicle in front braked.

How can we explain the PRP effect? Several theorists assume task performance involves three successive stages: (1) perceptual, (2) central (e.g., deciding which response to make) and (3) motor (preparing and executing a response). According to the central bottleneck theory (originally proposed by Welford, 1952), a bottleneck "prevents more than one central decision process from operating at any given moment" (Pashler et al., 2008, p. 313).

The notion of a central bottleneck remains the most influential explanation for the PRP effect. It can also explain many dual-task costs when individuals perform two tasks at the same time. However, other explanations of the PRP effect are possible. First, it may occur because participants in most studies receive insufficient practice to eliminate it. Second, the PRP effect may occur because people decide their performance will be better if they engage in serial rather than parallel processing.

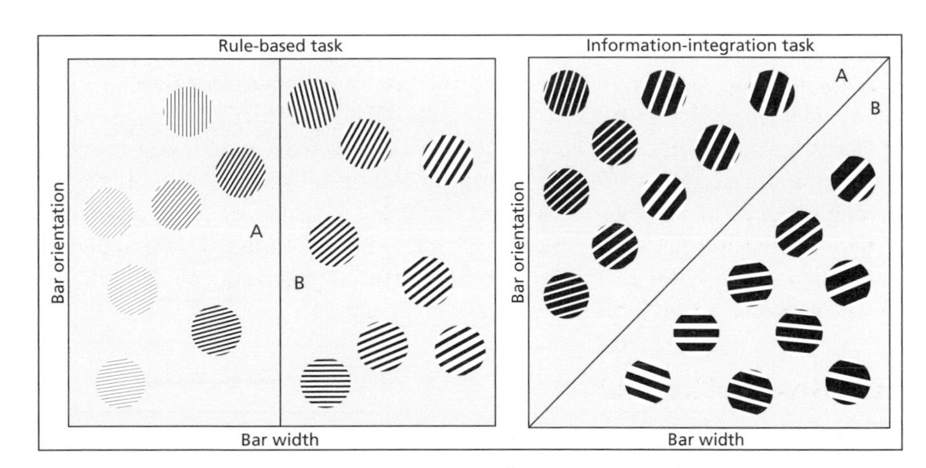

Figure 5.21
Examples of stimuli used to study rule-based (top) and information-integration (bottom) category learning. The boundaries between the A and B categories are indicated by solid lines. A simple verbal rule (e.g., respond "A" if the bars are narrow and "B" if they are wide) is sufficient on the rule-based task. In contrast, there is no simple verbal description of the categories with the information-integration task.

From Ashby and Crossley (2012). With permission of Wiley.

Findings

Hesselmann et al. (2011) used event-related potentials (ERPs; see Glossary) to clarify the processes involved in the PRP effect. They focused on the P300 component of the ERP, which probably reflects central decision processes. The amount of slowing of responses on the second task was closely matched by the amount of slowing in the onset of P300. However, there was *no* slowing of earlier ERP components reflecting perceptual processing. Thus, the PRP effect occurred because of a slowing of central decision processes rather than of perceptual processes, precisely as predicted by the central bottleneck theory.

Evidence apparently problematical for the notion of a bottleneck was reported by Schumacher et al. (2001). They used two tasks: (1) say "one", "two" or "three" to low-, medium- and high-pitched tones, respectively; and (2) press response keys corresponding to the position of a disc on a computer screen. These two tasks were performed together for over 2,000 trials, at the end of which some participants performed them as well together as singly. In general, those performing each task on its own especially well showed the smallest PRP effect.

Strobach et al. (2013) carried out a study that was very similar to that of Schumacher et al. (2001), with participants receiving over 5,000 trials involving single-task or dual-task conditions. However, they did not find evidence that dual-task costs were eliminated after extensive practice. As is shown in Figure 5.22, dual-task costs for the auditory task reduced from 185 to 60 ms with practice, and those for the visual task reduced from 83 to 20 ms.

Why did this difference in findings between Strobach et al. (2013) and Schumacher et al. (2001) occur? In both studies, participants were rewarded for fast responding on single-task and dual-task trials. However, the way the reward system was set up in the Schumacher et al. study may have led participants to exert more effort in dual-task than single-task trials. This potential bias was

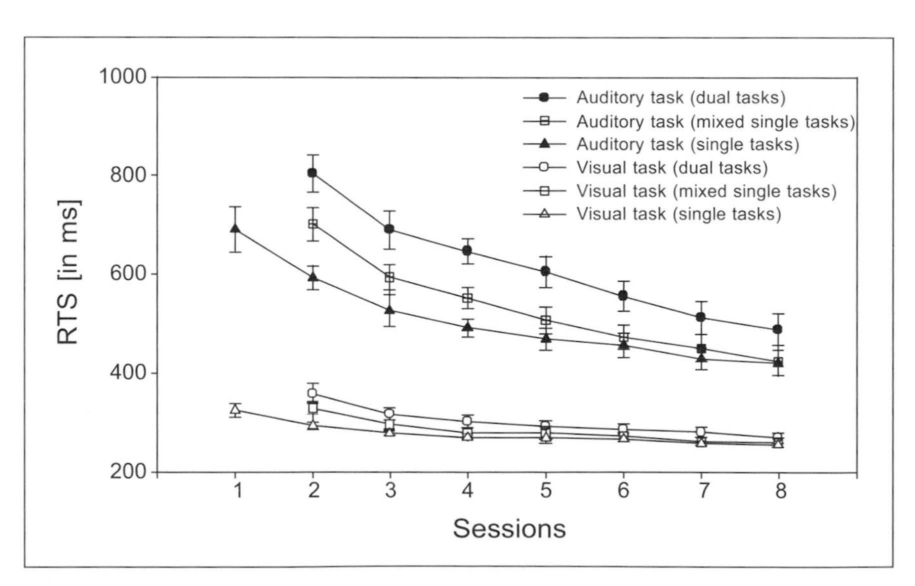

Figure 5.22
Reaction times on correct trials only over eight experimental sessions under dual-task (auditory and visual tasks) and single-task (auditory or visual task) conditions.
From Strobach et al. (2013). Reprinted with permission of Springer.

absent from the Strobach et al. study. This difference in reward structure may explain why there was much more evidence of dual-task costs in the Strobach et al. study.

How does dual-task practice benefit performance? This issue was addressed by Strobach et al. (2013). The main effect of practice was to speed up the central response-selection stage in both tasks. There was also an effect of practice on the perceptual stage of the auditory task. In contrast, practice had no effect at all on the motor or response stage on either task.

We have seen the central response-selection stage is of crucial importance in explaining interference effects between two tasks performed at the same time. There is much evidence suggesting the left posterior lateral prefrontal cortex plays an important role in response selection (Filmer et al., 2013). However, most research has obtained only correlational evidence to support that claim. Filmer et al. applied transcranial direct current cathodal stimulation to decrease excitability of that brain region. Dual-task costs (slower responding on dual-task trials compared to single-task trials) were significantly *reduced* by cathodal stimulation. The precise reasons why cathodal stimulation had this effect is unclear. However, the study is important in showing that the left posterior lateral prefrontal cortex is probably *causally* involved in response selection.

Finally, we return to the PRP effect. As mentioned earlier, it is possible the effect might disappear if participants received prolonged practice. In fact, practice typically reduces but rarely eliminates the effect. For example, Pashler (1993) found the PRP effect was still observable after over 10,000 practice trials.

Is it possible that participants typically engage in serial processing in PRP tasks because they *choose* to rather than because they *must* do so. Miller et al. (2009) argued that serial processing in PRP tasks generally leads to superior performance than parallel processing. However, their theoretical analysis indicated parallel processing would have the edge when the stimuli associated with the two tasks are mostly presented close together in time. As predicted, there was a shift from predominantly serial processing towards parallel processing when that was the case.

Miller et al. (2009) used very simple tasks, and it is likely that parallel processing is more likely to be found with simple than with complex tasks. In a study discussed earlier, Han and Marois (2013) used two tasks, one of which was relatively difficult. The participants engaged in serial processing even when the use of parallel processing was encouraged by financial rewards.

Summary and conclusions

The findings from most studies of the psychological refractory period effect and dual-task interference are consistent with the cognitive bottleneck theory. This is so for behavioural and neuroscience research. Practice typically produces a substantial reduction in the PRP effect and dual-task interference. However, these effects are rarely eliminated, which suggests central decision processes typically occur serially. However, there is some evidence for parallel processing when the two tasks are both easy. The predominance of serial processing over parallel processing may occur in part because it is generally associated with superior levels of performance (Miller et al., 2009).

Interactive exercise:
Definitions of attention

CHAPTER SUMMARY

- **Focused auditory attention**. The task of attending to one voice among several (the cocktail party problem) is a challenging one for automatic speech recognition systems. Human listeners use several top-down and bottom-up processes to select one voice. There is more limited processing of unattended than attended messages although unattended messages often receive some semantic processing. The restricted processing of unattended messages may reflect a bottleneck that can be found at various stages of processing.

- **Focused visual attention**. Visual attention can resemble a spotlight or zoom lens. However, it is very flexible and can also resemble multiple spotlights. Visual attention is typically object-based in everyday life. However, it can also be space-based or feature-based depending on the precise task requirements, recent experience and individual differences. According to Lavie's load theory, we are more susceptible to distraction when our current task involves low perceptual load and/or high cognitive load. There is much support for this theory, but the effects of perceptual and cognitive load are often not independent as predicted.

  There is a stimulus-driven ventral attention network and a goal-directed dorsal attention network involving different (but partially overlapping) brain networks. There is some lack of clarity concerning the precise brain regions associated with each network and little is currently known about how the two attentional systems interact.

- **Disorders of visual attention**. Neglect occurs when damage to the ventral attention network in the right hemisphere impairs the functioning of the undamaged dorsal attention network. This impaired functioning of the dorsal attention network is due to reduced activation and alertness within the left hemisphere. Extinction is due to biased competition for attention between the two hemispheres combined with reduced attentional capacity. Prism-adaptation and alertness training have both proved effective in treating the symptoms of neglect.

- **Visual search**. One problem with airport security checks is that there are numerous possible target objects. Another problem is the rarity of targets, which produces excessive caution in reporting targets. According to feature integration theory, object features are processed in parallel and are then combined by focused attention in visual search. In fact, there is more parallel processing than assumed by this theory. Much parallel processing occurs because much information is typically extracted from the peripheral visual field. In everyday life, general scene knowledge is used to focus visual search on areas of the scene most likely to contain the target object.

- **Cross-modal effects**. In the real world, we often coordinate information from two or more sense modalities. The ventriloquism effect shows vision dominates sound because an object's location is typically indicated more precisely by vision. Temporal ventriloquism shows temporal judgements can be dominated by auditory stimuli because the auditory modality is typically more precise than the visual modality at discriminating temporal relations. Auditory or vibrotactile warning signals informative about the direction of danger and/or time to collision speed up drivers' braking times in an emergency speed up braking reaction times.

- **Divided attention: dual-task performance**. Driving performance is impaired substantially by a secondary task (e.g., mobile-phone use). This is often due to inattentional blindness or reduced attention to peripheral objects.

  Multiple-resource theory and threaded cognition theory both assume that dual-task performance depends on several processing resources each of which has limited capacity. This permits two tasks to be performed together successfully provided they use different processing resources. This general approach has proved successful but de-emphasises high-level executive processes (e.g., monitoring and coordinating two tasks at the same time).

  Some neuroimaging studies have found underadditivity under dual-task conditions (less activation than for the two tasks performed separately). This may indicate that people have limited general processing resources. Other neuroimaging studies have found that dual-task conditions can introduce new processing demands of task coordination associated with activation within the dorsolateral prefrontal cortex and cerebellum.

- **Automatic processing**. Shiffrin and Schneider distinguished between slow, flexible controlled processes and fast, automatic ones. Automatic processes are generally goal-unrelated, unconscious, efficient and fast. This could occur because automatic processes require only the direct retrieval of relevant information from long-term memory. The typical existence of a psychological refractory period (PRP) effect can be explained by a processing bottleneck at the stage of response selection. However, massive practice may sometimes eliminate this bottleneck. Alternatively, the PRP effect may occur because participants choose to engage in serial processing rather than because they cannot use parallel processing.

Further reading

- Bartolomeo, P., de Schotten, M.T. & Chica, A.B. (2012). Brain networks of visuospatial attention and their disruption in visual neglect. *Frontiers in Human Neuroscience*, 6, Article 110. The authors provide a thorough account of theory and research on visual neglect.
- Chan, L.K.H. & Hayward, W.G. (2013). Visual search. *Wiley Interdisciplinary Review – Cognitive Science*, 4: 415–29. Louis Chan and William Hayward discuss the main theoretical approaches to visual search.
- Corbetta, M. & Shulman, G.L. (2011). Spatial neglect and attention networks. *Annual Review of Neuroscience*, 34: 569–99. The complexities of the brain mechanisms underlying visual neglect are discussed thoroughly in this review article.
- Kastner, S. & Nobre, A.C. (eds) (2014). *The Oxford handbook of attention*. Oxford: Oxford University Press. This edited book contains numerous chapters by leading authorities on the issues discussed in this chapter.
- McDermott, J.H. (2009). The cocktail party problem. *Current Biology*, 19: R1024–7. Josh McDermott provides an informative account of some of the main factors involved in focused auditory attention.
- Moors, A. (2013). Automaticity. In D. Reisberg (ed.), *The Oxford handbook of cognitive psychology*. Oxford: Oxford University Press. Issues relating to automaticity are discussed comprehensively by Agnes Moors.
- Wolfe, J.M., Võ, M.L.-H., Evans, K.K. & Greene, M.R. (2011). Visual search in scenes involves selective and nonselective pathways. *Trends in Cognitive Sciences*, 15: 77–84. Current theoretical models of visual search are discussed and evaluated by Jeremy Wolfe.
- Wu, W. (2014). *Attention*. Hove: Psychology Press. Wayne Wu considers attention from psychological, neuroscience and philosophical perspectives.

Memory

PART

How important is memory? Imagine if we were without it. We would not recognise anyone or anything as familiar. We would be unable to talk, read or write because we would remember nothing about language. We would have extremely limited personalities because we would have no recollection of the events of our own lives and therefore no sense of self. In sum, we would have the same lack of knowledge as a newborn baby.

We use memory for numerous purposes throughout every day of our lives. It allows us to keep track of conversations, to remember telephone numbers while we dial them, to write essays in examinations, to make sense of what we read, to recognise people's faces and to understand what we read in books or see on television.

The wonders of human memory are discussed in Chapters 6–8. Chapter 6 deals mainly with key issues regarded as important from the very beginnings of memory research. For example, we consider the overall architecture of human memory and the distinction between short-term and long-term memory. We also consider everyday uses of short-term memory. The notion of short-term memory has been largely superseded by that of a working memory system, which combines the functions of processing and short-term storage of information. There is extensive coverage of working memory in Chapter 6.

Another topic discussed in Chapter 6 is learning. Most learners devote their time to studying the to-be-remembered information. However, long-term memory is typically better (and sometimes much better) if a reasonable proportion of the learning period is spent in practising retrieval. Evidence suggesting some learning is implicit (i.e., does not depend on conscious processes) is also discussed. Finally, we deal with forgetting. Why do we tend to forget information as time goes by?

The scope of long-term memory is enormous. We have long-term memories for personal information about ourselves and those we know, knowledge about language, much knowledge about psychology (hopefully!) and knowledge about thousands of objects in the world around us. The key issue addressed in Chapter 7 is how to account for this incredible richness. It is almost universally acknowledged that there are several long-term memory systems. As we will see in Chapter 7, some of the most convincing support comes from patients whose brain damage has severely impaired their long-term memory.

Memory is important in everyday life in ways that historically were not the focus of much research. For example, autobiographical memory is of great significance to us. We would have no sense of self if we lacked memory for our own personal history. Autobiographical memory is discussed at length in Chapter 8.

The other topics on everyday memory considered in Chapter 8 are eyewitness testimony and prospective memory. Research into eyewitness testimony is of considerable importance with respect to the legal system. It has revealed that many assumptions we make about the accuracy of eyewitness testimony are mistaken. This matters because hundreds (or even thousands) of innocent people have been imprisoned solely on the basis of eyewitness testimony.

When we think about memory, we naturally focus on memory of the *past*. However, we also need to remember numerous *future* commitments (e.g., meeting a friend as arranged, turning up for a lecture), and such remembering involves prospective memory. We will consider how people try to ensure they carry out their future intentions in Chapter 8.

As will become apparent in the next three chapters, the study of human memory is fascinating and substantial progress has been made. However, human memory is undoubtedly complex. It depends on several different factors. Four kinds of factors are important in memory research: events, participants, encoding and retrieval (Roediger, 2008). Events range from words and pictures to texts and life events. The participants can vary in age, expertise, memory-specific disorders and so on. What happens at encoding varies as a function of task instructions, the immediate context and participants' strategies. Finally, memory performance at retrieval often varies considerably depending on the nature of the memory task (e.g., free recall, cued recall, recognition).

The crucial message is that memory findings are *context-sensitive* – they depend on *interactions* among the four factors. In other words, the effects of manipulating, say, what happens at encoding depend on the participants used, on the events to be remembered and on the conditions of retrieval. As a result, we should not expect to find many (if any) laws of memory that hold under all circumstances. How, then, do we make progress? As Baddeley (1978, p. 150) pointed out, what is required is "to develop ways of separating out and analysing more deeply the complex underlying processes".

Learning, memory and forgetting

CHAPTER

6

INTRODUCTION

This chapter and the next two focus on human memory. All three chapters deal with intact human memory, but Chapter 7 also considers amnesic patients in detail. Traditional laboratory-based research is the focus of this chapter and Chapter 7, with more naturalistic research being discussed in Chapter 8. There are important links among these different types of research. Many theoretical issues are relevant to brain-damaged and healthy individuals whether tested in the laboratory or the field.

Learning and memory involve several stages. Processes occurring during the presentation of the learning material are known as *encoding* and involve many of the processes involved in perception. This is the first stage. As a result of encoding, information is stored within the memory system. Thus, *storage* is the second stage. The third stage is *retrieval*, which involves recovering stored information from the memory system. Forgetting (discussed at length later in the chapter) occurs when our attempts at retrieval prove unsuccessful. These various processes occur within the overall structure or architecture of the memory system.

We have distinguished between architecture and process and among encoding, storage and process. Note, however, we cannot have architecture without process, or retrieval without previous encoding and storage.

ARCHITECTURE OF MEMORY

Many theorists distinguish between short-term and long-term memory. For example, there are enormous differences in capacity: a few items in short-term memory vs. essentially unlimited capacity for long-term memory. There are also massive differences in duration: a few seconds for short-term memory vs. up to several decades for long-term memory. The distinction between short-term and long-term memory stores is central to multi-store models. More recently, however, some theorists have proposed unitary-store models in which this distinction is much less clear-cut. Both types of models are discussed below.

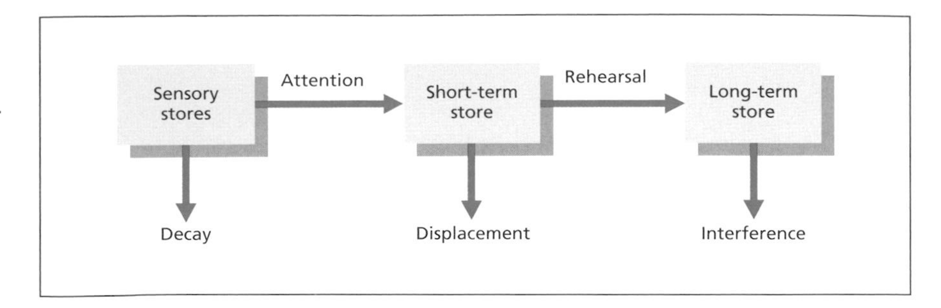

Figure 6.1
The multi-store model of memory as proposed by Atkinson and Shiffrin (1968).

Multi-store model

Atkinson and Shiffrin (1968) described the basic architecture of the memory system (see Figure 6.1):

- sensory stores each modality-specific (i.e., limited to one sensory modality) and holding information very briefly;
- short-term store of very limited capacity;
- long-term store of essentially unlimited capacity holding information over very long periods of time.

According to the multi-store model, environmental stimulation is initially processed by the sensory stores. These stores are modality-specific (e.g., vision, hearing). Information is held very briefly in the sensory stores, with some being attended to and processed further by the short-term store. Some information processed in the short-term store is transferred to the long-term store. There is a direct relationship between the amount of rehearsal in the short-term store and the strength of the stored memory trace in long-term memory.

Sensory stores

The visual store (**iconic memory**) holds visual information briefly. Sperling (1960) argued that information in iconic memory decays within about 500 milliseconds. However, this may be an underestimate. Iconic memory is very useful because the mechanisms responsible for visual perception always operate on the icon. More generally, the existence of iconic memory increases the time for which visual information is available to us (e.g., when reading).

It has typically been assumed that iconic memory is *preattentive*, meaning it does not depend on attention. This assumption was accepted by Atkinson and Shiffrin (1968) – in Figure 6.1, attention occurs only *after* information has been held in the sensory stores. Recent evidence suggests this assumption is incorrect. Persuh et al. (2012) found storage of information in iconic memory was severely disrupted if participants engaged in an attentionally demanding task at the same time. There is further discussion of iconic memory in Chapter 16.

Echoic memory, the auditory equivalent of iconic memory, holds auditory information for a few seconds. In everyday life, suppose someone asked you a question while your mind was elsewhere. Perhaps you replied, "What did you say?" just before realising you know what had been said. This "playback" facility depends on the echoic store. Ioannides et al. (2003) measured brain activation when tones were presented. The duration of echoic memory was longer in the left

KEY TERMS

Iconic memory
A sensory store that holds visual information for approximately 500 milliseconds or perhaps somewhat longer.

Echoic memory
A sensory store that holds auditory information for approximately two seconds.

hemisphere than the right (maximum of five seconds vs. two seconds, respectively). This hemispheric difference probably reflects the dominance of the left hemisphere in language processing.

There are sensory stores associated with each of the other senses (e.g., touch, taste). However, they are less important than iconic and echoic memory and have attracted much less research.

KEY TERM

Chunks
Stored units formed from integrating smaller pieces of information.

Short-term memory

Interactive exercise: Capacity of short-term memory

Interactive exercise: Duration of short-term memory

Short-term memory has very limited capacity. Consider digit span: participants listen to a random digit series and then repeat the digits back immediately in the correct order. There are also letter and word spans. The maximum number of items recalled without error is typically about seven (Miller, 1956).

There are two reasons for rejecting seven items as the capacity of short-term memory. First, we must distinguish between items and **chunks**, which are "groups of items that have been collected together and treated as a single unit" (Mathy & Feldman, 2012, p. 346). Memory span involves a *random* series of items and so the number of chunks corresponds to the number of items. In contrast, suppose you were given the following letters on a letter-span task: P S Y C H O L O G Y. There are ten letters but only one chunk and so your recall would be perfect (hopefully!). Second, estimates of short-term memory capacity are often inflated because participants' performance depends on rehearsal and long-term memory.

The concept of a "chunk" is rather vague. Mathy and Feldman (2012) argued that people process a string of items by compressing them into the smallest possible number of distinct sequences or chunks. The number of chunks so defined that were recalled immediately in order was three or four. A similar capacity limit has been obtained in several other studies. Chen and Cowan (2009) presented participants with chunks consisting of single words or pairs of words learned previously. Rehearsal was prevented by articulatory suppression (saying "the" repeatedly). Only three chunks were recalled in the absence of rehearsal.

Within the multi-store model, it is assumed that all items have equal importance. However, this is an oversimplification (Nee and Jonides, 2013). Suppose several items are presented, followed very rapidly by another, a probe item. Participants decide whether the probe item corresponds to any of the list items. Response to the probe is faster when it corresponds to the most recently rehearsed item than when it corresponds to any of the other items (McElree, 2006). Thus, the item within short-term memory that is the current focus of attention has a privileged position.

How is information lost from short-term memory? Two main answers have been proposed. First, information may *decay* over time in the absence of rehearsal. Second, there may be *interference*. This interference could come from items on previous trials and/or from information presented during the retention interval.

Berman et al. (2009) claimed that interference is more important than decay. Short-term memory performance on any given trial was disrupted by words presented on the previous trial. Suppose this disruption effect occurred because the words from the previous trial had not decayed sufficiently. If so, disruption would have been greatly reduced by *increasing* the time interval between trials. In fact, increasing the intertrial interval had no effect on performance. However, the disruption effect was largely eliminated when interference from previous trials was reduced.

Campoy (2012) pointed out that Berman et al.'s (2009) research was limited. Their experimental design did not allow them to observe any decay occurring within 3.3 seconds of an item being presented. Campoy discovered there were strong decay effects at time intervals shorter than 3.3 seconds. Thus, decay occurs mostly at short retention intervals and interference at longer ones.

Is short-term memory distinct from long-term memory? If they are separate, there should be some patients with impaired long-term memory but intact short-term memory and others showing the opposite pattern. This would produce a double dissociation (see Glossary). The findings are generally supportive. Patients with amnesia (discussed in Chapter 7) have severe long-term memory impairments, but typically have intact short-term memory (Spiers et al., 2001).

A few brain-damaged patients have severely impaired short-term memory but intact long-term memory. For example, KF had no problems with long-term learning and recall but had a very small digit span (Shallice & Warrington, 1970). Subsequent research indicated that his short-term memory problems focused mainly on recall of letters, words or digits rather than meaningful sounds or visual stimuli (e.g., Shallice & Warrington, 1974).

Evaluation

The multi-store approach has various strengths and has had enormous influence. It is still widely accepted (but see below) that there are important conceptual distinctions between three kinds of memory stores. Several kinds of experimental evidence provide strong support for the crucial distinction between short-term and long-term memory. However, the strongest evidence probably comes from brain-damaged patients having impairments only to short-term or long-term memory.

What are the model's limitations? First, it is very oversimplified. It is assumed the short-term and long-term stores are both unitary, that is, each store always operates in a single, uniform way. Shortly we will discuss an approach in which the single short-term store is replaced with a working memory system consisting of *four* components. In similar fashion, there are several long-term memory systems (see Chapter 7).

Second, it is assumed the short-term store acts as a *gateway* between the sensory stores and long-term memory (see Figure 6.1). This is incorrect, because the information processed in short-term memory has *already* made contact with information in long-term memory (Logie, 1999). Consider our ability to rehearse "IBM" as a single chunk in short-term memory. We can do this only because we have previously accessed relevant information in long-term memory.

Third, Atkinson and Shiffrin (1968) assumed that information in short-term memory represents the "contents of consciousness". This implies that only information processed consciously can be stored in long-term memory. However, implicit learning (learning without conscious awareness of what has been learned) appears to exist and leads to long-term memory (see later in the chapter).

Fourth, the assumption that all items within short-term memory have equal status is incorrect. In fact, the item currently receiving attention can be accessed more rapidly than the other items in short-term memory (McElree, 2006).

Fifth, it was assumed that most information is transferred to long-term memory via rehearsal. This greatly exaggerates the role of rehearsal – only a small fraction of the information we have stored in long-term memory was rehearsed during learning.

Unitary-store model

Jonides et al. (2008) argued that the multi-store model should be replaced by a unitary-store model. According to the unitary-store model, "STM [short-term memory] consists of temporary activations of LTM [long-term memory] representations or of representations of items that were recently perceived" (Jonides et al., 2008, p. 198). Such representations are especially likely to occur when they are the focus of attention.

Atkinson and Shiffrin (1968) emphasised the *differences* between short-term and long-term memory, whereas advocates of the unitary-store approach focus on the *similarities*. There are certainly close links between short-term and long-term memory. For example, word span is approximately seven words if the words are random. However, it can be 20 words if the words form sentences (Simon, 1974). This enhanced word span involves forming large chunks (integrated units), which depends heavily on long-term memory.

How can unitary-store models explain amnesic patients having essentially intact short-term memory but severely impaired long-term memory? Jonides et al. (2008) argued that they have special problems in forming novel relations (e.g., between items and their context) in both short-term and long-term memory. Amnesic patients perform well on short-term memory tasks because such tasks typically do not require storing *relational* information. Thus, amnesic patients should have impaired short-term memory performance on tasks requiring relational memory.

According to Jonides et al. (2008), the hippocampus and surrounding medial temporal lobes (damaged in amnesic patients) are crucial for forming novel relations. Multi-store theorists assume these structures are much more involved in long-term than short-term memory. However, unitary-store models predict the hippocampus and medial temporal lobes would be involved if a short-term memory task required forming novel relations.

Findings

Much relevant research involves amnesic patients with damage to the medial temporal lobes including the hippocampus (although other brain areas can be damaged). As predicted by the unitary-store approach, such patients often perform poorly on memory tasks with a fairly brief interval between study and test (Jeneson & Squire, 2012). In one study (Hannula et al., 2006), scenes were presented and then repeated exactly or with one object having been moved spatially. Amnesic patients with hippocampal damage and healthy controls decided whether each scene had been viewed previously. Amnesic patients performed worse than controls even with a very short retention interval, suggesting the hippocampus is needed even for relational short-term memory.

However, long-term memory may have been involved in the Hannula et al. study. Jeneson et al. (2011) used a similar task (but with reduced memory load to minimise the involvement of long-term memory). Amnesic patients (all with hippocampal damage) had comparable memory performance to controls. Thus, the hippocampus is *not* essential for good relational short-term memory.

Several neuroimaging studies have reported hippocampal involvement in short-term memory (Jeneson & Squire, 2012). However, it has generally been unclear whether hippocampal activation was due in part to encoding for long-term

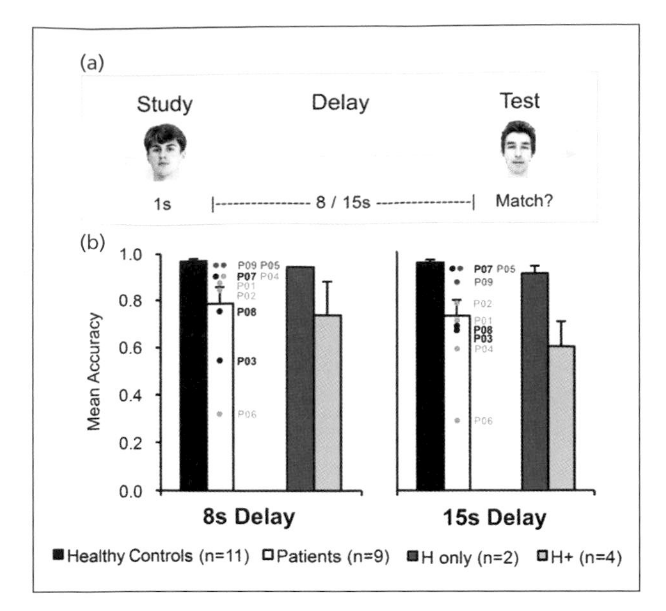

Figure 6.2
(a) Face recognition memory task with a retention interval of 8 or 15 seconds. (b) Memory performance at 8- and 15-second delay for healthy controls (black bars), the whole amnesic patient group (white bars), amnesic patients with damage limited to the hippocampus (H only; red bars) and amnesic patients with medial temporal lobe damage including the hippocampus (H+).

From Race et al. (2013). With permission of the American Psychological Association.

memory. An exception was a study by Bergmann et al. (2012), who assessed short-term and long-term memory for word pairs. The key evidence related to brain activation when short-term memory for word pairs was successful but subsequent long-term memory was not. Learning of these word pairs was *not* associated with hippocampal activation.

Clarification of the brain areas involved in short-term memory was obtained by Race et al. (2013). They assessed face recognition memory with an eight-second retention interval in amnesic patients and healthy controls. Patients with brain damage limited to the hippocampus had intact memory performance, whereas those with more extensive damage to the medial temporal lobes had impaired memory performance (see Figure 6.2).

Evaluation

As predicted by unitary-store models, activation of part of long-term memory typically plays an important role in short-term memory. There is also some (controversial) support for the notion that forming novel relations in short-term memory may involve the hippocampus. More promisingly, related areas of the medial temporal lobes may be involved in short-term as well as long-term memory (Race et al., 2013).

What are the limitations of the unitary-store approach? First, it is oversimplified to argue that short-term memory is *only* activated long-term memory. We can manipulate activated long-term memory in flexible ways going well beyond simply activating part of long-term memory. Two examples are backward digit recall (recalling digits in the opposite order to the one presented) and generating novel visual images (Logie & van der Meulen, 2009).

Second, most studies on amnesic patients suggest hippocampal involvement is far greater in long-term memory than short-term memory. Such findings are more consistent with the multi-store approach than the unitary-store approach.

Third, the findings of neuroimaging studies are not supportive of the unitary-store approach. There is little evidence of hippocampal involvement when attempts are made to separate out short-term and long-term memory processes (e.g., Bergmann et al., 2012).

WORKING MEMORY

Is short-term memory useful in everyday life? As textbook writers sometimes point out, it allows us to remember a telephone number for the few seconds required to dial it. However, that is now irrelevant – most people have mobile or cell phones that store all the phone numbers needed regularly.

Alan Baddeley and Graham Hitch (1974) (see photos) provided a convincing answer to the above question. They argued that we typically use short-term memory when performing complex tasks. With such tasks, you carry out various processes. However, you also have to store briefly information about the outcome of early processes in short-term memory as you move on to later ones. For example, this happens very often in mental arithmetic. One of Baddeley and Hitch's central insights was that short-term memory is essential in the performance of numerous tasks that are not explicitly memory tasks.

Alan Baddeley and Graham Hitch.

Courtesy of Alan Baddeley and Graham Hitch.

The above line of thinking led Baddeley and Hitch (1974) to replace the concept of the short-term store with that of working memory. Since then, the conceptualisation of the working memory system has become increasingly complex. The latest version of the working memory model has four components (Baddeley, 2012; see Figure 6.3):

1 A modality-free **central executive**, which "is an attentional system" (Baddeley, 2012, p. 22).
2 A **phonological loop** processing and storing information briefly in a phonological (speech-based) form.
3 A **visuo-spatial sketchpad** specialised for spatial and visual processing and temporary storage.
4 An **episodic buffer** providing temporary storage for integrated information coming from the visuo-spatial sketchpad and phonological loop. This component (added 25 years after the others) is discussed later.

The most important component is the central executive. It has limited capacity, resembles attention and deals with any cognitively demanding task. The phonological loop and the visuo-spatial sketchpad are slave systems used by the central executive for specific purposes. The phonological loop preserves the order in which words are presented, whereas the visuo-spatial sketchpad stores and manipulates spatial and visual information.

All three components discussed above have limited capacity and can function fairly independently of the others. Two key assumptions follow:

1 If two tasks use the same component, they cannot be performed successfully together.
2 If two tasks use different components, it should be possible to perform them as well together as separately.

Numerous dual-task studies have been carried out on the basis of these assumptions. For example, Robbins et al. (1996) considered the selection of chess moves by weaker and stronger players. The players selected continuation moves from various chess positions while also performing one of the following tasks:

- repetitive tapping: the control condition;
- random number generation: this involves the central executive;

KEY TERMS

Central executive
A modality-free, limited capacity, component of **working memory**.

Phonological loop
A component of **working memory** in which speech-based information is processed and stored and subvocal articulation occurs.

Visuo-spatial sketchpad
A component of **working memory** used to process visual and spatial information and to store this information briefly.

Episodic buffer
A component of **working memory**; it is essentially passive and stores integrated information briefly.

KEY TERM

Articulatory suppression
Rapid repetition of a simple sound (e.g., "the the the"), which uses the articulatory control process of the **phonological loop**.

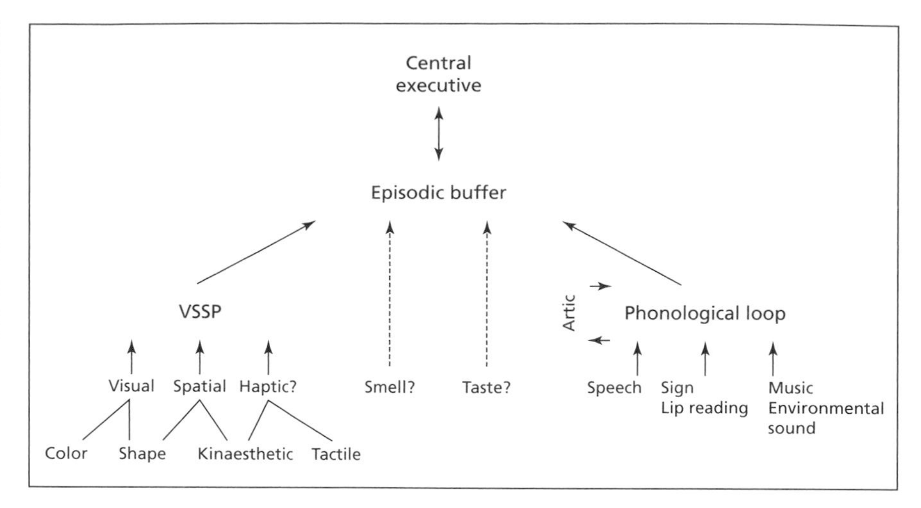

Figure 6.3
Baddeley's working memory model showing the flow of information from perception through working memory. VSSP = visuo-spatial sketchpad.
From Baddeley (2012). © Annual Reviews 2012. With permission of Annual Reviews.

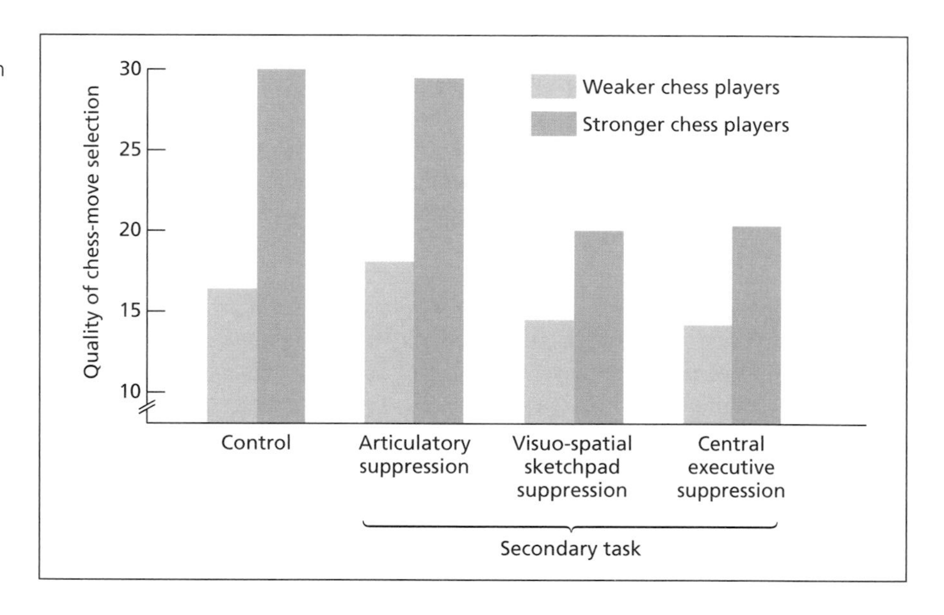

Figure 6.4
Effects of secondary tasks on quality of chess-move selection in stronger and weaker players.
Adapted from Robbins et al. (1996).

- pressing keys on a keypad in a clockwise fashion: this uses the visuo-spatial sketchpad;
- rapid repetition of the word "see-saw": this is **articulatory suppression** and uses the phonological loop.

Robbins et al. (1996) found that selecting chess moves involves the central executive and the visuo-spatial sketchpad but not the phonological loop (see Figure 6.4). The additional tasks had similar effects on stronger and weaker players, suggesting both groups used the working memory system in the same way.

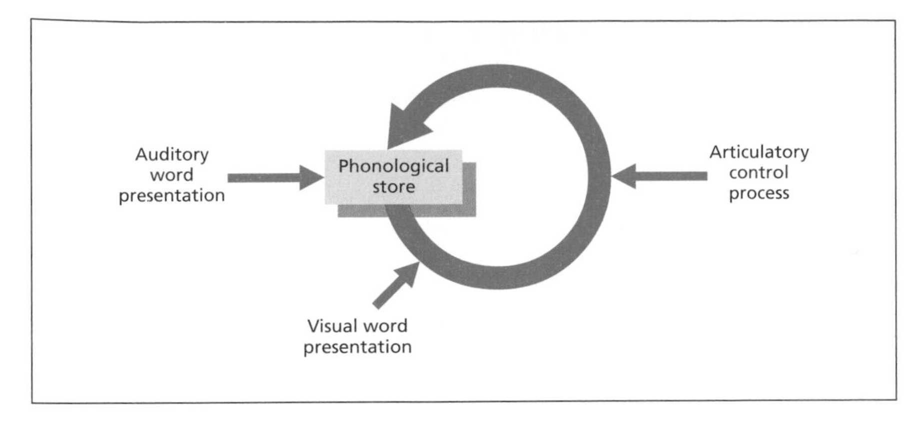

Figure 6.5
Phonological loop system as envisaged by Baddeley (1990).

KEY TERM

Phonological similarity effect
The finding that immediate serial recall of verbal material is reduced when the items sound similar.

Phonological loop

According to the working memory model, the phonological loop consists of two components (see Figure 6.5):

- a passive phonological store directly concerned with speech *perception*;
- an articulatory process linked to speech *production* (i.e., rehearsal) giving access to the phonological store.

Suppose we test people's memory span by presenting *visually* a series of words and requiring immediate recall in the correct order. Would they use the phonological loop to engage in verbal rehearsal (i.e., saying the words over and over to themselves) on this task? Two kinds of supporting evidence are discussed below.

First, there is the **phonological similarity effect**, which is reduced immediate serial recall when words are phonologically similar (i.e., having similar sounds). For example, FEE, HE, KNEE, LEE, ME and SHE form a list of phonologically similar words, whereas BAY, HOE, IT, ODD, SHY and UP form a list of phonologically dissimilar words. The ability to recall the words in order was 25% worse with the phonologically similar list (Larsen et al., 2000).

Research activity:
Phonemic similarity

Interactive exercise:
Encoding in STM

Research has revealed that the processes underlying the phonological similarity effect are more complex than originally assumed. Acheson et al. (2010) found the effect does not only involve the phonological loop – semantic processes also play a part. Schweppe et al. (2011) pointed out that the working memory model is underspecified. The emphasis in research has been on similarity at the phonemic level (phonemes are the basic units of sound). However, it is not clear whether the phonological similarity effect depends more on *acoustic* similarity (similar sounds) or on *articulatory* similarity (similar articulatory movements).

Schweppe et al. (2011) addressed the above issue. The phonological similarity effect depended more on acoustic than articulatory similarity. However, there was a significant effect of articulatory similarity when recall was *spoken* but not when it was *written*. These complexities are not predicted by the working memory model.

KEY TERM

Word-length effect
The finding that verbal memory span decreases when longer words are presented.

Second, there is the **word-length effect**: word span (number of words recalled immediately in the correct order) is greater for short than long words. There is much evidence for this effect (Baddeley, 2012). Baddeley et al. (1975) obtained the effect with visually and with auditorily presented words. In other conditions, participants engaged in articulatory suppression (repeating the digits 1 to 8) to prevent rehearsal within the phonological loop while being presented with word lists. This eliminated the word-length effect with visually presented words, suggesting the effect depends on rehearsal. This conclusion was supported by Jacquemot et al. (2011). They studied word span in a brain-damaged patient with greatly impaired ability to engage in verbal rehearsal. Theoretically, this should have prevented her from having a word-length effect. That was, indeed, what Jacquemot et al. found.

Jalbert et al. (2011) argued that there is an important confounding between word length and orthographic neighbourhood. A word's orthographic neighbourhood consists of words of the same length differing from it in only one letter. Short words generally have more neighbours than long ones, and so the so-called word-length effect may be due more to neighbourhood size than to word length itself. When short (one-syllable) and long (three-syllable) words were equated for neighbourhood size, the word-length effect disappeared (Jalbert et al., 2011). Thus, there are some doubts about the existence of the word-length effect.

What use is the phonological loop in everyday life? After all, we do not often try to remember lists of unrelated words in the correct order! We can address this issue by studying brain-damaged patients with a very impaired phonological loop. This was done by Baddeley et al. (1988). They tested a patient, PV, who had a digit span of only two items (much less than the population average of about seven). PV coped very well with everyday life, including running a shop and raising a family.

Baddeley et al. (1998) argued that the phonological loop is useful when learning a language. PV (a native Italian speaker) performed as well as healthy participants when learning to associate pairs of unrelated words in Italian. However, her performance was dramatically inferior to that of healthy controls when learning to associate Russian words with their Italian translations. Indeed, she showed no learning at all over ten trials!

In similar fashion, Papagno et al. (1991) found that articulatory suppression (which reduces use of the phonological loop) greatly slowed the learning of foreign vocabulary. However, it had little effect on the learning of Italian words.

You probably have experience of using your "inner voice" to resist temptation. This suggests the phonological loop can be used for action control. Tullett and Inzlicht (2010) used two versions of a simple task varying in their demands on action control. In one condition, use of the phonological loop on the task was reduced by articulatory suppression (saying the word *computer* repeatedly). As predicted, articulatory suppression reduced action control and increased the error rate considerably only when the demands on action control were high.

Visuo-spatial sketchpad

The visuo-spatial sketchpad is used for the temporary storage and manipulation of visual patterns and spatial movement. In essence, visual processing involves remembering *what* and spatial processing involves remembering *where*. The visuo-spatial sketchpad is very useful in everyday life – we use it to find the route when moving from one place to another or when watching television.

The most important issue is whether there is a *single* system combining visual and spatial processing or whether there are partially or completely *separate* visual and spatial systems. According to Logie (1995), the visuo-spatial sketchpad consists of two components:

- **Visual cache**: This stores information about visual form and colour.
- **Inner scribe**: This processes spatial and movement information. It is involved in the rehearsal of information in the visual cache and transfers information from the visual cache to the central executive.

Subsequent theoretical developments are discussed by Logie and van der Meulen (2009).

KEY TERMS

Visual cache
According to Logie, the part of the **visuo-spatial sketchpad** that stores information about visual form and colour.

Inner scribe
According to Logie, the part of the **visuo-spatial sketchpad** dealing with spatial and movement information.

Findings

Evidence supporting the notion of *separate* visual and spatial systems was reported by Smith and Jonides (1997). Two visual stimuli were presented together followed by a probe stimulus. Participants decided whether the probe was in the same location as one of the initial stimuli (spatial task) or had the same form (visual task). Even though the stimuli were identical in the two tasks, there were clear differences in patterns of brain activation. There was more activity in the *right* hemisphere during the spatial task than the visual task, but more activity in the *left* hemisphere during the visual task than the spatial task.

Zimmer (2008) reviewed research on the brain areas involved in visual and spatial processing. Areas within the occipital and temporal lobes were activated during visual processing. In contrast, areas within the parietal cortex (especially the intraparietal sulcus) were activated during spatial processing.

Klauer and Zhao (2004) also explored the issue of whether there are separate visual and spatial systems. They used two main tasks. One was a spatial task (memory for dot locations) and the other a visual task (memory for Chinese characters). Sometimes the main task was performed with a colour discrimination task to provide visual interference. At other times, the main task was performed with a movement discrimination task to provide spatial interference.

What would we predict if there are separate spatial and visual components? First, the spatial interference task should disrupt performance more on the spatial main task than the visual main task. Second, the visual interference task should disrupt performance more on the visual main task than the spatial main task. Both predictions were supported (see Figure 6.6).

In spite of the differences between visual and spatial processing, both can require the attentional resources of the central executive. Vergauwe et al. (2009) argued that the tasks used by Klauer and Zhao (2004) were too simple to require much attention. Accordingly, Vergauwe et al. used more demanding versions of Klauer and Zhao's tasks. Their findings were very different from those of Klauer and Zhao in that each type of interference had comparable effects on the spatial and visual main tasks.

What can we conclude? There are *general*, attentionally based interference effects when tasks are demanding, but interference effects are *specific* to the type of interference when tasks are relatively undemanding. The take-home message

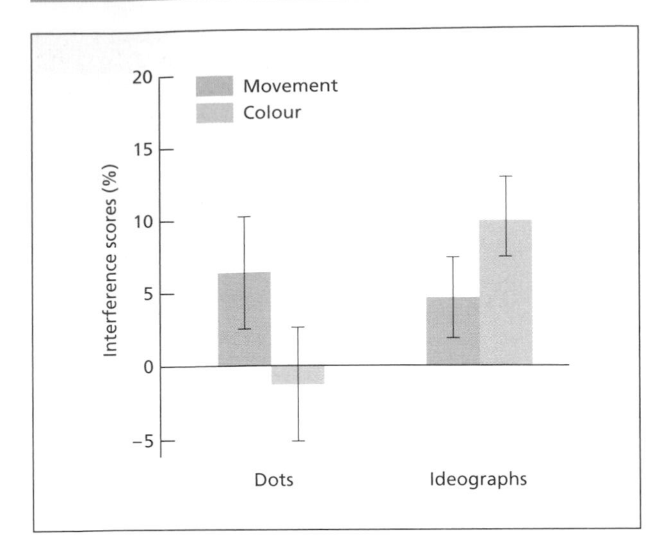

Figure 6.6
Amount of interference on a spatial task (dots) and a visual task (ideographs) as a function of secondary task (spatial: movement vs. visual: colour discrimination).

From Klauer and Zhao (2004). © 2000 American Psychological Association. Reproduced with permission.

is that the apparent separateness of the visual and spatial components of the visuo-spatial sketchpad depends on the extent to which general attentional processes are required.

Evaluation

Most research indicates that the visuo-spatial sketchpad consists of somewhat separable visual and spatial components. However, it remains for the future to understand more fully how processing and information from the two components are combined and integrated. In addition, much remains unknown about interactions between the workings of the visuo-spatial sketchpad and the episodic buffer. Finally, as Baddeley (2012) admitted, we know little about rehearsal processes within the visuo-spatial sketchpad.

Central executive

The central executive (which resembles an attentional system) is the most important and versatile component of working memory. It is heavily involved in almost all complex cognitive activities (e.g., solving a problem, carrying out two tasks at the same time) but does not store information.

It is generally assumed the prefrontal cortex is the brain region most involved in central executive functions. Mottaghy (2006) reviewed studies using repetitive transcranial magnetic stimulation (rTMS; see Glossary) to disrupt the dorsolateral prefrontal cortex (BA9/46). Performance on many complex tasks was impaired by this manipulation, indicating this region is involved in several central executive functions. However, executive processes do *not* depend solely on the prefrontal cortex. Many patients with illnesses or injuries such as diffuse trauma, multiple sclerosis and vascular cognitive impairment have poor executive functioning with little or no frontal damage (Stuss, 2011).

Baddeley has always recognised that the central executive is associated with several **executive processes** (processes that organise and coordinate the functioning of the cognitive system to achieve current goals). Baddeley (1996) speculatively identified four such processes: (1) focusing attention or concentration; (2) dividing attention between two stimulus streams; (3) switching attention between tasks; and (4) interfacing with long-term memory. In fact, it has proved very difficult to obtain consensus on the number and nature of executive processes. One of the most influential theoretical approaches is discussed below, but note that several different approaches have been proposed (Baddeley, 2012).

KEY TERM

Executive processes
Processes that organise and coordinate the functioning of the cognitive system to achieve current goals.

Miyake et al.'s executive functions

A crucial issue is to identify the number and nature of these executive processes. The approach advocated by Miyake et al. (2000) has been especially influential. They administered several executive tasks to their participants. Then they focused on positive correlations among tasks as the basis for identifying tasks all involving the same executive process.

Miyake et al. (2000) identified three related (but separable) executive processes or functions:

1 *Inhibition function*: used to deliberately override dominant responses and to resist distraction. For example, it is used on the **Stroop task**, which involves naming the colours in which words are printed. When the words are conflicting colour words (e.g., the word BLUE printed in red), it is necessary to inhibit saying the word instead of naming the colour.
2 *Shifting function*: used to switch flexibly between tasks or mental sets. Suppose you are presented with two numbers on each trial. Your task is to switch between *multiplying* the two numbers and *dividing* one by the other on alternate trials. Such task switching requires the shifting function.
3 *Updating function*: used to monitor and engage in rapid addition or deletion of working memory contents. For example, this function is used if you must keep track of the most recent member of each of several categories.

KEY TERM

Stroop task
A task on which participants have to name the ink colours in which colour words are printed; performance is slowed when the to-be-named colour (e.g., green) conflicts with the colour word (e.g., RED).

Interactive exercise: Stroop

Miyake and Friedman (2012) developed their theory into the unity/diversity framework. The basic idea is that each executive function consists of what is *common* to all three executive functions plus what is *unique* to that function (see Figure 6.7). Friedman et al. (2008) tested this framework. After accounting for what was common to all functions, there was no unique variance left for the inhibition function. In other words, the inhibition function correlates almost perfectly with the common executive function. What exactly is common to all executive functions? According to Miyake and Friedman (2012, p. 11), it is "one's ability to actively maintain task goals and goal-related information and use this information to effectively bias lower-level processing".

Friedman et al. (2008) obtained additional support for the unity/diversity framework. They studied monozygotic (identical) and dizygotic (fraternal) twins. The key finding was that genetic factors contributed substantially to individual differences at both unity and diversity levels.

Neuroimaging studies in which brain areas associated with each executive process or function are identified have provided some support for the unity/diversity framework. Collette et al. (2005) found all three of Miyake et al.'s (2000) functions were associated with activation in a different prefrontal area. This is consistent with the diversity notion. In addition, all tasks produced activation in other areas (e.g., the left lateral prefrontal cortex), which is consistent with the unity notion.

Hedden and Gabrieli (2010) carried out a similar study focusing on the inhibition and shifting functions. Their main findings are shown in Figure 6.8. First, several areas (e.g., dorsolateral prefrontal cortex, anterior cingulate cortex, basal ganglia) were fairly strongly associated

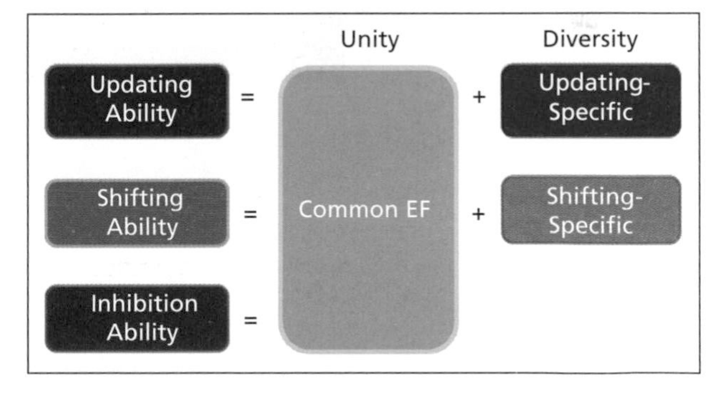

Figure 6.7
Schematic representation of the unity and diversity of three executive functions (EFs). Each executive function is a combination of what is common to all three and what is specific to that executive function. The inhibition-specific component is absent because the inhibition function correlates very highly with the common executive function.

From Miyake and Friedman (2012). Reprinted with permission of SAGE Publications.

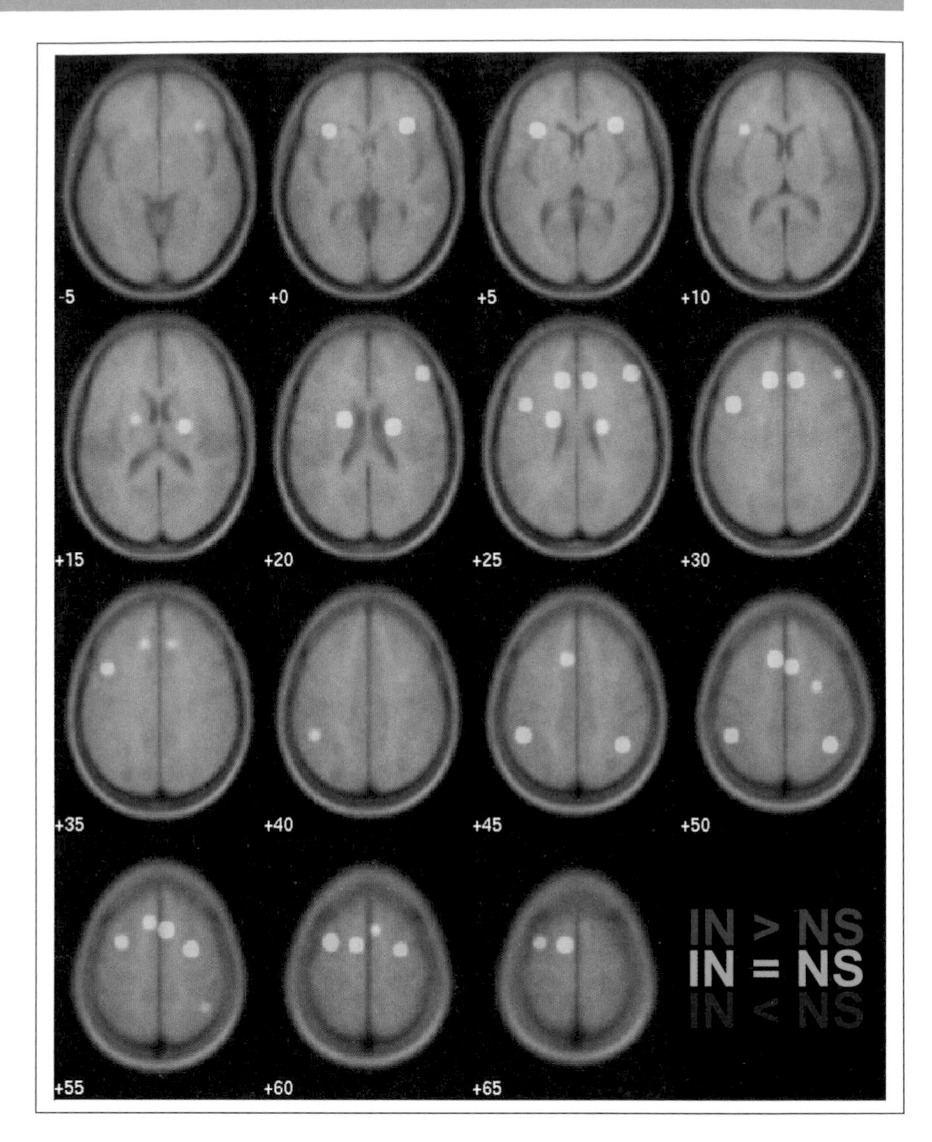

Figure 6.8
Brain areas having comparable activation on inhibition and shifting tasks (green), those having greater activation on inhibition than shifting tasks (red) and those having greater activation on shifting tasks than inhibition tasks (blue). Green areas include the dorsolateral prefrontal cortex and anterior cingulate cortex, red areas include the right middle and superior frontal gyrus, the right inferior parietal lobule and the left cerebellum, and blue areas include the inferior parietal lobe and the left dorsolateral prefrontal cortex.
From Hedden and Gabrieli (2010). Reproduced with permission from Elsevier.

with both functions. Second, other areas (e.g., right ventrolateral prefrontal cortex, bilateral temporo-parietal junction) were more activated by inhibition than shifting. Third, there was only modest evidence of brain areas more activated by shifting than inhibition. In sum, there was considerable overlap in the brain areas associated with inhibition and shifting. However, there was also evidence of diversity, especially with respect to the inhibition function.

Dysexecutive syndrome

Another approach to understanding the functions of the central executive is to study brain-damaged individuals whose central executive functioning is impaired. Such individuals suffer from **dysexecutive syndrome** (Baddeley, 1996). This syndrome involves numerous cognitive problems. Godefroy et al. (2010) identified impaired response inhibition, rule deduction and generation, maintenance and shifting of sets, and information generation as symptoms of dysexecutive syndrome. Unsurprisingly, patients with this syndrome typically have great problems in holding a job and functioning adequately in everyday life (Chamberlain, 2003).

KEY TERM

Dysexecutive syndrome A condition in which damage to the frontal lobes causes impairments to the **central executive** component of **working memory**.

Stuss and Alexander (2007) argued that the notion of a dysexecutive syndrome is flawed because it implies brain damage to the frontal lobes damages *all* central executive functions. They accepted that patients with widespread damage to the frontal lobes have a global dysexecutive syndrome. In their own research, however, they focused on patients with *limited* damage within prefrontal cortex and identified three executive processes:

1 *Task setting*: This involves planning; it is "the ability to set a stimulus-response relationship . . . necessary in the early stages of learning to drive a car or planning a wedding" (p. 906).
2 *Monitoring*: This involves checking the adequacy of one's task performance; deficient monitoring leads to increased variability of performance and increased errors.
3 *Energisation*: This involves sustained attention or concentration; deficient energisation leads to slow performance on all tasks requiring fast responding.

Each of the above processes was associated with a different region within the frontal cortex (Stuss & Alexander, 2007). While Stuss and Alexander's three processes are rather different from those previously identified by Miyake et al. (2000), there is reasonable overlap. For example, task setting and monitoring both involve aspects of cognitive control as do the processes of inhibition and shifting.

The importance of the three executive processes identified by Stuss and Alexander (2007) was confirmed by Stuss (2011). In addition, he argued for the existence of another executive process he called metacognition/integration. According to Stuss (2011, p. 761), "This function is integrative and coordinating-orchestrating . . . [it includes] recognising the differences between what one knows [and] what one believes." Evidence for this process has come from research on patients with damage to BA10 (frontopolar prefrontal cortex; Burgess et al., 2007).

Gläscher et al. (2012) administered many tasks (including some designed to assess inhibition and shifting) in brain-damaged patients. One was the Iowa Gambling Task, which assesses value-based decision making. It involves four virtual decks of cards from which participants choose cards and win or lose money as a result. Most participants gradually learn there are "good decks" that generally lead to winning money and "bad decks" that lead to losing money. Gläscher et al.'s key finding was the identification of two separate brain networks (see Figure 6.9):

Weblink:
Online Iowa Gambling Task demonstration

1 A *cognitive control* network including the dorsolateral prefrontal cortex and anterior cingulate cortex associated with response inhibition, conflict monitoring and switching.

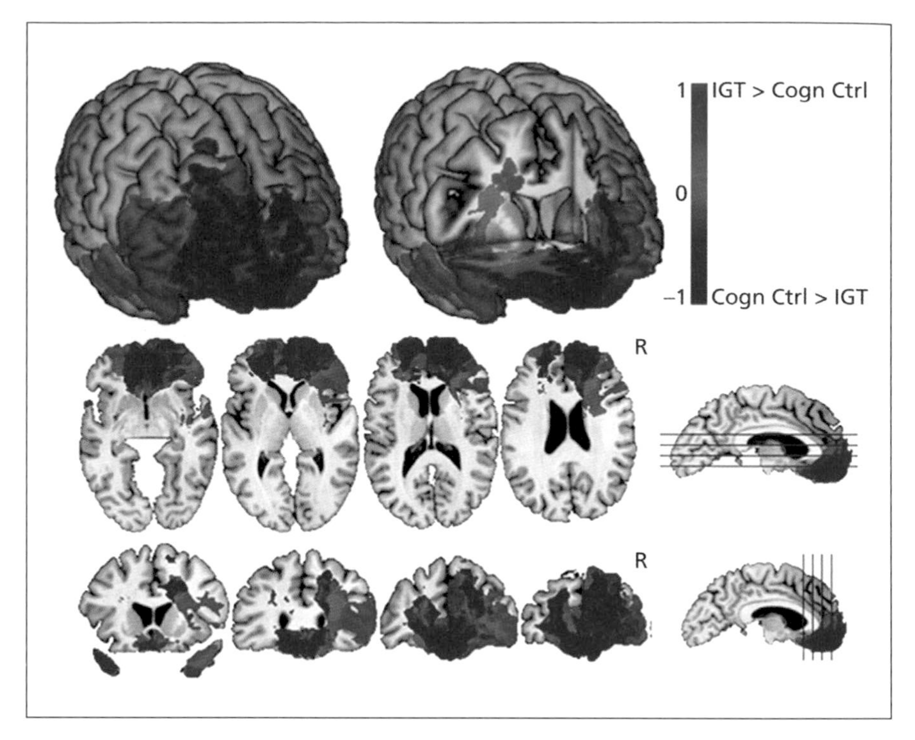

Figure 6.9
Findings from brain-damaged patients identifying two networks. The valuation network (shown in blue) includes the orbitofrontal and ventromedial cortex, and the cognitive control network (shown in red) includes the dorsolateral prefrontal cortex and anterior cingulate cortext.
From Gläscher et al. (2012). © National Academy of Sciences. Reproduced with permission.

2 A value-based decision-making network including the orbitofrontal, ventromedial and frontopolar cortex. This network has strong connections to the limbic system, which is involved in emotion and value judgements (see Chapter 15).

Evaluation

The central executive consists of various related (but separable) executive processes such as inhibition and shifting as proposed within the unity/diversity framework. This conclusion is based on both behavioural and neuroimaging evidence. The notion of a dysexecutive syndrome is misleading because it implies a *single* pattern of impairment. Instead, there are various executive processes associated with different parts of the prefrontal cortex.

What are the limitations of theory and research on the central executive? First, as Miyake and Friedman (2012) pointed out, research in this area is difficult because of the task-impurity problem (see Chapter 1). Most tasks require several different processes, making it hard to identify the contribution made by any specific executive process. Second, the number and nature of executive processes remain unclear. For example, should dual-task coordination, value-based decision making and metacognition/integration be regarded as executive processes?

Episodic buffer

As Baddeley (2012) pointed out, the function of the episodic buffer is suggested by its name. It is *episodic* because it holds integrated information (or chunks) about episodes or events in a multi-dimensional code combining visual, auditory and other sources of information. It acts as a *buffer* between the other components of the working memory system and also links working memory to perception and long-term memory. Baddeley (2012) suggested the capacity of the episodic buffer is approximately four chunks (integrated units of information).

Why did Baddeley (2000) add the episodic buffer to the working memory model? The original version of the model was limited because its components were too separate in their functioning. One of the useful features of the episodic buffer is that it provides storage for verbal information from the phonological loop and for visual and spatial information from the visuo-spatial sketchpad.

Another finding hard to explain within the original working memory model is that in immediate recall people can recall about five unrelated words but up to 16 words presented in sentences (Baddeley et al., 1987). This high level of immediate sentence recall is substantially beyond the capacity of the phonological loop. However, it can be accounted for by the proposed four-chunk capacity of the episodic buffer.

An important theoretical issue is the relationship between the episodic buffer and the central executive. Baddeley (2000) assumed that the central executive controls access to and from the episodic buffer. As a result, the central executive is needed to store integrated information (e.g., sentence chunks) in the episodic buffer. More recently, however, Baddeley (e.g., 2012) has argued that the links between the two components are less strong. His current position is that integrated information can be stored in the episodic buffer *without* the direct involvement of executive processes.

Findings

How can we explain our ability to produce immediate recall of sentences up to about 15 words long? Baddeley and Wilson (2002) argued that this ability depends on two factors: (1) the capacity of the episodic buffer; and (2) an efficiently functioning central executive to integrate or chunk sentence information. In essence, information is integrated within the episodic buffer with the assistance of the central executive. According to this argument, even severely amnesic patients with practically no delayed recall of prose should have good immediate prose recall provided they have an efficient central executive.

What did Baddeley and Wilson (2002) find? As predicted, immediate prose recall was much better in amnesics having little deficit in central executive functioning than those with a severe executive deficit. However, other research failed to confirm the importance of the central executive to good immediate prose recall (Baddeley, 2012). Suppose the presentation of sentences or random words is accompanied by a central executive task. This additional task should impair sentence recall more than word recall. However, Baddeley et al. (2009) found that the adverse effects of the additional task were similar for both types of material. Thus, the memory advantage for sentences over word lists is not crucially dependent on executive processes.

Allen et al. (2012) obtained similar findings with a different task. Participants were presented with visual stimuli and had to remember briefly a single feature (colour, shape) or colour–shape combinations. What was of interest was to observe the effects of performing a task requiring the central executive (counting backwards) at the same time. Counting backwards had comparable effects on performance regardless of whether or not feature combinations needed to be remembered. These findings suggest that combining visual features does not require the central executive but instead occurs automatically prior to information entering the episodic buffer.

Evaluation

The addition of the episodic buffer to the working memory model has extended its scope by providing a storage facility for information from the phonological loop and visuo-spatial sketchpad. There has been theoretical progress over the years – it is now clear the central executive is less crucially associated with the episodic buffer than was initially supposed. Here is the current position: "The episodic buffer [is] an essentially passive structure on which bindings [integration of information] achieved elsewhere can be displayed" (Baddeley, 2012, p. 17).

What are the limitations of research on the episodic buffer? First, there are separate inputs into the episodic buffer from the visuo-spatial sketchpad and the phonological loop (see Figure 6.3). It remains unclear precisely how information from these two components is combined to form unified representations in the episodic buffer. Second, as Figure 6.3 also shows, it is assumed that information from sensory modalities other than vision and hearing can be stored in the episodic buffer. However, relevant research on smell or taste is lacking.

Overall evaluation

The working memory model has several advantages over the short-term store proposed by Atkinson and Shiffrin (1968). First, the working memory system is concerned with both active processing and transient information storage, and so is involved in all complex cognitive tasks. Thus, its scope is much greater.

Second, the working memory model explains the partial deficits of short-term memory observed in brain-damaged patients. If brain damage affects only one component of working memory (e.g., the phonological loop), then selective deficits on short-term memory tasks would be expected.

Third, the working memory model incorporates verbal rehearsal as an optional process within the phonological loop. This is more realistic than the enormous significance of rehearsal within the multi-store model.

Fourth, theorising in cognitive psychology has changed dramatically over the 40 years since the original version of the working memory model was proposed. However, its major assumptions have stood the test of time remarkably well.

What are the limitations of the working memory model? First, it is oversimplified. Within the model, there are three components (phonological loop, visuo-spatial sketchpad, episodic buffer), which can briefly hold certain kinds of information and to which attention can be directed. However, there are numerous kinds of information not considered within the model (e.g., olfactory (smell), tactile (touch), gustatory (taste)). Spatial working memory is considered within the model, but there is evidence for somewhat separate eye-centred, hand-centred and foot-centred spatial working memory (Postle, 2006). As Postle (2006, p. 25) argued, "Followed to its logical extreme, the cognitive architecture of [Baddeley's]

Interactive exercise: Working memory

model would eventually depict a working memory system organised into hundreds . . . of domain-specific buffers, each responsible for the working memory processing of a different kind of information."

Second, as discussed earlier, it has proved difficult to identify the number and nature of the main executive processes associated with the central executive. One reason for the lack of clarity is that most complex tasks require more than one executive process, making it hard to establish the contribution each has made.

Second, we need more research on the *interactions* among the four components of working memory. For example, we lack a detailed account of how the episodic buffer integrates information from the other components and from long-term memory.

WORKING MEMORY CAPACITY

So far we have focused on Baddeley's working memory model with its four components. Other theorists have focused more on individual differences in working memory capacity. **Working memory capacity** refers to how much information an individual can process and store at the same time (see Chapter 10 on language comprehension).

Daneman and Carpenter (1980) devised a popular way of assessing working memory capacity. People read sentences for comprehension (processing task) and then recall the final word of each sentence (storage task). The largest number of sentences from which an individual can recall the final words more than 50% of the time is his/her **reading span**. This provides a measure of working memory capacity. Daneman and Carpenter assumed the processes used in comprehending the sentences require a small proportion of the available working memory capacity of large-capacity individuals. As a result, they have more capacity available for retaining the last words of the sentences.

Operation span is another measure of working memory capacity. Participants are presented with a series of items (e.g., IS (4 × 2) – 3 = 5? TABLE), answering each arithmetical question and trying to remember all the last words. Operation span is the maximum number of items for which participants can remember all the last words. It correlates highly with reading span.

It is important to note that any given individual's working memory capacity is not necessarily a fixed number. For example, there is much evidence that working memory capacity is reduced when someone is anxious or stressed (Eysenck et al., 2007). In contrast, relaxation training (perhaps in part because it reduces anxiety and stress) enhances working memory capacity (Kargar et al., 2013).

How important is working memory capacity? An indication of its importance is the correlation of +0.6 between working memory capacity and intelligence. The relationship can be clarified by identifying two types of intelligence: (1) **crystallised intelligence**, which depends on knowledge, skills and experience; and (2) fluid intelligence (see Glossary), which involves a rapid understanding of novel relationships. Working memory capacity correlates much more strongly with fluid intelligence (Unsworth, 2010). The correlation with crystallised intelligence is low because it involves acquired knowledge, whereas working memory capacity depends on cognitive processes and temporary information storage.

Most theories of working memory capacity assume that individuals with high capacity have superior executive and/or attentional processes to those with low

KEY TERMS

Working memory capacity
An assessment of how much information can be processed and stored at the same time; individuals with high capacity have higher intelligence and more attentional control.

Reading span
The largest number of sentences read for comprehension from which an individual can recall all the final words over 50% of the time.

Operation span
The maximum number of items (arithmetical questions + words) for which an individual can recall all the words more than 50% of the time.

Crystallised intelligence
The ability to use knowledge, skills and experience.

Weblink:
Online readings span task

Weblink:
Video of the operation span task

capacity. A very influential approach is Engle and Kane's (2004) two-factor theory. One factor involves the maintenance of task goals, and the other factor involves the resolution of response competition or conflict. Thus, high-capacity individuals are better at maintaining task goals and resolving conflict.

How does working memory capacity relate to Baddeley's working memory model? The greatest overlap is with the central executive: attentional control is of major importance to working memory capacity and the central executive. Why are the other components of the working memory model missing from the approach based on working memory capacity? Suppose individual differences in phonological loop and visuo-spatial sketchpad capacity are relatively small compared to individual differences in the central executive's capacity. As a result, individual differences in task performance would mostly reflect central executive functioning even if a task required the phonological loop and/or visuo-spatial sketchpad (Logie, 2011).

In view of the association between working memory capacity and intelligence, we would expect high-capacity individuals to outperform low-capacity ones on complex tasks. That is, indeed, the case (see Chapter 10). However, Engle and Kane's (2004) theory also predicts that high-capacity individuals might perform better than low-capacity ones even on relatively simple tasks if it were hard to maintain task goals.

Findings

Many studies have reported close links between working memory capacity and the executive functions of the central executive. For example, McCabe et al. (2010) obtained high correlations between measures of working memory capacity and of executive functioning. McCabe et al. argued that both types of measures reflect executive attention, which is required "to maintain task goals and resolve interference during complex cognition" (p. 237).

Individuals high in working memory capacity have greater attentional control than low scorers. For example, Sorqvist (2010) studied the effects of distraction caused by the sound of planes flying past. Recall of a prose passage was more adversely affected by distraction in low-capacity individuals. The effects of distracting stimuli can also be assessed by using event-related potentials (ERPs; see Glossary). High-capacity individuals had smaller ERPs than low-capacity ones to auditory distracting stimuli (Yurgil & Golob, 2013). Yurgil and Golob also found that high-capacity individuals had larger ERPs to target than to non-target tones, whereas low-capacity individuals had comparable ERPs to both types of tones. Thus, high-capacity individuals had better goal maintenance and early top-down control of processing.

We have just seen that goal maintenance in low-capacity individuals can be disrupted by *external* distraction. It can also be disrupted by *internal* task-unrelated thoughts (mind wandering). McVay and Kane (2012b) had participants complete a sustained-attention task in which they responded rapidly to frequent target words but withheld responses to rare non-targets. Low-capacity individuals performed worse than high-capacity ones on this task. Of most importance, low-capacity individuals engaged in more mind wandering than high-capacity individuals and this was a major reason for their inferior performance.

Suppose low-capacity individuals have poorer ability than high-capacity ones to maintain the current task goal. Such failures (known as goal neglect) would

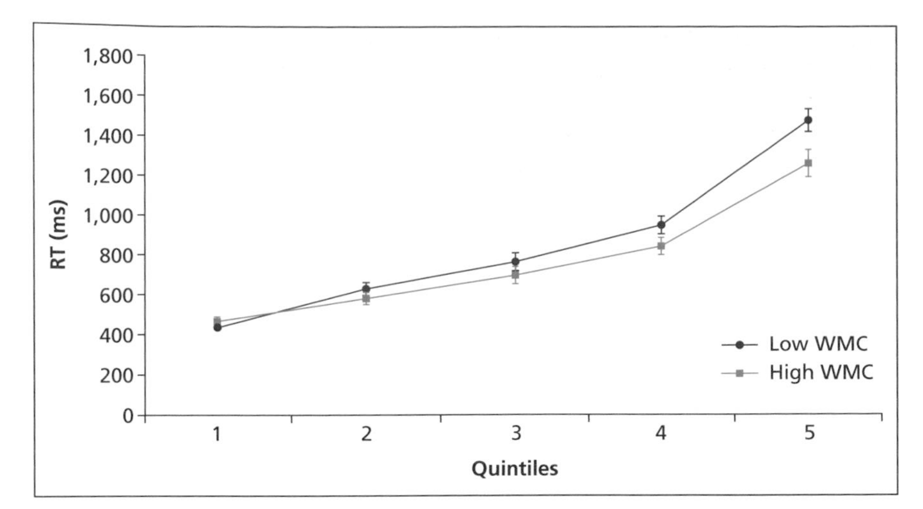

Figure 6.10
Mean reaction times (RTs) quintile-by-quintile on the anti-saccade task by groups high and low in working memory capacity.
From Unsworth et al. (2012).

presumably happen only on a small percentage of trials. Unsworth et al. (2012) obtained supporting evidence using the anti-saccade task. A flashing cue was presented to the left or right of fixation, followed by a cue presented in the *opposite* location. Reaction times to identify the target were recorded.

High-capacity individuals performed better than low-capacity ones on this task, suggesting they found it easier to inhibit a "natural" tendency to look at the flashing cue. This is a response-conflict explanation. In addition, Unsworth et al. (2012) divided each participant's reaction times into quintiles (five bins representing the fastest 20%, the next fastest 20% and so on). High-capacity individuals were significantly faster than the low-capacity ones only in the slowest quintile (see Figure 6.10). Thus, low-capacity individuals had a problem with goal maintenance on approximately 20% of trials.

Evaluation

Individuals high and low in working memory capacity differ in attentional control. More specifically, high-capacity individuals are better at controlling external and internal distracting information. In addition, they are less likely than low-capacity individuals to exhibit goal neglect. It is impressive that individual differences in working memory capacity are relevant to performance on numerous different tasks (see Chapter 10).

What are the limitations of research in this area? First, while there is much overlap between the notion of working memory capacity and Baddeley's working memory system, the former provides a less comprehensive account of working memory. Second, the fact that working memory capacity correlates highly with fluid intelligence means many findings that have been ascribed to individual differences in working memory capacity may actually reflect fluid intelligence instead.

LEVELS OF PROCESSING

What determines long-term memory? According to Craik and Lockhart (1972), what is crucial is how information is processed during learning. They argued in

Interactive exercise:
Levels of processing

their levels-of-processing approach that attentional and perceptual processes at learning determine what information is stored in long-term memory. Levels of processing range from shallow or physical analysis of a stimulus (e.g., detecting specific letters in words) to deep or semantic analysis. The greater the extent to which *meaning* is processed, the deeper the level of processing.

Here are Craik and Lockhart's (1972) main theoretical assumptions:

- The level or depth of stimulus processing has a large effect on its memorability.
- Deeper levels of analysis produce more elaborate, longer lasting and stronger memory traces than shallow levels.

Findings

Hundreds of studies support the levels-of-processing approach. For example, consider a study by Craik and Tulving (1975). They used incidental learning (the participants were not told there would be a memory test) and then assessed recognition memory as a function of the learning task:

1. *Shallow graphemic*: decide whether each word is in uppercase or lowercase letters.
2. *Intermediate phonemic*: decide whether each word rhymes with a target word.
3. *Deep semantic*: decide whether each word fits the blank in a sentence.

Depth of processing had impressive effects on memory – performance was more than *three* times higher with deep than with shallow processing. Craik and Tulving concluded that memory depends on the nature of task processing rather than the intention to learn.

Craik and Tulving (1975) argued that *elaboration* of processing (i.e., the amount of processing of a particular kind) is also important. Participants were presented with a word and a sentence containing a blank, and decided whether the word fitted into the blank space. Elaboration was manipulated by using simple (e.g., "She cooked the ____" and complex "The great bird swooped down and carried off the struggling ____") sentence frames. Cued recall was twice as high for words accompanying complex sentences.

Morris et al. (1977) argued that memory depends on the requirements of the memory test. Participants answered semantic or shallow (rhyme) questions for lists of words. Memory was tested by a standard recognition test (selected list words and reject non-list words) or by a rhyming recognition test. On this latter test, participants selected words rhyming with list words: the list words themselves were *not* presented.

There was the usual superiority of deep over shallow processing on the standard recognition test. However, the opposite result was reported with the rhyme test, which disproved the central prediction from levels-of-processing theory. According to Morris et al.'s (1977) transfer-appropriate processing theory, retrieval requires that the processing at the time of learning is *relevant* to the demands of the memory test. With the rhyming test, rhyme information is relevant but semantic information is irrelevant.

Mulligan and Picklesimer (2012) replicated Morris et al.'s (1977) findings. They extended those findings by discovering the effects of processing depth on the rhyme test depended on recollection (remembering contextual information about what happened at learning). Thus, the rhyme cues were more likely to activate contextual information for items receiving shallow processing at learning than those that had received deep processing.

Most research has used tests for **explicit memory** (e.g., recall, recognition) involving conscious recollection and has found strong effects of processing depth. It is also important to consider effects of processing depth on **implicit memory** (memory not involving conscious recollection; see Chapter 7). For example, on the word-fragment task, participants simply write down the first word they think of to complete each word fragment (e.g., c _ p p _ _). Implicit memory is shown when the fragments are completed by words presented previously.

Challis et al. (1996) used several explicit and implicit memory tasks. The levels-of-processing effect was generally greater in explicit memory than implicit memory and was especially small with word-fragment completion. Parks (2013) argued that we can explain this difference with reference to transfer-appropriate processing. Shallow processing differs from deep processing in involving more perceptual but less conceptual processing. Accordingly, levels-of-processing effects should generally be smaller when the memory task requires demanding perceptual processing (as is the case with most explicit memory tasks). Parks manipulated the perceptual demands of recognition-memory tasks. As predicted, the levels-of-processing effect decreased as perceptual demands increased.

KEY TERMS

Explicit memory
Memory that involves conscious recollection of information.

Implicit memory
Memory that does not depend on conscious recollection.

Distinctiveness
This characterises memory traces that are distinct or different from other memory traces stored in long-term memory.

Distinctiveness

Another factor important in determining long-term memory is distinctiveness. **Distinctiveness** means a memory trace differs from other memory traces because it was processed differently at the time of learning. According to Hunt (2013, p. 10), distinctive processing is "the processing of difference in the context of similarity". He gave as an example seeing a car painted purple with lemon-yellow polka dots in heavy traffic among conventionally coloured cars. The polka-dotted car is very distinctive and is likely to prove much more memorable than the other cars.

Eysenck and Eysenck (1980) used nouns having irregular pronunciations (e.g., *comb* has a silent "b"). In one condition, participants said these nouns in a distinctive way (e.g., pronouncing the "b" in *comb*). Thus, the processing was shallow (i.e., phonemic) but the memory traces were distinctive. As predicted, recognition memory was as good in this condition as in a deep or semantic condition in which meaning was processed.

Long-term memory is much better for learners having much relevant knowledge. Hunt and Rawson (2011) found that those knowledgeable about American football had better recognition memory for football items than those without that knowledge. Why is such knowledge useful? Hunt and Rawson found part of the answer was that it makes it easier for the learner to *organise* the to-be-remembered information. In addition, knowledge increases *distinctiveness* and so increases participants' ability to reject familiar but incorrect items.

Evaluation

Craik and Lockhart (1972) argued correctly that processes at learning have a major impact on subsequent long-term memory (Roediger, 2008). By so doing, they

KEY TERM

Testing effect
The finding that long-term memory is enhanced when some of the learning period is devoted to retrieving information to be learned rather than simply studying it.

issued a challenge to the then-dominant multi-store approach. Another strength is the central assumption that learning and remembering are by-products of perception, attention and comprehension. In addition, the approach led to the identification of elaboration and distinctiveness of processing as important factors in learning and memory. Finally, "The levels-of-processing approach has been fruitful and generative, providing a powerful set of experimental techniques for exploring the phenomena of memory" (Roediger & Gallo, 2001, p. 44).

The levels-of-processing approach has several limitations. First, Craik and Lockhart (1972) underestimated the importance of the retrieval environment in determining memory performance (e.g., Morris et al., 1977; Mulligan & Picklesimer, 2012). Second, the relative importance of processing depth, elaboration of processing and distinctiveness of processing to long-term memory remains unclear. Third, the terms "depth", "elaboration" and "distinctiveness" have not been defined or measured with any precision (Roediger & Gallo, 2001). Fourth, we do not know precisely why deep processing is so effective or why the levels-of-processing effect is small in implicit memory.

LEARNING THROUGH RETRIEVAL

Many people (including you?) agree with the following assumption: "Learning only occurs during study and . . . testing is useful only for evaluating the state of memory" (Pyc & Rawson, 2010, p. 335). In fact, practice in retrieving to-be-remembered information during the learning period can enhance long-term memory more than simply engaging in study and restudy. This is known as the **testing effect**. The testing effect is generally surprisingly strong (Karpicke, 2012).

Dunlosky et al. (2013) discussed ten learning techniques (e.g., writing summaries, forming images of texts, restudying texts) that have been claimed to enhance students' ability to perform successfully in examinations. They evaluated the research evidence relating to all ten techniques, concluding that repeated testing was the most effective technique of all.

Findings

Typical findings were reported by Roediger and Karpicke (2006). Students read and memorised a prose passage in one of three conditions:

1. *Repeated study*: the passage was read four times and there was no test.
2. *Single test*: the passage was read three times and then students recalled as much as possible.
3. *Repeated test*: the passage was read once and then students recalled as much as possible on three occasions.

Finally, memory for the prose passage was tested after five minutes or one week. Repeated study was the most effective strategy on the five-minute test. However, there was a dramatic reversal in the findings when the final test occurred after one week. There was a strong testing effect – average recall was 50% higher in the repeated test condition than the repeated study condition! This was the case even though students in the repeated study condition predicted they would recall more than those in the repeated test condition.

How can we explain the testing effect? Pyc and Rawson (2010) put forward the mediator effectiveness hypothesis, according to which testing promotes the use of more effective mediators. Suppose you are trying to learn the following pair of words: *wingu–cloud* (this is paired-associate learning). You might try to link the two words by using the mediator *plane*. When subsequently given the cue (*wingu*) and told to recall the target word (*cloud*), you might generate the sequence *wingu–plane–cloud*.

Pyc and Rawson (2010) obtained support for their mediator effectiveness hypothesis. Participants were instructed to learn Swahili–English pairs (e.g., *wingu–cloud*). In one learning condition, each trial after the initial study trial involved only restudy. In the other learning condition (test-restudy), each trial after the initial study trial involved a cued recall test followed by restudy. Participants generated and reported mediators on the study and restudy trials. There were three recall conditions on the final memory test one week after learning: (1) cue only; (2) cue + the mediator generated during learning; and (3) cue + prompt to try to generate the mediator.

The findings were straightforward (see Figure 6.11 (A)). First, memory performance in the cue only condition replicates the basic testing effect. Second, performance in the cue + mediator condition shows that test-restudy participants generated more effective mediators than restudy-only participants. Third, test-restudy participants performed much better than restudy-only ones in the cue + prompt condition. As is shown in Figure 6.11 (B), test-restudy participants were much better at remembering the mediators. Retrieving mediators was important for the high levels of recall achieved by the test-restudy participants – their performance was poor when they failed to recall mediators.

Pyc and Rawson (2012) developed some of the ideas in the mediator effectiveness hypothesis. Participants were more likely to change their mediators during test-restudy practice than restudy-only practice. Of most importance, participants engaged in test-restudy practice were more likely to change their mediators following retrieval failure than retrieval success. Thus, a key reason for the testing effect is that retrieval practice allows people to evaluate the effectiveness of their mediators and to replace ineffective ones with effective ones.

Pyc and Rawson (2009) tested the retrieval effort hypothesis – the notion that testing during the learning phase will be more effective when it is hard to retrieve the to-be-remembered information than when it is easy. They manipulated retrieval difficulty by varying the number of items between successive practice retrievals of any given item. Final recall was significantly better when several items intervened and so retrieval was difficult.

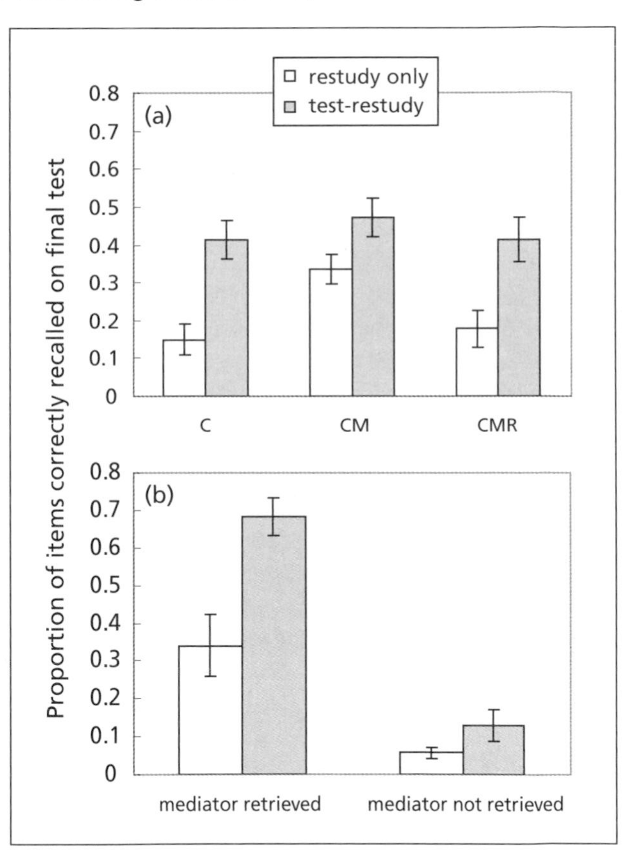

Figure 6.11
(a) Final recall for restudy-only and test-restudy group participants provided at test with cues (C), cues + the mediators generated during learning (CM) or cues + prompts to recall their mediators (CMR). (b) Recall performance in the CMR group as a function of whether the mediators were or were not retrieved.

From Pyc and Rawson (2010). © American Association for Advancement of Science. Reprinted with permission of AAAS.

It may make sense to combine the mediator effectiveness and retrieval effort hypotheses. When it is hard to retrieve the to-be-remembered information, this increases the need to generate and retrieve effective mediators. More generally, there is evidence that testing involves more effortful semantic processing than restudying. Several brain regions associated with language processing (e.g., left inferior frontal gyrus) are more active during testing than restudying (van den Broek et al., 2013).

Most research shows that testing enhances the learning of *specific* responses. There is also some evidence that testing promotes learning more *generally* (Carpenter, 2012). For example, participants who learned concepts through testing rather than restudying performed better on a test requiring inferences to be drawn based on those concepts (Butler, 2010).

However, other evidence (Peterson & Mulligan, 2013) suggests the learning produced by testing can be somewhat limited. Participants learned cue–target pairs, some of which are shown below:

Cue–Target	*Cue–Target*	*Cue–Target*	*Cue–Target*
Force–Horse	Tape–Grape	Wife–Knife	Swear–Bear
Cork–Fork	Vow–Cow	Teach–Peach	Moon–Spoon

Weblink:
Learning through testing

After initial studying of the cue–target pairs, some participants continued learning using restudying, whereas others engaged in testing or retrieval (producing the target to each cue word). Finally, the participants attempted free recall of all the target words in the absence of the cue words.

What do you think happened in this study by Peterson and Mulligan (2013)? You may have noticed that the target words belong to various categories (e.g., four-footed animals, fruit, kitchen utensils). Participants in the testing condition devoted so much processing effort to retrieving the target words they were less likely than restudying participants to notice and take advantage of the categorised nature of the target words (see Figure 6.12). Thus, the effort involved in retrieving information during *testing* can limit and constrain the kinds of information learned and remembered in that condition.

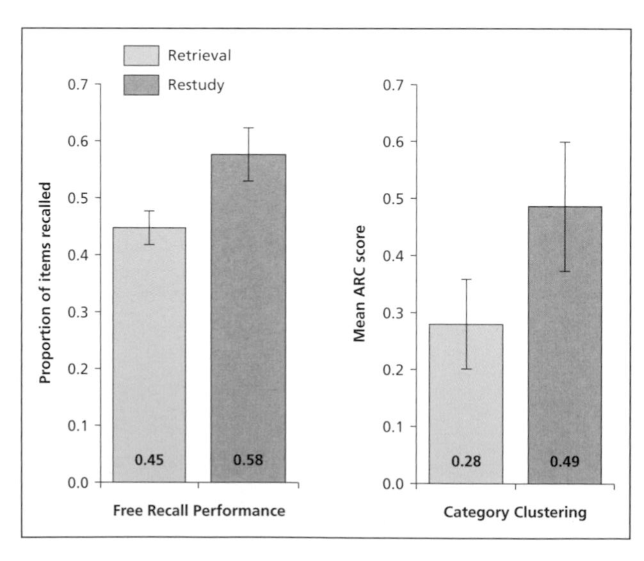

Figure 6.12
Free recall performance in the retrieval or testing and restudy conditions (left-hand side). Extent to which free recall exhibited categorical clustering or organisation for retrieval and restudy participants (right-hand side). From Peterson and Mulligan (2013). © American Psychological Association. Reproduced with permission.

Evaluation

The testing effect is strong and has been obtained in numerous studies. Testing during learning has the advantage that it can be used almost regardless of the nature of the to-be-learned material. It is an important phenomenon in part because the beneficial effects of retrieval practice are much larger than most people would have predicted. Progress has been made in identifying the processes underlying the testing effect. Retrieval practice leads learners to generate and retrieve increasingly effective mediators to link cues with to-be-remembered items. This process is especially effective when retrieval is difficult.

What are the limitations of theory and research in this area? First, most research on the mediator effectiveness hypothesis has involved paired-associate learning and so it is unclear whether the hypothesis is applicable to other learning tasks. Second, future research needs to establish whether factors other than mediator effectiveness and retrieval effort are also important in producing the testing effect. Third, most theoretical accounts assume that the testing effect will be found under almost any circumstances. Thus, the finding that testing is sometimes less effective than restudying (Peterson & Mulligan, 2013) provides a challenge for theorists.

IMPLICIT LEARNING

Do you think you could learn something without being aware of what you have learned? It sounds improbable. Even if we did learn something without realising, it seems unlikely we would make much use of it. Learning occurring in the absence of conscious awareness of what has been learned is known as **implicit learning**. Cleeremans and Jiménez (2002, p. 20) provided a fuller definition:

> Implicit learning is the process through which we become sensitive to certain regularities in the environment (1) in the absence of intention to learn about these regularities, (2) in the absence of awareness that one is learning, and (3) in such a way that the resulting knowledge is difficult to express.

Many of the issues of importance in research on implicit learning are also important with respect to implicit memory (memory not dependent on conscious recollection; see Chapter 7). Indeed, there is no clear distinction between the two areas. However, research on implicit learning generally uses fairly complex, novel learning tasks, whereas much research on implicit memory uses simple, familiar stimulus materials.

Reber (1993) made five assumptions concerning major differences between implicit and explicit learning (none has been established definitively):

1 *Age independence*: Implicit learning is little influenced by age or developmental level.
2 *IQ independence*: Performance on implicit tasks is relatively unaffected by IQ.
3 *Robustness*: Implicit systems are relatively unaffected by disorders (e.g., amnesia) affecting explicit systems.
4 *Low variability*: There are smaller individual differences in implicit learning than in explicit learning.
5 *Commonality of process*: Implicit systems are common to most species.

We will discuss the third assumption later. Here we will briefly consider the first and second ones. Several studies have reported that implicit learning is essentially intact in older adults compared to young ones (Simon et al., 2012). However, Simon et al. found in their study of implicit associative learning that

KEY TERM

Implicit learning
Learning complex information without conscious awareness of what has been learned.

IN THE REAL WORLD: SKILLED TYPISTS AND IMPLICIT LEARNING

Millions of people have highly developed typing skills. The typical American college student has ten years of typing experience and can type approximately 70 words a minute. In spite of such vast experience, many experienced typists claim that they find it hard to think exactly where the letters are on the keyboard. For example, the first author of this book has typed 7 million words for publication but has only vague conscious awareness of the locations of most letters on the keyboard! Such anecdotal evidence suggests considerable implicit learning and memory are involved in expert typing even if learning to type initially relies heavily on explicit learning.

Snyder et al. (2014) studied college typists with a mean of 11.4 years of typing experience. In the first experiment, they were presented with a blank keyboard and instructed to write the letters in their correct locations (see Figure 6.13). If you are a skilled typist, you might like to perform this task. The participants' performance was relatively poor: they located only 14.9 (57.3%) of the letters correctly. The correct answers are given in Figure 6.18 (page 241), which also shows the percentage of participants who located each letter accurately.

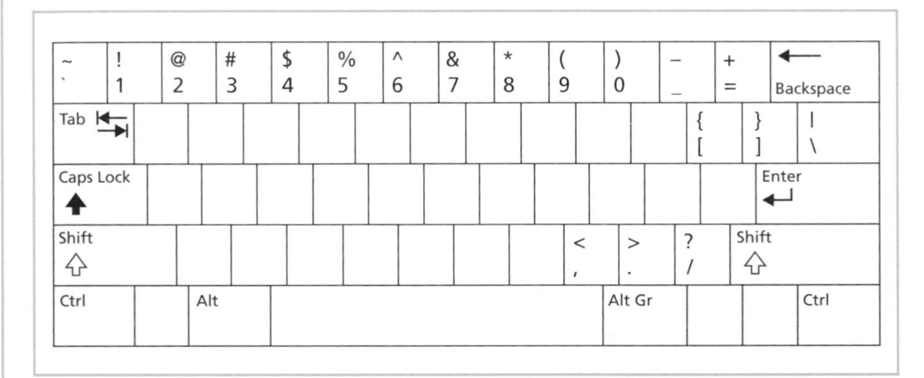

Figure 6.13
Schematic representation of the traditional keyboard.
From Snyder et al. (2014). © 2011 Psychonomic Society. Reprinted with permission from Springer.

Accurate identification of a letter's location on the keyboard could occur because typists possess relevant explicit learning and memory. Alternatively, it could occur because typists engage in simulated typing to enhance performance. In their second experiment, Snyder et al. (2014) found the ability to identify the keyboard locations of letters was significantly reduced when simulated typing was prevented by requiring typists to press a sequence of keys while performing the task. These findings indicate that explicit memory for letter locations is even lower than suggested by their first experiment.

In a final experiment, typists were given two hours' training on the Dvorak keyboard, on which the locations of the letters differs substantially from the traditional QWERTY keyboard. They were then given the same task as in the first experiment. Performance on the Dvorak and QWERTY keyboards was comparable, indicating that typists have no more explicit knowledge of letter locations on the keyboard after 10 or 11 years than after two hours.

In sum, typing provides a dramatic example of how expert performance based on vast experience can involve primarily implicit learning and memory. A great advantage of implicit learning is that relevant information can be accessed rapidly, which is essential for rapid touch-typing. In contrast, retrieval of letter locations from explicit memory would be far too slow to permit the production of five or six keystrokes per second.

the performance of older adults became increasingly inferior to that of young adults as training progressed. It is probably relevant that there was less activation of the striatum (a brain area strongly associated with implicit learning) in older adults.

With respect to the second assumption, Kaufman et al. (2010) found intelligence correlated +0.44 with explicit learning but only +0.16 with implicit learning. Janacsek and Nemeth (2013) reviewed research on working memory capacity (which correlates moderately highly with intelligence; see Glossary) and learning. There was typically a relationship between working memory capacity and explicit learning but not with implicit learning. These findings clearly support Reber's (1993) position.

KEY TERM

Process-dissociation procedure
On learning tasks, participants try to guess the next stimulus (inclusion condition) or *avoid* guessing the next stimulus accurately (exclusion condition); the difference between the two conditions indicates the amount of explicit learning.

Assessing implicit learning

You might imagine it would be fairly easy to decide whether implicit learning has occurred – we simply ask participants to perform a complex task without instructing them to engage in deliberate learning. Afterwards, they indicate their conscious awareness of what they have learned. Implicit learning is shown if learning occurs in the absence of conscious awareness of what has been learned.

The central problem with the above account is that there are several reasons why people fail to report conscious awareness of what they have learned (Shanks, 2010). For example, there is the "retrospective problem" (Shanks & St John, 1994) – participants may be consciously aware of what they are learning at the time but have forgotten it when questioned at the end of the experiment.

Shanks and St John (1994) put forward two criteria for implicit learning to be demonstrated:

1. *Information criterion*: The information participants are asked to provide on the awareness test must be the information responsible for the improved level of performance.
2. *Sensitivity criterion*: "We must be able to show that our test of awareness is sensitive to all of the relevant knowledge" (Shanks & St John, 1994, p. 374). We may underestimate participants' consciously accessible knowledge if we use an insensitive awareness test.

Before we turn to the experimental findings, we will discuss a technique for assessing whether learning is implicit or explicit: the **process-dissociation procedure**. Suppose participants carry out a task involving a repeating sequence of stimuli. Then they guess the next stimulus (inclusion condition) or try to avoid guessing accurately the next stimulus (exclusion condition). If learning is wholly implicit, participants should be unable to control how they use what they have learned, and so performance should be comparable in the two conditions. If learning is partly or wholly explicit, performance should be better in the inclusion condition than the exclusion condition.

The above procedure may be limited because it is based on the assumption that conscious and unconscious influences are *independent* rather than interactive. This issue is controversial, but Joordens et al. (2010) obtained evidence supporting the independence assumption.

Weblink:
Process-dissociation

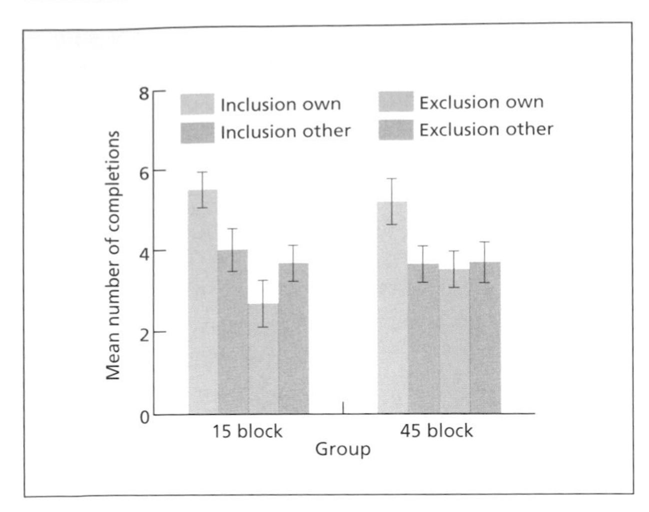

Figure 6.14
Mean number of completions (guessed locations) corresponding to the trained sequence (own) or the untrained sequence (other) in inclusion and exclusion conditions as a function of number of trials (15 vs. 45 blocks).

From Wilkinson and Shanks (2004). © 2004 American Psychological Association. Reproduced with permission.

Findings

The **serial reaction time task** has been much used in research on implicit learning. On each trial, a stimulus appears at one of several locations on a computer screen, and participants respond rapidly using the response key corresponding to its location. There is typically a complex, repeating sequence over trials but participants are not told this. Towards the end of the experiment, there is often a block of trials conforming to a novel sequence but this information is also not given to participants.

Participants speed up on the serial reaction time task over trials but respond much slower during the novel sequence (Shanks, 2010).When questioned at the end of the experiment, participants usually show no conscious awareness there was a repeating sequence or pattern in the stimuli presented to them.

Many participants performing the serial reaction time task often have at least partial awareness of what they have learned. For example, Wilkinson and Shanks (2004) gave participants 1,500 trials (15 blocks) or 4,500 trials (45 blocks) on the task and obtained strong sequence learning. This was followed by a test of explicit learning involving the process-dissociation procedure.

Participants' predictions were significantly better in the inclusion than the exclusion condition (see Figure 6.14), indicating some conscious or explicit knowledge was acquired. In a similar study, Gaillard et al. (2009) obtained comparable findings and conscious knowledge increased with practice.

Haider et al. (2011) argued that the best way to assess whether learning is explicit or implicit is to use several measures of conscious awareness. They used a form of the serial reaction time task (see Glossary) in which a colour word (the target) was written in the same (congruent trials) or a different (incongruent trials) ink. The task was to respond to the colour word rather than the ink. There were six different coloured squares below the target word and the participants' task was to press the coloured square corresponding to the colour word. Over each set of six trials, the correct coloured square followed a regular sequence (1–6–4–2–3–5) but the participants were not told this.

Haider et al. (2011) found 34% of the participants showed a sudden drop in reaction times at some point during the experiment. They hypothesised these RT-drop participants had engaged in explicit learning and were consciously aware of the regular sequence. The remaining 66% failed to show a sudden drop (the no-RT-drop participants) and were hypothesised to have engaged only in implicit learning. As you can see in Figure 6.15, the RT-drop participants showed much more learning during the course of the experiment.

Haider et al. (2011) tested the above hypotheses by using the process-dissociation procedure after the training trials. The RT-drop participants performed very well on this task: 80% correct on inclusion trials compared to only 18% correct on exclusion trials, suggesting the presence of considerable explicit learning. In contrast, the no-RT-drop participants showed no evidence of explicit learning – their performance was comparably low on inclusion and exclusion

KEY TERM

Serial reaction time task
Participants on this task respond as rapidly as possible to stimuli typically presented in a repeating sequence; it is used to assess **implicit learning**.

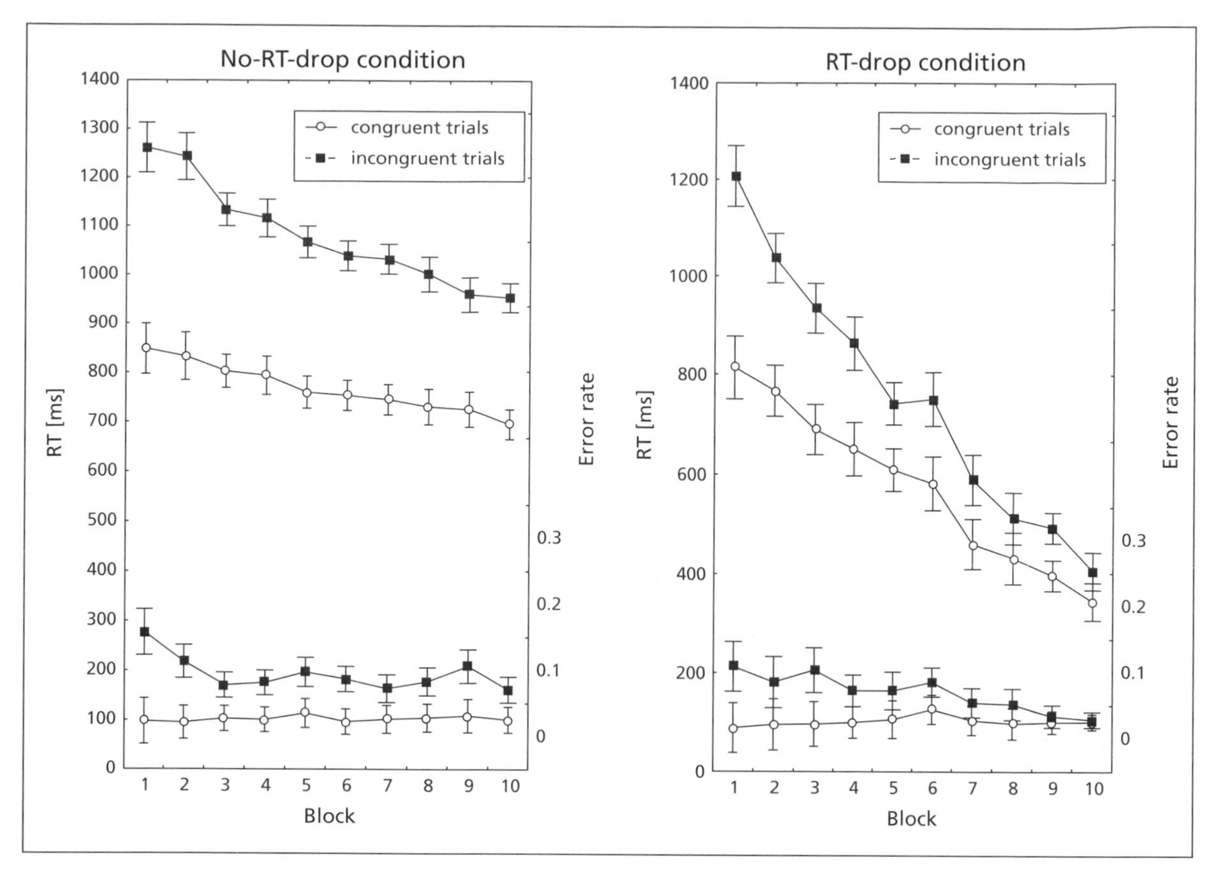

Figure 6.15
Response times (RTs) for participants showing a sudden drop in RTs (right-hand side) or not showing such a drop (left-hand side). The former group showed much greater learning than the latter group (especially on incongruent trials on which the colour word was in a different coloured ink).

From Haider et al. (2011). Reprinted with permission from Elsevier.

trials. Finally, all participants described the training sequence. Almost all the RT-drop participants (91%) did this perfectly compared to 0% of the no-RT-drop participants. Thus, the various findings all supported Haider et al.'s hypotheses.

It has often been assumed that implicit learning does not require cognitively demanding processes (e.g., attention). If so, people should be able to perform two implicit learning tasks at the same time without interference. Jiménez and Vázquez (2011) obtained support for this prediction. There was no interference when participants performed the serial reaction time task and a second implicit learning task. However, when the serial reaction time task became explicit, interference was present. This was expected because explicit learning involves limited attentional and other resources.

Neuroimaging studies

Different brain areas should be activated during implicit and explicit learning if they are genuinely different. Conscious awareness is most consistently associated with activation of the dorsolateral prefrontal cortex and the anterior cingulate (Dehaene & Naccache, 2001; see Chapter 16). Accordingly, these areas should be more active during explicit than implicit learning. In contrast, the striatum has been linked to implicit learning. The **striatum** is part of the basal ganglia and is located in the interior areas of the cerebral hemispheres and the upper region of the brainstem (see Figure 6.16).

KEY TERM

Striatum
It forms part of the basal ganglia and is located in the upper part of the brainstem and the inferior part of the cerebral hemispheres.

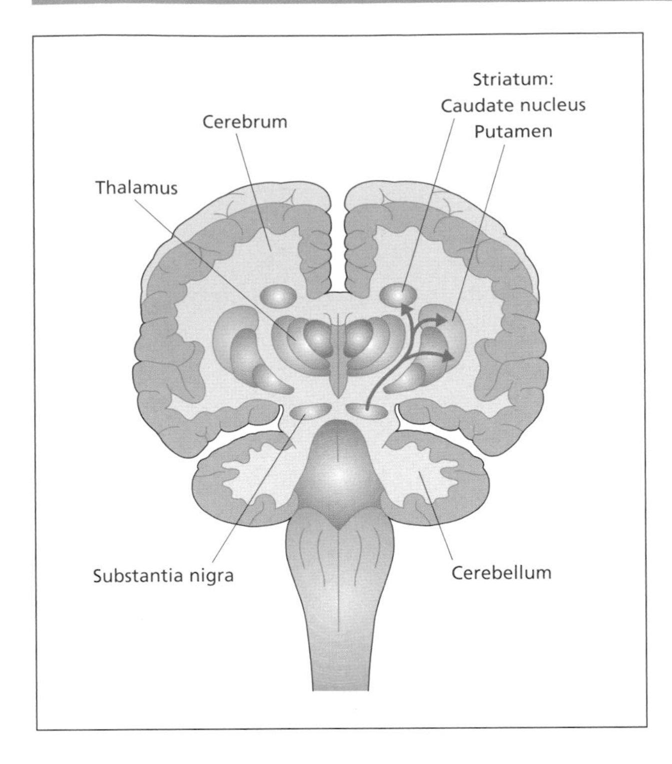

Figure 6.16
The striatum (which includes the caudate nucleus and the putamen) is of central importance in implicit learning.

Neuroimaging findings have been inconsistent (Shanks, 2010). One reason is that most so-called explicit or implicit learning tasks probably involve a mixture of explicit and implicit learnng. Destrebecqz et al. (2005) used the process-dissociation procedure with the serial reaction time task to distinguish between the explicit and implicit components of learning. As predicted, striatum activation was associated with the implicit component of learning whereas the prefrontal cortex and anterior cingulate were associated with the explicit component. Implicit perceptual sequence learning and implicit motor sequence learning using functional magnetic resonance imaging (fMRI; see Glossary) were studied by Gheysen et al. (2011). The striatum contributed to both types of learning. In addition, the hippocampus was involved in learning on the motor task.

Penhune and Steele (2012) put forward a model of motor sequence learning showing the main brain areas involved (see Figure 6.17). The striatum is involved in learning stimulus-response associations and motor chunking or organisation.

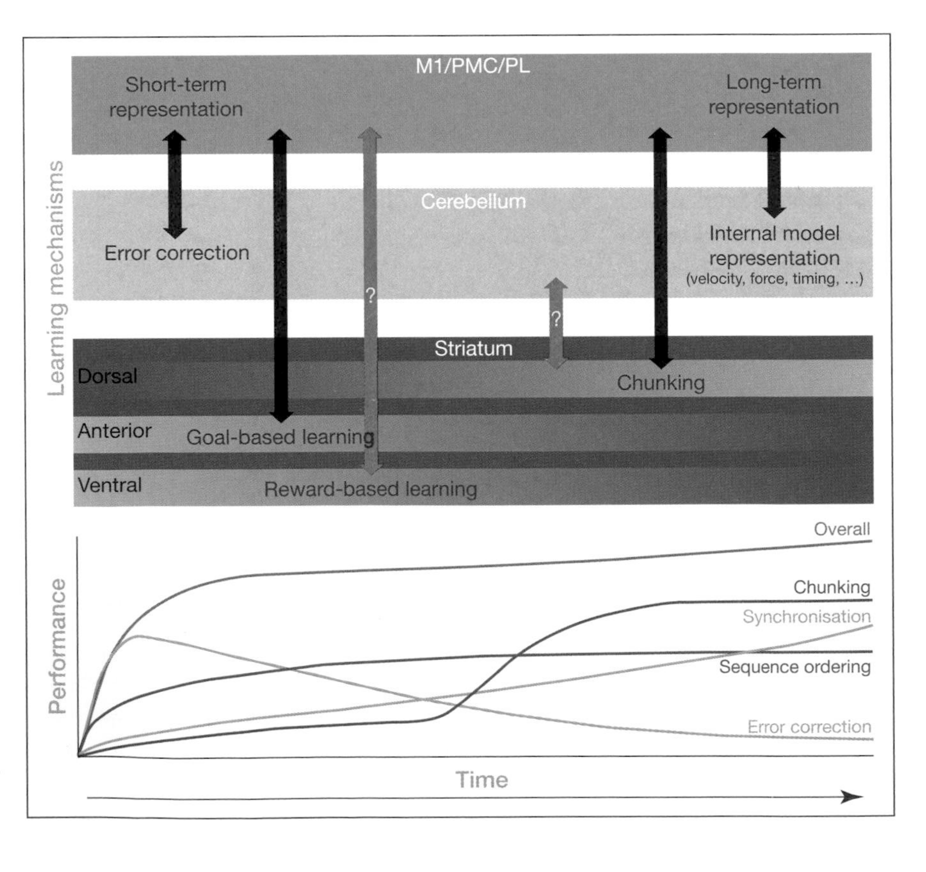

Figure 6.17
A model of motor sequence learning. The top panel shows the brain areas (PMC or M1 = primary motor cortex) and associated mechanisms involved in motor sequence learning. The bottom panel shows the changing involvement of different processing components (chunking, synchronisation, sequence ordering, error correction) in overall performance. Each component is colour-coded to its associated brain region.

From Penhune and Steele (2012). Reprinted with permission of Elsevier.

The cerebellum is involved in producing an internal model to aid sequence performance and error correction. Finally, the motor cortex is involved in storing the learned motor sequence. Of importance, the involvement of each brain area varies dependent on the stage of learning.

What happens when individuals show a transition from purely implicit learning to explicit learning? Wessel et al. (2012) provided an answer using a modified version of the serial reaction time task. They found 50% of participants showed clear evidence of explicit learning during training. Among these participants, an area of coordinated brain activity centred on the right prefrontal cortex became much larger around the onset of explicit learning, probably reflecting a state of conscious awareness.

KEY TERM

Parkinson's disease
A progressive disorder involving damage to the basal ganglia; the symptoms include muscle rigidity, limb tremor and mask-like facial expression.

Brain-damaged patients

Amnesic patients with damage to the medial temporal lobes typically perform very poorly on tests of explicit memory involving conscious recollection (Chapter 7). However, they often perform as well as healthy individuals on tests of implicit memory (on which conscious recollection is not needed; see Chapter 7). The notion that separate learning systems underlie implicit and explicit learning would be supported if amnesic patients showed intact levels of implicit learning combined with impaired explicit learning. That pattern of findings has been reported several times although amnesics' implicit learning performance is sometimes impaired (see Wilkinson et al. (2009) for a review). In more recent research, Van Tilborg et al. (2011) found that amnesic patients had comparable implicit learning to healthy controls on the serial reaction time task.

Earlier we discussed the hypothesis that the basal ganglia (especially the striatum) are of major importance in implicit learning. Patients with **Parkinson's disease** (a progressive neurological disorder) have damage to this brain region. As a result, we would expect them to show impaired implicit learning but not explicit learning. Wilkinson et al. (2009) studied explicit and implicit learning using the serial reaction time task. As predicted, patients with Parkinson's disease showed impaired implicit learning. However, they also showed impaired explicit learning, which was against prediction.

Foerde and Shohamy (2011) pointed out in a review that there are several studies in which Parkinson's patients have had impaired explicit learning. Their performance on implicit learning tasks was variable. Foerde and Shohamy reported that Parkinson's patients were especially likely to show poor implicit learning when participants were provided with error-correcting feedback. This suggests a function of the basal ganglia is to make effective use of feedback.

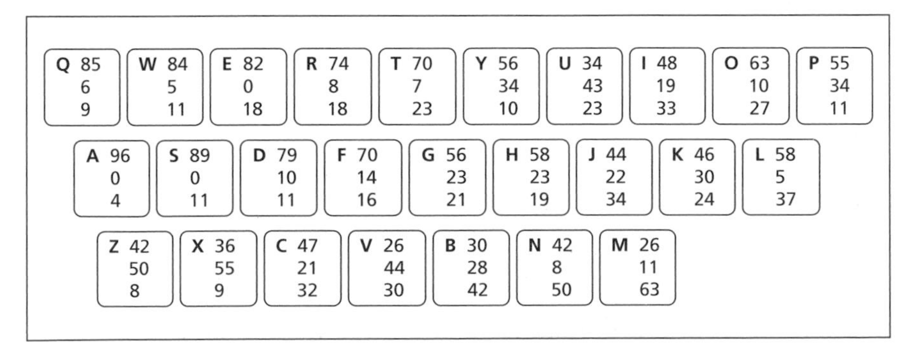

Figure 6.18
Percentages of experienced typists given an unfilled schematic keyboard (see Figure 6.13) who correctly located (top number), omitted (middle number) or misplaced (bottom number) each letter with respect to the standard keyboard.
From Snyder et al. (2014).
© 2011 Psychonomic Society. Reprinted with permission from Springer.

What conclusions can we draw from research on brain-damaged patients? According to Foerde and Shohamy (2011), the complexities in the findings indicate the notion of entirely *separate* systems underlying explicit and implicit learning is oversimplified. Key brain regions such as the medial temporal lobes (damaged in amnesia) and the basal ganglia (damaged in Parkinson's disease) often *interact* in their functioning in complex ways we are only starting to understand.

Evaluation

There has been much controversy surrounding research on implicit learning. However, research in this area has several strengths. First, the notion that implicit learning should be distinguished from explicit learning has obtained considerable support from behavioural and neuroimaging studies on healthy individuals and from research on brain-damaged patients.

Second, much evidence suggests the prefrontal cortex and anterior cingulate are more closely associated with explicit learning than implicit learning. In contrast, the striatum is more closely associated with implicit than with explicit learning. Recent research indicates that complex brain networks are involved in implicit learning (Penhune & Steele, 2012).

Third, progress has been made with assessing conscious awareness in studies on implicit learning. In view of the deficiencies of any *single* measure, it is preferable to use *several* measures. Thankfully, the extent of conscious awareness indicated by different measures is often comparable (e.g., Haider et al., 2011).

Fourth, learning typically involves implicit and explicit aspects (Sun et al., 2009). In addition, the extent to which learners are consciously aware of what they are learning varies across individuals and tasks and depends on the stage of training (e.g., Wessel et al., 2012). Researchers are increasingly rejecting the erroneous assumption that finding explicit learning plays some part in explaining task performance implies *no* implicit learning occurred.

What are the limitations of research on implicit learning? First, learning is often a complex mixture of implicit and explicit and it is hard to decide how much of that learning is implicit in nature. Second, the processes involved in implicit and explicit learning probably interact with each other in ways that remain unclear. Third, neuroimaging findings have been somewhat inconsistent. There is a tendency for the basal ganglia to be activated during implicit learning and areas within the prefrontal cortex to be activated during explicit learning. However, there are many exceptions due in part to the great variety of tasks involving implicit learning (Reber, 2013).

FORGETTING FROM LONG-TERM MEMORY

We discussed forgetting from short-term memory earlier in the chapter. Here the focus is on forgetting from long-term memory, first studied in detail by Hermann Ebbinghaus (1885/1913). He used himself as the only participant (not recommended!). Ebbinghaus initially learned lists of nonsense syllables lacking meaning and then relearned each list between 21 minutes and 31 days later. Ebbinghaus's basic measure of forgetting was the **savings method**, which involves seeing the *reduction* in the number of trials during relearning compared to original learning.

What did Ebbinghaus find? Forgetting was very rapid over the first hour after learning but then slowed considerably (see Figure 6.19), a pattern confirmed by

KEY TERM

Savings method
A measure of forgetting introduced by Ebbinghaus in which the number of trials for relearning is compared against the number for original learning.

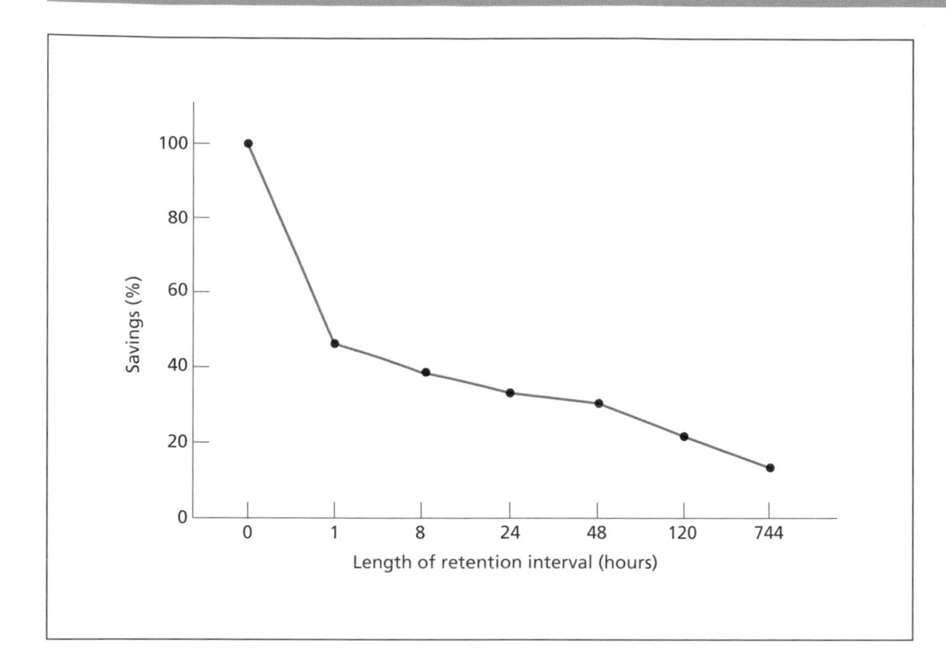

Figure 6.19
Forgetting over time as indexed by reduced savings.
Data from Ebbinghaus (1885/1913).

Rubin and Wenzel (1996) following analysis of numerous forgetting functions. Rubin and Wenzel argued that a *logarithmic* function describes forgetting over time. More recently, however, Averell and Heathcote (2011) provided arguments favouring a *power* function.

It is often assumed forgetting should be avoided. However, that is often *not* the case (Schacter et al., 2011; see "In the real world" box below). There are frequent changes in the information useful to us. It is not useful to remember last year's schedule of lectures or where your friends used to live. You need to *update* such information and forget what was previously the case.

Most studies of forgetting have focused on declarative or explicit memory, which involves conscious recollection (see Chapter 7). Comparisons of forgetting rates in explicit memory and implicit memory (not requiring conscious recollection) suggest forgetting is slower in implicit memory (e.g., Tulving et al., 1982).

Dramatic evidence of long-lasting implicit memories was reported by Mitchell (2006). Participants identified pictures from fragments having seen some of them in an experiment 17 years previously. Performance was better with the pictures seen before, providing evidence for very-long-term implicit memory. However, there was little explicit memory for the previous experiment. A 36-year-old male participant confessed, "I'm sorry – I don't really remember this experiment at all."

In what follows, we will discuss major theories of forgetting. These theories are not mutually exclusive – they all identify factors responsible for forgetting.

Decay

Perhaps the simplest explanation for the forgetting of long-term memories is decay, which is "forgetting due to a gradual loss of the substrate of memory" (Hardt et al., 2013, p. 111). According to this account, forgetting sometimes occurs

IN THE REAL WORLD: IS PERFECT MEMORY USEFUL?

What would it be like to have a perfect memory? Jorge Luis Borges (1964) answered this question in a story called "Funes the memorious". After falling from a horse, Funes remembers everything that happens to him in full detail. This may sound desirable but actually had several negative effects. When Funes recalled the events of a given day, it took him an entire day to do so! He found it very hard to think because his mind was full of incredibly detailed information. Here is an example of the problems he encountered:

> Not only was it difficult for him to comprehend that the generic symbol dog embraces so many unlike individuals of diverse size and form; it bothered him that the dog at three fourteen (seen from the side) should have the same name as the dog at three fifteen (seen from the front).
> (p. 153)

The closest real-life equivalent of Funes was a Russian called Solomon Shereshevskii. When he was working as a journalist, his editor noticed he could repeat anything that was said to him word for word. Accordingly, he sent Shereshevskii (often referred to as S) along to see the psychologist Luria. He found S rapidly learned complex material (e.g., lists of more than 100 digits), which he remembered perfectly several years later. According to Luria (1968), "There was no limit either to the *capacity* of S's memory or to the *durability of the traces he retained.*"

What was the secret of S's remarkable memory? He had exceptional imagery. Not only could he rapidly and easily create a wealth of visual images, he also had an amazing capacity for **synaesthesia**. This is the tendency for processing in one sense modality to evoke one or more other sense modalities. His synaesthesia often caused S problems: "Each word calls up images; they collide with one another, and the result is chaos. I can't make anything out of this. And then there's also your voice . . . another blur . . . then everything's a muddle."

S often found it hard to recognise the faces or voices of people he had known for some time because he processed so many details *specific* to each occurrence. His mind came to resemble "a junk heap of impressions" (Luria, 1968), which made it difficult for him to live a normal life. Eventually, he ended up in an asylum.

because of decay processes occurring within memory traces. In spite of its apparent plausibility, decay has been ignored as an explanation of forgetting by most theorists.

Hardt et al. (2013) argued that we form numerous trivial memories during the course of each day and so a process is required to remove them. According to their theoretical perspective, there is a decay process that does precisely this (mostly during sleep).

This decay process is especially active in the hippocampus (part of the medial temporal lobe involved in acquiring new memories; see Chapter 7). Detailed brain research supports this theoretical position (Hardt et al., 2013). However, as we will see, there is overwhelming evidence that several other factors make substantial contributions to forgetting.

KEY TERM

Synaesthesia
The tendency for one sense modality to evoke another.

Interference: proactive and retroactive

Interference theory was the dominant approach to forgetting during much of the twentieth century. According to this theory, there are two forms of interference that can impair long-term memory. First, there is **proactive interference**, which involves disruption of memory by previous learning. Second, there is **retroactive interference**, which involves disruption of memory for what was previously learned by other learning or processing during the retention interval.

Interference theory dates back to Hugo Munsterberg in the nineteenth century. Munsterberg kept his pocket watch in one particular pocket. When he started to keep it in a different pocket, he often fumbled around in confusion when asked the time. Munsterberg had initially learned an association between the stimulus, "What time is it, Hugo?", and the response of removing the watch from his pocket. Later on, a different response was associated with that stimulus, which led to proactive interference.

Research using methods such as those shown in Figure 6.20 indicates proactive and retroactive interference are both maximal when two different responses are associated with the *same* stimulus. Strong evidence of retroactive interference has been obtained in studies of eyewitness testimony in which memory of an event is interfered with by post-event information (Chapter 8).

KEY TERMS

Proactive interference
Disruption of memory by previous learning (often of similar material).

Retroactive interference
Disruption of memory for previously learned information by other learning or processing occurring during the retention interval.

Proactive interference

What causes proactive interference? There is typically *competition* between the correct response and one or more incorrect ones. There is more competition (and thus more proactive interference) when the incorrect response or responses are associated with the same stimulus as the correct response. Jacoby et al. (2001) pointed out that proactive interference might occur because the correct response

Proactive interference

Group	Learn	Learn	Test
Experimental	A–B (e.g., Cat–Dirt)	A–C (e.g., Cat–Tree)	A–C (e.g., Cat–Tree)
Control	–	A–C (e.g., Cat–Tree)	A–C (e.g., Cat–Tree)

Retroactive interference

Group	Learn	Learn	Test
Experimental	A–B (e.g., Cat–Tree)	A–C (e.g., Cat–Dirt)	A–B (e.g., Cat–Tree)
Control	A–B (e.g., Cat–Tree)	–	A–B (e.g., Cat–Tree)

Note: for both proactive and retroactive interference, the experimental group exhibits interference. On the test, only the first word is supplied, and the participants must provide the second word.

Figure 6.20
Methods of testing for proactive and retroactive interference.

is very weak or because the incorrect response is very strong. They found proactive interference was due much more to the strength of the incorrect response. Thus, a major cause of proactive interference is that it is hard to exclude incorrect responses from the retrieval process.

Bergström et al. (2012) used event-related potentials (ERPs; see Glossary). They discovered that proactive interference involves *automatic* and *controlled* retrieval processes. The automatic process was revealed by an early ERP component reflecting conflict between the correct and incorrect responses. It was followed by a controlled process reflecting intentional retrieval strategies.

Bäuml and Kliegl (2013) argued that proactive interference depends in large measure on retrieval processes. Rememberers' memory search is generally too broad, including material previously learned but currently irrelevant. It follows that proactive interference should be greatly reduced if steps were taken to restrict participants' memory search to relevant items.

Bäuml and Kliegl (2013) tested the above viewpoint. In two conditions, three lists were presented followed by free recall of the last one. In the remember (proactive interference) condition, participants were simply instructed to learn all three lists. In the forget condition, they were told after the first two lists to forget them. In the control (no proactive interference condition), participants learned and were tested on only one list.

What did Bäuml and Kliegl (2013) find? Participants in the no-proactive interference condition recalled 68% of the words, whereas those in the proactive interference condition recalled only 41%. Participants in the forget condition recalled 68% of the words and thus showed no proactive interference in spite of having learned two previous lists. The instruction to forget the first two lists made it easier for participants to limit their retrieval efforts to the third list. This interpretation was strengthened by the finding that speed of retrieval was as fast in the forget condition as in the control condition (see Figure 6.21).

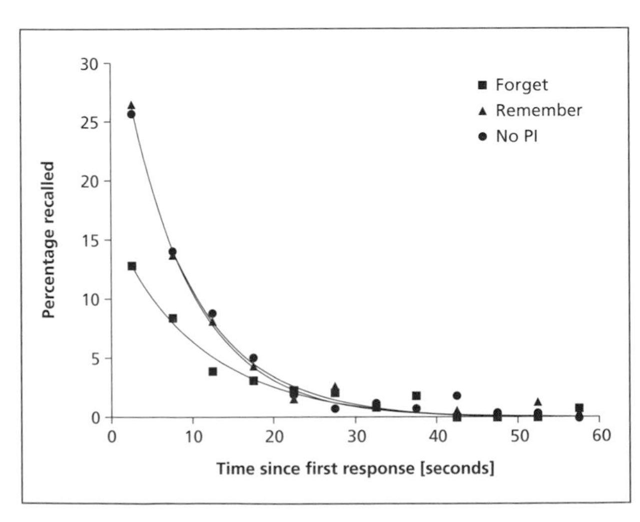

Figure 6.21
Percentage of items recalled over time for no proactive interference (PI); remember (proactive interference); and forget (forget previous lists) conditions.

From Bäuml & Kliegl (2013). Reprinted with permission of Elsevier.

In another experiment, Bäuml and Kliegl (2013) presented participants with two lists and tested their recall for the second list. In the crucial condition, participants spent the time between lists imagining their childhood home. This change in their mental context reduced proactive interference by almost 40% because it made it easier for them to exclude first-list items from the retrieval process.

Additional evidence that proactive interference can be partially controlled was reported by Wahlheim and Jacoby (2011). Participants became increasingly aware of proactive interference effects with practice. As a result, they devoted more learning time to items susceptible to proactive interference. They also focused their retrieval efforts more effectively, which reduced the tendency to recall incorrect responses.

Retroactive interference

Think of a friend you have known for several years. Try to form a clear visual image of what he/she looked like five years ago. We guess you found that hard to do because rich information about what they are like now interferes with your ability to remember what they were like then. This is a common example of retroactive interference.

Anecdotal evidence that retroactive interference can be important in everyday life comes from travellers who claim exposure to a foreign language reduces their ability to recall words in their own language. Misra et al. (2012) studied bilinguals whose native language was Chinese and second language was English. They named pictures in Chinese more slowly when they had previously named the same pictures in English. The evidence from event-related potentials (ERPs; see Glossary) suggested participants were inhibiting second-language names when naming pictures in Chinese.

Lustig et al. (2004) argued that retroactive interference in paired-associate learning might occur for two reasons: (1) the correct response is hard to retrieve; or (2) the incorrect response is highly accessible. They found retroactive interference was due mainly to the strength of the incorrect response.

Retroactive interference is generally greatest when the new learning resembles previous learning. However, Dewar et al. (2007) found retroactive interference even when no new learning occurred during the retention interval. Participants learned a list of words and were then exposed to various tasks during the retention interval before list memory was assessed. There was significant retroactive interference even when the intervening task involved detecting differences between pictures or detecting tones.

Dewar et al. (2007) concluded that retroactive interference can occur in two ways: (1) expenditure of mental effort during the retention interval; or (2) learning of material similar to the original learning material. The first cause of retroactive interference probably occurs more often in everyday life. Further support for the interfering effects of mental effort was reported by Dewar et al. (2010) in a study on amnesics' prose recall. Their recall was much better when the retention interval was unfilled rather than spent detecting tones.

The research discussed so far has involved explicit memory based on conscious recollection. As yet, there is very little research focusing on implicit memory (not involving conscious recollection). However, Eakin and Smith (2012) obtained clear evidence for retroactive interference in implicit memory with paired-associate learning.

Evaluation

There is strong evidence for both proactive and retroactive interference. Progress has been made in understanding the processes underlying interference effects. Of particular importance, the traditional view that individuals *passively* allow themselves to suffer from interference is too limited. In fact, people often adopt *active* strategies to minimise interference effects (e.g., Wahlheim & Jacoby, 2011).

What are the limitations of theory and research in this area? First, detailed information about interference effects in implicit memory is lacking. Second, interference theory explains why forgetting occurs but does not explain why

KEY TERMS

Repression
Motivated forgetting of traumatic or other threatening events (especially from childhood).

Recovered memories
Childhood traumatic memories forgotten for several years and then remembered in adult life.

Weblink:
Hopper's website

forgetting rate decreases over time. Third, we need to know more about the reasons why and how strategies can reduce interference effects. Simply asking participants to imagine their childhood home is effective in reducing proactive interference (Bäuml & Kliegel, 2013), and other strategies might be even more effective.

Repression

One of the best-known theories of forgetting owes its origins to the bearded Austrian psychologist Sigmund Freud (1856–1939). He claimed threatening or traumatic memories often cannot gain access to conscious awareness, and used the term **repression** to refer to this phenomenon. Freud argued that repression sometimes involves an active and intentional process and sometimes happens automatically.

How do we know people have repressed memories if they cannot recall them? What sometimes happens is that childhood traumatic memories that had been forgotten for many years are sometimes remembered in adult life. Freud found these **recovered memories** were often recalled in the course of therapy. Some experts (e.g., Loftus & Davis, 2006) argue that most recovered memories are false memories referring to events that did not happen.

Findings

How can we decide whether recovered memories are true or false? Lief and Fetkewicz (1995) provide relevant evidence. They found 80% of adult patients who admitted reporting false or imagined recovered memories had therapists who had made direct suggestions they had been subject to childhood sexual abuse. These findings suggest recovered memories recalled *inside* therapy are more likely to be false than those recalled *outside*.

Important evidence supporting the above suggestion was reported by Geraerts et al. (2007) in a study on three adult groups who had suffered childhood sexual abuse:

1 *Suggestive therapy group*: their recovered memories were recalled initially *inside* therapy.
2 *Spontaneous recovery group*: their recovered memories were recalled initially *outside* therapy.
3 *Continuous memory group*: they had continuous memories of abuse from childhood onwards.

Geraerts et al. (2007) argued that the genuineness of the memories produced could be assessed approximately by seeing how many had corroborating evidence (e.g., the abuser had confessed). Corroborating evidence was available for 45% of the continuous memory group and 37% of the outside therapy group but for 0% of the inside therapy group. The implication is that recovered memories recalled outside therapy are much more likely to be genuine than those recalled inside therapy.

Spontaneous recovery vs. recovered in therapy

According to Geraerts (2012), there are important differences in memory processes between women depending on whether their recovered memories were recalled spontaneously or in therapy. Women with spontaneous recovered memories can suppress unwanted memories and sometimes forget they have remembered something previously. In contrast, women whose recovered memories are recalled in therapy are susceptible to false memories.

Conclusions

It is hard to assess the genuineness of recovered memories of childhood sexual abuse. However, recovered memories seem to be of two different types. First, memories recovered *inside* therapy are often false memories occurring because of therapists' suggestions and the susceptibility to false memories of the women concerned. Second, memories recovered *outside* therapy are often genuine memories. Such memories occur because of relevant retrieval cues (e.g., returning to the scene of the abuse).

It may seem surprising that women recovering memories outside therapy failed for many years to remember childhood sexual abuse. However, it is so only if the memories are traumatic (as Freud assumed). In fact, only 8% of women with recovered memories regarded them as traumatic or sexual when they occurred (Clancy & McNally, 2005/2006). The great majority described them as confusing or uncomfortable – it seems reasonable that confusing or uncomfortable memories could be suppressed.

In sum, many assumptions about recovered memories are false. As McNally and Geraerts (2009, p. 132) concluded, "A genuine recovered CSA [childhood sexual abuse] memory does not require repression, trauma, or even complete forgetting."

Motivated forgetting

Freud focused on some aspects of motivated forgetting. However, his approach was narrowly focused on traumatic and other distressing memories. In recent years, a broader approach to motivated forgetting has been adopted.

Motivated forgetting of traumatic or other upsetting memories could fulfil a useful function (e.g., reducing anxiety). In addition, much information in long-term memory is outdated, making it useless for present purposes. For example, if you are looking for your car in a car park, there is no point remembering where you parked it previously. Thus, motivated or intentional forgetting can be adaptive. This approach is very different from the traditional one based on the assumption forgetting is *passive* and largely uninfluenced by our efforts to control it.

Directed forgetting

Directed forgetting is a phenomenon involving impaired long-term memory triggered by instructions to forget information that has been presented for learning. It is often studied using the item method: several words are presented, each followed immediately by an instruction to remember or forget it. Following presentation, participants are tested for recall or recognition of *all* the words. Memory performance is worse for the to-be-forgotten words than the to-be-remembered ones.

What causes directed forgetting? The forget instruction probably causes selective rehearsal of remember items (Geraerts & McNally, 2008). Inhibitory

KEY TERM

Directed forgetting
Reduced long-term memory caused by instructions to forget information that had been presented for learning.

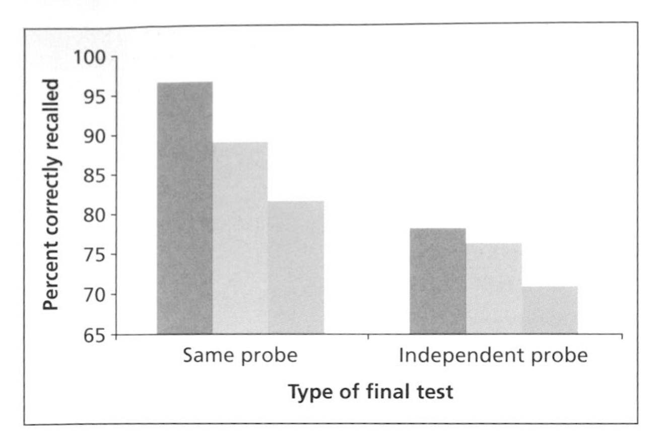

Figure 6.22
Percentage words correctly recalled across 32 articles in the respond, baseline and suppress conditions (in that order reading from left to right) with same probe and independent probe testing conditions.

From Anderson and Huddleston (2012). Reproduced with permission of Springer Science + Business Media.

processes also seem to be involved. Successful forgetting is associated with activation in areas within the right frontal cortex associated with inhibition (Rizio & Dennis, 2013).

Memory suppression: inhibition

Anderson and Green (2001) developed the think/no-think paradigm to assess the extent to which people can actively suppress memories (see Figure 6.22). Participants learn a list of cue–target word pairs (e.g., Ordeal–Roach, Steam–Train). Then they are presented with the cues studied earlier (e.g., Ordeal, Steam) and told to think of the associated words (e.g., Roach, Train) (respond condition) or to prevent them coming to mind (suppress condition). In addition, some cues are not presented at this stage (baseline condition). Finally, there are two testing conditions. In one condition (same probe), the original cues are presented (e.g., Ordeal) and participants recall the corresponding target words. In the other condition (independent probe), participants receive a novel category cue (e.g., Roach might be cued with Insect-R).

If people can suppress unwanted memories, recall should be lower in the suppress than the respond condition. In addition, recall should be lower in the suppress condition than the baseline condition. Anderson and Huddleston (2012) carried out a meta-analysis (see Glossary) of 47 experiments and found strong support for both predictions (see Figure 6.22).

What strategies do people use to produce successful suppression of unwanted memories? Thought substitution (associating a different, non-target word with each cue word) is very common. Another strategy is direct suppression (focusing on the cue word and blocking out the associated target word). Bergström et al. (2009) found both strategies were equally effective in reducing recall in the suppress condition. Other evidence suggested suppression of the unwanted memory traces was greater in the direct suppression condition.

How do suppression instructions cause forgetting? Anderson (e.g., Anderson & Huddleston, 2012) argues that negative control is of major importance – the learned response to the cue word must be inhibited. Depue et al. (2010) found suppression instructions led to *increased* activation in the dorsolateral prefrontal cortex but to *decreased* activation in the hippocampus. The dorsolateral prefrontal cortex is associated with inhibitory control processes and the hippocampus is involved in the formation of long-term memories (see Chapter 7). Thus, suppression instructions lead to inhibitory processes, some of which restrict the formation of new long-term memories.

M.C. Anderson et al. (2004) tested the executive deficit hypothesis, according to which the ability to suppress memories depends on individual differences in executive control abilities (especially inhibitory ones). Individuals having the greatest activation in bilateral dorsolateral and ventrolateral prefrontal cortex (areas associated with various executive control processes) were most successful at memory inhibition.

Anderson and Huddleston (2012) discussed research on depressed individuals. Such research is relevant to the executive deficit hypothesis because depression is associated with deficient executive control. As predicted, depressed individuals generally fail to suppress unwanted memories in the think/no-think paradigm.

Evaluation

There is convincing evidence that most people can *actively* suppress unwanted memories using various strategies. Progress has been made in identifying the underlying mechanisms. For example, neuroimaging evidence indicates successful inhibition typically involves increased activation in the dorsolateral prefrontal cortex combined with decreased hippocampal activation. As predicted, the ability to inhibit unwanted memories is low in depressed individuals.

What are the limitations of theory and research in this area? Anderson has probably exaggerated the role of inhibition in forgetting (Raaijmakers & Jakab, 2013). It is assumed within inhibition theory that suppression reduces the strength of unwanted memories. This may well de-emphasise the important role played by interference in forgetting – suppressed items may be hard to recall because of interference from other memories rather than because of inhibition.

KEY TERM

Encoding specificity principle
The notion that retrieval depends on the *overlap* between the information available at retrieval and the information in the memory trace.

Cue-dependent forgetting

We often attribute forgetting to the weakness of relevant memory traces. In fact, forgetting often occurs because we lack the appropriate cues (cue-dependent forgetting). For example, suppose you have forgotten the name of the street in which a friend lives. If someone gave you a short list of possible street names, you might well recognise the correct one.

Endel Tulving (e.g., 1979) (see photo) argued that forgetting typically occurs when there is a poor *match* or fit between the information in the memory trace and that available at retrieval. This led him to propose the **encoding specificity principle**: "The probability of successful retrieval of the target item is a monotonically increased function of informational overlap between the information present at retrieval and the information stored in memory" (p. 478). If you are bewildered, note that a "monotonically increasing function" is one that generally rises and doesn't decrease at any point.

The encoding specificity principle resembles the notion of transfer-appropriate processing (Morris et al., 1977; discussed earlier). The main difference between the two notions is that transfer-appropriate processing focuses more directly on the *processes* involved in memory.

Tulving (1979) assumed that when we store information about an event, we also store information about the *context* of that event. According to the encoding specificity principle, memory is better when the retrieval context is the same as that at learning. Note that context can be *external* (the environment in which learning and retrieval occur) or *internal* (e.g., mood state).

Endel Tulving. Courtesy of Anders Gade.

Eysenck (1979) pointed out that what we remember does *not* depend only on the informational overlap or match between information available at retrieval and stored information. The extent to which the retrieval information allows us to *discriminate* between the correct memory trace and incorrect ones is also important. These ideas are discussed more fully below.

Findings

Recognition memory is generally better than recall. We may be unable to recall an acquaintance's name. However, if someone mentions their name we instantly recognise it. A dramatic prediction from the encoding specificity principle is that recall can sometimes be better than recognition. This should happen when information in the recall cue overlaps more than that in the recognition cue with information in the memory trace.

Muter (1978) presented participants with people's names (e.g., DOYLE, THOMAS) and asked them to circle those they "recognised as a person who was famous before 1950". They were then given recall cues in the form of brief descriptions plus first names of the famous people whose surnames had appeared on the recognition test (e.g., author of the Sherlock Holmes stories: Sir Arthur Conan _____ ; Welsh poet: Dylan _____). Participants recognised only 29% of the names but recalled 42% of them.

Context is important in determining forgetting. For example, mood state is often stored in the memory trace. As a result, there should be less forgetting when the mood state at retrieval is the same as that at learning. There is much evidence for this phenomenon (known as mood-state-dependent memory) (see Chapter 15).

Godden and Baddeley (1975) showed the importance of context in a study on deep-sea divers. The divers listened to 40 words when they were on a beach or 10 feet underwater. They were then tested for recall of these words in the same or the other environment. As predicted, recall was much better when the environmental context was the same at test as at learning (see Figure 6.23). However, there was no effect of context when Godden and Baddeley (1980) repeated the experiment using recognition memory rather than recall. This probably happened because the presence of the learned items themselves on the recognition test provided powerful cues that outweighed any possible impact of context.

Brain-imaging evidence supporting the encoding specificity principle was reported by Park and Rugg (2008). Participants were presented with pictures and words. On a subsequent recognition test, each item was tested with a congruent cue (word–word and picture–picture conditions) or an incongruent cue (word–picture and picture–word conditions). As predicted by the encoding specificity principle, memory performance was better in the congruent condition.

Park and Rugg (2008) analysed brain activity at learning for items subsequently recognised. It should be more important for successful recognition for words to be processed at learning in a "word-like" way if tested by word cues rather than picture cues. In similar fashion, successful recognition of pictures should depend more on "picture-like" processing at study if tested by picture cues rather than word cues. Both predictions were supported, suggesting long-term memory is best when the processing at learning is similar to that at retrieval.

Bauch and Otten (2012) recorded event-related potentials (ERPs; see Glossary) in a study resembling that of Park and Rugg (2008). Overlap between encoding and retrieval brain activity was important when recognition memory for

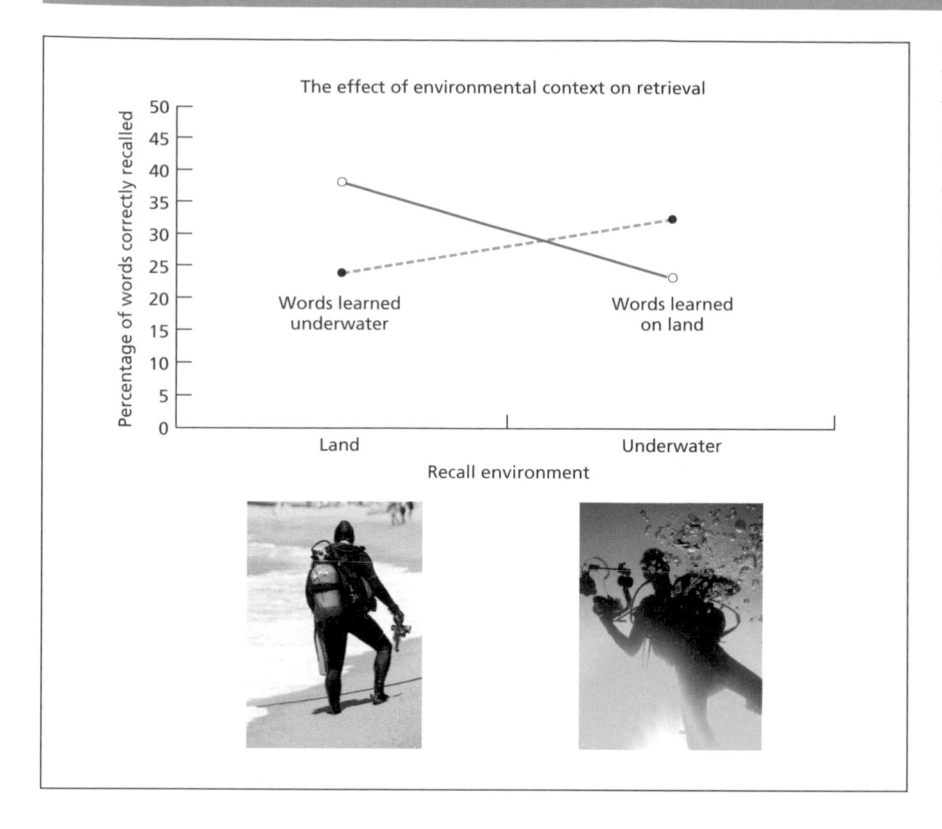

Figure 6.23
Words learned and tested in the same environment are better recalled than those items for which the environmental context varied between study and test.
Data from Godden and Baddeley (1975).

pictures was tested. However, this was not the case for recognition memory of words. They concluded that "encoding-retrieval overlap may not be a universal organising principle of neural correlates of memory" (p. 183).

Earlier we argued that *two* factors need to be considered when predicting a retrieval cue's effectiveness (Eysenck, 1979). First, there is the extent to which the retrieval cue provides information *overlapping* with that in the memory trace (i.e., the encoding specificity principle). Second, there is the extent to which the retrieval cue is *uniquely associated* with only one item.

Suppose you learn paired associates including *park–grove* and are later given the cue word *park* and asked to supply the target or response word (i.e., *grove*). The response words to the other paired associates are either associated with *park* (e.g., *tree*, *bench*, *playground*, *picnic*) or are not associated. In the latter case, the cue is *uniquely* associated with the target word and so your task should be easier. There is high overload when a cue is associated with several response words and low overload when it is only associated with one response word. The target word is more *distinctive* when there is low overload – the advantages of distinctiveness were discussed earlier in the chapter.

Goh and Lu (2012) tested the above predictions. Encoding-retrieval overlap was manipulated by using three types of items. There was maximal overlap when the same cue was presented at retrieval as at learning (e.g., *park–grove* followed by *park*–???); this was an intra-list cue. There was moderate overlap when the cue was a strong associate of the target word (e.g., *airplane–bird* followed by *feather*–???). Finally, there was little overlap when the cue was a weak associate of the target word e.g., *roof–tin* followed by *armour*–???).

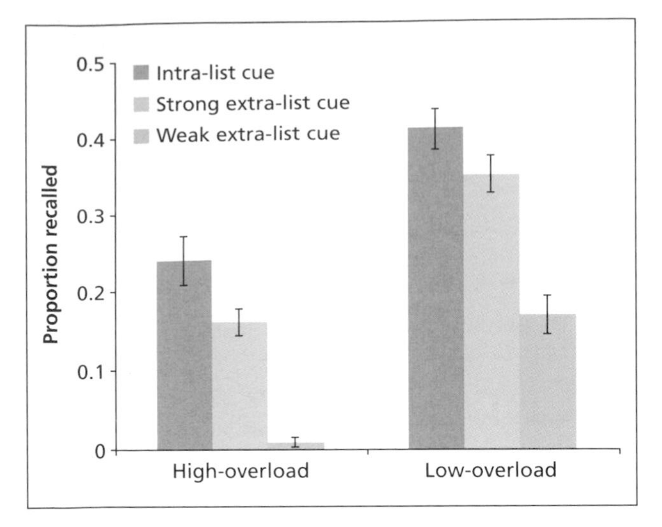

Figure 6.24
Proportion of words recalled in the high- and low-overload conditions with intra-list cues, strong extra-list cues and weak extra-list cues.

From Goh and Lu (2012). © 2011 Psychonomic Society, Inc. Reprinted with the permission of Springer.

What did Goh and Lu (2012) find? As predicted from the encoding specificity principle, encoding-retrieval overlap was important (see Figure 6.24). However, cue overload was also important – memory performance was much better when each cue was uniquely associated with a single response word. According to the encoding specificity principle, memory performance should be best when encoding-retrieval overlap is highest (i.e., with intra-list cues). However, that was *not* the case with high overload.

Evaluation

Tulving's approach has several strengths. The overlap between the information stored in the memory trace and that available in retrieval cues often determines retrieval success. The encoding specificity principle has received support from neuroimaging studies and from research on mood-state-dependent memory (see Chapter 15). The emphasis placed on the role of contextual information (external and internal) in influencing memory performance has proved correct.

What are the limitations with this approach? First, Tulving exaggerated the importance of encoding-retrieval overlap as the major determinant of remembering or forgetting. Remembering typically involves rejecting incorrect items as well as selecting correct ones. For this purpose, a cue's ability to *discriminate* among memory traces is important (Eysenck, 1979; Goh & Lu, 2012; Nairne, 2015, in press).

Second, Tulving's assumption that the information contained in retrieval cues is compared *directly* with that stored in memory is often inadequate. For example, suppose someone asked you, "What did you do six days ago?" You would probably use complex problem-solving strategies to answer the question. More generally, remembering is a more dynamic, reconstructive process than is implied by the notion that it simply involves matching retrieval environment and memory trace information (Nairne, 2015, in press).

Third, memory allegedly depends on "informational overlap", but this is rarely measured. Inferring the amount of informational overlap from memory performance is circular reasoning.

Fourth, it is not clear when matches between information in the environment and stored memory traces lead to conscious recollection and when they do not. As Nairne (2015, in press) pointed out, "Throughout the day, each of us regularly encounters events that 'match' prior episodes in our lives . . . but few of these events yield instances of conscious recollection." In other words, we seem to experience less conscious recollection than implied by the encoding specificity principle.

Fifth, Tulving originally assumed that context influences recall and recognition similarly. However, context effects are often greater on recall than recognition memory (e.g., Godden & Baddeley, 1975, 1980).

Consolidation and reconsolidation

No theory considered so far provides a wholly convincing account of forgetting over time. They identify factors causing forgetting but do not indicate clearly *why* the rate of forgetting decreases over time. The answer may well lie in consolidation theory. **Consolidation** is a long-lasting physiological process that fixes information in long-term memory.

It has been assumed the hippocampus plays a vital role in the consolidation of memories. Over time, however, memories are stored in the neocortex (including the temporal lobes). These assumptions receive support from neuroimaging studies (McKenzie & Eichenbaum, 2011). Activation of the hippocampus is greater during retrieval of recent memories than more remote ones, whereas the opposite is the case for cortical areas.

A central prediction of consolidation theory is that recently formed memories still being consolidated are especially vulnerable to interference and forgetting. Thus, "New memories are clear but fragile and old ones are faded but robust" (Wixted, 2004, p. 265).

KEY TERMS

Consolidation
A physiological process involved in establishing long-term memories; this process lasts several hours or more and newly formed memories are fragile.

Retrograde amnesia
Impaired ability of amnesic patients to remember information and events from the time period prior to the onset of **amnesia**.

Findings

Several lines of evidence support consolidation theory. First, consider the form of the forgetting curve. The decreasing rate of forgetting over time follows from the notion that recent memories are more vulnerable than older ones due to an ongoing process of consolidation.

Second, there is research on patients with **retrograde amnesia**, in which there is impaired memory for events occurring before amnesia onset. According to consolidation theory, patients with damage to the hippocampus should show greatest forgetting for memories formed shortly before amnesia onset and least for remote memories. The evidence generally supports that prediction (Manns et al., 2003). Some patients with retrograde amnesia do not show this time-graded pattern, but they typically have brain damage extending to the neocortex (Squire & Wixted, 2011).

Third, consider the effects of alcohol on memory. People who drink excessively sometimes suffer from "blackouts", an almost total loss of memory for all events occurring while they were very drunk. These blackouts probably indicate a failure to consolidate memories formed while intoxicated. Moulton et al. (2005) found that long-term memory was impaired in participants who drank alcohol shortly *before* learning.

An interesting (and surprising) finding is that alcohol consumption shortly *after* learning leads to improved memory (Moulton et al., 2005). Alcohol probably inhibits the formation of new memories that would interfere with the consolidation process of those formed just before alcohol consumption. Thus, alcohol protects previously formed memories from disruption.

Fourth, consolidation theory predicts that newly formed memories are more susceptible to retroactive interference than older memories. There is some support for this prediction. When the interfering material is dissimilar to that in the first learning task, there is often more retroactive interference when it is presented early in the retention interval (Wixted, 2004).

Fifth, there is evidence consolidation processes during sleep can enhance long-term memory (see Oudiette & Paller (2013) for a review). For example, previously

KEY TERM

Reconsolidation
This is a new consolidation process that occurs when a previously formed memory trace is reactivated; it allows that memory trace to be updated.

formed memories have been cued during sleep by auditory or olfactory cues (the latter relate to the sense of smell). Such cueing promotes consolidation and improves subsequent memory. Oudiette and Paller (2013, p. 142) concluded that, "Memory consolidation during sleep is instrumental for actively maintaining the storehouse of memories that individuals carry through their lives."

Reconsolidation

There have recently been exciting developments in consolidation theory. Several theorists (e.g., Hardt et al., 2010; Nadel et al., 2012) argue that reactivation of a memory trace previously consolidated puts it back into a fragile state. This leads to **reconsolidation** (a new consolidation process), with the fragility of the memory trace allowing it to be updated and altered.

Reconsolidation is very useful if we want to update our knowledge because previous learning is now irrelevant. However, it can cause us to misremember if we subsequently want to recall the information learned originally. This is how it happens. We learn some information at Time 1. At Time 2, we learn additional information. If the memory traces based on the information learned at Time 1 are activated at Time 2, they immediately become fragile. As a result, some information learned at Time 2 will mistakenly become incorporated into the memory traces of Time 1 information and thus cause misremembering.

Evidence of reconsolidation was reported by Hupbach et al. (2007, 2008). In one condition, participants' memory traces of their Time 1 learning were reactivated by reminding them of that learning just before the new learning at Time 2 (e.g., "Can you describe the general procedure of what you did on Monday?"). When participants were later asked to recall the Time 1 information, they misremembered some of the Time 2 information as having been learned at Time 1. This probably occurred because of reactivation of memory traces and reconsolidation. There was much less such misremembering when participants were *not* reminded of their Time 1 learning prior to Time 2 learning. This was because the Time 1 memory traces were less likely to be reactivated in this condition.

Further evidence that disrupting reconsolidation can cause forgetting was reported by Chan and LaPaglia (2013; see Figure 6.25). Participants watched a

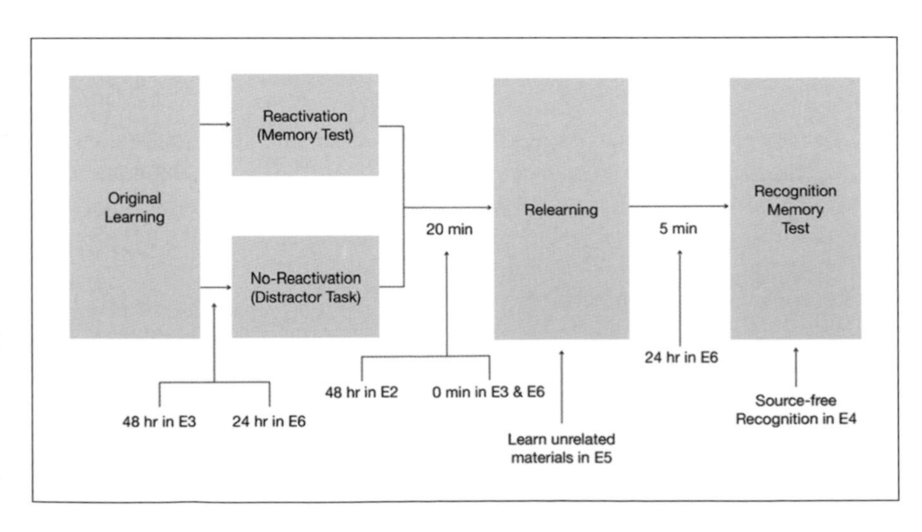

Figure 6.25
Experimental design in which original learning was followed by reactivation or no-reactivation of memories of the original learning. Later there was relearning involving misinformation or neutral information followed by a recognition-memory test.

From Chan and LaPaglia (2013). © National Academy of Sciences. Reproduced with permission.

movie about a fictional terrorist attack (original learning). Subsequently some of them recalled 24 specific details from the movie (e.g., a terrorist used a hypodermic needle on a flight attendant) to produce reconsolidation (reactivation), whereas others performed an irrelevant distractor task (no reactivation). After that, the participants encountered misinformation (e.g., the terrorist used a stun gun) or neutral information (relearning). Finally, there was a recognition-memory test for the information contained in the movie.

What did Chan and LaPaglia (2013) find? Misinformation during the relearning phase led to substantial forgetting of information from the movie in the reactivation/reconsolidation condition but not in the no-reactivation condition. Reactivating memory traces from the movie triggered reconsolidation, which made those memory traces vulnerable to disruption from misinformation. In contrast, memory traces not subjected to reconsolidation showed no disruption from misinformation.

Evaluation

Consolidation theory explains why the rate of forgetting decreases over time. In addition, it successfully predicts that retrograde amnesia is greater for recently formed memories and that retroactive interference effects are greatest shortly after learning. Consolidation processes during sleep may play an important role in promoting long-term memroy. Reconsolidation theory helps to explain how memories are updated. It serves as a useful corrective to the (perhaps excessive) emphasis of consolidation theory on the permanent storage of memory traces.

What are the limitations of this theoretical approach? First, forgetting does not depend solely on consolidation. For example, forgetting is greater when there is little informational overlap between the memory and the retrieval environment. Second, consolidation theory does not explain why proactive and retroactive interference are greatest when two different responses are associated with the same stimulus. Third, while progress has been made to relate consolidation and cognitive processes in forgetting, much remains to be done. Fourth, it is probably oversimplified to assume reconsolidation *always* occurs when a memory is retrieved. Reconsolidation may mostly occur when something can be learned during memory retrieval (Sevenster et al., 2012).

Weblink:
Consolidation theory

CHAPTER SUMMARY

- **Architecture of memory.** The multi-store model assumes there are separate sensory, short-term and long-term stores. Much evidence (e.g., from amnesic patients) provides general support for the model, but it is greatly oversimplified. According to the unitary-store model, short-term memory is the temporarily activated part of long-term memory. That is partially correct. However, neuroimaging studies and research on amnesic patients suggest the differences between short-term and long-term memory are greater than assumed by the unitary-store model.

- **Working memory**. Baddeley's original working memory model consists of three components: an attention-like central executive, a phonological loop holding speech-based information and a visuo-spatial sketchpad specialised for visual and spatial processing. The visual and spatial components of the visuo-spatial sketchpad are somewhat separate and both make use of attentional resources. More recently, Baddeley added an episodic buffer that stores integrated information from various sources. The central executive is used for executive functions such as inhibition, shifting and updating. The interrelationships of these functions can be understood within the unity-diversity framework, according to which each function consists of what is common to all functions plus processes unique to it.
- **Working memory capacity**. There is much overlap between the notions of working memory capacity and the executive functions of the central executive. High-capacity individuals differ from low-capacity ones in several ways. Of particular importance, however, high-capacity individuals have better attentional control than low-capacity ones. As a result, high-capacity individuals exhibit less goal neglect. Since individual differences in working memory capacity correlate highly with fluid intelligence, it is often hard to decide which ability is responsible for any given finding.
- **Levels of processing**. Craik and Lockhart (1972) focused on learning processes in their levels-of-processing theory. They identified depth of processing (the extent to which meaning is processed), elaboration of processing and distinctiveness of processing as key determinants of long-term memory. Insufficient attention was paid to the relationship between learning processes and those at retrieval. The theory is not explanatory, and the reasons why depth of processing influences explicit memory much more than implicit memory remain unclear.
- **Learning through retrieval**. Long-term memory is typically much better when much of the learning period is devoted to retrieval practice rather than study. This testing effect is greater when it is hard to retrieve the to-be-remembered information. A likely explanation for this finding is that difficult retrieval enhances the generation and retrieval of effective mediators. Testing can be less effective than restudying in enhancing long-term memory when it limits the types of information processed.
- **Implicit learning**. Behavioural findings from healthy and brain-damaged patients support the distinction between implicit and explicit learning. In addition, the brain areas activated during implicit learning (e.g., striatum) typically differ from those activated during explicit learning (e.g., prefrontal cortex). However, there are complexities

because much learning is a mixture of implicit and explicit and the systems underlying implicit and explicit learning probably interact with each other.

- **Forgetting**. Strong proactive and retroactive interference effects have been found inside and outside the laboratory. People use active control processes to minimise proactive interference. Recovered memories of childhood abuse are more likely to be genuine when recalled outside therapy than those recalled inside therapy. Memories can be suppressed with executive control processes within the prefrontal cortex playing a major role. Forgetting depends on encoding-retrieval overlap (encoding specificity principle) but cue overload is also important. However, decreased forgetting over time is hard to explain on the encoding specificity principle. Consolidation theory (which has been extended to include reconsolidation) explains the form of the forgetting curve. However, it de-emphasises the role of cognitive processes.

Further reading

- Baddeley, A.D. (2012). Working memory: Theories, models, and controversies. *Annual Review of Psychology*, 63: 1–29. Alan Baddeley provides an excellent comprehensive update of his very influential theoretical approach to working memory.
- Baddeley, A.D., Eysenck, M.W. & Anderson, M.C. (2015). *Memory* (2nd edn). Hove: Psychology Press. Chapters 2, 3, 4, 8 and 10 in this textbook provide coverage of most of the topics discussed in this chapter.
- Della Sala, S. (ed.) (2010). *Forgetting*. Hove: Psychology Press. This edited book provides a comprehensive discussion of theory and research on forgetting by some of the world's leading researchers.
- Karpicke, J.D. (2012). Retrieval-based learning: Active retrieval promotes meaningful learning. *Current Directions in Psychological Science*, 21: 157–63. This article provides a review of what is known about the processes underlying the testing effect.
- Reber, P.J. (2013). The neural basis of implicit learning and memory: A review of neuropsychological and neuroimaging research. *Neuropsychologia*, 51: 2026–42. Paul Reber argues that implicit learning is involved most of the time as we interact with the environment.
- Shanks, D.R. (2010). Learning: From association to cognition. *Annual Review of Psychology*, 61: 273–301. David Shanks provides an interesting historical account of the development of theory and research on implicit learning.

CHAPTER

7

Long-term memory systems

INTRODUCTION

We have an amazing variety of information stored in long-term memory. For example, long-term memory can contain details of our last summer holiday, the fact that Paris is the capital of France, information about how to ride a bicycle and so on. Much of this information is stored in the form of schemas or organised packets of knowledge and is used extensively during language comprehension. The relationship between schematic knowledge and language comprehension is discussed in Chapter 10.

In view of the remarkable variety of information stored in long-term memory, it is improbable that there is a *single* long-term memory store as proposed by Atkinson and Shiffrin (1968; see Chapter 6). Subsequently, it was accepted there are several major long-term memory systems. For example, Schacter and Tulving (1994) identified four major long-term memory systems: episodic memory, semantic memory, the perceptual representation system and procedural memory. The issue of the number and nature of long-term memory systems is considered by Squire (2009a) in the light of our knowledge of the brain. Various competing views are discussed later in this chapter.

Amnesia

Suggestive evidence that there may be several long-term memory systems comes from the study of brain-damaged patients with **amnesia**. Such patients have problems with long-term memory, but if you are a movie fan you may have mistaken ideas about the nature of amnesia (Baxendale, 2004). In the movies, serious head injuries typically cause characters to forget the past while still being fully able to engage in new learning. In the real world, however, new learning is generally greatly impaired. An exception is the movie *Memento* (2000) in which Leonard Shelby has amnesia that prevents him from learning and remembering new information.

There are several movies in which amnesic patients suffer a profound loss of identity or their personality changes completely. In the movie *Overboard* (1987), Goldie Hawn falls from her yacht and immediately switches from being a rich, spoilt socialite to being a loving mother. Such personality shifts are extremely rare in real life. Most bizarrely of all, the rule of thumb in the movies is that the best cure for amnesia caused by severe head injury is to suffer another massive blow to the head. This is *not* recommended medical practice!

There are various reasons why patients become amnesic. Bilateral stroke is one factor causing amnesia, but closed head injury is the most common cause. However, patients with closed head injury often have several cognitive impairments, making it hard to interpret their memory deficits. As a result, much experimental research (especially early research) has focused on patients whose amnesia is due to chronic alcohol abuse (**Korsakoff's syndrome**).

There are four problems with using Korsakoff patients to study amnesia. First, the amnesia typically has a *gradual* onset, being caused by an increasing deficiency of the vitamin thiamine associated with chronic alcoholism. This can make it hard to know whether certain past events occurred before or after the onset of amnesia.

Second, brain damage in Korsakoff patients is often rather widespread, although it typically involves the medial temporal lobes (especially the hippocampus; see Figure 7.1). There is frequently damage to the frontal lobes,

KEY TERMS

Amnesia
A condition caused by brain damage in which there is severe impairment of long-term memory.

Korsakoff's syndrome
Amnesia caused by chronic alcoholism.

Weblink:
Video about HM

IN THE REAL WORLD: THE FAMOUS CASE OF HM

HM (revealed to be Henry Gustav Molaison after his death in 2008) was the most-studied amnesic patient of all time. He suffered from very severe epilepsy starting when he was 10. Several years later on 23 August 1953, he received surgery for the condition that involved removal of the medial temporal lobes including the hippocampus.

The operation dramatically affected his memory. Corkin (1984, p. 255) reported many years later that HM, "does not know where he lives, who cares for him, or where he ate his last meal . . . In 1982 he did not recognise a picture of himself that had been taken on his fortieth birthday in 1966." When shown faces of individuals who became famous after the onset of his amnesia, HM could identify only John Kennedy and Ronald Reagan.

HM also had problems with the use of language. His brain damage meant he found it hard to form coherent sentence-level plans when speaking (Mackay et al., 2011).

Research on HM (starting with Scoville and Milner, 1957) transformed our understanding of long-term memory (Squire, 2009b; Eichenbaum, 2015, in press). Why is that the case? First, and most importantly, HM retained the ability to form many kinds of long-term memory. He showed reasonable learning on a mirror-tracing task (drawing objects seen only in reflection) and he retained some of this learning for one year (Corkin, 1968). He also showed learning on the pursuit rotor (manual tracking of a moving target). These findings indicate there is more than one long-term memory system.

Second, HM had good sustained attention and essentially intact performance on tasks involving short-term memory. These findings suggest there is an important distinction between short-term and long-term memory (see Chapter 6).

Third, the dramatic effects of surgery on many aspects of HM's memory indicate the involvement of the medial temporal lobes (including the hippocampus) in long-term memory. However, the fact that HM had generally good memory for events occurring a long time before his operation suggests memories are *not* stored permanently in the hippocampus.

which can produce various cognitive deficits not specific to the memory system. Interpreting findings from Korsakoff patients would be easier if the brain damage were more limited.

Third, the precise area of brain damage (and thus the pattern of memory impairment) varies from patient to patient. For example, Korsakoff's syndrome is generally (but not always) preceded by Wernicke's encephalopathy, which is characterised by confusion, lethargy and inattention (Fama et al., 2012). Such variations make it hard to generalise across patients.

Fourth, research on Korsakoff patients does not provide a *direct* assessment of the impact of brain damage on long-term memory. Brain plasticity and the learning of compensatory strategies mean patients can alleviate some of their memory symptoms over time (Fama et al., 2012).

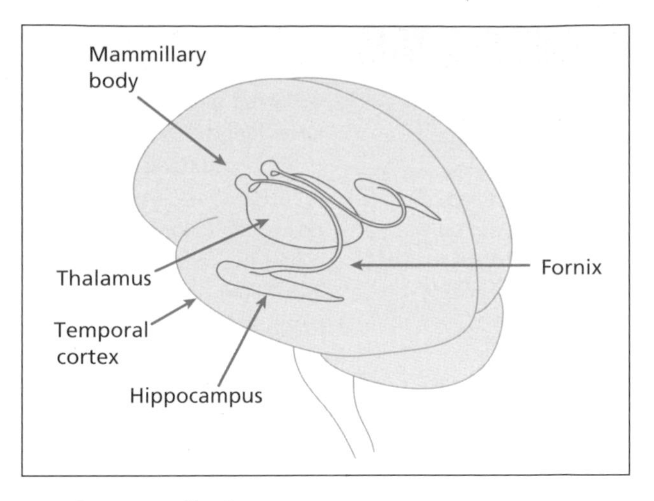

Figure 7.1
Brain structures involved in memory storage and consolidation.
From Groome et al. (2014).

Korsakoff patients are sometimes said to suffer from the "amnesic syndrome" consisting of the following features:

- **Anterograde amnesia**: a marked impairment in the ability to remember new information learned after the onset of amnesia. HM suffered severely from anterograde amnesia.
- Retrograde amnesia: problems in remembering events occurring prior to the onset of amnesia (see Chapter 6).
- Only slightly impaired short-term memory on measures such as digit span (repeating back a random string of digits).
- Some remaining learning ability (e.g., motor skills) after the onset of amnesia.

Weblink:
Amnesia

Do anterograde and retrograde amnesia depend on the same brain regions? Smith et al. (2013) assessed anterograde and retrograde amnesia in 11 patients with damage to the medial temporal lobes. There was a strong correlation ($r = +0.81$) between the extent of anterograde and retrograde amnesia, suggesting the same brain areas are involved. However, the correlation is often much lower when brain damage extends to other brain regions.

The study of amnesic patients has led to various theoretical developments (as in the case of HM). For example, distinctions such as that between declarative or explicit memory and non-declarative or implicit memory (discussed in the next section) were originally proposed in part because of data obtained from amnesic patients. Furthermore, such patients have provided some of the strongest evidence supporting these distinctions.

Declarative vs. non-declarative memory

It has often been argued that the most important distinction between different types of long-term memory is between declarative memory and non-declarative memory. **Declarative memory** involves conscious recollection of events and facts – it often refers to memories that can be "declared" or described but also includes memories that cannot be described verbally. Declarative memory is sometimes referred to as explicit memory and it involves knowing *that* something is the case.

KEY TERMS

Anterograde amnesia
Reduced ability to remember information acquired after the onset of **amnesia**.

Declarative memory
A form of long-term memory that involves knowing something is the case; it involves conscious recollection and includes memory for facts (**semantic memory**) and events (**episodic memory**); sometimes known as explicit memory.

KEY TERMS

Non-declarative memory
Forms of long-term memory that influence behaviour but do not involve conscious recollection (e.g., **priming, procedural memory**); also known as implicit memory.

Procedural memory
This is memory concerned with knowing how and it includes the knowledge required to perform skilled actions.

Priming
Facilitating the processing of (and response to) a target by presenting a stimulus related to it some time beforehand.

The two main forms of declarative memory are episodic memory and semantic memory. Episodic memory is concerned with personal experiences or events that occurred in a given place at a specific time. Semantic memory consists of general knowledge about the world, concepts, language and so on.

In contrast, **non-declarative memory** does not involve conscious recollection. Typically, we obtain evidence of non-declarative memory by observing changes in behaviour. For example, consider someone learning how to ride a bicycle. Their cycling performance improves over time even though they cannot consciously recollect what they have learned about cycling. Non-declarative memory is also known as implicit memory.

There are various forms of non-declarative memory. One is memory for skills (e.g., piano playing, bicycle riding). Such memory involves knowing *how* to perform certain actions and is sometimes known as **procedural memory**.

Another form of non-declarative memory is **priming**, in which the processing of a stimulus is influenced by the prior presentation of a stimulus related to it. For example, suppose a visual stimulus (e.g., of a cat) is presented very briefly. It is easier to identify the stimulus as a cat if a similar picture of a cat has been presented previously. The earlier picture acts as a *prime*, facilitating processing when the second cat picture is presented.

As mentioned already, evidence from amnesic patients is very relevant to the distinction between declarative and non-declarative memory. It appears such patients have great difficulties in forming declarative memories but can readily form non-declarative memories. For example, HM had extremely poor declarative memory for personal events occurring after the onset of amnesia and for faces of those who became famous in recent decades. However, he had reasonable learning ability on tasks such as mirror tracing, the pursuit rotor and perceptual identification (all involving non-declarative memory). As we will see later, the great majority of amnesic patients have patterns of memory performance similar to those of HM.

Most of this chapter is devoted to a detailed discussion of the various forms of declarative and non-declarative memory. A sketch-map of the ground we will cover is shown in Figure 7.2. It emphasises the distinction between declarative and non-declarative memory. The figure includes episodic and semantic memory as forms of declarative memory. It also includes procedural memory and priming as forms of non-declarative memory. It is assumed the various types of memory vary in terms of the brain areas most associated with them.

Limitations with the traditional memory systems approach

Figure 7.2 presents a standard view of thinking about memory systems. However, theorists increasingly argue that this view is incomplete and needs to be developed (e.g., Henke, 2010; Hannula & Greene, 2012; Cabeza & Moscovitch, 2013). These proposed theoretical developments are discussed later in the chapter.

The memory systems approach provides a valuable account of numerous memory phenomena and remains very influential. However, it is *oversimplified* – it is improbable each memory system has its own separate processes within a given brain area. However, it is certainly possible that a more complex memory systems approach might be able to account for most of the relevant findings.

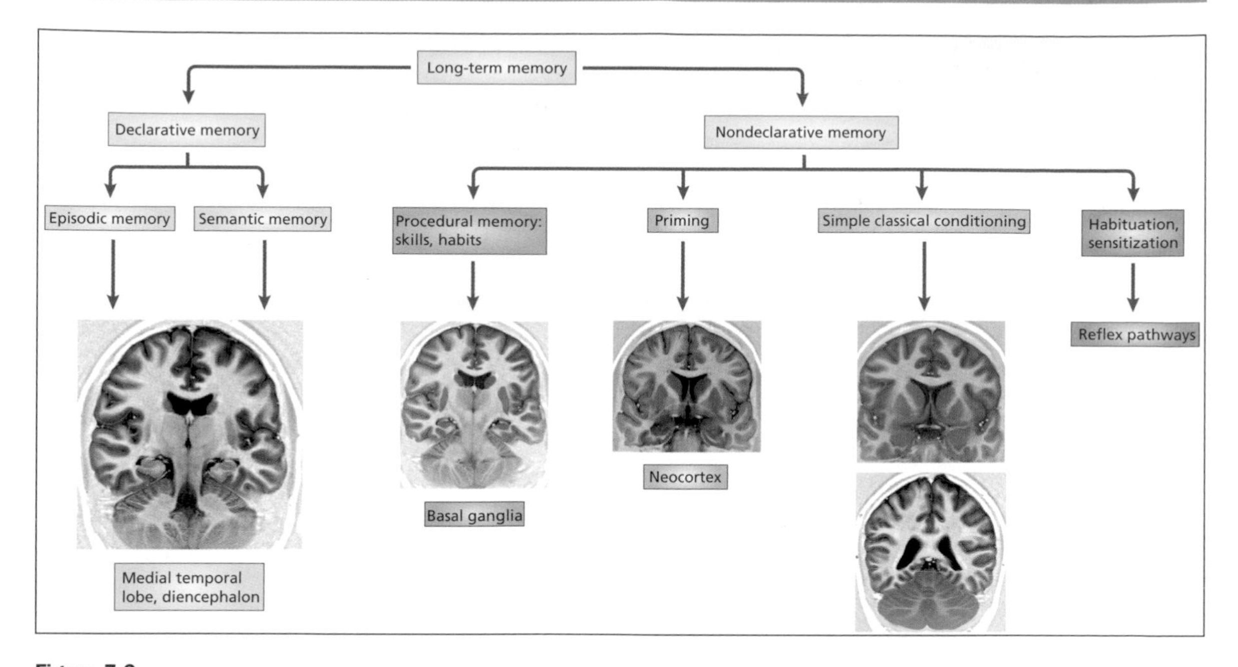

Figure 7.2
The standard account based on dividing long-term memory into two broad classes: declarative and non-declarative. Declarative memory is divided into episodic and semantic memory, whereas non-declarative memory is divided into procedural memory, priming, simple classical conditioning and habituation and sensitisation. The assumption that there are several forms of long-term memory is accompanied by the further assumption that different brain regions are associated with each one.
From Henke (2010). Reprinted with permission from Nature Publishing Group.

Cabeza and Moscovitch (2013) discussed a component process framework, which may prove preferable to the memory systems approach. According to this framework, there are numerous processing components that are used *flexibly* depending on the precise task demands.

The relevant issues are discussed at length later. Here we consider a single example of the rigidity of the traditional memory systems approach. According to that approach (see Figure 7.2), episodic memory depends on the medial temporal lobe (including the hippocampus) but not the basal ganglia (including the striatum).

Sadeh et al. (2011) reported findings apparently inconsistent with the above prediction. Successful recognition memory in episodic memory was preceded by enhanced activity in the striatum as well as the hippocampus at the time of learning. These findings could be taken to mean that effective learning was associated with *interactive* activity involving the hippocampus and striatum. However, the neuroimaging findings were only correlational and so cannot show that episodic learning requires the involvement of the striatum.

DECLARATIVE MEMORY

We all have declarative or explicit memory for many different kinds of memories. For example, we remember what we had for breakfast this morning and that "le petit déjeuner" is French for "breakfast". Tulving (1972) argued that these kinds of memories are very different. He introduced the terms "episodic memory" and "semantic memory" to refer to the difference (see Eysenck and Groome (2015, in press) for a review).

KEY TERMS

Episodic memory
A form of long-term memory concerned with personal experiences or episodes occurring in a given place at a specific time.

Semantic memory
A form of long-term memory consisting of general knowledge about the world, concepts, language and so on.

What is **episodic memory**? According to Tulving (2002, p. 5):

> [It] is a recently evolved, late-developing, and early-deteriorating past-oriented memory system, more vulnerable than other memory systems to neural dysfunction . . . It makes possible mental time travel through subjective time from the present to the past, thus allowing one to re-experience . . . one's own previous experiences.

Distinguishing features of episodic memory are that it allows us to access information concerning *where* and *when* personal events in our lives occurred.

What is **semantic memory**? According to Binder and Desai (2011, p. 527), it is "an individual's store of knowledge about the world. The content of semantic memory is abstracted from actual experience and is therefore said to be conceptual, that is, generalized and without reference to any specific experience."

There are similarities between episodic and semantic memory. Suppose you remember meeting your friend recently at a coffee shop. That clearly involves episodic memory because you are remembering an event at a given time in a given place. However, semantic memory is also involved – some of what you remember depends on your general knowledge about coffee shops, what coffee tastes like and so on.

What is the relationship between episodic memory and autobiographical memory (discussed in Chapter 8)? Both are forms of memory concerned with personal experiences from the past. However, much information in episodic memory is fairly trivial and is remembered fairly briefly. In contrast, autobiographical memory stores, for long periods of time, information about events and experiences having personal significance.

Episodic vs. semantic memory

If episodic and semantic memory form separate memory systems, there should be several important differences between them. Some of the strongest support for the separate-systems viewpoint comes from studies of brain-damaged patients (Greenberg & Verfaellie, 2010).

Much research has focused on the ability of amnesic patients to acquire episodic and semantic memories after the onset of amnesia. Thus, what was of interest was the extent of anterograde amnesia. Spiers et al. (2001) reviewed 147 cases of amnesia involving damage to the hippocampus or fornix. Episodic memory was impaired in *all* cases, whereas many patients had significantly less severe problems with semantic memory. The finding that the impact of hippocampal brain damage was much greater on episodic than on semantic memory suggests the two types of memory are distinctly different.

Note that the memory problems of amnesic patients are limited to long-term memory. According to Spiers et al. (2001, p. 359), "None of the cases was reported to have impaired short-term memory (typically tested using digit span – the immediate recall of verbally presented digits)."

We would have stronger evidence if we discovered amnesic patients with very poor episodic memory but essentially *intact* semantic memory. Such evidence was apparently obtained by Vargha-Khadem et al. (1997). Two of the patients they studied had suffered bilateral hippocampal damage at an early age before developing semantic memory. Beth suffered brain damage at birth and Jon at age 4.

Both patients (Beth and Jon) had very poor episodic memory for the day's activities, television programmes and telephone conversations. In spite of this, Beth and Jon both attended ordinary schools. Their semantic memory based on levels of speech and language development, literacy and factual knowledge (e.g., vocabulary) were within the normal range. However, healthy individuals with an intact hippocampus depend on it for semantic memory acquisition (Baddeley et al., 2015).

Subsequent research indicated Jon had some problems with semantic memory (Gardiner et al., 2008). When provided with various facts concerning geographical, historical and other kinds of knowledge, Jon's rate of learning was significantly slower than that of healthy controls.

Why did Jon show a good ability to acquire semantic information in semantic memory in his everyday life? Gardiner et al. (2008) suggested this occurred because Jon devoted much time to repeated study of such information.

Overall, Jon's semantic memory was somewhat impaired but his episodic memory was grossly deficient. How can we explain this difference? Vargha-Khadem et al. (1997) argued that episodic memory depends on the hippocampus whereas semantic memory depends on the underlying entorhinal, perirhinal and parahippocampal cortices. The brain damage suffered by Beth and Jon centred on the hippocampus.

Why do so many amnesics have great problems with both episodic and semantic memory? The answer may be that they have damage to the hippocampus *and* the underlying cortices. This is very likely given the two areas are adjacent.

Some support for the above viewpoint was reported by Bindschaedler et al. (2011). They reported the case of VJ, a boy with severe atrophy of the hippocampus but relatively preserved surrounding areas such as perirhinal and entorhinal cortex. VJ's performance on semantic memory tasks (e.g., vocabulary) increased over time at the same rate as that of healthy controls even though he showed severe impairment on 82% of episodic memory tasks.

Retrograde amnesia

So far we have focused on the ability of amnesic patients to acquire new episodic and semantic memories after the onset of amnesia. What about amnesic patients' retrograde amnesia (poor recall for memories formed *prior* to the onset of amnesia)?

Many amnesic patients show much greater retrograde amnesia for episodic than semantic memories. Consider KC. According to Tulving (2002, p. 13), "He cannot recollect any personally experienced events . . ., whereas his semantic knowledge acquired before the critical accident is still reasonably intact . . . his general knowledge of the world is not greatly different from others' at his educational level."

Retrograde amnesia for *episodic* memories in amnesic patients often spans several years. There is typically a temporal gradient with older memories showing less impairment than older ones (Bayley et al., 2006). In contrast, retrograde amnesia for *semantic* memories is generally small except for knowledge acquired shortly before the onset of amnesia (Manns et al., 2003).

Several theories have been put forward to explain retrograde amnesia (Kopelman & Bright, 2012). According to consolidation theory, there is a long-lasting physiological consolidation of episodic memories in the hippocampus.

KEY TERM

Semantic dementia
A condition involving damage to the anterior temporal lobes in which there is a widespread loss of information about the meanings of words and concepts; patients with this condition differ widely in symptoms and the pattern of brain damage. However, **episodic memory** and executive functioning are reasonably intact in the early stages.

Weblink:
Semantic dementia

After a period of several years, these memories are stored elsewhere, which protects them from the effects of hippocampal damage. This explains the temporal gradient, but the notion that consolidation lasts for several years is implausible.

An alternative theory is that episodic memories become more like semantic memories over time, thus protecting them from the effects of brain damage. According to this theory, remote semantic memories (e.g., for vocabulary) formed years before the onset of amnesia should be relatively intact but are often forgotten. Kopelman and Bright (2012, p. 2969) concluded that, "The problem is that the confusing and contradictory empirical data do not really support any of the main theories."

There is a final point. Episodic memories typically depend on a *single* learning experience, whereas most semantic memories (e.g., meanings of specific words) depend on *several* learning experiences. This reduced learning opportunity for episodic memories compared to semantic ones may explain at least in part greater retrograde amnesia for the former.

Semantic dementia

Are there brain-damaged patients having severe problems with semantic memory but with relatively intact episodic memory? The short answer is "Yes". Patients with **semantic dementia** have severe loss of concept knowledge from semantic memory even though their episodic memory and most cognitive functions are reasonably intact. Note, however, that patients with semantic dementia differ in terms of their precise symptoms.

Semantic dementia always involves degeneration of the anterior temporal lobe, so that area is of great importance to semantic memory. Areas such as perirhinal and entorhinal cortex are probably involved in the formation of semantic memories, whereas the anterior temporal lobes are where such memories are stored on a semi-permanent basis.

Patients with semantic dementia find it very difficult to access information about most concepts stored in semantic memory (Mayberry et al., 2011). However, their performance on several episodic memory tasks is good. For example, Adlam et al. (2009) asked patients with semantic dementia to remember what tasks they had performed 24 hours earlier, where those tasks were performed and when during the session they occurred. The patients as a group performed comparably to healthy controls.

In sum, the evidence points to a double dissociation (see Glossary). Amnesic patients have very poor episodic memory but often have fairly intact semantic memory. In contrast, patients with semantic dementia have very poor semantic memory but their episodic memory is reasonably intact.

Interdependence of episodic and semantic memory

So far we have focused mostly on the notion that there are separate episodic and semantic memory systems. However, some evidence suggests both involve similar brain regions. Burianova et al. (2010) compared patterns of brain activation during episodic, semantic and autobiographical memory retrieval. The same neural network was associated with retrieval of all these types of declarative memories. In addition, there was reduced activity in brain areas associated with attention to external stimuli.

Evidence showing that episodic and semantic memory can be *interdependent* in their functioning was shown by Kan et al. (2009) with respect to learning. Amnesic patients were given the episodic memory task of learning the prices of grocery items. Some items were congruent with participants' prior knowledge of the prices (semantic memory), whereas others were incongruent.

Healthy controls had better memory for grocery prices congruent with their prior knowledge than for those incongruent. Thus, their semantic knowledge provided a framework for the acquisition of new episodic memories. A similar pattern of findings was obtained from amnesic patients with fairly intact semantic memory. In contrast, amnesic patients with poor semantic memory were unable to use their semantic memory effectively and so showed no congruency effect.

As we have seen, Kan et al. (2009) found semantic memory can enhance *learning* on an episodic memory task. Greenberg et al. (2009) found episodic memory can facilitate *retrieval* on a semantic memory task. Amnesic patients and healthy controls were given the semantic memory task of generating as many category members as possible from various categories. Some categories (e.g., kitchen utensils, things given as birthday presents) were selected so performance would benefit from making use of episodic memory. Other categories (e.g., things that are typically red) seemed less likely to involve episodic memory.

What did Greenberg et al. (2009) find? Overall, amnesic patients performed worse than the healthy controls. However, the patients performed especially poorly on categories that would benefit from episodic memory. With those categories, the controls were much more likely than the amnesic patients to use episodic memory as an efficient organisational strategy to generate category members.

Evaluation

There are somewhat separate episodic and semantic memory systems. Amnesic patients with hippocampal damage always have severely impaired episodic memory but the impairment of semantic memory is often rather less. In contrast, patients with semantic dementia have very poor semantic memory but (at least in the early stages) reasonably intact episodic memory. Amnesic patients and those with semantic dementia thus provide an important double dissociation.

Most research is limited because it has focused on studying each type of memory in isolation. In fact, however, episodic and semantic memory are often *interdependent* at the time of learning and during retrieval. It is important for future research to discover in more detail how these two types of memory combine to enhance learning and retrieval.

Semanticisation of episodic memory

Finally, we consider the possibility that what are initially episodic memories can become semantic memories over time. Suppose you spent a childhood holiday at a place several miles from the sea. One day you went to a nearby seaside resort and formed episodic memories of your experiences there. Nowadays, however, while you remember visiting a seaside resort, you cannot remember the name of the resort, when you went there or any information about your experiences there. In essence, what was initially an episodic memory has become a semantic memory lacking the personal or contextual information it originally possessed. This change

KEY TERM

Semanticisation
Episodic memories changing into **semantic memories** over time.

is sometimes known as the **semanticisation** of episodic memory and it indicates that there is no sharp separation between episodic and semantic memories.

Evidence for semanticisation was reported by Harand et al. (2012). Almost 200 pictures were presented to participants and their memory for those pictures was then assessed three days and three months later. Some picture memories were episodic at both retention intervals (i.e., contextual information was recalled both times). Other picture memories were episodic at the short retention interval but had become semantic at the long interval (i.e., they were recognised but in the absence of any ability to recollect contextual information). The hippocampus (often thought to be crucial in the formation and retrieval of episodic memories) was much more activated at three months by episodic than semantic memories. This strengthens the argument that some episodic memories eventually change into semantic ones.

EPISODIC MEMORY

Most episodic memories exhibit substantial forgetting over time (see Chapter 6). However, there are exceptions. Bahrick et al. (1975) used photographs from high-school yearbooks. Ex-students showed remarkably little forgetting of information about their former classmates at retention intervals up to 25 years. Performance was 90% for recognising classmates' names, for recognising a classmate's photograph and for matching a classmate's name to his/her school photograph. Performance remained very high on the last two tests even after almost 50 years but declined on the name recognition task.

Bahrick et al. (2008) asked ex-college students to recall their academic grades. Distortions (mostly involving inflating the actual grade!) occurred shortly after graduation but thereafter remained fairly constant over retention intervals up to 54 years.

Bahrick (1984) used the term "permastore" to refer to very long-term stable memories. This term was based on permafrost (the permanently frozen subsoil found in Polar regions). The contents of the permastore consist mainly of information very well learned in the first place.

We now consider how we can assess someone's episodic memory following learning (e.g., a list of to-be-remembered items). Recognition and recall are the two main types of episodic-memory test. In essence, recognition-memory tests involve presenting a series of items with participants deciding whether each one was presented previously. As we will see, however, more complex forms of recognition-memory test have also been used.

There are three basic forms of recall test: free recall, serial recall and cued recall. Free recall involves producing list items in any order in the absence of any specific cues. Serial recall involves producing list items in the order in which they were presented. Cued recall involves producing list items in response to cues. For example, "cat – table" might be presented at learning and the cue, "cat – ???" might be given at test.

Recognition memory: familiarity and recollection

Recognition memory can involve recollection or familiarity. According to Diana et al. (2007, p. 379):

Recollection is the process of recognising an item on the basis of the retrieval of specific contextual details, whereas familiarity is the process of recognising an item on the basis of its perceived memory strength but without retrieval of any specific details about the study episode.

We can clarify the distinction between recollection and familiarity. Several years ago, the first author walked past a man in Wimbledon, and was immediately confident that he recognised him. However, he simply could not think of the situation in which he had seen the man previously. After some thought (this is the kind of thing academic psychologists think about!), he realised the man was a ticket-office clerk at Wimbledon railway station. Thus, initial recognition based on familiarity was replaced by recognition based on recollection.

An effective way of distinguishing between these two forms of recognition memory is the remember/know procedure (Migo et al., 2012). Participants indicate whether each item presented to them is "Old" or "New". An item identified as "Old" is followed by a *remember* response if recognition "is accompanied by a conscious recollection of its prior occurrence in the study" (Gardiner, 1988, p. 311). This corresponds to recollection. In contrast, participants give a *know* response following their "Old" response if they do not consciously recollect an item's prior occurrence. This corresponds to familiarity.

An important issue with the remember/know procedure is whether recollection and familiarity actually involve different processes. Sceptics have argued that the only real difference is that *strong* memory traces give rise to recollection judgements and *weak* memory traces to familiarity judgements. Dunn (2008) carried out a meta-analysis of 37 studies using the remember/know procedure. He claimed the findings could be explained by a *single* process based on memory strength.

Interactive exercise: Remember/know procedure

In spite of Dunn's findings, most evidence (some discussed in the next section) supports dual-process accounts. One experimental approach involves using event-related potentials (ERPs; see Glossary) to track the time course of recognition processes. We would expect the processes associated with recollection judgements to take longer than those associated with familiarity judgements because the former are more complex and depend on a greater variety of information.

Evidence confirming the above expectations has been obtained in several studies (Addante et al., 2012). Familiarity is associated with a negative ERP peak (FN400) between 400 and 600 ms after stimulus onset. In contrast, recollection is associated with a positive peak (late positive component) occurring 600–900 ms after stimulus onset. Note that it is not easy to interpret the ERP evidence because the FN400 may reflect implicit-memory mechanisms rather the explicit-memory mechanisms of interest to the researchers.

Familiarity and recollection: brain mechanisms

Diana et al. (2007) provided a theoretical account of the brain areas involved in recognition memory in their binding-of-item-and-context model (see Figure 7.3):

1 Perirhinal cortex receives information about specific items ("what" information needed for familiarity judgements).

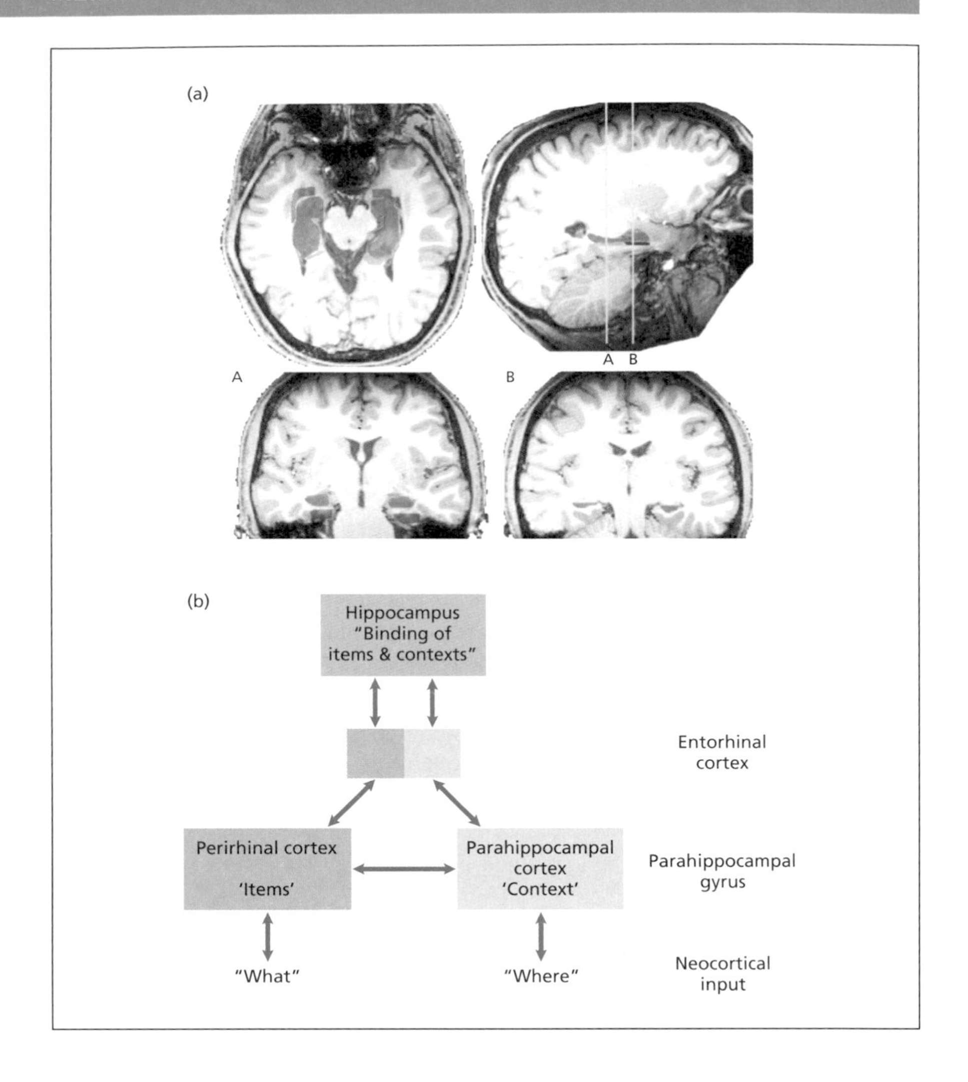

Figure 7.3
(a) Locations of the hippocampus (red), the perirhinal cortex (blue) and the parahippocampal cortex (green). (b) The binding-of-item-and-context model.

From Diana et al. (2007). Reprinted with permission of Elsevier.

2 Parahippocampal cortex receives information about context ("where" information useful for recollection judgements).
3 The hippocampus receives what and where information (both of great importance to episodic memory) and binds them to form item-context associations that permit recollection.

Findings

Functional neuroimaging studies support the above model. Diana et al. (2007) found using a meta-analytic approach that recollection was associated with more activation in parahippocampal cortex and the hippocampus than in the perirhinal cortex. In contrast, familiarity was associated with more activation in the perirhinal cortex than the parahippocampal cortex or hippocampus. De Vanssay-Maigne et al. (2011) replicated Diana et al.'s (2007) findings. For example, old words correctly recognised with a sense of familiarity were associated with greater bilateral activation in the perirhinal cortex than those not recognised. These brain areas were *not* associated with successful recollection performance.

There are two limitations with the neuroimaging evidence. First, it is correlational and does not show the hippocampus is actually more essential to recollection than familiarity. Second, there is typically a confounding between type of judgement (recollection vs. familiarity) and memory strength, with stronger memories being associated with recollection. When this confounding is avoided, hippocampal activation for recollection and familiarity judgements is usually comparable (Wixted & Squire, 2011).

In principle, we could obtain stronger evidence from brain-damaged patients. According to Diana et al.'s (2007) model, hippocampal damage should impair recollection more than familiarity. Bowles et al. (2010) studied amnesic patients who had undergone surgery involving the removal of much of the hippocampus and amygdala. As predicted, these patients had significantly impaired recollection but not familiarity. However, other research has typically found that amnesic patients with medial temporal lobe damage have a minor impairment in familiarity but a much larger impairment in recollection (Skinner & Fernandes, 2007).

Addante et al. (2012) also found that amnesic patients had severely impaired recollection but relatively intact familiarity in recognition memory. They used event-related potentials (ERPs; see Glossary) to shed light on the underlying processes. The amnesic patients showed the familiarity-related FN400 component (note that this may reflect the involvement of implicit-memory mechanisms as well). Importantly, however, they did not show the recollection-related late positive component.

According to the model, we would expect to find largely intact recollection but impaired familiarity in patients with damage to the perirhinal cortex. This prediction was tested by Bowles et al. (2007, 2011) with a female patient, NB, who had had surgery in which a large part of the perirhinal cortex (and adjacent entorhinal cortex) was removed. Her recollection performance was consistently at normal levels across a range of learning materials. In contrast, NB had impaired familiarity for verbal materials. Brandt et al. (submitted) studied a female patient, MR, who had brain damage limited to the entorhinal cortex. Recognition-memory tests indicated she had impaired familiarity for words but intact recollection.

Conclusions

There is much empirical support for the notion that recognition memory depends on rather separate processes of familiarity and recollection. Some evidence comes from brain neuroimaging studies, but the most convincing findings come from studying brain-damaged patients. A double dissociation (see Glossary) has been obtained – some patients have reasonably intact familiarity but impaired recollection, whereas a few patients exhibit the opposite pattern.

In essence, recollection involves accessing more information than does familiarity. This typically consists of contextual information, but may also involve information about the cognitive control processes used to access long-term memory. Thus, it may be necessary in future to distinguish among different forms of recollection (Moulin et al., 2013).

Recall memory

Some research on recall is discussed in Chapter 6. Here we will focus on the issue of whether the processes involved in free recall closely resemble those involved in recognition memory. Staresina and Davachi (2006) gave three memory tests to their participants: free recall, item recognition (familiarity) and associative recognition (recollection). Successful memory performance on all three tests was associated with increased activation at encoding in the left hippocampus and left ventrolateral prefrontal cortex. These associations were strongest with free recall and weakest with item recognition.

Only successful subsequent free recall was associated with increased activation in the dorsolateral prefrontal cortex and posterior parietal cortex. Why was this? The likeliest explanation is that successful free recall involves forming associations (between items and the colours in which they were studied), something that is not required for successful recognition memory.

What would happen if we used the remember/know procedure with free recall? Mickes et al. (2013) addressed this issue. Participants were presented with words and for each one answered an animacy question ("is this item animate or inanimate?") or a size question ("is this item bigger than a shoebox?"). After that, they recalled the words, made a *remember* or *know* judgement for each word recalled and indicated which question had been associated with each word.

Mickes et al.'s (2013) findings resembled those found in recognition memory. First, large numbers of recalled words received *remember* and *know* judgements, with approximately twice as many in the former category. Second, participants were more accurate at remembering which question was associated with recalled words when the words received *remember* judgements than when they received *know* judgements. This is very similar to recognition memory where participants access more contextual information for *remember* words than *know* ones.

Is episodic memory constructive?

We use episodic memory to remember past events we have experienced. You might think our episodic memory system should work like a video recorder, providing us with accurate and detailed information about past events. As you have probably discovered, that is *not* the case. As Schacter and Addis (2007, p. 773) pointed out, "Episodic memory is . . . a fundamentally constructive, rather than reproductive process that is prone to various kinds of errors and illusions."

Plentiful evidence for the above constructive view of episodic memory is discussed in other chapters. Research has shown how the constructive nature of episodic memory leads people to remember stories in distorted form (Chapter 10) and eyewitnesses to produce distorted memories of crimes (Chapter 8).

Why are we saddled with an episodic memory system so prone to error? Schacter and Addis (2007; see also Schacter, 2012) identified three reasons. First, it would require an incredible amount of processing to produce a semi-permanent record of every experience. Second, we generally want to access the gist or essence of our past experiences with the trivial details omitted.

Third, and perhaps most importantly, Schacter and Addis (2007) argued that we use our episodic memory system to imagine possible future events and scenarios, which is useful when forming plans for the future. Imagining the future is only possible because episodic memory is flexible and constructive rather than inflexible like a video recorder.

Findings

The tendency to remember the gist of what we have experienced increases throughout childhood (Brainerd et al., 2008). That is unsurprising. However, what is unexpected is that our increasing focus on remembering gist with age can produce errors in memory.

Brainerd and Mojardin (1998) asked children to listen to sets of three sentences (e.g., "The coffee is hotter than the tea"; "The tea is hotter than the cocoa"; "The cocoa is hotter than the soup"). On a subsequent memory test, participants decided whether test sentences had been presented previously in precisely that form. The key condition involved sentences having the same meaning as an original sentence but different wording (e.g., "The cocoa is cooler than the tea"). False recognition on these sentences was greater among older children than younger ones.

We turn now to the hypothesis that imagining future events involves the same (or similar) processes to those involved in remembering past events.

On that hypothesis, brain areas important to episodic memory (e.g., the hippocampus) should be activated when individuals imagine future events. Viard et al. (2012) reported a meta-analysis of relevant neuroimaging studies. Most studies reported hippocampal activation when people were imagining future events. There was greater hippocampal activation when individuals imagined future events in response to personally relevant cues rather than impersonal ones. There was also greater activation when the imagined events were regarded by the individual as vivid, emotional or having personal significance.

There is often more hippocampal activation during imagining future events than recalling past ones (Viard et al., 2012). Gaesser et al. (2013) argued that enhanced hippocampal activation was due to the demands of constructing coherent imaginary events. As predicted, there was more hippocampal activation when imagined events were constructed rather than re-imagined.

Neuroimaging evidence indicates hippocampal activation is generally *associated* with imagining future events. However, that does not show the hippocampus is *necessarily* involved in such imagining. We would have stronger evidence if we found that individuals with very poor episodic memory (e.g., amnesic patients with hippocampal damage) had an impaired ability to imagine future events.

Relevant evidence was reported by Hassabis et al. (2007). They asked amnesic patients and healthy controls to imagine future events (e.g., "Imagine you are lying on a white sandy beach in a beautiful tropical bay"). The amnesic patients' imaginary experiences consisted of isolated fragments lacking the richness and spatial coherence of the controls' experiences. Addis and Schacter (2012) reviewed research on amnesic patients with hippocampal damage. Most studies reported some adverse effects of amnesia on the ability to imagine future events.

Race et al. (2011) pointed out that hippocampal damage may be associated with impaired imagining of future events for two reasons. First, such damage may reduce the ability to access detailed information from episodic memory and then construct an imaginary future event. Second, such damage may reduce patients' ability to construct narratives describing imaginary events.

Race et al. (2011) used a condition in which amnesic patients simply constructed narratives from presented pictures *without* having to retrieve detailed information from episodic memory. Their performance was normal on this task, whereas it was severely impaired when they constructed narratives about future events. Thus, amnesics' ability to generate detailed narratives is preserved.

Evaluation

It has been assumed from Bartlett (1932) onwards that episodic memory relies heavily on constructive processes and this assumption has received substantial support (see Chapters 8 and 10). The further assumption that the same (or similar) constructive processes used in episodic memory for *past* events are also involved in imagining *future* events is an exciting development. Research using functional neuroimaging and amnesic patients has provided reasonable support.

What are the main limitations of research on imagining the future? First, we do not know in detail why there is generally more hippocampal activation when people imagine the future rather than remember the past. Second, more generally, imagining future events requires processes over and above those used in recalling the past. However, these processes remain ill-specified.

SEMANTIC MEMORY

Our organised general knowledge about the world is stored in semantic memory. Such knowledge can be extremely varied, including information about the French language, the rules of hockey, the names of capital cities and the authors of famous books. Much of this information is in the form of **concepts**, which are mental representations of categories (e.g., of objects) stored in semantic memory.

KEY TERM

Concepts
Mental representations of categories of objects or items.

Hierarchies of concepts

Suppose you are shown a photograph of a *chair* and asked what you are looking at. There are various answers you could provide based on information in semantic memory. You might say it is an *item of furniture*, a *chair* or an *easy chair*.

The above example suggests concepts are organised into hierarchies. Rosch et al. (1976) argued that there are three levels within such hierarchies: superordinate categories (e.g., *items of furniture*) at the top, basic-level categories (e.g., *chair*) in the middle and subordinate categories (e.g., *easy chair*) at the bottom.

Which level do we use most often? We sometimes talk about superordinate categories (e.g., "That furniture is expensive") and about subordinate categories (e.g., "I love my new iPhone"). However, we typically deal with objects at the intermediate, basic level.

Rosch et al. (1976) asked people to list concept attributes at each level in the hierarchy. Very few attributes were listed for the superordinate categories because these categories are abstract. Many attributes were listed for the categories at the other two levels. However, very similar attributes were listed for different categories at the lowest level. Thus, basic-level categories have the best balance between *informativeness* and *distinctiveness*. Informativeness is low at the highest level of the hierarchy and distinctiveness is low at the lowest level.

Basic-level categories also have other special properties not shared by categories at other levels. First, it is the most general level at which people use similar motor movements when interacting with category members. For example, nearly all chairs can be sat on in similar ways but this differs markedly from how we interact with tables. Second, the basic level is the one usually acquired first by young children (Bourdais & Pecheux, 2009).

Rosch et al. (1976) asked people to name pictures of objects. Basic-level names were used 1,595 times during the experiment. In contrast, subordinate names were used only 14 times, and superordinate names just once.

However, we do not always prefer basic-level categories. For example, we would expect a botanist to refer to the various different kinds of plants in a garden rather than simply describing them all as plants! Several exceptions to the rule that basic-level categories are preferred are discussed below.

Findings

Tanaka and Taylor (1991) studied the concepts of birdwatchers and dog experts shown pictures of birds and dogs. Both groups used subordinate names much more often in their expert domain than their novice domain. Bird experts used subordinate names 74% of the time with birds and dog experts used subordinate names 40% of the time with dogs. However, both groups used subordinate names only 24% of the time in their novice domain.

There is one type of object for which we mostly use subordinate categories – faces! For example, Anaki and Bentin (2009) presented participants with a category label at the superordinate, basic or subordinate level followed by the picture of a familiar face (i.e., a celebrity). Their task was to decide whether the face matched the label. Matching occurred faster at the subordinate or exemplar level than the basic level. It seems likely that this happened because we are nearly all experts at recognising faces.

Is expertise necessary for categorisation at the subordinate level to occur fastest? Anaki and Bentin (2009) argued that the answer is "No". They also presented their participants with photographs of familiar towers (e.g., Eiffel Tower, Leaning Tower of Pisa) preceded by labels at different levels in the hierarchy. Matching occurred faster at the subordinate level than at the basic level. Thus, individual familiarity with objects at the subordinate level can lead to very fast categorisation.

The fact that people generally *prefer* to categorise at the basic level does not necessarily mean they categorise *fastest* at that level. Prass et al. (2013) gave participants the task of categorising photographs of objects presented very briefly. Categorisation was at the superordinate level (animal or vehicle), the basic level (e.g., cat or dog) or the subordinate level (e.g., Siamese cat vs. Persian cat). Performance was most accurate and also fastest at the superordinate level and least accurate and slowest at the subordinate level (see Figure 7.4).

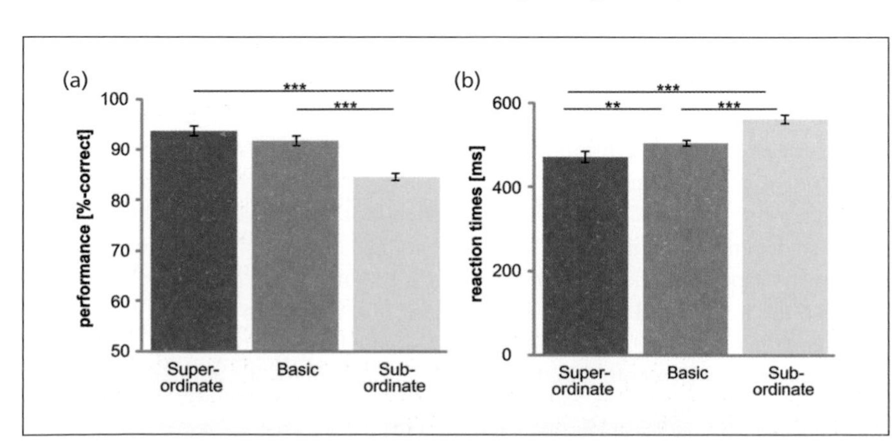

Figure 7.4
Accuracy of object categorisation ((a) left-hand side) and speed of categorisation ((b) right-hand side) at the superordinate, basic and subordinate levels.
From Prass et al. (2013). Reprinted with permission.

Why does categorisation often occur faster at the superordinate level than the basic level? Categorisation at the basic level is generally more informative than at the superordinate level and so requires more detailed processing (Close & Pothos, 2012).

Support for the above viewpoint was reported by Rogers and Patterson (2007). They studied patients with semantic dementia, a condition involving impairment of semantic memory (discussed at various points in this chapter). Patients with severe semantic dementia performed better at the superordinate level than the basic level.

Using concepts

What do the mental representations of concepts look like? This question has attracted much theoretical controversy (Kiefer & Pulvermüller, 2012; Meteyard et al., 2012). Most theorists until fairly recently assumed concept representations have the following characteristics:

- They are abstract in nature and are thus detached from input (sensory) and output (motor) processes.
- They are stable in that any given individual uses the same representation of a concept on different occasions.
- Different people generally have fairly similar representations of any given concept.

In sum, it has generally been assumed that concept representations, "have the flavour of detached encyclopaedia descriptions in a database of categorical knowledge about the world" (Barsalou, 2012, p. 247). This theoretical approach poses some problems. The notion of "detached encyclopaedia descriptions" seems remote from the realities of our lives. How, for example, do we make use of such descriptions when perceiving the visual world or deciding how to behave in a given situation?

Barsalou (2009, 2012) argued that *all* the major theoretical assumptions of the traditional approach are incorrect. In everyday life, we rarely process concepts in *isolation*. Instead, we process them in various different settings, and processing is influenced by the current context or setting. More generally, the representations of any given concept will vary across situations depending on the individual's current goals and the situation's major features.

Barsalou (2009) illustrated the limitations with previous theories by considering the concept of a *bicycle*. Traditionally, it was assumed a fairly complete abstract representation would always be activated resembling the *Chambers Dictionary* definition: "vehicle with two wheels one directly in front of the other, driven by pedals".

According to Barsalou (2009), the aspects of the bicycle concept that are activated depend on the individual's current *goals*. For example, information about the tyres is especially likely to be activated if you need to repair your bicycle. In contrast, the height of the saddle is important if you want to ride it.

Barsalou (e.g., 2009, 2012) put forward situated simulation theory. According to this theory, the perceptual and motor or action systems are typically involved in concept processing.

Findings

Wu and Barsalou (2009) provided evidence that conceptual processing can involve the perceptual system. Participants wrote down as many properties as they could for nouns or noun phrases. Those given the word *lawn* tended to focus on external properties (e.g., *plant*, *blades*), whereas those given *rolled-up lawn* focused more on internal properties (e.g., *dirt*, *soil*). The same pattern was found with other nouns. For example, *watermelon* generated external properties such as *rind* and *green*, whereas *half watermelon* generated internal properties such as *pips* and *red*.

What do the above findings mean? Concept processing can have a perceptual or imaginal quality about it. Object qualities not visible if you were actually looking at the object itself are harder to think of than those that would be visible.

Another way to assess concept processing is by using neuroimaging. Wang et al. (2010) carried out a meta-analysis (see Glossary) of neuroimaging studies focusing on concrete concepts (referring to objects we can see or hear). The processing of concrete concepts was associated with activation in brain regions (e.g., fusiform gyrus, posterior cingulate, parahippocampal gyrus) forming part of the perceptual system and also involved in imagery. In contrast, Wang et al. reported little evidence of perceptual processing with abstract concepts such as *truth*, *freedom* or *invention*.

Wilson-Mendenhall et al. (2013) argued that Wang et al.'s (2010) findings might simply reflect rather limited processing of abstract concepts. Accordingly, they instructed their participants to think deeply about two abstract concepts (*convince*, *arithmetic*). This produced more detailed processing than reported by Wang et al. Processing the concept *convince* led to activation in brain areas (e.g., medial prefrontal cortex) associated with social cognition. In contrast, processing *arithmetic* led to activation in brain areas (e.g., intraparietal sulcus) associated with numerical cognition.

Barsalou and Wiemer-Hastings (2005) asked people to list the characteristic properties of various abstract concepts. Many properties referred to settings or events associated with the concept (e.g., scientists working in a laboratory for *invention*) and others referred to relevant mental states. Thus, much of our knowledge of abstract concepts is relatively concrete and involves perceptual properties.

How can we test Barsalou's assumption that the motor system is often involved when we access concept information? Hauk et al. (2004) made use of the fact that tongue, finger and foot movements produce different patterns of activation along the motor strip. When they presented participants with words such as "lick", "pick" and "kick", these verbs activated parts of the motor strip overlapping with (or very close to) the corresponding part of the motor strip. Thus, for example, the word "lick" activated areas associated with tongue movements. Several other studies have reported similar findings (Pulvermüller, 2013).

Is the motor system involved in the processing of abstract concepts as well as concrete ones? There is evidence the answer is "Yes". Emotionally positive abstract concepts (e.g., *peace*) elicit approach tendencies, whereas emotionally negative ones (e.g., *hostility*) elicit avoidance tendencies. In several studies, people responded faster to positive stimuli with an approach movement but to negative ones with an avoidance movement (Pecher et al., 2011).

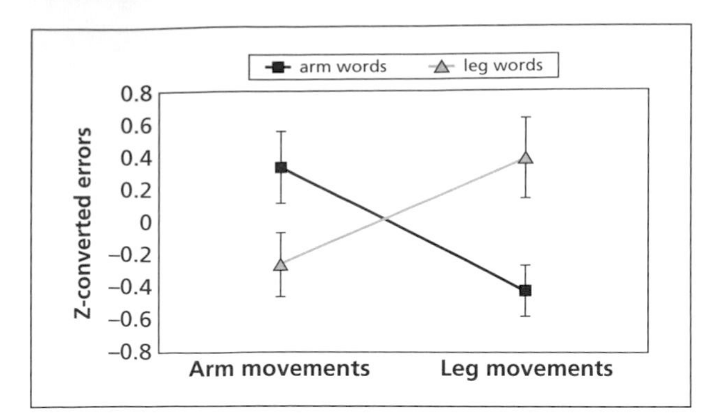

Figure 7.5
Memory errors over a short retention interval for arm words (e.g., wash) and leg words (e.g., stride) as a function of type of movements (arm or leg) made while processing the words.
From Shebani and Pulvermüller (2013). Reprinted with permission of Elsevier.

The above findings show the motor system is *associated* with the processing of action words. However, they do not show whether motor processing is *necessary* for understanding action concepts or whether such processing occurs only *after* concept meaning has been accessed. More convincing evidence has been obtained from patients with widespread damage to their motor system (e.g., those with motor neuron or Parkinson's disease). The key finding is that such patients have a deficit in processing action verbs (e.g., *hit*, *run*) but not other words.

In a study by Shebani and Pulvermüller (2013), participants processed leg-related words (e.g., *step*, *kick*) or arm-related words (e.g., *grasp*, *peel*). At the same time, they engaged in motor tapping of their legs or hands. Short-term memory was worse when there was concordance between word and movement type (e.g., leg-related words and leg movements) than when there was not (e.g., leg-related words and arm movements) (see Figure 7.5). These findings show the involvement of the motor system in processing action verbs. As Shebani and Pulvermüller (p. 222) concluded, the findings indicate "a genuine motor locus of semantic meaning".

Some of the strongest evidence that processing within the motor system is necessary for understanding action verbs was reported by Pulvermüller et al. (2005). Participants decided whether strings of letters formed words. Different parts of the motor system were stimulated with transcranial magnetic stimulation (TMS; see Glossary) while this task was performed.

The key conditions were those in which arm-related or leg-related words were presented while TMS was applied to parts of the left-hemisphere motor strip associated with arm or leg movements. Arm-related words were processed faster when TMS was applied to the arm site than to the leg site and the opposite effect occurred with leg-related words (see Figure 7.6).

Evaluation

There is much support for Barsalou's general theoretical approach. Our use of concept knowledge in everyday life typically involves the perceptual and motor systems even with abstract concepts. This helps to explain why concept processing varies across situations depending on the individual's goals. In other words, the precise way we process a concept depends on the situation and the perceptual and motor processes engaged by the current task.

What are the limitations of Barsalou's theoretical approach? First, he exaggerates how much concept processing varies across situations. The traditional view that concepts possess a stable, abstract core has not been disproved by Barsalou (Mazzone & Lalumera, 2010). In reality, both theoretical approaches are partially correct – concepts have a stable core *and* their structure is context-dependent.

Second, the finding that concept processing typically involves perceptual and/or motor features has various possible interpretations. As Barsalou argues,

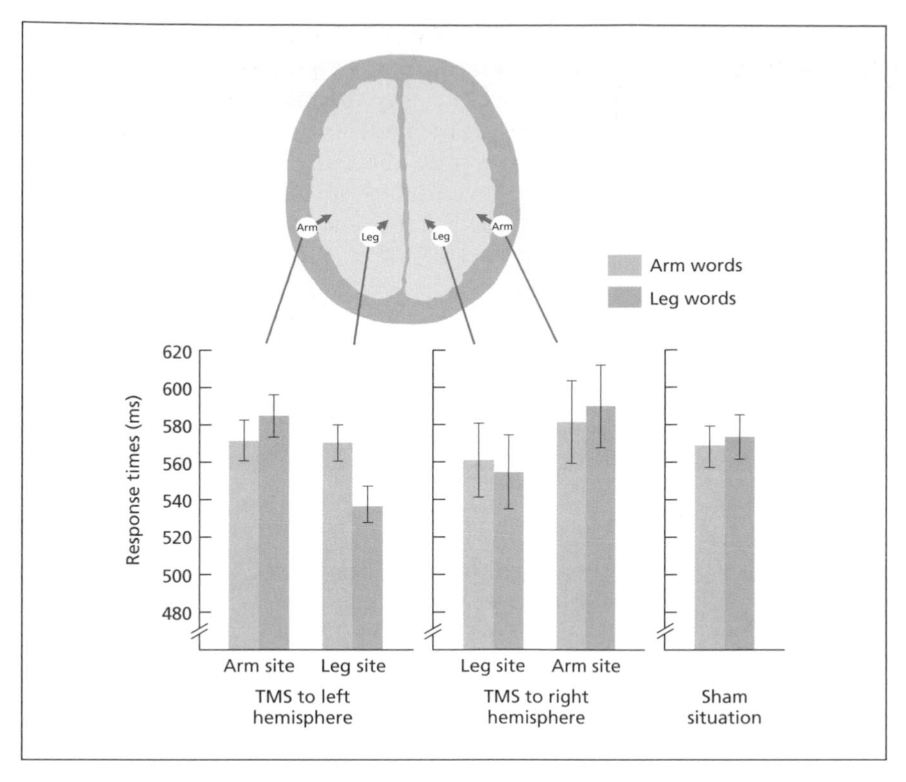

Figure 7.6
Top: sites to which TMS was applied. Bottom left: response times to make lexical (word vs. non-word) decisions on arm- and leg-related words when TMS was applied to the left language-dominant hemisphere. Bottom middle and right: findings from control experiments with TMS to the right hemisphere and during sham stimulation.

From Pulvermüller et al. (2005). © 2005 Federation of European Neuroscience Societies. Reprinted with permission of Wiley-Blackwell.

perceptual and motor processes may be of central relevance to understanding the meaning of concepts. Alternatively, these processes may occur only *after* concept meaning has been accessed. However, there is increasing evidence that such processes are necessary for achieving concept understanding (Pulvermüller, 2013).

Hub-and-spoke model

We have seen there is strong evidence that concept processing often involves the perceptual and motor systems. However, it is improbable concept processing involves nothing else. First, we would not have *coherent* concepts if our processing of any given concept varied considerably across occasions.

Second, we can detect similarities in concepts differing greatly in perceptual terms. For example, we know *scallops* and *prawns* belong to the same category (i.e., shellfish) even though they have different shapes, colours, forms of movement and so on (Patterson et al., 2007).

Such considerations led several researchers (e.g., Patterson et al., 2007; Pobric et al., 2010b) to propose a hub-and-spoke model (see Figure 7.7). The "spokes" consist of several modality-specific regions involving sensory and motor

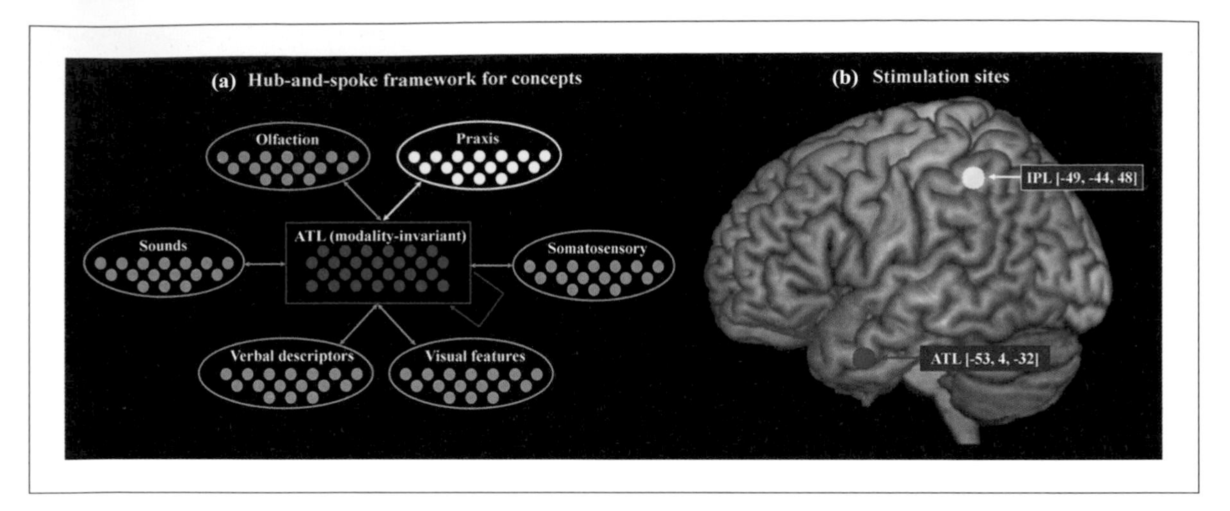

Figure 7.7
The hub-and-spoke model. The modality-invariant or modality-independent hub (shown in red) is in the anterior temporal lobe. The modality-specific spokes interact with the hub. There are separate spokes for sounds, olfaction (sense of smell), praxis (object manipulability; action-related), somatosensory (sensations such as pain or pressure relating to the skin or internal organs), visual features and verbal descriptors.
From Pobric et al. (2010b). Reprinted with permission.

processing. In addition, each concept has a "hub" – a modality-independent unified conceptual representation efficiently integrating our knowledge of any given concept.

It is assumed hubs are located within the anterior temporal lobes. As discussed earlier, patients with semantic dementia invariably have damage to the anterior temporal lobes and one of their main problems during the initial stages of semantic dementia is the extensive loss of conceptual knowledge (Patterson et al., 2007). For example, they cannot name objects when pictures of them are presented or when given a description of the object (e.g., "What do we call the African animal with black-and-white stripes?"). They also cannot identify objects when listening to their characteristic sounds (e.g., a dog barking).

In some ways, the hub-and-spoke model appears to give us the best of both worlds. The spokes facilitate our interactions (perceptual and motor) with the world around us. In contrast, the hubs provide conceptual coherence and integration of sensory and motor processing.

Findings

The findings from patients with semantic dementia suggest the anterior temporal lobes are the main brain area associated with "hubs". Supporting evidence has been provided by neuroimaging studies. Binder et al. (2009) carried out a meta-analysis (see Glossary) of 120 neuroimaging studies involving semantic memory. Several brain areas were consistently activated. Of most theoretical importance, those areas included the anterior temporal lobes and related regions.

Mayberry et al. (2011) asked semantic dementia patients to decide whether objects were members of a given category. They argued that semantic dementia involves a progressive loss of "hub" concept information and so involves a *blurring* of the boundary separating members of a category (e.g., birds) from non-members. This led them to predict patients with semantic dementia would have particular problems making accurate decisions with two kinds of stimuli: (1) atypical category members (e.g., *emu* is an atypical bird); and (2) pseudotypical items – non-category members resembling category members (e.g., *butterfly* is like a bird).

Both predictions were supported whether pictures or words were presented (see Figure 7.8). These findings suggest processing within the anterior temporal lobes is *general* and "hub-like" rather than modality-specific (e.g., confined to the visual modality).

We turn now to evidence concerning the role of modality-specific processes or "spokes" in concept identification. Many brain-damaged patients exhibit **category-specific deficits**, meaning they have problems with specific categories of objects.

Much greater difficulty in identifying pictures of living than non-living things is a very common type of category-specific deficit. It is hard to interpret such findings. Living things have greater contour overlap than non-living things and

KEY TERM

Category-specific deficits
Disorders caused by brain damage in which **semantic memory** is disrupted for certain semantic categories.

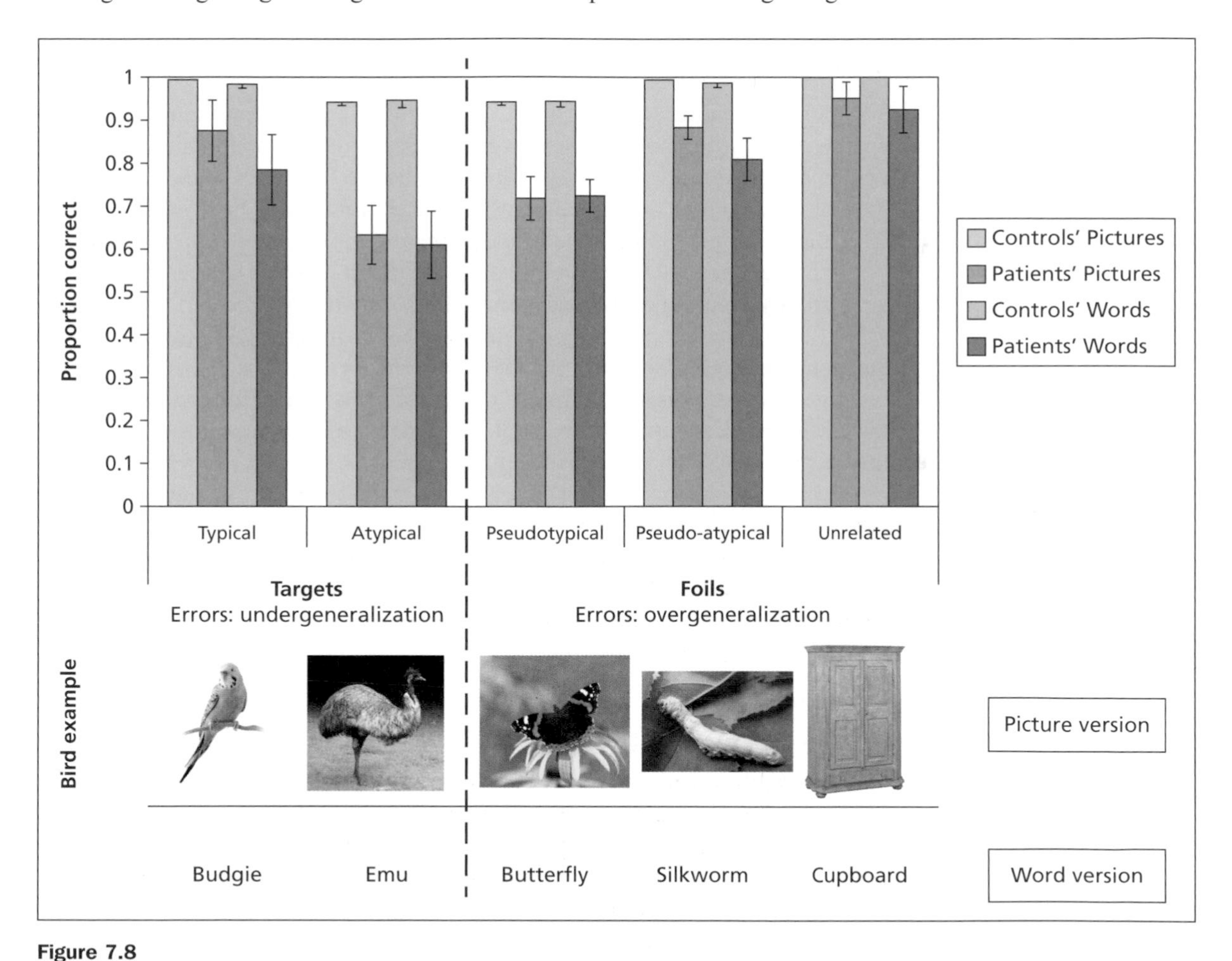

Figure 7.8
Categorisation performance for pictures and words by healthy controls and patients with semantic dementia. Performance on category members (targets) is shown to the left of the dotted line and performance on non-category members (foils) is shown to the right of the line.

From Mayberry et al. (2011). Photos from iStock.

KEY TERMS

Schema
Organised packet of information about the world, events or people stored in long-term memory.

Script
A form of **schema** containing information about a sequence of events (e.g., events during a typical restaurant meal).

are more complex structurally. In addition, non-living things activate motor information more often than living things. Patients have problems with identifying living things mainly because of factors such as these rather than simply because they are living things (Marques et al., 2013).

Cree and McRae (2003) identified seven different patterns of category-specific deficits following brain damage. Patients exhibiting each pattern differed in the concept features or properties most impaired. Across the seven categories, the most impaired properties included the following: colour, taste, smell, visual motion and function (i.e., object uses). Thus, concepts vary considerably in those properties (perhaps resembling spokes) of most importance.

Pobric et al. (2010a) applied transcranial magnetic stimulation (TMS; see Glossary) to interfere briefly with processing within the inferior parietal lobule (assumed to be involved in processing actions we can make towards objects). TMS slowed naming times for manipulable objects but not non-manipulable ones, indicating that the inferior parietal lobule (unlike the anterior temporal lobes) is involved in relatively *specific* concept processing.

Evaluation

The hub-and-spoke model is more comprehensive than previous theoretical approaches. The notion that concepts are represented by a combination of abstract core information and modality-specific information has much support. The brain areas associated with different aspects of concept processing have been identified (e.g., the anterior temporal lobes are of central importance to concept hubs).

What are the model's main limitations? First, it may not be correct that there are modality-independent or amodal hubs in the anterior temporal lobes. Mesulam et al. (2013) studied patients with damage primarily or exclusively to the left anterior temporal lobe. Their patients had much greater problems with verbal concepts than with visually triggered object concepts. These findings suggest that the left anterior temporal lobe forms an important part of a language network rather than a very general modality-independent hub.

Second it remains unclear precisely what information is contained within concept hubs. For example, is more information stored in the hubs of very familiar concepts than less familiar ones? Third, how is modality-specific "spoke" information integrated with modality-independent hub information? Fourth, the number and nature of concept "spokes" remain unclear.

Schemas

Our discussion of semantic memory may have created the misleading impression that nearly all the information in semantic memory is in the form of simple concepts. In fact, however, much of the knowledge stored in semantic memory consists of larger structures of information known as **schemas**. Schemas are well-integrated chunks of knowledge about the world, events, people or actions. Many schemas are in the form of **scripts** containing information about sequences of events. For example, your restaurant script is likely to include the following: being given the menu; ordering food and drink; eating and drinking; paying the bill; leaving the restaurant (Bower et al., 1979).

Scripts (and schemas more generally) are discussed at length in Chapter 10, where their role in language comprehension is emphasised. They are also considered in Chapter 8 in connection with understanding the memory errors made by eyewitnesses when trying to recall the details of crimes they have witnessed. Here we consider the important theoretical assumption that semantic memory contains two major types of information: (1) abstract concepts generally corresponding to individual words; and (2) broader and more flexible organisational structures based on schemas (e.g., scripts).

If the above assumption is correct, we might expect some brain-damaged patients would have greater problems accessing concept-based information than schema-based information. There should also be others who find it harder to use schema information than information about specific concepts. As we will see, there is some support for both predictions (especially the second one).

Findings

Bier et al. (2013) studied the script memory of three patients with semantic dementia. This condition (discussed earlier) involves severe problems in accessing word and object meanings but good executive functioning in the early stages of deterioration. The patients were asked what they would do if they had unknowingly invited two guests to lunch. The required script actions included dressing to go outdoors, going to the grocery store, shopping for food, preparing the meal and clearing up afterwards.

What did Bier et al. (2013) find? One patient, MG (a 68-year-old woman), successfully described all the above script actions accurately despite the severe problems patients with semantic dementia have with accessing concept information from semantic memory. The other patients needed assistance and had particular problems with planning the meal and then preparing it. However, they remembered script actions relating to dressing and shopping.

Which brain-damaged patients have greater problems with accessing script information than concept meanings? Scripts typically have a goal-directed quality (e.g., you use a script to achieve the goal of having an enjoyable restaurant meal). Since the prefrontal cortex is of major importance in forming and implementing goals, we might expect patients with damage to prefrontal cortex to have particular problems with script memory.

Sirigu et al. (1995) found patients with prefrontal damage could generate as many event-related actions as healthy controls. However, they made many more mistakes in ordering actions within a script – they lacked the ability to *assemble* information within a script into the optimal sequence.

Cosentino et al. (2006) studied patients with fronto-temporal dementia (involving damage to the prefrontal cortex as well as the temporal lobes). These patients (as well as others with semantic dementia and healthy controls) were presented with various scripts. Some scripts contained sequencing or script errors (e.g., dropping fish in a bucket *before* casting the fishing line). Other scripts contained semantic or meaning errors (e.g., placing a flower on a hook in a fishing story).

What did Cosentino et al. (2006) find? Patients with semantic dementia and healthy controls both detected as many sequencing errors as semantic ones. In contrast, the temporo-frontal patients with poor executive functioning failed to detect almost twice as many sequencing errors as semantic ones. Thus, these patients had relatively intact semantic knowledge of concepts combined with severe impairment of script-based knowledge relating to sequencing.

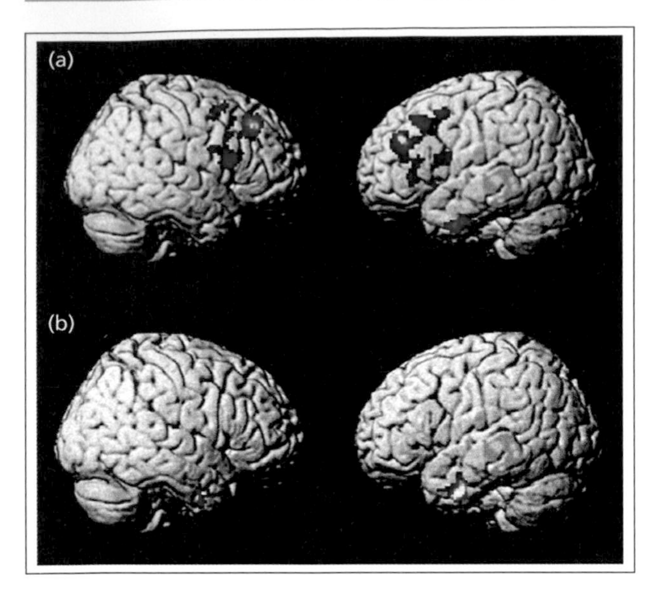

Figure 7.9
(a) Brain areas damaged in patients with fronto-temporal degeneration or progressive non-fluent aphasia. (b) Brain areas damaged in patients with semantic dementia or mild Alzheimer's disease.
From Farag et al. (2010). By permission of Oxford University Press.

Farag et al. (2010) argued that scripts can be broken down into various *clusters*. For example, the fishing script contains one cluster relating to worms (open can of worms; place worm on hook) and one relating to use of the fishing line (cast fishing line; reel line back in). Participants were given the task of judging the order of consecutive events in scripts.

Patients with semantic dementia and healthy controls showed sensitivity to the organisation of scripts by judging event order better *within* than *between* clusters. In contrast, patients with fronto-temporal dementia performed equally poorly on within- and between-cluster events.

Farag et al. (2010) identified the areas of brain damage in patients (including those with semantic dementia) showing sensitivity to script organisation and those (including fronto-temporal patients) insensitive to that organisation. The latter had damage in inferior and dorsolateral prefrontal areas, whereas there was no evidence of prefrontal damage in patients sensitive to script organisation (see Figure 7.9).

Conclusions

Research on brain-damaged patients supports the distinction between concept and script knowledge. For example, patients with damage to the prefrontal cortex often have greater problems with accessing script knowledge than concept knowledge. However, there are strong links between concept and script knowledge. When we use our script knowledge (e.g., preparing a meal), it is obviously very important to have access to relevant concept knowledge (e.g., knowledge about food ingredients). As a consequence, semantic dementia patients whose primary impairment is to concept knowledge also have great difficulties in accessing and using script knowledge.

NON-DECLARATIVE MEMORY

Non-declarative memory does *not* involve conscious recollection but instead reveals itself through behaviour. As discussed earlier, priming (facilitated processing of repeated stimuli; also known as repetition priming) and procedural memory (mainly skill learning) are two of the major forms of non-declarative memory. Note that procedural memory is involved in most research on implicit learning (discussed in Chapter 6).

There are two major differences between priming (also known as repetition priming) and procedural memory:

1 Priming often occurs rapidly, whereas procedural memory or skill learning is typically slow and gradual (Knowlton & Foerde, 2008).

2 Priming is tied to specific stimuli, whereas skill learning typically generalises to numerous stimuli. For example, it would not be of much use if you could hit good backhands at tennis only when the ball approached from a given direction at a given speed!

The single most important reason for distinguishing between declarative and non-declarative memory is that amnesic patients apparently have severely impaired declarative memory but almost intact non-declarative memory (but see next main section). Hayes et al. (2012) reviewed the research evidence on priming and procedural memory or skill learning in amnesic patients with Korsakoff's syndrome (see Glossary). Most studies reported intact (or nearly intact) non-declarative memory performance by the patients, but some found amnesic performance to be moderately impaired.

Why did amnesic patients sometimes perform poorly on non-declarative memory tasks in the studies reviewed by Hayes et al. (2012)? First, some tasks used probably required use of declarative as well as non-declarative memory. Second, some patients with Korsakoff's syndrome have fairly widespread brain damage that may include areas required for non-declarative memory. Third, the distinction between declarative and non-declarative memory may be less important than traditionally assumed (see later in the chapter).

KEY TERMS

Perceptual priming
A form of priming in which repeated presentations of a stimulus facilitate its perceptual processing.

Conceptual priming
A form or priming in which there is facilitated processing of stimulus meaning.

Repetition priming

We can distinguish between perceptual and conceptual priming. **Perceptual priming** occurs when repeated presentation of a stimulus leads to facilitated processing of its perceptual features. For example, it is easier to identify a degraded stimulus if it has recently been encountered. In contrast, **conceptual priming** occurs when repeated presentation of a stimulus leads to facilitated processing of its meaning. For example, we can decide faster whether an object is living or non-living if we saw it recently.

If repetition priming involves non-declarative memory, then amnesic patients should show intact repetition priming. There is much support for this prediction, although patients sometimes have a modest impairment of priming. Cermak et al. (1985) compared the performance of amnesic patients and non-amnesic alcoholics (controls) on perceptual priming. The amnesic patients showed as great a perceptual priming effect as the controls.

Levy et al. (2004) studied conceptual priming using a task that involved deciding whether words previously studied (or not studied) belonged to given categories. Two male amnesic patients (EP and GP) with large lesions in the medial temporal lobe had similar conceptual priming to healthy controls. In contrast, the amnesic patients performed much worse than the controls on recognition memory (involving declarative memory).

Much additional research was carried out on EP, who had very extensive damage to the perirhinal cortex as well as the medial temporal lobes (see Insausti et al. (2013) for a review). His long-term declarative memory was generally even worse than that of HM, the most famous amnesic patient ever studied (see page 262). For example, he had a very modest ability to identify names, words and faces that only became familiar after the onset of his amnesia.

In spite of his very deficient declarative memory, EP's performance was intact on non-declarative tasks such as perceptual priming and visuo-motor skill learning.

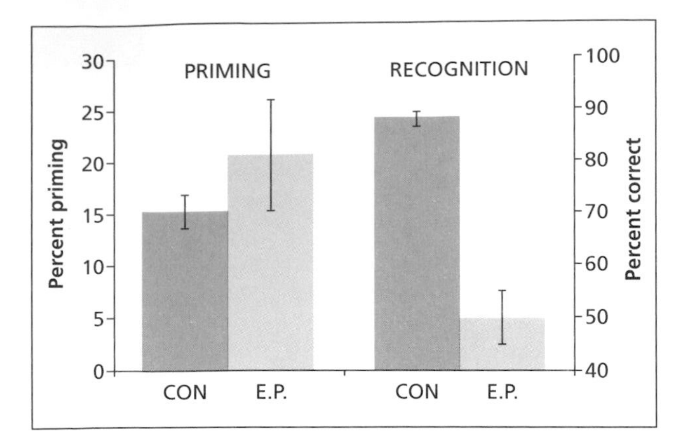

Figure 7.10
Percentages of priming effect (left-hand side) and recognition-memory performance of healthy controls (CON) and patient (EP).

From Insausti et al. (2013).
© National Academy of Sciences. Reproduced with permission.

Illustrative findings from EP are shown in Figure 7.10. His performance was at chance level on recognition memory but was at least as good as that of healthy controls on perceptual priming.

Further evidence that amnesic patients have intact perceptual priming was reported by Schacter and Church (1995). Participants initially heard words all spoken in the same voice. Then they identified the same words passed through an auditory filter. Priming was shown by the finding that identification performance was better when the words were spoken in the same voice as initially.

The notion that priming depends on memory systems different from those involved in declarative memory would be strengthened if we found patients having intact declarative memory but impaired priming. This would be a double dissociation when considered with amnesics having intact priming but impaired declarative memory. Gabrieli et al. (1995) studied a patient, MS, who had a right occipital lobe lesion. MS had normal levels of performance on the declarative-memory tests of recognition and cued recall but impaired performance on perceptual priming using certain visual tasks.

Everything so far seems neat and tidy. However, other research reveals complications. Schacter et al. (1995) used a similar experimental design to that of Schacter and Church (1995) but obtained very different findings. They also studied perceptual priming based on auditory word identification. However, the words were initially presented in *six* different voices. On the word-identification test, half the words were presented in the same voice as initially and the other half were spoken by one of the other voices (re-paired condition). Healthy controls showed more priming for words presented in the same voice, but the amnesic patients did not.

How can we explain Schacter et al.'s (1995) findings? In both the same voice and re-paired voice conditions, the participants were exposed to words and voices they had heard before. The only advantage in the same voice condition was that the pairing of word and voice was the same as before. However, only those participants who had linked or associated words and voices at the original presentation would benefit from that fact. The implication is that amnesics are poor at binding together different kinds of information even on priming tasks apparently involving non-declarative memory. This issue is discussed more fully later in the chapter (see also Hannula & Greene, 2012).

Priming processes

KEY TERM

Repetition suppression
The finding that stimulus repetition often leads to reduced brain activity (typically with enhanced performance via **priming**).

What processes are involved in priming? One popular view is based on perceptual fluency: repeated presentation of a stimulus means it can be processed more efficiently using fewer resources. This view is supported by the frequent finding that brain activity decreases with stimulus repetition: this is known as **repetition suppression**.

The precise brain regions showing repetition suppression vary depending on whether perceptual or conceptual priming is involved. Early visual areas in the occipital lobe at the back of the brain often show reduced activity with perceptual priming (Schacter et al., 2007). Different brain areas are associated with conceptual priming. In contrast, Voss et al. (2008) found repetition suppression was associated with reduced activity in the left prefrontal cortex.

Why is repetition suppression associated with priming effects? Several theoretical answers have been put forward of which the synchrony model is perhaps the most promising (Gotts et al., 2012). According to this model, repeated stimuli cause cells in the brain to fire at lower rates, as a result of which they fire more synchronously with one another. This enhanced synchrony leads to more efficient neural processing.

The finding that repetition of a stimulus causes priming and reduced brain activity does not show there is a *causal* link between patterns of brain activation and priming. More direct evidence was reported by Wig et al. (2005) who studied conceptual priming (the task was to classify objects as living or non-living). Wig et al. tested the involvement of the left inferior frontal gyrus in conceptual priming by delivering transcranial magnetic stimulation (TMS; see Glossary) to interfere with processing. Subsequent classification of objects that had been accompanied by TMS showed an absence of both conceptual priming and repetition suppression. These findings suggest left inferior temporal cortex plays a causal role in producing conceptual priming.

Some complexities disturb the picture presented so far. For example, several studies reported *enhanced* rather than *reduced* neural activity when stimuli are repeated (Segaert et al., 2013). Such enhancement effects are likely to depend on cognitive processes such as attention and expectation.

Another complexity was discovered by Kessler and Moscovitch (2013). Participants performed a lexical decision task (deciding rapidly whether strings of letters formed words). Some words on this task had been studied a few minutes earlier. Previous research had shown that lexical decisions were made faster for words previously presented. It had been assumed this effect was due to priming involving implicit or non-declarative memory.

According to the above account, a priming effect should *always* be obtained on the lexical decision task because it depends on relatively automatic and implicit processes. However, Kessler and Moscovitch (2013) found this was *not* the case. In previous research, only words were initially presented prior to the lexical decision task. As a result, participants could use the simple (explicit) strategy of deciding that every item on the lexical decision task recognised as having been presented before was a word. When Kessler and Moscovitch prevented use of this strategy by presenting an equal number of words and non-words for study prior to the lexical decision task, there was no priming effect (see Figure 7.11).

What conclusions can we draw from Kessler and Moscovitch's (2013) study? Their findings suggest that most of the typical priming effect obtained in lexical decision tasks is due to a strategic (explicit) process rather than implicit memory. This is important in part because it makes it more complicated to interpret the findings from priming studies involving lexical decision.

Procedural memory or skill learning

Motor skills are important in everyday life – examples include word processing, writing and playing a musical instrument. Foerde and Poldrack (2009) identified many types of skill learning or procedural memory, including sequence learning, mirror tracing, perceptual skill learning, mirror reading and artificial grammar

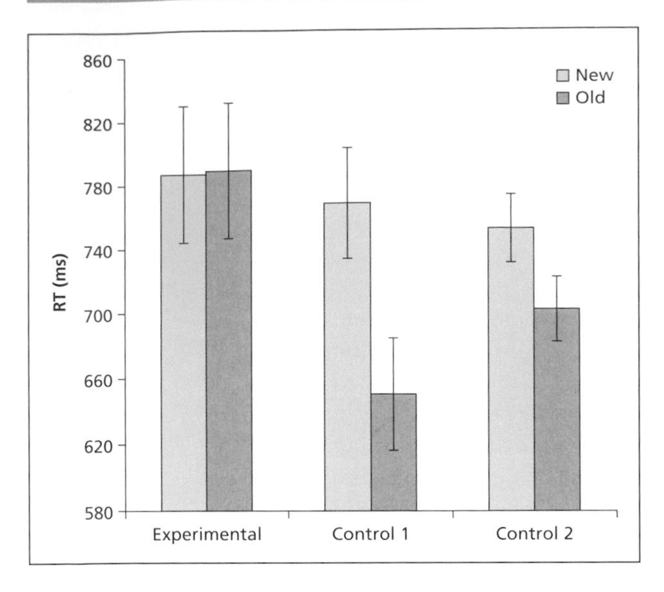

Figure 7.11
Mean response times on a lexical decision task (deciding whether letter strings form words) for words that had been presented previously (old words) or not presented previously (new). Words and non-words had been presented previously for participants in the experimental group but only words had previously been presented in the two control groups.

From Kessler and Moscovitch (2013). With permission from Taylor & Francis.

learning (see Chapter 6). Note that while these tasks have been categorised as involving skill learning, they undoubtedly differ considerably in terms of the precise cognitive processes involved.

Here we will consider whether the above tasks involve non-declarative or procedural memory and thus involve different memory systems from those underlying episodic and semantic memory. We will focus on skill learning in amnesic patients. If such patients have essentially intact skill learning but severely impaired declarative memory, that would provide evidence that different memory systems are involved.

Before we turn to the relevant evidence, we must address an important issue. It is easy (but sometimes incorrect) to assume that any given task is always performed using non-declarative or declarative memory. Consider a task in which participants use various cues to predict whether the weather will be sunny or rainy (the weather prediction task). Reber et al. (1996) found amnesics learned this task as rapidly as healthy controls, suggesting it involves procedural (non-declarative) memory.

Foerde et al. (2006) had participants perform the weather prediction task on its own or with a demanding secondary task. Performance was comparable in the two conditions, but the participants used different processes. Task performance in the single-task condition correlated with activity in the medial temporal lobe, an area associated with declarative memory. In contrast, performance in dual-task conditions correlated with activity in the striatum (striatum part of the basal ganglia in the upper region of the brainstem), an area associated with non-declarative memory.

In similar fashion, Schwabe and Wolf (2012) found using the weather prediction task that non-stressed participants relied mostly on declarative memory (the hippocampus). In contrast, stressed ones relied more on non-declarative memory (the striatum). Thus, a given task can involve primarily declarative or non-declarative memory depending on the precise conditions (e.g., single- vs. dual-task) and participant characteristics (e.g., stressed vs. non-stressed).

Findings

Amnesics often have intact (or nearly intact) rates of skill learning across numerous tasks. Spiers et al. (2001) considered the memory performance of 147 amnesic patients. They concluded: "None of the cases was reported to . . . be impaired on tasks which involved learning skills or habits, priming, simple classical conditioning and simple category learning" (Spiers et al., 2001, p. 359). As mentioned earlier, Hayes et al. (2012) reported similar findings in their review, but some studies showed modest impairment in procedural memory for amnesic patients.

Consider, for example, a study by Tranel et al. (1994). They used the pursuit rotor (which involves manual tracking of a moving target) with 28 amnesic patients. All showed comparable learning on the pursuit rotor to healthy controls. Of particular note was a patient, Boswell, who had unusually extensive brain damage to areas (e.g., medial and lateral temporal lobes) strongly associated with declarative memory. In spite of this, his learning on the pursuit rotor and retention over a two-year period were comparable to healthy controls.

Much research on implicit learning and non-declarative memory has used the serial reaction time task (see Chapter 6). On this task, a stimulus can appear at various locations and participants respond as rapidly as possible using the closest response key. There is a repeating sequence over trials, and non-declarative memory is shown by progressively faster responding. More specifically, the speed-up is faster for the repeating sequence than non-repeating sequences.

Two main conclusions emerged from the discussion of amnesics' performance on this task in Chapter 6. First, their performance is typically intact or slightly impaired. Second, the serial reaction time task does not depend solely on non-declarative memory – in healthy individuals, there is often some consciously accessible knowledge (Gaillard et al., 2009).

Cavaco et al. (2004) pointed out that most tasks used to assess skill learning in amnesics require learning far removed from everyday life. Accordingly, they used five skill-learning tasks requiring skills similar to those needed in the real world. For example, there was a weaving task and a control stick task requiring movements similar to those involved in operating machinery. Amnesic patients showed comparable rates of learning to healthy individuals despite significantly impaired declarative memory for the same tasks assessed by recall and recognition tests.

Anderson et al. (2007) studied the motor skill of car driving in two severely amnesic patients. Their steering, speed control, safety errors and driving with distraction were comparable to those of healthy controls.

Interacting systems

A central theme of this chapter is that traditional theoretical views were very oversimplified. For example, it used to be assumed that skill learning and related tasks involve implicit memory depending heavily on the striatum, whereas declarative memory involves the hippocampus. We have already discussed evidence inconsistent with that assumption – there is less involvement of the striatum and greater involvement of the medial temporal lobes when participants perform a secondary task at the same time (Foerde et al., 2006) or when they are stressed (Schwabe & Wolf, 2012).

There is accumulating evidence that skill learning typically involves complex brain circuitry including the hippocampus (traditionally associated exclusively with episodic memory). Albouy et al. (2013) discuss relevant research on motor sequence learning. The hippocampus played a crucial role in the acquisition and storage of procedural memories, and there were numerous interactions between hippocampal-cortical and striato-cortical systems. Note that Albouy et al. argue that the involvement of the hippocampus in motor sequence learning does *not* necessarily mean explicit learning and memory occurred.

Robertson (2012) argued that there are functional connections between implicit and explicit memory. Brown and Robertson (2007) gave participants a motor-skill procedural learning task and a declarative task (word-list learning). Performance on the motor-skill task was reduced by 25% when the declarative task occurred during the retention interval. Performance on the word-list task was reduced by 10% when the motor-skill task was performed during the retention interval. Thus, there can be *interactions* between the two memory systems.

How different are priming and skill learning?

Various kinds of experimental evidence can in principle clarify the extent to which priming and skill learning involve different memory systems. For example, if different memory systems are involved, there is no particular reason why individuals good at skill learning should also be good at priming. Schwartz and Hashtroudi (1991) used a word-identification task to assess priming and an inverted-text reading task to assess skill learning. There was no correlation between priming and skill learning.

In principle, neuroimaging evidence could be used to shed light on the similarities and differences between priming and skill learning. In practice, however, the wide range of tasks used to assess priming and skill learning means numerous brain regions are sometimes activated. In spite of the complexities we will consider relevant evidence, starting with skill learning.

Research on implicit learning provides relevant evidence concerning the brain areas most associated with skill learning (see Chapter 6). As discussed already, the striatum is often involved in skill learning. Practice in skill learning is often associated with decreased activation in the prefrontal cortex but increased activation in the basal ganglia. Debaere et al. (2004) found decreases in activation within the right dorsolateral prefrontal cortex, the right premotor cortex and the bilateral superior parietal cortex during acquisition of a skill requiring hand coordination. At the same time, there were increases in activation within the cerebellum and basal ganglia.

The role of the basal ganglia in skill learning has been assessed by studying patients with Parkinson's disease (see Glossary). Parkinson's disease is a progressive neurological disorder involving severe damage to the basal ganglia. Such patients typically have impaired skill learning but they also often have impaired explicit learning (Foerde & Shohamy, 2011; see Chapter 6). Some of these learning deficits may depend in part on reduced motivation in Parkinson patients.

Osman et al. (2008) reviewed several studies in which Parkinson's patients had good levels of skill learning. In their own experiment, participants learned about and controlled a complex system (e.g., water-tank system). Patients with Parkinson's disease showed the same level of procedural learning as healthy controls. This suggests the striatum is *not* needed for all forms of skill learning.

Numerous brain areas are sometimes associated with perceptual and conceptual priming. Schacter et al. (2007) reviewed the literature. Perceptual priming with visual stimuli often involves early visual areas in the occipital lobe. Conceptual priming often involves the lateral temporal cortex. In addition, there is frequently increased synchronisation of prefrontal activity with that in other regions. In contrast to Schacter et al.'s emphasis on brain areas showing reduced activation with priming, Segaert et al. (2013) focused on those areas showing increased activation. They reviewed 29 studies and concluded that, "repetition enhancement effects have been found all over the brain" (p. 60).

In sum, there is evidence that priming and skill learning typically involve different brain areas and that perceptual priming involves different areas from conceptual priming. However, it is hard to draw definitive conclusions because of the numerous brain areas associated with priming.

Evaluation

Most of the evidence suggests repetition priming and skill learning are forms of non-declarative memory. They often (but by no means always) involve different processes and brain areas from those involved in declarative memory. The strongest findings are those obtained from amnesic patients who typically have intact (or nearly intact) priming and skill learning. In spite of this similarity between priming and skill learning, they differ in terms of the brain areas involved.

What are the main limitations of research in this area? First, many different tasks have been used to assess priming (perceptual and conceptual) and skill learning. More attention needs to be paid to task differences in the precise cognitive processes involved. Second, the neuroimaging findings are rather variable and inconsistent, in part as a direct consequence of the use of diverse tasks.

Third, there was until recently an excessive emphasis on the role of the striatum in priming and skill learning. As we saw in Chapter 1, greater understanding of the processes involved in most cognitive tasks is achieved by focusing on brain *networks* rather than *specific* areas. For example, motor sequence learning involves a striato-cortical system rather than simply the striatum, and this system interacts with a hippocampal-cortical system (Albouy et al., 2013).

BEYOND DECLARATIVE AND NON-DECLARATIVE MEMORY

Most memory researchers until fairly recently claimed that the distinction between declarative/explicit memory and non-declarative/implicit memory was of major theoretical importance. Advocates of this distinction assume a crucial difference between memory systems is whether or not they support conscious access to stored information. They also often assume memory systems involving conscious access depend heavily on the hippocampus, whereas memory systems not involving conscious access do not.

These assumptions have had an enormous influence on memory research and the findings obtained have provided reasonable support for those assumptions. However, the rapid increase in findings inconsistent with these assumptions means more complex theorising is required. It is possible the traditional memory systems approach can be developed to explain these inconsistent findings. Alternatively, a new theoretical approach may be required.

We will first discuss limitations (some mentioned earlier) with the standard or traditional approach. After that, we consider more recent theoretical accounts de-emphasising the distinction between conscious (explicit) and non-conscious (implicit) memory.

Explicit vs. implicit memory

If the major dividing line in long-term memory is between declarative (explicit) memory and non-declarative (implicit) memory, it is important to devise tasks involving only *one* type of memory. In principle, this may seem relatively simple. Declarative memory is involved when the instructions explicitly tell participants to remember previously presented information, whereas non-declarative memory is involved when the instructions do not.

Reality is more complex than that (Dew & Cabeza, 2011). Consider the word-completion task. Participants are presented with a list of words. Subsequently they perform an apparently unrelated task: word fragments (e.g., STR ___) are presented and they recall the first word they think of starting with those letters. Implicit memory is revealed by the extent to which the word completions correspond to words from the initial list. Since the instructions make no reference to recalling list words, this task apparently qualifies as an implicit/non-declarative task. However, participants who become aware of the connection between the word list and the word-completion task perform better than those who do not (e.g., Mace, 2003).

Research activity:
Word stem completion task

Autobiographical memory is often assessed by presenting people with cues and asking them to recall personal memories associated with the cues. On the face of it, this is a declarative memory task because it involves the intention to recall. However, many of the memories people produce on this task are retrieved involuntarily and spontaneously (e.g., Uzer et al., 2012; see Chapter 8).

Another way of distinguishing between declarative/explicit memory and non-declarative/implicit memory is in terms of patterns of brain activation. As discussed earlier, it used to be assumed that the striatum is closely associated with non-declarative/implicit memory and the hippocampus with declarative/explicit memory. However, we have seen there are many studies in which allegedly non-declarative/implicit memory involved the hippocampus (e.g., Foerde et al., 2006; Schwabe & Wolf, 2012; Albouy et al., 2013).

There are also several studies in which there was greater activity in the striatum on episodic memory tasks for items subsequently remembered than those forgotten (see Sadeh et al. (2011) for a review). In Sadeh et al.'s own study (discussed earlier), effective learning in episodic memory was associated with *interactive* activity between the hippocampus and striatum.

A final problem with the distinction between declarative and non-declarative memory is that it is based on consciousness and awareness, neither of which is clearly understood (see Chapter 16). As Ortu and Vaidya (2013, p. 1) pointed out, "Grounding an entire taxonomy [classificatory system] of learning and memory on consciousness-based criteria might complicate, instead of simplifying, scientific interpretations, and progress."

Processing-based theoretical accounts

In recent years, several theorists (e.g., Henke, 2010; Dew & Cabeza, 2011; Cabeza & Moscovitch, 2013) have argued that the traditional theoretical approach based on the declarative–non-declarative distinction should be replaced. We will discuss these newer theoretical approaches within the context of an alternative model for memory systems developed by Henke (2010). She rejected the notion that consciousness is an important criterion for distinguishing among memory systems. Henke argued instead for a model in which memory systems are identified on the basis of the types of processing involved.

The essence of Henke's (2010) processing-based model can be seen in Figure 7.12, which can be compared to the standard model (shown in Figure 7.2, page 265). There are *three* basic processing modes:

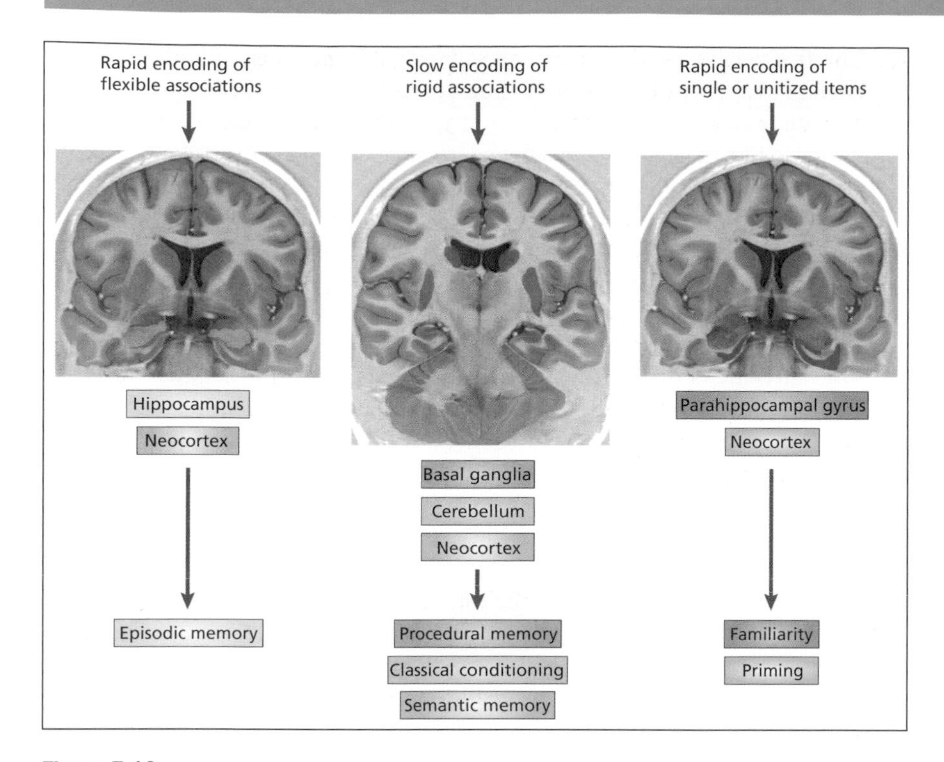

Figure 7.12
A processing-based memory model. There are three basic processing modes: (1) rapid encoding of flexible associations; (2) slow encoding of rigid associations; and (3) rapid encoding of single or unitised items formed into a single unit. The brain areas associated with each of these processing modes are indicated towards the bottom of the figure.
From Henke (2010). Reproduced with permission from Nature Publishing Group.

1 Rapid encoding of flexible associations: This involves episodic memory and depends on the hippocampus. Figure 7.12 does not show this, but it is assumed within the model that semantic memory often involves the hippocampus.
2 Slow encoding of rigid associations: This involves procedural memory, semantic memory and classical conditioning and depends on the basal ganglia (e.g., the striatum) and cerebellum.
3 Rapid encoding of single or unitised items (formed into a single unit): This involves familiarity in recognition memory and priming and depends on the parahippocampal gyrus.

Henke's (2010) model and the traditional declarative/non-declarative theory share several predictions. For example, amnesic patients with hippocampal damage should often have poor episodic memory but intact procedural memory and priming. It is more important, however, to consider cases in which the two theoretical approaches make different predictions. Here are three examples:

1 Henke's model predicts that the hippocampus is involved in the encoding of flexible associations with unconscious learning as well as with conscious learning. In contrast, the traditional theoretical assumption is that the hippocampus is involved only in conscious learning.

2 The first prediction can be extended to amnesic patients with hippocampal damage. These patients should find it hard to form flexible associations regardless of whether learning is conscious or unconscious. The traditional theory assumes that only conscious learning should be adversely affected.
3 Henke's model predicts the hippocampus is not directly involved in familiarity judgements in recognition memory. In contrast, the traditional theory assumes all forms of episodic memory depend on the hippocampus.

Findings

We will start with the first prediction above. Hannula and Greene (2012) pointed out that it is often hard to be sure that learning has occurred in the absence of conscious awareness. In spite of that, they discussed several studies showing associative or relational learning can occur without conscious awareness. Duss et al. (2011) presented face–occupation pairs below the level of conscious awareness. When the same faces were presented above the level of conscious awareness, participants showed some ability to classify them on regularity of income and length of education consistent with their occupation.

Of most relevance here is whether the hippocampus is activated during non-conscious encoding and retrieval of the face–occupation pairs. Henke et al. (2003) presented participants with face–occupation pairs that could not be seen at the conscious level. There were two main findings. First, there was hippocampal activation during non-conscious *encoding* of the face–occupation pairs. Second, there was also hippocampal activation during non-conscious *retrieval* of occupations associated with faces on the memory test.

We turn now to the second prediction. Ryan et al. (2000) used a task involving forming associations through implicit/unconscious learning. Amnesics should perform poorly on this task according to Henke (2010), but should have intact performance according to the traditional viewpoint.

Ryan et al. (2000) presented amnesic patients and healthy controls with colour images of real-world scenes in three conditions:

1 *Novel scenes*: the scene had not been presented before.
2 *Repeated old scenes*: an identical scene had been presented before.
3 *Manipulated old scenes*: the scene had been presented before, but the positions of some objects had been altered.

Participants' eye movements were recorded. The key measure was the proportion of eye fixations in the critical region (the area altered in the manipulation condition). The healthy controls had more eye movements in the critical region in the manipulated condition than in the other two conditions (see Figure 7.13). In contrast, the amnesic patients did not devote more fixations to the critical region in the manipulated condition. This was because they had failed to form associations between objects and their locations.

While most of the available evidence supports the second prediction (Henke, 2010), there are exceptions. For example, consider a study by Verfaellie et al. (2013). Amnesic patients were presented with word pairs (e.g., *mall–rain*). In one condition of the subsequent implicit-memory test, the first word was re-presented (e.g., *mall*) together with a category name (e.g., *weather phenomena*). The task was to generate four members of the category. Implicit relational memory was

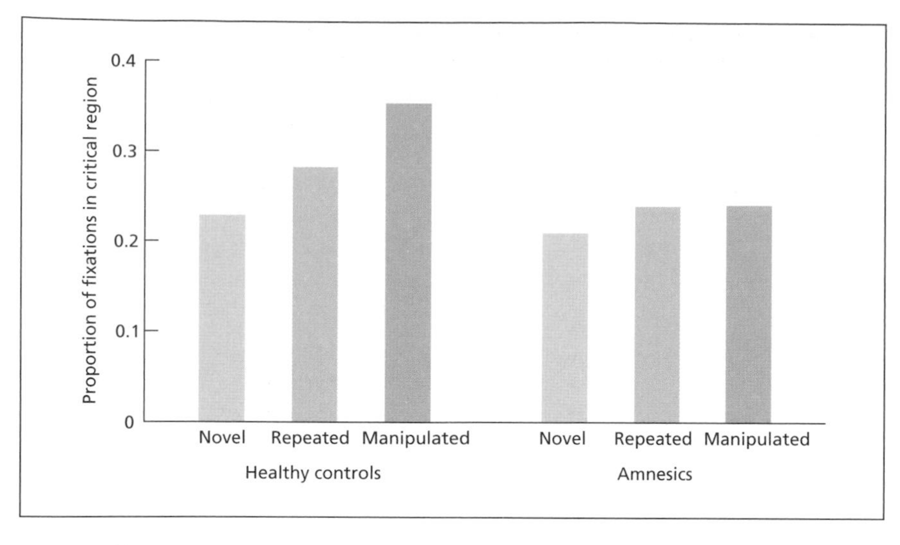

Figure 7.13
Proportion of eye fixations in the critical region in healthy controls and amnesic patients as a function of condition (novel, repeated, manipulated).
Data from Ryan et al. (2000).

shown by an increased probability of producing the target word (e.g., *rain*) when the word previously associated with it (e.g., *mall*) was presented at test.

What did Verfaellie et al. (2013) find? The amnesic patients showed as much implicit relational memory as healthy controls. It is not known why their findings are discrepant from previous ones. However, it may be relevant that they studied implicit memory for *verbal* associations. In contrast, previous studies focused on other kinds of relational memory. For example, Ryan et al. (2000) studied implicit memory for *scenes*.

Finally, we turn to Henke's third prediction, namely, that the hippocampus is not required for familiarity judgements in recognition memory. We saw earlier there is evidence that amnesic patients with hippocampal damage have reasonably intact familiarity judgements but impaired recollection judgements (Bowles et al., 2010). However, the typical finding is that recognition memory based on familiarity is significantly impaired in amnesic patients but much less than recognition memory based on recollection (Skinner & Fernandes, 2007).

How can we reconcile the above findings with Henke's prediction? The most likely explanation is that amnesics' brain damage often extends beyond the hippocampus to adjacent areas, including those associated with familiarity (perirhinal cortex). Aggleton et al. (2005) tested this prediction in a male amnesic patient, KN, with hippocampal damage but no perirhinal damage. KN's recognition performance as assessed by recollection was greatly inferior to that of healthy controls. Of greater theoretical importance, his familiarity performance was comparable to that of healthy controls (see Figure 7.14).

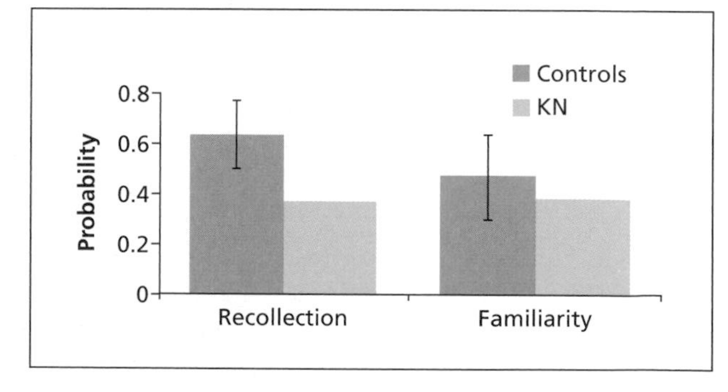

Figure 7.14
Recollection and familiarity performance on a recognition-memory test by healthy controls and amnesic patient KN.
From Aggleton et al. (2005). Reprinted with permission from Elsevier.

Processing components: Cabeza and Moscovitch (2013)

As mentioned earlier, Cabeza and Moscovitch (2013) discussed a processing-component approach to long-term memory. This approach resembles that of Henke (2010) in that the emphasis is on processes rather than memory systems. However, it is a more flexible approach. It is assumed there are numerous processing components and that these components can be combined and re-combined for specific learning purposes. Thus, memory systems are "considered as ad hoc coalitions of computational modules that are recruited per task" (Dudai & Morris, 2013, p. 747).

A major motivation for this theoretical approach is the accumulating neuroimaging evidence. Of particular importance, "Brain regions attributed to one memory system can contribute to tasks associated with other memory systems" (Cabeza & Moscovitch, 2013, p. 49).

Dew and Cabeza (2011) suggested a theoretical model in which the emphasis is on linking processes to brain regions (see Figure 7.15). Five brain areas are identified varying along three dimensions:

1 *cognitive process*: perceptually or conceptually driven;
2 *stimulus representation*: item or relational;
3 *level of intention*: controlled vs. automatic.

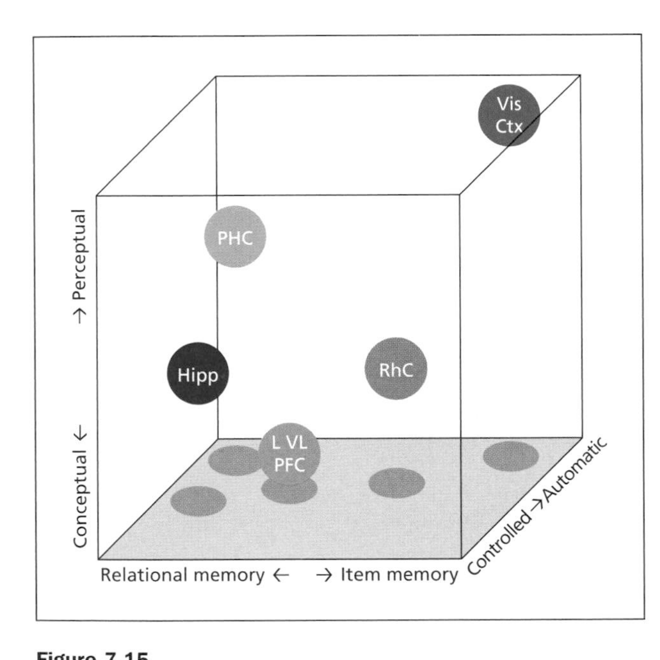

Figure 7.15
A three-dimensional model of memory: (1) conceptually or perceptually driven; (2) relational or item stimulus representation; (3) controlled or automatic/involuntary intention. The brain areas are the visual cortex (Vis Ctx), parahippocampal cortex (PHC), hippocampus (Hipp), rhinal cortex (RhC) and left ventrolateral prefrontal cortex (L VL PFC).

From Dew and Cabeza (2011). © 2011 New York Academy of Sciences. Reprinted with permission of Wiley & Sons.

Evaluation

The component process approach has various strengths. First, it is more consistent with the neuroimaging evidence than is the traditional memory systems approach. Second, the approach avoids the excessive focus on the declarative–non-declarative distinction found in many previous theories. Third, its *flexibility* helps to explain why any given memory task can be performed using different processes depending on the individual performing the task and the precise task conditions (e.g., Foerde et al., 2006; Schwabe & Wolf, 2012).

The main limitation of the component process approach is, as Cabeza and Moscovitch (2013) admitted, that it is "fuzzy" and often fails to make specific predictions. As a result, it is hard to devise strong tests of the approach. However, the notion that people learn and remember using numerous different combinations of specific processes is a powerful one and may point the way for future theorists.

Overall evaluation

The assumption that there is a fundamental distinction between declarative memory (requiring the hippocampus) and non-declarative memory (not dependent on the hippocampus) is clearly oversimplified. According to that assumption, amnesic patients should have intact non-declarative/implicit relational memory, but that is not the case. It appears that the hippocampus is required for relational or associative processing rather than conscious processing.

More generally, the traditional view that the main function of the hippocampus is to facilitate episodic memory is too narrow. The hippocampus is connected to many other brain areas (e.g., dorsolateral prefrontal cortex, temporal cortex, visual cortex, striatum). This helps explain why it seems to be involved in several cognitive processes including perception, inference drawing, imagining the future and decision making (Shohamy & Turk-Browne, 2013).

Theoretical approaches based on processing modes (Henke, 2010) or processing components (Cabeza & Moscovitch, 2013) can readily accommodate several findings problematical for the traditional memory systems approach. In addition, they are more consistent with neuroimaging evidence indicating the involvement of several brain areas during learning. However, the flexible theoretical assumptions of these newer processing-based approaches are hard to put to stringent empirical test. This limitation may be overcome as these approaches are developed over time. Finally, it should be borne in mind (as mentioned earlier) that the traditional memory systems approach could perhaps be developed to account for most of the relevant findings.

CHAPTER SUMMARY

- **Introduction.** The notion that there are several memory systems is very influential. Within that approach, the crucial distinction is between declarative memory (involving conscious recollection) and non-declarative memory (not involving conscious recollection). This distinction receives its strongest support from amnesic patients having severely impaired declarative memory but almost intact non-declarative memory. Declarative memory is divided into semantic and episodic/autobiographical memory, whereas non-declarative memory is divided into priming and skill learning or procedural memory. The component processing framework suggests the memory systems approach is oversimplified.

- **Declarative memory.** Evidence from patients supports the distinction between episodic and semantic memory. Amnesia patients with damage to the medial temporal lobe, including the hippocampus, typically have more extensive impairment of episodic than semantic memory in anterograde and retrograde amnesia. In contrast, patients with semantic dementia (involving damage to the anterior temporal lobe) have more extensive impairment of semantic than of episodic memory. However, the performance of many long-term memory tasks involves combining episodic and semantic memory processes. In addition, similar brain regions are often activated on so-called episodic and semantic memory tasks. There is evidence that some episodic memories change into semantic memories (semanticisation).

- **Episodic memory**. Episodic memory is often assessed by means of recognition tests. Recognition memory can involve familiarity or recollection. Familiarity is associated with a relatively early ERP component, whereas recollection is associated with a later component. Evidence supports the binding-of-item-and-context model, according to which familiarity judgements depend on perirhinal cortex and recollection judgements depend on binding what and where information in the hippocampus. In similar fashion, words produced in free recall can involve familiarity or recollection with the latter being associated with better recall of contextual information. Episodic memory is basically constructive rather than reproductive, and so we remember mostly the gist of our past experiences rather than the detail. Constructive processes associated with episodic memory are used to imagine future events.

- **Semantic memory**. Most objects can be described at three levels: superordinate category, basic-level category and subordinate-level category. Basic-level categories are typically used in everyday life. However, experts often use subordinate-level categories for objects in their area of expertise. Categorisation is often faster at the superordinate level than at the basic level because less information needs to be processed at the former level.

  According to Barsalou's situated simulation theory, concept processing involves perceptual and motor information. There is support for the involvement of perceptual and motor processes even with abstract concepts. However, it has not been shown clearly that perceptual and motor information is both necessary and sufficient for concept understanding. Indeed, it is probable that concepts have an abstract central core of meaning de-emphasised by Barsalou.

  According to the hub-and-spoke model, concepts consist of hubs (unified abstract representations) and spokes (modality-specific information). The existence of patients with category-specific deficits supports the notion of spokes. Evidence from patients with semantic dementia indicates that hubs are stored in the anterior temporal lobes. It is not very clear how information from hubs and spokes is combined and integrated.

- **Non-declarative memory**. Priming is tied to specific stimuli and occurs rapidly. It has been argued that priming depends on enhanced neural efficiency, which is shown by repetition suppression of brain activity. Skill learning occurs slowly and generalises to stimuli in addition to those presented during learning. Amnesic patients typically have intact (or nearly intact) performance on priming and skill-learning tasks, suggesting that these tasks involve non-declarative memory. However, skill learning often involves some declarative memory as well as non-declarative memory. The striatum is typically associated with skill learning but not declarative memory, but there are many exceptions. There is evidence that priming and skill learning involve different brain areas.

- **Beyond declarative and non-declarative memory**. The distinction between declarative and non-declarative memory is oversimplified. It is inadequate to explain amnesics' memory deficits. The hippocampus (which is severely damaged in most amnesic patients) is involved in relational or associative learning regardless of whether that learning is conscious or unconscious. Learning and memory involve numerous processes used in flexible combinations rather than a much smaller number of memory systems. The main limitation of the processing-component approach is that its flexibility makes it hard to test.

Further reading

- Baddeley, A.D., Eysenck, M.W. & Anderson, M.C. (2015). *Memory* (2nd edn). Hove: Psychology Press. Several chapters (especially 5, 6 and 11) are of direct relevance to the topics covered in this chapter.
- Cabeza, R. & Moscovitch, M. (2013). Memory systems, processing modes, and components: Functional neuroimaging evidence. *Perspectives on Psychological Science*, 8: 49–55. Roberto Cabeza and Morris Moscovitch provide an excellent discussion of the advantages and disadvantages of various theoretical approaches to long-term memory, including those based on memory systems and those based on processing components.
- Henke, K. (2010). A model for memory systems based on processing modes rather than consciousness. *Nature Reviews Neuroscience*, 11: 523–32. Katharina Henke identifies clearly the major differences between the traditional declarative/non-declarative account and the more recent processing-based account.
- Eysenck, M.W. & Groome, D. (2015, in press). Memory systems: Beyond Tulving's (1972) episodic and semantic memory. In M.W. Eysenck & D. Groome (eds), *Cognitive psychology: Revisiting the classic studies*. London: SAGE. This chapter provides an authoritative account of how theorising about episodic and semantic memory has developed since Tulving introduced the terms.
- Mulligan, N.W. & Besken, M. (2013). Implicit memory. In D. Reisberg (ed.), *The Oxford handbook of cognitive psychology*. Oxford: Oxford University Press. Theory and research on implicit memory are discussed at length by Neil Mulligan and Miri Besken.
- Pulvermüller, F. (2013). Semantic embodiment, disembodiment or misembodiment? In search of meaning in modules and neuron circuits. *Brain*

& Language, 127(1): 86–103. Friedemann Pulvermüller discusses theoretical accounts of concept processing with a focus on the role of the motor or action system.

- Schacter, D.L. (2012). Adaptive constructive processes and the future of memory. *American Psychologist*, 67: 603–13. Dan Schacter discusses in detail the role of episodic memory in imagining possible future events.

CHAPTER

8

Everyday memory

INTRODUCTION

Over the past 35 years, there has been a rapid increase in research on everyday memory. The study of everyday memory is concerned with how we use memory in our daily lives. Everyday memory differs in some important ways from the kinds of memory traditionally studied in the laboratory and discussed in Chapters 6 and 7. Much of it relates to our goals and motives (Cohen, 2008). This can be seen most clearly with prospective memory (remembering to carry out intended actions). Our intended actions are designed to assist us in achieving our current goals. For example, the first author often intends to track down an article to achieve the goal of completing a chapter in one of his textbooks.

Traditional memory research vs. everyday memory research

What are the main differences between the traditional approach to memory and the one based on everyday memory phenomena? First, everyday memories are often of events that happened a long time ago and have frequently been thought about or rehearsed during that time. As a result, "Naturally occurring memories are very often memories of memories rather than memories of the originally perceived objects and events" (Cohen, 2008, p. 2). In contrast, participants in laboratory studies usually remember information presented shortly beforehand.

Second, learning in most everyday memory research is *incidental* (not deliberate), with people learning information relevant to their goals or interests. In most traditional memory research, however, learning is *intentional*. What individuals learn is determined largely by the instructions they have been given.

Third, *social* factors are often important in everyday memory but are typically absent in traditional memory research. Fourth, we turn to a crucial difference between memory as traditionally studied and memory in everyday life. Participants in traditional memory studies are generally motivated to be as *accurate* as possible in their memory performance. In contrast, everyday memory research is typically based on the notion that, "Remembering is a form of purposeful action" (Neisser, 1996, p. 204). This approach involves three assumptions about everyday memory:

KEY TERM

Saying-is-believing effect
Tailoring a message about an event to suit a given audience causes subsequent inaccuracies in memory for that event.

1 It is purposeful (i.e., motivated).
2 It has a personal quality about it, meaning it is influenced by the individual's personality and other characteristics.
3 It is influenced by situational demands (e.g., the wish to impress one's audience).

The essence of Neisser's (1996) argument is this: what we remember in everyday life is determined by our personal goals, whereas what we remember in traditional memory research is mostly determined by the experimenter's demands for accuracy. Sometimes we strive for maximal accuracy in our recall in our everyday life (e.g., during an examination), but accuracy is typically *not* our main goal.

Findings

Evidence that the memories we report in everyday life are sometimes deliberately distorted was reported by Marsh and Tversky (2004). Students kept a record of their retelling of personal memories over a period of a month, and admitted that 42% were inaccurate.

If what you say about an event is deliberately distorted, does this change your memory and make your subsequent recall inaccurate? Very often the answer is "Yes". Dudokovic et al. (2004) asked people to read a story and then recall it three times accurately (as in traditional memory research) or entertainingly (as in the real world). Unsurprisingly, entertaining retellings were more emotional but contained fewer details than accurate retellings.

The participants subsequently tried to recall the story accurately. Those who had previously provided entertaining retellings recalled fewer story events and fewer details, and were less accurate than those who had provided accurate retellings. This is an example of the **saying-is-believing effect** – tailoring a message about an event to suit a given audience causes subsequent inaccuracies in memory for that event.

Further evidence of the saying-is-believing effect was reported by Hellmann et al. (2011). Participants saw a video of a pub brawl involving two men. They then described the brawl to a student whom they had been told believed that person A was (or was not) responsible for what happened. The participants' retelling of the event reflected the student's biased views. Finally, the participants were given an unexpected test of free recall for the crime event. Their recall was systematically influenced by their earlier retelling of the event. Free recall was most distorted in those participants whose retelling of the event had been most biased.

What should be done?

Research on human memory should ideally possess ecological validity (i.e., applicability to real life; see Glossary). Ecological validity consists of two aspects: (1) *representativeness* and (2) *generalisability*. Representativeness refers to the naturalness of the experimental situation, stimuli and task. In contrast, generalisability refers to the extent to which a study's findings apply to the real world.

Generalisability is more important than representativeness. It is often (mistakenly) assumed that everyday memory research always has more ecological validity than traditional laboratory research. In fact, research having high ecological validity can be carried out by devising well-controlled naturalistic experiments in which the task and conditions resemble those found in real life.

It has been argued that traditional memory research and everyday memory research are mutually antagonistic. That argument is incorrect in two ways. First, the distinction between these two types of research is actually blurred and indistinct. Second, there is much *cross-fertilisation*, with the insights from both kinds of memory research enhancing our understanding of human memory.

KEY TERM

Autobiographical memory
Long-term memory for the events of one's own life.

AUTOBIOGRAPHICAL MEMORY: INTRODUCTION

We have hundreds of thousands of memories relating to an endless variety of things. However, those relating to the experiences we have had and to those important to us have special significance and form our **autobiographical memory** (memory for the events of one's own life). What is the relationship between autobiographical memory and episodic memory (concerned with events occurring at a given time in a specific place; see Chapter 7)? One important similarity is that both types of memory relate to personally experienced events.

However, there are also several differences between autobiographical and episodic memory. First, autobiographical memory relates to events of personal significance, whereas episodic memory (sometimes termed "laboratory memory") often relates to trivial events (e.g., was the word "chair" presented in the first list?).

Second, autobiographical memory typically deals with complex memories selected from a huge collection of personal experiences. In contrast, episodic memory is much more limited in scope.

Third, autobiographical memory extends back over years or decades. In contrast, episodic memory (at least for laboratory events) often extends back only for minutes or hours.

Fourth, some aspects of autobiographical memory involve semantic memory (general knowledge; see Glossary) rather than episodic memory (Prebble et al., 2013). For example, some brain-damaged patients with little or no episodic memory can nevertheless recall information about themselves (e.g., knowledge about their own personality; Klein & Lax, 2010).

Gilboa (2004) discussed meta-analytic evidence that autobiographical and episodic memory differ in brain activity. There was much more activation in the right mid-dorsolateral prefrontal cortex in episodic than autobiographical memory (see Figure 8.1). This probably occurred because episodic memory requires conscious monitoring to minimise errors. In contrast, there was much more activation in the left ventromedial prefrontal cortex in autobiographical memory than in episodic memory – autobiographical memory involves monitoring the accuracy of retrieved memories in relation to activated knowledge of the self.

Burianova et al. (2010) carried out a study using the same pictures in all conditions but varying the retrieval demands. For example, participants shown a photograph of a tent might be asked to think of a personal camping experience (autobiographical memory), to remember the colour of the tent (episodic memory) or to show knowledge of the number of campsites in a given area (semantic memory). All three types of memory were associated with activation in a common network involving frontal, temporal and parietal brain areas. These findings suggest there are important similarities between episodic and autobiographical memory.

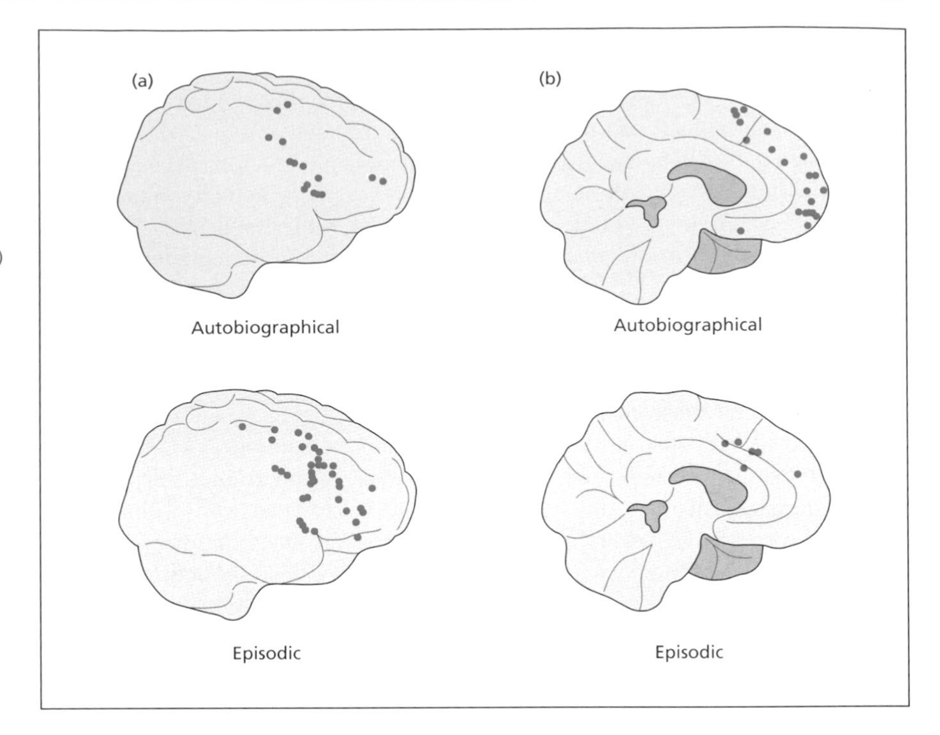

Figure 8.1
(a) Shows more activation in the right mid-dorsolateral (top and to the side) prefrontal cortex in episodic than in autobiographical memory. (b) Shows more activation in the left ventromedial (bottom middle) prefrontal cortex in autobiographical than in episodic memory.
Both reprinted from Gilboa (2004). Reprinted with permission from Elsevier.

Why do we spend much of our time recalling autobiographical memories from our past? Bluck and Alea (2009) identified three key reasons:

1 maintenance of social bonds (e.g., shared memories);
2 directing future behaviour: using the past as a guide to the future;
3 creating a sense of self-continuity over time.

What is to come

In the following sections we will discuss major topics within autobiographical memory. First, we consider unusually vivid autobiographical memories for dramatic events. Second, we focus on those periods in people's lives from which disproportionately many or few autobiographical memories come, with an emphasis on the underlying reasons. Third, we discuss major theoretical approaches to understanding autobiographical memory, including those within neuroscience. Note that research on autobiographical memories for traumatic childhood experiences is discussed in Chapter 7.

KEY TERMS

Flashbulb memories
Vivid and detailed memories of dramatic events (e.g., 9/11).

Hyperthymestic syndrome
An exceptional ability to remember the events of one's own life.

Flashbulb memories

Most people think they have very clear, long-lasting autobiographical memories for important and dramatic public events (e.g., the terrorist attacks on the United States on 11 September 2001 – see photo). Such memories were termed **flashbulb memories** by Brown and Kulik (1977). They argued that dramatic events perceived as surprising and as having real consequences for the individual activate a special neural mechanism. This mechanism "prints" the details of such events permanently in the memory system.

IN THE REAL WORLD: EXCEPTIONAL AUTOBIOGRAPHICAL MEMORY

Jill Price. Getty Images.

Most people regret their inability to remember autobiographical memories of important past experiences. However, a few people have remarkably few such memory failures. Parker et al. (2006) reported the fascinating case of Jill Price (see photo), a woman born in 1965. She has an incredible ability to recall detailed information about almost every day of her life over the past several decades. Parker et al. coined the term **hyperthymestic syndrome** (formed from Greek words meaning "remembering" and "more than usual") to describe her ability.

It might seem advantageous to have access to incredibly detailed information about your own autobiographical memory. However, Jill Price regards it as a disadvantage: "Most have called it a gift, but I call it a burden. I run my entire life through my head every day and it drives me crazy!!!" (Parker et al., 2006, p. 35). Strangely, her memory generally is very ordinary. For example, her ability to recall lists of words is average and she finds it very hard to remember which locks fit each of the five keys on her keyring.

Why is Jill Price's autobiographical memory so outstanding? First, she has obsessional tendencies and spends most of her time thinking about herself and her past. When she was asked about her excessive focus on her personal past, Jill Price said, "This is OCD [obsessive-compulsive disorder]. I have OCD of my memories." Second, she has poor inhibitory processes and so finds it very hard to switch her personal memories off. Third, Jill Price makes the passage of time seem more concrete by representing it in spatial form (e.g., drawing January in the 11 o'clock position on a circle and working anticlockwise from there). Such linkage of time and space is often associated with very good memory (Simner et al., 2009).

LePort et al. (2012) carried out a thorough investigation of 11 individuals having hyperthymestic syndrome. These individuals performed eight times better than controls in thinking of autobiographical experiences associated with various random dates. About 80% of them showed similar obsessional characteristics to Jill Price. However, their performance was only average on several standard memory tasks, which is also the case with Jill Price. Other research (Patihis et al., 2013) has shown that individuals with hyperthymestic syndrome are as prone to false memories as ordinary controls.

Of most theoretical importance, LePort et al. (2012) found that individuals with hyperthymestic syndrome showed structural differences from controls in brain regions (e.g., parahippocampal gyrus, anterior insula) associated with an autobiographical memory network. Another individual with hyperthymestic syndrome is HK, a blind man who was tested when he was 20 years old (Ally et al., 2013). Long-term memory of emotional material is enhanced by amygdala activation (the amygdala is strongly involved in emotional processing; see Chapter 15), and HK's right amygdala was approximately 20% larger than in most other people. In addition he had enhanced connectivity between the amygdala and the hippocampus (centrally involved in the formation of long-term memories). It remains to be established whether the structural and functional differences found in individuals with hyperthymestic syndrome partially cause the remarkable autobiographical memory ability or are a consequence of it.

Weblink:
Article on flashbulb memories

According to Brown and Kulik (1977), flashbulb memories often include the following information:

- informant (person who supplied the information);
- place where the news was heard;
- ongoing event;
- individual's own emotional state;
- emotional state of others;
- consequences of the event for the individual.

World Trade Center attacks on 9/11.
iStock/Dan Howl.

It is often thought that Brown and Kulik (1977) argued that flashbulb memories are very different from other memories because of their longevity, accuracy and reliance on a special neural mechanism. In fact, their approach was less extreme (Curci & Conway, 2013). For example, they stated that, "A flashbulb memory is only somewhat indiscriminate and is very far from complete" (p. 75).

Some individuals experiencing traumatic events (e.g., war, terrorist attacks) develop post-traumatic stress disorder in which the traumatic event is re-experienced in the form of intrusive memories. Of particular interest are **flashbacks**, which are "vivid, sensory-perceptual . . . emotional memories from a traumatic event that intrude involuntarily into consciousness" (Bourne et al., 2013, p. 1521). Flashbacks may be an intense form of flashbulb memory.

Findings

It has sometimes been assumed that flashbulb memories should be very accurate but this is often not the case. Pezdek (2003) asked American students the following question: "On September 11, did you see the videotape on television of the first plane striking the first tower?" In fact, only the videotape of the *second* tower being hit was available on that day, but 73% of the participants said "Yes".

It is often impossible to assess the accuracy of people's flashbulb memories (e.g., their emotional reaction on first hearing about the event). However, if such memories involve permanent storage, they might show *consistency* (lack of change) over time. Talarico and Rubin (2003) compared the consistency of students' memories for the events of 9/11 and an everyday event over a period of 32 weeks. The reported vividness of flashbulb memories remained much higher than that of everyday memories throughout the 32-week period. However, flashbulb memories showed no more consistency or lack of change than everyday memories. Thus, there was a major discrepancy between people's beliefs in the strength of their flashbulb memories and the actual accuracy of those memories.

In contrast, Kvavilashvili et al. (2009) found that most people's memories for 9/11 were reasonably consistent for up to three years after the event. However, a very small number of participants showed major memory distortions because they heard the news about 9/11 from multiple sources and became confused among them.

Rimmele et al. (2012) compared participants' 9/11 memories one week and three years after the event. Consistency of memory varied across features. There was high consistency for remembering the location at which they heard about 9/11 (83%), but lower consistency for informant (70%), ongoing activity (62%) and their own immediate reaction (34%).

Rimmele et al. (2012) also studied memory for emotionally negative and neutral scenes with added coloured dots in the centre. There was good memory for time and place with the negative scenes but poorer memory for the coloured dots than with neutral scenes. Thus, strong negative emotions may *selectively* enhance memory for only some features. However, this is sufficient to produce the illusion that the entire scene has been remembered clearly and vividly.

Sharot et al. (2007) argued that it may require intense emotional experience to produce genuine flashbulb memories. They compared the memories of individuals close to the World Trade Center (about 2 miles) on 9/11 with those who were somewhat further away (about 4½ miles) three years after the event. The flashbulb memories of those close to the event were more vivid and involved more activation of the amygdala (strongly involved in emotion) than the memories of those further away. Their memories were also more detailed. These findings indicate the importance of the intensity of the emotional reaction to a dramatic event.

Berntsen (2001) studied students who had had a traumatic experience more than five years ago or within the past year and who all satisfied the criteria for post-traumatic stress disorder. Both groups had comparably frequent, vivid flashbacks of the traumatic event indicating that trauma memories are incredibly persistent over time. These findings suggest that flashbacks and flashbulb memories resemble each other in some ways.

Bourne et al. (2013) asked healthy participants to watch a traumatic movie. The processing of scenes that later caused flashbacks was associated with increased activation in several areas including the amygdala (involved in emotional processing) and the ventral occipital cortex (involved in higher-level visual processing and imagery). Thus, flashbacks are more likely when there is intense emotional processing when the traumatic event is experienced.

KEY TERM

Flashbacks
Intense emotional memories of traumatic events that are recalled involuntarily by patients suffering from post-traumatic stress disorder.

Interactive exercise:
Flashbulb memories

KEY TERMS

Childhood amnesia
The inability of adults to recall autobiographical memories from early childhood; also known as infantile amnesia.

Reminiscence bump
The tendency of older people to recall a disproportionate number of autobiographical memories from early adulthood.

Conclusions

The evidence is mixed concerning the claim that flashbulb memories are special. On the one hand, so-called flashbulb memories are often remembered no better than ordinary memories and show only moderate consistency over time. On the other hand, there is generally very good consistency over time for some details (e.g., where the news was heard). Thus, there may be selective enhancement of some kinds of information in flashbulb memories. Flashbulb memories may also benefit from being distinctive and from having being retrieved many times (Bob Logie, personal communication). Flashbulb memories are more detailed and long-lasting if there was an intense emotional experience when they were formed – see Chapter 15 for a discussion of the effects of emotional stimuli on memory. Finally, there may be important similarities between flashbulb memories and flashbacks relating to personally experienced traumatic events.

MEMORIES ACROSS THE LIFETIME

Suppose we ask 70-year-olds to recall personal memories suggested by cue words (e.g., nouns referring to common objects). From which points in their lives would most memories come? Rubin et al. (1986) answered this question by combining findings from several studies. Two findings were of theoretical interest:

- **Childhood amnesia** (or infantile amnesia) shown by the almost total lack of memories from the first three years of life.
- **Reminiscence bump**, consisting of a surprisingly large number of memories coming from the years between 10 and 30 (especially between 15 and 25).

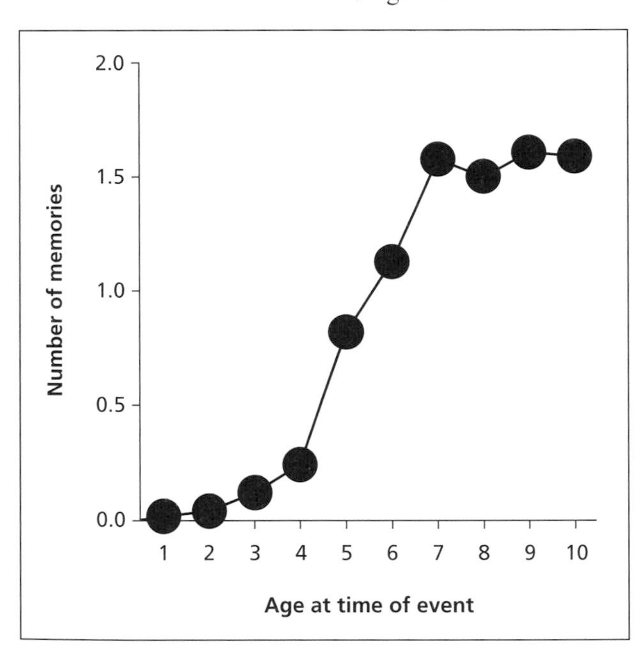

Figure 8.2
Childhood amnesia based on data reported by Rubin and Schulkind (1997). Participants (20, 35 and 70 years of age) reported very few autobiographical memories before the age of 3 and there was later a levelling off between the ages of 7 and 10.

From Josselyn and Frankland (2012). © 2012 Cold Spring Harbor Laboratory Press. Reproduced with permission of author and Cold Spring Harbor Laboratory Press.

Childhood amnesia

Adults report very few autobiographical memories from before the age of 3 and show limited recall for events occurring between the ages of 3 and 6 (see Figure 8.2). How can we explain this phenomenon (known as childhood amnesia)? The most famous (or notorious!) account was provided by Sigmund Freud (1915/1957). He attributed it to repression, with threat-related thoughts and experiences being consigned to the unconscious. This dramatic theory fails to explain why adults cannot remember *positive* and *neutral* events from early childhood.

Cognitive self

Howe and Courage (1997) argued that children can only form autobiographical memories *after* developing a sense that some events have personal significance. According to Howe and Courage's theory:

> The development of the cognitive self late in the second year of life (as indexed by visual self-recognition [in a mirror]) provides a new framework around which memories can be organised. With this cognitive advance . . . we witness the emergence of autobiographical memory and the end of infantile amnesia.
>
> (1997, p. 499)

Evidence that the cognitive self plays a role in the onset of autobiographical memory around or shortly after a child's second birthday was reported by Howe et al. (2003). Young children only showed good performance on a memory test for personal events *after* having achieved self-recognition. However, it is entirely possible that other factors also contribute to the onset of autobiographical memory.

Social-cultural developmental theory

The social-cultural developmental theory (Fivush & Nelson, 2004; Fivush, 2010) provides another plausible account. According to this theory, language and culture are both central in the early development of autobiographical memory. Language is important in part because we use it to communicate our memories. Experiences occurring before children develop language are hard to express in language later on.

Mothers differ considerably in how they reminisce about the past with their young children. Some have a very elaborate reminiscing style whereas others do not. As predicted, the age of first memory reported by 12-year-olds was earlier in those whose mothers had had a very elaborate reminiscing style when they were preschoolers (Jack et al., 2009).

An individual's culture influences his/her autobiographical memories. Individuals from individualistic cultures that emphasise personal achievement recollect personal experiences and feelings (e.g., successes, fears). In contrast, those from collectivistic cultures emphasising group cohesion recall memories involving interpersonal relations (Ross & Wang, 2010).

Two-stage theory

Jack and Hayne (2010) argued that the common assumption of a gradual decline in childhood amnesia during the preschool period is incorrect. In their study, the participants' earliest memory dated from 23 months of age. However, their memories for the first four–six years of life were sparse. Thus, childhood amnesia is a two-stage process: there is *absolute* amnesia for the first two years of life followed by *relative* amnesia for the remaining preschool years.

How can we account for these two stages? According to Jack and Hayne (2010), the period of absolute amnesia ends with the onset of the cognitive self. After that, the development of language leads to the end of relative amnesia. There was a strong tendency for the amount of information recalled about a childhood event to increase as the participant's age at the time of the event increased. This may well reflect children's rapid development of language over the early years of life.

KEY TERM

Neurogenesis
The process of generating new neurons in the brain.

Neurogenic hypothesis

Josselyn and Frankland (2012) pointed out that childhood amnesia has been observed in several non-human species. Thus, it probably cannot be explained fully using human concepts (e.g., the cognitive self, language development). Josselyn and Frankland pointed out that the hippocampus (crucially involved in declarative memory, including autobiographical memory) shows protracted postnatal development. Of special importance, there is a process of **neurogenesis** in which new neurons are generated in the hippocampus (especially the dentate gyrus) during the early years of life.

According to Josselyn and Frankland's (2012) neurogenic hypothesis, "High neurogenesis levels negatively regulate the ability to form enduring memories, most likely by replacing synaptic connections in pre-existing hippocampal memory circuits" (p. 423). There is indirect supporting evidence for this hypothesis. For example, mice with high levels of neurogenesis in the dentate gyrus have especially fast rates of forgetting (see Josselyn & Frankland, 2012). Conversely, it has been found in several species that the ability to form long-lasting memories increases substantially when neurogenesis declines.

In sum, there is as yet little or no definitive evidence to support the neurogenic hypothesis. However, the central role of the hippocampus in the formation of long-term declarative memories means that it provides a very plausible explanation of the almost complete absence of long-term memories for the first three years of life.

Overall evaluation

Significant progress has been made in understanding childhood amnesia. Absolute amnesia can probably be explained by the neurogenic hypothesis. After that, the *onset* of autobiographical memory in infants probably depends on the reducing neurogenesis plus the emergence of the self. Its *subsequent* expression depends heavily on social and cultural factors and the child's development of language. Other factors may also be involved. For example, children's development of semantic memory may be important (anonymous reviewer). There are dramatic changes in children's understanding of the world during the early years, and these changes may limit access to our early autobiographical memories.

What are the main limitations of research in this area? First, it is predominantly *correlational*. For example, an association between the emergence of the cognitive self and the end of childhood amnesia does not prove that the former causes the latter.

Second, most studies have focused on *adults'* memories from early childhood. Tustin and Hayne (2010) asked children and adolescents to provide early memories. The earliest memories of children between the ages of 5 and 9 were from about 1½ years on average, those of adolescents were from 2½ years, and those of adults were from just over 3 years. Thus, childhood amnesia depends in part on forgetting over the years rather than the factors emphasised by the theories discussed above.

Reminiscence bump

As mentioned earlier, older people asked to recall personal memories recall numerous events from adolescence and early adulthood (the reminiscence bump).

Conway et al. (2005) asked older people from America, China, Japan, England and Bangladesh to recall autobiographical memories. There was a reminiscence bump in all five cultures.

Conway et al. (2005) found the Chinese were more likely than others to recall events with a social or group orientation because theirs is a collectivistic culture emphasising group cohesion. In contrast, Americans were more likely to recall events relating directly to themselves as individuals – America is an individualistic culture emphasising personal responsibility and achievement.

How can we explain the existence of the reminiscence bump? Rubin and Berntsen's (2003) influential theory is based on the notion of a **life script** (cultural expectations about the major life events in most people's lives). Examples of such events are falling in love, marriage and having children. Most of these events are emotionally positive and generally occur between the ages of 15 and 30. According to the theory, the life script guides and organises the retrieval of autobiographical memories.

KEY TERM

Life script
Cultural expectations concerning the nature and order of major life events in a typical person's life.

Findings

Bohn and Berntsen (2011) discovered that children aged between 10 and 14 possess a life script. When the children wrote their *future* life stories, 79% of the events they listed were life script events. In addition, there was a stronger reminiscence bump for life script events than for events not forming part of the life script. Bohn and Berntsen obtained further support for the notion that the reminiscence bump depends in part on the life script in a second study. When young people described future events in such a way as not to activate the life script, the reminiscence bump disappeared.

Further support for life-script theory was reported by Berntsen et al. (2011). Older people identified the most positive and the most negative event in their lives. Negative events did not exhibit a reminiscence bump. In contrast, positive life script events (but not positive non-life script events) showed a strong reminiscence bump (see Figure 8.3).

Interactive exercise:
Reminiscence bump

Weblink:
Modelling the reminiscence bump

As predicted, Berntsen et al. (2011) found 68% of the positive events related to the life script: having children (34%), marriage (22%), college (6%) and falling in love (1%).In contrast, few of the negative events (e.g., someone's death, life-threatening illness) related to the life script. Finally, the positive events recalled were rated as much more central to the participants' life story and identity than the negative ones.

Additional support for life-script theory was reported by Scherman (2013). In four different countries (Denmark, USA, Turkey, the Netherlands), life scripts had a lifespan distribution resembling the reminiscence bump.

As Dickson et al. (2011) pointed out, the emphasis in life-script theory is on autobiographical memories referring to personal events *predictable* within any given culture. Thus, older people should show a reminiscence bump for very

Figure 8.3
Percentage of positive life script events and positive non-life script events as a function of age at the time of the event.
From Berntsen et al. (2011). © 2011 American Psychological Association.

expected personal events. That prediction was supported. Recall of very *unexpected* personal events also showed a strong reminiscence bump, which is less consistent with the notion of a life script guiding retrieval. However, it can be explained on the basis that our strongest autobiographical memories tend to be those of direct relevance to our self-identity (Conway, 2005). Most people's self-identity develops substantially during adolescence and early adulthood, and this provides a potential explanation for the reminiscence bump.

Evaluation

The finding that the reminiscence bump is generally much stronger for positive memories than for negative ones provides support for the life-script theory. However, the late teens and twenties differ in several ways from the life periods that precede and follow them (e.g., establishment of self-identity; novel or first-time experiences). As a result, it is likely that several factors contribute to the reminiscence bump.

THEORETICAL APPROACHES TO AUTOBIOGRAPHICAL MEMORY

Several theories of autobiographical memory have been proposed over the years. Here we will focus mostly on Conway and Pleydell-Pearce's (2000) self-memory system model. After that, we will consider the contribution cognitive neuroscience has made to our understanding of autobiographical memory. Finally, we consider how our understanding of depression can be enhanced through the study of autobiographical memory.

Self-memory system model

According to Conway and Pleydell-Pearce's (2000) theory, we possess a self-memory system with two major components:

1. *Autobiographical memory knowledge base*: This contains personal information at three levels of specificity:
   - lifetime periods: these generally cover substantial periods of time defined by major ongoing situations (e.g., time spent living with someone);
   - general events: these include repeated events (e.g., visits to a sports club) and single events (e.g., a holiday in Australia); general events are often related to each other as well as to lifetime periods;
   - event-specific knowledge: this knowledge consists of images, feelings and other details relating to general events, and spanning time periods from seconds to hours; knowledge about an event is usually organised in the correct temporal order.

Research activity:
Memory for personal events

2. *Working self*: This is concerned with the self, what it may become in the future and with the individual's current goals. The working self's goals influence the kinds of memories stored within the autobiographical memory knowledge base, and the autobiographical memories we recall. As a result, "Autobiographical memories are primarily records of success or failure in goal attainment" (Conway & Pleydell-Pearce, 2000, p. 266).

According to the theory, autobiographical memories can be accessed through generative or direct retrieval. **Generative retrieval** involves deliberately constructing autobiographical memories by combining the resources of the working self with information in the autobiographical knowledge base. Autobiographical memories produced via generative retrieval often relate to the individual's goals within the working self.

In contrast, **direct retrieval** does not involve the working self. Autobiographical memories produced by direct retrieval are triggered spontaneously by specific cues (e.g., hearing the word "Paris" on the radio may trigger retrieval of a holiday there). Direct retrieval is less effortful than generative retrieval and involves less active involvement of the rememberer.

Conway (2005) developed the above theory (see Figure 8.4). The knowledge structures in autobiographical memory are divided into the conceptual self and episodic memories (previously called event-specific knowledge). At the top of the

KEY TERMS

Generative retrieval
Deliberate or voluntary construction of autobiographical memories based on an individual's current goals.

Direct retrieval
Involuntary recall of autobiographical memories triggered by a specific cue (e.g., being in the same place as the original event).

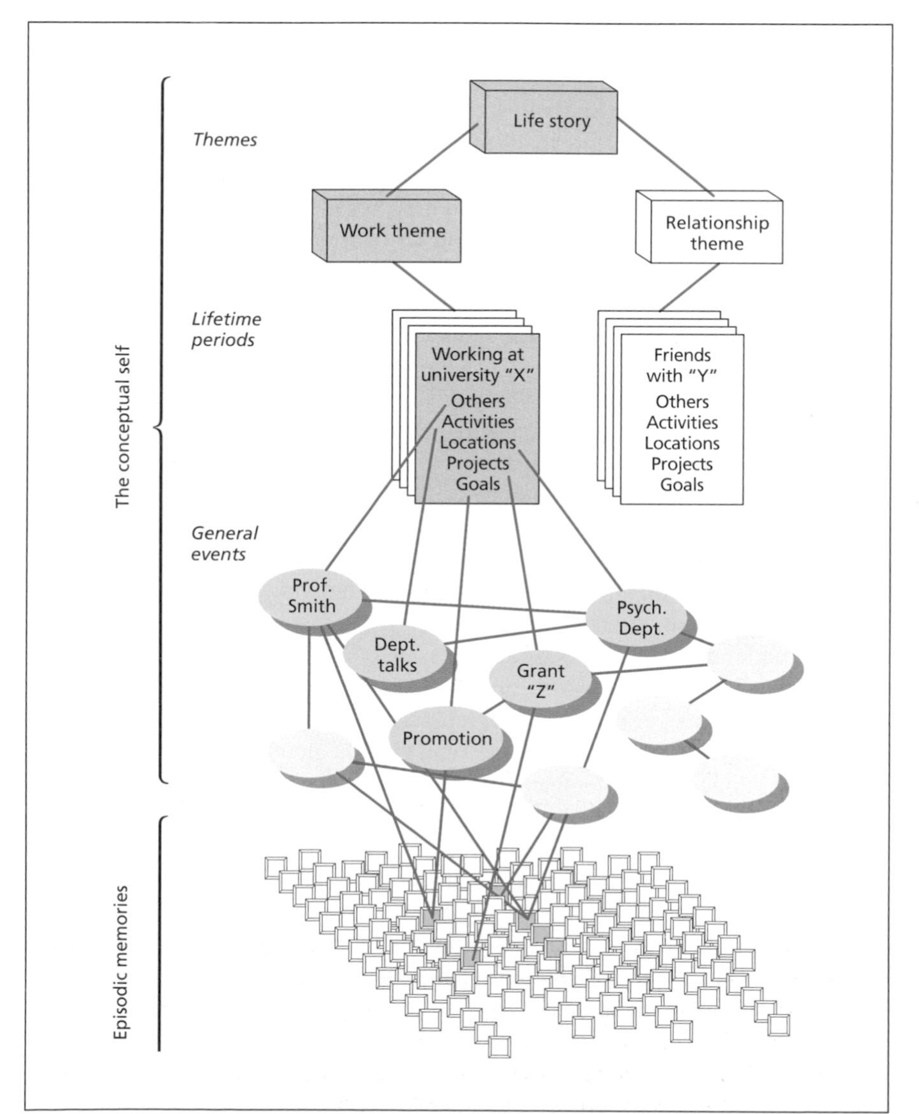

Figure 8.4
The knowledge structures within autobiographical memory, as proposed by Conway (2005).

Reprinted from Conway (2005). Reprinted with permission of Elsevier.

hierarchy, the life story and themes have been added. The life story consists of very general factual and evaluative knowledge we possess about ourselves. Themes refer to major life domains (e.g., work, relationships).

Conway (2005) argued that we want our autobiographical memories to exhibit *coherence* (consistency with our current goals and beliefs). However, we also often want them to exhibit *correspondence* (being accurate). Over time, coherence tends to win out over correspondence.

Findings

Research on patients with retrograde amnesia (widespread forgetting of events preceding brain injury; see Chapter 7) supports the notion there are different types of autobiographical knowledge. These patients often have great difficulty in recalling episodic memories, but their ability to recall general events and lifetime periods is less impaired (Conway & Pleydell-Pearce, 2000). Rosenbaum et al. (2005) studied an amnesic patient, KC, who had no episodic memories. However, he could access some general autobiographical knowledge about his own life. As mentioned earlier, several brain-damaged patients with practically no episodic memory can still recall the kind of personality they have. This is the case even in patients with severe deficits in semantic memory as well as episodic memory (Klein & Lax, 2010) showing the resilience of self-knowledge about one's personality.

Autobiographical memory and the self are closely related. Woike et al. (1999) distinguished between two personality types:

1 *agentic*, with an emphasis on independence, achievement and personal power;
2 *communal*, with an emphasis on interdependence and similarity to others.

Woike et al. asked participants with agentic and communal personality types to write about a positive or negative personal experience. When the experience was positive, 65% of the agentic participants recalled agentic memories (e.g., involving success), whereas 90% of the communal participants recalled communal memories (e.g., involving love or friendship). The same pattern was found for negative personal experiences: 47% of the agentic individuals recalled agentic memories (e.g., involving failure), but 90% of the communal individuals recalled communal memories (e.g., involving betrayal of trust).

The model distinguishes between generative or effortful retrieval and direct or spontaneous retrieval. Support for this distinction was reported by Uzer et al. (2012). Participants recalled autobiographical memories when presented with emotion words (e.g., *frustrated*, *amused*) and thought aloud while doing so. Direct retrieval was three times faster than generative retrieval, which is as expected given its automatic nature. Also as predicted, direct retrieval was associated with much less vocalisation than generative retrieval.

How different are the autobiographical memories produced via generative and direct retrieval? Memories elicited by direct retrieval are more specific, less significant and less relevant to the individual's personal identity than those involving generative retrieval (Johannessen & Berntsen, 2010). Thus, as predicted, the individual's working self and goals were more involved in generative than direct retrieval.

Addis et al. (2012) compared patterns of brain activation when autobiographical memories were accessed by direct or generative retrieval. Generative retrieval was associated with more activation in parts of the prefrontal cortex thought to be involved in strategic search for autobiographical information. Other areas (e.g., left hippocampus) were more activated during direct than generative retrieval. These findings confirm there are important differences between direct and generative retrieval.

Conway (2005) argued that autobiographical memories are often inaccurate because we want them to be consistent with the working self's goals. For example, people often claim aspects of their lives (e.g., the self, marital relationship) are better now than in the past. However, this "improvement" is typically due to misremembering their past selves in a negatively biased way (see Newman and Lindsay (2009) for a review). Such inaccuracies can enhance our self-image and our social relationships with other people.

Evaluation

The theoretical approach of Conway and Pleydell-Pearce (2000) and Conway (2005) provides a reasonably comprehensive account of autobiographical memory. Several of their major theoretical assumptions (e.g., the hierarchical structure of autobiographical memory; the intimate relationship between autobiographical memory and the self; the importance of goals in autobiographical memory) are well supported. There is also good support for the distinction between generative and direct retrieval.

What are the limitations with the self-memory system model? First, as we will see in the next section, the retrieval of autobiographical memories involves several brain areas and processes, and the model does not capture all this complexity. Second, we need to know more about *how* the working self *interacts* with the autobiographical knowledge base to produce recall of specific autobiographical memories. Third, autobiographical memories vary in the extent to which they contain episodic information (e.g., contextual details) and semantic information (e.g., world knowledge). However, this is not addressed fully within the model.

Cognitive neuroscience

The prefrontal cortex plays a major role in the retrieval of autobiographical memories. Svoboda et al. (2006) found in a meta-analysis of functional neuroimaging studies that the medial and ventromedial prefrontal cortex were nearly always activated during autobiographical retrieval as were medial and lateral temporal cortex. Summerfield et al. (2009) studied the involvement of the prefrontal cortex in more detail. Participants produced real and imagined autobiographical events. Only recall of real autobiographical events was associated with activation in the ventromedial prefrontal cortex and the posterior cingulate cortex.

Autobiographical memories are often of personally significant events and so are associated with emotion. The amygdala, which is buried deep within the temporal lobe (see Figure 15.3, page 638) is strongly associated with emotion, and so we would expect it to be activated during autobiographical retrieval. As predicted, among patients with damage to the medial temporal lobes, those who also have damage to the amygdala find it harder to retrieve emotional autobiographical memories (Buchanan et al., 2006). Markowitsch and Staniloiu (2011)

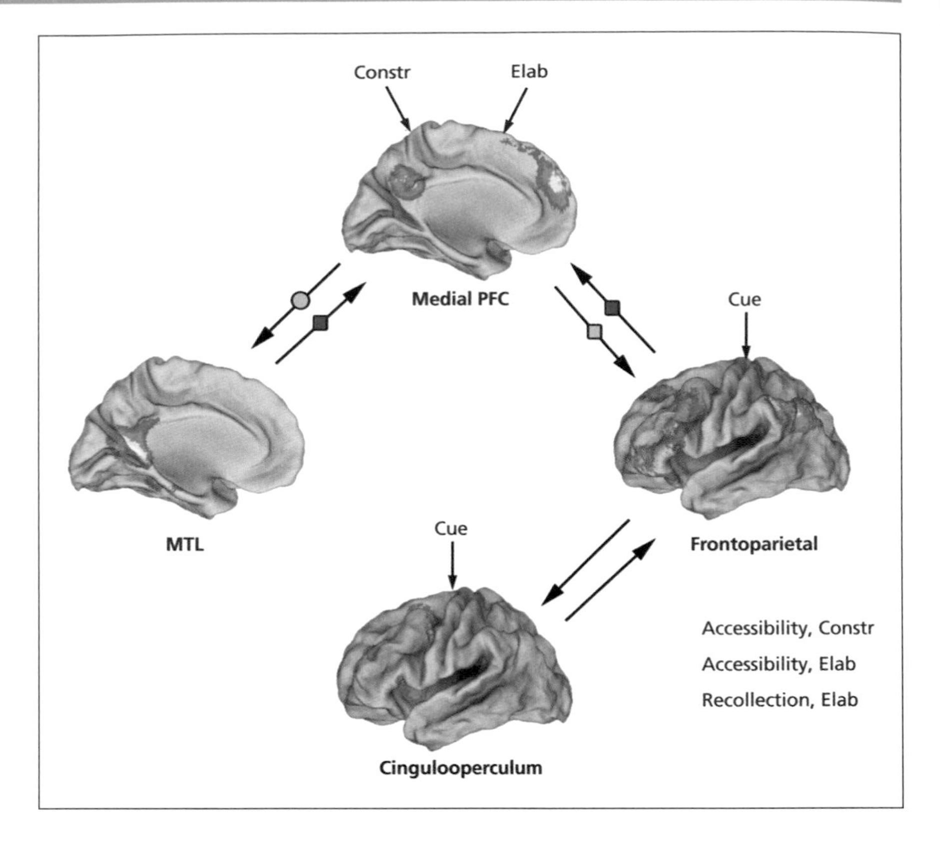

Figure 8.5
A model of the bi-directional relationships among neural networks involved in the construction and/or elaboration of autobiographical memories. MTL = medial temporal lobe network; Medial PFC = medial prefrontal cortex.
From St Jacques et al. (2011). Reprinted with permission of Elsevier.

discussed research in which autobiographical retrieval (but not recall of fictitious material) was associated with amygdala activation.

St Jacques et al. (2011) assessed the brain areas activated when people produced autobiographical memories to emotionally arousing words by generative retrieval. They identified four brain networks (see Figure 8.5):

1 *Fronto-parietal network*: This is involved in the construction of autobiographical memories; it is associated with adaptive controlled processes and is probably involved in verbal retrieval.
2 *Cinguloopercululum network*: This is also involved in the construction of autobiographical memories; it is associated with goal maintenance.
3 *Medial prefrontal cortex network*: This is involved in the construction and subsequent elaboration of autobiographical memories; it is involved in self-referential processing.
4 *Medial temporal lobe network*: This is involved in the construction and subsequent elaboration of autobiographical memories; it is associated with declarative memory (conscious recollection).

There are two important additional points with reference to Figure 8.5. First, there are strong bi-directional connections between brain networks and so they do not operate in isolation. Second, all four networks are involved in the initial construction of autobiographical memories. However, only the medial prefrontal cortex and medial temporal lobes are involved in the subsequent elaboration of those memories.

Depression

We have seen there are clear-cut individual differences in autobiographical memory. Important research in this area has focused on patients with major depressive disorder or on healthy individuals high in depression. In general terms, it is assumed within the self-memory system model that the information stored in autobiographical memory reflects the individual's personality and his/her sense of self. Accordingly, our understanding of the nature of depression can be increased by considering in detail how autobiographical memory differs in depressed and non-depressed individuals.

A much-used task involves participants recalling autobiographical memories of events lasting less than one day in response to word cues. Depressed individuals show reduced autobiographical memory *specificity* compared to non-depressed ones. In other words, they are much more likely to produce over-general memories. For example, when given the cue "angry", a depressed person might say, "Arguing with other people" (see Liu et al. (2013) for a meta-analysis of studies on depressed patients).

Most evidence shows only an *association* or correlation between depression and reduced memory specificity. As a result, it does not demonstrate this reduced memory specificity is important. More convincing evidence was reported by Stange et al. (2013) in a study on Caucasian adolescents. The extent of over-general autobiographical memory predicted increases in depressive symptoms eight months later in those exposed to high levels of familial emotional abuse. Thus, over-general autobiographical memory made adolescents especially vulnerable to the adverse effects of emotional abuse.

Additional evidence for the importance of over-general autobiographical memory comes from longitudinal studies on depressed patients. For example, Brittlebank et al. (1993) found increased autobiographical memory specificity predicted recovery from major depressive disorder.

What processes are involved in over-general autobiographical memory? According to the affect regulation hypothesis, a cognitive avoidance strategy may be involved. More specifically, depressed individuals may avoid retrieving specific negative memories because such memories are associated with intense negative emotions. Support for this hypothesis was reported by Debeer et al. (2011), who considered the effect of threat instructions (i.e., retrieval of autobiographical memories may have negative side effects). These threat instructions led to an increase in over-general memories only among individuals high in avoidant coping. Not that all depressed individuals have avoidant coping strategies.

Structure of autobiographical memory

Dalgleish et al. (2011) studied autobiographical memory in patients with current major depressive disorder, patients in remission from major depressive disorder and healthy controls. The participants listed their most important lifetime periods or life chapters, with all three groups identifying between nine and ten lifetime periods on average. They then decided which positive and negative items (words or phrases) applied to each lifetime period.

Several measures were obtained for each participant. First, there was the proportion of the selected items that was negative. Second, there was compartmentalisation (the extent to which the proportion of items that was negative varied

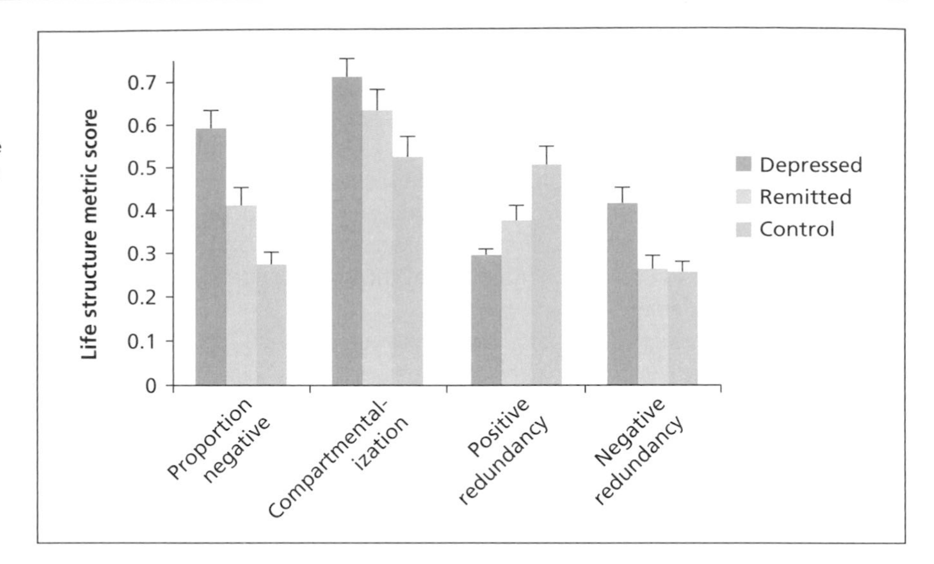

Figure 8.6
Life structure scores (proportion negative, compartmentalisation, positive redundancy, negative redundancy) for patients with major depressive disorder, patients in remission from major depressive disorder and healthy controls.

From Dalgleish et al. (2011). © 2010 American Psychological Association.

across lifetime periods). Third, there was positive redundancy (the extent to which the same positive terms were used across lifetime periods). Fourth, there was negative redundancy (the extent to which the same negative terms were used across lifetime periods).

The proportion of selected terms that was negative was much greater for current depressed patients than for controls (see Figure 8.6). In addition, current patients had a less integrated sense of self as indicated by greater *compartmentalisation*. This greater compartmentalisation occurred in part because current depressed patients showed little consistency in their use of positive terms across lifetime periods (i.e., low positive redundancy). Finally, depressed patients in remission were intermediate between current patients and controls on most measures.

What do these findings mean? First, the organisation of autobiographical knowledge in currently depressed patients is revealing concerning their working self as described by Conway and Pleydell-Pearce (2000). More generally, current patients' perceived self is revealed in the predominantly negative and non-integrated structure of their autobiographical knowledge.

Second, the structure of autobiographical knowledge is more integrated and less pervasively negative in patients in remission than current patients. This suggests part of the process of recovery from major depressive disorder involves having a "healthier" perspective on one's life history.

Third, patients in remission nevertheless had a more negative and less integrated view of their life histories than did the healthy controls. These findings suggest these patients were at risk of a subsequent depressive episode.

Conclusions

Depressed individuals produce over-general autobiographical memories in part because of avoidant coping strategies. Their autobiographical memories reveal depressed individuals' negative and poorly integrated sense of self. Individuals having over-general memories are at risk of developing depression, and increased specificity of memories in clinically depressed individuals predicts recovery from depression.

EYEWITNESS TESTIMONY

Cornelius Dupree. PA Photos.

The accuracy (or otherwise) of an individual's memory is sometimes of enormous importance. Suppose you are the only eyewitness to a very serious crime. Subsequently the person you identify as the murderer on a line-up is found guilty even though there is no other strong evidence. Such cases raise the question: is it safe to rely on eyewitness testimony?

Many people answer "Yes" to the above question. Simons and Chabris (2011) found 37% of Americans believe the testimony of a single confident eyewitness should be enough to convict a criminal defendant. DNA testing is relevant to answering the above question. These tests can often help to establish whether the convicted person was actually the culprit. Note, however, that such tests generally only indicate a given individual was present at the crime scene.

In the United States, 200 convicted individuals have been shown to be innocent by DNA tests, mostly on the basis of mistaken eyewitness identification. In 2011, DNA testing led to the release of Cornelius Dupree, 51 (see photo), who spent 30 years in prison for the alleged rape of a 26-year-old Dallas woman. He was convicted because he was identified as the culprit by the victim.

Unfortunately, most jurors and judges underestimate problems with eyewitness testimony. Benton et al. (2006) found judges disagreed with eyewitness experts on 60% of eyewitness issues, and jurors disagreed with the experts on 87% of them!

Eyewitness testimony can be distorted via **confirmation bias**, that is, event memory is influenced by the observer's expectations. In one study (Lindholm & Christianson, 1998), Swedish and immigrant students saw a simulated robbery in which the culprit seriously wounded a cashier. Afterwards, participants saw colour photographs of eight men (four Swedes and four immigrants). The participants were twice as likely to select an innocent immigrant as an innocent Swede. Immigrants are overrepresented in Swedish crime statistics, and this influenced participants' expectations about the criminal's likely ethnicity.

Weblink:
Bartlett's War of the Ghosts story

Bartlett (1932) argued that we have numerous schemas or packets of knowledge stored in long-term memory. These schemas lead us to form certain expectations. They can distort our memory by causing us to reconstruct an event's details based on "what must have been true" (see Chapter 10). Most people's bank-robbery schema includes information that robbers are typically male, wear disguises and dark clothes, make demands for money and have a getaway car with a driver (Tuckey & Brewer, 2003a). Tuckey and Brewer showed eyewitnesses a video of a simulated bank robbery followed by a memory test. As predicted by Bartlett's theory, eyewitnesses recalled information relevant to the bank-robbery schema better than information irrelevant to it (e.g., the colour of the getaway car).

KEY TERM

Confirmation bias
A tendency for eyewitness memory to be distorted by the eyewitness's prior expectations.

Tuckey and Brewer (2003b) focused on how eyewitnesses remembered ambiguous information about a simulated crime. For example, some eyewitnesses saw a robber's head covered by a balaclava (ski mask) so the robber's gender was

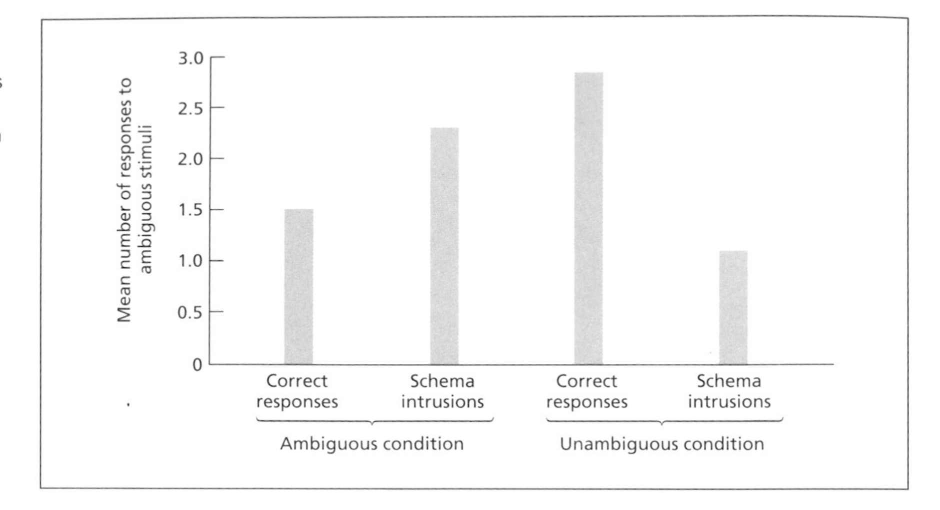

Figure 8.7
Mean correct responses and schema-consistent intrusions in the ambiguous and unambiguous conditions with cued recall.

Data from Tuckey and Brewer (2003b).

ambiguous. Eyewitnesses mostly interpreted the ambiguous information as being consistent with their bank-robbery schema (see Figure 8.7). Thus, their recall was systematically distorted by including information from their bank-robbery schema even though it did not correspond to what they had observed.

Post- and pre-event information

The most obvious explanation for eyewitnesses' inaccurate memories is that they often fail to attend fully to the crime situation. After all, it typically occurs suddenly and unexpectedly. However, Loftus and Palmer (1974) argued that eyewitness memories are fragile and can – surprisingly easily – be distorted by misleading information presented *afterwards*. This is known as the **misinformation effect**.

Findings

Loftus and Palmer (1974) showed eyewitnesses a film of a multiple-car accident. Afterwards, the eyewitnesses described what had happened and answered specific questions. Some were asked, "About how fast were the cars going when they smashed into each other?" For other participants, the word "hit" was substituted for "smashed into". The estimated speed averaged 41 mph when the verb "smashed" was used vs. 34 mph when "hit" was used. Thus, the information implicit in the question affected how the accident was remembered.

One week later, all the eyewitnesses were asked, "Did you see any broken glass?" In fact, there was no broken glass, but 32% of those previously asked about speed said they had seen broken glass. In contrast, only 14% of those asked using the verb "hit" said they had seen broken glass, and the figure was 12% for controls. Thus, our fragile event memory can be distorted by changing one word!

Ecker et al. (2010) discovered the misinformation effect was still present even when eyewitnesses were explicitly warned beforehand to avoid being influenced by misleading information. However, such warnings did serve to reduce the size of the misinformation effect.

Weblink:
Loftus and Palmer

KEY TERM

Misinformation effect
The distorting effect on eyewitness memory of misleading information presented after a crime or other event.

Eyewitness memory can also be distorted by misleading information presented *before* an event. Lindsay et al. (2004) showed eyewitnesses a video of a museum burglary. On the previous day, they listened to a narrative thematically similar (a palace burglary) or thematically dissimilar (a school field-trip to a palace) to the video. Eyewitnesses made many more errors when recalling information from the video when the narrative was thematically similar. This is potentially important, because eyewitnesses often have relevant past experiences that may distort their memory for a crime.

However, the distorting effects of misinformation may be less damaging than might be imagined. Most research has focused on distortions for peripheral or minor details (e.g., presence of broken glass) rather than central features. Memory distortions are more common following misinformation about peripheral features than about central features (Dalton & Daneman, 2006).

Theoretical explanations

How does misleading post-event information distort what eyewitnesses report? Various processes are involved. For example, there is source misattribution (Johnson et al., 1993; Lindsay, 2008). In essence, a memory probe (e.g., a question) activates memory traces overlapping with it in the information they contain. The eyewitness decides on the *source* of any activated memory on the basis of the information it contains. Source misattribution is most likely when the memories from one source resemble those from a second source. Supporting evidence was reported by Lindsay et al. (2004) in a study discussed above. Many participants showed source misattribution by intruding information from the narrative into their memory of the video. As predicted by the source misattribution account, such intrusions were much more common when the two events were similar.

Prull and Yockelson (2013) obtained a robust misinformation effect when a slide sequence was followed by a narrative containing misleading information. However, the misinformation effect was much smaller when participants were given a source-recognition test encouraging them to retrieve source information. This latter finding suggests that source misattribution is important in explaining the typical misinformation effect.

There is much evidence that consolidation (a long-lasting physiological process) leads to the formation of long-lasting memories. Reactivation of a memory trace that has undergone consolidation makes it fragile and can lead to a new consolidation process known as reconsolidation (see Chapter 6). This reconsolidation process allows the original memory trace to be altered and updated. In a study by Chan and LaPaglia (2013; see Chapter 6), some participants recalled details from a movie about a terrorist attack before receiving misleading information, whereas others did not. There was a strong misinformation effect among participants who had recalled movie details previously, but not among those who had not.

How can we explain the above findings? Reactivating memory traces from the movie led to reconsolidation in which the original memory traces were updated and perhaps "overwritten" by the misleading information. Those participants who did not recall movie details prior to receiving misleading information had no reconsolidation process and so did not exhibit a misinformation effect.

KEY TERM

Weapon focus
The finding that eyewitnesses pay so much attention to some crucial aspect of the situation (e.g., the weapon) that they ignore other details.

Related findings were reported by Edelson et al. (2011). Eyewitnesses watched a crime scene on a large screen in groups of five but all subsequent memory tests were carried out individually. When tested three days later, they showed accurate memory for the crime events. Four days after that, they were misinformed their fellow participants remembered several events differently. This was followed immediately by a memory test (Test 2) during which their brain activity was recorded. Seven days later, the participants were told the answers allegedly given by their co-observers had actually been generated at random. After that, they received another memory test (Test 3).

There are two possible reasons why participants went along with group pressure on Test 2: (1) they pretended to agree with the group; or (2) their memories had genuinely changed. Which reason is more applicable can be ascertained by considering whether participants maintained their incorrect answers on Test 3. Brain activity during Test 2 indicated that enhanced connectivity between the amygdala and the hippocampus (both centrally involved in memory formation) was associated with memories that had genuinely changed but not those that had not. These findings may well indicate that a long-lasting misinformation effect occurred only when there was a reconsolidation process that "modified the neural representation of memory" (Edelson et al., 2011, p. 108).

In sum, two of the most important factors causing the misinformation effect are source misattribution and reconsolidation. However, other factors can also be involved (Wright & Loftus, 2008). One example is the vacant slot explanation (misinformation is more likely to be accepted when related information from the original event was not stored in memory). Another example is the blend explanation (misinformation and information from the original event are integrated in memory).

Anxiety and violence

What are the effects of anxiety and violence on eyewitness memory? There is evidence for **weapon focus** – eyewitnesses attend to the criminal's weapon, which reduces their memory for other information. Loftus et al. (1987) asked participants to watch a person pointing a gun at (or handing a cheque to) a cashier and receiving cash. The participants looked more at the gun than the cheque and their memory for details unrelated to the gun/cheque was worse in the weapon condition. Biggs et al. (2013) carried out a similar study. Weapons were fixated more times than neutral objects and this was at the expense of fixating faces less often in the weapon conditions. These findings indicate weapon focus, but note that on average faces were fixated more often than weapons.

Pickel (2009) pointed out that people often attend to stimuli that are *unexpected* in the current situation (inconsistent with their schema of that situation). This impairs their memory for other stimuli. She argued that the weapon focus effect will be greater when the presence of a weapon is very unexpected. As predicted, there was a strong weapon focus effect when a criminal carrying a folding knife was female because it is unexpected to see a woman with a knife.

Fawcett et al. (2013) carried out a meta-analysis (see Glossary) of studies on weapon focus. There was a moderate effect on eyewitness memory of weapon focus. Of importance, the size of this effect was similar regardless of whether the event occurred in the laboratory or in the real world.

What are the effects of stress and anxiety on eyewitness memory? Deffenbacher et al. (2004) carried out a meta-analysis. Culprits' faces were identified 54% of the time in low-anxiety or low-stress conditions vs. 42% for high-anxiety or high-stress conditions. The average proportion of details recalled correctly was 64% in low-stress conditions and 52% in high-stress conditions. Thus, stress and anxiety generally impair eyewitness memory.

Deffenbacher et al.'s (2004) findings were supported by Valentine and Mesout (2009). Participants encountered somebody in the Horror Labyrinth at the London Dungeon. Their subsequent memory performance for the person encountered was worse among those participants experiencing most anxiety while in the Labyrinth.

Why does stress impair memory? According to Easterbrook's (1959) hypothesis, stress causes a narrowing of attention on central or important stimuli, which causes a reduction in people's ability to remember peripheral details (see Chapter 15). Yegiyan and Lang (2010) presented people with distressing pictures. As picture stressfulness increased, recognition memory for the central details improved progressively. In contrast, memory for peripheral details was much worse with highly stressful pictures than with moderately stressful ones. Thus, the findings supported Easterbrook's hypothesis.

KEY TERM

Own-age bias
The tendency for eyewitnesses to identify the culprit more often when he/she is of similar age to the eyewitness than when he/she is of a different age.

Ageing and memory

Older eyewitnesses' memory is less accurate than that of younger adults and misinformation effects are often much greater on older than on younger adults. Jacoby et al. (2005) presented misleading information to younger and older adults. The older adults had a 43% chance of producing false memories on a later recall test compared to only 4% for the younger adults.

Wright and Stroud (2002) considered differences between younger and older adults identifying the culprits after being presented with crime videos. They found an **own-age bias** – both groups had more accurate identification when the culprit was of a similar age to themselves.

What causes own-age bias? Harrison and Hole (2009) found it was due to the greater *exposure* most people have to people of their own age. Teachers (who spend hours a day exposed to children's faces) showed no evidence of own-age bias – they recognised children's faces as well as those of people of their own age. Wiese et al. (2013) found young geriatric nurses also had no own-age bias because they recognised old faces much better than did young controls as a result of their experience with older people. Using event-related potentials (ERPs; see Glossary), Wiese et al. found experience with old faces influenced later stages of face processing but not early perceptual processing.

Eyewitness identification: face recognition

The police often ask eyewitnesses to identify the person responsible for a crime from various people physically present or shown in photographs. Eyewitness identification from such line-ups is often very fallible. Valentine et al. (2003) studied the evidence from 640 eyewitnesses trying to identify suspects in 314 real line-ups. About 20% of witnesses identified a non-suspect, 40% identified the suspect and 40% failed to make an identification.

Eyewitnesses who are very confident about face identification tend to be more accurate than those less confident (Brewer & Wells, 2011). For example, Odinot et al. (2009) studied eyewitness memory for an actual supermarket robbery in the Netherlands. There was a moderate correlation of +0.38 between eyewitness confidence and accuracy.

KEY TERMS

Unconscious transference
The tendency of eyewitnesses to misidentify a familiar (but innocent) face as being the person responsible for a crime.

Other-race effect
The finding that recognition memory for same-race faces is generally more accurate than for other-race faces.

Face recognition

Eyewitness identification typically depends largely on face recognition. Face recognition is discussed in Chapter 3, but here we will discuss aspects of particular relevance to eyewitness identification. For example, eyewitnesses sometimes remember a face but fail to remember the precise circumstances in which they saw it. Ross et al. (1994) had eyewitnesses observe an event in which a bystander and the culprit were present. Eyewitnesses were three times more likely to select the bystander from a line-up than someone else not seen before from a line-up excluding the culprit. This effect is known as **unconscious transference** – a face is correctly recognised as having been seen before but incorrectly judged to be responsible for a crime.

Another finding of relevance to eyewitness identification is the **other-race effect** – the tendency for same-race faces to be identified better than other-race faces. What causes this effect? We tend to process the faces of individuals belonging to a group with which we identify (an ingroup) more than those of individuals belonging to outgroups. Shriver et al. (2008) found the usual other-race effect mostly disappeared when white American students saw photographs of men in impoverished contexts (e.g., ramshackle housing). This happened because these white faces were not regarded as belonging to the students' ingroup.

The other-race effect may occur because we find it hard to *remember* the faces of individuals belonging to different races. However, that is not a complete explanation. Megreya et al. (2011) found *perceptual* processes are also involved. British and Egyptian participants were presented with a target face and an array of ten faces (see Figure 8.8). They had to decide whether the target face was in

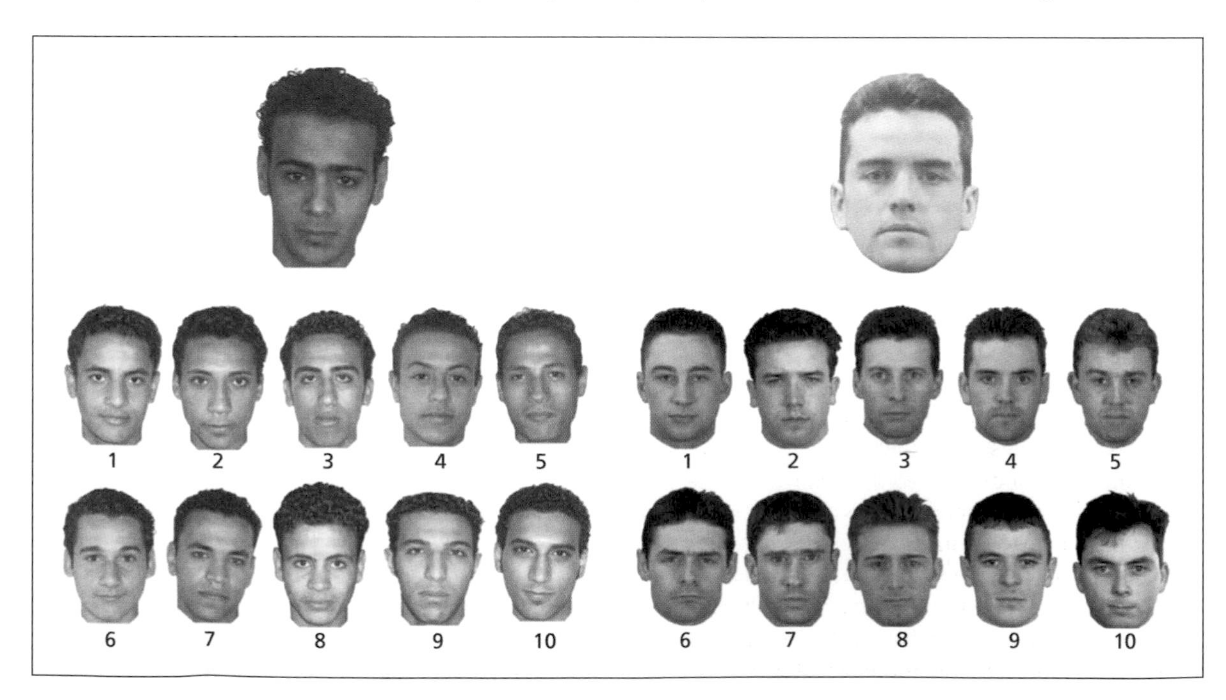

Figure 8.8
Examples of Egyptian (left) and UK (right) face-matching arrays. The task was to decide whether the person shown at the top was present in the array underneath.

From Megreya et al. (2011). © Taylor & Francis.

the array and, if so, to identify it. There were minimal demands on memory because all the photographs remained in view.

Megreya et al. (2011) found the other-race effect. Correct identifications of the target face when present in the array were 70% for same-race faces vs. 64% for other-race faces. When the target face was not present, there was mistaken identification of a non-target face 34% of the time with same-sex faces vs. 47% of the time with other-race faces.

It is much harder to recognise unfamiliar faces than familiar ones, but research has often failed to show this clearly. For example, most studies that have involved matching unfamiliar faces have used photographs taken on the same day. Megreya et al. (2013) found participants' ability to match unfamiliar faces was much worse when the photographs had been taken months apart rather than on the same day.

Jenkins et al. (2011) obtained striking evidence of the complexities of matching unfamiliar faces. They presented British participants with 40 photographs (20 of each of two Dutch celebrities unknown in the UK). The participants sorted the photographs into piles for each person shown in the photographs. On average, participants thought 7.5 different individuals were shown in the photographs! This study is discussed further in Chapter 3.

The above findings mean that photographs of the same face can show considerable *variability*. This means it is hard for eyewitnesses to make an identification on the basis of a *single* photograph as typically happens. Jenkins and Burton (2011) argued that the way forward is to *combine* information from multiple photographs of the same face to create an average face. They found with familiar faces that averaged ones were recognised significantly faster than single photographs.

Jenkins et al. (2011) made use of a computer-based system to study face recognition. It recognised 100% of faces with averaged faces compared to only 54% with individual photographs. Thus, detectives should use averaged faces (wherever possible) to maximise the ability of eyewitnesses to make accurate identifications.

From laboratory to courtroom

Can we apply findings from laboratory studies to real-life crimes? There are several differences. First, eyewitnesses are much more likely to be the victims in real life than in the laboratory. Second, it is much less stressful to watch a video of a violent crime than actually to experience it. Third, in laboratory research the consequences of an eyewitness making a mistake are trivial. However, they can literally be a matter of life or death in an American court of law.

In spite of these differences, there are important similarities. Ihlebaek et al. (2003) used a staged robbery involving two robbers with handguns. In the live condition, eyewitnesses were ordered repeatedly to "Stay down!" A video taken during the live condition was presented to eyewitnesses in the video condition. Participants in both conditions exaggerated the duration of the event and they showed similar patterns in terms of what was remembered. However, eyewitnesses in the video condition recalled more information. In another study (Pozzulo et al., 2008), eyewitnesses observed a staged theft live or via video. Correct identification of the culprit was comparable in the two conditions. However, eyewitnesses in the live condition reported more stress and arousal.

Tollestrup et al. (1994) analysed police records concerning the identifications by eyewitnesses to crimes involving fraud and robbery. Factors important in laboratory studies (e.g., weapon focus, retention interval) were also important in real-life crimes.

In sum, artificial laboratory conditions typically distort the findings only modestly. If anything, the errors in eyewitness memory obtained under laboratory conditions *underestimate* memory deficiencies for real-life events. The optimal approach is for researchers to use diverse approaches and then to combine the findings (Chae, 2010). Overall, laboratory research is relevant to the legal system.

ENHANCING EYEWITNESS MEMORY

Weblink:
The Eyewitness Identification Research Laboratory at the University of Texas

How can we increase the usefulness of the information obtained from eyewitnesses? There are several ways this can be done. Here we will initially consider how to maximise eyewitnesses' identification performance on line-ups. After that, we focus on the development of optimal interviewing techniques.

Line-ups

Line-ups can be *simultaneous* (the eyewitness sees everyone at the same time) or *sequential* (the eyewitness sees only one person at a time). Which is more effective? Steblay et al. (2011) carried out a meta-analysis (see Glossary). When the culprit was present, he/she was selected 52% of the time with simultaneous line-ups compared to 44% with sequential ones. When the culprit was absent, eyewitnesses mistakenly selected someone with simultaneous line-ups more often than with sequential ones (54% vs. 32%, respectively). Thus, eyewitnesses adopt a more stringent criterion for identification with sequential than with simultaneous line-ups.

Overall, the sequential line-up is probably preferable. The small reduction in the number of correct identifications (8%) is outweighed by the substantial reduction in the number of misidentifications (22%). Misidentifications with sequential line-ups can be further reduced by explicitly providing eyewitnesses with a not-sure option. This reduced misidentifications from 22% to only 12% (Steblay & Phillips, 2011).

Another way of minimising identification errors is to warn eyewitnesses the culprit may not be in the line-up. Steblay (1997) found in a meta-analysis that such warnings reduced mistaken identification rates in culprit-absent line-ups by 42% while reducing accurate identification rates in culprit-present line-ups by only 2%.

Cognitive interview

The police want to maximise the amount of information provided by eyewitnesses when interviewed. Psychologists have contributed substantially to achieving that goal by developing the cognitive interview (e.g., Geiselman & Fisher, 1997) based on four retrieval rules:

1 Mental reinstatement of the environment and any personal contact experience during the crime.
2 Encouraging the reporting of *every* detail including minor ones.

3 Describing the incident in several different orders (e.g., backwards in time).
4 Reporting the incident from different viewpoints, including those of other eyewitnesses. Anderson and Pichert (1978) found this strategy useful (see Chapter 10).

As we will see, the cognitive interview increases the information obtained from eyewitnesses. It is effective because it is based on our knowledge of human memory. The first two rules derive from the encoding specificity principle (Tulving, 1979; see Chapter 7). According to this principle, recall depends on the overlap or match between the *context* in which an event is witnessed and that at recall. The third and fourth rules are based on the assumption that memory traces are complex and contain several kinds of information. As a result, crime information can be retrieved using different retrieval routes.

There have been two major developments in the cognitive interview over the years (Memon et al., 2010). First, researchers developed an enhanced cognitive interview (e.g., Fisher & Geiselman, 1992). This differed from the basic cognitive interview by emphasising the importance of creating *rapport* between the interviewer and the eyewitness. Roy (1991, p. 399) indicated how this can be achieved:

> Investigators should minimise distractions, induce the eyewitness to speak slowly, allow a pause between the response and next question, tailor language to suit the individual eyewitness, follow up with interpretive comment, try to reduce eyewitness anxiety, and avoid judgmental and personal comments.

Second, the police typically use a shortened version of the cognitive interview, focusing on the first two retrieval rules discussed earlier and ignoring the third and fourth ones. This is done in part because the entire cognitive interview can be very time-consuming.

Findings

Memon et al. (2010) carried out a meta-analysis comparing the effectiveness of the cognitive interview with the standard police interview. There was a large increase in the number of details correctly recalled by eyewitnesses with the cognitive interview (basic or enhanced) compared to the standard interview. This increase was comparable whether the crime or incident was viewed live or via videotape.

Memon et al. (2010) found beneficial effects of the cognitive interview were reduced when the situation was highly arousing. They were also reduced when there was a long retention interval between the incident and the interview. However, the cognitive interview remained effective even with high arousal and a long retention interval.

The cognitive interview had only one negative effect on eyewitness performance. There was a fairly small but significant increase in recall of incorrect details compared to the standard interview.

Advocates of the cognitive interview often recommend the eyewitness recalls the event with his/her eyes closed. Vredeveldt et al. (2011) obtained evidence this enhances recall. Why is eye-closure beneficial? It reduces cognitive load on the eyewitness and reduces distraction.

KEY TERMS

Retrospective memory
Memory for events, people and so on experienced in the past.

Prospective memory
Remembering to carry out some intended action in the absence of an explicit reminder to do so.

Does the cognitive interview reduce the adverse effects of misleading information on eyewitness memory? Memon et al. (2009) found it did not when the misleading information was presented *before* the cognitive interview. However, the impact of misleading information on eyewitness memory was reduced when presented *after* the cognitive interview.

Is it essential to use all components of the cognitive interview? The answer is "No". Colomb and Ginet (2012) found mental reinstatement of the situation and reporting all the details both enhanced recall. However, altering the eyewitness's perspective and changing the order in which the information was recalled were ineffective. Dando et al. (2011) found requiring eyewitnesses to recall information in a backward temporal order *reduced* the number of correct details recalled and *increased* recall errors. This happened because it disrupted the temporal organisation of eyewitnesses' memory for the crime.

Evaluation

The cognitive interview has the advantage of having a well-established theoretical and empirical basis. There is compelling evidence it is an effective method for obtaining as much accurate information as possible from eyewitnesses under most circumstances. Some progress has been made in identifying the components of the cognitive interview that are most responsible for its effectiveness.

What are the limitations with the cognitive interview? First, the small increased amount of incorrect eyewitness recall can lead detectives to misinterpret the evidence.

Second, recreating the context at the time of the incident is a key ingredient in the cognitive interview. However, context reinstatement can have a negative effect on *recognition* memory by increasing the perceived familiarity of non-target faces (Wong & Read, 2011).

Case study:
Cognitive interview and eyewitness confidence

Third, the cognitive interview is less effective when the event was stressful than when it was not. It is also less effective when there is a long delay between the event and the interview.

PROSPECTIVE MEMORY

Most memory studies have focused on **retrospective memory**, in which the emphasis is on the past, especially on people's ability to remember events they have experienced or knowledge acquired previously. In contrast, **prospective memory** is "the cognitive function we use for formulating plans and promises, for retaining them, and for recollecting them subsequently either at the right time or on the occurrence of appropriate cues" (Graf, 2012, pp. 7–8). Examples include remembering to meet a friend at a coffee shop or attend a revision session for a course in psychology.

We can see the importance of prospective memory by considering a tragic case discussed by Einstein and McDaniel (2005, p. 286):

> After a change in his usual routine, an adoring father forgot to turn toward the daycare centre and instead drove his usual route to work at the university. Several hours later, his infant son, who had been quietly asleep in the back seat, was dead.

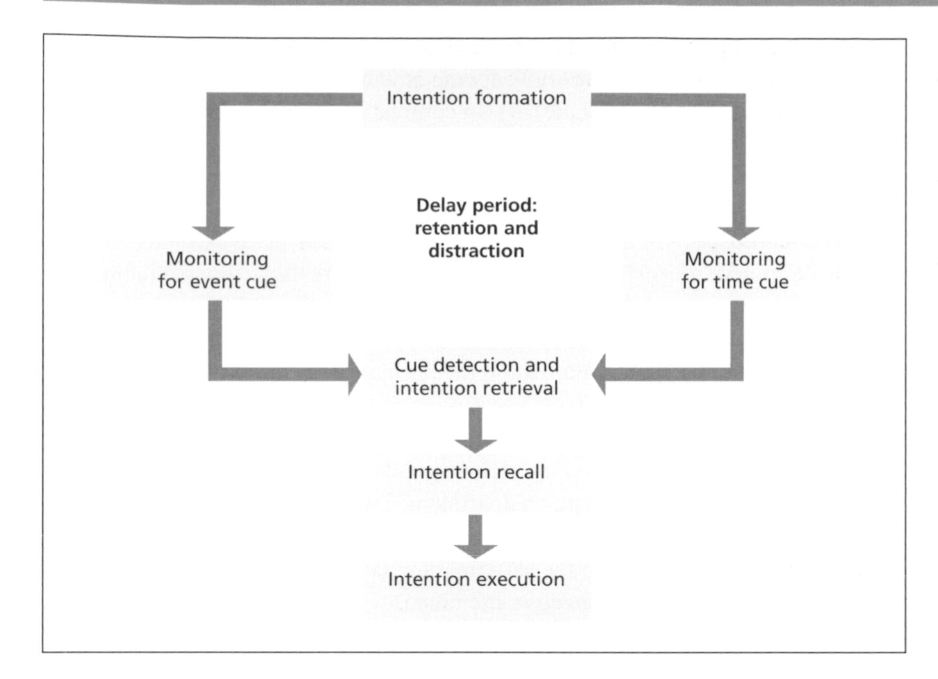

Figure 8.9
A model of the component processes involved in prospective memory. Intention formation is followed by monitoring for event and/or time cues. Successful monitoring leads to cue detection and intention retrieval, intention recall and intention execution.

From Zogg et al. (2012). Reprinted with permission of Springer Science + Business Media.

Stages in prospective memory

Prospective memory involves several separate processes or stages and so there are various ways prospective memory can fail. Zogg et al. (2012) summarised the views of several theorists (see Figure 8.9):

1 *Intention formation*: At this stage, the individual forms or encodes an intention linked to a specific cue (e.g., "I will talk to my friend when I see him").
2 *Retention interval*: There is a delay between intention formation and intention execution of between minutes and weeks. During that time, there is typically some environmental monitoring for task-relevant cues (e.g., sighting your friend).
3 *Cue detection and intention retrieval*: The individual detects and recognises the relevant cue; this is followed by self-initiated retrieval of the appropriate intention.
4 *Intention recall*: The individual retrieves the intention from retrospective memory. There may be problems because of the intention's complexity, its relationship to other stored intentions, or the presence of competing intentions.
5 *Intention execution*: This is typically fairly automatic and undemanding.

Prospective memory vs. retrospective memory

How different are retrospective memory and prospective memory? People certainly interpret failures of the two types of memory differently. They interpret failures of prospective memory involving promises to another person as indicating poor motivation and reliability (Graf, 2012). In contrast, failures of retrospective memory are attributed to a poor memory. Thus, deficient prospective memory means "flaky person", whereas deficient retrospective memory means "faulty brain" (Graf, 2012).

KEY TERMS

Time-based prospective memory
A form of **prospective memory** that involves remembering to carry out an intended action at the appropriate time.

Event-based prospective memory
A form of **prospective memory** that involves remembering to perform an intended action (e.g., buying groceries) when the circumstances are appropriate.

There are several other differences. First, retrospective memory generally involves remembering *what* we know about something and can be high in informational content (Baddeley et al., 2015). In contrast, prospective memory typically focuses on *when* to do something and has low informational content. This low informational content helps to ensure non-performance of the prospective-memory task is *not* due to retrospective memory failure.

Second, prospective memory is more relevant to the plans or goals we form for our daily activities. Third, more external cues are typically available with retrospective memory than prospective memory. Fourth, as Moscovitch (2008, p. 309) pointed out, "Research on prospective memory is about the only major enterprise in memory research in which the problem is not memory itself, but the uses to which memory is put."

Remembering and forgetting often involve prospective *and* retrospective memory. Suppose you agree to buy various goods at the supermarket for yourself and friends with whom you share an apartment. Two things need to happen. First, you must remember your intention to go to the supermarket (prospective memory). Even if you remember to go to the supermarket, you then have to remember what you had agreed to buy (retrospective memory).

Crawford et al. (2003) identified separate prospective and retrospective memory factors from a questionnaire designed to assess prospective and retrospective memory. There was also a general memory factor based on elements of prospective and retrospective memory.

Event-based vs. time-based prospective memory

There is an important distinction between time-based and event-based prospective memory. **Time-based prospective memory** is assessed by tasks that involve remembering to perform a given action at a particular time (e.g., phone a friend at 8 pm). In contrast, **event-based prospective memory** is assessed by tasks that involve remembering to perform an action in the appropriate circumstances (e.g., passing on a message when you see someone).

There is much more research on event-based prospective memory. With event-based tasks, researchers can manipulate the precise nature and timing of cues indicating participants should perform the intended action. That provides more control over the conditions of retrieval than is possible with time-based tasks. In the real world, the requirement to use prospective memory typically occurs while individuals are busily involved in performing some unrelated task. The set-up in most laboratory research is similar in that participants are generally engaged in an unrelated ongoing task at the same time as performing a prospective-memory task.

Sellen et al. (1997) compared time-based and event-based prospective memory in a work environment in which participants had badges containing buttons. They were told to press their button at a pre-arranged time (time-based task) or when in a pre-specified place (event-based task). Performance was better in the event-based task than the time-based task (52% vs. 33%, respectively). Sellen et al. argued that event-based tasks are easier because the intended actions are more likely to be triggered by external cues. Kim and Mayhorn (2008) supported that argument, finding event-based prospective memory was superior under laboratory and naturalistic conditions.

Hicks et al. (2005) confirmed event-based tasks are less demanding than time-based ones. However, both kinds of tasks were more demanding when the task was ill-specified (e.g., detect animal words) than when it was well-specified (e.g., detect the words "nice" and "hit"). A well-specified time-based task was no more demanding than an ill-specified event-based task.

The strategies used on time-based and event-based tasks often differ considerably. An important difference is that the occurrence of the prospective-memory cues is typically much more *predictable* on time-based tasks. As a result, people generally engage in only sporadic monitoring of prospective-memory cues on time-based tasks, with this monitoring increasing as the occurrence of the cue approaches (Tarantino et al., submitted). In contrast, there was much more evidence of continuous monitoring on event-based tasks because of the unpredictability concerning the occurrence of the cue.

Cona et al. (2012) also reported clear-cut differences between event-based and time-based tasks. On the ongoing task, five letters were presented and participants decided whether the second and fourth letters were the same or different. At the same time, they performed an event-based task (detect the letter "B" in the second or fourth position) or a time-based task (respond every five minutes). Cona et al. (2012) used event-related potentials (ERPs; see Glossary) to assess the patterns of brain activity on each trial.

What did Cona et al. (2012) find? First, the greater amplitude of the ERPs 130–180 ms after stimulus onset in the event-based condition probably reflected the greater use of attentional resources in that condition (see Figure 8.10). Second, the greater amplitude of the ERPs 400–600 ms after stimulus onset in the event-based condition was probably due to the greater frequency of target checking in that condition. Overall, there was greater processing activity in the event-based condition.

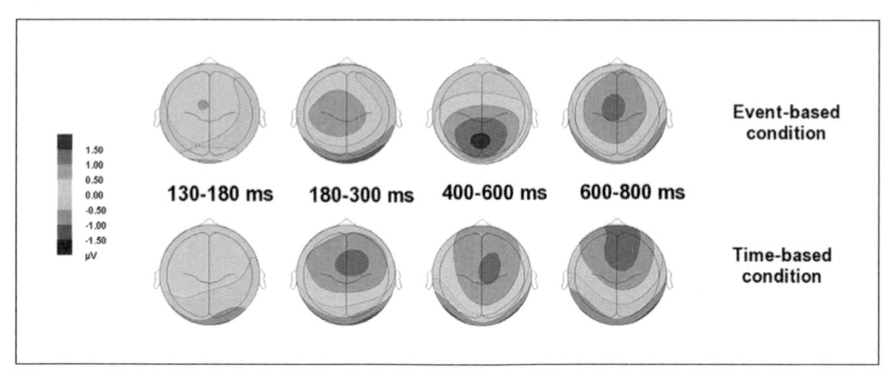

Figure 8.10
Event-related potential (ERP) amplitudes at various post-stimulus time intervals in event-based and time-based conditions. Areas exhibiting high ERP amplitudes are shown in dark red.

From Cona et al. (2012). Reprinted with permission.

Prospective memory in real life

In this section, prospective memory in various groups of people will be discussed. In the box below, we consider people (e.g., pilots, air traffic controllers) for whom forgetting of intended actions can easily prove fatal. We also consider people regarded as having poor prospective memory.

IN THE REAL WORLD: PLANE CRASHES – PILOTS AND AIR TRAFFIC CONTROLLERS

Dismukes and Nowinski (2006) studied pilot errors involving memory failures. Out of 75 incidents or accidents, there were failures of prospective memory in 74 cases! There was only one failure of retrospective memory because air pilots have excellent knowledge and memory of the operations needed to fly a plane.

Here is a concrete example of a plane crash due to failure of prospective memory. On 31 August 1988, a Boeing 727 (Flight 1141) was held in a long queue awaiting departure from Dallas-Fort Worth airport. The air traffic controller unexpectedly told the crew to move up past the other planes to the runway. This caused the crew to forget to set the wing flaps and leading edge slat to 15 degrees (a failure of prospective memory). As a result, the plane crashed beyond the end of the runway leading to several deaths.

Dismukes and Nowinski (2006) found pilots were most likely to show failures of prospective memory if interrupted while carrying out a plan of action. Unsurprisingly, commercial pilots interrupted while flying a simulator made 53% more errors than those who were not interrupted (Latorella, 1998).

Dodhia and Dismukes (2009) found interruptions can seriously impair prospective memory. Participants were instructed to return to an interrupted task after completing a different task. When there was a ten-second pause after the interruption, 88% of participants returned to the interrupted task. The comparable figure was 65% when there was a four-second pause just before the interruption, but only 48% when there was no pause before or after the interruption.

What do the above findings mean? People benefit from having a few seconds to form a new plan when an interruption changes the situation, but pilots often do not have that amount of time available. It is also important to have a few seconds at the end of the interruption to retrieve the intention of returning to the interrupted task. Trafton and Monk (2007) discussed research showing that individuals interrupted when performing a task often engage in prospective rehearsal (e.g., "What was I about to do?"). Such rehearsal maintains the intention or goal in an active state and so enhances performance after the interruption but is hard to use when time is very limited.

Air traffic control is an excellent example of an occupation in which individuals must remember to perform intended actions while monitoring a display (Loft et al., 2011). It is thus no surprise that 38% of the memory errors reported by controllers involve failures to complete intentions (Shorrock, 2005).

Here is a case of air traffic controller error causing a fatal aircraft accident (Dismukes & Nowinski, 2006). At Los Angeles International airport one evening in 1991, a tower controller cleared one aircraft to position and hold on runway 24L while clearing other aircraft to cross the other end of the runway. Unfortunately, there were various communication delays and visibility was poor because of the haze and glare. The tower controller forgot to clear the first aircraft to take off but did clear another aircraft to land on runway 24L. This aircraft crashed into the stationary plane on that runway, destroying both planes and killing 34 people.

Loft and Remington (2010) used a simulated air traffic control task and distinguished between well-practised or strong routines and less practised weak routines. Prospective memory errors were more common when participants had to deviate from strong rather than weak routines. This effect is known as *habit capture* – we are much more likely to carry out well-practised routines in a fairly automatic fashion. Pilots and air traffic controllers devote much of their time to habitual tasks, which can cause prospective memory failures when something unexpected happens. In contrast, there is very little emphasis on habitual tasks in most laboratory studies (Dismukes, 2012).

Loft et al. (2013) used a simulated air traffic control situation in which participants had to deviate from the normal routine when dealing with certain target planes. Performance on this prospective-memory task improved when flashing visual aids accompanied the appearance of the target planes. However, these flashing visual aids sometimes led to impaired performance in dealing with non-target planes, possibly because they reduced the allocation of attention to those planes.

Obsessive-compulsive disorder and checking behaviour

Most patients with obsessive-compulsive disorder have checking compulsions. They check repeatedly they have locked their front door, that the gas has been turned off and so on. In spite of this repeated checking, they are uncertain whether they have actually performed their intended actions.

How can we explain checking behaviour? Perhaps obsessional individuals have poor *retrospective* memory ability that causes them to forget whether they have recently engaged in checking behaviour. In fact, however, most findings indicate compulsive checkers do *not* differ from controls in retrospective memory (Cuttler & Graf, 2009a). Cuttler and Graf also considered **meta-memory** (knowledge and beliefs about one's own memory). Meta-memory concerning retrospective memory was generally comparable for compulsive checkers and controls.

An alternative explanation is that checkers have poor *prospective* memory. Checkers have impaired performance on event-based and time-based prospective-memory tasks (Cuttler & Graf, 2009b). What causes such performance impairments? One important factor is meta-memory in the form of confidence about one's prospective memory. Cuttler et al. (2013) provided participants with fake feedback indicating their prospective memory performance was poor. This caused diminished confidence in their prospective memory ability and an increased urge to engage in checking behaviour.

It is possible poor prospective memory leads obsessionals to engage in excessive checking. However, it is also possible excessive checking leads to poor prospective memory. Suppose you check several times every day you have locked your front door. You would obviously remember you have checked it hundreds or thousands of times. However, you might well be unsure whether you have checked your front door *today* because of all the competing memories.

Van den Hout and Kindt (2004) asked some (but not all) participants to engage in repeated checking of a virtual gas stove. Those who had checked repeatedly had less vivid and detailed memories of what had happened on the final trial. Linkovski et al. (2013) carried out a similar study. They also assessed participants' level of inhibitory control. They did this because obsessional patients have deficient inhibitory control, which may lead to intrusive thoughts and memory problems.

What did Linkovski et al. (2013) find? Repeated checking did not impair prospective memory performance but did reduce memory vividness and detail and

KEY TERM

Meta-memory
Beliefs and knowledge about one's own memory including strategies for learning and memory.

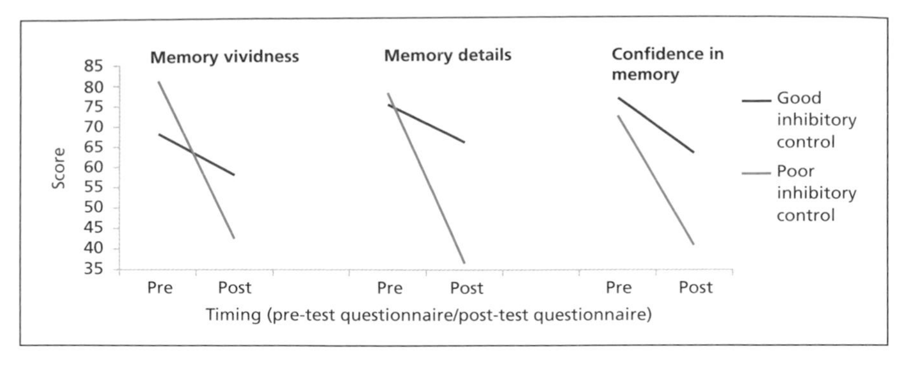

Figure 8.11
Self-reported memory vividness, memory details and confidence in memory for individuals with good and poor inhibitory control before (pre-) and after (post-) repeated checking.
From Linkovski et al. (2013). Reprinted with permission of Elsevier.

also lowered participants' confidence in their memory. These effects were all much stronger in participants with poor inhibitory control (see Figure 8.11).

In sum, several factors explain why obsessionals engage in compulsive checking. They have poor prospective memory, low confidence in their own memory and deficient inhibitory control. Their repeated checking further diminishes their confidence in their memory.

THEORETICAL PERSPECTIVES ON PROSPECTIVE MEMORY

Does successful prospective memory performance *always* involve active and capacity-consuming monitoring (e.g., attention)? According to some theorists (e.g., Smith & Bayen, 2005), the answer is "Yes", whereas for others (e.g., Einstein & McDaniel, 2005) the answer is "Sometimes".

We start with Smith and Bayen's (2005) preparatory attentional and memory processes (PAM) theory, according to which prospective memory requires two processes:

1. A capacity-consuming monitoring process, which starts when an individual forms an intention and is maintained until the required action is performed.
2. Retrospective-memory processes that ensure we remember what action is to be performed on the prospective-memory task.

It is implausible we *always* use preparatory attentional processes when trying to remember some future action. Smith et al. (2007) accepted we are not constantly engaged in preparatory attentional processing over long periods of time. However, they argued that retrieval of intentions on prospective-memory tasks always incurs a cost and is never automatic.

Einstein and McDaniel (2005) put forward a multi-process theory, according to which various cognitive processes (including attentional processes) can be used to perform prospective-memory tasks. However, the detection of cues for response will typically be automatic (and thus not involve attentional processes) when the following four criteria (especially the first one) are fulfilled:

1 The ongoing task (performed at the same time as the prospective-memory task) stimulates processing of the target event on the prospective-memory task.
2 The cue and the to-be-performed action are highly associated.
3 The cue is conspicuous or salient.
4 The intended action is simple.

Einstein and McDaniel (2005) distinguished between ongoing tasks that encourage processing of the target event on the prospective-memory task (focal tasks) and those that do not (non-focal tasks). According to McDaniel and Einstein (2011), frontal brain systems involved in planning or monitoring for cues are much more important with non-focal ongoing tasks. Ageing especially impairs frontal functioning (higher-level cognitive processes) and so ageing should have a greater negative impact on prospective memory with non-focal tasks. Indeed, there should be little age-related decline with focal tasks. However, Uttl (2011) found in a meta-analysis (see Glossary) there was a substantial age-related decline in prospective memory with focal tasks. Why was this? The most likely answer is that even focal tasks generally require the use of cognitive resources (e.g., retrieval of the intention). Uttl's findings provide very little support for McDaniel and Einstein's (2011) prediction.

Scullin et al. (2013) developed Einstein and McDaniel's (2005) theory in their dynamic multi-process framework. According to Scullin et al., two different cognitive processes can underlie successful prospective memory performance:

1 *Monitoring*: This involves top-down attentional control to search for cues indicating the prospective memory action should be performed.
2 *Spontaneous retrieval*: This involves bottom-up processing triggered by processing a cue.

What determines which process is used? Scullin et al. (2013) argued that monitoring is used primarily when prospective-memory cues are *expected*. The essence of their approach is shown in Figure 8.12. Suppose someone wants to post a package after work. Cues present at work (e.g., spotting a letter on a colleague's desk) may cause spontaneous retrieval of the intention. However, this does not lead to monitoring because there is no opportunity at work to send the package. It is only after work that spontaneous retrieval leads to monitoring (Examples 1 and 2). In Example 3, an individual intends to deliver a message to a colleague when seeing him. There is no monitoring when the colleague is not expected (e.g., in the coffee shop). However, the intention is spontaneously retrieved when she walks past the colleague's cubicle and this triggers monitoring and a search for the colleague.

Findings

It is generally agreed monitoring processes associated with prospective memory are cognitively demanding. As a result, performance on an ongoing task should typically be disrupted by a prospective-memory task requiring monitoring performed at the same time. Smith (2003) found performance on an ongoing task was 45% slower for participants also performing a prospective-memory task than for those only performing the ongoing task. Monitoring is likely to fail on some trials. When that happens, the cognitive demands of monitoring are absent and so

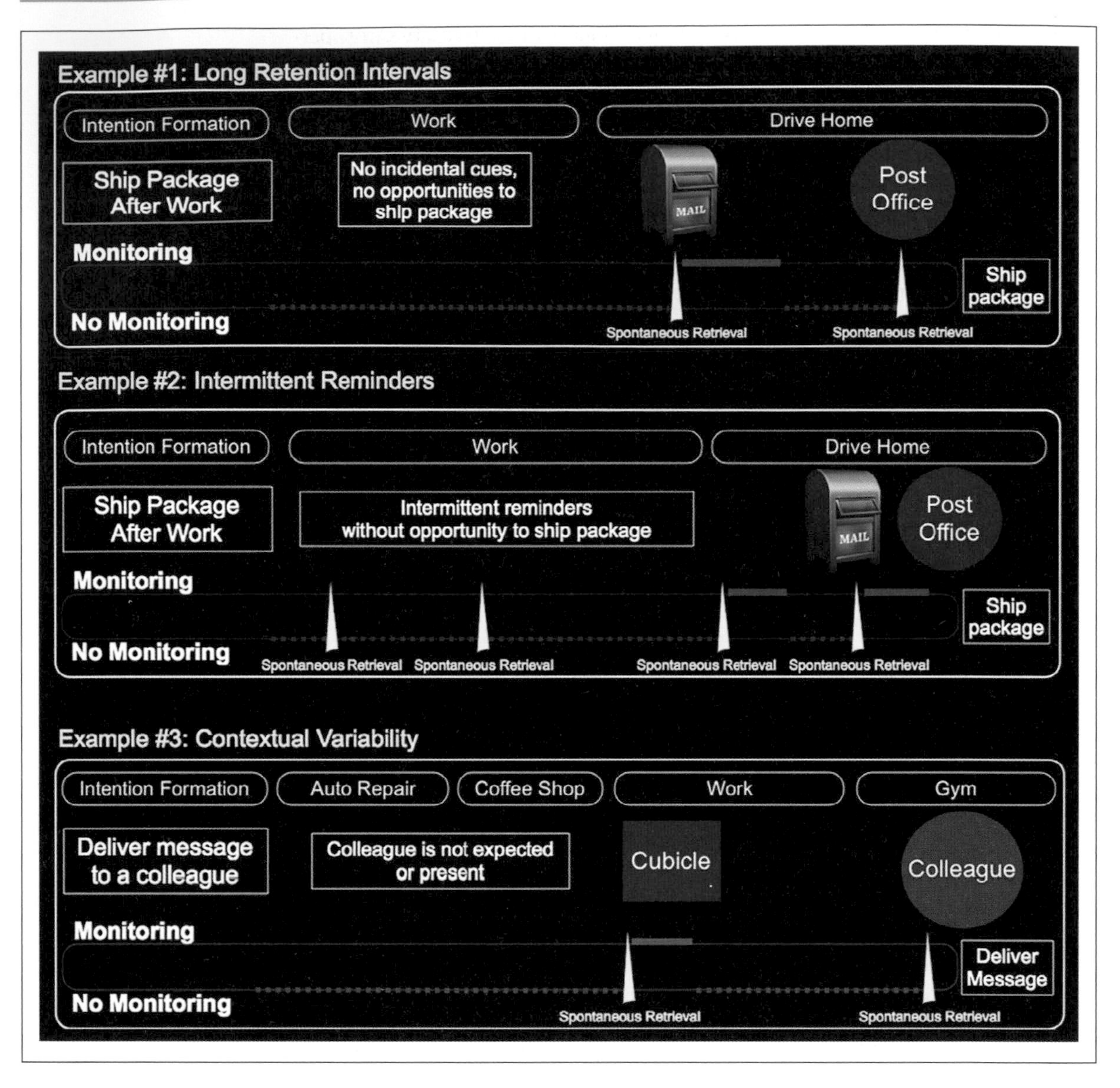

Figure 8.12
The dynamic multi-process framework. The three examples illustrate various ways in which active monitoring and spontaneous retrieval support carrying out prospective-memory intentions. See additional information in the text.
From Scullin et al. (2013). Reprinted with permission of Elsevier.

performance on the ongoing task should improve. That is precisely what Gilbert et al. (2013) found.

Does automatic cue detection occur in prospective memory with focal tasks? We will consider research of direct relevance to Smith et al.'s (2007, p. 735) statement: "Successful performance of a prospective-memory task accompanied by convincing evidence of no disruption of a sufficiently sensitive and demanding background task . . . would falsify the PAM theory." Smith et al. used a very simple prospective-memory task (pressing the "P" key when a pink stimulus was presented). In spite of its simplicity, this task had a disruptive effect on performance speed of the ongoing task. This apparently supports the PAM theory's assumption that prospective memory always requires some processing capacity.

Knight et al. (2011) reported findings supportive of multi-process theory. The ongoing task involved lexical decision, and the prospective-memory task was to detect animal names starting with "C". The novel twist was that participants were told the prospective-memory task would *only* be required later in the experiment. This was done to see what would happen when monitoring and attentional processes were not involved.

What did Knight et al. (2011) find? Knowing a prospective-memory task would be required later had no effect on overall performance speed on the ongoing lexical decision task. Thus, there was no active monitoring of the letter strings on the lexical decision task. However, targets from the subsequent prospective-memory task (e.g., *cougar*) were spontaneously noticed and recognised on a recognition-memory test. Thus, as predicted by multi-process theory, prospective-memory cues can be noticed without conscious monitoring.

Support for the notion that prospective memory can involve top-down monitoring or bottom-up spontaneous retrieval was reported by McDaniel et al. (2013). The ongoing task involved semantic processing and was performed at the same time as a prospective-memory task. There were two such tasks:

1 Respond to a given syllable (e.g., *tor* as in *tornado* or *history*); it was assumed to require top-down monitoring because its demands differed substantially from those of the ongoing task. This was the non-focal condition.
2 Respond to a specific word (e.g., *table*); this task was assumed to depend on bottom-up spontaneous retrieval because its demands resembled those of the ongoing task (i.e., process word meaning). This was the focal condition.

McDaniel et al. (2013) argued that the monitoring required to perform non-focal task (1) would involve top-down attentional control. As a result, there would be *sustained* activity in the anterior prefrontal cortex, an area associated with attentional control. In contrast, the lesser demands of focal task (2) would mean there would be only *transient* activation in the relevant brain areas (e.g., anterior prefrontal cortex). That is precisely what they found (see Figure 8.13). These findings support the multi-process theory.

Scullin et al. (2013) tested their dynamic multi-process framework. Participants were given the prospective-memory task of responding whenever the word *table* or *horse* was presented on any of three separate ongoing tasks. According to their framework, participants should engage in monitoring much more often in contexts in which prospective-memory cues were *expected* than in contexts in which such cues were not expected. As predicted, participants showed more monitoring on any given ongoing task if they detected the first prospective-memory cue on that task (and so expected further cues) than if they failed to detect the first cue.

Evaluation

Much theoretical progress has been made. There is good support for multi-process theory, especially the assumption that prospective memory can involve either spontaneous retrieval or monitoring. As predicted by multi-process theory,

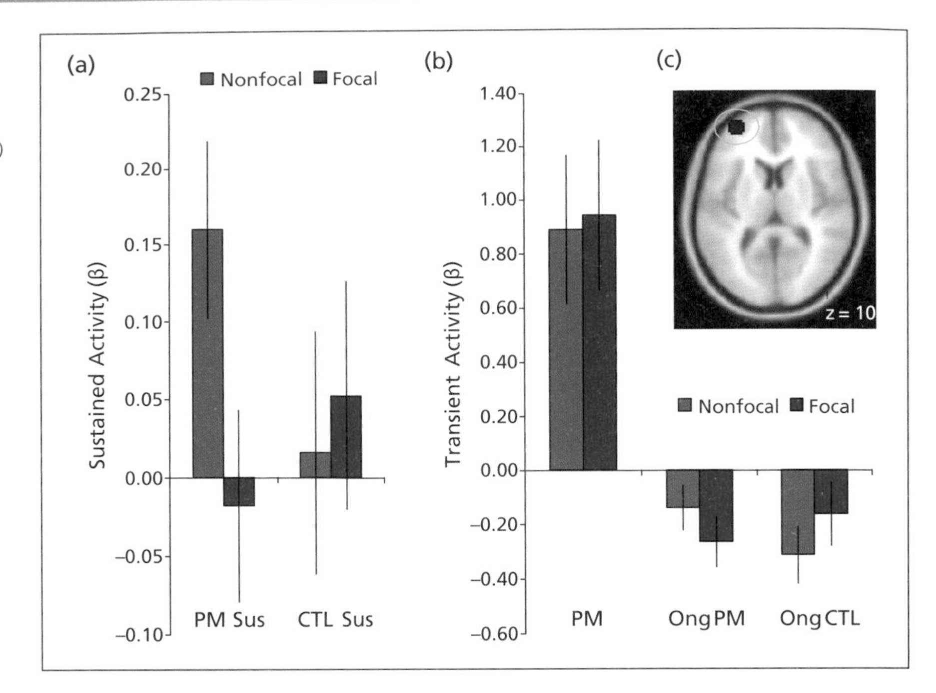

Figure 8.13
(a) Sustained (PM Sus) and (b) transient (PM) activity in the left anterior prefrontal cortex (c) for non-focal (blue) and focal (red) prospective memory (PM) tasks. The other conditions shown (i.e., CTL, Ong PM and Ong CTL) are not of theoretical relevance.

From McDaniel (2013). Reprinted with permission of the Association for Psychological Science.

spontaneous retrieval occurs when the prospective-memory task is easy, and is sometimes relatively automatic (e.g., Knight et al., 2011). Of importance, the dynamic multi-process framework indicates monitoring occurs much more often when prospective-memory cues are expected rather than unexpected. General limitations of theory and research on prospective memory are discussed shortly.

Cognitive neuroscience: prefrontal cortex

We have already seen the prefrontal cortex is involved in prospective memory (especially when monitoring is involved). Burgess et al. (2000) considered 65 brain-damaged patients having problems with prospective memory, finding various frontal regions were damaged. Of importance, BA10 (located at the front of the brain and also known as rostral prefrontal cortex) was involved in the maintenance of intentions. In contrast, the retrospective-memory component of prospective-memory tasks (i.e., remembering which action needs to be carried out) was based in the anterior and posterior cingulate.

Gilbert et al. (2006) carried out a meta-analysis (see Glossary). They identified the regions within BA10 associated with three processes relevant to prospective memory. First, episodic memory retrieval was associated with lateral BA10 activations. Second, coordinating two processing demands involved anterior (at the front) BA10. Third, self-reflection involved activation within medial BA10. Thus, several cognitive processes involved in prospective memory depend on BA10.

In another review, Burgess et al. (2011) confirmed the importance of BA10. They emphasised it would be "exceptionally inefficient" if prospective memory involved unique processes not shared with other cognitive activities. For example, anterior BA10, which is consistently activated on prospective-memory tasks, is also typically activated in studies of future thinking or mental time travel.

Improving prospective memory

There are several ways of improving prospective memory. Failures of prospective memory occurring when we are interrupted during task performance can be reduced by forming an explicit intention to resume the interrupted task as soon as possible (Dodhia & Dismukes, 2009). Dismukes (2012) identified several other practical measures such as creating distinctive reminder cues and placing them in locations so they will be seen at the appropriate time to carry out the intention. For example, if you need to take a book into college tomorrow, you could leave it close to your keys the evening before.

One of the most-used techniques for enhancing prospective memory involves **implementation intentions**. Implementation intentions "specify the when, where, and how of responses leading to goal attainment" (Gollwitzer, 1999, p. 494). For example, you might find it easier to remember to take your medicine every day if you formed the intention to take it immediately after brushing your teeth at night.

Gollwitzer and Sheeran (2006) found in a meta-analysis that implementation intentions greatly increased the probability of successfully completing intentions. Gollwitzer (1999) argued that forming an implementation intention is like forming an "instant habit". As a result, implementation intentions should reduce the processing costs when intentions are retrieved on a prospective-memory task.

McFarland and Glisky (2012) tested the above prediction. Participants were asked trivia questions as their main task, and prospective memory involved detecting occasional usage of the word "state" in these questions. In addition, participants listened to digits and responded when they heard two consecutive odd ones. Performance on the prospective-memory task was better in the implementation intention than the control condition (54% detection rate vs. 31%, respectively). In addition, participants in the implementation intention condition detected more pairs of odd digits than controls (59% vs. 35%, respectively). Thus, implementation intentions led to relatively automatic identification of targets on the prospective-memory task, thereby freeing up processing resources to detect pairs of odd digits.

Rummel et al. (2012) found participants who had received implementation intention instructions performed better on a prospective-memory task (e.g., detecting *peach* or *tennis* within an ongoing task). They hypothesised this occurred because implementation intentions produced relatively *automatic* retrieval of intentions. This hypothesis was tested by having trials on which participants were told *not* to respond to target words from the prospective-memory task. These target words caused more disruption to the ongoing task for participants previously given implementation intentions because they were more likely to retrieve their intentions spontaneously and automatically.

KEY TERM

Implementation intentions
Action plans designed consciously to achieve some goal (e.g., healthier eating) based on specific information concerning where, when and how the goal will be achieved.

Overall evaluation

Impressive progress has been made in understanding prospective memory in several ways. First, the number and nature of the processes of prospective memory have been identified with increasing clarity. Second, reasons for prospective memory failures in various groups, including pilots, air traffic controllers and obsessional individuals, have been identified.

Third, there has been much theoretical progress. Most research is consistent with multi-process theory, including its assumption that spontaneous detection of target cues is possible. As indicated by the dynamic multi-process framework, monitoring typically occurs in contexts in which individuals expect prospective-memory cues. Fourth, the cognitive neuroscience approach is increasingly identifying the brain areas associated with different prospective-memory processes. Fifth, researchers are developing a new field of "prospection" or future thinking including prospective memory.

What are the limitations of research on prospective memory? First, participants in most laboratory experiments lack any strong incentive to perform intended actions as instructed by the experimenter. In contrast, the incentives in real life can include preserving friendships and even saving lives (e.g., air traffic controllers).

Second, the differences between prospective and retrospective memory are sometimes exaggerated. The two types of memory share common features (e.g., responding in the light of what has been learned previously) and many prospective-memory tasks also involve retrospective memory.

Third, there are important differences between prospective memory in real life and in the laboratory. First, we often need to maintain our intentions for much longer periods of time in everyday life. This matters because attentional and monitoring processes are less important (and long-term memory much more important) when the retention interval is long (e.g., Kvavilashvili & Fisher, 2007). Second, participants in laboratory studies typically know the task context in which prospective-memory cues will be presented. In the real world, in contrast, we often do not know for sure the context in which we will need to carry out our prospective-memory intention.

CHAPTER SUMMARY

- **Introduction.** What people remember in traditional memory research is largely determined by the experimenter's demands for accuracy. In contrast, what we remember in everyday life is determined by our personal goals. Tailoring our message to create an impression can cause subsequent memory distortions. Memory research should strive for generalisability and representativeness. The distinction between traditional and everyday memory research is imprecise.
- **Autobiographical memory: introduction.** Autobiographical memories generally have greater personal significance and complexity than episodic memories. Autobiographical memory helps to maintain social bonds and a sense of self-continuity. Flashbulb memories are perceived as being more vivid than other memories, even though such memories are often inaccurate and exhibit only moderate consistency. Most evidence suggests flashbulb memories resemble other memories in their susceptibility to interference and forgetting.
- **Memories across the lifetime.** The first stage of childhood amnesia is absolute amnesia (i.e., no recall) for memories of the first two years of life, which probably occurs because the cognitive self only emerges towards the end of the second year of life. Absolute amnesia

is followed by relative amnesia for the preschool years, which comes to an end when children have a good command of language. The reminiscence bump is much stronger for positive memories than negative ones, which occurs because the retrieval of autobiographical memories is often guided by the life script.

- **Theoretical approaches to autobiographical memory**. According to the self-memory system model, autobiographical information is stored hierarchically. An individual's goals and personality influence the retrieval of autobiographical memories. Autobiographical memories can be accessed via direct or generative retrieval. The prefrontal cortex (associated with controlled processing) and the amygdala (involved in emotional processing) are activated during autobiographical retrieval. Several interconnected brain networks involved in autobiographical retrieval have been identified. Depressed individuals exhibit over-general autobiographical memory, which is due in part to avoidant coping. Non-depressed individuals with over-general autobiographical memory are at risk of developing depression.
- **Eyewitness testimony**. Eyewitness memory is influenced by several factors, including confirmation bias, stress and ageing. Weapons attract attention because they are threatening and/or unexpected (weapon focus). The misinformation effect is due in part to source misattribution and memory updating. Eyewitness memory for faces is affected by the cross-race effect. It is also affected by difficulties in recognising a given unfamiliar face from different photographs of the same person.
- **Improving eyewitness memory**. Culprits are slightly more likely to be identified from simultaneous than from sequential line-ups, but there are many more false alarms with simultaneous line-ups. The cognitive interview leads eyewitnesses to produce many more detailed memories at the expense of a small increase in inaccurate memories. Mental reinstatement and the requirement to report all details are both crucial to the success of the cognitive interview.
- **Prospective memory**. Prospective memory involves successive stages of intention formation, monitoring, cue detection, intention retrieval and retrieval execution. Event-based prospective memory is often better than time-based prospective memory because the intended actions are more likely to be triggered by external cues. Many failures of prospective memory occur when individuals are interrupted while carrying out an action plan and have insufficient time to form a new plan. Obsessional individuals engage in compulsive checking in part because they have problems with prospective memory. They lack confidence in their own prospective

memory, and this lack of confidence becomes more marked as a result of repeated checking.

- **Theoretical perspectives on prospective memory.** According to PAM theory, successful prospective memory performance always requires monitoring for targets. In contrast, multi-process theory claims prospective memory can involve top-down monitoring or bottom-up spontaneous retrieval. The evidence favours the multi-process approach. Evidence from brain-damaged patients and functional neuroimaging indicates that the frontal lobes (especially BA10) have a central role in prospective memory. Implementation intentions enhance prospective memory performance in part by facilitating relatively automatic retrieval of intentions.

Further reading

- Baddeley, A., Eysenck, M.W. & Anderson, M.C. (2015). *Memory* (2nd edn). Hove: Psychology Press. This textbook provides detailed coverage of research and theory on all the main topics discussed in this chapter.
- Berntsen, D. & Rubin, D.C. (eds) (2012). *Understanding autobiographical memory: Theories and approaches*. Cambridge: Cambridge University Press. This edited volume has interesting contributions by leading memory experts including Martin Conway, Alan Baddeley, Morris Moscovitch and Dorthe Berntsen.
- Dismukes, R.K. (2012). Prospective memory in workplace and everyday situations. *Current Directions in Psychological Science*, 21: 215–20. Key Dismukes provides a brief introduction to research on prospective memory in the real world.
- Frenda, S.J., Nichols, R.M. & Loftus, E.F. (2011). Current issues and advances in misinformation research. *Current Directions in Psychological Science*, 20: 20–3. Some of the major factors causing eyewitness testimony to be distorted are discussed in this article by Elizabeth Loftus and her colleagues.
- Magnussen, S. & Helstrup, T. (eds) (2007). *Everyday memory*. Hove: Psychology Press. The contributors to this edited book discuss a wide range of topics on everyday memory.
- Prebble, S.C., Addis, D.R. & Tippett, L.J. (2013). Autobiographical memory and sense of self. *Psychological Bulletin*, 139: 815–40. Sally Prebble and her colleagues provide a framework for understanding the relationship between our autobiographical memory and our sense of self.

Language

PART

Our lives would be remarkably limited without language. Our social interactions rely very heavily on language, and all students need a good command of it. We are considerably more knowledgeable than people of previous generations because knowledge is passed on from one generation to the next via language.

What is language? According to Harley (2013, p. 5), language "is a system of symbols and rules that enable us to communicate. Symbols stand for other things: Words, either written or spoken, are symbols. The rules specify how words are ordered to form sentences." Communication *is* the primary function of language, but Crystal (1997) identified eight different functions. In addition to communication, we use language for thinking, to record information, to express emotion (e.g., "I love you"), to pretend to be animals (e.g., "Woof! Woof!"), to express identity with a group (e.g., singing in church) and so on.

It is somewhat surprising there was little research on language prior to the late 1950s. The behaviourists (e.g., Skinner, 1957) argued that the language we produce consists of conditioned responses that have been rewarded. According to this analysis, there is nothing special about language and no reason why other species should not be able to develop language.

The situation changed dramatically with the work of Noam Chomsky (1957, 1959). He argued that the behaviourist approach to language was woefully inadequate. According to him, language possesses several unique features (e.g., grammar or syntax) and can only be acquired by humans. Chomsky's ideas led to a dramatic increase in language research (Harley & McAndrews, 2015, in press). As a result, language research has been of central importance within cognitive psychology ever since.

Is language unique to humans?

Impressive evidence for learning in other species came from Savage-Rumbaugh's research with a bonobo great ape called Panbanisha (born in 1985). Panbanisha, who died in 2012, spent her entire life in captivity receiving language training. She used a specially designed keypad with about 400 geometric patterns or lexigrams on it. When she pressed a sequence of keys, a computer translated the sequence into a synthetic voice.

Panbanisha learned a vocabulary of 3,000 words by the age of 14 years, and became very good at combining a series of symbols in the grammatically correct order (e.g., "Please can I have an iced coffee?"). Lyn (2007) studied Panbanisha and her half-brother Kanzi. They understood English at the level of a 2½-year-old child. However, they had little grasp of grammar.

It has often been argued that chimpanzees' and apes' language responses lack spontaneity and refer only to the present. However, that was not the case in a study by Lyn et al. (2011) on three great apes (including Panbanisha and Kanzi). They found 74% of the apes' utterances were spontaneous. In addition, the apes referred to the past as often as young children and produced more responses referring to future intentions.

In sum, great apes can acquire many aspects of language and sometimes refer to the past and the future. However, they do not produce many novel sentences, their sentences are generally very simple and they have little or no understanding of grammar. Thus, chimpanzees cannot acquire language as humans do.

Noam Chomsky (quoted in Atkinson et al., 1993) made the following telling point: "If animals had a capacity as biologically advantageous as language but somehow hadn't used it until now, it would be an evolutionary miracle, like finding an island of humans who could be taught to fly."

Is language innate?

There has been fierce controversy (with Chomsky as a key figure) concerning the extent to which language is innate. Chomsky claims there is an innate Universal Grammar (a set of grammatical principles found in all human languages). In Chomsky's own words, "Whatever universal grammar is, it's just the name for [our] genetic structure" (Baptista, 2012, pp. 362–3).

Possible linguistic universals that might form a Universal Grammar include lexical categories (nouns, verbs, adjectives), word order (subject-verb-object or subject-object-verb) and recursion (embedding clauses within sentences to generate an infinite number of sentences).

Recursion can be shown by taking the sentence, "John met Mary in Brighton." This can be expanded as follows: "John, who was a very handsome man, met Mary in Brighton." This can be expanded in turn: "John, who was a very handsome man, met Mary, who was a vivacious woman, in Brighton." And so on for ever.

Hauser et al. (2002) provided a clear account of Chomsky's ideas. They distinguished between a *narrow* and a *broad* language faculty. The former consists of unlearned capacities specific to language (including the Universal Grammar). The broad language faculty consists of the narrow language faculty plus an auditory system, a motor system, working memory, attention, intelligence and so on. These additional abilities and systems are necessary for language acquisition but are not *specific* to language.

Chomsky's ideas have changed over time. Of special importance, the scope of the Universal Grammar has shrunk dramatically over time and now consists mainly of recursion.

Why did Chomsky propose the notion of an innate Universal Grammar? First, he argued that it explains why only humans develop language fully. Second, it explains the broad similarities among the world's languages if there is a Universal Grammar. Third, Chomsky claimed the spoken language young children experience is too limited to allow them to develop language with the breathtaking speed they display.

Christiansen and Chater (2008) totally disagreed with Chomsky's approach. Their five main points were as follows:

1 Languages differ enormously, which is inconsistent with the notions of Universal Grammar and linguistic universals.
2 The notion that natural selection has provided us with genes that can respond to abstract features of languages we have never encountered is mystifying.
3 Languages change amazingly rapidly. For example, the entire range of Indo-European languages emerged from a common source in under 10,000 years (Baronchelli et al., 2012). Natural selection could not have kept pace with the changes.
4 "Language has been shaped by the brain: language reflects pre-existing, and hence non-language-specific, human learning and processing mechanisms" (Christiansen & Chater, 2008, p. 491).
5 Children find it easy to acquire language because it was invented by humans to take account of human abilities.

Findings

How different are the world's languages? The main European languages are very similar, but large differences appear when all the world's 6,000 to 8,000 languages are considered. Evans and Levinson (2009, p. 429) did precisely that and concluded, "There are vanishingly few universals of language in the direct sense that all languages exhibit them."

Remember that Hauser et al. (2002) identified recursion as forming a major part of the Universal Grammar. Everett (2005) claimed recursion was lacking in the Amazonian language Pirahã. However, this claim was rejected by Nevins et al. (2009) and the outcome of this disagreement is unclear.

Evans and Levinson (2009) concluded some languages lack one or more of the lexical categories of noun, verbs and adjectives. One was Charrosso, an Austronesian language. Chung (2012) analysed this language in considerable detail and concluded it does actually have nouns, verbs and adjectives! She concluded that the failure to identify the three main lexical categories in some languages occurs simply because they are understudied.

Word order has some claim to be almost a linguistic universal. Greenberg (1963) found the subject preceded the object in 98% of numerous languages. It makes much sense to start with the central focus of the sentence (i.e., the subject). The word order subject-verb-object (S-V-O) was most common, followed by subject-object-verb (S-O-V).

Sandler et al. (2005) studied the Al-Sayyid group living in a desert region of Israel. There is much congenital deafness in this isolated community, which

KEY TERM

Child-directed speech
The short, simple, slowly spoken sentences used by parents and others when talking to young children.

led them in recent generations to develop Bedouin Sign Language. The Al-Sayyid use the S-O-V word order, which differs from that found in the other languages to which they are exposed.

What do the above findings mean? Grammatical structures can form very rapidly because communication is facilitated when there is agreement on word order. The human tendency to *impose structure* on language was shown by Culbertson et al. (2012). Learners were exposed to a miniature artificial language having an inconsistent mixture of word-order patterns. Most learners inferred grammatical structures more regular than the linguistic input.

Bickerton (1984) put forward the language bioprogram hypothesis, which is closely related to Chomsky's views. According to this hypothesis, children will create a grammar even if hardly exposed to a proper language. Relevant evidence was reported by Senghas et al. (2004), who studied deaf Nicaraguan children at special schools. These deaf children developed a new system of gestures that expanded into a basic sign language passed on to successive groups of children. Since this sign language does not resemble Spanish or the gestures of hearing children, it appears to be a genuinely new language owing remarkably little to other languages.

The above findings certainly suggest humans have a strong innate motivation to acquire language (including grammatical rules) and to communicate with others. However, the findings do *not* provide strong support for a Universal Grammar.

The genetic approach shows innate factors are important in language acquisition (Graham & Fisher, 2013). There are large individual differences in language ability, some dependent on genetic factors. Consider the KE family in London. Across three generations of this family, about 50% of its members have suffered from severe language problems (e.g., difficulties in understanding speech; slow and ungrammatical speech; a poor ability to assess grammaticality).

Detailed genetic research indicated their complex language disorder was controlled by a specific gene named FOXP2 (Lai et al., 2001). More specifically, mutations of this gene were found only in affected family members.

Why does FOXP2 cause these language impairments? FOXP2 is probably a hub in various gene networks leading to impaired functioning of brain areas directly involved in language. However, we must not exaggerate the importance of FOXP2. Other genes such as ATP2C2 and CMIP are associated with specific language impairment (Graham & Fisher, 2013). In addition, the FOXP2 sequence is found in numerous vertebrate species. The take-home message is that FOXP2 plays a role in language but is far from being "the language gene".

Chomsky claimed children's rapid acquisition of language cannot be fully explained on the basis of their exposure to language alone. However, he minimised the richness of children's linguistic input. Children are exposed to **child-directed speech** that is easy for them to understand (Eysenck, 2013). Child-directed speech involves very short, simple sentences, a slow rate of speaking and use of a restricted vocabulary. The children of parents who use much child-directed speech show more rapid language development than other children (Rowe, 2008).

Chomsky exaggerated the speed with which children master language. Children's speech for the first two years after they start to speak is remarkably limited (Bannard et al., 2009). For example, young children use a small set of familiar verbs and often repeat back what they have just heard.

Evaluation

Chomsky's theoretical approach is supported by evidence strongly suggesting language is uniquely human (Berwick et al., 2013). His general approach also receives some support from the identification of specific genes influencing language acquisition. Finally, the existence of brain areas (especially in the left hemisphere) heavily associated with language processing is consistent with Chomsky's general approach (Berwick et al., 2013).

What are the limitations of Chomsky's approach? First, the world's languages differ far more than he predicted. Second, Chomsky now admits the Universal Grammar is very restricted in scope and so there are very few linguistic universals. This greatly weakens his initial theory. Third, the notion that children's linguistic input is too impoverished to produce language acquisition has received little support. Fourth, as Christiansen and Chater (2008) argued, the nature of language probably directly reflects non-language cognitive processes (e.g., perception, attention). Fifth, languages probably possess grammatical structure because they facilitate human communication rather than because there is a Universal Grammar.

KEY TERMS

Whorfian hypothesis The notion that language determines (or at least influences) thinking.

Linguistic relativity The notion that speakers of different languages think differently.

Whorfian hypothesis

The best-known theory about the interrelationship between language and thought was put forward by Benjamin Lee Whorf (1956). He was a fire prevention officer for an insurance company whose hobby was linguistics. According to the **Whorfian hypothesis**, language determines or influences thinking. Of central importance is the notion of **linguistic relativity** – the ways in which speakers of any given language think are influenced by the language they speak.

There are numerous ways language might influence thinking (Wolff & Holmes, 2011). The extreme "strong" position is that differences in language inevitably cause differences in thought. An intermediate position is that language influences certain aspects of cognition such as perception and memory. Finally, language may cause preferences for certain ways of thinking, but these preferences are easily eliminated if not useful. As we will see, the evidence suggests language's effects on thinking are typically rather weak and easily overcome if necessary.

Findings

We start with perception. Perceivers often exhibit categorical perception – they find it easier to discriminate between stimuli belonging to *different* categories than those within the *same* category (see Chapter 9 and Glossary). The relevance of categorical perception is that it is assumed to depend in part on language. Winawer et al. (2007) studied categorical perception in Russian- and English-speaking participants. They took advantage of the fact that the Russian language has separate words for dark blue (*siniy*) and light blue (*goluboy*). The participants decided which of two test colours matched a *siniy* (dark blue) target. The Russian participants showed clear evidence of categorical perception – they performed faster when the distractor was *goluboy* rather than a different shade of *siniy*. English speakers (who would simply describe all the stimuli as "blue") did not show this effect. Roberson and Hanley (2010) provide an overview of research on the effects of language on colour processing.

Casasanto (2008) pointed out that English speakers use *distance* metaphors to describe an event's duration (e.g., long meeting). However, Greek speakers use *amount* metaphors (e.g., *synantisis pou diekese poli*, meaning "meeting that lasts much"). Casasanto studied the effects of this difference using two tasks. On one task, participants saw a line "growing" across the screen. On the other task, participants viewed a drawing of a container filling with liquid. The participants estimated how long the lengthening or filling had taken.

Casasanto (2008) assumed English speakers naturally think of duration in terms of distance and so would produce longer estimates when the line was long. In contrast, Greek speakers should be strongly influenced by amount (i.e., extent of the fill) but not by distance. The findings supported these predictions.

Manner of motion (e.g., hopping, running) is expressed more prominently in English than in Spanish. As a result, Kersten et al. (2010) argued that English speakers should outperform Spanish ones on a task in which novel animated objects were categorised on the basis of manner of motion. The findings were as predicted (see Figure III.1), suggesting language can influence thinking and performance.

It is important to avoid exaggerating the impact of language on thinking. Consider a study by Li et al. (2009). They presented participants with objects made of a given substance (e.g., a plastic whisk). English speakers focused on the object itself (whisk) rather than the substance (plastic), whereas Mandarin and Japanese speakers focused on the substances.

It could be argued that the above differences reflect differences in the nature of the three languages and so Li et al.'s (2009) findings are consistent with the Whorfian hypothesis. However, this was not the case with another experiment of theirs. When participants simply indicated how likely they would be to think of various objects as objects or as substances, there were no differences between English, Mandarin and Japanese speakers. The effects of language were very task-specific and far smaller than predicted by the Whorfian hypothesis.

Frank et al. (2008) studied the Pirahã, an Amazonian tribe. They have no words to express precise quantities or numbers, not even "one". Nevertheless, the Pirahã could perform exact quantitative matches even with large numbers of objects. However, their performance was inaccurate when information

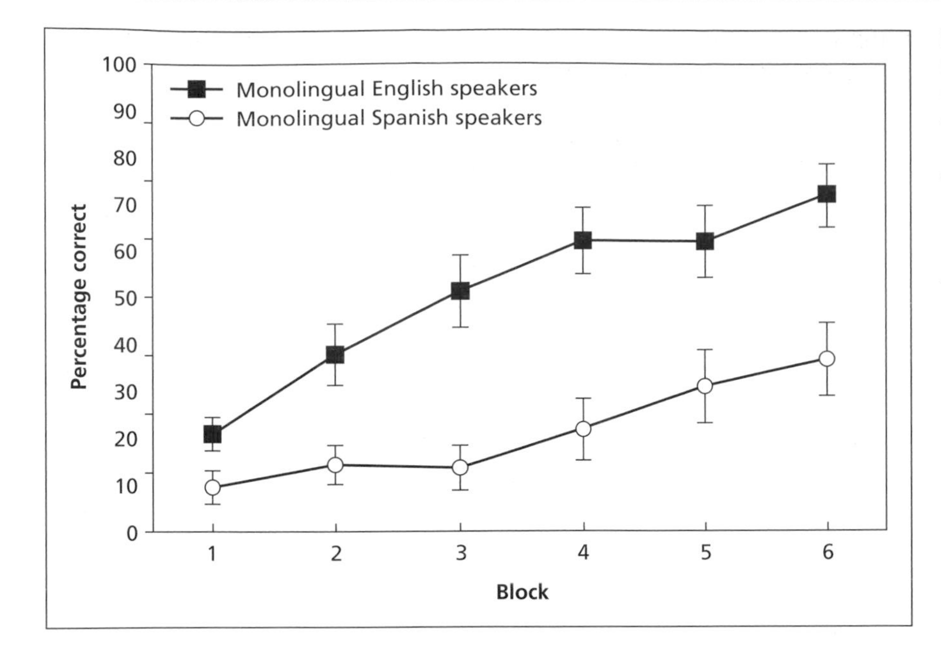

Figure III.1
Percentage correct by monolinguals English and Spanish speakers on a task involving objects being categorised on the basis of manner of motion.

From Kersten et al. (2010). © American Psychological Association.

needed to be remembered. Thus, language is not essential for certain numerical tasks. However, it provides an efficient way of encoding information and so boosts performance when memory is required.

Evaluation

People's native language influences their performance on various tasks (e.g., colour discrimination, temporal estimation, categorisation). Wolff and Holmes (2011, p. 261) summarised such influence as follows: "We did not find empirical support for the view that language . . . 'closes doors' . . . however, while it may not close doors, it may fling others wide open." For example, it can enhance memory (Frank et al., 2008) and increase categorical perception (Winawer et al., 2007).

Language frequently influences thinking. However, there is little or no support for a strong version of the Whorfian hypothesis according to which language necessarily determines thinking. Instead, language causes a *tendency* for people to attend to, perceive or remember information in certain ways. However, such tendencies are often no more than *preferences* and as such often disappear with changing task requirements (e.g., Li et al., 2009). The take-home message is that the available evidence supports only a rather weak version of the Whorfian hypothesis.

Language chapters

We possess four main language skills (listening to speech, reading, speaking and writing). It is perhaps natural to assume any given person will have generally strong or weak language skills. That assumption is often incorrect with respect to people's first language – for example, many people talk fluently and coherently but find writing difficult. The assumption is even more incorrect with respect to people's second language. The first author has spent numerous summer holidays in France and can just about read newspapers and easy novels in French. However, he finds if agonisingly hard to understand rapid spoken French and his ability to speak French is poor.

The three chapters in this section (Chapters 9–11) focus on the four main language skills. Chapter 9 deals with the basic processes involved in reading and listening to speech. The emphasis is on how readers and listeners identify and make sense of individual *words*. As we will see, the study of brain-damaged patients has clarified the complex processes underlying reading and speech perception.

Chapter 10 deals mostly with the processes involved in the comprehension of sentences and discourse (connected text or speech). Most of these processes are common to text and speech. An important part of sentence understanding involves parsing (working out the sentence's grammatical structure). Understanding discourse involves drawing numerous inferences and often forming a mental model of the situation described.

Chapter 11 deals with the remaining two main language abilities: speaking and writing. We spend much more of our time speaking than writing. This helps to explain why we know much more about speech production than writing. Research on writing has been somewhat neglected until recently, which is regrettable given the importance of writing skills in many cultures.

The processes discussed in these three chapters are *interdependent*. Speakers use comprehension processes to monitor what they are saying. In addition, listeners use language production processes to predict what speakers will say next (Pickering & Garrod, 2007).

Reading and speech perception

CHAPTER

9

INTRODUCTION

Human beings excel in their command of language. Indeed, language is so important that this chapter and the following two are devoted to it. In this chapter, we consider the basic processes involved in reading words and recognising spoken words. It often does not matter whether a message is presented to our eyes or to our ears. You would understand the sentence, "You have done exceptionally well in your cognitive psychology examination", in much the same way whether you read or heard it. Thus, many comprehension processes are very similar whether we read a text or listen to someone talking.

However, reading and speech perception differ in several ways. In reading, each word can be seen as a whole, whereas spoken words are spread out in time and are transitory. More importantly, it is harder to tell where one word ends and the next starts with speech than with text.

Speech generally provides a more *ambiguous* signal than printed text. For example, when words were spliced out of spoken sentences and presented on their own, they were recognised only half the time (Lieberman, 1963).

The conditions under which speech perception occurs in everyday life are generally less optimal than is the case with reading. For example, our ability to hear what a speaker is saying is often impaired by other speakers close by and/or irrelevant noises. In contrast, readers are rarely distracted by other visual stimuli. Finally, demands are greater when listening to speech than reading a text because previous words are no longer accessible.

So far we have indicated why listening to speech can be harder than reading. However, there are also reasons why speech perception can be easier. Speech often contains prosodic cues, which are hints to sentence structure and intended meaning via the speaker's pitch, intonation, stress and timing (see Glossary and Chapter 10). For example, questions typically have a rising intonation on the last word in the sentence. In contrast, the main cues to sentence structure are punctuation marks (e.g., commas, semi-colons). These are often (but not always) less informative than prosodic cues in speech. In addition, speakers often accompany their speech with gestures providing very useful information.

Research on adult brain-damaged patients has shown that some understand spoken language but cannot read. Other patients have good reading skills but cannot understand the spoken word. Thus, reading and speech perception involve somewhat different brain areas and cognitive processes.

Basic processes specific to reading are dealt with first in this chapter. These processes are involved in recognising and reading individual words and guiding our eye movements. After that, we consider basic processes specific to speech, including those required to divide the speech signal into separate words and to recognise those words.

In Chapter 10, we discuss comprehension processes common to reading and listening. The emphasis in that chapter is on larger units of language consisting of several sentences. However, the processes discussed in this chapter play an important role in our comprehension of texts or long speech utterances.

READING: INTRODUCTION

It is important to study reading because adults lacking effective reading skills are very disadvantaged. That means we need to understand the processes involved in reading to help poor readers. Reading requires several perceptual and other cognitive processes plus a good knowledge of language and grammar.

The overwhelming majority of studies on reading have only considered the English language. Does this matter? Share (2008) argued strongly that the "Anglocentricities" of reading research do matter. The reason is that the relationship between spelling (orthography) and sound (phonology) is much less *consistent* in the English language than most others. Caravolas et al. (2013) studied young children learning English or a much more consistent language (Spanish or Czech). The English children learned to read more slowly than the others because of the inconsistencies of the English language (see Figure 9.1).

The relationship between orthography and phonology is unusually inconsistent in English. However, it does *not* necessarily follow that the processes involved in reading English differ substantially from those involved in reading other

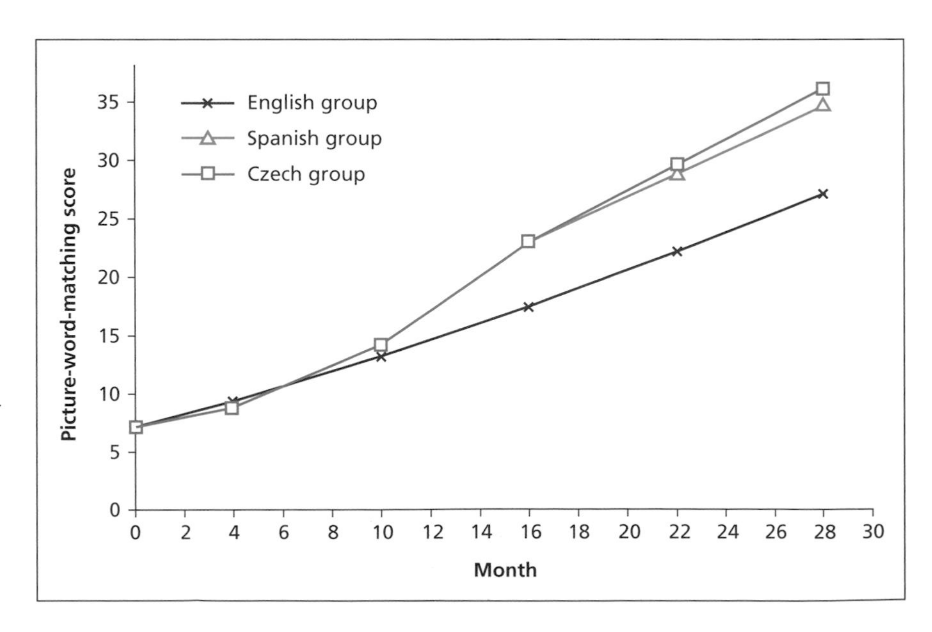

Figure 9.1
Estimated reading ability over a 30-month period with initial testing at a mean age of 66 months for English, Spanish and Czech children.

From Caravolas et al. (2013). Reprinted by permission of SAGE Publications.

languages. Caravolas et al. (2013) found factors such as letter-sound knowledge and phoneme awareness were comparably strong predictors of speed of reading development in English, Czech and Spanish.

Research methods

Several methods are available for studying reading. For example, consider ways of assessing the time taken for word identification or recognition (e.g., deciding a word is familiar; accessing its meaning). The **lexical decision task** involves deciding rapidly whether a string of letters forms a word. The **naming task** involves saying a printed word out loud as rapidly as possible. Both tasks have limitations. Normal reading times are disrupted by the requirement to respond to task demands, and it is hard to identify the processes underlying performance.

Balota et al. (1999) argued that reading involves several kinds of processing: **orthography** (the spelling of words); **phonology** (the sound of words); **semantics** (word meaning); syntax or grammar; and higher-level discourse integration. The involvement of these kinds of processing varies across tasks. The naming task emphasises links between orthography and phonology. In contrast, the lexical decision task emphasises links between orthography and semantics. Normal reading also involves processing of syntax and higher-level integration, processes of little or no relevance to naming or lexical decision.

Recording eye movements during reading is useful. It provides an *unobtrusive* and detailed on-line record of attention-related processes. The main problem is deciding *what* processing occurs during each fixation (period of time when the eye remains still).

Next, there is priming (see Glossary), in which a prime word is presented shortly before the target word. This prime word is related to the target word in spelling, meaning or sound. What is of interest is to see the effects of the prime on processing of (and response to) the target word. For example, when reading *clip*, do you access information about its pronunciation? The answer appears to be "Yes". A word preceded by a non-word having identical pronunciation (*klip*) presented below the level of conscious awareness is processed faster (Rastle & Brysbaert, 2006).

Finally, there has been a dramatic increase in research assessing brain activity. Event-related potentials (ERPs; see Glossary) are of special interest and importance (Hagoort & van Berkum, 2007). They provide a precise measure of the time taken for certain processes to occur. For example, consider the N400, a negative wave with a peak at about 400 ms. A large N400 in sentence processing typically means there is a mismatch between the meaning of the word currently being processed and its context.

Phonological processes

You are currently reading this sentence. Did you access the relevant sounds when identifying the words in it? In more technical terms, did you engage in phonological processing of the words?

Two main answers have been provided to the above question. According to the weak phonological model (e.g., Coltheart et al., 2001), phonological processing is fairly slow and inessential for word identification. In contrast, phonological processing has a much more central role in the strong phonological model:

KEY TERMS

Lexical decision task
Participants presented with a string of letters decide rapidly whether it forms a word.

Naming task
A task in which visually presented words are pronounced aloud rapidly.

Orthography
The study of letters and word spellings.

Phonology
The study of the sounds of words and parts of words.

Semantics
The study of the meaning conveyed by words, phrases and sentences.

Weblink:
Lexical decision task

> A phonological representation is a necessary product of processing printed words, even though the explicit pronunciation of their phonological structure is not required. Thus, the strong phonological model would predict that phonological processing will be mandatory [obligatory], perhaps automatic.
> (Frost, 1998, p. 76)

Why might we expect phonological processing to play an important role in reading? Children start speaking several years before they can read. They are often taught to read using the phonics approach, which involves forming connections between letters or groups of letters and the sounds of spoken English (Share, 2008). Children's early phonemic skills predict (and are probably causally related to) their future word-reading skills (Melby-Lervåg et al., 2012).

Even if readers typically engage in phonological processing, it may occur too slowly to influence word recognition. Sliwinska et al. (2012) addressed this issue using transcranial magnetic stimulation (TMS; see Glossary) to create a transient "lesion". They applied TMS to the supramarginal gyrus (an area associated with phonological processing) 80 and 120 ms after word onset. This impaired performance on a phonological task, suggesting that phonological processing starts within 80–120 ms. This would be fast enough for such processing to influence word recognition.

KEY TERMS

Homophones
Words pronounced in the same way but that differ in their spellings (e.g., *pain–pane*, *sale–sail*).

Phonological neighbourhood
Words are phonological neighbours if they differ in only one **phoneme**.

Case study:
Phonological processes

Findings

Evidence that phonological processing is important was reported by Van Orden (1987) in a study using **homophones** (words with one pronunciation but two spellings). Participants made many more errors when asked, "Is it a flower? ROWS", than when asked, "Is it a flower? ROBS". The errors occurred because participants engaged in phonological processing of the word "ROWS", which is homophonic with the flower name "ROSE".

We now consider the notion of **phonological neighbourhood**. Two words are phonological neighbours if they differ in only one phoneme (e.g., *gate* has *bait* and *get* as neighbours). If reading involves phonological processing, words with many phonological neighbours should have an advantage. Within sentences, as predicted, words having many phonological neighbours are fixated for less time than those with few neighbours (Yates et al., 2008). When the phonological neighbours are closely related to each other in sound, however, this can slow down word recognition rather than facilitate it (Yates, 2013). This occurs because the phonological neighbours receive activation from each other and so compete with the target word.

Many researchers have used phonological priming to assess the role of phonology in word processing (mentioned earlier). A word (e.g., *clip*) is immediately preceded by a phonologically identical non-word prime (e.g., *klip*). This prime is masked and presented very briefly so it is not consciously perceived. In a control condition, the non-word primes are less similar phonologically to the words.

Rastle and Brysbaert (2006) carried out a meta-analysis (see Glossary). Words were processed faster when preceded by phonological identical non-word primes than by control primes. This finding suggests phonological processing occurs rapidly and automatically as predicted by the strong phonological model.

Kinoshita and Norris (2012) noted previous research on phonological priming had typically obtained small and somewhat inconsistent effects. They used very carefully selected words and obtained a larger phonological priming effect than previous studies. They also found priming effects were greater when the prime was orthographically as well as phonologically identical to the word. Thus, word processing combines orthographic and phonological information.

Research using masked phonological priming indicates readers typically use phonological information during word processing. However, it does not prove that visual word recognition *must* depend on prior phonological processing. Evidence that word meaning can be accessed without access to phonology was reported by Hanley and McDonnell (1997). They studied a patient, PS, who could not gain access to the other meanings of homophones when he saw one of the spellings (e.g., "air") and could not pronounce written words accurately.

In spite of his severe problems, PS provided accurate definitions of printed words. This suggests he had full access to the meanings of words for which he could not supply the appropriate phonology. Han and Bi (2009) studied another brain-damaged patient, YGA, whose phonological processing was very impaired. However, YGA's ability to understand the meaning of visually presented words was intact.

When you are reading, you probably sometimes experience inner speech (saying the printed words to yourself). This phenomenon of inner speech is of relevance to the role of phonological processing in reading.

Filik and Barber (2012) wondered whether our inner speech resembles our own speaking voice. They compared groups from the North and South of England having different dialects. For example, the vowel in the word *path* is pronounced with a longer sound by Southerners than by Northerners. The participants read limericks. There was disruption of eye movements when the limerick's final word did not rhyme based on the reader's accent. Thus, inner speech is very similar to our speaking voice.

In sum, the evidence supports the notion that phonological processing is involved in reading. Most research is consistent with the strong phonological model. However, the findings from patients with severely impaired phonological processing suggest such processing is not essential for effective reading. Finally, some phonological processing during reading resembles the dialect we use when speaking.

WORD RECOGNITION

College students typically read at about 300 words a minute, thus averaging only 200 ms per word. How long does word recognition take? That is hard to say, in part because of imprecision about the meaning of "word recognition". The term can refer to deciding that a word is familiar, accessing a word's name or accessing its meaning. As a result, estimates of the time taken for word recognition vary.

Interactive activation model

McClelland and Rumelhart (1981) proposed an influential interactive activation model of visual word processing. It is a computational model involving considerable parallel processing and based on the assumption that bottom-up and top-down processes interact (see Figure 9.2):

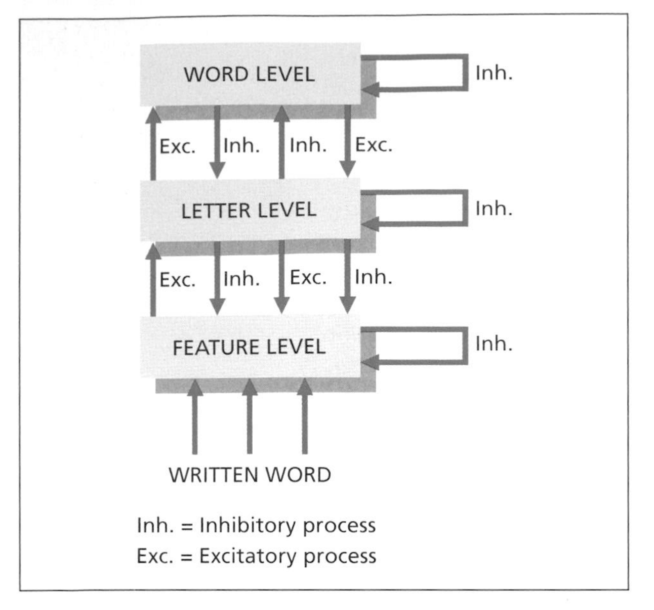

Figure 9.2
McClelland and Rumelhart's (1981) interactive activation model of visual word recognition.
Adapted from Ellis (1984).

- There are recognition units at three levels: the feature level at the bottom; the letter level in the middle; and the word level at the top.
- When a feature in a letter is detected (e.g., vertical line at the right-hand side of a letter), activation goes to all letter units containing that feature (e.g., H, M, N), and inhibition goes to all other letter units.
- Letters are identified at the letter level. When a letter within a word is identified, activation is sent to the word level for all four-letter word units containing that letter in that position within the word, and inhibition is sent to all other word units.
- Words are recognised at the word level. Activated word units increase the level of activation in the letter-level units for that word's letters.

Findings

Much research has used the following task. A letter string is presented very briefly followed by a pattern mask and participants decide which of two letters was presented in a given position (e.g., the third letter). Performance on this task is better when the letter string forms a word – this is the **word superiority effect**.

The model accounts for the word superiority effect by assuming there are top-down processes from the word level to the letter level. Suppose the word SEAT is presented and participants decide whether the third letter is an A or an N. If the word unit for SEAT is activated, this increases activation of the letter A and inhibits activation of the letter N. These top-down processes from the word level occurred about 200 ms after word onset (Martin et al., 2006).

Much research has considered **orthographic neighbours**, which are the words formed by changing one of a target word's letters. For example, the word *stem* has several orthographic neighbours including *seem*, *step* and *stew*. When a word is presented, its orthographic neighbours become activated and influence its recognition time.

The effects of orthographic neighbours on word recognition were reviewed by Chen and Mirman (2012). Orthographic neighbours typically *facilitate* word recognition if they are less frequent in the language than the word itself. However, they have an *inhibitory* effect if they are more frequent than the target word.

Chen and Mirman (2012) developed a computational model based on the interactive activation model's assumptions. This computational model produced *facilitative* effects when the orthographic neighbours were weakly activated but *inhibitory* effects when they were strongly activated. These findings fit neatly with the empirical data on the assumption that high-frequency words are generally more activated than low-frequency ones.

The model assumes each letter in a word is rigidly assigned to a specific position. As a result, "WROD is no more like WORD than is WXYD" (Norris &

KEY TERMS

Word superiority effect
A target letter is more readily detected in a letter string when the string forms a word than when it does not.

Orthographic neighbours
With reference to a target word, the number of words that can be formed by changing one of its letters.

Kinoshita, 2012, p. 517). It follows that readers should have great problems in reading the "Cambridge email":

> Aoccrdnig to a rscheearch at Cmabrigde Uinervtisy it deosn't mttaer in waht oredr the ltteers in a wrod are. The olny iprmoatnt tihng is that the frist and lsat ltteer be at the rghit pclae. The rset can be a toatl mses and you can still raed it wouthit porbelm. This is bcusease the huamn mnid deos not raed ervey lteter by istlef but the wroad as a wlohe.

We imagine you found it fairly easy to read the email even though numerous letters are in the wrong positions. Velan and Frost (2007) asked readers to repeat sentences in English presented one word at a time. These sentences were presented with normal spelling or with numerous letter transpositions. Strikingly, there was practically no difference between conditions in the percentage of words read correctly (86% with normal spelling vs. 84% with transpositions). Note that it is much easier for readers to cope with transposed letters when the first and last letters of each word are in the correct place (Norris & Kinoshita, 2012).

Evaluation

The interactive activation model has been very influential (Harley, 2013). It was an early example of how a connectionist model (see Chapter 1) could be applied to visual word processing. It can account for the word superiority effect and the effects of orthographic neighbours on word recognition. More generally, its emphasis on the importance of top-down processes has received much support.

What are the model's limitations? First, the model provides no account of the role of meaning in visual word recognition. Second, phonological processing is often involved in word recognition, but this is not considered within the model. Third, the model attaches too much importance to letter order and so cannot provide a convincing account of efficient reading with numerous transposed letters within words. Fourth, it was designed to account for processing four-letter words and its applicability to word recognition for longer words is unclear.

Semantic priming

Many words within any given sentence are related in meaning, and this facilitates word recognition. One process involved is **semantic priming** – a word is recognised or identified more rapidly if immediately preceded by a semantically related word. For example, people decide faster that DOCTOR is a word when preceded by a semantically related word (e.g., NURSE) than by a semantically unrelated word such as LIBRARY (Meyer & Schvaneveldt, 1971).

Why does semantic priming occur? Perhaps the context or priming word *automatically* activates the stored representations of all words related to it due to massive previous learning. Alternatively, *controlled processes* may be involved, with a prime such as NURSE leading people to *expect* a semantically related word will follow.

Both of the above explanations of semantic priming are valid. However, Neely (1977) found an ingenious way of distinguishing between them. The priming word was a category name (e.g., BIRD), followed by a letter string at 250, 400 or 700 ms. The participant's task was to decide whether the letter string (target) formed

KEY TERM

Semantic priming
The finding that word recognition is facilitated by the prior presentation of a semantically related word.

Weblink:
Word superiority effect

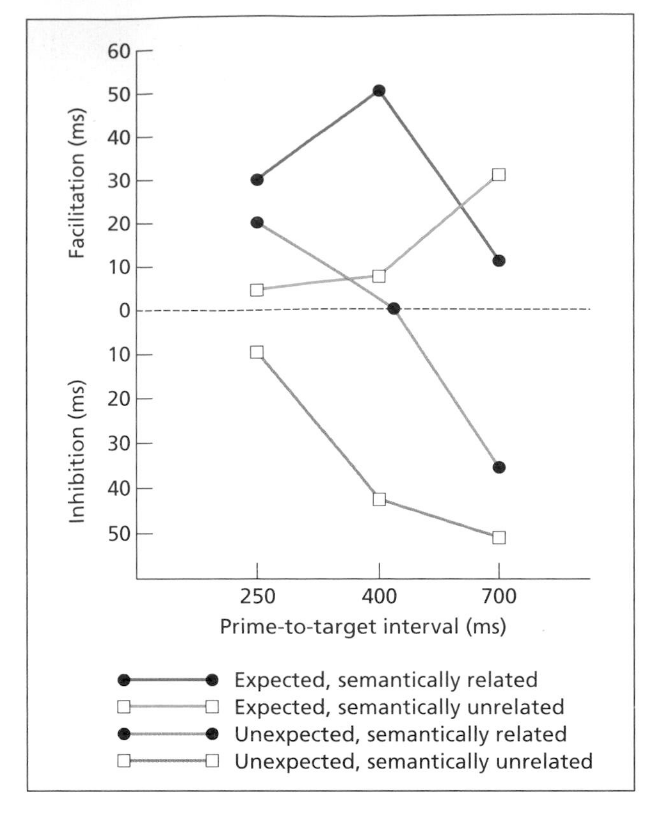

Figure 9.3
The time course of inhibitory and facilitatory effects of priming as a function of whether or not the target word was related semantically to the prime, and of whether or not the target word belonged to the expected category.
Data from Neely (1977). © American Psychological Association.

a word (lexical decision task). Participants were instructed that the prime BIRD would mostly be followed by a type of bird. However, the prime BODY would mostly be followed by a part of a building. This gives us four conditions with respect to the relationship between the prime and the target word:

1 expected, semantically related (e.g., BIRD–robin);
2 expected, semantically unrelated (e.g., BODY–door);
3 unexpected, semantically related (e.g., BODY–heart);
4 unexpected, semantically unrelated (e.g., BIRD–arm).

It was assumed automatic facilitatory processes would be activated if the target were semantically related to the prime but not if it were semantically unrelated. In contrast, controlled processes might be involved if the target was expected but not if it was unexpected.

What did Neely (1977) find? There were two priming or context effects (see Figure 9.3). First, there was a rapid, short-lived facilitatory effect based on semantic relatedness. Second, there was a slower but more long-lasting effect based on expectations, with expected target words showing facilitation and unexpected showing a negative or inhibitory effect.

Sanchez-Casas et al. (2012) confirmed semantic priming can occur automatically in the absence of conscious awareness. Participants were presented with a masked word (e.g., *table*) followed by a strongly associated word (e.g., *chair*). There was semantic priming even though the masked word was not visible.

Sentential context effects

How do readers use preceding sentence context when reading a word? Perhaps they use context to predict the next word and so context affects the *early* processing of that word. Alternatively, readers may adopt a more passive approach and use contextual information only *after* accessing the next word's meaning. The first possibility has received increasing support in recent years (Kutas et al., 2011; see Chapter 10).

Evidence that context can influence lexical access was reported by Penolazzi et al. (2007) using event-related potentials (ERPs; see Glossary). The target word (shown here in bold) was expected (when preceded by *around*) or not expected (when preceded by *near*):

He was just around/near the **corner**.

ERPs within 200 ms of the onset of the target word differed depending on whether the word was expected or unexpected. The finding that context affected the processing of the target word so rapidly suggests context can influence lexical access to the target word.

Convincing evidence that readers predict what will be presented next was reported by DeLong et al. (2005) using event-related potentials (ERPs; see Glossary). Here is an example of the sentences they used:

> The day was breezy so the boy went outside to fly [a kite/an airplane] in the park.

In the example, *a kite* is highly predictable whereas *an airplane* is not. They were especially interested in the N400 component of the ERP, which reflects the extent to which a word's meaning matches the context.

What did DeLong et al. (2005) find? First, there was a larger N400 to the less predictable noun (e.g., *airplane*) than the more predictable one (e.g., *kite*). This finding has two possible interpretations: (1) readers predicted beforehand that *kite* would be presented; (2) readers found it easier to integrate *kite* than *airplane* after it was presented. Second, there was a larger N400 to the article *an* (preceding *airplane*) than to *a* (preceding *kite*). This finding occurred because readers were predicting the most likely noun would follow.

DeLong et al. (2005) showed readers anticipate a specific word (e.g., *kite*) when the context is highly constraining. However, that situation is relatively rare in everyday reading. Szewczyk and Schriefers (2013) found readers also predict that a noun will belong to a broad category (e.g., inanimate objects). Thus, context can lead to the production of specific or general expectations.

Dikker and Pylkkänen (2013) studied the processes involved in prediction in detail. Participants viewed a drawing followed by a noun phrase. On some trials (e.g., a drawing of an apple followed by the noun phrase *the apple*), the participants could predict which noun would be presented. On these trials, there was significant activation in brain areas associated with several kinds of word processing (e.g., semantic processing, visual word form processing) before the noun was presented. These findings support the view predictive context can trigger widespread top-down processing.

READING ALOUD

Read aloud the following words and non-words (pronounceable non-words are **pseudowords** but we will generally use the term non-words):

CAT FOG COMB PINT MANTINESS FASS

You probably regarded that as a simple task even though it involves hidden complexities. For example, how do you know the "b" in "comb" is silent and that "pint" does not rhyme with "hint"? Presumably you have specific information stored in long-term memory about how to pronounce these words. However, that does not explain your ability to pronounce non-words such as "mantiness" and "fass". Perhaps non-words are pronounced by analogy with real words (e.g., "fass" is pronounced to rhyme with "mass"). Another possibility is that rules governing the translation of letter strings into sounds generate pronunciations for non-words.

KEY TERM

Pseudowords
Non-words consisting of strings of letters that can be pronounced (e.g., mantiness).

KEY TERM

Cascade model
A model in which information passes from one level to the next *before* completion of processing at the first level.

The above description of the reading of words and non-words is incomplete. Studies on brain-damaged patients indicate there are different reading disorders depending on which parts of the language system are damaged. We turn now to two major theoretical approaches focusing on reading aloud in healthy and brain-damaged individuals. First, there is the dual-route cascaded model (Coltheart et al., 2001). Second, there is the distributed connectionist approach or triangle model (Plaut et al., 1996; Harm & Seidenberg, 2004).

Both models adopt a computational approach. Why is this? The processes involved in skilled reading are very complex and interactive, and computational models are well suited to handling such complexity. Of particular importance, computational models make it easier to predict what follows from various theoretical assumptions (Norris, 2013).

At the risk of oversimplification, we can identify various key differences between the dual-route and connectionist triangle approaches. According to the dual-route approach, reading words and non-words involves different processes. These processes are relatively neat and tidy and some are rule-based. However, the dual-route approach has become less neat and tidy over time!

According to the connectionist triangle approach, reading processes are used more *flexibly* than assumed within the dual-route model. Reading involves interactive processes – all the relevant knowledge we possess about word sounds, word spellings and word meanings is used in parallel (at the same time) whether reading words or non-words.

In what follows, we first consider each model's major assumptions plus relevant supporting evidence. After that, we directly compare the two models with respect to controversial issues where the two models make different predictions.

Dual-route cascaded model

Coltheart et al. (2001) put forward a dual-route cascaded model of reading (see Figure 9.4; see also Coltheart (2012) for a review of dual-route theories). It accounts for reading aloud and for silent reading. There are two main routes between printed words and speech, both starting with orthographic analysis (used for identifying and grouping letters in words). The crucial distinction is between a non-lexical route that involves converting letters into sounds and a lexical or dictionary lookup route. In Figure 9.4, the non-lexical route is Route 1 and the lexical route is divided into two sub-routes (Routes 2 and 3).

Healthy individuals use both routes in parallel when reading aloud and these two routes do not function independently. In practice, however, naming visually presented words typically depends mostly on the lexical route because it operates faster than the non-lexical route.

It is a **cascade model** because activation at one level is passed on to the next level before processing at the first level is complete. Cascaded models differ from thresholded models in which activation at one level is only passed on to other levels after a given threshold of activation is reached.

Earlier we discussed the role of phonological processing in visual word identification. Coltheart et al. (2001) argued for a weak phonological model in which word identification generally does not depend on phonological processing.

Coltheart et al. (2001) produced a detailed computational model to test their dual-route cascaded model. They started with 7,981 one-syllable words and used McClelland and Rumelhart's (1981) interactive activation model (discussed

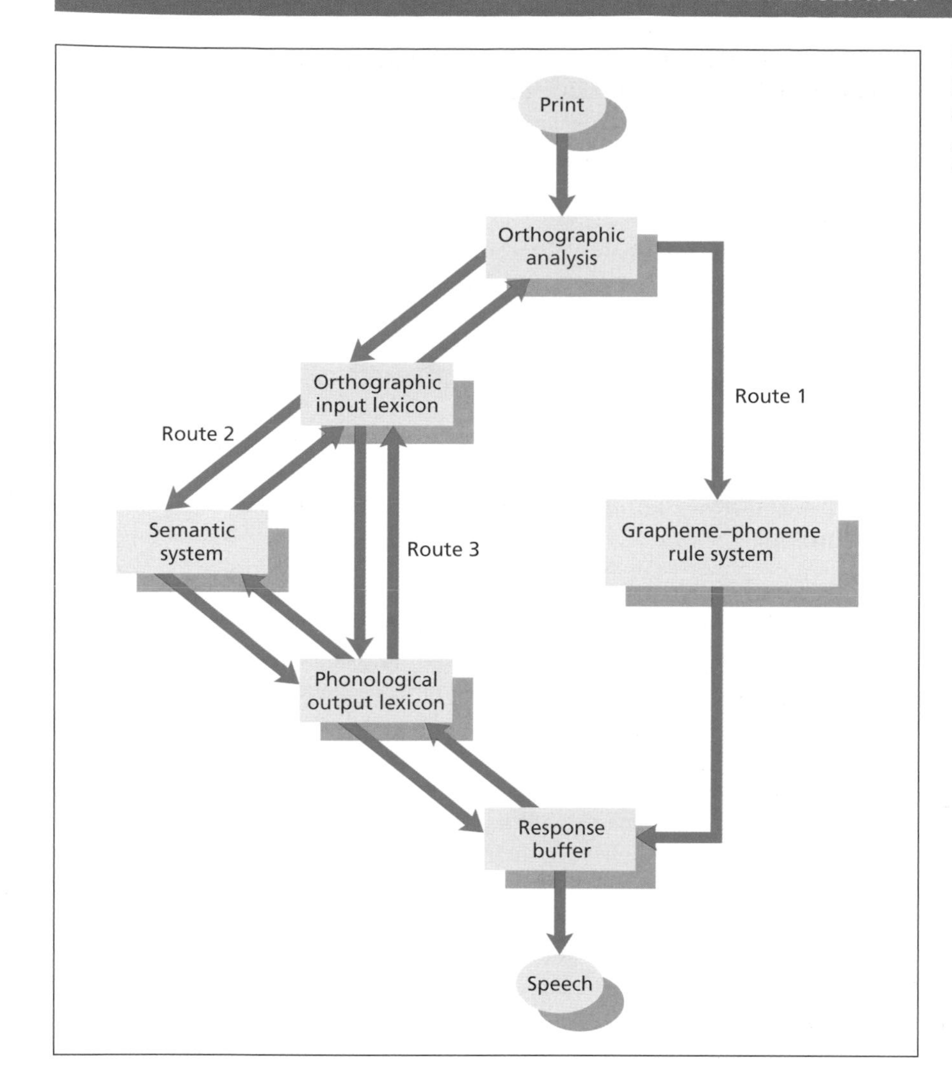

Figure 9.4
Basic architecture of the dual-route cascaded model.
Adapted from Coltheart et al. (2001).

earlier) as the basis for the orthographic component of their model. They predicted the pronunciation most activated by processing in the lexical and non-lexical routes would determine the naming response.

Coltheart et al. (2001) tested their computational model with all 7,981 words and found 99% were read accurately. When the model was presented with 7,000 one-syllable non-words, it read 98.9% of them correctly.

Interactive exercsie:
Dual route cascade model

Route 1 (grapheme–phoneme conversion)

Route 1 differs from the other routes in using grapheme–phoneme conversion, which involves converting spelling (graphemes) into sound (phonemes). A **grapheme** is a basic unit of written language and a **phoneme** is a basic unit of spoken language. Examples of graphemes are the *i* in *pig*, the *ng* in *ping* and the *igh* in *high* (Coltheart et al., 2001).

If a brain-damaged patient used only Route 1, what would we find? Grapheme–phoneme conversion rules (converting each grapheme into the phoneme most closely associated with it) should permit accurate pronunciations

KEY TERMS

Grapheme
A small unit of written language corresponding to a **phoneme**.

Phoneme
The basic unit of sound; words consist of one or more phonemes.

of words with regular spelling–sound correspondences. However, they would *not* permit accurate pronunciation of irregular words not conforming to the conversion rules. For example, if the irregular word *pint* has grapheme–phoneme conversions rules applied to it, it would be pronounced to rhyme with *hint*. This is known as regularisation. Finally, grapheme–phoneme conversion rules can provide pronunciations of non-words.

Patients apparently largely reliant on Route 1 are surface dyslexics. **Surface dyslexia** is a condition involving special problems in reading irregular words. For example, the surface dyslexic, KT, read 100% of non-words accurately and 81% of regular words, but succeeded with only 41% of irregular words (McCarthy & Warrington, 1984). Over 70% of KT's errors on irregular words were due to regularisation.

Route 2 (lexicon + semantic knowledge) and Route 3 (lexicon only)

The basic idea behind Route 2 is that representations of thousands of familiar words are stored in an orthographic output **lexicon**. Visual presentation of a word produces activation in this lexicon. This is followed by obtaining its meaning from the semantic system, after which its sound pattern is generated by the phonological output lexicon. Route 3 also involves the orthographic input and phonological output lexicons but it bypasses the semantic system.

What would we find if a patient used Route 2 or 3 but not Route 1? Their intact orthographic input lexicon means they could pronounce familiar words (regular or irregular). However, their inability to use grapheme–phoneme conversion rules means they should find it very hard to pronounce unfamiliar words and non-words.

Phonological dyslexics fit this predicted pattern fairly well. **Phonological dyslexia** involves special problems with reading unfamiliar words and non-words. Caccappolo-van Vliet et al. (2004) studied two phonological dyslexics. Both patients showed the typical pattern associated with phonological dyslexia – their performance on reading regular and irregular words exceeded 90% compared to under 60% with non-words.

Deep dyslexia

Deep dyslexia is a condition involving problems in reading unfamiliar words and an inability to read non-words. However, the most striking symptom is semantic reading errors (e.g., *ship* read as *boat*). According to Coltheart et al. (2001), deep dyslexics use a completely different reading system based in the right hemisphere. In contrast, the great majority of people have language primarily based in the left hemisphere. Coltheart et al. (2001, p. 246) concluded, "the explanation of any symptom of deep dyslexia is outside the scope of the DRC [dual-route cascaded] model".

Evidence consistent with the right-hemisphere hypothesis was reported by Patterson et al. (1989). They studied a girl, NI, whose left hemisphere was removed. Two years later, NI had all the symptoms of deep dyslexia.

KEY TERMS

Surface dyslexia
A condition in which regular words can be read but there is impaired ability to read irregular or exception words.

Lexicon
A store of detailed information (e.g., orthographic, phonological, semantic, syntactic) about words.

Phonological dyslexia
A condition in which familiar words can be read but there is impaired ability to read unfamiliar words and pseudowords.

Deep dyslexia
A condition in which reading unfamiliar words and non-words is impaired and there are semantic errors (e.g., reading *missile* as *rocket*).

Two routes?

We have seen that findings from brain-damaged patients provide support for the notion of two different routes (one lexical and one non-lexical) in reading aloud. Additional support for this notion has come from neuroimaging studies (discussed later).

Neuroimaging studies have also revealed individual differences in reading aloud. Jobard et al. (2011) studied silent reading of familiar words by highly educated participants. Fewer brain areas were activated during reading by those with high working memory capacity (ability to process and store information at the same time; see Glossary) than those with low capacity because of their more efficient processing. Of most interest, only those with low capacity had activation in areas associated with grapheme–phoneme conversion.

According to the dual-route model, the non-lexical route to reading involves grapheme–phoneme conversion. This requires *serial* left-to-right processing and so the time taken to start saying pseudowords should depend on their length. In contrast, the lexical route involves *parallel* processing and so there should be little or no effect of length on the time taken to start saying words. As predicted, length generally has much more effect on the pronunciation of non-words than that of words (Rastle et al., 2009).

Juphard et al. (2011) obtained similar findings. The time to start saying three-syllable non-words was 26% longer than for one-syllable ones. In contrast, the difference between three- and one-syllable words was only 11%. Juphard et al. compared brain activation during the processing of non-words and words. Syllabic length of non-words (but not words) influenced the duration of brain activity in areas associated with phonological processing. These findings suggest producing phonological representations of non-words is a slow, serial process, whereas it is fast and parallel for words.

Preliminary evaluation

The dual-route cascaded model represents an ambitious and original attempt to account for basic reading processes in brain-damaged individuals. The notion there are two routes in reading has been very influential, as has the model's explanation of reading disorders such as surface dyslexia and phonological dyslexia.

The assumption there are separate lexical and non-lexical routes involving parallel and serial processing respectively has received support from studies on healthy individuals. Some of this research has focused on behavioural data (Rastle et al., 2009) and some has focused on brain activity (Juphard et al., 2011; Taylor et al., 2013, discussed later).

Perry et al. (2007) developed a new connectionist dual-process model (the CDP+ model) based in part on the dual-route cascaded model. This model includes a lexical and a sublexical route, and eliminates some problems with the dual-route cascaded model (e.g., its inability to learn).

What are the limitations of the dual-route cascaded model? First, the model's account of the involvement of semantic processes in reading is vague. The semantic system can play an important role via Route 2, but how this operates remains unclear.

The above is a serious problem. There is compelling evidence (discussed later) that semantic processes are often very important in reading. For example, Cattinelli et al. (2013) carried out a meta-analysis of functional imaging studies. Word processing during reading was associated with brain areas (e.g., regions of the temporal lobe, the anterior fusiform region) involved in semantic processing.

Second, the model does not exhibit learning. As a result, it does not explain how children acquire grapheme–phoneme rules in the first place.

Third, the model assumes phonological processing of words typically occurs fairly slowly and has little effect on word recognition and reading. As we saw earlier, however, phonological processing often occurs rapidly and automatically (Rastle & Brysbaert, 2006).

Fourth, Adelman et al. (2014) tested the model by focusing on individual differences. The model did not provide an adequate account of individual differences. In addition, the model's assumption that readers have perfect knowledge of the positions of letters within words was shown to be incorrect.

Fifth, it is more impressive when a computational model accounts for numerous findings using relatively few parameters (values free to change) rather than many. The model has over 30 parameters, so it is unsurprising it fits the data well.

Sixth, the dual-route model cannot be applied universally. As Coltheart et al. (2001, p. 236) admitted, "Monosyllabic nonwords cannot even be written in the Chinese script or in Japanese kanji, so the distinction between a lexical and non-lexical route for reading cannot even arise."

Connectionist triangle model

Within the dual-route model, it is assumed pronouncing irregular words and non-words involves different routes. This contrasts somewhat with the connectionist triangle approach advocated by Plaut et al. (1996) and Harm and Seidenberg (2004). According to this approach:

> All of the system's knowledge of spelling–sound correspondences is brought to bear in pronouncing all types of letter strings [words and non-words]. Conflicts among possible alternative pronunciations of a letter string are resolved . . . by co-operative and competitive interactions based on how the letter string relates to all known words and their pronunciations.
>
> (Plaut et al., 1996, p. 58)

As the above quotation makes clear, the model is based on a highly interactive system. In other words, word processing involves "all hands to the pump".

The triangle model (which has been instantiated in distributed connectionist form) is shown in Figure 9.5. The three sides of the triangle are orthography (spelling), phonology (sound) and semantics (meaning). There are two routes from

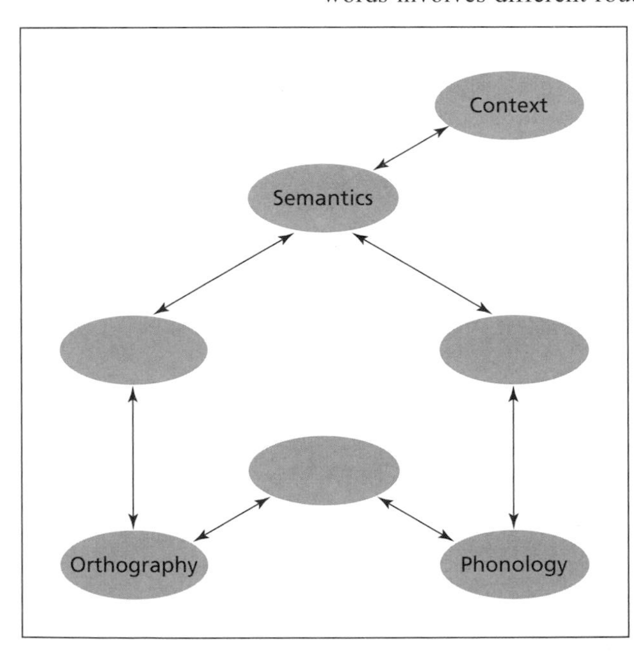

Figure 9.5
The triangle model of reading showing two routes from orthography to phonology.
From Harley (2010).

spelling to sound: (1) a direct pathway from orthography to phonology; and (2) an indirect pathway from orthography to phonology that proceeds via word meanings. If you compare this figure with Figure 9.4, it is clear semantics plays a greater role in reading in the triangle than the dual-route model.

According to the triangle model, words and non-words vary in *consistency* – the extent to which their pronunciation agrees with those of similarly spelled words (known as neighbours). Harley (2010) gives the examples of TAZE and TAVE. TAZE has consistent neighbours (*gaze*, *laze*, *maze*), whereas TAVE does not (*have* as well as *gave*, *rave*, *save*). The prediction (to which we will return) is that consistent words and non-words should be said faster than inconsistent ones. In contrast, the dual-route model focuses on dividing words into regular ones (conforming to grapheme–phoneme rules) and irregular (not conforming to those rules).

How does the triangle model account for the dyslexias? It is assumed surface dyslexia occurs mainly because of damage to the semantic system. Plaut et al. (1996) damaged their connectionist model to reduce or eliminate the contribution of semantics. Its performance remained very good on consistent high- and low-frequency words and on non-words, worse on inconsistent high-frequency words, and worst on inconsistent low-frequency words. This matches the pattern with surface dyslexics.

The model assumes phonological dyslexia (involving problems in reading unfamiliar words and pseudowords) is due to a *general* impairment of phonological processing. Evidence relevant to this assumption is discussed later. Finally, there is deep dyslexia (involving problems in reading unfamiliar words and non-words plus semantic errors). The fact it shares several symptoms with phonological dyslexia suggests it may represent a more serious form of phonological dyslexia. Within the triangle model, deep dyslexia may involve severely impaired phonological processing leading to increased reliance on semantic processing.

Findings

Plaut et al. (1996) trained the model to pronounce words accurately. Learning occurred via back-propagation (see Glossary) in which the system's actual outputs or responses were compared against the correct ones (see Chapter 1). The network received prolonged training with 2,998 words. After this, its performance resembled that of adult readers in various ways:

- Inconsistent words took longer to name than consistent ones.
- Rare words took longer to name than common ones.
- The effects of consistency were much greater for rare words than common ones.
- The network pronounced over 90% of non-words "correctly", which is comparable to adult readers. This is impressive given the network received no direct training on non-words.

According to the model, semantic factors can be important in reading aloud, especially when the words (or non-words) are irregular or inconsistent and so are more difficult to read. McKay et al. (2008) tested this prediction by training participants to read aloud non-words (e.g., *bink*). Some had consistent (or expected) pronunciations, whereas others had inconsistent pronunciations. Participants learned the meanings of some of these non-words.

McKay et al.'s (2008) findings were as predicted by the model. Reading aloud was faster for non-words in the semantic condition (learning pronunciations) than the non-semantic condition when the non-words were inconsistent. However, speed of reading aloud was the same in the semantic and non-semantic conditions with consistent non-words.

Preliminary evaluation

The triangle model has several successes to its credit. First, the overarching assumption that the orthographic, semantic and phonological systems are used in a parallel, interactive fashion during reading has received much support. Second, the assumption the semantic system is often important in reading aloud appears correct (e.g., McKay et al., 2008). Third, the triangle approach includes an explicit mechanism to simulate how we learn to pronounce words, whereas the dual-route model has less to say about learning.

What are the triangle model's limitations? First, as Harley (2013) pointed out, the model has "focused on the recognition of morphologically simple, often monosyllabic words".

Second, as Plaut et al. (1996, p. 108) admitted, "The nature of processing within the semantic pathway has been characterised in only the coarsest way." However, Harm and Seidenberg (2004) largely filled that gap within the triangle model by implementing its semantic component to map orthography and phonology on to semantics.

Third, the model's explanations of phonological dyslexia and surface dyslexia are oversimplified. Phonological dyslexia is supposed to be due to a general phonological impairment, but some phonological dyslexics do not show that general impairment (e.g., Caccappolo-van Vliet et al., 2004). This issue is discussed further shortly.

Controversial topics

We turn now to a discussion of controversial topics for which the two models make different predictions. Bear in mind, however, that both models have evolved over time, and so some predictions have changed.

Surface dyslexia

Remember that surface dyslexics have problems in reading exception words (irregular or inconsistent words) but perform reasonably well with regular or consistent words and with non-words. According to the dual-route cascaded model, surface dyslexics have damage to Routes 2 and 3, and so must rely heavily or exclusively on Route 1 (grapheme–phoneme conversion). In contrast, the connectionist triangle model argues that the major problem in surface dyslexia is extensive damage to the semantic system.

Woollams et al. (2007) assessed the importance of semantic information in reading aloud by studying 51 patients with semantic dementia. It is a condition involving severe loss of knowledge about word meanings (see Chapter 7). Surface dyslexia was present in 48 of the 51 patients, and the remaining three patients became surface dyslexic as their semantic knowledge deteriorated over time. Of crucial importance, there was a large negative correlation between the ability to read low-frequency exception words and the extent of patients' semantic knowledge.

In sum, both models provide reasonable accounts of surface dyslexia. Problems within the semantic system are of great importance to surface dyslexia. It can be argued that the triangle model offers the simpler explanation.

Phonological dyslexia

Phonological dyslexia involves severe difficulties in reading unfamiliar words and pseudowords. According to the dual-route cascaded model, the central problem in phonological dyslexia is the patient's inability to use Route 1 (grapheme–phoneme conversion). In contrast, it is assumed within the connectionist triangle model that phonological dyslexics have a general phonological deficit. Thus, an important issue is whether the problems of phonological dyslexics are *specific* to reading (the dual-route model) or are more *general* (the triangle model).

The evidence is mixed. Support for the dual-route model comes from a study by Caccappolo-van Vliet et al. (2004), discussed earlier. Their two phonological dyslexics showed essentially intact performance on various non-reading phonological tasks. In contrast, Coltheart (1996) found many cases in which phonological dyslexia was associated with a general phonological impairment. This is more consistent with the triangle model.

There are various types of phonological dyslexia. Nickels et al. (2008) used computer modelling and data from phonological dyslexics. No single locus of impairment (e.g., the phonological system) could account for the various impairments found in patients.

In sum, both models can explain the findings from some (but not all) patients with phonological dyslexia. However, many (or even most) phonological dyslexics have fairly general phonological impairments.

Deep dyslexia

The dual-route model emphasises reading processes within the left hemisphere. Coltheart et al. (2001) argued that deep dyslexics (who make many semantic errors when reading aloud) predominantly use the *right* hemisphere when reading. As a result, an account of deep dyslexia is outside the scope of the dual-route model. In contrast, it is assumed within the general triangle approach that deep dyslexia and phonological dyslexia both involve severe impairments in phonological processing with no clear dividing line between the two conditions.

There is support for the assumptions based on the triangle model approach. Jefferies et al. (2007) found deep dyslexics performed poorly on various phonologically based tasks (e.g., phoneme addition, phoneme subtraction). They concluded deep dyslexics have a general phonological impairment as do phonological dyslexics. Crisp et al. (2011) studied patients diagnosed with deep dyslexia or phonological dyslexia. The two groups were similar in that they both had substantially impaired ability to translate orthography (spelling) into phonology as predicted by the triangle approach. It is plausible the semantic errors made by deep dyslexics occur because their very severe problems with phonological processing force them to rely heavily on the semantic system.

In sum, the triangle model provides a generally persuasive account of deep dyslexia. However, it is probably not applicable to *all* cases (Harley, 2013).

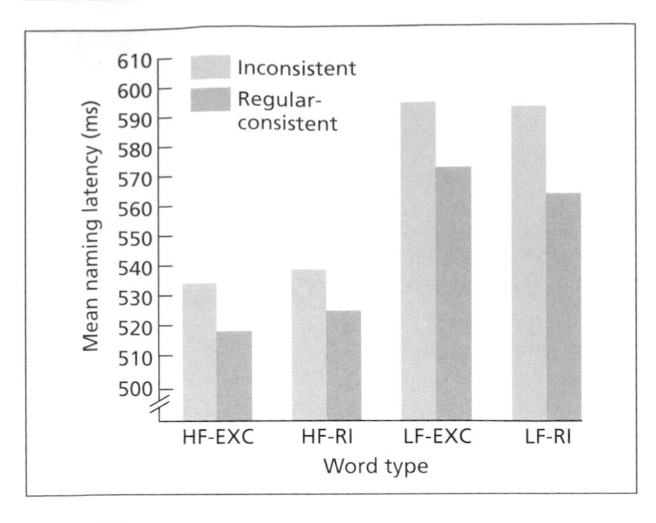

Figure 9.6
Mean naming latencies for high-frequency (HF) and low-frequency (LF) words that were irregular (exception words: EXC) or regular and inconsistent (RI). Mean naming latencies of regular consistent words matched with each of these word types are also shown. The differences between consistent and inconsistent words were much greater than those between regular and irregular words (EXC compared to RI).

From Jared (2002). Reprinted with permission from Elsevier.

Word regularity vs. word consistency

According to the dual-route model, *regular* words (those conforming to the grapheme–phoneme rules in Route 1) can often be named faster than irregular words. According to the triangle approach, what matters is *consistency*. Consistent words have letter patterns always pronounced the same in all words in which they appear and are assumed to be faster to name than inconsistent words. Irregular words tend to be inconsistent, and so we need to decide whether *regularity* or *consistency* is more important.

Jared (2002) presented words belonging to the four following categories:

1. regular consistent (e.g., *bean*);
2. regular inconsistent (e.g., *beak*);
3. irregular consistent (e.g., *both*);
4. irregular inconsistent (e.g., *bear*).

The findings were reasonably clear-cut: word naming times were affected more by consistency than by regularity (see Figure 9.6). This finding, which supports the triangle model but not the dual-route model, has been replicated in other studies (Harley, 2013).

Pronouncing non-words

The dual-route model assumes the processes involved in reading non-words are *inflexible*. As Pritchard et al. (2012, p. 1278) pointed out, the dual-route model is designed to account for a "skilled reader, and thus only produces a single, ideal response to each nonword". This contrasts with the triangle model, which argues that the pronunciations of inconsistent non-words should be more variable than those of consistent ones. Zevin and Seidenberg (2006) obtained findings supportive of the triangle model rather than the dual-route model.

Pritchard et al. (2012) asked 47 participants to read 1,475 non-words. There were two main findings. First, the mean number of different pronunciations produced for each non-word was 8.4. Second, the mean percentage of participants giving the most frequent response to a non-word was 61.2%. Thus, there was substantially more flexibility in non-word pronunciation than can be accommodated by the dual-route model.

Evidence of flexibility in the pronunciation of non-words due to language context was reported by Buetler et al. (2014). The relationship between spelling and sound is much more *consistent* in German than French and so the non-lexical route involving grapheme-to-phoneme conversion should be easier to use in German. In contrast, the lexical or dictionary lookup route should be more suitable in French given the difficulty in using the non-lexical route.

Buetler et al. (2014) tested the above predictions using German/French bilinguals presented with non-words presented in a context of German or

French words. As predicted, the non-lexical route was used more often in the German context than the French one, whereas the opposite was the case for the lexical route. This responsiveness to language context is harder to explain on the dual-route model than the triangle model.

KEY TERM

Orthographic lexicon
Part of long-term memory in which learned word spellings are stored.

Converging models

The dual-route and triangle models have evolved to account more precisely for the data. As a consequence, the predictions of the two models differ less nowadays than in the past. We will discuss similarities between them in the context of a meta-analysis of neuroimaging studies of reading carried out by Taylor et al. (2013).

According to both models, different processes are used with words and non-words. Thus, some brain areas should be more activated during the processing of words than non-words, and other brain areas should show the opposite pattern. The evidence strongly supported these predictions. Words produced more activation than non-words in the anterior fusiform gyrus, an area associated with the **orthographic lexicon** and/or the semantic system. Words also produced more activation than pseudowords in the angular and middle temporal gyri, areas associated with the phonological lexicon and/or semantic system. Unsurprisingly, words engage semantic processes and the orthographic and phonological lexicons more than non-words.

Interactive exercise:
Dual route reading

Non-words produced more activation than words in the posterior fusiform and occipito-temporal cortex, areas involved in basic orthographic processing. Non-words also produced more activation than words in the inferior parietal and inferior parietal cortex and inferior frontal gyrus, areas involved in converting orthographic information into sound-based information. These findings appear consistent with the dual-route model.

Finally, irregular words produced more activation than regular ones in the inferior frontal gyrus. This finding reflects the greater effort involved in deciding how to pronounce irregular words.

Taylor et al. (2013) used the findings from their meta-analysis to identify the brain areas associated with the processes involved in reading (see Figure 9.7). They also indicated how these processes can be related to the dual-route and triangle models.

In sum, neuroimaging findings are broadly consistent with both models, but are perhaps more consistent with the more detailed assumptions incorporated into the dual-route model. However, a note of caution is in order. Discovering a given brain area is activated more during word than non-word processing, say, does not necessarily mean that area is necessarily more crucial for word processing. This is because the correlational nature of neuroimaging evidence precludes drawing conclusions about causality.

READING: EYE-MOVEMENT RESEARCH

Eye movements are of fundamental importance to reading. Most text information we process at any given moment relates to the word currently being fixated. However, some information from other words close to fixation may also be processed.

KEY TERM

Saccades
Rapid eye movements separated by eye fixations lasting about 250 milliseconds.

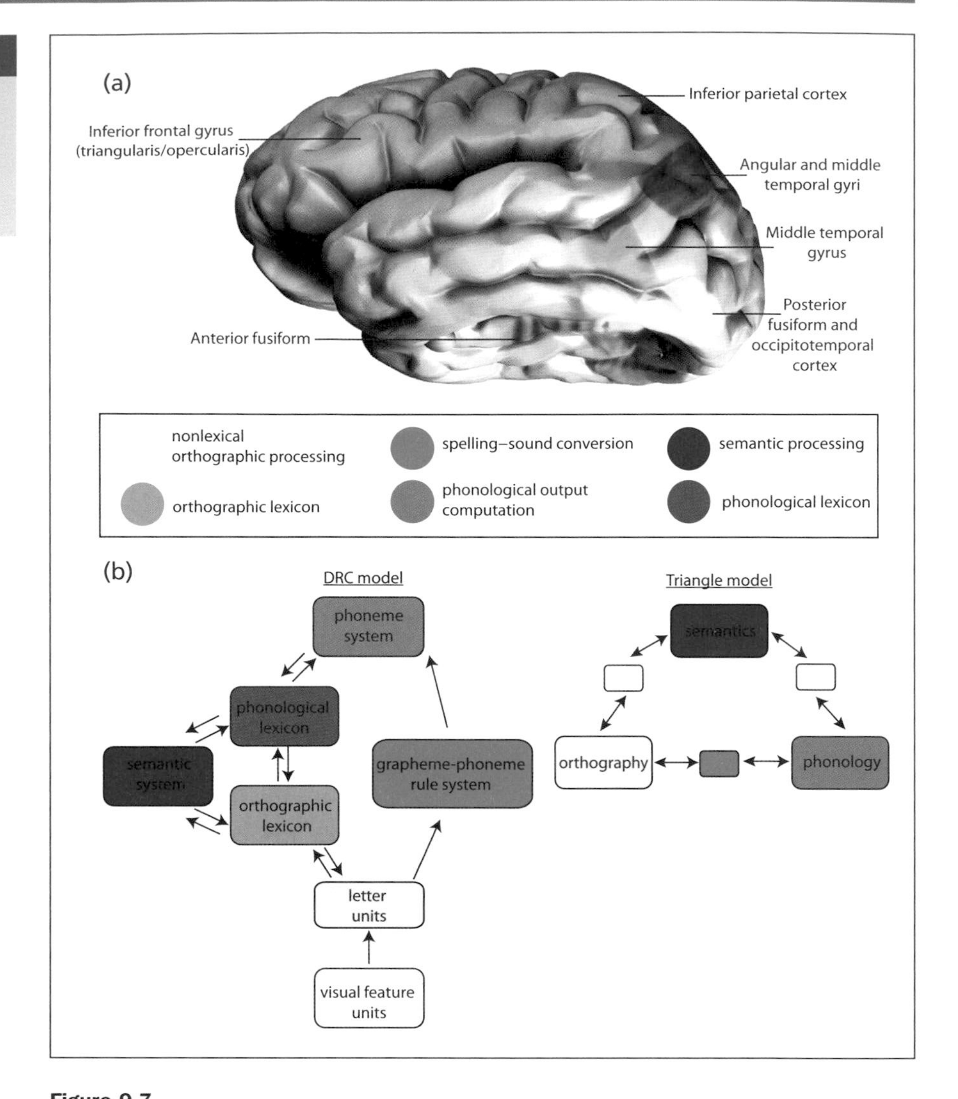

Figure 9.7
(a) Brain areas associated with non-lexical orthographic processing (yellow), spelling–sound conversion (green), semantic processing (red), orthographic lexicon (orange), phonological output computation (blue) and phonological lexicon (purple). (b) The components shown in (a) related to the dual-route cascaded (DRC) model (left) and the triangle model (right).
From Taylor et al. (2013). © American Psychological Association.

Our eyes seem to move smoothly while reading. However, they actually move in rapid jerks (**saccades**). Saccades are ballistic (once initiated their directions cannot be changed). Regressions (the eyes moving backwards in the text) account for 10% of saccades.

Saccades take 20–30 ms to complete and are separated by fixations lasting 200–250 ms. The length of each saccade is about eight letters or spaces. Information is extracted from the text *only* during each fixation.

The amount of text from which useful information can be obtained on each fixation has been assessed with the "moving window" technique (Rayner et al., 2012). The text is mutilated except for an experimenter-defined area or window surrounding the reader's fixation point. When the reader moves his/her eyes, different parts of the text are mutilated to permit normal reading only within the window region. The effects of different-sized windows on reading performance can be compared.

The **perceptual span** (effective field of view) is affected by text difficulty and print size. It extends three or four letters to the left of fixation and up to 15 letters to the right in English, which is read in a left-to-right fashion. Note that there are other languages (e.g., Hebrew) in which reading is right-to-left. The size of the perceptual span varies across languages. In Chinese, it only extends one character to the left of fixation and two or three characters to the right (Inhoff & Liu, 1998), reflecting the complexity of Chinese characters.

The size of the perceptual span means parafoveal information (from the area surrounding the foveal region of high visual acuity) is used in reading. Convincing evidence comes from the boundary technique in which there is a preview word just to the right of fixation. When readers make a saccade to this word, it changes into the target word (the reader is unaware of the change). The fixation time on the target word is less when it is the same as the preview word because visual and phonological information is extracted during parafoveal processing (Rayner et al., 2012).

Readers fixate 80% of content words (nouns, verbs, adjectives) but only 20% of function words (articles such as *a* and *the*; conjunctions such as *and* and *or*). Words not fixated tend to be common, short or predictable. Thus, easily processed words are most likely to be skipped. Finally, there is the **spillover effect**: the fixation time on a word preceded by a rare word is longer.

There are numerous theoretical accounts of reading based on eye-movement data (Rayner & Reichle, 2010). However, we will focus on the most influential theoretical approach: the E-Z Reader model.

KEY TERMS

Perceptual span
The effective field of view in reading (letters to the left and right of fixation that can be processed).

Spillover effect
Any given word is fixated longer during reading when preceded by a rare word rather than a common one.

Weblink:
Eye movements when reading

E-Z Reader model

Several versions of the E-Z Reader model, starting with Reichle et al. (1998), have been put forward (Rayner et al., 2012). The model is designed to account for the pattern of eye movements in reading.

The most obvious model would assume we fixate a word until we have processed it adequately, after which we immediately fixate the next word until it has been adequately processed. Alas, there are two major problems with such a model. First, it takes 85–200 ms to execute an eye-movement programme and so readers would waste time waiting for their eyes to move to the next word.

Second, readers sometimes skip words. It is hard to see how this could happen within the above model because readers would know nothing about the next word until they had fixated it. How, then, could readers decide which words to skip?

The E-Z Reader model provides an elegant solution to the above problems. A crucial assumption is the next eye movement is programmed after only *partial* processing of the current word. This assumption greatly reduces the time between completing processing of the current word and eye movement to the next word. There is typically less spare time available with rare words than common ones – this accounts for the spillover effect. If the processing of the next word is completed rapidly enough (e.g., it is highly predictable in the sentence context), it is skipped.

KEY TERM

Lexical access
Accessing detailed information about a given word by entering the **lexicon**.

According to the model, readers can attend to two words (the currently fixated one and the next one) during a single fixation. However, it is a *serial* processing model – at any given moment only *one* word is processed.

The E-Z Reader model differs from *parallel* processing models such as the SWIFT (Saccade-generation With Inhibition by Foveal Targets) model (Engbert et al., 2005; Engbert & Kliegl, 2011). This model assumes the durations of eye fixations in reading are influenced by the previous and next words as well as the current one. The typical perceptual span of about 18 letters can often accommodate all three words (prior, current and next) provided they are of average length. We will compare these models later.

Here are the six major assumptions of the E-Z Reader model:

1. Readers check the familiarity of the word currently fixated.
2. Completion of frequency checking of a word (the first stage of lexical access) is the signal to initiate an eye-movement programme.
3. Readers then engage in the second stage of **lexical access**, which involves accessing the current word's semantic and phonological forms.
4. Completion of the second stage signals a shift of covert (internal) attention to the next word.
5. Frequency checking and lexical access are completed faster for common words than rare ones (more so for lexical access).
6. Frequency checking and lexical access are completed faster for predictable than unpredictable words.

The above theoretical assumptions lead to various predictions (see Figure 9.8). Assumptions 2 and 5 together predict common words will be fixated for less time than rare words: this has been found repeatedly. According to the model, readers spend the time between completion of lexical access to one word and the next eye movement in parafoveal processing of the next word. There is less parafoveal processing when the fixated word is rare (see Figure 9.8). Thus, the word following a rare word is fixated longer than one following a common word (the spillover effect described earlier).

Why are common, predictable or short words most likely to be skipped or not fixated? A word is skipped when its lexical access has been completed during fixation on the current word. This is most likely with common, predictable or short words because lexical access is fastest for these words (assumptions 5 and 6).

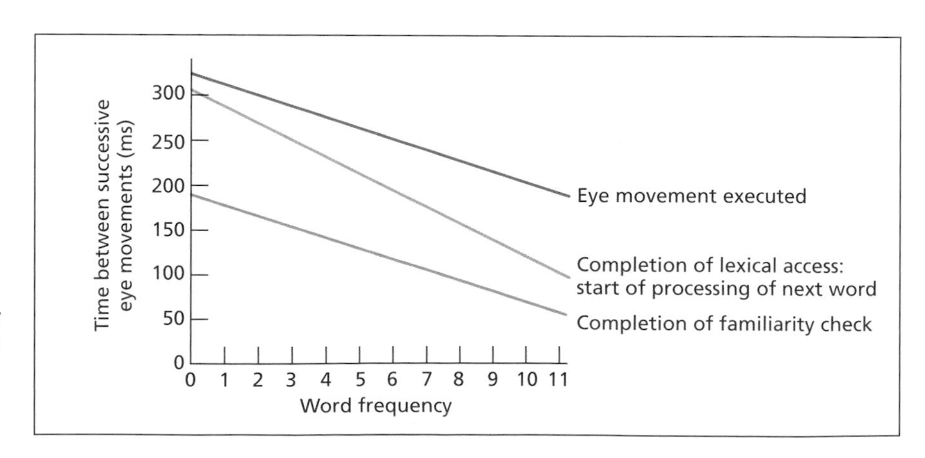

Figure 9.8
The effects of word frequency on eye movements according to the E-Z Reader model.
Adapted from Reichle et al. (1998).

Findings

The model's major assumptions have all received much support (Rayner et al., 2012). For example, the model assumes word-frequency information is accessed rapidly during word processing. Reichle et al. (2011) used event-related potentials (ERPs; see Glossary) and found word frequency influenced brain activity within 110 ms of word onset.

A central assumption of the model is that there are two stages of lexical processing for words: (1) checking word frequency; and (2) lexical access (accessing semantic and phonological information about the word). Sheridan and Reingold (2013) argued that presenting words faintly disrupts stage 1 but not stage 2. In contrast, case alternation (e.g., tAbLe) disrupts only stage 2. Their findings were as predicted and strengthen support for the notion that lexical processing occurs in two stages.

The assumption readers use parafoveal processing to extract information from the next word before fixating it was tested by Reingold et al. (2012). One of the sentences read by participants was *John decided to sell the table in the garage sale*. On some trials, as they made a saccade towards the word *table*, it was replaced by the word *banjo*. As predicted by the model, participants fixated longer on *banjo* than on *table* because it had not benefited from extrafoveal processing.

The reading strategies used by English readers (the focus of most research) may not be universal. Rayner et al. (2007) studied eye movements in Chinese individuals reading Chinese text. Chinese differs from English in that it is written without spaces between characters and most words consist of two characters. In spite of these differences, the pattern of eye movements resembled that previously found for readers of English. Other research has shown that reading rates in English and Chinese are comparable (Reilly & Radach, 2012).

The E-Z Reader model assumes words are processed serially (one at a time). We will focus on **parafoveal-on-foveal effects** – it sounds complicated but simply means that characteristics of the *next* word influence the fixation duration on the *current* word. If such effects exist, they suggest the current and the next word are processed at the same time. Thus, these effects would support the existence of parallel processing as predicted by the SWIFT model but not the E-Z Reader model.

The findings are mixed (Schotter et al., 2012). Orthographic information in the parafoveal word can apparently produce parafoveal-on-foveal effects. For example, Pynte et al. (2004) found the fixation on a word was shorter when the next, parafoveal word contained a spelling mistake. Lexical information (word frequency) of a parafoveal word can also produce parafoveal-on-foveal effects (Harley, 2013). Parafoveal-on-foveal effects are typically small and sometimes non-significant. Overall, the findings suggest processing during reading is predominantly serial but with some limited parallel processing.

Most versions of the E-Z Reader model (other than the most recent ones) assume readers fixate and process words in the "correct" order (although occasional words may be skipped). If readers deviate from the "correct" order, the model predicts they would struggle to understand what they are reading. Readers often fail to read texts in a totally orderly way (10% of eye movements are regressions). However, failures to read words in the correct order have only limited and short-term effects (Kennedy & Pynte, 2008).

KEY TERM

Parafoveal-on-foveal effects
The finding that fixation duration on the *current* word is influenced by characteristics of the next word.

Evaluation

The model has proved very successful in several ways. First, it specifies several major factors (e.g., word frequency, word predictability) determining eye fixations in reading. Second, there is support for the assumption that lexical processing occurs in two separate stages. Third, the model has identified close connections between eye (fixations) and mind (cognitive processes) during reading. We can see this more clearly by considering what happens when readers engage in mind wandering. This produced a decoupling of eyes and mind in which fixations were longer and erratic and were less influenced by factors such as word frequency (Reichle et al., 2010). Fourth, the model performs well against rival models (Rayner & Reichle, 2010) and is applicable to languages other than English.

What are the model's limitations? First, its emphasis is on early reading processes (e.g., lexical access). As a result, the model has little to say about higher-level processes (e.g., integration of information across a sentence).

Second, the existence of parafoveal-on-foveal effects suggests parallel processing can occur. Even though the effects are mostly small, they are inconsistent with the model's serial processing assumption.

Third, the finding that most readers fail to process the words within a text strictly in the "correct" order is inconsistent with the model. The fact that readers generally cope well with reading in an "incorrect" order is also not predicted by the model.

Fourth, context influences reading in complex ways not predicted by the model. For example, word predictability and word frequency sometimes have *additive* effects on fixation times and sometimes have *interactive* effects (Hand et al., 2010). The E-Z Reader model does not make clear predictions about the relationship between these factors.

Fifth, the model probably focuses too much on explaining eye-movement data. What is needed is to *integrate* the findings from eye-movement studies more closely with general theories of reading.

Sixth, we saw earlier that word presentation often triggers the activation of other, related words (Chen & Mirman, 2012). However, the model does not readily accommodate these findings.

SPEECH PERCEPTION: INTRODUCTION

Speech perception is easily the most important form of auditory perception. However, other kinds (e.g., music perception) are also of significance. There has been controversy concerning the relationship between speech perception and auditory perception in general. One possibility (Trout, 2001) is that humans are born with specially designed speech-perception mechanisms. However, many theorists argue for a *general* mechanism used to process both speech and non-speech sounds.

An interesting (but controversial) view was expressed by Brandt et al. (2012). They claimed we can "describe spoken language as a special type of music" (p. 1). We will briefly mention two kinds of relevant evidence. First, adults typically use child-directed speech when talking to children. Child-directed speech is high-pitched, slow and rhythmical and so has a musical quality about it. Second, if you listen repeatedly to the same looped recording of speech it often starts to sound like singing as you cease to attend to the meaning of what is being said (Tierney et al., 2013). Brain areas associated with music perception were more activated by repeated speech perceived as song than repeated speech not perceived as song.

Further evidence on the relationship between speech perception and music perception is discussed briefly below. After that, we discuss the main processing stages involved in speech perception.

KEY TERM

Categorical perception
A sound intermediate between two **phonemes** is perceived as being one or other of the phonemes.

Categorical perception

Suppose listeners are presented with a series of sounds starting with /ba/ and gradually moving towards /da/ and report what sound they hear. We might expect listeners to report a gradual change from perceiving one phoneme to the other. In fact, however, there is typically **categorical perception** – speech stimuli intermediate between two phonemes are categorised as one of those phonemes. Below we address the issue of whether categorical perception is unique to speech perception.

Raizada and Poldrack (2007) studied brain processes associated with categorical perception. Two auditory stimuli were presented together, and listeners decided whether they represented the same phoneme. The listeners showed categorical perception. Of interest, differences in brain activation of the two stimuli were strongly *amplified* when they were on opposite sides of the boundary between the two phonemes.

We must not exaggerate the extent of categorical perception with speech sounds. Categorical perception is more evident with consonants than vowels and depends to some extent on the particular task demands (Scott & Evans, 2010).

Case study:
ASL

Categorical perception is *not* confined to speech perception. Locke and Kellar (1973) studied chord identification. Musicians showed much clearer evidence of categorical perception than non-musicians when categorising chords as A minor or A major. This finding may help to explain why categorical perception of phonemes is so strong – we are all expert listeners to phonemes. McMurray et al. (2008) confirmed musicians show categorical perception.

Cognitive neuroscience

Much overlap in the brain areas associated with the processing of speech and non-speech sounds has often been reported. For example, Husain et al. (2006) found various speech and non-speech sounds activated similar regions in the primary and non-primary areas of the temporal cortex, intraparietal cortex and frontal lobe. In addition, there were only minor differences in *patterns* of brain activity when speech and non-speech sounds were processed.

This overlap in the brain areas associated with speech and music perception occurs in part because there are close connections between them. These connections are found at three levels of analysis: sound, structure and meaning (Slevc, 2012).

Rogalsky et al. (2011b) obtained rather different findings from those of Husain et al. (2006). They assessed brain activation while participants listened to sentences, scrambled sentences and novel melodies. Speech and music perception both activated the superior temporal lobe and there was overlap in parts of the auditory cortex. However, the patterns of activation produced by speech and by music were distinguishable even in the overlapping regions. There were also several non-overlapping areas. For example, a temporal lobe network was activated during the processing of sentences (but not scrambled sentences). This network was not activated at all by music perception.

Why did previous research suggest greater overlap in the brain areas involved in speech and music perception than found by Rogalsky et al. (2011b)? The complex nature of the tasks used by other researchers meant that higher-order cognitive processes (e.g., working memory) were required for both speech and music perception.

Research on brain-damaged individuals has also revealed important differences between speech and music perception. Some patients have intact speech perception but impaired music perception, whereas others have intact music perception but impaired speech perception (Peretz & Coltheart, 2003).

The speech-production system is typically activated during speech perception. There is much evidence (discussed later) indicating this system plays an important role in speech perception (Möttönen & Watkins, 2012). Möttönen et al. (2013) wondered whether the motor cortex was also important in the perception of non-speech sounds (piano tones). They used transcranial magnetic stimulation (TMS; see Glossary) to disrupt motor lip representations in the motor cortex. This impaired the processing of speech sounds but not non-speech sounds. Thus, motor processes are probably more important in speech than non-speech perception.

Processing stages

The main processes involved in listening to speech are shown in Figure 9.9. Initially, we often have to select out the speech signal of interest from several other irrelevant auditory inputs (e.g., other voices). Decoding involves extracting discrete elements (e.g., phonemes or basic speech sounds) from the speech signal.

There is controversy as to whether the second stage of speech perception involves identifying phonemes or syllables. Goldinger and Azuma (2003) argued that the perceptual unit varies flexibly. Participants listened to lists of non-words recorded by speakers who had been told phonemes or syllables were the basic units of speech perception.

Listeners detected phoneme targets faster than syllable targets when the speaker believed phonemes were the fundamental units in speech. However, the opposite was the case when the speaker believed syllables were the fundamental units. Thus, either phonemes or syllables can form the perceptual units in speech perception.

The third stage (word identification) is of special importance. Various problems in word identification are discussed shortly. However, one problem will be mentioned here. All the English words we know are formed from only about 35 phonemes. As a result, most spoken words resemble many other words at the phonemic level, making them hard to distinguish.

The fourth and fifth stages both emphasise speech comprehension. The focus in the fourth stage is on *interpretation* of the utterance. This involves constructing a coherent meaning for each sentence on the basis of information about individual words and their order in the sentence. Finally, in the fifth stage, the meaning of the current sentence is integrated with preceding speech to construct an overall model of the speaker's message.

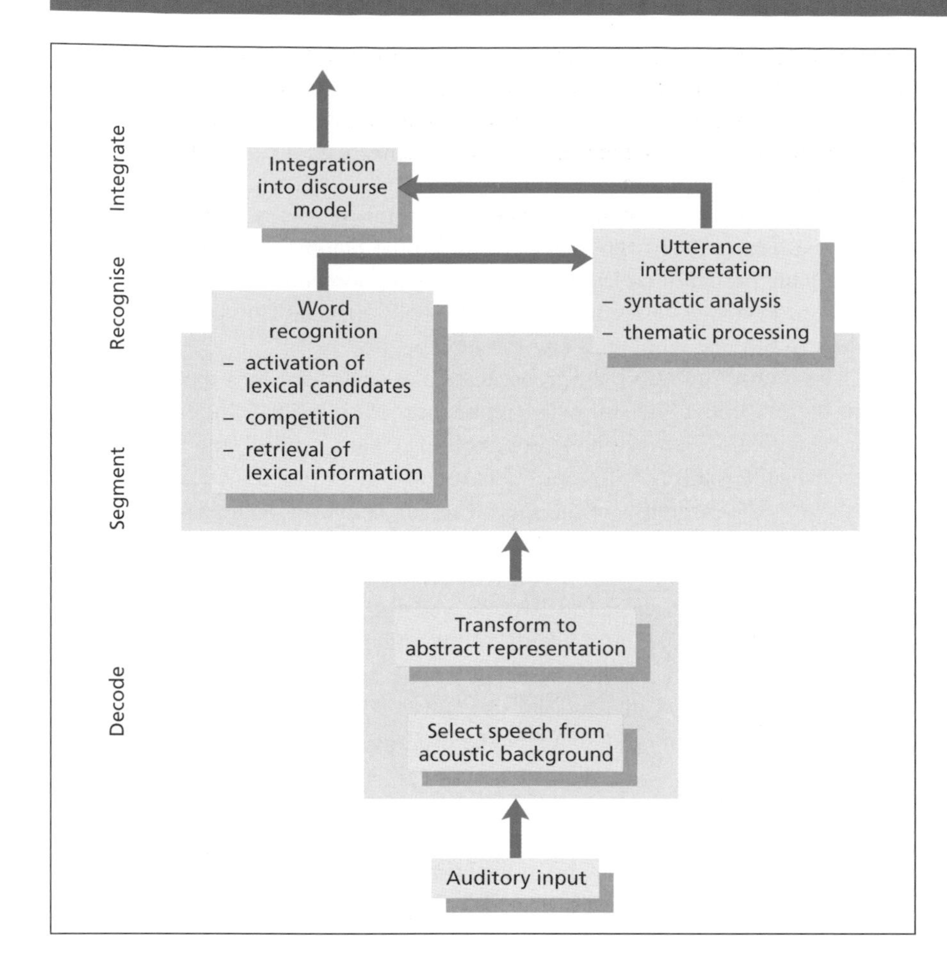

Figure 9.9
The main processes involved in speech perception and comprehension.

From Cutler and Clifton (1999). By permission of Oxford University Press.

LISTENING TO SPEECH

Understanding speech is much less straightforward than we might imagine. At the most general level, listeners have to contend with considerable *variability* in the speech signal. In other words, any given phoneme (basic unit of sound) or word can be pronounced in several different ways.

Listeners in everyday life also have to cope with perceiving speech under various adverse conditions. Mattys et al. (2012, p. 953) defined an *adverse condition* as, "any factor leading to a decrease in speech intelligibility on a given task relative to the level of intelligibility when the same task is performed in optimal listening situations".

Mattys et al. (2009) distinguished between two major types of adverse conditions. First, there is *energetic* masking, in which distracting sounds cause the intelligibility of target words to be degraded. Energetic masking primarily affects bottom-up processing and is a serious problem for listeners in everyday life. There are often several people talking at the same time and/or there are distracting sounds (e.g., traffic noise). Until fairly recently, listeners in the laboratory were rarely confronted by these problems. This led Mattys and Liss (2008, p. 1235) to argue that, "Laboratory-generated phenomena reflect what the speech perception system can do with highly constrained input."

KEY TERMS

Segmentation
Dividing the almost continuous sounds of speech into separate **phonemes** and words.

Coarticulation
A speaker's production of a **phoneme** is influenced by his/her production of the previous sound and by preparations for the next sound.

Second, there is *informational* masking, in which cognitive load (e.g., performing a second task while listening to speech) makes speech perception harder. Informational masking mainly affects top-down processing.

Here are some specific problems faced by listeners:

- There is the issue of **segmentation**, which involves separating out or distinguishing phonemes and words from the pattern of speech sounds. As you have probably noticed when listening to someone speak an unfamiliar foreign language, speech has few periods of silence. This makes it hard to know when one word ends and the next begins.
- There is **coarticulation**: the pronunciation of a phoneme by a speaker depends on the preceding and following phonemes. Harley (2010, p. 148) provides an example: "The /b/ phonemes in 'bill', 'ball', 'able', and 'rub' are all acoustically slightly different." Coarticulation is problematical because it increases the variability of the speech signal. However, it can also be a useful cue, because it allows listeners to predict to some extent the next phoneme.
- Speakers differ from each other in several ways (e.g., their dialect, rate of speaking), and yet we generally cope well with such variability. How do we do it? Kraljic et al. (2008) identified two main answers. First, listeners may be responsive to acoustic invariants in the speech signal across different speakers. Second, listeners may use active cognitive processes to produce perceptual learning and so understand a speaker with an unusual speech pattern.

  Kraljic et al. (2008) argued that *perceptual learning* is important. However, it is not *always* used. Suppose a friend gets drunk and starts slurring his words. Since this is not characteristic of his normal speech, it would not make sense to learn to perceive his drunken speech. Similarly, Kraljic et al. found listeners did not show perceptual learning when the speaker spoke oddly because she had a pen in her mouth.

  Magnuson and Nusbaum (2007) argued that listeners' *expectations* are important. Some listeners to a speech signal expected to hear two speakers with similar voices whereas others expected to hear one speaker. In fact, there was only one speaker. Those expecting two speakers showed worse listening performance because they devoted cognitive resources to identifying and coping with two voices.
- Language is spoken at about ten phonemes (basic speech sounds) per second and so requires rapid processing.

Coping with listening problems

We have seen that listeners experience various problems and complexities when understanding speech. How do they cope? They use multiple sources of information and these sources are used *flexibly* depending on the immediate situation.

There are bottom-up processes stemming directly from the acoustic signal. There are also top-down processes based on the listener's past knowledge and contextual information (e.g., the speaker's previous utterance). We will see below how these processes aid speech perception.

Segmentation

Dividing the speech they hear into its constituent words (i.e., segmentation) is a crucial task for listeners. Segmentation involves using several cues. Some are acoustic-phonetic (e.g., coarticulaton, stress) whereas others depend on the listener's knowledge (e.g., of words) and the immediate context (Mattys et al., 2012).

Segmentation is influenced by the constraints on what words are possible. For example, a stretch of speech lacking a vowel is not a possible word in English. Listeners found it hard to identify the word *apple* in *fapple* because the [f] could not possibly be an English word (Norris et al., 1997). In contrast, listeners easily detected the word *apple* in *wuffapple* because *wuff* could be an English word.

Stress is an important acoustic cue. In English, the initial syllable of most content words (e.g., nouns, verbs) is typically stressed. Strings of words without the stress on the first syllable are misperceived (e.g., "conduct ascents uphill" is perceived as "A duck descends some pill").

There are other acoustic cues. For example, coarticulation helps listeners to anticipate the next phoneme and there is generally more coarticulation *within* words than *between* them. In addition, segments and syllables at the start and end of words are lengthened relative to those in the middle (Kim et al., 2012).

Finally, listeners sometimes use sentence context rather than acoustic cues to facilitate segmentation. In a study by Kim et al. (2012), speakers pronounced the following italicised words almost identically: "Lovers are meant to *adore* each other" and "The hallway leads to *a door* at the end." In the absence of acoustic cues, listeners relied very heavily on sentence context to decide whether the italicised part of a sentence consisted of one or two words.

Mattys et al. (2005) argued that we need to go beyond simply identifying individual cues that assist word segmentation. According to his hierarchical approach, there are *three* main categories of cues: lexical (e.g., syntax, word knowledge), segmental (e.g., coarticulation) and metrical prosody (e.g., word stress) (see Figure 9.10).

We prefer to use lexical cues (Tier 1) when all cues are available. When lexical information is lacking or is impoverished, we use segmental cues such as coarticulation and **allophony** (one phoneme may be associated with two or more similar sounds or allophones) (Tier 2). For example, the phoneme /p/ is pronounced differently in "pit" and "spit".

Finally, if it is difficult to use Tier 1 or Tier 2 cues, we resort to metrical prosody cues (e.g., stress) (Tier 3). Why do we generally prefer to avoid stress cues? One reason is that stress information is misleading when a word's initial syllable is not stressed (see Cutler & Butterfield, 1992).

The above hierarchical approach has received support. Mattys (2004) found coarticulation (Tier 2) was more useful than stress (Tier 3) for identifying word boundaries when the speech signal was intact. However, when the speech signal was impoverished so it was hard to use Tier 1 or Tier 2 cues, stress was more useful than coarticulation.

Mattys et al. (2005) found that lexical cues (i.e., word context vs. non-word context) were more useful than stress in facilitating word segmentation in a no-noise condition. However, stress was more useful than lexical cues in noise.

KEY TERM

Allophony
An allophone is one of two or more similar sounds associated with the same **phoneme**.

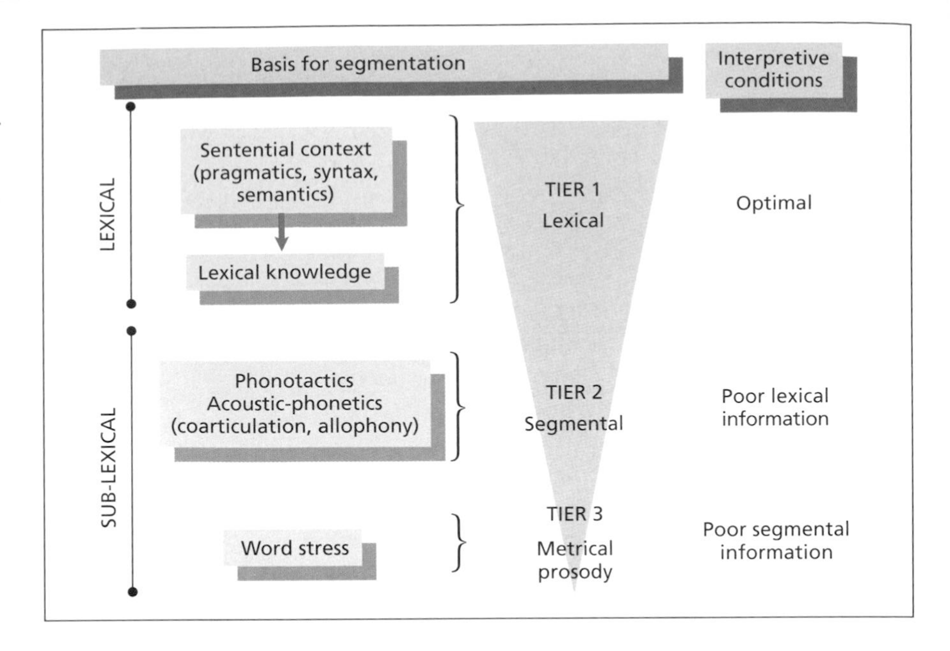

Figure 9.10
A hierarchical approach to speech segmentation involving three levels or tiers. The relative importance of the different types of cue is indicated by the width of the purple triangle.

From Mattys et al. (2005). © American Psychological Association.

Speech perception is harder when there is energetic masking (e.g., distracting sounds) or informational masking (e.g., cognitive load). We might assume both types of masking would have similar effects on speech segmentation. In fact, that is often *not* the case. Consider the effects of coarticulation and transitional probabilities between syllables (low probabilities often indicate a word boundary) on segmentation. Segmentation is determined more by coarticulation than transitional probabilities with an intact speech signal (Fernandes et al., 2007).

What are the effects of energetic and informational masking on segmentation? Fernandes et al. (2007) found energetic masking impaired the usefulness of coarticulation much more than transitional probabilities. In contrast, Fernandes et al. (2010) found informational masking impaired the usefulness of transitional-probability information more than coarticulation. The take-home message is that the effects on speech perception of disrupting bottom-up processes (i.e., energetic masking) differ from those of disrupting top-down processes (i.e., informational masking).

McGurk effect

Weblink:
McGurk effect

Weblink:
Demonstrations of the McGurk effect

Listeners (even with intact hearing) often make extensive use of lip-reading when hearing speech. McGurk and MacDonald (1976) provided a striking demonstration. They prepared a videotape of someone saying "ba" repeatedly. Then the sound channel changed so there was a voice saying "ga" repeatedly in synchronisation with lip movements still indicating "ba". Listeners reported hearing "da", a blending of the visual and auditory information. There is a video of the McGurk effect on YouTube: McGurk effect (with explanation).

It has often been assumed the McGurk effect depends on fairly automatic bottom-up processes triggered directly by the discrepant visual and auditory signals. However, the reality is more complex. The McGurk effect is stronger when the crucial word is presented in a semantically congruent rather than a semantically incongruent sentence (Windmann, 2004). Thus, top-down processes are important.

Soto-Faraco and Alsius (2009) disputed the assumption that the McGurk effect involves *automatic* processes. They discussed their research in which there was a temporal mismatch between the visual and auditory input (one started before the other). The McGurk effect was still found even when participants were aware of the temporal mismatch. Thus, the processes involved are not necessarily entirely automatic.

In sum, the McGurk effect shows listeners often use visual information even when it impairs speech perception. Under normal listening conditions, however, visual information typically enhances speech perception.

CONTEXT EFFECTS

Context essentially consists of relevant information not contained directly in the auditory signal currently available to listeners. There are several types of contextual information including that provided by previous input (e.g., earlier parts of a sentence) and that provided by our knowledge of language and words.

As we will see, context typically influences spoken word recognition (Samuel, 2011). However, it has proved difficult to clarify *when* and *how* context exerts its influence. Harley (2013) identified two extreme positions. According to the *interactionist* account, contextual information can influence processing at an *early* stage and may influence word perception. In contrast, the *autonomous* account claims context has its effects *late* in processing. According to this account, "context cannot have an effect prior to word recognition. It can only contribute to the evaluation and integration of the output of lexical processing, not its generation" (Harley, 2013).

Evidence that context can have a rapid influence on spoken word recognition was provided by Brock and Nation (2014). Participants viewed a display containing four objects and then heard a sentence in various conditions. Their task was to click on any object mentioned in the sentence. In the first three conditions, the object in the sentence was *not* in the display but a critical object (indicated below) was present:

1 Competitor constraining (e.g., "Alex fastened the button"; butter in display).
2 Competitor neutral (e.g., "Alex chose the button"; butter in display).
3 Unrelated neutral (e.g., "Alex chose the button"; lettuce in display).
4 Target neutral (e.g., "Joe chose the button"; button in display).

Brock and Nation (2014) recorded eye movements in the above conditions (see Figure 9.11). When the sentence context made the critical object improbable (condition 1), participants were far less likely to fixate it than when the sentence context was less constraining (condition 2). This difference was apparent early on, and indicates that sentence context has almost immediate effects on word processing. This is consistent with the interactionist account.

In what follows, we will discuss various context effects. Research relevant to the interactionist and autonomous accounts will be considered at various points.

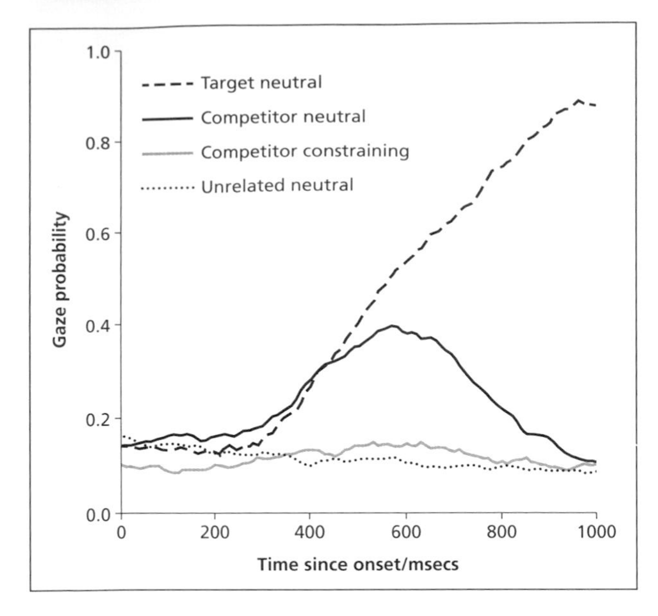

Figure 9.11
Gaze probability for critical objects over the first 1,000 ms since target word onset for target neutral, competitor neutral, competitor constraining and unrelated neutral conditions (described in text).
From Brock and Nelson (2014).

Phonemic restoration effect

Warren and Warren (1970) reported strong evidence that sentence context can influence phoneme perception in the **phonemic restoration effect**. Listeners heard a sentence in which a phoneme had been removed and replaced with a meaningless sound (cough). The sentences used were as follows (the asterisk indicates the deleted phoneme):

- It was found that the *eel was on the axle.
- It was found that the *eel was on the shoe.
- It was found that the *eel was on the table.
- It was found that the *eel was on the orange.

The perception of the crucial element in the sentence (i.e., **eel*) was influenced by the sentence in which it appeared. Participants listening to the first sentence heard *wheel*, those listening to the second sentence heard *heel* and those exposed to the third and fourth sentences heard *meal* and *peel*, respectively. The crucial auditory stimulus (i.e., **eel)* was always the same, so all that differed was the contextual information.

What causes the phonemic restoration effect? There has been much controversy on this issue (Samuel, 2011). Samuel (1981, 1996) found there was a greater restoration effect with real words than non-words. Thus, higher-order lexical information (information about words) can be used to enhance restoration.

Shahin et al. (2009, 2012) shed light on the phonemic restoration effect by assessing brain activity. They found two different processes were involved. First, there is sensory repair, which is a largely unconscious process. Successful phoneme restoration (but not failed restoration) was accompanied by suppression of activation in the auditory cortex to the onset and offset of the interrupting noise. Second, there is subjective continuity: listeners use their prior top-down expectations so they appear to "perceive" the missing phoneme.

KEY TERMS

Phonemic restoration effect
The finding that listeners are unaware that a phoneme has been deleted and replaced by a non-speech sound (e.g., cough) within a sentence.

Ganong effect
The finding that perception of an ambiguous **phoneme** is biased towards a sound that produces a word rather than a non-word.

Ganong effect

Earlier we saw that listeners often show categorical perception, with speech signals intermediate between two phonemes being categorised as one phoneme or the other. Ganong (1980) wondered whether categorical perception of phonemes would be influenced by the immediate context. Accordingly, he presented listeners with various sounds ranging between a word (e.g., *dash*) and a non-word (e.g., *tash*). There was a context effect – an ambiguous initial phoneme was more likely to be assigned to a given phoneme category when it produced a word. This is the **Ganong effect** or lexical identification shift.

There are at least two possible reasons why lexical context influences phoneme perception. First, such context may exert a *direct* influence on perceptual processes. Second, context may influence decision or other processes occurring *after* perceptual processing is complete but prior to a response being made.

Myers and Blumstein (2008) obtained findings supportive of both the above possibilities. The Ganong effect was associated with increased activation in the superior temporal gyri (a brain area associated with auditory perceptual processing). This suggests perceptual processes are involved and is consistent with the interactionist account. It was also associated with increased activation in frontal and midline areas associated with executive processes. Thus, post-perceptual decision processes are also probably involved, which is consistent with the autonomous account.

Interactionist vs. autonomous accounts

Listeners can use contextual information very rapidly to anticipate what word(s) will be presented next (Kutas et al., 2011). Van Berkum et al. (2005) presented listeners with Dutch stories. An important feature of the Dutch language is its use of gender-marked adjectives (i.e., an adjective linked to a noun has the same gender as the noun). Consider the following:

> The burglar had no trouble locating the secret family safe. Of course, it was situated behind a . . .

It is a reasonable prediction the following noun will be *painting*, which has the neuter gender in Dutch. The word *a* was followed by the Dutch adjective *big* in the neuter gender or common gender. The key finding was that event-related potentials (ERPs; see Glossary) to the adjective differed depending on whether the adjective's gender was or was not consistent with the predicted noun (i.e., *painting*). Thus, story context can influence speech processing even before the predicted word has been presented.

Strong evidence favouring the interactionist account was reported by Wild et al. (2012). Listeners heard sentences presented in clear speech or in degraded but potentially intelligible speech. Each sentence was accompanied by context consisting of text matching the spoken words or random strings of consonants.

The rated perceptual clarity of the heard sentences in degraded but potentially intelligible speech was greater when accompanied by matching text rather than random consonants. What caused this context effect? According to the interactionist position, context might influence the *early* stages of spoken word processing within primary auditory cortex. In contrast, it follows from the autonomous position that context should influence only *later* processing stages and so should have no effect on processing in the primary auditory cortex. Context was associated with activation within primary auditory cortex as predicted by the interactionist position.

There was some support for the autonomous position with regard to the findings when sentences were presented in clear speech. With these sentences, there was *no* effect of context on activation within primary motor cortex. Why do these findings differ from those with degraded speech? Suppose it takes some time for contextual information to influence processing in primary auditory cortex. The delay in speech perception produced by presenting degraded speech allows sufficient time for this to occur. In contrast, speech perception occurs rapidly with clear speech and so there are no effects of context on activation in primary auditory cortex.

Sohoglu et al. (2014) found that the perceived clarity of a degraded spoken word was greater when preceded by written text containing that word. What would happen if the written text was presented *after* the spoken word? According to the autonomous account, context has its effects only late in processing, and so the beneficial effect of written text should still be found. In contrast, according to the interactionist account, context has beneficial effects on speech perception by influencing acoustic processing. As a result, context presented some time after a spoken word should have little or no effect on perceived clarity of a degraded word. The findings were much more supportive of the interactionist account.

Summary and conclusions

It has proved hard to distinguish between the interactionist and autonomous accounts. Research on the phonemic restoration and Ganong effects provides some support for both positions. However, increasing evidence suggests context can influence relatively early stages of speech perception (e.g., van Berkum et al., 2005; Wild et al., 2012; Sohoglu et al., 2014), which favours the interactionist position. This issue is discussed again later when we consider theories of speech perception.

There is support for the assumption that top-down effects of context on the early stages of speech perception are much more likely to be found when speech is degraded than when it is clear and unambiguous (e.g., Wild et al., 2012). There is less evidence of such effects with clear speech because top-down effects occur too slowly (Mattys et al., 2012). In addition, top-down processes may simply be unnecessary when bottom-up processes provide ample information for word recognition.

THEORIES OF SPEECH PERCEPTION

In this section, we consider theoretical accounts of the processes involved in identifying spoken words. These accounts are designed in part to explain some of the findings on segmentation and context effects discussed already.

As we have seen, phonological processing plays a major role in speech perception. However, it seems implausible that orthographic processing (processing related to word spellings) is involved. We start by considering evidence on this topic.

After that, we consider major theories of spoken word recognition. First, we consider the motor theory of speech perception originally proposed by Liberman et al. (1967). After that, the focus switches to the TRACE and cohort models. The TRACE model (McClelland & Elman, 1986) argues that word recognition involves interactive top-down and bottom-up processes. The original cohort model (Marslen-Wilson & Tyler, 1980) also emphasised interactions between bottom-up and top-down processes in spoken word recognition. However, Marslen-Wilson (e.g., 1990) later revised his cohort model to increase the emphasis on bottom-up processes driven by the auditory stimulus. As we will see, the cohort model provides a more complex and comprehensive account of spoken word recognition.

Orthographic influences

Suppose you listen to spoken words. Would this activate the *spellings* of those words? It seems unlikely. However, there is increasing evidence that orthography (word spelling) *is* involved.

Perre and Ziegler (2008) gave listeners a lexical decision task (deciding whether auditory stimuli were words or non-words). The words varied in the consistency between their orthography or spelling and their phonology. Listeners performed the lexical decision task slower when the words were inconsistent. Thus, spoken word processing is disrupted when there is a *mismatch* between phonological and orthographic information.

How does orthography influence speech perception? Perhaps hearing a word leads fairly automatically to activation of its orthographic codes and so influences lexical access (see Glossary). Alternatively, a spoken word's orthography may influence its processing only *after* lexical access. This issue has been addressed by using event-related potentials (ERPs; see Glossary) to assess the timing of orthographic effects.

Perre et al. (2009) found an orthographic consistency effect in spoken word recognition. Brain activation assessed by ERPs showed differences between consistent and inconsistent words 330 ms after word onset. This is sufficiently early enough for it to be plausible (but not certain) that orthography influenced lexical access. Pattamadilok et al. (2011) asked listeners to decide whether spoken words had a given final syllable. Orthographic consistency influenced ERPs at 175–250 ms. This finding also suggests orthography can influence the early processing of spoken words prior to lexical access.

Motor theory

Liberman et al. (1967) argued that a key issue is to explain how listeners perceive spoken words accurately even though the speech signal provides variable information. In their motor theory of speech perception, they proposed that listeners *mimic* the speaker's articulatory movements. It was claimed this motor signal provides much less variable and inconsistent information about the speaker's words than the speech signal itself. Thus, our recruitment of the motor system facilitates speech perception.

Pulvermüller and Fadiga (2010) argued along similar lines that language processing (including speech perception) involves action-perception circuits. These circuits include various auditory areas plus premotor and motor areas. Of most relevance here, it was assumed premotor and motor areas are typically involved in speech perception.

It is relevant to consider the mirror neuron system (see Glossary and Chapter 4) at this point. It is assumed the same neurons within the motor neuron system are activated whether someone performs an action or observes someone else perform the same action. Activity within the mirror neuron system (which includes premotor areas) provides the basis for understanding others' actions. By extension, the mirror neuron system may play an important role in speech perception.

Findings

In a study discussed earlier, Möttönen et al. (2013) applied transcranial magnetic stimulation (TMS; see Glossary) to the area of motor cortex associated with lip representations while listeners heard speech sounds. They used event-related potentials (ERPs; see Glossary) to assess the effects of TMS on auditory processing. TMS impaired auditory processing of changes in speech sounds as indicated by ERPs.

D'Ausilio et al. (2012) pointed out that most previous research showing involvement of the motor cortex in speech perception had used demanding conditions (i.e., noisy environment). They compared undemanding (no noise) and demanding (noise) conditions while listeners identified consonants pronounced using lip or tongue movements. They applied transcranial magnetic stimulation (TMS) to motor areas associated with lip or tongue movements. Note that TMS's effects on processing can be facilitatory (rather than disruptive) depending on the precise pattern of stimulation, intensity of stimulation and so on.

What did D'Ausilio et al. (2012) find? TMS had no effect on speech perception in the no-noise condition. In the noise condition, however, consonant detection was faster when TMS was applied to a motor area *matching* that required for its articulation. Thus, motor areas facilitated speech perception under noise but not no-noise conditions.

Findings consistent with those of D'Ausilio et al. (2011) were reported by Osnes et al. (2011). There was much more activation of premotor cortex when speech sounds were degraded than when they were clearly perceivable.

If speech perception causally depends on the motor speech system, damage to that system should impair speech perception. Hickok et al. (2011) reported evidence inconsistent with that prediction. They studied brain-damaged patients with Broca's aphasia (see Glossary), which involves severe problems with speech production. The patients performed well on simple speech-perception tasks such as deciding whether two syllables were the same or different. In a similar study, Rogalsky et al. (2011a) found speech comprehension performance was good in patients with damage to the mirror neuron system.

Dramatic evidence was reported by Hickok et al. (2008). They made use of the fact that the motor speech system (unlike the auditory speech system) has strong left-hemisphere dominance. Anaesthesia of the entire left hemisphere almost totally inactivated the motor speech system so the participants were unable to speak. In spite of that, they performed reasonably well on a task in which heard words had to be matched to pictures.

Krieger-Redwood et al. (2013) studied performance on a phonemic and a semantic task. Transcranial magnetic stimulation (TMS) was applied to premotor cortex, to the posterior superior temporal gyrus (an area involved in auditory and speech processing) or to the occipital pole (involved in visual processing).

What did Krieger-Redwood et al. (2013) find? First, TMS to premotor cortex disrupted performance on the phonemic task but had no effect on the semantic task (see Figure 9.12). Second, TMS to the posterior superior temporal gyrus disrupted performance on both tasks. Thus, speech comprehension depends more on non-motor areas such as the superior temporal gyrus than on motor areas. They also indicated that motor areas have a limited role in facilitating phoneme processing in speech perception.

Evaluation

There is some support for the motor theory of speech perception. First, motor areas (e.g., premotor cortex) have been shown to be important when explicit

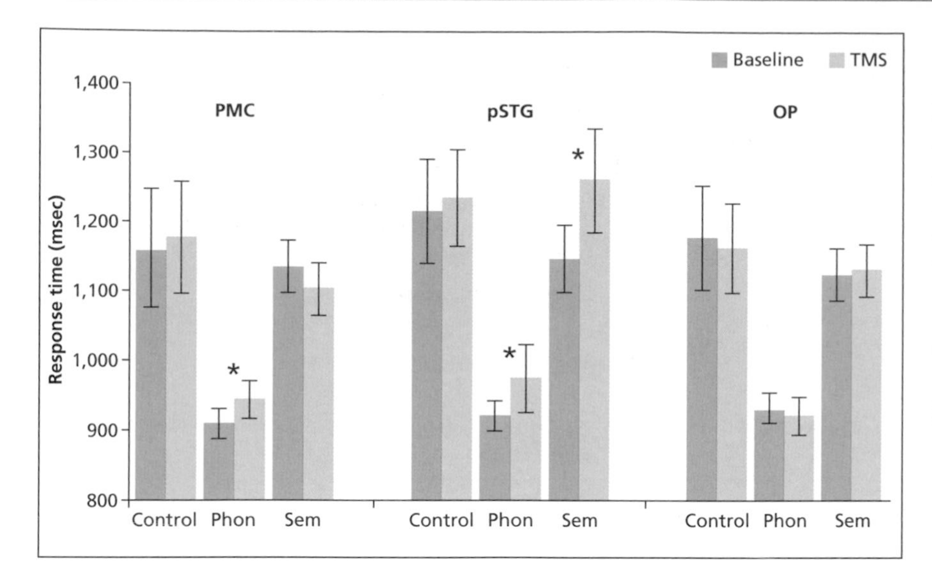

Figure 9.12
Response times on a visual control task, a phonological task and a semantic task when transcranial magnetic stimulation (TMS) was applied to the premotor cortex (PMC), posterior superior temporal gyrus (pSTG) and occipital pole (OP).

From Krieger-Redwood et al. (2013). © Massachusetts Institute of Technology, by permission of The MIT Press.

perception or manipulation of phonemes is required. Second, motor areas generally play a greater role when task conditions are demanding than when they are undemanding.

What are the limitations of the motor theory approach? First, when the speech input is clear, comprehension can be achieved with practically no involvement of the motor speech system. That limits the applicability of the motor theory to speech perception in typical conditions.

Second, our understanding of the brain networks involved in speech perception suggests non-motor areas are much more important than motor ones. More specifically, there is evidence for a dual-stream model of speech perception (Specht, 2014; see Figure 9.13). The ventral or "what" stream (including areas such as the superior temporal gyrus and the middle temporal gyrus) is strongly involved in most aspects of speech perception (e.g., phoneme processing, speech comprehension). In contrast, the dorsal or "how" stream (including premotor areas and Broca's area) has a much more limited role. However, there are interactions between the two streams (see Figure 9.13).

Third, it remains unclear precisely *how* listeners use auditory information to produce useful motor processing. As Harley (2013) pointed out, "There is no apparent way of translating the articulatory hypothesis generated by the production system into the same format as the heard speech in order for the potential match to be assessed."

TRACE model

McClelland and Elman (1986) put forward a network model of speech perception based on connectionist principles (see Chapter 1). Their TRACE model of speech perception assumes bottom-up and top-down processes interact flexibly in spoken word recognition. Thus, all sources of information are used at the same time.

The TRACE model is based on the following assumptions (see Figure 9.14):

- There are individual processing units or nodes at three different levels: features (e.g., voicing, manner of production), phonemes and words.

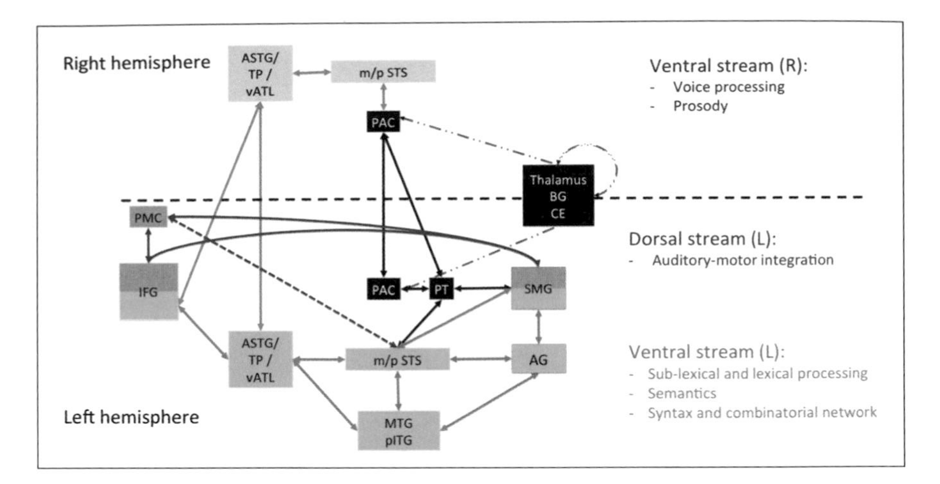

Figure 9.13
A dual-stream model for speech comprehension showing a left-hemisphere dorsal stream involved in auditory-motor integration and two distinct ventral streams (one in each hemisphere) involved in voice processing, prosody, sub-lexical and lexical processing, semantics and syntax. Brain areas include supramarginal gyrus (SMG), anterior superior temporal gyrus/temporal pole (ASTG/TP), superior temporal gyrus (STS), premotor cortex (PMC), angular gyrus (AG), inferior frontal gyrus (IFG) and middle temporal gyrus (MTG).
From Specht et al. (2014). Reprinted with permission from Elsevier.

- Feature nodes are connected to phoneme nodes, and phoneme nodes are connected to word nodes.
- Connections between levels operate in both directions and are always *facilitatory*.
- There are connections among units or nodes at the *same* level; these connections are *inhibitory*.

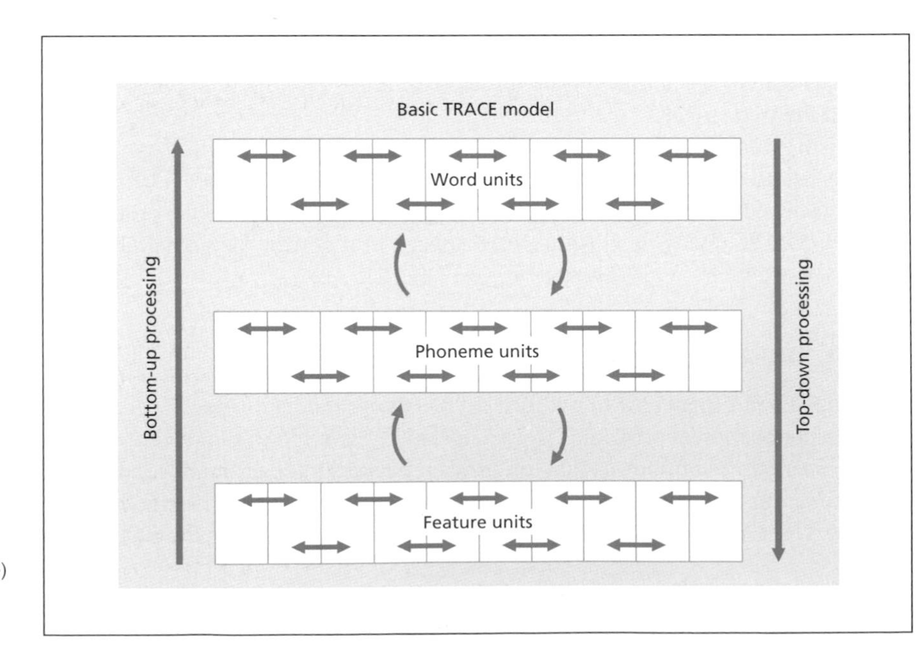

Figure 9.14
The basic TRACE model, showing how activation among the three levels (word, phoneme and feature) is influenced by bottom-up and top-down processing.

- Nodes influence each other in proportion to their activation levels and the strengths of their interconnections.
- As excitation and inhibition spread among nodes, a pattern of activation develops.
- The word recognised or identified by the listener is determined by the activation level of the possible candidate words.

The TRACE model assumes bottom-up and top-down processes *interact* throughout speech perception. Bottom-up activation proceeds upwards from the feature level to the phoneme level and on to the word level, whereas top-down activation proceeds in the opposite direction from the word level to the phoneme level and on to the feature level.

Findings

Suppose we asked listeners to detect target phonemes presented in words and non-words. According to the TRACE model, performance should be better in the word condition. Why is that? In that condition, activation going from the word level proceeding to the phoneme level would facilitate phoneme detection.

Mirman et al. (2008) asked listeners to detect a target phoneme (/t/ or /k/) in words and non-words. Words were presented on 80% or 20% of the trials. The argument was that attention to (and activation at) the word level would be greater when most auditory stimuli were words, which would increase the word superiority effect.

What did Mirman et al. (2008) find? First, the predicted word superiority effect was found in all conditions (see Figure 9.15). Second, the magnitude of the effect was greater when 80% of the auditory stimuli were words than when only 20% were. These findings indicate the involvement of top-down processes in speech perception.

The TRACE model can explain the basic Ganong effect. In this effect (discussed earlier), there is a bias towards perceiving an ambiguous phoneme so that a word is formed. According to the TRACE model, top-down activation from the word level is responsible for this effect.

Additional evidence that phoneme identification can be influenced directly by top-down processing was reported by Norris et al. (2003). Listeners categorised ambiguous phonemes as /f/ or /s/. Those who had previously heard this phoneme in the context of /f/-ending words favoured the /f/ categorisation. In contrast, those who had heard it in /s/-ending words favoured the /s/ categorisation. Thus, top-down learning affected phoneme categorisation as predicted by the model.

The TRACE model explains categorical speech perception (discussed earlier). According to the model, the discrimination boundary between phonemes becomes sharper because of mutual

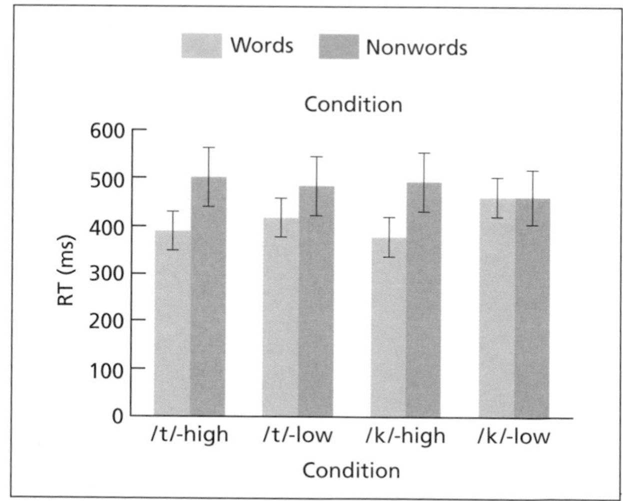

Figure 9.15
Mean reaction times (in ms) for recognition of /t/ and /k/ phonemes in words and non-words when words were presented on a high (80%) or low (20%) proportion of trials.

From Mirman et al. (2008). Reprinted with permission of the Cognitive Science Society Inc.

inhibition between phoneme units at the phoneme level. These inhibitory processes produce a "winner takes all" situation with one phoneme becoming increasingly activated while other phonemes are inhibited, thus producing categorical perception.

High-frequency words (those often encountered) are generally recognised faster than low-frequency ones (Harley, 2013). It would be consistent with the TRACE model's approach to assume this happens because they have higher resting activation levels. If so, word frequency should influence even early stages of word processing. Supporting evidence was reported by Dufour et al. (2013) in a study on spoken word recognition for high- and low-frequency words using event-related potentials (ERPs; see Glossary). There was a clear word-frequency effect as early as 350 ms from word onset. This finding suggests word frequency affects early word processing consistent with the TRACE model.

We turn now to research that is problematical for the model. It attaches excessive importance to top-down processes in spoken word recognition. Frauenfelder et al. (1990) asked listeners to detect a given phoneme. In the key condition, a non-word closely resembling an actual word was presented (e.g., *vocabutaire* instead of *vocabulaire*). The model predicts that top-down effects from the word node corresponding to *vocabulaire* should have impaired the task of identifying the *t* in *vocabutaire* but they did not.

McQueen (1991) asked listeners to categorise ambiguous phonemes at the end of auditory stimuli. Each ambiguous phoneme could be perceived as completing a word or non-word. The TRACE model predicts that listeners should have shown a preference for perceiving the phonemes as completing words. This prediction was confirmed when the stimulus was degraded but not when it was not degraded.

The TRACE model considers only some contextual factors influencing spoken word recognition. For example, Rohde and Ettlinger (2012) presented listeners with sentences such as the following (___ corresponds to an ambiguous phoneme interpretable as *he* or *she*):

1 Abigail annoyed Bruce because ___ was in a bad mood
2 Luis reproached Heidi because ___ was getting grouchy.

Listeners indicated whether they thought each sentence had contained the word *he* or *she*. Rohde and Ettlinger predicted that listeners would hear the ambiguous phoneme as *she* in both sentences. *Annoyed* is typically followed by a pronoun referring to the subject, whereas *reproached* is followed by a pronoun referring to the object. The findings were as predicted, indicating that contextual information contained in verbs can be used to make inferences.

Davis et al. (2002) challenged the TRACE model's assumption that recognising a spoken word necessarily involves identifying its phonemes. Listeners decided whether they had heard the only syllable of a short word (e.g., *cap*) or the first syllable of a longer word (e.g., *captain*). Since they could not use phonemic information, the task should have been very hard according to the model. In fact, performance was good. Listeners used non-phonemic information (e.g., syllable duration) ignored by the TRACE model to discriminate between short and longer words.

Earlier we discussed evidence that listeners' spoken word identification is influenced by orthographic (spelling) information (e.g., Perre & Ziegler, 2008; Pattamadilok et al., 2011). This points to a limitation in the TRACE model, which makes no allowance for the involvement of orthography in speech perception.

Evaluation

The TRACE model has several successes to its credit. First, it provides reasonable accounts of phenomena such as the phonemic restoration effect, categorical perception, the Ganong effect and the word superiority effect in phoneme monitoring. Second, a strength of the model is the notion that bottom-up and top-down processes both contribute to spoken word recognition, combined with explicit assumptions concerning the processes involved.

Third, the model predicts accurately some effects of word frequency on auditory word processing (e.g., Dahan et al., 2001). Fourth, the TRACE model "copes extremely well with noisy input – which is a considerable advantage given the noise present in natural language" (Harley, 2008, p. 274). This is achieved through its emphasis on top-down processes, which become more important when the speech input is degraded and provides only limited information. Further evidence that top-down processes become more important with degraded speech input was discussed earlier (e.g., Wild et al., 2012; Sohoglu et al., 2014).

What are the model's limitations? First, its focus is rather narrow in that it has relatively little to say about the main processes involved in comprehending speech. Second, the model exaggerates the importance of top-down effects on speech perception (e.g., Frauenfelder et al., 1990; McQueen, 1991). Suppose listeners hear a mispronunciation. According to the model, top-down activation from the word level will generally lead listeners to perceive the word best fitting the presented phonemes rather than the mispronunciation itself. However, mispronunciations can have a strong adverse effect on speech perception (Gaskell & Marslen-Wilson, 1998).

Third, the TRACE model incorporates many different theoretical assumptions. This allows it to account for many findings. However, there is a suspicion it makes the model "too powerful, in that it can accommodate any result" (Harley, 2013).

Fourth, the model ignores factors influencing auditory word recognition. As we have seen, orthographic information plays a significant role in speech perception (e.g., Perre & Ziegler, 2008). In addition, non-phonemic information (e.g., syllable duration) also influences auditory word perception (Davis et al., 2002).

Fifth, spoken word recognition is influenced by several contextual factors. The TRACE model has an emphasis on top-down processes and so accounts for many context effects. However, there are many exceptions (e.g., use of verb information within sentences: Rohde and Ettlinger, 2012).

Cohort model

The cohort model focuses on the processes involved over time during spoken word recognition. This model differs from the TRACE model in that it focuses more on bottom-up processes and less on top-down ones. Several versions have been put forward over the years, starting with Marslen-Wilson and Tyler (1980). Here are the main assumptions of the original version:

KEY TERM

Uniqueness point
The point in time during spoken word recognition at which the available perceptual information is consistent with only one word.

- Early in the auditory presentation of a word, all words conforming to the sound sequence heard so far become active; this set of words is the cohort. There is *competition* among these words to be selected.
- Words within the cohort are eliminated if they cease to match further information from the presented word or because they are inconsistent with the semantic or other context. For example, *crocodile* and *crockery* might both belong to the initial cohort with the latter word being excluded when the sound /d/ is heard.
- Processing continues until information from the word itself and contextual information are sufficient to permit elimination of all but one of the cohort words. The **uniqueness point** is the point at which only one word is consistent with the acoustic signal.

How do later versions of the cohort model differ from the original version? In the original model, it was assumed that any word was in or out of the cohort at a given point. This assumption is too extreme. In revised versions (e.g., Marslen-Wilson, 1990), it is assumed words vary in their level of activation and so membership of the word cohort is a matter of degree. In addition, Marslen-Wilson assumed the word-initial cohort may contain words having *similar* initial phonemes rather than only words having the *same* initial phoneme as the presented word.

The more recent assumptions are clearly superior. According to the original assumption, spoken words would not be recognised if their initial phoneme was unclear or ambiguous. Contrary evidence was reported by Frauenfelder et al. (2001). French-speaking listeners activated words even when the initial phoneme of spoken words was distorted (e.g., hearing *focabulaire* activated the word *vocabulaire*). However, the listeners took some time to overcome the effects of the mismatch in the initial phoneme.

Three processing stages are identified within the cohort model. First, there is the *access* stage during which a word cohort is activated. Second, there is the *selection* stage during which one word is chosen from the cohort. Third, there is the *integration* stage during which the word's semantic and syntactic properties are integrated within the sentence. A major difference between the original and revised versions of the model concerns the stage at which context (e.g., preceding words) influences word processing. In the original version, context influences the selection stage. In contrast, context only influences the later integration stage in the revised version.

Findings

O'Rourke and Holcomb (2002) tested the assumption that a spoken word is identified when its uniqueness point (i.e., the point at which only *one* word is consistent with the acoustic signal) is reached. Listeners decided whether spoken words and pseudowords were words. Some words had an early uniqueness point (average of 427 ms after word onset), whereas others had a late uniqueness point (533 ms after word onset). The N400 (a component of the event-related potential; see Glossary) was used to assess the speed of word processing.

O'Rourke and Holcomb (2002) found the N400 occurred 100 ms earlier for words having an early uniqueness point than those having a late uniqueness point. This suggests the uniqueness point is important.

Radeau et al. (2000) cast some doubt on the general importance of the uniqueness point. Listeners heard nouns having early or late uniqueness points. The uniqueness point influenced performance when the nouns were presented slowly (2.2 syllables/sec) or at a medium rate (3.6 syllables/sec) but not when presented fast (5.6 syllables/sec). Note that the fast rate is close to the typical conversational speaking rate.

The revised version of the model assumes listeners form an initial word cohort of words, and context influences only the later stages of word recognition. Support for these assumptions was reported by Zwitserlood (1989). Listeners performed a lexical decision task (deciding whether visually presented letter strings were words) immediately after hearing part of a word. When only *cap*___ had been presented, it was consistent with *captain* and *capital*. Lexical decision performance was faster when the presented word was related in meaning to either word (e.g., *ship*, *money*). Of greatest importance was what happened when the part word was preceded by a biasing context (e.g., *With dampened spirits the men stood around the grave. They mourned the loss of their cap*___). As predicted by the model, such context did not prevent activation of *capital* even though it was inconsistent with the context.

Friedrich and Kotz (2007) carried out a study resembling that of Zwitserlood (1989). Listeners heard sentences ending with incomplete words (e.g., *To light up the dark she needed her can*___). Immediately afterwards, listeners saw a visual word matched to the incomplete word in form and meaning (e.g., *candle)* in meaning only (e.g., *lantern*), in form only (e.g., *candy*) or in neither (e.g., *number*). Event-related potentials (ERPs; see Glossary) were recorded to assess the early stages of word processing. There was evidence for a form-based cohort 220 ms after word presentation. In other words, *candy* was activated even though it was inconsistent with the context.

Van Petten et al. (1999) found sentence context can influence word processing ahead of its uniqueness point. Listeners heard a sentence frame (e.g., *Sir Lancelot spared the man's life when he begged for* ___), followed after 500 ms by a congruent (e.g., *mercy*) or incongruent (e.g., *mermaid*) word. There were significant differences in the N400 to the contextually congruent and incongruent words 200 ms *before* the uniqueness point was reached. Thus, context can influence spoken word processing earlier than expected within the cohort model.

Why were Van Petten et al.'s (1999) findings different from those of Zwitserlood (1989) and Friedrich and Kotz (2007)? The most likely reason is that the contexts used by Van Petten et al. very strongly predicted the final word in the sentence.

More evidence that context can exert a very early influence was reported by Weber and Crocker (2012). Listeners heard sentences in German such as *The woman irons the* ___. *Bluse* (the German word for *blouse*) is a likely final word, whereas the similar-sounding word *Blume* (meaning *flower*) is implausible. Weber and Crocker studied eye fixations to pictures of the target word (e.g., *Bluse*), the similar-sounding word (e.g., *Blume*) and an irrelevant distractor (e.g., *Wolke* meaning *cloud*).

What did Weber and Crocker (2012) find? Context had a very strong effect. More fixations were directed at the target object than the other two objects *before* the final word was presented and this tendency increased during and after its presentation (see Figure 9.16). In addition, similar-sounding words were fixated more than irrelevant distractors shortly after the final word in the sentence was

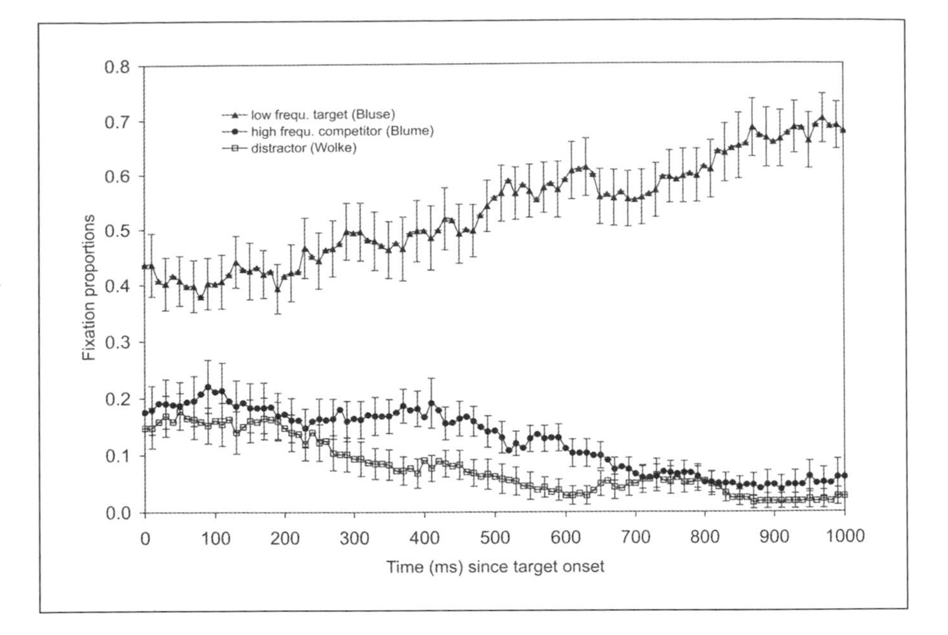

Figure 9.16
Fixation proportions to high-frequency target words, high-frequency competitors phonologically similar to target words and unrelated distractor words during the first 1,000 ms after target onset.

From Weber and Crocker (2012). With kind permission from Springer Science + Business Media.

presented. Thus, as predicted by the model, words phonologically related to a spoken word are activated to some extent even when inconsistent with the context.

Gagnepain et al. (2012) distinguished between two processes possibly involved in auditory word recognition. First, there may be competition between the words in the word cohort with those failing to match the incoming auditory signal being inhibited or *losing* activation. Second, listeners may predict upcoming speech segments. Words associated with successful predictions have *increased* activation.

The cohort model is based on the first possibility above. However, Gagnepain et al. found patterns of activation in auditory cortex were more consistent with the second possibility. These findings are potentially important because they suggest the mechanism underlying spoken word recognition may not be the one identified within the cohort model.

Evaluation

The cohort model possesses several strengths. First, the assumption that accurate perception of a spoken word involves processing several competitor words is generally correct. Second, the processing of spoken words is sequential and changes considerably during the course of their presentation. Third, the uniqueness point is of great importance in spoken word recognition. Fourth, context effects often (but not always) occur during the integration stage following word identification as predicted by the model. Fifth, the revised versions of the model are an improvement compared to the original version. For example, the assumption that membership of the word cohort is a matter of degree rather than being all-or-none is in line with the evidence.

What are the model's limitations? First, context sometimes influences word processing earlier than the integration stage. This is especially the case when the context is strongly predictive (e.g., Van Petten et al., 1999; van Berkum et al.,

2005; Weber & Crocker, 2012) or the speech input is degraded (Wild et al., 2012). Note, however, that Gaskell and Marslen-Wilson (2002) emphasised the notion of "continuous integration" of speech input and contextual information and so can handle the finding that context sometimes has early effects.

Second, the revised cohort model de-emphasises the role of word meaning in spoken word recognition. Tyler et al. (2000) focused on word meaning in terms of imageability (ease of forming an image of a word's referent). Word recognition was facilitated for high-imageability words only when there were many words in the word cohort. Zhuang et al. (2011) found greater activation in brain areas involved in speech perception for high-imageability than low-imageability words when there were many words in the word cohort. Thus, word selection depends on semantic factors as well as phonological ones.

Third, there is intriguing evidence that the mechanism responsible for spoken word recognition may differ from that assumed within the cohort model. More specifically, prediction of upcoming speech segments may be of major importance although de-emphasised by the cohort model (Gagnepaine et al., 2012).

KEY TERM

Pure word deafness
A condition involving severely impaired speech perception but intact speech production, reading, writing and perception of non-speech sounds.

COGNITIVE NEUROPSYCHOLOGY

So far we have focused mainly on the processes used by listeners to achieve word recognition. Here we consider briefly how research on brain-damaged patients has shed light on processes involved in speech perception. Our focus will be on repeating a spoken word immediately after hearing it.

Our discussion will revolve around the theoretical framework suggested by Ellis and Young (1988; see Figure 9.17). There are five components:

1. The *auditory analysis system* extracts phonemes or other sounds from the speech wave.
2. The *auditory input lexicon* contains information about spoken words known to the listener but not about their meaning.
3. Word meanings are stored in the *semantic system*.
4. The *speech output lexicon* provides the spoken form of words.
5. The *phoneme response buffer* provides distinctive speech sounds.

The framework's most striking feature is the assumption that *three* different routes can be used to say spoken words. We will discuss these routes after considering the auditory analysis system.

Auditory analysis system

Patients with damage only to the auditory analysis system would have impaired phonemic processing. As a result, they would have impaired speech perception for words and non-words. However, they would have intact speech production, reading and writing, unimpaired hearing and normal perception of non-verbal sounds (e.g., coughs, whistles) not containing phonemes. Patients with these symptoms suffer from **pure word deafness**.

A crucial part of the definition of pure word deafness is that auditory perception problems are *selective* to speech and do not apply to non-speech sounds. The evidence is mixed. Pinard et al. (2002) identified impairments of music and/or environmental sound perception in 94% of 63 patients.

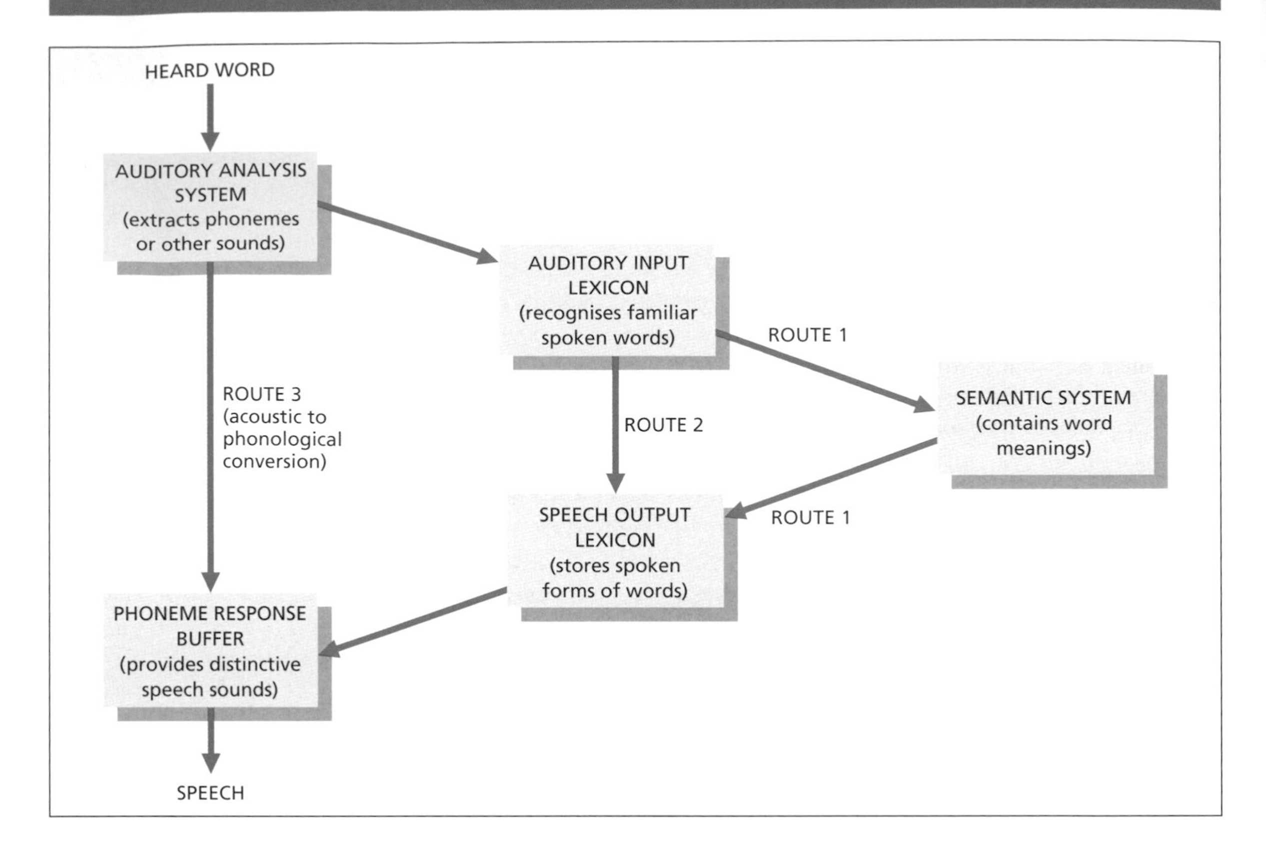

Figure 9.17
Processing and repetition of spoken words according to the three-route framework.
Adapted from Ellis and Young (1988).

Speech perception differs from the perception of most non-speech sounds in that coping with rapid stimulus changes is much more important. It is thus possible that individuals with pure word deafness have specific problems when confronted by rapid temporal changes in auditory stimuli. Supporting evidence was reported by Slevc et al. (2011). NL, a patient with pure word deafness, had particular difficulties in discriminating sounds (speech or non-speech) differing in rapid temporal changes.

Three-route framework

Ellis and Young's (1988) framework specifies three ways (or routes) used when individuals process and repeat words they have just heard (see Figure 9.17). All three routes involve the auditory analysis system and the phonemic response buffer. Route 1 also involves the other three components (auditory input lexicon, semantic system, speech output lexicon). Route 2 involves two additional components (auditory input lexicon, speech output lexicon) and Route 3 involves an additional rule-based system that converts acoustic information into words that can be spoken.

According to the three-route framework, Routes 1 and 2 are designed to be used with unfamiliar words, whereas Route 3 is designed to be used with unfamiliar words and non-words. When Route 1 is used, a heard word activates its relevant stored information (e.g., meaning, spoken form). Route 2 resembles Route 1 except that information about the meaning of heard words is *not* accessed.

As a result, someone using Route 2 would say familiar words accurately without knowing their meaning. Finally, Route 3 involves using rules about the conversion of the acoustic information in heard words into their spoken forms. Such conversion processes allow listeners to repeat back unfamiliar words and non-words.

Findings

Patients using predominantly Route 2 should recognise familiar words but not understand their meaning. Since they can use the input lexicon, they should distinguish between words and non-words. Finally, they should have problems saying unfamiliar words and non-words.

Patients with **word meaning deafness** fit the above description. Only a few such patients have been identified. Franklin et al. (1996) studied Dr O. He had reasonable use of the input lexicon as shown by his excellent ability to distinguish between words and non-words. His ability to repeat words was dramatically better than his ability to repeat non-words (80% vs. 7%, respectively). Dr O. had impaired auditory comprehension but intact written word comprehension – this latter finding indicates his semantic system was probably not damaged.

Bormann and Weiller (2012) studied a female patient, BB, who had word meaning deafness. She could distinguish between words and non-words, but was severely impaired in identifying pictures matching spoken words. However, her performance was intact when identifying the appropriate picture in response to a *written* word. Thus, BB could not access the meanings of spoken words even though her semantic processing ability was intact.

If patients used Route 3 primarily or exclusively, they would be able to repeat spoken words and non-words but should have very poor comprehension of the words. Patients with **transcortical sensory aphasia** exhibit this pattern. Kim et al. (2009) studied a male patient who could repeat spoken words and sentences. However, his auditory and reading comprehension was severely impaired, suggesting he had damage within the semantic system.

Patients with **deep dysphasia** have extensive problems with speech perception and production. They make semantic errors when repeating spoken words by producing words related in meaning to those spoken (e.g., saying *sky* instead of *cloud*). They also have a very poor ability to repeat words and non-words. Ablinger et al. (2008) discussed findings from JR, a man with deep dysphasia. In spite of severely impaired speech perception, he was only slightly impaired at reading aloud words and non-words.

We could explain deep dysphasia with respect to Figure 9.17 by arguing that all three routes are damaged. However, Jefferies et al. (2007) argued plausibly that the central problem in deep dysphasia is a general phonological impairment (i.e., impaired processing of word sounds). This leads to semantic errors because it increases patients' reliance on word meanings when repeating spoken words.

Jefferies et al. (2007) found deep dysphasics suffered from poor phonological production on word repetition, reading aloud and spoken picture naming. As predicted, they also performed very poorly on tasks involving the manipulation of phonology such as the phoneme subtraction task (e.g., remove the initial phoneme from "cat"). Furthermore, they had speech perception problems (e.g., impaired performance when deciding whether words rhymed).

KEY TERMS

Word meaning deafness
A condition in which there is selective impairment of the ability to understand spoken (but not written) language.

Transcortical sensory aphasia
A condition in which spoken words can be repeated but comprehension of spoken and written language is severely impaired.

Deep dysphasia
A condition involving semantic errors when trying to repeat spoken words and a generally poor ability to repeat spoken words and non-words.

Evaluation

The three-route framework is along the right lines. Patients have various problems with speech perception (and speech production), and evidence exists for all three routes. Conditions such as pure word deafness, word meaning deafness and transcortical aphasia can readily be related to the framework.

Interactive exercise:
Ellis and Young's (1988) three-route model

What are the limitations with this theoretical approach? First, it is sometimes hard to relate patients' symptoms to the framework. For example, there are disagreements as to whether deep dysphasia involves impairments to all three routes or whether it mainly reflects a general phonological impairment. Second, the approach identifies crucial components involved in speech perception but does not fully explain their functioning (e.g., what are the detailed processes occurring within the semantic or auditory analysis systems?).

CHAPTER SUMMARY

- **Reading: introduction**. It is harder to read English than most other languages because the relationship between spelling and sound is very inconsistent. Lexical decision, naming and priming tasks have been used to assess word identification. Studies of masked phonological priming suggest that visual word recognition typically depends on prior phonological processing. However, phonological activation is probably not essential for word recognition.

- **Word recognition**. According to the interactive activation model, bottom-up and top-down processes interact during word recognition. The model accounts for the word superiority effect and the effects of orthographic neighbours on word recognition. However, it does not account for the roles of meaning and sound.

  Semantic priming can facilitate word recognition automatically or in a more controlled fashion. Sentence context can influence the early stages of word processing, with readers sometimes forming specific or more general predictions about future words.

- **Reading aloud**. According to the dual-route model, lexical and non-lexical routes are used to read words and non-words, respectively. Surface dyslexics rely mainly on the non-lexical route, whereas phonological dyslexics use mostly the lexical route. Neuroimaging evidence supports this model. However, it emphasises the importance of word regularity but word consistency is more important.

  The triangle model consists of orthographic, phonological and semantic systems. Surface dyslexia is attributed to damage within the semantic system, whereas phonological dyslexia stems from a general phonological impairment. The original triangle model failed to consider the semantic system in detail, and its accounts of phonological and surface dyslexia are oversimplified.

- **Reading: eye-movement research**. According to the E-Z Reader model, the next eye movement is planned when only part of the processing of the currently fixated word has occurred. Completion of frequency checking of a word is the signal to initiate an eye-movement programme, and completion of lexical access is the signal to shift attention covertly to the next word. The model exaggerates the extent of serial processing and the disruptive effects of failing to read words in the correct order. The model is not well integrated with other theories of reading.
- **Speech perception: introduction**. Speech perception resembles music perception in that they both involve categorical perception. However, motor processes are probably more important in speech than music perception, and some patients have selective impairment of speech or music perception. Speech perception involves a series of stages, starting with selection of speech from the acoustic background and including word recognition and utterance interpretation.
- **Listening to speech**. Among the problems faced by listeners are the speed of spoken language, the segmentation problem, coarticulation, individual differences in speech patterns and degraded speech. Listeners prefer to use lexical (e.g., syntax) information to achieve word segmentation but can also use coarticulation, allophony and syllable stress. The McGurk effect shows listeners often make use of visual information (i.e., lip-reading) during speech perception.
- **Context effects**. There is much controversy concerning the ways in which context influences speech perception. The main divide is between those who argue that such effects occur late in processing (autonomous position) and those who argue that they can also occur early in processing (interactionist position). The interactionist position has received additional support recently, but is more applicable when speech is degraded than when it is clear and unambiguous.
- **Theories of speech perception**. According to the motor theory, motor processes can facilitate speech perception. Research using transcranial magnetic stimulation (TMS) provides reasonable support for the theory, especially when the listening conditions are demanding. There is some evidence that patients with damage to motor areas have impaired speech perception.

  The TRACE model assumes bottom-up and top-down processes interact flexibly in spoken word recognition. The model provides reasonable accounts of several phenomena, including the word superiority effect, the Ganong effect, categorical perception and the phonemic restoration effect. However, the model exaggerates the importance of top-down processes and provides a limited account of the ways in which context influences spoken word recognition.

The cohort model is based on the assumption that perceiving a spoken word involves rejecting competitors in a sequential process. It also assumes that context effects occur during the integration stage following word identification. This is often the case, but context effects sometimes occur earlier in processing. Spoken word recognition depends in part on listeners predicting upcoming speech segments, but this process is de-emphasised within the model.

- **Cognitive neuropsychology**. Patients varying in brain damage exhibit different patterns of impairment in speech perception. It has been argued that some of these patterns can be explained by assuming the existence of three routes between sound and speech. Support for this argument has been obtained by studying patients with pure word deafness, word meaning deafness and transcranial sensory aphasia.

Further reading

- Carreiras, M., Armstrong, B.C., Perea, M. & Frost, R. (2014). The what, when, where, and how of visual word recognition. *Trends in Cognitive Sciences*, 18: 90–8. Manuel Carreiras and his colleagues provide a valuable, succinct account of the processes involved in recognising words while reading.
- Harley, T.A. (2013). *The psychology of language: From data to theory* (4th edn). Hove: Psychology Press. The most recent edition of Trevor Harley's outstanding textbook provides excellent coverage of research and theory on basic reading processes and speech perception.
- Magnuson, J.S., Mirman, D. & Myers, E. (2013). Spoken word perception. In D. Reisberg (ed.), *The Oxford handbook of cognitive psychology*. Oxford: Oxford University Press. The basic processes involved in recognising spoken words are discussed fully.
- Mattys, S.L., Davis, M.H., Bradlow, A.R. & Scott, S.K. (2012). Speech recognition in adverse conditions: A review. *Language and Cognitive Processes*, 27: 953–78. Sven Mattys and colleagues focus on the problems experienced by listeners engaged in speech perception under the demanding conditions often experienced in everyday life.
- Rayner, K., Pollatsek, A., Ashby, J. & Clifton, C. (2012). *Psychology of reading* (2nd edn). Hove: Psychology Press. The basic processes involved in reading are discussed at length in this book by Keith Rayner and his colleagues.
- Taylor, J.S.H., Rastle, K. & Davis, M.H. (2013). Can cognitive models explain brain activation during word and pseudoword reading? A meta-analysis of 36 neuroimaging studies. *Psychological Bulletin*, 139: 766–91. This article shows how our understanding of the cognitive processes involved in reading can be enhanced by cognitive neuroscience.

CHAPTER

10

Language comprehension

INTRODUCTION

Basic processes involved in the initial stages of reading and listening to speech were discussed in Chapter 9. The focus was on the identification of individual words. In this chapter, we discuss how phrases, sentences and entire stories are processed and understood during reading and listening.

The previous chapter dealt mainly with aspects of language processing *differing* between reading and listening to speech. In contrast the higher-level processes involved in comprehension are *similar* whether a story is being listened to or read. There has been much more research on comprehension processes in reading than listening, and so our emphasis will be on reading. However, what is true of reading is mostly also true of listening to speech.

What is the structure of this chapter? We start by considering comprehension at the sentence level and finish by focusing on comprehension processes with larger language units (e.g., complete texts). A more detailed indication of this chapter's coverage is given below.

There are two main levels of analysis in sentence comprehension. First, there is an analysis of the syntactical structure of each sentence. **Syntax** involves a study of the rules for the formation of grammatical sentences in any given language. It often involves close attention to word order. **Grammar** is similar to syntax but somewhat broader in meaning. It includes a focus on sentence structure, punctuation, parts of speech and so on.

Second, there is an analysis of sentence meaning. The intended meaning of a sentence often differs from its literal meaning as in irony, sarcasm or metaphor. For example, someone may say, "Don't overdo it!", when talking to a notoriously lazy co-worker. The study of intended meaning is pragmatics. The *context* in which a sentence is spoken can also influence its intended meaning in various ways. Issues concerning pragmatics are discussed immediately following the section on parsing.

Most theories of sentence processing have ignored individual differences even though individuals differ substantially in their comprehension processes and abilities. Individual differences in language comprehension are discussed in the third section of the chapter.

KEY TERMS

Syntax
The set of rules concerning word order within sentences in a language.

Grammar
The set of rules concerning which word orders are acceptable and which are unacceptable and on parts of speech.

Parsing
An analysis of the syntactical or grammatical structure of sentences.

Inflection
Grammatical changes to nouns or verbs (e.g., adding –s to a noun to indicate the plural).

In the fourth section, we consider processes involved when individuals are presented with a text or speech consisting of several sentences. Our focus will mainly be on the inferences readers and listeners draw during comprehension. The major theoretical issue is the following: what determines which inferences are (and are not) drawn during language comprehension?

In the fifth section, we consider processing involving larger units of language. When we read a text or story, we typically try to integrate the information within it. Such integration often involves drawing inferences, identifying the main themes in the text and so on. These integrative processes (and theories put forward to explain them) are discussed in this section.

PARSING: OVERVIEW

This section is devoted to **parsing** (analysis of the syntactical or grammatical structure of sentences) and the processes readers and listeners use to comprehend the sentences they read or hear. A fundamental issue is to work out *when* different kinds of information are used. Much research on parsing concerns the relationship between syntactic and semantic analysis. There are at least four major possibilities:

1 Syntactic analysis generally precedes (and influences) semantic analysis.
2 Semantic analysis usually occurs *prior* to syntactic analysis.
3 Syntactic and semantic analysis occur at the same time.
4 Syntax and semantics are very closely associated and have a hand-in-glove relationship (Gerry Altmann, personal communication).

We will address the above possibilities shortly. Note that most studies on parsing have considered only the English language. Does this matter? It probably does. Information about syntax or grammar can be provided by word order or **inflection**. Inflection involves modifying nouns or verbs to indicate grammatical changes (e.g., adding –ed to a verb to indicate the past tense). Word order is more important to parsing in English than in more inflectional languages (e.g., German) permitting greater flexibility of word order (Harley, 2013). These differences may explain why German parsers perform worse than English ones (Kübler, 2006).

Syntax and grammar

It is possible to produce an infinite number of systematic and organised sentences in any language. Linguists (e.g., Chomsky, 1957) have produced rules explaining the productivity and regularity of language. A set of rules forms a grammar. Ideally, we should be able to use a grammar to generate all the permissible sentences in a given language while rejecting all the unacceptable ones.

Numerous sentences are ambiguous. Some are ambiguous at the *global* level, meaning the whole sentence has two or more possible interpretations. An example is, "Kids make nutritious snacks." Other sentences are ambiguous at the *local* level, meaning various interpretations are possible at some point during parsing.

Why are so many written and spoken sentences ambiguous? It would be very demanding for writers and speakers to produce only totally unambiguous sentences. In fact, a certain amount of ambiguity is actually desirable (Piantadosi et al., 2012). The *context* typically provides useful information about meaning, and it would be inefficient (and very boring for readers and listeners!) if written or spoken language duplicated that information.

Much research on parsing has used ambiguous sentences. Why is this? Parsing operations generally occur very rapidly, making it hard to study the processes involved. Observing the problems encountered by listeners and readers struggling with ambiguous sentences provides revealing information about parsing processes.

Prosodic cues

One way listeners work out the syntactic or grammatical structure of spoken language is by using prosodic cues (e.g., stress, intonation, rhythm, word duration). When each syllable is spoken with equal weight in a monotone (i.e., without prosodic cues), listeners struggle to understand the speaker (Duffy & Pisoni, 1992). The use of prosodic cues by speakers and writers is discussed in Chapter 11.

Suppose a spoken sentence contains a prosodic cue (pause) that occurs misleadingly at a place in conflict with its syntactic structure. Pauker et al. (2012) found this made the sentence much harder to understand, thus showing the impact of prosodic cues. There is a more detailed discussion of this experiment shortly.

Prosodic cues are of most value with *ambiguous* spoken sentences. Consider the ambiguous sentence, "The old men and women sat on the bench." If the women are not old, the spoken duration of "men" will be relatively long and the stressed syllable in "women" will have a steep rise in pitch contour.

Listeners often make very rapid use of prosodic cues to facilitate the understanding of ambiguous sentences. Holzgrefe et al. (2013) presented ambiguous word strings such as *Mona oder Lena und Lola* (*Mona or Lena and Lola*) auditorily with a pause and other prosodic cues occurring after the word *Mona* (early pause) or after *Lena* (late pause) (see Figure 10.1).

When the pause came after the word *Lena* to indicate it was Mona or Lena as well as Lola, listeners immediately integrated the prosodic information into the parsing of the utterance. In a study by Nakamura et al. (2012), listeners' interpretations of ambiguous sentences were influenced by prosodic cues *before* the disambiguating information had been presented.

Prosodic cues are used during silent reading to facilitate comprehension. In one study (Steinhauer & Friederici, 2001), participants listened to (or read) various sentences. These sentences contained intonational boundaries (speech) or commas (text). The key finding was that event-related potentials (ERPs; see Glossary) were similar in both cases. This is consistent with the hypothesis that the mechanisms underlying speech comprehension play a role in comprehension of written sentences.

Further supporting evidence for the above hypothesis was reported by Hirotani et al. (2006). Consider this sentence:

John, go to the library for me.

If that sentence were spoken, there would be a pause after the word "John". This pause is a prosodic cue and makes it easier to understand the sentence. Hirotani et al. measured fixation time on the word "John" when the same sentence was presented visually. Fixation on the word "John" was longer when there was a comma after it, which is very similar to the pause at that point in spoken language.

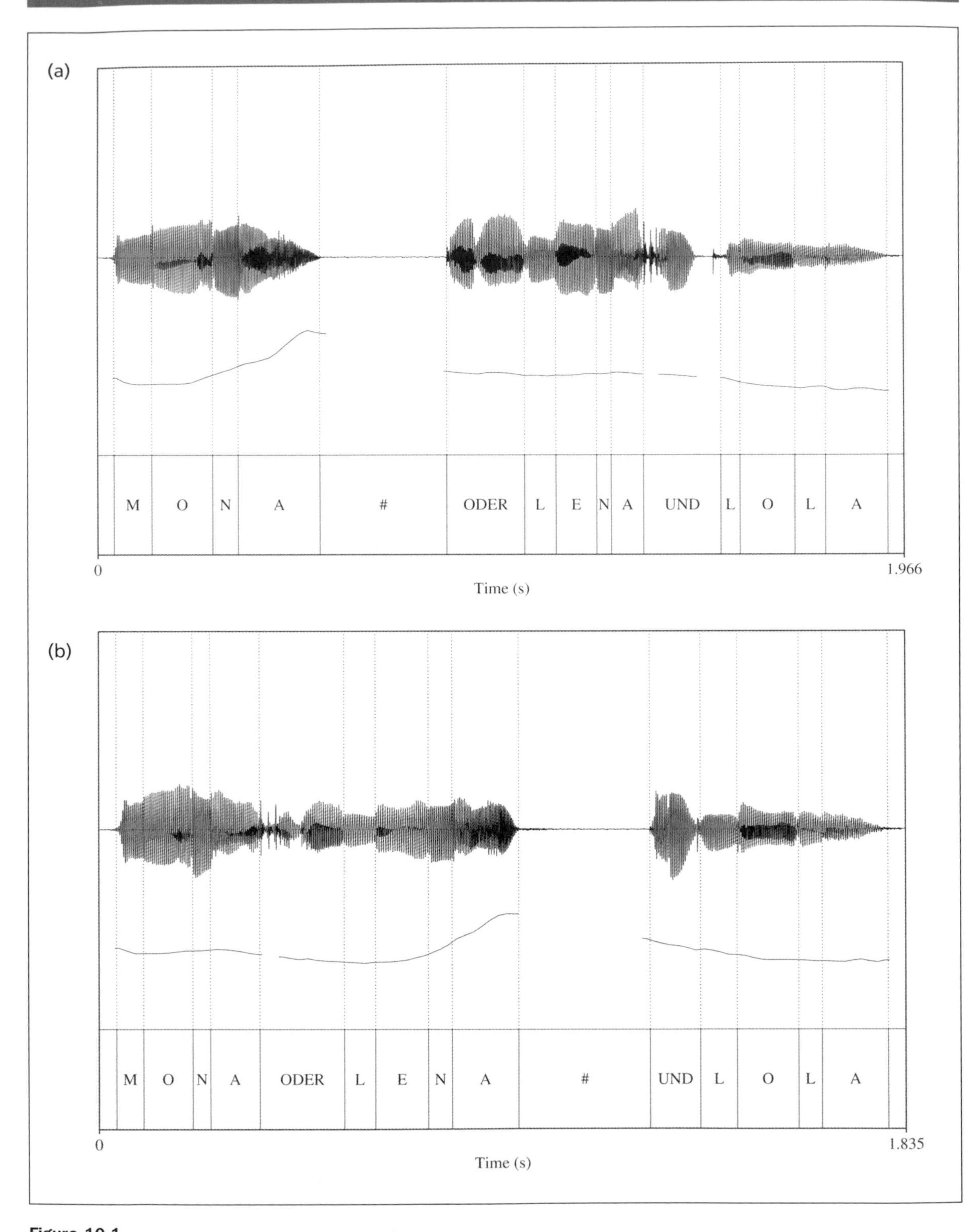

Figure 10.1
Spectrum of sound frequencies when (a) the intonation phrase boundary occurred early in the utterance and (b) when it occurred late in the utterance. The silent pause is indicated by #.
From Holzgrefe et al. (2013). Courtesy Julia Holzgrefe.

Frazier et al. (2006) argued that we should consider the overall *pattern* of prosodic phrasing within a sentence rather than simply what happens at *one* particular point. Consider the following ambiguous sentence:

I met the daughter (#1) of the colonel (#2) who was on the balcony.

There was an intermediate phrase boundary at (#2), and the phrase boundary at (1#) was larger, the same size or smaller. What determined sentence interpretation was the *relationship* between the phrase boundaries. Listeners were most likely to assume the colonel was on the balcony when the first boundary was greater than the second one, and least likely to when the first boundary was smaller than the second.

The above findings conflict with the traditional view. According to this view, a prosodic boundary (#2) immediately before the phrase "who was on the balcony" indicates it should *not* be attached to the most recent potential candidate (i.e., the colonel). This view is limited because it minimises the importance of the *pattern* of boundaries.

In sum, prosody is important in language comprehension. As Frazier et al. (2006, p. 248) concluded, "Perhaps prosody provides the structure within which utterance comprehension take place (in speech and even in silent reading)."

MODELS OF PARSING

There are more models of parsing than you can shake a stick at. However, many models can be divided into two categories: (1) two-stage, serial processing theories and (2) one-stage, parallel processing models. The garden-path model (Frazier & Rayner, 1982) is the most influential one in the first category. It is based on the assumption that the initial attempt to parse a sentence involves using only syntactic information.

MacDonald et al.'s (1994) constraint-based model is the most influential example of a one-stage, parallel processing model. It is based on the assumption that *all* sources of information (syntactic, semantic, contextual) are used from the outset to construct a syntactic model of each sentence.

We will initially consider the above two models. After that, we turn to the unrestricted race model, which combines aspects of the garden-path and constraint-based models. As we will see, there are many apparent inconsistencies in research findings in this area. Why is that? A major reason is that most people are very sensitive to the subtleties of language. As a result, sentence parsing often varies as a function of apparently minor differences in the sentences presented.

Garden-path model

Frazier and Rayner's (1982) garden-path model is so called because readers or listeners can be misled or "led up the garden path" by ambiguous sentences. A famous (or notorious!) example of such a sentence is, "The horse raced past the barn fell." It is infamous because it is very hard to understand. This is perhaps unsurprising given that such sentences occur exceptionally rarely in naturally produced language (McKoon & Ratcliff, 2003). However, numerous other more commonly encountered ambiguous sentences have shed much light on parsing processes.

The garden-path model is based on the following assumptions:

- Only *one* syntactical structure is initially considered for any sentence.
- Meaning is *not* involved in the selection of the initial syntactical structure.
- The simplest syntactical structure is chosen, making use of two general principles: minimal attachment and late closure.
- According to the principle of minimal attachment, the grammatical structure producing the fewest nodes (major parts of a sentence such as noun phrase and verb phrase) is preferred.
- The principle of late closure is that new words encountered in a sentence are attached to the current phrase or clause if grammatically permissible.
- Conflict between the above two principles is resolved in favour of the minimal attachment principle.
- If the initial syntactic structure a reader constructs for a sentence is incompatible with additional information (e.g., semantic) generated by a thematic processor, there is a second processing stage in which it is revised.

The relevance of the principle of minimal attachment was shown by Frazier and Rayner (1982). Consider the following sentences:

1 The girl knew the answer by heart.
2 The girl knew the answer was wrong.

The minimal attachment principle produces a grammatical structure in which "the answer" is treated as the direct object of the verb "knew". This is appropriate only for the first sentence. As predicted, Frazier and Rayner found eye fixations were longer with the second sentence.

Frazier and Rayner (1982) also showed the importance of the principle of late closure. Consider the following sentences:

1 Since Jay always jogs a mile it seems like a short distance to him.
2 Since Jay always jogs a mile seems like a short distance to him.

Use of the principle of late closure leads "a mile" to be included in the first clause as the object of "jogs". This is appropriate only for the first sentence. Frazier and Rayner (1982) found readers had very long fixations on the word "seems" in the second sentence when it became clear the principle of late closure did not apply to it. However, the second sentence would be much easier to read if we insert a comma (a prosodic cue) after "jogs" (Rayner et al., 2012).

We have just seen that the principles of minimal attachment and late closure can lead readers and listeners to construct incorrect grammatical structures for sentences. However, it can be argued that this is efficient because use of these principles minimises the demands on short-term memory. In addition, a sentence's correct grammatical structure is often constructed rapidly via use of these two principles.

Findings

The principles of minimal attachment and late closure are used very often by readers and listeners (Rayner et al., 2012). For example, readers' use of late closure was shown by van Gompel and Pickering (2001). Consider the following sentence: "After the child had sneezed the doctor prescribed a course of injections." Eye-movement data indicated that readers experienced a difficulty after the word "sneezed" because they mistakenly used the principle of late closure to try to make "the doctor" the direct object of "sneezed". This shows the powerful influence exerted by the principle of late closure because the verb "sneezed" cannot take a direct object.

A distinctive assumption of the garden-path model is that the syntactic structure of sentences can often be worked out in the almost complete absence of semantic information. Findings consistent with that assumption were reported by Breedin and Saffran (1999). They studied a patient, DM, with semantic dementia, a condition involving loss of knowledge of word meanings (see Chapter 7). DM performed at essentially normal levels on tasks involving the detection of grammatical violations or selecting the subject and object in sentences. Garrard et al. (2004) found that a patient with semantic dementia showed intact performance on a task involving grammaticality judgements.

Semantic dementia (see Glossary) involves damage to the anterior temporal lobe. Wilson et al. (2012) reviewed research on the brain regions associated with syntactical processing. Patients with impaired ability to process syntax often have damage to the left inferior and middle frontal gyri (see Figure 10.2).

A crucial assumption of the garden-path model is that semantic factors do *not* influence the construction of the initial syntactic structure. The findings are somewhat inconsistent and depend on the precise sentences used. Trueswell et al. (1994) recorded eye movements while readers read sentences such as the following:

1 The defendant examined by the lawyer turned out to be unreliable.
2 The evidence examined by the lawyer turned out to be unreliable.

According to the principle of minimal attachment, readers should initially treat the verb *examined* as the main verb and so experience ambiguity for both sentences. However, if readers rapidly make use of semantic information, they would experience more ambiguity for the first sentence. Readers took longer to disambiguate the first sentence, which is inconsistent with the garden-path model.

Pauker et al. (2012) studied sentences such as, "When a bear is approaching the people the dogs come running." Listeners heard such sentences with prosodic cues (pauses, indicated by #) introduced at different points:

1 When a bear is approaching the people # the dogs come running.
2 When a bear is approaching # the people # the dogs come running.

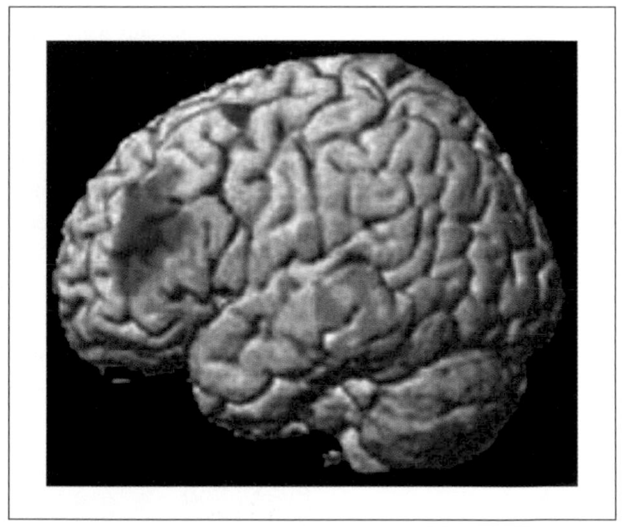

Figure 10.2
Brain areas (left inferior and middle frontal gyri) associated with impaired comprehension of complex syntax in brain-damaged patients.
From Wilson et al. (2012). Reprinted with permission from Elsevier.

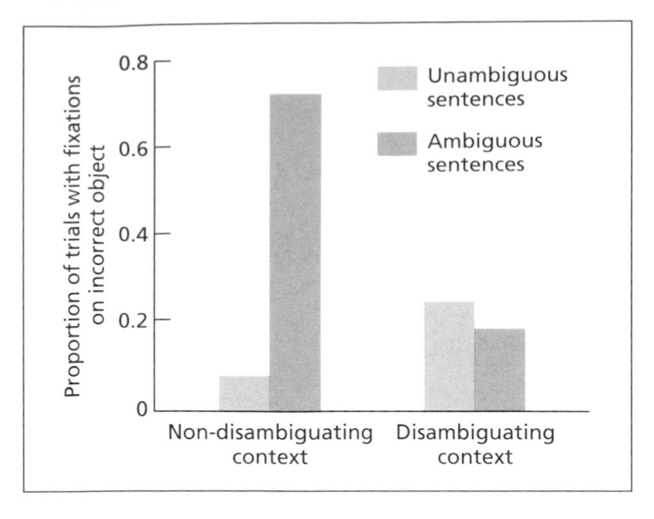

Figure 10.3
Proportion of trials with eye fixations on the incorrect object as a function of sentence type (unambiguous vs. ambiguous) and context (non-disambiguating vs. disambiguating).
Based on data in Spivey et al. (2002). With permission from Elsevier.

According to the garden-path model, listeners should apply the principle of late closure and so find it fairly easy to identify the syntactical structure of such sentences. Sentences such as (1) in which the location of the pause coincided with the syntactic structure of the sentence were accepted 87% of the time. In contrast, sentences such as (2) in which there was a misleading pause (i.e., between *approaching* and *the people*) were accepted only 28% of the time. Thus, listeners' adherence to the principle of late closure can be greatly disrupted by misleading prosodic cues.

According to the garden-path model, visual context should *not* influence the initial parsing of an ambiguous sentence. However, much research using the visual world paradigm indicates that is not always the case. In a study by Spivey et al. (2002), participants heard ambiguous sentences (e.g., "Put the apple on the towel in the box") and their eye movements were recorded.

According to the garden-path model, "on the towel" should initially be understood as the place where the apple should be put because that is the simplest syntactic structure. That was the case when the visual context did not remove the ambiguity and so these findings supported the garden-path model. However, when the visual context consisted of two apples, one on a towel and the other on a napkin, the participants used that context to identify which apple to move. There were far fewer eye movements to the incorrect object (e.g., the towel on its own) when the context disambiguated the sentence (see Figure 10.3).

An important aspect of the Spivey et al. (2002) study was that participants had several seconds to process the visual context before the spoken instruction. Ferreira et al. (2013) essentially replicated Spivey et al.'s findings using a similar experimental situation when the visual context preceded the spoken instruction. When the visual display appeared at the same time as the spoken instruction, however, participants found it much harder to use disambiguating context to inhibit eye movements to the incorrect object.

What conclusions should we draw? First, the processes used by participants depend very much on the precise task demands. Second, disambiguating context is only used effectively when it is presented ahead of the spoken instruction. Ferreira et al. (2013) found that this was the case because prior context allowed participants to predict reasonably accurately the type of spoken instruction they would hear.

Evaluation

The model provides a simple and coherent account of key processes in sentence processing. The principles of minimal attachment and late closure often influence the selection of an initial syntactic structure for sentences. The model is plausible in that use of these two principles reduces processing demands on the reader or listener.

What are the model's limitations? First, the assumption that the meanings of words within sentences do not influence the initial assignment of grammatical structure is inconsistent with some of the evidence (e.g., Trueswell et al., 1994). We will see later that semantic information about word meanings and the world has a rapid influence on sentence processing.

Second, several factors can prevent readers and listeners from adhering to the principles of minimal attachment and late closure. These factors include misleading prosody (Pauker et al., 2012) and prior context (e.g., Spivey et al., 2002). Other factors are discussed in the next section.

Third, it is hard to provide a definitive test of the model. Evidence that non-syntactic information is used early in sentence processing seems inconsistent with the model. However, it is possible the second stage of parsing (which follows the first, syntactic stage) starts very rapidly.

Fourth, the model does not take account of differences among languages. For example, there is a preference for early rather than late closure in various languages including Spanish, Dutch and French (Harley, 2013).

Constraint-based model

According to MacDonald et al.'s (1994) constraint-based model, a sentence's initial interpretation depends on multiple information sources (e.g., syntactic, semantic, general world knowledge) called constraints. These constraints limit, or constrain, the number of possible interpretations.

The constraint-based model is based on a connectionist architecture (see Chapter 1). It is assumed *all* relevant sources of information are available immediately to the parser. Competing analyses of the current sentence are activated at the same time. The syntactic structure receiving most support from the various constraints is highly activated, with other syntactic structures being less activated. Readers become confused when reading ambiguous sentences if the correct syntactic structure is less activated than one or more incorrect structures.

According to the model, the processing system uses four language characteristics to resolve sentence ambiguities:

1. Grammatical knowledge constrains possible sentence interpretations.
2. The various forms of information associated with any given word are typically not independent of each other.
3. A word may be less ambiguous in some ways than in others (e.g., ambiguous tense but not grammatical category).
4. The various interpretations permissible according to grammatical rules generally differ considerably in frequency and probability on the basis of past experience. The syntactic interpretation most consistent with past experience is typically selected.

MacDonald (2013) developed her constraint-based model in a production–distribution–comprehension account. She started by assuming speakers use various strategies to reduce processing demands (see also Chapter 11). One strategy is easy – start with common words and syntactically simple phrases while the rest of the utterance is planned. Another strategy is plan reuse – favour more practised and easy sentence plans. The central assumption is that listeners' comprehension processes are sensitive to these strategies and this assists them in predicting the

KEY TERM

Verb bias
An imbalance in the frequency with which a verb is associated with different syntactic structures.

speaker's next utterance. This account goes beyond the constraint-based model in assuming that many of the constraints used by listeners to facilitate comprehension depend on their knowledge of the language strategies used by speakers.

Findings

It is assumed within the constraint-based model that several kinds of non-syntactic information are used very early in sentence processing. Within the garden-path model, in contrast, this occurs only *after* an initial stage of syntactic processing. Earlier we discussed research by Trueswell et al. (1994) in which contextual information was used very rapidly. There are many other studies in which semantic information was used very rapidly after sentence presentation and these are discussed by Harley (2013) and van Berkum (2009).

A major difference between the constraint-based model and the garden-path model is that the former assumes sentence processing is *parallel* whereas the latter assumes it is *serial*. Cai et al. (2012) compared the predictions of the two models by considering the processing of ambiguous sentences such as the following:

> Because it was John that Ralph threatened the neighbour recorded their conversation.

This sentence is temporally ambiguous. It is not initially clear whether *the neighbour* is the subject of the main clause *recorded their conversation* (subject analysis) or the object of the preceding verb *threatened* (object analysis).

Readers interpreted the sentence in line with the subject analysis. According to the garden-path model, the alternative interpretation is not considered. In contrast, the constraint-based model assumes readers can process both analyses at the same time in parallel. Cai et al.'s (2012) key finding was that the object analysis disrupted sentence processing even though that analysis was not adopted. This finding is more consistent with the constraint-based model.

According to the model, verbs are an important constraint that can strongly influence initial attempts at parsing. Many verbs can occur within two different syntactic structures but are more often encountered within one syntactic structure than the other. This is known as **verb bias**. The verb *read* is an example. Consider the following two sentences:

1 The professor read the newspaper had been destroyed.
2 The professor read the newspaper during his break.

Which of the above sentences was easier to read? Most people find the second sentence easier. The verb *read* is most often followed by a direct object (as in (2)) but is sometimes followed by an embedded clause (as in (1)). It follows from the constraint-based model that readers should find it easier to resolve ambiguities and identify the correct syntactic structure when the sentence structure is *consistent* with the verb bias. According to the garden-path model, in contrast, verb bias should have no effect.

Wilson and Garnsey (2009) studied the effects of verb bias on ambiguous sentences involving a direct object or embedded clause. The findings were as predicted by the constraint-based model (see Figure 10.4). The time taken to resolve the ambiguity was greater when the sentence structure was *inconsistent* with the verb bias. Thus, readers' previous experience with verbs has an immediate effect on sentence processing.

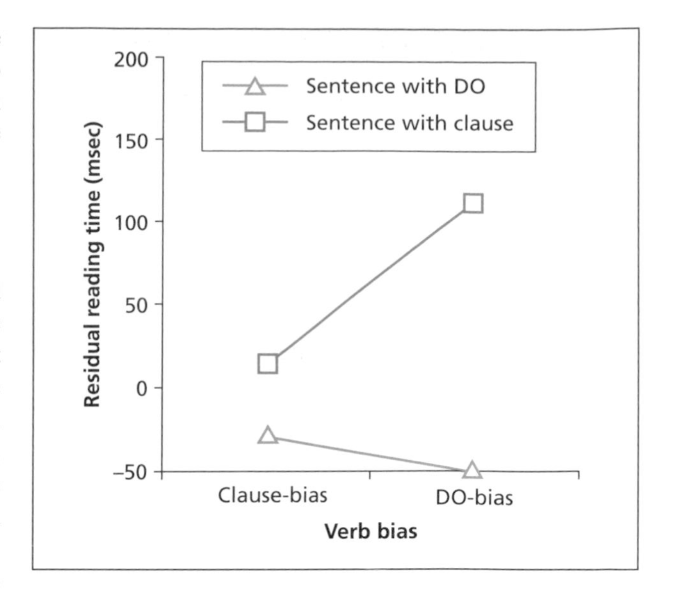

Figure 10.4
Mean reading time in milliseconds for the disambiguating region of sentences having a direct object (DO) or embedded clause with verbs biasing an embedded-clause or direct-object interpretation.
From Wilson and Garnsey (2009). With permission from Elsevier.

Evaluation

What are the strengths of the constraint-based model? First, it seems efficient (as assumed by the model) that readers should use *all* relevant information from the outset when working out the syntactic structure of a sentence. As we have seen, non-syntactic factors such as word meaning (e.g., Trueswell et al., 1994; Wilson & Garnsey, 2009) and context (e.g., Spivey et al., 2002) are often used rapidly during sentence processing.

Second, we can consider more than one syntactic analysis at a time (e.g., Cai et al., 2012). This is as predicted by the constraint-based model, which assumes there is parallel processing. However, it appears inconsistent with the garden-path model, which assumes processing is serial.

Third, the constraint-based model assumes there is some *flexibility* in parsing decisions because the information to which we attend depends on our past linguistic experience. In contrast, there is little scope for flexibility within the garden-path model. Brysbaert and Mitchell (1996) found there were substantial individual differences among Dutch people in their parsing decisions, which is more consistent with the constraint-based model.

What are the limitations of the constraint-based model? First, it often fails to make precise predictions about parsing. As Rayner et al. (2012, p. 229) pointed out, "It is difficult if not impossible to falsify the general claim that parsing is interactive and constraint-based . . . it does not by itself make any clear predictions about which things actually matter, or how and when they have their influence."

Second, much experimental support for the constraint-based model consists of findings showing that non-syntactic factors have an early influence on sentence processing. Such findings are clearly consistent with the model. However, some of them can be accounted for by the garden-path model on the assumption that the second, non-syntactic, stage of parsing starts very rapidly.

Unrestricted race model

Van Gompel et al. (2000) put forward the unrestricted race model, which combines aspects of the garden-path and constraint-based models. Its three main assumptions are as follows:

1 All sources of information (semantic as well as syntactic) are used to identify a syntactic structure, as assumed by the constraint-based model.

2 All other possible syntactic structures are ignored unless the favoured syntactic structure is disconfirmed by subsequent information.
3 If the initially chosen syntactic structure has to be discarded, there is an extensive reanalysis before a different syntactic structure is chosen. This assumption makes the model similar to the garden-path model, in that parsing often involves two distinct stages.

Findings

Van Gompel et al. (2001) compared the unrestricted race model against other models. Participants read three kinds of sentences (sample sentences provided):

1 *Ambiguous sentences*: The burglar stabbed only the guy with the dagger during the night. (It could be either the burglar or the guy who had the dagger.)
2 *Verb-phrase attachment*: The burglar stabbed only the dog with the dagger during the night. (This sentence involves verb-phrase attachment because it was the burglar who stabbed with the dagger.)
3 *Noun-phrase attachment*: The burglar stabbed only the dog with the collar during the night. (This sentence involves noun-phrase attachment because the dog had the collar.)

According to the garden-path model, the principle of minimal attachment means readers should always adopt the verb-phrase analysis. This will lead to rapid processing of sentences such as (2) but slow processing of sentences such as (3). Ambiguous sentences can be processed rapidly because the verb-phrase analysis is acceptable.

According to the constraint-based theory, sentences such as (2) and (3) will be processed rapidly, because the meanings of the words support only the correct interpretation. However, there will be serious competition between the two possible interpretations of sentence (1) and so processing will be slow.

In fact, the ambiguous sentences were processed *faster* than either of the other types of sentences, which did not differ (see Figure 10.5). According to van Gompel et al. (2001), these findings support the unrestricted race model. With the ambiguous sentences, readers rapidly use syntactic and semantic information to form a syntactic structure. Since both syntactic structures are possible, no reanalysis is necessary. In contrast, reanalysis is sometimes needed with noun-phrase and verb-phrase sentences.

Mohamed and Clifton (2011) compared the same three models. Participants read temporarily ambiguous sentences such as the following:

The second wife will claim the entire family inheritance for herself.

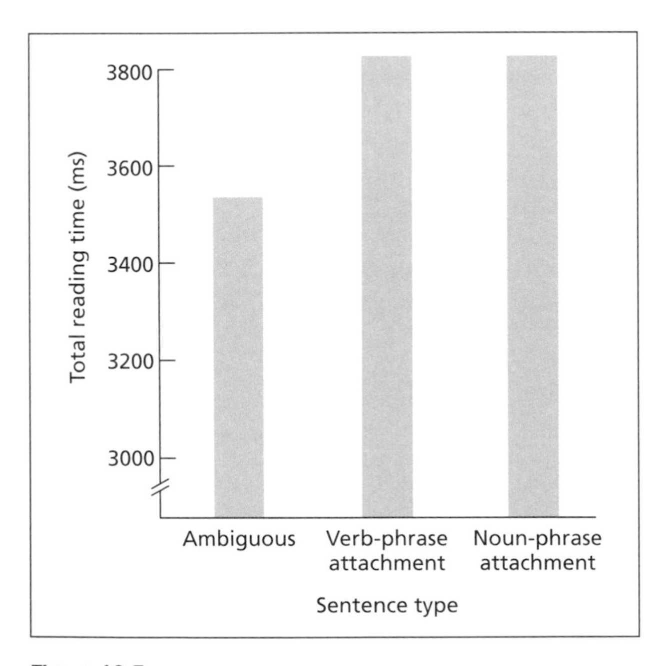

Figure 10.5
Total sentence processing time as a function of sentence type (ambiguous, verb-phrase attachment, noun-phrase attachment).
Data from van Gompel et al. (2001). With kind permission from Springer Science + Business Media.

This sentence has an ambiguous region (*the entire family inheritance*) and a disambiguating region (*for herself*). The sentence was sometimes preceded by a context biasing the *incorrect* syntactic structure.

What are the predictions of the three parsing models? We start with the garden-path model. Since the actual syntactic structure is the simplest possible, it predicts readers will not be slowed down in the ambiguous or disambiguating regions.

According to the constraint-based theory, both syntactic structures are activated in the ambiguous region, which slows down reading. Readers then need to select one of these syntactic structures in the disambiguating region, which also slows reading time.

Finally, according to the unrestricted race model, only *one* syntactic structure is produced in the ambiguous region and so reading is not slowed at that point. However, it will often be the *incorrect* syntactic structure, and so reading is slowed in the disambiguating region.

Which model was the winner? Reading times in the ambiguous and disambiguating regions were most consistent with the predictions of the unrestricted race model.

Evaluation

The unrestricted race model in some ways combines the best features of the garden-path and constraint-based models. It seems reasonable that all sources of information (including world knowledge) are used from the outset to construct a syntactic structure. This syntactic structure is then retained unless subsequent evidence is inconsistent with it.

More research is needed before we can provide a proper assessment of the unrestricted race model. However, the model seems to be based on the assumption that readers will sooner or later identify the correct syntactic structure. As we will see shortly, this is by no means always the case.

Good-enough representations

Until recently, nearly all theories of sentence processing (including those discussed above) possessed an important limitation. They were based on the assumption that the language processor "generates representations of the linguistic input that are complete, detailed, and accurate" (Ferreira et al., 2002, p. 11).

An alternative viewpoint is based on the assumption of "good-enough" representations. According to this viewpoint, a reader's or listener's typical comprehension goal is "to get a parse [sentence analysis] of the input that is 'good enough' to generate a response given the current task" (Swets et al., 2008, p. 211).

The Moses illusion is an example of inaccurate comprehension. When asked, "How many animals of each sort did Moses put on the ark?", many people reply "Two". In fact, the correct answer is "None" (think about it!). Ferreira (2003) found representations of heard sentences are sometimes inaccurate rather than rich and complete. For example, "The mouse was eaten by the cheese" was sometimes misinterpreted as meaning the mouse ate the cheese.

Explanations

Why are we so prone to error when processing anomalous sentences? According to Ferreira (2003), we use heuristics (see Glossary) or rules of thumb to simplify sentence understanding. A very common heuristic (the NVN strategy) is to assume the subject of a sentence is the agent of some action, whereas the object of the sentence is the recipient or theme. We use this heuristic because most English sentences conform to this pattern.

Christianson et al. (2010) made a similar point. They argued that listeners in the study by Ferreira (2003) faced a *conflict* between the syntactic structure of the passive sentences and their semantic knowledge of what is typically the case in the real world. Sometimes that conflict is resolved by favouring semantic knowledge over syntactic information.

Christianson et al. (2010) tested their viewpoint. Some listeners heard plausible passive sentences, such as "The fish was caught by the angler", and then described an unrelated line drawing. Listeners tended to produce passive sentences in their description, suggesting they were influenced by the syntactic structure of the original sentences.

Other listeners heard implausible passive sentences, such as "The angler was caught by the fish." These listeners tended *not* to produce passive sentences in their descriptions of line drawings, suggesting they paid little attention to the syntactic structure of the original sentences.

How can we persuade readers and listeners to process sentences more thoroughly and so reduce their misinterpretations? Swets et al. (2008) argued that readers should process sentences more thoroughly if they anticipate detailed comprehension questions rather than superficial ones. Thus, the extent to which sentences are processed depends on the reader's or listener's specific goals.

As predicted, participants read sentences (especially syntactically ambiguous ones) more slowly in the former case than in the latter case (see Figure 10.6). Ambiguous sentences were read *more* rapidly than non-ambiguous ones when superficial questions were asked. However, this ambiguity advantage disappeared when more challenging comprehension questions were anticipated.

Other findings indicate it can be hard to persuade people to process sentences thoroughly. For example, Dwivedi (2013) gave participants pairs of sentences such as the following:

1 Every kid climbed that tree.
2 The tree was in the park.

Even though they knew they would be asked questions about the meaning of each pair of sentences, approximately one-third of participants incorrectly claimed that several trees were climbed. Thus, readers and listeners very often engage in shallow or heuristic processing leading to misinterpretations of the presented sentences.

Cognitive neuroscience: event-related potentials

Cognitive neuroscience has made substantial contributions to our understanding of parsing and sentence comprehension. Since the precise *timing* of different processes is so important, much use has been made of event-related potentials

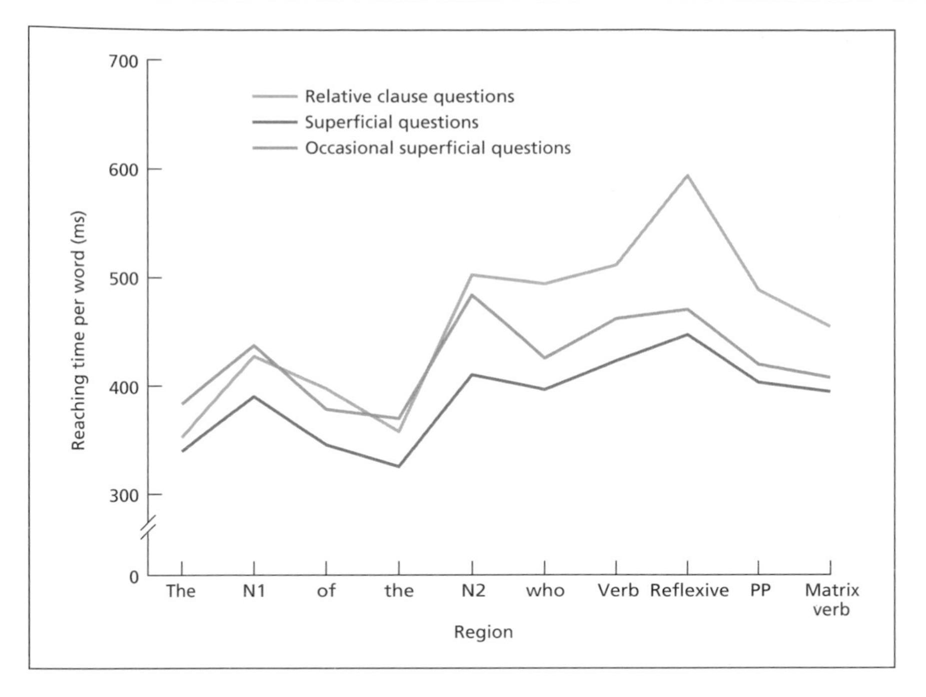

Figure 10.6
Sentence reading times as a function of the way in which comprehension was assessed: detailed (relative clause) questions; superficial questions on all trials; or occasional superficial questions. Sample sentence: The maid of the princess who scratched herself in public was terribly humiliated.

From Swets et al. (2008). With kind permission from Springer Science + Business Media.

(ERPs; see Glossary). As we will see, semantic information of various kinds is actively processed very early on, which is broadly consistent with predictions from the constraint-based theory and the unrestricted race model. There are several reviews of the evidence (e.g., Kutas et al., 2011; Van Petten & Luka, 2012).

The N400 component in the ERP waveform is of particular importance in research on sentence comprehension. It is a negative wave with an onset at 250 ms and a peak at 400 ms. The N400 to a sentence word is smaller when there is a match between its meaning and that provided by the sentence context. Thus, N400 reflects aspects of semantic processing.

To what extent do readers (and listeners) try to predict what they will read (or hear) next? Historically, it was generally assumed prediction is inefficient: "Natural language is not considered to be very constraining, certainly not constraining enough for a predictive system to be accurate a majority of the time. In principle, such errors should result in processing costs" (Kutas et al., 2011, p. 192). However, as we will see, research within cognitive neuroscience has provided evidence for top-down predictive processes in sentence processing. These issues with respect to reading and speech perception are also discussed in Chapter 9.

Findings

How does meaning influence initial sentence construction? The traditional view is that initially we process only the meanings of the words in a sentence. Other

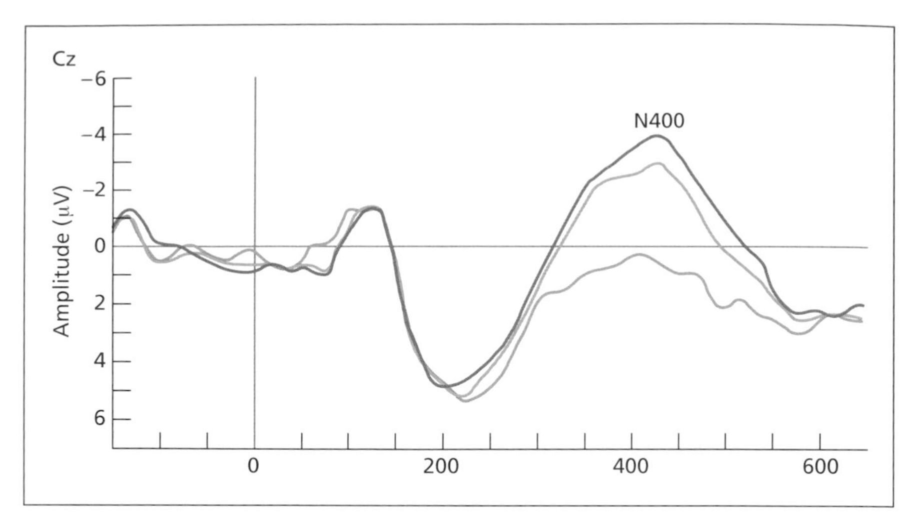

Figure 10.7
The N400 response to the critical word in a correct sentence ("The Dutch trains are yellow": green line), a sentence incorrect on the basis of world knowledge ("The Dutch trains are white": orange line) and a sentence incorrect on the basis of word meanings ("The Dutch trains are sour": purple line). The N400 response was very similar with both incorrect sentences.

From Hagoort et al. (2004). Reprinted with permission from AAAS.

aspects of meaning going beyond the sentence itself (e.g., our world knowledge) are considered subsequently. Contrary evidence was reported by Hagoort et al. (2004). Dutch participants read sentences such as the following (the critical words are in italics):

1 The Dutch trains are *yellow* and very crowded. (This sentence is true.)
2 The Dutch trains are *sour* and very crowded. (This sentence is false because of the meaning of the word "sour".)
3 The Dutch trains are *white* and very crowded. (This sentence is false because of world knowledge – Dutch trains are yellow.)

According to the traditional view, the semantic mismatch in a sentence such as (3) should have taken longer to detect than the mismatch in a sentence such as (2). In fact, however, the effects of these different kinds of semantic mismatch on N400 were very similar (see Figure 10.7).

What do these findings mean? First, "While reading a sentence, the brain retrieves and integrates word meanings and world knowledge at the same time" (Hagoort et al., 2004, p. 440). Thus, the traditional view that we process word meaning *before* information about world knowledge may be wrong. Second, word meaning and world knowledge are both accessed and integrated into the reader's sentence comprehension within about 400 ms. This suggests (but does not prove) that sentence processing involves making almost immediate use of all relevant information as assumed by MacDonald et al.'s (1994) constraint-based theory.

The traditional view also assumed contextual information is processed *after* information concerning the meanings of words within a sentence. Evidence against this view was reported by Nieuwland and van Berkum (2006a). Here is an example of the materials they used:

> A woman saw a dancing peanut who had a big smile on his face. The peanut was singing about a girl he had just met. And judging from the song, the peanut was totally crazy about her. The woman thought it was really cute to see the peanut singing and dancing like that. The peanut was *salted/in love*, and by the sound of it, this was definitely mutual.

Some listeners heard "salted", which was appropriate in terms of word meanings but inappropriate in the story context. Others heard "in love", which was appropriate in the story context but inappropriate in terms of word meanings. The key finding was that the N400 was greater for "salted" than for "in love" because it did not fit the story context. Thus, contextual information can have a very rapid major impact on sentence processing.

Van den Brink et al. (2012) argued that listeners often draw inferences going beyond the content of the speaker's message. Suppose you heard someone with an upper-class accent saying, "I have a large tattoo on my back." There would be a conflict between what the person was saying and your stereotyped inferences about the speaker. In contrast, you would probably not perceive a conflict if the speaker had a working-class accent.

Van den Brink et al. (2012) tested the above assumptions. They argued that detection of a conflict or mismatch between the message content and the speaker's characteristics should be reflected in N400. As predicted, there was a much larger N400 to the word "tattoo" spoken in an upper-class accent than a working-class one. However, this was found only in women. Why was this? They had greater skills of empathy than the male participants and so rapidly processed voice-based inferences about the speaker.

Evaluation

Behavioural measures (e.g., time to read a sentence) generally provide rather indirect evidence concerning the nature and timing of the underlying processes involved in sentence comprehension. In contrast, research using event-related potentials has indicated clearly that we make use of our world knowledge of the speaker and contextual knowledge at an early stage of processing. Such findings are more supportive of constraint-based theories than the garden-path model.

More generally, the evidence based on event-related potentials suggests readers and listeners typically try to anticipate what will be read or heard next. As Van Petten and Luka (2012, p. 186) concluded in their review, "Readers and listeners interpret input continuously and incrementally and that interpretation leads to general expectations about the semantic content that will occur later."

What are the limitations of research in this area? First, a small N400 to a predictable word in a sentence is consistent with successful prediction, but is also consistent with easy integration of that word into the developing sentence meaning. It is typically hard to distinguish between these possibilities.

Second, if readers and listeners make specific predictions as to what will be presented next, we would expect significant costs when these predictions are incorrect. However, it has proved difficult to identify such costs. As a result, Van Petten and Luka (2012) argued that readers and listeners form "general expectations" rather than specific predictions.

PRAGMATICS

Pragmatics is concerned with practical language use and comprehension. It relates to the *intended* rather than *literal* meaning as expressed by speakers and understood by listeners, and often involves drawing inferences. For example, we assume someone who says, "The weather's really great!", when it has been raining non-stop for several days, actually thinks the weather is terrible.

Pragmatics is "meaning minus semantics". Suppose someone says something in an unfamiliar language. Using a dictionary would clarify what the speaker intended to communicate. What the dictionary (plus knowledge of the language's grammatical structure) *fails* to tell you about the speaker's intended meaning is the field of pragmatics. A full understanding of intended meaning often requires taking account of *contextual* information (e.g., the speaker's tone, the speaker's relevant behaviour, the current environment).

An important area within pragmatics is **figurative language**, which is language not intended to be taken literally. For example, there is metaphor in which a word or phrase is used figuratively to mean something it resembles (e.g., "Time is a thief"). There is also irony, in which the intended meaning differs substantially from the literal meaning. Here is an example from the film *Dr Strangelove*: "Gentlemen, you can't fight in here! This is the War Room." There are also idioms, which are common figurative expressions (e.g., "kick the bucket").

Bohrn et al. (2012) carried out a meta-analysis (see Glossary) comparing brain activation with figurative and ordinary literal language processing. There were two main findings. First, figurative language processing involved essentially the same brain network as literal processing. Second, several areas in the inferior frontal gyrus (BA45/46/47/13) (especially in the left hemisphere) were more activated during figurative than literal language processing. Thus, figurative processing often requires more cognitive resources (e.g., to work out word meanings and produce semantic integration).

Pragmatics covers numerous topics. Here we will briefly discuss two of the most important ones. First, we consider figurative language (especially metaphor). Second, we focus on the extent to which listeners are able to adopt the speaker's perspective when comprehending what he/she is saying.

KEY TERMS

Pragmatics
The study of the ways language is used and understood in the real world, including a consideration of its intended meaning; meaning minus semantics.

Figurative language
Language that is not intended to be taken literally; examples include metaphor, irony and idiom.

Autistic spectrum disorders
Disorders involving difficulties in social interaction and communication and repetitive patterns of behaviour and thinking.

Central coherence
The ability to make use of all the information when interpreting an utterance or situation.

Weblink:
Pragmatics

IN THE REAL WORLD: AUTISTIC SPECTRUM DISORDERS AND PRAGMATICS

We can assess the importance of pragmatics by studying people poor at distinguishing between literal and intended meanings. For example, consider individuals with **autistic spectrum disorders**. They are very poor at understanding others' intentions and beliefs and so find social communication very difficult. In addition, they have weak **central coherence** (the ability to integrate information from different sources). It follows that individuals with autistic spectrum disorders should have severe problems in working out the intended meaning of figurative language.

Most individuals with autistic spectrum disorders have general learning difficulties and so all aspects of language develop more slowly than they do for other children. In contrast, individuals with **Asperger syndrome** (a relatively mild autistic spectrum disorder) develop language normally but still have difficulties with social communication. Suppose such individuals have impaired pragmatic language comprehension in spite of normal language comprehension generally. That would strengthen the argument that the processes involved in pragmatic language comprehension differ from those involved in basic language comprehension.

Loukusa and Moilanen (2009) reviewed studies of pragmatic comprehension and inference ability in individuals with Asperger syndrome. These individuals had impaired pragmatic language comprehension on several tasks. For example, Kaland et al. (2005) found children and adolescents with Asperger syndrome were poor at drawing the appropriate inferences when presented with jokes, white lies, figurative language, irony and misunderstandings. Here is an example involving irony:

> Ann's mother has spent a long time cooking Ann's favourite meal: fish and chips. But when she brings it to Ann, she is watching TV, and she doesn't even say thank you. Ann's mother is cross and says, "Well, that's very nice, isn't it! That is what I call politeness!"

Individuals with Asperger syndrome were less able than healthy controls to explain why Ann's mother said what she did. This illustrates their general inability to understand what other people are thinking. Of importance, Asperger's individuals were comparable to controls when drawing inferences *not* requiring social understanding.

As mentioned already, one reason individuals with Asperger syndrome have deficient pragmatic language comprehension is because they have weak central coherence and so fail to use all the available information. Supporting evidence was reported by Zalla et al. (2014). Participants decided whether a speaker's compliments to another person were literal or ironic. The speaker's occupation was one stereotypically associated with use of irony and sarcasm (e.g., comedian, chat show host) or not associated with irony and sarcasm (e.g., accountant, clergyman).

Healthy controls were influenced by the speaker's occupation: they correctly recognised that a speaker was being ironic when he/she had a sarcastic/ironic occupation. In contrast, individuals with Asperger syndrome ignored information about the speaker's occupation.

In sum, individuals with Asperger syndrome have special difficulty in inferring correctly the intentions and motivations of other people. As a result, in spite of generally normal language ability, they exhibit impaired pragmatic language comprehension in social contexts.

Figurative language: metaphors

Our processing of metaphors depends on many factors (Gibbs, 2013). These include individual differences in the listener's language ability, the nature of the metaphor (e.g., its familiarity) and the listener's goal (e.g., understanding a metaphor, judging a metaphor's appropriateness in context). We need to take these complexities into account when interpreting the findings of metaphor research.

Traditionally, it was assumed that it is more effortful to understand metaphorical statements than literal ones. According to the standard pragmatic model (e.g., Grice, 1975), three stages are involved in processing metaphorical and other figurative statements:

KEY TERM

Asperger syndrome
An autistic spectrum disorder involving problems with social communication in spite of at least average intelligence and no delays in language development.

1. the literal meaning is accessed;
2. the reader or listener decides whether the literal meaning makes sense in the current context;
3. if the literal meaning is inadequate, there is a search for a suitable non-literal meaning.

The standard pragmatic model has proved inadequate. It predicts that figurative or metaphorical meanings should be accessed more slowly than literal ones. The findings are somewhat inconsistent, but it has often been found that metaphors are understood as rapidly or even faster than literal statements (Gibbs, 2013).

Suppose we gave participants the task of deciding whether various sentences are literally true or false. According to the standard pragmatic model, participants should not access the figurative meanings of metaphors on this task and so should respond rapidly. However, when Glucksberg (2003) used this task, participants took *longer* to respond with metaphorical statements than literally false ones. The participants responded slowly to metaphors because they experienced conflict between their "true" non-literal meaning and their false literal meaning.

Glucksberg's (2003) findings suggest metaphorical meanings are accessed fairly automatically. In a similar study, Kazmerski et al. (2003) found that high-IQ individuals accessed metaphorical meaning automatically whereas low-IQ ones did not.

Several theorists (e.g., Barsalou, 2012; Gibbs, 2013) have argued that sensory experience is relevant to the processing of metaphors and other forms of language. Lacey et al. (2012) tested this viewpoint by presenting participants with metaphorical (e.g., "Sam had a rough day") and literal (e.g., "Sam had a bad day") sentences. All the metaphorical sentences referred to texture. There were non-significant differences in activation in language and visual areas between these two types of sentences. Of most importance, however, somatosensory brain areas associated with texture processing were activated only with the metaphorical sentences. These findings suggest comprehension of metaphors is perceptually grounded.

Predication model

Kintsch (2000) put forward a predication model of metaphor understanding consisting of two components:

1. The *latent semantic analysis component*: This represents the meanings of words based on their relations with other words.
2. The *construction–integration component*: This uses the information from the first component to construct interpretations of statements. Consider a statement such as "Lawyers are sharks." It consists of an argument (lawyers) and a predicate or assertion (sharks). This component of the model *selects* predicate features relevant to the argument and *inhibits* irrelevant predicate features. In this case, features of sharks such as *vicious* and *aggressive* are relevant, whereas having fins and swimming are not.

Wolff and Gentner (2011) agreed with Kintsch that metaphors involve a *directional* process with information from the argument (e.g., *lawyers*) being projected on to the predicate (e.g., *sharks*). However, this directional process is preceded by a *non-directional* process that involves finding commonalities in meaning between the argument and predicate.

Findings

The non-reversibility of metaphors is an important phenomenon (Chiappe & Chiappe, 2007). For example, "My surgeon is a butcher" has a very different meaning from "My butcher is a surgeon." This non-reversibility is explained by Kintsch's predication model. According to the model, only those features of the predicate (second noun) relevant to the argument (first noun) are selected. Thus, changing the argument changes the features selected.

Kintsch's model explains an interesting finding reported by McGlone and Manfredi (2001). Suppose we try to understand a metaphor such as "My lawyer was a shark." According to the model, it should be harder to understand when literal properties of sharks (e.g., *can swim*) irrelevant to its metaphorical meaning have recently been activated. As predicted, the above metaphor took longer to understand when preceded by a contextual sentence emphasising the literal meaning of *shark* (e.g., "Sharks can swim").

According to Kintsch's predication model, our understanding of metaphors depends on our ability to *inhibit* semantic properties of the predicate irrelevant to the argument. Individuals high in working memory capacity (ability to process and store information at the same time; see Glossary) are better than low-capacity individuals at inhibiting irrelevant information (see Chapter 6). Chiappe and Chiappe (2007) found, as predicted, that high-capacity individuals interpreted metaphors 23% faster than low-capacity ones.

Inhibitory processes are also important when people are presented with metaphors (e.g., *an insult is a razor*) and decide whether they are literally false. What needs to be inhibited is the fact that they are true metaphorically. Individuals with high working memory capacity performed better than low-capacity individuals on this task, thus showing more effective inhibitory processes (Pierce et al., 2010).

Finally, we turn to Wolff and Gentner's (2011) notion that the first stage of metaphor comprehension consists of a non-directional process that involves finding overlapping meaning between the argument and predicate. This non-directional process is the same whether participants see forward metaphors (e.g., *Some giraffes are skyscrapers*) or reversed metaphors (e.g., *Some skyscrapers are giraffes*). This leads to the prediction that comprehensibility ratings should be the same for forward and reversed metaphors if participants must respond rapidly. In contrast, forward metaphors should be rated as much more comprehensible than reversed ones if participants have sufficient time to process the metaphors thoroughly using the directional process.

What did Wolff and Gentner (2011) find? As predicted, there was no difference in comprehensibility between forward and reversed metaphors when participants responded after 500 ms (see Figure 10.8). However, forward metaphors were much more comprehensible than reversed ones after 1,600 ms.

Evaluation

Figurative language processing typically requires the use of more cognitive resources than literal language processing. There is support for the assumption

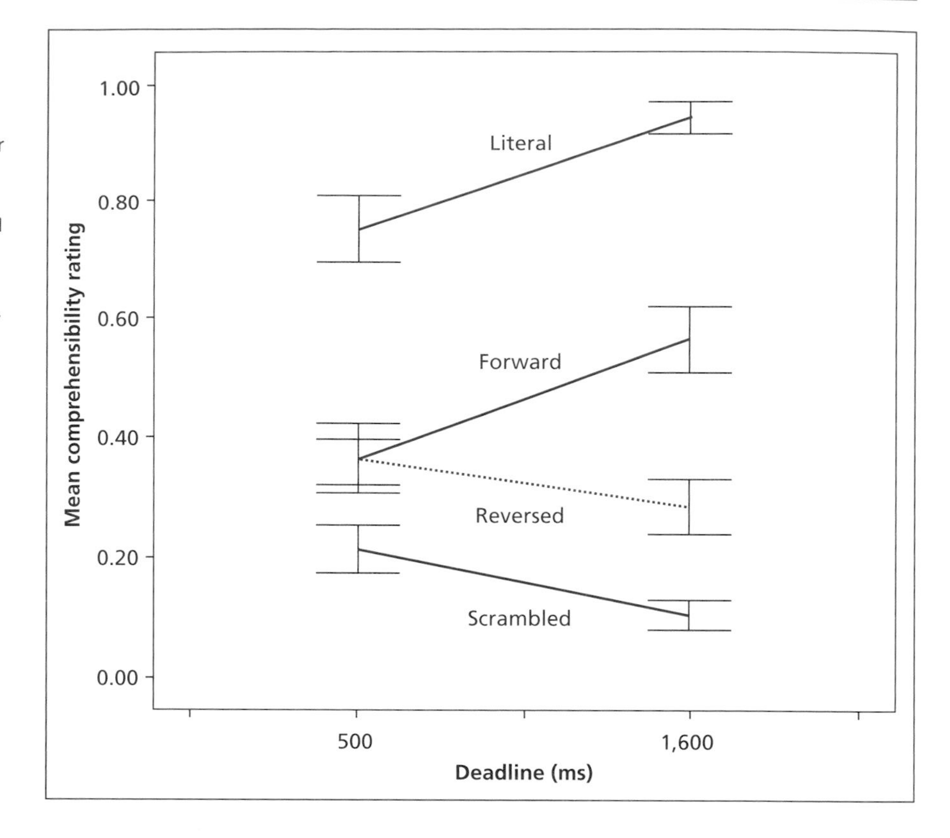

Figure 10.8
Mean proportion of statements rated comprehensible with a response deadline of 500 or 1600 ms. There were four statement types: literal, forward metaphors, reversed metaphors and scrambled metaphors.
From Wolff and Gentner (2011).

that metaphor comprehension involves a non-directional process followed by a directional one. There is also support for the assumption that individuals with high working memory capacity process metaphors faster than low-capacity individuals in part because they have more effective inhibitory processes. The notion that perceptual processing is involved in the processing of most metaphors (e.g., Lacey et al., 2012) is of potential theoretical importance.

Insufficient attention has been paid to possible processing differences between various types of metaphors. For example, we can distinguish between "A is B" metaphors and what are sometimes called correlation metaphors (Gibbs, 2013). "Lawyers are sharks" is an example of an "A is B" metaphor and "My research is off to a great start" is an example of a correlation metaphor. Kintsch's (2000) predication model is more applicable to the former type of metaphor than the latter.

Common ground

Grice (1975) argued that speakers and listeners generally conform to the cooperativeness principle – they work together to ensure mutual understanding. In that connection, it is important for speakers and listeners to have **common ground** (shared knowledge and beliefs between speaker and listener). Listeners expect that speakers will mostly refer to information and knowledge in the common ground and often experience comprehension difficulties if that is not the case.

Our discussion of common ground here should be considered in conjunction with our coverage of the extent to which *speakers* typically use the common ground in Chapter 11. It is important to note that use of common ground is not

KEY TERM

Common ground
Shared knowledge and beliefs possessed by a speaker and a listener; its use facilitates communication.

static. A major goal of conversation is to exchange information so that the common ground between those involved is increased and extended (Brown-Schmidt & Heller, 2014).

Theoretical approaches

Keysar et al. (2000) argued that it can be very effortful for listeners to work out the common ground existing between them and the speaker. Accordingly, they generally use a rapid and non-effortful egocentric heuristic. The **egocentric heuristic** is "a tendency to consider as potential referents objects that are not in the common ground, but are potential referents from one's own perspective" (Keysar et al., 2000, p. 32).

Use of the egocentric heuristic will often cause listeners to misunderstand what the speaker is trying to communicate. Accordingly, Keysar et al. (2000) argued that listeners sometimes follow use of the egocentric heuristic with the effortful and demanding process of trying to adopt the speaker's perspective.

Several theorists (e.g., Bezuidenhout, 2013, 2014; Brown-Schmidt & Heller, 2014) have argued that listeners rarely use the egocentric heuristic. According to them, listeners typically take account of the speaker's perspective very early in processing.

KEY TERM

Egocentric heuristic
A strategy used by listeners in which they interpret what they hear based on their own knowledge rather than knowledge shared with the speaker.

Findings

Keysar et al. (2000) obtained evidence consistent with use of the egocentric heuristic. A sample experimental set-up is shown in Figure 10.9. The listener (addressee) could see *three* candles of different sizes but the speaker (director) could see only *two*. The task was to move the small candle. If listeners used

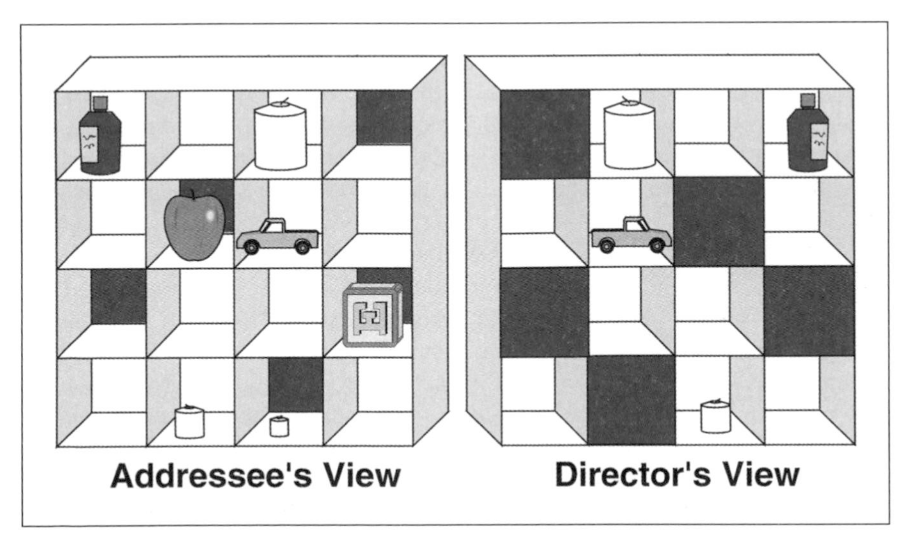

Figure 10.9
An example showing differences in what can be seen by the director (speaker) and the addressee (listener) because some of the slots are closed up. As is discussed in the text, the speaker's instruction to move "the small candle" identifies a different candle from each person's perspective.
From Keysar et al. (2000). Reprinted by permission of SAGE Publications.

common ground information, they would move the smaller of the two candles the speaker could see. However, if they used the egocentric heuristic, they would initially consider the candle the speaker could not see. Listeners' initial eye movements were often directed to the candle only they could see.

Keysar et al.'s (2000) study was biased because the object only the listener could see was a better fit to the speaker's instructions than the intended target. When Heller et al. (2008) eliminated that bias, participants rapidly fixated the target object regardless of the presence of an object only the listener could see. Thus, participants had no trouble using the common ground early in processing.

People living in Western cultures are allegedly more individualistic and self-focused than those living in Eastern cultures. As a result, there may be cultural differences in use of the egocentric heuristic. Luk et al. (2012) addressed this issue using Keysar et al.'s (2000) paradigm. Chinese–English bilinguals were initially exposed to icons of the Chinese culture (e.g., Chinese dragon, Confucius) or American culture (e.g., American flag, Superman).

What did Luk et al. (2012) find? Of those primed with the American culture, 45% showed egocentric bias at least once when responding to a speaker's instructions. In contrast, only 5% of those primed with the Chinese culture made any egocentric errors. Subsequent research (S. Wu et al., 2013) found Chinese individuals showed comparable egocentric bias to Americans early in processing. However, Chinese individuals showed more rapid correction of their initially egocentric processing than did Americans later in processing.

Why do listeners use the egocentric heuristic? It is often too attentionally demanding to use the common ground to understand the speaker's intentions. Consider a study by Lin et al. (2010) using Keysar et al.'s (2000) paradigm with listeners moving a target object on each trial. On some trials, only the listeners could see a non-target object resembling the target object. The tendency to fixate this competitor object (which was not part of the common ground) was greater when participants performed an attentionally demanding task at the same time (see Figure 10.10).

We have seen there is some support for the notion (Keysar et al., 2000) that it is cognitively demanding for listeners to take the common ground into account. However, listeners can sometimes use the common ground relatively rapidly and effortlessly (Horton & Slaten, 2012). Participants were presented with pairs of pictures (e.g., *a cat drinking milk*, *a cat sitting up*). On different trials, one speaker always described *the cat drinking milk* whereas a second one always described *the cat sitting up*. This caused participants to form strong associations between speaker and picture – when a speaker said, "the cat that's ___", they rapidly fixated the appropriate picture.

What do these findings mean? They indicate that common ground can occur through *memory*

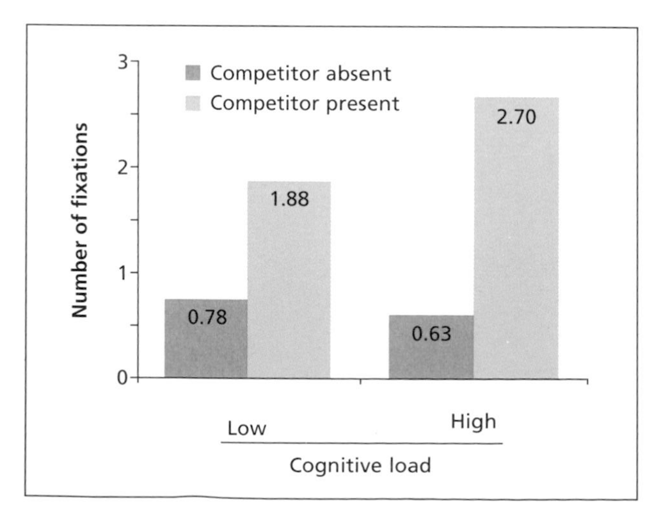

Figure 10.10
Mean number of fixations on the competitor object (not part of the common ground) as a function of cognitive load (low or high) and presence of a competitor.
From Lin et al. (2010). With permission from Elsevier.

associations between speakers and pictures. Such memory associations offer a much less effortful mechanism for common ground than the deliberate construction of common ground emphasised by Keysar et al. (2000).

Brown-Schmidt (2012) pointed out that most research is limited in that the focus is on whether specific pieces of information are (or are not) in common ground. This ignores the potential richness of common ground representation, which can include cultural and community information shared by speaker and listener. Brown-Schmidt used a task in which two individuals worked together to move various game pieces. The participants' interactive discussions led to the formation and maintenance of rich common ground representations.

Nearly all research in this area has involved speakers and listeners who are strangers. It is often assumed that people communicate better with close friends than with strangers because friends share much more common ground. It follows that the egocentric heuristic would be used less often by listeners who were friends with the speaker than those who were not. In fact, Savitsky et al. (2011) obtained precisely the *opposite* finding because friends overestimated how well they communicated with friends.

Evaluation

Several factors that jointly determine whether listeners will establish common ground with speakers have been identified. First, it can be effortful and attentionally demanding to do so, and so listeners sometimes rely on the egocentric heuristic. Second, there are cultural factors with less use of the common ground in individualistic than in collectivistic cultures. Third, common ground can sometimes be achieved rapidly and fairly effortlessly via forming simple associations in long-term memory.

What are the limitations of research in this area? First, most research has failed to address the potential richness of common ground and has instead focused on very specific aspects of it. Second, the findings from the overwhelming majority of studies based on listener–speaker pairs who are strangers may not generalise to listeners who are friends with speakers (Savitsky et al., 2011).

Third, the situations used in many studies are very artificial. For example, it is unusual in everyday life for objects present immediately in front of a speaker and a listener to differ in their perceptual accessibility as happened in the studies by Keysar et al. (2000) and Heller et al. (2008). In addition, as Bezuidenhout (2014, p. 285) pointed out, real life involves "multiple turns in an evolving conversation, as opposed to just reactions to a single utterance or to repeated utterances of the same sort".

INDIVIDUAL DIFFERENCES: WORKING MEMORY CAPACITY

There are considerable individual differences in almost all complex cognitive activities. Accordingly, theories based on the assumption that everyone comprehends text similarly are unlikely to be correct. Just and Carpenter (1992) argued that there are individual differences in working memory capacity (the ability to process and store information at the same time) and that these individual differences influence language comprehension.

Engle and Kane (2004) put forward an influential theory of working memory capacity (see Chapter 6). According to their theory, individuals with high working memory capacity have superior executive attention or attentional control than low-capacity individuals. This manifests itself in superior monitoring of task goals and ability to resolve response competition.

Findings

How well do individual differences in working memory capacity predict comprehension performance? Daneman and Merikle (1996) considered *global* measures of comprehension ability (e.g., vocabulary) and *specific* measures (e.g., making inferences, detecting ambiguity) in a meta-analysis. Working memory capacity correlated approximately +0.35 with global measures and +0.50 with specific measures. Thus, comprehension is moderately strongly associated with individual differences in working memory capacity.

There is an issue concerning interpretation of the above findings because working memory capacity correlates highly with IQ (intelligence). However, Christopher et al. (2012) found working memory capacity continued to predict comprehension performance even when the impact of intelligence was controlled for.

Later in the chapter we discuss the controversy concerning the extent to which readers draw elaborative inferences that add details not contained in the text. Barreyro et al. (2012) considered the role of working memory capacity. Their key finding was that high-capacity individuals were more likely than low-capacity ones to draw elaborative causal inferences on a reading task.

Thorough text comprehension often involves forming a situation model of the state of affairs described by the text (discussed at length later in the chapter). Readers high in working memory capacity formed a more complete situation model of a text than low-capacity individuals (Dutke & von Hecker, 2011).

Theoretical explanations

Why do high-capacity individuals perform better than low-capacity ones on many tasks relating to language comprehension? Earlier we discussed the hypothesis that high-capacity individuals are better at maintaining task goals than low-capacity ones (Engle & Kane, 2004). It follows that high-capacity individuals should have less mind wandering (task-unrelated thoughts) while engaged in reading comprehension.

McVay and Kane (2012a) tested the above prediction. High-capacity individuals had superior reading comprehension and less mind wandering than low-capacity ones. Of most importance, the beneficial effects of high working memory capacity on comprehension performance were due in part to low levels of mind wandering. Unsworth and McMillan (2013) confirmed that high working memory capacity produces superior reading comprehension partly because of reduced mind wandering. In addition, mind wandering was influenced by readers' motivation to perform the reading task and topic interest.

An alternative explanation for the comprehension superiority of individuals high in working memory capacity is that they are better than low-capacity individuals at *discriminating* between relevant and irrelevant information.

Kaakinen et al. (2003) had participants read a text on rare diseases containing a mixture of relevant and irrelevant information. Only high-capacity individuals allocated extra time to reading the relevant information during the initial reading of the text.

Sanchez and Wiley (2006) studied the seductive details effect (e.g., the tendency for reduced comprehension of text if accompanied by irrelevant illustrations). Low-capacity individuals showed a greater seductive details effect. This occurred in part because they looked at the irrelevant illustrations for longer periods of time as shown by their pattern of eye movements.

KEY TERM

Discourse
Language that is a minimum of several sentences in length; it includes written text and connected speech.

Evaluation

There is strong empirical support for Just and Carpenter's (1992) assumption that individual differences in working memory capacity have a substantial impact on language comprehension. High-capacity individuals differ from low-capacity ones in several ways, including greater vocabulary, superior ability to detect ambiguities, generation of more elaborative inferences and formation of more effective situation models. Progress has been made in understanding *why* high-capacity individuals outperform low-capacity ones: (1) they have greater attentional control and so engage in less mind wandering; and (2) they are better at discriminating between more and less relevant information and inhibiting the processing of irrelevant information.

What are the limitations of research in this area? First, individual differences in working memory capacity correlate fairly strongly with several other variables (e.g., intelligence, vocabulary). This often makes it hard to decide whether individual differences in language comprehension are actually due to working memory capacity rather than these other variables.

Second, the cognitive processing of high- and low-capacity individuals differs in several ways (see Chapter 6). Thus, it is entirely possible that the comprehension superiority of high-capacity individuals depends in part on processes additional to those studied so far.

DISCOURSE PROCESSING: INFERENCES

So far we have focused primarily on the processes involved in understanding individual sentences. In real life, however, we mostly encounter connected **discourse** (speech or written speech at least several sentences long). What are the main differences between single sentences and those within discourse? First, single sentences are much more likely to be ambiguous. Second, discourse processing typically involves drawing *inferences* to make sense of what we are listening to or reading.

We draw inferences most of the time when reading or listening to someone, even though we are generally unaware of doing so. Indeed, if a writer or speaker spelled everything out in incredible detail, you would probably be bored to tears! Here is an example of inference drawing (Rumelhart & Ortony, 1977):

1 Mary heard the ice-cream van coming.
2 She remembered the pocket money.
3 She rushed into the house.

KEY TERMS

Bridging inferences
Inferences or conclusions drawn to increase coherence between the current and preceding parts of a text; also known as backward inferences.

Elaborative inferences
Inferences based on our knowledge of the world that involve adding details to a text that is being read.

Mental model
An internal representation of some possible situation or event in the world.

You probably made various inferences while reading the above story. For example, Mary wanted to buy some ice-cream; buying ice-cream costs money; Mary had some pocket money in the house; and Mary had only a limited amount of time to get hold of some money before the ice-cream van appeared. None of these inferences is explicitly stated.

There are three main types of inferences: logical inferences, bridging inferences and elaborative inferences. Logical inferences depend only on the meanings of words. For example, we infer that anyone who is a widow is female. **Bridging inferences** establish coherence between the current part of the text and the preceding text, and so are also known as backward inferences.

Elaborative inferences embellish or add details to the text by using world knowledge to expand on the information it contains. Forward (or predictive) inferences are an important type of elaborative inference that involves anticipating the future. It is a major theoretical problem to decide how we typically access *relevant* information from our huge store of world knowledge when forming elaborative inferences (Harley, 2013).

The differences between bridging and elaborative inferences are not always clear-cut. Consider the following scenario adapted from Kuperberg et al. (2011):

1 Jill had very fair skin.
2 She forgot to put sunscreen on.
3 She had sunburn on Monday.

When readers read the second sentence, they could draw the elaborative inference that Jill had sunburn. When they read the third sentence, they could draw the bridging or backward inference that the sunburn has resulted from forgetting to put on sunscreen.

Theoretical perspectives

Readers typically draw logical and bridging inferences because they are generally essential for understanding. However, there has been theoretical controversy concerning the number and nature of the elaborative inferences typically drawn. Two extreme positions on this issue are the constructionist approach proposed by Bransford (e.g., Bransford et al., 1972) and the minimalist hypothesis (McKoon & Ratcliff, 1992).

Bransford et al. (1972) argued that readers typically construct a relatively complete "**mental model**" of the situation and the events described in the text. A key implication of the constructionist approach is that numerous elaborative inferences are drawn during reading even when such inferences are not required to understand the text.

McKoon and Ratcliff (1992, p. 440) challenged the constructionist position with their minimalist hypothesis:

> In the absence of specific, goal-directed strategic processes, inferences of only two kinds are constructed: those that establish locally coherent representations of the parts of a text that are processed concurrently and those that rely on information that is quickly and easily available.

Here are McKoon and Ratcliff's (1992) main assumptions:

- Inferences are either automatic or strategic (goal directed).
- Some automatic inferences establish local coherence (two or three sentences making sense on their own or in combination with easily available general knowledge). These inferences involve parts of the text in working memory at the same time.
- Other automatic inferences rely on information readily available because it is explicitly stated in the text.
- Strategic inferences are formed in pursuit of the reader's goals; they sometimes serve to produce local coherence.
- Most elaborative inferences are made at recall rather than during reading.

KEY TERM

Anaphor
A word (especially pronoun) whose referent is a previously mentioned noun or noun phrase.

The greatest difference between the minimalist hypothesis and the constructionist position concerns the number of automatic inferences formed. According to the minimalist hypothesis, far fewer automatic inferences are drawn in reading than is assumed by constructionists.

The minimalist hypothesis was subsequently developed into a memory-based theoretical framework that was more specific about the underlying mechanisms. According to this framework, incoming text "serves as a signal to all of long-term memory, including both the inactive portion of the discourse representation [for the text currently being read] as well as general world knowledge. The signal proceeds autonomously [independently] and is unrestricted . . . activation builds and . . . the most active elements" become part of the reader's understanding of the text (Gerrig & O'Brien, 2005, p. 229).

Graesser et al. (1994) argued in their search-after-meaning theory that there is much *flexibility* in the number of inferences drawn by readers. The extent to which the reader's goals include a search after meaning is of special importance in determining how many inferences readers will draw. For example, someone proofreading a text focuses relatively little on meaning and thus draws few inferences.

Case study:
Search-after-meaning

Findings: anaphor resolution

Perhaps the simplest form of bridging inference is **anaphor** resolution, in which a pronoun or noun has to be identified with a previous noun or noun phrase. Here is an example:

> Fred sold John his lawn mower, and then he sold him his garden hose.

It requires a bridging inference to realise the referent for "he" is Fred rather than John.

How do people make the appropriate anaphoric inference? Gender information can be very helpful. For example, contrast ease of anaphor resolution with the following sentence compared to the one above:

> Juliet sold John her lawn mower, and then she sold him her garden hose.

Research activity:
Text comprehension

Supportive evidence was reported by Arnold et al. (2000). Participants looked at pictures while listening to text. Gender information ("he" or "she") was used faster to look at the appropriate picture when it contained a male and a female character than when it contained two same-sex characters.

Anaphor resolution is also facilitated by having pronouns in the expected order. Harley (2013) provided the following example:

1 Vlad sold Dirk his broomstick because he hated it.
2 Vlad sold Dirk his broomstick because he needed it.

The first sentence is easy to understand because "he" refers to the first-named man (i.e., Vlad). The second sentence is harder to understand because "he" refers to the second-named man (i.e., Dirk).

Another factor influencing anaphor resolution is working memory capacity (discussed in the previous section). Nieuwland and van Berkum (2006b) presented sentences containing pronouns whose referents were ambiguous. Readers high in working memory capacity were more likely than low-capacity ones to take account of the two possible referents for the pronouns, indicating they were more sensitive to language subtleties.

Pronouns presented within a text often only have a single possible referent and thus are unambiguous. It has frequently been assumed that readers *automatically* identify the correct referent with unambiguous pronouns. This was the case when readers had a high level of engagement with the text but not when their engagement was less (Love & McKoon, 2011). Thus, automatic anaphor resolution occurs only when the meaning of a text is processed fairly thoroughly by readers.

Most of the above findings are consistent with the theoretical approach developed by Kaiser (e.g., Kaiser et al., 2009). In essence, it is assumed anaphor resolution depends on the interaction of multiple constraints such as gender and meaning. These constraints operate together and in parallel.

Findings: more complex inferences

Causal inferences are a very common form of bridging inference. They require readers to work out the causal relationship between the sentence they are currently reading and one or more previous sentences. Garrod and Terras (2000) studied the processes involved in drawing such inferences. Consider the following two sentences:

1 Ken drove to London yesterday.
2 The car kept overheating.

You had no trouble (hopefully!) in linking these sentences based on the assumption that Keith drove to London in a car that kept overheating.

Garrod and Terras (2000) identified two possible ways bridging inferences could be made. First, reading the verb "drove" in the first sentence may activate concepts related to driving (especially "car"). Second, readers may form a representation of the entire situation described in the first sentence and then relate information in the second sentence to that representation. The crucial difference is that the sentential context is irrelevant in the first explanation but is very relevant in the second.

Garrod and Terras (2000) reported evidence for both possibilities. They found there are *two* stages in forming bridging inferences. The first stage is *bonding*, a low-level process involving the automatic activation of words from the preceding sentence. The second stage is *resolution*, which involves ensuring the overall interpretation is consistent with the contextual information. Resolution is influenced by context but bonding is not.

According to the minimalist hypothesis and the search-after-meaning theory, the precise inferences drawn depend on the reader's goals. There is much support for that prediction. Calvo et al. (2006) instructed some participants to read sentences for comprehension, whereas others were explicitly told to anticipate what might happen next. Participants in the latter condition drew more predictive inferences. Even when participants reading for comprehension drew elaborative inferences, they did so more slowly than those in the anticipation condition.

The extent to which inferences are drawn also depends on individual differences. As we saw earlier, individuals high in working memory capacity are more likely than low-capacity individuals to draw causal inferences. Murray and Burke (2003) considered inference drawing in participants with high, moderate or low reading skill. They were tested on predictive inferences (e.g., inferring "break" when presented with a sentence such as "The angry husband threw the fragile vase against the wall"). All three groups showed some evidence of drawing these predictive inferences. However, these inferences were only drawn automatically by participants with high reading skill.

Findings: underlying processes

The minimalist hypothesis is consistent with the assumption that predictive inferences are drawn automatically rather than through controlled processing. This issue was addressed by Gras et al. (2012) using short texts such as the following:

> Charlotte was having her breakfast on the terrace when the bees started flying about the pot of jam. She made a movement to brush them away but one of them succeeded in landing on her arm.

The predictive inference is that Charlotte felt a sting.

Gras et al. (2012) followed the text with the word *sting* presented in blue, red or green 350, 750 or 1,000 milliseconds after the text with instructions to name the colour. The speed of colour naming was slowed only at 1,000 ms (see Figure 10.11). This finding suggests it took approximately one second for the predictive inference to be drawn. The fact that participants could not prevent it from interfering with colour naming suggests the inference was drawn automatically.

Kuperberg et al. (2011) also investigated the automaticity of inference drawing using short scenarios such as one discussed earlier:

1 Jill had very fair skin.
2 She forgot to put sunscreen on.
3 She had sunburn on Monday.

Kuperberg et al. recorded event-related potentials (ERPs; see Glossary) to assess readers' processing of these scenarios. Of particular interest was the N400 component, which is larger when the meaning of the word currently being processed does not match its context.

What did Kuperberg et al. (2011) find? Consider the above scenario in which the word "sunburn" in the third sentence is highly causally related to its context. There was only a small N400 to this word. Thus, processing of the causal inference

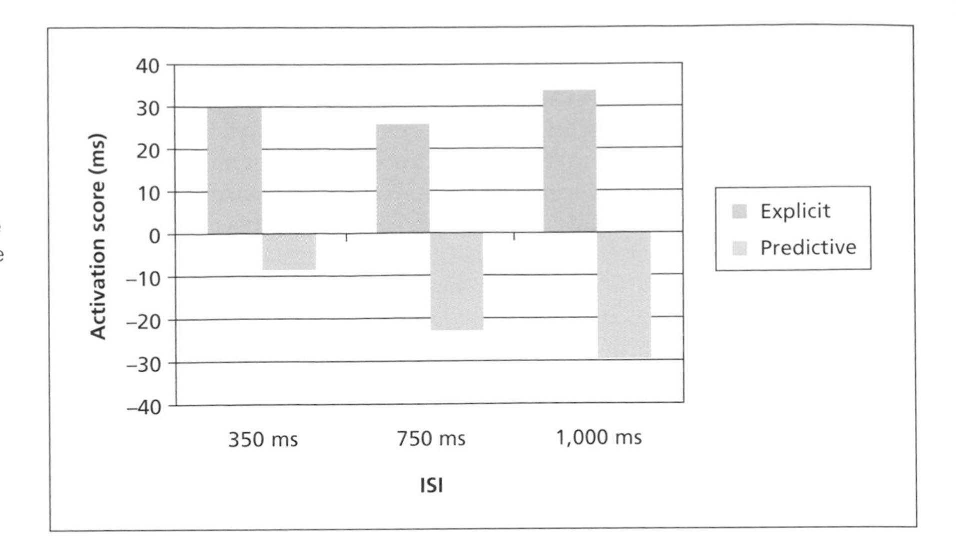

Figure 10.11
Reaction times to name colours when the word presented in colour was predictable from the preceding text compared to a control condition (scores below 0 ms indicate a slowing effect of predictive inferences). Performance in the explicit condition is not relevant here.
From Gras et al. (2012). © American Psychological Association.

explaining Jill's sunburn in terms of her fair skin and failure to use suncream started very rapidly. Such findings suggest some processes involved in inference drawing occur fairly automatically.

Kuperberg et al. (2011) wondered what would happen if readers drew complex causal inferences. They explored this issue by using short scenarios such as the following:

1 Jill had very fair skin.
2 She usually remembered to wear sunscreen.
3 She had sunburn on Monday.

Kuperberg et al. found there was a small N400 to the word "sunburn", but it was not as small as in the previous case. Thus, some inference processing is initiated very rapidly even with complex causal inferences.

There is convincing evidence that readers produce predictive inferences when strongly supported by the preceding context (Lassonde & O'Brien, 2009). What happens when the preceding context is weaker and less specific? Perhaps readers do not form predictive inferences in such circumstances. Another possibility is that they form a flexible, general inference consistent with more than one specific inference. Lassonde and O'Brien obtained support for the latter possibility. They also found readers formed specific inferences when the preceding context strongly supported a given inference.

As we saw earlier, listeners' stereotypical inferences about the speaker can influence sentence processing. For example, there was a large N400 when the sentence, "I have a large tattoo on my back", was spoken in an upper-class accent (van den Brink et al., 2012). Thus, listeners rapidly draw inferences about the kinds of statement a given speaker is likely (or unlikely) to make.

Overall evaluation

There is a growing consensus on several issues. First, readers (and listeners) typically form bridging inferences (including causal inferences) to make coherent sense of what they are reading or listening to. Second, people rapidly use contextual information and their knowledge of the world to form inferences. Third, many inferences (including causal and predictive ones) are often drawn automatically, but this depends on various factors (e.g., working memory capacity, engagement with the text). Fourth, readers' goals are important in determining whether predictive inferences are drawn. Fifth, readers with superior reading skills (including those having high working memory capacity) draw more inferences than other readers.

As Graesser et al. (1997, p. 183) pointed out, the major theories work well in certain circumstances:

> The minimalist hypothesis is probably correct when the reader is very quickly reading the text, when the text lacks global coherence, and when the reader has very little background knowledge. The constructionist theory is on the mark when the reader is attempting to comprehend the text for enjoyment or mastery at a more leisurely pace.

Thus, the number and nature of the inferences drawn by readers are very *flexible*.

What are the limitations of theory and research in this area? First, it is often hard to predict accurately *which* inferences will be drawn. This is due partly to the fact that inference drawing depends on several factors that interact in complex ways. In addition, there is theoretical imprecision. For example, according to the minimalist hypothesis, automatic inferences are drawn if the necessary information is "readily available". How do we establish the precise degree of availability of some piece of information?

Second, the measures typically used to assess inference drawing are limited. For example, N400 indicates whether readers have detected a mismatch between the current word and the context. This is clearly only *one* aspect of inference drawing.

Research activity:
Inferences

Third, the range of inferences drawn may be greater than generally assumed. As we have seen, listeners sometimes infer that what the speaker is saying is improbable given his/her assumed characteristics. In similar fashion, you might be surprised if the authors of this book included colloquial passages written in cockney slang.

DISCOURSE COMPREHENSION: THEORETICAL APPROACHES

If someone asks us to describe a story or book we have read recently, we discuss the main events and themes and leave out the minor details. Thus, our description is highly *selective* based on the meaning extracted from the story while reading it and on selective processes operating at retrieval. Imagine our questioner's reaction if our description wasn't selective but simply involved recalling random sentences from the story!

Gomulicki (1956) showed how selectively stories are comprehended and remembered. One group of participants wrote a précis (a summary) of a story visible in front of them and a second group recalled the story from memory. A third group was given each précis and recall and found it very hard to tell them apart. Thus, story memory resembles a précis in that we focus on important information.

What determines whether any given information in a story is regarded as important? Trabasso and Sperry (1985) addressed this issue. Statements causally connected to several other statements were judged to be much more important than those lacking causal connections. Later we will discuss various theories that have considered the centrality of different kinds of information within stories.

Unsurprisingly, nearly all research on reading comprehension has presented readers with paper-based texts. In the real world, however, readers increasingly make use of e-readers (e.g., Kindle) or computers (e.g., when accessing information from the internet). Margolin et al. (2013) presented readers with narrative texts (telling a story) and expository texts (conveying facts and information) using all three methods for presenting text.

What did Margolin et al. (2013) find? Comprehension was comparable regardless of the presentation method (paper, e-reader, computer). In addition, the presentation method had only modest effects on reading activities (e.g., rereading, note-taking). Thus, the findings obtained with paper-based texts are likely to generalise to other methods of presenting texts.

In what follows, we discuss several theories or models of language comprehension. We start with Bartlett's (1932) very influential schema-based approach. Numerous theories of comprehension have been put forward over the past 20–30 years (McNamara and Magliano (2009) discuss the most prominent ones). We will be discussing key features of some of them.

Schema theory: Bartlett

Our processing of stories or other texts involves relating the information in the text to relevant structured knowledge stored in long-term memory. What we process in stories, how we process story information and what we remember from stories we have read all depend on such stored information.

Much of our stored knowledge is in the form of schemas. Schemas are well-integrated packets of knowledge about the world, events, people and actions (see Chapter 7). Schemas include what are often referred to as *scripts* and *frames*. Scripts deal with knowledge about events and consequences of events. Frames are knowledge structures referring to some aspect of the world (e.g., building).

Ghosh and Gilboa (2014) argued that schemas possess four necessary and sufficient features:

1 *Associative structure*: Schemas consist of interconnected units.
2 *Basis in multiple episodes*: Schemas consist of integrated information based on several similar events.
3 *Lack of unit detail*: This follows from the variability of events from which any given schema is formed.
4 *Adaptability*: Schemas change and adapt over time as they are updated in the light of new information.

As Ghosh and Gilboa pointed out, several different definitions of "schema" have been used by theorists. Of interest, Bartlett (1932) attached great importance to adaptability, but it is probably the feature of the four above that is least often found in recent definitions.

Why are schemas important? First, they contain much of the information needed to understand what we hear and read. Second, schemas allow us to form *expectations* (e.g., of the typical sequence of events in a restaurant). They make the world relatively predictable because our expectations are generally confirmed.

Evidence that schemas can influence story comprehension was reported by Bransford and Johnson (1972, p. 722). Here is part of the story they used:

> The procedure is quite simple. First, you arrange items into different groups. Of course one pile may be sufficient depending on how much there is to do. If you have to go somewhere else due to lack of facilities that is the next step; otherwise, you are pretty well set. It is important not to overdo things. That is, it is better to do too few things at once than too many.

What on earth was that all about? Participants hearing the passage in the absence of a title rated it as incomprehensible and recalled an average of only 2.8 idea units. In contrast, those supplied beforehand with the title "Washing clothes" found it easy to understand and recalled 5.8 idea units on average. Relevant schema knowledge helped passage comprehension rather than simply acting as a retrieval cue – participants receiving the title *after* hearing the passage but *before* recall recalled only 2.6 idea units on average.

Bartlett (1932) argued persuasively that schemas play an important role in determining how we remember stories. According to him, memory is affected not only by the presented story but also by the reader's store of relevant prior schematic knowledge. Thus, comprehension of (and memory for) discourse depend on top-down processes triggered by schemas.

Bartlett (1932) had the ingenious idea of presenting people with stories producing a *conflict* between the story itself and their prior knowledge. Suppose people read a story from a different culture. Prior knowledge might produce *distortions* in the remembered version of the story, making it more conventional and acceptable from their own cultural background. Thus, what was remembered would be inaccurate because it would include some schematic knowledge not included in the story.

Bartlett (1932) focused on three types of error. First, and most important, there is **rationalisation**, which involves distortions designed to make recall more rational and in line with the reader's own cultural expectations. Second, there is *levelling* (omitting unfamiliar details from recall). Third, there is *sharpening* (selecting certain details for embellishment).

There are two main ways schematic knowledge may cause rationalisations. First, schematic knowledge may distort *comprehension* processes when someone is reading a story. Second, schematic knowledge may distort *retrieval* processes. Bartlett (1932) favoured the latter explanation, arguing that story recall is a *reconstructive* process in which story and schema information is combined.

Bartlett (1932) claimed the information presented in discourse shows fairly rapid forgetting but our schematic knowledge does not. As a result, the tendency for schematic knowledge to produce distortions in discourse memory should increase over time.

KEY TERM

Rationalisation
In Bartlett's theory, errors in story recall that conform to the rememberer's cultural expectations.

Case study:
Bartlett

Findings

Bartlett (1932) tested his theoretical ideas using stories from North American Indian culture. The most famous of these stories was "The War of the Ghosts". Unfortunately, his studies were poorly controlled (Roediger, 2010). For example, he failed to provide specific instructions: "I thought it best, for the purposes of

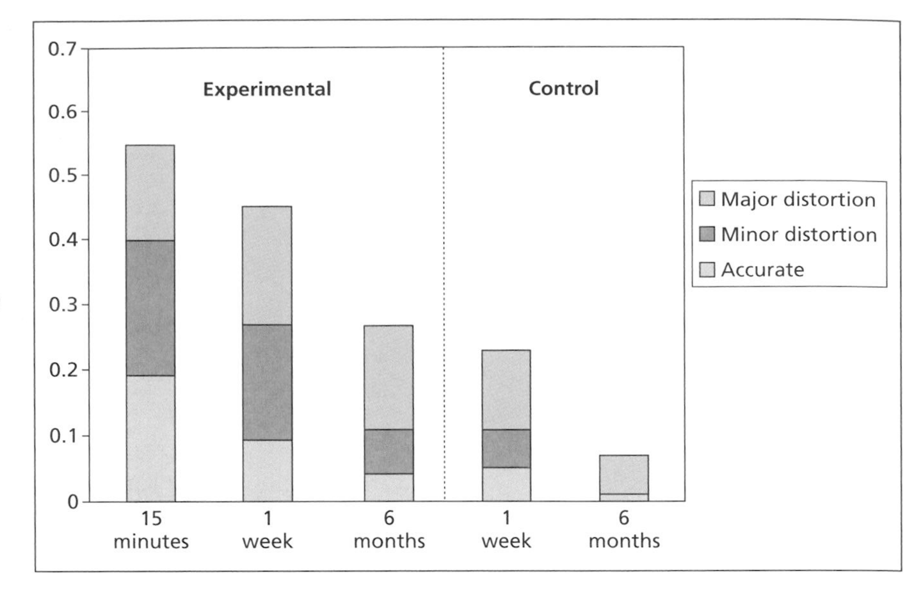

Figure 10.12
Mean proportions of propositions recalled (out of 42) that were accurate or distorted in a major or minor way on the first, second and third recall sessions (experimental conditions on left-hand side). The two control conditions showed memory performance on the second and third recalls for participants who had no initial recall.

From Bergman and Roediger (1999). With kind permission from Springer Science + Business Media.

these experiments, to try to influence the subjects' procedure as little as possible" (Bartlett, 1932, p. 78).

Such vague instructions meant that many distortions observed by Bartlett were due to conscious guessing rather than deficient memory. This was shown by Gauld and Stephenson (1967), also using "The War of the Ghosts". Instructions stressing the need for accurate recall (designed to reduce deliberate guessing) eliminated almost half the errors obtained using Bartlett's instructions.

Bartlett (1932) claimed systematic distortions *increased* over time when the same story was recalled repeatedly. There have been several failures to obtain supporting evidence (Roediger, 2010). An exception is a study by Bergman and Roediger (1999). They used "The War of the Ghosts" and tested participants' recall after 15 minutes, one week and six months. The proportion of recall involving major distortions increased progressively from 27% at the shortest retention interval to 59% at the longest (see Figure 10.12).

Sulin and Dooling (1974) also supported Bartlett's theory. They presented participants with a story about a ruthless dictator identified as Gerald Martin or Adolf Hitler. It was assumed participants told the story was about Adolf Hitler would activate their schematic knowledge of him. After a short or long retention interval, participants were given a recognition-memory test including the sentence, "He hated the Jews particularly and so persecuted them."

What did Sulin and Dooling (1974) find? Participants told the story was about Hitler tended to falsely recognise the above Hitler-relevant sentence at the long (but not the short) retention interval. Thus, the influence of schematic knowledge in producing memory distortions increased over time.

Bartlett (1932) assumed memorial distortions occur mainly because of schema-driven reconstructive processes operating at retrieval. Supportive evidence was reported by Anderson and Pichert (1978). Participants read a story from the perspective of a burglar or potential homebuyer. After story recall, participants recalled the story again from the alternative perspective. This time, participants recalled more information important only to the second perspective or schema than on the first recall. Remember, however, that schemas can also influence *compre-*

hension processes (e.g., Bransford and Johnson, 1972; discussed earlier).

Altering the perspective changed the schematic knowledge accessed by the participants (e.g., from knowledge of what burglars are interested in to knowledge of what potential house buyers are interested in). Accessing different schematic knowledge enhanced recall, and so Anderson and Pichert's (1978) findings provide support for the notion of schema-driven retrieval.

Brewer and Treyens (1981) pointed out that much research on schemas had used artificially constructed texts with participants *intentionally* learning the material. In contrast, they focused on the *incidental* acquisition of information in a more naturalistic study. Participants spent 35 seconds in a room resembling a graduate student's office prior to an experiment (see Figure 10.13). After the participants moved to another room, they were unexpectedly tested on their memory for objects in the first room.

Figure 10.13
The "graduate student's room" used by Brewer and Treyens (1981) in their experiment.
With permission from Elsevier.

Brewer and Treyens (1981) obtained much evidence for the importance of schemas. First, participants recalled more schema-consistent objects (e.g., desk, calendar, pencils) than schema-inconsistent ones (e.g., skull, toy shop).

Second, objects *not* present in the room but "recognised" with high confidence were nearly all highly schema-consistent (e.g., books, filing cabinet). Similar findings have been obtained in research on eyewitness testimony (see Chapter 8). Eyewitnesses have a bank-robbery schema (e.g., robbers are typically male and in disguise). As a result, their recall of crimes can include schema-consistent details that do not correspond to what actually happened (Tuckey & Brewer, 2003a, b).

Steyvers and Hemmer (2012) argued that previous research had exaggerated the negative effects of schemas on memory. Consider Brewer and Treyens' (1981) study. In the real world, guessing that a graduate student's office contained books and a filing cabinet is very likely to prove accurate. In contrast, Brewer and Treyens deliberately manipulated the office environment by omitting such objects.

Steyvers and Hemmer (2012) studied memory for various naturalistic scenes (e.g., kitchen). The objects in each scene varied in schema-consistency. For example, a *stove* was a highly schema-consistent object for the kitchen scene whereas a *small wooden sailing boat* was very inconsistent. In one experiment, they found (in contrast to Brewer and Treyens, 1981) that the false recall rate was much lower for high-schema-consistent objects than low-schema-consistent ones (9% vs. 18%, respectively). This happened in part because participants' guesses were more likely to be correct with high-schema-consistent objects. These findings show that schemas can be very beneficial when remembering scenes and events in the real world.

Steyvers and Hemmer (2012) carried out a second, similar experiment. There were two main findings (see Figure 10.14). First, very schema-consistent objects were better recalled than any others. Second, very schema-inconsistent objects

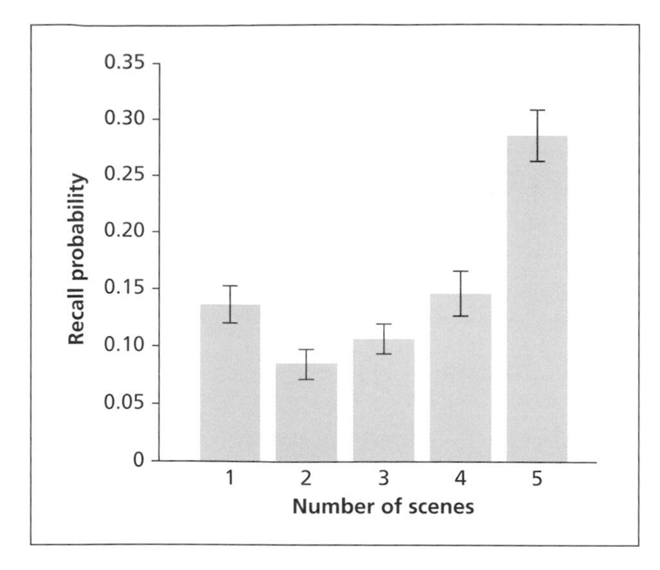

Figure 10.14
Mean recall probability for objects as a function of schema-consistency. Objects appearing in all five scenes of a given type (e.g., kitchens) were regarded as high in schema-consistency, whereas those appearing in only one were low in schema-consistency.

From Steyvers and Hemmer (2012). With permission from Elsevier.

were reasonably well recalled. These objects attracted attention because they were unexpected within the scenes in which they were present.

How can we explain high levels of recall for both schema-consistent and schema-inconsistent information? Van Kesteren et al. (2012) put forward a neuroscience theory based on two main assumptions. First, schema-inconsistent information is generally thoroughly processed within the medial temporal lobe (a brain area of central importance to long-term memory; see Chapter 7). As a result, it is well remembered.

Second, schema-consistent information is processed by the medial prefrontal cortex. This facilitates the storage of *direct* connections between the presented information and relevant information in long-term memory and thus leads to enhanced memory. Ghosh and Gilboa (2014) discussed several studies showing that schema processing was associated with activation in the ventromedial prefrontal cortex.

At the most general level, this approach emphasises the role of the prefrontal cortex in schema-related processing. Evidence that patients with damage to the prefrontal cortex have particular difficulties in processing schematic information (e.g., Cosentino et al., 2006; Farag et al., 2010; see Chapter 7) supports this approach.

Evaluation

Our organised schematic knowledge of the world assists text comprehension and recall. In addition, many errors and distortion in memory for stories or other texts are due to the influence of schematic information. Such distortions are very common in the laboratory. More generally, schema theory emphasises the role of top-down processes in discourse comprehension and memory (see Wagoner (2013) for a historical review). There is accumulating evidence that effective processing of schema-related information involves the prefrontal cortex.

What are the limitations with schema theories? First, there are disagreements about the definition of "schema" (Ghosh & Gilboa, 2014), and it is hard to ascertain the precise information stored within any given schema.

Second, schema theories are hard to test. If we want to explain text comprehension and memory in terms of schema activation, we need *independent* evidence of the existence (and appropriate activation) of those schemas. However, such evidence is generally not available. As Harley (2013) pointed out, "The primary accusation against schema and script-based approaches is that they are nothing more than re-descriptions of the data."

Third, the conditions determining *when* a given schema will be activated are unclear. According to schema theory, top-down processes should generate numerous inferences during story comprehension. However, as we saw earlier, such inferences are often not drawn.

Fourth, it is not entirely clear *how* schemas are activated. For example, the phrase "the five-hour journey from London to New York" would probably activate the "plane flight script" for most people (Harley, 2013). However, none of the words in the phrase has strong associations with flying by plane.

Fifth, schema theories exaggerate how error prone we are in our everyday lives, as we saw in the research of Steyvers and Hemmer (2012). Similar findings were reported by Wynn and Logie (1998), who tested students' recall of "real-life" events experienced during their first week at university. Recall was generally accurate up to six months later, providing little evidence of error-producing reconstructive processes.

Sixth, Bartlett (1932) argued that schemas exert their influence at retrieval rather than during comprehension. In fact, however, schemas often affect comprehension processes (e.g., Bransford & Johnson, 1972).

KEY TERM

Proposition
A statement making an assertion or denial that can be true or false.

Kintsch's construction–integration model

Walter Kintsch's views on language comprehension have been extremely influential. In his construction–integration model, Kintsch (e.g., 1998) combined elements of schema-based theories and Johnson-Laird's mental model approach (see Chapter 14).

Here are the main assumptions of the construction–integration model (see Figure 10.15):

1. Readers turn sentences in the text into **propositions** (statements that are true or false) representing its meaning.
2. The propositions constructed from the text are stored briefly along with associatively related propositions (e.g., inferences). At this stage, many irrelevant propositions are stored.
3. A spreading-activation process selects propositions for the text representation. In this integration process, clusters of highly interconnected propositions attract most activation and have the greatest probability of inclusion in the text representation. Within the text representation, it is hard to distinguish between propositions based directly on the text and those based on inferences.
4. As a result of the above processes, three levels of text representation are constructed:

   i surface representation (the text itself);
   ii propositional representation or textbase (propositions formed from the text);
   iii situation representation (a mental model describing the situation referred to in the text). This is the only representation depending mostly on the integration process.

The construction–integration model sounds rather (very?) complex. However, its major assumptions are straightforward. The processes involved in the initial construction of many propositions are relatively *inefficient* with many irrelevant propositions being included. At this stage, context provided by the overall theme of the text is ignored. After that, the integration process uses contextual information from the text to weed out irrelevant propositions.

How does the construction–integration model differ from schema theory? Schema theory emphasises the importance of top-down processes in discourse

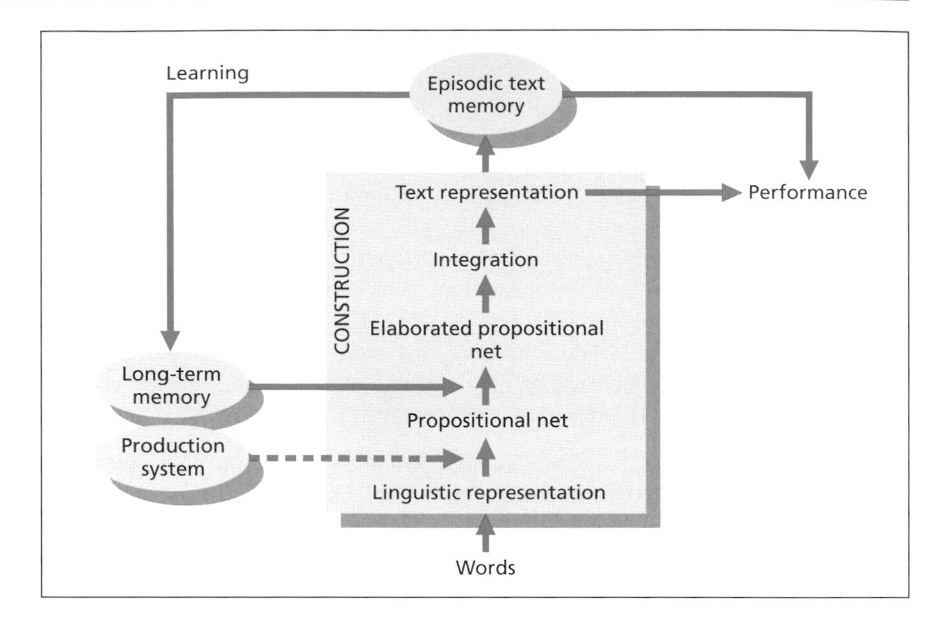

Figure 10.15
The construction–integration model.
Adapted from Kintsch (1992).

comprehension and memory. This differs substantially from the assumptions incorporated within the construction–integration model: "During the construction phase, the text input launches a dumb bottom-up process in the reader's knowledge base . . . top-down factors, such as reading perspective or reading goal, exert their influence at the integration phase" (Kaakinen & Hyönä, 2007, p. 1323).

Findings

Much research supports the model's assumptions. For example, it predicts readers and listeners will often find it hard to discriminate between text information and inferences based on that information. As we saw earlier, that prediction has often been supported (e.g., Sulin & Dooling, 1974).

Kintsch et al. (1990) tested the assumption that text processing produces three levels of representation as described above. Participants read brief descriptions of various situations and then their recognition memory was tested immediately or at times ranging up to four days later.

The forgetting functions for the surface, propositional or textbase, and situational representations were distinctively different (see Figure 10.16). There was rapid forgetting of the surface representation, whereas information from the situational representation showed no forgetting. As predicted, the most complete representation of the text's meaning (i.e., the situational representation) was best remembered. Also as predicted, the least complete representation (i.e., the surface representation) was the worst remembered.

Dixon and Bortolussi (2013) presented participants with an interesting text (*Interview with the Vampire*) and a less interesting text (*The History of Pendennis*). Participants provided ratings of their engagement with the text or ratings of their on-task attention to the task. Subsequently, the extent to which they had formed a situation model (which requires integrative processes) was assessed on a recall test.

Dixon and Bortolussi (2013) predicted that recall performance would be strongly predicted by engagement ratings, because those ratings reflect fairly

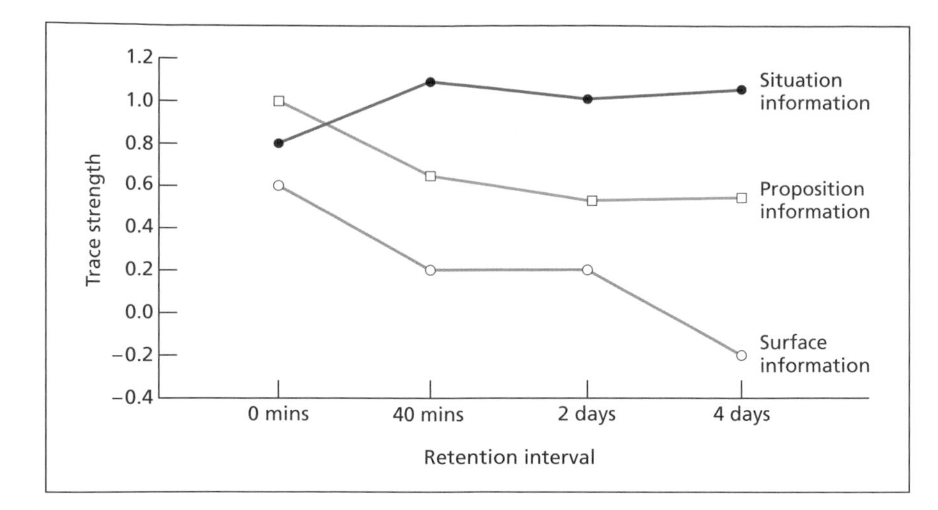

Figure 10.16
Forgetting functions for situation, proposition and surface information over a four-day period.

Adapted from Kintsch et al. (1990).

directly participants' use of integrative processes. In contrast, ratings of on-line attention reflect a mixture of constructive and integrative processes, and so those ratings should be less predictive of recall performance. The findings were exactly as predicted, and so provide evidence in support of the distinction between constructive and integrative processes.

Mulder and Sanders (2012) assessed recognition memory for causal relations within discourse. Their findings suggested causal relations were represented within the situation representation but not the propositional or surface representations. Thus, readers may not *always* form three levels of text representation even for important information such as causal relations.

It is assumed within the construction–integration model that the reader's goal in reading influences the integration stage rather than the earlier construction stage. It is implausible that this is what *always* happens. Imagine you read a text discussing four rare diseases knowing a close friend has been diagnosed with one of those diseases. Your task is to inform your common friends about that disease.

Kaakinen and Hyönä (2007) carried out a study on the above lines. Participants spent most of their time processing relevant sentences (those dealing with their friend's disease) and relatively little time processing irrelevant sentences. Thus, the reader's goals can influence the construction phase, which is inconsistent with the model.

According to the construction–integration model, textual information is linked with general world or semantic knowledge *before* it is linked to contextual information from the rest of the text. Cook and Myers (2004) tested this assumption using various passages. Here is an excerpt from one passage:

> The movie was being filmed on location in the Sahara Desert. It was a small independent film with a low budget and small staff, *so everyone involved had to take on extra jobs and responsibilities*. On the first day of filming, "Action!" was called by the actress so that shooting could begin . . .

What was of interest was how long the readers fixated the word *actress*. This word is inappropriate in terms of our general knowledge, which tells us it is the director who says, "Action!" However, the context (in italics) provides a reason why there might not be a director in charge. According to the construction–integration model, readers' knowledge that actresses do not direct films should have caused them to dwell a long time on the unexpected word "actress".

What did Cook and Myers (2004) find? Contrary to the construction–integration model, the word was *not* fixated for long. Presumably readers immediately used the contextual justification for someone other than the director being in charge. Thus, in opposition to the model, contextual information can be accessed *before* general world knowledge. Similar findings were reported by Nieuwland and van Berkum (2006a) in a study discussed earlier.

Evaluation

The construction–integration model has the advantage over preceding theories in that how text information is combined with the reader's knowledge is spelled out in more detail. For example, the notion that propositions for the text representation are selected by spreading activation operating on propositions drawn from the text and stored knowledge is plausible. There is also reasonable evidence for the three levels of representation (surface, propositional, situational) specified in the model. There is some support for the distinction between constructive and integrative processes. Finally, the model predicts accurately that readers often find it hard to discriminate between text information and inferences based on that information.

What are the model's limitations? At the most general level, it is unlikely the initial construction process always involves inefficient, bottom-up processes. This criticism is at the heart of the first two limitations discussed below.

First, the assumption that only bottom-up processes are used during the construction phase of text processing is dubious. The finding that readers' goals can lead them to allocate attention selectively very early in text processing (Kaakinen & Hyönä, 2007) indicates text processing is more flexible than assumed by Kintsch.

Second, it is assumed only general world and semantic knowledge is used in addition to text information during the formation of propositions in the construction phase. However, the notion that other sources of information are used *only* at the integration stage has been disproved (Cook & Myers, 2004; Nieuwland & van Berkum, 2006a).

Third, several factors relevant to comprehension are de-emphasised within the construction–integration model. These factors include the reader's goals when reading, the reader's emotional response to the text and the reader's use of imagery (McNamara & Magliano, 2009).

Fourth, Graesser et al. (1997) argued that Kintsch ignored two levels of discourse representation. One is the *text genre level* (e.g., narrative, description, jokes, exposition). The other is the *communication level*, which is how the writer communicates with his/her readers (e.g., some writers present themselves as invisible storytellers).

Interactive exercise: Construction–integration model

Fifth, the model correctly predicts that inferences will sometimes be confused with text information. However, the model does not spell out which inferences will and will not be drawn.

Sixth, the model is not specific about the processes involved in the construction of situation models. This omission was remedied in the event-indexing model to which we turn next.

Event-indexing model and event-segmentation theory

We turn now to approaches to discourse comprehension emphasising the importance of *events*. Why are events important? According to Radvansky and Zacks (2011, p. 608), "Events are fundamental to human experience. They seem to be the elements that constitute the stream of experience."

One theoretical approach we will be discussing is the event-indexing model (Zwaan et al., 1995). The other is event-segmentation theory (Zacks et al., 2007), which represents a development and extension of the event-indexing model.

The event-indexing model (Zwaan et al., 1995) accounts for comprehension processes when someone reads a *narrative* text (e.g., a story or novel). Thus, its scope differs from that of the construction–integration model in which the focus is mostly on comprehension of *expository* texts designed to describe and/or inform. However, there are some similarities such as the emphasis on the notion that readers construct situation models when reading text.

As McNamara and Magliano (2009, p. 321) pointed out, a fundamental assumption of the event-indexing model is that "the cognitive system is more attuned to perceive dynamic events (changes in states) rather than static information". According to the event-indexing model, readers monitor five situational aspects to decide whether their situation model needs to be updated:

1. *Protagonist*: the central character or actor in the present event compared to the previous one.
2. *Temporality*: the relationship between the times at which the present and previous events occurred.
3. *Causality*: the causal relationship of the current event to the previous one.
4. *Spatiality*: the relationship between the spatial setting of the current event and a previous event.
5. *Intentionality*: the relationship between the character's goals and the present event.

Discontinuity (unexpected change) in any of the five aspects of a situation (e.g., a change in the spatial setting, a flashback in time) leads to more processing effort than when all five aspects or indexes remain the same. It is also assumed the five aspects are monitored independently of each other. As a result, processing effort should be greater when two aspects change at the same time rather than only one.

Zwaan and Madden (2004) distinguished between two views on what happens to outdated information when situation models are updated. One is the *here-and-now view*: the most current information is more available than outdated information. This view forms part of the event-indexing model.

The alternative position is the *resonance view*: new information in a text resonates with *all* text-related information stored in memory. As a result, outdated or incorrect information can influence the comprehension process.

According to event-segmentation theory (Zacks et al., 2007), updating of a situation model can take two main forms:

1. Incremental updating of individual situational dimensions (the "brick by brick" approach emphasised within the event-indexing model).
2. Global updating in which an old situational model is replaced by a new one (the "from scratch" approach emphasised by event-segmentation theory).

When do readers engage in global updating? It is assumed we try to *predict* the near future as we read a text or observe a scene. Such predictions become harder to make as we approach the boundary between one event and the next, which can trigger construction of a new model.

Support for the above viewpoint was reported by Zacks et al. (2011). Observers watched movies of everyday events (e.g., washing a car). When the movie was stopped, observers' ability to predict what would happen five seconds later was significantly worse close to an event boundary than in the middle of an event.

Findings

According to the event-indexing model, it is effortful for readers to adjust to changes in any of the five aspects by *updating* their situation model. As predicted, reading speed decreased by 35% when one aspect changed compared to when there was no change (Rinck & Weber, 2003).

Curiel and Radvansky (2014) obtained similar findings when they considered the time taken to update spatial or protagonist information. As predicted by the event-indexing model, updating time was greater when both dimensions required updating than when only one did. This finding is consistent with the notion that each aspect of the situation model is processed independently or separately.

The probability of updating occurring varies across the different situational aspects. Readers generally update information on intentionality, time and protagonist, but are less likely to do so with spatial information (Smith & O'Brien, 2012). However, Smith and O'Brien found spatial information was more likely to be updated when cues made previously mentioned spatial information more accessible.

McNerney et al. (2011) pointed out that most studies on the event-indexing model had involved several unrelated short texts. They studied reading times while readers read a novel (*The Stone Diaries* by Carol Shields). As with short texts, reading time increased significantly when information about the protagonist or causality required updating. Surprisingly, however, reading times were *reduced* when spatial or temporal information required updating. Perhaps readers' engagement with the novel was so great it facilitated the task of updating such information.

O'Brien et al. (2010) investigated whether outdated information disrupts current processing. Some readers were given a passage in which it was decided that a given tree would not be cut down. After that, however, the tree was struck by lightning and had to be cut down. Then came the following sentence: "All that remained of the tree was the stump." Updated information had a disruptive effect on comprehension of the final sentence as predicted by the resonance view discussed earlier.

Kendeou et al. (2013) argued that it would be disadvantageous for readers if outdated information *always* had an interfering effect. They discovered the provision of *causal explanations* supporting the updating process eliminated any interference effect. For example, one story involved Mary, who had been a vegetarian for ten years. This sentence was presented later in the story: "Mary ordered a cheeseburger and fries." There was no interference from the earlier part of the story for readers who had been given a causal explanation why Mary was no longer vegetarian (she had insufficient vitamins and so her doctor told her to eat meat).

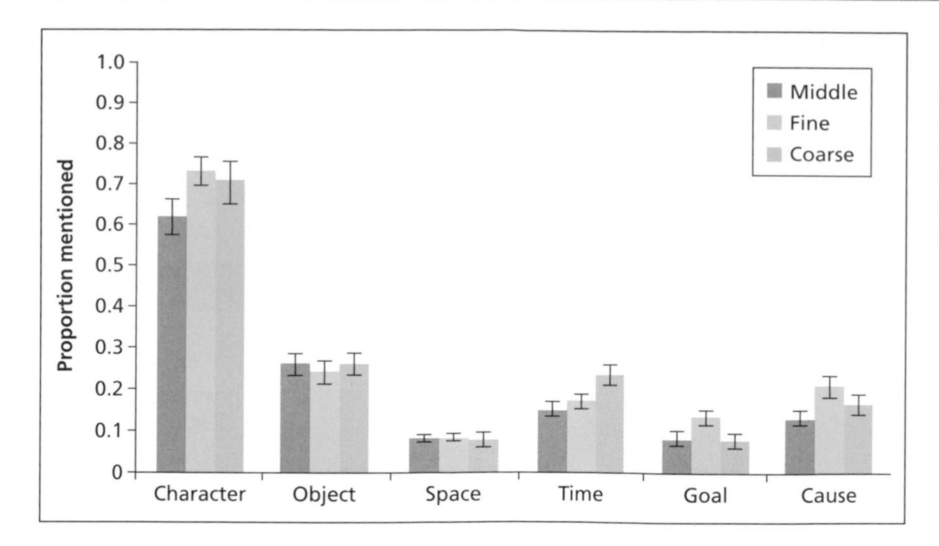

Figure 10.17
Proportion mention scores for six dimensions (character, object, space, time, goal, cause) when they changed vs. when they did not change.
From Kurby and Zacks (2012).

Ezzyat and Davachi (2011) tested the assumption of the event-segmentation theory that continuous actions are segmented into events. Participants read narratives containing event boundaries (signalled by the phrase "a while later". A subsequent memory test indicated their memory for information *across* event boundaries was lower than that for information *within* an event. These findings provide support for the existence of event segmentation.

The notions that situation model updating can be incremental (as emphasised by the event-indexing model) or global (as emphasised by event-segmentation theory) were investigated by Kurby and Zacks (2012). Readers indicated what they were thinking while reading an extended narrative. Readers showed evidence of incremental updating by increased mentions of the character, object, space, time and goal, when the relevant situational aspect changed (see Figure 10.17). They also showed evidence of global updating – the presence of an event boundary was associated with increased mentions of the character, cause, goal and time. Thus, these findings provided some support for both theoretical approaches.

Evaluation

The greatest strength of the event-indexing model is that it identifies key aspects of situation models ignored by other theoretical approaches. Of particular importance, the model (and event-segmentation theory) focus on gradual and global updating of situation models in response to changes within and between events. Some factors influencing whether outdated information has a disruptive effect on reading have been identified.

What are the limitations of this theoretical approach? First, it is fully applicable only to narrative texts describing event sequences and is of little relevance to expository texts providing information and/or explanations.

Second, the approach works better when the comprehension task involves reading a simple text rather than a complex one. For example, it is assumed readers will form situation models. However, most readers failed to do that when they read a complex account of a murder scene (Zwaan & van Oostendorp, 1993).

Third, the theoretical approach de-emphasises important determinants of comprehension such as the reader's goals and reading skills (McNamara &

Magliano, 2009) and adequate motivation for successfully monitoring the five different dimensions of protagonist, temporality, causality, spatial relationships and intentionality.

Fourth, most research has focused on the comprehension of relatively short texts. However, preliminary evidence suggests some comprehension processes may differ between long and short texts (McNerney et al., 2011).

CHAPTER SUMMARY

- **Parsing: overview**. Many sentences are ambiguous. Listeners often make use of prosodic cues provided by the speaker to interpret sentences correctly. Readers seem to use similar processes triggered by punctuation and by silent reading.

- **Models of parsing**. The garden-path model is a two-stage model in which only syntactic information is used at the first stage. In fact, however, various kinds of non-syntactic information are used earlier in sentence processing than predicted by the model. According to the constraint-based model, all sources of information (e.g., context) are available immediately to someone processing a sentence. Competing sentence analyses are activated in parallel, with several language characteristics (e.g., verb bias) being used to resolve ambiguities. There is much support for this model but its predictions are sometimes imprecise. According to the unrestricted race model, all information sources are used to identify a single syntactic structure for a sentence. If this structure is disconfirmed, there is extensive reanalysis.

  Most parsing models assume sentences are eventually interpreted correctly. In fact, we sometimes process sentences rather superficially and so are prone to error. ERP studies support the view that several sources of information (including word meanings and context) influence sentence processing at an early stage. There is evidence that top-down processes generate predictions as to what will be read or heard next.

- **Pragmatics**. Pragmatics is concerned with intended rather than literal meanings. The processing of figurative language (e.g., metaphor, irony) is more cognitively demanding than literal language processing. Understanding metaphors involves selecting predicate features relevant to the argument and inhibiting irrelevant predicate features.

  Listeners generally understand better what a speaker is saying if they make use of the common ground (shared knowledge and beliefs). When it is effortful to use the common ground, listeners often fail to use it and rely on the egocentric heuristic. However, basic memory processes sometimes allow listeners to use the common ground in a fairly automatic and effort-free fashion.

- **Individual differences: working memory capacity.** Individuals high in working memory capacity outperform low-capacity individuals with respect to several aspects of language comprehension (e.g., generating elaborative inferences, forming situation models). These differences occur in part because high-capacity individuals have better attentional control and discriminate better between relevant and irrelevant information. Working memory capacity correlates highly with IQ, making it hard to disentangle these individual-difference dimensions.

- **Discourse processing: inferences.** Readers typically make logical and bridging inferences (e.g., anaphor resolution). According to the constructionist approach, numerous elaborative inferences are typically drawn when we read a text. According to the minimalist hypothesis, in contrast, only a few inferences are drawn automatically. According to search-after-meaning theory, the number of inferences drawn is flexible and depends on the extent to which the reader's goals include a search after meaning. The evidence is more supportive of the minimalist and search-after-meaning approaches than the constructionist one.

- **Discourse comprehension: theoretical approaches.** According to schema theory, schemas or organised packets of knowledge influence our comprehension of (and memory for) discourse in a top-down fashion. Comprehension and memory are less error-prone that assumed by the theory and it lacks strong explanatory power. According to Kintsch's construction–integration model, three levels of text representation are constructed. It is assumed bottom-up processes during the construction stage are followed by top-down processes during the integration stage. In fact, top-down processes occur earlier than assumed by the model. The event-indexing model and event-segmentation theory focus on how readers update their situation models in response to changes within and between events. This general approach works well with simple narrative texts but is less applicable to complex and/or expository texts.

Further reading

- Ghosh, V.E. & Gilboa, A. (2014). What is a memory schema? A historical perspective on current neuroscience literature. *Neuropsychologia*, 53: 104–14. Varying definitions of "schema" are discussed, as is neuroscience research on schemas.
- Graesser, A.C. & Forsyth, C. (2013). Discourse comprehension. In D. Reisberg (ed.), *The Oxford handbook of cognitive psychology*. Oxford: Oxford University Press. Theory and research on language comprehension are discussed in detail by Arthur Graesser and Carol Forsyth.

- Harley, T.A. (2013). *The psychology of language: From data to theory* (4th edn). Hove: Psychology Press. Trevor Harley has (as with the previous editions) produced an outstanding account of what is currently known about the psychology of language.
- Kutas, M., DeLong, K.A. & Smith, N.J. (2011). A look around at what lies ahead: Prediction and predictability in language processing. In M. Bar (ed.), *Predictions in the brain: Using our past to generate a future* (pp. 190–207). Oxford: Oxford University Press. Marta Kutas and her colleagues review the growing evidence for the importance of top-down processes in language comprehension.
- McNamara, D.S. & Magliano, J. (2009). Toward a comprehensive model of comprehension. In B. Ross (ed.), *The psychology of learning and motivation, vol. 51* (pp. 297–384). New York: Elsevier Science. The authors provide detailed critical evaluations of several major theories of comprehension.
- Rayner, K., Pollatsek, A., Ashby, J. & Clifton, C. (2012). *Psychology of reading* (2nd edn). Hove: Psychology Press. Keith Rayner and his colleagues provide a comprehensive review of theory and research on reading.
- Vasishth, S., von der Malsburg, T. & Engelmann, F. (2013). What eye movements can tell us about sentence comprehension. *Wiley Interdisciplinary Reviews – Cognitive Science*, 4: 125–34. Shravan Vasishth and colleagues discuss the ways in which eye-movement research has enhanced our understanding of comprehension processes.

CHAPTER

11

Language production

INTRODUCTION

We know more about language comprehension than language production. Why is this? We can control the material to be comprehended, but it is harder to constrain an individual's language production. A further problem in accounting for language production (shared with language comprehension) is that more than a theory of language is needed. Language production is basically a goal-directed activity having *communication* as its main goal. People speak and write to impart information, to be friendly and so on. Thus, motivational and social factors need to be considered in addition to purely linguistic ones.

The two major topics considered in this chapter are speech production and writing, including coverage of the effects of brain damage on these language processes. More is known about speech production than about writing. Nearly everyone spends more time talking than writing. As a result, it is more important to understand the processes involved in talking. Nevertheless, writing is an important skill.

How similar are the processes involved in spoken and written language? Both have as their central function the communication of information about people and the world. In addition, both depend on the same knowledge base. However, children and adults nearly all find writing much harder than speaking, which suggests there are important differences between them. The main similarities and differences are discussed in more detail below.

Similarities

The view that speaking and writing are similar receives some support from theoretical approaches to speech production and writing. It is assumed there is an initial attempt to decide on the overall meaning to be communicated (e.g., Dell et al., 1997, on speech production; Hayes & Flower, 1986, on writing). At this stage, the actual words to be spoken or written are not considered. This is followed by language production, which often proceeds on a clause-by-clause basis.

Hartley et al. (2003) studied an individual (Eric Sotto) who word processed academic letters or used a voice-recognition system. He had much less experience of dictating letters than word processing them. However, the letters produced in these two ways were comparable in readability and grammatical errors.

Gould (1978) found that even those highly practised at dictation rarely dictated more than 35% faster than they wrote. This is notable given that people can speak five or six times faster than they can write. Gould (1980) videotaped people while they composed letters. Planning took up two-thirds of the total time for both dictated and written letters – this is why dictation was only slightly faster than writing.

Differences

There are several important differences between speaking and writing (Cleland and Pickering, 2006). Written language uses longer and more complex constructions as well as longer words and a larger vocabulary. Writers make more use than speakers of words or phrases signalling what is coming next (e.g., *but, on the other hand*). This helps to compensate for the lack of prosody (rhythm, intonation and so on; discussed shortly) that is important in spoken language.

Four differences between speaking and writing are as follows:

1. Speakers generally know precisely who is receiving their communication.
2. Speakers mostly receive moment-by-moment verbal and non-verbal feedback (e.g., expressions of bewilderment) from the listener(s) and adapt what they say in response based on that feedback.
3. Speakers generally have much less time than writers to plan their language production. This explains why spoken language is shorter and less complex than written language.
4. Writers typically have direct access to what they have produced so far whereas speakers do not. However, Olive and Piolat (2002) found no difference in the quality of texts produced by writers having (or not having) access to what they had written.

What are the consequences of the above differences between speaking and writing? Spoken language is often informal and simple in structure with information communicated rapidly. In contrast, written language is more formal and more complex. Writers need to write clearly because they do not receive immediate feedback.

Some brain-damaged patients have writing skills that are largely intact despite an almost total inability to speak and a lack of inner speech (e.g., EB, studied by Levine et al., 1982). Other brain-damaged patients can speak fluently but find writing very hard (Kolb & Whishaw, 2003). In spite of such patients, the higher-level processes involved in language production (e.g., planning, use of knowledge) are very similar in speaking and writing.

How easy is speech production?

On the face of it (by the sound of it?), speech production is straightforward. It seems almost effortless as we chat with friends and acquaintances. We typically speak at 2–3 words a second or about 150 words a minute, and this rapid speech rate fits the notion that speaking requires few processing resources.

The reality of speech production is often very different from the above account. We use various strategies when talking to reduce processing demands while planning what to say next. One example is **preformulation**, which involves reducing processing costs by producing phrases used before. About 70% of our speech consists of word combinations we use repeatedly (Altenberg, 1990). Kuiper (1996) analysed the speech of auctioneers and sports commentators, who often need to speak very rapidly. They make very extensive use of preformulations (e.g., "They are on their way", "They are off and racing now").

Another strategy we use to make speech production easier is **underspecification**. This involves using simplified expressions in which the full meaning is not explicit. Underspecification and preformulation often go together – many expressions used repeatedly by speakers are simplified ones. De Cock (2004) provides several examples of such expressions (e.g., "or something", "and things like that").

We can obtain some idea of the complexities of speech production by considering the adverse effects of alcohol. Alcohol impairs several cognitive processes (e.g., attention, short-term memory, thinking) and so we would expect speech to be affected adversely in intoxicated individuals.

Hollien et al. (2001) compared speech production in individuals when sober and when intoxicated. When intoxicated, they produced three times more dysfluencies (e.g., tripping on their words, stammering, stuttering) than when sober. In addition, intoxication slowed speaking rate and the pitch of the voice became higher.

Reichel and Kisler (2012) analysed the speech of 162 speakers recorded twice, once while sober and once while intoxicated. Among male speakers, the richness and creativity of their speech were reduced when intoxicated. More specifically, word variety and phoneme combinations were both reduced in the intoxicated state. Of interest, this was *not* the case for female speakers because they exerted more effort to compensate for the adverse effects of alcohol.

KEY TERMS

Preformulation
The production by speakers of phrases used frequently before; it reduces the demands of speech production.

Underspecification
A strategy used to reduce processing costs in speech production by using simplified expressions.

Morphemes
The basic units of meaning; words consist of one or more morphemes.

Stages in speech production

Speech production involves several general stages or processes. Dell (1986), in his spreading-activation theory (discussed later), argued that speech production consists of four levels:

1 *Semantic level*: the meaning of what is to be said or the message to be communicated; this is the planning level.
2 *Syntactic level*: the grammatical structure of the words in the planned utterance.
3 *Morphological level*: the **morphemes** (basic units of meaning).
4 *Phonological level*: the phonemes (basic units of sound).

It makes sense to assume the above four levels or stages occur in the order described. Thus, we engage in planning, followed by working out the grammatical structure of the sentence and the basic units of meaning, and finally work out the sounds to be produced. In fact, as we will see later, speech production is actually much less neat and tidy than that: "later" processes can occur at the same time as (or even ahead of) some "earlier" processes.

IN THE REAL WORLD: IMPOVERISHMENT OF SPONTANEOUS SPEECH

It is cognitively demanding to produce coherent spontaneous speech. As a result, individuals suffering from **Alzheimer's disease** (a disease involving progressive mental deterioration caused by brain degeneration) typically exhibit clear signs of impaired spontaneous speech. Alzheimer's disease is often preceded by mild cognitive impairment, a condition involving minor problems with memory and thinking. It is of practical and theoretical interest to consider which aspects of speech production are impaired in individuals with mild cognitive impairment.

Relevant evidence was reported by Butterworth (1984). He analysed Ronald Reagan's speeches before he was re-elected American President in 1984. There were subtle signs of impairment in those speeches (e.g., use of vocabulary) a full ten years before Reagan was diagnosed with Alzheimer's disease.

Ahmed et al. (2013) carried out a longitudinal study in which they studied individuals progressing from mild cognitive impairment through mild Alzheimer's disease to moderate Alzheimer's disease. They assessed the patients' speech performance in several ways:

1 *Speech production*: speech rate, distortions and production of non-words.
2 *Fluency errors*: false starts, filled pauses and incomplete sentences.
3 *Lexical content*: relative frequency of content words (e.g., nouns, verbs) providing most of an utterance's meaning.
4 *Syntactic complexity*: length of utterance, syntactic errors and so on.
5 *Semantic content*: the extent to which full information is provided in an utterance.

What did Ahmed et al. (2013) find? Disease progression had relatively minor (and non-significant) effects on speech production and fluency (see Figure 11.1). In contrast, there were significant declines in lexical content and semantic content even during the stage of mild cognitive impairment, with syntactic complexity declining later in the disease. Ahmed et al. (p. 3735) concluded early Alzheimer's disease "is characterised by 'empty' speech containing a high proportion of words and utterances that communicate little or no information".

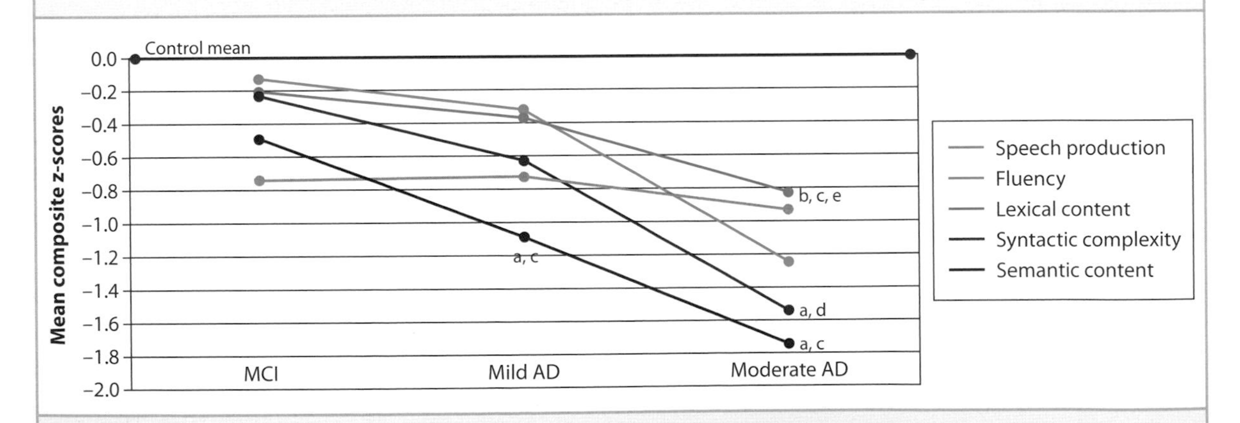

Figure 11.1
Changes in several aspects of speech production (fluency, lexical content, syntactic complexity, semantic content) across three clinical stages of Alzheimer's disease.
From Ahmed et al. (2013). By permission of Oxford University Press.

The take-home message is that individuals with mild cognitive impairment speak fluently and make relatively few speech errors but nevertheless communicate less information than healthy controls. This reduction in semantic content provides a way of monitoring disease progression.

SPEECH PLANNING

Most of the time, we plan what we are going to say before speaking (the first stage in speech production). In other words, we engage our brain before speaking.

Lee et al. (2013) wondered whether speech planning is influenced by the syntactic structure of planned utterances. Consider the following sentence:

The student of the teacher who is raising her hand.

This sentence is ambiguous. With the simpler syntactic structure, it is the teacher who is raising her hand. With the more complex structure, it is the student who is raising her hand. Lee et al. found the time to speech onset was longer when speakers produced sentences with a more complex syntactic structure. This suggests they prepared at least part of the syntactic structure of what they were about to say in advance.

What is the scope of speakers' planning? Planning might occur at the level of the **clause** (a part of a sentence containing a subject and a verb). Alternatively, it might occur at the level of the **phrase** (a group of words expressing a single idea). In the sentence, "Failing the exam was a major disappointment to him", the first three words form a phrase.

Some support for the notion speech planning often extends over an entire clause comes from the study of speech errors. Consider, for example, word-exchange errors in which two words in a sentence are swapped. Of importance, the words exchanged often come from different phrases but belong to the same clause (e.g., "My chair seems empty without my room").

Additional evidence that planning can occur at the clause level was reported by Holmes (1988). Speakers talking spontaneously about various topics often had hesitations and pauses immediately before the start of a clause. This suggests they were planning the forthcoming clause.

Martin et al. (2004) found planning can occur at the phrase level. Participants described moving pictures. The sentences they produced had a simple initial phrase (e.g., "The ball moves above the tree and the finger") or a complex initial phrase (e.g., "The ball and the tree move above the finger"). Speakers took longer to initiate speech when using complex initial phrases, suggesting they were planning the initial phrase before speaking.

The extent of advance speech planning often differs in extent at the semantic, syntactic and phonological levels. For example, consider sound-exchange errors (two sounds in a sentence are swapped) and word-exchange errors (discussed earlier). Sound-exchange errors occur over shorter distances than word-exchange errors, suggesting the sounds of words to be spoken are planned only shortly in advance.

KEY TERMS

Alzheimer's disease
A condition in which there is a progressive deterioration in mental abilities caused by a general degeneration of the brain.

Clause
A group of words within a sentence that contains a subject and a verb.

Phrase
A group of words within a sentence expressing a single idea.

Flexibility

How can we account for the somewhat mixed findings discussed above? Speakers generally want to start communicating rapidly, which implies little forward planning. However, they also want to talk fluently, which implies much forward planning. Speakers resolve this conflict *flexibly* depending on their immediate goals and situational demands.

Ferreira and Swets (2002) obtained support for the notion that speakers' planning varies flexibly. Participants answered mathematical problems. With no time pressure, task difficulty affected the time taken to start speaking but not that spent speaking. These findings suggest participants planned their responses before starting to speak.

In a second experiment, Ferreira and Swets (2002) asked participants to start producing their answers very rapidly. In these circumstances, speakers engaged in some planning before starting to speak with additional planning occurring during speaking. Thus, speakers did as much planning as was feasible before starting to speak.

Wagner et al. (2010) agreed speech planning is flexible. They identified several factors determining the extent of grammatical advance planning. First, individuals who spoke fairly slowly engaged in more planning than those who spoke rapidly. Second, speakers engaged in more planning before producing simple sentences than more complex ones. Third, speakers under low cognitive load showed more planning than those burdened with a high cognitive load.

How can we account for the flexibility of speakers' advance planning? Speakers are faced with a *tradeoff* between avoiding errors and cognitive demands. If they focus on avoiding errors, the cognitive demands will be substantial. On the other hand, if they try to minimise cognitive demands, their speech will contain many errors. In practice, speakers mostly engage in extensive planning only when such planning is not very cognitively demanding (e.g., the to-be-produced sentence is simple; there is no additional task). In sum, "speech planning processes flexibly adapt to external task goals" (Swets et al., 2013).

SPEECH ERRORS

Our speech is generally accurate and coherent. However, we are all prone to error. It has been estimated that the average person makes a speech error every 500 sentences (Vigliocco & Hartsuiker, 2002). One reason why there are several kinds of speech errors is because they can occur at any of the several stages of speech production mentioned earlier.

In spite of their relative rarity, the study of speech errors is important. We can gain insights into how the complex cognitive system involved in speech production works by focusing on what happens when it malfunctions. This would *not* be the case if speech errors were *random* and thus unpredictable. In fact, however, the great majority of speech errors are *systematic*. The speech errors even of brain-damaged patients are generally similar to the correct words (Dell et al., 2014). As Dell et al. concluded, "Slips [speech errors] are more right than wrong."

How do we know what errors are made in speech? Much of the evidence consists of speech errors written down immediately after being heard by a researcher. Ferber (1995) compared such errors against those based on tape recordings of speech. There were major differences between speech errors obtained in these two ways because those noticed spontaneously by researchers are incomplete. This has become less important because research on speech errors increasingly focuses on errors deliberately produced under laboratory conditions.

Error types

There are several types of speech error in addition to those mentioned already. For example, there is the **spoonerism**, which occurs when the initial letter(s) of two words are switched. It is named after the Reverend William Archibald Spooner, who is credited with several memorable examples (e.g., "You have hissed all my mystery lectures"). Alas, most of his gems resulted from painstaking effort.

The **Freudian slip** is a famous type of error revealing the speaker's true sexual desires. Motley (1980) studied Freudian slips by trying to produce sex-related spoonerisms. Male participants said out loud pairs of items such as *goxi furl* and *bine foddy*. The experimenter was a female who was "attractive, personable, very provocatively attired, and seductive in behaviour" (Motley, 1980, p. 140).

Motley (1980) predicted (and found) that the number of spoonerisms (e.g., *goxi furl* turning into *foxy girl*) was greater when the passions of the male participants were inflamed by the female experimenter. In other experiments (see Motley et al., 1983), male participants received word pairs such as *tool kits* and *fast luck*. There were more sexual spoonerisms when the situation produced sexual arousal.

Semantic substitution errors occur when the correct word is replaced by a word of similar meaning (e.g., "Where is my tennis bat?" instead of "Where is my tennis racquet?"). In 99% of cases, the substituted word is the same part of speech as the correct word (e.g., nouns substituted for nouns). These errors suggest speakers often plan the grammatical structure of their next utterance before finding the precise words to insert into that structure.

Morpheme-exchange errors involve inflections or suffixes remaining in place but attached to the wrong words (e.g., "He has already trunked two packs"). An implication of morpheme-exchange errors is that the positioning of inflections is dealt with by a rather separate process from the one responsible for positioning word stems (e.g., *trunk*, *pack*).

The word stems (e.g., *trunk*, *pack*) seem to be worked out *before* the inflections are added because the spoken inflections or suffixes are generally altered to fit with the *new* word stems. For example, the "s" sound in the phrase "the forks of a prong" is pronounced in a way appropriate within the word "forks". However, this differs from the "s" sound in the original word "prongs".

Finally, we consider *number-agreement errors*, in which singular verbs are mistakenly used with plural subjects or vice versa. We have problems with collective nouns (e.g., government, team) that are actually singular but resemble plural nouns. We should say, "The government has made a mess of things", but sometimes say "The government have made a mess of things."

Why do we make number-agreement errors? McDonald (2008) asked participants to decide whether various sentences were grammatically correct. Those with an externally imposed load on working memory found it especially difficult to make accurate decisions concerning subject–verb agreement. Thus, we require considerable processing resources to avoid number-agreement errors.

KEY TERMS

Spoonerism
A speech error in which the initial letter or letters of two words (typically close together) are switched to form two different words.

Freudian slip
A speech error that reveals the speaker's (often unconscious) sexual desires.

Weblink:
Fun spoonerisms

According to Haskell and MacDonald (2003), we use several sources of information. For example, consider the two sentence fragments, "The family of mice . . ." and "The family of rats . . .". The verb should be singular in both cases. However, many participants used a plural verb. This tendency was greater when the noun closest to the verb was more obviously plural (e.g., *rats* ends in –s, which is a strong predictor of a plural noun).

Recent experience is one source of information used by speakers. When speakers had recently encountered phrases (e.g., *a trio of violinists*) paired with plural verbs, they were more likely to produce plural verbs with other, similar phrases (e.g., a class of children) (Haskell et al., 2010).

Mirković and MacDonald (2013) found semantic factors influence number–verb decisions. Participants were presented with verbs plus phrases (in Serbian) such as the following:

1 (to jump) Many wolves . . .
2 (to jump) Several wolves . . .

What was of interest was whether participants would say jump or jumps (both of which are grammatically acceptable in Serbian). Mirković and MacDonald argued that *several* is more suggestive than *many* of a collection of distinct individuals. As a result, speakers should be more likely to use plural verbs with phrases containing several than in those containing many. That is what was found.

In sum, speakers make several different types of speech error. We will shortly be discussing other types of speech error within the context of a theoretical approach (Dell's (1986) spreading-activation theory), which provides an explanation of most types of speech error.

Error detection

So far we have focused on speakers' errors. However, they often successfully detect and rapidly correct their errors. Below we consider two major theories of error detection.

In his perceptual loop theory, Levelt (1983) argued that speakers detect their own speech errors by listening to themselves and discovering that what they say sometimes differs from what they intended. Thus, speakers use the *comprehension* system to detect their own speech errors in ways resembling those used to detect errors in other people's speech.

Nozari et al. (2011) favoured an alternative conflict-based theoretical account. They argued that error detection relies on information generated by the speech-production system itself rather than the comprehension system. Their theory assumes speakers engage in conflict monitoring during competition among various possible words at the time of response selection.

The two theories make different predictions. First, the perceptual loop theory predicts speakers' success at detecting their own speech errors should depend mostly on their comprehension ability. In contrast, Nozari et al.'s (2011) conflict-based account predicts speakers' ability to detect their speech errors should depend on the quality of their speech production system.

Second, the theories differ with respect to how rapidly speech errors will be detected. Speakers' error detection should occur relatively rapidly if it depends on detecting conflict *prior* to producing an error. In contrast, error detection will be slow if it depends on speakers monitoring their own overt speech. Admittedly, error detection would be faster if speakers monitored their own inner speech. However, Huettig and Hartsuiker (2010) found speakers monitored their overt rather than inner speech.

Findings

Nozari et al. (2011) tested 29 aphasic patients having various language problems to see whether their ability to detect their own speech errors depended more on their comprehension ability or speech-production ability. Overall, there was practically no correlation between comprehension ability and error-detection performance ($r = -0.01$). In contrast, speech-production ability predicted error detection (see Figure 11.2). Patients making many semantic speech errors were much worse than other patients at detecting their own semantic errors ($r = -0.59$). Those who made many phonological speech errors were poorer at detecting their own phonological errors ($r = -0.43$).

Evidence concerning the speed of error detection was reported by Blackmer and Mitton (1991) in a study on callers to a radio chat show. Many errors were detected very rapidly (e.g., 19% of the overt corrections of what a caller had just said occurred immediately). For example, one caller said "willfiddily" and without any pause added "fully". These findings are more consistent with the conflict-based theory than the perceptual loop theory.

According to Nozari et al. (2011), speakers should find it easiest to detect speech errors that are the result of much conflict during speech planning and production. Such speech errors should have low perceptual clarity because they combine correct and incorrect sounds. Nooteboom and Quené (2013b) found support for this prediction with errors detected late by speakers. However, errors detected early by speakers had *high* perceptual clarity. This finding suggests conflict during speech planning and production may not account for all speech errors.

Evaluation

It is probable speakers detect some of their speech errors by listening to and monitoring their own speech and others by conflict monitoring within the speech-production system itself. However, the evidence is more supportive of the latter position in two ways. First, the success of brain-damaged patients in detecting their own speech errors depends much more on their speech-production ability than on their comprehension ability.

Second, the finding that speakers often detect their own errors very rapidly is consistent with the notion that speech monitoring occurs within the speech-production system. In contrast, it would seem likely error detection based on the comprehension system would take longer. However, the finding that speech errors detected early are typically perceptually clear suggests conflict monitoring may not explain all speech errors.

What are the limitations of research in this area? First, it is hard to carry out systematic research when the occurrence of speech errors and their correction is hard to predict. Second, the processes involved in error detection occur rapidly

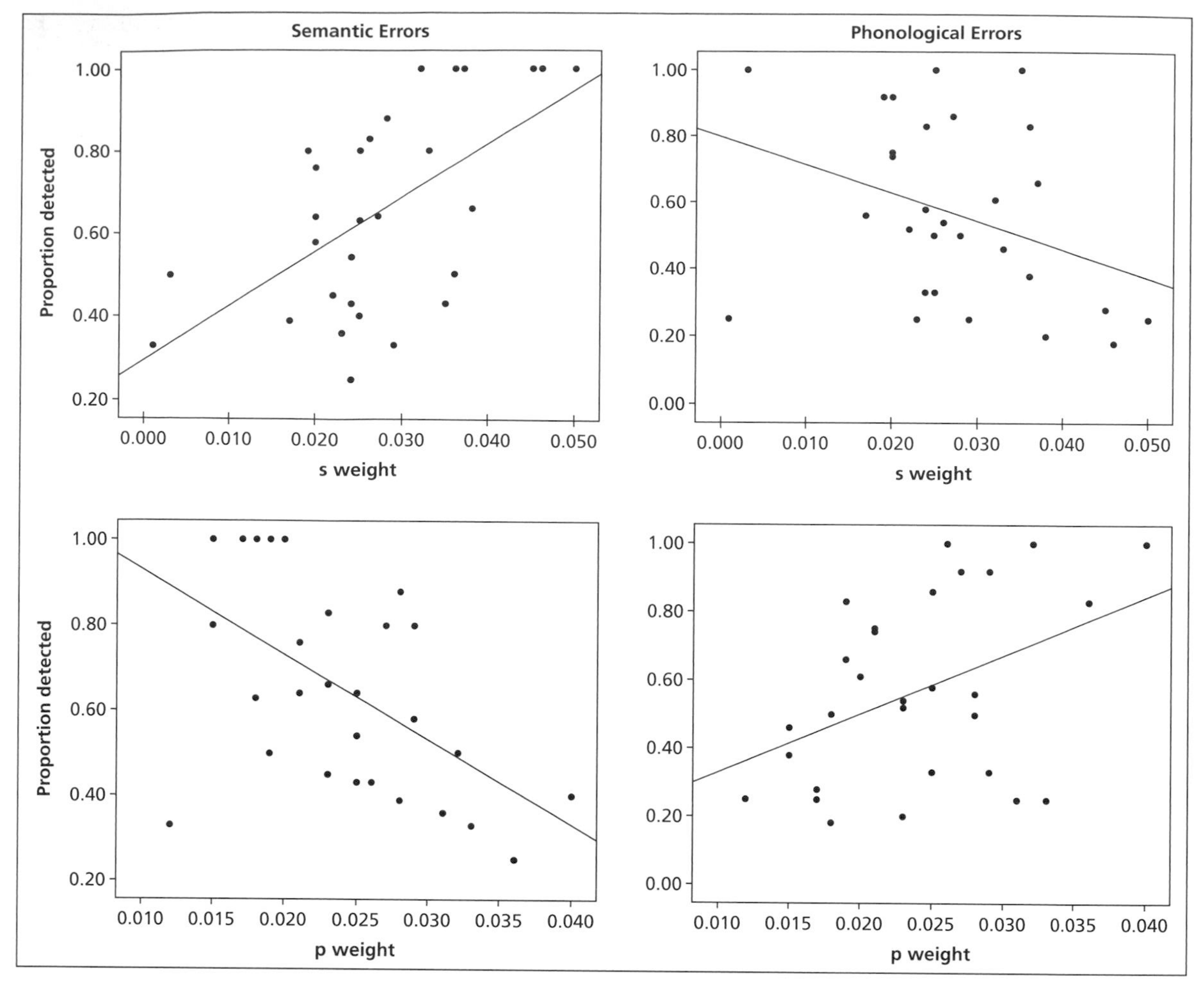

Figure 11.2
Correlations between aphasic patients' speech-production abilities and their ability to detect their own speech-production errors. Top row: ability to avoid semantic errors when speaking (s weight) was positively correlated with ability to detect their own semantic errors (left) but not with ability to detect their own phonological errors. Bottom row: ability to avoid phonological errors when speaking (p weight) was not positively correlated with ability to detect their own semantic errors (left) but was positively correlated with ability to detect their own phonological errors (right).
From Nozari et al. (2011). Reprinted with permission from Elsevier.

and are extremely difficult to assess with any precision. Third, it is probable various processes can be involved in the detection of speech errors, but the factors determining when each process is used remain unclear.

THEORIES OF SPEECH PRODUCTION

Earlier in the chapter we mentioned four levels or stages of processing involved in speech production: semantic, syntactic, morphological and phonological. There has been controversy concerning *how* these levels or stages of processing relate to each other in speech production. Two highly influential theories of speech production are Dell's (1986) spreading-activation theory and Levelt et al.'s (1999) WEAVER++ model. We will discuss both theories in detail shortly. However, we will provide a brief overview of the differences between them here to orientate the reader.

According to Dell's (1986) spreading-activation theory, processing occurs in *parallel* (at the same time) at different levels (e.g., semantic, syntactic). In addition, processing is *interactive*, meaning processes at one level can influence processes at any other level.

In contrast, Levelt et al. (1999) argued that word production involves various processing stages following each other in *serial* (i.e., one at a time) fashion. The key notion here is that each processing stage is completed before the next one starts. In addition, their WEAVER++ model assumes speech production involves a *feedforward* system with processing proceeding in a strictly forward direction (i.e., from meaning to sound).

In sum, the main assumptions of spreading-activation theory imply the processes involved in speech production are (if not chaotic) then at least very flexible. In contrast, the main assumptions of WEAVER++ imply that speech-production processes are highly regimented and structured. In fact, the theoretical differences are not so extreme. Dell (1986) accepted processing at any given point in time is generally more advanced at some levels (e.g., semantic) than others (e.g., phonological). Thus, the notions that initial processing is mainly at the semantic and phonological levels, while later processing is mostly at the morphological and phonological levels, are common to both theories.

There are two final points before we discuss the spreading-activation and WEAVER++ theoretical approaches in more detail. First, a compromise position is appropriate. In his research review, Goldrick (2006) concluded that there is "limited interaction" in speech production. This makes sense – too much interaction would lead to numerous speech errors, whereas too little interaction would inhibit speakers' ability to produce interesting new sentences and new ideas.

Second, spreading-activation theory was initially based mainly on evidence from speech errors. In contrast, WEAVER++ was based mostly on laboratory studies of the time taken to speak words accurately in different contexts. There is stronger evidence of interactive effects in speech-error data than response-time data (Goldrick, 2006).

Spreading-activation theory

Unsurprisingly, the notion of **spreading activation** is central to Dell's (1986) spreading-activation theory. It is assumed the nodes within a network (nodes correspond to words or concepts) vary in activation or energy. When a node or word is activated, activation or energy spreads from it to other related nodes or words. For example, strong activation of the node corresponding to "tree" may cause some activation of the node corresponding to "plant". According to the theory, spreading activation can occur for sounds as well as words.

It is assumed within the theory that there are *categorical rules* at the semantic, syntactic, morphological and phonological levels of speech production. These rules impose constraints on the categories of items and combinations of categories that are acceptable. The rules at each level define categories appropriate to that level. For example, the categorical rules at the syntactic level specify the syntactic categories of items within a sentence.

KEY TERM

Spreading activation
The notion that activation of a node (corresponding to a word or concept) in the brain causes some activation to spread to several related nodes or words.

KEY TERMS

Mixed-error effect
A form of speech error in which the incorrect word spoken is related to the correct one in terms of meaning and sound.

Lexical bias effect
The tendency for speech errors to form words rather than non-words.

In addition to the categorical rules, there is a *lexicon* (dictionary) in the form of a connectionist network. It contains nodes for concepts, words, morphemes and phonemes (see Glossary). When a node is activated, it sends activation to all the nodes connected to it (see Chapter 1).

Insertion rules select items for inclusion in the representation of the to-be-spoken sentence according to the following criterion: the most highly activated node belonging to the appropriate category is chosen. For example, if the categorical rules at the syntactic level dictate that a verb is required at a particular point, then the verb whose node is most activated will be selected. After an item has been selected, its activation level immediately reduces to zero, thus preventing it from being selected repeatedly.

Dell et al. (2008) focused on why we replace a noun with a noun and a verb with a verb when we make mistakes while speaking. They argued that through learning we possess a "syntactic traffic cop". It monitors what we intend to say, and inhibits words not belonging to the appropriate syntactical category.

According to spreading-activation theory, speech errors occur because an incorrect item is sometimes more activated than the correct one. The existence of spreading activation means several nodes are all activated at the same time, which increases the likelihood of errors being made in speech. Dell et al. (2014) provide an excellent account of the processes responsible for the occurrence of several major speech errors (e.g., anticipatory errors, exchange errors).

Findings

What kinds of errors are predicted by spreading-activation theory? First, and of particular importance, there is the **mixed-error effect**. The mixed-error effect occurs when an incorrect spoken word is semantically and phonemically related to the correct word. The existence of this effect suggests the various levels of processing *interact* flexibly with each other. More specifically, the mixed-error effect suggests semantic and phonological factors can both influence word selection at the same time. Alternatively, there may be a monitoring system that inhibits production of words phonologically dissimilar to the intended word (Levelt et al., 1999).

It is hard to work out how many incorrect words would be phonologically related to the correct word by chance and thus to assess the strength of the mixed-error effect. However, convincing evidence was provided by Ferreira and Griffin (2003). Participants were presented with an incomplete sentence, such as "I thought that there would still be some cookies left, but there were . . ." followed by picture naming (e.g., of a priest). Participants tended to produce the wrong word "none". This was due to the semantic similarity between *priest* and *nun* combining with the phonological identity of *nun* and *none*.

Second, speech errors tend to consist of actual words rather than non-words (the **lexical bias effect**). According to spreading-activation theory (e.g., Dell et al., 2008), this effect occurs because it is easier for words than for non-words to become activated because they have representations in the lexicon. An alternative explanation is that we monitor our internal speech and edit out non-words.

There is support for both above explanations (Dell et al., 2014). Nooteboom and Quené (2008) found evidence for self-monitoring in that speakers would often correct themselves just before producing an incorrect word. For example, they might see *BARN-DOOR* and say *D . . . BARN DOOR*.

Corley et al. (2011) asked people to say tongue twisters rapidly. They carried out several experiments but what is of most relevance here is an experiment in which there were two conditions. In the first condition, all the stimuli were real words. In contrast, only half of the stimuli presented in the second condition were real words with the others being pronounceable non-words (e.g., gulk; bish; nabe). Corley et al. found that there was the typical lexical bias effect in the first condition. However, the lexical bias effect disappeared in the second condition.

Why was there no lexical bias effect in the second condition? The reason was that 50% of the stimuli in this condition were non-words and as a result non-words were not edited out.

Third, spreading-activation theory predicts speakers should make anticipatory errors in which a speech sound is made too early in the sentence (e.g., "a Tanadian from Toronto" instead of "a Canadian from Toronto"). This prediction has been confirmed (e.g., Nooteboom & Quené, 2013a). Anticipatory errors occur because many of the words in a sentence become activated during speech planning and sometimes a later word is more activated than the one that should be spoken.

Fourth, many errors should be exchange errors in which two words within a sentence are swapped (e.g., "I must send a wife to my email"). That is, indeed, the case (Nooteboom & Quené, 2013a). Remember that the activation level of a selected word immediately reduces to zero. If "wife" is selected too early, it is unlikely to be selected in its correct place in the sentence. This allows a previously unselected but highly activated word such as "email" to be spoken in the wrong place.

Fifth, anticipation and exchange errors generally involve words moving only a relatively short distance within the sentence. Those words relevant to the part of the sentence under current consideration are generally more activated than those relevant to more distant parts of the sentence. Thus, the findings accord with the predictions of spreading-activation theory.

Evaluation

Spreading-activation theory has various strengths:

- The mixed-error and lexical bias effects indicate that the processing associated with speech production can be highly interactive as predicted theoretically.
- Several other types of speech error (e.g., exchange errors, anticipatory errors) can be accounted for.
- The theory's emphasis on spreading activation provides links between speech production and other cognitive activities (e.g., word recognition: McClelland & Rumelhart, 1981).
- Our ability to produce novel sentences may owe much to the flexibility resulting from widespread activation between processing levels assumed within the theory.
- The original version of the theory was vulnerable to the charge that it predicted more speech errors than are actually found. However, Nozari et al. (2011; discussed earlier) have provided plausible mechanisms for monitoring and editing out errors early in the process of speech production.

What are the theory's limitations?

- It de-emphasises the processes involved in the construction of a message and its intended meaning.
- While the theory predicts many errors occurring in speech production, it does not predict the time taken to produce correct and incorrect spoken words.
- The interactive processes emphasised by the theory are less apparent in error-free data than speech-error data (Goldrick, 2006).
- There is insufficient focus in the theory on the factors determining the *extent* of interactive processes during speech production. As we will see shortly, interactive processing occurs less often when overall processing demands are high than when they are low (Mädebach et al., 2011).

Anticipatory and perseveration errors

Dell et al. (1997) developed spreading-activation theory. They argued that most speech errors belong to two categories:

1. *Anticipatory*: As discussed earlier, sounds or words that are spoken ahead of their time (e.g., "caff of coffee" instead of "cup of coffee"). These errors mainly reflect inexpert planning.
2. *Perseveratory*: Sounds of words are spoken later than they should have been (e.g., "beef needle" instead of "beef noodle"). These errors reflect planning failure or a failure to monitor what one is about to say.

Dell et al.'s (1997) key assumption was that expert speakers plan ahead more than non-expert ones. As a result, a higher proportion of their speech errors will be anticipatory. In their own words, "Practice enhances the activation of the *present* and *future* at the expense of the *past*. So, as performance gets better, perseverations become relatively less common" (p. 140; original italics). The increasing activation levels of present and future sounds and words with practice prevent the past from intruding into present speech.

Dell et al. (1997) assessed the effects of practice on the anticipatory proportion (the proportion of total errors (anticipation + perseveration) that is anticipatory). Participants received extensive practice at saying several tongue twisters (e.g., *five frantic fat frogs*; *thirty-three throbbing thumbs*). As expected, the number of errors decreased with practice. However, the anticipatory proportion increased from 0.37 early in practice to 0.59 at the end of practice.

Dell et al. (1997) argued that speech errors are most likely when the speaker has not formed a coherent speech plan. In such circumstances, there will be relatively few anticipatory errors, and so the anticipatory proportion will be low. Thus, the overall error rate (anticipatory + perseverative) should correlate *negatively* with the anticipatory proportion. Dell et al. worked out the overall error rate and the anticipatory proportion for several sets of published data. The anticipatory proportion decreased from 0.75 with low overall error rates to about 0.40 with high overall error rates (see Figure 11.3).

Vousden and Maylor (2006) tested the theory by assessing speech errors in 8-year-olds, 11-year-olds and young adults who said tongue twisters aloud slowly or fast. There were two main findings. First, the anticipatory proportion increased with age. This is predicted by the theory, because older children and young adults have had more practice at producing language.

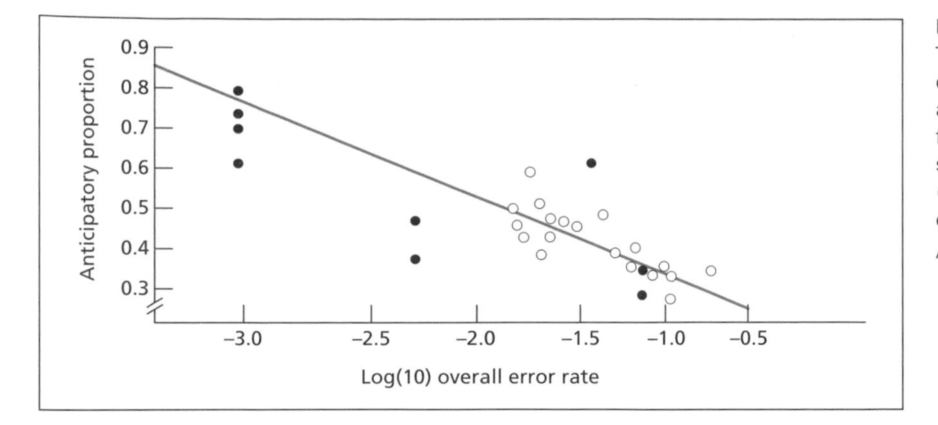

Figure 11.3
The relationship between overall error rate and the anticipatory proportion. The filled circles come from studies reported by Dell et al. (1997) and unfilled circles come from other studies.
Adapted from Dell et al. (1997).

Second, fast speech produced a higher error rate than slow speech and also resulted in a lower anticipatory proportion. This confirms the prediction that a higher overall error rate should be associated with a reduced anticipatory proportion.

Wutzler et al. (2013) assessed the anticipatory proportion in elderly individuals. Those who had significant cognitive impairment had a significantly lower anticipatory proportion than those without such impairment, presumably because they were less able to plan their utterances.

Levelt's theoretical approach and WEAVER

Levelt et al. (1999) put forward a computational model called WEAVER++ (WEAVER stands for Word-form Encoding by Activation and VERification: see Figure 11.4). It focuses on the processes involved in producing individual spoken words. The model is based on the following assumptions:

- There is a feedforward activation-spreading network meaning that activation proceeds forwards through the network but not backwards. Of particular importance, processing proceeds from meaning to sound.
- There are *three* main levels within the network:

  i At the highest level are nodes representing lexical concepts.
  ii At the second level are nodes representing **lemmas** from the mental lexicon. Lemmas are word representations that "are specified syntactically and semantically but not phonologically" (Harley, 2013). Thus, if you know the meaning of a word you are about to say and that it is a noun, but you do not know its pronunciation, you have accessed its lemma.
  iii At the lowest level are nodes representing word forms in terms of morphemes (basic units of meaning) and their phonemic segments.

- Lexical (word) selection depends on a competitive process based on the number of lexical units activated.
- Speech production following lexical selection involves various processing states following each other in serial fashion (one at a time).
- Speech errors are avoided by means of a checking mechanism based on the speaker monitoring what he/she says (discussed earlier).

KEY TERM

Lemmas
Abstract words possessing syntactic and semantic features but not phonological ones.

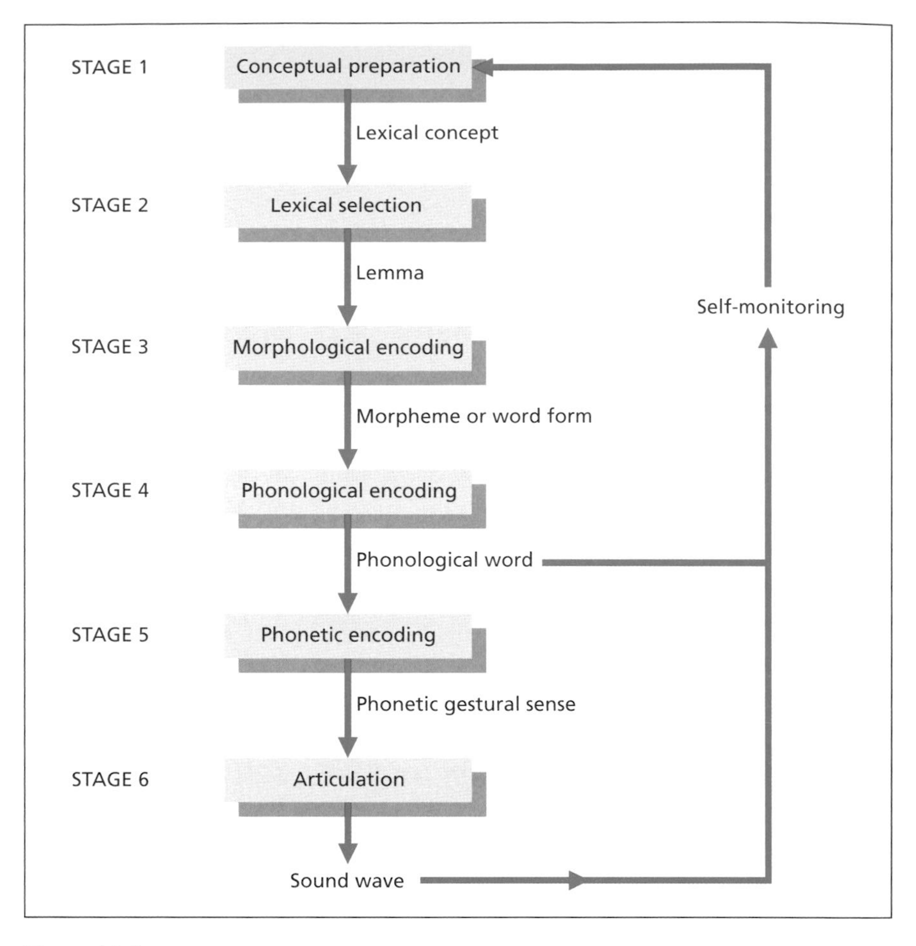

Figure 11.4
The WEAVER++ computational model.
Adapted from Levelt et al. (1999).

It is easy to get lost in the model's complexities (agreed?). Note, however, the model is mainly designed to show how word production proceeds from *meaning* (lexical concepts and lemmas) to *sound* (e.g., phonological words). There is a stage of lexical selection at which a lemma (representing word meaning + syntax) is selected. A given lemma is generally selected because it is more activated than other lemmas.

Weblink:
WEAVER on the web

Then there is morphological encoding during which the basic word form of the selected lemma is activated. This is followed by phonological encoding during which the word's syllables are computed. What happens is known as **lexicalisation**, which is "the process in speech production whereby we turn the thoughts underlying words into sounds" (Harley, 2013).

KEY TERM

Lexicalisation
The process of translating a word's meaning into its sound representation during speech production.

In sum, WEAVER++ is a discrete, feedforward model. Processing is discrete (separate), because the speed-production system identifies the correct lemma or abstract word *before* starting to work out the sound of the selected word. It is feedforward, because processing proceeds in a strictly forward (from meaning to sound) direction.

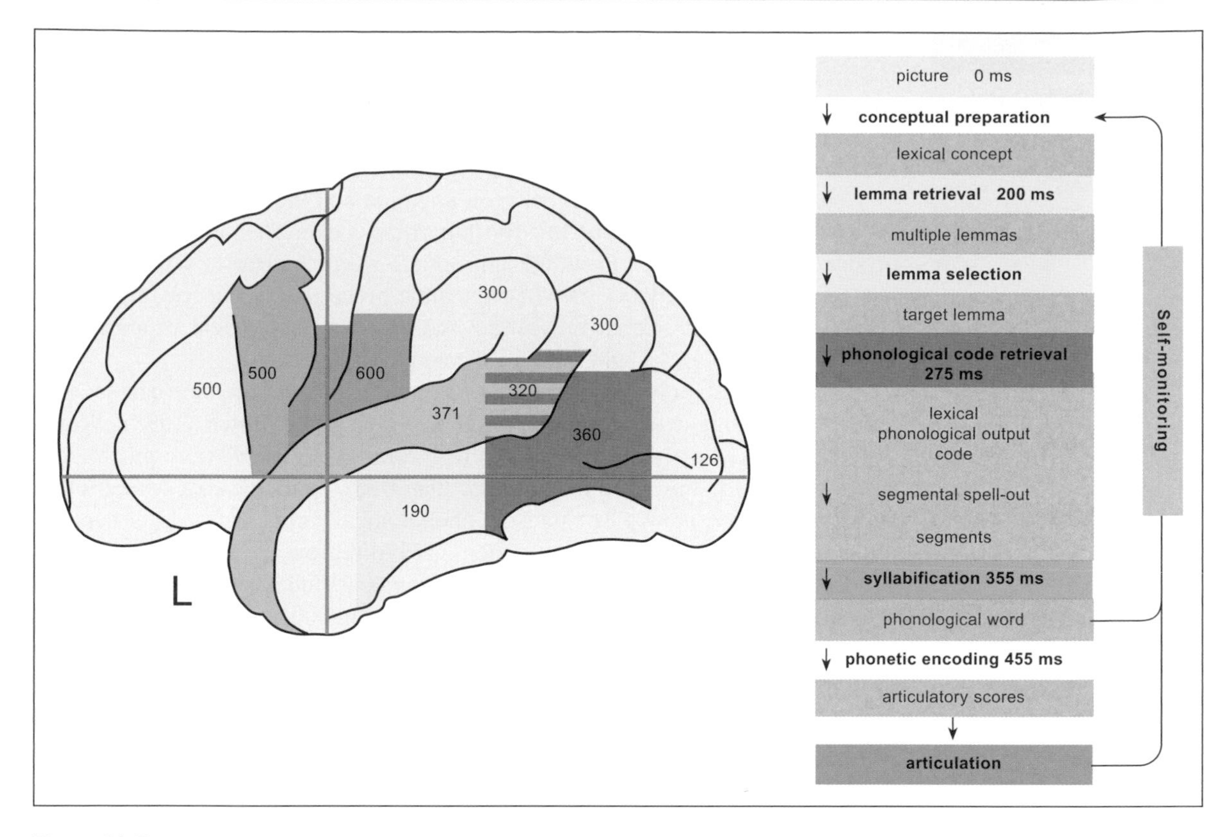

Figure 11.5
The right side of the figure indicates the sequence of processes (and their timings) for picture naming. Identical colours on the left side of the figure indicate the brain regions associated with each process (the numbers within regions are the median peak activation times in msec after picture onset).

From Indefrey (2011). Copyright © 2011 Indefrey.

Findings

The theoretical assumption that speakers have access to semantic and syntactic information about words *before* their phonological information has been tested using event-related potentials (ERPs; see Glossary). For example, van Turennout et al. (1998) found, using ERPs with Dutch participants, that syntactic information about a noun's gender was available 40 ms before its initial phoneme. This is consistent with Levelt's theoretical approach.

Indefrey (2011) carried out a meta-analysis (see Glossary) based on many studies involving ERPs and other techniques for assessing brain activity. The right column of Figure 11.5 provides approximate timings for the various processes involved in speech production. Conceptual preparation takes about 200 ms. After that, lemma retrieval takes 75 ms, and phonological code retrieval takes 20 ms per phoneme and 50–55 ms per syllable. Finally, there is phonetic encoding with articulation typically starting about 600 ms after the initiation of processing. The left-hand side of Figure 11.5 is colour coded to indicate the various brain regions in the left hemisphere associated with each of these stages.

Indefrey's (2011) meta-analysis provides an excellent overview. However, the research on which it is based is limited because it mostly involved picture

KEY TERM

Tip-of-the-tongue state
The frustrating experience of being unable to find the correct word to describe a given concept or idea.

naming. In addition, as Riès et al. (2013) pointed out, the timings provided by Indefrey are with respect to the presentation of a stimulus (e.g., picture). However, speech production is more concerned with *action* than with *perception*. As a result, it would make more sense to focus on how long a given process occurs prior to speech onset.

We can see the distinction between a lemma and the word itself in the tip-of-the-tongue state. The **tip-of-the-tongue state** occurs when we have a concept or idea in mind but cannot find the appropriate word. As Harley (2013) pointed out, this state generally occurs when semantic processing is successful (i.e., we activate the correct lemma or abstract word) but phonological processing is unsuccessful (i.e., we cannot produce the sound of the word).

Evidence that problems with accessing phonological information can underlie the tip-of-the-tongue state was reported by Harley and Bown (1998). Words sounding unlike nearly all other words (e.g., *apron*, *vineyard*) were much more susceptible to the tip-of-the-tongue state than those sounding like several other words (e.g., *litter*, *pawn*). The unusual phonological forms of words susceptible to the tip-of-the-tongue state makes them hard to retrieve.

Levelt et al. (1999) argued that the lemma includes syntactic as well as semantic information. Accordingly, individuals in the tip-of-the-tongue state should have access to syntactic information. In many languages (e.g., Italian, German), grammatical gender (e.g., masculine, feminine) is part of the syntactic information relating to nouns. As predicted, Italian participants in the tip-of-the-tongue state for nouns guessed the grammatical gender correctly 85% of the time (Vigliocco et al., 1997).

Findings less supportive of WEAVER++ were reported by Biedermann et al. (2008). German speakers guessed the grammatical gender and initial phoneme of nouns when in a tip-of-the-tongue state. Theoretically, access to grammatical gender *precedes* access to phonological information. As a result, participants should have guessed the first phoneme more often when they had access to accurate gender information. That was *not* the case, suggesting syntactic information is *not* available prior to phonological information.

Levelt et al. (1999) claim lexical (word) selection is a *competitive* process. For example, consider the picture–word interference task in which participants name pictures while ignoring distractor words presented at the same time. Distractors from the same semantic category as the word describing the picture slow picture naming (Melinger & Rahman, 2013). This interference effect may be due to a competitive process.

Piai et al. (2014) studied the processes involved in the picture–word interference task in more detail. Pictures (e.g., of a *dog*) were presented for naming in the presence of a semantically related distractor word (e.g., *cat*), an unrelated distractor word (e.g., *pin*) or an identical distractor word (e.g., *dog*).

According to Levelt et al. (1999), possible words are activated initially. This is followed by a top-down competitive process involving the frontal cortex to select the correct word. Piai et al. (2014) reported two main findings. First, activity in the left temporal cortex (reflecting activation of words) was greater with unrelated and related distractors than identical distractors. This makes sense given that only one word was activated in the identical distractor condition.

Second, Piai et al. (2014) considered activation in the left superior frontal gyrus reflecting the processing effort involved in resolving the competition among competing words. There was greatest activation on trials with related distractors and least on trials with identical distractors. This is exactly as predicted – competition is greatest with related distractors and minimal with identical distractors.

According to WEAVER++, abstract word or lemma selection is completed *before* phonological information about the word is accessed. In contrast, it is assumed within Dell's spreading-activation theory that phonological processing can start before lemma or word selection is completed.

Most evidence is inconsistent with the above prediction from WEAVER++. Meyer and Damian (2007) asked participants to name target pictures while ignoring simultaneously presented distractor pictures. The picture names were phonologically related (e.g., *dog–doll*, *ball–wall*) or unrelated. According to Levelt et al.'s model, the phonological features of the names for distractor pictures should not have been activated. Thus, speed of naming target pictures should *not* have been influenced by whether the picture names were phonologically related. In fact, target pictures were named faster when accompanied by phonologically related distractors. These findings are consistent with spreading-activation theory.

Oppermann et al. (2014) carried out a similar study involving pairs of pictures. The target picture had to be named and the other picture was a distractor. They discovered the distractor object was processed phonologically when it was attended, which is inconsistent with WEAVER++. This effect depended on attention because it was not found when the distractor object did not capture attention.

Mädebach et al. (2011) found picture naming was slowed in the presence of a phonologically similar distractor word when the demands on processing resources were relatively low. However, there was *no* effect of phonological similarity when processing demands were high. What do these findings mean? Serial processing (as predicted by Levelt) is found when processing demands are high. In contrast, processing is more interactive (as predicted by Dell) when processing demands are low.

Evaluation

WEAVER++ has various successes to its credit. First, the notion that word production involves a series of stages moving from lexical selection to morphological encoding to phonological encoding is reasonably accurate (Indefrey, 2011). Second, Levelt's theoretical approach has served to shift the balance of research away from speech errors and towards precise timing of word-production processes under laboratory conditions. Third, WEAVER++ is a simple and elegant model making many testable predictions. It is arguably easier to test WEAVER++ than more interactive theories such as Dell's spreading-activation theory. Fourth, lexical or word selection often involves a competitive process as assumed by the model.

We turn now to the main limitations of WEAVER++:

- It has a narrow focus on the processes involved in the production of single words. As a result, several processes involved in planning and producing entire sentences are relatively ignored.
- There is much more *interaction* between different processing levels than assumed within WEAVER++ (e.g., Meyer & Damian, 2007).

Interactive exercsie:
WEAVER++

KEY TERMS

Aphasia
Severe problems in the comprehension and/or production of language caused by brain damage.

Broca's aphasia
A form of **aphasia** involving non-fluent speech and grammatical errors.

Wernicke's aphasia
A form of **aphasia** involving fluent speech with many content words missing and impaired comprehension.

Weblink:
Broca's aphasia video

Weblink:
Wernicke's aphasia video

- The evidence from speech errors such as the mixed-error effect, the lexical bias effect, word-exchange errors and sound-exchange errors suggests parallel processing during speech production occurs to a greater extent than predicted by WEAVER++.
- As Harley (2013, p. 418) pointed out, "It is not clear that the need for lemmas is strongly motivated by the data. Most of the evidence really only demands a distinction between the semantic and the phonological levels."
- WEAVER++ provides an explanation of anomia (a condition in which brain-damaged patients have severe problems in naming objects). Research on anomia (discussed later in the chapter) provides reasonable support for the model but some findings appear inconsistent with it.

COGNITIVE NEUROPSYCHOLOGY: SPEECH PRODUCTION

The cognitive neuropsychological approach to language started in the nineteenth century. The focus was on brain-damaged patients suffering from **aphasia**, a condition involving severe impairments of language comprehension and/or production.

The most important outcome of early research was the distinction between Broca's and Wernicke's aphasia. Patients with **Broca's aphasia** have slow, non-fluent speech. They also have a poor ability to produce syntactically correct sentences although their sentence comprehension is relatively intact. This form of aphasia involves BA44 and BA45 in the inferior frontal gyrus (see Figure 11.6).

In contrast, patients with **Wernicke's aphasia** have fluent and apparently grammatical speech that often lacks meaning. In addition, they have severe problems with speech comprehension. This form of aphasia involves the posterior part of BA22 in the superior temporal gyrus (see Figure 11.6). The take-home message from the traditional approach was that impaired language production is of central importance in Broca's aphasia, whereas language comprehension is at the heart of Wernicke's aphasia.

There is a grain of truth in the distinction between Broca's and Wernicke's aphasia. For example, Yang et al. (2008) found in stroke patients that most of those with damage to Broca's area had language deficits associated with Broca's aphasia. In similar fashion, those with damage to Wernicke's area mostly had language problems associated with Wernicke's aphasia.

The central problem with the distinction between Broca's and Wernicke's aphasia is that it is oversimplified. We will consider five ways in which that is the case. First, the terms Broca's aphasia and Wernicke's aphasia imply that numerous brain-damaged patients all have very similar patterns of language impairment. In fact, patients with allegedly the same form of aphasia exhibit very different symptoms (Harley, 2013).

Second, several brain areas are involved in language processing, and these areas are interconnected in complex ways (see Figure 11.6). According to Berwick et al. (2013), one pathway (blue) is associated with basic syntactic processing, a second pathway (purple) connects sensory and motor processes, while the other two pathways are involved in semantic processing. Note that two of these pathways involve Broca's area *and* Wernicke's area. We will return to a discussion of brain areas involved in syntactic processing shortly.

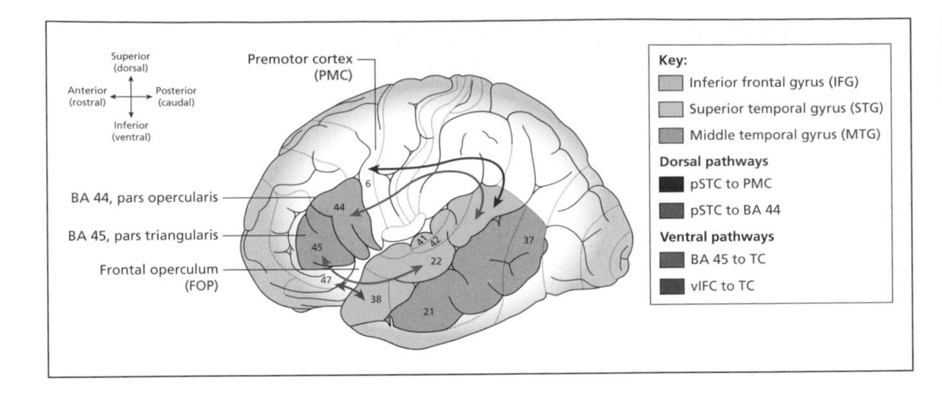

Figure 11.6
Language-related regions and their connections in the left hemisphere. Abbreviations: PMC, premotor cortex; STC, superior temporal cortex; p, posterior.
From Berwick et al. (2013). Reprinted with permission from Elsevier.

KEY TERM

Anomia
A condition caused by brain damage in which there is an impaired ability to name objects.

Third, patients with Broca's aphasia often have damage to Wernicke's area and those with Wernicke's aphasia sometimes have damage to Broca's area (De Bleser, 1988). This is unsurprising given the complexities of the brain systems involved in language processing.

Fourth, the finding that Broca's patients have much greater difficulty than Wernicke's patients in speaking grammatically is more common in English-speaking than German- or Italian-speaking patients. According to Dick et al. (2001), this difference occurs because languages differ in terms of how inflected they are (inflected languages are those in which grammatical changes to nouns and verbs are indicated by changes to the words themselves). English is a less inflected language than German or Italian. As a result, the grammatical limitations of English-speaking patients with Wernicke's aphasia are less obvious than those of patients who speak more inflected languages.

Fifth, McNeil et al. (2010) claimed the traditional centres-and-pathways view focuses too much on *specific* language impairments. They argued that aphasic patients also have more *general* problems relating to attention and memory. The common finding that the language performance of aphasic patients often varies from occasion to occasion is consistent with that argument.

Weblink:
Aphasia characteristics

Hodgson and Lambon Ralph (2008) reported further supporting evidence. When healthy participants had only 500 ms to name pictures, they made errors closely resembling those of stroke aphasics with semantic impairments. These findings suggest many errors made by aphasics on picture-naming tasks occur because of reduced processing resources and/or semantic control.

In sum, the traditional approach is both oversimplified and limited. As a result, the emphasis has shifted towards systematic attempts to understand relatively specific cognitive impairments. These more specific impairments include anomia, agrammatism and jargon aphasia (all discussed below).

Anomia

Nearly all aphasics (regardless of the type of aphasia) suffer from **anomia**, which is an impaired ability to name objects. According to Levelt et al.'s (1999)

WEAVER++ model, there are two reasons why aphasics might have problems with lexicalisation (translating a word's meaning into its sound):

1 There could be problems at the *semantic* level (e.g., selecting the appropriate lemma or abstract word). In that case, naming errors would resemble the correct word in meaning.
2 There could be problems at the phonological level, in which case patients would be unable to find the appropriate form of the word.

Findings

Howard and Orchard-Lisle (1984) studied an aphasic patient, JCU, who had a semantic impairment. When she named objects shown in pictures, she often produced the wrong answer when given the first sound of a word closely related to the target object. However, if she produced a name very different in meaning from the object depicted, she rejected it 86% of the time. Thus, she had limited access to semantic information.

Kay and Ellis (1987) studied an aphasic patient, EST, who could apparently select the correct abstract word or lemma but not the word's phonological form. There seemed to be no significant impairment of his semantic system but he had great problems in finding words other than very common ones. Kay and Ellis argued that his condition resembled in magnified form the everyday tip-of-the-tongue state.

Laganaro et al. (2008) divided aphasic patients into semantic and phonological groups based on their main cognitive impairment on various tasks. Both groups were then given a picture-naming task and event-related potentials (ERPs; see Glossary) were recorded to assess the time course of processing. The semantic group had ERP abnormalities early (100–250 ms after picture onset). In contrast, the phonological group only had later abnormalities (300–450 ms after picture onset). The brain areas associated with these abnormal ERPs differed between the two groups. The take-home message is that anomia can result from an early semantic stage (finding the correct word) or a later phonological stage (generating the word's phonological form).

We have seen anomia can result from difficulties at the semantic and/or phonological levels. This is consistent with *serial* models (e.g., Levelt et al.'s WEAVER++). However, it does not rule out *interactive* models such as Dell's spreading-activation theory. Soni et al. (2009) provided relevant evidence in a study on aphasics. They used a picture-naming task under three conditions. Some pictures were presented with a correct cue (e.g., picture of a *lion* with the cue *l*). Others were presented with an incorrect cue (e.g., picture of a *lion* with the cue *t*, which misleadingly suggests tiger). In the third condition, there was no cue.

What would we expect to find? According to Levelt's model, speakers determine the name of each object *before* making use of phonological information generated by the cues. Thus, an incorrect phonological cue should not impair performance. Interactive models make the opposite prediction. Word selection can be influenced by phonological activation and this can enhance or impair performance depending on whether the cue is correct or incorrect. The findings supported interactive models over serial ones.

Soni et al. (2011) extended their earlier research. Aphasics were presented with pictures accompanied by a sound and named the picture. There were four conditions determined by the relationship between the sound and the picture. Suppose the picture was of a candle. The sound could be *l* (related category – suggests lamp), *w* (associate word – suggests wax) or neutral (*g*). The key finding was that naming performance was worse in these conditions than when the sound was *k* (suggesting the correct answer). These findings indicate (contrary to Levelt et al., 1999) that semantic processing is not necessarily complete before phonological processing starts.

KEY TERM

Agrammatism
A condition in which speech production lacks grammatical structure and many function words and word endings are omitted.

Evaluation

Much research on anomia is consistent with Levelt et al.'s (1999) notion that problems with word retrieval can occur at two different stages: (1) abstract word selection or lemma selection; and (2) accessing the phonological form of the word. However, there are two potential problems with that notion. First, a simpler explanation may well be preferable. According to this explanation, anomia occurs in patients as a fairly direct consequence of their semantic and phonological impairments. Second, there is suggestive evidence (Soni et al., 2009) that there is more interaction between semantic and phonological processing than is assumed by Levelt et al. (1999).

Agrammatism

It is often assumed that speaking involves separate stages of working out the syntax or grammatical structure of utterances and producing content words to fit that grammatical structure (e.g., Dell, 1986). Patients who can apparently find the appropriate words but not order them grammatically suffer from **agrammatism**. Patients with agrammatism typically produce short sentences containing content words (e.g., nouns, verbs) but lacking function words (e.g., the, in, and) and word endings. This is important because function words play a key role in producing a grammatical structure for sentences. In addition, patients with agrammatism often have problems with the comprehension of syntactically complex sentences.

Use of the term "agrammatism" implies it forms a syndrome in which all those with the condition have the same symptoms. It follows that we might expect syntax or grammar to be localised within the brain. There is indirect support for this expectation in that there is a relatively strong correlation between agrammatism and damage to Broca's area (BA44/45) (Cappa, 2012; see Figure 11.6). However, agrammatism is *not* a syndrome. Many patients show dissociations in which they possess some (but not all) the symptoms typical of agrammatism (Harley, 2013).

Findings

The diversity in symptoms shown by agrammatic patients can be partially explained with reference to Grodzinsky and Friederici's (2006) model of syntactic processing (see Figure 11.7). They identified three phases of syntactic processing occurring in different brain areas:

1 Local phrase structures are formed after word category information (e.g., noun; verb) has been obtained. This phase involves the frontal operculum and anterior superior temporal gyrus.

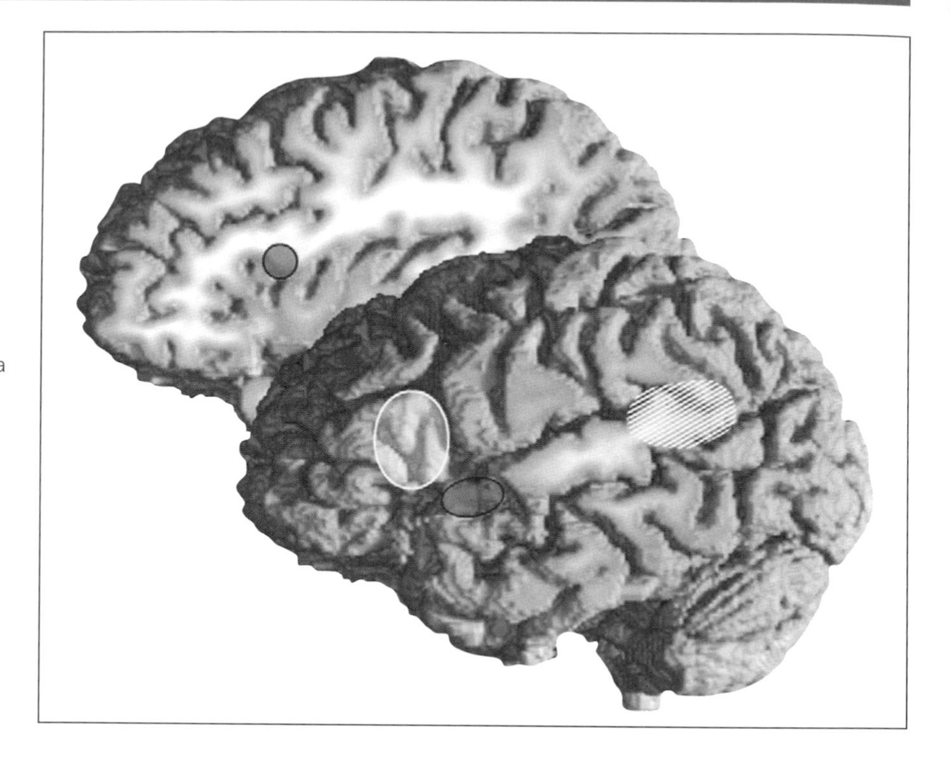

Figure 11.7
The main brain areas involved in syntactic processing. Pink areas (frontal operculum and anterior superior temporal gyrus) are involved in the build-up of local phrase structures; the yellow area (BA33/45) is involved in the computation of dependency relations between sentence components; the striped area (posterior superior temporal gyrus and sulcus) is involved in integration processes.
From Grodzinsky and Friederici (2006). Reprinted with permission from Elsevier.

2 Dependency relationships among the various sentence elements are calculated (i.e., who is doing what to whom?). This phase occurs in Broca's area (BA44/45). Friederici et al. (2006) found that activation in this area was greater with syntactically complex sentences than simple ones. Broca's area is typically damaged in patients with agrammatism.
3 Syntactic and lexical information is integrated in the posterior superior temporal gyrus and sulcus.

Agrammatic patients' speech may be ungrammatical because they lack the competence or ability to speak grammatically. Another possibility is that agrammatic patients may possess competence or ability but find it hard to use that competence to produce accurate speech. Both factors are almost certainly involved. As we will see, however, there has recently been increasing interest in the latter explanation.

Beeke et al. (2007) argued that the artificial tasks (e.g., picture descriptions) used in most research may have led researchers to *underestimate* the grammatical abilities of agrammatic patients. They studied an agrammatic patient in the laboratory and while having a conversation at home with a family member. His speech was more grammatical in the more naturalistic situation.

Burkhardt et al. (2008) wondered whether agrammatic patients have limited processing capacity specifically affecting syntactic processing. The patients were reasonably successful at resolving syntactic complexities in sentences but took a long time to do so. These findings suggest they had a processing limitation rather than loss of the necessary syntactic knowledge.

Rhys et al. (2013) studied an agrammatic patient whose language production was extremely limited. Of particular note, she made extensive use of variants

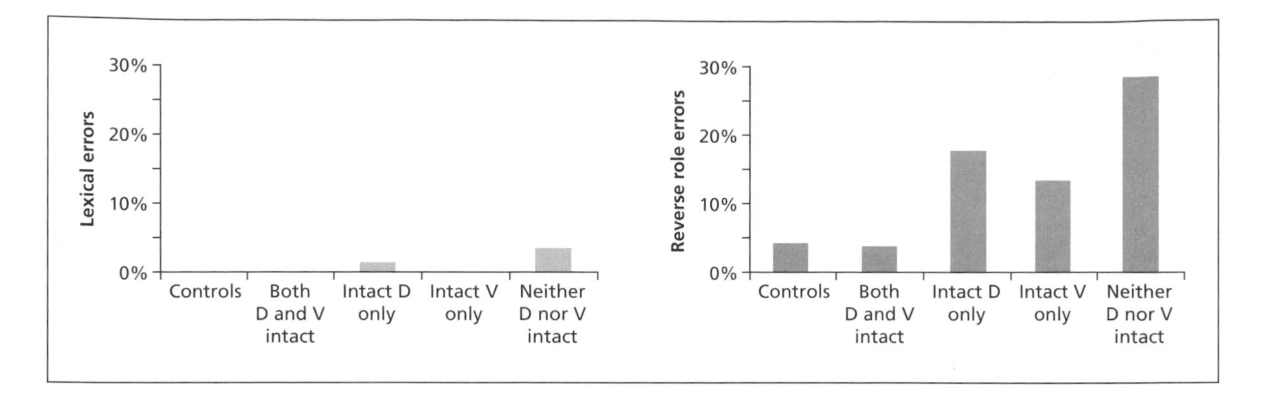

Figure 11.8
Semantic errors (left) and syntactic (right) errors made by healthy controls, patients with no damage to the dorsal (D) or ventral (V) pathway, damage to the ventral pathway only, damage to the dorsal pathway only and damage to both pathways.

From Griffiths et al. (2013). By permission of Oxford University Press.

of the phrase "very good". Close examination indicated she used prosodic cues (e.g., stress, intonation) to communicate various meanings and grammatical structures.

It has nearly always been assumed the problems of agrammatic patients relate specifically to language. However, that assumption may be incorrect. Christianson et al. (2010) found agrammatic patients showed impaired sequence learning as well as grammaticality. A deficit in sequence learning could easily lead to the production of ungrammatical sentences given the great dependence of grammaticality on appropriate word order. Thus, the deficits of agrammatic patients may be relatively *general* and not limited *specifically* to language (at least in some patients).

Griffiths et al. (2013) clarified the brain pathways involved in syntactic processing. They studied patients with damage to the dorsal pathway shown in blue in Figure 11.6 and/or to a ventral pathway also connecting Broca's area with Wernicke's area. Participants listened to sentences (e.g., "The woman is hugged by the man") and then selected one of three drawings: (1) the correct one, (2) a syntactic distractor (e.g., a woman hugging a man) and (3) a semantic distractor (e.g., a man painting a woman).

What did Griffiths et al. (2013) find? Patients with damage to either pathway or to both made many more syntactic errors than controls or patients with damage to neither pathway (see Figure 11.8). However, all patient groups made very few semantic errors and the same was the case on other semantic comprehension tasks. The take-home message is that syntactic processing for comprehension (and probably also speech production) involves two pathways linking the major language regions (Broca's area and Wernicke's area).

Evaluation

Research on agrammatism provides some support for the notion that speech production involves a syntactic level at which the grammatical structure of a sentence is formed. In addition, there is preliminary evidence (Burkhardt et al., 2008) that reduced processing resources may be involved. The research of Griffiths et al. (2013) indicates two brain pathways are necessary for effective syntactic processing.

What are the limitations of research on agrammatism? First, the symptoms of those diagnosed with agrammatism are too diverse for it to form a syndrome. Second, agrammatic patients may possess more grammatical competence than

KEY TERMS

Jargon aphasia
A brain-damaged condition in which speech is reasonably correct grammatically but there are severe problems in accessing the appropriate words.

Neologisms
Made-up words produced by patients suffering from **jargon aphasia**.

used to be assumed. Third, there is preliminary evidence (Christiansen et al., 2010) that the impairments of agrammatic patients are broader than assumed traditionally.

Jargon aphasia

Jargon aphasia "is an extreme form of fluent aphasia in which syntax is primarily intact, but speech is marked by gross word-finding difficulties" (Harley, 2013, p. 437). This pattern is apparently the opposite to that of patients with agrammatism, who can find the correct content words but cannot produce grammatically correct sentences. Jargon aphasics often substitute one word for another and also produce **neologisms**, which are made-up words. Finally, jargon aphasics have deficient self-monitoring – they are typically unaware their speech contains numerous errors and become irritated when others do not understand them.

Here is how a jargon aphasic described a picture (Sampson & Faroqui-Shah, 2011, p. 508):

> It's not a large house, it's small, unless an awful lot of it goes back behind the hose. They are whiking what they are doing in the front part which must be peeving . . . leeling . . . weeding . . . there is a nicoverit spotole for the changer.

Findings

How grammatical is the speech of jargon aphasics? If they engage in syntactic processing, their neologisms or made-up words might possess appropriate prefixes or suffixes to fit the syntactic structure of sentences. Jargon aphasics do seem to modify their neologisms in this way (Butterworth, 1985).

What determines the specific form of jargon aphasics' neologisms? Several factors are involved. First, some neologisms are phonologically related to the target word. In such cases, the target word was accessed and it is probable that such neologisms arise during subsequent phonological processing. Second, Robson et al. (2003) found the neologisms of an English-speaking jargon aphasic, LT, consisted mostly of consonants common in the English language. Third, Goldman et al. (2001) found jargon aphasics often included recently used phonemes in their neologisms – presumably these phonemes still retained some activation.

Other neologisms are almost unrelated phonologically to the target word. It is unclear whether the same mechanism is involved with neologisms related and unrelated phonologically to the target. Olson et al. (2007) studied VS, an 84-year-old woman with jargon aphasia. Her neologisms (regardless of how related phonologically they were to target words) were affected in similar ways by word frequency, imageability and word length. These findings suggest (but certainly do not prove) there may be a single underlying deficit.

How important is deficient self-monitoring in jargon aphasia? It is generally assumed it plays a major role. Sampson and Faroqi-Shah (2011) obtained two relevant findings with five jargon aphasics. First, there was a strong negative correlation between self-monitoring and their production of jargon (neologisms + real words unrelated phonologically to the target word). Second, masking noise that prevented the patients from hearing the sound of their own voice led to reduced self-monitoring and increased use of jargon. These findings suggest much of the jargon produced by jargon aphasics occurs in part because of their inadequate monitoring of what they are saying.

Eaton et al. (2011) studied the role of self-monitoring in a jargon aphasic, TK, who was studied over a 21-month period. His performance on single-word production tasks (e.g., word naming) improved over time. Of most importance, this improved performance correlated highly with increased self-monitoring. This suggests inadequate self-monitoring played a role in TK's initially poor performance.

Impaired phonological processing often plays a major role in jargon aphasia (Harley, 2013). If that is the case, then therapy designed to enhance phonological processing might improve the accuracy of speech production. Bose (2013) used such therapy (focused on generating and analysing phonological features of words) with FF, a 77-year-old man with jargon aphasia. As predicted, this therapy increased FF's naming ability and reduced the number of neologisms he produced.

Evaluation

Many neologisms produced by jargon aphasics occur because their ability to monitor their own speech is severely deficient. Their neologisms sometimes incorporate phonemes from the target word or phonemes used very recently.

What are the limitations of research in this area? First, jargon aphasia may occur because of phonological and/or semantic deficits (Harley, 2013), but the precise importance of each type of deficit remains unclear. Second, more research is needed to establish the extent of the sentences produced by jargon aphasics. Third, it is not known whether the same underlying processes are responsible for neologisms resembling or not resembling the target word phonologically. The grammaticality of the sentences produced by jargon aphasics is also unclear.

SPEECH AS COMMUNICATION

Most theories and research discussed so far possess the same limitation. This limitation was expressed succinctly by Pickering and Garrod (2004, p. 169): "Traditional mechanistic accounts of language processing derive almost entirely from the study of monologue. Yet, the most natural and basic form of language use is dialogue." In other words, speech production and speech comprehension are interwoven (Pickering & Garrod, 2013).

For most people (unless they are mentally ill), speech nearly always occurs as conversation in a social context. That has led many theorists to emphasise the importance of partner-specific processing or audience design, in which speakers tailor *what* they say and *how* they say it to the listener's needs.

Grice (1967) considered the requirements of successful communication. He proposed the Cooperative Principle, according to which speakers and listeners should try to be cooperative.

In addition, Grice (1967) proposed four maxims a speaker should heed:

1. *Maxim of relevance*: the speaker should say things relevant to the situation.
2. *Maxim of quantity*: the speaker should be as informative as necessary.
3. *Maxim of quality*: the speaker should be truthful.
4. *Maxim of manner*: the speaker should make his/her contribution easy to understand.

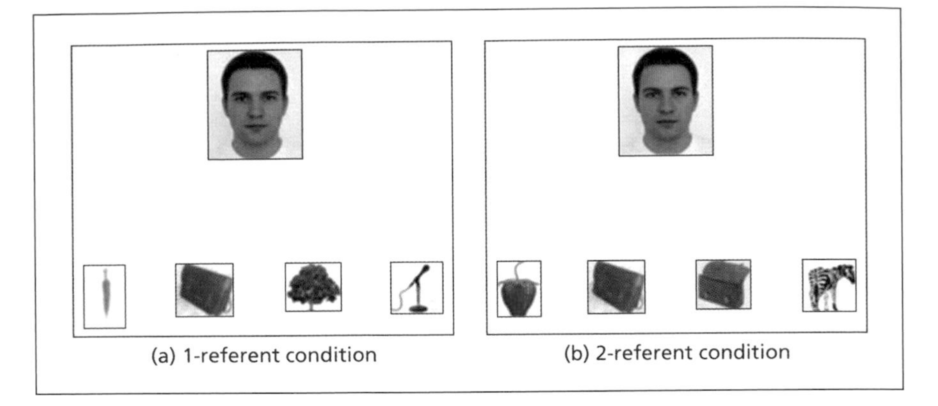

Figure 11.9
The task involved asking a hypothetical listener (shown in the photograph) to pass them a given object (here the second item from the left). The task is more complex when a second bag is visible ((b) 2-referent condition) than when only one bag is visible ((a) 1-referent condition).

From Davies and Katsos (2013). Reprinted with permission from Elsevier.

Grice's approach is reasonable. However, there are two issues with it. First, it is not clear we need four maxims – the other three maxims are implied by the maxim of relevance. Second, in the real world, some individuals (e.g., second-hand car salesmen, politicians) are guided by self-interest and so ignore one or more of the maxims (Faulkner, 2008). Thus, individuals' motives and goals may distort what they say.

Speakers (even those not guided by self-interest) often fail to adhere to Grice's four maxims. Suppose a speaker wants his/her listener to put an apple in a box. If only one apple is present, it follows from the maxim of quantity that speakers should say something like, "Put the apple in the box." In fact, in one study 30% of the time speakers produced an unnecessarily detailed sentence (e.g., "Put the apple on the towel in the box") (Engelhardt et al., 2006).

Davies and Katsos (2013) argued that the visual displays used by Engelhardt et al. (2006) were relatively complex, and this may have led speakers to be overinformative. In their own study, Davies and Katsos (2013) used simpler arrays (see Figure 11.9). The participants were instructed to ask a hypothetical listener to pass them a given item. Adherence to the maxim of quantity would have led speakers to say, "Pass me the bag" in the 1-referent condition and "Pass me the closed bag" in the 2-referent condition. That is what happened on 90% of trials in both conditions. In sharp contrast to Engelhardt et al.'s findings, speakers displayed overinformativeness on only 8% of trials.

Audience design and common ground

Speakers need to take account of the specific needs of their listener(s) for communication to be maximally effective. This is known as **audience design**. For example, communication can be facilitated by establishing and extending common ground (see Glossary and Chapter 9). Common ground "includes representations of information that is physically co-present (e.g., both partners can see it), information that is linguistically co-present (e.g., information that was mentioned in the discourse), as well as information about cultural or community membership" (Brown-Schmidt, 2012, p. 63).

Speakers typically make various assumptions about the listener when establishing common ground. There are *global* assumptions (e.g., the listener's preferred language, the listener's general knowledge, shared personal experiences). There are also *local* assumptions concerning what the listener knows (or is

KEY TERM

Audience design
This involves speakers tailoring what they say to the specific needs of their audience.

attending to) at any given moment. Speakers are more likely to make incorrect local assumptions than global ones because the former keep changing (Arnold, 2008).

There is controversy concerning the extent to which speakers actually use audience design and common ground. Horton and Keysar (1996) proposed the monitoring and adjustment model. According to this model, speakers plan their utterances initially using information available to them *without* considering the listener's perspective or knowledge. These plans are then monitored and corrected to incorporate the common ground.

Horton and Keysar (1996) assumed it is often computationally difficult for speakers to focus on the listener's perspective while planning what to say next. If so, how do speakers generally communicate reasonably effectively? According to Shintel and Keysar (2009, p. 21), speakers do so "by relying on powerful, simple, and cheap cues". One such cue is whether the listener is new or old – if the listener is new, the speaker can express information more clearly than if the listener is old. Another cue (often not used deliberately) is for speakers to fixate the object they are talking about.

Findings

Speakers sometimes fail to use audience design, simply producing utterances that are easy for them to say (Ferreira, 2008). Fukumura and van Gompel (2012) reported evidence that speakers do not always take account of listeners' knowledge. Speakers typically use a noun phrase (e.g., "the red desk") the first time an object is mentioned but a pronoun (e.g., "it") in the next sentence. However, it is only appropriate to use a pronoun in the second sentence provided the listener has heard the previous sentence.

Fukumura and van Gompel (2012) found speakers generally used a pronoun in the second sentence even when the listener had *not* heard the previous sentence. Thus, the speakers focused on their own speaker-centred processes and paid little or no attention to audience design.

It is often cognitively demanding to take account of the listener's perspective. Accordingly, we might expect that the ability to do so would depend on speakers' inhibitory control (an executive function related to intelligence; see Chapter 6). Wardlow (2013) obtained a correlation of +0.42 between perspective-taking ability and inhibitory control.

We have focused so far on problems speakers have in communicating effectively. However, there are various simple strategies they can (and do) use. Speakers often copy words, phrases and ideas they heard when the other person was speaking. Thus, the other person's words serve as a prime or prompt.

A very common example of speakers copying aspects of what the other person said previously is **syntactic priming**. Syntactic priming occurs when a previously experienced syntactic structure influences the speaker's current processing. If you have just heard a passive sentence (e.g., "The man was bitten by the dog"), this increases the chance you will produce a passive sentence. Syntactic priming occurs even when you are talking about a different topic and it does not require conscious awareness of copying a previous syntactic structure (Pickering & Ferreira, 2008).

Why do speakers make extensive use of syntactic priming? One reason is that it reduces demands on speech production. Another reason was identified by

KEY TERM

Syntactic priming
The tendency for a speaker's utterances to have the same syntactic structure as those they have heard shortly beforehand.

Jaeger and Snider (2013). Speakers were most likely to show syntactic priming when the last sentence they heard contained an *unexpected* syntactic structure. Speakers strive to "get on the same wavelength" as the person with whom they are talking and this helps to achieve that goal.

Galati and Brennan (2010) argued that the probability of speakers focusing on audience design is highest when the listener's needs are clear and simple. For example, bilingual speakers in conversation with a monolingual listener generally find it very easy to confine themselves to speaking the language their listener understands.

Galati and Brennan (2010) asked speakers to tell the same cartoon story twice to one listener and once to a different listener. They predicted speakers would be responsive to the listener's needs because it was so easy for them to tell whether he/she had heard the story before. As predicted, speakers used fewer words and included less detail when the listeners had heard the story before than when they had not. In addition, speakers spoke more intelligibly when telling the story to listeners to whom it was new. Thus, speakers can show a high level of audience design in what they say and the way they say it.

Gesture

Most speakers use various gestures. It is generally assumed they do this because they believe it will increase their ability to communicate with their listener(s). This belief is correct (see Chapter 9).

Human communication probably depended on gestures in our ancestral past and it was only much later that vocalisation emerged. The fact primate gestures resemble human language much more closely than do primate vocalisations supports that viewpoint (Cartmill et al., 2012).

Findings

If speakers use gestures to communicate, we might assume they would gesture more frequently when they can see the listener than when they cannot. In fact, 50% of studies obtained this finding but the effects of listener visibility were non-significant in the other 50% (Bavelas & Healing, 2013).

Gerwing and Allison (2011) asked speakers to describe an elaborate dress to a listener who was visible or not visible (on the telephone). The number of gestures did not vary in the two conditions, but the gestures used by speakers in the face-to-face situation were much more informative. In that situation, 74% of the information communicated by speakers was in the form of gestures and only 26% via speech. In contrast, only 27% of the information communicated in the telephone situation was gestural with the remaining 73% coming from speech.

How responsive are speakers to feedback from listeners? Holler and Wilkin (2011) compared speakers' gestures before and after listener feedback. There were two main findings:

1 The number of gestures reduced when the listener indicated understanding of what had been said.
2 Feedback encouraging clarification, elaboration or correction was followed by more precise, larger or more visually prominent gestures.

We have seen that speakers are *flexible* in terms of how much information they communicate via gestures and are also *responsive* to the listener's needs. Why do speakers use gestures when their listener cannot see those gestures? The mystery deepens with the additional finding that speakers blind since birth use gestures even when speaking to blind listeners (Iverson & Goldin-Meadow, 1998). Gestures make it easier for speakers to communicate what they want to say. Frick-Horbury and Guttentag (1998) presented participants with the definitions of relatively uncommon words (e.g., *tambourine*) and they said the word defined. When it was hard to use gestures, 21% fewer words were produced compared to a condition in which speakers were free to use gestures.

In sum, gestures often form an important accompaniment to speech. Speakers use gestures because they make it easier to work out what they want to say and also because they facilitate communication with their listener. As we saw in Chapter 9, listeners generally find it easier to understand speakers when they use gestures.

KEY TERM

Prosodic cues
Features of spoken language such as stress, intonation and duration that make it easier for listeners to work out grammatical structure and meaning.

Prosodic cues

Some information that speakers communicate to listeners does not depend directly on the words themselves but rather on *how* those words are uttered. This is prosody, which describes "systematic modifications to the way that speakers utter words in order to specify or disambiguate the meaning of an utterance" (Cvejic et al., 2012, p. 442).

Prosodic cues include rhythm, stress and intonation. For example, in the ambiguous sentence, "The old men and women sat on the bench", the women may or may not be old. If the women aren't old, the spoken duration of the word "men" should be relatively long and the stressed syllable in "women" will have a steep rise in pitch contour. Neither prosodic feature will be present if the sentence means the women are old. The extent to which listeners' comprehension of spoken language is enhanced by prosodic cues is discussed in Chapter 9.

Snedeker and Trueswell (2003) argued that prosodic cues are much more likely to be provided when the meaning of an ambiguous sentence is not clarified by the context. Speakers said ambiguous sentences (e.g., "Tap the frog with the flower": you either use the flower to tap the frog or you tap the frog that has the flower). They provided many more prosodic cues when the context was consistent with both interpretations.

Suppose speakers produce prosodic cues that resolve syntactic ambiguities. Does that necessarily mean speakers are responsive to their listeners' needs? According to Kraljic and Brennan (2005), it does not. In their study, speakers made extensive use of prosodic cues, and listeners successfully used these cues to disambiguate what they heard. However, speakers consistently produced prosodic cues regardless of whether the listener needed them and whether they realised the listener needed disambiguating cues.

What do the above findings mean? First, speakers' use of prosodic cues did *not* indicate any particular responsiveness to their listener (i.e., audience design). Second, prosodic cues were probably used because they emerged out of speaker-centred processes while speakers planned what they wanted to communicate.

In sum, speakers often make considerable use of prosodic cues. This often reflects audience design, but sometimes it depends mostly on speaker-centred planning processes (Wagner & Watson, 2010).

KEY TERM

Discourse markers
Spoken words and phrases that do not contribute directly to the content of what is being said but still serve various functions (e.g., clarifying the speaker's intentions).

Research activity:
Discourse markers

Discourse markers

A final way speakers enhance listener comprehension is with discourse markers. **Discourse markers** are words or phrases that assist communication even though they are only indirectly relevant to the speaker's message.

Listeners' interpretations of discourse markers are generally accurate. For example, speakers use the discourse markers *oh* and *um* to indicate problems in deciding what to say next. Listeners realise that is what speakers mean (Tree, 2007). In similar fashion, listeners understand that speakers say *you know* when they wish to check for understanding and to connect with them.

Bolden (2006) considered which of the discourse markers *oh* and *so* speakers use when moving on to a new conversational topic. The word *oh* was used 98.5% of the time when the new topic directly concerned the *speaker*. In contrast, *so* was used 96% of the time when of most relevance to the *listener*. You almost certainly do the same, but probably without realising. There are several other uses of the word *so*, including to indicate the consequences of what has just been said (Buysse, 2012).

WRITING: THE MAIN PROCESSES

Writing is an important topic in its own right (no pun intended!), but it is important to realise it is not separate from other cognitive activities. As Kellogg and Whiteford (2012, p. 111) pointed out:

> Composing extended texts is at once a severe test of memory, language, and thinking ability. It depends on the rapid retrieval of domain-specific knowledge about the topic from long-term memory. It depends on a high degree of verbal ability . . . It depends on the ability to think clearly.

It is thus probable writing expertise correlates at least moderately with general intelligence or IQ.

Key processes

Writing extended texts involves several processes. There have been minor disagreements about the nature and number of these processes (Hayes & Chenoweth, 2006; Hayes, 2012). However, most theorists agree with Hayes and Flower (1986) that writing involves the following three processes:

1. a *planning* process that involves producing ideas and organising them to satisfy the writer's goals;
2. a *sentence-generation* process that involves turning the writing plan into the actual production of sentences;
3. a *revision process* that involves evaluating what has been written or word processed so far and revising it as and when necessary.

Chenoweth and Hayes (2003) developed Hayes and Flower's (1986) theoretical approach. Their model identifies four processes:

1. *Proposer*: This proposes ideas for expression and is engaged in higher-level processes of planning.

IN THE REAL WORLD: EFFECTS OF ALZHEIMER'S DISEASE ON NOVEL WRITING

Iris Murdoch. © Sophie Bassouls/Sygma/Corbis.

We saw earlier in the chapter that mild cognitive impairment (often a precursor to Alzheimer's disease – see Glossary) is associated with various problems in speech production. In view of the cognitive complexities of effective writing, it seems probable that mild cognitive impairment would also impair writing performance.

Research has been carried out on Iris Murdoch (see photo), the renowned Irish novelist who was diagnosed with Alzheimer's disease. Garrard et al. (2005) compared her first published work, a novel written during her prime and her final novel. Iris Murdoch's vocabulary became progressively less sophisticated (e.g., smaller vocabulary, more common words) across these three works, but changes in syntax were less clear-cut. Subsequent research by Pakhomov et al. (2011) provided some evidence that the syntactic complexity of Irish Murdoch's writing decreased over time. Thus, aspects of Iris Murdoch's writing were adversely affected several years before she was diagnosed with Alzheimer's disease during a period in which she probably had mild cognitive impairment.

Le et al. (2011) carried out a detailed longitudinal analysis of the writings of Iris Murdoch, Agatha Christie (who was suspected of having Alzheimer's disease towards the end of her life) and P.D. James (a novelist with no signs of cognitive impairment or Alzheimer's disease). They confirmed previous findings that there were signs of impairment in Iris Murdoch's writing a considerable time before she was diagnosed with Alzheimer's disease.

Le et al. (2011) also found Agatha Christie's last novels indicated that she probably suffered the onset of Alzheimer's disease. The writing impairments of Agatha Christie and Iris Murdoch both involved vocabulary much more than syntax. More specifically, they both showed a sharp decrease in vocabulary size, increased repetition of phrases and irrelevant filler words or phrases.

In sum, there are detectable impairments in the writing of novelists probably suffering from mild cognitive impairment. These impairments can provide an early indication of Alzheimer's disease, and probably reflect in part the cognitive complexity of writing. Note, however, that even the onset of Alzheimer's disease has only modest effects on syntax. Thus, cognitive impairment affects the *content* of what is written more than its grammatical *structure*.

2 *Translator*: This converts the message formed by the proposer into word strings (e.g., sentences).
3 *Transcriber*: This converts the word strings into written or word-processed text.
4 *Evaluator/reviser*: This monitors and evaluates what has been produced and engages in revision of deficiencies.

The main difference between the two approaches above is that Chenoweth and Hayes (2003) added a transcriber to Hayes and Flower's (1986) theory.

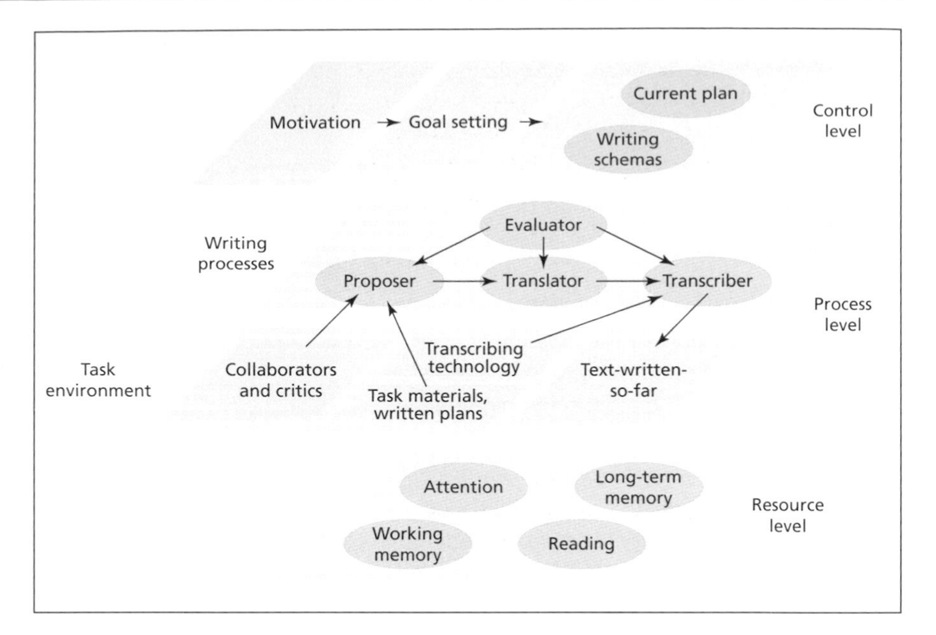

Figure 11.10
Hayes' (2012) writing model. It consists of three levels: (1) control level (including motivation and goal setting); (2) writing process level (including proposer, evaluator, translator and transcriber); and (3) resource level (including working memory, attention and long-term memory).

From Hayes (2012). Reprinted by permission of SAGE Publications.

Why did they do that? Hayes and Flower assumed transcribing (writing sentences already composed) required practically no processing resources and so had no impact on other writing processes. However, there is much evidence that assumption is incorrect. For example, Hayes and Chenoweth (2006) asked participants to transcribe or copy texts from one computer window to another. They transcribed more slowly and made more errors when performing a very simple task (saying *tap* repeatedly) at the same time.

The latest version of Hayes' writing model is shown in Figure 11.10. It incorporates the four writing processes identified by Chenoweth and Hayes (2003). It is more comprehensive than previous versions in that it includes a control level, task environment and resource level in addition to the process level. Of importance, the current version includes motivation as a factor. Writing effectively is so demanding (as the authors of this book know to their cost!) that high motivation is required to engage in prolonged evaluation and revision of what has been written.

The "natural" sequence of the four main writing processes is obviously the order described above. However, as we will see, writers surprisingly often deviate from this sequence, switching rapidly between processes.

Findings

We can identify the processes used in writing by using **directed retrospection**. Writers are stopped at various times during the writing process and indicate what they were just doing (e.g., planning). Kellogg (1994) reviewed studies involving directed retrospection. On average, writers devoted 30% of their time to planning, 50% to sentence generation and 20% to revision. Kellogg (1988) found writers who produced an outline focusing on the main themes spent more time in sentence generation than no-outline writers. However, they spent less time in planning and reviewing or revising.

KEY TERM

Directed retrospection
A technique in which individuals (e.g., writers) categorise their immediately preceding thoughts.

Kaufer et al. (1986) asked writers to think aloud. Expert and average writers accepted 75% of the sentence parts they verbalised. Average sentence part was 11.2 words for expert writers compared to 7.3 words for average writers. Thus, good writers use larger units or "building blocks".

Levy and Ransdell (1995) asked writers to verbalise what they were doing and also obtained video recordings as they wrote essays on computers. The time spent on any given process before switching to a different one was often very short. It averaged 7.5 seconds for text generation, but was only 2.5 seconds for planning, reviewing and revising.

Levy and Ransdell (1995) found writers were only partially aware of how they allocated time. Most underestimated the time spent on generating text and overestimated time spent on reviewing and revising (estimate = 30%; actual = 5%!).

Beauvais et al. (2011) also found writers switch rapidly between different processes. Participants wrote a narrative and an argumentative text. The narrative text involved telling a story about six coloured pictures and the argumentative text required writers to defend their opinion concerning a law banning smoking in public places.

Writers on average switched writing processes about eight times a minute with narrative texts and six times a minute with argumentative texts. Each episode of translating lasted on average 16 seconds (narrative text) or 17 seconds (argumentative text), planning 8 seconds (narrative text) or 12 seconds (argumentative text) and revision (4 seconds for both texts). Thus, as Levy and Ransdell (1995) found, episodes of planning and revising were shorter than those of translating or text generation.

How do writers make decisions about switching processes? According to Hayes and Flower (1980), writers have a *monitor* controlling their processing activities. This monitor closely resembles the central executive component of the working memory model (see Chapter 6). Two functions of the central executive are to switch attention between tasks and to inhibit unwanted responses.

Quinlan et al. (2012) argued that the monitor requires working-memory resources. As a result, it is less likely to trigger a switch in the current task when overall processing demands are high. In the first experiment, participants chose whether to complete a sentence before correcting an error or interrupt sentence composing to focus on the error. The great majority of the participants completed the sentence first, and this tendency was increased when the total processing demands were high.

Evaluation

Processes resembling planning, sentence generation and revision are all crucial in writing. However, these processes cannot be neatly separated because writers typically move rapidly among these processes (Levy & Ransdell, 1995; Beauvais et al., 2011). Writers probably possess a monitor that is more likely to initiate processing shifts when overall processing demands are relatively low (Quinlan et al., 2012).

What are the limitations with research in this area? First, little is known about the factors determining when writers shift from one process to another. Second, most research has de-emphasised the social aspect of much writing. As is discussed shortly, writers need to take account of the intended readership for the texts they

KEY TERM

Knowledge effect
The tendency to assume others possess the same knowledge as us.

produce during every stage of writing. Third, the processes involved in writing and the precise ways they interact are not specified with any precision in most models. For example, Hayes (2012; Figure 11.10) fails to indicate how the four resources relate to writing processes.

Writing expertise

Why are some writers more skilful than others? As with any complex cognitive skill, extensive and deliberate practice is essential (see Chapter 12). In the next section, we will see the working memory system (see Chapter 6) is very important in writing. All its components have limited capacity, and the demands of writing on these components generally decrease with practice. That provides experienced writers with spare processing capacity to enhance their writing quality.

Unsurprisingly, individuals with high levels of writing expertise generally have more reading experience. They also have higher reading ability as assessed by comprehension tests (Daane, 1991). There are various reasons for this. First, reading allows writers to learn much about the structure and style of good writing. Second, it enhances their vocabulary and knowledge, which can then be incorporated into the texts they write. However, most evidence is correlational, so the extent to which writing expertise is *caused* by reading experience remains unclear.

Bereiter and Scardamalia (1987) identified two major strategies used by writers. First, there is the knowledge-telling strategy, which involves them simply writing down all they know about a topic with minimal planning. The text already produced provides retrieval cues for generating subsequent text.

Second, there is the knowledge-transforming strategy. This involves using a rhetorical problem space and a content problem space. Rhetorical problems relate to the achievement of the goals of the writing task (e.g., "Can I strengthen the argument?"). In contrast, content problems relate to the specific information to be written down (e.g., "The case of Smith vs. Jones strengthens the argument"). Information should move in both directions between the rhetorical and content spaces.

Bereiter and Scardamalia (1987) argued that expert writers make increased use of the knowledge-transforming strategy. Kellogg (2008) and Kellogg and Whiteford (2012) developed this approach (see Figure 11.11). They argued that really expert writers move beyond the knowledge-transforming strategy to use a knowledge-crafting strategy. With this strategy, "The writer shapes what to say and how to say it with the potential reader fully in mind. The writer tries to anticipate different ways that the reader might interpret the text and takes these into account in revising it" (Kellogg & Whiteford, 2012, p. 116).

The knowledge-crafting stage focuses on the reader's needs. One reason this is important is because of the **knowledge effect** – writers tend to assume other people share the knowledge they possess. Hayes and Bajzek (2008) found individuals familiar with technical terms greatly overestimated other people's knowledge of these terms (does this failing afflict the authors of this book?).

Findings

Expert writers are more likely than non-expert ones to use the knowledge-transforming strategy (Kellogg & Whiteford, 2012). Why is this strategy

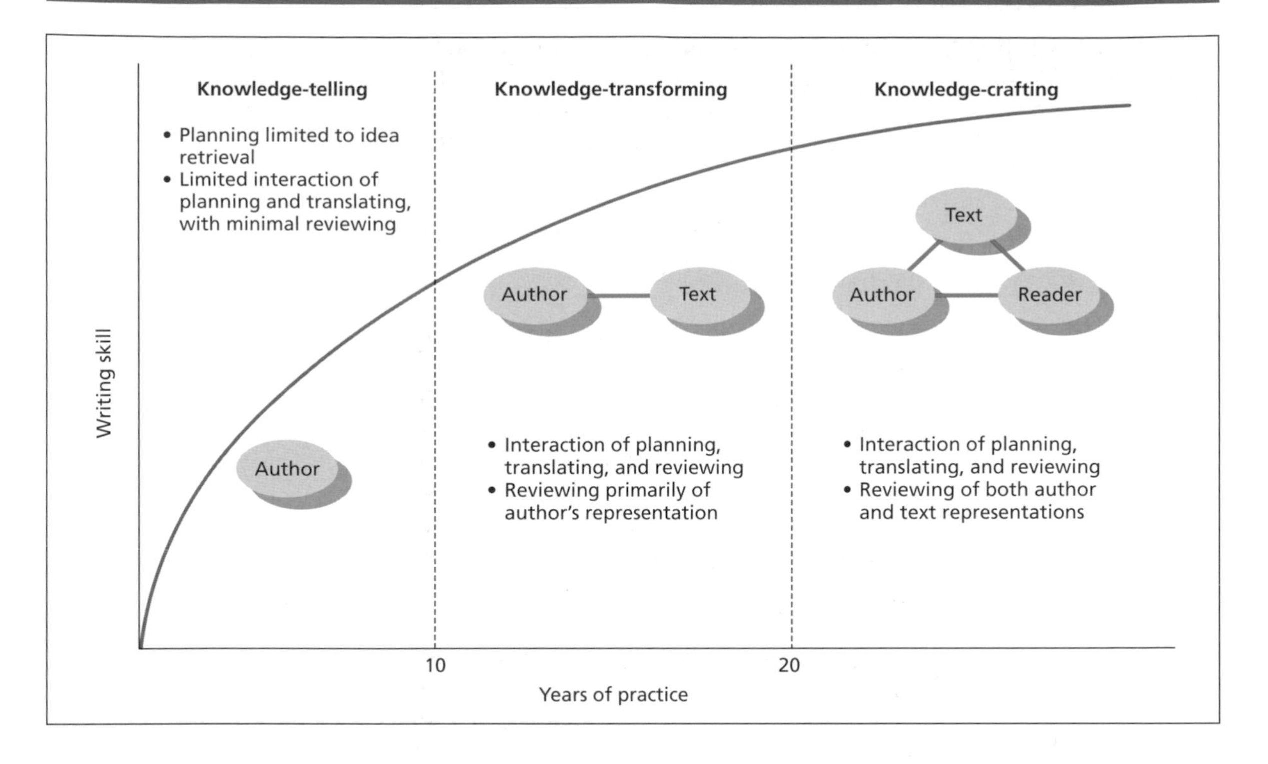

Figure 11.11
Kellogg's three-stage theory of the development of writing skill.

From Kellogg (2008). Reprinted with permission of the *Journal of Writing Research*, www.jowr.org.

successful? Writers using it show extensive *interactions* among planning, language generation and reviewing. In addition, writers using the knowledge-transforming strategy produce more high-level main points capturing important themes (Bereiter et al., 1988). This provides what they write with more structure and coherence.

Chuy et al. (2012) pointed out that the knowledge-transforming strategy involves a content problem space. Accordingly, they argued that writers would benefit from the opportunity to enhance their knowledge. This was achieved by having a Knowledge Forum, allowing students to write down their own ideas, comment on others' ideas and raise challenging questions. Writers with access to the Knowledge Forum produced essays that were more coherent and easier to read and understand.

Kellogg and Whiteford (2012, p. 109) argued that "there is no such thing as an expert writer, when conceived as a generalist capable of writing across any number of domains". Two reasons support this argument. First, expert writing depends partly on the amount of relevant knowledge a writer possesses.

Second, the requirements of expert writing vary depending on the type of text (e.g., an advanced textbook vs. a children's story). Earlier we discussed a study by Beauvais et al. (2011) in which moderately expert writers produced narrative and argumentative texts. They engaged in more knowledge-telling with the narrative than the argumentative texts, while the opposite was the case with the argumentative text.

Expert writers spend more time revising than non-expert ones and identify problems more successfully. Levy and Ransdell (1995) found writers producing the best essays spent 40% more of their time in reviewing and revising their essays than those producing the worst essays. Expert writers detected 60% more problems in a text than non-experts (Hayes et al., 1985).

Research activity:
Knowledge telling

Weblink:
Olive (2003)

The most expert writers use knowledge-crafting, which involves being responsive to the reader's needs. Such responsiveness can be improved. Holliway and McCutcheon (2004) found text revisions made by students were improved by the instruction to "read as the reader". Sato and Matsushima (2006) found a more effective approach was to provide student writers with feedback from readers about the comprehension problems they had experienced.

Working memory

Most people find writing difficult and effortful because it involves several different cognitive processes (e.g., attention, thinking, memory). Several theorists claim writers make extensive use of working memory (see Chapter 6 and Figure 6.3) to deal with these complexities. Kellogg and Whiteford (2012) and Olive (2012) have provided reviews of research on working memory and writing performance.

Working memory is used when a task requires temporary storage of some information while other information is processed. That is clearly the case with writing – writers have to remember what they have just written while planning what they are going to write next.

The key component of the working memory system is the central executive, an attention-like process involved in organising and coordinating cognitive activities. Other components of the working memory system are the visuo-spatial sketchpad (involved in visual and spatial processing) and the phonological loop (involved in verbal rehearsal). All these components have limited capacity. This can easily cause problems with the writing process, which is often very cognitively demanding.

Writing can involve any (or all) of these working memory components. Kellogg (2001) linked these components to five processes involved in writing (see Table 11.1). These processes overlap with those identified by Chenoweth and Hayes (2003; described earlier). Planning corresponds to the proposing process, translating to the translating process, programming is part of the transcribing process, and reading and editing together form the evaluating/revising process (reading involves going back over what has been written so far).

Findings

As you can see from Table 11.1, Kellogg (2001) assumed the central executive is the component of working memory of greatest importance for writing performance. How can we assess the involvement of the central executive in writing? We can measure reaction times to auditory probes presented in isolation (control condition) or while participants are engaged in writing. If writing uses much of the capacity of the central executive, reaction times should be longer in the writing condition. Kellogg found probe reaction times were much slower for planning, translating, programming and reviewing than under control conditions, and this was especially the case for the reading component of reviewing.

Kellogg et al. (2013) reconsidered the information contained in Table 11.1 and decided the phonological loop is actually involved in the editing process. Research by Hayes and Chenoweth (2006; discussed earlier) showed that error correction while copying text was slowed down when the phonological loop was required for another task. However, research since 2001 has amply confirmed the key role of the central executive in writing.

TABLE 11.1 INVOLVEMENT OF WORKING MEMORY COMPONENTS IN VARIOUS WRITING PROCESSES

Process	Visuo-spatial sketchpad	Central executive	Phonological loop
Planning	yes	yes	–
Translating	–	yes	yes
Programming	–	yes	–
Reading	–	yes	yes
Editing	yes	–	–

Source: based on Kellogg (2001).

KEY TERM

Dysexecutive agraphia Severely impaired writing abilities in individuals with damage to the frontal lobes whose central executive functioning is generally impaired.

Vanderberg and Swanson (2007) adopted an individual-difference approach to assess the involvement of the central executive in writing. Students wrote stories and their performance was divided into *general* writing skills (e.g., planning, translating, and revision) and *specific* skills (e.g., grammar, punctuation).

What did Vanderberg and Swanson (2007) find? Individuals with the most effective central executive functioning had the best writing performance at the general and specific levels. In contrast, individual differences in the functioning of the visuo-spatial sketchpad and the phonological loop did not significantly affect performance.

Connelly et al. (2012) studied essay-writing performance in children assessed for working memory capacity (an approximate measure of central executive functioning; see Glossary). Essay quality was predicted by working memory capacity.

Another approach is to study brain-damaged individuals with impaired central executive functioning. Such individuals (who typically have damage to the frontal lobes) are said to have dysexecutive syndrome (see Glossary and Chapter 6). Ardila and Surloff (2006) argued with supporting evidence that many patients with dysexecutive syndrome have difficulties planning and organising their ideas on writing tasks and in maintaining attention. They proposed the term **dysexecutive agraphia** to refer to such patients.

Sitek et al. (2014) studied two pairs of siblings with fronto-temporal dementia, a disease involving severe cognitive impairment. All four participants had dysexecutive agraphia. It was noteworthy that progressive deterioration in their writing skills was closely linked to increasing impairment in more general cognitive abilities.

What role does the phonological loop play in writing? Chenoweth and Hayes (2003) asked participants to perform the task of typing sentences to describe cartoons on its own or while repeating a syllable continuously. Syllable repetition is an articulatory suppression task using the resources of the phonological loop. It caused writers to produce shorter sequences of words, suggesting it suppressed their "inner voice".

Earlier we discussed a study by Hayes and Chenoweth (2006) in which participants transcribed or copied texts. When this was performed while they performed an articulatory suppression task, task performance slowed down. This suggests transcription (including editing for errors) makes use of the phonological loop.

Participants in a study by Colombo et al. (2009) wrote down three- and four-syllable words presented auditorily or visually. Their ability to produce the component parts of each word in the correct serial order was impaired when performing an articulatory suppression task at the same time.

The above findings show the phonological loop is often used on writing tasks. However, it is unclear that writing performance *necessarily* depends on the involvement of the phonological loop. For example, some patients with a severely impaired phonological loop nevertheless have essentially intact written language (Gathercole & Baddeley, 1993).

What role does the visuo-spatial sketchpad play in writing? Relevant research was reviewed by Olive & Passerault (2012). Kellogg et al. (2007) asked students to write descriptions of concrete (e.g., *house*, *pencil*) and abstract (e.g., *freedom*, *duty*) nouns while detecting visual stimuli. The writing task slowed detection times only when concrete words were being described, indicating the visuo-spatial sketchpad is more involved when writers are thinking about concrete objects.

The evidence indicates relatively separate visual and spatial processes occur within the visuo-spatial sketchpad (see Chapter 6). This raises the issue of whether both processes are involved in writing. Olive et al. (2008) asked students to write a text while performing a visual or spatial task. The findings indicated visual and spatial processes were both involved in writing.

As mentioned earlier, Kellogg (2001) argued that the visuo-spatial sketchpad is used during planning and editing. Galbraith et al. (2005) tested this hypothesis. Participants searched for ideas, structured those ideas into a plan and finally generated texts. Performance of a spatial task reduced the number of ideas generated and impaired the structuring of ideas more than performance of a visual task.

Evaluation

The main writing processes are very demanding and effortful and make substantial demands on working memory. Individuals with high working memory capacity have good general and specific writing skills. The central executive is heavily involved in most writing processes. There is also convincing evidence that the visuo-spatial sketchpad and phonological loop are both involved in the writing process. The visuo-spatial sketchpad is involved in planning and editing and the phonological loop seems to be of relevance to various writing processes.

What are the limitations of theory and research on working memory in writing? First, it is not entirely clear *why* processes such as planning, sentence generation and revising are so demanding of processing resources. Second, very little research has focused on the role of working memory in determining *when* and *why* writers shift from one writing process to another. Preliminary evidence (Quinlan et al., 2012; discussed earlier) suggests switching of processes is less likely when overall demands on working memory are high. Third, it would be useful to know more about how the various components of working memory *interact* in the writing process.

Word processing

Word processing using computers has increased substantially in recent years. This has proved beneficial because it promotes use of the revision process (Lee &

Stankov, 2012). Goldberg et al. (2003) carried out meta-analyses (combining findings from many studies) to compare writing performance when students used word processors or wrote in longhand. Here are their conclusions: "Students who use computers when learning to write are not only more engaged in their writing but they produce work that is of greater length and higher quality" (Goldberg et al., 2003, p. 1).

Are there any disadvantages associated with word processing? Kellogg and Mueller (1993) found word processing involves more effortful planning and revision (but not sentence generation) than writing in longhand. Those using word processors were much less likely than those writing in longhand to make notes (12% vs. 69%, respectively), which may explain the findings.

SPELLING

Spelling is an important aspect of writing and has attracted considerable research interest. Brain areas involved were identified by Planton et al. (2013) using a meta-analytic approach (see Figure 11.12). Three main areas were consistently activated during handwriting tasks:

Weblink:
Improve your essay writing

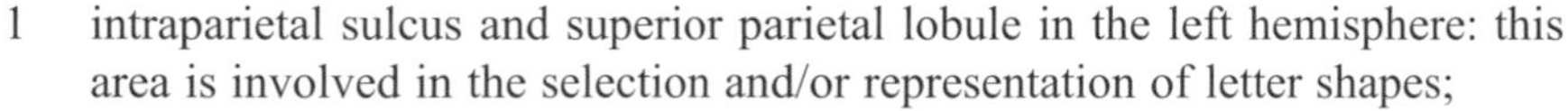

1. intraparietal sulcus and superior parietal lobule in the left hemisphere: this area is involved in the selection and/or representation of letter shapes;

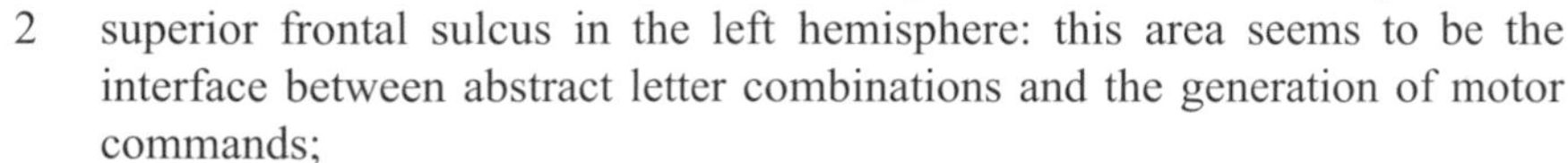

2. superior frontal sulcus in the left hemisphere: this area seems to be the interface between abstract letter combinations and the generation of motor commands;
3. posterior cerebellum in the right hemisphere: this area is probably most involved in motor activity.

As Planton et al. (2013) pointed out, the above areas probably form part of various much more extensive brain networks associated with handwriting.

Rapp and Dufor (2011) provided a fairly detailed theoretical sketch map of the main processes and structures involved in spelling heard words (see Figure 11.13):

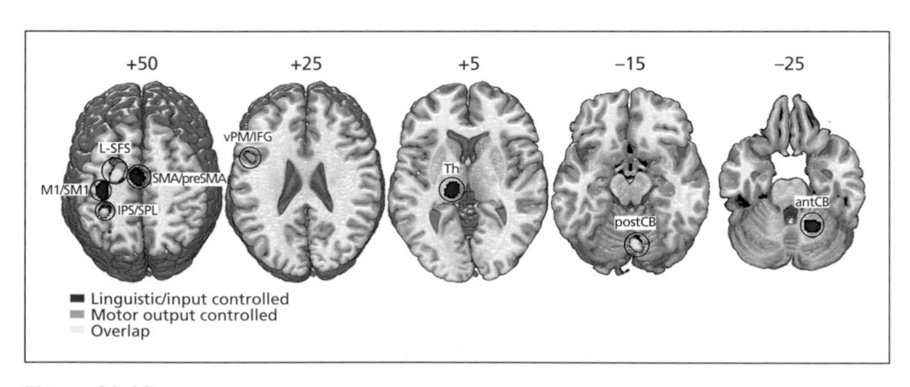

Figure 11.12
Brain areas activated during handwriting tasks controlling for verbal or linguistic input (red) or motor output (green). The areas in yellow are controlled for both and so provide an indication of handwriting-specific brain regions. Abbreviations: IPS, intraparietal sulcus; SPL, superior parietal lobe; SFS, superior frontal sulcus; post CB, posterior cerebellum.

From Planton et al. (2013). Reprinted with permission from Elsevier.

KEY TERMS

Graphemic buffer
A store in which graphemic information about the individual letters in a word is held immediately prior to spelling the word.

Phonological dysgraphia
A condition caused by brain damage in which familiar words can be spelled reasonably well but non-words cannot.

- There are two main routes between hearing a word and spelling it:
  1. the lexical route (left-hand side of the figure);
  2. the non-lexical route (right-hand side).
- The lexical route contains the information needed to relate phonological (sound), semantic (meaning), and orthographic (reading) representations of words to each other. This route to spelling a heard word involves accessing detailed information about all features of the word. Orthographic information (information about spellings) is contained in orthographic long-term memory (often called the orthographic lexicon).

  It is the main route we use with familiar words regardless of whether the relationship between the sound units (phonemes) and units of written language (graphemes) is regular (e.g., *cat*) or irregular (e.g., *yacht*).
- The non-lexical route does *not* involve gaining access to detailed information about the sound, meaning and spelling of heard words. Instead, this route uses stored rules to convert sounds or phonemes into groups of letters or graphemes. We use this route when spelling unfamiliar words or non-words. It produces correct spellings when the relationship between phonemes and graphemes is regular or common (e.g., *cat*). However, it produces systematic spelling errors when the relationship is irregular or uncommon (e.g., *yacht*, *comb*).
- Both routes involve orthographic working memory (the **graphemic buffer**). This briefly holds graphemic representations consisting of abstract letters or letter groups just before they are written or typed.

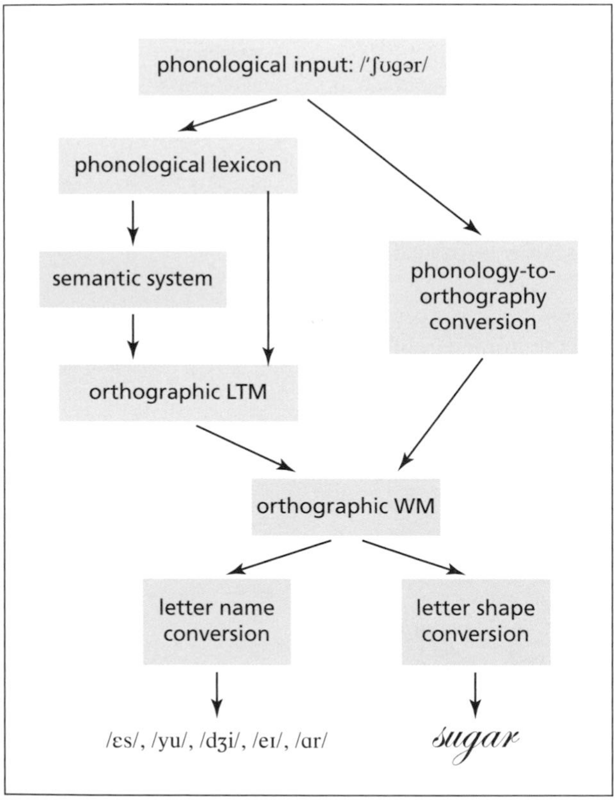

phonological input: /ˈʃʊgər/
phonological lexicon
semantic system
orthographic LTM
phonology-to-orthography conversion
orthographic WM
letter name conversion
letter shape conversion
/ɛs/, /yu/, /dʒi/, /eɪ/, /ɑr/
sugar

Figure 11.13
The functional architecture of the spelling process. The lexical route (left-hand side) involves the phonological lexicon, the semantic system and orthographic long-term memory. The non-lexical route (right-hand side) involves phonology-to-orthography conversion. Both routes converge on orthographic working memory.

From Rapp and Dufor (2011). © Massachusetts Institute of Technology, by permission of The MIT Press.

Lexical route: phonological dysgraphia

What would happen if a brain-damaged patient could make very little use of the non-lexical route but the lexical route was essentially intact? He/she would spell known words accurately because their spellings would be available in the orthographic lexicon (orthographic long-term memory). However, there would be great problems with unfamiliar words and non-words for which relevant information is not contained in the orthographic lexicon. The term **phonological dysgraphia** refers to such patients.

Several patients with phonological dysgraphia have been studied. Shelton and Weinrich (1997) studied a patient, EA, who could not write correctly any of 55 non-words to dictation. In contrast, the patient wrote 50% of regular words and 45% of irregular words correctly. Cholewa et al. (2010) found children with phonological dysgraphia performed much worse than healthy controls at writing non-words and irregular words (especially the former).

A plausible hypothesis to explain the spelling problems of patients with phonological dysgraphia is that they have a severe deficit with phonological processing (processing involving the sounds of words). According to this hypothesis, such patients should have difficulties on any task involving phonological processing even if it did not involve spelling.

Cholewa et al. (2010) tested this hypothesis. They gave children with phonological dysgraphia various tests of phonological processing. One test involved deciding whether two spoken non-words sounded the same and another involved repeating a non-word with a given consonant removed. As predicted, children with phonological dysgraphia performed considerably worse than healthy controls on all these tests of phonological processing.

KEY TERM

Surface dysgraphia
A condition caused by brain damage in which there is poor spelling of irregular words, reasonable spelling of regular words and some success in spelling non-words.

Non-lexical route: surface dysgraphia

What would happen if a patient had damage to the lexical route and so relied mostly on the phoneme-conversion system? Apart from producing misspellings sounding like the relevant word, such a patient would have some success in generating appropriate spellings of non-words. In addition, he/she would be more accurate at spelling regular or consistent words (i.e., words where the spelling can be worked out from the sound) than irregular or inconsistent words.

Weblink:
Fun brain

Patients fitting the above pattern suffer from **surface dysgraphia**. Macoir and Bernier (2002) studied a patient, MK, who spelled 92% of regular words correctly but only 52% of irregular words. Cholewa et al. (2010) found children with surface dysgraphia spelled 56% of irregular or inconsistent words wrongly but only 19% of non-words.

According to the two-route approach, surface dysgraphics have problems accessing information about words. We might thus predict surface dysgraphics would find it much easier to spell those words for which they could access some semantic information. Precisely this was found by Macoir and Bernier (2002) in a study already mentioned. Bormann et al. (2009) found a male surface dysgraphic, MO, had very poor access to word information. When he heard two words (e.g., *lass das* meaning *leave it*), he often wrote them as a single meaningless word (e.g., *lasdas*).

A further prediction from the two-route approach is that surface dysgraphics should not have a particular problem with phonological processing. Relevant evidence was obtained in the study by Cholewa et al. (2010) discussed earlier. Children with surface dysgraphia performed much better than those with phonological dysgraphia on several phonological tasks. However, their performance was still clearly worse than that of healthy controls.

Are the two routes independent?

Are the lexical and non-lexical routes independent or do they interact? There is increasing evidence that they often interact. Rapp et al. (2002) studied LAT, a patient with Alzheimer's disease. He made many errors in spelling. However, he used the non-lexical route reasonably well as shown by his good spelling of non-words. Some of his incorrect spellings indicated he was integrating

Interactive exercise:
Rapp and Dafour (2011)

information from both routes. For example, he spelled *bouquet* as BOUKET and *knowledge* as KNOLIGE. These spellings suggest some use of the non-lexical route. However, he could only have known that *bouquet* ends in *t* and that *knowledge* starts with *k* by using information in the orthographic lexicon.

According to the two-route approach, the spelling of non-words should involve *only* the non-lexical route. Suppose you heard the non-word /vi:m/ and wrote it down. Would you write VEAM or VEME? Most people write VEAM if the word *dream* has just been presented auditorily and VEME if it is immediately preceded by *theme* (Martin & Barry, 2012). This shows an influence of the lexical route on non-word spellings.

Delattre et al. (2006) pointed out that irregular words produce a *conflict* between the outputs of the lexical and non-lexical routes whereas regular ones do not. If the two routes interact, we might expect it would take longer to write irregular than regular words. That is what Delattre et al. found.

Overall evaluation

Research has revealed surprising complexity in spelling processes. Evidence from individuals with phonological dysgraphia and surface dysgraphia provides reasonable evidence that the spelling of heard words can involve a lexical route or a non-lexical route. It has also been established that there are important interactions between the two routes.

What are the limitations of theory and research in this area? First, the notion that phonological dysgraphia involves a *specific* problem with turning sounds into groups of letters may be incorrect. It often involves a much more *general* problem with phonological processing. Second, little is known about the interactions between the two spelling routes. Third, the precise rules used in phoneme–grapheme conversion are unclear. Fourth, we do not know in detail how the three components of the lexical route combine to produce spellings of heard words.

One or two orthographic lexicons?

Knowledge of word spellings is important in reading and writing. The simplest (and most plausible) assumption is that a *single* orthographic lexicon is used for reading and spelling. An alternative assumption is that an input lexicon is used in reading and a separate orthographic output lexicon is used in spelling. Below we discuss relevant evidence.

Findings

What evidence suggests there are two orthographic lexicons? Much of it comes from the study of brain-damaged patients. Tainturier et al. (2006) reported the case of CWS, a 58-year-old man who had had a stroke. His ability to spell words was severely impaired, whereas his ability to read words was almost intact. For example, he was very good at deciding which of two homophones (e.g., *obey–obay*) was correct. Many other brain-damaged patients have much better reading than spelling and others show the opposite pattern of much better spelling than reading.

The evidence from brain-damaged patients falls far short of showing there are two orthographical lexicons (Rapp & Lipka, 2011). Patients having greater problems with reading than with spelling generally have damage to brain areas associated with visual perception (e.g., BA17/18). In contrast, patients whose spelling is much worse than their reading typically have damage to premotor areas (e.g., BA6).

The above findings reflect the fact perception is more important in reading than spelling, whereas motor processes are more important in spelling than reading. They tell us little about the number of orthographic lexicons there are.

What findings suggest there is only one orthographic lexicon? First, most brain-damaged patients with a reading impairment (**dyslexia**) generally also have impaired writing and spelling (**dysgraphia**). Patients with dyslexia and dysgraphia typically have damage to brain areas such as the fusiform temporal gyrus (BA37) and the inferior frontal gyrus (BA44/45) (Rapp & Lipka, 2011). As we will see shortly, other evidence suggests these areas are of great relevance for the orthographic lexicon. Additional support for a single orthographic lexicon comes from patients having problems with the same specific words in both reading and writing (Rapp & Lipka, 2011).

Second, there are behavioural studies on healthy individuals. Holmes and Carruthers (1998) presented healthy participants with five versions of words they could not spell, including the correct version and their own misspelling. They showed no ability to select the correct spelling over their own misspelling.

Third, there are neuroimaging studies on healthy individuals. Rapp and Lipka (2011) gave their participants spelling and reading tasks. Their key finding was that the mid-fusiform gyrus and the inferior frontal gyrus were strongly activated during both tasks (see Figure 11.14). Of particular importance, the activation peaks for reading and spelling in each area were very close to each other.

Rapp and Dufor (2011) used different spelling tasks but obtained very similar findings. The relevance of the left fusiform gyrus was further shown by Tsapkini and Rapp (2010). They studied a patient, DPT, with damage to the left fusiform gyrus. He had severely impaired spelling and reading in spite of having intact processing of spoken language.

The available evidence suggests parts of the left fusiform gyrus are of central importance with respect to the orthographic lexicon. The inferior frontal gyrus is used during spelling and writing but its precise function is unclear.

Evaluation

The issue of one vs. two orthographic lexicons is still unresolved. However, converging evidence from brain-damaged patients and from behavioural and neuroimaging studies on healthy

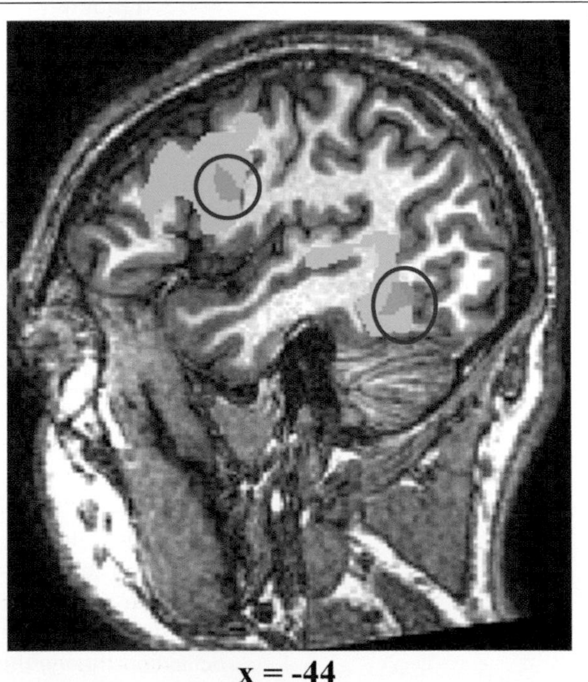

Figure 11.14
Brain areas activated by reading (in blue) and by spelling (in green). The red circles indicate the regions of overlap between reading and spelling in the left mid-fusiform area and the left inferior frontal gyrus.

From Rapp and Lipka (2011). © Massachusetts Institute of Technology, by permission of The MIT Press.

KEY TERMS

Dyslexia
Impaired ability to read that is not attributable to low intelligence.

Dysgraphia
Impaired ability to write (including spelling).

individuals suggests there is a single orthographic lexicon. The brain area most closely associated with the orthographic lexicon seems to be the fusiform temporal gyrus (BA37).

What are the limitations of research in this area? First, the issue of one vs. two orthographic lexicons is so complex it is hard to obtain convincing evidence. Second, neuroimaging studies on healthy individuals suggest *some* processes and/or structures are shared by reading and spelling. However, it does not necessarily follow that a single orthographic lexicon is involved in both language activities. Third, while it might be efficient for us to have only a single orthographic lexicon, there are other relevant considerations. For example, reading and spelling are typically taught to children as separate skills. That suggests some caution before completely rejecting the notion of two orthographic lexicons.

CHAPTER SUMMARY

- **Introduction**. The same knowledge base and similar planning skills are used in speaking and writing. However, spoken language is more informal and simple than written language because there is less time for planning and it is more interactive. The complexities involved in speech production lead speakers to make use of preformulation and underspecification. The notion there are important differences between speaking and writing receives support from the study of brain-damaged patients who perform well with one form of language production but not the other. Speech production involves four levels: semantic, syntactic, morphological and phonological.

- **Speech planning**. Speech planning can extend over a phrase or over a clause. Forward planning is fairly extensive when speakers have relative freedom about what to say and when to say it. However, there is much less planning when speakers are under time pressure. Speakers decide to focus on accurate speech, which involves cognitively demanding planning, or on cognitively undemanding planning leading to errors.

- **Speech errors**. The study of speech errors can provide insights into the processes (e.g., planning) underlying speech production. There are numerous types of speech error, including spoonerisms, Freudian slips, semantic substitutions, exchange errors and number-agreement errors. Rival theories attribute the ability to detect one's own speech errors mainly to the comprehension system or the speech-production system itself. The evidence mostly favours the latter position. Aphasic patients' ability to detect their own speech errors depends far more on the extent of impairment in their speech-production system than their comprehension system.

- **Theories of speech production**. According to Dell's spreading-activation theory, the processing associated with speech production is parallel and interactive. The theory accounts for most speech errors but is in danger of exaggerating processing interactivity. WEAVER++ is a discrete, feedforward model based on the assumption of serial processing. Patterns of brain activation provide some support for this model, as does some research on the tip-of-the-tongue state. However, processing during speech production is much more interactive than assumed within WEAVER++. In addition, the model exaggerates the role of comprehension processes in the detection of one's own speech errors.

- **Cognitive neuropsychology: speech production**. There is a traditional distinction between Broca's aphasia (slow, ungrammatical and non-fluent speech) and Wernicke's aphasia (fluent speech often lacking meaning) involving damage to different brain areas. This distinction greatly oversimplifies the complexities of language processing and of the underlying brain systems, some of which connect Broca's area with Wernicke's area. Anomia (the impaired ability to name objects) can involve semantic impairments early in processing or subsequent phonological impairments. Patients with agrammatism produce sentences lacking grammatical structure and with few function words. They seem to have reduced processes for syntactic processing, and may have more general problems with sequence learning. Two brain pathways are important for syntactic processing. The speech of jargon aphasics is reasonably grammatical. However, they produce many neologisms and are generally unaware of doing so. They often have deficient self-monitoring of their speech.

- **Speech as communication**. The key purpose of speech is communication, and speakers are often sensitive to the needs of their listener when those needs are clear and straightforward. Otherwise, speakers often simply produce utterances easy for them to say. Speakers use gestures in flexible ways that are generally responsive to the listener. However, speakers continue to make gestures even when the listener cannot see those gestures. This occurs because the use of gestures makes it easier for speakers to plan what they are going to say. Other ways speakers facilitate communication are by using prosodic cues (e.g., rhythm, stress) and discourse markers (words or phrases indirectly assisting the listener's comprehension).

- **Writing: the main processes**. Writing involves proposing or planning, translating, transcribing, and evaluating and revising the text that has been produced. Shifts from one writing process to another depend on a monitor or control system. Good writers use a knowledge-transforming rather than knowledge-telling strategy and devote more time to revision. Expert writers attain a knowledge-crafting stage emphasising the reader's needs. The working memory system (especially the central executive) is heavily involved in the writing process.

- **Spelling.** It is often claimed there are separate lexical and non-lexical routes in spelling, with the former used to spell familiar words and the latter to spell unfamiliar words and non-words. Patients with phonological dysgraphia have damage to the lexical route whereas those with surface dysgraphia have damage to the non-lexical route. However, some evidence suggests phonological dysgraphics have a general impairment in phonological processing. The two routes often interact with each other. Reading and spelling probably both depend on the same orthographic lexicon.

Further reading

- Chang, F. & Fitz, H. (2014). Computational models of sentence production. In M. Goldrick, V. Ferreira and M. Miozzo (eds), *The Oxford handbook of language production: A dual-path approach*. Oxford: Oxford University Press. Franklin Chang and Hartmut Fitz discuss major theoretical approaches to spoken sentence production in detail.
- Dell, G.S., Nozari, N. & Oppenheim, G.M. (2014). Word production: Behavioural and computational considerations. In M. Goldrick, V. Ferreira & M. Miozzo (eds), *The Oxford handbook of language production*. Oxford: Oxford University Press. Gary Dell and his colleagues provide a comprehensive account of theory and research on spoken word production.
- Harley, T.A. (2013). *The psychology of language: From data to theory* (4th edn). Hove: Psychology Press. Chapter 13 in Trevor Harley's excellent textbook is devoted to language production in its various forms.
- Hayes, J.R. (2012). Modelling and remodelling writing. *Written Communication*, 29: 369–88. John Hayes presents a revised version of his influential theory of writing.
- Kellogg, R.T., Whiteford, A.P., Turner, C.E., Cahill, M. & Mertens, A. (2013). Working memory in written composition: An evaluation of the 1996 model. *Journal of Writing Research*, 5: 159–90. Ronald Kellogg discusses the role of the various components of the working memory system in writing.
- Konopka, A. & Brown-Schmidt, S. (2014). Message encoding. In M. Goldrick, V. Ferreira & M. Miozzo (eds), *The Oxford handbook of language production*. Oxford: Oxford University Press. The processes involved in planning speech utterances are discussed in this chapter.
- Olive, T. (2012). Writing and working memory: A summary of theories and findings. In E.L. Grigorenko, E. Mambrino & D.D. Preiss (eds), *Writing: A mosaic of perspectives* (pp. 125–40). Hove: Psychology Press. The influential theoretical attempts to explain writing performance in terms of working memory are discussed and evaluated by Thierry Olive.

Thinking and reasoning

IV

Our ability to reflect in complex ways on our lives (e.g., to plan and solve our daily problems) is the bedrock of thinking behaviour. However, as in all things human, the ways we think (and reason and make decisions) are many and varied. They range from solving newspaper puzzles to troubleshooting (or not!) when our car breaks down to developing a new theory of the universe. Below we consider a sample of the sorts of things to which we apply the term "thinking".

First, a fragment of Molly Bloom's sleep thoughts in James Joyce's *Ulysses* (1922/1960, pp. 871–2) about Mrs Riordan:

> God help the world if all women in the world were her sort down on bathingsuits and lownecks of course nobody wanted her to wear I suppose she was pious because no man would look at her twice I hope I'll never be like her a wonder she didn't want us to cover our faces but she was a well educated woman certainly and her gabby talk about Mr. Riordan here and Mr. Riordan there I suppose he was glad to get shut of her.

Second, here is the first author trying to use PowerPoint:

> Why has the Artwork put the title in the wrong part of the slide? Suppose I try to put a frame around it so I can drag it up to where I want it. Ah-ha, now if I just summon up the arrows I can move the top bit up, and then I do the same with the bottom bit. If I move the bottom bit up more than the top bit, then the title will fit in okay.

These two examples illustrate several general aspects of thinking. First, they both involve individuals being *conscious* of their thoughts. Clearly, thinking typically involves conscious awareness. However, we tend to be aware of the products of thinking rather than the processes themselves (see Chapter 16). Furthermore, even when we can introspect on our thoughts, our recollections of them are often inaccurate. Joyce reconstructs well the nature of idle, associative thought in Molly Bloom's internal monologue. However, if we asked her to tell us her thoughts from the previous five minutes, little of it would be recalled.

Second, thinking varies in the extent to which it is directed. It can be relatively undirected as in the case of Molly Bloom letting one thought slide into another as she is on the point of slipping into a dream. In the other case, the goal is much clearer and better defined.

Third, the amount and nature of the knowledge used in different thinking tasks vary enormously. The knowledge required in the PowerPoint case is quite limited even though it took the first author considerable time to acquire it. In contrast, Molly Bloom is using a vast amount of her knowledge of people and of life.

The next three chapters (12–14) are concerned with the higher-level cognitive processes involved in thinking and reasoning (see the box below). Note that we use the *same* cognitive system to deal with all these types of thinking. As a result, many distinctions among different forms of thinking and reasoning are somewhat arbitrary and camouflage underlying similarities in cognitive processes.

From the above viewpoint it is unsurprising the same (or similar) brain areas are typically involved in most problem-solving and reasoning tasks (see Chapter 14). It is also worth mentioning there has recently been a major shift in research from deductive reasoning to informal reasoning. Informal reasoning is closer than deductive reasoning to research on judgement and

FORMS OF THINKING

Problem solving	Cognitive activity that involves moving from the recognition that there is a problem through a series of steps to the solution. Most other forms of thinking involve some problem solving.
Decision making	Selecting one out of a number of presented options or possibilities, with the decision having personal consequences.
Judgement	A component of decision making that involves calculating the likelihood of various possible events; the emphasis is on accuracy.
Deductive reasoning	Deciding what conclusions follow necessarily, provided that various statements are assumed to be true; a form of reasoning that is supposed to be based on logic.
Inductive reasoning	Deciding whether certain statements or hypotheses are true on the basis of the available information. It is used by scientists and detectives but is not guaranteed to produce valid conclusions.
Informal reasoning	Evaluating the strength of arguments by taking account of one's knowledge and experience.

decision making because it makes much more use of an individual's knowledge and experience.

We will briefly describe the structure of this section. Chapter 12 is concerned primarily with the processes involved in problem solving. There is an emphasis on the role of learning in problem solving and on the skills possessed by experts.

Chapter 13 deals with judgement and decision making with an emphasis on the errors and biases that are often involved. A central theme is that most people make extensive use of heuristics (rules of thumb) that are simple to use but prone to error.

Chapter 14 deals with the major forms of reasoning (inductive, deductive and informal) and the errors to which they are prone. There is also discussion of the key (but very tricky!) question, "Are humans rational?" As you might expect, many psychologists answer that question "Yes and no", rather than a definite "Yes" or "No"!

CHAPTER 12

Problem solving and expertise

INTRODUCTION

Life presents us with plenty of problems, although thankfully the great majority are fairly trivial. Here are three examples. First, you have an urgent meeting in another city and so must get there rapidly. However, the trains generally run late, your car is old and unreliable and the buses are slow.

Second, you are struggling to work out the correct sequence of operations on your computer to perform a given task. You try to remember what you needed to do with your previous computer.

Third, you are an expert chess player in the middle of a competitive match against a strong opponent. The time clock is ticking away and you must decide rapidly on your move in a complicated position.

The above examples relate to the three main topics of this chapter. The first topic is *problem solving*. What do we mean by problem solving? It requires the following (Goel, 2010, p. 613):

> (1) there are two states of affairs; (2) the agent is in one state and wants to be in the other state; (3) it is not apparent to the agent how the gap between the two states is to be bridged; and (4) bridging the gap is a consciously guided multi-step process.

The second topic is *analogical problem solving*. In our everyday lives, we constantly use past experience and knowledge to assist us in our current task. Often we detect (and make effective use of) analogies or similarities between a current problem and ones solved in the past.

The third topic is *expertise*. Individuals possessing expertise have considerable specialist knowledge in some given area or domain. There is much overlap between expertise and problem solving in that experts are very efficient at solving numerous problems in their area of expertise. However, there are also important differences. Knowledge is typically more important in research on expertise than research on problem solving. There is more focus on individual differences in expertise research than research on problem solving. Indeed, a central issue in expertise is to identify the main differences (e.g., in knowledge, in strategic processing) between experts and novices.

KEY TERMS

Well-defined problems
Problems in which the initial state, the goal and the methods available for solving them are clearly laid out.

Ill-defined problems
Problems that are imprecisely specified; for example, the initial state, goal state and the methods available to solve the problem may be unclear.

Knowledge-rich problems
Problems that can only be solved by those having considerable relevant background knowledge.

Knowledge-lean problems
Problems that can be solved by individuals in the absence of specific relevant prior knowledge.

PROBLEM SOLVING: INTRODUCTION

There are three major aspects to problem solving:

1 It is purposeful (i.e., goal-directed).
2 It involves controlled processes and is not totally reliant on "automatic" processes.
3 A problem exists when someone lacks the relevant knowledge to produce an immediate solution. Thus, a problem for most people (e.g., a mathematical calculation) may not be so for a professional mathematician.

There are important differences among problems. **Well-defined problems** are ones in which *all* aspects of the problem are clearly specified, including the initial state or situation, the range of possible moves or strategies and the goal or solution. The goal is well specified because it is clear when it has been reached (e.g., the centre of a maze). Chess is a well-defined (although very complex) problem – there is a standard initial state, the rules specify all legitimate rules and the goal is to achieve checkmate.

Ill-defined problems are underspecified. Suppose you set yourself the goal of becoming happier. There are endless strategies you could adopt and it is very hard to know ahead of time which would be most effective. Since happiness varies over time and is hard to define, how are you going to decide whether you have solved the problem of becoming happier?

Most everyday problems are ill-defined, but psychologists have focused on well-defined problems (Goel, 2010). Why is this? One major reason is that well-defined problems have an optimal strategy for their solution. Another reason is that the researcher knows the right answer. As a result, he/she can easily identify the errors and deficiencies in the strategies used by problem solvers.

The importance of the above distinction was shown by Goel and Grafman (2000). They studied PF, a man with brain damage to the right prefrontal cortex. He had an IQ of 128 (considerably above average) and he performed at a high level on well-defined laboratory tasks. However, he coped very poorly with the ill-defined problems of everyday life. Why was this? PF found it very hard to work out preliminary *plans* to impose some structure on such problems and so could not solve them. Such planning is much less necessary with well-defined problems.

Interactive exercise:
Brain regions in reasoning

We must also distinguish between knowledge-rich and knowledge-lean problems. **Knowledge-rich problems** (e.g., chess problems) can only be solved by those having much relevant specific knowledge. In contrast, **knowledge-lean problems** do not require such knowledge because most of the information needed to solve the problem is contained in the initial problem statement. Most traditional research on problem solving involved knowledge-lean problems because such problems minimise individual differences in relevant knowledge.

IN THE REAL WORLD: MONTY HALL PROBLEM

Monty Hall. ZUMA Press, Inc./Alamy.

We can illustrate key issues in problem solving with the notorious Monty Hall problem, which formed an important part of Monty Hall's (see photo) show on American television:

> Suppose you're on a game show and you're given the choice of three doors. Behind one door is a car, behind the others, goats. You pick a door, say, Number 1, and the host, who knows what's behind the doors, opens another door, say Number 3, which has a goat. He then says to you, "Do you want to switch to door Number 2?" Is it to your advantage to switch your choice?

If you stayed with your first choice, you are in good company. About 85% of people make that decision (Burns & Wieth, 2004). Unfortunately, it is wrong! There is actually a two-thirds chance of being correct if you switch.

Many people (including you?) furiously dispute the above answer. Let us work it through in two ways. First, when you initially pick one door at random, you clearly only had a

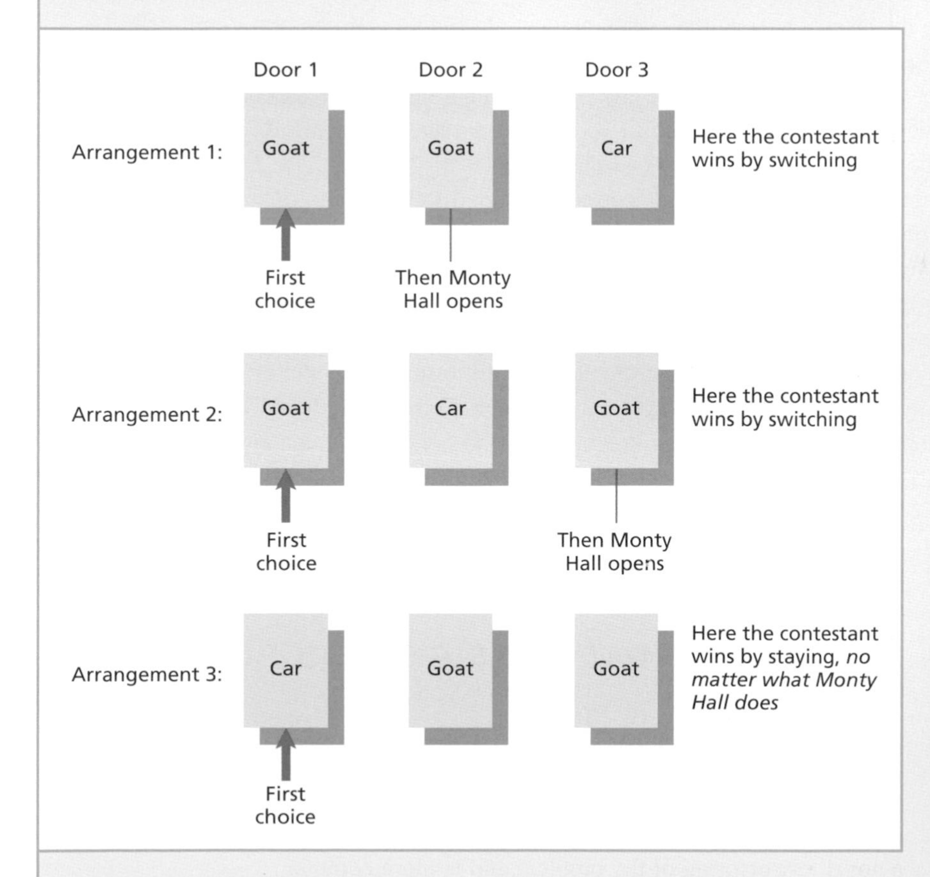

Weblink:
Monty Hall problem

Figure 12.1 Explanation of the solution to the Monty Hall problem: in two out of three possible car–goat arrangements, the contestant would win by switching; therefore she should switch.

From Krauss and Wang (2003). © 2003 American Psychological Association.

one-third chance of winning the car. Regardless of whether your initial choice was correct, the host can open a door that does not have the prize behind it. Thus, the host's action sheds *no light at all* on the correctness of your initial choice.

Second, there are only three possible scenarios with the Monty Hall problem (Krauss & Wang, 2003; see Figure 12.1). With scenarios 1 and 2, your first choice is incorrect, and so Monty Hall opens the only remaining door with a goat behind it. As a result, switching is certain to succeed. With scenario 3, your first choice is correct and you would win by refusing to switch. Overall, switching succeeds two-thirds of the time and fails only with scenario 3.

Human performance on the Monty Hall problem is very poor. Herbranson and Schroeder (2010) found it was much worse than that of Silver King pigeons! After extensive practice, humans switched on 66% of trials with the Monty Hall problem. In contrast, pigeons switched on 96% of trials. The pigeons performed well because they simply maximised the reward they received, whereas humans adopted more complex strategies.

Why do people perform so poorly on this problem? First, we typically use a heuristic or rule of thumb known as the *uniformity fallacy* (Falk & Lann, 2008). This fallacy involves assuming all available options are equally likely whether they are or not.

Second, the problem places substantial demands on the central executive (an attention-like component of working memory; see Chapter 6). Participants were much less likely to solve the Monty Hall problem if they performed a demanding task involving the central executive task at the same time (8% vs. 22%; De Neys & Verschueren, 2006).

Third, most people mistakenly believe the host's actions are *random*. Burns and Wieth (2004) made the causal structure of the problem clearer. There are three boxers, one of whom was so good he was certain to win any bout. You select one boxer and then the other two boxers fight each other. The winner of this bout then fights the boxer you selected initially. You win if you choose the winner of this second bout.

With the above version of the problem, 51% correctly decided to switch vs. only 15% with the standard three-door problem. This occurred because it is easy to see that the boxer who won the first bout did so because of skill rather than any random factor.

In sum, the Monty Hall problem shows our fallibility as problem solvers. We produce wrong answers because we use heuristics or rules of thumb (see Chapter 13), because our processing capacity is limited and because we misrepresent problems (e.g., misunderstanding their causal structure). A final reason is that we know that hosts on television shows sometimes play tricks – perhaps the host only opened the door because he/she knew the contestant's initial choice was correct (Schuller, 2012).

GESTALT APPROACH: INSIGHT AND ROLE OF EXPERIENCE

Early research on problem solving was dominated by the Gestaltists, German psychologists flourishing between the 1920s and 1940s. They distinguished between reproductive and productive thinking. *Reproductive thinking* involves the systematic reuse of previous experiences. In contrast, *productive thinking* involves a novel restructuring of the problem and is more complex.

Insight

The Gestaltists argued that problems requiring productive thinking are often solved using insight. **Insight** involves a sudden restructuring of a problem and is sometimes accompanied by the "ah-ha experience". More technically, insight is "any sudden comprehension, realisation, or problem solution that involves a reorganisation of the elements of a person's mental representation of a stimulus, situation, or event to yield a nonobvious or nondominant interpretation" (Kounios & Beeman, 2014, p. 74).

The mutilated draughtboard (or checkerboard) problem (see Figure 12.2) is an insight problem. The board is initially covered by 32 dominoes occupying two squares each. Then two squares are removed from diagonally opposite corners. Can the remaining 62 squares be filled by 31 dominoes? Think what your answer is before reading on.

Nearly everyone starts by mentally covering squares with dominoes. Alas, this strategy is not terribly effective – there are 758,148 possible permutations of the dominoes! Since very few people solve the mutilated draughtboard problem without assistance, we will assume you are in that large majority (our apologies if you are not!). You may well rapidly solve the problem using insight if we tell you something you already know – each domino covers one white and one black square. If that clue does not work, think about the colours of the two removed squares – they *must* have the same colour. Thus, the 31 dominoes cannot cover the mutilated board.

Theoretically, there has been controversy as to whether insight is a special process or whether it involves the same processes as other thinking tasks (the "business-as-usual" view). We will shortly be discussing evidence relevant to this controversy. Note, however, that it is probably the case that insight problems involve a mixture of both processes (see Weisberg (2014) for an excellent discussion).

KEY TERMS

Insight
The experience of suddenly realising how to solve a problem.

Remote Associates Test
This involves finding a word that is related to three given words.

Findings

Metcalfe and Wiebe (1987) recorded participants' feelings of "warmth" (closeness to solution) during insight and non-insight problems. Warmth increased progressively during non-insight problems (as expected if they involve a sequence of processes). With insight problems, in contrast, the warmth ratings remained at the same low level until suddenly increasing dramatically just before the solution was reached.

Weblink:
Mutilated draughtboard problem

Much research has considered whether insight is associated with a particular pattern of brain activity (Kounios & Beeman, 2014). For example, Bowden et al. (2005) used the **Remote Associates Test**. Three words were presented (e.g., *fence*, *card*, *master*) and participants thought of a word (e.g., *post*) going with each one to form compound words. The participants indicated insight was involved on some trials but not others. Differences in brain activity between insight and non-insight trials centred in the right hemisphere. More specifically, the anterior superior temporal

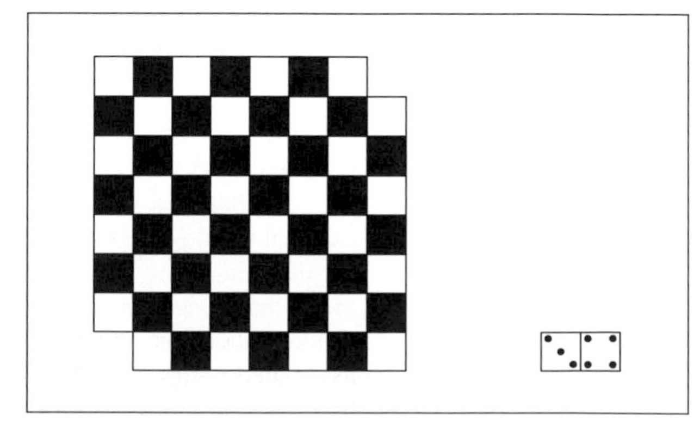

Figure 12.2
The mutilated draughtboard problem.

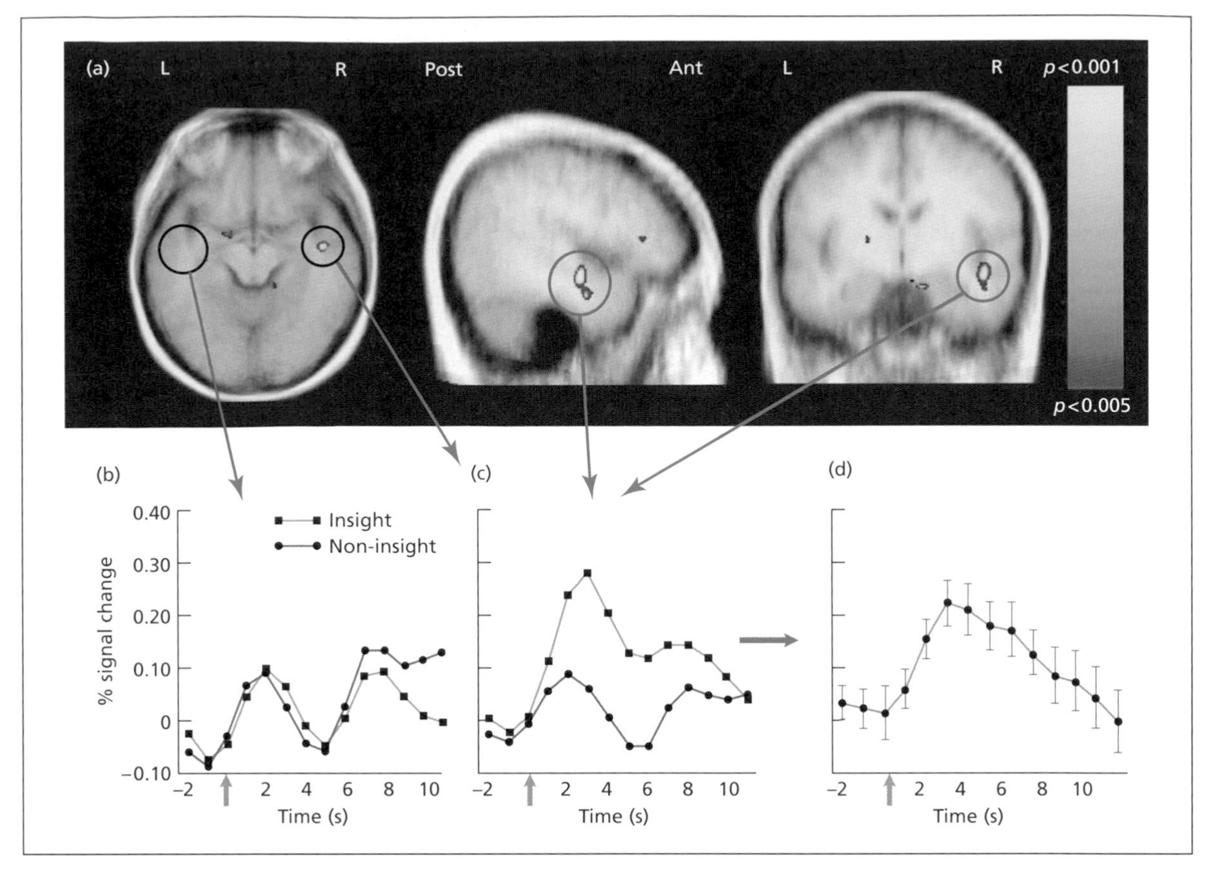

Figure 12.3
Activation in the right hemisphere anterior superior temporal gyrus (RH-aSTG). (a) Areas within the aSTG showing greater activation for insight than non-insight problems; (b) mean signal change following solution for insight and non-insight solutions in left hemisphere (b) and right hemisphere (c); (d) difference between changes shown in (c).
Reprinted from Bowden et al. (2005). With permission from Elsevier.

Weblink:
Remote associates test

gyrus (ridge) (see Figure 12.3) was activated only when solutions involved insight. This is a brain area associated with processing distant semantic relations between words as well as reinterpretation and semantic integration.

Why is the right hemisphere more associated with insight than the left hemisphere? Integration of weakly active and distant associations occurs mostly in the right hemisphere (Bowden & Jung-Beeman, 2007). Such processing activities are very relevant for producing insight. In contrast, strong activation of closely connected associations occurs mostly in the left hemisphere.

Another area often associated with insight is the anterior cingulate cortex (located within BA24, BA32 and BA33; see Figure 1.4). This area is involved in the detection of cognitive conflict and the breaking of mindsets. This is important given that insight involves replacing one way of thinking about a problem with a new and more efficient way. In addition, several studies found insight was associated with activation of the prefrontal cortex (involved in higher cognitive processes) (Kounios & Beeman, 2014). Note the neuroscience evidence discussed here is correlational and so does not show that any given brain area is necessary for insightful problem solving.

Our subjective experience tells us insight occurs *suddenly* and unexpectedly. However, the same is *not* true of the underlying processes. Ellis et al. (2011) used an anagram task in which four consonants and a vowel were presented in a circular pattern. Four of the letters formed a word and there was an additional distractor consonant (e.g., K A F M S).

Ellis et al. (2011) recorded eye movements during the anagram task. On most trials, participants reported they had suddenly solved the anagram (insight trials). However, the eye-movement data told a different story. During each insight trial, participants spent a gradually decreasing percentage of their time fixating the distractor consonant. Thus, the eye-movement findings indicated participants were gradually accumulating knowledge relevant to anagram solution even though they were unaware that was happening. We could explain this on the basis that insight depends on processes operating below the level of conscious awareness.

Further relevant evidence was reported by Cushen and Wiley (2012). Participants were divided into insight and non-insight groups on the basis of the processes used during problem solving. There was no relationship between these processes and the subjective insightfulness of solutions presumably because participants had little or no access to information about their solution processes.

Weblink:
Two-string problem

Facilitating insight: Hints

How can insight be facilitated? Unsurprisingly, hints increase the number of solutions produced on insight problems. However, what *is* surprising is that even *subtle* hints are useful. For example, consider Maier's (1931) pendulum problem. Participants were brought into a room containing various objects (e.g., poles, pliers, extension cords), plus two strings hanging from the ceiling (see Figure 12.4).

The task was to tie the two strings together. However, they were too far apart for participants to reach one string while holding the other. The most "insightful"

Figure 12.4
The two-string problem in which it is not possible to reach one string while holding the other.

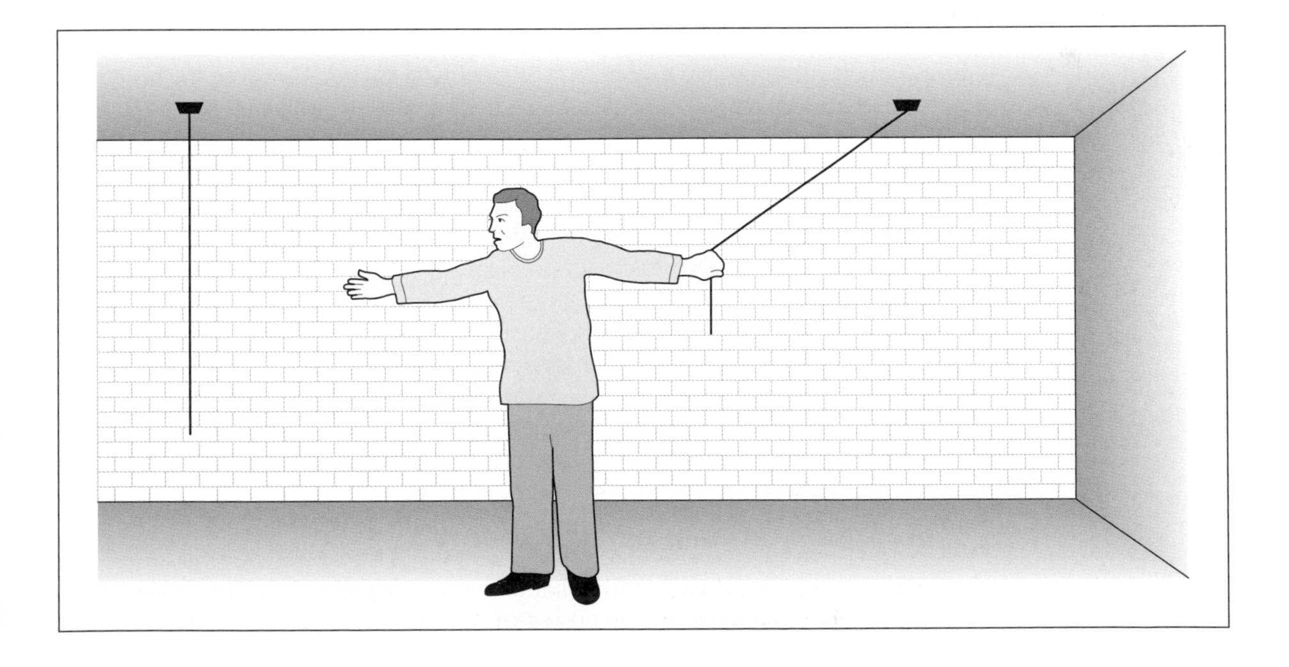

KEY TERM

Incubation
A stage of problem solving in which the problem is put to one side for some time; it is claimed to facilitate problem solving.

(but rare) solution was to tie the pliers to one string and swing it like a pendulum. Participants could hold one string and catch the other on its upswing.

Thomas and Lleras (2009) used the pendulum problem with occasional exercise breaks in which participants swung or stretched their arms. Those moving their arms in a solution-relevant way (i.e., swinging) were more likely to solve the problem than those stretching their arms, although they were unaware of the relationship between their arm movements and the task. Thus, hints can be effective without conscious awareness of their task relevance.

Facilitating insight: incubation and sleep

Wallas (1926) argued for the importance of **incubation**, in which a problem is put aside for some time. He claimed the subconscious mind continues to work towards a solution during incubation and so incubation facilitates problem solution.

Research on incubation typically involves comparing an experimental group having an incubation period away from an unsolved problem with a control group working continuously. Sio and Ormerod (2009) reported three findings in a meta-analysis:

1. Incubation effects (generally fairly small) were reported in 73% of the studies.
2. Incubation effects were stronger with creative problems having multiple solutions than linguistic and verbal problems having a single solution. Incubation often widens the search for knowledge, which may be more useful with multiple-solution problems.
3. The effects were larger when there was a fairly long preparation time prior to incubation. This may have occurred because an impasse or block in thinking is more likely to develop when preparation time is long.

It is often claimed "sleeping on a problem" is an effective form of incubation. Wagner et al. (2004) tested this claim. Participants solved mathematical problems and were then retested several hours later. Each problem had a simple (but hard to find) short cut. Of those who slept between training and testing, 59% found the short cut, compared to only 25% of those who did not. However, the beneficial effects of sleep may be somewhat limited. Sio et al. (2013) found using the Remote Associates Test (see Glossary) that sleep enhanced performance on difficult problems but not on easy ones.

Why is incubation beneficial? Simon (1966) argued that *control* information relating to the strategies tried by the problem solver is forgotten during incubation. This forgetting makes it easier for problem solvers to adopt a new approach after the incubation period.

Penaloza and Calvillo (2012) obtained evidence that forgetting misleading information is important. Participants solved insight problems in the presence or absence of misleading clues. One group worked continuously while the other group had a two-minute incubation period. There was a beneficial effect of incubation only when the break allowed misleading information to be forgotten.

Representational change theory

Ohlsson (1992) argued that we often encounter a block or impasse when solving a problem because we have *represented* it wrongly (e.g., consider the mutilated

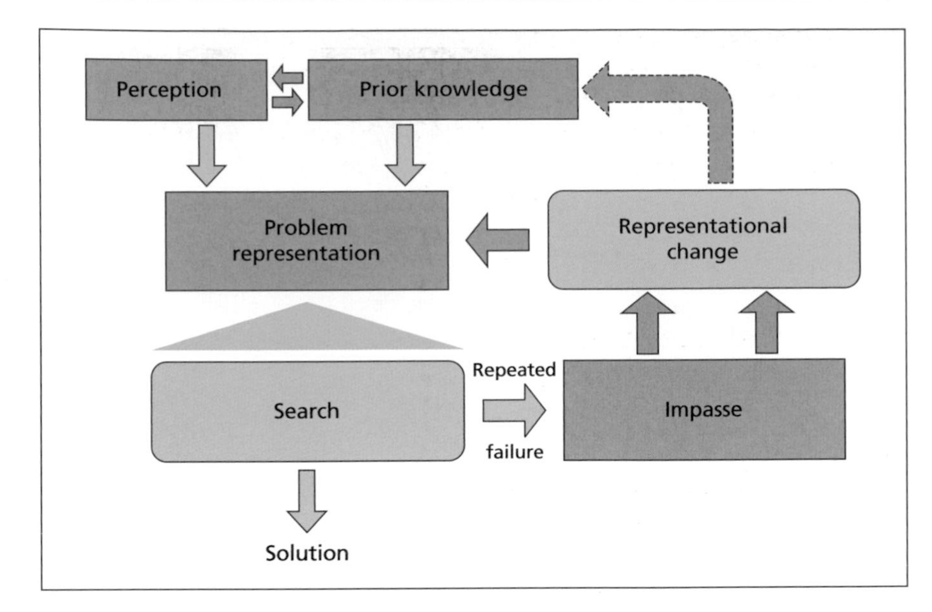

Figure 12.5
Flow chart of insight problem solving. Initially, a problem representation is established using prior knowledge and perceptual processes. The problem representation is searched by heuristics (rules of thumb). If this proves unsuccessful, an impasse is encountered. This leads to a change in the problem representation and this new representation is also searched by heuristics. This process is continued until a solution is found or the problem is abandoned.
From Öllinger et al. (2014).

draughtboard problem discussed earlier). According to his representational change theory, we typically need to change the problem representation for insight to occur. This can happen in three ways:

1. *Constraint relaxation*: inhibitions on what is regarded as permissible are removed.
2. *Re-encoding*: some aspect of the problem representation is reinterpreted.
3. *Elaboration*: new problem information is added to the representation.

Changing the problem representation in Ohlsson's theory is very similar to restructuring in the Gestalt approach. However, Ohlsson specified more precisely the processes leading to insight. Öllinger et al. (2014) developed Ohlsson's theory (see Figure 12.5). Prior knowledge and perceptual aspects of a problem lead to the formation of a problem representation. This is followed by a search process. If this search process is repeatedly unsuccessful, there is an impasse or block. A new problem representation is formed to try to overcome the impasse and this is followed by another search process. What is new about this theory is the assumption that a search process may be necessary even after an impasse has been overcome by insight.

Findings

Earlier we discussed the mutilated draughtboard problem. Solving it requires representing each domino as an object covering one white and one black square (re-encoding) and representing the draughtboard as having lost two black (or white) squares (elaboration).

The importance of constraint relaxation was shown by Knoblich et al. (1999). Participants were given problems such as those shown in Figure 12.6. As you can see, you would need to know all about Roman numerals to solve the problems! Each problem involved moving a *single* stick to produce a true statement to replace the initial false one.

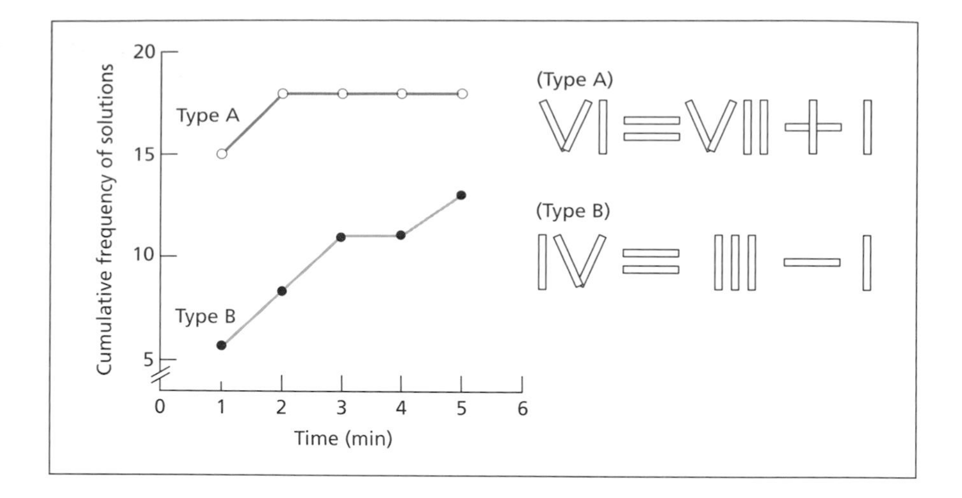

Figure 12.6
Two of the matchstick problems used by Knoblich et al. (1999), and the cumulative solution rates produced to these types of problem in their study.

© American Psychological Association.

Some problems (Type A) only required changing two values in the equation (e.g., VI = VII + 1 (6 = 7 + 1) becomes VII = VI + 1 (7 = 6 + 1)). In contrast, other problems (Type B) involved a less obvious change in the representation of the equation (e.g., IV = III – I (4 = 3 – 1) becomes IV – III = 1 (4 – 3 = 1)).

Knoblich et al. (1999) argued that our experience of arithmetic tells us that many operations change the values (numbers) in an equation (as with Type A problems). In contrast, relatively few operations change the operators (i.e., +, – and =) as is required in type B problems. As predicted, it was much harder to relax the normal constraints of arithmetic (and so show insight) for Type B problems (see Figure 12.6).

Knoblich et al. (2001) expanded their earlier research by recording eye movements. Participants initially spent much more time fixating the values than the operators for both types of problem. Thus, their initial representation was based on the assumption that values had to be changed.

Reverberi et al. (2005) argued that individuals' processing constraints when on insight problems involve the lateral prefrontal cortex. Patients with damage to that brain area should *not* impose artificial constraints when solving insight problems and so might perform better than healthy individuals. As predicted, brain-damaged patients solved 82% of the hardest matchstick arithmetic problems compared to only 43% of healthy controls.

Chi and Snyder (2011) used the same problems as Reverberi et al. (2005). For some participants, they used brain stimulation to *reduce* the excitability of the left lateral prefrontal cortex but to *increase* that of the comparable area on the right side. This had a dramatic effect: 60% solved the hardest matchstick problem compared to only 20% of control participants.

What do the above findings mean? Decreased excitability of the left lateral prefrontal cortex probably reduced inhibitions about constraint relaxation. Increased excitability on the right side may have enhanced insight processes.

According to representational change theory, solution hints are most useful when individuals have just reached a block or impasse. At that point, they have formed a problem representation (which is not the case earlier). However, they have not become excessively fixated on it (as happens after reaching an impasse). As predicted, hints before or after an impasse improved performance less than those given at the point of impasse (Moss et al., 2011).

IN THE REAL WORLD: CONSTRAINT RELAXATION: MAGIC TRICKS

Figure 12.7
(a) Screenshot from the beginning of the ice cube trick; (b) screenshot from the end of the trick.
From Danek et al. (2014). Reprinted with permission from Elsevier.

Danek et al. (2014) argued that representational change and insight are important in working out how magicians achieve their tricks. Consider a trick in which the magician pours water from a glass into an empty mug. He then turns the mug upside down and a large ice cube drops out (see Figure 12.7; visit www.youtube.com/watch?v=3B6ZxNROuNw). This seems impossible on the basis of reasonable assumptions such as the following: (1) the mug and glass are ordinary objects; (2) it is real water; (3) the mug is empty; (4) it is a real ice cube.

In fact, the "empty" mug is filled with a white napkin glued to the bottom of the mug and the ice cube. The water is fully absorbed by the napkin and so only the ice cube falls out. When participants were given a verbal cue designed to relax incorrect assumption (3), performance improved significantly.

Öllinger et al. (2014) tested their development of representational change theory using the nine-dot problem. It involves drawing four straight lines that go through all nine dots without lifting your pencil off the page (see Figure 12.8). Most people initially assume that the lines must remain within the confines of the square formed by the dots and so the key insight is to realise that this constraint must be relaxed.

In the past, researchers have been puzzled by the finding that the success rate on the nine-dot problem is typically not very high even when participants are explicitly told they can draw lines outside the square. Öllinger et al. argued that the insight is useful but still leaves an incredibly large number of possible combinations of four lines. As predicted by their theory, Öllinger et al. found the insight needed to be followed by an efficient search process for the problem to be solved.

Evaluation

Representational change theory extended the Gestalt approach by specifying the mechanisms underlying insight more precisely. This theory involves a fruitful combination of Gestalt ideas with the information-processing approach. Öllinger et al.'s (2014) extension of this theory has improved it by emphasising that efficient search processes are often needed *after* as well as *before* an impasse leading to insight.

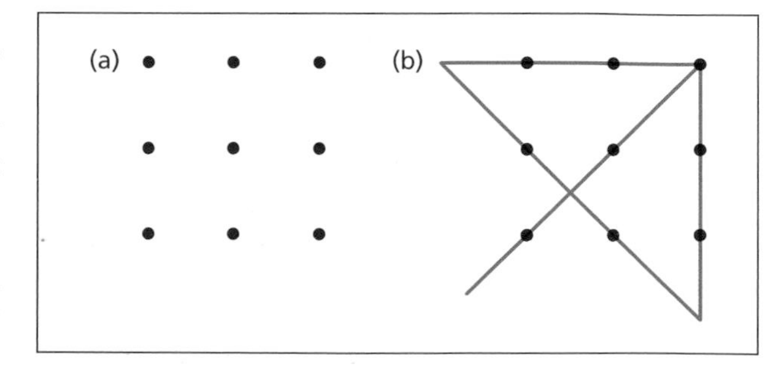

Figure 12.8
The nine-dot problem (a) and its solution (b).

What are the theory's limitations? First, we often cannot predict when (or why) a problem's

KEY TERM

Functional fixedness
The inflexible focus on the usual function(s) of an object in problem solving.

representation will change. Second, Ohlsson de-emphasised important individual differences in problem-solving skills (e.g., working memory capacity, discussed later).

Third, the theory mistakenly implies that constraint relaxation is typically sufficient to solve insight problems. However, we have seen that this is not the case with respect to the nine-dot problem (Öllinger et al., 2014).

Past experience: functional fixedness

Past experience generally increases our ability to solve problems. However, the Gestaltists argued persuasively that this is not always the case. Indeed, numerous failures on insight problems occur because we are misled by our past experience. Negative effects of past experience are shown clearly in the phenomenon of **functional fixedness**. Functional fixedness occurs when we mistakenly assume that any given object has only a limited number of uses.

Duncker (1945) carried out a classic study on functional fixedness. Participants were given a candle, a book of matches, tacks in a box and several other objects (see Figure 12.9). Their task was to attach the candle to a wall by the table so it did not drip on to the table below.

Most participants tried to nail the candle directly to the wall or glue it to the wall by melting it. Only a few produced the correct answer – use the inside of the tack box as a candle holder and then nail it to the wall with tacks.

According to Duncker (1945), his participants "fixated" on the tack box's function as a container rather than a platform. More correct solutions were produced when the box containing the tacks was empty at the start of the experiment because that made it appear less like a container.

More direct evidence that past experience can produce functional fixedness was obtained by Ye et al. (2009). Participants decided whether each of nine objects could be used for a given function (e.g., packable-with – usable as packing material to pack an egg in a box). Immediately afterwards, they decided whether the same objects could be used for a different function (e.g., play catch-with over a distance of 15 feet). Some objects (e.g., ski cap, pillow) could be used for both functions. Deciding an object possessed the first function reduced the probability of detecting it also possessed the second function.

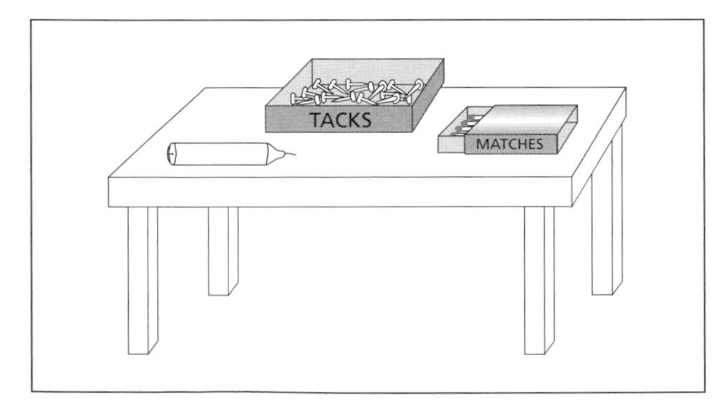

Figure 12.9
Some of the materials provided for participants instructed to mount a candle on a vertical wall in the study by Duncker (1945).

How can we overcome the negative effects of functional fixedness? Challoner (2009) answered that question. He studied the creation of 1,001 important inventions and the solutions to insight problems. In almost every case, two steps were involved:

1 Notice an infrequently noticed or new feature.
2 Form a solution based on that obscure feature.

McCaffrey (2012) argued that crucial obscure features are ignored because people focus on the typical functions of objects based on their shape, size, material of which they made and so on. This functional fixedness can be reduced by the generic-parts technique: (1) function-free descriptions of each part of an object are produced; (2) people decide whether each description implies a use.

McCaffrey (2012) gave some participants training in the generic-parts technique. These participants solved 83% of insight problems (e.g., Duncker's candle problem) compared to only 49% in the control group.

Chrysikou et al. (2013) argued that high levels of cognitive control can produce functional fixedness. They tested this hypothesis in a study in which participants generated a common or uncommon use for objects. In one condition, transcranial stimulation was applied to the left prefrontal cortex to reduce cognitive control. As predicted, this facilitated performance only when uncommon uses for objects had to be produced.

KEY TERM

Mental set
The tendency to use a familiar problem-solving strategy that has proved successful in the past even when it is not appropriate.

Past experience: mental set

There is another way past experience can impair problem solving: **mental set**. Mental set involves continuing to use a previously successful problem-solving strategy even when it is inappropriate or sub-optimal. Mental set is often useful in spite of its drawbacks – it allows successive problems of the same type to be solved rapidly and with few processing demands.

Classic research on mental set was carried out by Luchins (1942) using problems involving three water jars of varying capacity. Here is a sample problem. Jar A can hold 28 quarts of water, Jar B 76 quarts and Jar C 3 quarts. You must end up with exactly 25 quarts in one of the jars. The solution is easy: Jar A is filled, and then Jar C is filled from it, leaving 25 quarts in Jar A.

Of participants previously given similar problems, 95% solved it. Other participants had previously been trained on problems all having the same complex three-jar solution (fill Jar B and use the contents to fill Jar C twice and Jar A once). Of these participants, only 36% solved the easy final problem!

It seems plausible that experts given a problem in their area of expertise would be relatively immune from the damaging effects of mental set. In fact, this is *not* the case. When chess experts tried to find the most rapid way to win a chess game, most failed to identify the shortest solution. Instead, they used a longer solution based on a familiar strategy (Bilalić et al., 2008a).

Why are chess experts susceptible to the damaging effects of mental set? Bilalić et al. (2008b) studied chess experts who had found the familiar solution but were looking hard for a better one. Their eye movements revealed they were still looking at features of the chessboard position related to the familiar solution. Thus, their direction of attention remained partly under the control of processes producing the initial familiar solution.

How can we minimise the damaging effects of mental set? Vallée-Tourangeau et al. (2011) presented Luchins' water-jar problems on paper (as in the original research) or using actual water jars at a sink. Participants received several problems all requiring the same complex three-jar solution. After that, they were given a problem that could only be solved using a much simpler solution. Only 40% of those given problems on paper solved that problem compared to 68% using actual water jars. The beneficial effect of using actual water jars probably occurred because of "the rich and dynamic nature of the perceptual input" (Vallée-Tourangeau et al., 2011, p. 1894).

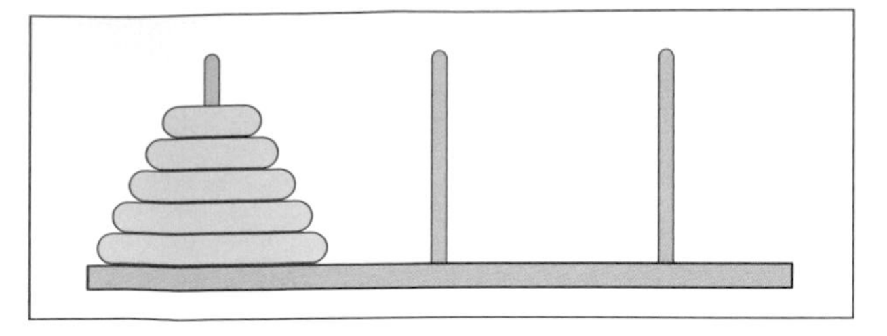

Figure 12.10
The initial state of the five-disc version of the Tower of Hanoi problem.

PROBLEM-SOLVING STRATEGIES

Major landmarks in problem-solving research were an article by Newell et al. (1958), followed in 1972 by Allen Newell and Herb Simon's book entitled *Human Problem Solving*. Their central insight was that the strategies we use when tackling complex problems take account of our limited ability to process and store information. Newell and Simon (1972) assumed we have very limited short-term memory capacity and that complex information processing is typically serial (one process at a time). These assumptions were included in their General Problem Solver (a computer program designed to solve well-defined problems). The successes (and limitations) of this theoretical approach are discussed by Gobet and Lane (2015, in press).

Weblink:
Tower of Hanoi

Newell and Simon (1972) used various well-defined, knowledge-lean problems. An example is the Tower of Hanoi (see Figure 12.10). The initial state of the problem consists of up to five discs piled in decreasing size on the first of three pegs. When all the discs are placed in the same order on the last peg, the problem has been solved. Only one disc can be moved at a time and a larger disc cannot be placed on top of a smaller one.

Newell and Simon (1972) identified a **problem space** for each problem. A problem space consists of the initial state of the problem, the goal state, all possible mental operators (e.g., moves) that can be applied to any state to change it into a different state, and all the intermediate problem states.

How do we solve well-defined problems with our limited processing capacity? According to Newell and Simon (1972), we rely heavily on **heuristics**. Heuristics are rules of thumb that are easy to use and often produce reasonably accurate answers. Heuristics can be contrasted with **algorithms**, which are generally complex methods or procedures guaranteed to lead to problem solution.

In this section, we consider some heuristics identified by Newell and Simon (1972). We will also discuss other heuristics and strategies for problem solving discovered by other researchers.

KEY TERMS

Problem space
An abstract description of all the possible states that can occur within a given problem.

Heuristics
Rules of thumb that are cognitively undemanding and often produce approximately accurate answers.

Algorithm
A computational procedure providing a specified set of steps to problem solution.

Means–ends analysis
A heuristic method for solving problems based on creating a subgoal to reduce the difference between the current state and the goal state.

Means–ends analysis

According to Newell and Simon (1972), the most important heuristic method is **means–ends analysis**:

- Note the difference between the current problem state and the goal state.
- Form a subgoal to reduce the difference between the current and goal states.
- Select a mental operator (e.g., move or moves) that permits attainment of the subgoal.

Means–ends analysis is generally very useful and assists problem solution. However, dramatic evidence that people sometimes persist with that heuristic even when it severely impairs performance was reported by Sweller and Levine (1982). Participants were given the maze shown in Figure 12.11, but most of it was not visible. Some participants could see the goal state (goal-information group) whereas others could not (no-goal-information group).

What do you think happened on this fairly simple problem? Use of means–ends analysis requires knowledge of goal location, and so only the goal-information group could use that heuristic. However, the problem was designed so means–ends analysis would not be useful – every correct move involved turning *away* from the goal. Participants in this group performed very poorly – only 10% solved the problem in 298 moves! In contrast, those in the other group solved the problem in only 38 moves on average.

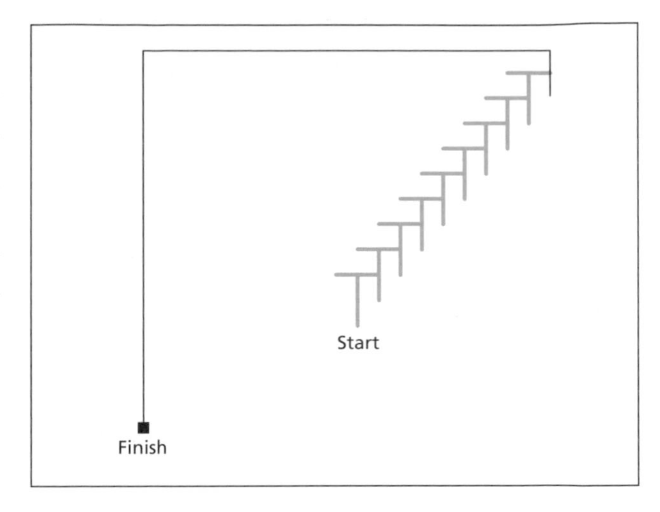

Figure 12.11
The maze used in the study by Sweller and Levine (1982).
Adapted from Sweller and Levine (1982).

Hill climbing

Newell and Simon (1972) also identified the **hill-climbing** heuristic. Hill climbing involves changing the present state within the problem into one closer to the goal. It is simpler than means–ends analysis and is mostly used when the problem solver has no clear understanding of the problem structure.

The hill-climbing heuristic involves a focus on *short-term goals*, and so often does not lead to problem solution. Someone using this heuristic is like a climber who tries to reach the highest mountain peak in the area by using the strategy of always moving upwards. This may work, but it is likely that the climber will find himself/herself trapped on a hill separated by several valleys from the highest peak.

Progress monitoring

MacGregor et al. (2001) argued that individuals engaged in problem solving use a heuristic known as **progress monitoring**. This involves assessing their rate of progress towards the goal. If progress is too slow to solve the problem within the maximum number of moves allowed, people adopt a different strategy.

MacGregor et al. (2001) obtained evidence for progress monitoring using the nine-dot problem (see Figure 12.8). Participants were given one line of the solution to assist them. Performance was worse in a condition in which participants had the illusion of making progress (and so were slow to switch strategies) than in another condition where it was more obvious that little progress was being made.

Payne and Duggan (2011) extended the general notion of progress monitoring. They gave participants an unsolvable water-jar problem (discussed earlier). The problem had a small or a large number of possible problem states. In the former condition, participants were more likely to repeat moves and thus to perceive progress towards a solution was not possible. As predicted, participants abandoned the problem in fewer moves when the problem had a small number of problem states.

Planning

It is generally assumed most people presented with complex problems will engage in some preliminary planning. If that is correct, areas within the prefrontal cortex

KEY TERMS

Hill climbing
A simple **heuristic** used by problem solvers in which they focus on making moves that will apparently put them closer to the goal.

Progress monitoring
A heuristic or rule of thumb in which slow progress towards problem solution triggers a change of strategy.

associated with planning and other complex cognitive processes should be activated during problem solving.

Evidence indicating the involvement of the prefrontal cortex comes from brain-damaged patients. Goel and Grafman (1995) found patients with prefrontal damage performed worse than healthy controls on the Tower of Hanoi task (see Figure 12.10) even though both groups used basically the same strategy. The patients were especially at a disadvantage compared to the controls on a difficult move involving moving away from the goal. Thus, patients with prefrontal damage find it harder to plan ahead.

Similar findings using water-jar problems were reported by Colvin et al. (2001). Patients with prefrontal damage and healthy controls used a relatively unsophisticated hill-climbing strategy. However, the patients performed worse because they found it harder to make moves in conflict with the strategy. Patients with damage to the left dorsolateral prefrontal cortex performed worse than those with right damage. As we will see later, there is neuroimaging evidence suggesting the left dorsolateral prefrontal cortex is involved in initial planning.

Prefrontal damage can also produce general problems in everyday life. As discussed earlier, Goel and Grafman (2000) studied a patient with damage to the right prefrontal cortex. He had very poor planning ability in spite of a high level of intelligence and so found it extremely difficult to cope with life. Goel et al. (2013) used a real-world travel planning task in which participants had to organise a trip to Italy for an American couple. Patients with right prefrontal damage had impaired planning in part because they made premature commitments to various decisions.

Dagher et al. (1999) used the Tower of London task in which coloured discs must be moved one by one from an initial state to match the goal state (see Figure 12.12) and participants are often instructed to plan the whole sequence of moves mentally before moving the discs. Dagher et al. found that the more complex versions of the task were associated with increased activity in several brain areas. Of particular note, the dorsolateral prefrontal cortex was more active when participants were engaged in solving complex versions of the Tower of London task.

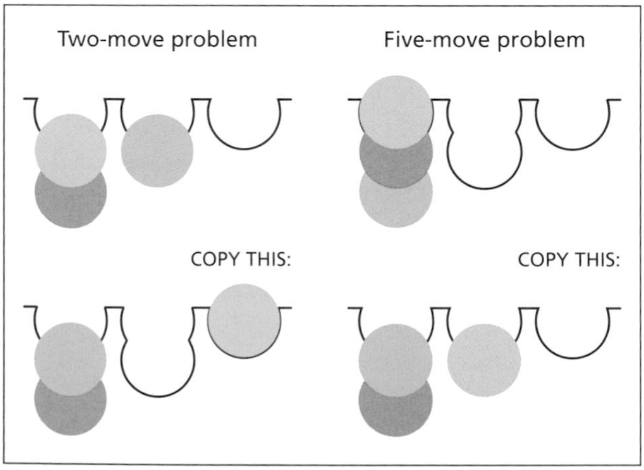

Figure 12.12
Tower of London task (two-move and five-move problems). The balls in the bottom half must be rearranged to match the arrangement in the top half.
From Dagher et al. (1999). By permission of Oxford University Press.

Sequential processing stages

Tasks such as the Tower of Hanoi (see Figure 12.10) and the Tower of London require planning the sequence of moves to be made. However, planning is only part of a sequence of processing stages including plan production and plan execution. With complex tasks, only some moves are typically planned, so executing the initial plan is followed by generating a further plan and then its execution.

Evidence supporting the distinction between plan production and plan execution was reported by Crescentini et al. (2012) using simple versions of the Tower of Hanoi task. The dorsolateral prefrontal cortex was more active during initial planning than plan execution. In contrast, posterior temporal areas, inferior frontal regions and dorsolateral premotor cortex were more activated during plan execution.

Nitschke et al. (2012) argued that Tower of London problems require participants to engage in problem representation followed by planning. They supported this view by obtaining eye-movement data. On problems placing high demands on forming a problem representation, participants alternated their gaze more often between the start and goal state. On problems imposing high demands on planning, in contrast, the last fixation of the start state was unusually prolonged. These findings are consistent with an initial stage of problem representation followed by planning.

Further support for separate stages of problem representation and planning was reported by Ruh et al. (2012), also using the Tower of London task. Activation in the *left* dorsolateral prefrontal cortex was greatest during problem representation. In contrast, activation in the *right* dorsolateral prefrontal cortex was greatest during planning itself.

How much planning?

How much explicit planning do most people use on complex problems? Newell and Simon (1972) assumed most problem solvers engage in only a modest amount of planning because of limited short-term memory capacity. Delaney et al. (2004) found participants solving water-jar problems showed little evidence of planning when free to choose their preferred strategy. However, participants instructed to generate the complete solution before making any moves showed clear evidence of being able to plan and solved the problem much faster than the controls.

Koppenol-Gonzalez et al. (2010) studied individual differences in students performing the Tower of London task. Some students engaged in efficient planning – they spent a long time in preplanning their moves and exhibited high levels of performance. Other participants showed little or no evidence of effective planning. They devoted a short period of time to preplanning and made numerous errors.

If problem solvers engage in deliberate planning, it seems likely they would be consciously aware of it. Evidence suggesting important problem-solving processes occur below the level of conscious awareness was reported by Paynter et al. (2010). They recorded event-related potentials (ERPs; see Glossary) during complex problem solving. Paynter et al. focused on early trials when there was no behavioural evidence participants were making any progress towards problem solution. However, there were clear differences in the ERPs associated with correct and incorrect moves. Thus, there are non-conscious learning mechanisms owing little or nothing to explicit plans.

Patsenko and Altmann (2010) provided some of the strongest evidence that most problem solvers may engage in little planning. Participants solved Tower of Hanoi problems. In the key condition, they added, deleted or moved discs during participants' saccades (eye movements) so they were not directly aware of the change. If participants had been using plans, such changes should have had a very disruptive effect on performance. In fact, there was minimal disruption, suggesting that performance was determined by immediate perceptual and attentional processes. Thus, the next move was mostly triggered by the *current* state of the problem rather than by a pre-formed plan.

KEY TERM

Cognitive miser
Someone who is economical with their time and effort when performing a thinking task.

In sum, the evidence suggests problem solvers engage in deliberate pre-planning some of the time. However, some problem-solving processes occur below the level of conscious awareness and many people often make little use of pre-planning.

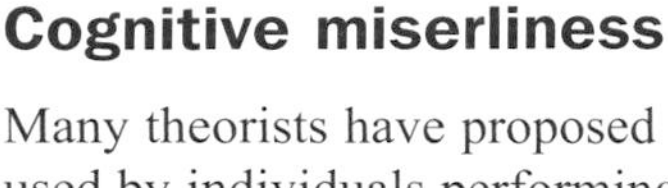

Cognitive miserliness

Many theorists have proposed dual-process theories to account for the strategies used by individuals performing cognitive tasks such as judgement and reasoning (Evans, 2008). For example, Kahneman (2003) distinguished between System 1 thinking (which is fast and effortless) and System 2 thinking (which is slow and effortful) (see Chapter 13).

Most dual-process theorists argue that many people are **cognitive misers**. A cognitive miser is someone who is typically economical with his/her time and effort on tasks requiring thinking. For example, Kahneman (2003) claimed System 2 thinking monitors or evaluates answers generated by System 1. However, this often fails to happen even when the generated answer is incorrect.

The Cognitive Reflection Test (see box below) provides evidence of the extent to which people are cognitive misers (Frederick, 2005). Why don't you take this very short test and then see how many of your answers are correct?

COMPANION @ WEBSITE

Weblink:
Cognitive reflection test

IN THE REAL WORLD: COGNITIVE REFLECTION TEST

1 A bat and a ball cost $1.10 in total. The bat costs $1.00 more than the ball. How much does the ball cost?

___ cents

2 If it takes 5 machines 5 minutes to make 5 widgets, how long would it take 100 machines to make 100 widgets?

___ minutes

3 In a lake, there is a patch of lily pads. Every day, the patch doubles in size. If it takes 48 days for the patch to cover the entire lake, how long would it take for the patch to cover half the lake?

___ days

The correct answers are 5 cents (problem 1), 5 minutes (problem 2) and 47 days (problem 3). Do not worry if you did not get them all right. When this test was administered at Harvard and Princeton Universities, 75% of the participants failed on at least one question and 20% were wrong on every question!

The most common wrong answers on the Cognitive Reflection Test are 10 cents (problem 1), 100 minutes (problem 2) and 24 days (problem 2). These answers strongly suggest people behave like cognitive misers. Consider the first problem. You probably rapidly thought of the answer "10 cents". However, it would follow that the bat cost $1.10, and so the total would be $1.20 rather than $1.10 as required.

Low scorers on the Cognitive Reflection Test perform relatively poorly on a wide range of judgement and reasoning tasks (Toplak et al., 2011). This occurs in part because low scorers are cognitive misers. However, it is also due partly to the fact that performance on the Cognitive Reflection Test correlates positively with intelligence (Toplak et al., 2011). Toplak et al. (2014) investigated this issue using an expanded version of the Cognitive Reflection Test. Scores on the test predicted performance on several thinking tasks even when the effects of intelligence were removed statistically.

There is overlap between the notion of cognitive miser and Newell and Simon's (1972) focus on problem solvers' use of heuristics or rules of thumb. In both cases, individuals resort to simple (and sometimes inaccurate) strategies. However, there is a difference. Newell and Simon assumed we use heuristics because we are forced to by our limited processing capacity. In contrast, cognitive misers use heuristics because they are *reluctant* to engage in effortful processing rather than because they cannot.

KEY TERM

Analogy
A comparison between two objects (or between a current and previous problem) that emphasises similarities between them.

ANALOGICAL PROBLEM SOLVING

Analogical problem solving involves solving problems by using analogies. An **analogy** is "a comparison between two objects, or systems of objects, that highlights respects in which they are thought to be similar" (*Stanford Encyclopedia of Philosophy*, 2013). It is extremely important in everyday life. Much of the time, we cope successfully with novel situations by relating them to situations we have encountered previously.

Analogical problem solving has proved valuable in the history of science. For example, the physicist Ernest Rutherford used a solar system analogy to understand the structure of the atom. He argued that electrons revolve around the nucleus as the planets revolve around the sun.

When do scientists make use of analogies? Chan et al. (2012) recorded group discussions among scientists working on the Mars Rover Mission. Uncertainty about scientific issues was a good predictor of the use of analogies. Analogies were useful – they reduced uncertainty and facilitated rapid, approximate problem solving.

If we are to use a previous problem to solve the current one, we must detect *similarities* between them. Chen (2002) identified three main types of similarity between problems:

1 *Superficial similarity*: Solution-irrelevant details (e.g., specific objects) are common to the two problems.
2 *Structural similarity*: Causal relations among some of the main components are shared by both problems.
3 *Procedural similarity*: Procedures for turning the solution principle into concrete operations are common to both problems.

Chen (2002) presented participants with a problem. To assist them, they were presented with an analogy having structural and procedural similarity with the problem or one having only structural similarity. Performance was significantly better in the former condition because those participants were more likely to find the correct procedures or actions to solve the problem.

Initially, we will consider factors determining *whether* people use relevant analogies when solving a problem. Then we will consider the processes involved when individuals solve an *explicit* analogical problem. Finally, we will consider individual differences in analogical problem solving.

Weblink:
Analogy

Findings: analogy detection

If you were given a problem, would you use a relevant analogy to solve it? Some findings are discouraging. Gick and Holyoak (1980) used a problem in which a patient with a malignant stomach tumour can only be saved by a special kind of ray. However, a ray strong enough to destroy the tumour will also destroy the healthy tissue, whereas a ray that does not harm healthy tissue will be too weak to destroy the tumour. Only 10% of participants solved this problem when presented on its own.

If you are puzzled as to the correct answer, here is an analogy. A general wants to capture a fortress. However, the roads to it are mined, making it too dangerous for the entire army to march along any one of them. However, the mines were set so small numbers of men could pass over safely. The general had his army converge at the same time on the fortress by walking along several different roads. The participants had previously memorised this story.

Gick and Holyoak (1980) found 80% of participants solved the radiation problem when informed the above story was relevant. However, only 40% did so when *not* informed of its relevance.

Why did Gick and Holyoak's (1980) participants fail to make spontaneous use of the relevant, memorised story? The lack of *superficial* similarities between the story and the problem was important. When the story was superficially similar to the problem (it involved a surgeon using rays on a cancer), 88% of participants spontaneously recalled it when given the radiation problem (Keane, 1987).

Gick and Holyoak's (1980) research involved the *reception paradigm*, in which participants received detailed information about a possible analogy before receiving a problem. In contrast, people in everyday life generally produce their own analogies: the *production paradigm*. Blanchette and Dunbar (2000) confirmed previous findings showing that participants given the reception paradigm often selected analogies based on superficial similarities. However, those given the production paradigm mostly produced analogies sharing structural features with the current problem.

Dunbar and Blanchette (2001) studied what leading molecular biologists and immunologists said during laboratory meetings. When they used analogies to fix experimental problems, the previous problem was often superficially similar to the current one. When scientists *generated* hypotheses, the analogies they used involved fewer superficial similarities and considerably more structural similarities. The take-home message is that the types of analogies people use depend importantly on their current goal.

How can people use analogies to solve problems when there are substantial dissimilarities between the current problem and a previous analogous problem? Day and Goldstone (2011) argued that this often happens in everyday life when people *interact* extensively with the first problem and are able to form a *concrete* mental model of it.

Day and Goldstone (2011) obtained empirical support for the above argument. Participants who interacted with a task involving the oscillating motion of a ball suspended between two elastic bands were reasonably successful at solving a subsequent task involving regulating the population of a city.

How can we increase people's ability to use analogies? We should consider *memory* processes because retrieval of a relevant analogy is required (Loewenstein, 2010). Loewenstein argued that analogy retrieval is more likely if the underlying structure of a current problem is made clear. Kurtz and Loewenstein (2007) did this by asking some participants to *compare* the underlying structure of two similar problems (one was Duncker's radiation problem). Other participants considered the two problems *separately*. Participants in all conditions had previously been presented with the fortress story.

What did Kurtz and Loewenstein (2007) find? Participants who had compared the two problems were more likely to solve the tumour problem than those who considered the two problems separately (54% vs. 38%). This advantage was due to better retrieval of the fortress story analogy. Thus, effective *encoding* of the to-be-solved problem is important.

Gentner et al. (2009) used a similar approach in a study on management consultants. These consultants studied two examples of a type of contract structure one example at a time or with instructions to compare them. After that, they retrieved a similar example from their past experience. There were two main findings. First, the comparison group found it easier to recall a relevant example. Second, the *quality* of retrieved examples in terms of embodying the key principle common to the two presented examples was significantly higher in the comparison group.

In sum, it is important for problem solvers to form a complete description of the underlying structure of the current problem. This increases the probability of retrieving a relevant analogy and also increases its quality.

Findings: processes

What processes are involved in analogical problem solving or reasoning? Much relevant research has used four-term analogy problems taking the form A:B::C:D. Here is an example taken from Schmidt et al. (2012, p. 1374): FLAME: CANDLE::STEEPLE:CHURCH. Participants decided whether the two word pairs expressed the same relationship (i.e., is it true that flame is to candle as steeple is to church?).

Why are four-term analogy problems used so often? They are tightly controlled – all the necessary information is presented explicitly and there is a single correct answer. This facilitates the task of understanding the underlying processes.

Some processes involved in such problems may occur below the level of conscious awareness. Reber et al. (2014) presented participants with word pairs (e.g., *desk–bus*) and asked them to judge how closely related the words were semantically. The words were judged to be more closely related when participants had previously been presented subliminally (below the level of conscious awareness) with a word pair expressing the same semantic relation (e.g., *table–car*). These findings suggest analogies can be detected unconsciously.

Sequential processing stages

Four-term analogy problems involve three sequential processing stages:

1 *encoding* of the first pair of words based on the relationship between them;
2 *mapping* (a connection is formed between the first words of each pair and an inference drawn as to the fourth word);
3 *response* (decision concerning the correctness of the fourth word).

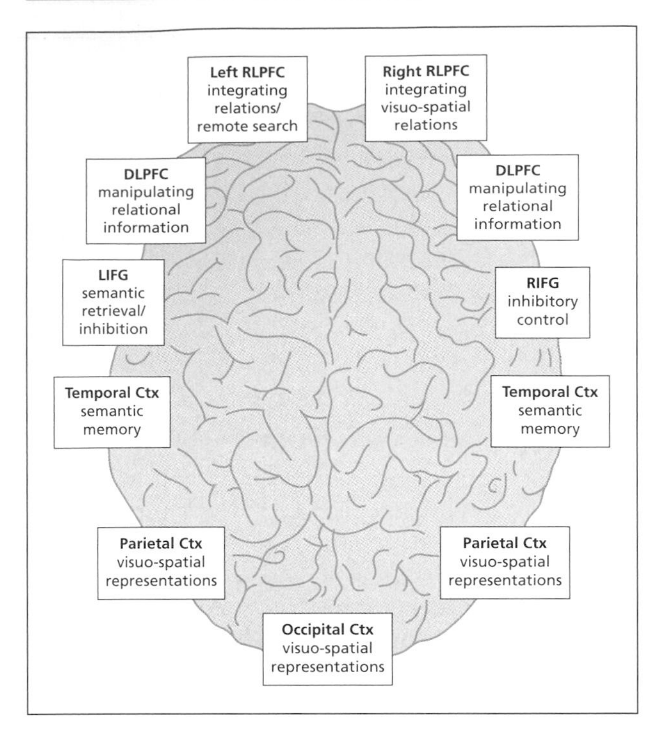

Figure 12.13
Summary of key brain regions and their associated functions in relational reasoning based on patient and neuroimaging studies. Abbreviations: RLPFC, rostolateral prefrontal cortex; DLPFC, dorsolateral prefrontal cortex; LIFG, left inferior frontal gyrus; Ctx, cortex.

From Krawczyk (2012). Reprinted with permission from Elsevier.

Knowlton et al. (2012) discussed computational models based on the notion that analogical reasoning involves sequential stages. They argued that it has to involve serial processing (one process at a time) because of the processing demands involved. In their theoretical approach, they identify sequential stages of analogue retrieval, mapping, analogical inference and schema induction. These schemas are abstract and are formed on the basis of comparisons drawn between the analogy and the current problem.

Knowlton et al. (2012) pointed out that there had previously been a large gap between computational models and the cognitive neuroscience approach to analogical reasoning. However, this gap is rapidly narrowing because of developments within cognitive neuroscience.

Krawczyk et al. (2010) assessed brain activity using functional magnetic resonance imaging (fMRI; see Glossary) during analogical reasoning at each of the above three stages. Encoding involved several frontal regions including the inferior frontal gyrus, the dorsolateral prefrontal cortex (BA9/46) and the rostrolateral prefrontal cortex (BA10; shown in Figure 12.13). All these areas are known to be associated with complex cognitive processing. Similar brain regions (centred on the inferior frontal gyrus and rostrolateral prefrontal cortex) were engaged by mapping. There was less prefrontal activation during the response stage because most cognitive processing required by the task had occurred prior to this stage.

Maguire et al. (2012) obtained similar findings using event-related potentials (ERPs; see Glossary). Considerable processing occurred during the encoding stage with similar (but shorter-lasting) processing occurring during mapping. Processing was more limited during the response stage. The ERPs indicated participants often distinguished between correct and incorrect fourth terms within about 400 ms because most required cognitive processing had occurred earlier.

Krawczyk (2012) summarised neuroimaging and patient research on the brain areas involved in analogical reasoning (see Figure 12.13). Occipital and parietal regions are used for visual and spatial processing, followed by extensive involvement of the prefrontal cortex. Rostral prefrontal cortex (approximately BA10) is involved in integrating information within analogical problems. One region within BA10 is activated throughout analogical reasoning whereas a second region is only activated during mapping and response (Volle et al., 2010).

The dorsolateral prefrontal cortex and the inferior frontal gyrus are involved in inhibitory processes to prevent distraction and interference. Finally, the temporal lobes are involved because they contain information about the meanings of concepts within semantic memory.

Krawczyk et al. (2008) argued that successful analogical problem solving often requires executive processes *inhibiting* responding to relevant distractors. Consider the following picture analogy:

sandwich:lunchbox::hammer:????

Possible answers are *toolbox* (correct), *nail* (semantic distractor), *gavel* (auctioneer's hammer: perceptual distractor) and *ribbon* (irrelevant distractor).

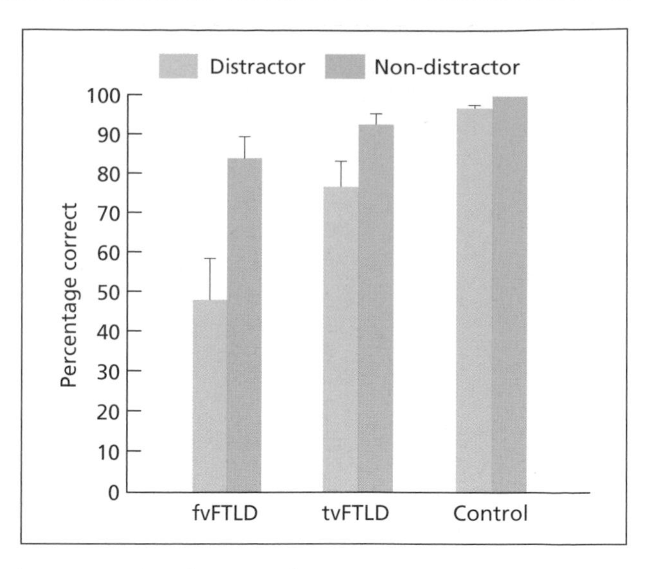

Figure 12.14
Mean percentage correct responses on analogical problems with and without relevant distractors. Abbreviations: fvFTLD = fronto-temporal lobar degeneration; tvFTLD = temporal-variant fronto-temporal lobar degeneration.

Reprinted from Krawczyk et al. (2008). With permission from Elsevier.

Krawczyk et al. (2008) gave the above task to patients with damage to the prefrontal cortex, patients with damage to the temporal area and healthy controls. They hypothesised that inhibitory processes involve the prefrontal cortex. As predicted, the frontal patients were more likely than the temporal patients to give incorrect responses involving relevant semantic or perceptual distractors. In addition, only the frontal patients showed enhanced performance when no relevant distractors were present (see Figure 12.14). Thus, an intact prefrontal cortex is needed to inhibit answers related to the correct answer.

Cho et al. (2010) identified more precisely the prefrontal regions involved in inhibitory control. Activity in the inferior frontal gyrus increased when the amount of interfering information increased and so there was greater need for inhibitory control.

Schmidt et al. (2012) argued that processes (and brain areas) involved in analogical processing depend on the precise *nature* of the analogy. They distinguished between *associative* analogies (e.g., CAR:TRAILER::DONKEY:CART) and *categorical* analogies (e.g., RODENT:MOUSE::APPLIANCE:TOASTER). They argued that the relationships in associative analogies can be experienced directly whereas those in categorical analogies are more abstract.

Schmidt et al. (2012) found patients with left hemisphere damage performed equally poorly with associative and categorical analogies. This is as expected given the dominance of the left hemisphere for language processes and the verbal nature of the analogies. However, patients with right hemisphere damage were more impaired with categorical than associative analogies reflecting the more complex and abstract nature of categorical relationships.

Working memory

The working memory system (see Chapter 6) is involved in analogical problem solving. This was shown clearly by Morrison et al. (2001). Participants received verbal analogies (e.g., BLACK:WHITE::NOISY:QUIET) and decided whether they were true or false. They also received picture-based analogies involving cartoon characters. These tasks were performed on their own or while participants performed an additional task imposing demands on one component of the working memory system.

Interactive exercise:
Brain regions in reasoning

What did Morrison et al. (2001) find? First, performance on verbal and pictorial analogies was impaired when the additional task involved the central executive (an attention-like system). Thus, solving analogies requires the limited capacity of the central executive. Second, performance on verbal analogies was impaired when the additional task involved the phonological loop (used for verbal rehearsal). This happened because both tasks involved verbal processing. Third, performance on pictorial analogies suffered when the additional task involved the visuo-spatial sketchpad (used for basic visual and spatial processing).

Cho et al. (2007) obtained further support for the involvement of working memory in analogical problems. They manipulated the complexity of the problem and the need for interference resolution. Analogical performance was especially poor when participants faced the combination of high problem complexity and interference resolution because this overloaded the central executive.

Individual differences

Analogical reasoning performance correlates about +0.7 with intelligence (Spearman, 1927), which suggests higher-level cognitive processes are important. This conclusion is also suggested by the research discussed above on the role of working memory (see Morrison (2005) for a review).

The association between analogical reasoning and intelligence becomes even closer when we consider research on the Raven's Progressive Matrices (Raven et al., 1998). A sample item resembling those in Raven's Progressive Matrices is shown in Figure 12.15.

The Raven's test is used as a measure of fluid intelligence (non-verbal intelligence applied to novel problems). In addition, however, it is a test involving geometrical analogies (the correct answer is chosen based on analogical reasoning). As such, it is theoretically important to determine dimensions of individual differences influencing test performance.

Several studies have assessed the relationship between Raven's Advanced Progressive Matrices and working memory capacity (the ability to process and store information at the same time; see Glossary). Ackerman et al. (2005) found in a meta-analysis that the overall correlation between those two measures was +0.50. This relationship is due mainly to Raven's items involving new rule combinations rather than the same rules as previous items (Wiley et al., 2011).

Individuals high in working memory capacity may have superior Raven's performance because they have superior attentional or executive *control* than low scorers or because they have greater

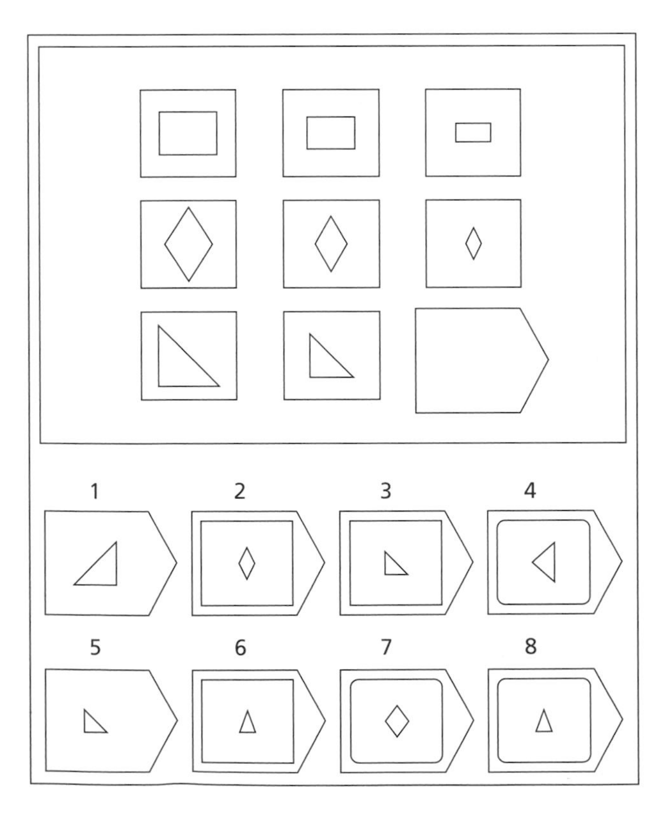

Figure 12.15
A sample matrix problem similar to those in Raven's Progressive Matrices. The task is to look along the rows and down the columns to decide which of the eight options underneath completes the overall pattern.
From Wiley et al. (2011). © American Psychological Association.

attentional *capacity*. Jarosz and Wiley (2012) obtained support for the attentional control explanation using eye tracking. Individuals high in working memory capacity spent less time than low scorers fixated on the most common incorrect response on Raven's problems. This finding suggests they have greater attentional control than low-capacity individuals and so are less susceptible to distraction by the most common incorrect response.

Chuderski and Nęcka (2012) obtained measures of attentional capacity and attentional control. Attentional capacity correlated highly with performance on the Raven's Matrices. Attentional control also correlated with Raven's performance but to a lesser extent. Attentional capacity and attentional control made separate contributions to Raven's performance, indicating that both contribute to the solving of geometrical analogies.

KEY TERM

Expertise
The high level of knowledge and performance in a given domain that an expert has achieved through years of systematic practice.

EXPERTISE

So far we have mostly discussed studies in which the time available for learning was short, the tasks were relatively limited and prior specific knowledge was not required. In the real world, however, people often spend several years acquiring knowledge and skills in a given area (e.g., psychology, law, medicine, journalism). The end point of such long-term learning is the development of **expertise**. Expertise involves a very high level of thinking and performance in a given domain (e.g., chess) as a result of many years of practice.

The development of expertise resembles problem solving in that experts are extremely efficient at solving numerous problems in their area of expertise. As mentioned in the Introduction, however, most traditional research on problem solving involved "knowledge-lean" problems requiring no special knowledge or training. In contrast, studies on expertise have typically used "knowledge-rich" problems requiring much knowledge beyond that contained in the problem.

In this section, we first consider chess expertise. There are several advantages to studying chess playing (Gobet et al., 2004). First, the ELO ranking system (named after the chess master Arpad Elo) provides a precise assessment of individual players' level of expertise. Second, expert chess players develop specific cognitive skills (e.g., pattern recognition, selective search) useful in other areas of expertise. Third, information about chess experts' remarkable memory for chess positions generalises very well to most other forms of expertise.

After discussing chess expertise, we turn to medical expertise (especially medical diagnosis). After that, we consider the possible role of brain plasticity in expertise. Finally, we consider Ericsson's theoretical approach, according to which deliberate practice is the main requirement for the development of expertise.

CHESS-PLAYING EXPERTISE

As already indicated, there are various reasons why it is valuable to study chess-playing expertise. For example, unlike many other sports and games, we can measure chess players' levels of skill very precisely based on their results against other players. In addition, the fact that permanent records are kept of chess players' tournament performance over their entire career means that detailed longitudinal data are available for analysis.

Why are some people much better than others at playing chess? The obvious answer is that they have devoted far more time to *practice* – it takes about 10,000

KEY TERM

Template
As applied to chess, an abstract schematic structure consisting of a mixture of fixed and variable information about chess pieces and positions.

hours to become a grandmaster. Of special importance, expert chess players have much more detailed information about chess positions stored in long-term memory than non-experts.

In classic research, De Groot (1965) presented chess players with brief presentations of board positions from actual games. After removing the board, they reconstructed the positions. Chess masters recalled the positions much more accurately than less expert players (91% vs. 43%, respectively). This finding is due to differences in stored chess positions rather than in memory ability – there were no group differences in remembering random board positions.

We will shortly consider the strategies used by human expert chess players. These strategies are totally different from those used by chess-playing computers. Consider, for example, the computer Deep Blue, which beat the then World Chess Champion, Garry Kasparov, in May 1997. It evaluated up to 200 million positions per second and processed up to about six moves ahead.

Template theory

Weblink:
Article about Deep Blue

It is obvious that expert chess players possess much more chess-related information in long-term memory than novices. However, it is harder to identify the precise nature of such information. Fernand Gobet (see photo) (e.g., Gobet & Waters, 2003) made an influential attempt to do so in his template theory. According to the theory, much of this information is in the form of templates.

A **template** is an abstract, schematic structure more general than an actual board position. Each template consists of a *core* (fixed information) plus *slots* (containing variable information about pieces and locations). Each template typically stores information relating to about ten pieces although it can be larger than that. Their possession of slots makes templates adaptable and flexible.

Fernand Gobet. Courtesy Fernand Gobet.

Template theory makes several testable predictions. First, it predicts that chess positions are stored in three templates, some of which are relatively large.

Second, it is assumed that outstanding chess players owe their excellence mostly to their superior template-based knowledge of chess rather than their use of slow, strategy-based processes. This template-based knowledge can be accessed rapidly and allows expert players to narrow down the possible moves they need to consider. If these assumptions are correct, the performance of outstanding players should remain very high even when making their moves under considerable time pressure.

Third, it is assumed that expert chess players store away the precise board locations of pieces after studying a board position. In addition, it is assumed that chess pieces close together are most likely to be found in the same template (Gobet & Simon, 2000).

Fourth, it is predicted that expert chess players will have better recall of apparently random chess positions than non-experts. This is because some patterns occur by chance even in random positions, and these patterns relate to template-based information.

Findings

Support for the first prediction was reported by Gobet and Clarkson (2004). Expert players recalled chess board positions much better than novices. However, the number of templates did not vary as a function of playing strength, averaging out at about 2. The maximum template size was 13–15 for masters compared to only about 6 for novices.

Case study:
Recording eye movement

Evidence relating to the second prediction is more inconsistent. If greater expertise is associated with *rapid* access to relevant information in long-term memory, we would expect this to be evident in eye-movement data. Supportive evidence was reported by Charness et al. (2001), who asked expert and intermediate chess players to identify the best move in various chess positions. Their first five eye fixations (lasting a total of only about one second) were recorded. Even at this early stage, the experts were more likely than intermediate players to fixate on tactically relevant pieces (80% vs. 64% of fixations, respectively).

Further support for the second prediction was reported by Burns (2004) who considered chess performance in blitz chess, in which the entire game must be completed in five minutes (less than 5% of the time normally available). It was assumed that performance in blitz chess must depend mainly on players' template-based knowledge because there is too little time to engage in slow searching through possible moves. As predicted, performance in blitz chess correlated highly (between +0.78 and +0.90) with performance in normal chess.

Evidence apparently inconsistent with the second prediction was reported by van Harreveld et al. (2007). Skill differences between players were less predictive of game outcome as the time available decreased. This finding suggests slow processes are more important for strong players than for weak ones.

Moxley et al. (2012) gave experts and tournament players five minutes to select the best possible move with several problems. The players thought aloud while performing this task, which allowed the researchers to compare the first move mentioned against the one finally chosen. The final move was generally much stronger than the first move for both experts and tournament players and across the various levels of task difficulty (see Figure 12.16). These findings indicate that slow, strategy-based processes are very important in determining chess performance.

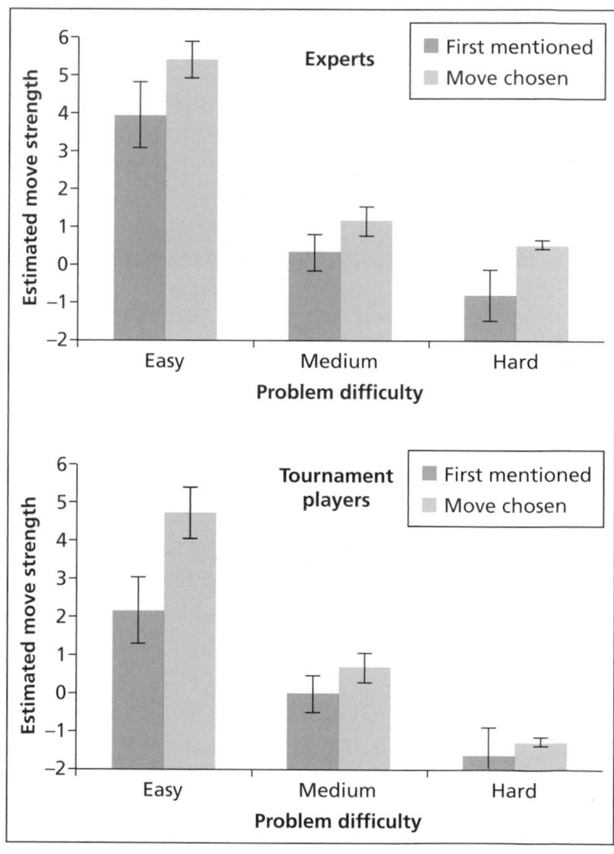

Figure 12.16
Mean strength of the first-mentioned move and the move chosen as a function of problem difficulty by experts (top panel) and tournament players (bottom panel).
From Moxley et al. (2012). With permission from Elsevier.

We turn now to the third prediction. Most studies indicate chess players typically recall the precise squares on the board occupied by given pieces within a template that are close together on the board. However, McGregor and Howes (2002) pointed out that participants in previous research had generally been asked to *memorise* board positions. In contrast, actual chess playing focuses much more on *evaluating* board positions.

McGregor and Howes (2002) asked expert and non-skilled players to evaluate various chess positions (e.g., decide which colour was winning). After that, the players decided on a test of recognition memory whether they had seen board positions before. Some board positions were *identical* to those presented previously, whereas others were *shifted* (all pieces moved one square horizontally). Still others were *distorted* (only one piece was moved one square but this changed the attack/defence relations).

What did McGregor and Howes (2002) find? Expert players had much better memory for attack/defence relations than precise board locations of the pieces. In similar fashion, Linhares et al. (2012) distinguished between errors in reconstructing chess positions that involved abstract features reflecting the strategic situation and those involving superficial features (e.g., specific board locations). Masters differed from grandmasters more with respect to memory failures for abstract features (e.g., strategically significant attacks or defences) than superficial features.

The fourth prediction is that expert players will have better recall than non-experts of *random* chess positions. Gobet and Simon (1996) found a small effect of skill on memory for random-board positions in a meta-analysis. However, Gobet and Waters (2003) pointed out that the random-board positions used in these studies were not totally random. More specifically, the pieces placed on the board were *not* selected at random (e.g., two kings were always present).

Gobet and Waters (2003) used truly random positions and pieces. The findings were as predicted – the number of pieces recalled varied from 14.8 for the most expert players to 12 for the least expert.

Evaluation

Template theory has several successes to its credit. First, much of the information experts store from a board position is in the form of a few large templates (McGregor & Howes, 2002). Second, outstanding chess players possess much more knowledge about chess positions than experts, and this gives them a substantial advantage when playing chess. Third, the tendency of experts to win at blitz chess is due mainly to their superior template-based knowledge (Burns, 2004). Fourth, experts have better recall than non-experts of random-board positions (Gobet & Waters, 2003).

What are the limitations of template theory? First, slow search processes are more important to expert players than assumed by the theory. For example, they look ahead more moves than non-expert players (Charness, 1981) and skill level is less predictive of outcome with reduced time available per move (van Harreveld et al., 2007).

Second, the most expert players are more skilled at using strategies allowing them to go beyond stored knowledge of chess positions. Bilalić et al. (2008a) presented chess players with a problem solvable in five moves using a familiar strategy but in only three moves using a less familiar solution. No candidate masters found the shorter solution, whereas 50% of the international masters did. Thus, the international masters were much better at going beyond the familiar, template-based solution.

Third, the precise nature of the information stored in long-term memory remains controversial. It is assumed within template theory that precise locations of individual pieces are typically stored. However, there is evidence that attack/defence relations may be more important (McGregor & Howes, 2002; Linhares et al., 2012).

MEDICAL EXPERTISE

We turn now to medical expertise, and the ability of medical experts to make rapid and accurate diagnoses. This ability is important because medical decision making is often a matter of life or death. In this section, we will focus mostly on radiology and the impact of expertise on diagnoses based on X-ray evidence. Even expert radiologists are prone to error and the false negative rate (i.e., failures to detect disease) can reach 30% in some areas (Krupinski, 2011). Research on expertise in dermatology (skin diseases) will also be discussed.

How do the strategies used by medical experts differ from those of unskilled ones? Theorists differ in their answers. However, the distinction between explicit and implicit reasoning is central to many theoretical viewpoints (Engel, 2008). Explicit reasoning is slow, deliberate and associated with conscious awareness. In contrast, implicit reasoning is fast, automatic, and not associated with conscious awareness. The crucial assumption is that medical experts engage mainly in implicit reasoning while novices rely mostly on explicit reasoning. Note that dual-process theories of judgement (see Chapter 13) and reasoning (see Chapter 14) involve rather similar distinctions between deliberate, explicit processes and rapid, implicit ones.

We will shortly examine evidence relevant to the above theoretical position. This evidence is more relevant to *visual* specialities such as pathology, radiology and dermatology than more technical specialities such as surgery or anaesthesiology (Engel, 2008). In addition, even when medical experts start with fast, automatic processes, they generally *cross-check* their diagnoses with slow, deliberate processes (McLaughlin et al., 2008).

Findings

How can we identify the diagnostic strategies used by medical experts and novices? Eye tracking is a useful technique that provides information about doctors' focus of attention while examining case slides. Krupinski et al. (2013) carried out a longitudinal study of pathologists viewing breast biopsies at the start of their first, second, third and fourth years of residency. The findings from one participant are shown in Figure 12.17. They show that there was a substantial reduction in the number of fixations per slide and there was less examination of non-diagnostic regions.

Kundel et al. (2007) tracked eye movements while doctors experienced in mammography examined difficult mammograms showing or not showing breast cancer. The mean search time with mammograms showing cancer was 27 seconds. However, the median time to *fixate* a cancer was 1.13 seconds, and was typically less than one second for the experts. There was a correlation of about –0.9

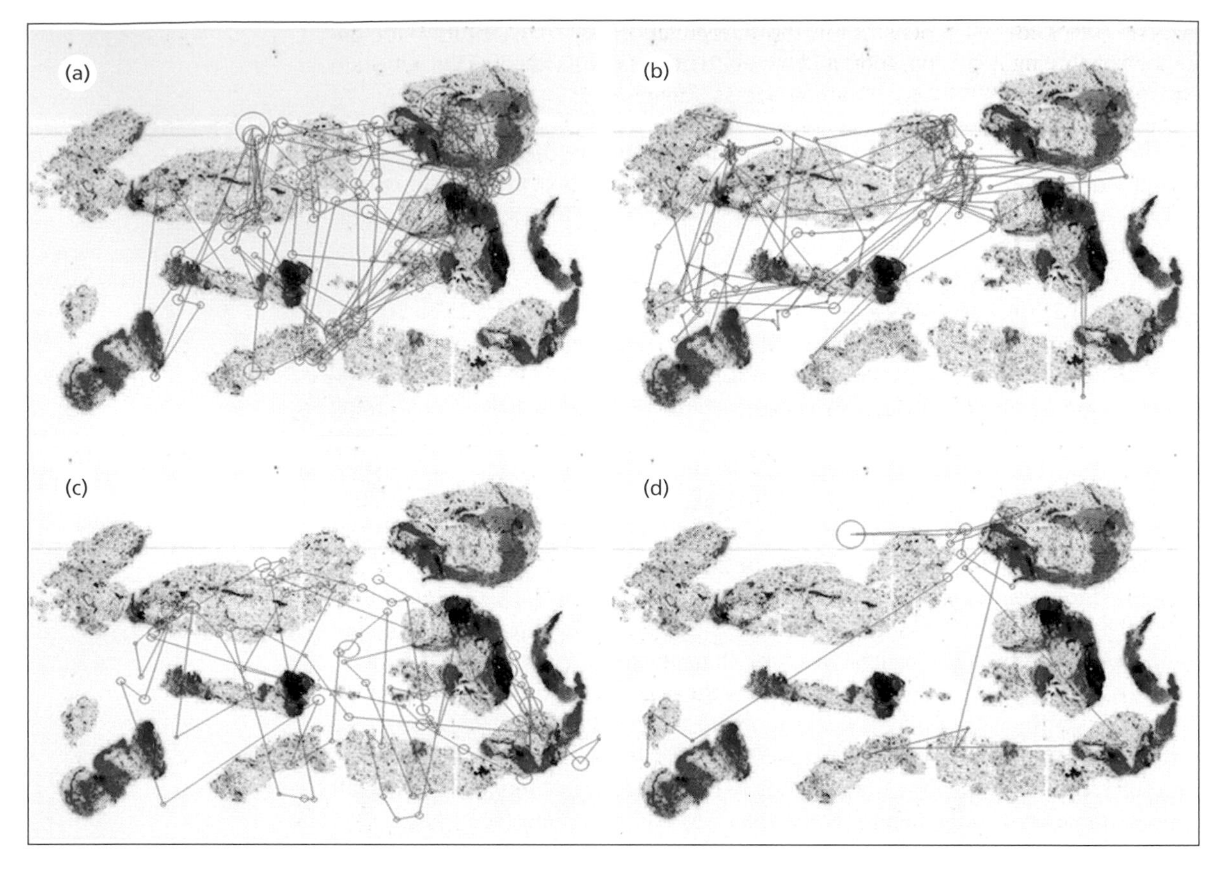

Figure 12.17
Eye fixations of a pathologist given the same biopsy whole-slide image starting in year 1 (a) and ending in year 4 (d). Larger circles indicate longer fixation times.
From Krupinski et al. (2013). Reprinted with permission from Elsevier.

between time of first fixation on the cancer and performance (i.e., accurately detecting breast cancer), meaning fast fixation was an excellent predictor of high performance. The most expert doctors typically fixated on the cancer almost immediately, suggesting they used holistic or global processes. In contrast, the least expert doctors relied on a slower processing strategy.

Early evidence that medical experts can detect abnormalities very rapidly was reported by Kundel and Nodine (1975). Chest radiographs were presented for only 200 milliseconds to prevent visual search. Experienced radiologists interpreted the radiographs correctly 70% of the time.

Expertise is not the only factor influencing patterns of eye movements. The type of image is also important. Kok et al. (2012) compared images showing focal or localised diseases (e.g., tumours) and those showing diffuse diseases. Experts and non-experts both showed similarly long fixations with focal diseases but shorter, more dispersed ones with diffuse diseases. The main reason experts outperformed the non-experts in diagnostic accuracy was because of their superior knowledge.

Are the effects of expertise on eye movements similar across different domains of expertise? Gegenfurtner et al. (2011) addressed this issue in a meta-analysis (see Glossary) focusing on the interpretation of visual information in domains including medicine, sport and transportation. Several differences between experts and non-experts were common across domains: (1) shorter fixations; (2) faster first fixations on task-relevant information; (3) more fixations on task-relevant information; (4) fewer fixations on task-irrelevant areas; and (5) longer saccades (rapid eye movements).

The above findings are consistent with two theoretical approaches. First, there is the information-reduction hypothesis (Haider & Frensch, 1999). According to this hypothesis, the development of expertise is associated with an increasingly efficient and selective allocation of attention. Second, there is the holistic model (Kundel et al., 2007), according to which experts can extract information from a wider area than non-experts with each fixation. As predicted by this model, experts fixated task-relevant areas faster than non-experts and successive fixations were further apart.

What cognitive processes do experts use when diagnosing diseases from X-rays? The speed and accuracy of their performance resemble our ability to perceive the gist of visual scenes. For example, Prass et al. (2013; see Chapter 7) presented photographs for only 30 milliseconds and found observers could detect whether an animal or a vehicle had been presented on more than 90% of trials. It is tempting to conclude "automatic" processes not requiring attention underlie such impressive performance. However, the evidence (e.g., Cohen et al., 2011; see Chapter 16) suggests some attention is needed for conscious perception of the gist of natural scenes.

Melo et al. (2012) tested the above notion that medical experts use similar processes to those we all use when perceiving visual scenes. They found comparably fast times to diagnose lesions in chest X-ray images and to name animals (1.33 vs. 1.23 seconds, respectively). Of most importance, diagnosing and naming animals involved activation in very similar brain regions (see Figure 12.18). However, diagnosing lesions was associated with greater activation in the frontal sulcus and posterior cingulate cortex, suggesting diagnosing is more cognitively demanding than naming animals. Naming letters involved similar brain regions to diagnosing lesions and naming animals but with less activation.

How can we explain the above findings? Melo et al. (2012) suggested medical experts engage in rapid pattern recognition: each slide is compared against stored patterns from the past. In other words, they use a predominantly *visual* strategy. In contrast, non-experts may use a more analytic approach in which they consider the various clinical features prior to offering a diagnosis.

Kulatunga-Moruzi et al. (2004) tested the above assumptions in a study in which three groups varying in expertise diagnosed skin diseases from case photographs. Some participants made their decisions purely on the basis of the photographs, whereas others were given a comprehensive verbal description before each photograph.

The obvious prediction is that all groups should have produced more accurate diagnoses when given verbal descriptions as well as case photographs. That was, indeed, the case with the least expert group. In striking contrast, the more expert groups (including dermatologists) performed better when *not* given the verbal descriptions. Experts used a rapid visual strategy and the verbal descriptions interfered with their ability to use that strategy effectively.

Most of the research discussed so far is consistent with the notion that experts can make accurate diagnoses without relying on slow, analytic processes. That is

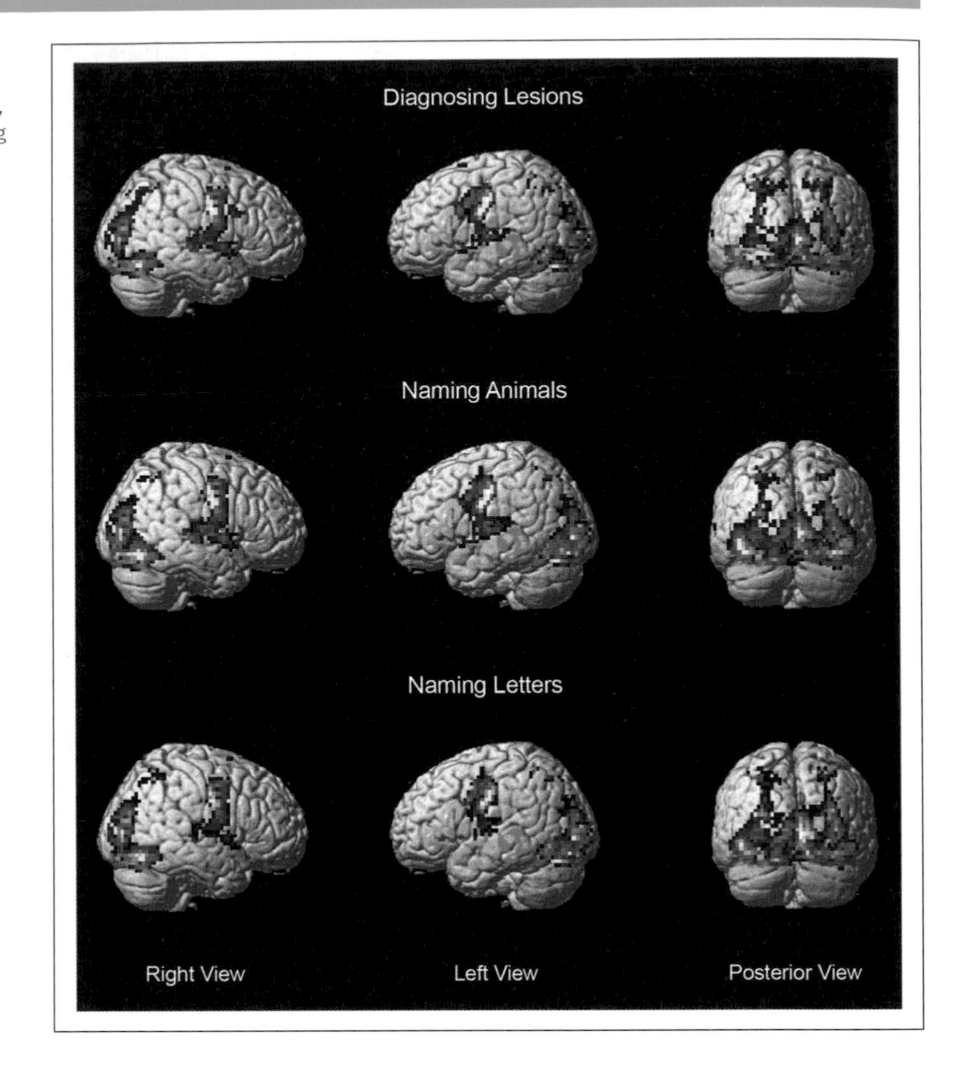

Figure 12.18
Brain activation while diagnosing lesions in X-rays, naming animals and naming letters. The first column provides a right view, the middle column a left view and the last column a posterior view.
From Melo et al. (2012).

an oversimplification. Mamede et al. (2010) compared the performance of medical experts and non-experts providing diagnoses immediately or after a process of analytic thinking. Analytic thinking enhanced the diagnostic performance of experts with complex cases but not simple ones. In contrast, non-experts derived no benefit from engaging in analytic thinking.

Evaluation

The diagnostic strategies used by medical experts and non-experts often differ considerably. Eye-tracking studies have provided support for the notion that experts use fast (almost automatic) processes more effectively than non-experts. There is also support for the notion that there is an important distinction between such processes and deliberate, analytic processes. Finally, there is interesting evidence that the processes used by experts in diagnosis resemble those used in visual recognition of everyday objects.

What are the limitations of theory and research on medical expertise? First, most studies involve comparisons between experts and non-experts. This approach is valuable but is uninformative about the learning processes responsible for the development of expertise.

Second, more research is needed to understand what happens when experts and non-experts use a combination of fast and analytic processes. For example, Kulatunga-Moruzi et al. (2011) found non-experts benefited from this combination when fast processes preceded analytic ones but not when analytic processes came first. This issue is important given that doctors in real-life settings typically combine both types of processing during diagnosis.

Third, it has been claimed that the fast processes often used by medical experts are "automatic". However, the notion of "automaticity" is complex and imprecise (see Chapter 5), and there is as yet no compelling evidence that medical experts use automatic processes.

KEY TERM

Plasticity
Changes in brain structure and function dependent on experience that affect behaviour.

Chess expertise vs. medical expertise

Chess and medical expertise have several similarities. First, several years of intensive training are needed to attain genuine expertise. Second, extensive training leads to the acquisition of huge amounts of relevant stored knowledge that can be accessed rapidly. Third, experts in both areas are superior to non-experts at using rapid (possibly "automatic") processes. Fourth, experts in both areas make flexible use of analytic or strategy-based processes when necessary.

What are the differences between chess and medical expertise? First, the form in which knowledge is stored may differ between the two kinds of expertise. Much of the knowledge possessed by chess experts consists of fairly abstract templates. In contrast, the knowledge possessed by medical experts is probably less abstract and more visual in nature. Second, chess experts have to relate a current chess position to their stored knowledge and then consider their subsequent moves and those of their opponent. In contrast, the task of medical experts is more *narrowly* focused on relating information about a specific case to their stored knowledge.

BRAIN PLASTICITY

We know the development of expertise involves acquiring huge amounts of knowledge and specialised cognitive processes. What is more controversial is whether the development of expertise also causes *modifications* within the brain. The key concept here is **plasticity**, which refers to "changes in structure and function of the brain that affect behaviour and that are related to experience or training" (Herholz & Zatorre, 2012, p. 486). It is likely that structural changes resulting from plasticity facilitate further learning and the enhancement of expertise.

Important research has been carried out on London taxi or cab drivers. To obtain a licence to drive black cabs, they must acquire "The Knowledge". This consists of detailed knowledge of the 25,000 streets within six miles of Charing Cross and of the locations of thousands of hospitals, tube stations and so on. Unsurprisingly, it takes three years to acquire all this information.

How do cab drivers develop this extraordinary knowledge and expertise? High intelligence is certainly not essential – the mean IQ of London cab drivers is around the average in the population at large. However, the hippocampus (an area within the medial temporal lobes) is of major importance. This is unsurprising given its crucial role in long-term memory (see Chapter 6).

Maguire et al. (2006) tested an older patient, TT, who had recently suffered extensive hippocampal damage. He still possessed a good knowledge of London landmarks and their spatial relationships. However, his navigation skills had deteriorated considerably. He relied excessively on main roads and became lost when using minor roads.

Does acquisition of The Knowledge have a direct effect on the hippocampus? The answer is likely to be "Yes". Experienced London cab drivers have a greater volume of grey matter in the *posterior* hippocampus than novice drivers or other control groups, and older full-time cab drivers have greater grey matter volume in this area than those of the same age who have retired (Woollett et al., 2009).

There are disadvantages associated with learning huge amounts of spatial knowledge about London streets. Taxi drivers performed poorly on tasks requiring them to learn and remember *new* word–word or object–place associations (Woollett & Maguire, 2009). Of interest, these drivers had a smaller volume of grey matter than other people in the *anterior* hippocampus, which is important for processing novel stimuli and encoding information. The very extensive involvement of the hippocampus in learning The Knowledge may impair the ability to acquire new information.

Causality

The findings discussed so far are *correlational* and so cannot show that acquiring The Knowledge *causes* hippocampal changes. Less indirect evidence was reported by Woollett and Maguire (2011). They studied adults who had spent several years acquiring The Knowledge. Those who qualified to become London taxi drivers had a selective increase in grey matter in their posterior hippocampus whereas those who failed did not.

More convincing evidence that developing expertise can modify the brain was reported in a longitudinal study by Scholz et al. (2009). Individuals learning to juggle showed a 5% increase in grey and white matter in the visual motion area over a 6-week training period, and this increase was mostly still present at follow-up.

Several studies have assessed the effects of musical training on changes in brain structure and function (Herholz and Zatorre, 2012; Zatorre, 2013). Such changes (e.g., greater volume or thickness of auditory cortex) are present at all ages. However, they are generally greater among children and young adults than older adults. In a study by Hyde et al. (2009), 6-year-old children who received 15 months of instrumental musical training showed significant changes in voxel size (a voxel is a small cube of brain tissue) in the primary motor area (see Figure 12.19) and the primary auditory area (see Figure 12.20). In addition, those children with the greatest brain changes showed the greatest improvement in musical skills.

Foster and Zatorre (2010) found cortex volume was greatest in adults with the most musical practice (up to 58,000 hours). However, cortical structure still predicted musical performance even when eliminating statistically the effects of musical training. This finding suggests *pre-existing* anatomical features can influence the rate of musical learning.

Evaluation

Numerous studies have shown predictable differences in brain structure between individuals with varying levels of training in a given domain (Zatorre, 2013).

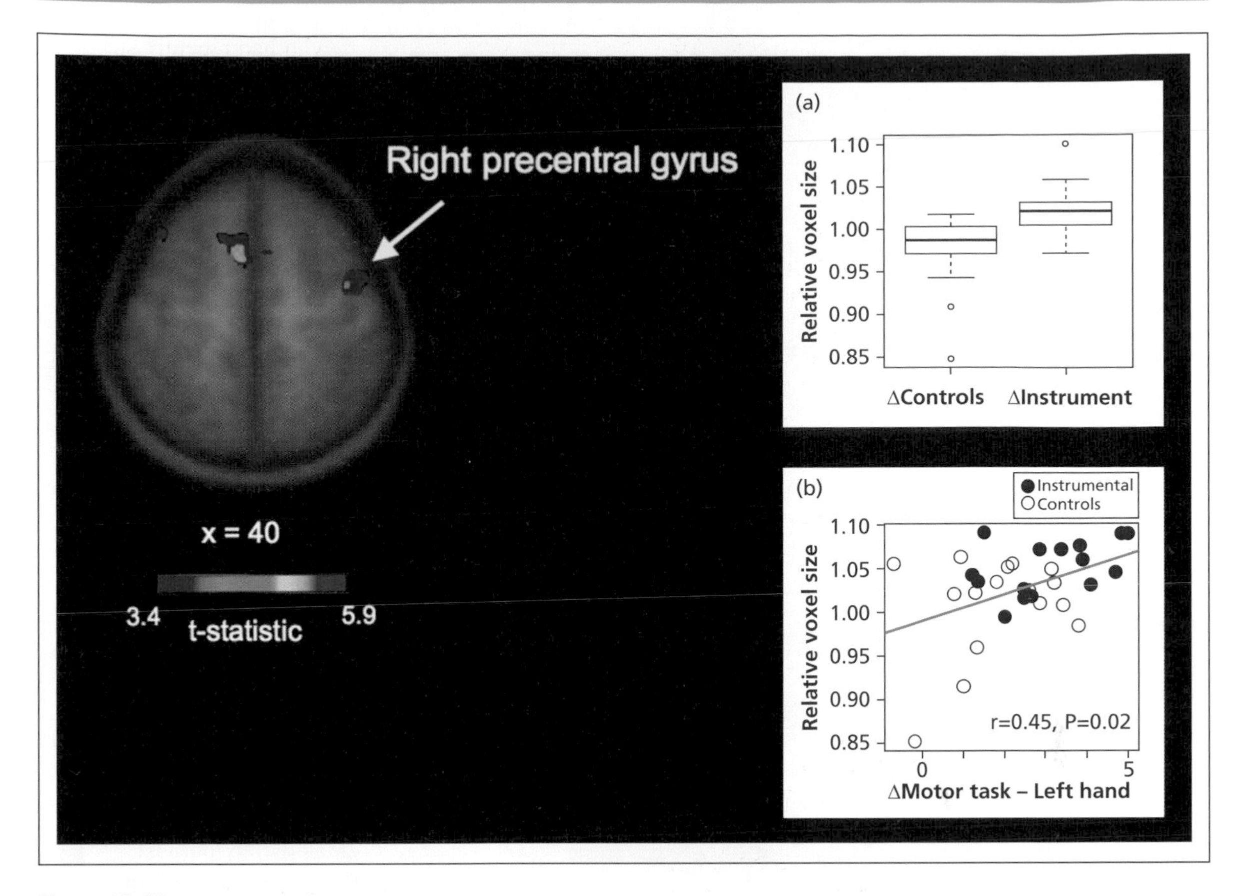

Figure 12.19

The brain image shows areas in the primary motor cortex with differences in relative voxel size (a voxel is a small cube of brain tissue) between children receiving 15 months of instrumental music training and non-trained controls. (a) Changes in relative voxel size over time in trained and non-trained groups (a value of 1.00 indicates no change). (b) Correlation between amount of improvement in motor-test performance and change in relative voxel size for all participants.

From Hyde et al. (2009). Republished with permission of The Society for Neuroscience. Permission conveyed through Copyright Clearance Center, Inc.

Reasonable support for the hypothesis that developing expertise can *cause* changes in brain structure has come from controlled training studies in which brain structure was assessed before, during and after training. The finding that brain plasticity is greatest in the young may be of relevance when comparing the rate at which expertise develops at different ages.

What are the limitations of research on plasticity and expertise? First, it is hard to show definitely that practice has caused changes in brain structure of relevance to performance improvements. Second, while there is much evidence that musical training is associated with plasticity (Herholz & Zatorre, 2012), it is less clear whether the same is true with other forms of expertise.

Third, there is no coherent theoretical understanding of the effects of plasticity on expertise development. Cognitive neuroscientists (e.g., Bullmore & Sporns, 2012; see Chapter 1) have established the importance of complex brain networks in cognition. However, the links between specific changes to brain structure and such networks remain unclear.

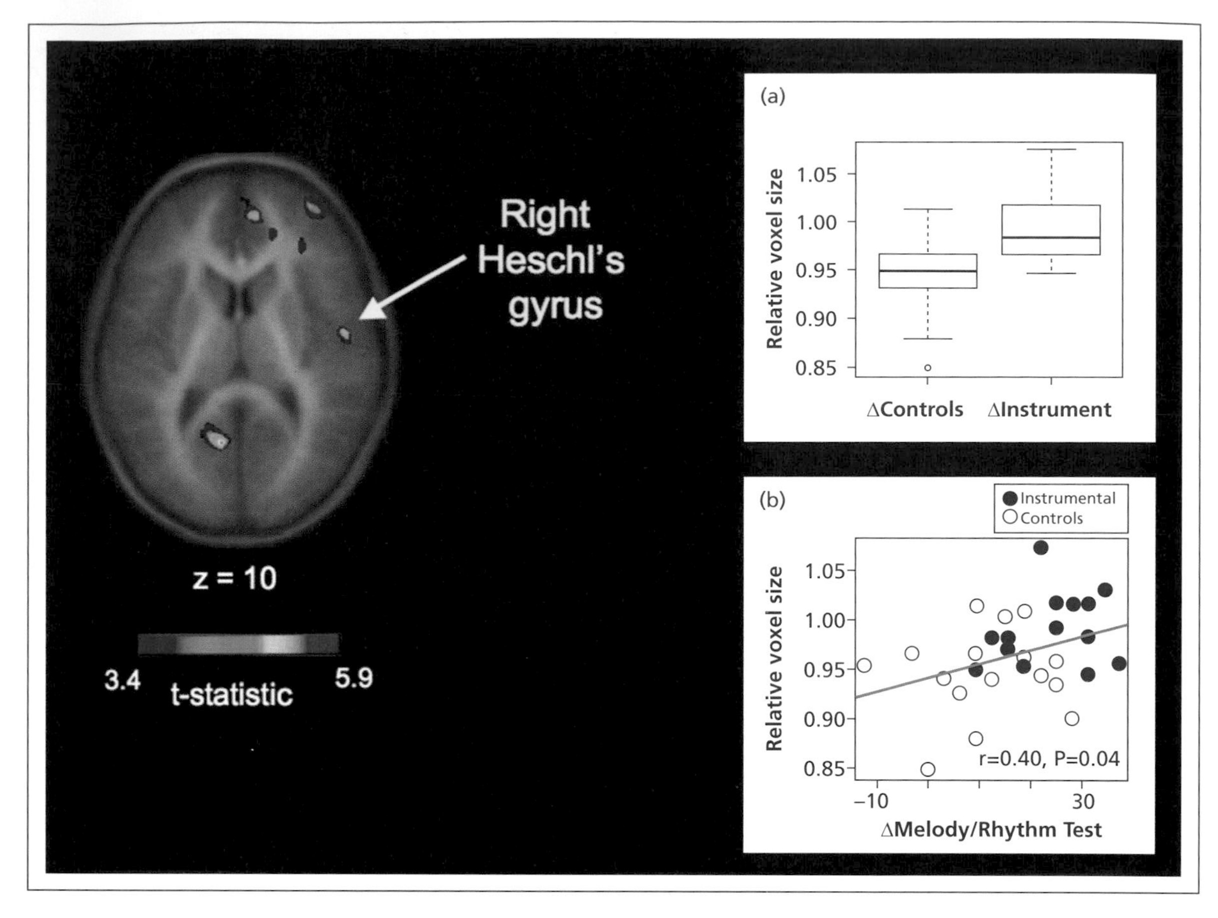

Figure 12.20
The brain image shows areas in the primary auditory area with differences in relative voxel size (a voxel is a small cube of brain tissue) between children receiving instrumental music training and those receiving no training. (a) Changes in relative voxel size over time in training (instrument) and non-trained (control) groups. (b) Correlation between improvement on a melody-rhythm test and change in relative voxel size.

From Hyde et al. (2009). Republished with permission of The Society for Neuroscience. Permission conveyed through Copyright Clearance Center, Inc.

DELIBERATE PRACTICE

We have seen that prolonged practice over a period of several years is essential for anyone aspiring to become an expert chess player and the same is true for every type of expertise. However, what we really need is a theory spelling out the details of what is involved in effective practice. Precisely that was done by Ericsson (e.g., Ericsson & Towne, 2010), who argued that expertise can be developed through **deliberate practice**.

Deliberate practice has four aspects:

1 The task is at an appropriate level of difficulty (not too easy or hard).
2 The learner is given informative feedback about his/her performance.
3 The learner has adequate chances to repeat the task.
4 The learner has the opportunity to correct his/her errors.

KEY TERM

Deliberate practice
This form of practice involves the learner being provided with informative feedback and having the chance to correct his/her errors.

What exactly happens as a result of prolonged deliberate practice? According to Ericsson and Kintsch (1995), experts can reduce the negative effects of having limited working memory capacity. They put forward the notion of **long-term working memory**. The crucial notion is that "fast . . . transfer to LTM [long-term memory] becomes possible with expertise via knowledge structures, which enables LTM to be used during working memory tasks, thus giving the appearance of expanding individuals' WM capacity" (Guida et al., 2013, p. 1).

Here is an example to show the nature of long-term working memory. Suppose an expert and novice chess player try to learn the positions of chess pieces on a board. The novice must rely very largely on working memory (a system of limited capacity that processes and stores information briefly; see Chapter 6). In contrast, the expert player can use his/her huge relevant knowledge to store much of the information *directly* in long-term memory and thus enhance his/her recall of the board positions. In other words, the expert uses long-term working memory but the novice does not.

This theoretically predicts that the acquisition of expertise depends more on the amount of deliberate practice than simply on the number of hours devoted to practice. A second major prediction (and much more controversial) is that deliberate practice is *all* that is needed to develop expert performance. Thus, deliberate practice is necessary and sufficient for the development of outstanding expert performance. It follows that innate talent or ability is of little or no relevance to the development of expertise.

KEY TERM

Long-term working memory
Used by experts to store relevant information rapidly in long-term memory and to access it through retrieval cues in **working memory**.

Findings: positive

There is reasonable support for the notion that experts use long-term working memory to enhance their ability to remember task-relevant information. Ericsson and Chase (1982) studied SF, an American student. He received extensive practice (one hour a day for two years) on the digit-span task in which random digits are recalled immediately in the correct order. His initial digit span was seven digits, but this increased dramatically to 80 digits at the end of practice. This is ten times the average performance level!

Research activity:
Skill acquisition

How did SF do it? He started by using his great knowledge of running times. For example, if the first few digits were "3594" he would note this was Bannister's world-record time for the mile and so store these four digits as a single unit or chunk. After that, he organised chunks into a hierarchical retrieval structure. Thus, SF made very effective use of long-term working memory.

Guida et al. (2012, 2013) reviewed neuroimaging findings in studies of experts performing tasks involving use of working memory. There were two main findings. First, the experts showed *decreased* activation in prefrontal and parietal areas as chunks were created and retrieved. Second, experts showed *increased* activation in medial temporal regions strongly associated with long-term memory as knowledge structures were created and retrieved. This pattern of findings differed from that of non-experts and suggests only experts used long-term working memory extensively.

The performance level of experts is highly correlated with the amount of deliberate practice they have had. For example, Campitelli and Gobet (2011) reviewed evidence from studies on chess-playing expertise. In all studies, the correlation between total practice hours and chess skill was above +0.50. On average, players without international standing had devoted fewer than 10,000 hours to practice (slackers!). In contrast, international masters had devoted over 25,000 hours on average to practice.

Deliberate practice is also strongly correlated with expertise in many other areas. For example, Tuffiash et al. (2007) studied tournament-rated Scrabble players. Elite players spent much more time than average players on deliberate practice activities (e.g., analysis of their own previous games, solving anagrams). Overall, lifetime accumulated study of Scrabble was a good predictor of Scrabble-playing expertise.

Surprisingly little research has compared more and less deliberate practice. An exception is a study by Coughlan et al. (2014). Expert and intermediate Gaelic football players chose how to practise. Compared to the intermediate players, the experts focused more on their weaker skill and found practice more effortful and less enjoyable, strongly suggesting their practice was more deliberate. As predicted theoretically, only those using deliberate practice (i.e., the experts) showed any benefit from practice after a 6-week retention interval.

Some individuals who have developed a high level of expertise decide to abandon their area of expertise. Why does this happen? According to Ericsson and Moxley (2012) the main reason is a reduction in the amount of deliberate practice. This causes a reduction in performance level, which in turn leads to drop out. Evidence supportive of this proposed sequence was reported in a study on elite young chess players who had dropped out of competitive chess (de Bruin et al., 2008).

Findings: negative

Are you convinced expertise depends only on deliberate practice? We hope not! Studies on chess-playing and music performance were reanalysed by Hambrick et al. (2014). On average, variations in deliberate practice accounted for only 34% of chess-playing performance and 29.9% of music performance.

It is important to note that the existence of a positive correlation between deliberate practice and expert performances does not establish causality. Note also that the amount of time any individual devotes to deliberate practice is typically not under experimental control. Individuals having high levels of innate talent and/or encountering early success are generally the ones most motivated to engage in substantial amounts of deliberate practice. Thus, correlations between amount of practice and skill level probably depend on two factors:

1 deliberate practice enhances skill level;
2 early success leads to greater subsequent practice.

Campitelli and Gobet (2011) identified three predictions from deliberate practice theory:

1 All individuals who engage in massive deliberate practice should achieve very high skill levels.
2 The variability across individuals in the number of hours required to achieve high expertise should be relatively small.
3 Everyone's skill level should benefit comparably from any given amount of deliberate practice.

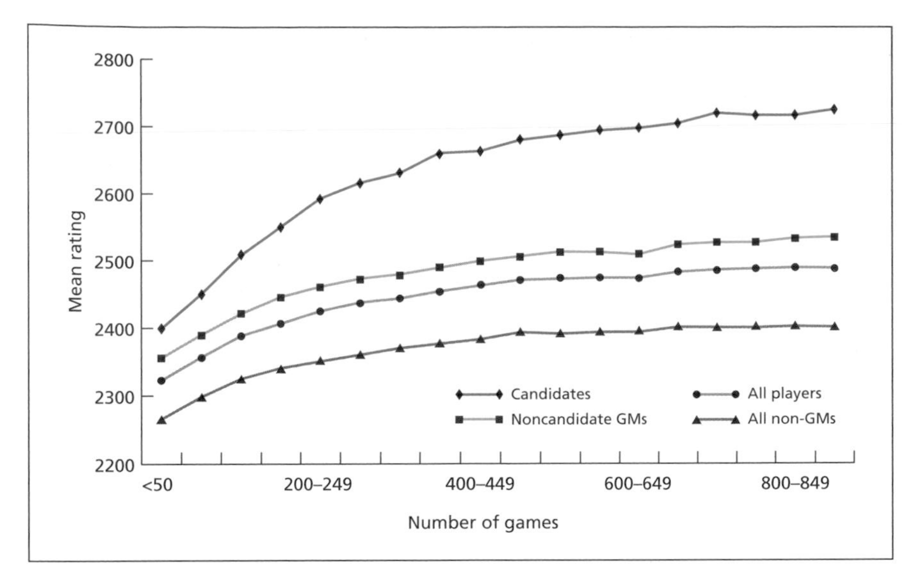

Figure 12.21
Mean chess ratings of candidates, non-candidate grandmasters (GMs) and all non-grandmasters as a function of number of games played.
From Howard (2009). With kind permission from Springer Science + Business Media.

Campitelli and Gobet (2011) considered the above three predictions with reference to chess-playing expertise. None was supported. So far as the first prediction is concerned, there are several chess players who have devoted over 20,000 hours to practice without becoming masters.

With respect to the second prediction, the total numbers of practice hours required to achieve master level varied between 3,000 and 23,600 hours. This indicates the existence of substantial individual differences unaccounted for by deliberate practice theory.

Evidence against the third prediction was reported by Howard (2009). He studied chess experts in three categories: candidates (elite players who have competed for the right to challenge the world champion); non-candidate grandmasters (elite players but less expert than candidates); and non-grandmasters.

The skill ratings of these three groups as a function of the number of games played are shown in Figure 12.21. There are two points of interest. First, there were clear performance differences among these three groups early on and these differences increased over games. Second, the ratings of players in all groups showed no improvement after they had played about 750 games.

Howard (2009) found additional evidence of a performance ceiling among five players who had played over 2,300 games (representing more than 8,000 hours' playing time!). These players showed no improvement at all over the last 1,000(+) games they played. Thus, there are definite limits on the beneficial effects of deliberate practice.

The above findings suggest it is possible early in their careers to identify those who will eventually become top players, and that they have very high natural talent. Precisely the same is true in sports such as tennis and golf (think of Federer, Woods and the Williams sisters). The findings also suggest there is a ceiling on the performance level any individual can attain based on his/her natural talent.

How can we identify those with high vs. low levels of natural talent or ability? When expertise is very broad (e.g., career expertise), intelligence is of major importance. Gottfredson (1997) reviewed the literature on intelligence and occupational success. The correlation between intelligence and work performance was +0.58 for high-complexity jobs (e.g., biologist, city circulation manager). The mean IQ of those in very complex jobs (e.g., accountants, lawyers, doctors) is about 120–130, which is much higher than the population mean of 100.

In similar fashion, Grabner et al. (2007) found none of the chess masters they studied had a verbal IQ below 110 or a non-verbal IQ below 115. In addition, intelligence correlated significantly with the players' rated skill level.

Meinz and Hambrick (2010) studied factors influencing piano-playing skill. Sight-reading performance correlated +0.67 with total amount of deliberate practice. In addition, they considered individual differences in working memory capacity (a dimension of individual differences correlating highly with intelligence). Working memory capacity correlated +0.28 with sight-reading performance, and this *increased* to +0.37 when controlling for individual differences in deliberate practice. Thus, talent or ability (as well as amount of deliberate practice) predicted musical performance.

Intelligence is less important when it comes to very specific skills. For example, Ceci and Liker (1986) studied experts at calculating the odds in harness racing. These experts worked out probable odds, which involved taking account of complex interactions among up to seven variables (e.g., track size, each horse's lifetime speed). The experts' IQs ranged from 81 to 128, and there was no correlation between performance and IQ.

Evaluation

There is much support for the notion that memory in a domain of expertise can be developed via the use of long-term working memory. Most experts develop superior long-term working memory, which reduces limitations on processing capacity. There is also strong evidence that deliberate practice is necessary for the achievement of outstanding levels of expertise.

What are the limitations of deliberate practice theory? First, it has proved hard to assess deliberate practice with precision. Study hours are often used as a measure of deliberate practice, but it is clearly possible to spend much time practising in a non-deliberate way. The number of hours chess players devote to study is determined in part by how many competitive games they play. Howard (2012) compared two groups who had played a similar number of games but who differed *fivefold* in the number of study hours. The two groups had comparable performance, suggesting the number of study hours is relatively unimportant.

Second, a key finding claimed to support the theory is that level of expertise is strongly correlated with amount of deliberate practice. Such evidence cannot establish *causality*. The correlation could arise because naturally talented individuals are more motivated to devote substantial time to practice than are those lacking in natural talent.

Third, the evidence suggests deliberate practice is necessary (but *not* sufficient) to produce high levels of expertise. There are substantial performance differences between individuals in the same domain who have spent comparable amounts of time in deliberate practice (Howard, 2009).

Fourth, the notion that innate talent is unimportant is unconvincing. As Sternberg and Ben-Zeev (2001, p. 302) argued, "Is one to believe that anyone could become a Mozart if only he or she put in the time?" It is far more likely talent sets a *ceiling* on what anyone can achieve, and the amount of deliberate practice they put in determines how close they come to realising their potential (Howard, 2009).

Fifth, individual differences in talent as assessed by intelligence tests are important. This is especially the case with the development of broad and complex skills (e.g., becoming an outstanding lawyer).

Sixth, what is required is detailed longitudinal research. There are probably causal links among deliberate practice, talent and motivation. At present, however, the strengths (and directions) of these links have not been clearly established.

CHAPTER SUMMARY

- **Introduction**. This chapter is devoted to problem solving, analogical problem solving and reasoning, and expertise. Most research on problem solving focuses on problems requiring no special knowledge. In contrast, research on expertise typically involves problems requiring considerable background knowledge. Analogical problem solving focuses on the use of previous knowledge and experience on a current problem, whereas expertise research is concerned with what differentiates experts from novices in a given area.

- **Gestalt approach: insight and role of experience**. There is behavioural, neuroimaging and verbal report evidence for the existence of insight. It can be facilitated by subtle hints. Incubation often benefits problem solving because misleading information or ineffective strategies are forgotten. There is evidence supporting the assumptions of representational change theory that solving insight problems often requires constraint relaxation and/or re-encoding of the problem representation. However, constraint relaxation is often insufficient on its own. The phenomena of functional fixedness and mental set show past experience can have negative effects on problem solving. Functional fixedness can be reduced by focusing on obscure features of an object and basing solutions on those features.

- **Problem-solving strategies**. Problem solvers make extensive use of heuristics or rules of thumb such as hill climbing, means–ends analysis, and progress monitoring. Much problem solving involves successive stages of problem representation, planning and plan execution. Evidence from brain-damaged patients and neuroimaging indicates that the prefrontal cortex (especially the dorsolateral prefrontal cortex) is heavily involved in planning and problem solving generally. Many problem solvers rely relatively little on deliberate pre-planning but make use of non-conscious learning processes. Cognitive misers fail to solve problems they have the ability to solve through a reluctance to engage in effortful processing.

- **Analogical problem solving**. Analogical problem solving depends on three kinds of similarity: superficial, structural and procedural. Failures to use analogies often occur through failures of memory retrieval. Such failures can be reduced if problem solvers identify the underlying structure of the current problem. Four-term analogy problems have three sequential stages of encoding, mapping or inference, and response. Several brain regions (especially within the prefrontal cortex) are involved in analogical reasoning. Individuals high in working memory capacity perform better than those low in capacity on analogical reasoning because they have great attentional control and attentional capacity.
- **Chess-playing expertise**. Expertise is typically assessed by using knowledge-rich problems. Expert chess players differ from non-expert ones in possessing far more templates containing knowledge of chess positions. These templates permit expert players to identify good moves rapidly. However, the precise information contained in templates remains unclear. In addition, the template approach de-emphasises the importance to chess performance of slow search processes and complex strategies.
- **Medical expertise**. Medical experts (e.g., radiologists) often rely more than non-experts on fast, automatic processes in diagnosis. This is revealed by eye-movement data indicating that experts rapidly fixate relevant information and ignore task-irrelevant information. Slow, analytic processes can enhance diagnostic performance but the precise circumstances in which this is the case remain to be determined. Medical expertise involves more visual and less abstract knowledge than chess expertise. It is also more narrowly focused than chess expertise in that the primary goal is diagnosis rather than "diagnosis" of the current position plus complex planning of future moves.
- **Brain plasticity**. There is accumulating evidence that there are differences in brain structure between experts and non-experts. Training studies (especially in music) have shown these changes in brain structure are often caused by experience and reflect brain plasticity. The structural changes associated with brain plasticity probably provide experts with an additional benefit compared to non-experts.
- **Deliberate practice**. According to Ericsson, the development of expertise depends on deliberate practice involving informative

feedback and the opportunity to correct errors. Deliberate practice is necessary (but not sufficient) for the development of expertise. The importance of innate talent is suggested by the variability in the amount of practice required to achieve high expertise and individual differences in the benefits of a given amount of practice. Individual differences in innate ability are especially important in broad domains (e.g., career success). It may be mainly individuals of high innate ability who are motivated to devote thousands of hours to deliberate practice.

Further reading

- Feltovich, P.J., Prietula, M.J. & Ericsson, K.A. (2013). Studies of expertise from psychological perspectives. In K.A. Ericsson, N. Charness, P.J. Feltovich & R.R. Hoffman (eds), *The Cambridge handbook of expertise and expert performance*. Cambridge: Cambridge University Press. This chapter provides an up-to-date account of theory and research on expertise. Other chapters in this handbook focus on specific types of expertise.
- Gentner, D. & Smith, L.A. (2013). Analogical learning and reasoning. In D. Reisberg (ed.), *The Oxford handbook of thinking and reasoning*. Oxford: Oxford University Press. Theory and research on analogical thinking and problem solving are discussed in this chapter.
- Hambrick, D.Z., Oswald, F.L., Altmann, M., Meinz, E.J., Gobet, F. & Campitelli, G. (2014). Deliberate practice: Is that all it takes to become an expert? *Intelligence*, 45(July–August): 34–45. David Hambrick and his colleagues show convincingly that deliberate practice is not sufficient to account for individual differences in expertise.
- Kounios, J. & Beeman, M. (2014). The cognitive neuroscience of insight. *Annual Review of Psychology*, 65: 71–93. John Kounios and Mark Beeman review cognitive neuroscience approaches to human insight.
- Mayer, R.E. (2013). Problem solving. In D. Reisberg (ed.), *The Oxford handbook of thinking and reasoning*. Oxford: Oxford University Press. Richard Mayer discusses our current knowledge and understanding of problem solving.
- Morrison, R.G. & Knowlton, B.J. (2012). Neural substrate of thinking. In K.J. Holyoak and R.G. Morrison (eds), *The Oxford handbook of thinking and reasoning*. Oxford: Oxford University Press. The rapidly expanding cognitive neuroscience approach to thinking is discussed at length.
- Zatorre, R.J. (2013). Predispositions and plasticity in music and speech learning: Neural correlates and implications. *Science*, 342: 585–9. Robert Zatorre discusses evidence addressing the role of brain plasticity in learning and the development of expertise.

CHAPTER 13

Judgement and decision making

INTRODUCTION

In this chapter, our focus is on the overlapping areas of judgement and decision making. **Judgement** involves deciding on the likelihood of various events using incomplete information. For example, you might use information about your previous examination performance to work out the probability you will succeed in your next examination. What matters in judgement is *accuracy*.

Decision making involves selecting one option from several possibilities. You probably had to decide which university to attend, which courses to study and so on. The factors involved in decision making depend on the *importance* of the decision. For example, the processes involved in deciding which career path to follow are much more complex and time-consuming than those involved in deciding whether to drink Coca-Cola or Pepsi-Cola!

We typically assess the quality of our decisions in terms of *consequences* – are we happy with our choice of university or course? However, this is sometimes unfair. There is the story of a surgeon saying, "The operation was a success. Unfortunately, the patient died." This sounds like a sick joke in every sense. In fact, however, a decision can be good on the information available when it is made even if it seems poor in terms of its consequences.

Judgement often forms an important initial part of the decision-making process. For example, someone deciding which car to buy might make judgements about how much various cars would cost to run, how reliable they would be and how much they would enjoy owning each one.

What does research on judgement and decision making tell us about human rationality? That issue is part of a broader one concerning human rationality and logicality in general. That broader issue (which includes consideration of research on judgement and decision making) is discussed in Chapter 14.

JUDGEMENT RESEARCH

We often change our opinion of the likelihood of something based on new information. Suppose you are 90% confident someone has lied to you. However, their version of events is later confirmed by another person, leading you to believe

KEY TERMS

Judgement
An assessment of the probability of a given event occurred based on incomplete information.

Decision making
Making a selection from various options; if full information is unavailable, **judgement** is required.

Base-rate information
The relative frequency of an event within a given population.

there is only a 60% chance you have been lied to. In everyday life, the strength of our beliefs is very often increased or decreased by new information.

The Rev. Thomas Bayes provided a precise way of thinking about such cases. He focused on situations in which there are two possible beliefs or hypotheses (e.g., X is lying vs. X is not lying), and showed how new data or information change the probabilities of each hypothesis being correct.

According to Bayes' theorem, we need to assess the relative probabilities of the two hypotheses *before* the data are obtained (prior odds). We also need to calculate the relative probabilities of obtaining the observed data under each hypothesis (likelihood ratio). Bayesian methods evaluate the probability of observing the data, D, if hypothesis A is correct, written $p(D/H_A)$, and if hypothesis B is correct, written $p(D/H_B)$. Bayes' theorem is expressed as an odds ratio:

$$\frac{p(H_A/D)}{p(H_B/D)} = \frac{p(H_A)}{p(H_B)} \times \frac{p(D/H_A)}{p(D/H_B)}$$

Interactive exercise:
Taxi-cab problem

The above formula may look intimidating and offputting, but is not really so (honestly!). On the left side of the equation are the relative probabilities of hypotheses A and B in the light of the new data. These are the probabilities we want to work out. On the right side of the equation, we have the prior odds of each hypothesis being correct *before* the data were collected multiplied by the likelihood ratio based on the probability of the data given each hypothesis.

We will apply Bayes' theorem to Kahneman and Tversky's (1972) taxi-cab problem. A cab was involved in an accident one night. Of the city's cabs, 85% belonged to the Green company and 15% to the Blue company. An eyewitness identified the cab as a Blue cab. However, when her ability to identify cabs under similar visibility conditions was tested, she was wrong 20% of the time. What is the probability the cab was Blue?

The hypothesis the cab was Blue is H_A and the hypothesis it was Green is H_B. The prior probability for H_A is 0.15 and for H_B it is 0.85 because 15% of the cabs are blue and 85% are green. The probability of the eyewitness identifying the cab as Blue when it was Blue, $p(D/H_A)$, is 0.80. Finally, the probability that the eyewitness identifies the cab as Blue when it was Green, $p(D/H_B)$, is 0.20. According to the formula:

$$\frac{0.15}{0.85} \times \frac{0.80}{0.20} = \frac{0.12}{0.17}$$

Thus, the odds ratio is 12:17 and there is a 41% (12/29) chance the taxi-cab was Blue. As we will see, this is *not* the most popular answer.

Neglecting base rates

According to Bayes' theorem, people making judgements should take account of **base-rate information** (the relative frequency with which an event occurs within a population). However, such information is often ignored or de-emphasised. In the taxi-cab problem, most participants ignored the base-rate information about the relative numbers of Green and Blue cabs. They considered *only* the witness's evidence, and so concluded there was an 80% likelihood the taxi was Blue rather than Green.

Kahneman and Tversky (1973) provided another example of people not attending to base-rate information. Participants were given the lawyer–engineer problem:

> Jack is a 45-year-old man. He is married and has four children. He is generally conservative, careful and ambitious. He shows no interest in political and social issues and spends most of his free time on his many hobbies, which include home carpentry, sailing and numerical puzzles.

The participants were told the description had been selected at random from 100 descriptions. Half were told 70 descriptions were of engineers and 30 of lawyers, whereas the others were told 70 were of lawyers and 30 of engineers.

On average, the participants decided there was a 0.90 probability Jack was an engineer regardless of whether most of the 100 descriptions were of lawyers or engineers. Thus, participants ignored the base-rate information (i.e., the 70:30 split in the 100 descriptions).

KEY TERMS

Representativeness heuristic
The assumption that an object or individual belongs to a specified category because it is representative (typical) of that category.

Conjunction fallacy
The mistaken assumption that the probability of a conjunction of two events is greater than the probability of one of them.

Heuristics

According to Amos Tversky and Daniel Kahneman (e.g., 1974), most people given judgement tasks make considerable use of rules of thumb or heuristics. Heuristics (see Glossary) are "strategies that ignore part of the information, with the goal of making decisions more quickly, frugally, and/or accurately than more complex methods" (Gigerenzer & Gaissmaier, 2011, p. 454). As Shah and Oppenheimer (2008, p. 207) pointed out, "Heuristics primarily serve the purpose of reducing the effort associated with a task."

Case study:
Base rate

Representativeness heuristic

Our liking for heuristics can lead us to ignore base-rate information. More specifically, we use the **representativeness heuristic**, which involves deciding an object or person belongs to a given category because it/he/she appears typical or representative of that category. Thus, for example, Jack's description sounds like that of a typical engineer.

Tversky and Kahneman (1983) obtained more evidence of people using the representativeness heuristic. They studied the **conjunction fallacy**, the mistaken belief that the conjunction or combination of two events (A and B) is more likely than one event (A or B) on its own. Tversky and Kahneman used the following description:

> Linda is 31 years old, single, outspoken and very bright. She majored in philosophy. As a student, she was deeply concerned with issues of discrimination and social justice, and also participated in anti-nuclear demonstrations.

Is it more likely that Linda is a bank teller or a bank teller active in the feminist movement? Most people (including you?) argue it is more likely she is a feminist bank teller than that she is a bank teller. They seem to rely on the representativeness heuristic – the description sounds more like that of a feminist bank teller than of a bank teller. This is the conjunction fallacy: all feminist bank tellers belong to the larger category of bank tellers!

Many people misinterpret the statement, "Linda is a bank teller", as implying she is not active in the feminist movement (Manktelow, 2012). However, the conjunction fallacy is still found even when almost everything possible is done to ensure participants interpret the problem correctly (Sides et al., 2002).

Standard explanations of the conjunction fallacy (including those based on the representativeness heuristic) assume it depends mostly on the high perceived *probability* of the additional information (i.e., she is a feminist activist) given the description. In contrast, Tentori et al. (2013) argued for a subtly different explanation: the *hypothesis* that Linda is a feminist activist is strongly supported by her description.

Tentori et al. (2013) contrasted these explanations by considering a further additional scenario: "Linda is a bank teller and owns a pair of black shoes." It is more probable that Linda owns a pair of black shoes than that she is an activist feminist. However, the information that she owns a pair of black shoes is hardly supported by her description. Thus, standard explanations would predict that Linda owning a pair of black shoes would be rated as likelier than her being an activist feminist, whether the hypothesis explanation predicts the opposite. Tentori et al.'s findings supported the hypothesis explanation. These findings suggest it is harder to explain the conjunction fallacy than is generally assumed.

Pat Croskerry. Courtesy Pat Croskerry.

IN THE REAL WORLD: REPRESENTATIVENESS HEURISTIC IN MEDICAL DIAGNOSIS

The importance of the representativeness heuristic would be greatly increased if we discovered experts in real life sometimes mistakenly make use of it. Evidence that this is, indeed, the case was discussed by Groopman (2007). Evan McKinley was a forest ranger in his early forties. He was slim and very fit. While hiking in the woods, he experienced severe discomfort in his chest so that it hurt every time he took a breath. Accordingly, he went to see a doctor (Pat Croskerry – see photo). He ascertained McKinley had never smoked, he was not under stress, his blood pressure was normal and no problems were revealed by electrocardiogram and chest X-ray.

Dr Croskerry concluded, "I'm not at all worried about your chest pain. You probably overexerted yourself in the field and strained a muscle. My suspicion that this is coming from your heart is about zero." Shortly afterwards, it turned out that McKinley had had a heart attack. This led Croskerry to admit, "I missed it because my thinking was overly influenced by how healthy this man looked, and the absence of risk factors." In other words, McKinley seemed very representative of healthy people with an extremely low risk of having a heart attack.

Heeding base rates

In spite of the findings discussed so far, base-rate information is sometimes both relevant and generally used. Krynski and Tenenbaum (2007) argued that we possess valuable *causal knowledge* that allows us make accurate judgements using base-rate information in everyday life. In the laboratory, however, the judgement problems we confront often fail to provide such knowledge.

Krynski and Tenenbaum (2007) gave some participants the following judgement task (the false positive scenario):

- The following statistics are known about women at age 60 who participate in a routine mammogram screening, an X-ray of the breast tissue that detects tumours:

  1. 2% of women have breast cancer at the time of screening. Most of them will receive a positive result on the mammogram.
  2. There is a 6% chance that a woman without breast cancer will receive a positive result on the mammogram.

- Suppose a woman at age 60 gets a positive result during a routine mammogram screening. Without knowing any other symptoms, what are the chances she has breast cancer?

The base rate of cancer in the population was often neglected by participants given this task. This may have happened because breast cancer is the *only* cause of positive mammograms explicitly mentioned. Suppose the problem is reworded slightly to indicate an alternative cause of positive mammograms. Krynski and Tenenbaum (2007) did this by changing the wording of point 2:

> There is a 6% chance that a woman without breast cancer will have a dense but harmless cyst that looks like a cancerous tumour and causes a positive result on the mammogram.

Participants given the benign cyst scenario were far more likely to take full account of the base-rate information than those given the standard false positive scenario (see Figure 13.1). Krynski and Tenenbaum (2007) argued that the reasonably full causal knowledge available to participants with the benign cyst scenario allowed them to solve the problem. It also corresponds to real life.

In Kahneman and Tversky's (1972) taxi-cab problem (discussed earlier), most participants ignored the base-rate information about the numbers of Green and Blue cabs. Krynski and Tenenbaum (2007) argued that this happened because it was hard for participants to see the causal structure. Accordingly, they devised a version providing a *reason* why the witness might have made a mistake. Here is the crucial addition to the problem:

> When testing a sample of cabs, only 80% of the Blue Co. cabs appeared blue in colour, and only 80% of the Green Co. cabs appeared green in colour. Due to faded paint, 20% of Blue Co. cabs appeared green in colour, and 20% of Green Co. cabs appeared blue in colour.

Only 8% of participants showed base-rate neglect with the faded paint version compared to 43% with the standard version. Correct answers increased from 8%

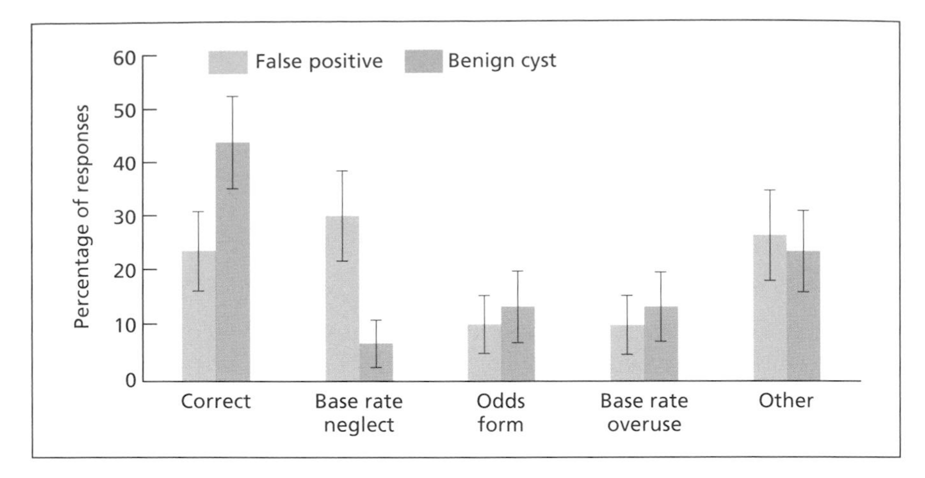

Figure 13.1
Percentages of correct responses and various incorrect responses (based on base-rate neglect, odds form, base-rate overuse, and other) with the false-positive and benign cyst scenarios.

From Krynski and Tenenbaum (2007). Copyright © 2007, American Psychological Association. Reproduced with permission.

with the standard version to 46% with the faded paint version. Thus, many people use base-rate information when they understand the underlying causal factors.

We also use base-rate information when strongly *motivated* to do so. Suppose you were asked to put some saliva on a strip of paper. If it turned blue, that would mean you had an enzyme deficiency indicating a health problem. However, there was a 1/10 probability the test was misleading. Unfortunately, the paper turned blue.

Ditto et al. (1998) gave participants the above task. Most used the base-rate information (i.e., 1/10 probability of a misleading result) to argue that the test was inaccurate. In contrast, participants told the paper turning blue meant they did not have a health problem perceived the test as accurate – they were not motivated to take account of the base-rate information.

In sum, we often use base-rate information in everyday life when we possess relevant causal knowledge. We also use such information when it is advantageous to us but ignore it when it is disadvantageous to us.

Availability heuristic

We have spent some time discussing the representativeness heuristic. Another common heuristic identified by Tversky and Kahneman (1974) is the **availability heuristic** – the frequencies of events can be estimated on the basis of how easy or hard it is subjectively to retrieve them from long-term memory.

Lichtenstein et al. (1978) asked people to judge the relative likelihood of different causes of death. Causes of death that attract much publicity (e.g., murder) were judged more likely than those that do not (e.g., suicide) even when the opposite was the case. These findings suggest people use the availability heuristic.

Pachur et al. (2012) argued that there are three ways of explaining people's judged probabilities or frequencies of various causes of death. First, people may use an availability heuristic based on their own direct experiences. Second, they may use an availability heuristic based on media coverage of causes of death as well as their own experience (availability by total experience). Third, they may use the **affect heuristic**, which they defined as follows: "Gauge your feeling of dread that Risk A and Risk B, respectively, evoke and infer that risk to be more prevalent in the population for which the dread is higher" (Pachur et al., 2012, p. 316).

KEY TERMS

Availability heuristic
The rule of thumb that the frequencies of events can be estimated accurately by the subjective ease with which they can be retrieved.

Affect heuristic
Using one's emotional responses to influence rapid judgements or decisions.

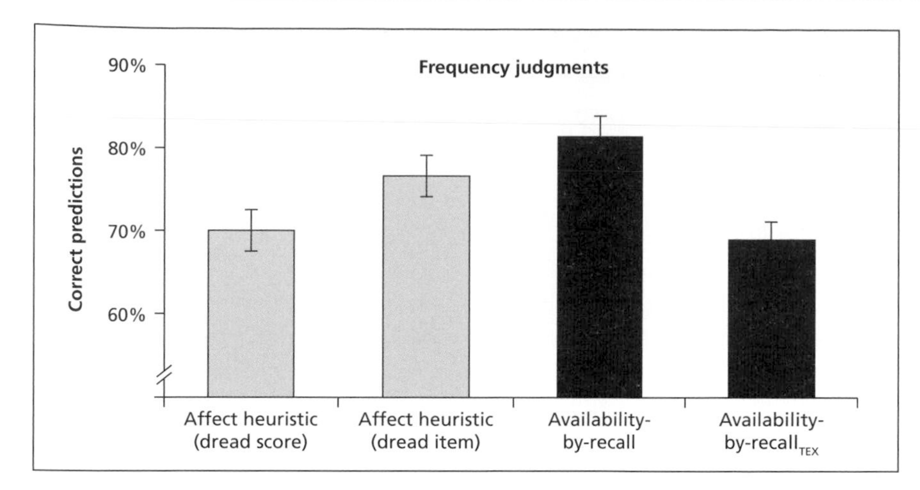

Figure 13.2
Percentage correct predictions of the judged frequencies of different causes of death based on the affect heuristic (overall dread score), affect heuristic (single dread item), availability-by-recall (direct experience) and availability-by-total-experience (TEX: direct experience + media).
From Pachur et al. (2012). © American Psychological Association.

Pachur et al. (2012) found availability based on recall of direct experiences was the best predictor of the judged frequencies of different causes of death (see Figure 13.2). Judged risks were also predicted by the affect heuristic. Availability based on media coverage was the least successful predictor.

The availability heuristic is sometimes overridden (Oppenheimer, 2004). American participants were presented with pairs of names (one famous, one non-famous) and indicated which surname was more common in the United States. If participants had relied on the availability heuristic, they would have selected the famous names. In fact, they mostly selected the non-famous names (correctly because the non-famous names were slightly more common).

The above findings occurred because the participants used deliberate thought to override the availability heuristic. When participants decided which surname was more common under cognitive load, they used the availability heuristic and so the famous name was mistakenly selected 80% of the time (Oppenheimer & Monin, 2009).

Overall evaluation

Kahneman and Tversky showed several general heuristics or rules of thumb (e.g., representativeness heuristic, availability heuristic) underlie judgements in many different contexts. They were instrumental in establishing the field of judgement research. Their ideas have been hugely influential within psychology but also outside (e.g., economics, philosophy). There is plentiful evidence that most people prefer to minimise the cognitive demands on them by using heuristics (e.g., Kool et al., 2010; Fiedler & von Sydow, 2015, in press).

It is easy to imagine Kahneman and Tversky's approach is more applicable to less intelligent individuals than to more intelligent ones. In fact, intelligence or cognitive ability is almost unrelated to performance on most judgement tasks (e.g., the Linda problem, the lawyer–engineer problem) (Stanovich, 2012; see Chapter 14).

There are several limitations with the original heuristics-and-biases approach. First, the heuristics identified by Kahneman and Tversky are vaguely defined. As Fiedler and von Sydow (2015, in press) point out, "One-word labels like 'representativeness' are theory surrogates [substitutes] that fail to place any testable constraints on the cognitive decision process."

IN THE REAL WORLD: AVAILABILITY HEURISTIC IN MEDICAL DIAGNOSIS

An example of poor medical decision making triggered by use of the availability heuristic was discussed by Groopman (2007). When Dr Harrison Alter was working in A&E at a hospital in Arizona, he saw dozens of patients in a three-week period suffering from viral pneumonia. One day, Blanche Begaye, a Navajo woman, arrived in A&E complaining of having trouble breathing. She had taken a few aspirin and was breathing at almost twice the normal rate.

Dr Alter diagnosed viral pneumonia even though she did not have the white streaks in her lungs or rhonchi (harsh sounds in the lungs characteristic of that disease). However, her blood had become slightly acidic, which can occur when someone has a major infection. A few minutes later, an internist argued correctly that Blanche Begaye had aspirin toxicity, which occurs when patients overdose on that drug. Dr Alter used the availability heuristic because he was overly influenced by the numerous recent cases of viral pneumonia, which made that disease spring to mind. He admitted, "She was an absolutely classic case – the rapid breathing, the shift in her blood electrolytes – and I missed it."

Second, theorising based on the heuristics-and-biases approach has been limited (but see later discussion). According to Fiedler and von Sydow (2015, in press), "What is disillusioning and disappointing . . . is how little precision, refinement, and progress has been obtained at the theoretical level." For example, Kahneman and Tversky failed to indicate the precise conditions eliciting the various heuristics or the relationships among different heuristics.

Third, it is sometimes unfair to conclude people's judgements are biased and error-prone. For example, most people judge skin cancer to be a more common cause of death than cancer of the mouth and throat, whereas the opposite is actually the case (Hertwig et al., 2004). People make this "error" simply because skin cancer has attracted considerable media attention in recent years. More generally, the heuristics-and-biases approach focuses on biased processing, but the problem is often with the quality of the available information (Juslin et al., 2007; Le Mens & Denrell, 2011).

Fourth, much research is detached from the realities of everyday life. Emotional and motivational factors often influence our judgements in the real world but were rarely studied in the laboratory until fairly recently (see Chapter 15). For example, the estimated probability of future terrorist attacks was higher in fearful individuals than those who were sad or angry (Lerner et al., 2003).

JUDGEMENT THEORIES

Kahneman and Tversky included various theoretical ideas in their early research on judgement. In the years since then, however, they and other theorists have enhanced our understanding of the processes underlying judgement and its biases.

Support theory

Tversky and Koehler (1994) put forward their support theory based partly on the availability heuristic (discussed earlier). Their key assumption was that an event appears more or less likely depending on how it is described. Thus, we must distinguish between events themselves and the descriptions of those events.

You almost certainly assume the probability you will die on your next summer holiday is extremely low. However, it might seem more likely if you were asked, "What is the probability you will die on your next summer holiday from a disease, a car accident, a plane crash, or from any other cause?"

Why is the subjective probability of death on holiday greater in the second case? According to support theory, more *explicit* event descriptions have greater subjective probability for two main reasons:

1 An explicit description often draws attention to aspects of the event less obvious in the non-explicit description.
2 Memory limitations may prevent people remembering all the relevant information if it is not supplied.

Findings

Mandel (2005) asked some participants to judge the risk of a terrorist attack over the following six months. Other participants judged the probability of an attack plotted by al-Qaeda or not plotted by al-Qaeda. The mean estimated probabilities were 0.30 (terrorist attack), 0.30 for an al-Qaeda attack and 0.18 for a non al-Qaeda attack. Thus, as predicted by support theory, the overall estimated probability of a terrorist attack was greater (0.30 + 0.18) when the two major possibilities were made explicit than when they were not (0.30).

Are experts' probability estimates influenced by the explicitness of the descriptions they receive? It seems plausible the answer is "No", because they can presumably fill in any missing details from their own knowledge. However, Redelmeier et al. (1995) found expert doctors *did* show the effect. They were given a description of a woman with abdominal pain. Half assessed the probabilities of two specified diagnoses (gastroenteritis and ectopic pregnancy) and a residual category of everything else. The other half assigned probabilities to five specified diagnoses (including gastroenteritis and ectopic pregnancy) and everything else.

The key comparison was the subjective probability of all diagnoses other than gastroenteritis and ectopic pregnancy. This probability was 0.50 with the non-explicit description but 0.69 with the explicit one. Thus, subjective probabilities were higher for explicit descriptions even with experts.

Sloman et al. (2004) obtained findings directly opposite those predicted by support theory. Participants decided the probability an American person selected at random would die of disease rather than some other cause. When no examples of diseases were presented, the average estimated probability was 0.55. The subjective probability was similar when three *typical* diseases (i.e., heart disease, cancer, stroke) were explicitly mentioned. However, when three *atypical* diseases (i.e., pneumonia, diabetes, cirrhosis) were mentioned, the subjective probability was only 0.40. Thus, an explicit description can *reduce* subjective probability if it leads us to focus on low-probability causes.

Redden and Frederick (2011) argued that providing an explicit description can reduce subjective probability by making it more *effortful* to comprehend an event. Some participants decided the likelihood of throwing an even number with a die, whereas others decided the likelihood of throwing a 2, 4 or 6. The latter description is more explicit. However, it was associated with a lower subjective likelihood because the calculations required were more demanding.

KEY TERM

Recognition heuristic
Using the knowledge that only one out of two objects is recognised as the basis for making a judgement.

Evaluation

The theory's main predictions have received empirical support. It shows how the availability heuristic can lead to errors in judgement. It is also impressive (and somewhat surprising) that experts' judgements can be influenced by the explicitness of the information provided.

Support theory has various limitations. First, the precise reasons why providing an explicit description generally increases an event's subjective probability are not clear. Second, explicit descriptions can reduce subjective probability if they lead individuals to focus on low-probability causes (Sloman et al., 2004). Third, explicit descriptions can also reduce subjective probability if they are hard to understand (Redden & Frederick, 2011). Fourth, the theory is oversimplified. It assumes the perceived support for a given hypothesis provided by relevant evidence is *independent* of the rival hypothesis or hypotheses. In fact, however, people often *compare* hypotheses and so this independence assumption is incorrect (Pleskac, 2012).

Fast-and-frugal heuristics

We have seen our judgements are often inaccurate because we rely on various heuristics or rules of thumb. Such findings led Glymour (2001, p. 8) to ask the question, "If we're so dumb, how come we're so smart?" Gigerenzer and his colleagues (e.g., Gigerenzer & Gaissmaier, 2011) argue that heuristics are often very valuable. Their central focus is on fast-and-frugal heuristics involving rapid processing of relatively little information. It is assumed we possess an "adaptive toolbox" consisting of several such heuristics. It is also assumed these heuristics are often surprisingly accurate.

The take-the-best heuristic is a key fast-and-frugal heuristic. It is based on "take the best, ignore the rest". For example, suppose you must decide which of two German cities (*Cologne* and *Herne*) has the larger population. You might assume the most valid cue to city size is that cities whose names you recognise typically have larger populations than other unrecognised cities. However, you recognise both names.

Then you think of another valid cue to city size (e.g., cities with cathedrals tend to be larger than those without). Since you know *Cologne* has a cathedral but are unsure about Herne, you say "Cologne".

The take-the-best strategy has three components:

1 *search rule*: search cues (e.g., name recognition, cathedral) in order of validity;
2 *stopping rule*: stop after finding a discriminatory cue (i.e., the cue applies to only one of the options);
3 *decision rule*: choose outcome.

The most researched example of the take-the-best strategy is the **recognition heuristic**. The recognition heuristic involves selecting the object that is recognised in preference to the one not recognised. In the example above, if you recognise the name *Cologne* but not *Herne*, you guess (correctly) that Cologne is the larger city and ignore other information. Goldstein and Gigerenzer (2002) argued controversially that when individuals recognise one object but not the other, no other information influences the judgement.

Weblink:
Todd and Gigerenzer

How do people decide which heuristic to use on judgement tasks? Kruglanski and Gigerenzer (2011) argued that there is a two-step process. First, the nature of the task and individual memory limit the number of available heuristics. Second, people select one of them based on the likely outcome of using it and its processing demands.

KEY TERM

Hiatus heuristic
The rule of thumb that only customers who have purchased goods fairly recently remain active customers.

Findings

Evidence the recognition heuristic is important was reported by Goldstein and Gigerenzer (2002). American students were presented with pairs of German cities and decided which was larger. When only one city name was recognised, participants apparently used the recognition heuristic 90% of the time. There is a tricky issue here (and in much other research). Selecting the recognised object does *not* necessarily mean the recognition heuristic was used – it could have been chosen for other reasons.

Research activity: Smart heuristics

In another study, Goldstein and Gigerenzer (2002) told participants that German cities with football teams tend to be larger than those without. When participants decided whether a recognised city without a football team was larger or smaller than an unrecognised city, they apparently used the recognition heuristic 92% of the time. Thus, as predicted theoretically, they mostly ignored the conflicting information about the absence of a football team.

The recognition heuristic has obvious limitations. For example, suppose you decide which of two cities in another country is further north. It would not make much sense to choose the one you recognise! In fact, people are much more likely to use the recognition heuristic when it is valid than when it is not. Pachur et al. (2012) found in a meta-analysis (see Glossary) there was a correlation of +0.64 between usage of the recognition heuristic and its validity.

It is unsurprising simple heuristics can be moderately effective. What *is* surprising is that such heuristics sometimes outperform judgements based on much more complex calculations. For example, Wübben and van Wangenheim (2008) considered how managers of clothes shops decide whether customers are active (i.e., likely to buy again) or inactive. The **hiatus heuristic** is a very simple strategy – only customers who have purchased fairly recently are deemed to be active. Another approach is to use a complex model based on all the available information.

What did Wübben and Wangenheim (2008) find? The hiatus heuristic correctly categorised 83% of customers, whereas the comparable figure for the complex model was only 75%. This is a less-is-more effect – the approach based on less information was more successful.

People do not always rely on simple heuristics even when they are reasonably valid. Richter and Späth (2006) asked German students to decide which in each pair of American cities was larger. For some recognised cities, the students were told it had an international airport, whereas for others they were told it did not.

The recognised city was chosen 98% of the time when it had an international airport but only 82% of the time when it did not. Thus, the recognition heuristic was often *not* used when participants had access to inconsistent information. They believed the presence or absence of an international airport is a valid cue to city size.

The take-the-best strategy is used less often than predicted theoretically. Newell et al. (2003) asked participants to choose between the shares of two

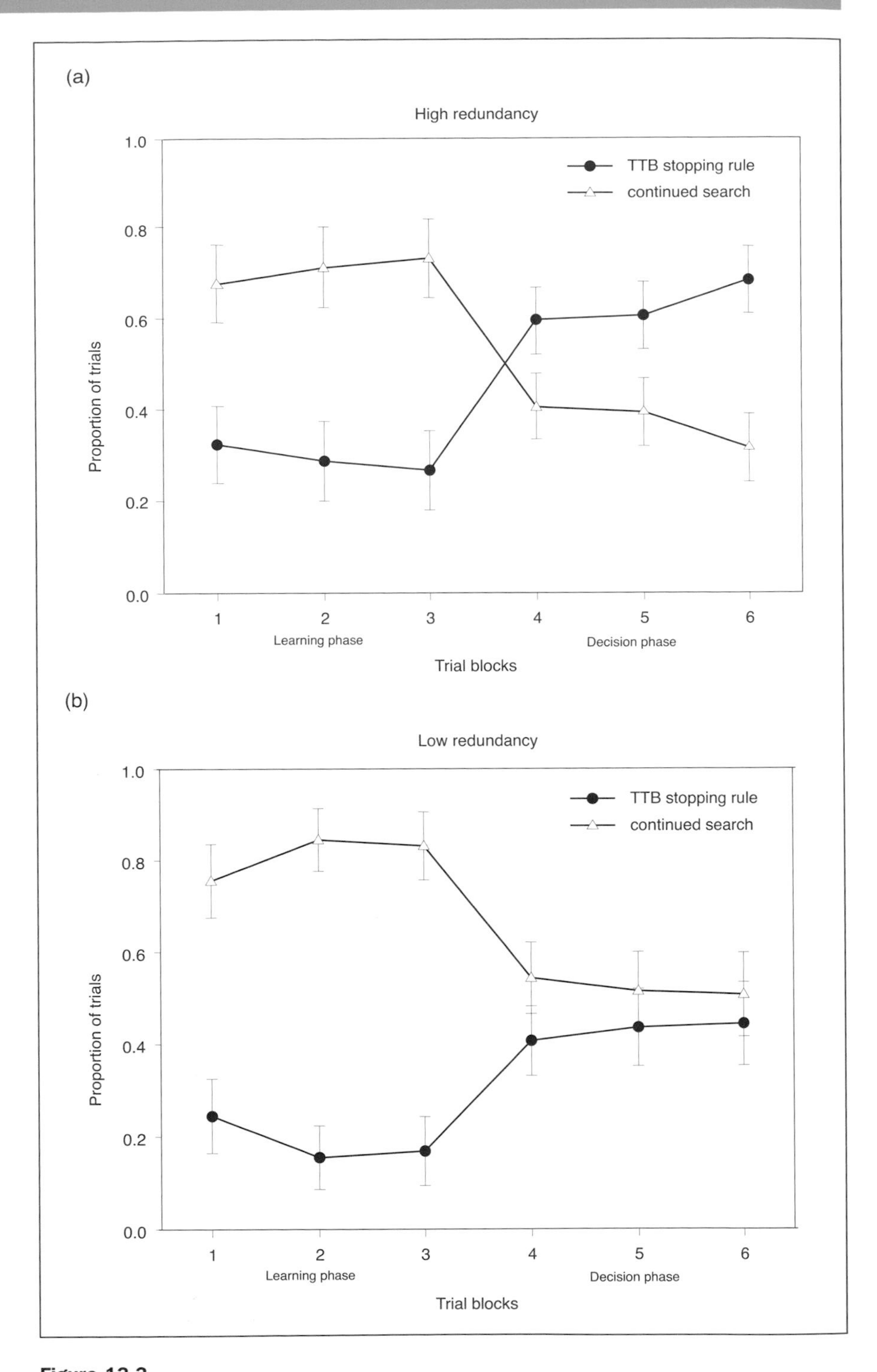

Figure 13.3
Proportions of trials on which a simple strategy (take-the-best) or a more complex continued search strategy was used during learning and a subsequent decision phase (during which information had to be paid for) in conditions of high redundancy (a) and low redundancy (b).

From Dieckmann and Rieskamp (2007). Republished with permission of the Psychonomic Society. Permission conveyed through Copyright Clearance Center, Inc.

fictitious companies on the basis of various cues. Only 33% of the participants used all three components of the take-the-best strategy. The take-the-best strategy was least likely to be used when the cost of obtaining information was low and cue validities were unknown. In those circumstances, participants engaged in more detailed processes than those associated with the take-the-best strategy.

Individual differences have often been ignored. Bröder (2003) used a task involving choosing between shares. More intelligent participants were more likely than less intelligent ones to use the take-the-best strategy when it was the best one to use.

Finally, we consider the factors determining which processing strategy is used on judgement tasks. Dieckmann and Rieskamp (2007) focused on *information redundancy* – redundancy is high when different cues provide similar information but low when cues provide different information. They argued that simple heuristics (e.g., the take-the-best strategy) are more effective in conditions of high than low redundancy. In crude terms, simple strategies work best (and are more likely to be used) when environmental information is simple.

Dieckmann and Rieskamp (2007) tested the above hypothesis. There was an initial learning phase followed by a decision phase in which participants had to pay for information. As predicted, the take-the-best strategy was more likely to be used than a more complex strategy with high information redundancy but the opposite with low information redundancy (see Figure 13.3).

Evaluation

People often use fast-and-frugal heuristics such as the recognition heuristic and the take-the-best strategy. These heuristics can be surprisingly effective in spite of their simplicity. It is impressive that individuals with little knowledge can sometimes outperform those with greater knowledge. Some progress has been made in identifying the factors determining strategy selection on judgement tasks (Dieckmann & Rieskamp, 2007; Kruglanski & Gigerenzer, 2011).

What are the limitations of this theoretical approach? First, the greatest problem was expressed clearly by Evans and Over (2010, p. 174): "The suggestion that we are always better off following intuitions and 'gut feelings' is an extraordinary claim. Why would we have the capacity for logical reasoning if it was of no value to us?"

Second, use of the recognition heuristic is more complex than traditionally assumed. Gigerenzer originally claimed this heuristic was used whenever one out of two objects was recognised. However, people generally also consider *why* they recognise an object and only then decide whether to use the recognition heuristic (Newell, 2011).

Third, using the take-the-best heuristic is also more complex than suggested by Gigerenzer. This heuristic requires us to organise the various cues hierarchically based on their validity. However, we often do not have sufficient knowledge of cue validities.

Fourth, when the approach is applied to decision making, it de-emphasises the importance of the decision. Decision making may stop after finding a single discriminatory cue when deciding which of two cities is larger. However, most women want to consider *all* the relevant evidence before deciding which of two men to marry!

Natural frequency hypothesis

As Gigerenzer and Hoffrage (1999) pointed out, most people in their everyday lives are rarely presented with summary statistics providing base-rate information. What typically happens in our everyday experience is *natural sampling* – this is "the process of encountering instances in a population sequentially" (p. 425).

What follows from the above arguments? Gigerenzer and Hoffrage (1999) claimed our evolutionary history makes it easy for us to work out the *frequencies* of different kinds of events. In contrast, we are ill-equipped to deal with fractions and percentages, which helps to explain why many people perform so poorly on judgement problems involving base rates. The central prediction is that performance on such problems would be greatly enhanced if natural frequencies were used.

This theoretical approach poses some problems. First, the emphasis is on the "natural" or objective frequencies of certain kinds of events. Such frequencies can in principle provide valuable information. In the real world, however, we encounter only a *sample* of events, and the frequencies of such events may differ substantially from natural or objective samples. For example, the frequencies of highly intelligent and less intelligent people encountered by most university students differ from those in the general population.

Second, we must distinguish between natural frequencies and the word problems actually used in research. In most word problems, participants receive frequency information and do not have to grapple with the complexities of natural sampling.

Findings

Judgement performance is often much better when problems are presented in frequencies rather than probabilities or percentages. For example, Fiedler (1988) compared standard and frequency versions of the Linda problem discussed earlier. The percentage of participants showing the conjunction fallacy (arguing she was more likely to be a feminist bank teller than a bank teller) dropped by two-thirds with the frequency version.

Even experts benefit from having problems expressed in frequency terms. Hoffrage et al. (2000) used four realistic diagnostic tasks in probability or frequency versions with advanced medical students. These experts performed much better (and with much more use of base-rate information) with the frequency versions.

Lesage et al. (2013) also presented base-rate problems in probability or frequency versions. The information was expressed in relatively straightforward absolute terms (natural frequencies) or more complex relative terms. Correct answers based on full use of base-rate information were much more common with the frequency versions than the probability ones. Lesage et al. found even the frequency versions required the use of cognitive resources: individuals of higher cognitive ability performed better than those of lower ability on these versions.

We must not exaggerate the advantages of presenting frequency information. Evans et al. (2000) pointed out that frequency versions of problems often make their underlying structure much more obvious. When this confounding was avoided, performance was typically no better on frequency versions of problems than on probability versions. Participants exposed to frequency versions were more likely than those exposed to probability versions to focus exclusively on base-rate information and ignore specific, diagnostic information.

Fiedler et al. (2000) tested the prediction that frequency sampling increases use of base rates. In their problem, there was an 80% chance that a woman with breast cancer would have a positive mammogram compared to 9.6% for a woman without. The base rate of breast cancer in women is 1%. Participants decided whether the woman had breast cancer given a positive mammogram. Participants selected cards from files organised into the categories of women with breast cancer and those without.

Participants' sampling was heavily biased towards women with breast cancer because they mistakenly believed that category was more informative. As a result, the participants produced an average estimate of 63% a woman has breast cancer given a positive mammogram (the correct answer is 7.8%).

Fiedler (2008) considered the effects of natural sampling on a decision-making task. The use of natural sampling often meant participants had insufficient information about infrequent categories of items, which led to biased decisions.

Evaluation

There are two major apparent strengths of the natural frequency hypothesis. First, it seems reasonable that use of natural or objective sampling could enhance the accuracy of many of our judgements. Second, judgements based on frequency information are often superior to those based on probability information.

What are the limitations with the natural sampling hypothesis? First, the frequency version of a problem is generally not easier than the probability version when steps are taken to avoid making the underlying problem structure much more obvious in the former version (Evans et al., 2000; Manktelow, 2012). Thus, the benefits of frequency formats probably do not occur because people are naturally equipped to think about frequencies rather than probabilities.

Second, there is often a yawning chasm between people's actual sampling behaviour and the neat-and-tidy frequency data provided in laboratory experiments (e.g., Fiedler et al., 2000).

Third, "Truly natural sampling may not be possible at all. At any point in time or space, information about different objects is not equally available" (Fiedler, 2008, p. 201).

Fourth, people sometimes find it harder to think in frequencies than in probabilities. Keeping track of frequency information in the real world can impose considerable demands on memory (Amitani, 2008).

Dual-process theory: Kahneman (2003)

As we have seen, most people rely on heuristics or rules of thumb when making judgements because they can be used rapidly and fairly effortlessly. However, individuals do sometimes use complex cognitive processes. This has led several theorists (e.g., Kahneman, 2003; De Neys, 2012) to propose dual-process models. Such models have also been applied to performance on reasoning problems (see Chapter 14).

According to Kahneman (2003, p. 698), probability judgements depend on processing within two systems:

- *System 1*: "The operations of System 1 are typically fast, automatic, effortless, implicit (not open to introspection) and often emotionally charged; they are also difficult to control or modify."
- *System 2*: "The operations of System 2 are slower, serial [one at a time], effortful, more likely to be consciously monitored and deliberately controlled; they are relatively flexible and potentially rule-governed."

How are these two systems related? System 1 rapidly generates intuitive answers to judgement problems (e.g., based on the representativeness heuristic). These answers are then monitored or evaluated by System 2, which may correct them. Thus, judgement involves *serial* processing starting with System 1 and sometimes being followed by System 2.

Findings

De Neys (2006) presented participants with the Linda problem (discussed earlier) and another very similar one. Those who produced the correct answers (and so presumably used System 2) took almost 40% longer than those apparently using only System 1. This is consistent with the assumption that it takes longer to use System 2.

De Neys (2006) also compared performance on the same problems performed on their own or with a demanding secondary task requiring use of the central executive (see Glossary). Participants performed worse on the problems when accompanied by the secondary task (9.5% correct vs. 17%, respectively). This is as predicted given that System 2 involves use of cognitively demanding processes.

Kahneman's dual-process theory is oversimplified in several ways. Consider the assumption we make judgement errors because we fail to monitor our intuitive responses. De Neys et al. (2011) used standard base-rate problems. On 80% of trials, participants produced incorrect intuitive or heuristic answers neglecting the base-rate information.

The above findings suggest most participants totally ignored base-rate information. However, participants were less *confident* about their responses when they produced incorrect intuitive answers than when they produced correct answers. Thus, there is some processing of base-rate information even when it does not influence people's judgements. Other research suggests this processing occurs below the level of conscious awareness (De Neys & Glumicic, 2008).

De Neys et al. (2008) also focused on people whose answers on judgement problems involved heuristic processing and who apparently did not use base-rate information. They argued that these people nevertheless processed the base-rate information and detected a *conflict* between their answers and base-rate information. De Neys et al. tested this hypothesis by measuring activity in the anterior cingulate cortex, an area associated with conflict detection. As predicted, there was increased activation in this area.

Earlier we discussed the lawyer–engineer problem (Kahneman & Tversky, 1973) on which most people ignore relevant base-rate information. Pennycook and Thompson (2012) used similar problems, of which this is an example (p. 528):

> In a study 1,000 people were tested. Among the participants there were 995 nurses and five doctors. Paul is a randomly chosen participant of this study.

> Paul is 34 years old. He lives in a beautiful home in a posh suburb. He is well spoken and very interested in politics. He invests a lot of time in his career. What is the probability that Paul is a nurse?

The essence of this problem is the conflict between the base-rate information (suggesting Paul is probably a nurse) and the personality description (which seems much more consistent with him being a doctor). Use of System 1 processing might lead participants to focus on the personality description using the representativeness heuristic and decide Paul was probably a doctor. The participants answered each problem twice: initially with the first answer that came to mind and then with a more deliberate answer.

On Kahneman's theory, people need to use System 2 processing for their answers to reflect base-rate information. That leads to two predictions. First, initial answers should rarely reflect base-rate information but instead should involve the representativeness heuristic. Second, base-rate information should be used much more often in deliberate than initial answers.

Of theoretical importance, neither prediction was supported. Approximately half the initial answers were based primarily on base-rate information. Of the participants who changed their responses, 30% took more account of base-rate information in their deliberate answer than their initial one. However, an almost equal number (23%) took *less* account of base-rate information in their deliberate answer.

What is going on here? The assumptions that answers based on base-rate information always involve System 2 processing whereas those based on personality descriptions involve System 1 processing are incorrect. As we will see shortly, processing is more *flexible* than these assumptions suggest.

Relevant evidence was obtained by Chun and Kruglanski (2006) using various versions of the lawyer–engineer problem discussed earlier. Some information (base-rate or personality) was easy to process because it was presented briefly, whereas the remainder (base-rate or personality) was presented at length. Chun and Kruglanski manipulated cognitive load to assess its effect on the answers produced. According to dual-process theory, cognitive load should reduce System 2 processing and so lead to answers making less use of base-rate information than answers produced without cognitive load.

What did Chun and Kruglanski (2006) find? Cognitive load led to increased use of the information presented briefly. This was so regardless of whether this information referred to base rate or personality. Thus, usage of System 1 and System 2 processing depends more on *how* information is presented (e.g., briefly vs. lengthily) than on its *content* (i.e., base-rate vs. personality description).

Evaluation

There is reasonable support for the existence of two different processing systems. Of importance, System 2 processing is more demanding and effortful than System 1 processing. The notion that people's judgements are typically determined by System 1 rather than System 2 accords with most findings. Note that similar two-process theories have proved reasonably successful in accounting for decision making (this chapter) and reasoning (Chapter 14).

What are the limitations of dual-process theory? First, it is based on the assumption that people often rely almost exclusively on System 1 and so totally ignore base-rate information. However, the existence of rapid, non-conscious processing of base-rate information (De Neys & Glumicic, 2008; De Neys et al., 2008, 2011) indicates that is an oversimplification.

Second, there is a danger of assuming error-prone performance reflects exclusive use of System 1, whereas accurate performance reflects use of System 2. In fact, people can show strong biases on judgement tasks even when they use effortful, conscious and controlled strategies typically associated with System 2 processing (Le Mens & Denrell, 2011).

Third, it is assumed base-rate information will influence judgements only when the conditions favour the use of effortful System 2 processing. That assumption increasingly appears to be incorrect or at least oversimplified (Chun & Kruglanski, 2006; Pennycook & Thompson, 2012).

Fourth, there is a tricky problem associated with a *serial* processing theory such as that of Kahneman. How can we detect rapidly that the response produced by System 1 is wrong given that System 2 has not been used up to that point (De Neys, 2012)?

Fifth, the assumption the processes used on judgement tasks can be divided into heuristic and controlled ones is too neat and tidy (Keren & Schul, 2009). As Fiedler and von Sydow (2015, in press) pointed out, the two processes or systems "are pretended to differ in too many attributes at the same time". System 1 allegedly involves automatic processes and has few capacity constraints, a lack of conscious awareness and so on. In contrast, System 2 is allegedly rule based and requires high cognitive capacity and effort expenditure and so on. There is very little evidence that all these attributes are nearly as highly correlated as is assumed theoretically.

The way forward?

We have seen various findings conflict with Kahneman's dual-process theory. How can we account for these findings? De Neys (2012) has suggested an answer in his logical intuition model (see Figure 14.6 and accompanying discussion, pages 608–611). In essence, he argued that there is rapid, intuitive processing (System 1) of heuristic information *and* intuitive logical processing (e.g., of base-rate information). This initial processing is sometimes followed by deliberate or System 2 processing.

What are the advantages of this model over Kahneman's dual-process theory? First, heuristic and base-rate information can both be rapidly accessed through intuitive processing, which is consistent with recent evidence (Pennycook & Thompson, 2012). Second, the finding that easily processed base-rate information is used more often under cognitive load (Chun & Kruglanski, 2006) is consistent with De Neys' model but not dual-process theory. Third, it is much easier to understand how conflicts between heuristic and base-rate information are rapidly detected (e.g., De Neys et al., 2008, 2011).

DECISION MAKING UNDER RISK

Life is full of decisions. Which movie will I see tonight? Would I prefer to date Dick or Harry? Who will I share an apartment with next year? At one time, it was assumed people behave rationally (at least most of the time) and so generally select the best option. This assumption was built into normative theories, which focused more on how people *should* make decisions rather than how they *actually* make them.

Here we will consider the views of von Neumann and Morgenstern (1944). Their utility theory was not a psychological theory of decision making. However, they suggested we try to maximise *utility* (the subjective value we attach to an outcome). When we choose between simple options, we assess the expected utility or expected value of each one via the following formula:

Expected utility = (probability of a given outcome) × (utility of the outcome)

One of von Neumann and Morgenstern's (1944) important contributions was to treat decisions as if they were gambles. As Manktelow (2012) pointed out, this approach was subsequently coupled with Savage's (1954) mathematical approach based on using information from people's preferences to combine subjective utilities and subjective probabilities. This led to the development of subjective expected utility theory.

In the real world, various factors are generally associated with each option. For example, one holiday option may be preferable to another because it is in a more interesting area with better weather. However, the first holiday is more expensive and more time would be spent travelling. In such circumstances, people allegedly calculate the expected utility or disutility (cost) of each factor to work out the overall expected value or utility of each option. In fact, people's choices and decisions are often decided by factors other than simply utility.

Decisions differ enormously in their complexity. It is more difficult to decide what to do with your entire life than which brand of cereal to have for breakfast. We will start with relatively simple decision making (i.e., relatively little information needs to be considered). The most influential such theory (prospect theory) will be discussed in detail, followed by other theoretical approaches putting more emphasis on emotional and/or social factors. After that, we will consider more complex decision making.

Losses and gains

It is reasonable to assume we make decisions to maximise the chances of making a gain and minimise the chances of making a loss. Suppose someone offered you $200 if a tossed coin came up heads but a loss of $100 if it came up tails. You would jump at the chance (would you not?) given the bet provides an average expected gain of $50 per throw.

Here are two more decisions. Would you prefer a sure gain of $800 or an 85% chance of gaining $1,000 and a 15% probability of gaining nothing? Since the expected value of the latter decision is greater than that of the former ($850 vs. $800, respectively), you might well choose the latter option. Finally, would you prefer a sure loss of $800 or an 85% probability of losing $1,000 with a 15% probability of avoiding any loss? The average expected loss is $800 for the former choice and $850 for the latter one, so you go with the former choice, do you not?

The first problem was from Tversky and Shafir (1992) and the other two from Kahneman and Tversky (1984). In all three cases, most participants did *not* make

Nik Wallenda at the Grand Canyon.
Tim Boyes/Getty Images.

IN THE REAL WORLD: NIK WALLENDA'S DECISION MAKING UNDER RISK

Individuals differ enormously in their willingness to take risky decisions. Consider the case of Nik Wallenda (see photo), the American tightrope walker known as "the King of the Wire" (Newell, 2015, in press). On 23 June 2013, he embarked on a walk along a wire suspended 1,500 feet above the Grand Canyon without a safety harness or safety net. The conditions were windy and at one point during his walk Wallenda said, "Winds are way worse than I expected." In spite of that, he successfully reached the other side in 22 minutes and 54 seconds.

The authors of this book would certainly never consider making Nik Wallenda's life-threatening decision and we guess the same is true of you. How can we explain his decision making? He focused very much on the gains: "I do this because I love what I do . . . Walking the wire to me is life." Most importantly, his strong Christian faith allowed him to minimise the potential losses: "I know where I'm going to go when I die . . . I'm not scared of dying."

what appears to be the best choice. Two-thirds refused to bet on the coin toss and a majority preferred the choices with the *smaller* expected gain and the *larger* expected loss! The rest of this section is concerned with attempts to understand most people's seemingly irrational decision making.

Prospect theory

Kahneman and Tversky (1979, 1984) developed prospect theory to explain apparently paradoxical findings such as those discussed above. Two of its main assumptions are as follows:

1 Individuals identify a reference point generally representing their current state.
2 Individuals are much more sensitive to potential losses than potential gains; this is **loss aversion**. This explains why most people are unwilling to accept a 50:50 bet unless the amount they might win is about twice the amount they might lose (Kahneman, 2003).

KEY TERM

Loss aversion
The greater sensitivity to potential losses than potential gains shown by most people engaged in decision making.

The above assumptions are represented in Figure 13.4. The reference point is where the line labelled losses and gains intersects the line labelled value. The positive value associated with gains increases relatively slowly as gains become greater. Thus, winning £2,000 (2,400 euros) instead of £1,000 (1,200 euros) does not double the subjective value of the money won. In contrast, the negative value associated with losses increases relatively rapidly as losses become greater.

How does prospect theory account for the findings discussed earlier? If people are much more sensitive to losses than gains, they should be unwilling to accept bets involving potential losses even when the potential gains outweigh the potential losses. They should also prefer a sure gain to a risky but potentially greater gain. The theory does *not* predict people will always avoid risky decisions. If offered a chance to avoid a loss, most people will take it because they are so concerned to avoid losses.

It is assumed within prospect theory that people *overweight* low-probability events – rare events receive more weight than they should based on their actual probability of occurrence. This assumption may help to explain why people bet on the National Lottery where the chances of winning the jackpot are 1 in 14 million.

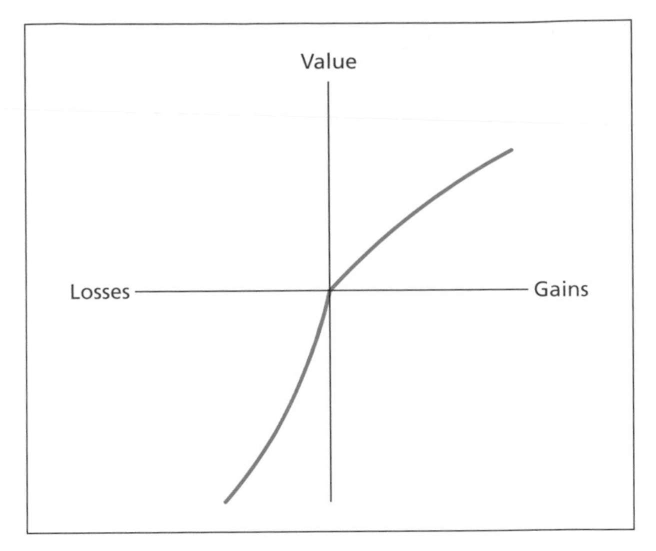

Figure 13.4
A hypothetical value function.
From Kahneman and Tversky (1984). © American Psychological Association.

Findings: framing effect

Much research has involved the **framing effect** in which decisions are influenced by irrelevant aspects of the situation. Tversky and Kahneman (1981) used the Asian disease problem to study the framing effect. All participants were given the following information:

Weblink:
Prospect theory

> Imagine that the US is preparing for the outbreak of an unusual Asian disease, which is expected to kill 600 people. Two alternative programmes to combat the disease have been proposed. Assume that the exact scientific estimate of the consequences of the program are as follows . . .

In the gain-frame condition, participants chose between the following prospects:

> If programme A is adopted, 200 people will be saved.
> If programme B is adopted, there is a 1 in 3 probability 600 people will be saved, and a 2 in 3 probability that no people will be saved.

In this condition, 72% chose the certain gain (programme A) even though the two programmes (if implemented several times) would on average both lead to the saving of 200 lives.

In the loss-frame condition, participants chose between the following prospects:

> If programme C is adopted, 400 people will die.
> If programme D is adopted, there is a 1 in 3 probability that nobody will die, and 2 in 3 probability that 600 people will die.

KEY TERM

Framing effect
The finding that decisions can be influenced by situational aspects (e.g., problem wording) irrelevant to good decision making.

KEY TERM

Sunk-cost effect
Investing additional resources to justify a previous commitment that has so far proved unsuccessful.

In this condition, 78% of participants chose programme D because they were strongly motivated by loss aversion. There was this strong preference even though the two programmes would have the same effect if implemented several times.

The above findings provide less support for prospect theory than initially appears. The certain option is always more ambiguous than the risky option with which it is paired. Some participants probably interpreted programme A as meaning *at least* 200 people would be saved and programme C as meaning *at least* 400 people will die. This appears to be the case. When all the programmes were completely described (or all incompletely described), the framing effect disappeared (Mandel & Vartanian, 2011).

Wang (1996) argued that social and moral factors not considered by prospect theory can influence performance on the Asian disease problem. Participants chose between definite survival of two-thirds of the patients (the deterministic option) and a 1/3 probability of all patients surviving and a 2/3 probability of none surviving (the probabilistic option).

The deterministic option leads, on average, to the survival of twice as many patients. However, the probabilistic option seems fairer because all patients share the same fate. Participants strongly preferred the *deterministic* option when the problem related to six unknown patients. However, they preferred the *probabilistic* option when it related to six close relatives because participants were especially concerned about fairness in that condition.

How can we eliminate the framing effect? Almashat et al. (2008) presented medical scenarios involving cancer treatments. The framing effect disappeared when participants listed the advantages and disadvantages of each option and justified their decision. Thus, the framing effect can be eliminated when individuals think carefully about the available options.

Findings: Sunk-cost effect

A phenomenon resembling loss aversion is the **sunk-cost effect**. This is "a tendency for people to pursue a course of action even after it has proved to be suboptimal, because resources have been invested in that course of action" (Braverman & Blumenthal-Barby, 2012, p. 186). This effect is captured by the expression "throwing good money after bad".

Dawes (1988) discussed a study in which participants were told two people had paid a $100 non-refundable deposit for a weekend at a resort. On the way there, they both became slightly unwell and felt they would probably have a more pleasurable time at home. Many participants argued that the two people should drive on to avoid wasting the $100 – the sunk-cost effect. This decision involves extra costs (money spent at the resort) and is less preferred than being at home!

How can the sunk-cost effect be overcome? First, Baliga and Ely (2011) argued that individuals with complete *memory* of all the relevant information should be immune from the effect. This information would prevent them from focusing excessively on the costs incurred so far. As predicted, MBA students given an investment problem with full access to information showed the opposite of the sunk-cost effect.

Second, experts may possess *knowledge* allowing them to avoid the sunk-cost effect. Expert healthcare providers who made treatment recommendations based on clinical scenarios showed no overall sunk-cost effect (Braverman & Blumenthal-Barby, 2012).

Findings: overweighting rare events

Several studies have obtained support for prospect theory's prediction that people *overweight* the probability of rare events when making decisions. However, participants were generally given a neat summary description of the possible outcomes and their associated probabilities. In the real world, in contrast, people often make decisions based on their limited personal experience.

Hertwig et al. (2004) compared decision making based on descriptions with that based on experience (i.e., personal experience of events and their outcomes). When decisions were based on descriptions, participants *overweighted* the probability of rare events as predicted by prospect theory. When decisions were based on experience via sequential sampling, however, participants *underweighted* the probability of rare events. This happened because participants in the sequential sampling or experience condition often failed to encounter the rare event at all.

How could we produce appropriate weighting of rare events? Hilbig and Glöckner (2011) argued that this could be done by rapidly presenting participants with a large amount of detailed information (open sampling). They also used conditions involving descriptions and sequential sampling. As in previous research, descriptions led to overweighting of rare events and sequential sampling led to underweighting (see Figure 13.5). As predicted, rapid access of detailed information in the open sampling condition produced accurate weighting of rare events.

What can we conclude from the above study? First, the weighting of rare events in decision making depends on the precise information provided to participants. Second, the findings from the sequential and open sampling conditions are inconsistent with predictions from prospect theory.

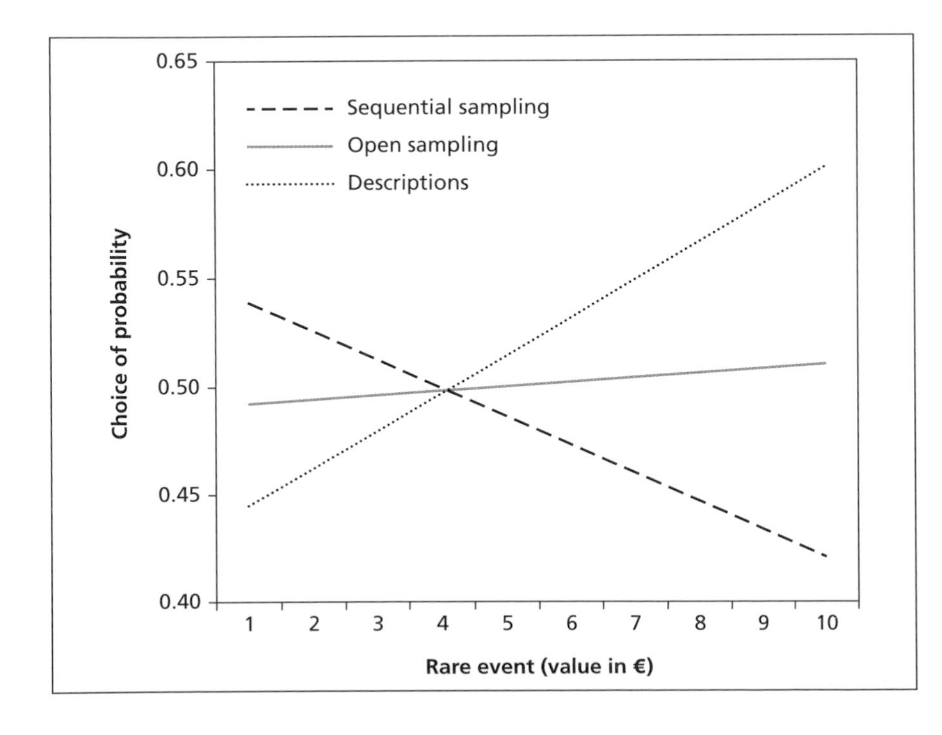

Figure 13.5
Probabilities of choosing a gamble involving a rare event as a function of its desirability (value in euros) and on the presentation format of information (sequential sampling, open sampling or descriptions).
From Hilbig & Glöckner (2011). With permission from Elsevier.

IN THE REAL WORLD: RISK TAKING BY EXPERTS

Most research on prospect theory is laboratory-based. As a result, there are doubts about the theory's applicability in the real world. In particular, it seems likely experts would have learned how to prevent biases such as loss aversion from influencing their behaviour and reducing their income. Here we will briefly consider a few real-world examples.

For professional golfers, birdie (one under par) on a hole is a gain whereas bogey (one over par) is a loss. Loss aversion would lead them to be more cautious when putting for birdie than for par. In the latter case, failure to hole the putt would lead to a bogey and thus a loss.

Pope and Schweitzer (2011) studied 2½ million putts made by professional golfers. Par putts were less likely than same-length birdie putts to stop short of the hole (indicative of loss aversion). Pope and Schweitzer found 94% of golfers (including Tiger Woods) showed evidence of loss aversion.

Smith et al. (2009) studied experienced poker players (including many professionals) playing high-stakes poker. The stakes were high – 50% of the players studied won or lost more than

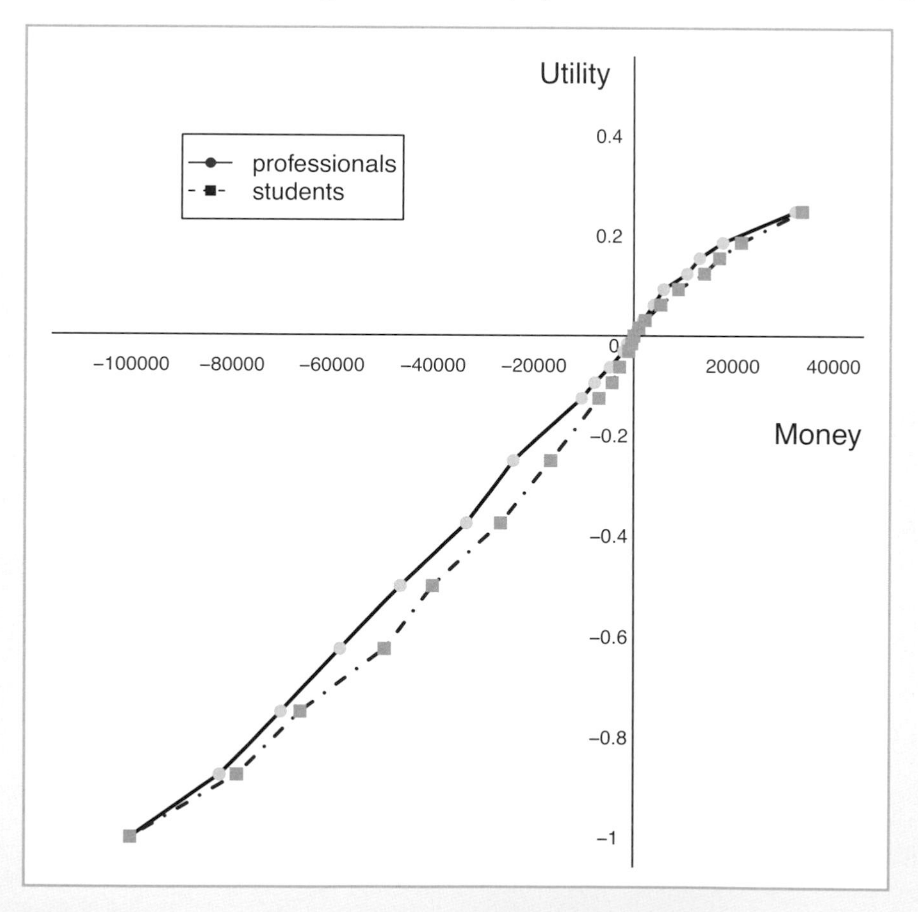

Figure 13.6
Risk aversion for gains and risk seeking for losses on a money-based task by financial professionals and students.

From Abdellaoui et al. (2013). With kind permission from Springer Science + Business Media.

$200,000 (£130,000)! These expert poker players typically played more aggressively (i.e., betting and raising more often) following a big loss, which is as predicted if players were motivated by loss aversion.

Abdellaoui et al. (2013) studied financial professionals handling an average of £200 million (240 million euros) each. As prospect theory predicts, they were risk averse for gains and risk seeking for losses on a money-based task. Their risk aversiveness for gains was comparable to students but they were less loss averse than students (see Figure 13.6).

In sum, even experts whose income depends on accurate decision making show loss aversion. Thus, prospect theory is applicable in the real world. However, there is some evidence (e.g., Abdellaoui et al., 2013) that experts are less loss averse than non-experts.

Loss neutrality

Suppose you were given the following choice:

1 50% to win £1 (1.20 euro); 50% to lose £1 (1.20 euro).
2 50% to win £5 (6 euros); 50% to lose £5 (6 euros).

According to prospect theory, people are loss averse and so should choose (1) because it reduces potential losses. In fact, however, the typical finding across several studies using similar choices is loss neutrality – overall, participants do not favour one option over the other unless the stakes are high (Yechiam & Hochman, 2013). This consistent finding is contrary to prospect theory.

Why was there loss neutrality in the above studies but loss aversion in many other kinds of studies? Yechiam and Hochman (2013) put forward an attentional model. They argued that losses produce a brief increase in arousal. This directs attention to on-task events and makes the individual more sensitive to task reinforcements (losses and gains). These processes lead to loss neutrality when information about potential gains and losses is presented at the same time. In contrast, loss aversion is typically found on tasks where an individual's attention is directed to gains or losses rather than both together.

Findings: individual differences

Prospect theory de-emphasises individual differences (see earlier discussion of the tightrope walker Nik Wallenda). Consider research on the television show *Deal or No Deal*, a game of chance on which contestants can win or lose large sums of money. As predicted by prospect theory, most participants were risk averse, especially when the stakes were high (Brooks et al., 2009). However, there were large individual differences in willingness to take risks even with very high stakes.

Personality influences individuals' attitudes to risk. Those high in self-esteem are more likely to prefer risky gambles than those low in self-esteem (Josephs et al., 1992). This is because they have a strong self-protective system that helps them to maintain self-esteem when confronted by threat or loss. Narcissism, a personality dimension related to self-esteem but involving excessive self-regard, was studied by Foster et al. (2011). Individuals high in narcissism engaged in riskier stock-market investing because they have high sensitivity to reward but low sensitivity to punishment.

Evaluation

Prospect theory provides a more adequate account of decision making than previous approaches (e.g., subjective expected utility theory). The value function (especially the assumption people attach more weight to losses than gains) allows us to explain many phenomena (e.g., loss aversion, sunk-cost effect, framing effects). Professional golfers, experienced poker players and financiers all show loss aversion in the real world, thus demonstrating the wide applicability of the theory.

What are the limitations of prospect theory? First, Kahneman and Tversky failed to provide a detailed explicit rationale for the value function. It is possible its origins lie in our evolutionary history (McDermott et al., 2008). For example, engaging in risky behaviour may be the optimal strategy for someone facing starvation, whereas it may be sensible to minimise risk when resources are abundant.

Second, prospect theory is oversimplified. For example, the reference point represents the current situation (see Figure 13.4). In fact, however, its meaning varies depending on the context. Winning nothing (the current reference point) would seem far worse if you had been given a 90% chance to win $1 million than if you had had one chance in a million (Newell, 2015, in press). In addition, the theory pays relatively little attention to the effects of social and emotional factors on decision making (Wang, 1996; see the next section).

Third, the predicted overweighting of rare events sometimes fails to materialise. This is especially the case when people obtain information about different events through experience based on sequential sampling.

Weblink:
Thinking of making a risky decision

Case study:
Full fat milk

Fourth, loss aversion occurs less often than predicted by the theory. Loss neutrality is sometimes found, especially when information about potentials gains and losses is available at the same time.

Fifth, our everyday experience tells us people vary enormously in their willingness to make risky decisions. However, such individual differences are de-emphasised in the theory.

Sixth, prospect theory pays little attention to the effects of social and emotional factors on decision making (e.g., Wang, 1996). However, there is much research on such factors (see next section).

DECISION MAKING: EMOTIONAL AND SOCIAL FACTORS

Emotional factors are important in decision making given that winning and losing both have emotional consequences. We would expect individuals who are more emotionally affected by winning than by losing to take more risks than individuals showing the opposite tendency. We have already discussed some supportive research (Foster et al., 2011).

Laboratory decisions are rarely taken in a social context, but we often need to justify our decisions to others in our everyday lives. Consider a contestant on

Who Wants To Be A Millionaire? deciding whether to attempt a question when there are two possible answers. If she answers correctly, she gains £75,000 (90,000 euros), but she loses £25,000 (30,000 euros) if she is wrong. In strict financial terms, the balance of advantage lies with answering the question. Suppose, however, the contestant's family is poor and their lives would be transformed by taking home the money won already. In that case, the social context indicates she should take the money.

Emotional factors

Emotional factors play a significant role in decision making. More specifically, anticipated or actual losses may cause individuals to experience negative emotions (e.g., anxiety) leading to loss aversion. Much of the relevant research lies within **neuroeconomics**, in which cognitive neuroscience is used to increase our understanding of economic decision making.

Kermer et al. (2006) found people often exaggerate how negative the impact of a loss is likely to be. Participants were initially given $5 (£3.50) and predicted how they would feel if they won $5 or lost $3 (£2.10) on a coin toss. They predicted losing $3 would have more impact on their happiness immediately and ten minutes later than gaining $5, which is suggestive of loss aversion.

In fact, participants who lost felt happier than they had predicted at both time intervals and the actual impact on happiness of losing $3 was no greater than the actual impact of gaining $5. Overestimation of the intensity and duration of negative emotional reactions to loss is known as **impact bias** and has been found with predictions about losses such as losing one's job or a romantic partner (Kermer et al., 2006).

We can distinguish between *anticipated* emotions (those predicted to follow possible outcomes of a decision) and *immediate* emotions (those actually experienced just before making a decision). Schlösser et al. (2013) found the riskiness of decision making was predicted by both anticipated and immediate emotions.

The effects of emotion on decision making are fairly complex. Giorgetta et al. (2013) used a gambling situation in which the choices were made by the participant or a computer. When the participant lost, it was experienced as regret if he/she had made the decision, but as disappointment if the computer had. Regret was followed by riskier choices than was disappointment (see Figure 13.7). Wins were experienced as rejoicing (personal choices) or as elation (computer choices), with elation being followed by riskier choices. Overall, the findings are more consistent with prospect theory when participants had a sense of personal agency (i.e., regret and rejoicing conditions).

Which brain areas are associated with emotion processing during decision making? Several areas are involved but the amygdala and ventromedial prefrontal cortex have been the focus of most research (see Figures 15.3 and 15.19). The amygdala is in the limbic system and is associated with several emotional states including fear or anxiety.

Weller et al. (2007) found patients with damage to the ventromedial prefrontal cortex had elevated risk-seeking behaviour with respect to both potential gains and losses. This was especially the case when the probability of success was low. Patients with amygdala damage also showed elevated risk-seeking behaviour with potential gains but not potential losses.

KEY TERMS

Neuroeconomics
An approach in which economic decision making is understood within the framework of **cognitive neuroscience**.

Impact bias
Overestimation of the intensity and duration of negative emotional reactions to loss.

KEY TERM

Omission bias
A biased preference for risking harm through inaction compared to risking harm through action.

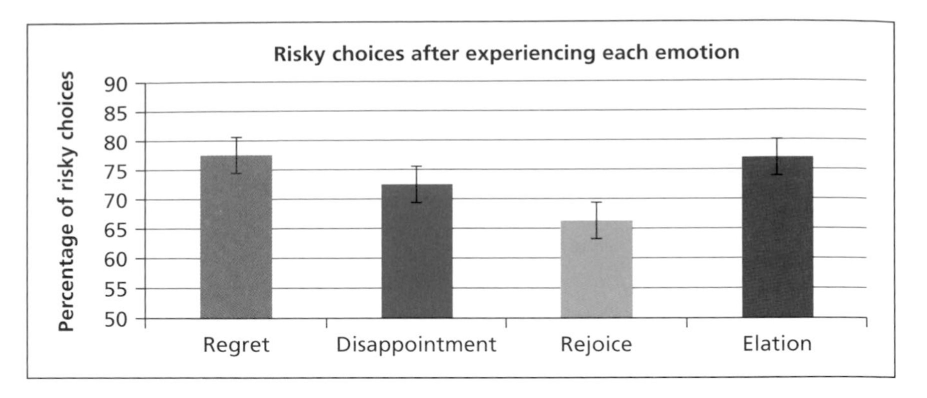

Figure 13.7
Percentage of risky choices made after having experienced regret, disappointment, rejoicing or elation. Regret and disappointment were both associated with losses, and rejoicing and elation with wins. Regret and rejoicing were associated with personally chosen gambles, whereas disappointment and elation were associated with computer-chosen gambles.
From Giorgetta et al. (2013). With permission from Elsevier.

De Martino et al. (2010) studied loss aversion in two women, SP and AP, who had suffered severe damage to the amygdala. Neither woman showed evidence of loss aversion. In the words of De Martino et al. (2010), the amygdala may act as a "cautionary brake".

Sokol-Hessner et al. (2013) studied the effects of emotion on risky financial decision making. When participants were instructed to engage in emotion regulation (designed to reduce their emotional involvement in the task), they showed reduced loss aversion. Other findings suggested this happened because emotion regulation led to decreased amygdala responses to losses.

Koscik and Tranel (2013) explored the role of the ventromedial prefrontal cortex. Participants invested money with hypothetical investors who had made money through their own efforts (e.g., "because he is highly motivated and ambitious") or because of a favourable situation (e.g., "due to economic growth in China"). Healthy individuals make dispositional attributions about others' behaviour (attributing it to their internal characteristics in most circumstances). As a result, they invested comparable amounts of money with both investors. In contrast, patients with damage to the ventromedial prefrontal cortex invested more with investors whose success depended on their own efforts than with those who had benefited from the situation.

What do the above findings mean? The bias towards dispositional attributions depends on the processing of social information in the ventromedial prefrontal cortex, and so is no longer present in those having damage to that area. Intriguingly, the brain-damaged patients made more financially advantageous investments than the healthy controls, given that it makes more sense to invest with those who have made money from their own efforts rather than because they were lucky.

Omission bias and status quo bias

There is other evidence that emotional factors influence decision making. For example, consider **omission bias**, a preference for inaction to action when engaged in risky decision making.

IN THE REAL WORLD: CAN BRAIN DAMAGE IMPROVE DECISION MAKING?

Shiv et al. (2005a, b) argued that emotions can make us excessively cautious and loss averse. That led them to the counterintuitive prediction that brain-damaged patients would outperform healthy participants on a gambling task provided the brain damage reduced their emotional experience.

There were three groups of participants in the study by Shiv et al. (2005b). One group consisted of patients with brain damage in areas related to emotion (amygdala, orbitofrontal cortex, insula or somatosensory cortex). The other groups were healthy controls and patients with brain damage.

Initially, Shiv et al. provided participants with $20. On each of 20 rounds, they decided whether to invest $1. If they did, they lost the $1 if a coin came up heads but won $1.50 if it came up tails. Participants had an average gain of 25 cents per round if they invested compared to simply retaining the $1. Thus, the most profitable strategy was to invest on every single round.

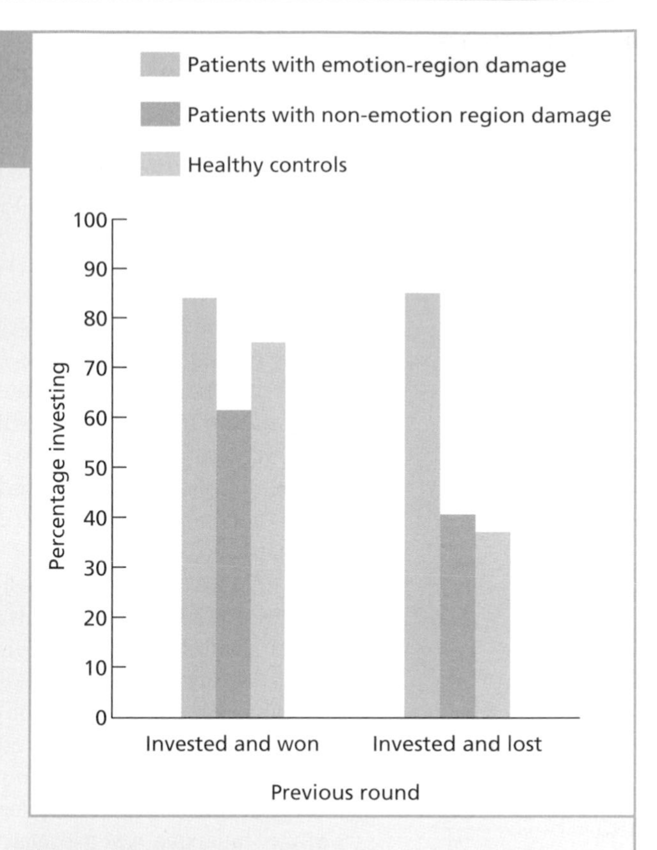

Figure 13.8
Percentage of rounds in which patients with damage to emotion regions of the brain, patients with damage to other regions of the brain and healthy controls decided to invest $1 having won or lost on the previous round.

Data from Shiv et al. (2005a). Reprinted by permission of SAGE Publications.

Patients with damage to emotion regions invested in 84% of the rounds compared to only 61% for the other patient group and 58% for healthy controls. Thus, the patients with restricted emotions performed best. Why was this? Patients with brain damage unrelated to emotion and healthy controls were much less likely to invest following loss on the previous round than following gain. In contrast, patients with brain damage related to emotion were totally unaffected in their investment decisions by the outcome of the previous round (see Figure 13.8).

What can we conclude? An emotion such as anxiety can prevent us from maximising profit by making us unduly concerned about possible losses and therefore excessively afraid of taking risks. However, that does not mean emotional involvement necessarily impairs decision making. Seo and Barrett (2007) found, using an internet-based stock investment simulation, that those stock investors experiencing more intense feelings had superior decision-making performance than those with less intense feelings. The stock investors who performed the best had a good understanding of their emotions and prevented them from directly influencing their decision making.

KEY TERM

Status quo bias
A preference for maintaining the status quo (present state) rather than acting to change one's decision.

Omission bias has been found in numerous situations. For example, British parents were asked questions about having their children vaccinated against various diseases (Brown et al., 2010). They were willing to accept a higher risk of their children having a disease than of their children suffering adverse reactions to vaccination (this is omission bias). In a similar study (Wroe et al., 2005), parents argued that the level of anticipated responsibility and regret would potentially be higher if they had their child vaccinated than if they did not.

Even experts exhibit omission bias. Aberegg et al. (2005) gave pulmonologists (experts in treating lung disease) scenarios involving evaluation of pulmonary embolism and treatment of septic shock. When these experts had the option of doing nothing, they were less likely to select the best management strategy than when this option was unavailable (40% vs. 59%, respectively). Thus, these experts showed strong evidence of omission bias.

Not everyone shows omission bias. In one vaccination study (Baron & Ritov, 2004), 58% of participants showed omission bias but 22% showed the opposite bias: "action bias". Those susceptible to action bias used the heuristic, "Don't just sit there. Do something!"

Another example of decision avoidance often caused by emotional factors is **status quo bias** – individuals often prefer to accept the status quo (current state) rather than change their decision. For example, many people keep the same allocation of retirement funds year after year even when they would not incur any costs by changing (Samuelson & Zeckhauser, 1988).

Nicolle et al. (2011) found status quo bias on a difficult perceptual decision task. Mistaken rejection of the status quo was accompanied by stronger feelings of regret than mistaken acceptance of the status quo. In addition, mistaken rejection of the status quo was associated with greater activation in brain regions (medial prefrontal cortex, insula) associated with regret.

Anderson (2003) proposed a rational-emotional model to account for decision avoidance including omission bias and status quo bias. Within the model, both biases are explained in terms of regret and fear. We have seen regret is important. Fear is relevant because it can be reduced when someone decides not to make a decision for the time being.

There are some issues with this model. First, we have seen that individuals often experience more regret for errors of action than inaction shortly afterwards. However, the opposite is frequently the case in the long term (Leach & Plaks, 2009), which is hard for the model to explain.

Second, status quo bias is found even with trivial decisions such as whether or not to switch television channels (Esteves-Sorenson & Perretti, 2012). It is hard to believe regret or fear lies behind people's decision to remain on the same television channel rather than switching!

Social factors

Tetlock (2002) emphasised the importance of social factors in his social functionalist approach. He argued that people often act like intuitive politicians, in that "They are accountable to a variety of constituencies . . . their long-term success at managing impressions hinges on their skill at anticipating objections that others are likely to raise to alternative courses of action" (p. 454).

Simonson and Staw (1992) studied the effects of accountability on decision making in a study on the sunk-cost effect (see Glossary). Some participants were told their decisions would be shared with other students and instructors (high-accountability condition), whereas others were told their decisions would be confidential (low-accountability condition). High-accountability participants were more likely to continue with their previously ineffective course of action. They showed a stronger sunk-cost effect because they experienced a greater need to justify their previous decisions.

Accountability pressures also influence experts' decisions. Schwartz et al. (2004) asked medical experts to choose treatment for a patient with osteoarthritis. Their decision making was more biased when they were made accountable for their decision by writing an explanation for it and agreeing to be contacted later to discuss it.

What are the limitations with the social functionalist approach? First, individual differences in the extent to which people feel the need to justify themselves to others are de-emphasised. Second, most research has involved laboratory tasks not making any real demands on social responsibility.

COMPLEX DECISION MAKING

So far we have focused on decision making with fairly simple problems. In real life, however, we are sometimes confronted by important and complex decisions. For example, medical experts make diagnostic decisions that can literally be a matter of life or death (see Chapter 12). Other decisions are both important and complex (e.g., Shall I marry John?, Shall I move to Australia?). How do we deal with such decisions?

Before proceeding, note there are two important differences between decision making in the laboratory and the real world. First, decision making generally has much more serious *consequences* in the real world. Second, laboratory-based decision makers typically make a *single* decision. In contrast, in real life we often make a *series* of decisions over time as we strive towards important goals (e.g., establishing a career).

The focus in this section is on the strategies we use when making complex decisions. We will start by considering an approximation to an ideal strategy. According to multi-attribute utility theory (Wright, 1984), decision makers should go through the following stages:

1 Identify attributes relevant to the decision.
2 Decide how to weight those attributes.
3 List all options under consideration.
4 Rate each option on each attribute.
5 Obtain a total utility (i.e., subjective desirability for each option by summing its weighted attribute values) and select the one with the highest weighted total.

We can see how this theory works in practice by considering someone deciding which flat to rent. First, the relevant attributes (e.g., number of rooms, location, rent per week) are identified. Second, the relative utility of each attribute is calculated. Third, the flats under consideration are compared for total utility and the one with the highest utility is chosen.

Decision makers adopting the above approach will often make the best decision provided *all* options are listed and the criteria are independent of each other. However, there are various reasons why people rarely adopt the above decision-making procedure in real life. First, it can be very complex. Second, the sets of relevant dimensions cannot always be worked out. Third, the dimensions themselves may not be clearly separate from each other.

Simon (1957) proposed a much more realistic approach to complex decision making. He argued that our decision-making ability is constrained by processing limitations (e.g., small short-term memory capacity). This led him to develop the notion of **bounded rationality** – our decision making is "bounded" by environmental constraints (e.g., information costs) and by cognitive constraints (e.g., limited attention).

In essence, bounded rationality means we are as rational as the constraints of the environment and the mind permit (this issue is discussed more fully in Chapter 14). In practical terms, bounded rationality leads to **satisficing** (formed from the words satisfactory and sufficing). Satisficing is not guaranteed to produce the best decision. However, it is especially useful when options become available at different times (e.g., potential romantic partners).

Schwartz et al. (2002) distinguished between *satisficers* (content with making reasonably good decisions) and *maximisers* (perfectionists). There were various advantages associated with being a satisficer. Satisficers were happier and more optimistic than maximisers, had greater life satisfaction and experienced less regret and self-blame.

The study by Schwartz et al. (2002) was carried out only on American participants. In China, maximisers and satisficers do not differ in psychological well-being (Roets et al., 2012). Chinese society places less emphasis than American society on making optimal choices and decisions.

KEY TERMS

Bounded rationality
The notion that people are as rational as the environment and their limited processing capacity permit.

Satisficing
In decision making, the strategy of choosing the first option that satisfies the individual's minimum requirements.

Weblink:
Bounded rationality

Elimination by aspects

Tversky (1972) put forward a theory of decision making resembling Simon's (1957) approach. According to his elimination-by-aspects theory, decision makers eliminate options by considering one relevant attribute or aspect after another. For example, someone buying a house may initially consider geographical location, eliminating all houses not lying within a given area. They may then consider the attribute of price, eliminating all properties costing above a certain figure. This process continues attribute by attribute until only one option remains.

One problem with elimination by aspects is that the option selected varies as a function of the order in which the attributes are considered. As a result, the choice made may not be the best one.

Kaplan et al. (2011) put forward a modified version of Tversky's (1972) theory. In their two-stage theory, there is an initial stage resembling elimination by aspects, in which only options meeting certain criteria are retained. This stage reduces the options being considered to a manageable number. In the second stage, there are detailed comparisons of the patterns of attributes of the retained options. It is often only feasible to engage in such detailed comparisons of a relatively small number of options.

Findings

Payne (1976) asked students to decide among flats on the basis of information about various attributes (e.g., rent, distance from campus). When there were many flats to consider, the students typically started with a simple strategy such as satisficing or elimination by aspects. When only a few flats remained for consideration, they often switched to a more complex strategy corresponding to the assumptions of multi-attribute utility theory.

Kaplan et al. (2011) obtained support for their two-stage theory. Student participants selected an apartment after having searched through information about 600 apartments. In the first stage, the three most popular criteria for retaining or eliminating apartments were location, walking time to the university and rental price.

In the second stage, participants engaged in more complex calculations. For example, the importance attached to a low rental price depended on several other factors such as price knowledge, frequency of going to the university and experience of searching for apartments. More specifically, low rent was most important when participants had little price knowledge, went frequently to the university and had often searched for apartments in recent years.

Similar findings were obtained by Lenton and Stewart (2008) when single women made selections from a real dating website with 4, 24 or 64 potential mates. Unsurprisingly, the women shifted from complex to simple strategies with increased potential mates. The weighted averaging strategy assumed by multi-attribute utility theory was used by 81% of the women with 4 potential mates but by only 41% choosing from 64. The respective figures for the elimination-by-aspects strategy were 39% and 69%, respectively, and for the satisficing strategy were 6% and 16%. Note that the numbers exceed 100% because many women used multiple strategies.

Which attributes most influence mate choice depends on how easily they are assessed. Speed-dating decisions at large events were determined mostly by easily assessable attributes (e.g., age, height, weight) rather than those harder to assess (e.g., occupation, academic achievements) (Lenton and Francesconi (2010). The opposite was the case at small events. These findings probably reflect the increased cognitive load at large events.

Evaluation

Elimination-by-aspects theory has proved reasonably successful when individuals have to choose between numerous options. However, individuals often adopt a more complex approach resembling that of multi-attribute utility theory when there are relatively few options. In other words, elimination by aspects is a useful filter at an early stage of decision making but is less valuable at later stages.

Another limitation of elimination-by-aspects theory is that it does not take account of our preference for options sharing many attributes with other options. Won (2012) showed that adding this preference to the elimination-by-aspects approach enhances its predictive power.

Changing preferences and facts

Most theories assume a given individual's assessment of the utility or preference (desirability × importance) of any given attribute remains constant. Simon et al. (2004) tested this assumption. Participants decided between job offers from two department store chains on the basis of four attributes (e.g., salary, commuting time).

KEY TERM

Selective exposure
A preference for information that strengthens pre-existing views and avoidance of information conflicting with those views.

After the participants had assessed their preferences, they were told one job was in a much better location than the other. This often led them to choose the job in the better location. The participants then reassessed their preferences. Preferences for desirable attributes of the chosen job increased and those for undesirable attributes of that job decreased, which is inconsistent with the notion that preferences remain constant.

Decisions can even cause people to misremember factual information used during decision making. Advanced nursing students prioritised a male or female patient for surgery because there were only sufficient resources for one operation (Svenson et al., 2009). After they had made their decision, their memory for the objective facts (e.g., life expectancy without surgery, probability of surviving surgery) was distorted to increase the apparent support for that decision.

Selective exposure

An important factor in poor decision making is **selective exposure** – the tendency in decision making to prefer information consistent with one's beliefs over inconsistent information. Fischer and Greitemeyer (2010) proposed a model according to which increased selective exposure is predicted when there is high defence motivation (i.e., a need to define one's personal position) (see Figure 13.9). Increased selective exposure should also be found when decision makers have high accuracy motivation but are only permitted to access a restricted amount of

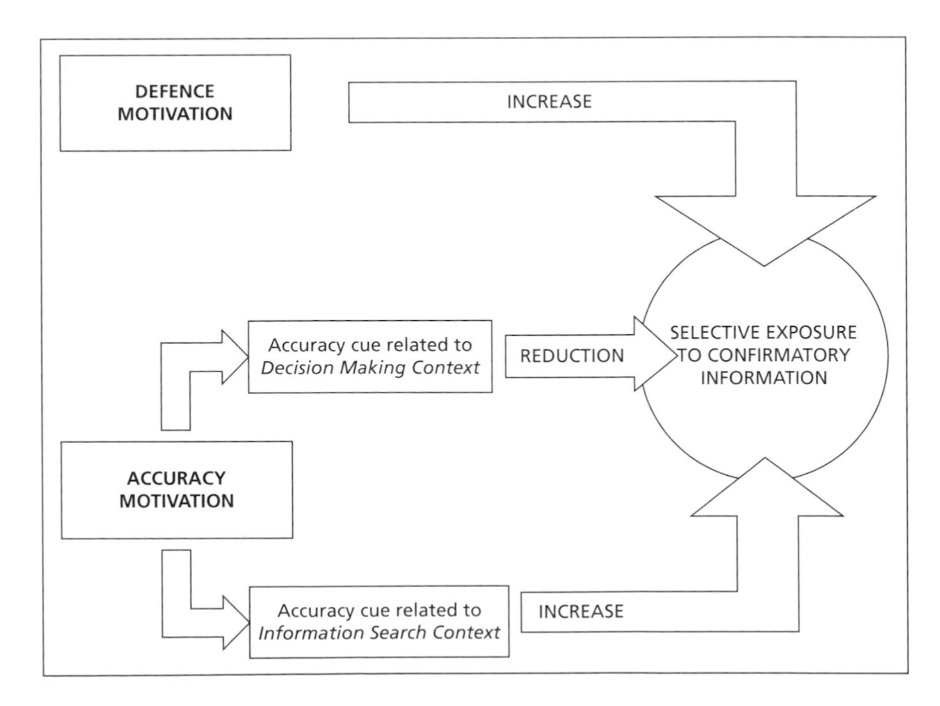

Figure 13.9
A model of selective exposure. Defence motivation (a need to define one's own position) increases the individual's selective exposure to confirmatory information. Accuracy motivation reduces selective exposure when it is triggered by the goal of making the optimal decision, but increases it when it is triggered during the search for information.
From Fischer and Greiemeyer (2010). Reprinted by permission of SAGE Publications.

information. The opposite effect of reduced selective exposure occurs when there is high accuracy motivation produced by instructing decision makers to make the best choice. All these findings were reported in a meta-analysis by Hart et al. (2009).

Naturalistic decision making

In view of the artificiality of much laboratory research, there has been much interest in naturalistic decision making. This approach is designed to identify the processes involved in real-life decision making.

Galotti (2002) put forward a theory of naturalistic decision making involving five phases: setting goals, gathering information, structuring the decision (i.e., listing options + the criteria for deciding among them), making a final choice and evaluating the decision. As Figure 13.10 shows, there is *flexibility* in phase order with many decision makers returning to previous phases if struggling to make a decision.

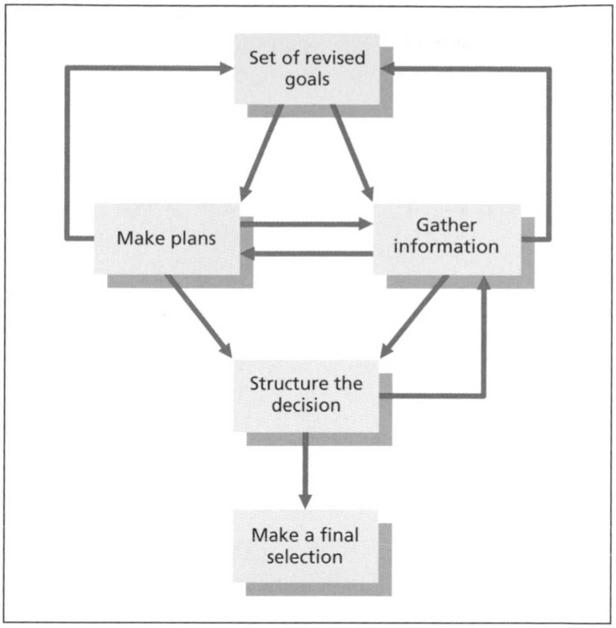

Set of revised goals

Make plans

Gather information

Structure the decision

Make a final selection

Figure 13.10
The five phases of decision making according to Galotti's theory. Note the flexibility in the ordering of the phases.
From Galotti (2002).

A key phase in Galotti's theory is that of decision structuring. Galotti (2007) discussed five studies concerned with important real-life decisions (e.g., students choosing a college, college students choosing their main subject). There were several findings:

1. Decision makers constrained the amount of information they considered, focusing on between two and five options (mean = four) at any given time.
2. The number of options considered decreased over time.
3. The number of attributes considered at any given time was between three and nine (mean = six).
4. The number of attributes did not decrease over time; sometimes it actually increased.
5. Individuals of higher ability and/or more education considered more attributes.
6. Most of the decisions makers' real-life decisions were assessed as good.

What can we conclude from Galotti's (2007) study? The most striking finding is that people consistently limited the amount of information (options and attributes) considered. This is inconsistent with multi-attribute utility theory but is consistent with Simon's (1957) notion of bounded rationality.

In addition, Galotti (2007) found the number of options considered decreased by 18% over a period of several months. A reduction (but larger than the one obtained) is predicted by Tversky's (1972) elimination-by-aspects theory.

Similar findings to those of Galotti (2007) were reported by Galotti and Tinkelenberg (2009). They studied parents choosing a first-grade school placement for their child. The parents focused on a restricted number of options (typically three out of the eight or more potentially available), and generally considered only about five criteria or attributes at any given time. However, the parents' decision making was *dynamic* – over a six-month period, one-third of the options and over half the criteria changed on average.

Individual differences

There are marked individual differences in the strategies used in naturalistic decision making. For example, Crossley and Highhouse (2005) studied the approaches taken by individuals searching for and choosing a job. They identified three distinct information-search strategies:

1. *Focused search*: This involved a focus on a small number of carefully selected potential employers.
2. *Exploratory search*: This involved taking into account several job options and making use of several information sources (e.g., friends, employment centres).
3. *Haphazard search*: This was a rather non-strategic approach resembling trial and error.

Which approach was most successful? Focused search correlated positively with satisfaction with the process of job search and with job satisfaction. In contrast, haphazard search correlated negatively with both measures of satisfaction.

Expert decision making

How do experts make work decisions? An influential approach is the recognition-primed decision model put forward by Klein (e.g., 1998, 2008), which is especially relevant when decisions must be made rapidly (e.g., there is a forest fire).

The model is shown in Figure 13.11. When the situation is perceived as familiar or typical, experts *match* the situation to learned patterns of information stored in long-term memory using pattern recognition. This rapid automatic

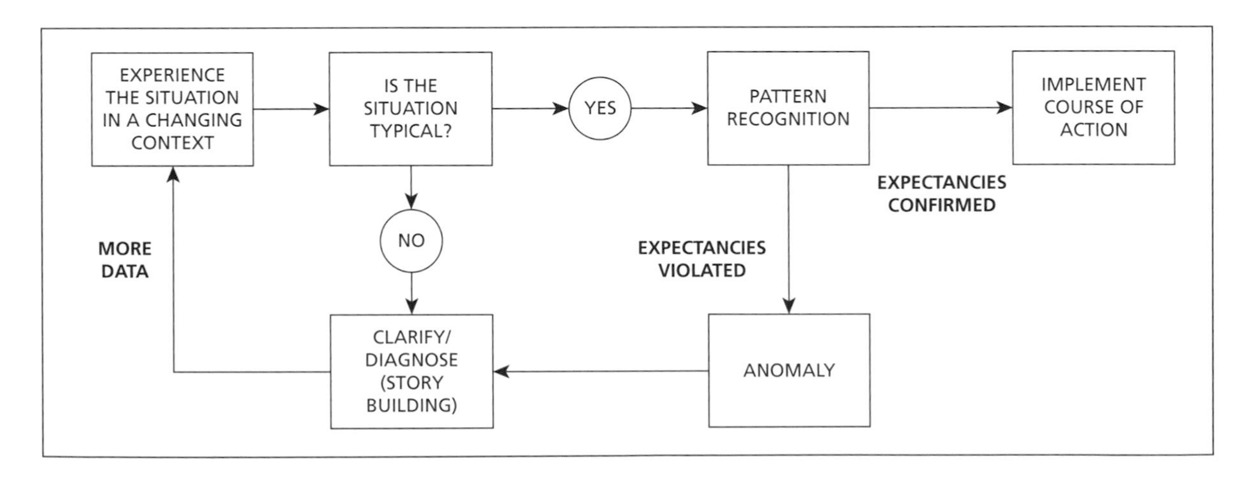

Figure 13.11
Klein's recognition-primed decision model. Decision making is easy if the situation is typical; pattern recognition based on information in long-term memory generates a decision that confirms expectancies. Decision making is more complex if the decision maker's expectancies are violated or if the situation is perceived as not typical. In either case, there is a process of clarifying and diagnosing the situation and collecting more data.
From Patterson et al. (2009). British Computer Society.

process typically leads to retrieval of a *single* option. It is followed by *mental simulation* (i.e., imagining what would happen if the expert acted on the retrieved option). If the imagined outcome is satisfactory (as it generally is with experts), that option rapidly determines his/her actions.

The situation is more complex if the situation is *not* perceived as familiar or if the expert's expectancies are violated (see Figure 13.11). In such circumstances, experts diagnose the situation further. This can include story building and considering more data prior to making a decision.

There is much support for the model. Klein (1998) found in an analysis of over 600 decisions that various kinds of experts (e.g., fire commanders, military commanders) generally considered only one option at time. Experts typically rapidly categorised even a novel situation as an example of a familiar type of situation. After that, they simply retrieved the appropriate decision from long-term memory.

Turpin and Marais (2004) held interviews with six prominent decision makers. The approaches taken to decision making by three of these decision makers were consistent with the model in that they relied heavily on intuition. However, the approaches taken by the other decision makers were less supportive. These decision makers preferred a reasonable decision today over a better decision in the future, which can be regarded as a satisficing approach.

Kahneman and Klein (2009) pointed out that the recognition-primed decision model emphasises the accuracy of human judgement and decision making. In contrast, Kahneman's heuristics-and-biases approach focuses more on human *error*. This difference occurs because the recognition-primed decision model applies to experts while the heuristics-and-biases does not. On average, experts make superior decisions to non-experts.

What are the model's limitations? First, it was explicitly designed to explain the behaviour of experts confronted by crisis situations with severe time constraints. That helps to explain why it did not predict the decision-making behaviour of some of the prominent decision makers interviewed by Turpin and Marais (2004).

Second, the model provides a general outline of what is involved but provides few specific details For example, when a crisis situation is perceived as unfamiliar it is assumed experts engage in clarification and diagnosis. However, the precise forms of information processing involved will differ substantially depending on the nature of the crisis and the personality and relevant knowledge of the expert.

Unconscious thought theory

Most people assume conscious thinking is more effective than unconscious thinking with complex decision making. In contrast, unconscious thinking (if useful at all) is so with respect to simple decision making. However, Dijksterhuis and Nordgren (2006) argued the opposite in their unconscious thought theory. They claimed conscious thinking is constrained by the limited capacity of consciousness. As a result, unconscious thinking is better than conscious thinking at *integrating* large amounts of information. However, only conscious thought can follow strict rules and so is well suited to rule-based problems (e.g., in mathematics).

Findings

Dijksterhuis et al. (2006) tested unconscious thought theory. All participants read information about four hypothetical cars. In the simple condition, each car was described by four attributes. In the complex condition, each car was described by 12 attributes. Participants spent four minutes thinking about the cars (conscious thought condition) or solved anagrams for four minutes before choosing a car (unconscious thought condition). As predicted, performance was higher in the unconscious thought condition than the conscious thought condition when the decision was complex but the opposite was the case when the decision was simple.

Nieuwenstein and van Rijn (2012) reviewed research similar to that of Dijksterhuis et al. (2006). A superiority of unconscious thought over conscious thought was found in only 45% of experiments.

Nordgren et al. (2011) argued that complex decision making should be best if it involved conscious *and* unconscious thought. Participants selected the best apartment from 12 apartments. Of participants using only conscious thought, 26% selected one of the best apartments as did 28% of those using unconscious thought. As predicted, performance was much better (57% success rate) for those using conscious thought followed by unconscious thought.

Do the positive findings in this area show unconscious thought is superior to conscious thought? There are reasons for doubt (Newell & Shanks, 2014). In most studies, participants in the conscious thought condition spent several minutes thinking about their decision while relying on their fragmentary memory for the previously presented information. This probably *underestimates* the value of conscious thought.

Evidence consistent with the above viewpoint was reported by Payne et al. (2008). Some participants spent four minutes engaged in conscious thought whereas others decided how long to engage in conscious thought (self-paced). Self-paced participants (devoting 20 seconds on average to conscious thought) outperformed those in the four-minute conscious thought group and performed as well as those in the unconscious thought condition. Thus, devoting a long time to conscious thought has detrimental effects on decision making.

Most research has involved decisions made by non-experts. Mamede et al. (2010) asked medical experts to diagnose simple and complex cases immediately or following conscious or unconscious thought. Diagnostic accuracy with simple cases did not vary across conditions. However, with complex cases it was best after conscious thought (see Figure 13.12), which is contrary to unconscious thought theory.

Mamede et al. (2010) argued that experts have much relevant, well-organised knowledge they can access effectively by conscious searching through long-term memory. As a result, conscious thought sometimes produces much better decision making than unconscious thought.

Evaluation

Unconscious thought theory has focused attention on the strengths and limitations of conscious and unconscious thought. Unconscious thought sometimes produces superior decision making to conscious thought. Decision making can be optimal when people combine conscious and unconscious thought (Nordgren et al., 2011).

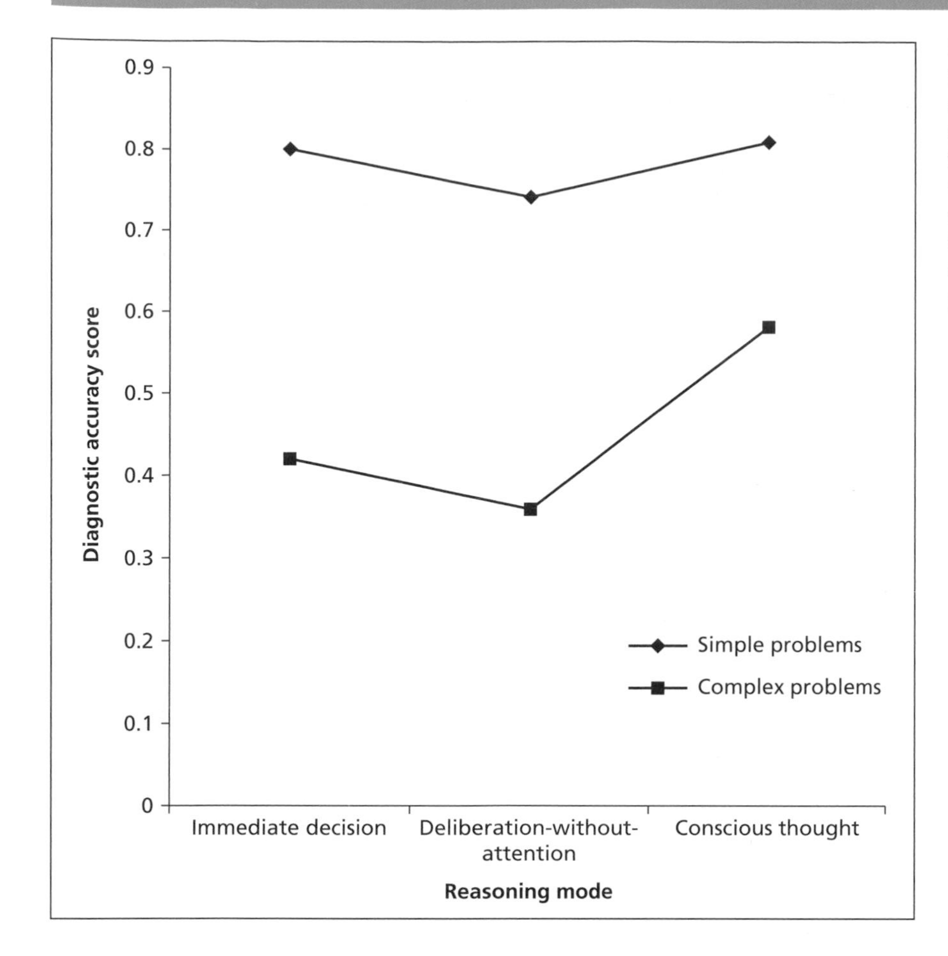

Figure 13.12
Doctors' mean diagnostic accuracy on simple and complex problems as a function of reasoning type (immediate decision; deliberation-without-attention involving distraction; and conscious thought).
From Mamede et al. (2010).

What are the theory's limitations? First, the relevant findings are inconsistent (Nieuwenstein & van Rijn, 2012). Second, forcing participants to spend several minutes engaged in conscious thought probably diminishes its value. Third, conscious thought can be much more useful than unconscious thought when experts engage in complex decision making (Mamede et al., 2010).

Fourth, it is assumed unconscious-thought participants rely heavily on intuitive processes in decision making. However, such participants claim to rely mostly on conscious memory (Aczel et al., 2011).

CHAPTER SUMMARY

- **Introduction.** There are close relationships between the areas of judgement and decision making. Decision-making research covers all the processes involved in deciding on a course of action. In contrast, judgement research focuses mainly on those aspects of decision making concerned with estimating the probability of various events. Judgements are evaluated in terms of their accuracy while decisions are evaluated on the basis of their consequences.

- **Judgement research**. Our estimates of the probability of something happening change in the light of new evidence. When making such estimates, people often fail to take full account of base-rate information in part because of their reliance on the representativeness heuristic. Base-rate information is used more often when people are strongly motivated to use such information or when full causal knowledge is available. Some judgement errors depend on use of the availability heuristic. The representativeness and availability heuristics are sometimes used in real life.
- **Judgement theories**. According to support theory, an event's subjective probability increases as its description becomes more explicit and detailed. This is often the case, but the opposite finding has sometimes been obtained (e.g., when the problem focuses people's attention on low-probability causes). The recognition and take-the-best heuristics are rules of thumb that are often useful. However, these heuristics are more complex than usually assumed and are only useful in certain limited conditions. According to the natural frequency hypothesis, judgements are more accurate when based on natural sampling and frequencies rather than probabilities. In fact, the reasons for the superiority of frequency formats are varied and complex. According to Kahneman's dual-process theory, initial intuitive processing (System 1) is sometimes followed by more conscious and controlled processing (System 2). This serial processing assumption is oversimplified as is the theory in general.
- **Decision making under risk**. According to prospect theory, people are much more sensitive to potential losses than potential gains. As a result, they are willing to take risks to avoid losses. The theory is supported by research on phenomena such as the framing and sunk-cost effects, and there is evidence of loss aversion in professional golfers, experienced poker players and financial experts. The theory de-emphasises individual differences, emotional and social factors in decision making under risk, and loss aversion is sometimes not found.
- **Decision making: emotional and social factors**. One reason people show loss aversion is because they overestimate the negative impact of losses. Reduced loss aversion and superior performance on a gambling task are shown by patients with damage to brain areas involved in emotion. Brain areas of relevance to risky decision making include the amygdala and the ventromedial prefrontal cortex. The emotion of regret helps to explain the existence of the omission and status quo effects. According to Tetlock's social functionalist approach, people's need to justify their decisions to others accounts for some biases in decision making.

- **Complex decision making.** Decision makers in the laboratory and in the real world often start by reducing the number of options considered by eliminating aspects, followed by detailed comparisons of the retained options. However, experts often consider a single option and make rapid intuitive decisions. Making a decision can cause decision makers to misremember relevant factual information to increase the apparent support for that decision. According to Dijksterhuis's unconscious thought theory, unconscious thinking is more useful than conscious thinking with complex decision making. Unconscious thinking is generally less useful than the theory suggests. However, decision making is sometimes best when individuals combine conscious and unconscious thinking.

Further reading

- De Neys, W. (2012). Bias and conflict: A case for logical intuitions. *Perspectives on Psychological Science*, 7: 26–38. Wim De Neys compares and contrasts opposing theoretical approaches in judgement research.
- Fiedler, K. & von Sydow, M. (2015, in press). Heuristics and biases: Beyond Tversky and Kahneman's (1974) judgment under uncertainty. In M.W. Eysenck & D. Groome (eds), *Cognitive psychology: Revisiting the classic studies*. London: SAGE. The strengths and limitations of Kahneman and Tversky's theoretical approach to judgement are discussed by Klaus Fiedler and Momme von Sydow.
- Gigerenzer, G. & Gaissmaier, W. (2011). Heuristic decision making. *Annual Review of Psychology*, 62: 451–82. This chapter provides a comprehensive account of research on the role of heuristics in judgement and decision making.
- Kahneman, D. (2011). *Thinking, fast and slow*. London: Penguin Books. Several chapters in this fascinating book by Danny Kahneman focus on judgement and decision making.
- Manktelow, K. (2012). *Thinking and reasoning: An introduction to the psychology of reason, judgment and decision making*. Hove: Psychology Press. Chapters 1, 8 and 9 of this readable introductory textbook provide coverage of most of the topics discussed in this chapter.
- Marchionni, C. & Vromen, J. (eds) (2012). *Neuroeconomics: Hype or hope?* London: Routledge. This edited volume contains a thorough evaluation of neuroeconomics from several different perspectives.
- Newell, B.R. (2015, in press). Decision making under risk: Beyond Kahneman and Tversky's (1979) prospect theory. In M.W. Eysenck & D. Groome (eds), *Cognitive psychology: Revisiting the classic studies*. London: SAGE. Kahneman's highly influential theory of decision making under risk is discussed analytically by Ben Newell.
- Pachur, T. & Bröder, A. (2013). Judgment: A cognitive processing perspective. *WIREs Cognitive Science*, 4: 665–81. The authors provide a

comprehensive account of judgement research and identify the main cognitive processes involved.

- Pammi, V.S.C. & Srinivasan, N. (eds) (2013). *Decision making: Neural and behavioural approaches*. Amsterdam: Elsevier. This edited book has several chapters on the strengths and limitations of the cognitive neuroscience approach to decision making.

CHAPTER

14

Reasoning and hypothesis testing

INTRODUCTION

For hundreds of years, philosophers have distinguished between two kinds of reasoning. One is **inductive reasoning**, which involves drawing general conclusion from premises (statements) referring to particular instances. A key feature of inductive reasoning is that the conclusions of inductively valid arguments are probably (but not necessarily) true.

The philosopher Bertrand Russell provided the following example. A turkey might use inductive reasoning to draw the conclusion, "Each day I am fed", because that has always been the case in the past. However, there is no *certainty* the turkey will be fed tomorrow. Indeed, if tomorrow is Christmas Eve, it is likely to be proven false.

As we will see, scientists very often make use of inductive reasoning in a very similar way to Russell's hypothetical turkey. For example, a psychologist may conduct numerous experiments and consistently find that reinforcement is required for learning. This might lead him/her to use inductive reasoning to propose the hypothesis that reinforcement is essential for learning. However, this conclusion is not necessarily true because he/she does not know for sure that future experiments will produce similar findings to past ones.

The other kind of reasoning identified by philosophers from Aristotle onwards is **deductive reasoning**. Deductive reasoning allows us to draw conclusions that are definitely or certainly valid provided other statements are assumed to be true. For example, if we assume Tom is taller than Dick and that Dick is taller than Harry, the conclusion that Tom is taller than Harry is necessarily true.

Deductive reasoning is related to problem solving, because people trying to solve a deductive reasoning task have a definite goal and the solution is not obvious. However, an important difference is that deductive reasoning problems owe their origins to formal logic. Note that the fact most deductive reasoning problems are based on formal logic does *not* necessarily mean people actually use formal logic to solve them. Indeed, as we will see, most people rarely or never use traditional logic with such problems.

Finally in this chapter, we consider informal reasoning. There is increasing concern at the apparently wide chasm between everyday reasoning in the form of

KEY TERMS

Inductive reasoning
Forming generalisations (that may be probable but are not certain) from examples or sample phenomena.

Deductive reasoning
Reasoning to a conclusion from a set of premises or statements where that conclusion follows necessarily from the assumption that the premises are true.

Falsification
Proposing hypotheses and then trying to falsify them by experimental tests; the logically correct means by which science should work, according to Popper (1968).

Confirmation bias
In hypothesis testing, seeking evidence that supports one's beliefs.

Weblink:
Karl Popper

Weblink:
Video of 2–4–6 task

argumentation and the artificial reasoning tasks used in the laboratory. That has led to the emergence of research on informal reasoning, focusing on the processes of everyday reasoning.

Evans (2012) provided an excellent account of the shift in research from deductive to informal reasoning. This shift has been so profound that Evans refers to "a *new paradigm* psychology of reasoning" (p. 7) in which there is much less focus on deductive reasoning and logic.

What are the consequences of this shift? It is becoming increasingly clear the processes involved in reasoning often resemble those used in judgement and decision making. As a result, theoretical ideas developed to account for judgement and decision making are also applicable to reasoning. For example, consider the Bayesian approach (see Chapter 13). According to this approach, our subjective probabilities (e.g., that X is dishonest) are adjusted upwards or downwards in the light of new or additional information. This approach sheds much light on reasoning performance as well as judgement and decision making.

HYPOTHESIS TESTING

Karl Popper (1968) argued that there is an important distinction between confirmation and falsification. Confirmation involves the attempt to obtain evidence confirming the correctness of one's hypothesis. In contrast, **falsification** involves the attempt to falsify hypotheses by experimental tests. According to Popper, we cannot achieve confirmation via hypothesis testing. Even if all the available evidence supports a hypothesis, future evidence may disprove it. In Popper's opinion, *falsifiability* (the potential for falsification) separates scientific from unscientific activities such as religion and pseudo-science (e.g., psychoanalysis).

It follows from Popper's analysis that scientists should focus on falsification as their preferred strategy. In fact, as discussed later, they often seek confirmatory rather than disconfirmatory evidence when testing their hypotheses! It has also been claimed that the same excessive focus on confirmatory evidence is found in laboratory studies on hypothesis testing, to which we now turn.

Wason's 2–4–6 task

Peter Wason (1960) devised a hypothesis-testing task that has attracted much interest (Manktelow, 2012). Participants were told three numbers, 2–4–6, conformed to a simple relational rule. Their task was to generate sets of three numbers and provide reasons for each choice. After each choice, the experimenter indicated whether the set of numbers conformed to the experimenter's rule. Here is the rule: "Three numbers in ascending order of magnitude". The participants could announce on any trial what they believed to be the rule and were told whether it was correct.

The rule sounds simple. However, it took most university students a long time to discover it. Only 21% were correct with their first attempt, and 28% never discovered the rule (Wason, 1960). Similar low levels of performance have been obtained in most subsequent research.

Why is performance so poor on the 2–4–6 problem? It has often been argued that most people show **confirmation bias** – they seek information confirming their hypothesis. For example, participants whose original hypothesis or rule was that the second number is twice the first, and the third number is three times the first number, generated sets of numbers consistent with that hypothesis (e.g., 6–12–18, 50–100–150). It has often been claimed that Wason (1960) focused on confirmation bias as an explanation for people's poor performance. That is actually a myth – it was only several years later that he used the equivalent term "verification bias", arguing that this bias prevented participants from replacing their initial hypothesis (which was too narrow and specific) with the correct general rule.

Wason's analysis was limited because he did not take account of people's *expectations*. We can see the limitation by drawing a distinction between confirmation and positive testing. Positive testing means generating numbers that are an instance of your hypothesis. This is confirmatory *only* if you believe your hypothesis is correct. If you believe your hypothesis is wrong, then generating numbers not conforming to your hypothesis can be regarded as confirming behaviour!

Findings

Cowley and Byrne (2005) argued that people show confirmation bias because they are loath to abandon their own initial hypothesis. They suggested people might be much more willing to try to falsify the same hypothesis if told it was someone else's. This prediction was supported: 62% of participants abandoned the other person's hypothesis compared to only 25% who abandoned their own hypothesis.

Tweney et al. (1980) discovered an effective way of enhancing performance on the 2–4–6 task. Participants were told the experimenter had *two* rules in mind and they had to identify both of them. One rule generated DAX triples and the other generated MED triples. They were also told 2–4–6 was a DAX triple. Whenever the participants generated a set of three numbers, they were informed whether the set fitted the DAX rule or MED rule. The DAX rule was any three numbers in ascending order and the MED rule covered all other sets of numbers.

Over 50% of participants produced the correct answer on their first attempt (much higher than with the standard 2–4–6 problem). Participants in the Tweney et al. (1980) study could use positive testing and did not have to focus on disconfirmation of hypotheses. They could identify the DAX rule by confirming the MED rule, and so they did not have to try to disconfirm the DAX rule.

Gale and Ball (2012) carried out a study similar to that of Tweney et al. (1980). They argued that what was crucial was how easily participants could identify the relevant dimensions of ascending vs. descending numbers. They always used 2–4–6 as an example of a DAX triple, but the example of a MED triple could be 6–4–2 or 4–4–4. Success in identifying the DAX rule was much greater when the MED example was 6–4–2 (75%) than when it was 4–4–4 (23%). Overall, the only clear difference between solvers and non-solvers of the DAX rule was the number of descending triples they produced. These findings indicate the importance of persuading participants to focus on *the ascending–descending dimension*, which was hard to do when the MED example was 4–4–4.

Performance on the 2–4–6 task involves separable processes of hypothesis *generation* and hypothesis *testing*. Most research has focused on the latter. An exception is a study by Cherubini et al. (2005). They argued that participants try to preserve as much of the information contained in the example triple (i.e., 2–4–6) as possible in their initial hypothesis. As a result, this hypothesis is typically much more *specific* than the correct rule. When participants generate sets of numbers fitting their specific hypothesis, those numbers are almost bound to fit the rule as well. This prevents them from discovering the correct rule.

Cherubini et al. (2005) tested their ideas by presenting participants with two initial examples of the rule. When they were given two triples such as 6–8–10 and 16–18–20, their initial hypothesis tended to be "increasing by twos" and the success rate was only 30%. In contrast, when the information in the two triples appeared less rich (e.g., 6–8–10, 9–14–15), participants generated more general hypotheses and their success rate was 70%.

How can people be persuaded to generate more hypotheses on the 2–4–6 task? Russo and Meloy (2008) compared conditions in which feedback was given on every trial (as in most previous research) vs. only after each block of five trials. On average, 4.6 hypotheses were tested in the former condition and 9.4 in the latter. The percentage of participants discovering the rule was greater with less frequent feedback (62% vs. 39%). Less frequent feedback led participants to think more flexibly about the possible nature of the rule.

Theoretical analysis

Most hypotheses are *sparse* or narrow in that they apply to less than half the possible entities in any given domain (Navarro & Perfors, 2011). For example, Perfors and Navarro (2009) asked participants to generate all the rules or hypotheses applying to numbers in a given domain (numbers 1 to 1,000). The key finding was that 83% of the rules (e.g., two-digit numbers, prime numbers) applied to fewer than 20% of the numbers.

What follows from the fact that most hypotheses are sparse? Positive testing is optimal with such hypotheses "because there are so many ways to be wrong and so few to be right". In such instances, the learner will discover "the world has a bias towards saying 'no', and asking for 'yes' is the best way to overcome it" (Perfors & Navarro, 2009, p. 2746). Thus, positive testing is typically a successful strategy. However, this is *not* the case with the 2–4–6 task – it penalises positive testing because the target rule is so general.

Evaluation

Wason's 2–4–6 task has fascinated psychologists ever since 1960. Research on this task has shed much light on the strengths and limitations of human inductive reasoning. The processes involved in the 2–4–6 task are of relevance to understanding scientists' hypothesis testing.

What are the limitations of Wason's approach? First, the 2–4–6 task differs from real-life hypothesis testing. Participants given the 2–4–6 task receive immediate accurate feedback but are not told *why* the numbers they produced attracted a "yes" or "no" response. In the real world (e.g., scientists testing hypotheses), the feedback is much more informative. However, it is often delayed in time and may not be accurate.

Second, the correct rule or hypothesis in the 2–4–6 task (three numbers in ascending order of magnitude) is very general in that it applies to a fairly high proportion of sets of three numbers. In contrast, most rules or hypotheses apply to only a smallish proportion of possible objects or events. Positive testing works poorly on the 2–4–6 task but not with most other forms of hypothesis testing.

Third, Wason argued that most people show confirmation bias on the 2–4–6 task. However, there is much less evidence of confirmation bias if the hypothesis being tested is someone else's (Cowley & Byrne, 2005). This is consistent with scientists' behaviour. In 1977, the first author participated in a conference on the levels-of-processing approach to memory (see Chapter 6). Nearly all the research presented was designed to identify limitations and problems with that approach.

Hypothesis testing: simulated and real research environments

Remember Popper (1968) argued that a crucial feature of all truly scientific theories is falsifiability. He also argued that scientists should focus on falsification rather than confirmation because the latter is impossible to achieve fully.

Most experts argue that Popper's views are partially correct but somewhat simplistic (Okasha, 2002). Suppose a scientist carries out an experiment producing findings apparently inconsistent with his/her hypothesis. There are various possible interpretations of these findings. The findings may mean the hypothesis is incorrect. Alternatively, however, the findings may be due to problems with the experimental design or the accuracy of the data.

Before discussing research directly on scientific hypothesis testing, we will briefly consider more broadly what scientists do (e.g., how they generate hypotheses). There is a popular view that "scientific discovery is the result of genius, inspiration, and sudden insight" (Trickett & Trafton, 2007, p. 868). That view is largely incorrect. Scientists typically use what Klahr and Simon (2001) described as weak methods. These methods are very general and can be applied to almost any scientific problem. Several weak methods (e.g., trial and error; means–ends analysis – see Glossary) are also used in everyday problem solving.

Numerous studies have considered the weak methods used by scientists. Kulkarni and Simon (1988) found scientists make extensive use of the **unusualness heuristic** or rule of thumb. This involves focusing on unusual or unexpected findings and then using them to guide future theorising and research.

Zelko et al. (2010) asked leading biomedical scientists in several countries to identify their research strategies. Every researcher had a main heuristic he/she used much of the time. The heuristics included the following: challenge conventional wisdom; adopt a step-by-step approach; carry out many experiments on a trial-and-error basis.

Trickett and Trafton (2007) argued that scientists make much use of "what if" reasoning in which they work out what would happen in various imaginary circumstances. A famous example involves Albert Einstein. At the age of 16, he imagined himself riding a beam of light, which led eventually to his theory of relativity. Trickett et al. (2009) also found evidence of "what if" reasoning among experts in astronomy and computational fluid dynamics faced with anomalous findings. This reasoning involved conceptual simulations that allowed the scientists to work out the detailed implications of some hypotheses.

Dunbar (1993) found evidence of confirmation bias using a simulated research environment. Participants had to explain how genes are controlled by other genes using a computer-based molecular genetics laboratory. The problem was so difficult that solving it in real life led to the award of the Nobel prize! The participants were led to focus on the hypothesis that the gene control was by *activation* while it was actually by *inhibition*.

Those participants who simply tried to find data consistent with their activation hypothesis failed to solve the problem. In contrast, the 20% of

KEY TERM

Unusualness heuristic
A rule of thumb used by scientists in which unexpected findings are used to develop new hypotheses and lines of research.

Alexander Graham Bell.
Mondadori/Getty Images.

IN THE REAL WORLD: HYPOTHESIS TESTING BY SCIENTISTS

What actually happens in real-life science? Do scientists focus on confirmation or falsification? In fact, scientists very often adopt the strategy of "confirm early and disconfirm late" (Manktelow, 2012, p. 183). This strategy is frequently optimal. Initial confirmation shows a hypothesis can account for a range of experimental findings. Subsequent disconfirmation/falsification can lead the way to a superior hypothesis explaining more findings.

Gorman (1995) studied Alexander Graham Bell's research on the development of the telephone. Bell (see photo) showed evidence of confirmation bias because he continued to focus on undulating current and electromagnets even after he and others had obtained good results with liquid devices. Indeed, he abandoned liquid devices, leaving the way open for Edison to develop the forerunner of today's phones.

Mitroff (1974) studied experts in lunar geology involved in the Apollo space programme. They spent most of their time trying to confirm their hypotheses and were very reluctant to abandon them. This happened for two main reasons. First, the experts emphasised the value of commitment to a given position as a motivating factor. Second, they often attributed negative findings to deficiencies in the measuring instruments.

Fuselsang et al. (2004) studied professional scientists working on issues in molecular biology relating to how genes control and promote replication in bacteria, parasites and viruses. Of 417 experimental results, over half (223) were inconsistent with the scientists' predictions. They responded to 88% of these inconsistent findings by blaming problems with their methods (e.g., wrong incubation temperature). In only 12% of cases did the scientists modify their theories. Thus, the scientists showed considerable reluctance to change their original theoretical position.

Approximately two-thirds of the inconsistent findings were followed up, generally by changing the methods used. In 55% of cases, the inconsistent findings were replicated. The scientists' reactions were very different this time – in 61% of cases, they changed their theoretical assumptions.

How defensible was the scientists' behaviour? Note almost half of the inconsistent findings were not replicated when a second study was carried out. Thus, it was reasonable for the scientists to avoid prematurely accepting findings that might be spurious.

participants who solved the problem tried to explain the *discrepant* findings. Most participants started with the general hypothesis that activation was the key controlling process. They then applied this hypothesis, focusing on one gene after another as the potential activator. It was typically only when every activation hypothesis had been disconfirmed that some participants focused on explaining the data inconsistent with activation hypotheses.

KEY TERM

Conditional reasoning
A form of **deductive reasoning** based on "if . . . then" propositions.

Evaluation

There is convincing evidence that scientists make extensive use of heuristics or rules of thumb in scientific discovery. This evidence sheds some doubt on the notion that scientific discovery typically requires genius or inspiration.

The evidence from simulated and real research environments indicates that Popper's emphasis on falsification is oversimplified (Dunbar & Klahr, 2012). Confirmation is often appropriate (e.g., when developing a new theory). Popper's approach is impractical because it is based on the assumption that research findings can provide *decisive* evidence falsifying a hypothesis. In fact, as we have seen, findings apparently falsifying hypotheses in molecular biology often cannot be replicated (Fugelsang et al., 2004). Such variability in findings is likely to be greater in a statistical science such as psychology.

Findings in simulated research environments have various limitations. First, the *commitment* motivating real scientists to defend their own theories and disprove those of other scientists is lacking. Second, real scientists typically work in teams, whereas participants in simulated research environments sometimes work on their own (e.g., Dunbar, 1993). Okada and Simon (1997) found, using Dunbar's genetic control task, that pairs performed better than individuals. Pairs entertained hypotheses more often, considered alternative ideas more frequently and discussed more ways of justifying ideas. In sum, real research is typically influenced by major motivational and social factors largely absent from simulated research environments.

DEDUCTIVE REASONING

In deductive reasoning, conclusions can be drawn with certainty. Researchers have used numerous deductive reasoning problems. However, we will mostly consider conditional and syllogistic reasoning problems based on traditional logic. After that, we consider theoretical explanations.

Conditional reasoning

Conditional reasoning (basically, reasoning with "if") had its origins in propositional logic, in which logical operators such as *or*, *and*, *if . . . then*, *if and only if* are included in sentences or propositions. In this logical system, symbols stand for sentences and logical operators are applied to them to reach conclusions. Thus, in propositional logic we might use *P* to stand for the proposition "It is raining", and *Q* to stand for "Nancy gets wet", and then use the logical operator *if . . . then* to relate these two propositions: *if P then Q*.

The meanings of words and propositions in propositional logic differ from natural language meanings. For example, propositions can have only one of two truth values: true or false. If *P* stands for "It is raining", then *P* is true (in which case it is raining) or *P* is false (it is not raining). Propositional logic does not admit any uncertainty about the truth of *P* (where it is so misty you could almost call it raining).

Many people produce incorrect answers when given certain conditional reasoning problems. Consider the following, which involves *affirmation of the consequent*:

Premises

If Susan is angry, then I am upset.
I am upset.

Conclusion

Therefore, Susan is angry.

Interactive exercise:
Conditional reasoning

Do you accept the above conclusion as valid? Many people do, but it is *not* valid according to propositional logic – I may be upset for some other reason (e.g., I have lost my job).

Here is another concrete problem in conditional reasoning:

Premises

If it is raining, then Nancy gets wet.
It is raining.

Conclusion

Nancy gets wet.

This conclusion is valid. It illustrates the rule of inference known as *modus ponens*: "If *P*, then *Q*" and also given "*P*", we can validly infer *Q*.

Another major rule of inference is *modus tollens*: from the premise "If *P*, then *Q*" and the premise "*Q* is false", the conclusion "*P* is false" necessarily follows. Here is an example:

Premises

If it is raining, then Nancy gets wet.
Nancy does not get wet.

Conclusion

It is not raining.

People consistently perform much better with modus ponens than modus tollens, with many people arguing that the conclusion to the above problem is invalid.

Another inference involves *denial of the antecedent*:

Premises

If it is raining, then Nancy gets wet.
It is not raining.

Conclusion

Therefore, Nancy does not get wet.

Many people argue that the above conclusion is valid, but it is actually invalid. It does not have to be raining for Nancy to get wet (e.g., she might have jumped into a swimming pool).

Traditionally, research on conditional reasoning was limited in that it focused on *disinterested* reasoning. This is reasoning in which goals and preferences are irrelevant and which therefore contrasts greatly with everyday life. For example, denial of the antecedent is invalid in traditional logic. In natural language, however, "If *P*, then *Q*" often means "If and only if *P*, then *Q*." If someone says to you, "If you mow the lawn, I will give you five dollars", you are likely to interpret it to imply, "If you don't mow the lawn, I won't give you five dollars."

Findings

Nearly everyone makes the valid modus ponens inference, but far fewer make the valid modus tollens inference. Invalid inferences (denial of the consequent, affirmation of the consequent) are accepted much of the time, the former typically more often (Evans et al., 1993).

De Neys et al. (2005) carried out research on conditional reasoning using counterexamples appearing to invalidate a given conclusion. Counterexamples that conflict with a valid conclusion (modus ponens and modus tollens) should be ignored according to classical logic, even though they provide additional information. The number of counterexamples was low or high, and participants were low or high in working memory capacity (see Glossary).

What did De Neys et al. (2005) find? First, the number of counterexamples had a major impact on participants' willingness to accept valid inferences (modus ponens, modus tollens) (see Figure 14.1), which is contrary to traditional logic. Second, the reasoning performance of participants high in working memory capacity was better than those low in working memory capacity.

Bonnefon et al. (2012) argued that reasoners draw *inferences* when presented with conditional reasoning problems. For example, consider the premise, "If she eats oysters then she will be very sick." Most people draw the inference, "She is

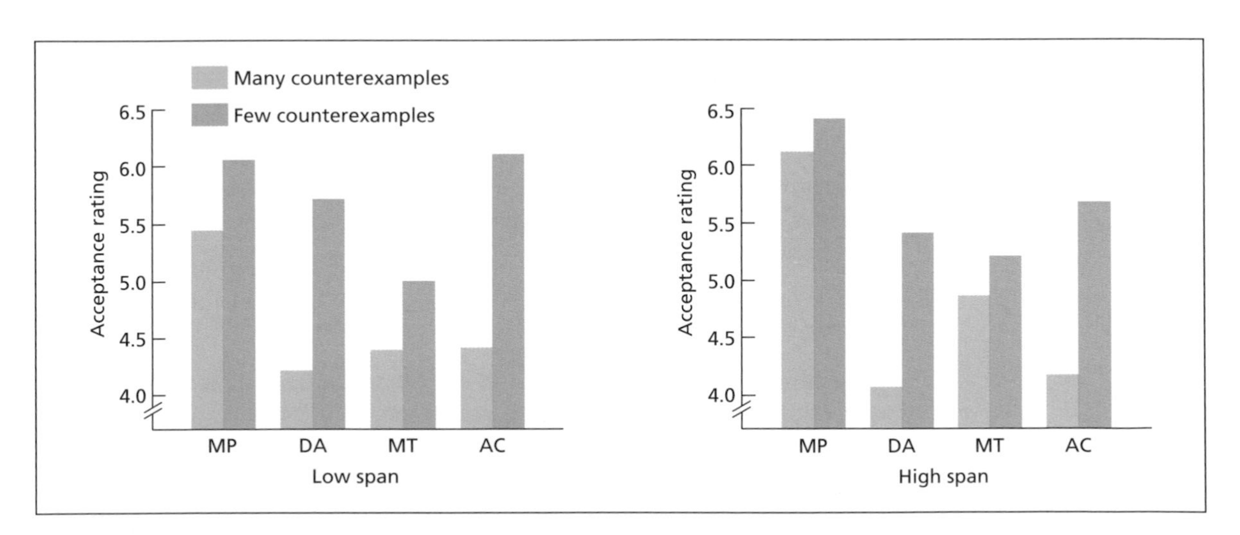

Figure 14.1
Acceptance ratings for valid syllogisms (MP = modus ponens; MT = modus tollens) and invalid syllogisms (DA = denial of the antecedent; AC = affirmation of the consequent) as a function of the number of counterexamples (few vs. many) and working memory capacity (low vs. high).
From De Neys et al. (2005).

not going to eat oysters." Such inferences are derived from folk axioms (e.g., people engage in self-interested behaviour) and often lead reasoners to accept invalid conclusions. However, such inferences are not included within classical logic, which takes no account of people's knowledge and experience.

Markovits et al. (2013) studied the processes relating to affirmation of the consequent. Consider the following problems:

1. If a rock is thrown at a window, then the window will break. A window is broken. Therefore, a rock was thrown at the window.
2. If a finger is cut, then it will bleed. A finger is bleeding. Therefore, the finger was cut.

In both cases, the conclusion is invalid. However, people are much more likely to accept the conclusion in problem (2) than (1). According to Markovits et al. (2013), there are two strategies people can use with problems such as those above. First, there is a statistical strategy, which is contrary to the dictates of traditional logic. It is basically intuitive and involves estimating the probability that the conclusion is true given what the individuals knows about the world. The subjective probability, that "If a finger is bleeding, it was cut", is higher than the probability that, "If a window is broken, it was broken by a rock." As a result, the invalid conclusion is accepted more often in problem (2) than problem (1).

Second, there is the counterexample strategy, which is more cognitively demanding. This strategy involves trying to think of a counterexample contradicting the conclusion and accepting the conclusion if no counterexamples come to mind. It is easy to find counterexamples with respect to the conclusion of problem (1) (the window might have been broken by several objects other than a rock) but more difficult with problem (2). However, reasoners using this strategy will correctly reject invalid conclusions with affirmation of the consequent problems provided a counterexample is identified.

Markovits et al. (2013) used affirmation of the consequent problems with limited or unlimited time. Since the counterexample strategy is more cognitively demanding than the statistical strategy, they predicted that it would be used less often with limited than with unlimited time. The findings provided strong support for this prediction: the counterexample strategy was used on 49% of trials with unlimited time but on only 1.7% of trials with limited time. In contrast, the less demanding statistical strategy was used on 55% of limited-time trials but only 19% of unlimited-time trials.

Summary

Weblink: Common facilities

Research activity: Deductive reasoning

People rarely think logically on conditional reasoning tasks as is shown by their poor performance on arguments such as affirmation of the consequent and denial of the antecedent. Of major importance, reasoners use their knowledge of other people's goals and preferences to draw inferences. They also use their general knowledge of causal factors (e.g., fingers typically bleed because they are cut). Using one's available knowledge makes good sense in the real world but produces allegedly "illogical" thinking.

Performance on conditional reasoning tasks depends in part on individuals' ability and preference for using relatively demanding and effortful forms of processing. It also depends on the time available for reasoning. Much conditional reasoning is closer to decision making than to classical logic (Bonnefon et al., 2012).

Figure 14.2
Rule: If there is an R on one side of the card, then there is a 2 on the other.

Wason selection task

The Wason selection task was invented by the aforementioned British psychologist Peter Wason. It has often been investigated by researchers primarily interested in deductive reasoning. However, it is more accurately described as a task involving hypothesis testing using a conditional rule.

In the standard version, four cards lie on a table (R, G, 2, 7; see Figure 14.2). Each card has a letter on one side and a number on the other. Participants are told a rule applies to the four cards (e.g., "If there is an R on one side of the cards, then there is a 2 on the other side of the card"). The task is to select *only* those cards that need to be turned over to decide whether or not the rule is correct. What is your answer to the question? Most people select the R and 2 cards. If you did the same, you are wrong!

Weblink:
Online Wason selection task

You need to see whether any cards *fail* to obey the rule when turned over. From this perspective, the 2 card is irrelevant. If there is an R on the other side of it, this only tells us the rule *might* be correct. If there is any other letter on the other side, we have discovered nothing about the rule's validity. The correct answer is to select the R and 7 cards, an answer given by only about 5–10% of university students. The 7 is necessary because it would definitely disprove the rule if it had an R on the other side.

Evans (e.g., 1998) identified **matching bias** as an important factor. Matching bias is the tendency for participants to select cards matching the items named in the rule. Evans and Ball (2010) reanalysed data from a previous study using several versions of the selection task: If T then 4; If R then not 1; If not M then 5; and If not G then not 1. There was substantial evidence of matching bias with all versions.

Stenning and van Lambalgen (2004) argued that participants may not fully realise they must make *all* their choices before receiving feedback. Only 3.7% of participants given the standard instructions produced the correct answer. In contrast, 18% of those explicitly warned they wouldn't receive any feedback before making all their choices got the answer right.

Oaksford (1997) argued that the logical answer to the Wason selection task conflicts with what typically makes most sense in everyday life. Consider testing the rule, "All swans are white." According to formal logic, we should try to find swans and non-white birds. However, in the real world, only a few birds are swans, and the overwhelming majority of birds are non-white. Thus, the pursuit of non-white birds may be extremely time-consuming. In the real world, it is more informative to look for white birds to see if they are swans. Thus, it is usually best to adopt a *probabilistic* approach that takes account of the likely probabilities of different kinds of events or objects.

The problem of testing the rule that all swans are white resembles the Wason selection task, which has the form, "If *P*, then *Q*". According to the probabilistic approach, people should choose *Q* cards (e.g., 2) when the expected probability of *Q* is low but not-*Q* cards when *Q*'s expected probability is high. This approach maximises information gain. Oaksford et al. (1997) carried out an experiment in

KEY TERM

Matching bias
The tendency on the Wason selection task to select cards matching the items explicitly mentioned in the rule.

which the percentage of *Q* cards was 17%, 50% or 83%. As predicted, far more *Q* cards were selected when the percentage of *Q* cards was low than when it was high.

Improving performance

The traditional Wason selection task involves an indicative rule (e.g., "If there is a *P*, then there is a *Q*"). However, it is also possible to use a deontic rule (e.g., "If there is a *P*, then you *must* do *Q*"). Deontic rules are concerned with detection of rule violation (e.g., cheating). They are typically easier for people to understand because the underlying structure of the problem is more explicit (e.g., the emphasis on disproving the rule).

Sperber and Girotto (2002) gave some participants a version of the selection task involving a deontic rule. Paolo buys things through the internet but is concerned he will be cheated. For each order, he fills out a card. On one side, he indicates whether he has received the item ordered, and on the other side he indicates whether he has paid for the items ordered. He places four orders, and what is visible on the four cards is as follows: "item paid for", "item not paid for", "item received" and "item not received".

Which cards does Paolo need to turn over to decide whether he has been cheated? Sperber and Girotto found 68% of their participants made the correct choices (i.e., "item paid for", "item not received").

Another way of improving performance is to *motivate* participants to disprove the rule. Dawson et al. (2002) gave some participants the rule that individuals high in emotional lability experience an early death. The four cards were showing: "low emotional lability", "high emotional lability", "early death" and "late death".

The correct answer for testing the rule was to select the "high emotional lability" and "late death" cards. Of participants led to believe they were low in emotional lability (and so having no powerful motive to disprove the rule), only 9% solved the problem. In contrast, of those led to believe they were high in emotional lability, 38% solved the problem because they were highly motivated to disprove the rule.

Summary

A small percentage of individuals (mostly of high intelligence) use deductive reasoning and provide the correct answer on the standard Wason selection task. However, the great majority produce incorrect answers because they use simple strategies such as matching bias and/or because they do not understand fully what the task involves.

Performance is substantially better with deontic rules than indicative ones because the former rules direct people's attention to the importance of disproving the rule. Performance also improves if individuals are personally motivated to disprove the rule.

KEY TERM

Syllogism
A type of problem used in **deductive reasoning;** there are two statements or premises and a conclusion that may or may not follow logically from the premises.

Syllogistic reasoning

Syllogistic reasoning has been studied for over 2,000 years. A **syllogism** consists of two premises or statements followed by a conclusion. Here is an example of a syllogism: "All A are B; All B are C. Therefore, all A are C". A syllogism contains three items (A, B and C), with one (B) occurring in both premises. The premises and conclusion each contain one of the following quantifiers: all, some, no, and some . . . not.

When presented with a syllogism, you must decide whether the conclusion is valid in the light of the premises. The validity (or otherwise) of the conclusion depends *only* on whether it follows logically from the premises. The truth or falsity of the conclusion in the real world is irrelevant. Consider the following example:

Premises

All children are obedient.
All girl guides are children.

Conclusion

Therefore, all girl guides are obedient.

The conclusion follows logically from the premises. Thus, it is valid regardless of your views about the obedience of children.

KEY TERM

Belief bias
In syllogistic reasoning, the tendency to accept invalid but believable conclusions and reject valid but unbelievable ones.

Findings

Various biases cause errors in syllogistic reasoning. For example, there is **belief bias**: a tendency to accept invalid conclusions if they are believable and reject valid (but unbelievable) conclusions. This bias was investigated by Klauer et al. (2000). Half the conclusions of their syllogisms were believable (e.g., "Some fish are not trout"), whereas the others were unbelievable ("e.g., "Some trout are not fish"). In addition, half the syllogisms were valid and the remainder invalid. However, some participants were told only one-sixth of the syllogisms were valid while others were told five-sixths were.

What did Klauer et al. (2000) find? First, they obtained a base-rate effect: syllogistic reasoning performance was influenced by the perceived probability of syllogisms being valid. Second, there was strong evidence for belief bias. Third, there was a belief-by-logic interaction. Performance on syllogisms with valid conclusions was *better* when the conclusions were believable, whereas performance on syllogisms with invalid conclusions was *worse* when the conclusions were believable (see Figure 14.3). All three findings indicate participants' decisions on the validity of syllogism conclusions were influenced by factors irrelevant to logic.

Stupple and Ball (2008) found with syllogistic reasoning that people took longer to process unbelievable premises than believable ones. This suggests participants experienced conflict between their beliefs and what they were asked to assume, and resolving this conflict was time consuming.

With some syllogisms, the conclusions match the premises with respect to their surface features (e.g., No A are not B, No B are not C, Therefore, No C are not A). With other syllogisms, the conclusions do not match the premises (e.g., All A are B, All B are C, Therefore No A are not C). From the perspective of logic, it does not matter whether the surface features of conclusions and premises match or do not match. However, Stupple et al. (2013) found participants were more likely to accept conclusions that matched the premises in surface features than those not matching. With valid syllogisms, the acceptance rates were 84% and 76%, respectively. With invalid syllogisms, the acceptance rates were 62% and 57%, respectively. In contrast to belief bias, this matching bias shows

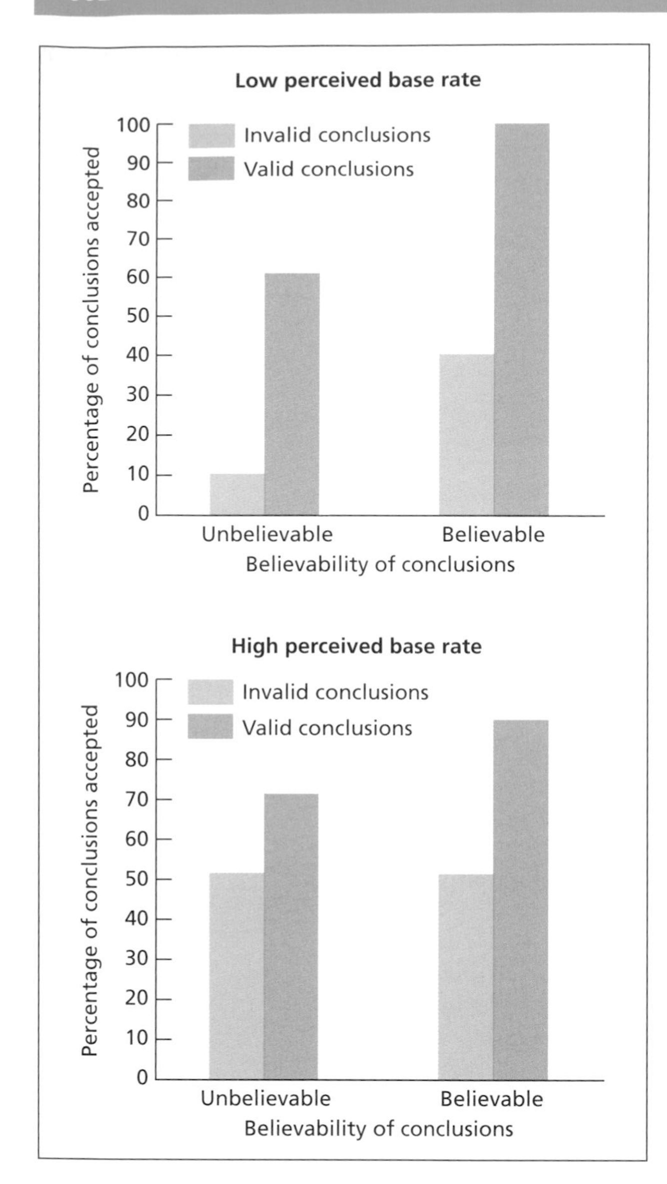

Figure 14.3
Percentage acceptance of conclusions as a function of perceived base rate (low vs. high), believability of conclusions and validity of conclusions.

Based on data in Klauer et al. (2000). © American Psychological Association.

syllogistic reasoning can be influenced by non-logical factors that do not depend on relevant knowledge and experience.

Finally, difficulties are caused by differences between the meanings of expressions in formal logic and everyday life. For example, we often assume that "All As are Bs" means that "All Bs are As", and that "Some As are not Bs" means that "Some Bs are not As". Ceraso and Provitera (1971) tried to prevent these misinterpretations by spelling out the premises unambiguously (e.g., All As are Bs, but some Bs are not As). This produced a substantial improvement in performance.

Schmidt and Thompson (2008) pointed out that "some" means "at least one and possibly all" in formal logic but "some but not all" in everyday usage. Performance on a syllogistic reasoning task improved when the meaning of "some" in formal logic was made explicit.

Summary

Most people find it hard to reason logically on syllogistic reasoning problems. Their knowledge of the real world strongly influences their willingness to accept or reject the conclusions of such problems. They are also influenced by whether the surface features of conclusions match those of the premises (matching bias). Finally, syllogistic reasoning is often inaccurate because the meanings of various words and expressions in formal logic differ from their everyday meanings. We turn now to theoretical accounts of the processes involved in conditional and syllogistic reasoning.

THEORIES OF DEDUCTIVE REASONING

Here we will discuss two very influential theoretical approaches to deductive reasoning. First, there is Johnson-Laird's mental model theory. Second, we turn our attention to the increasingly popular dual-system approach (also discussed in Chapter 13). There are several dual-system theories, all based on the assumption reasoning can involve two very different processing systems.

Mental models

Johnson-Laird (e.g., 1983, 2010, 2013) argues that reasoning involves constructing mental models. What is a mental model? According to Johnson-Laird (2004,

p. 170), "Each mental model represents a possibility, capturing what is common to the different ways in which the possibility could occur." For example, a tossed coin has an infinite number of trajectories. However, there are only two mental models: heads, tails.

Here is a concrete example of a mental model:

Premises

The lamp is on the right of the pad.
The book is on the left of the pad.
The clock is in front of the book.
The vase is in front of the lamp.

Conclusion

The clock is to the left of the vase.

According to Johnson-Laird (1983), people use the information contained in the premises to construct a mental model like this:

book	pad	lamp
clock		vase

The conclusion that the clock is to the left of the vase clearly follows from the mental model. The fact we cannot construct a mental model consistent with the premises but inconsistent with the conclusion indicates it is valid.

Here are the main assumptions of mental model theory:

- A mental model describing the given situation is constructed and the conclusions that follow are generated. The model is iconic (its structure corresponds to what it represents).
- An attempt is made to construct alternative models to falsify the conclusion by finding *counterexamples* to the conclusion. If a counterexample model is not found, the conclusion is assumed to be valid.
- The construction of mental models involves the limited resources of working memory (see Chapter 6).
- Reasoning problems requiring the construction of several mental models are harder to solve than those requiring only one mental model because of increased demands on working memory.
- The **principle of truth**: "Individuals minimise the load on working memory by tending to construct mental models that represent explicitly only what is true, and not what is false" (Johnson-Laird, 1999, p. 116).

KEY TERM

Principle of truth
The notion that we represent assertions by forming **mental models** concerning what is true but ignoring what is false.

Findings

Mental models are iconic in that their structure corresponds to what they represent. Thus, mental models preserve *spatial* relationships. Mental models may also involve *visual* imagery. However, Knauff et al. (2003) found deductive reasoning was slower when it involved visual imagery. Why was that? Reasoners generated visual images including irrelevant details, and these details made effective reasoning harder.

Theoretically, people's ability to construct mental models is constrained by the limited capacity of working memory. Copeland and Radvansky (2004) tested this assumption. Participants indicated what conclusions followed validly from sets of premises, and the demands on working memory were varied by manipulating the number of mental models consistent with the premises. A total of 86% of participants drew the valid conclusion when the premises allowed the generation of one mental model but only 31% with three mental models.

Copeland and Radvansky (2004) tested the hypothesis that reasoning performance depends on the limitations of working memory in a second study. Working memory capacity correlated +0.42 with syllogistic reasoning performance.

Legrenzi et al. (2003) tested the principle of truth. Participants decided whether descriptions of everyday objects (e.g., a chair) were consistent or inconsistent. Some descriptions were constructed so participants would be lured into error (illusory inferences) if they adhered to the principle of truth. Here is an example of an inference typically interpreted as consistent (valid) although it is inconsistent (invalid):

> Only one of the following assertions is true:
>
> > The tray is heavy or elegant, or both.
> >
> > The tray is elegant and portable.
>
> The following assertion is definitely true:
>
> > The tray is elegant and portable.

Why is the inference inconsistent or invalid? Suppose the final assertion is true. It follows the second assertion is also true, since the two assertions are identical. If the final assertion is true, it also follows that the first assertion is true – the fact that the tray is elegant is enough to make that assertion true. However, the problem starts by stating, "Only one of the following assertions is true." If the final assertion is true, both the first two assertions are also true, but only one is allowed to be true (sorry this is so complicated!). Therefore, the inference is inconsistent and invalid.

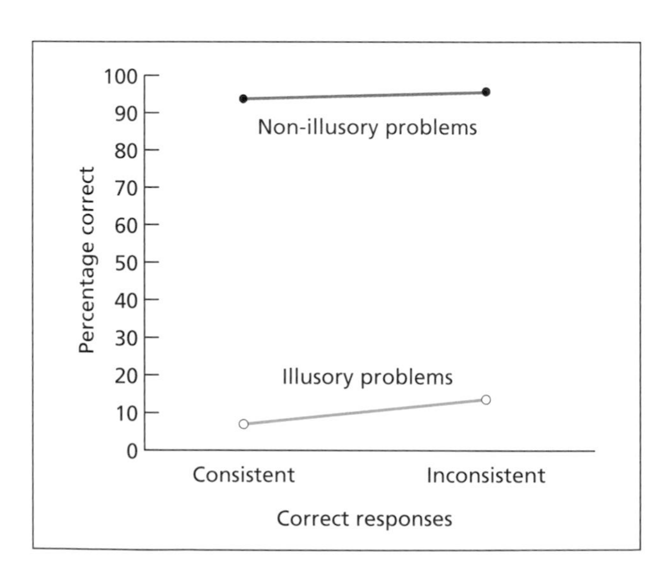

Figure 14.4
Percentage of correct responses to problems that were predicted to be susceptible (illusory problems) or not susceptible (non-illusory problems) to illusory inferences.

Data from Legrenzi et al. (2003). Reprinted by permission of SAGE Publications.

There was convincing evidence for the predicted illusory inferences (see Figure 14.4) when the principle of truth did not permit the correct inferences to be drawn. In contrast, performance was very high on control problems where adherence to the principle of truth was sufficient. Reasoners' excessive adherence to the principle of truth produces incorrect reasoning with several other types of problems (Johnson-Laird et al., 2012).

Theoretically, individuals make illusory inferences because they fail to think about what is false. As predicted, people are less susceptible to such inferences if explicitly instructed to falsify the premises of reasoning problems (Newsome & Johnson-Laird, 2006).

According to Johnson-Laird's theory, people search for counterexamples after having constructed their initial mental model and generated a conclusion. As a result, they may construct several mental models and consider several conclusions. Newstead et al. (1999) found no support for this conclusion – the average number of conclusions considered with multiple- and single-model syllogisms was very similar (1.12 vs. 1.05, respectively).

More evidence that reasoners find it hard to generate counterexamples was reported by Khemlani et al. (2012). Participants were given the following task:

They're not living adult males. So, who could they be?

There are actually *seven* possibilities (e.g., dead adult males, living adult females, living boys). In spite of the task's apparent simplicity, participants listed only *four* possibilities on average.

Mental model theory focuses on the *general* approach taken by reasoners, and so de-emphasises individual differences. Bucciarelli and Johnson-Laird (1999) asked participants to evaluate valid and invalid syllogisms. Some initially formed a mental model of the first premise to which they then added information based on the second premise. Other participants proceeded in the opposite direction, and still others constructed an initial mental model satisfying the conclusion.

Evaluation

Most of the theory's predictions have been confirmed experimentally. First, mental models represent what is common to a set of possibilities and seem to be iconic. Second, many errors on deductive reasoning tasks occur because people use the principle of truth and ignore what is false (e.g., Legrenzi et al., 2003). Third, even when people seek counterexamples, they often find it hard to do so (Khemlani et al., 2012). Fourth, our reasoning ability is often limited by working-memory constraints.

Khemlani and Johnson-Laird (2012) carried out a meta-analysis (see Glossary) on studies of syllogistic reasoning to compare the predictive accuracy of seven theories. The mental model theory was best at predicting participants' responses, having a 95% success rate. However, it was relatively weak at rejecting responses participants do *not* produce.

The theory has various limitations. First, it assumes people engage in deductive reasoning more than they do. As Khemlani and Johnson-Laird (2012, p. 445) admitted, "[The theory] originally postulated that individuals search for counterexamples as a matter of course. They do not." Most people find deductive reasoning very difficult and so generally engage in easier forms of processing (discussed shortly).

Second, the processes involved in forming mental models are *underspecified*. It is assumed people use background knowledge when forming mental models. However, the theory does not spell out how we decide *which* information to include in a mental model.

Third, the theory does not provide an adequate account of the mental model formed with ambiguous reasoning problems. Here is an example (Ragni & Knauff, 2013):

The Porsche is to the right of the Ferrari.
The Beetle is to the left of the Porsche.

The Dodge is in front of the Beetle.
The Volvo is in front of the Porsche.

Which relation holds between the Beetle and the Ferrari?

There is no definite answer to the above problem because the second premise is ambiguous: the Beetle could be placed to the left or the right of the Ferrari. Participants' responses on such ambiguous problems are not predicted by mental model theory.

In contrast, Ragni and Knauff (2013) argued that it is easier to interpret the second premise as meaning that the Beetle is placed to the left of the Ferrari rather than having to remember it has been squeezed in between the Ferrari and the Porsche. As predicted, most reasoners answered incorrectly that the Beetle is to the left of the Ferrari.

Ragni and Knauff (2013) obtained much support for their theoretical assumption that reasoners generally have a preference for mental models that are easy to construct. They also argued that reasoners typically only construct a single mental model (as in the example above), whereas it is assumed within mental model theory that additional mental models will often be constructed. Their experimental findings supported their assumption over that of mental model theory.

Dual-system theories

Several researchers (e.g., Kahneman, 2003; see Chapter 13) have put forward dual-system theories to account for human reasoning and other aspects of higher-level cognition (Evans, 2008). System 1 emerged early in evolution, is based on unconscious processes, involves parallel processing and is independent of general intelligence. System 2 emerged recently in evolutionary history, is based on conscious processes and involves rule-based serial processing. It has limited capacity and is linked to general intelligence.

Evans (2006; see Figure 14.5) put forward a heuristic–analytic theory of reasoning. Heuristic processes are located within System 1 and analytic processes within System 2. When someone is presented with a reasoning problem, heuristic processes uses task features, the current goal and background knowledge to construct a *single* hypothetical possibility or mental model.

After that, time-consuming and effortful analytic processes may intervene to revise or replace this mental model. Such interventions are most likely when:

- task instructions tell participants to use abstract or logical reasoning;
- participants are highly intelligent;
- sufficient time is available for effortful analytic processing;
- participants need to justify their reasoning.

The analytic system evaluates mental models, and should *not* be regarded simply as a system based on logic. Involvement of the analytic system often (but not always) improves reasoning performance. For example, conclusions that could be true but are not necessarily so are often mistakenly accepted by the analytic system because of its reliance on the satisficing principle (see below and Chapter 13).

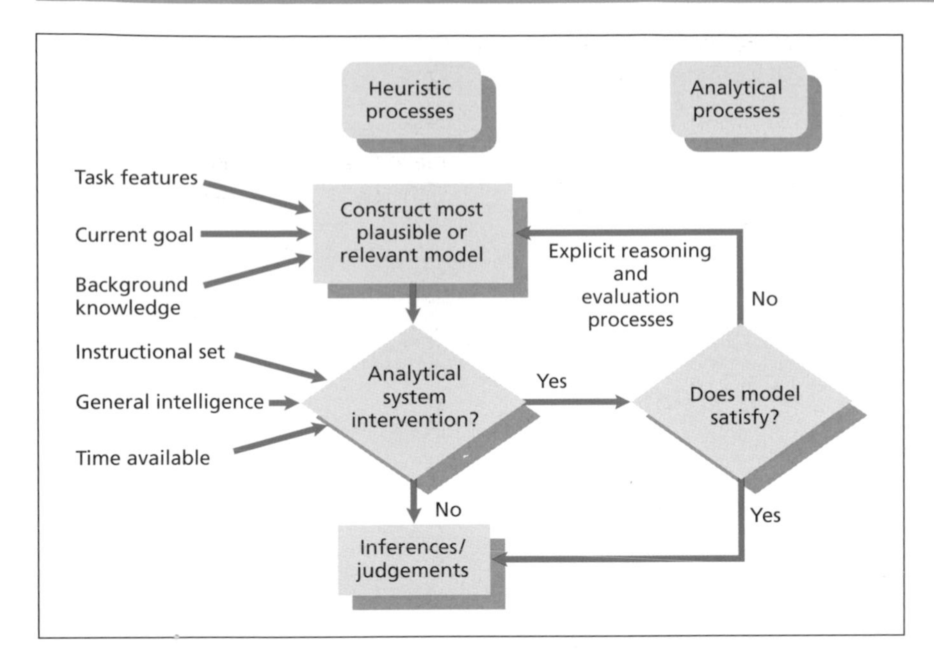

Figure 14.5
The heuristic–analytic theory of reasoning put forward by Evans (2006).
With kind permission from Springer Science + Business Media.

According to Evans (2006), human reasoning (and hypothetical thinking generally) is based on three principles:

1. *Singularity principle*: Only a *single* mental model is considered at any given time.
2. *Relevance principle*: The most relevant (i.e., plausible or probable) mental model based on prior knowledge and the current context is considered.
3. *Satisficing principle*: The current mental model is evaluated by the analytic system and accepted if adequate. Use of this principle often leads people to accept conclusions that are not necessarily true.

This theory is very different from Johnson-Laird's mental model theory. The latter theory assumes people initially use deductive reasoning, which may then be affected by real-world knowledge. The sequence is basically the *opposite* in heuristic–analytic theory: people initially use their world knowledge and the immediate context in their reasoning, which may then be affected by deductive reasoning within the analytic system. Thus, deductive reasoning is less important in heuristic–analytic theory than mental model theory.

The assumption that rapid heuristic or intuitive processes are used initially and may be followed by slower analytic processes is oversimplified (Handley et al., 2011; De Neys, 2012; Evans, 2012). First, different types of processing may occur in parallel rather than serially. Second, logical processing is not confined to the analytic system but may also occur within the heuristic or intuitive system (see Chapter 13).

Three models based on the above assumptions are shown in Figure 14.6 (see also discussion in Chapter 13, pages 561–564):

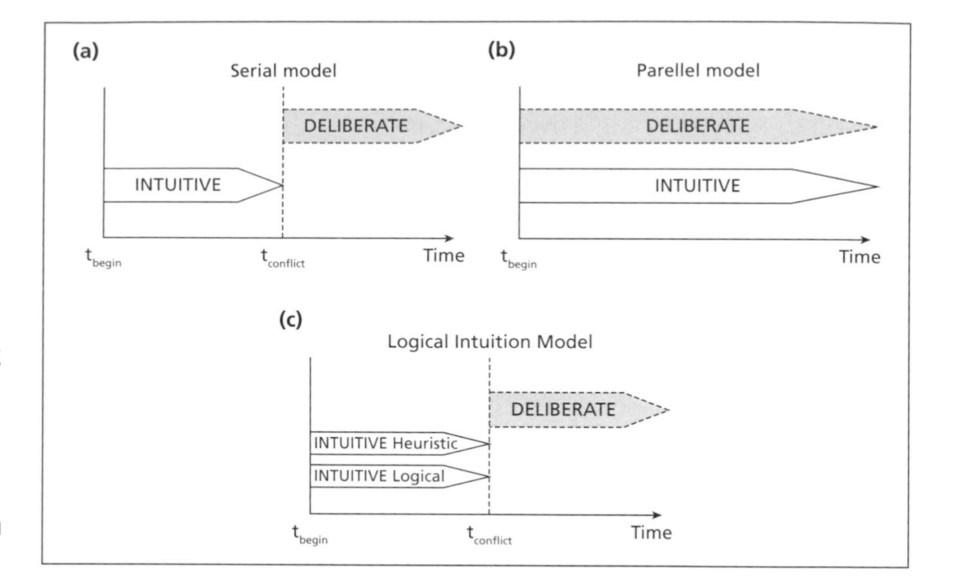

Figure 14.6
Three models of the relationship between the intuitive and deliberate systems. (a) Serial model: intuitive processing may or may not be followed by deliberate processing. (b) Parallel model: intuitive and deliberate processing are both involved from the outset. (c) Logical intuition model: deliberate processing is triggered if there is a conflict between initial intuitive heuristic and intuitive logical responses produced in parallel.

From De Neys (2012). Reprinted by permission of SAGE Publications.

1 According to the "traditional" serial model (e.g., Evans, 2006), there is serial processing with deliberate or analytic processing *following* intuitive processing.
2 According to the parallel model, intuitive and deliberate processes occur at the same time. This model is wasteful of cognitive resources because effortful deliberate processes are always used.
3 According to the logical intuition model (advocated by De Neys, 2012, 2014), two types of intuitive responses are activated in parallel: heuristic or intuitive and logical. If these two responses are in conflict, deliberate processes then resolve matters. The notion of intuitive logical processing sounds puzzling, but De Neys argued that traditional logical principles can be activated fairly automatically.

Findings

Case study:
Deductive reasoning

The heuristic system uses various heuristics depending on the precise problem. For example, as we saw earlier, an important heuristic used on the Wason selection task is matching bias. This bias leads people to select the cards stated in the rule regardless of relevance. A similar matching bias has also been found in syllogistic reasoning (Stupple et al., 2013).

A very useful phenomenon for distinguishing between heuristic and analytic processes is belief bias (discussed earlier and in a later section on brain systems). This bias occurs when a logically valid conclusion that is not believable is rejected as invalid, or a conclusion that is logically invalid but believable is accepted as valid. Belief bias is stronger when only heuristic processes are used than when analytic ones are also used.

According to heuristic–analytic theory, analytic processes are more likely to be used (and performance will be better) when instructions stress the importance of logical reasoning. As predicted, Evans (2000) found reduced belief bias when the instructions emphasised logical reasoning.

Stupple et al. (2011) compared groups of participants who showed much evidence of belief bias and those showing little belief bias. Those with high levels of belief bias responded faster on syllogistic reasoning problems (especially those involving invalid but believable conclusions) than those with low levels of belief bias. These findings are consistent with the assumption that the former group was more likely to use heuristic processing (which is more rapid than analytic processing).

Intelligence correlates highly with working memory capacity (see Glossary) as was shown in a review by Conway et al. (2003). As a result, individuals high in working memory capacity should make more extensive use of analytic processes than those having low capacity. Another prediction is that use of analytic processes while reasoning should be reduced by requiring participants to perform a demanding secondary task during the reasoning task.

De Neys (2006) tested the above predictions. Participants varying in working memory capacity were given a reasoning task. The task included belief-bias problems involving a conflict between validity and believability of the conclusion and requiring analytic processing for successful reasoning. There were also non-conflict problems requiring only heuristic processes. The reasoning problems were presented on their own or with a secondary task low or high in its demands.

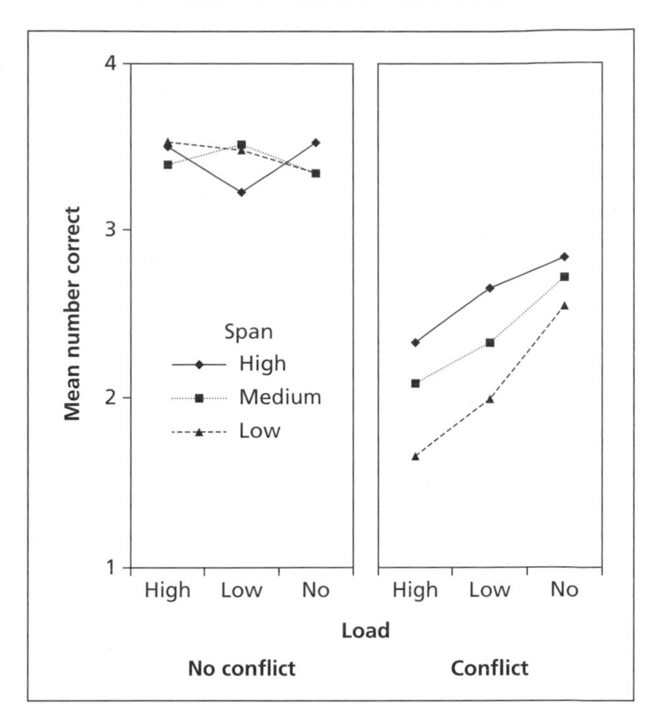

Figure 14.7
Reasoning performance as a function of high, low or no cognitive load and working memory capacity (high, medium or low) no conflict (left-hand side) or conflict (right-hand side) problems.
From De Neys (2006). Reprinted by permission of SAGE Publications.

De Neys' (2006) findings are shown in Figure 14.7. As predicted, high working memory capacity was an advantage only on conflict problems requiring analytic processes. Also as predicted, a demanding secondary task impaired performance on conflict problems but not non-conflict ones. This latter finding was replicated by Tsujii and Watanabe (2009; see later in chapter).

According to the theory, belief bias should be stronger when the time for thinking is strictly limited, so making it hard to use analytic processes. Evans and Curtis-Holmes (2005) obtained support for this prediction. In similar fashion, errors in conditional reasoning occur more often when participants must respond rapidly (Markovits et al., 2013).

What determines whether a reasoner uses the output of heuristic/intuitive processing to determine their response or whether they additionally engage analytic processes? The heuristic–analytic theory provides only a partial answer. Thompson et al. (2011) addressed this issue using syllogistic and conditioning reasoning tasks. Participants provided an initial answer as soon as they had read each problem (intuitive answer), followed by an assessment of that answer's correctness (feeling of rightness). After that, participants had unlimited time to reconsider their initial answer and provide a final answer (analytic or deliberate answer).

Interactive exercise:
Heuristic-analytic model

Thompson et al. (2011) argued that we possess a *monitoring system* (assessed by the feeling-of-rightness ratings) that evaluates the output of heuristic or intuitive processes. Low feelings of rightness should lead participants to spend much time reconsidering their intuitive answer and then often changing it with their analytic answer. In contrast, high feelings of rightness should mean participants generally decide fairly rapidly to make their analytic answer the same as their initial, intuitive answer. The findings were as predicted.

Thompson et al. (2011) reported another important finding. The use of analytic processes was no guarantee the correct answer would be produced. For example, the analytic answers to conditional reasoning problems were correct only about 65% of the time.

The processes individuals use when solving reasoning problems are typically inferred mainly on the basis of their performance. For example, it is assumed someone making many errors has failed to detect the logical structure of reasoning problems. However, performance accuracy may be a fairly insensitive measure of internal processing (De Neys, 2012, 2014).

Evidence that people are more responsive to the logical structure of reasoning problems than suggested by performance accuracy was reported by De Neys et al. (2010). Participants received syllogisms involving conflict or no conflict between the logical validity and believability of the conclusions and decided whether the conclusion was logically valid. There was strong belief bias – accuracy was only 52% on conflict trials compared to 89% on no-conflict trials.

The very poor performance on conflict trials (only slightly greater than chance) suggests participants failed to detect the logical structure of the problems. However, the picture looks different when we consider additional findings. De Neys et al. (2010) recorded skin conductance responses (which assess physiological arousal) during reasoning problems. All participants had greater physiological arousal on conflict trials than no-conflict trials. Thus, the presence of conflict was registered within the processing system below the conscious level, possibly as a "gut" feeling.

What can we conclude from De Neys et al.'s (2010) findings? They are more consistent with the logical intuition model than the heuristic–analytic theory and other serial models (see Figure 14.6). More specifically, the findings suggest some logical processing can be intuitive rather than analytic.

Morsanyi and Handley (2012) obtained support for the above conclusion. Participants provided rapid, intuitive ratings of how much they liked the conclusions of syllogistic reasoning problems. Participants liked valid conclusions much more than invalid ones and this was associated with slight changes in their affective state. This suggests intuitive processing can possess some logical characteristics. However, other research suggests logical processing may not have been involved. Klauer and Singmann (2013) obtained evidence suggesting Morsanyi and Handley's findings occurred simply because there were pre-existing differences in the mean liking of different conclusions.

Evaluation

Evans' (2006) heuristic–analytic theory of reasoning has achieved several successes. First, the overarching notion that the cognitive processes (e.g., heuristic processes, analytic processes) used by individuals to solve reasoning problems resemble those used in numerous other cognitive tasks is essentially correct.

Second, the notion that thinking (including reasoning) is based on the singularity, relevance and satisficing principles has received empirical support. Most errors people make on reasoning problems can be explained by their adherence to these principles at the expense of logic-based deductive reasoning.

Third, there is support for the distinction between heuristic and analytic processes, and for the notion that the latter are more effortful (e.g., De Neys, 2006). Phenomena such as belief bias and matching bias indicate the importance of heuristic processes.

Fourth, the theory accounts for some individual differences in performance on reasoning problems. For example, individuals high in working memory capacity or intelligence perform better than those low in working memory capacity or intelligence in part because they are more likely to use analytic processes.

There are various limitations with heuristic–analytic theory and the dual-process approach in general. First, the distinction between heuristic and analytic processes is too neat and tidy (Keren & Schul, 2009). However, it can nevertheless be argued that it has proved very fruitful in practice (Evans & Stanovich, 2013).

Second, the distinction between heuristic and analytic processes poses the problem of working out exactly *how* these two different kinds of processes interact. In that connection, the notion that the decision whether to use analytic processes depends on a monitoring mechanism (Thompson et al., 2011) is useful.

Third, it is assumed analytic processes vary in how closely they approximate to logic-based, deductive reasoning (Evans, 2006). However, it is not very clear precisely what these processes are or how individuals decide which ones to use.

Fourth, the theory assumes logical processing depends on conscious, analytic processes. However, some evidence (De Neys et al., 2010; Morsanyi & Handley, 2012; but see Klauer & Singmann, 2013) suggests logical processing can involve heuristic or intuitive processes occurring below the conscious level.

Fifth, the assumption that heuristic processing is followed by analytic processing in a serial fashion may not be entirely correct. There may be more parallel processing than assumed within the theory.

BRAIN SYSTEMS IN REASONING

In recent years, there has been a substantial increase in research designed to identify the brain regions associated with deductive reasoning. Here we will discuss the main findings, including a consideration of brain activity associated with individual differences in reasoning.

Prado et al. (2011) carried out a meta-analysis of 28 neuroimaging studies on deductive reasoning (see Figure 14.8). They obtained evidence for a brain system centred in the left hemisphere involving frontal and parietal areas. Specific brain areas activated during deductive reasoning included the inferior frontal gyrus, the middle frontal gyrus, the medial frontal gyrus, the precentral gyrus and the basal ganglia.

The left-hemisphere dominance reported by Prado et al. (2011) has also been found in patient data. Goel et al. (2007) studied patients having damage to left or right parietal cortex. Those with left-side damage performed worse than those with right-side damage on reasoning tasks in which complete information was provided.

How can we explain the role of the left hemisphere in deductive reasoning? Gazzaniga et al. (e.g., 2008) argue that there is a single conscious system based

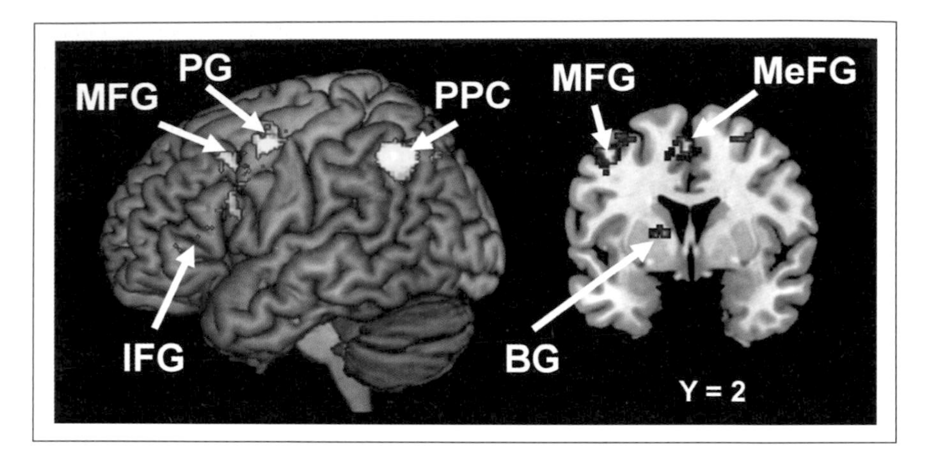

Figure 14.8
Brain regions most consistently activated across 28 studies of deductive reasoning. Abbreviations: PG = precentral gyrus; MFG = middle frontal gyrus; PPC = posterior parietal cortex; IFG = inferior frontal gyrus; BG = basal ganglia; MeFG = medial frontal gyrus.
From Prado et al. (2011). © Massachusetts Institute of Technology, by permission of The MIT Press.

in the left hemisphere. This system is the interpreter, and it tries to make coherent sense of the information available to it. Left-hemisphere dominance in deductive reasoning may depend at least in part on this interpreter.

Type of task

Prado et al. (2011) found the precise brain areas associated with deductive reasoning depended to a large extent on the nature of the task. Some tasks involve *relational* arguments (e.g., A is to the left of B; B is to the left of C; therefore, A is to the left of C). Others involve *categorical* arguments (e.g., All As are Bs; all Bs are Cs; therefore, all As are Cs) and still others involve *propositional* arguments (e.g., If there is an A, then there is a B; there is an A; therefore, there is a B).

Prado et al. (2011) compared patterns of brain activation associated with these three types of deductive reasoning in a meta-analysis (see Glossary). Relational reasoning was more associated with activation in parietal cortex in both hemispheres than were the other two types of reasoning.

Additional evidence that parietal cortex is of major importance in relational reasoning was reported by Waechter et al. (2013). They studied patients with damage to parietal cortex (BA7, BA40) or anterior prefrontal cortex (BA10). Only those with parietal damage performed worse than healthy controls on relational reasoning.

Why is parietal cortex important in relational reasoning? Look back at the examples given of the three types of deductive reasoning. Relational arguments lend themselves best to spatial processing and representation (e.g., you might form an image something like this: A B C). The relevance of this is that spatial processing depends mostly on parietal cortex. For example, Sack et al. (2002) applied transcranial magnetic stimulation (TMS; see Glossary) to the right posterior parietal cortex. This impaired visuo-spatial processing.

Prado et al. (2011) also found the left inferior frontal gyrus (BA9/44) was more activated during the processing of categorical arguments than relational or propositional ones. This region is associated with various rule-based processes, and it is plausible that rule-based processing is of particular importance in categorical reasoning.

Prado et al. (2011) found that the left precentral gyrus (BA6) was more activated with propositional reasoning than with categorical or relational reasoning. The involvement of the precentral gyrus may reflect the additional use of attentional and motor processes with this type of reasoning. In general, however, the findings with propositional reasoning were less clear-cut and harder to interpret than those with the other forms of reasoning.

In sum, the findings of Prado et al. (2011, p. 3494) point to the following conclusion: "Deductive reasoning does not rely on a unitary brain system . . . This is inconsistent with any cognitive theory that would posit that the same cognitive mechanism underlies these three forms of reasoning [relational, propositional, categorical]."

What is the role of language in deductive reasoning? Monti and Osherson (2012) addressed this issue in a review of the literature. Language is heavily involved in the initial reading and encoding of the verbal information presented on deductive reasoning tasks. However, language seems to play little or no role later in processing.

In sum, the evidence suggests deductive reasoning does not involve a single cognitive system. Language is typically confined to an early stage of processing. After that, processing is mainly visuo-spatial or rule-based depending on the nature of the reasoning task.

Individual differences

There are important individual differences in the strategies used on deductive reasoning problems. Earlier we discussed evidence supporting that conclusion (e.g., De Neys et al., 2005; De Neys, 2006). Reverberi et al. (2012) identified three strategies used in categorical reasoning:

1 sensitivity to the logical form of problems;
2 sensitivity to the validity of conclusions (i.e., accurate performance);
3 use of heuristic strategies.

Individuals using the first strategy had greater activation in the left inferior lateral frontal (BA44/45) and superior medial frontal (BA6/8) areas. These areas seem to be involved in the extraction and representation of problem structure. Individuals using the second strategy had greater activation in the left ventro-lateral frontal (BA47) area, which is involved in the selection and application of relevant inferential rules. There was no specific pattern of brain activation associated with use of heuristic strategies.

What do the above findings mean? According to Reverberi et al. (2012, p. 1763), they suggest that deductive reasoning consists of "several subcomponents that interact in complex ways".

Large individual differences have been found in belief bias (the tendency to accept invalid but believable conclusions and to reject valid but unbelievable ones). As we saw earlier, more intelligent individuals exhibit less belief bias because they make more use of analytic processing strategies (De Neys, 2006).

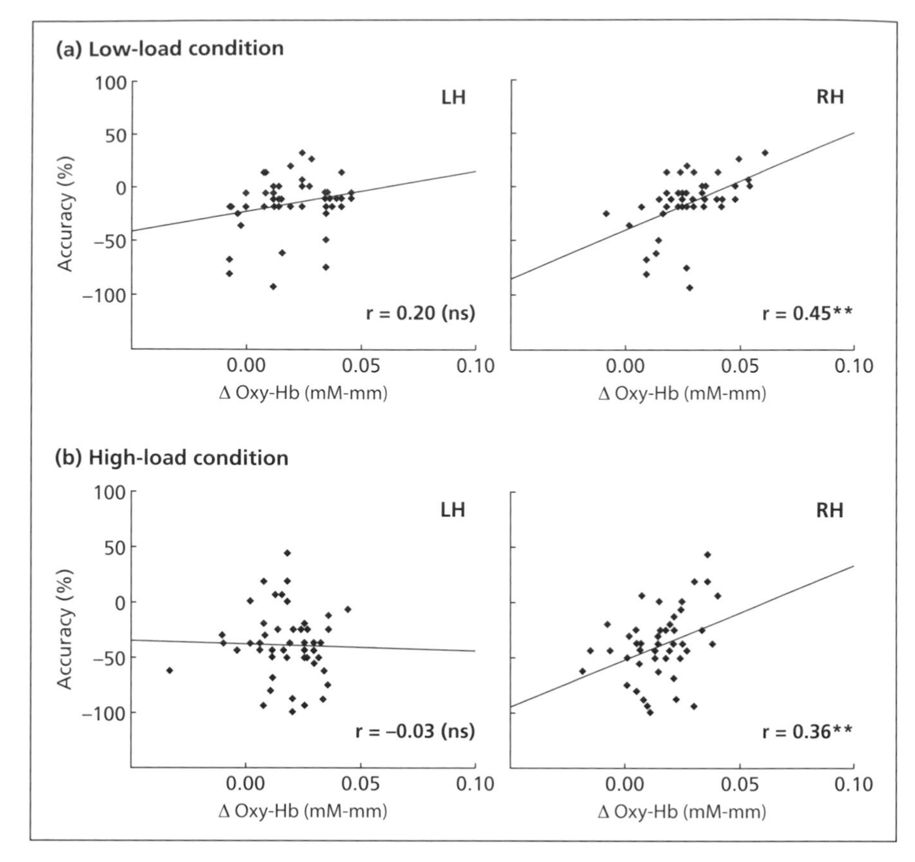

Figure 14.9 Relationships between reasoning task performance (accuracy) and inferior frontal cortex activity in the left hemisphere (LH) and the right hemisphere (RH) in (a) the low-load condition and (b) the high-load condition.

From Tsujii and Watanabe (2009). Reprinted with permission from Elsevier.

Tsujii and Watanabe (2009) pointed out that the right inferior frontal cortex seems to be involved in inhibiting incorrect responses triggered by the heuristic system. Accordingly, they predicted individuals with high levels of activation in that area would show less belief bias in deductive reasoning than those with low activation. They tested this hypothesis using conditions in which participants performed an additional task at the same time involving low or high cognitive load.

What did Tsujii and Watanabe (2009) find? There was much support for their hypothesis (see Figure 14.9). Individual differences in performance accuracy (and thus low belief bias) were strongly associated with activation in the right inferior frontal cortex under low and high cognitive load conditions. There was additional evidence of the key role played by this brain region – it was less activated under high- than low-load conditions and there was much more belief bias in the high-load condition.

Sequence of processes

The neuroimaging data reported in most studies indicate brain areas activated during the course of a reasoning task. However, such data fail to indicate *when* each brain area was activated. Fangmeier et al. (2006) used mental model theory as the basis for assuming the existence of three stages of processing in relational reasoning. Different brain areas were associated with each stage:

1. *Premise processing*: At this stage, there was substantial temporo-occipital activation reflecting the use of visuo-spatial processing.
2. *Premise integration*: At this stage, there was much activation in the anterior prefrontal cortex (e.g., BA10), an area associated with executive processing.
3. *Validation*: At this stage, the posterior parietal cortex was activated, as were areas within the prefrontal cortex (BA6, BA8) and the dorsal cingulate cortex. Why was this? First, modality-independent representations are held in the parietal cortex, and could be useful for validation purposes. Second, the involvement of the prefrontal cortex reflects cognitively demanding processes during validation of the conclusion.

The study by Fangmeier et al. (2006) involved *visual* presentation of each problem. Fangmeier and Knauff (2009) used essentially the same task but with *auditory* presentation. They replicated the finding that the anterior prefrontal cortex is associated with the premise integration stage and parietal cortex with the validation phase.

Bonnefond et al. (2013) studied the brain processes associated with conditional reasoning focusing on modus ponens (If *P* then *Q*; *P*//Therefore *Q*). There were two main findings. First, participants *expected* the second premise to match the first one (e.g., *P* following If *P* then *Q*). There was enhanced brain activity 300 ms after presentation of the second premise when it failed to match the first one.

Second, when the second premise matched the first one, participants generated the inference that followed validly from the two premises (activation in the parieto-frontal network at 400 ms). This occurred sometime *before* the conclusion was presented. Thus, participants engaged in much *anticipatory* processing before the second premise and the conclusion were presented.

Overall evaluation

Limited progress has been made in identifying the brain systems involved in deductive reasoning. For example, Goel (2007, p. 435) pointed out that the findings from neuroimaging studies of reasoning "might seem chaotic and inconsistent". However, there is an increased understanding of the reasons for these inconsistencies. For example, the pattern of brain activation differs somewhat depending on the type of deductive reasoning problem (Prado et al., 2011). Another reason is there are substantial individual differences in the strategies used (and the brain areas activated) during reasoning (e.g., Reverberi et al., 2012).

Research in this area has focused mostly on complex tasks involving several different cognitive processes. Such tasks almost invariably involve many brain areas, making it hard to make coherent sense of the findings. One solution is to assess *when* different brain regions are involved in reasoning (e.g., Fangmeier et al., 2006). Another solution is to focus on more specific issues (e.g., brain areas involved in belief bias).

Finally, Bonnefond et al.'s (2013) finding that individuals performing a conditional reasoning task often engage in anticipatory processing is potentially of importance. This finding contradicts the typical assumption that virtually all processing on reasoning tasks is triggered by the presentation of each premise.

KEY TERMS

Informal reasoning
A form of reasoning based on one's relevant knowledge and experience rather than logic.

Straw man fallacy
Refuting an opponent's views by misrepresenting them in some way.

INFORMAL REASONING

Research on deductive reasoning is *narrow* because of its emphasis on problems based on formal logic in which past knowledge is of no relevance. As such, it appears far removed from the **informal reasoning** typically found in everyday life. Informal reasoning is a form of reasoning based on one's knowledge and experience. Knowledge and experience are often used to argue persuasively in favour of (or against) some statement. Such reasoning typically has little (or nothing) to do with logic.

The *content* of an argument is generally important in informal reasoning. However, it is (at least in principle) irrelevant in formal deductive reasoning. For example, consider the two following superficially similar arguments (Hahn & Oaksford, 2007):

1 Ghosts exist because no one has proved they do not.
2 The drug is safe because we have found no evidence that it is not.

The implausibility of ghosts existing means most people find (1) much less persuasive than (2).

Another difference between informal reasoning and deductive reasoning is that *contextual factors* are important in informal reasoning. Thus, for example, we are more persuaded by the arguments on a given topic put forward by an expert than the same arguments proposed by a non-expert (Walton, 2010).

We turn now to possibly the most important difference between deductive and informal reasoning. As Evans (2012) emphasised, traditional research on deductive reasoning focuses on *binary logic* – every proposition is assumed to be true or false. In contrast, informal reasoning is all about *probabilities* – we regard most statements or arguments as possibly or probably true rather than certainly true or certainly false.

We can see the importance of the above differences by considering fallacies (Hahn & Oaksford, 2014). An example is the **straw man fallacy** in which someone else's views are misrepresented by weakening or distorting them. According to classical logic, such fallacies are totally inadequate forms of argument because they are not supported by logic. However, that position is too extreme if we think in terms of probabilities. As Aikin and Casey (2011) pointed out, one version of the straw man fallacy involves selecting one's opponent's weakest arguments and then trying to demolish them. This version can genuinely reduce the probability that the opponent's position is correct. There is more on fallacies shortly.

Finally, the reasoner's *motives* often differ between deductive reasoning and informal reasoning. People trying to solve deductive reasoning problems are supposed to be motivated to reason as logically and accurately as possible. In contrast, the motives of those engaged in informal reasoning are often very different. According to Mercier and Sperber (2011, p. 57), "The function of informal reasoning is . . . to devise and evaluate arguments intended to persuade . . . Skilled arguers are not after the truth but after arguments supporting their views." This viewpoint is somewhat narrow. In fact, we also use reasoning for thinking generally and for anticipating and planning the future (Evans, 2011).

Note the differences we have identified between informal and deductive reasoning refer mostly to what has historically been assumed to be the case.

IN THE REAL WORLD: INFORMAL REASONING CAN BE UNDULY INFLUENCED BY NEUROSCIENCE CONTENT: "NEUROIMAGING ILLUSION"

How do we decide whether the explanations of findings given by cognitive psychologists or cognitive neuroscientists are convincing? Perhaps you are most likely to be convinced when there is evidence from functional neuroimaging showing the brain areas that seem to be most involved. Weisberg et al. (2008) addressed this issue in a study on students taking an introductory course in cognitive neuroscience. The students were provided with a mixture of good and bad explanations for various psychological phenomena. Some explanations were accompanied by neuroscience evidence irrelevant to the quality of the explanation. The students indicated how satisfying they found each explanation.

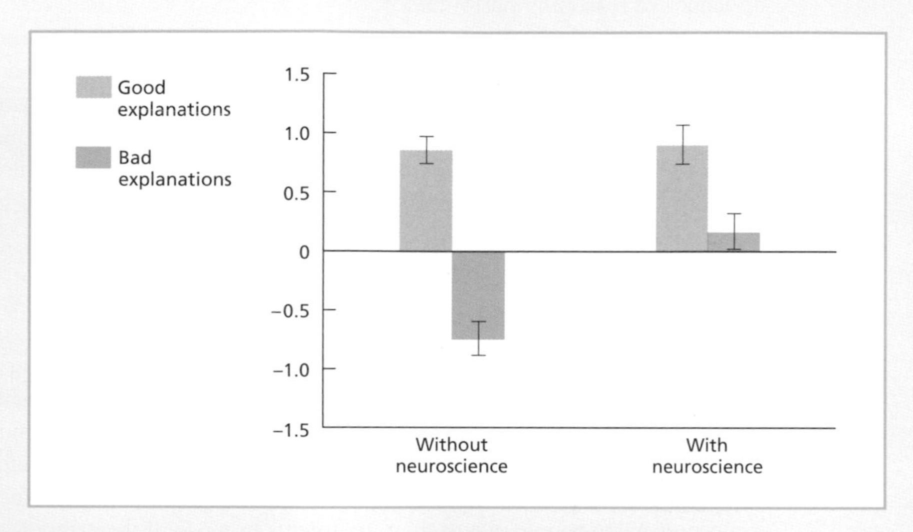

Figure 14.10
Mean ratings of good and bad explanations of scientific phenomena with and without neuroscience information.
From Weisberg et al. (2008). © Massachusetts Institute of Technology, by permission of The MIT Press.

The students were more impressed by explanations accompanied by neuroscience evidence, especially with bad explanations (see Figure 14.10). This is a clear example of content having a disproportionate impact on informal reasoning. *Why* were the students so impressed by neuroscience evidence irrelevant to the quality of the explanation? First, neuroscientific findings often seem more "scientific" than purely psychological ones because they involve complex and expensive technology. Second, it is easy to assume information about brain activity provides fairly direct access to information about underlying psychological processes.

In sum, this study provides an illustration of the "neuroimaging illusion" (see Chapter 1). The take-home message is that you need to evaluate neuroscientific evidence as carefully as psychological evidence.

KEY TERM

Myside bias
In informal reasoning, the tendency to evaluate statements in terms of one's own beliefs or to generate reasons or arguments supporting those beliefs.

In fact, as was emphasised earlier in the chapter, most people make some use of their knowledge and experience when performing deductive reasoning tasks. They also often think in terms of probabilities rather than binary logic. Thus, most individuals make much use of informal reasoning even on deductive reasoning tasks.

If the processes involved in informal reasoning resemble those used on deductive reasoning tasks, we might expect to find individuals who perform well on one type of task will also tend to perform well on the other type of task. Ricco (2007) identified common informal fallacies. Examples are *irrelevance* (seeking to support a claim with an irrelevant reason) and *slippery slope* (claiming an innocent-looking first step will lead to bad consequences without providing reasons). He found the ability to detect such informal fallacies was associated with deductive reasoning performance.

Most people confronted by formal deductive reasoning tasks make extensive use of informal reasoning *processes* (e.g., their prior knowledge and beliefs). For example, many reasoners exhibit belief bias with syllogistic reasoning – they accept invalid conclusions if they are believable and reject valid conclusions that are unbelievable (see earlier in chapter). This suggests the value of studying informal reasoning processes *directly* by using informal reasoning tasks rather than *indirectly* via the errors made on formal tasks.

Findings: motivation

There is compelling evidence that many people's informal reasoning and thinking are seriously flawed. For example, tens of millions of Americans believe humans did not evolve from apes, that the moon landing was a hoax and that global warming is not a problem. Why do intelligent people have such beliefs? According to Thagard (2011, pp. 156–7), the answer lies in motivated inference, which "occurs when people distort their judgments because of their underlying personal goals . . . motivated inference is based on wishes, not facts".

The notion of motivated inference is very similar to that of **myside bias**. Myside bias is the tendency to evaluate statements with respect to one's own beliefs rather than solely on their merits. Evidence of myside bias was reported by Stanovich and West (2007). College students rated the accuracy of contentious (but factually correct) propositions such as the following:

1 College students who drink alcohol while in college are more likely to become alcoholic in later life.
2 The gap in salary between men and women generally disappears when they are employed in the same position.

What did Stanovich and West (2007) find? Students who regularly drank alcohol rated the accuracy of proposition (1) lower than those who did not. Women rated the accuracy of proposition (2) lower than men. Thus, there was strong myside bias. Stanovich and West (2008) also found evidence of myside bias with the strength of participants' prior beliefs predicting the extent of myside bias. Of interest, the extent of myside bias was *unrelated* to individual differences in cognitive ability or intelligence. This suggests participants made little use of System 2 or analytic thinking.

IN THE REAL WORLD: DOES CLIMATE CHANGE EXIST?

The notion that motivational factors often distort informal reasoning can be considered with reference to climate change. For example, Howe and Leiserowitz (2013) tested Americans' memories of the previous summer (which had been unusually hot) and winter (which had been unusually cold). Those most dismissive of the notion of global warming were only half as likely as those most alarmed by global warming to remember the preceding summer had been warmer than normal (see Figure 14.11).

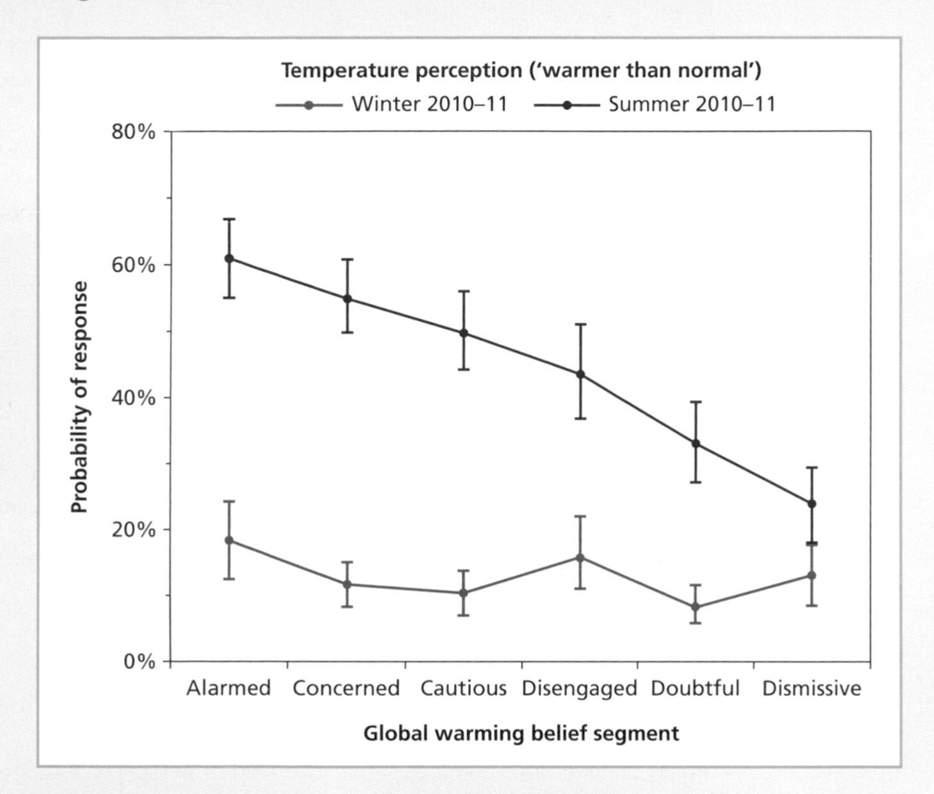

Figure 14.11
Probability of responding that winter 2010–11 and summer 2010 in the United States were warmer than normal as a function of belief in global warming (ranging from alarmed to dismissive).

From Howe and Leiserowitz (2013). With permission from Elsevier.

Leviston et al. (2013) obtained evidence of another distortion. Australian participants provided their opinion on climate change and also estimated the views of the general population. Disbelievers in climate change grossly overestimated the percentage of other people whose views were the same as theirs: this is an example of the false consensus effect.

We might expect individuals with high levels of science literacy and numeracy to be most concerned about climate change. In fact, cultural values are much more important. Kahan et al. (2012) identified two groups differing in their values: (1) egalitarian communitarians believing in equality and the value of society; (2) hierarchical individualists believing in a hierarchical society and personal responsibility. Both groups provided an estimate of the risks of climate change.

What did Kahan et al. (2012) find? First, the impact of science literacy and numeracy was small (see Figure 14.12). Second, egalitarian communitarians perceived the risks of climate change to be considerably greater than did hierarchical individualists. Similar findings relating to individual differences in values were reported by Capstick and Pidgeon (2014). Individualism correlated +0.42 with scepticism about climate change, whereas egalitarianism correlated –0.22.

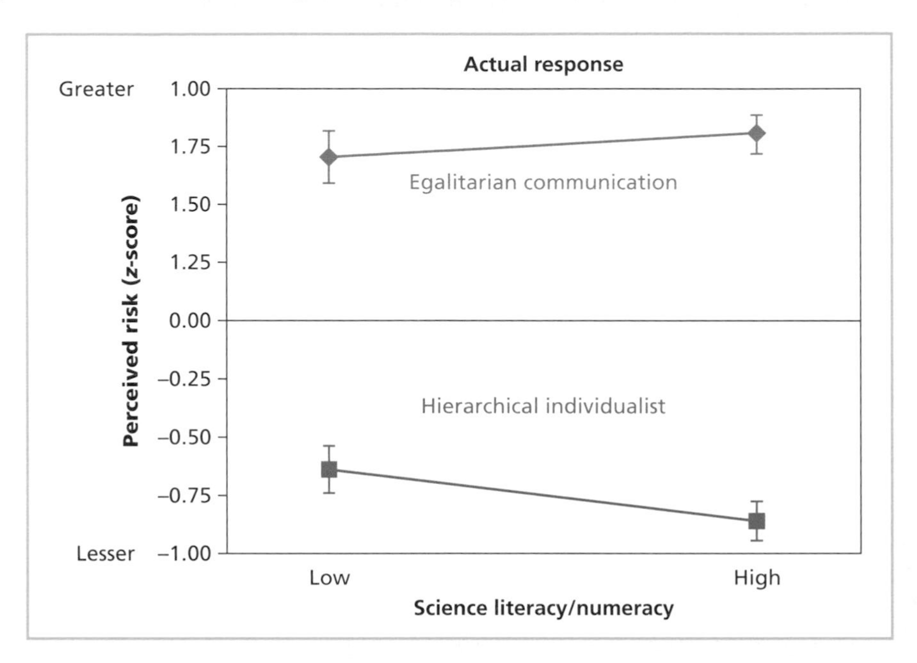

Figure 14.12
Mean responses to the question, "How much risk to you believe climate change poses to human health, safety or prosperity?" by individuals low or high in science literacy/numeracy who were egalitarian communitarians or hierarchical individualists.
From Kahan et al. (2012).

In sum, "Positions on climate change have come to signify the kind of person one is. People whose beliefs are at odds with those of the people with whom they share their basic cultural commitments risk being labelled as weird" (Kahan, 2012, p. 255). This motivation to appear as a particular kind of person helps to explain why most people's reasoning about climate change focuses very little on the relevant scientific evidence. It also helps to explain why disbelievers in climate change show a false consensus effect and distorted memory for past weather patterns.

The motivation to find support for one's own beliefs or views sometimes *improves* reasoning performance. We saw earlier that reasoning on the Wason selection task is influenced by the personal relevance of the rule. Individuals strongly motivated to disprove the rule because it implied they would die young showed much more accurate reasoning than those lacking such motivation (Dawson et al., 2002).

Findings: probabilities

As pointed out earlier, probabilities are much more important in informal than deductive reasoning (e.g., we believe statements are possibly or probably true). In contrast, statements in formal logic are true or false – there is no half-way house.

Support for the probabilistic approach was reported by Hahn and Oaksford (2007). They identified several factors influencing the perceived strength of a conclusion:

- degree of previous conviction or belief;
- positive arguments have more impact than negative arguments;
- strength of the evidence.

Hahn and Oaksford (2007) studied these factors using scenarios such as the following:

Barbara: Are you taking digesterole for it?
Adam: Yes, why?
Barbara: Well, because I strongly believe that it does have side-effects.
Adam: It does have side-effects.
Barbara: How do you know?
Adam: Because I know of an experiment in which they found side-effects.

This scenario presents strong prior belief (i.e., strongly believe), a positive belief (i.e., it does have side effects) and weak evidence (i.e., one experiment). There were several versions of this scenario, some involving a weak prior belief, negative belief (i.e., does not have side effects) or 50 experiments rather than one. Participants decided how strongly Barbara should now believe the conclusion that the drug has side effects.

All three factors had the predicted effects (see Figure 14.13). Argument strength was regarded as greater when the prior belief was positive rather than

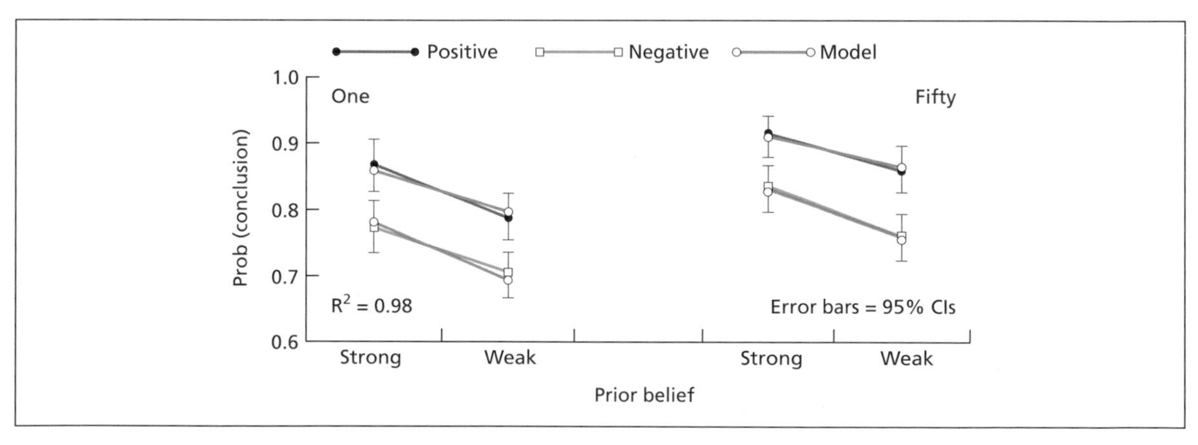

Figure 14.13
Mean acceptance ratings of arguments as a function of prior belief (weak vs. strong), amount of evidence (1 vs. 50 experiments) and whether the arguments are positive or negative. From a study by Oaksford and Hahn (2004), discussed in Hahn and Oaksford (2007). The predictions of their model are shown with green lines.

From Hahn and Oaksford (2007). © American Psychological Association.

KEY TERM

Slippery slope argument
The claim that an innocuous first step will lead to an undesirable outcome; sometimes regarded as a fallacy.

negative, when it was strong rather than weak and when the evidence was strong rather than weak. Thus, participants' ratings of argument strength took account of the strength and nature of Barbara's beliefs prior to receiving new evidence and were also influenced appropriately by the strength of the new evidence.

Figure 14.13 also shows the excellent fit to the data of a model based on the Bayesian approach. This approach (also discussed in Chapter 13 and later in this chapter) emphasises the notion that the subjective probabilities associated with our beliefs based on our knowledge and experience are altered (increased or decreased) by new evidence. As predicted by this approach, factors such as the strength of prior belief and strength of the evidence have a major impact on subjective probabilities.

Within the framework of traditional reasoning research, several types of arguments were identified as "fallacies". For example, consider the **slippery slope argument** in which it is argued a fairly small first step will lead to a chain of events producing an undesirable outcome. One such argument (from Corner et al., 2011) is as follows: "If voluntary euthanasia is legalised, then in the future there will be more cases of 'medical murder'."

According to the Bayesian approach, we should not reject all slippery slope arguments. Such arguments vary in strength, with strong arguments being regarded as more persuasive than weak ones. From within this approach, two important factors determine argument strength: (1) the probability of the negative outcome; (2) how negative the outcome would be. Thus, strong slippery slope arguments are those in which the negative outcome is both highly probable and very undesirable.

Corner et al. (2011) tested the above predictions using various topics, including the legalisation of euthanasia and the introduction of ID cards. The findings showed the two factors identified as important within the Bayesian approach both influenced the assessment of argument strength (see Figure 14.14).

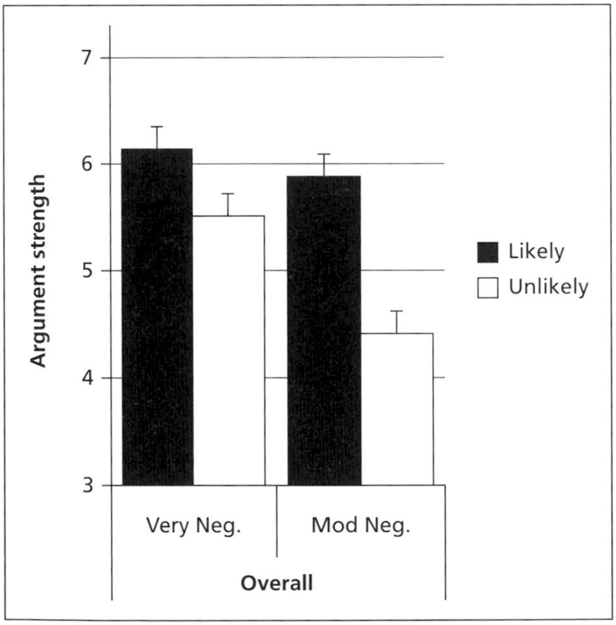

Figure 14.14
Mean rated argument strength as a function of the probability of the outcome (likely vs. unlikely) and how negative the outcome would be (very negative vs. moderately negative).
From Corner et al. (2011). With permission from Elsevier.

Evaluation

Informal reasoning is far more important than deductive reasoning in everyday life. It has been clearly established that motivational factors (e.g., myside biases) play a major role in informal reasoning. The Bayesian approach based on the assumption that *prior* subjective probabilities are modified by new information to produce *posterior* subjective probabilities provides a very useful framework within which to understand human informal reasoning. It is also applicable to research using deductive reasoning problems. Several factors (e.g., strength of prior beliefs, strength of evidence) influencing the rated strength of informal arguments have been identified. In addition, Hahn and Oaksford (2007) found a Bayesian model predicted informal reasoning performance very well (see Figure 14.13).

What are the limitations of the Bayesian approach? Bowers and Davis (2012) argued that the Bayesian approach is too flexible and thus hard to falsify. For example, there is often no precise assessment of the strength of prior beliefs.

Griffiths et al. (2012) replied that we must consider the distinction between a theoretical framework and specific models. The Bayesian approach is a general theoretical framework, and frameworks are not falsifiable. However, many specific Bayesian models have been proposed, and such models are readily falsifiable. Harris et al. (2012) studied the *ad hominem* argument (disregarding a proposition because of the negative characteristics of the person putting if forward). They measured the factors deemed crucial by Bayesian theorists and obtained good support for the Bayesian approach with precise quantitative tests of it.

Another limitation is that relatively little has been discovered about individual differences in informal reasoning ability. Sá et al. (2005) found unsophisticated reasoning was more common among those of lower cognitive ability. However the details of what is involved are unclear.

ARE HUMANS RATIONAL?

Much research discussed in this chapter and the previous two seems to indicate human thinking and reasoning are often inadequate. It is apparently the case that most people are simply *not* rational in their thinking. For example, we fail to solve fairly simple problems (e.g., on Frederick's Cognitive Reflection Test), we often ignore base-rate information when making judgements, 90% of people produce the wrong answer on the Wason selection task and we are very prone to belief bias in syllogistic reasoning.

Research activity:
Cognitive Reflection Test

The above findings apparently reveal a paradox. Most people (but not all!) cope reasonably well with the problems and challenges of everyday life and yet seem irrational and illogical when given thinking and reasoning problems in the laboratory. However, that overstates the differences between everyday life and the laboratory. Our everyday thinking is less rational and effective than we like to believe and our thinking and reasoning in the laboratory are less inadequate than is often supposed.

Why human reasoning is not limited

There are several reasons why many apparent inadequacies and limitations of human thinking and reasoning should *not* be taken at face value. First, it is often misleading to describe people's use of heuristics as "errors". Heuristics allow us to make rapid, reasonably accurate, judgements and decisions. As Maule and Hodgkinson (2002, p. 71) pointed out:

> Often . . . people have to judge situations or objects that change over time, making it inappropriate to expend a good deal of time to make a precise judgment . . . an approximate judgment based on a simpler, less effortful heuristic may be much more appropriate.

Second, performance on tasks is often poor because it is unclear *which* information is important. On many judgement problems, people ignore base-rate information because its relevance is not explicit. When problems are reworded so people can use their intuitive causal knowledge to understand why base-rate

KEY TERM

Dunning–Kruger effect
The finding that less skilled individuals overestimate their abilities more than those who are more skilled.

information is relevant, their performance is much better (e.g., Krynski & Tenenbaum, 2007).

Third, many so-called "errors" in human decision making only appear as such when we think of people operating in a social vacuum. As we saw in Chapter 13, the decisions that people make are often influenced by *accountability* – the need to justify those decisions to others.

Fourth, "errors" on deductive reasoning problems often mostly reflect the artificiality of such problems. For example, the validity of the conclusions on syllogistic reasoning problems does not depend on whether they are believable or unbelievable. It is hard to think of real-world situations requiring reasoning in which background knowledge is totally irrelevant.

Laboratory deductive reasoning tasks are also artificial in that conclusions are definitely valid or invalid. In contrast, reasoning in everyday life nearly always involves varying levels of probability rather than certainties.

Thus, performance on many judgement and reasoning tasks *underestimates* people's ability to think effectively. However, we must beware of the temptation to go further and claim that *all* our difficulties stem from inadequacies in the problems themselves or because the problems fail to motivate people (see below).

Why human reasoning is limited

There are several reasons for believing human reasoning is limited. Here we will briefly consider five such reasons.

First, Camerer and Hogarth (1999) reviewed 74 studies concerned with the effects of motivation on thinking and reasoning. The provision of incentives rarely led to improved performance, suggesting poor motivation is not responsible for people's low levels of performance.

Second, poor performance is sometimes due to limitations within the participants rather than the problems themselves. For example, Brase et al. (2006) used a complex judgement task involving use of base-rate information. Students from a leading university were much more likely than those from a second-tier university (40% vs. 19%) to produce the correct answer.

Third, many participants fail to solve problems even when strenuous steps are taken to ensure they fully understand them. For example, Tversky and Kahneman (1983) studied the conjunction fallacy (see Chapter 13). Participants decided from a description of Linda whether it was more likely she was a feminist bank teller than that she was a bank teller. There was still a strong (although somewhat reduced) conjunction fallacy when the category of bank teller was made explicit: "Linda is a bank teller whether or not she is active in the feminist movement."

Fourth, we would expect experts to interpret problems correctly and avoid cognitive biases in their thinking. In fact, medical experts make biased judgements and decisions (e.g., Redelmeier et al., 1995; Schwartz et al., 2004).

Fifth, there is the **Dunning–Kruger effect**: "those who are incompetent . . . have little insight into their incompetence" (Dunning, 2011, p. 260). Individuals largely unaware of their own thinking mistakes are unlikely to show much improvement over time and so continue to exhibit signs of "irrationality".

Why does the Dunning–Kruger effect exist? Evaluating the correctness of one's own responses on cognitively demanding tasks often requires very similar

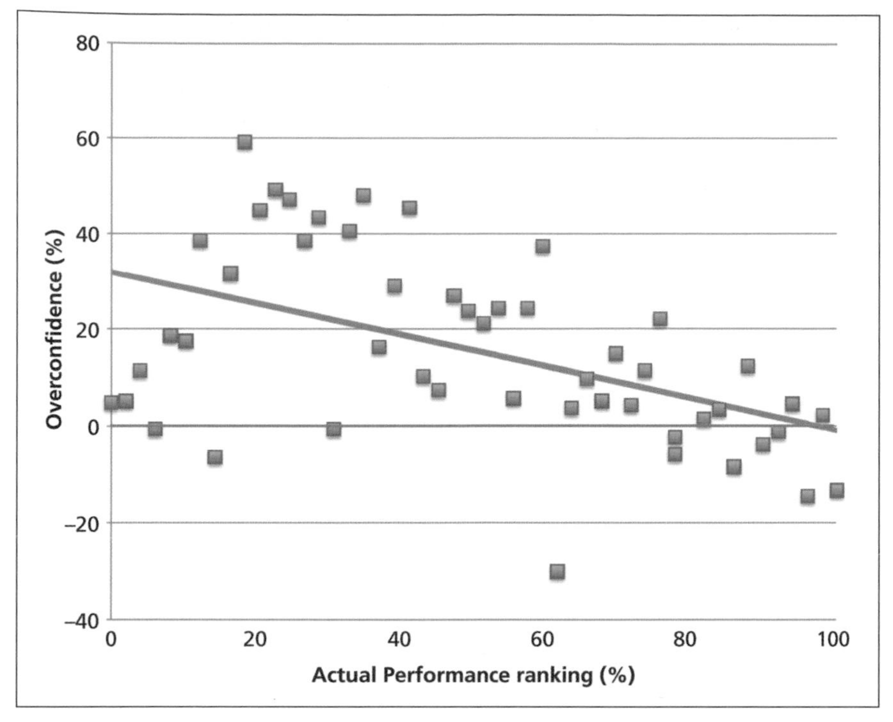

Figure 14.15
Overconfidence (%) as a function of actual performance (increasing from left to right on the horizontal axis) shown by the blue line. The green line indicates the absence of overconfidence or underconfidence. Each square represents an individual player.
From Simons (2013). With kind permission from Springer Science + Business Media.

knowledge and expertise to those necessary to produce the correct responses in the first place. The effect can be dramatic. Dunning (2011) considered an experiment of his on the Wason selection task (discussed earlier). Some participants used the same *correct* rule across different versions of this task and so had a success rate of 100%. Other participants used the same *incorrect* rule consistently, and so had a 0% success rate. Both groups thought they had solved between 80 and 90% of the problems correctly!

Simons (2013) found the Dunning–Kruger effect is unexpectedly robust. Bridge players were given feedback about their performance following each session at a bridge club. In spite of that, weaker players still overestimated their future performance (see Figure 14.15).

What is rationality?

Deciding whether humans are rational depends on how we define "rationality". A very popular viewpoint (championed by Piaget, Wason and many others) used to be that rational thought is governed by logic. It follows that deductive reasoning (which seems to require logical thinking) is very relevant for assessing human rationality. Sadly, most people perform relatively poorly on complex deductive reasoning tasks. As a result, humans are not very rational if we define rationality as reasoning according to the rules of logic.

KEY TERM

Normativism
The notion that human thinking should be regarded as "correct" or "incorrect", depending on how closely it follows certain norms or standards (e.g., those of classical logic).

The approach discussed above is an example of **normativism**. Normativism "is the idea that human thinking reflects a normative system [one conforming to norms or standards] against which it should be measured and judged" (Elqayam & Evans, 2011, p. 233). Thus, human thinking is "correct" if it conforms to classical logic but "incorrect" otherwise.

There are serious doubts as to whether logic (and deductive reasoning) provide a suitable normative system against which to evaluate human thinking. Why is that? As Sternberg (2011, p. 270) pointed out, "Few problems of consequence in our lives had a deductive or even any meaningful kind of 'correct' solution. Try to think of three, or even one!"

An alternative (and preferable) approach is that human rationality involves effective use of probabilities rather than logic. This makes sense (and can be regarded as rational) given that we live in a world typically characterised by uncertainty and imprecise information rather than the certainties of logic.

Oaksford and Chater (e.g., 2009) put forward an influential probabilistic approach to human reasoning. The emphasis in this approach is on probability (subjective degree of belief). The central hypothesis is that *prior* subjective probabilities are modified on the basis of new information to produce *posterior* subjective probabilities. This hypothesis originated in the work of the Rev. Thomas Bayes (see Chapter 13). It has received support from research in several areas including informal reasoning.

In what follows, we will address the following crucial question: *why* does actual human thinking and reasoning often fall short of the standards laid down by normative theories?

Bounded rationality

Herb Simon devoted much of his research career to the issue of human rationality (Heukelom, 2007). According to Simon (1945, p. 5), behaviour is rational, "in so far as it selects alternatives which are conductive to the achievement of the previously selected goals". Thus, for example, an individual's informal reasoning is rational if it achieves his/her goal of arguing persuasively, even if it differs from the experimenter's prior expectations (e.g., by demonstrating myside bias: see Glossary).

Simon (1957) argued that we possess bounded rationality (see Glossary). This means we produce workable solutions to problems in spite of limited processing ability by using various short-cut strategies (e.g., heuristics). More specifically, our thinking is "bounded" or constrained by the environment and constraints in the mind (e.g., limited attention, limited short-term memory).

What matters is the degree of fit or match between the mind and the environment. According to Simon (1990, p. 7), "Human rational behaviour is shaped like a scissors whose blades are the structure of task environments and the computational capabilities of the actor." If we consider only one of these two blades, we will have a partial understanding of human thinking.

In sum, many "errors" in human thinking are due to limited processing capacity rather than irrationality. As Stich (1990, p. 27) argued, "It seems simply perverse to judge that subjects are doing a bad job because they are not using a strategy that required a brain the size of a blimp [airship]."

Individual differences: intelligence

Even though *average* performance on most judgement, decision making and reasoning tasks is relatively poor, it is still possible highly intelligent individuals perform consistently well. That is only partially true (Stanovich, 2012). Students with high IQs perform better than those with lower IQs on many deductive reasoning tasks. However, there is often only a modest effect of intelligence on judgement tasks (e.g., framing problems, sunk-cost effect, omission bias). Nevertheless, Toplak et al. (2011) reported a correlation of +0.32 between cognitive ability and performance across 15 judgement and decision tasks.

How can we explain the impact of intelligence on thinking and reasoning? Stanovich (2012) answered this question within his tripartite model (see Figure 14.16), which extended previous dual-process models. At the bottom is Type 1 processing (e.g., use of heuristics) within the autonomous mind. It is rapid and fairly automatic. Above that is Type 2 processing (also called System 2 processing), which is slow and effortful.

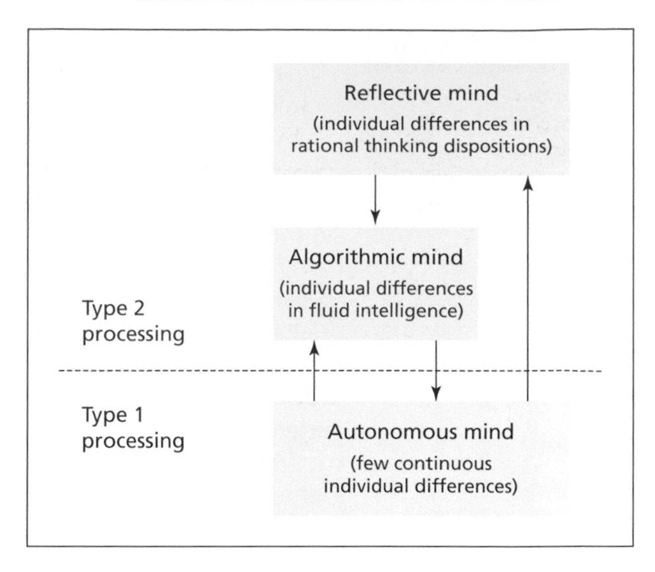

Figure 14.16
Stanovich's tripartite model of reasoning. According to the model, Type 1 processing within the autonomous mind is typically fast and fairly automatic. There are two major forms of Type 2 processing: (1) the algorithmic mind, which contains information about rules, strategies and procedures; and (2) the reflective mind, which makes use of the individual's goals and beliefs. Individual differences in reasoning are generally much greater with respect to the reflective mind and the algorithmic mind than the autonomous mind.

From Stanovich (2012). By permission of Oxford University Press.

Stanovich's (2012) model has two major novel features. First, there are two levels of cognitive control at the higher level. One consists of Type 2 or System 2 processes (the algorithmic mind). The algorithmic mind contains *mindware*, which consists of "the rules, knowledge, procedures, and strategies that a person can retrieve from memory in order to aid decision making and problem solving" (Stanovich, 2012, p. 355). The algorithmic mind can override the (often incorrect) heuristic responses generated by the autonomous mind.

Type 2 processes are *only* used when the individual realises they are necessary and has the necessary motivation to initiate them. The other level of control involves the reflective mind, which has access to the individual's goals, beliefs and general knowledge. It is involved in the decision whether or not to use Type 2 processes.

Second, the model considers the role of individual differences in intelligence. **Fluid intelligence** (which corresponds approximately to non-verbal reasoning ability) is of direct relevance to the functioning of the algorithmic mind. Individuals with high levels of fluid intelligence have a greater range of Type 2 processes and can use them more efficiently.

KEY TERM

Fluid intelligence
Non-verbal reasoning ability applied to novel problems.

Predictions

What follows from this tripartite theory? Of greatest importance, there are *three* different reasons why individuals produce incorrect responses when confronted by problems:

KEY TERM

Dysrationalia
The failure of reasonably intelligent individuals to think and reason in a rational way.

1. They may lack the appropriate mindware within the algorithmic mind to override incorrect heuristic responses.
2. They may have the necessary mindware but have insufficient processing capacity to override incorrect Type 1 processing.
3. They may have the necessary mindware but fail to use it because its use is not triggered by the reflective mind.

These theoretical ideas have direct relevance to the issue of human rationality. Stanovich (2009, p. 35) used the term **dysrationalia** to refer to "the inability to think and behave rationally despite having adequate intelligence". Why does this occur? Most people (including those with high IQs) are cognitive misers, preferring to solve problems with fast, easy strategies than with more accurate effortful ones.

The tendency to be a cognitive miser (and thus to make limited use of the reflective mind) can be assessed by the Cognitive Reflection Test (Frederick, 2005; see Chapter 12). Toplak et al. (2011) found low scorers on the Cognitive Reflection Test performed relatively poorly on many judgement and reasoning tasks.

Conclusions

Discussions of human rationality can become too philosophical and detached from empirical evidence. Accordingly, we will evaluate the theoretical views discussed earlier with respect to how they explain apparent failures of human rationality.

Theorists believing in human rationality have put forward several arguments to support their position. First, they argue that humans have limited processing capacity (Simon, 1957). This limited capacity (rather than deficient rationality) explains why people often think and reason in moderately effective but suboptimal ways.

Second, many theorists (e.g., Oaksford & Chater, 2009; Evans, 2012) argue that classical logic is an inappropriate normative system against which to evaluate human reasoning. In essence, classical logic is almost totally irrelevant to our everyday lives because it deals in certainties. Our lives involve constant uncertainties, and so it is unsurprising that we appear much more "rational" if our thinking and reasoning are evaluated against models of probabilistic thinking.

Third, it is often argued (e.g., Simon, 1945; Mercier & Sperber, 2011) that our thinking and reasoning are rational when used to achieve our goals (this is *instrumental* rationality). Thus, for example, we may appear irrational because we are influenced by wishful thinking (Thagard, 2011), by the desire to avoid losses (Kahneman & Tversky, 1979) or by the need to be accountable to others (Tetlock, 2002).

What are the arguments against human rationality? First, many humans are cognitive misers. In other words, even when they possess the necessary knowledge and skills to reason effectively, they often fail to do so and thus exhibit dysrationalia. Second, numerous studies indicate there is a widespread tendency on judgement tasks to de-emphasise base-rate information, which shows a failure to reason in conformity with Bayes' theorem. Third, people often fail to think rationally because they are unaware of limitations and errors in their thinking (the Dunning–Kruger effect).

Research activity:
Are humans rational?

CHAPTER SUMMARY

- **Introduction**. Inductive reasoning involves drawing general conclusions from statements referring to particular instances. These conclusions can never be shown to be definitely valid. Inductive reasoning is often applied to scientific hypotheses. Deductive reasoning allows us to draw conclusions that are definitely valid provided other statements are assumed to be true. Deductive reasoning problems owe their origins to formal logic. Deductive reasoning is of little relevance to everyday life. As a result, there has been a rapid increase in research on informal reasoning based on probabilities rather than formal logic.
- **Hypothesis testing**. Wason argued that performance was poor on his 2–4–6 task because people show confirmation bias. In fact, it is more accurate to claim people engage in confirmatory or positive testing. Positive testing works much better when hypotheses apply to a relatively small fraction of the entities in a domain than when they are much more general, as is the case on the 2–4–6 task. Scientists make extensive use of heuristics in the process of scientific discovery. They generally focus on confirmation rather than falsification of their hypotheses. However, they often change their theoretical assumptions if findings inconsistent with their hypotheses are obtained twice.
- **Deductive reasoning**. Performance is generally poor on conditional reasoning problems, which have their origins in propositional logic. Reasoners use their knowledge of the world on such problems to draw inferences, which often leads to logical "errors". With Wason's selection task, reasoners typically perform poorly unless the rule is deontic rather than indicative or they are motivated to disprove the rule. Syllogistic reasoning is based on propositional logic. Performance is often poor because reasoners interpret problems differently from the dictates of logic and also use their knowledge of the world.
- **Theories of deductive reasoning**. According to Johnson-Laird's mental model theory, people form mental models representing what is common to a set of possibilities. As predicted, reasoners often reduce the load on working memory by forming mental models representing explicitly only what is true. There is much less search for counterexamples than assumed by the theory, the processes involved in forming mental models are underspecified and the theory is somewhat narrow in scope.

  According to Evans' heuristic–analytic theory, heuristic processes are used to construct a single mental model and effortful analytic processes may be used subsequently to revise or replace it. This theory is based on the singularity, relevance and satisficing principles and attaches less importance than mental model theory to deductive reasoning. There is substantial evidence to support the theory's predictions, and it helps to explain individual differences in reasoning performance. However, the notion there is serial processing with analytic processes following heuristic ones may well be oversimplified.

- **Brain systems in reasoning**. Neuroimaging studies of reasoning often produce apparently inconsistent findings. However, the situation is becoming clearer. Each type of deductive reasoning problem produces its own pattern of brain activation. In addition, different reasoning strategies are associated with different patterns of activation. Finally, research assessing when different brain areas are activated makes it easier to interpret the brain activity associated with reasoning.
- **Informal reasoning**. Informal reasoning involves use of the individual's knowledge and experience and the content of arguments and contextual factors are important. Motivational factors are often important, with individuals seeking support for their previous beliefs. The Bayesian approach, based on the assumption that new information changes the probabilities of various beliefs, provides a more adequate theoretical approach than the traditional approach based on binary logic.
- **Are humans rational?** Human rationality is greater than appears to be the case on many thinking and reasoning tasks. Apparent "failures" of rationality often occur because people have limited processing capacity or the goals for which they strive differ from those expected by the experimenter. Other "failures" occur when human reasoning is compared against the dictates of classical logic, which is of negligible usefulness in everyday life. However, human reasoning is often deficient because we have limited awareness of our own cognitive incompetence. Human rationality involves effective use of probabilities rather than logic. We possess bounded rationality, which allows us to produce workable solutions to problems in spite of limited processing ability. More intelligent individuals perform better than less intelligent ones on reasoning (especially deductive reasoning) tasks. However, some intelligent individuals fail to think rationally because they are cognitive misers who are economical with the effort they exert on reasoning problems.

Further reading

- De Neys, W. & Osman, M. (eds) (2013). *New approaches in reasoning research*. Hove: Psychology Press. Leading experts indicate how reasoning research has broadened and deepened in recent years.
- Evans, J.St.B.T. (2012). Questions and challenges for the new psychology of reasoning. *Thinking & Reasoning*, 18: 5–31. This article by Jonathan Evans provides an excellent account of the recent major changes in theorising about human reasoning.
- Hahn, U. & Oaksford, M. (2014). *The fallacies explained*. Oxford: Oxford University Press. Ulrike Hahn and Mike Oaksford provide a very informative account of the processes involved in informal reasoning.
- Halpern, D.F. (2013). *Thought and knowledge: An introduction to critical thinking* (5th edn). New York: Psychology Press. Diane Halpern discusses deductive and informal reasoning and focuses on ways of enhancing these reasoning abilities.
- Manktelow, K. (2012). *Thinking and reasoning: An introduction to the psychology of reason, judgement and decision making*. Hove: Psychology Press. Chapters 2–6 of this introductory textbook provide extensive coverage of the main topics in reasoning.
- Mercier, H. & Sperber, D. (2011). Why do humans reason? Arguments for an argumentative theory. *Behavioral and Brain Sciences*, 34: 57–111. The central theme of this article is that human reasoning is designed to persuade others rather than establish what is true.
- Schaeken, W., De Vooght, G., Vandierendonck, A. & d'Ydewalle, G. (eds) (2014). *Deductive reasoning and strategies*. Hove: Psychology Press. This edited book focuses on the variety of strategies individuals use on deductive reasoning problems.
- Stanovich, K.E. (2012). On the distinction between rationality and intelligence: Implications for understanding individual differences in reasoning. In K.J. Holyoak & R.G. Morrison (eds). *The Oxford handbook of thinking and reasoning*. Oxford: Oxford University Press. Keith Stanovich discusses key issues relating to human rationality with reference to research on individual differences.

Broadening horizons

PART

V

One of the most refreshing developments within cognitive psychology in recent years has been a broadening of its horizons. In this section of the book, we consider two of the most important manifestations of that broadening. First, there is the issue of the ways in which emotion and mood are related to human cognition (Chapter 15). Second, there is the issue of consciousness (Chapter 16).

It is appropriate to place these two topics at the end of the book, because both are relevant to most topics within cognitive psychology. Emotional factors influence our perception, our memory, our interpretation of language and our decision making. In addition, many cognitive processes influence our current mood state. So far as consciousness is concerned, distinguishing between conscious and unconscious processes is important when studying almost any aspect of human cognition.

COGNITION AND EMOTION

The origins of the notion that our emotional states are determined in part by our cognitions go back at least as far as Aristotle over two thousand years ago. Aristotle (who may have been the cleverest person who ever lived) had this to say: "Let fear, then, be a kind of pain or disturbance resulting from the imagination of impending danger" (quoted by Power & Dalgleish, 2008, p. 35). The key word in that sentence is "imagining" – how much fear we experience depends on our expectations. Aristotle developed this point: "Those in great prosperity . . . would not expect to suffer; nor those who reckon they have already suffered everything terrible and are numbed as regards the future, such as those who are actually being crucified" (quoted by Power & Dalgleish, 2008, p. 35).

Aristotle emphasised the impact of cognitions on emotion. In addition, however, there is compelling evidence that emotional states influence many cognitive processes, as we will see in Chapter 15. However, it has proved hard to predict the circumstances in which such effects will occur.

Finally, note that some research on emotion and cognition has already been discussed in this book. For example, emotional states can have a substantial effect on eyewitness testimony and autobiographical memory (Chapter 8) and can impair decision making (Chapter 13).

KEY TERM

Introspection
A careful examination and description of one's own mental thoughts.

CONSCIOUSNESS

The topic of consciousness did not fare well during most of the twentieth century. As is well-known, the behaviourists such as John Watson argued strongly that the concept of "consciousness" should be eliminated from psychology. He was also scathing about the value of **introspection**, which involves an examination and description of one's own internal thoughts. Consider, however, this quotation from Watson (1920): "The present writer has felt that a good deal more can be learned about the psychology of thinking by making subjects think aloud about definite problems, than by trusting to the unscientific method of introspection." This quotation is somewhat bizarre given that "thinking aloud" is essentially synonymous with introspection! Watson's view was that thinking aloud is acceptable because it can simply be regarded as verbal behaviour.

It is increasingly accepted that consciousness is an extremely important topic. In that connection, the first author remembers clearly a conversation with Endel Tulving in the late 1980s. Tulving said one criterion he used when evaluating a textbook on cognitive psychology was the amount of coverage of consciousness. Reference back to the fourth edition of this textbook revealed consciousness was discussed on only two out of 525 pages of text. Accordingly, that edition clearly failed the Tulving test! The burgeoning research in consciousness was reflected in an increase to 22 pages in the sixth edition.

Cognitive psychologists in recent decades have carried out numerous studies showing the importance of unconscious processes. For example, subliminal perception and blindness are discussed in Chapter 2, automatic processes are analysed in Chapter 5, implicit memory is dealt with in Chapter 7 and the potential importance of unconscious thinking in decision making is discussed in Chapter 13. Such research has increased interest in studying consciousness – if some processes are conscious and others are unconscious, we clearly need to identify the crucial differences between them.

Finally, several concepts used by cognitive psychologists are clearly of much relevance to consciousness. Examples include many theoretical ideas about attention (Chapter 5), controlled processing in the Shiffrin and Schneider (1977) theory (Chapter 5) and the central executive of Baddeley's working memory system (Chapter 6).

Cognition and emotion

CHAPTER

15

INTRODUCTION

Cognitive psychology is still somewhat influenced by the computer analogy or metaphor (although much less than used to be the case) as can be seen in the emphasis on information-processing models. This approach does not lend itself to an examination of the relationship between cognition and emotion because it is hard to think of computers as having emotional states.

Most cognitive psychologists ignore the effects of emotion on cognition by trying to ensure their participants are in a neutral emotional state. However, there has been a substantial increase in research in the area of emotion and cognition. Examples include research on everyday memory (Chapter 8) and decision making (Chapter 13).

Two issues are central to cognition and emotion. First, how do cognitive processes influence our emotional experience? Second, how does emotion influence cognitive processes? For example, how does any emotion influence learning and memory? In other words, we need to consider the effects of cognition on emotion and those of emotion on cognition.

We will discuss four major topics in this chapter. First, we consider how our emotional experience is influenced by our cognitive appraisals or interpretations of our current situation. Second, we move on to a broader discussion of issues relating to emotion regulation. Emotion regulation is concerned with the processes (mostly deliberate) involved in *managing* our emotions and so allowing us to be relatively happy and to achieve our goals.

Third, we consider the effects of emotion on cognition. As we will see, emotional states influence attention, memory, judgement and decision making. Of practical and theoretical importance, each emotional state produces a different pattern of effects.

Fourth, we discuss various cognitive biases (e.g., a tendency to interpret ambiguous situations in a threatening way) associated with anxiety and depression in healthy individuals and clinical patients. A key issue is whether cognitive biases influence the *development* of anxiety and depression or whether they are merely a *consequence* of being anxious or depressed. We will address this issue by considering research designed to reduce or eliminate these biases. Such research has high societal relevance.

KEY TERM

Valence
The positive or negative character of emotional experience.

Emotion, mood and affect

A distinction is often drawn between emotions and moods. How do they differ? First, emotions typically last for less time. Second, emotions are more intense than moods and so are more likely to attract our attention. Third, emotions are generally caused by a specific event (e.g., passing an exam), whereas the reason for being in a given mood is often unclear.

In spite of these differences, emotions can create moods and moods can turn into emotions. Thus, there is no sharp distinction between them. In what follows, we often use the broader term *affect*, which encompasses both emotions and moods. Positive affect refers to positive emotions and moods and negative affect refers to negative emotions and moods. The term **valence** refers to a dimension running from very negative to very positive affect.

Structure of emotions

There has been controversy concerning the structure of emotions. There are two main schools of thought (Fox, 2008). Some theorists (e.g., Izard, 2007) argue that we should adopt a *categorical* approach, according to which there are several distinct emotions such as happiness, anger, fear, disgust and sadness. This approach probably fits your subjective experience.

Other theorists prefer a *dimensional* approach. Barrett and Russell (1998) argued for two uncorrelated dimensions of misery–pleasure (valence) and arousal–sleep. In contrast, Watson and Tellegen (1985) favoured two uncorrelated dimensions of positive and negative affect. In spite of their apparent differences, both approaches refer to the same two-dimensional space (see Figure 15.1).

There is much support for the dimensional approach. Watson and Tellegen (1985) analysed the data from several self-report measures of mood. They found 50–65% of the variance in the data was accounted for by dimensions of negative and positive affect. Baucom et al. (2012) had participants view numerous emotional pictures. The patterns of brain activity were consistent with the assumption of independent arousal and valence dimensions.

How can we reconcile the categorical and dimensional approaches? First, most emotional states fit within the two-dimensional space shown in Figure 15.1. Emotions such as *happy* and *excited* fall in the top-right quadrant, *contented*, *relaxed* and *calm* are in the bottom-right quadrant, *depressed* and *bored* are in the bottom-left quadrant and *stressed* and *tense* are in the top-left quadrant.

Second, our ability to move beyond the dimensions of arousal and valence to experience specific emotions depends largely on various

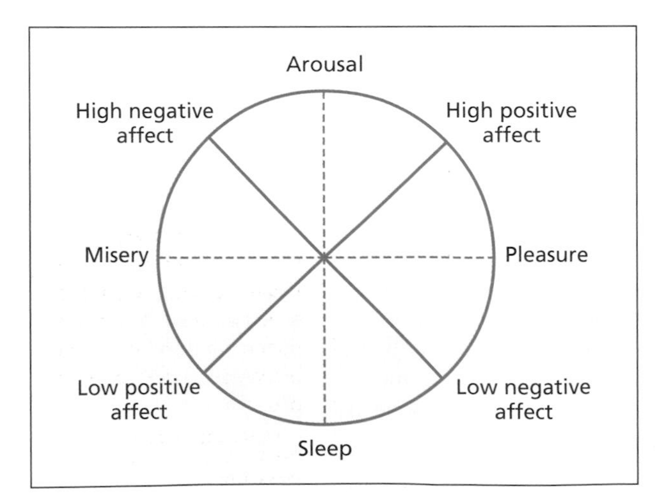

Figure 15.1
The two-dimensional framework for emotion showing the two dimensions of pleasure–misery and arousal–sleep (Barrett & Russell, 1998) and the two dimensions of positive affect and negative affect (Watson & Tellegen, 1985).

Based on Barrett and Russell (1998). © American Psychological Association.

cognitive processes. In a meta-analysis (see Glossary) of neuroimaging studies, Lindquist et al. (2012) found areas associated with attentional processes, language and long-term memory were activated across several emotions.

Convincing evidence of the importance of language to emotion perception was reported by Lindquist et al. (2014). They studied patients with semantic dementia, a condition involving substantial impairments of concept knowledge (see Chapter 7). These patients viewed photographs of faces showing anger, sadness, fear, disgust, happiness or a neutral expression and were instructed to sort them into meaningful piles. The patients distinguished clearly between positive and negative emotions. However, they showed little ability to discriminate among the four negative emotions even though the task did not require the use of language. The findings suggest that emotion perception involves core affect (i.e., positive vs. negative valence) plus a more specific categorisation based on language.

Bottom-up and top-down processes

Emotional experience depends on bottom-up (or stimulus-driven) processes involving attention and perception. It also depends on top-down processes involving appraisal of the situation drawing on stored knowledge of similar situations. Ochsner et al. (2009) used brain imaging to explore these two processes. In the bottom-up condition, participants were presented with aversive photographs and told to respond naturally to the images. In the top-down condition, participants were told to interpret neutral photographs as if they were aversive.

What did Ochsner et al. (2009) find? The answer is shown in Figure 15.2. The brain areas activated in the bottom-up condition included those in the occipital,

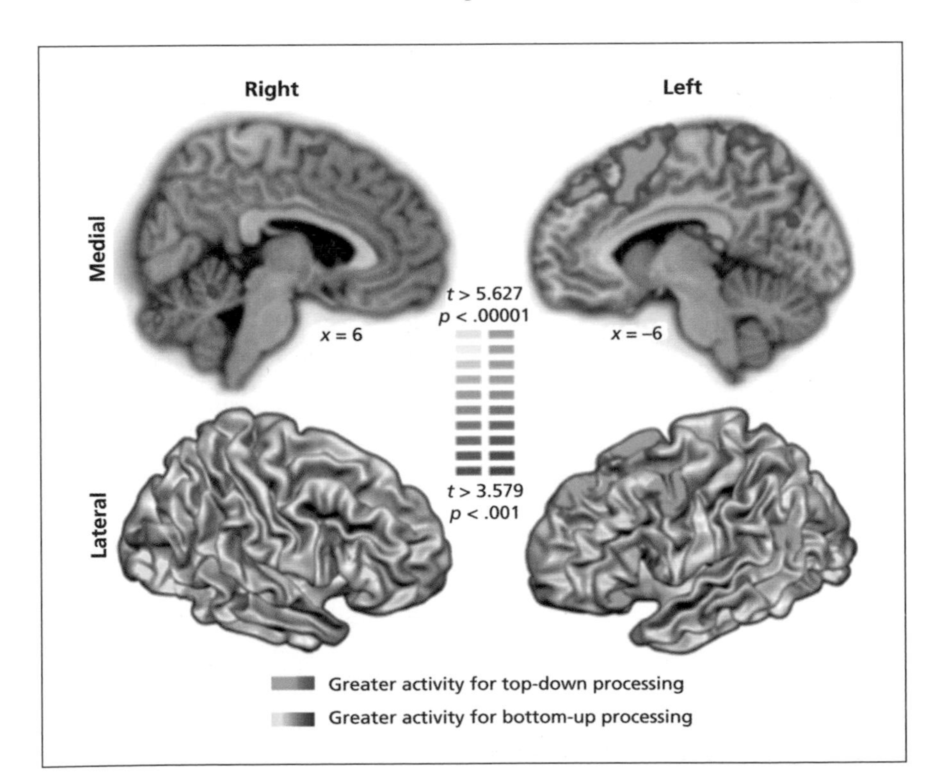

Figure 15.2
Brain areas showing greater activity for top-down than for bottom-up processing (shades of blue) and those showing greater activity for bottom-up than for top-down processes (shades of yellow and red).

From Ochsner et al. (2009). Reprinted by permission of SAGE Publications.

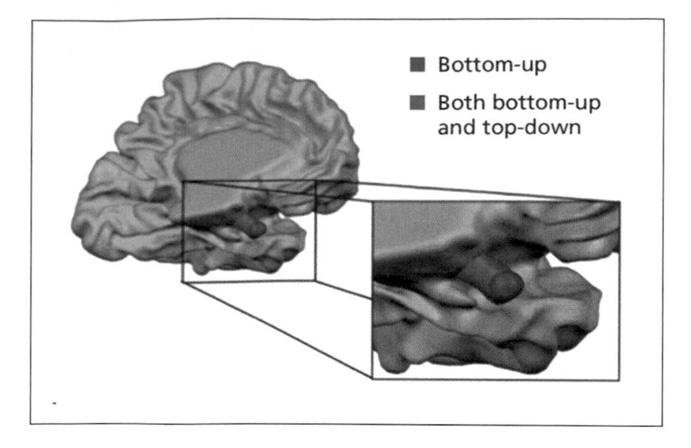

Figure 15.3
Amygdala activation during bottom-up (red) and both bottom-up and top-down (blue) emotional processing.
From Ochsner et al. (2009). Reprinted by permission of SAGE Publications.

temporal and parietal lobes associated with visual perceptual processing. In addition, there was a high level of activation within the **amygdala** (see Figure 15.3). This is a structure located deep within the temporal lobe. Self-reported negative affect was associated most closely with amygdala activation.

Somewhat different areas were activated in the top-down condition. Top-down processing involved the dorsolateral prefrontal cortex and medial prefrontal cortex, areas associated with high-level cognitive processes. The anterior cingulate and amygdala were also activated. Self-reported negative affect was associated most strongly with activation of the medial prefrontal cortex (associated with producing cognitive representations of stimulus meaning).

Inhibitory control is one of the most important top-down processes in human cognition (see Chapter 5). Individuals with good inhibitory control showed smaller increases in anger and anxiety than those with poor control when those emotions were induced (Tang & Schmeichel, 2014). Thus, inhibitory control is a top-down process that can reduce the experience of negative emotional states.

In sum, there are substantial differences between bottom-up and top-down processes in emotion. Many theories (e.g., appraisal theories) emphasise the role of top-down processes in emotional experience. In considering the factors causing emotional experience, we must not neglect the role of bottom-up processes. Note that the distinction between bottom-up and top-down processes oversimplifies a complex reality and that there may be other, intermediate processes as well (Viviani, 2013).

APPRAISAL THEORIES

Cognitive processes influence *when* we experience emotional states and *what* emotional state we experience in any given situation. The most important of these cognitive processes involve *appraisal* of the situation. According to Brosch (2013, p. 370), appraisal theories assume "emotional responses are elicited as the organism evaluates the relevance of environmental changes for its well-being".

There are more appraisal theories than you can shake a stick at. However, most assume each emotion is elicited by its own specific and distinctive appraisal pattern, and thus top-down processes play a crucial role. Scherer and Ellsworth (2009) identified possible appraisal profiles for major emotions. For example, you experience anger if you blame someone else for the current situation and you appraise the situation as one offering you control and power. In contrast, you experience sadness if you appraise the situation as one permitting very little control or power.

Appraisal theories typically assume appraisal is the most important determinant of emotional states. They also assume appraisal often leads to other components of emotion (e.g., bodily sensations, action tendencies). However, other theories assign a less crucial role to appraisal (Moors & Scherer, 2013).

KEY TERM

Amygdala
A part of the brain strongly associated with several emotions including fear; it is located towards the front of the temporal lobe.

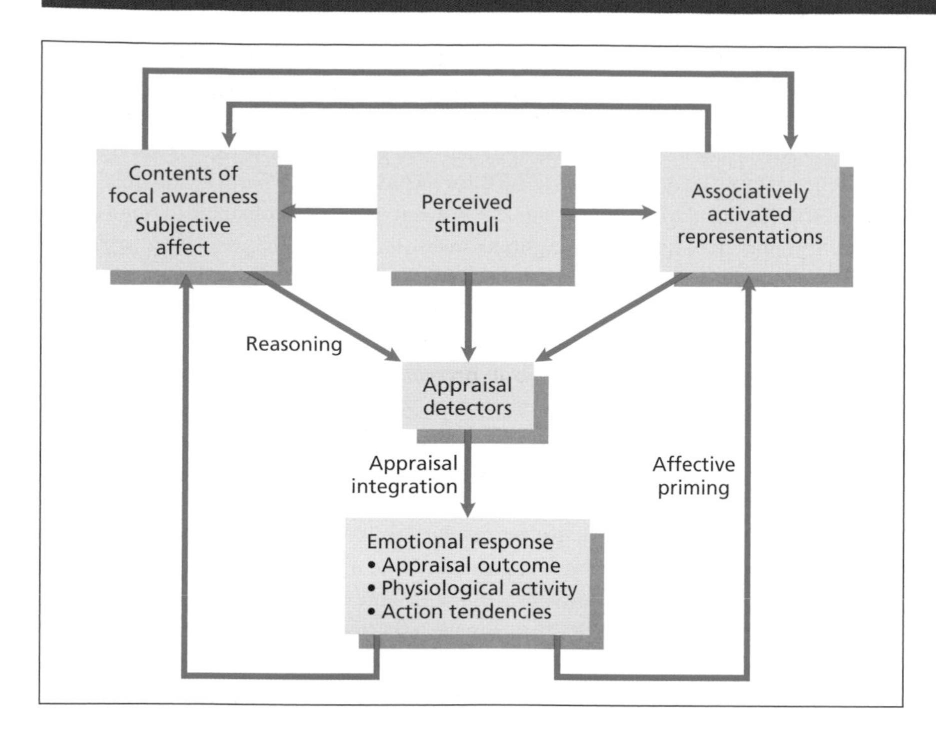

Figure 15.4
Mechanisms involved in the appraisal process.
From Smith and Kirby (2001). By permission of Oxford University Press.

Fontaine et al. (2013) tested the centrality of appraisal to emotion. Participants from 27 countries indicated for various emotion words the probability with which features of appraisal and other components of emotion would apply to someone experiencing each emotion. Emotions were correctly classified solely on the basis of appraisal features in 71% of cases. All other components (e.g., bodily sensations, motor expressions, action tendencies) improved classification accuracy only slightly. These findings suggest appraisal is vitally important in determining emotional states.

So far it may seem appraisal always involves deliberate conscious processing. However, most theorists argue that appraisal can also occur *automatically* without conscious awareness. Smith and Kirby (2001, 2009) distinguished between appraisal based on reasoning (involving deliberate thinking) and appraisal based on activation of memories (involving automatic processes) (see Figure 15.4). Appraisal based on reasoning is slower and more flexible.

Findings: conscious appraisals

Most research has used scenarios in which participants identify with the central character. These scenarios differ in the appraisals to which they give rise and the emotional experiences they generate. One scenario used by Smith and Lazarus (1993) involved a student who had performed poorly in an examination. Participants reported he would experience anger when he blamed the unhelpful teaching assistants but guilt when he blamed himself (e.g., for doing work at the last minute). These findings are predicted by the appraisal approach.

Smith and Lazarus (1993) found appraisal manipulations generally had the predicted effects on participants' emotional states. However, Parkinson (2001) was unimpressed by their findings. He pointed out that under 30% of the variance in emotion ratings was accounted for by participants' appraisal manipulations.

Any given emotion can result from several different combinations of appraisals. Kuppens et al. (2003) studied four appraisals (goal obstacle; other accountability: someone else is to blame; unfairness; and control) relevant to anger. No appraisal component was essential for the experience of anger in recently experienced unpleasant situations. Thus, for example, some participants felt angry *without* the appraisal of unfairness or the presence of a goal obstacle. Tong (2010) studied four negative emotions (anger, sadness, fear and guilt). No *single* appraisal (or combination of appraisals) was necessary or sufficient for the experience of any emotional state.

Much research (including that of Smith and Lazarus (1993)) has involved manipulated situations and appraisals at the same time. As a result, it is often hard to know whether participants' emotional reactions occurred *directly* as a response to situations or *indirectly* as a response to appraisals. Siemer et al. (2007) used a *single* situation in which the experimenter's behaviour towards the participants was rude, condescending and very critical. Afterwards, participants gave emotion ratings on six emotions and five appraisals (e.g., controllability, other-responsibility, self-responsibility). The key finding was that appraisals predicted the intensity of the various emotions. For example, the appraisal of personal control was negatively associated with guilt, shame and sadness but not anger.

Participants are typically presented with hypothetical scenarios and so experience little genuine emotion. Bennett and Lowe (2008) rectified this by having hospital nurses identify their most stressful work-related incident experienced recently. Anger and frustration were the emotions most strongly experienced. The emotions were predicted reasonably well by the nurses' appraisals of the stressful situations. The exception was sadness, perhaps because it is often used very generally to refer to negative emotional experience.

The appraisal approach can explain some individual differences in emotional reactions to a given situation. In one study (Ceulemans et al., 2012) participants read brief scenarios (e.g., "A friend spreads gossip about you") and indicated the appraisals they would make. Individual differences in the amount of anger triggered by the scenarios depended on two factors: (1) the appraisals activated by each scenario; and (2) the specific pattern of appraisal components necessary for the individual to experience anger.

Most research reports associations or correlations between cognitive appraisals and emotional states and so cannot shed direct light on causality. If appraisals cause emotions (rather than emotions causing appraisals), appraisal judgements should be made *faster* than emotion judgements. In fact, however, appraisal judgements are generally made *slower* (Siemer & Reisenzein, 2007). However, it is possible that appraisal judgements are made very rapidly and automatically, but that it is time-consuming to make explicit appraisal judgements. Siemer and Reisenzein (2007) obtained some support for this viewpoint.

We can decide whether appraisals help to cause emotional states by *manipulating* people's cognitive appraisals when individuals are confronted by emotional stimuli. These manipulations should influence experienced emotion. Schartau et al. (2009) used this approach. Participants viewed films of humans and animals experiencing marked distress. Some participants received training in positive cognitive appraisal (e.g., "silver lining: there are usually some good aspects to every situation" (p. 19)). This training reduced horror, distress and physiological arousal as indexed by the galvanic skin response (see Figure 15.5).

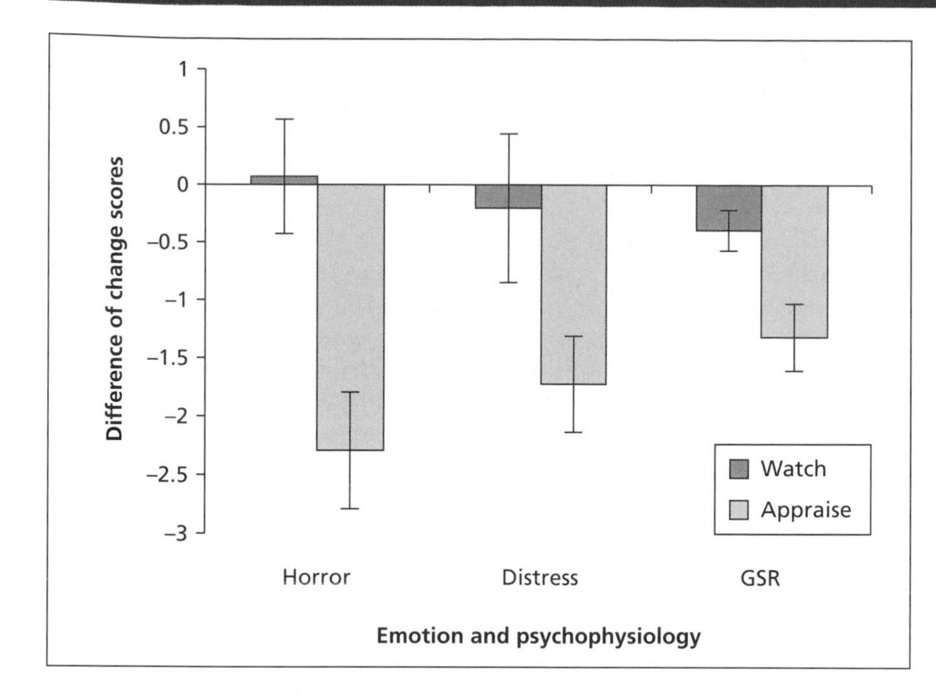

Figure 15.5
Changes in self-reported horror and distress and in galvanic skin response (GSR) between pre-training and post-training for individuals instructed to simply watch the films (watch condition) and those training in positive cognitive appraisal (appraisal condition).

From Schartau et al. (2009). © American Psychological Association.

Similar research has focused on interpretive bias (the tendency to interpret ambiguous situations as threatening). The existence of interpretive bias (discussed more fully later) in anxious individuals suggests their appraisals are unduly negative. We could show such appraisals influence emotional reactions by using training to reduce interpretive bias. As predicted, there are generally reductions in experienced anxiety (Mathews, 2012; see later in chapter).

Weblink:
Appraisal article

Findings: non-conscious emotional processing

Processes below the level of conscious awareness can produce emotional reactions. For example, consider a study by Öhman and Soares (1994). They presented snake and spider phobics with pictures of snakes, spiders, flowers and mushrooms so rapidly they could not be identified consciously. The spider phobics reacted emotionally to the spider pictures, as did the snake phobics to the snake pictures. More specifically, there were greater physiological responses (in the form of skin conductance responses) to the phobia-relevant pictures. In addition, the participants experienced more arousal and felt more negative when exposed to those pictures.

Winkielman et al. (2005) presented happy and angry faces subliminally (below the conscious level) to thirsty participants. Those presented with subliminal happy faces poured and drank approximately twice as much liquid as those presented with subliminal angry faces (see Figure 15.6). In a further experiment, thirsty participants were willing to pay an average of 38 cents for a drink after being presented with happy faces but only 10 cents following presentation of angry faces. These findings indicate affective reactions can be unconscious.

In Chapter 2, we discussed patients with damage to primary visual cortex who nevertheless show some ability to respond appropriately to visual stimuli for which they lack conscious awareness – this is blindsight. Several of these patients show

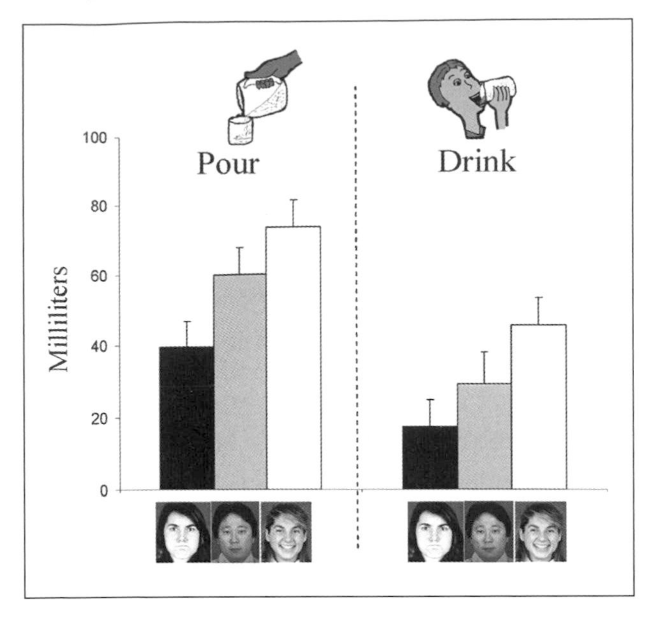

Figure 15.6
Mean volume of liquid poured and drunk by participants exposed to subliminal angry, neutral or happy faces.

From Winkielman et al. (2005). Reprinted by permission of SAGE Publications.

affective blindsight, in which emotional stimuli can be discriminated without conscious perception (Tamietto & de Gelder, 2010).

Interesting research on two patients with blindsight was reported by Tamietto et al. (2009). The patients viewed pictures of facial or bodily expressions indicating fear or happiness in their intact or blind visual field. The researchers considered the effects of these pictures on the zygomaticus major muscle (involved in smiling) and the corrugator supercilli (involved in frowning).

What did Tamietto et al. (2009) find? First, the zygomaticus major muscle was activated more by happy expressions (whether conscious or non-conscious) than fearful ones, whereas the opposite was the case with the corrugator supercilli. Second, these facial reactions occurred 200–300 ms faster for non-consciously perceived expressions than consciously perceived ones. Emotional processing may be faster below the level of conscious awareness because it bypasses the cortex.

Evaluation

Cognitive appraisal often strongly influences emotional experience. Appraisal processes determine *whether* we experience emotion and influence *which* emotion is experienced. Individual differences in emotional experience in a given situation can be partially explained by appraisals varying from person to person. The distinction between conscious appraisal processes and more automatic ones (Smith & Kirby, 2001) has proved of value. Research showing manipulating cognitive appraisals alters emotional experience suggests appraisals have causal effects on emotion.

Research activity: Appraisals in every day life

KEY TERM

Affective blindsight
The ability of brain-damaged patients to discriminate among different emotional stimuli in spite of the absence of conscious perception.

What are the limitations of appraisal theory? First, the assumption that situational appraisal is *always* crucial in determining emotional experience is too strong. The emotions individuals experience are typically only moderately well predicted by their situational appraisals. Appraisal theories often exaggerate the importance of top-down processes and de-emphasise bottom-up processes (Ochsner et al., 2009).

Second, most research focuses on *passive* individuals on their own presented with an emotional situation. In the real world, our emotions mostly emerge out of *active* social interaction and are strongly influenced by others' emotional reactions (Parkinson, 2011).

Third, appraisal theories focus on emotional experience as determined by the *current* situation. However, emotions often relate to the past or the future. Someone may experience anger because they blame another person for a past event. In addition, their anger may indicate they expect the other person to make amends in the *future* (Parkinson, 2011).

Fourth, it is assumed theoretically that appraisals cause emotional experiences. In practice, however, appraisals and emotional experiences often blur into each other (McEachrane, 2009) – there is no sharp distinction between cognition and emotion.

EMOTION REGULATION

So far we have focused on a one-stage approach in which an individual encounters a situation and responds with an emotional experience. This process is **emotion generation**, which involves a spontaneous emotional response to a situation.

In the real world, however, matters are often more complex. For example, someone in authority makes you angry by saying something unpleasant. However, you make strong efforts to inhibit your anger and pretend all is well. This illustrates the two-stage approach in which an initial emotional reaction is followed by attempts to change that emotional reaction.

The above example involves **emotion regulation**. Emotion regulation "requires the activation of a goal to up- or down-regulate either the magnitude or duration of the emotional response" (Gross, 2013, p. 359). Thus, emotion regulation occurs when someone *overrides* their initial, spontaneous emotional response.

The distinction between emotion generation and emotion regulation is intuitively appealing and can be studied in the laboratory. In essence, two groups of participants are presented with the same emotional situation. One group is instructed to react naturally (emotion generation). The other group is told to regulate their emotional responses using a specified strategy (emotion regulation). Emotional responding (e.g., self-reported emotion, brain activation) in the two conditions can then be compared.

The distinction between emotion generation and emotion regulation is often blurred (Gross et al., 2011). Emotion-generative and emotion-regulatory processes interact and involve overlapping brain systems (Ochsner et al., 2009). Emotion-generative processes are *auto-regulatory*, meaning they are self-correcting (Kappas, 2011). Emotion-generative processes lead to behaviour that changes the situation and thus the emotional response. Thus, emotion generation is often combined with emotion regulation in the absence of specific instructions. Nevertheless, the research evidence shows convincingly that emotion regulation often differs in several ways from emotion generation.

Process model

A process model of emotion regulation put forward by Gross and his colleagues is very influential (e.g., Gross & Thompson, 2007; see Figure 15.7). The basic processes involved in emotion generation are shown along the horizontal line. Of importance, it is assumed emotional intensity generally increases over time as we move from left to right.

Figure 15.7 also incorporates the crucial assumption that emotion-regulation strategies can be used at various points in time. For example, individuals with social anxiety can regulate their emotional state by avoiding potentially stressful situations (situation selection).

Socially anxious individuals can use other emotion-regulation strategies. For example, they can change social situations by asking a friend to accompany them (situation modification). Alternatively, they can use attentional processes by focusing on distracting thoughts (attention deployment).

KEY TERMS

Emotion generation
The immediate and spontaneous emotional response to a given situation.

Emotion regulation
The use of deliberate and effortful processes to change the spontaneous emotional state (usually a negative one) produced by the emotion-generation process.

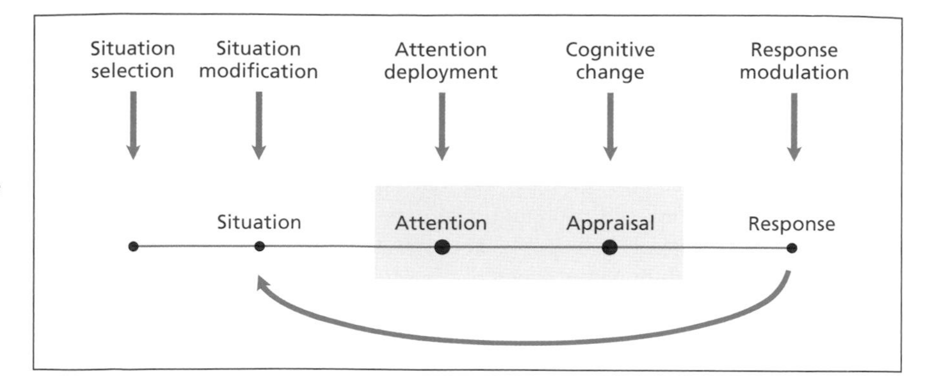

Figure 15.7
A process model of emotion regulation based on five major types of strategy (situation selection, situation modification, attention deployment, cognitive change and response modulation).
From Gross and Thompson (2007). Guilford Press.

Socially anxious individuals can also use cognitive reappraisal to reinterpret the current situation (cognitive change). For example, socially anxious individuals might tell themselves most people are friendly and will not judge them harshly if they say or do something inappropriate.

Finally, there is response modulation. For example, it is commonly believed you should express your angry feelings to get them "out of your system". Alas, expressing anger *increases* rather than decreases anger because it facilitates the retrieval of angry thoughts (Bushman, 2002). Another form of response modulation involves suppression of emotionally expressive behaviour (e.g., hiding your angry feelings).

Strategies involving situation selection, situation modification, attentional deployment and cognitive change are all *antecedent*-focused – they occur before appraisals produce a full-blown emotional response. In contrast, response-modulation strategies are *response*-focused – they occur after emotional responses have been generated.

Most emotion-regulation strategies are used at the attentional deployment stage (e.g., **distraction** – disengaging attention from emotional processing) or the cognitive change stage (e.g., **reappraisal** – elaborating emotional information and then changing its meaning). According to Sheppes et al. (2014), the emotional intensity of an event tends to increase over time if not subject to emotion regulation. Distraction is less cognitively demanding than reappraisal and can be used early to control negative emotion and so "nip it in the bud". Reappraisal is more cognitively demanding but it has the advantage that re-evaluating emotional information can produce long-lasting benefits.

KEY TERMS

Distraction
A strategy used in **emotion regulation** in which the individual disengages attention from emotional processing and focuses on neutral information.

Reappraisal
A strategy used in **emotion regulation** in which the individual elaborates emotional information from an event prior to changing its meaning.

Sheppes et al. (2014) used the above analysis to predict when distraction and reappraisal are most likely to be used. First, distraction will be used more than reappraisal in high negative intensity situations because it can block emotional information before it intensifies. Second, reappraisal will be used more often with emotional stimuli that are likely to be encountered many times than those encountered only once. The reason is that the reinterpretation of these stimuli produced by reappraisal serves to reduce their subsequent emotional impact.

So far the emphasis has been on deliberate and conscious processes involved in emotion regulation (explicit emotion regulation). Gyurak et al. (2011) argued that *implicit* emotion regulation is also important. According to their theoretical approach, "Implicit processes are believed to be *evoked automatically* by the stimulus itself and run to completion *without monitoring* and can happen *without insight* and *awareness*" (p. 401). Using a given emotion-regulation strategy repeatedly often leads to the development of implicit processes.

Why is implicit emotion regulation necessary? It would require excessive cognitive resources to use explicit emotion-regulation strategies to deal with every emotionally negative situation we encounter.

Findings

Which are the most effective emotion-regulation strategies? In a meta-analysis (see Glossary), Augustine and Hemenover (2009) distinguished between cognitive strategies (involving thinking) and behavioural strategies (involving physical action). Cognitive strategies (especially reappraisal and distraction) were more effective than behavioural strategies.

Patients with anxiety disorders or major depressive disorder have difficulties in emotion regulation (e.g., Campbell-Sills & Barlow, 2007). The role of various emotion-regulation strategies in changing the symptoms of anxiety and depression over time was assessed in a meta-analytic review by Aldao et al. (2010). Acceptance, problem solving and reappraisal had beneficial effects on anxiety and depression. However, rumination (obsessive thinking about issues) and avoidance both *increased* the symptoms of anxiety and depression.

The most thorough attempt to assess the effectiveness of different strategies to regulate emotion was by Webb et al. (2012). They carried out a meta-analysis based on 306 experimental comparisons of different strategies using the process model shown in Figure 15.7. Overall, strategies involving cognitive change had a moderate effect on emotion, strategies involving response modulation had a small effect and strategies involving attentional deployment had a non-significant effect.

Webb et al. (2012) argued that combining several different strategies in the same category is very limited. For example, although attentional deployment strategies overall had a non-significant effect, distraction had clearly beneficial effects. With respect to cognitive-change strategies, reappraising the emotional situation was more beneficial than reappraising the emotional response. With response modulation, suppressing emotional expression had a moderate effect on emotion but suppressing emotional experience had no effect. In sum, what matters is the *specific* strategy rather than the broad category.

There is an important qualification on the findings discussed so far – the effectiveness of any given emotion-regulation strategy varies from situation to situation. For example, consider a study by Troy et al. (2013). They argued that reappraisal would be effective in situations in which stress was uncontrollable. However, it would be ineffective in situations in which stress was controllable and the optimal strategy would probably be problem-focused coping rather than changing one's emotional state. Troy et al. assessed participants' reappraisal ability, the stressfulness of participants' recent negative life experiences and the controllability of those experiences.

What did Troy et al. (2013) find? Participants with high appraisal ability had *less* depression than those with low ability when high stress was uncontrollable (see Figure 15.8).

In contrast, high appraisal ability was associated with *greater* depression when high stress was controllable. Thus, the effectiveness of reappraisal ability depended very much on the controllability vs. uncontrollability of stressful life events.

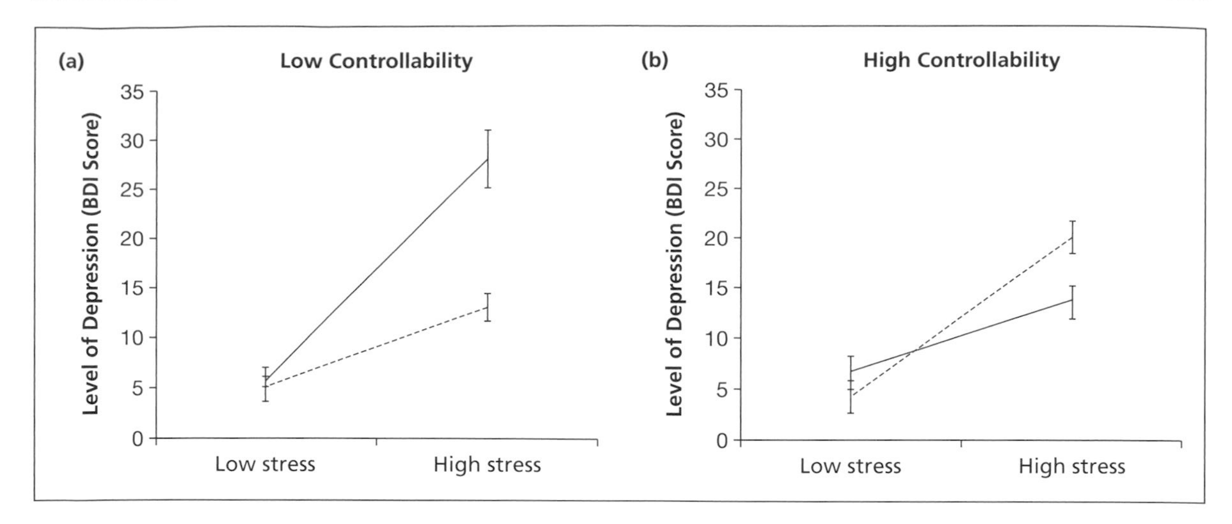

Figure 15.8

Mean level of depression as a function of stress severity and cognitive reappraisal ability (high = - - - - ; low = ———) when the situation was low in controllability (left-hand side) and high in controllability (right-hand side).

From Troy et al. (2013). Reprinted by permission of SAGE Publications.

Much research on emotion regulation has focused on the brain mechanisms involved (Ochsner & Gross, 2008). Most effective strategies for emotion regulation involve effortful cognitive processes associated with activation within the prefrontal cortex. These effortful processes cause reduced activation in the amygdala (strongly implicated in emotional responding) and reduced negative affect.

Weblink:
Article, Ochsner and Gross

In a meta-analysis, Kohn et al. (2014) identified several brain areas associated with emotion regulation. Their findings were consistent with a three-stage neural network model (see Figure 15.9):

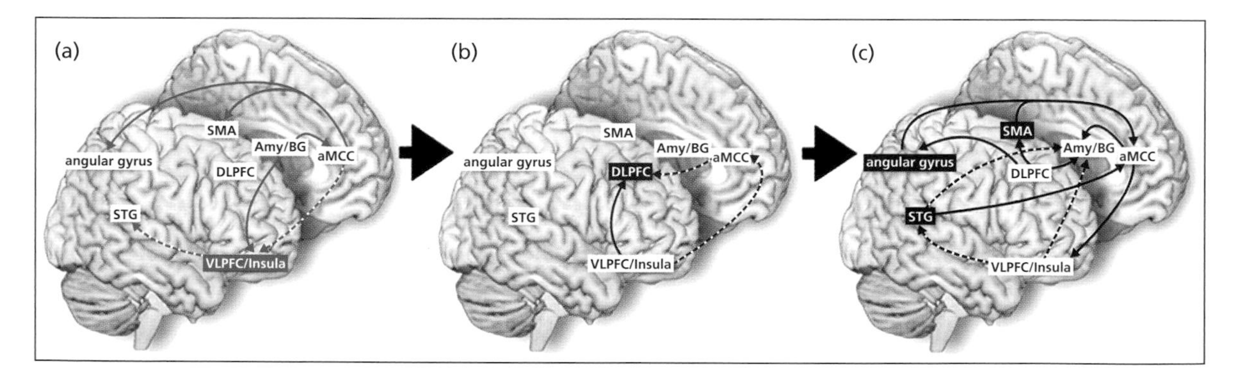

Figure 15.9

A three-stage neural network model of emotion regulation. (a) In the emotion evaluation network, affective arousal is relayed via the amygdala (Amy) and basal ganglia (BG) to the ventrolateral prefrontal cortex (VLPFC). (b) In the initiation-of-regulation network, the dorsolateral prefrontal cortex (DLPFC) is involved in processing the emotion regulation. (c) The execution-of-regulation network centring on the superior temporal gyrus (STG), the supplementary motor area (SMA) and the angular gyrus generates a regulated emotional state.

From Kohn et al. (2014). Reprinted with permission from Elsevier.

1. *Emotion evaluation*: This network centres on the ventrolateral prefrontal cortex (VLPFC) and is involved in initiating appraisal and signalling the need to regulate emotion.
2. *Initiation of regulation*: This network centres on the dorsolateral prefrontal cortex (DLPFC) and is involved in processing the regulation of emotion.
3. *Execution of regulation*: this network regulates affective arousal by changing the emotional state.

The cognitive neuroscience approach has shed light on differences in the effectiveness of emotion-regulation strategies. Consider a study by McRae et al. (2010). Participants presented with very negative pictures used reappraisal (reinterpret the picture more positively) or distraction (remember a six-letter string). Reappraisal was associated with greater increases in activation within the medial prefrontal cortex and anterior temporal regions (associated with processing affective meaning). It was also more effective in reducing negative affect. This suggests reappraisal was associated with greater *control* of the individual's emotional state.

Evidence supporting the hypothesis that processes within the prefrontal cortex cause reduced amygdala activation and negative affect was reported by S.-H. Lee et al. (2012). Participants used reappraisal to reduce negative affect while viewing very negative pictures. Lee et al. predicted (and found) individuals with the strongest links between prefrontal areas and the amygdala would show the most effective use of reappraisal.

Earlier we discussed the views of Sheppes et al. (2014). They predicted distraction is used more often than reappraisal when people are confronted by situations having high emotional intensity or when negative situations are unlikely to be re-encountered. They obtained support for both predictions.

Sheppes and Gross (2011) adopted a similar perspective to that of Sheppes et al. (2014) to predict the effectiveness of emotion-regulation strategies. They assumed the intensity of the emotional response to threatening or unpleasant stimuli generally increases over time. This is unimportant if a strategy does not require much effortful cognitive processing (e.g., distraction). However, cognitively demanding strategies (e.g., reappraisal) will be more effective if used early on while emotional intensity remains low.

Sheppes and Gross (2011) reviewed the relevant research. As predicted, distraction was equally effective in reducing negative affect at low (early on) and high (later on) levels of emotional intensity. Also as predicted, reappraisal worked well at low levels of emotional intensity but was counterproductive at high levels.

Next, we consider evidence relating to the use of *implicit* processes in emotion regulation. Mauss et al. (2007) exposed participants to an anger-provocation experience in which the experimenter was impatient and irritated. Some participants had previously been exposed to reappraisal-relevant words (e.g., *restrains*, *stable*) during a task in which words were rearranged to form sentences. These participants experienced less anger and general negative emotions than controls because of the implicit processes they used when provoked.

In a similar study, Williams et al. (2009) compared implicit and explicit reappraisal processes in an anxiety-provoking situation (preparing to give a speech). Both were equally effective in holding down physiological activity in the emotional situation.

Evaluation

Several advances have been made in our understanding of emotion regulation. First, we know effective strategies often involve effortful cognitive processing in prefrontal cortex leading to reduced amygdala activation. Second, reasons why strategies may (or may not) be less effective when used later rather than sooner in processing of emotional stimuli have been identified. Third, the processes involved in strategy use can be explicit or implicit. Fourth, some of the factors influencing which emotion-regulation strategy is selected in a given emotional situation have been identified.

What are the limitations of theory and research in this area? First, several theorists doubt whether there is a clear-cut distinction between emotion generation and emotion regulation (Gross et al., 2011). Second, most of the emphasis has been on emotion-regulation strategies occurring within the individual. However, people often use more behavioural strategies such as drinking alcohol, arguing with others and avoiding situations. These behavioural strategies are associated with the symptoms of mental disorder such as social phobia and eating disorders (Aldao & Dixon-Gordon, 2014). Third, the effectiveness of any given emotion-regulation strategy probably depends on the situation involved (e.g., whether stress is controllable or not), but the interaction between strategy and situation has seldom been studied.

Fourth, much remains to be discovered about the detailed processes involved in implementing complex strategies such as reappraisal. Fifth, little is known about individual differences in the ability to use any given strategy. However, McRae et al. (2012) made a start. Individuals who used the reappraisal strategy successfully tended to have higher well-being and greater working memory capacity (see Glossary) than others.

AFFECT AND COGNITION: ATTENTION AND MEMORY

As mentioned in the Introduction, most research in cognitive psychology involves assessing the cognitive processes and performance of participants in a *neutral* state. This contrasts strongly with everyday life in which we are often happy, sad, angry or anxious when engaged in cognitive activities (e.g., thinking, problem solving, decision making).

Affect often influences people's behaviour in everyday life. Consider driving behaviour. Pêcher et al. (2009) used a simulator to study the effects of music on car driving. Sad music had no effect on drivers' ability to keep the car in its lane but there was a slight reduction in speed. However, happy music had a distracting effect. There was a reduced ability to keep the car in its lane and an 8 mph decrease in speed relative to the neutral music condition.

Many people believe in "road rage", the notion that frustrated drivers become angry and drive dangerously as a consequence. In a study by Stephens and Groeger (2011), drivers performing a simulated driving task were made angry by being trapped behind a slow-moving vehicle. After that, they showed poor decision making by engaging in dangerous overtaking manoeuvres and approaching hazards recklessly.

Our emotional state influences numerous aspects of cognition including perception, attention, interpretation, learning, memory, judgement, decision making and reasoning (Blanchette & Richards, 2010). We will be considering the main findings on attention and memory in this section. The next section focuses on judgement and decision making.

Lench et al. (2011) assessed the frequency with which different techniques have been used to manipulate participants' affect (especially mood state). The most common technique (24% of studies) involved presenting emotional films. Another very popular technique (20% of studies) involved autobiographical recall with participants describing or writing about an intense emotional experience. Other techniques involve staged real-life situations (15%) and emotional music (7% of studies).

Attention

When we look at the world around us, we have some *flexibility* in the scope of focal attention (see Chapter 5). Some theorists (e.g., Eriksen & St James, 1986) compare visual attention to a zoom lens, in which the attended area can be increased or decreased. This issue is important in enhancing our understanding of attention but is also relevant to long-term memory. What we remember of an event is strongly influenced by what we attended to at the time.

How does affect influence the breadth of attention? An influential answer with reference to negative affect was provided by Easterbrook (1959). He hypothesised that the range of cues processed (i.e., the breadth of attention) decreases as arousal or anxiety increases. This "will reduce the proportion of irrelevant cues employed, and so improve performance . . . further reduction in the number of cues employed can only affect relevant cues, and proficiency will fall" (Easterbrook, 1959, p. 193). Thus, high negative affect produces "tunnel vision".

Easterbrook's hypothesis has potential practical importance. For example, it may help us understand eyewitness memory (see Chapter 8) given that eyewitnesses are often highly stressed when they observe a crime. There is also some evidence (e.g., Janelle et al., 1999) that anxious car drivers attend less than non-anxious ones to peripheral information.

What about the effects of *positive* affect on the breadth of attention? According to Fredrickson and Branigan (2005, p. 315), positive emotions "widen the array of percepts, thoughts, and actions presently in mind". Thus, positive affect produces broadening of attention in contrast to the narrowing of attention assumed for negative affect by Easterbrook (1959).

Harmon-Jones et al. (2011) argued that both approaches above are limited because they consider only whether the affect is negative or positive. They claimed we should also consider *motivational intensity* (i.e., having the goal of approaching or avoiding a stimulus). Positive affect can be produced by listening to pleasant music (low motivational intensity) or by seeing an attractive member of the opposite sex (high motivational intensity). Negative affect can be produced by being exposed to sad situations (low motivational intensity) or by threatening stimuli or situations (high emotional intensity).

What conclusions did Harmon-Jones et al. (2011) draw? They argued that positive and negative affective states of high motivational intensity produce attentional narrowing because this helps people to acquire desirable objects and avoid unpleasant ones. In contrast, there is attentional broadening with positive and negative affective states of low motivational intensity because this leaves people open to encountering new opportunities.

Lee et al. (2014) identified a different way in which emotional states influence visual information processing. Fear is associated with widening of the eyes, whereas disgust is associated with narrowing of the eyes. Eye widening enhanced the ability to detect visual stimuli but reduced visual acuity, while eye narrowing had the opposite effect. These effects may be functional: fear facilitates detection and localisation of threat, whereas disgust assists in identifying the object triggering disgust (e.g., contaminated food).

Findings

We will start by considering the effects of negative affect on breadth of attention. Anxiety or fear has high motivational intensity. Thus, Easterbrook's (1959) hypothesis and the theoretical perspective of Harmon-Jones et al. (2011) both predict it should produce attentional narrowing.

The above prediction has often been tested using a dual-task paradigm in which a primary task is presented in the centre of the visual field and a secondary task in the periphery. If anxiety causes attentional narrowing, we would expect it to impair performance on the secondary task more than the primary task. That prediction has been supported in several studies (Eysenck et al., 2007).

Gable and Harmon-Jones (2010b) considered the effects of two other negative mood states (disgust and sadness) on attentional narrowing. Disgust (a mood state involving high motivational intensity) produced attentional narrowing. In contrast, sadness (a mood state involving low motivational intensity) led to attentional broadening. These findings are consistent with Harmon-Jones et al.'s (2011) assumption that high motivational intensity produces narrowing of attention, whereas low motivational intensity produces broadening.

What are the effects of positive affect on the breadth of attention? Fredrickson and Branigan (2005) predicted positive affect consistently leads to a broadening of attention. There is much support for that prediction, as was shown in a review by Friedman and Förster (2010). Bear in mind, however, that Harmon-Jones et al. (2011) argued that positive affect should produce attentional *narrowing* if there is high motivational intensity.

Gable and Harmon-Jones (2011) assessed the effects of positive affect on the breadth of attention under conditions of high and low motivational intensity. Positive high motivational intensity was created by providing the opportunity to win money on a game. Positive low motivational intensity was created by indicating money had been won. As predicted by both theories, positive affect of low motivational intensity was associated with attentional broadening. However, positive affect with high motivational intensity produced attentional narrowing. Thus, the findings supported Harmon-Jones et al. (2011) rather than Frederick and Brannigan (2005).

The breadth of attention is of relevance to the effects of mood on memory. Emotion increases memory for information central to our current goals but reduces it for peripheral or unimportant information (Levine & Edelstein, 2009). Some of the evidence comes from studies on weapon focus. This is the tendency for eyewitnesses to attend narrowly to a gun or other weapon and thus fail to remember peripheral details (see Chapter 8).

It is tempting to link these findings to Easterbrook's (1959) hypothesis by arguing that the "memory narrowing" associated with emotional states is due to

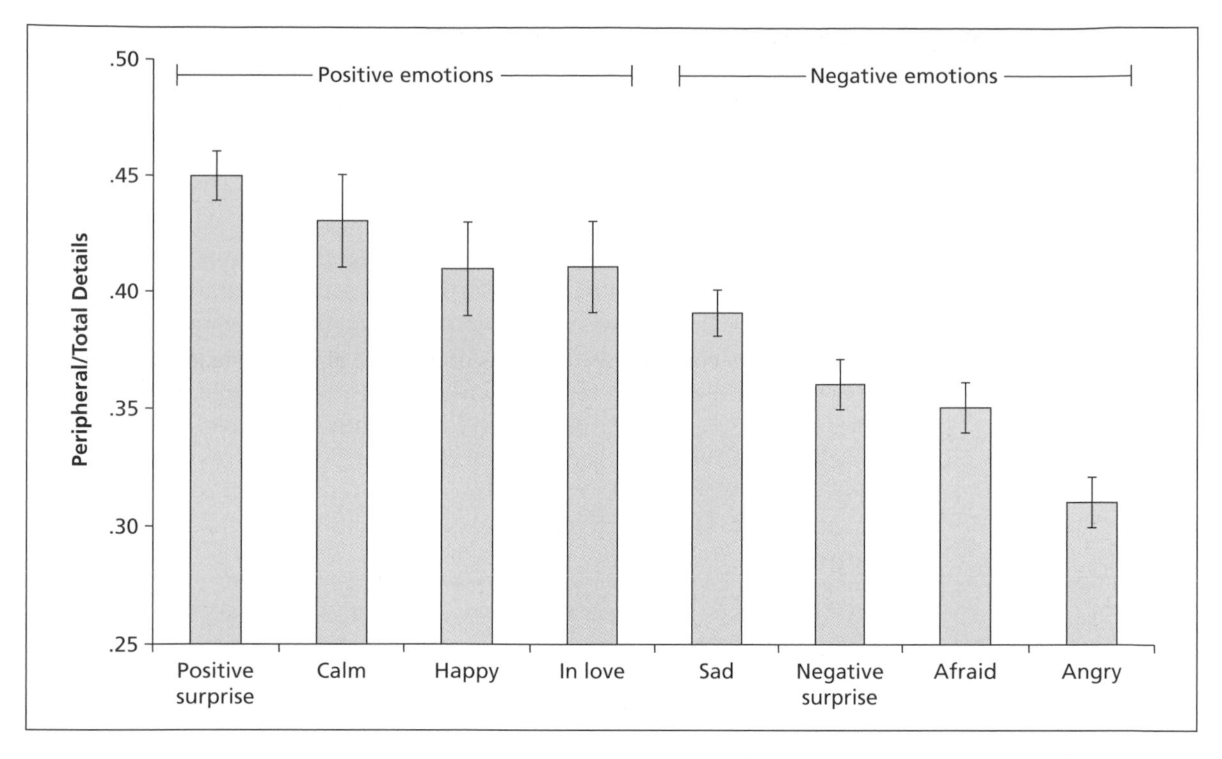

Figure 15.10
Mean proportion of total details rated as peripheral for autobiographical memories associated with eight different emotions. The emotions are ranked from the highest to the lowest proportion of peripheral details.
From Talarico et al. (2009).

attentional narrowing at the time of learning. However, there are two problems with this argument. First, very few studies have assessed attentional and memory narrowing. Riggs et al. (2011) did this and found evidence for both attentional and memory narrowing. However, memory narrowing could *not* be explained fully by attentional narrowing. As predicted, centrally presented emotional stimuli led to reduced eye fixations towards neutral peripheral stimuli. However, poor memory for peripheral information was *not* due directly to reduced attention. The processing of emotional stimuli may be more distinctive and/or focus more on meaning than that of neutral stimuli regardless of the amount of attention they receive.

Second, it follows from Harmon-Jones et al.'s (2011) theory that attention (and perhaps memory) depend on the motivational intensity of an emotional state. As a result, there should be memory *broadening* if the emotional state has low motivational intensity. Talarico et al. (2009) asked participants to recall eight emotional autobiographical memories. Peripheral details were poorly recalled with memories associated with anger, fear and negative surprise (see Figure 15.10), as predicted by Easterbrook's hypothesis. Sad memories were associated with reasonably good recall of peripheral details, perhaps because of the low motivational intensity of that emotional state.

Talarico et al. (2009) found good recall of peripheral details for all types of positive memories (see Figure 15.10). This fits Harmon-Jones et al.'s (2011) theory if we assume most positive mood states occur with low motivational intensity.

Of relevance, Gable and Harmon-Jones (2010a) found positive affect enhanced memory for peripheral details when there was low motivational intensity but failed to do so when there was high motivational intensity.

Conclusions

The findings predominantly support Harmon-Jones et al.'s (2011) theoretical account (see Harmon-Jones et al. (2013) for a review). In other words, affect (positive vs. negative) and motivational intensity generally influence attentional breadth as predicted. However, the breadth of attention is more *flexible* than implied by this theory. There is evidence (reviewed by Huntsinger, 2013) that the breadth of attention depends on currently accessible thoughts and response tendencies as well as on affect and motivational intensity. The various findings can be used to determine how individuals will respond to real-life situations when in a given emotional state.

Memory

Affect influences learning and memory in several ways. Imagine you are in a negative mood state because you have a serious personal problem. What types of memory would spring to your mind? People generally recall predominantly negative or unpleasant memories in such circumstances. In contrast, we typically recall happy memories when in a good mood. These examples illustrate **mood congruity** – emotionally toned material is learned and retrieved best when its affective value matches the learner's (or rememberer's) mood state. Mood congruity may help to explain why negative mood states in everyday life are sometimes prolonged – the negative mood state makes it easier to learn and to retrieve negative information.

Mood-congruity effects based on mood at the time of learning were studied by Hills et al. (2011). Participants induced into a happy mood showed better subsequent recognition memory for happy than sad faces. In contrast, those induced into a sad mood had slightly (but non-significantly) better recognition memory for sad than for happy faces.

Mood-congruity effects have also been found in daily life (Loeffler et al., 2013) but were found to depend on the level of physiological arousal at the time of learning. Mood congruity for emotionally negative words was greater when physiological arousal was high. In contrast, mood congruity for emotionally positive words was greater when physiological arousal was low. These findings indicate the importance of considering the learner's arousal at the time of learning as well as his/her mood state.

Miranda and Kihlstrom (2005) asked adults to recall childhood and recent autobiographical memories to pleasant, unpleasant and neutral word cues. They did this in a musically induced happy, sad or neutral mood. There was mood congruity – the retrieval of happy memories was facilitated when participants were in a happy mood and retrieval of sad memories was enhanced by a sad mood.

Research on mood and autobiographical memory was reviewed by Holland and Kensinger (2010). There was clear evidence of mood congruity when people were in a positive mood, but mood congruity was less often found when people were in a negative mood. Similar findings have been reported in studies of mood congruity with non-autobiographical material (Rusting & DeHart, 2000).

KEY TERMS

Mood congruity
Learning and memory of emotional material are better when the learner's/rememberer's mood state matches the affective value of the material.

Case study:
Hills et al. (2011)

The most plausible explanation for the frequent failure to obtain mood congruity in a negative mood state is that people are motivated to change it into a positive mood state. The resultant reduction in negative mood state caused by emotion regulation reduces the accessibility of negative memories. Rusting and DeHart (2000) obtained support for this explanation. Participants were presented with positive, negative and neutral words. Then there was a negative mood induction. Those who claimed to be successful at reducing negative moods showed less evidence of mood congruity than other participants.

How can we explain mood congruity? The effect can be explained with respect to Tulving's (1979) encoding specificity principle (see Chapter 6). According to this principle, memory depends on the *overlap* between the information available at retrieval and that in the memory trace. This overlap is greater when the to-be-remembered material is congruent with the rememberer's mood state than when it is not. Danker and Anderson (2010, p. 87) discussed an extension of this viewpoint focusing on brain states: "Remembering an episode involves literally returning to the brain state . . . present during that episode." They reviewed supportive evidence.

The above assumption was tested by Lewis et al. (2005) in the context of mood congruity. Participants learned positive and negative words and then received a recognition-memory test in a happy or sad mood. There was mood congruity in memory performance. One brain region (the subgenual cingulate) was activated when positive stimuli were presented and was reactivated when participants were in a positive mood at test. In similar fashion, a different brain region (the posteriolateral orbitofrontal cortex) was activated when negative stimuli were presented and was reactivated when participants' mood at test was negative.

Another effect of mood on memory is **mood-state-dependent memory**. This is the finding that memory is better when the mood state at retrieval *matches* that at learning than when it does not. Ucros (1989) reported moderate evidence for mood-state-dependent memory in a review. The effect was stronger when participants were in a positive mood rather than a negative one. This probably occurred because individuals experiencing a negative mood state are motivated to change it into a more positive mood.

Kenealy (1997) studied mood-state-dependent memory. Participants looked at a map and learned a set of instructions concerning a given route. The next day they had tests of free recall and cued recall (the cue consisted of the map's visual outline). Mood was manipulated by using music to create happy or sad mood states at learning and test. There was strong evidence for mood-state-dependent memory in free recall but not cued recall (see Figure 15.11).

How can we explain these apparently conflicting findings? The existence of mood-state-dependent memory can be understood by the encoding specificity principle. Assume information about mood state is stored at the time of learning. If so, the overlap between information at retrieval and information in the memory trace will clearly be greater when the mood state is the same at learning and test.

Kenealy's (1997) finding that there was no mood-state-dependent memory with cued recall cannot easily be explained by encoding specificity. Eich (1995) argued that mood state has less influence when crucial information (the to-be-remembered information or retrieval cues) is presented explicitly as happens with

KEY TERM

Mood-state-dependent memory
Memory performance is better when the individual's mood state is the same at learning and retrieval than when it differs.

Weblink:
Article on mood-state-dependent memory

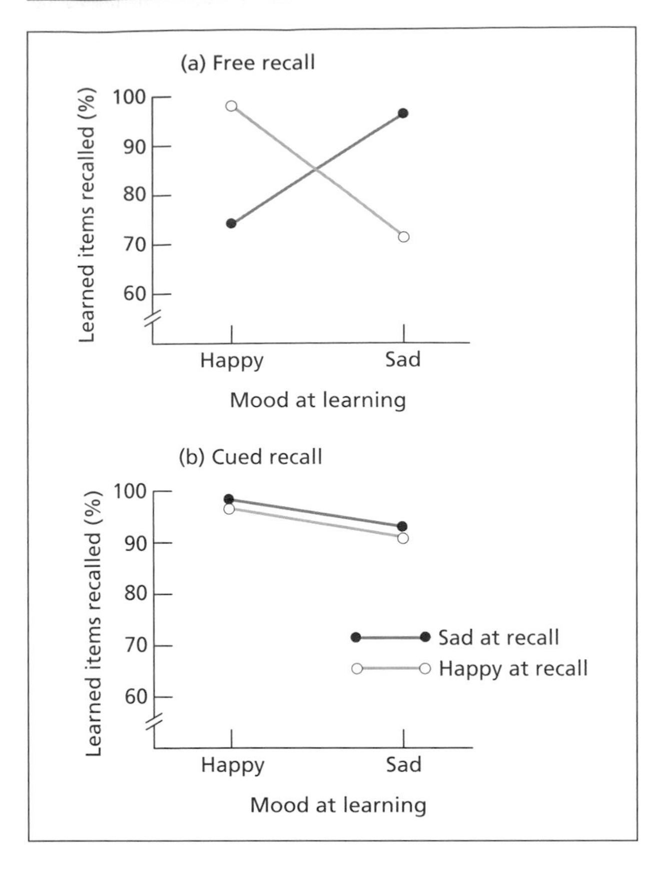

Figure 15.11
(a) Free and (b) cued recall as a function of mood state (happy or sad) at learning and at recall.

Based on data in Kenealy (1997).

cued recall. Eich discussed a "do-it-yourself principle" – memory is most likely to be mood-dependent when *effortful* processing at learning and/or retrieval is required.

Support for the "do-it-yourself principle" was obtained by Eich and Metcalfe (1989). At learning, participants were assigned to read (e.g., *river-valley*) or generate (e.g., *river-v____*) conditions. In the generate condition, they completed the second word in each pair during learning and so engaged in effortful processing. The mood-state-dependent effect was four times greater in the generate condition.

Amygdala involvement

The effects of mood or emotion on long-term memory depend on activation within several brain regions. A brain area centrally involved is the amygdala (see Figure 15.3, page 638), which is associated with several emotions (especially fear). A major reason for the importance of the amygdala is that it acts as a *hub* – it has numerous connections to 90% of cortical areas.

It is a reasonable prediction that the probability of emotional items being remembered is greater when associated with high levels of amygdala activation at learning. Support for this prediction was reported by Murty et al. (2010) in a meta-analysis (see Glossary). Good long-term memory for emotional material was associated with greater activation during learning in a network of brain regions including the amygdala and temporal lobe regions involved in memory.

Another approach is to study patients with damage to the amygdala. Adolphs et al. (2005) found healthy controls showed enhanced memory for gist when the encoding context was emotional rather than neutral. In contrast, patients with amygdala damage showed a *specific* impairment of gist memory only with an emotional context at encoding. Of interest, amygdala damage was not associated with impaired memory for background details of the stimuli. These findings suggest the amygdala (much involved in emotion and arousal) is required for focused attention on important information, and are thus consistent with Easterbrook's (1959) hypothesis (discussed earlier).

Some research has involved the study of patients with **Urbach–Wiethe disease**. This is a disease in which the amygdala and nearby areas are destroyed. Cahill et al. (1995) studied BP, a patient with the disease. His recall of a very emotional event in a story was poorer than his recall of an emotionally neutral event. In contrast, healthy controls showed much better recall of the emotional event than a neutral event. In similar fashion, Siebert et al. (2003) found the memory impairment for Urbach–Wiethe patients was greater for emotional pictures (positive and negative) than neutral ones.

KEY TERM

Urbach–Wiethe disease
A disease in which the **amygdala** and adjacent areas are destroyed.

Why is the amygdala so important in enhancing memory for emotional information? It is connected to brain regions (e.g., hippocampus, prefrontal cortex) strongly involved in memory processes (LaBar & Cabeza, 2006). Of special importance, the amygdala is linked to brain areas involved in long-term consolidation of memories.

It is important to note superior memory for emotional information depends on cognitive processes as well as amygdala activation. As Talmi (2013, p. 432) argued with supporting evidence, "Emotional events recruit cognitive resources such as attention, distinctive processing, and organisation more than do neutral events, resulting in a memory advantage for emotional stimuli."

Evaluation

Several effects of mood state on attention and memory have been established. Mood states involving high motivational intensity typically produce attentional narrowing. In contrast, mood states involving low motivational intensity produce attentional broadening. These effects on attention have some impact on long-term memory. There is convincing evidence for mood congruity and mood-state-dependent memory, and these effects can often be explained by the encoding specificity principle. Finally, there is an increasing understanding of the role played by the amygdala in determining the effects of mood state on memory.

What are the limitations of research in this area? First, the notion that attentional narrowing or broadening has direct effects on long-term memory is only partially correct. Second, it has proved harder to find evidence for mood congruity and mood-state-dependent memory with negative mood states than positive ones. This is due mainly to participants' attempts to reduce (or eliminate) their negative mood state. Third, stronger mood-state-dependent memory effects are found with some memory tasks than others but the reasons are not fully understood. Finally, the relative importance of enhanced amygdala activation and various cognitive processes in producing a memory advantage for emotional stimuli over neutral ones remains unclear.

AFFECT AND COGNITION: JUDGEMENT AND DECISION MAKING

Research and theory on judgement and decision making were discussed in Chapter 13. Decision making involves choosing among various options. These decisions vary between the trivial (e.g., deciding which movie to see tonight) and the enormously important (e.g., deciding which career path to follow).

Judgement is an important component of decision making. It involves assessing the probability of various events occurring and then deciding how we would feel if each one actually happened. The decisions made by those whose judgements about the future are pessimistic would probably differ from those whose judgements are optimistic.

Angie et al. (2011) came to two general conclusions from their review of research in this area. First, major mood states (sadness, anger, fear or anxiety, happiness) have significant (and somewhat different) effects on judgement and decision making. Second, the average effects of mood are greater with respect to decision making than judgement.

KEY TERM

Interoception
Sensitivity to bodily stimuli at the conscious or non-conscious level.

In this section, we consider the influence of mood on judgement and decision making (see also Chapter 13). In addition, we will discuss relevant research concerned with the effects of personality on judgement and decision making. Why have we done this? The main reason is that there are moderately strong links between personality and mood. For example, consider the personality dimension of trait anxiety (see Glossary) which relates to individual differences in susceptibility to anxiety. Unsurprisingly, individuals high in trait anxiety are in an anxious mood state much more often than those low in trait anxiety.

Predictions

Various predictions seem reasonable. First, we might expect mood valence (positive vs. negative) to be of major importance. More specifically, individuals experiencing negative moods (e.g., fear, anger, sadness) should be pessimistic and risk averse, whereas those experiencing positive moods should be optimistic and inclined to take risks.

Second, we might expect any given mood state to be associated with a tendency towards risky or cautious decision making regardless of the situation or the nature of the decision. As we will see, both assumptions are only partially correct.

Integral vs. incidental emotions

We need to distinguish between integral emotions and incidental emotions (Han & Lerner, 2009). *Integral* emotions are triggered by considering the consequences of a decision. For example, gambling a lot of money on a risky project is likely to trigger anxiety. In contrast, *incidental* emotions arise from past events totally *unrelated* to the present decision. For example, hearing you have passed an important examination may influence your subsequent judgements and decisions on other matters.

Most research on emotion and decision making has involved incidental emotions (Lench et al., 2011). For example, participants write about a very emotional experience and then perform a completely unrelated task. However, decision making in the real world very often involves integral emotions (e.g., we make decisions about what to do in order to reduce our sad or depressed state).

Damasio (1994) put forward a somatic marker hypothesis explaining how integral emotions may be of value. According to this hypothesis, automatic bodily arousal responses (somatic markers) are triggered by emotional events and mark them with an emotional signal. These somatic markers influence decision making. Of key importance is **interoception**, which is the ability to detect subtle bodily changes. Interoception sometimes (but by no means always) involves conscious detection of bodily changes.

Evidence supporting the above theoretical approach was reported by Dunn et al. (2010) using a version of the Iowa gambling task (Bechara et al., 1994). Participants chose a card from one of four decks of playing cards. Two decks were profitable (on average participants would gain money by selecting from them), while the other two were unprofitable. Decision-making performance on this task improved over time although the participants had little conscious understanding of how the decks differed. Bodily changes prior to choosing from an unprofitable or a profitable deck were recorded. Finally, participants' interoceptive ability was assessed by their accuracy in counting their own heartbeats.

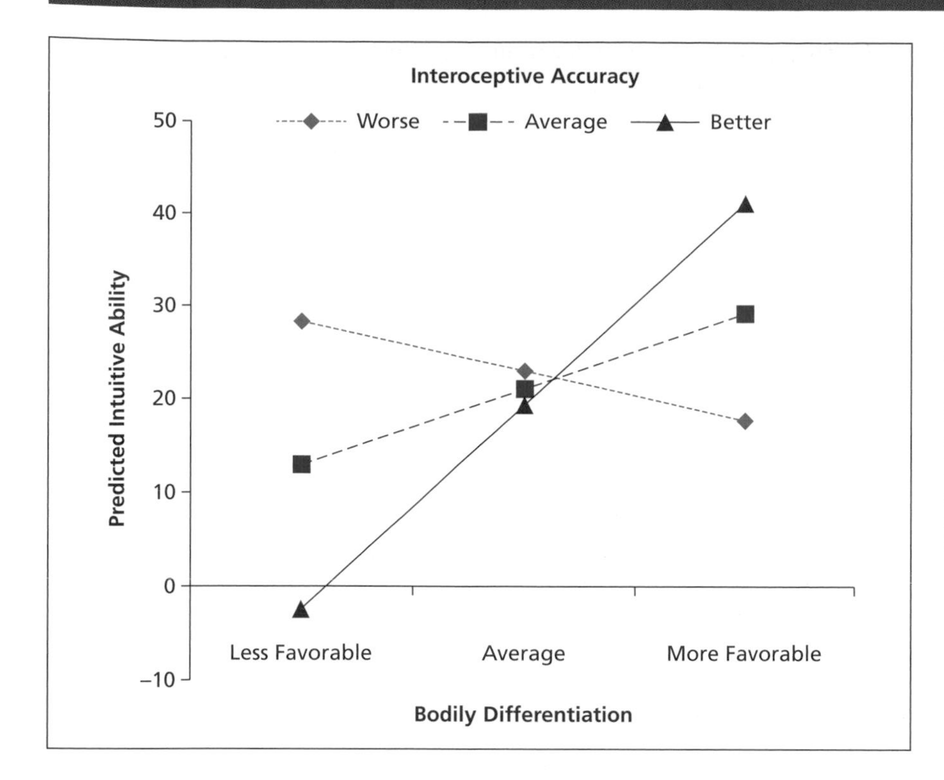

Figure 15.12
Intuitive ability (total number of profitable-deck selections minus total number of unprofitable-deck selections) as a function of bodily responses to unprofitable decks minus bodily responses to profitable decks (more favourable = large difference). There were three groups defined by their interoceptive ability: worse than average (blue), average (red) and better than average (black).

From Dunn et al. (2010). Reprinted by permission of SAGE Publications.

What did Dunn et al. (2010) find? First, there were significant differences in bodily responses *prior* to selecting from profitable and unprofitable decks. Participants having the largest differences exhibited superior decision making to those with the smallest differences. Second, individuals high in interoceptive ability made much more use of information from their bodily responses than those low in such ability (see Figure 15.12). Thus, perception of emotional bodily responses can influence decision making.

Other research has focused on the brain regions critically involved in the processes linking interoception with decision making. Werner et al. (2013) found the right anterior insula was such a region. They also reviewed previous research indicating the involvement of other brain regions such as the ventromedial prefrontal cortex and the amygdala.

Anxiety

Of all the negative emotional states, fear or anxiety is most consistently associated with pessimistic judgements about the future. Lerner et al. (2003) carried out a study very shortly after the 9/11 terrorist attacks. Participants focused on aspects of the attacks that made them afraid, angry or sad. The estimated probability of future terrorist attacks was higher in fearful participants than sad or angry ones.

Most people have what is known as an **optimism bias**. This bias involves individuals believing they are more likely than other people to experience positive events but less likely to experience negative events. This is what Shepperd et al. (2013) call *unrealistic comparative optimism*. This can be contrasted with the less frequently studied *unrealistic absolute optimism*, which relates an individual's

KEY TERM

Optimism bias
The tendency to exaggerate our chances of experiencing positive events and to minimise our chances of experiencing negative events relative to other people.

judgements to some objective standard (e.g., someone thinks they have a 4% chance of contracting a given disease but objectively there is a 7% chance).

Anxious individuals have less of an optimism bias than other people. Lench and Levine (2005) asked college participants to make judgements of the likelihood of various events happening to them compared to the average college student. Participants put into a fearful mood were more pessimistic than those put into a happy or neutral mood.

Similar findings at the level of personality were reported by Harris et al. (2008). Most individuals perceive others to be more vulnerable to future risks than themselves. However, this tendency was weaker among those high in trait anxiety, a personality dimension relating to anxiety susceptibility. This may, at least in part, reflect reality. Individuals with an anxious personality actually experience more negative life events than those with a non-anxious personality (van Os et al., 2001).

Decision making and anxiety

Anxious individuals typically make less risky decisions than non-anxious ones. Lorian and Grisham (2011) studied risk taking in patients with anxiety disorders who completed the Domain-Specific Risk-Taking Scale. This scale consists of 30 items assessing an individual's likelihood of engaging in risky activities (e.g., "Betting a day's income at the horse races"; "Engaging in unprotected sex"). The anxious patients had lower risk-taking scores than healthy controls.

Raghunathan and Pham (1999) asked participants to decide whether to accept job A (high salary + low job security) or job B (average salary + high job security). Participants in an anxious mood state were much less likely than those in a neutral state to choose the high-risk option (job A) (see Figure 15.13).

Gambetti and Giusberti (2012) studied real-life financial decision making in individuals having anxious or non-anxious personalities. Anxious participants had made safer or more conservative financial decisions than non-anxious ones. They were more likely to have put their money into interest-bearing accounts but less likely to have invested large sums of money in stocks, shares and so on.

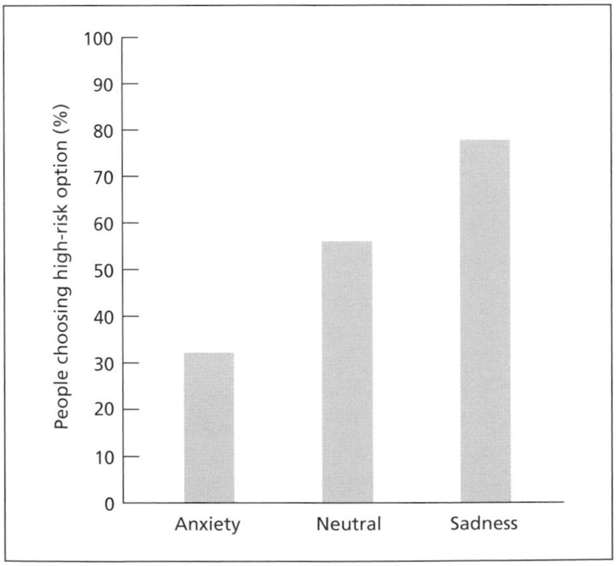

Figure 15.13
Effects of mood manipulation (anxiety, sadness or neutral) on percentages of people choosing the high-risk job option.
Based on data in Raghunathan and Pham (1999). With permission from Elsevier.

Sadness

Sadness and anxiety are both negative emotional states. However, sadness (which turns into depression when intense) is more strongly associated with an absence of positive affect. As a result, sad individuals experience the environment as relatively unrewarding and so may be especially motivated to obtain rewards even if risks are involved.

Waters (2008) reviewed studies on the effects of mood state on likelihood estimates of health hazards and life events. Those of sad individuals were more pessimistic than those of individuals in a positive mood state. Several studies found sad or depressed individuals have a smaller optimism bias than non-depressed ones. This has often been referred to as *depressive realism*, meaning sad or depressed individuals are more realistic about the future than other people. However, the existence of depressive realism is problematic because it is generally hard to decide *accurately* how optimistic any given individual is about his/her future (Harris & Hahn, 2011).

KEY TERM

Misery-is-not-miserly effect
The tendency for sad individuals to be willing to pay more for some commodity than other people.

Decision making and sadness

Earlier we discussed a study by Raghunathan and Pham (1999) in which anxious participants tended to choose a low-risk job rather than a high-risk one. Raghunathan and Pham also considered the effects of sadness. Most sad participants differed from anxious ones in selecting the high-risk job (see Figure 15.13). Why was this? According to Raghunathan and Pham, sad individuals experience the environment as relatively unrewarding and so are especially motivated to obtain rewards.

Cryder et al. (2008) investigated the **misery-is-not-miserly effect** – sad individuals will pay more than others to acquire a given commodity. Why does this effect occur? Cryder et al. argued that sad individuals have a diminished sense of self (especially when engaging in self-focus). This increases their motivation to acquire possessions to enhance the self. Sad individuals were willing to pay almost *four* times as much as those in a neutral mood for a sporty, insulated water bottle. However, the key finding was that sad individuals high in self-focus were willing to pay much more than sad individuals low in self-focus (see Figure 15.14). Thus, the misery-is-not-miserly effect depends on sad individuals' desire to enhance the self.

Much research supports the "sadder-but-wiser" hypothesis, namely, that sad individuals make wiser decisions. For example, there is the controversial notion (discussed earlier) that they show depressive realism. Lerner et al. (submitted) wondered whether this hypothesis has general applicability. They studied the well-known phenomenon that most people are impatient and prefer immediate rewards to larger but later ones. The median participant in a neutral mood regarded receiving \$19 today as comparable to receiving \$100 in a year. The median sad participant was even more impatient regarding \$4 today as comparable to \$100 in a year!

What do these findings mean? Sad individuals experienced a need to enhance the self by obtaining an immediate reward. Of relevance, many sad individuals focused on possible purchases before deciding between immediate and delayed reward.

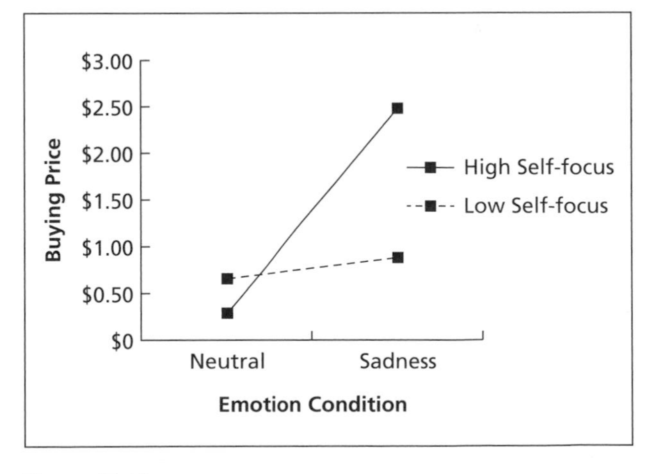

Figure 15.14
Mean amount of money that individuals were willing to pay for a water bottle as a function of induced emotional state (neutral vs. sad) and self-focus (low vs. high).
From Cryder et al. (2008). Reprinted by permission of SAGE Publications.

Anger

Anger is typically regarded as a negative affect. However, it can be experienced as relatively pleasant because it leads individuals to believe they can control the situation and dominate those whom they dislike (Lerner & Tiedens, 2006). *Schadenfreude* (experiencing pleasure at the misfortune of disliked others) is increased by anger (Hareli & Weiner, 2002). However, the events triggering anger are remembered as unpleasant, and this can lead to behaviour (e.g., aggression, violence) causing substantial negative affect (Litvak et al., 2010).

How does anger influence judgement? There are striking differences between the effects of anger and other negative emotional states. Anger is associated with relatively optimistic judgements about the likelihood of negative events, whereas anxiety and sadness are both associated with pessimistic judgements (Waters, 2008). Angry people rate themselves as *less* at risk than other people, although they are actually *more* likely to experience divorce, have problems at work and suffer from heart disease (Lerner & Keltner, 2001).

Why is anger associated with optimistic judgements rather than the pessimistic ones associated with other negative mood states? Anger differs from other negative moods in being associated with a sense of certainty about what has happened and with *perceived control* over the situation (Litvak et al., 2010). These unique features of anger (especially high perceived control) explain why anger produces optimistic judgements.

Decision making and anger

Since angry people perceive themselves to have high control over situations, we might expect them to make riskier decisions than others. There is support for this prediction. Lerner and Keltner (2001) used the Asian disease problem on which most people exhibit risk-averse decision making (see Chapter 13). Fearful participants were risk averse but angry ones were risk seeking. Earlier we discussed a study by Gambetti and Giusberti (2012) in which they found anxious individuals had made less risky real-life financial decisions than those low in anxiety. Gambetti and Giusberti also found individuals with angry personalities had made risker financial decisions (e.g., more likely to have invested money in stocks and shares; more likely to have invested relatively large sums of money) than non-angry ones.

Research by Kugler et al. (2012) suggests the effects of anger on decision making are more complex than stated so far. First they replicated the finding that angry participants on their own were much less risk averse than happy or fearful ones on a lottery task involving large real-money payoffs. However, they obtained the *opposite* findings when participants were in pairs. Each individual chose between a risk-free option in which the outcome did not depend on the other person's choice and a risky option in which it did. Angry participants were much less likely than fearful ones (56% vs. 93%, respectively) to choose the risky option. Angry individuals did not want to lose control of the situation by making the risky choice.

Most people assume anger impairs our ability to think straight. According to the American Ralph Waldo Emerson, anger "blows out the light of reason". This viewpoint was supported by Bright and Goodman-Delahunty (2006). Some mock jurors were shown gruesome photographs of a murdered woman. Those shown the photographs were far more likely to find the husband guilty (41% vs. 9%). The photographs' distorting effect occurred in part because they increased jurors' anger towards the husband.

In a study discussed earlier, Stephens and Groeger (2011) also found anger impaired decision making using a simulated driving task. More specifically, angry drivers drove in a dangerous and reckless manner.

Why does anger often impair decision making? It can lead to shallow processing based on heuristics (rules of thumb) rather than systematic or analytic processing (Litvak et al., 2010). Supporting evidence was reported by Coget et al. (2011) in a study of seven film directors. They mostly resorted to intuitive decision making when moderately or very angry, whereas moderate anxiety led to analytic processing.

Small and Lerner (2008) presented participants with the fictitious case of Patricia Smith, a young divorced mother with three children. Participants put into an angry mood decided she should receive less welfare assistance than those put into a neutral or sad mood. In another condition, participants were given a second task (cognitive load) to perform at the same time as the decision-making task. This was done to reduce participants' use of systematic or analytic processing on the decision-making task. The added cognitive load did not influence the angry participants' *decisions*, suggesting they made little use of analytic processing in either condition.

Anger causes *judgements* as well as decisions to be made using heuristic processing. Ask and Granhag (2007) asked angry or sad police investigators to read the summary of a criminal case and two witness statements. They then judged the witnesses on several measures (e.g., trustworthiness) and judged how likely it was the defendant was guilty. The angry participants processed the case information more superficially than the sad ones (e.g., their judgements were less influenced by the content of the witness statements).

Positive mood

As discussed earlier, there has been much interest in optimism bias (the tendency for people to judge they will experience more positive but fewer negative events than others). We would expect optimism bias to be stronger among those in a positive mood than those in a negative or neutral mood.

Lench and Levine (2005) presented participants with several hypothetical positive and negative events. Those in a happy mood showed a stronger optimism bias than fearful participants. However, they were not more optimistic than participants in a neutral mood.

Drace et al. (2009) argued that most people show an optimism bias regardless of mood. They manipulated mood using pictures and music in several experiments. Optimism bias was comparable regardless of whether participants were in a positive, neutral or negative mood. Why did Drace et al.'s findings differ from those of most earlier studies? In many of those studies, participants' mood states were measured shortly before assessing optimism. Thus, some participants may have guessed the experimenter was interested in the relationship between mood and optimism and altered their judgements accordingly. In contrast, Drace et al. minimised the chance of such distortions occurring.

Decision making and positive mood

Positive mood states are typically associated with a risk-averse approach to decision making (Blanchette & Richards, 2010). For example, Mustanski (2007) found the prevalence of HIV risk behaviours among gay men is less among those having high levels of positive affect. In one study (Cahir & Thomas, 2010), participants in a positive mood made less-risky decisions than those in a neutral mood when betting on hypothetical horse races. Those in a positive mood were probably risk averse because they were motivated to maintain their current happy feeling.

Positive affect is associated with increased use of heuristic or low-effort processing and decreased use of analytic processing (Griskevicius et al., 2010). De Vries et al. (2012) asked participants on each trial to decide between two gambles: (1) 50% chance of winning 1.20 euro and 50% chance of winning nothing; (2) 50% chance of winning 1.00 euro and 50% chance of winning nothing. Analytic thinking would lead participants to choose the first gamble on every trial. Happy participants were less likely than sad ones to use the analytic process consistently. Instead, happy participants were more likely than sad ones to engage in heuristic processing (e.g., switching gambles if the current one had proved unsuccessful on recent trials).

De Vries et al. (2008) argued that people are most satisfied with their decision making when using their *preferred* processing strategy. Participants put into a happy or sad mood were required to use heuristic/intuitive or analytic/deliberative processing when making a decision.

De Vries et al.'s findings supported their predictions (see Figure 15.15). Happy participants were more satisfied with their decision following heuristic/intuitive processing than analytic/deliberative processing. The findings for sad participants were precisely the opposite. Thus, people are most content when their decision-making strategy matches their mood.

There is a puzzling difference between research on negative and on positive affect. *Three* different kinds of negative affect (anxiety, sadness, anger) have been emphasised but only a *single* broad positive affect. In fact, however, there is evidence for eight different positive moods: awe, amusement, interest, pride, gratitude, joy, love and contentment (Campos et al., 2013).

Griskevicius et al. (2010) considered the effects of several positive mood states on the ability to assess the persuasiveness of strong and weak arguments. Participants experiencing three positive emotions (anticipatory enthusiasm, amusement, attachment love) exhibited heuristic or shallow processing – they were persuaded by weak arguments (see Figure 15.16). However, two other positive emotions (awe, nurturant love) were associated with *less* heuristic or shallow processing than a neutral mood state. It is for future research to explain why positive mood states differ in their effects on processing.

Figure 15.15
Subjective value associated with decision as a function of mood (happy vs. sad) and decision strategy (intuitive vs. deliberative).
From de Vries et al. (2008).

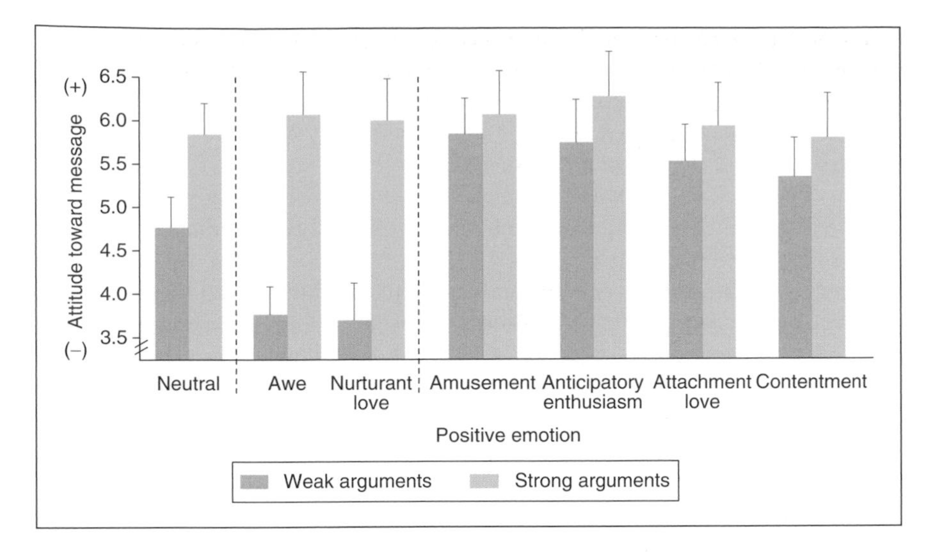

Figure 15.16
Effects of six positive emotions on persuasiveness of arguments (weak vs. strong).

From Griskevicius et al. (2010). © American Psychological Association.

Overall conclusions and evaluation

Several mood states have significant effects on judgement and decision making. Of theoretical importance, the pattern of effects varies across mood states (see Figure 15.17). It is especially noteworthy that the pattern varies across the three negative mood states of anxiety, sadness, and anger.

How can we make sense of Figure 15.17? Anxiety occurs in threatening situations involving uncertainty and unpredictability. Accordingly, anxious individuals are motivated to reduce anxiety by increasing certainty and unpredictability, which can be achieved by minimising risk taking and choosing non-risky options.

Individuals become sad or depressed when they discover a desired goal is unattainable. Sadness or depression leads individuals to abandon the unachievable goal and engage in extensive thinking to focus on new goals (Andrews & Thomson, 2009). Focusing on what to do next involves analytic processing. This helps us to understand why sadness is the only mood state associated with analytic processing.

Anger has the function of overcoming some obstacle to an important goal by taking direct and aggressive action. This approach is most likely to be found when individuals feel they have personal control and are thus optimistic the goal can be achieved. This perception of personal control also persuades angry individuals to take risks to achieve their goals.

	Anxiety	**Sadness**	**Anger**	**Positive mood**
Judgement	Pessimistic	Pessimistic	Optimistic	Optimistic?
Attitude to risk	Risk averse	Risk taking	Risk taking	Risk averse
Processing	Inefficient	Analytic	Heuristic	Heuristic

Figure 15.17
Effects of mood states on judgement and decision making.

An important function of positive mood states is to maintain the current mood (Oatley & Johnson-Laird, 1987). This leads happy individuals to engage in shallow or heuristic processing and to avoid taking risks that might endanger the positive mood state.

What are the main limitations of research in this area? First, most research has involved incidental emotional states of no direct relevance to the judgement or decision-making task. Such research may be relatively uninformative about the effects of integral mood states.

Second, most laboratory research has involved relatively trivial judgements and decisions having no implications outside the laboratory. It is unsurprising that people use predominantly heuristic processing with such tasks. However, the situation may be very different in real life when people in an intense emotional state make major decisions.

Third, many findings have been explained using the distinction between heuristic or shallow processing and analytic or deliberate processing. This distinction is oversimplified and ignores the likelihood that many cognitive processes involve a combination of both types of process (Keren & Schul, 2009).

Moral dilemmas: emotion vs. cognition

Most research discussed so far has involved *mild* mood manipulations. In the real world, however, strong emotion can be involved when we make complex judgements and decisions (e.g., with moral dilemmas).

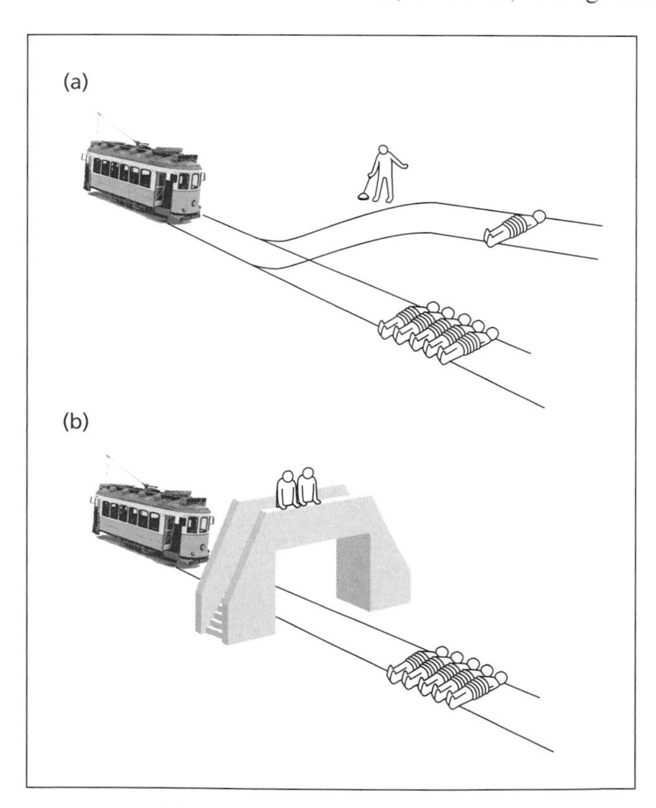

Figure 15.18
Two well-known moral dilemma problems: (a) the trolley problem; and (b) the footbridge problem.

The *trolley problem* is an example of a moral dilemma. You must decide whether to divert a runaway trolley threatening the lives of five people on to a side-track where it will kill only one person (see Figure 15.18A). The *footbridge problem* is another example. You must decide whether to push a fat person over a bridge causing the death of the person pushed but saving the lives of five other people (see Figure 15.18B).

What did you decide? In experimental studies, 90% of participants decide to divert the trolley but only 10% decide to push the person off the footbridge (Hauser, 2006). Greene et al. (2008) argued that the footbridge problem is an example of a *personal* moral dilemma because we might *directly* harm or kill one or more people by our actions. In contrast, the trolley problem is an *impersonal* moral dilemma because the harm that might be done results less directly and immediately from our actions. Most research has focused on personal moral dilemmas.

According to Greene et al. (2008), personal moral dilemmas trigger a strong emotional response. With the footbridge problem, we face a severe conflict. There is a powerful *emotional* argument not to kill another person. On the other hand, there is a strong *cognitive* argument that more lives will be saved (five vs. one) if you push the person over the bridge.

In their dual-process model, Greene et al. (2008) distinguished between two systems: (1) a fast, automatic and affective system; and (2) a slower, effortful and more "cognitive" system. With personal moral dilemmas, those making **deontological judgements** based on moral rules or obligations (e.g., do not kill) respond mainly on the basis of the first, affective system. In contrast, those making practical or **utilitarian judgements** based on saving as many lives as possible use the second, cognitive system. In crude terms, you can use your head (utilitarian judgements) or your heart (deontological judgements) when resolving a moral dilemma.

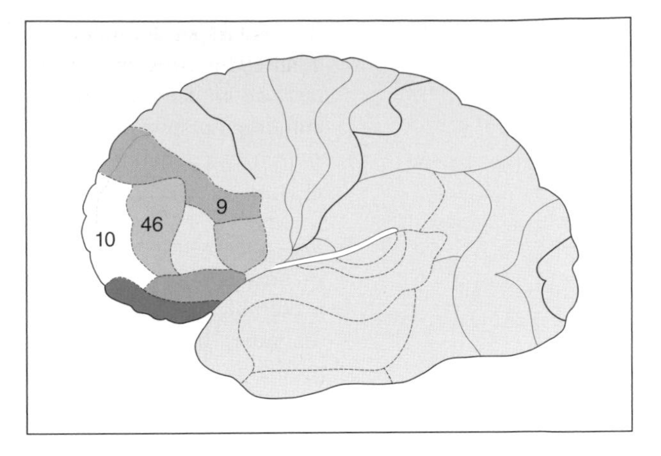

Figure 15.19
The dorsolateral prefrontal cortex is located approximately in Brodmann areas 9 and 46; the parts of the ventromedial prefrontal cortex is located approximately in Brodmann area 10 and 11 (shown in blue).
From Ward (2010).

Different brain areas have been associated with the two systems (see Figure 15.19). The dorsolateral prefrontal cortex (DLPFC) and anterior cingulate cortex (ACC) are involved in cognitive control (see also Figure 16.6, page 697). In contrast, the ventromedial prefrontal cortex (VMPFC) is involved in the generation of emotions.

Findings: positive

According to the two-process model, utilitarian judgements with personal moral dilemmas typically involve much use of the cognitive system. Suppose participants performed a demanding cognitive task reducing accessibility of cognitive resources while making moral judgements. This task should increase the time taken to make utilitarian judgements (which generally involve much cognitive processing) more than that for deontological judgements. That is precisely what Greene et al. (2008) found.

It is assumed theoretically that deontological judgements depend much more on emotional processing than do utilitarian ones with personal moral dilemmas but not impersonal ones. We can test this assumption by giving an anti-anxiety drug to participants to reduce the impact of emotion on judgements. This was done by Perkins et al. (2013). As predicted, anti-anxiety drugs increased utilitarian judgements (and reduced deontological ones) with personal moral dilemmas but did not affect judgements with impersonal ones.

According to the model, individuals making utilitarian judgements should show more activity in the dorsolateral prefrontal cortex (DLPFC) than those making deontological judgements. This finding was obtained by Greene et al. (2004). Further support for the importance of the DLPFC was reported by Tassy et al. (2012). They applied repetitive transcranial magnetic stimulation (rTMS; see Glossary) to the DLPFC to inhibit its functioning. This reduced utilitarian judgements with moral dilemmas of high emotional intensity.

Thomas et al. (2011) studied patients with damage to the ventromedial prefrontal cortex (VMPFC). Such patients have reduced emotional responsiveness. As a result, they should be less influenced than healthy controls by emotional

KEY TERMS

Deontological judgements
Judgements based on moral rules and/or obligations when resolving moral dilemmas.

Utilitarian judgements
Judgements based on practical and pragmatic considerations when resolving moral dilemmas.

factors. As predicted, they made more utilitarian judgements than other brain-damaged patients or healthy controls. Other research (Young & Dungan, 2012) has shown the utilitarian judgements of VMPFC patients are due to reduced emotional responsiveness rather than impaired cognitive functioning.

Findings: negative

We turn now to potential problems with the dual-process model. As Bartels and Pizarro (2011) noted, the model seems to assume utilitarian judgements are preferable to deontological ones. They found individuals without a clinical diagnosis but high on psychopathy (anti-social personality) produced more utilitarian judgements than low scorers. These findings suggest utilitarian judgements can stem from inhibited reactions to harm, and thus can be undesirable.

According to Broeders et al. (2011), the assumption that utilitarian judgements with personal moral dilemmas are based on pragmatic considerations while deontological judgements are based on moral rules is oversimplified. They tested this assumption in a study in which participants were presented with information designed to focus their attention on the moral rules "Do not kill" or "Saving lives" prior to the footbridge problem. Participants for whom the rule "Saving lives" was more accessible produced more utilitarian judgements than those given the rule "Do not kill". Thus, utilitarian judgements (as well as deontological ones) can be based on moral rules and the differences between the two types of judgements may be less than generally assumed.

Kahane et al. (2012) pointed out that utilitarian judgements in most previous research were *counterintuitive* or opposed to common sense. The reason such judgements involve cognitive control within the DLPFC and take longer than deontological judgements could be because they are counterintuitive rather than because they are utilitarian.

We can see what Kahane et al. (2012) meant by considering a personal moral dilemma in which a utilitarian judgement is *not* counterintuitive. Suppose you are a waiter and a customer you know well tells you he is determined to infect as many people as possible with HIV before he goes to prison in 48 hours. You know he has a very strong allergy to poppy seeds and so if you put some in his food he would be hospitalised for at least 48 hours. What would you do? In this case, the utilitarian judgement (i.e., give him the poppy seeds) is intuitively appealing.

Kahane et al. (2012) studied utilitarian and deontological judgements that were intuitive or counterintuitive. There were three main findings. First, counterintuitive judgements were regarded as more difficult than intuitive ones regardless of whether those judgements were utilitarian or deontological. Second, in contrast to previous research, utilitarian judgements were *not* associated with DLPFC activation nor were deontological judgements associated with VMPFC activation. Third, there was greater activation in the anterior cingulate cortex (ACC) with counterintuitive judgements than intuitive ones, suggesting only the former involved emotional conflict. Thus, the distinction between intuitive and counter-intuitive judgements seemed more fundamental than that between utilitarian and deontological ones.

Evaluation

Research on moral dilemmas focuses on complex emotional issues of relevance to everyday life. There is much support for the theoretical assumption that people confronting a moral dilemma can use fast affective processes and/or slow cognitive ones. Progress has been made in identifying the brain areas associated with those two types of process based on neuroimaging studies and studies on brain-damaged patients.

What are the limitations of the dual-process model? First, the assumption that utilitarian judgements are "better" seems dubious given the tendency of individuals with an anti-social personality to prefer such judgements. Second, the notion that moral rules are used with deontological judgements but not utilitarian ones is oversimplified. Utilitarian judgements can also be based on moral rules. Third, the distinction between utilitarian and deontological judgements may be of less fundamental importance than that between intuitive and counterintuitive judgements.

KEY TERMS

Trait anxiety
A personality dimension based on individual differences in susceptibility to anxiety.

Comorbidity
The presence of two or more mental disorders in a given patient at the same time.

ANXIETY, DEPRESSION AND COGNITIVE BIASES

Most of the research discussed in the previous section dealt with the effects of mood manipulations on cognitive processing and performance. It is also possible to focus on cognitive processing in individuals who are generally in a given mood state (e.g., patients suffering from an anxiety disorder or major depressive disorder). Alternatively, we can study healthy individuals having anxious or depressive personalities. For example, anxious individuals can be selected by using questionnaires assessing **trait anxiety** (susceptibility to experiencing anxiety).

The above may sound like easy research strategies to adopt. However, anxious individuals also tend to be depressed, and vice versa. **Comorbidity** is the term used to indicate a patient has two or more mental disorders at the same time; it is very common in patients with an anxiety disorder or major depressive disorder. It is also the case that healthy individuals with anxious personalities (high in trait anxiety) also tend to have depressive personalities.

In spite of the overlap between anxiety and depression, there are important differences between them. For example, past losses are associated mainly with depression whereas future threats are associated more with anxiety. Eysenck et al. (2006) presented participants with scenarios referring to several negative events (e.g., the diagnosis of a serious illness). Each scenario had three versions depending on whether it referred to a past event, a future possible event or a future probable event. Participants indicated how anxious or depressed each event would make them. Anxiety was associated more with future than past events, whereas the opposite was the case for depression.

There is further support for the above notions if we consider the symptoms of anxiety and depression. *Worry* about possible future events is a major symptom of several anxiety disorders (Hirsch & Mathews, 2012). Indeed, it is the central symptom of generalised anxiety disorder in which patients have excessive concerns across various domains (e.g., work, interpersonal relationships). In contrast, *rumination* (which involves dwelling on negative feelings and experiences from the past) is a very common symptom in depressed patients.

Why is it important to study cognitive processes in anxious and depressed people? Patients with clinical anxiety or depression differ from healthy individuals in several ways (e.g., cognitively, behaviourally, physiologically, perhaps biochemically). Therapies differ in terms of which type of symptom is the central focus in treatment (Kring et al., 2012). Within this context, it is of major theoretical importance to establish the role played by cognitive factors.

KEY TERMS

Attentional bias
Selective allocation of attention to threat-related stimuli when presented simultaneously with neutral stimuli.

Interpretive bias
The tendency when presented with ambiguous stimuli or situations to interpret them in a threatening way.

Explicit memory bias
The retrieval of relatively more negative information than positive or neutral information on tests of **explicit memory**.

Implicit memory bias
Relatively better memory performance for negative than for neutral or positive information on tests of **implicit memory**.

Many theorists (e.g., Beck & Dozois, 2011) assume vulnerability to clinical anxiety and depression depends in part on various cognitive biases. A second key assumption is that cognitive therapy (and cognitive-behaviour therapy) should focus on reducing or eliminating these cognitive biases as a major goal of treatment.

The most important cognitive biases are as follows:

- **Attentional bias**: selective attention to threat-related stimuli presented at the same time as neutral stimuli; this can involve rapid attentional *engagement* with threat stimuli and/or slow attentional *disengagement*.
- **Interpretive bias**: the tendency to interpret ambiguous stimuli and situations in a threatening fashion.
- **Explicit memory bias**: the tendency to retrieve mostly negative or unpleasant rather than positive or neutral information on memory tests involving conscious recollection.
- **Implicit memory bias**: the tendency to exhibit superior performance for negative or threatening than neutral or positive information on memory tests not involving conscious recollection.

Someone possessing all the above cognitive biases would attend excessively to environmental threat, interpret most ambiguous situations as threatening, and thus would perceive themselves as having experienced numerous unpleasant past events. As a result, it seems reasonable he/she would be more likely than most people to develop an anxiety disorder or depression. However, we need to consider the causality issue. Suppose, for example, most anxious patients possess both cognitive biases. Did the cognitive biases play a role in triggering the anxiety disorder, did the anxiety disorder enhance the cognitive biases, or is causality bi-directional?

Theoretical positions

Which cognitive biases would we expect anxious and depressed individuals to possess? Williams et al. (1997) put forward an influential answer, which we will consider after discussing their distinction between perceptual and conceptual processes. Perceptual processes are essentially data-driven and are often fast and "automatic". They are used in basic attentional processes and implicit memory. In contrast, conceptual processes are top-down and are generally slower and more controlled than perceptual processes. They are involved in explicit memory, but can also be involved in attentional processes and implicit memory.

Williams et al. (1997) argued that anxiety and depression fulfil different functions, and these different functions have important consequences for information processing. Anxiety has the function of anticipating danger or future threat. As a result, anxiety facilitates the perceptual processing of threat-related stimuli. Depression has the function of replacing failed goals. This implies that, "the conceptual processing of internally generated material related to failure or loss may be more relevant to this function than perceptual vigilance" (p. 315).

The above assumptions generate the following four predictions:

1 Anxious individuals should have an attentional bias for threatening stimuli when perceptual processes are involved. Depressed individuals should have an attentional bias only when conceptual processing is involved.

2. Anxious and depressed individuals should have an interpretive bias for ambiguous stimuli and situations.
3. Depressed individuals should have an explicit memory bias but anxious ones should not.
4. Anxious individuals should have an implicit memory bias but depressed ones should not when only perceptual processes are involved.

There have been various important theoretical developments in the years since Williams et al. (1997) put forward their theory. Two such developments are discussed below.

Combined cognitive bias hypothesis

Most theorists have treated the various cognitive biases as if they were entirely *separate*. This approach was challenged by Hirsch et al. (2006). According to their combined cognitive bias hypothesis, "cognitive biases do not operate in isolation, but rather can influence each other and/or can interact so that the impact of each on another variable is influenced by the other" (p. 224).

Hirsch et al. (2006) focused on cognitive processes in social phobia (excessive fear of social situations). Everaert et al. (2012) argued that this hypothesis is equally applicable to depression and identified several questions raised by it. First, are different cognitive biases interrelated? Second, can changes in one cognitive bias cause changes in another one? Third, do multiple biases have *additive* effects on patients' symptoms or are the effects greater than that?

Cognitive control

Joormann (e.g., Joorman et al., 2007; Gotlib & Joormann, 2010) argued that executive or control processes are important to an understanding of cognitive biases in depression. Consider inhibitory control (see Chapter 6). If depressed individuals have deficient inhibitory control, they might have difficulty in disengaging attention from negative stimuli. More generally, inhibitory control is an executive process involving the resources of working memory (see Chapter 6) and there is evidence that depression is associated with reduced working-memory resources (Kircanski et al., 2012).

According to Joormann's theoretical approach, depressed individuals have impaired cognitive control (see Figure 15.20). As just discussed, this impaired control causes problems in disengaging attention from negative information. Depressed individuals are likely to elaborate on this information during the additional time they attend to it. This can lead to enhanced memory for such information (i.e., a memory bias).

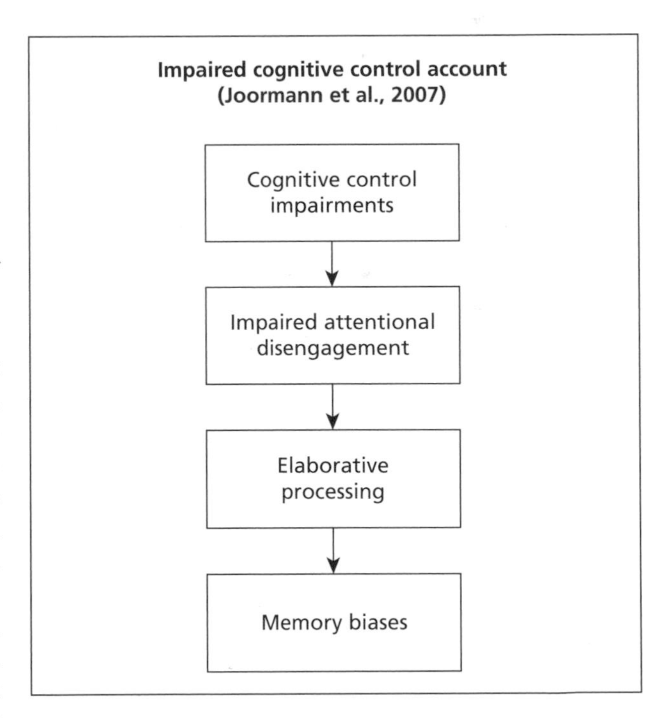

Figure 15.20
According to the impaired cognitive control account put forward by Joormann et al. (2007), depression is associated with cognitive control impairments that lead to impaired attentional disengagement, elaborative processing and memory biases.
From Everaert et al. (2012). With permission from Elsevier.

There is much evidence that depressed individuals are slower than non-depressed people to disengage attention from negative emotional stimuli (De Raedt & Koster, 2010). Zetsche and Joormann (2012) studied the role of inhibitory control in depression. Poor inhibitory control was associated with a greater number of depressive symptoms. In addition, poor inhibitory control predicted the maintenance of depressive symptoms and rumination over the following six months.

Impaired attentional control is also relevant to understanding the effects of anxiety on cognitive processing. According to attentional control theory (Eysenck et al., 2007), anxiety reduces the available capacity of working memory. This impairs the efficiency of attentional control (which depends on working memory) in two ways. First, it impairs inhibitory control including the ability to avoid processing task-irrelevant stimuli (negative attentional control). Second, it impairs the ability to shift attention optimally within and between tasks (positive attentional control).

Eysenck et al. (2007) reviewed numerous studies showing anxious individuals are impaired in their ability to inhibit and to shift attention. In subsequent research, Calvo et al. (2012) studied the interference effect of threat distractors on task performance. High-anxiety individuals showed delayed inhibitory control relative to low-anxiety ones.

Impaired attentional control in anxious individuals is of potential relevance to their cognitive biases. For example, anxious individuals should often have problems in disengaging attention from threatening stimuli (discussed shortly). It also means anxious individuals should spend longer periods of time than non-anxious ones attending to and thinking about their worries (Hirsch & Mathews, 2012).

Attentional bias

Various tasks assess attentional bias (Yiend et al., 2013). First, there is the dot-probe task (see Figure 15.21). Two stimuli are presented at the same time to different locations on a computer screen. On critical trials, one stimulus is emotionally negative (e.g., the word *failure*, an *angry face*) and the other neutral.

Weblink:
Dot-probe task

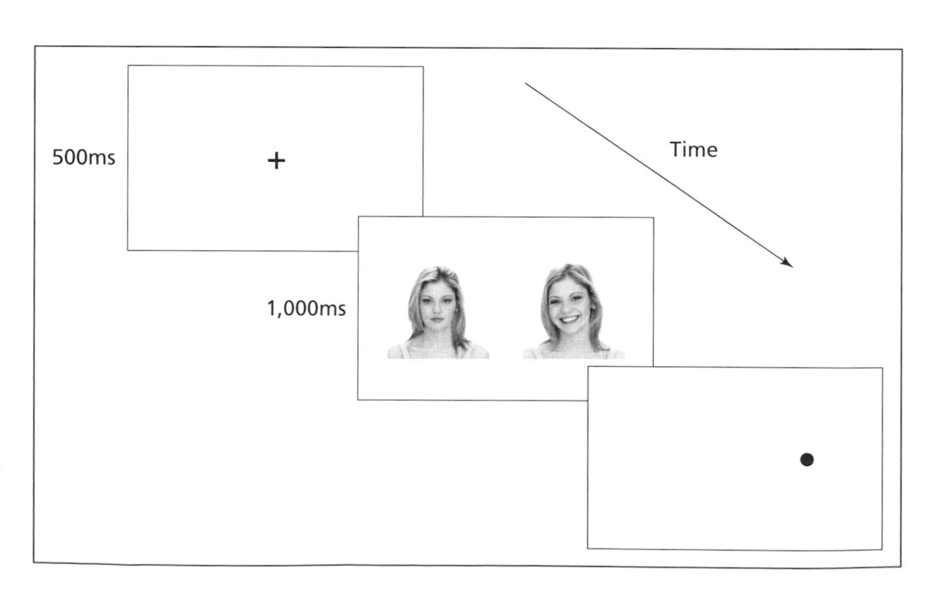

Figure 15.21
This is the dot-probe task. Participants initially focus the central +, then view two stimuli varying in emotion and then respond rapidly to a dot that replaces one of the stimuli.

© ZoneCreative/iStock.

The allocation of attention is assessed by recording the speed of detection of a dot that replaces one stimulus. It is assumed detection latencies are shorter in attended areas. Therefore, attentional bias is shown by a consistent tendency for detection latencies to be shorter when the dot replaces the negative stimulus.

Second, there is the emotional Stroop task (see Glossary) on which participants name the colour in which words are printed as rapidly as possible (see Figure 15.22). Some words are emotionally negative while others are neutral. It is claimed attentional bias is shown if participants take longer to name the colours of emotional than those of neutral words (but see below).

HATE	CHAMPION
DEPRESSED	EXAM
CRYING	SKY
BULLY	CARWASH
SUICIDE	WIKIPEDIA

Figure 15.22
The emotional Stroop task. Participants name the colours in which emotional or neutral words are printed. Attentional bias is allegedly shown if participants take longer to name the colours of emotional words than those of neutral words.

Findings

Bar-Haim et al. (2007) carried out a meta-analysis (see Glossary) on studies of attentional bias in anxious individuals. They distinguished between studies involving subliminal stimuli (i.e., presented below the level of conscious awareness) and those involving supraliminal stimuli (i.e., presented above the level of conscious awareness).

What did Bar-Haim et al. (2007) find? There was strong evidence of attentional bias with subliminal and supraliminal stimuli. The magnitude of the attentional bias effect was comparable across all anxiety disorders and high trait-anxious healthy individuals. The existence of attentional bias with both subliminal and supraliminal stimuli suggests this bias can involve various preattentive and attentional processes.

Rudaizky et al. (2014) found high trait anxiety (see Glossary) was associated with facilitated attentional *engagement* with negative stimuli and also with slowed attentional *disengagement* from such stimuli. These two biases were uncorrelated with each other. This suggests vulnerability to anxiety depends on *separate* contributions from attentional engagement bias and attentional disengagement bias.

Cisler and Koster (2010) reviewed research on attentional bias and attentional disengagement in the anxiety disorders. The evidence suggested attentional bias depends in part on a threat-detection mechanism that is largely automatic and is activated by threat stimuli presented subliminally. Anxiety also produces difficulty in disengaging attention from threat stimuli that is mostly due to poor attentional control.

Is depression associated with attentional bias? In a meta-analysis, Peckham et al. (2010) found clear evidence for attentional bias with depressed patients and healthy samples using the dot-probe task. However, the effect was only marginally significant when the emotional Stroop task was used, probably because it provides a more indirect assessment of attentional processes.

The dot-probe and emotional Stroop tasks provide us with reaction-time data. Such data are of limited value in tracking the time course of attentional bias. Indeed, such data make it hard to decide whether anxiety (or depression) is affecting attentional engagement or attentional disengagement (Clarke et al., 2013).

How can we clarify the effects of anxiety and depression on attentional processes? Eye tracking provides a fairly direct and continuous assessment of visual attention. This technique has been used in studies on *visual search* (finding a target stimulus among several distractors).

Armstrong and Olatunji (2012) used meta-analysis to assess the effects of anxiety and depression on eye movements during visual search. Anxious individuals had increased vigilance for threat (attentional bias) compared to controls, and also found it harder to disengage from threat. There was much less evidence that depressed individuals were susceptible to these attentional biases.

Free viewing involves participants viewing a display with complete freedom to choose which stimuli to attend to. It has the advantage of closely resembling what is typically the case in everyday life. Armstrong and Olatunji (2012) found the effects of depression were greater than those of anxiety. More specifically, depressed individuals (but not anxious ones) took longer than controls to fixate positive (i.e., pleasant) stimuli and maintained gaze on them for less time.

What can we conclude from the above findings? Anxious individuals have heightened sensitivity to threatening stimuli but depressed ones do not. In contrast, depressed individuals have decreased sensitivity to positive stimuli but this is not found in anxious individuals.

Evaluation

The findings are reasonably consistent with predictions from the theory of Williams et al. (1997). More specifically, anxious individuals show attentional bias in terms of rapid engagement with threat stimuli and slow disengagement with supraliminal stimuli. They also show attentional bias with subliminal stimuli. This fits with Williams et al.'s assumption that anxious individuals should have an attentional bias when fast and "automatic" perceptual processes are involved. As predicted, attentional bias is less commonly found with depressed individuals than with anxious ones.

What are the limitations of research in this area? First, the two major paradigms (dot-probe, emotional Stroop) provide limited information concerning the time course of attentional processing. However, more detailed information is available from eye-tracking studies.

Second, there may be an additional uncertainty concerning the appropriate interpretation of findings from the emotional Stroop task. Rapid *avoidance* is the natural reaction to threat in everyday life. On the emotional Stroop task, in contrast, participants produce an *approach* response (e.g., pressing the appropriate lever), which may explain why responding is slow when threatening stimuli are presented. Chajut et al. (2010) found faster responding to threatening stimuli than neutral ones on the emotional Stroop task when participants produced avoidance responses (i.e., pushing a joystick).

Interpretive bias

In our everyday lives we often encounter ambiguous situations. For example, if someone walks past you without acknowledging your presence, does this mean they dislike you or simply that they failed to notice you? Individuals who generally interpret ambiguous situations in a threatening manner have an interpretive bias.

Anxious individuals have an interpretive bias. Eysenck et al. (1987) asked participants varying in their level of trait anxiety (see Glossary) to write down the spellings of auditorily presented words. Some words were homophones (words with the same pronunciation but different spellings) having separate threat-related and neutral interpretations (e.g., *die*, *dye*; *pain*, *pane*). Trait anxiety correlated +0.60 with the number of threatening homophone interpretations. These findings suggest individuals with anxious personalities have interpretive bias.

Individuals high in trait anxiety do not have an interpretive bias for every potentially threatening situation. Walsh et al. (submitted) found high trait anxiety was associated with interpretive bias for ambiguous situations potentially involving social or intellectual threat. However, trait anxiety did not affect the interpretation of situations potentially involving physical or health threat. Thus, interpretive bias in high-anxiety normal individuals is limited to *interpersonal* threats (i.e., negative reactions of other people to one's behaviour).

Eysenck et al. (1991) studied patients with generalised anxiety disorder, a condition characterised by excessive worrying about numerous issues. The patients listened to ambiguous sentences such as the following:

1 At the refugee camp, the weak/week would soon be finished.
2 The doctor examined little Emma's growth.
3 They discussed the priest's convictions.

Patients with generalised anxiety disorder were more likely than healthy controls to interpret such sentences in a threatening way. Thus, they exhibited interpretive bias.

The evidence that depressed individuals have an interpretive bias is less strong than in the case of anxiety (Mathews, 2012). Several researchers (e.g., Gupta & Kar, 2008) have used the Cognitive Bias Questionnaire. Ambiguous events are described briefly and participants select one of four possible interpretations of each one. Depressed patients typically select more negative interpretations than healthy controls. These findings rely entirely on self-report data, which may be distorted.

Mogg et al. (2006) avoided self-report in a study on interpretive bias in patients meeting criteria for major depressive disorder. In one experiment, participants wrote down the spellings of auditorily presented homophones. Depressed patients interpreted 81% of the homophones in a threatening way compared to only 63% for healthy controls. These findings suggest there is an interpretive bias associated with depression.

Does interpretive bias depend mostly on rapid, automatic processes or on slower, strategic processes? Both kinds of processes are involved (Mathews, 2012). Evidence that strategic processes are involved was reported by Calvo and Castillo (1997), who presented ambiguous sentences relating to personal social threat. Individuals high in trait anxiety showed an interpretive bias 1,250 ms after the sentence but not at 500 ms.

Evidence suggesting that interpretive bias can occur fairly rapidly was reported by Moser et al. (2012b). Participants were presented with ambiguous scenarios resolved positively or negatively by the final word. Interpretive bias would be found if positive resolutions of the scenarios were regarded as *unexpected* by the participants, an effect associated with the N4 component of event-related potentials (ERPs; see Glossary).

Participants meeting the criteria for social phobia (excessive fear of social situations) or major depressive disorder had larger N4s than healthy controls to positive resolutions. Thus, interpretive bias had developed within about 400 ms (the time period after stimulus onset associated with N4). It is probably harder to inhibit interpretive biases that occur rapidly than those depending more on controlled processing.

Memory biases

KEY TERM

Memory bias
The retrieval of relatively more negative or unpleasant information than positive or neutral information on a memory test.

Why is it important to study **memory bias** in anxious and depressed individuals? The existence of such biases may well play a role in maintaining negative mood states via relatively automatic processes (implicit memory bias) or processes of which the individual is aware (explicit memory bias).

Williams et al. (1997) predicted explicit memory bias would be found more often in depressed than anxious individuals, whereas the opposite would be the case for implicit memory bias. In their literature review, they identified numerous studies showing explicit memory bias in depressed individuals. Similar findings have been reported in subsequent research (e.g., Rinck & Becker, 2005).

Several studies have focused on implicit memory bias. Phillips et al. (2010) found in a meta-analysis that there was a small but significant positive relationship between depression and implicit memory bias. Williams et al. (1997) argued that this would not be found when perceptual processes were involved. However, Phillips et al. (2010) found evidence for implicit memory bias associated with depression even when perceptual processing occurred at encoding or learning and at retrieval.

What are the effects of anxiety on memory biases? In a meta-analysis, Mitte (2008) found anxiety was not associated with implicit memory bias, which is directly contrary to the prediction of Williams et al. (1997). The findings for explicit memory bias depended on the type of memory test used. Anxiety was associated with memory bias with recall tests but not recognition-memory tests. This difference probably occurred because more extensive retrieval processes are required for recall than for recognition, which provides more scope for the involvement of emotion.

In sum, the effects of depression and anxiety on memory are different. This is especially clear with respect to implicit memory bias (typically found in depressed individuals but not anxious ones). Explicit memory bias is found more strongly and more often in depressed individuals than in anxious ones. These findings are consistent with the notion that depression (more than anxiety) is associated with an inward focus and disengagement from the environment. The findings also suggest depression is more associated than is anxiety with negative past events (Eysenck et al., 2006).

Combined cognitive bias hypothesis

According to the combined cognitive bias hypothesis (discussed earlier), cognitive biases influence each other. How can we show this is the case? The best approach is to increase (or decrease) one cognitive bias using cognitive bias modification techniques (discussed later). According to the hypothesis, this should have predictable effects on a different cognitive bias.

White et al. (2011) used a training procedure to increase attentional bias. This increased participants' tendency to interpret ambiguous information in a threatening way. Amir et al. (2010) found training to reduce interpretive bias made it easier for participants to disengage attention from threat. These findings suggest attentional and interpretive biases reflect (at least in part) the operation of shared selective processing mechanisms.

Salemink et al. (2010) presented participants with ambiguous scenarios to which they provided endings based on their own interpretations of the scenarios. After that, they received training designed to increase or decrease interpretive bias for other ambiguous situations. Finally, participants recalled the initial scenarios and the endings they had provided. Training to produce negative interpretations led to memory for endings that was more negative in emotional tone than occurred following training to produce positive interpretations.

Cognitive vulnerability hypothesis

Cognitive therapists (e.g., Williams et al., 1997; Beck & Dozois, 2011) assume healthy individuals possessing various cognitive biases are more vulnerable than other people to developing anxiety disorders or depression. According to this cognitive vulnerability hypothesis, negative life events (e.g., losing one's job) should have greater adverse effects on the well-being of individuals with cognitive biases. We will briefly discuss two studies supporting this hypothesis.

Lewinsohn et al. (2001) assessed interpretive bias in adolescents. One year later, they recorded the negative life events experienced by the participants over the 12-month period. Those most likely to have developed major depressive disorder over that period experienced many negative life events and had a strong interpretive bias initially. In contrast, the number of negative life events experienced did *not* influence the likelihood of developing major depressive disorder in participants initially low in interpretive bias. The take-home message is that cognitive vulnerability (i.e., strong interpretive bias) increased the adverse effects of negative life events on depressive symptoms.

J.R. Cohen et al. (2012) assessed children's self-reported reactions to negative events. Interpretive bias was shown by pessimistic views of the consequences of such events and the effects of such events on the self. Cohen et al. then assessed the effects of *actual* negative events over a 7-week period on depressive symptoms. As can be seen in Figure 15.23, a high number of negative events led to a greater increase in depressive symptoms in cognitively vulnerable children (i.e., those with interpretive bias).

Conclusions

Four main conclusions follow from the research we have discussed. First, anxious and depressed individuals differ in the nature (and strength) of their cognitive biases (see Figure 15.24). These findings contribute to our basic understanding of the differences between anxiety and depression.

Second, the findings are of considerable theoretical importance. As mentioned earlier, a major function of anxiety is to anticipate future threats, while a major function of depression is to think about past failures and produce new goals. As a result, anxiety should be strongly associated with an *external* focus and attentional bias. In contrast, depression should be strongly associated with an

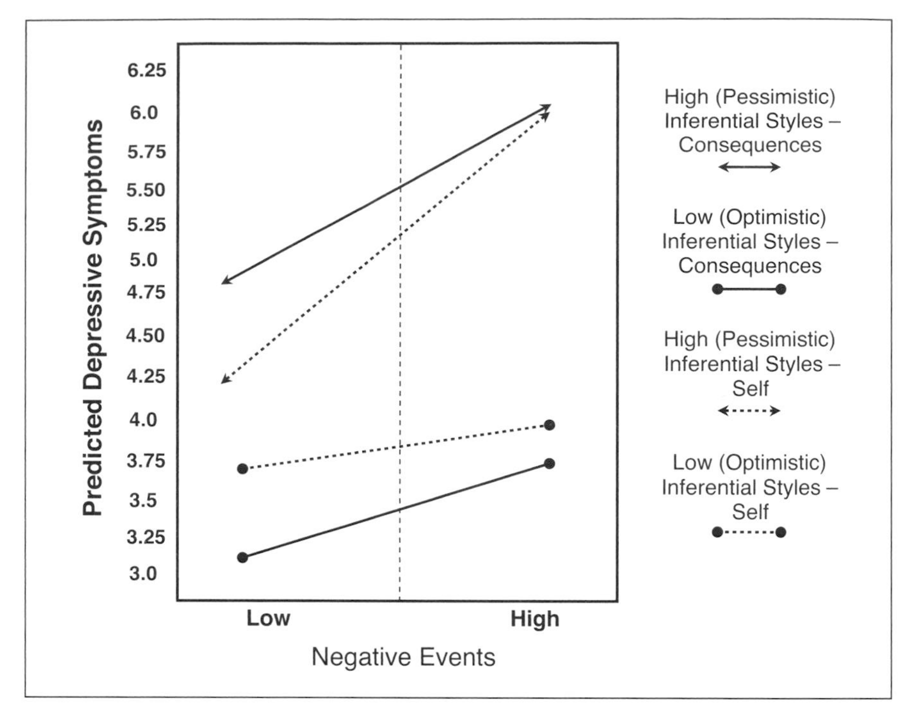

Figure 15.23
Effects of negative events (low vs. high) on depressive symptoms in children with interpretive bias (pessimistic beliefs about the consequences of such events or their effects on the self) and without interpretive bias (optimistic beliefs about the effects of negative events).
From J.R. Cohen et al. (2012). © Springer Science + Business Media.

internal focus and memory biases. The pattern of biases associated with anxiety and depression (see Figure 15.24) corresponds approximately to predictions.

Third, the existence of cognitive biases in anxiety and depression is of value to therapeutic interventions. It suggests a major focus of therapy should be on reducing or eliminating the individual patient's cognitive biases. The progress of therapy can be assessed by the extent to which those cognitive biases are reduced.

Fourth, progress has been made in understanding the *interconnections* among the various cognitive biases. So far this has mostly consisted of showing that producing changes in one cognitive bias often leads to changes in other cognitive biases. The common underlying mechanisms remain to be identified.

	Anxiety	Depression
Attentional bias	***	*
Interpretive bias	**	*
Memory bias (explicit)	*	***
Memory bias (implicit)	–	*

Figure 15.24
Strength of various cognitive biases associated with anxiety and depression: – = no association; * = weak association; ** = moderate association; *** = strong association.

COGNITIVE BIAS MODIFICATION

We have seen anxiety and depression are both associated with the presence of various cognitive biases. As mentioned earlier, the direction of causality is crucial. Do cognitive biases make individuals vulnerable to developing anxiety or depression, or does having anxiety or depression lead to the development of cognitive biases? The optimal way of addressing this issue is by **cognitive bias modification**, which is an "experimental paradigm that uses training to induce maladaptive or adaptive cognitive biases" (Hallion & Ruscio, 2011, p. 940).

KEY TERM

Cognitive bias modification
Training typically designed to reduce **attentional bias** and/or **interpretive bias.**

IN THE REAL WORLD: REDUCING ANXIETY AND DEPRESSION THROUGH COGNITIVE BIAS MODIFICATION

If cognitive biases make individuals more susceptible to anxiety and depression, then cognitive bias modification might have therapeutic value as a way of reducing those negative emotional states. Cognitive bias modification has typically consisted of attempts to *reduce* attentional bias and/or interpretive bias (MacLeod & Clarke, 2013). A common form of training to reduce attentional bias involves the dot-probe task (see Figure 15.21, page 670). This task is altered so the dot *always* appears in the location in which the neutral stimulus had been presented. As a result, participants learn to avoid allocating attention to the threatening stimulus.

A common way of reducing interpretive bias involves initial presentation of a **homograph**. This is a word having only one spelling but at least two meanings. The homograph (e.g., *choke*) has a negative and a benign meaning and is followed by a word fragment to be completed using the homograph as a clue. Each word fragment can only be completed with a positive or neutral

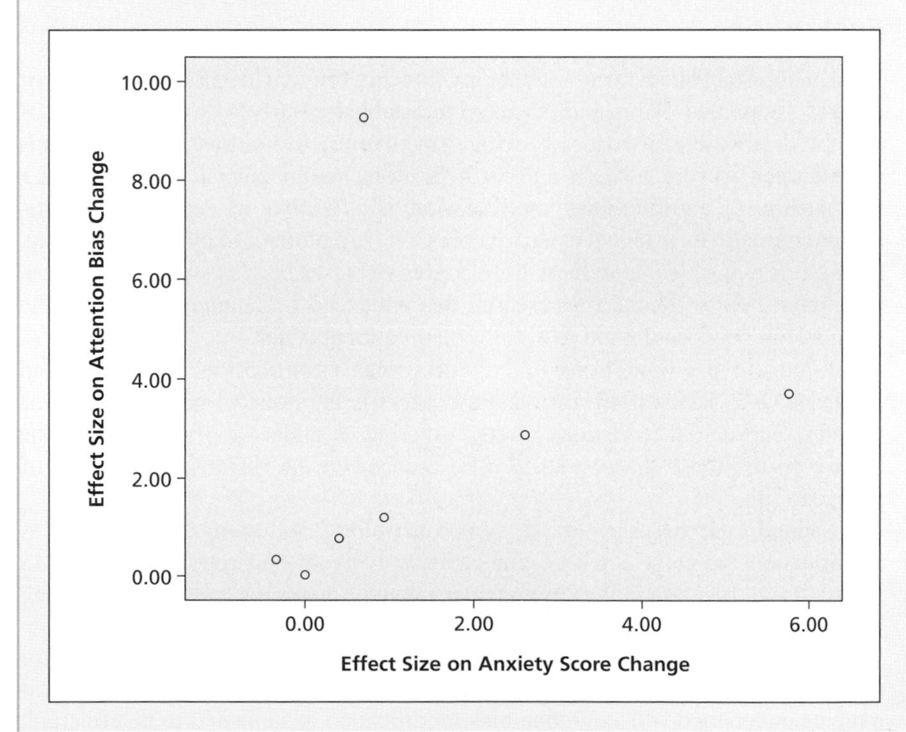

Figure 15.25
Findings from seven studies on attention bias modification showing the relationship between the amount of reduction in attention bias and reductions in self-reported anxiety.
From Hakamata et al. (2010) with permission from Elsevier.

word (e.g., *eng-n-*). Participants learn to focus on the positive or neutral interpretation of each homophone.

How effective is cognitive bias modification? Hakamata et al. (2010) considered the effects of attention bias modification on anxiety across several studies. There were three main findings. First, there was a correlation of +0.75 between the amount of reduction in attention bias and the reduction in anxiety (see Figure 15.25). Second, the effects of attention bias modification were greater with patient than non-patient groups. Third, there were clear effects on trait anxiety, suggesting the technique may produce enduring changes to personality.

Hallion and Ruscio (2011) carried out a meta-analysis (see Glossary) to assess the effects of cognitive bias modification on individuals high in anxiety or depression. Training reduced attentional and interpretive biases but the reduction was greater for interpretive bias. When participants experienced a stressor, cognitive bias modification significantly reduced anxiety but not depression. Most research has targeted only *one* cognitive bias and it is likely stronger effects would have been obtained if training had focused on attentional and interpretive biases.

Haeffel et al. (2012) studied the effects of attentional bias modification designed to decrease attention to depression-relevant adjectives (e.g., *failure*, *unlovable*, *worthless*). Participants with the greatest reduction in attentional bias had few depressive symptoms. They also spent longer on a difficult laboratory task, which is a behavioural indication of low depression.

There is a final point on cognitive bias modification. As we saw earlier, training designed to reduce one cognitive bias often leads to reductions in another cognitive bias. As a result, the beneficial effects can extend *beyond* the specific focus of training.

Evaluation

Most well-established forms of therapy for anxiety and depression consist of several components. This makes it hard to establish clearly why a given form of therapy is effective in reducing clinical symptoms. In contrast, cognitive bias modification is very *focused* and so it is easier to understand the underlying mechanisms. Cognitive bias modification is effective in reducing anxious symptoms and (to a lesser extent) depressive symptoms (MacLeod & Clarke, 2013). It is plausible that reductions in cognitive biases play a causal role in these beneficial effects. Thus, this research has enhanced our understanding of the relationship between cognitive biases and emotional states.

What are the limitations of cognitive bias modification? MacLeod and Mathews (2012) identified several. First, there is the issue of *generalisation* or transfer. Substantial reductions in cognitive biases under laboratory conditions do not ensure these biases will also be reduced in the different conditions of everyday life.

Second, the assessment of symptomatology following cognitive bias modification typically consists almost exclusively of self-report measures. In future, it will be important to use a wider range of measures (e.g., physiological, behavioural) to discover the full extent of changes produced.

Third, the reasons behind cognitive bias modification are often unclear to anxious and depressed individuals. It is probable it would be more effective if patients understood *why* cognitive bias modification is supposed to be effective.

KEY TERM

Homograph
Word having a single spelling but two or more different meanings (e.g., *bank*, *patient*).

CHAPTER SUMMARY

- **Appraisal theories**. Appraisal theories assume that emotional experience is determined mostly by cognitive appraisals of the current situation. They also assume each emotion is elicited by a specific pattern of appraisal and that appraisal can involve automatic processes as well as more controlled ones. It is hard to decide whether appraisals *cause* emotional experience.

- **Emotion regulation**. The main types of emotion-regulation strategies are attention deployment, cognitive change and response modulation. Cognitive change is the most effective type of strategy in reducing negative affect and response modulation the least effective. Many successful strategies are associated with activation in the prefrontal cortex, which leads to reduced amygdala activation. Effortful emotion-regulation strategies are most effective when used early in processing of negative emotional situations. In contrast, timing matters less for less demanding strategies. Emotion-regulation strategies can involve explicit and/or implicit processes. The effectiveness of any given emotion-regulation strategy depends on the precise situation.

- **Affect and cognition: attention and memory**. Emotional states involving high motivational intensity are associated with attentional narrowing, whereas those involving low motivational intensity are associated with attentional broadening. Attentional narrowing and broadening partially determine what is remembered in long-term memory. Mood states also influence memory through mood congruity and mood-state-dependent memory. These effects, which are consistent with the encoding specificity principle, are stronger with positive mood states than negative ones. Research on patients with Urbach–Wiethe disease has shown the importance of the amygdala in influencing the effects of emotion on memory.

- **Affect and cognition: judgement and decision making**. Anxiety, sadness, anger and positive affect all have different patterns of effects on judgement and decision making. Many effects can be explained on the basis that anxiety increases the need to reduce uncertainty, sadness increases the need to rethink priorities, anger creates a sense of personal control and positive affect creates a desire to maintain the current mood state. An important limitation of research in this area is the use of problems irrelevant to participants' lives.

  The two-process model provides an account of judgement and decision making with moral dilemmas involving severe conflicts. According to the model, deontological judgements are based on affective processing, whereas utilitarian ones are based more on cognitive processing. There is support for this model from neuroimaging studies. However, the model is oversimplified and de-emphasises the importance of whether judgements are intuitive or counterintuitive.

- **Anxiety, depression and cognitive biases.** Anxiety and depression have been associated with four cognitive biases: attentional bias, interpretive bias, explicit memory bias and implicit memory bias. Changes in one cognitive bias often change other cognitive biases. Attentional bias is stronger in anxiety than depression, while the opposite is the case with memory biases. These differences are understandable given that anxiety has the function of anticipating future threat and depression has the function of replacing failed goals with new ones. Healthy individuals possessing cognitive biases are more vulnerable than other people to developing clinical anxiety and depression in the face of negative life events.
- **Cognitive bias modification.** Most cognitive bias modification techniques are designed to reduce attentional or interpretive bias. These techniques have proved successful in reducing cognitive biases and symptoms in anxious and depressed individuals, but more so in anxious ones. The greatest strength of these techniques is that they are very focused, which makes it easier to identify the underlying mechanisms. More research is needed to increase the effectiveness of these techniques and to promote *generalisation* of positive effects from laboratory settings to everyday life.

Further reading

- Angie, A.D., Connelly, S., Waples, E.P. & Kligyte, V. (2011). The influence of discrete emotions on judgment and decision-making: A meta-analytic review. *Cognition & Emotion*, 25: 1393–422. This article contains a comprehensive review of the effects of several major mood states on judgement and decision making.
- Blanchette, I. & Richards, A. (2010). The influence of affect on higher level cognition: A review of research on interpretation, judgment, decision making and reasoning. *Cognition & Emotion*, 24: 561–95. Isabelle Blanchette and Anne Richards provide a comprehensive review of the effects of different mood states on cognition.
- Forgas, J.P. & Koch, A.S. (2013). Mood effects on cognition. In M.D. Robinson, E. Watkins & E. Harmon-Jones (eds), *Handbook of cognition and emotion*. New York: Guilford Publications. The main ways in which cognition is influenced by different mood states are discussed in this comprehensive chapter.

- Gross, J.J. (2013). Emotion regulation: Taking stock and moving forward. *Emotion*, 13: 359–65. James Gross discusses ten fundamental questions relating to emotion regulation.
- Gross, J.J. (2014). *Handbook of emotion regulation*. Hove: Psychology Press. Theory and research on emotion regulation are discussed by leading experts in the field.
- MacLeod, C. & Clarke, P.J.F. (2013). Cognitive bias modification: A new frontier in cognition and emotion research. In M.D. Robinson, E. Watkins & E. Harmon-Jones (eds), *Handbook of cognition and emotion*. New York: Guilford Publications. Colin MacLeod and Patrick Clarke demonstrate the exciting potential of cognitive bias modification as a therapeutic technique.
- Moors, A. & Scherer, K.R. (2013). The role of appraisal in emotion. In M.D. Robinson, E. Watkins & E. Harmon-Jones (eds), *Handbook of cognition emotion*. New York: Guilford Publications. This chapter provides good coverage of the ways in which emotion is influenced by appraisal processes.

CHAPTER

16

Consciousness

INTRODUCTION

What exactly is "consciousness"? There is an important distinction between conscious content and conscious level (Bor & Seth, 2012). Conscious content refers to the information of which we are aware at any given moment. Consciousness in this sense is "characterised by the experience of perceptions, thoughts, feelings, awareness of the external world, and often in humans . . . self-awareness" (Colman, 2001, p. 160). The limitation of this definition is that it leads us to ponder the exact meaning of the words "experience" and "self-awareness".

In contrast, conscious level refers to the state of consciousness. It runs from the total unconsciousness found in coma through to alert wakefulness. These two aspects of consciousness are related – a non-zero conscious level is required for an individual to experience conscious content or awareness.

In this chapter, we will focus mostly on consciousness in the former sense of conscious awareness. Several theorists have distinguished between two forms of consciousness. For example, Block (e.g., 2012) identified access and phenomenal consciousness. Access consciousness can be reported and its contents are available for use by other cognitive processes (e.g., attention, memory). In contrast, phenomenal consciousness is our raw, private experience.

Baumeister and Masicampo (2010) proposed a different distinction. First, there is phenomenal consciousness, which "describes feelings, sensations, and orienting to the present moment" (Baumeister & Masicampo, 2010, p. 945). It is a basic form of consciousness. Second, there is a higher form of consciousness probably not available to other species (although definitive evidence is lacking). It "involves the ability to reason, to reflect on one's experiences, and have a sense of self, especially one that extends beyond the current moment" (Baumeister & Masicampo, 2010, p. 945). Pinker (1997) provided an example of this form of consciousness: "I cannot only feel pain and see red, but think to myself, 'Hey, here I am, Steve Pinker, feeling pain and seeing red!'."

Cognitive neuroscientists and cognitive psychologists have shed little light on the *origins* of our subjective experience (phenomenal consciousness). This is what is often known as the "hard problem" of consciousness. It was described by Chalmers (2007, p. 226): "Experience arises from a physical basis, but we have no good explanation of why and how it so arises. Why should physical processing give rise to a rich inner life at all? It seems objectively unreasonable that it should, and yet it does."

The good news is that much progress has been made with what Chalmers (2007) described as the "easy problems". These include understanding our ability to discriminate and categorise environmental stimuli, the integration of information, our ability to access our own internal states and the deliberate control of behaviour. As you can imagine, these problems are actually extremely difficult, but it is somewhat easier to make progress with them than with the so-called "hard problem".

Weblink:
What is consciousness?

FUNCTIONS OF CONSCIOUSNESS

What are the functions of consciousness? There has been much controversy on this issue. However, there is reasonable agreement on some of its functions:

- It is associated with perceiving the environment.
- It plays a crucial role in social communication and understanding what other people are thinking.
- It has a role in controlling our actions.
- It allows us to think about events and issues far removed from the here-and-now. This is a common occurrence – Kane et al. (2007) found people's conscious thoughts wander away from their current activity 30% of the time on average.
- Tononi and Koch (2008, p. 253) argued that "The most important property of consciousness is that it is extraordinarily informative. This is because, whenever you experience a particular conscious state, it rules out a huge number of alternative experiences." In other words, consciousness involves integrating and combining numerous types of information.

There has been much controversy concerning the extent and usefulness of unconscious processes. It has often been argued that unconscious processes are of limited value and suffer from inflexibility (see Chapter 5). In contrast, Sigmund Freud famously emphasised the massive power of the unconscious. We have seen in this book that unconscious processes fulfil many purposes. For example, perceptual processes (Chapter 2), learning (Chapter 6), memory (Chapter 7) and possibly (but controversially) decision making (Chapter 13) can occur in the absence of conscious awareness.

In a provocative article, Hassin (2013) proposed the "Yes It Can" principle. According to this principle, unconscious processes can perform the same high-level cognitive functions (e.g., goal pursuit, cognitive control, reasoning) as conscious processes.

Support for the "Yes It Can" principle was reported by Marien et al. (2012). Participants performed a proofreading task in which they detected errors in a text. Marien et al. induced the unconscious goal of socialisation in some participants by presenting socialisation-relevant words (*socialisation*, *partying*, *dancing*, *celebrating*) below the level of conscious awareness. This unconscious socialisation goal impaired proofreading performance in participants for whom socialisation is an important goal (see Figure 16.1).

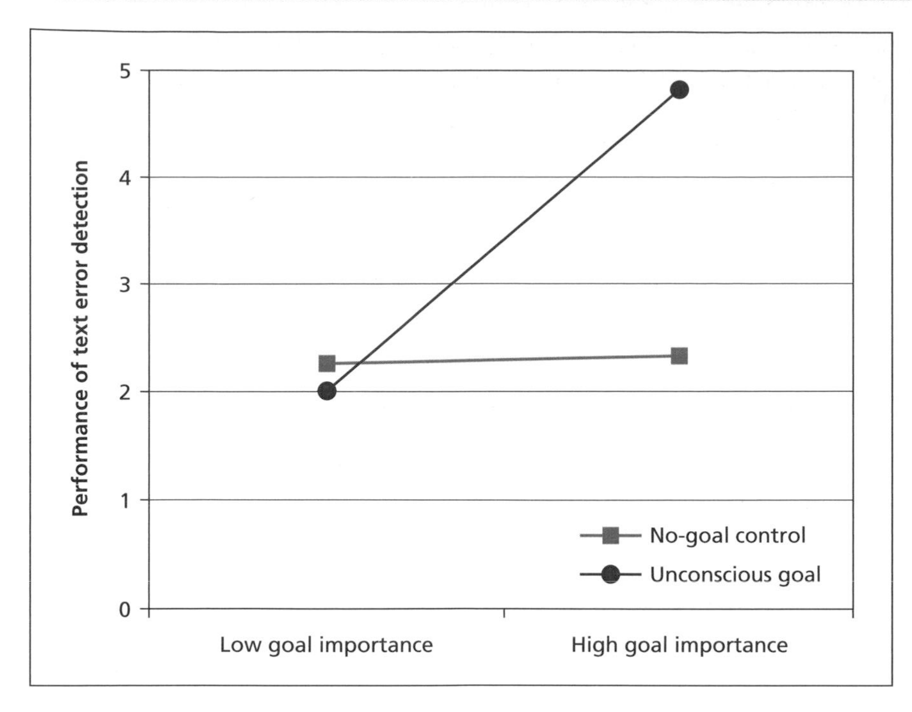

Figure 16.1
Mean scores for error detection on a proofreading task as a function of whether the goal of socialisation had been induced unconsciously (unconscious goal vs. no-goal control) and the importance of the goal of socialisation to the participants (low vs. high goal importance). Scores closer to zero indicate better error-detection performance.

From Marien et al. (2012). © American Psychological Association.

Some caution is required in interpreting such findings. There is evidence that many cognitive functions can occur at the unconscious level. However, these cognitive functions are much more limited in scope than is the case for conscious processing.

A popular view among sceptics of the value of consciousness is that it is often used to provide a misleading interpretation or rationalisation of some event after it has happened. Classic research supporting this viewpoint was reported by Nisbett and Wilson (1977). In one experiment, participants decided which of five essentially identical pairs of stockings was the best. Most chose the rightmost pair and so their decisions were influenced by spatial position. However, the participants vehemently denied it had played any part in their decision! Instead, they referred to slight differences in colour, texture and so on among the pairs of stockings.

We turn now to a consideration of two of the major functions of consciousness. Social communication is discussed first, followed by controlling action.

Social communication

According to Humphrey (1983, 2002), the main function of consciousness is *social*. Humans have lived in social groups for tens of thousands of years and so have needed to predict, understand and manipulate others' behaviour. This is much easier to do if you can imagine yourself in their position. Humans developed conscious awareness of themselves and this helped them to understand others.

Graziano and Kastner (2011, p. 98) also emphasised the social nature of consciousness: "The machinery that computes information about other people's

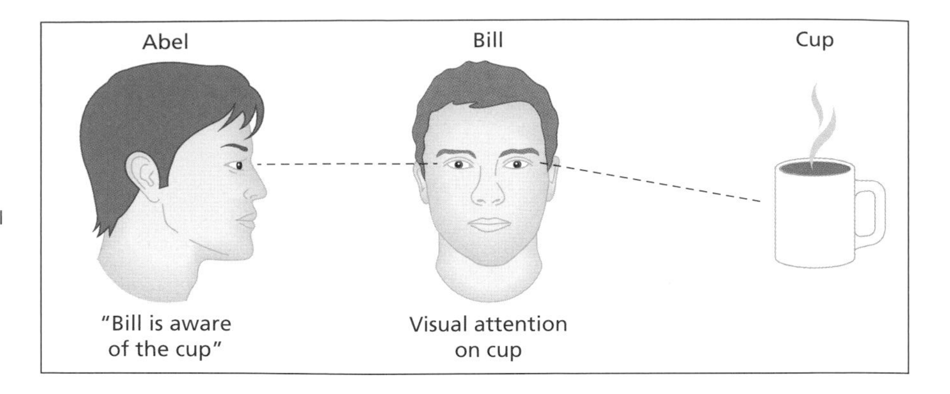

Figure 16.2
Awareness as a social perceptual model of attention. Abel observes Bill and constructs a model of Bill's mental state using mechanisms specialised for social perception. This model includes the notion that Bill is aware of the cup. The mechanisms of social perception used to perceive awareness in other people may be used to perceive awareness in ourselves.
From Graziano & Kastner (2011).

awareness is the same machinery that computes information about our own awareness." Within this theory, "Awareness . . . is one's social intelligence perceiving one's focus of attention" (p. 98).

Key aspects of the theory are illustrated in Figure 16.2. Abel forms a model of Bill's mental state ("Bill is aware of the cup") using neuronal machinery specialised for social perception. This machinery is also used to perceive awareness in ourselves. It is possible awareness originally developed to understand others and only later did humans develop self-awareness.

According to Graziano and Kastner (2011), this social machinery depends crucially on the temporo-parietal junction (where the temporal and parietal lobes meet). There is support for this view. For example, transcranial magnetic stimulation (TMS; see Glossary) applied to this area impaired people's ability to switch between representations of the self and those of another person (Sowden & Catmur, 2014).

If perceiving someone else's awareness and perceiving our own awareness both depend on the same neuronal mechanisms, we might sometimes be confused as to the *source* of our awareness. This is, indeed, the case with **out-of-body experiences**, which are "sensations in which a person's consciousness seems to become detached from the body and take up a remote viewing position" (Blanke et al., 2002, p. 269). When electrical stimulation was applied to the temporo-parietal junction of a 43-year-old woman, she reported out-of-body experiences (e.g., "I see myself lying in bed from above").

There is another way conscious thoughts contribute to social communication. This was expressed elegantly by Baumeister et al. (2011a, p. 74): "Many investigators operationally define conscious thought as those thoughts the person can report to others . . . the purpose of conscious thought is precisely for enabling people to tell their thoughts to one another." Thus, much of conscious thinking is for talking.

KEY TERMS

Out-of-body experiences
Vivid feelings of being outside of (and detached from) one's own body.

Free will
The notion that we freely or voluntarily choose what to do from various options.

Controlling our actions?

Numerous times every day we think of doing something followed by doing it. For example, "I will get myself a coffee" is followed by finding ourselves in a café drinking coffee. Thus, our experience suggests we have **free will**, which is "the ability to make choices and to determine one's own outcomes free from constraints" (Aarts & van den Bos, 2011, p. 532).

There has been much controversy over the centuries concerning the existence (or otherwise) of free will. For example, Thomas Huxley (1874) put forward the "steam whistle hypothesis", according to which conscious thought resembles the steam whistle on a train locomotive. The whistle tells us something about what is happening inside the engine but has no *causal* impact on the train's movement.

In similar fashion, Wegner (2003) claimed we have only the *illusion* of conscious or free will. Our actions are actually caused by unconscious processes However, we mistakenly infer our actions are determined by our conscious intentions.

Wegner (2003, p. 67) argued that the principles of priority, consistency and exclusivity jointly lead us to believe our actions are caused by our conscious thoughts:

> When a thought appears in consciousness just before an action (priority), is consistent with the action (consistency), and is not accompanied by conspicuous alternative causes of the action (exclusivity), we experience conscious will and ascribe authorship to ourselves for the action.

We turn now to research evidence on the role of consciousness in influencing our actions. This evidence includes behavioural and neuroimaging studies.

Findings: behavioural research

Baumeister et al. (2011b) argued that an individual's behaviour generally depends crucially on his/her conscious thoughts even though those thoughts may have been preceded by various unconscious processes. They reviewed much supportive evidence, but we will consider only a small fraction.

Gollwitzer (1999) focused on implementation intentions (see Glossary), which "specify the when, where, and how of responses leading to goal attainment" (Gollwitzer, 1999, p. 494). Gollwitzer assumed conscious implementation intentions create "instant habits", making it much easier for us to achieve our goals (e.g., passing exams) and to avoid being distracted by irrelevant activities.

Gollwitzer and Sheeran (2006) carried out a meta-analysis (see Glossary) of studies on implementation intentions. Goal achievement was much more likely with implementation intentions than less specific goal intentions (e.g., "I will achieve my goal"). This suggests conscious intentions can influence behaviour. However, the typically long delay between conscious manipulation of intentions and subsequent behaviour makes it hard to establish the precise causal factors.

The probability of goal achievement is often reduced by our habits. For example, a student may habitually turn on the television when he/she needs to study to pass an important examination. Adriaanse et al. (2011) found implementation intentions made alternatives to habitual responses more consciously accessible and so reduced habitual responding.

Evidence against free will was reported by Wegner and Wheatley (1999). Two participants placed their fingers on a small board. When they moved the board, a cursor moved over a screen showing numerous pictures of small objects. Every 30 seconds or so, the participants were told to stop the cursor and indicate whether they had consciously intended the cursor to stop where it did.

Both participants wore headphones. One was genuine but the other was the experimenter's confederate. The genuine participants thought they were both hearing different words through the headphones. In fact, the confederate was actually receiving instructions to make certain movements. On crucial trials, the confederate was told to stop on a given object (e.g., *cat*) and the genuine participants heard the word "cat" 30 seconds before, 5 seconds before, 1 second before or 1 second after the confederate stopped the cursor.

Genuine participants wrongly believed they had caused the cursor to stop where it did when hearing the object name one or five seconds beforehand. Thus, the participants mistakenly believed their conscious intention had caused the action, which can be explained by the principles of priority, consistency and exclusivity.

Consider a situation in which a rapid sequence of word strings is stopped by participants pressing a key in response to a stop cue. The sequence stops at a word (e.g., *glass*) determined by the computer, although the participants are not told this (van der Weiden et al., 2013). Perception of self-agency (the belief one has caused a given outcome) was high when the stopped word matched a participant's goal (i.e., it was the one he/she intended to stop at). Perceptions of self-agency were also high when the stopped word matched an earlier prime word presented below the level of conscious awareness. Thus, there are various ways in which people can be misled into thinking they have caused a given outcome.

There are various limitations with the research discussed in this section. First, the effects are weak. For example, only 60% of the participants in the Wegner and Wheatley (1999) study believed their conscious intention caused the cursor to move even when all three principles applied.

Second, the studies involved artificial set-ups designed to make it hard for participants to realise their conscious intentions had not caused certain actions. By analogy, no one would argue that visual perception is hopelessly fallible simply because we misidentify objects in a thick fog!

Findings: cognitive neuroscience

Thought-provoking research of relevance to free will was reported by Libet et al. (1983). Participants bent their wrist and fingers at a time of their choosing, and indicated when they were consciously aware of their intention to perform those movements. Libet et al. also recorded event-related potentials (ERPs; see Glossary) to assess the readiness potential (thought to reflect pre-planning of a bodily movement). The readiness potential occurred 350 ms *before* participants reported having conscious awareness of the intention to bend the wrist and fingers. In turn, conscious awareness preceded the actual hand movement by about 200 ms.

Superficially, the above findings suggest much processing associated with deciding when to make a movement occurs ahead of conscious awareness. However, it is hard to study conscious intentions with precision, because "the conscious experience of intending is quite thin and evasive" (Haggard, 2005, p. 291).

Weblink:
Libet's free will study

Evidence supportive of Haggard's views was reported by Banks and Isham (2009) in a study in which some participants saw their hand movement at a 120-ms delay in a delayed video image. The reported decision time was 44 ms later in this condition than when the participant's hand was in full view.

IN THE REAL WORLD: BRAIN READING AND FREE WILL

Libet et al.'s (1983) research was limited because it focused on the *late* stages of motor preparation in the supplementary motor area rather than on *earlier* high-level decision processes. Another limitation is that Libet et al. (1983) focused on *when* decisions (when shall I move my hand?) and ignored *what* decisions (e.g., what movement shall I make?).

Soon et al. (2008) addressed these limitations by assessing brain activation in the prefrontal and parietal cortex (areas associated with decision making) before participants consciously decided whether to move their left or right index finger. The findings were dramatic. Participants' decisions could be predicted on the basis of brain activity in frontopolar cortex (BA10) and an area of parietal cortex a full *seven seconds* before they were consciously aware of their decision!

In addition, activity in the supplemental and presupplemental motor areas *five seconds* before conscious awareness of their decision predicted the timing of participants' responses. These findings suggest the processing of *what* decisions occurs prior to the processing of *when* decisions.

A study similar to that of Soon et al. (2008) was reported by Bode et al. (2011) using a more powerful scanner to provide better temporal and spatial resolution of brain activity. Participants decided whether to respond with their left or right index finger. On the basis of Soon et al.'s (2008) findings, they focused on anterior frontopolar cortex.

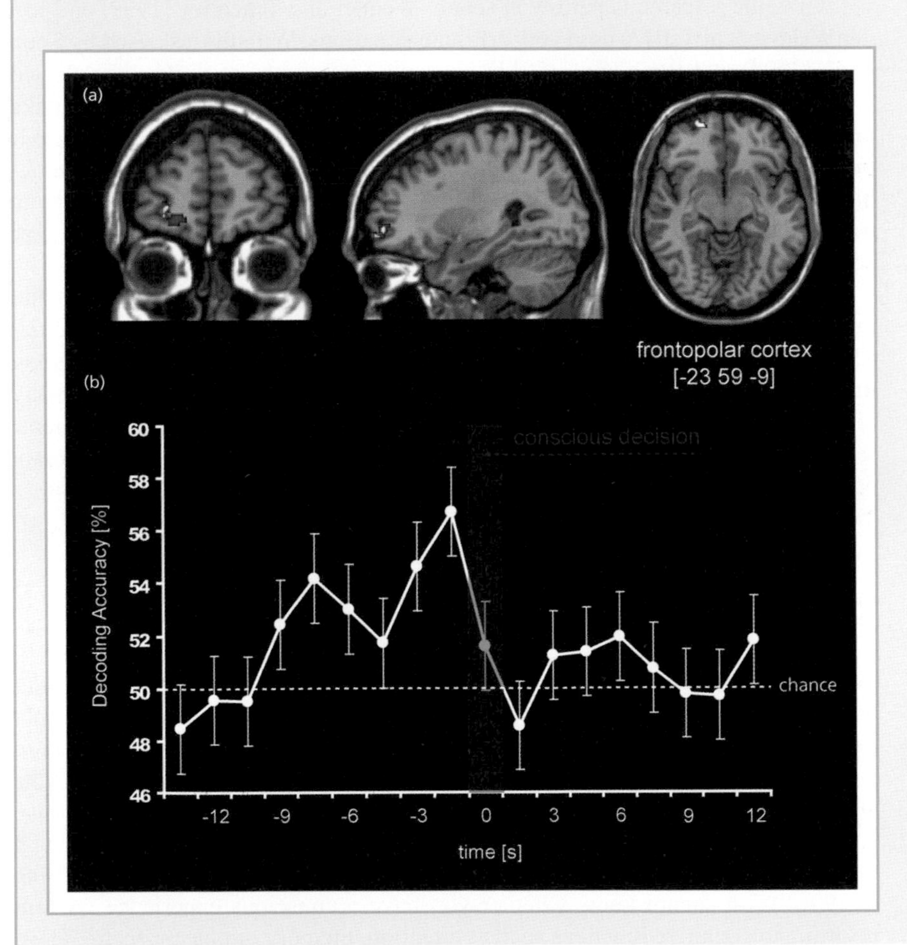

Research activity: Libet's experiment

Figure 16.3
(a) Region in left frontopolar cortex for which decoding of upcoming motor decisions was possible. (b) Decoding accuracy of these decisions (times preceding conscious awareness of the intention are labelled as negative numbers). Chance performance = 50%.
From Bode et al. (2011).

What did Bode et al. (2011) find? Participants' decisions could be predicted on the basis of activity in the left frontopolar cortex up to 7½ seconds before they were consciously aware of their decision (see Figure 16.3). However, predictive accuracy was rarely above 55% except very shortly before the conscious decision (chance = 50%).

There is another issue. Participants indicated when they had reached a conscious *decision*. As a result, decision-relevant thoughts, such as "I have a slight preference for moving my left hand", were probably ignored. A convincing demonstration that brain activity can predict subsequent conscious decisions requires that we take account of such decision-relevant thoughts (Fahle et al., 2011).

Overall evaluation

Various strands of research apparently converge on the counterintuitive conclusion that at least some of our decisions are prepared preconsciously before we are aware of them. However, we must be very cautious about accepting that conclusion for various reasons.

First, the research is narrow in scope. Wegner and Wheatley (1999) and van der Weiden et al. (2013) used very artificial situations. With the task used by Soon et al. (2008) and Bode et al. (2011), there was no reason to prefer the selected response to the non-selected one (Mele, 2013). The requirement to make unpredictable and random responses probably reduces any pre-decision conscious processing to a minimum by encouraging participants to use "automatic tie-breaking mechanisms" (Mele, 2013, p. 781). In contrast, most people engage in much conscious thinking prior to important decisions, such as whether to marry someone or commit a crime.

Second, the cognitive neuroscience research is less informative about whether humans possess free will than sometimes claimed. In the study by Bode et al. (2011), the researchers' ability to predict participants' decisions from preceding brain activity was only slightly above chance. That leaves open the possibility that conscious processing was *very* important in determining participants' actions. It is entirely possible participants' actions in that study depended on early brain activity *and* conscious processing – the two are not mutually exclusive.

ASSESSING CONSCIOUSNESS AND CONSCIOUS EXPERIENCE

How can we assess conscious experience? Overwhelmingly, the most popular answer has been that we should use behavioural measures. For example, we could decide whether people have conscious experience of an object by asking them to provide verbal reports of their visual experience. Alternatively, they could make yes/no decisions concerning the presence of a target object.

Lamme (2010) argued that our *actual* conscious experience is often much richer than our *report* of that experience. Why is that? According to Lamme (2006, p. 499), "You cannot know whether you have a conscious experience without resorting to cognitive functions such as attention, memory or inner speech." Thus, reports of our conscious experience may be limited due to processes intervening between the experience and its report rather than limitations in the experience itself. This view implies verbal reports of conscious experience may often be very inadequate.

Another problem with using behavioural measures to assess conscious awareness is that different measures often disagree. For example, consider research on subliminal perception (see Chapter 2). Observers sometimes show "awareness" of visual stimuli when making forced-choice decisions about them (objective threshold) but not when reporting their experience (subjective threshold).

What is the alternative to assessing conscious awareness by behavioural measures such as self-report? Increasingly, it is argued that we should make more use of the neural correlates of consciousness (e.g., Lamme, 2010; van Gaal & Lamme, 2012). In essence, this approach involves relating behavioural measures of conscious awareness to associated patterns of brain activity.

Two main advantages are claimed for the above approach. First, it is theoretically important to compare the findings from behavioural and neuroimaging measures to identify their similarities and differences. Second, neuroimaging measures may provide a more direct assessment of consciousness uncontaminated by additional processes such as attention and memory.

Under-reporting of conscious experience?

Classic evidence suggesting accounts of our conscious experience *underestimate* our actual experience was reported by Sperling (1960; see Chapter 6). He presented a visual array containing three rows of four letters each for 50 ms. Participants could usually report only four–five letters, but claimed to have seen many more.

Sperling (1960) assumed this under-reporting occurred because visual information had faded before most of it could be reported. He tested this by asking participants to recall only *part* of the information presented. As predicted, part recall was high provided the to-be-recalled information was cued very soon after the offset of the visual display.

Much subsequent research has confirmed Sperling's (1960) findings. Lamme (2010) discussed several experiments in which an array of objects was presented briefly followed by a blank interval of several seconds. Finally, the array was presented again with a cue pointing at one object with participants deciding whether that object has changed. Performance was poor in this condition. However, it was very good when the cue was presented within about two seconds of the first array's disappearance and ahead of the presentation of the second array. Thus, it appears participants have access (possibly conscious) to a considerable amount of information for some time after the disappearance of the first array.

Block (2012) has used evidence such as that just discussed to support his distinction between access and phenomenal consciousness. The essence of this distinction (discussed earlier in the chapter) is that only access consciousness can be reported. Our belief that our conscious experience is richer than our reported experience occurs because phenomenal consciousness is more extensive than access consciousness.

Kouider et al. (e.g., 2010, 2012) argued that there is no phenomenal consciousness separate from access consciousness. Our belief that our conscious experience is very rich may be largely illusory. Consider, for example, change blindness, which is the inability to detect a changed aspect of the visual environ-

KEY TERM

Vegetative state
A condition produced by brain damage in which there is some wakefulness but an apparent lack of awareness and purposeful behaviour.

ment (see Chapter 4). Most people substantially overestimate their ability to avoid change blindness (Levin et al., 2002).

Observers may exaggerate the richness of their conscious experience because what they claim to experience is influenced by their *expectations* as well as by the visual information presented to them. Supportive evidence was reported by de Gardelle et al. (2009) using a modified version of the Sperling task. Participants expected letters to be presented but sometimes pseudo-letters were presented (real letters were rotated and flipped). Participants rarely detected the presence of pseudo-letters but believed that only real letters had been presented. Thus, their conscious experience was less accurate and detailed than they believed it to be.

In sum, most people believe they have much richer conscious visual experience than they are able to report. It is likely (but not certain) that this richness is illusory and depends on the involvement of top-down processes (e.g., expectations). Thus, individuals' self-reports of their visual experience are more likely to involve misreporting than under-reporting.

Consciousness in brain-damaged patients

Three stages of degraded consciousness have been identified in brain-damaged patients. The most severe stage is coma, in which there is no conscious awareness and no wakefulness. The next stage is the **vegetative state** in which there is "wakefulness without conscious awareness". The third stage is the minimally conscious state involving some evidence of consciousness.

Most research interest has focused on patients in the vegetative state, which involves "no awareness of self or environment, no response to external stimuli of

IN THE REAL WORLD: VEGETATIVE-STATE PATIENTS

What tasks should we use to show patients in the vegetative state have conscious awareness? It is important to use *active* tasks in which participants cannot respond automatically but instead must generate the responses themselves (Owen, 2013). Accordingly, we will focus on findings using active tasks.

Owen et al. (2006) studied a 23-year-old woman in the vegetative state due to a very serious road accident. She was asked to imagine playing a game of tennis or visiting the rooms of her house. These two tasks were associated with different patterns of brain activity (e.g., imagining playing tennis was associated with activation in the supplementary motor area). The patterns of brain activity were very similar to those shown by healthy participants.

More dramatic findings were reported by Monti et al. (2010) with a patient in the vegetative state. He was asked yes-or-no questions such as "Is your father's name Thomas?", having been instructed to imagine playing tennis if the answer was "Yes" but to imagine navigating his house if the answer was "No". The patient's patterns of brain activity corresponded to the correct answers.

Interesting findings were reported by Cruse et al. (2011) in a study on 16 vegetative state patients. Cruse et al. tested their ability to respond to two commands ("squeeze your right hand"; "squeeze your toes"). In healthy participants, these commands produce activation in the hand and toe motor areas, respectively. Three of the patients showed very similar patterns of brain activation (see Figure 16.4).

The above findings are perhaps more impressive than they initially seem. Successful task performance requires sustained attention, language comprehension (of the task instructions), working memory (to remember which task to perform) and response selection (between the two imagery tasks).

Monti et al. (2013) found a patient with a severe disorder of consciousness could shift his attention between two competing stimuli. He was presented with superimposed pictures of faces and houses. In healthy participants, different brain regions are activated depending on whether they attend to the face or the house. The patient had very similar patterns of brain activation to the healthy controls when instructed to shift attention from the face to the house or vice versa. Note that these changes in brain activation were driven by the patient's *intentions* rather than by the stimulus itself (it remained unchanged).

Suppose neuroimaging evidence assesses validly the extent of conscious awareness in patients with severe disorders of consciousness. If so, such evidence might predict future behavioural recovery. Coleman et al. (2009) addressed this issue in a study of 41 patients. At the start of the study, neuroimaging signs of consciousness failed to correlate with behavioural assessment. As predicted, however, there was a high correlation between neuroimaging signs of consciousness initially and behavioural recovery six months later.

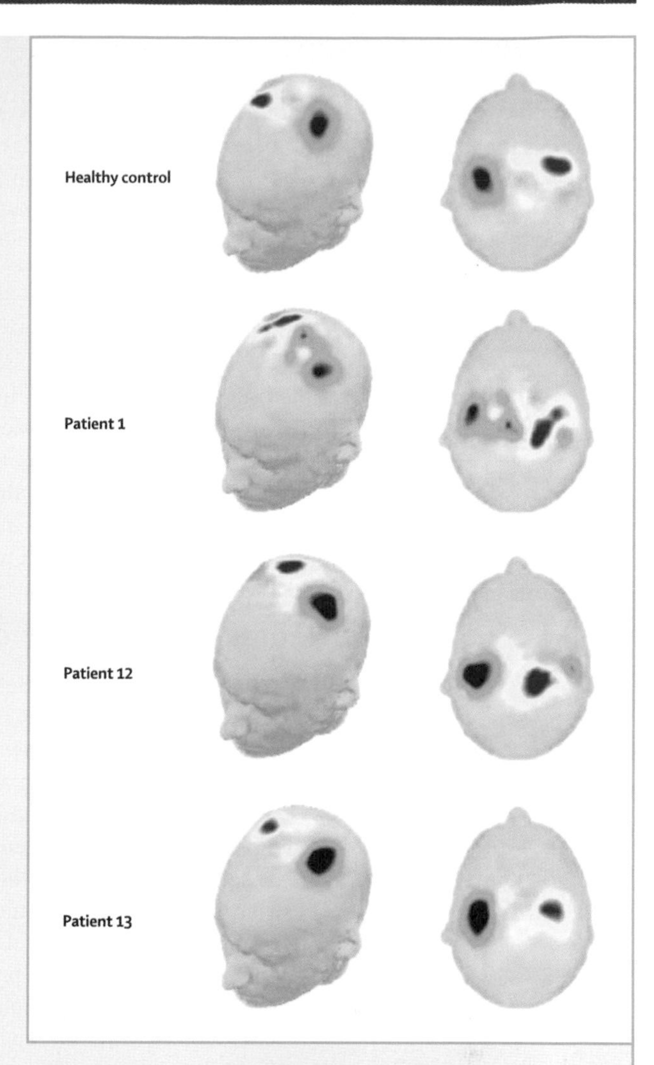

Figure 16.4
Modulation of the appropriate frequency bands of the EEG signal associated with motor imagery in one healthy control and three patients. Red colours show values more than zero, while blue colours show values less than zero. There are clear focal areas over the hand and toe motor areas (directly relevant to the task) for all four participants.
From Cruse et al. (2011). Reprinted with permission from Elsevier.

We have seen vegetative-state patients produce several cognitive processes generally thought to involve conscious awareness. These processes include language comprehension, sustained attention, switching attention, use of imagery and question answering. In addition, patients showing the most neuroimaging evidence of consciousness generally show the greatest behavioural recovery thereafter.

What are the limitations of research in this area? First, most patients in the vegetative state (81% in the Cruse et al. (2011) study) have *not* shown signs of consciousness as assessed by neuroimaging responses on cognitive tasks. It remains unknown whether these findings are genuine or simply reflect insensitivity of measurement/assessment.

Second, much remains unknown about the conscious mental states of those patients exhibiting signs of consciousness. As Owen (2013, p. 128) pointed out, "Are they [patients] depressed? Are they in pain? Do they want to live or die? We cannot presume to know the answers to these questions."

a kind suggesting volition or purpose, and no evidence of language comprehension or expression" (Owen & Coleman, 2008, p. 235). Thus, behavioural measures provide no evidence patients in the vegetative state have conscious awareness. However, exciting recent studies using neuroimaging measures indicate at least some vegetative state patients *do* have some conscious awareness when performing various cognitive tasks (see Owen (2013) for a review).

Neural correlates of consciousness

Weblink:
More information about vegetative states

Weblink:
Lamme's lecture slides

In recent years, there has been a marked increase in research on the neural correlates of consciousness. In essence, experimental conditions in which participants are consciously aware or unaware of what stimulus has been presented are compared with respect to associated brain activity.

As mentioned earlier, Lamme (e.g., 2010) has argued that it may be preferable to define consciousness in neural rather than behavioural terms. He has focused on visual consciousness, that is, conscious experience of visual objects. Presentation of a visual stimulus leads to extremely rapid (essentially automatic) processing at successive levels of the visual cortex. This processing starts with early visual cortex and then proceeds to higher levels (see Chapter 2). This fast "feedforward sweep" is completed within about 100–150 ms.

The feedforward sweep is typically followed by recurrent processing. Recurrent processing (a form of top-down processing) involves feedback from higher to lower brain areas producing extensive interactions among different areas. According to Lamme (2010), its relevance to conscious experience is very direct – recurrent processing is accompanied by conscious experience, while the feedforward sweep is not.

Why is conscious experience associated with recurrent processing rather than the feedforward sweep? First, the feedforward sweep involves the somewhat fragmented processing of different kinds of information (e.g., shape, colour, motion). In contrast, recurrent processing is associated with *integrated* processing of this information. Such integrated processing is of central importance to the high level of informativeness of conscious experience (Tononi & Koch, 2008).

Second, conscious visual experience is typically coherent and unambiguous even when the visual environment is ambiguous and some objects partly obscure others. The top-down processes (e.g., expectations) associated with recurrent processing are important in producing this coherence (O'Reilly et al., 2013).

KEY TERM

Masking
Suppression of the processing (and conscious perception of) a stimulus by presenting a second, masking stimulus very shortly thereafter.

How can we prevent (or reduce) recurrent processing so as to assess its importance for conscious perception? One method involves **masking**. Masking involves blocking the processing and perception of a stimulus by following it rapidly with a second, masking stimulus. Another method is to use transcranial magnetic stimulation (TMS; see Glossary) to cause interference with task processing. We can apply TMS to early visual cortex sufficiently long after stimulus presentation to ensure it disrupts recurrent processing rather than the feedforward sweep.

Findings

Fahrenfort et al. (2007) used non-masked and masked conditions and asked observers to decide whether a given target (a texture-defined square) had been presented. Evidence from the electroencephalogram (EEG; see Glossary) indicated that feedforward processing was intact under masked conditions even when observers' target-detection performance was at chance level. In contrast, there was practically no evidence of recurrent processing in the masked condition. These findings suggest conscious visual perception depends on recurrent more than feedforward processing.

Fahrenfort et al.'s (2007) findings were essentially correlational. Thus, they do not show recurrent processing is *essential* for visual consciousness. Koivisto et al. (2011) addressed the causality issue by using transcranial magnetic stimulation (TMS; see Glossary). Observers decided whether natural scenes contained animals. Feedforward processing progresses from early visual cortex (V1/V2) to lateral occipital cortex and is followed by recurrent processing progressing from lateral occipital cortex back to V1/V2. Koivisto et al. disrupted recurrent processing by applying transcranial magnetic stimulation *after* processing had started in lateral occipital cortex.

What did Koivisto et al. (2011) find? As predicted, conscious visual perception was reduced by TMS that disrupted recurrent processing. This finding suggests conscious visual perception depends at least in part on recurrent processing.

Boly et al. (2011) studied brain activity in minimally conscious patients, patients in the vegetative state and healthy controls when presented with expected and unexpected tones. Feedforward processes were comparable in all three groups. However, only the vegetative state patients had impaired top-down connectivity from frontal to temporal areas indicative of reduced recurrent processing. These findings are consistent with Lamme's (2010) view that recurrent processing is essential for conscious awareness.

In spite of the above findings, some evidence suggests conscious visual perception can occur without recurrent processing provided the visual task is easy. Koivisto et al. (2014) presented photographs briefly, some of which were followed by masking to prevent recurrent processing. The task was to respond to those photographs containing an animal. Detection of animals was comparable with and without masking (86% and 88%, respectively). However, participants reported less awareness of what was shown on each photograph under masked than unmasked conditions (see Figure 16.5). Thus, recurrent processing is not always required for conscious visual perception but it enhances perceptual experience.

Recurrent processing *without* conscious awareness was reported by Scholte et al. (2006). Observers detected white vowels in a stream of black and white letters. Sometimes unexpected square figures were also presented. These figures produced recurrent processing, but 50% of participants reported afterwards they had not seen them. It was only when there was widespread recurrent processing

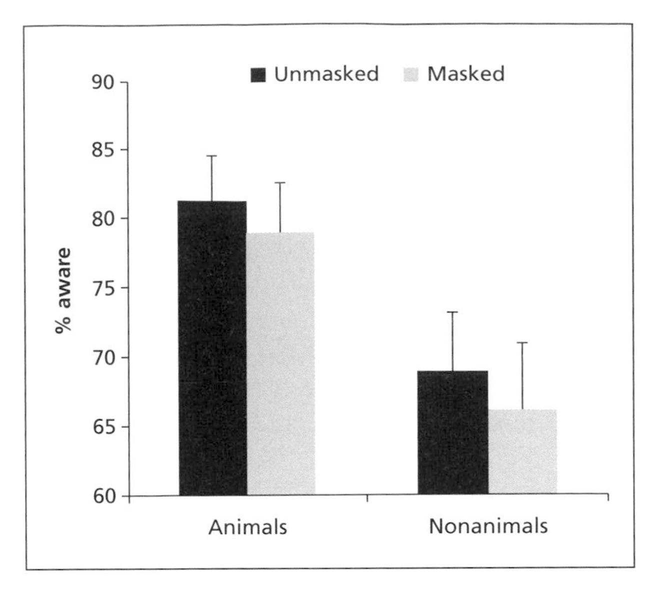

Figure 16.5
Percentage of trials on which participants reported awareness of the content of photographs under masked and unmasked conditions for animal and non-animal (e.g., landscapes, vehicles) photographs.

From Koivisto et al. (2014). © Massachusetts Institute of Technology, by permission of The MIT Press.

that the figures were consistently seen. Thus, inattention to the square figures meant fairly extensive recurrent processing was required for them to be consciously perceived.

Similar findings were reported by Thakral (2011). Unexpected visual stimuli that were not consciously perceived were nevertheless associated with extensive neural activity in brain areas (e.g., prefrontal cortex) involved in recurrent processing.

Evaluation

There is much support for the notion that conscious visual perception is generally associated with the presence of recurrent processing. Feedforward processing in the absence of recurrent processing typically does not lead to conscious perception. In principle, then, recurrent processing could be regarded as a neural index or marker of consciousness.

What are the limitations with this approach? First, the emphasis has been primarily on *visual* consciousness. As a result, little is known about the processes involved when we are consciously aware of past or future events.

Second, the extent to which recurrent processing plays a necessary role in conscious perception probably depends very much on the complexity of the visual environment and the difficulty of the visual task. Thus, recurrent processing may not be *necessary* for conscious perception if the visual task is sufficiently easy (e.g., Koivisto et al., 2014).

Third, there is evidence (e.g.,Scholte et al., 2006; Thakral, 2011) that there can be fairly extensive recurrent processing in the absence of conscious awareness. Thus, there are circumstances (e.g., inattention) in which recurrent processing is not *sufficient* for conscious awareness.

Fourth, we must not overstate the potential usefulness of recurrent processing as an index of conscious experience. Recurrent processing appears to be a useful measure largely because it typically correlates highly with self-report and other behavioural measures of consciousness. An approach in which brain-activation and behavioural measures of consciousness are combined is preferable to one attaching excessive importance to brain-activation measures.

GLOBAL WORKSPACE THEORETICAL APPROACH

Many theories of consciousness have been put forward. Here we will focus on the very influential global workspace approach identified with two rather similar theories. First, there is the global workspace theory proposed by Baars (1988) and by Baars and Franklin (2007) in which the emphasis is on behavioural data.

Second, there is the global neuronal workspace theory of Dehaene and Naccache (2001) developed by Dehaene and Changeux (2011). This theory differs mostly from global workspace theory in its emphasis on identifying the main brain areas associated with conscious awareness.

Major predictions

Here are some of the main assumptions of the two theories. First, it is argued that much human information processing involves numerous special-purpose unconscious processors operating in parallel. These processors are distributed in numerous brain areas with each processor carrying out specialised functions (e.g., colour processing, motion processing). The assumption follows that *early* processing should be very similar regardless of whether a stimulus is or is not consciously perceived.

Second, it is assumed consciousness is associated with *integrating* information from several special-purpose processors relatively late in processing. As a result, "Conscious contents evoke widespread brain activation" (Baars & Franklin, 2007, p. 956). More specifically, a combination of bottom-up processing and top-down attentional control produces "ignition" leading to synchronised activity across large areas of the brain. This makes information globally available and corresponds to conscious experience.

Third, it is assumed the brain areas associated with consciousness vary as a function of the *content* of conscious awareness. However, some brain areas are much more likely than others to be activated during conscious awareness. Dehaene and Naccache (2001) emphasised the role of the dorsolateral prefrontal cortex and the anterior cingulate (see Figure 16.6). In similar fashion, Dehaene and Changeux (2011, p. 210) emphasise the role of "prefrontal, cingulate, and parietal regions" in conscious experience. Involvement of these brain areas is associated with widespread synchronised brain activity. Of importance, this brain activity is often relatively long-lasting.

Fourth, it is assumed there are very close links between attention and consciousness. Consider sentences such as, "We look in order to see" or "We listen in order to hear." According to Baars (1997, p. 363), "The distinction is between selecting an experience and being conscious of the selected event . . . the first word of each pair ['look'; 'listen'] involves attention; the second word ['see'; 'hear'] involves consciousness." Thus, attention resembles choosing a television channel and consciousness resembles the picture on the screen.

The nature of the relationship between attention and consciousness was described by Baars and Franklin (2007, p. 957) using a theatre metaphor: "Unconscious processors in the theatre audience receive broadcasts from a conscious 'bright spot' on the stage. Control of the bright spot corresponds to selective attention."

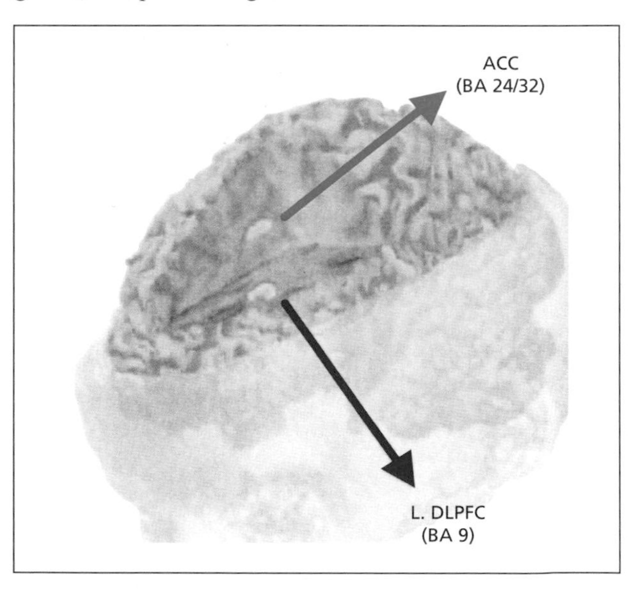

Figure 16.6
The anterior cingulate cortex (ACC) and the dorsolateral prefrontal cortex (DLPFC), regions that are strongly associated with consciousness.

Adapted from MacDonald et al. (2000). Reprinted with permission from AAAS.

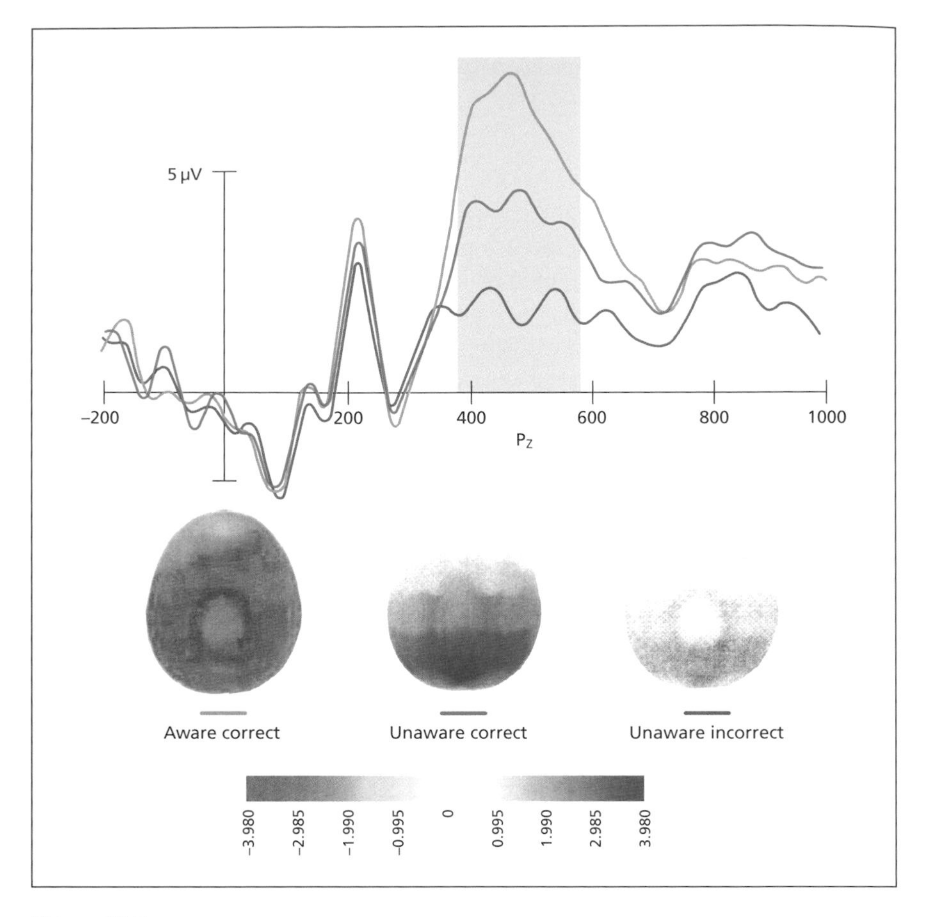

Figure 16.7
Event-related potential (ERP) waveforms in the aware-correct, unaware-correct and unaware-incorrect conditions. The greatest differences among the conditions occurred for the P3 component (shown in light grey). In the bottom part of the figure, the extent of brain positivity in the three conditions is shown in red.

From Lamy et al. (2009). © Massachusetts Institute of Technology, by permission of The MIT Press.

Findings: early processing

The first assumption is that early stimulus processing is not influenced by whether it is subsequently consciously perceived. There is much empirical support for this assumption. Lamy et al. (2009) asked participants to indicate the location of a target stimulus and report on their subjective awareness of its presence (see Figure 16.7). Event-related potentials (ERPs; see Glossary) were recorded to compare brain activity on trials on which there was or was not conscious awareness of the target stimulus.

As you can see in Figure 16.7, the amplitude of early ERP components was unaffected by whether or not there was conscious awareness. However, conscious awareness was associated with a late wave of activity (P3) between 400 and 600 ms after stimulus onset spread widely across the brain. Figure 16.7 also shows brain positivity was far more widespread in the presence rather than the absence of conscious awareness.

Weblink:
Baars' article

If a stimulus is expected, participants might be able to use top-down processes to speed up the time taken for conscious awareness to occur. Melloni et al. (2011) found support for this prediction. Differences between the ERPs to seen and unseen stimuli started at 200 ms with expected stimuli but at 300 ms with stimuli for which no expectations could be formed. However, the key finding was that the early stages of processing for seen and unseen stimuli were very similar regardless of whether these stimuli were expected.

Findings: integrated brain functioning

The notion (second assumption) that integrated brain functioning is crucial to conscious awareness is appealing. One reason is that what we are consciously aware of is nearly always integrated information. For example, it is almost impossible to perceive an object while ignoring its colour.

Melloni et al. (2007) tested the above assumption. They presented words that were hard to perceive, and compared brain activity for those consciously perceived or not consciously perceived. There was sufficient EEG activation to words not consciously perceived to suggest they were thoroughly processed. In spite of that, *only* consciously perceived words produced synchronised neural activity involving frontal, parietal and occipital areas, especially between 40 and 182 ms (see Figure 16.8).

Gaillard et al. (2009) studied epileptic patients with electrodes implanted in their brains. These electrodes were used to record event-related potentials (ERPs; see Glossary). This approach has the advantage that neural activity could be recorded *directly* from the brain with more precision than is typically possible.

These patients were presented with unmasked visual stimuli that were consciously perceived and masked stimuli that were not consciously perceived. Gaillard et al. (2009) found there was far more synchronised brain activity in the unmasked or conscious condition than the masked or unconscious condition 300–500 ms after stimulus onset (time period during which conscious perception typically occurs).

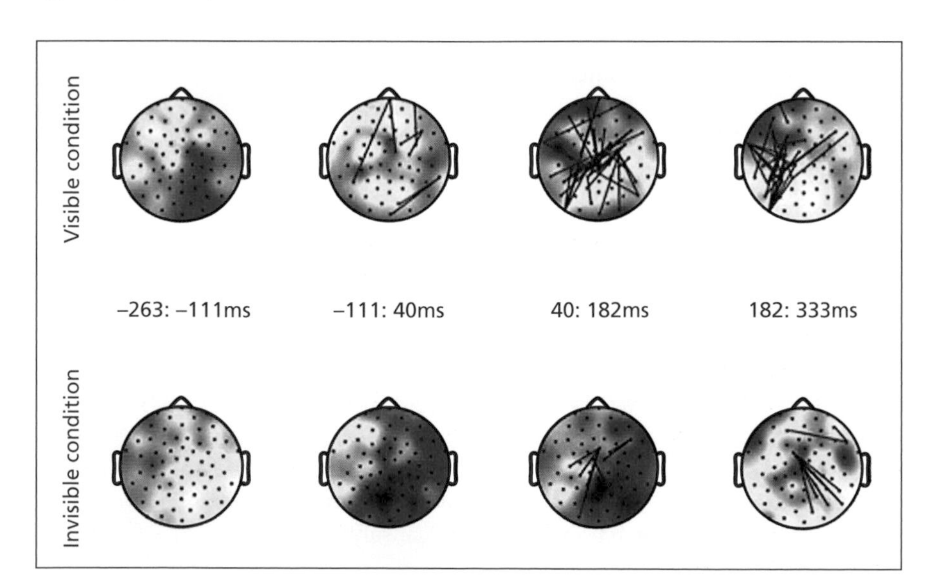

Figure 16.8
Synchronisation of neural activity across cortical areas (shown by connecting lines) for consciously perceived words (visible condition) and non-perceived words (invisible condition) during different time periods. 0 ms = stimulus onset.

From Melloni et al. (2007). Republished with permission of The Society for Neuroscience. Permission conveyed through Copyright Clearance Center, Inc.

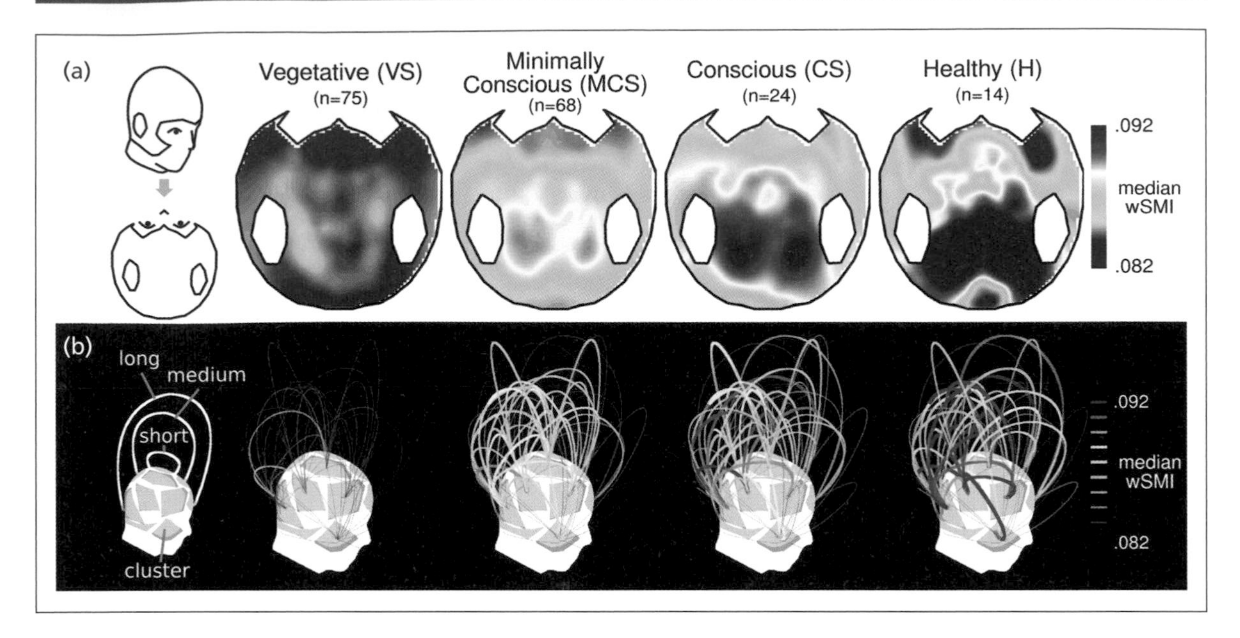

Figure 16.9
(a) Overall information sharing or integration across the brain for vegetative state, minimally conscious, conscious brain-damaged patients and healthy controls (blue = low integration; red/brown = high integration). (b) Information sharing (integration) across short, medium and long distances within the brain for the four groups.
From King et al. (2013). Reprinted with permission from Elsevier.

King et al. (2013) used electroencephalography (EEG; see Glossary) to assess integrated brain functioning in response to auditory stimuli using a measure known as weighted symbolic mutual information (wSMI). There were four groups of participants having varying levels of conscious awareness:

1 patients in a vegetative state (no conscious awareness; see earlier in the chapter);
2 minimally conscious patients;
3 conscious patients with brain damage (often recovering from a vegetative state or a state of minimal consciousness);
4 healthy participants.

What did King et al. (2013) find? There were dramatic differences in the extent of integrated brain activity across these four groups (see Figure 16.9). As predicted, there was much more integrated brain activity in groups having high levels of conscious awareness than in those having little or no awareness.

The findings discussed in this section are as predicted by global workspace theory. However, there is a tricky issue concerning causality. Synchronised neural activity may directly reflect conscious awareness. However, it is possible synchronised neural activity *precedes* and influences conscious awareness or that it occurs merely as a *consequence* of conscious awareness (de Graaf et al., 2012). It remains for future research to clarify this causality issue.

Findings: prefrontal cortex and anterior cingulate

The third assumption is that the prefrontal cortex and anterior cingulate are especially likely to be associated with conscious awareness. This assumption has received much empirical support. For example, Eriksson et al. (2006) presented auditory stimuli (sounds of objects) and visual stimuli (pictures of objects) under conditions making it hard to identify the stimulus. Activation in the lateral prefrontal cortex and the anterior cingulate was associated with both auditory and visual conscious awareness.

Further support for the third assumption was reported by Gaillard et al. (2009) in a study on epileptic patients discussed earlier. They assessed the proportion of EEG electrodes in various brain areas activated at different time periods for unmasked (conscious) and masked (unconscious) stimuli (see Figure 16.10).

What did Gaillard et al. (2009) find? First, as predicted, conscious awareness (from about 350 ms) was associated with much greater effects on activation in the frontal cortex than any other brain region. Second, the *duration* of brain activity was considerably longer for seen than unseen stimuli.

The findings discussed so far are limited because they are basically *correlational*. That means activation of the prefrontal cortex may not be causally related to conscious awareness. For example, there is much evidence (discussed shortly) that attention is a necessary prerequisite for conscious experience. As a result, it is hard to distinguish between brain activity associated with attention and that associated with conscious awareness (de Graaf et al., 2012). That is especially so since attentional processes are generally associated with activation of the prefrontal cortex (see Chapter 5).

In spite of the above issues, Wyart and Tallon-Baudry (2008) had some success in distinguishing between the neural correlates of attention and conscious awareness. Participants attended towards or away from faint stimuli that were perceived consciously only 50% of the time. Attention and conscious awareness were both associated with activity in parietal and occipital regions. However, the key finding was that brain activities associated with attention and conscious awareness were independent of each other.

How can we deal with the above causality issue? One approach is to study patients with brain damage to prefrontal cortex, as was done by Del Cul et al. (2009). On each trial, a digit was followed by a masking stimulus and participants indicated whether they had seen the masking number. The masking stimulus had to be delayed longer for brain-damaged patients than healthy controls for the digit to be consciously perceived. Thus, damage to prefrontal cortex makes it harder to achieve conscious perception. The magnitude of this effect was greater in patients having the most damage to the prefrontal cortex.

Another approach to the causality issue is to apply transcranial magnetic stimulation (TMS; see Glossary). This was done by Rounis et al. (2010) in a study in which participants discriminated between correct and incorrect stimulus judgements. TMS had no effect on participants' performance but led to lower visibility levels for correctly identified stimulus judgements. Thus, disrupting prefrontal processing via TMS made participants less aware of the quality of their visual information processing.

We have seen consciousness is associated with activation of the prefrontal cortex. However, there is increasing evidence that the prefrontal cortex can also

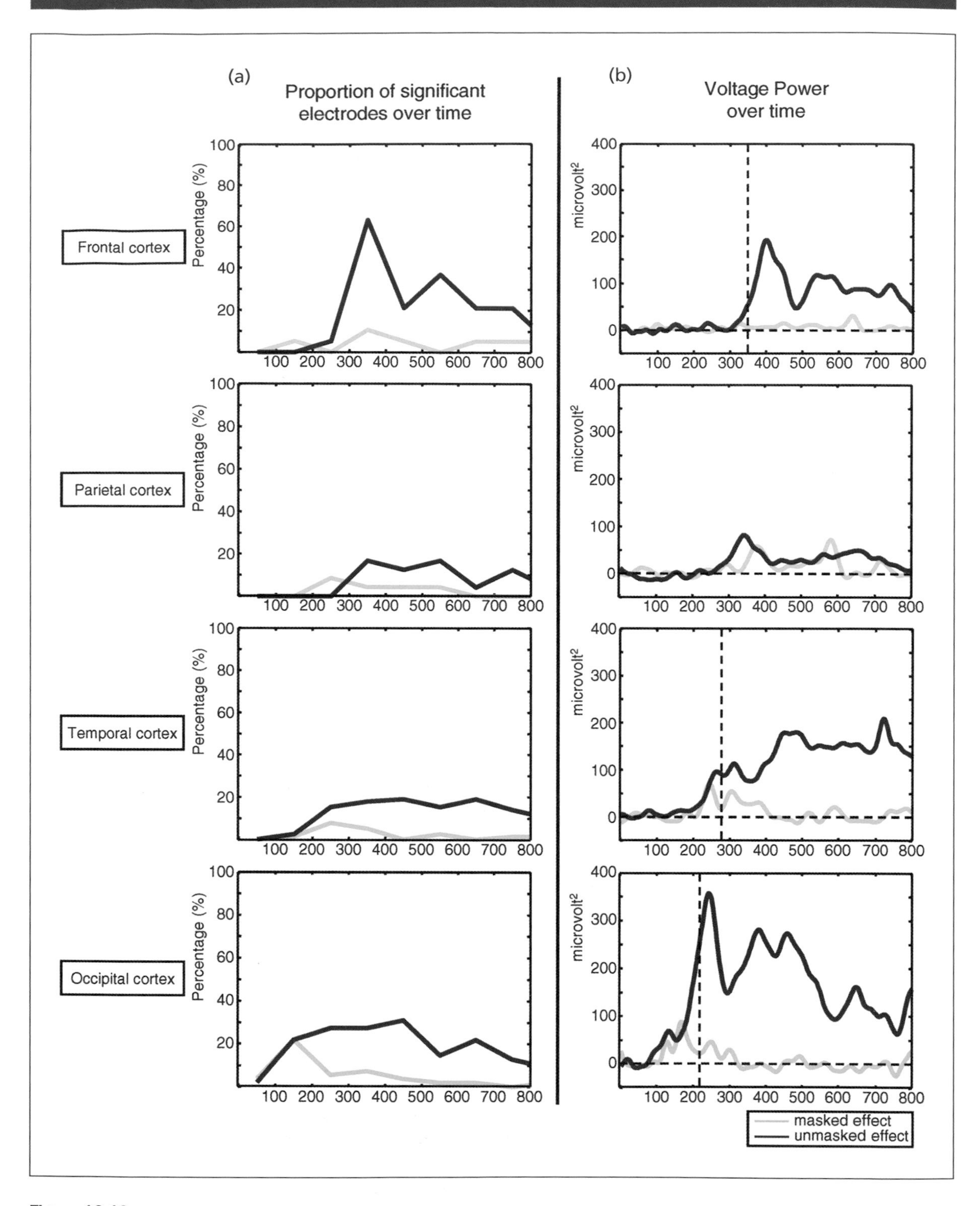

Figure 16.10

(a) percentage of electrodes and (b) voltage power of electrodes in the frontal cortex, parietal cortex, temporal cortex and occipital cortex activated by unmasked stimuli for which there was conscious awareness (dark blue) and by masked stimuli for which there was no conscious awareness (greenish-blue) over the first 800 ms since stimulus onset.

From Gaillard et al. (2009).

be activated during *unconscious* processing (van Gaal & Lamme, 2012). For example, van Gaal et al. (2010) told participants to respond to a given visible stimulus unless it was preceded by a small white square. When the small white square was visible, participants showed good inhibitory control associated with extensive prefrontal activation. Of more theoretical importance were the findings when the small white square was presented at the unconscious level. This led to a slowing of responding and some activation in the inferior frontal cortex and the presupplementary motor area. Thus, there were unconscious attempts to exercise inhibitory control and these attempts were associated with some prefrontal activation.

Findings: attention and consciousness

The fourth assumption is that consciousness depends on prior selective attention. That probably sounds reasonable to you, but several theorists have argued it is wrong. For example, Koch and Tsuchiya (2012) argued that attention without consciousness is possible and so is consciousness without attention.

Attention can influence behaviour in the absence of conscious awareness. For example, Jiang et al. (2006) presented pictures of male and female nudes that were invisible to the participants. This was achieved by presenting these nude pictures to the non-dominant eye while participants performed a task on noise patches presented to the dominant eye. Direction of attention was assessed by assessing performance on a stimulus presented after the displays. High performance implied attention was directed to the location of the stimulus, whereas poor performance implied attention was directed elsewhere.

The key finding was that the invisible nude pictures influenced participants' attentional processes. Heterosexual males attended to invisible female nudes, whereas heterosexual females attended to invisible male nudes.

How can unseen emotional stimuli influence attention? Relevant evidence was reported by Troiani et al. (2014). Unseen fearful faces produced increased amygdala activation (associated with emotional processing), which was associated with activation of brain areas associated with an attentional network.

Further evidence was reported by Naccache et al. (2002). Participants decided as rapidly as possible whether a target digit was greater or smaller than 5. Another digit that was invisible was presented immediately before the target digit. The two digits were congruent (i.e., both below or above 5) or incongruent (i.e., one below and one above 5). Attention to the visual display was manipulated by having a cue present or absent.

Naccache et al.'s (2002) findings are shown in Figure 16.11. Information about the nature of the invisible digit had no effect on uncued trials but a highly significant effect on cued ones. Thus, attentional processes amplified the information extracted from the invisible digit but did so without producing conscious awareness of that digit.

The assumption within the global workspace approach that conscious awareness is always preceded by attention has proved very controversial. Some experts (e.g., Koch & Tsuchiya, 2007, 2012) argue that consciousness does not depend on prior attention, while others (e.g., Bor & Seth, 2012) argue the opposite. Of relevance are change blindness and inattentional blindness (see Glossary; see Chapter 4). These phenomena suggest novel objects (or changes to objects) within a visual scene are not detected consciously in the absence of attention.

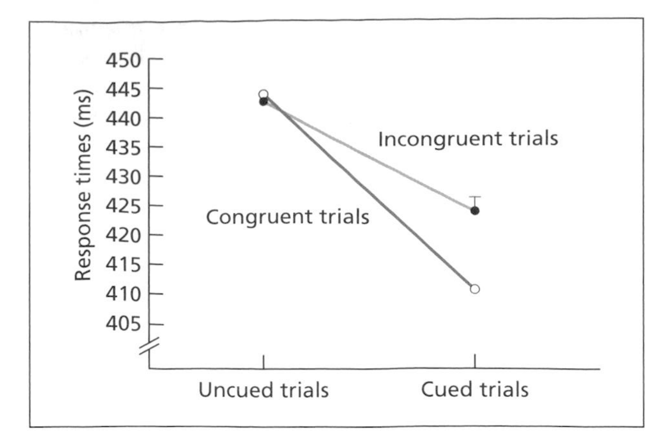

Figure 16.11
Mean reaction times for congruent and incongruent trials that were cued or uncued.

From Naccache et al. (2002). Reprinted by permission of SAGE Publications.

Koch and Tsuchiya (2007) identified various phenomena they claimed showed consciousness in the absence of attention. Two are discussed below: (1) natural-scene perception and (2) visual pop-out.

We seem to perceive the gist of natural scenes without attention. However, that may be illusory. Cohen et al. (2011) investigated this issue. Participants saw rapidly presented digits and letters against changing chessboard masks and counted the number of digits presented. Unexpectedly, a natural scene containing an animal or a vehicle replaced one of the masks.

What did Cohen et al. (2011) find? Only 23% of the participants could immediately identify the object contained within the scene and 50% reported no conscious perception of the scene. Subsequently, the participants were instructed to attend to the background and to ignore the digits and letters. In this condition, participants perceived and classified the natural scenes accurately 93% of the time. These findings strongly suggest attention is required for conscious perception of the gist of natural scenes.

Visual pop-out occurs when a target stimulus can be detected rapidly when it differs in some obvious way (e.g., colour, orientation) from surrounding distractor stimuli. It has often been assumed attention is not required to detect such target stimuli. M.A. Cohen et al. (2012) reviewed the relevant evidence. Pop-out typically fails to occur when observers' attention is engaged in another task. Thus, it appears that the pop-out effect requires attention.

Attention and unconscious processes

There is still no consensus concerning the relationship between consciousness and attention. However, most of the evidence is consistent with the assumption that attention is necessary (but not sufficient) for conscious awareness. M.A. Cohen et al. (2012) provided a sketch-map of what may be involved (see Figure 16.12). It shows prior attention is required for information to reach conscious

Figure 16.12
Representation of the relationship between attention and consciousness. A: information can only reach conscious awareness if attention operates on it. B: some attended items do not reach consciousness. Such items can nevertheless influence behaviour (e.g., priming) and produce neural changes. C: information that is not attended can produce modest priming effects and some neural activation.

From M.A. Cohen et al. (2012). With permission from Elsevier.

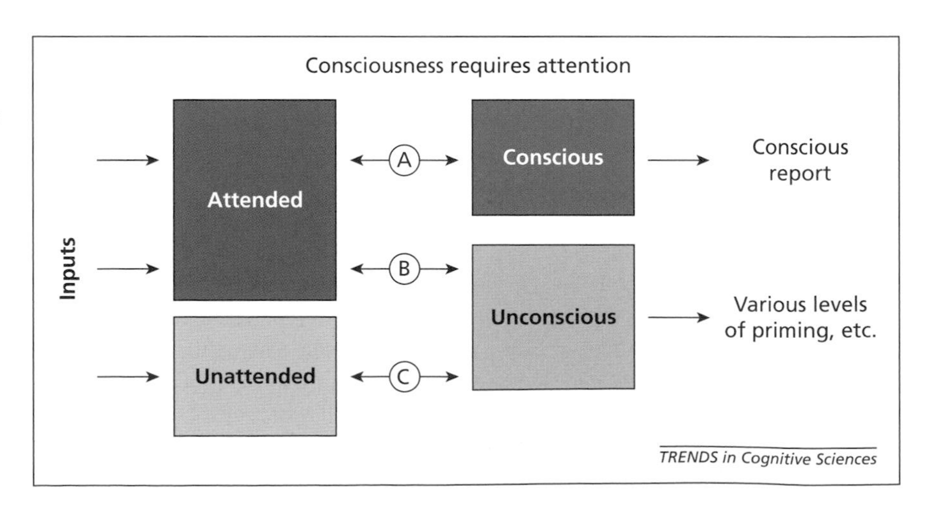

awareness (route A in the figure). However, attention is not necessarily followed by conscious awareness, but sometimes influences only unconscious processes (route B in the figure).

There has been a recent increase in studies showing unconscious processes can be strongly influenced by attention. We have discussed some of them in this section. In addition, there are studies discussed earlier in the chapter. For example, Marien et al. (2012) showed unconscious goals can influence task performance. Van Gaal et al. (2010) found inhibitory control can be exercised at the unconscious level.

KEY TERM

Split-brain patients
Patients in whom most of the direct links between the two hemispheres of the brain have been severed.

Overall evaluation

All the major assumptions of the global workspace approach have received support. As predicted, early processing of seen stimuli typically does not differ from that of unseen ones in patterns of brain activity. It is also correct that conscious awareness is generally associated with widespread integrated or synchronised brain activity, including the prefrontal cortex and the anterior cingulate. Finally, there are close links between attention and conscious awareness. It is plausible (although controversial) that conscious awareness is mostly or always preceded by attention.

What are the limitations of the global workspace approach? First, it focuses narrowly on the processes (e.g., integration of information) responsible for conscious visual perception. Such an approach tells us little or nothing about more complex forms of consciousness such as those involved in self-knowledge (Timmermans et al., 2012).

Second, the integrated brain functioning associated with conscious awareness is not necessarily the neural substrate of conscious awareness. Other possibilities are that integrated brain functioning is a *prerequisite* or *consequence* of conscious experience (de Graaf et al., 2012).

Third, identifying the brain areas and patterns of brain activity associated with conscious awareness is of value. However, this focus on cognitive neuroscience has led to a relative neglect of the associated psychological processes.

IS CONSCIOUSNESS UNITARY?

Most people assume they have a single, unitary consciousness, although a few are in two minds on the issue. However, this assumption has become controversial because of research on **split-brain patients**, who have few connections between the two brain hemispheres following surgery (see Figure 16.13). In most cases, the corpus callosum (bridge) between the two brain hemispheres was cut surgically to contain epileptic seizures within one hemisphere. This structure is a collection of 250 million axons connecting sites in one hemisphere with sites in the other.

The evidence suggests there are some remaining *interactions* between the two hemispheres in split-brain patients. Uddin et al. (2008) studied a split-brain patient whose entire corpus callosum had been cut through. In spite of that, functional neuroimaging revealed coordination of networks in both hemispheres through subcortical mechanisms.

Weblink:
Split-brain patients video

Tyszka et al. (2011) studied eight patients lacking a corpus callosum because of abnormalities in development rather than through surgical intervention.

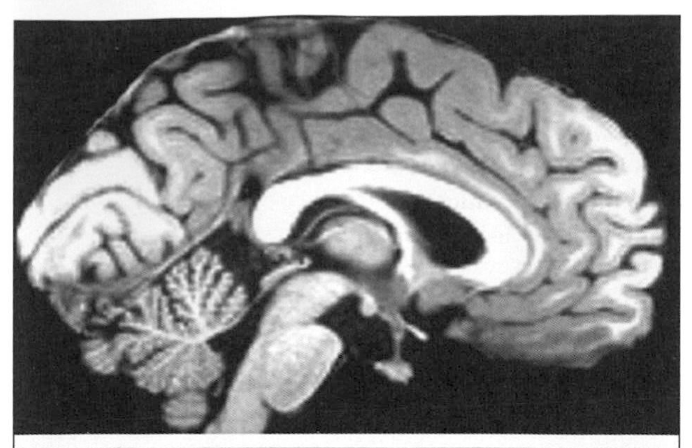

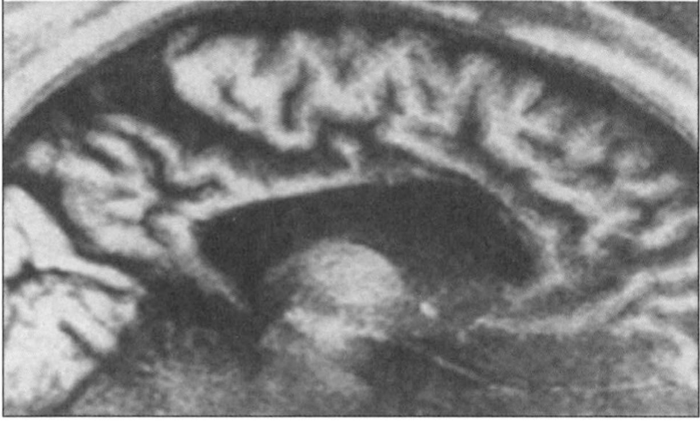

Figure 16.13
A normal brain (top) and that of a split-brain patient, JW (bottom). The normal brain shows an intact corpus callosum while that of JW shows its total absence.

From Gazzaniga (2013). Republished with permission of Annual Reviews. Permission conveyed through Copyright Clearance Center, Inc.

Surprisingly, the patients had largely normal functional networks in both hemispheres. This may have been the case because the patients' brains had undergone extensive functional reorganisation early in life. Thus, there may be important differences in cognitive functioning between these patients and patients lacking a corpus callosum due to surgery.

It is sometimes believed split-brain patients have great difficulty in functioning effectively in everyday life. This is typically *not* the case, although they sometimes find it hard to carry out complex sequences of actions as in cooking (Ferguson et al., 1985). It was not realised initially that cutting the corpus callosum caused problems. This is because split-brain patients ensure environmental information reaches both hemispheres by moving their eyes around. Impaired performance in split-brain patients is produced by presenting visual stimuli briefly to only one hemisphere so the information is not available to the other hemisphere.

There are other strategies that split-brain patients use. For example, a split-brain patient, VP, was presented with *break* to the right hemisphere and *fast* to the left hemisphere. She started to say, "bre-" as in *brake*, but then instantly corrected herself saying "breck". What happened here was that the left hemisphere used the auditory input from the right hemisphere to produce a correct pronunciation. This is an example of what is known as self-cueing.

Weblink:
Split-brain experiments

Weblink:
Dual consciousness in split-brain patients

Do split-brain patients have two minds, each with its own consciousness? Contrasting answers have been offered by experts. Roger Sperry argued that these patients have two consciousnesses: "The minor hemisphere [the right one] constitutes a second conscious entity that . . . runs along in parallel with the more dominant stream of consciousness in the major hemisphere [the left one]" (1968, p. 723). He regarded the left hemisphere as dominant because language processing is typically centred there.

In contrast, Gazzaniga (e.g., 2013) argued that split-brain patients have only a *single* conscious system based in the left hemisphere known as the interpreter. It "tries to make sense out of the many independent functions we have going on at any one time" (p. 13). The interpreter continues to function even when provided with very limited information, as occurs with many brain-damaged patients. According to Cooney and Gazzaniga (2003, p. 162), "This [system] generates a causal understanding of events that is subjectively complete and seemingly self-evident, even when that understanding is incomplete."

Bayne's (2008, 2010) switch model differs from both theories just discussed. According to the switch model, there is a single stream of consciousness that *switches* between the two hemispheres. The hemisphere in which consciousness resides at any given moment depends on the allocation of attentional resources. As we saw earlier, there is much support for the general view that conscious experience depends on prior selective attention.

It is not clear that split-brain patients have a truly *single* stream of consciousness. After all, most experiments are designed to ensure each hemisphere has access to different information. It seems more likely split-brain patients have *two* distinct streams of activity even if only one stream is accessible to consciousness at any given moment (Schechter, 2012).

An advantage of Bayne's switch model is that it can explain why there are relatively few disagreements between the two hemispheres. However, there is a significant disadvantage with the model. It would seem to predict that split-brain patients would report rapid *changes* in the contents of consciousness. In fact, that occurs very rarely.

Findings

Before we discuss the research, note that information from the left visual field goes to the right hemisphere, whereas information from the right visual field goes to the left hemisphere (see Chapter 2). More generally, the left half of the body is controlled by the right hemisphere and the right half by the left hemisphere. Note also that it is hard to know whether the right hemisphere of split-brain patients has its own consciousness because that hemisphere has limited language ability.

Two streams

What evidence supports Sperry's view that split-brain patients have two streams of consciousness? On that view we might expect *disagreements* between the two hemispheres. Such disagreements have occasionally been reported. Mark (1996, p. 191) discussed a patient having speech in both hemispheres:

> She mentioned that she did not have feelings in her left hand. When I echoed the statement, she said that she was not numb, and then the torrent of alternating "Yes!" and "No!" replies ensued, followed by a despairing "I don't know!"

Weblink:
Split-brain patients

Baynes and Gazzaniga (2000) studied VJ, a split-brain patient whose writing is controlled by the right hemisphere, while her speech is controlled by the left hemisphere. According to Baynes and Gazzaniga (2000, p. 1362):

> She [VJ] is the first split . . . who is frequently dismayed by the independent performance of her right and left hands. She is discomfited by the fluent writing of her left hand to unseen stimuli and distressed by the inability of her right hand to write out words she can read out loud and spell.

Speculatively, we could interpret the evidence from VJ as suggesting limited dual consciousness.

Evidence that the two hemispheres of split-brain patients can function simultaneously and independently was reported by Schiffer et al. (1998). Two patients responded to emotionally sensitive questions. Their hands were hidden from view behind a screen as they responded at the same time with each hand separately. The right hemisphere produced more emotional answers to the questions. This is consistent with the notion that the right hemisphere plays a key role in emotional experience.

Trevarthen (2004) discussed studies on the abilities of the two hemispheres in split-brain patients. The right hemisphere outperformed the left on tasks involving visual or touch perception of complex shapes, manipulations of geometric patterns and judgements involving hand explorations of shapes.

The ability to recognise one's own face has often been regarded as an indication of reasonable self-awareness. Uddin et al. (2005) found NG, a 70-year-old split-brain patient, could recognise her own face equally well whether presented to her left or right hemisphere. Her self-recognition performance was close to that of healthy individuals, suggesting the existence of some basic self-awareness in both hemispheres.

A review of neuroimaging studies by Keenan and Gorman (2007) indicated self-awareness is generally associated with greater right hemisphere than left hemisphere activation. Thus, some aspects of conscious experience may depend more on the right hemisphere than assumed by Gazzaniga (2013).

One stream

Gazzaniga (e.g., 2013) emphasised the importance of a stream of conscious centred in the dominant left hemisphere, although he accepted much processing also occurs in the right hemisphere. What evidence supports his viewpoint? The subjective experiences of split-brain patients are relevant. According to Colvin and Gazzaniga (2007, p. 189), "No split-brain patient has ever woken up following callostomy [cutting of the corpus callosum] and felt as though his/her experience of self had fundamentally changed or that two selves now inhabited the same body."

The fact that the right hemisphere of most split-brain patients lacks speech makes it hard to know whether it possesses its own consciousness. Accordingly, it is important to study patients with reasonable right-hemisphere language abilities.

Gazzaniga and Ledoux (1978) studied Paul S, a split-brain patient with unusually well-developed right-hemisphere language abilities. He showed limited evidence of right-hemisphere consciousness by responding appropriately to questions using Scrabble letters with his left hand. For example, he could spell out his own name, that of his girlfriend, his hobbies, his current mood and so on. There were some interesting differences between Paul S's hemispheres. For example, his right hemisphere said he wanted to be a racing driver, whereas his left hemisphere wanted to be a draughtsman.

Gazzaniga (1992, 2013) discussed other studies on Paul S. He was presented with a chicken claw to his left hemisphere and a snow scene to his right hemisphere. When asked to select relevant pictures from an array, he chose a picture of a chicken with his right hand (connected to the left hemisphere) and a shovel with his left hand (connected to the right hemisphere).

The above findings may suggest Paul S had a separate consciousness in each hemisphere. However, here is how he explained his choices: "The chicken claw goes with the chicken and you need a shovel to clean out the chicken shed" (Gazzaniga, 1992, p. 124). Thus, Paul S's left hemisphere was *interpreting* behaviour initiated by the right hemisphere with little contribution from the right hemisphere. Similarly, Paul S obeyed when his right hemisphere was given the command to walk. However, his left hemisphere explained his behaviour by saying something such as that he wanted a Coke.

Verleger et al. (2011) studied GH, a 69-year-old man. His corpus callosum was damaged, which led to **anarchic-hand syndrome**. This is a condition in which one hand (the left in GH's case) does not act as intended and sometimes counteracts the right hand. Sometimes in a shop GH would put money on the counter with his right hand but his left hand would take the money back.

GH was instructed to respond to a stimulus presented to his left or right hemisphere. His performance in terms of response speed and errors was significantly worse when he responded with his left hand (i.e., following stimulus presentation to his right hemisphere). Event-related potentials (ERPs; see Glossary) indicated GH had a much smaller P3 component (at about 300–400 ms) to stimuli presented to his right hemisphere than those presented to his left hemisphere. These P3 findings suggest the patient's ability to pay attention to stimuli and to control processing was much less in the right hemisphere than the left. Of interest, GH's experiences in everyday life strongly suggested his consciousness resided within his left hemisphere.

Similar findings were reported by Hesselmann et al. (2013) in a study on a male patient, AC, who had severe damage to his corpus callosum. Two stimuli were presented 100, 300 or 800 ms apart, one to the left hemisphere and the other to the right hemisphere. AC responded as rapidly as possible to both stimuli. We will focus on the ERP responses to the first stimulus. AC had a pronounced P3 component to left-hemisphere stimuli but no P3 component to *right*-hemisphere stimuli (see Figure 16.14). These findings suggest AC had conscious access to information about stimuli presented to the left hemisphere but much delayed and/or reduced conscious access to stimuli presented to the right hemisphere.

KEY TERM

Anarchic-hand syndrome
Complex, goal-directed hand movements that the patient does not initiate voluntarily and cannot interpret.

Summary and evaluation

Research has not fully resolved the issue of whether it is possible to have two separate consciousnesses. The commonest view is that the left hemisphere in split-brain patients plays the dominant role in conscious awareness because it is the location of an interpreter or self-supervisory system providing coherent interpretations of events. This view is supported by findings showing the left hemisphere overruling the right hemisphere and by the persistent failure to observe genuine dialogues between the hemispheres. In the words of Gazzaniga (2013, p. 16), "Dazzling unitary speech behaviour is the product of discrete modules [specialised processors] that are massively self-cued to appear coherent despite being isolated and rather independent modules."

In contrast, the right hemisphere engages in various processing activities (e.g., basic self-awareness, emotional processing, aspects of visual or touch perception). Consciousness within the right hemisphere is hard to assess because it possesses very limited language abilities. However, recent evidence using event-related potentials supports the view that there is much less conscious awareness in the right hemisphere than in the left hemisphere.

What is needed for the future? As we saw earlier in the chapter, considerable advances have been made in identifying the neural correlates of consciousness. It would be of great theoretical relevance to discover the presence (or absence) of these neural correlates within the right hemisphere.

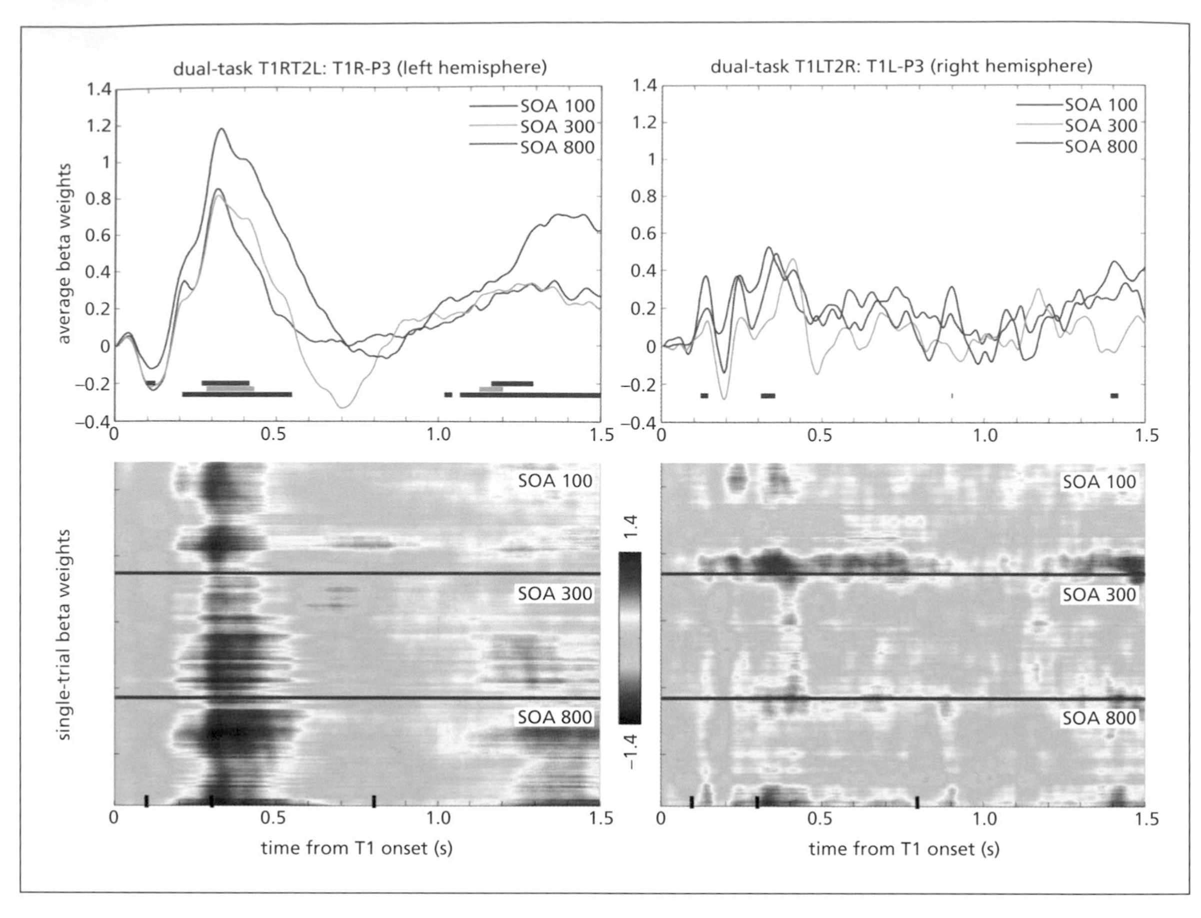

Figure 16.14

Event-related potentials (ERPs) in the left hemisphere (left-hand figure) and the right hemisphere (right-hand figure) to the first of two stimuli by AC (a patient with severe corpus callosum damage). The time course of the ERPs is shown on the horizontal axis in seconds. The second stimulus was presented 100 ms (red line), 300 ms (green line) or 800 ms (blue line) after the first stimulus (SOA = stimulus onset asynchrony).

From Hesselmann et al. (2013). Reprinted with permission from Elsevier.

CHAPTER SUMMARY

- **Introduction.** There is a distinction between conscious content and conscious level or state of consciousness. There is also an important distinction between phenomenal or basic consciousness tied to perception and higher-level consciousness that is not restricted to the here-and-now.
- **Functions of consciousness.** The functions claimed for conscious awareness include perception, social communication, action control, thinking beyond the here-and-now and a very informative integration of information. The machinery used to compute information about

other people's awareness is also used to compute information about their own awareness. Some behavioural evidence suggests the notion of conscious control of action is an illusion driven by the principles of priority, consistency and exclusivity. Neuroimaging studies indicate some decision-relevant processing occurs prior to conscious awareness. However, the tasks used are artificial and trivial, and a major role for conscious awareness has not been ruled out.

- **Assessing consciousness and conscious experience**. It has been claimed our actual conscious experience is often much richer than our verbal reports of that experience. The main reason is that attention and memory limit our verbal reports. However, this alleged richness of experience may be illusory and may reflect the involvement of top-down processes (e.g., expectations).

  Patients in the vegetative state show no behavioural signs of consciousness. However, a few show evidence of conscious awareness based on neuroimaging data obtained while they perform cognitive tasks. The cognitive processes they exhibit include language comprehension, sustained attention, switching attention, use of imagery and question answering.

  Lamme argues that recurrent processing (but not feedforward processing) is associated with conscious visual perception. The main reason is that recurrent processing is associated with integrated processing. There is support for the importance of recurrent processing. However, it remains unclear whether recurrent processing is necessary or sufficient for conscious experience.

- **Global workspace theoretical approach**. According to global workspace theory, selective attention influences the information of which we become consciously aware. Another key assumption is that conscious awareness is associated with integrated, synchronous activity. This activity involves many brain areas, especially prefrontal cortex, the anterior cingulate and parts of the parietal cortex. There is reasonable support for all the major assumptions of global workspace theory. However, research focuses on conscious and unconscious visual perception and the theory de-emphasises consciousness based on self-awareness and self-knowledge. Another issue is whether integrated brain functioning reflects conscious awareness or is a prerequisite or consequence of conscious awareness.

- **Is consciousness unitary?** Evidence from split-brain patients indicates their behaviour can be controlled to some extent by each hemisphere. However, the left hemisphere is dominant in determining conscious awareness and behaviour and can be regarded as an interpreter of internal and external events. This hypothesis is supported by the fact that split-brain patients rarely report disagreements between the two hemispheres. However, the very limited language abilities of the right hemisphere make it hard to assess the extent to which it is conscious. Nevertheless, electrophysiological evidence suggests the right hemisphere has only limited consciousness.

Further reading

- Baumeister, R.F. & Masicampo, E.J. (2010). Conscious thought is for facilitating social and cultural interactions: How mental simulations serve the animal-culture interface. *Psychological Review*, 117: 945–71. Roy Baumeister and Emer Masicampo discuss the functions of consciousness in a thorough and insightful way.
- Blackmore, S. (2010). *Consciousness: An introduction* (2nd edn). London: Hodder Education. Susan Blackmore's book provides an entertaining and accessible introduction to the complexities of human consciousness.
- Cohen, M.A., Cavanagh, P., Chun, M.M. & Nakayama, K. (2012). The attentional requirements of consciousness. *Trends in Cognitive Sciences*, 16: 411–17. The authors provide a useful theoretical framework within which to understand the relationship between attention and consciousness.
- de Graaf, T.A., Hsieh, P.-J. & Sack, A.T. (2012). The "correlates" in neural correlates of consciousness. *Neuroscience and Biobehavioral Reviews*, 16: 191–7. This article provides an excellent discussion of the issues involved in trying to establish the neural correlates of consciousness.
- Gazzaniga, M.S. (2013). Shifting gears: Seeking new approaches for mind/brain mechanisms. *Annual Review of Psychology*, 64: 1–20. Michael Gazzaniga (a leading expert) discusses theoretical developments in our understanding of split-brain patients.
- Owen, A.M. (2013). Detecting consciousness: A unique role for neuroimaging. *Annual Review of Psychology*, 64: 109–33. Adrian Owen discusses the nature of consciousness in the light of neuroimaging research on non-responsive patients.
- Seager, W. (2015). *Theories of consciousness: An introduction and assessment* (2nd edn). Hove: Psychology Press. William Seeger provides a well-informed discussion of major theoretical approaches to consciousness.

Glossary

accommodation: a depth cue based on changes in optical power produced by thickening of the eye's lens when an observer focuses on close objects.

achromatopsia: a condition involving brain damage in which there is little or no colour perception but form and motion perception are relatively intact.

affect heuristic: using one's emotional responses to influence rapid judgements or decisions.

affective blindsight: the ability of brain-damaged patients to discriminate among different emotional stimuli in spite of the absence of conscious perception.

affordances: the potential uses of an object, which Gibson claimed are perceived directly.

agrammatism: a condition in which speech production lacks grammatical structure and many function words and word endings are omitted.

akinetopsia: a brain-damaged condition in which motion perception is severely impaired even though stationary objects are perceived reasonably well.

algorithm: a computational procedure providing a specified set of steps to problem solution.

allocentric coding: visual coding that is independent of the observer's perspective; *see also* **egocentric coding**.

allophony: an allophone is one of two or more similar sounds associated with the same **phoneme**.

Alzheimer's disease: a condition in which there is a progressive deterioration in mental abilities caused by a general degeneration of the brain.

amnesia: a condition caused by brain damage in which there is severe impairment of long-term memory.

amygdala: a part of the brain strongly associated with several emotions including fear; it is located towards the front of the temporal lobe.

analogy: a comparison between two objects (or between a current and previous problem) that emphasises similarities between them.

anaphor: a word (especially pronoun) whose referent is a previously mentioned noun or noun phrase.

anarchic-hand syndrome: complex, goal-directed hand movements that the patient does not initiate voluntarily and cannot interpret.

anomia: a condition caused by brain damage in which there is an impaired ability to name objects.

anterior *see* **rostral**

anterograde amnesia: reduced ability to remember information acquired after the onset of **amnesia**.

Anton's syndrome: a condition found in some blind people in which they misinterpret their visual imagery as visual perception.

aphasia: severe problems in the comprehension and/or production of language caused by brain damage.

articulatory suppression: rapid repetition of a simple sound (e.g., "the the the"), which uses the articulatory control process of the **phonological loop**.

artificial intelligence: this involves developing computer programs that produce intelligent outcomes.

Asperger syndrome: an autistic spectrum disorder involving problems with social communication in spite of at least average intelligence and no delays in language development.

association: the finding that certain symptoms or performance impairments are consistently found together in numerous brain-damaged patients.

attentional bias: selective allocation of attention to threat-related stimuli when presented simultaneously with neutral stimuli.

audience design: this involves speakers tailoring what they say to the specific needs of their audience.

autistic spectrum disorders: disorders involving difficulties in social interaction and communication and repetitive patterns of behaviour and thinking.

autobiographical memory: long-term memory for the events of one's own life.

autostereogram: a complex two-dimensional image perceived as three-dimensional when not focused on for a period of time.

availability heuristic: the rule of thumb that the frequencies of events can be estimated accurately by the subjective ease with which they can be retrieved.

back-propagation: a learning mechanism in connectionist models based on comparing actual responses to correct ones.

base-rate information: the relative frequency of an event within a given population.

belief bias: in syllogistic reasoning, the tendency to accept invalid but believable conclusions and reject valid but unbelievable ones.

binding problem: the issue of integrating different types of information to produce coherent visual perception.

binocular cues: cues to depth that require both eyes to be used together.

binocular disparity: a depth cue based on the slight disparity in the two retinal images when an observer views a scene; it is the basis for **stereopsis**.

binocular rivalry: when two different visual stimuli are presented one to each eye, only one stimulus is seen; the seen stimulus alternates over time.

blindsight: the ability to respond appropriately to visual stimuli in the absence of conscious visual experience in patients with damage to the primary visual cortex.

body size effect: an illusion in which misperception of one's own bodily size causes the perceived size of objects to be misjudged.

BOLD: blood oxygen level-dependent contrast; this is the signal measured by **functional magnetic resonance imaging (fMRI)**.

bottom-up processing: processing that is directly influenced by environmental stimuli; *see also* **top-down processing**.

bounded rationality: the notion that people are as rational as the environment and their limited processing capacity permit.

bridging inferences: inferences or conclusions drawn to increase coherence between the current and preceding parts of a text; also known as backward inferences.

Broca's aphasia: a form of **aphasia** involving non-fluent speech and grammatical errors.

cascade model: a model in which information passes from one level to the next *before* completion of processing at the first level.

case-series study: a study in which several patients with similar cognitive impairments are tested; this allows consideration of individual data and of variation across individuals.

categorical perception: a sound intermediate between two **phonemes** is perceived as being one or other of the phonemes.

category-specific deficits: disorders caused by brain damage in which **semantic memory** is disrupted for certain semantic categories.

central coherence: the ability to make use of all the information when interpreting an utterance or situation.

central executive: a modality-free, limited capacity, component of **working memory**.

change blindness: failure to detect various changes (e.g., in objects) in the visual environment.

change blindness blindness: the tendency of observers to overestimate greatly the extent to which they can detect visual changes and so avoid **change blindness**.

Charles Bonnet syndrome: a condition in which individuals with eye disease form vivid and detailed visual hallucinations sometimes mistaken for visual perception.

child-directed speech: the short, simple, slowly spoken sentences used by parents and others when talking to young children.

childhood amnesia: the inability of adults to recall autobiographical memories from early childhood; also known as infantile amnesia.

chromatic adaptation: changes in visual sensitivity to colour stimuli when the illumination alters.

chunks: stored units formed from integrating smaller pieces of information.

clause: a group of words within a sentence that contains a subject and a verb.

coarticulation: a speaker's production of a **phoneme** is influenced by his/her production of the previous sound and by preparations for the next sound.

cocktail party problem: the difficulties involved in attending to one voice when two or more people are speaking at the same time.

cognitive architecture: a comprehensive framework for understanding human cognition in the form of a computer programs.

cognitive bias modification: training typically designed to reduce **attentional bias** and/or **interpretive bias**.

cognitive miser: someone who is economical with their time and effort when performing a thinking task.

cognitive neuroscience: an approach that aims to understand human cognition by combining information from behaviour and the brain.

cognitive psychology: an approach that aims to understand human cognition by the study of behaviour; a broader definition also includes the study of brain activity and structure.

colour constancy: the tendency for an object to be perceived as having the same colour under widely varying viewing conditions.

common ground: shared knowledge and beliefs possessed by a speaker and a listener; its use facilitates communication.

comorbidity: the presence of two or more mental disorders in a given patient at the same time.

computational modelling: this involves constructing computer programs that simulate or mimic human cognitive processes.

concepts: mental representations of categories of objects or items.

conceptual priming: a form or priming in which there is facilitated processing of stimulus meaning.

conditional reasoning: a form of **deductive reasoning** based on "if . . . then" propositions.

confirmation bias: (1) a tendency for eyewitness memory to be distorted by the eyewitness's prior expectations; (2) in hypothesis testing, seeking evidence that supports one's beliefs.

conjunction fallacy: the mistaken assumption that the probability of a conjunction of two events is greater than the probability of one of them.

connectionist models: models in computational cognitive science consisting of interconnected networks of simple units; the networks exhibit learning through experience and specific items of knowledge are distributed across numerous units.

consolidation: a physiological process involved in establishing long-term memories; this process lasts several hours or more and newly formed memories are fragile.

converging operations: an approach in which several methods with different strengths and limitations are used to address a given issue.

covert attention: attention to an object in the absence of an eye movement towards it.

cross-modal attention: the coordination of attention across two or more modalities (e.g., vision and audition).

crystallised intelligence: the ability to use knowledge, skills and experience.

decision making: making a selection from various options; if full information is unavailable, **judgement** is required.

declarative memory: a form of long-term memory that involves knowing something is the case; it involves conscious recollection and includes memory for facts (**semantic memory**) and events (**episodic memory**); sometimes known as explicit memory.

deductive reasoning: reasoning to a conclusion from a set of premises or statements where that conclusion follows necessarily from the assumption that the premises are true; *see also* **inductive reasoning**.

deep dyslexia: a condition in which reading unfamiliar words and non-words is impaired and there are semantic errors (e.g., reading *missile* as *rocket*).

deep dysphasia: a condition involving semantic errors when trying to repeat spoken words and a generally poor ability to repeat spoken words and non-words.

deliberate practice: this form of practice involves the learner being provided with informative feedback and having the chance to correct his/her errors.

deontological judgements: judgements based on moral rules and/or obligations when resolving moral dilemmas; *see also* **utilitarian judgements**.

depictive representations: representations (e.g., visual images) resembling pictures in that objects within them are organised spatially.

dichotic listening task: a different auditory message is presented to each ear and attention has to be directed to one message.

dichromacy: a deficiency in colour vision in which one of the three cone classes is missing.

direct retrieval: involuntary recall of autobiographical memories triggered by a specific cue (e.g., being in the same place as the original event); *see also* **generative retrieval**.

directed forgetting: reduced long-term memory caused by instructions to forget information that had been presented for learning.

directed retrospection: a technique in which individuals (e.g., writers) categorise their immediately preceding thoughts.

discourse: language that is a minimum of several sentences in length; it includes written text and connected speech.

discourse markers: spoken words and phrases that do not contribute directly to the content of what is being said but still serve various functions (e.g., clarifying the speaker's intentions).

dissociation: as applied to brain-damaged patients, intact performance on one task but severely impaired performance on a different task.

distinctiveness: this characterises memory traces that are distinct or different from other memory traces stored in long-term memory.

distraction: a strategy used in **emotion regulation** in which the individual disengages attention from emotional processing and focuses on neutral information.

divided attention: a situation in which two tasks are performed at the same time; also known as multitasking.

domain specificity: the notion that a given module responds selectively to certain types of stimuli (e.g., faces) but not others.

dorsal: superior, or towards the top of the brain.

dorsal stream: the part of the visual processing system most involved in visually guided action.

double dissociation: the finding that some brain-damaged individuals have intact performance on one task but poor performance on another task, whereas other individuals exhibit the opposite pattern.

Dunning–Kruger effect: the finding that less skilled individuals overestimate their abilities more than those who are more skilled.

dysexecutive agraphia: severely impaired writing abilities in individuals with damage to the frontal lobes whose central executive functioning is generally impaired.

dysexecutive syndrome: a condition in which damage to the frontal lobes causes impairments to the **central executive** component of **working memory**.

dysgraphia: impaired ability to write (including spelling).

dyslexia: impaired ability to read that is not attributable to low intelligence.

dysrationalia: the failure of reasonably intelligent individuals to think and reason in a rational way.

echoic memory: a sensory store that holds auditory information for approximately two seconds.

ecological validity: the applicability (or otherwise) of the findings of laboratory studies to everyday settings.

EEG *see* **electroencephalography**

efference copy: an internal copy of a motor command (e.g., to the eyes); it can be used to compare actual with desired movement.

efMRI *see* **event-related functional magnetic resonance imaging**

egocentric coding: visual coding that is dependent on the observer's perspective; *see also* **allocentric coding**.

egocentric heuristic: a strategy used by listeners in which they interpret what they hear based on their own knowledge rather than knowledge shared with the speaker.

elaborative inferences: inferences based on our knowledge of the world that involve adding details to a text that is being read.

electroencephalography (EEG): recording the brain's electrical potentials through a series of scalp electrodes.

emotion generation: the immediate and spontaneous emotional response to a given situation; *see also* **emotion regulation**.

emotion regulation: the use of deliberate and effortful processes to change the spontaneous emotional state (usually a negative one) produced by the emotion-generation process.

encoding-specificity principle: the notion that retrieval depends on the *overlap* between the information available at retrieval and the information in the memory trace.

endogenous spatial attention: attention to a stimulus controlled by intentions or goal-directed mechanisms.

episodic buffer: a component of **working memory**; it is essentially passive and stores integrated information briefly.

episodic memory: a form of long-term memory concerned with personal experiences or episodes occurring in a given place at a specific time.

ERPs *see* **event-related potentials**

event-based prospective memory: a form of prospective memory that involves remembering to perform an intended action (e.g., buying groceries) when the circumstances are appropriate.

event-related functional magnetic resonance imaging (efMRI): this is a form of functional magnetic resonance imaging in which patterns of brain activity associated with specific events (e.g., correct vs. incorrect responses on a memory test) are compared.

event-related potentials (ERPs): the pattern of electroencephalograph (EEG) activity obtained by averaging the brain responses to the same stimulus (or very similar stimuli) presented repeatedly.

executive processes: processes that organise and coordinate the functioning of the cognitive system to achieve current goals.

exogenous spatial attention: attention to a given spatial location determined by "automatic" processes.

expertise: the high level of knowledge and performance in a given domain that an expert has achieved through years of systematic practice.

explicit memory: memory that involves conscious recollection of information; *see also* **implicit memory**.

explicit memory bias: the retrieval of relatively more negative information than positive or neutral information on tests of **explicit memory**.

extinction: a disorder of visual attention in which a stimulus presented to the side opposite the brain damage is not detected when another stimulus is presented at the same time to the side of the brain damage.

face inversion effect: the finding that faces are much harder to recognise when presented upside down; the effect of inversion is less marked (or absent) with other objects.

falsification: proposing hypotheses and then trying to falsify them by experimental tests; the logically correct means by which science should work, according to Popper (1968).

figurative language: language that is not intended to be taken literally; examples include metaphor, irony and idiom.

figure–ground segregation: the perceptual organisation of the visual field into a figure (object of central interest) and a ground (less important background).

flashbacks: intense emotional memories of traumatic events that are recalled involuntarily by patients suffering from post-traumatic stress disorder.

flashbulb memories: vivid and detailed memories of dramatic events (e.g., 9/11).

fluid intelligence: non-verbal reasoning ability applied to novel problems.

fMRI *see* **functional magnetic resonance imaging**

focused attention: a situation in which individuals try to attend to only one source of information while ignoring other stimuli; also known as selective attention.

focus of expansion: the point towards which someone in motion is moving; it does not appear to move but the surrounding visual environment apparently moves away from it.

framing effect: the finding that decisions can be influenced by situational aspects (e.g., problem wording) irrelevant to good decision making.

free will: the notion that we freely or voluntarily choose what to do from various options.

Freudian slip: a speech error that reveals the speaker's (often unconscious) sexual desires.

functional fixedness: the inflexible focus on the usual function(s) of an object in problem solving.

functional magnetic resonance imaging (fMRI): a technique based on imaging blood oxygenation using an MRI machine; it provides information about the location and time course of brain processes.

functional specialisation: the assumption that each brain area or region is specialised for a specific function (e.g., colour processing, face processing).

fusiform face area: an area that is associated with face processing; the term is somewhat misleading given that the area is also associated with processing other categories of objects.

Ganong effect: the finding that perception of an ambiguous **phoneme** is biased towards a sound that produces a word rather than a non-word.

generative retrieval: deliberate or voluntary construction of autobiographical memories based on an individual's current goals; *see also* **direct retrieval**.

grammar: the set of rules concerning which word orders are acceptable and which are unacceptable and on parts of speech.

grapheme: a small unit of written language corresponding to a **phoneme** (e.g., the *ph* in *photo*).

graphemic buffer: a store in which graphemic information about the individual letters in a word is held immediately prior to spelling the word.

gyri: prominent elevated areas or ridges on the brain's surface ("gyrus" is the singular).

haptic: relating to the sense of touch.

heuristics: rules of thumb that are cognitively undemanding and often produce approximately accurate answers.

hiatus heuristic: the rule of thumb that only customers who have purchased goods fairly recently remain active customers.

hill climbing: a simple **heuristic** used by problem solvers in which they focus on making moves that will apparently put them closer to the goal.

holistic processing: processing that involves *integrating* information from an entire object (especially faces).

homograph: word having a single spelling but two or more different meanings (e.g., *bank*, *patient*).

homophones: words pronounced in the same way but that differ in their spellings (e.g., *pain–pane*, *sale–sail*).

hyperthymestic syndrome: an exceptional ability to remember the events of one's own life.

iconic memory: a sensory store that holds visual information for approximately 500 milliseconds or perhaps somewhat longer.

ideomotor apraxia: a condition caused by brain damage in which patients have difficulty in planning and carrying out learned movements.

ill-defined problems: problems that are imprecisely specified; for example, the initial state, goal state and the methods available to solve the problem may be unclear.

illuminant: a source of light illuminating a surface or object.

illusory conjunction: mistakenly combining features from two different stimuli to perceive an object that is not present.

impact bias: overestimation of the intensity and duration of negative emotional reactions to loss.

implacable experimenter: the situation in experimental research in which the experimenter's behaviour is uninfluenced by the participant's behaviour.

implementation intentions: action plans designed consciously to achieve some goal (e.g., healthier eating) based on specific information concerning where, when and how the goal will be achieved.

implicit learning: learning complex information without conscious awareness of what has been learned.

implicit memory: memory that does not depend on conscious recollection.

implicit memory bias: relatively better memory performance for negative than for neutral or positive information on tests of **implicit memory**.

inattentional blindness: failure to detect an unexpected object appearing in the visual environment.

incubation: a stage of problem solving in which the problem is put to one side for some time; it is claimed to facilitate problem solving.

inductive reasoning: forming generalisations (that may be probable but are not certain) from examples or sample phenomena; *see also* **deductive reasoning**.

inferior *see* **ventral**

inflection: grammatical changes to nouns or verbs (e.g., adding *–s* to a noun to indicate the plural).

informal reasoning: a form of reasoning based on one's relevant knowledge and experience rather than logic.

inhibition of return: a reduced probability of visual attention returning to a recently attended location or object.

inner scribe: according to Logie, the part of the **visuo-spatial sketchpad** dealing with spatial and movement information.

insight: the experience of suddenly realising how to solve a problem.

interoception: sensitivity to bodily stimuli at the conscious or non-conscious level.

interpretive bias: the tendency when presented with ambiguous stimuli or situations to interpret them in a threatening way.

introspection: a careful examination and description of one's own mental thoughts.

invariants: properties of the optic array that remain constant even though other aspects vary; part of Gibson's theory.

jargon aphasia: a brain-damaged condition in which speech is reasonably correct grammatically but there are severe problems in accessing the appropriate words.

judgement: an assessment of the probability of a given event occurred based on incomplete information.

knowledge effect: the tendency to assume others possess the same knowledge as us.

knowledge-lean problems: problems that can be solved by individuals in the absence of specific relevant prior knowledge.

knowledge-rich problems: problems that can only be solved by those having considerable relevant background knowledge.

Korsakoff's syndrome: **amnesia** caused by chronic alcoholism.

lateral: situated at the side of the brain.

lateral inhibition: reduction of activity in one neuron caused by activity in a neighbouring neuron.

law of Prägnanz: the notion that the simplest possible organisation of the visual environment is perceived; proposed by the Gestaltists.

lemmas: abstract words possessing syntactic and semantic features but not phonological ones.

lesions: structural alterations within the brain caused by disease or injury.

lexical access: accessing detailed information about a given word by entering the **lexicon**.

lexical bias effect: the tendency for speech errors to form words rather than non-words.

lexical decision task: participants presented with a string of letters or auditory stimulus decide rapidly whether it forms a word.

lexicalisation: the process of translating a word's meaning into its sound representation during speech production.

lexicon: a store of detailed information (orthographic, phonological, semantic, syntactic) about words.

life script: cultural expectations concerning the nature and order of major life events in a typical person's life.

linguistic relativity: the notion that speakers of different languages think differently.

long-term working memory: used by experts to store relevant information rapidly in long-term memory and to access it through retrieval cues in **working memory**.

loss aversion: the greater sensitivity to potential losses than potential gains shown by most people engaged in decision making.

magneto-encephalography (MEG): a non-invasive brain-scanning technique based on recording the magnetic fields generated by brain activity.

masking: suppression of the processing (and conscious perception of) a stimulus by presenting a second, masking stimulus very shortly thereafter.

matching bias: the tendency on the Wason selection task to select cards matching the items explicitly mentioned in the rule.

means–ends analysis: a heuristic method for solving problems based on creating a subgoal to reduce the difference between the current state and the goal state.

medial: situated in the middle of the brain.

MEG *see* **magneto-encephalography**

memory bias: the retrieval of relatively more negative or unpleasant information than positive or neutral information on a memory test.

mental model: an internal representation of some possible situation or event in the world.

mental set: the tendency to use a familiar problem-solving strategy that has proved successful in the past even when it is not appropriate.

meta-analysis: a form of statistical analysis based on combining the findings from numerous studies on a given issue.

meta-memory: beliefs and knowledge about one's own memory including strategies for learning and memory.

mirror neuron system: neurons that respond to actions whether performed by oneself or someone else; it is claimed these neurons assist in imitating and understanding others' actions.

misery-is-not-miserly effect: the tendency for sad individuals to be willing to pay more for some commodity than other people.

misinformation effect: the distorting effect on eyewitness memory of misleading information presented after a crime or other event.

mixed-error effect: a form of speech error in which the incorrect word spoken is related to the correct one in terms of meaning and sound.

modularity: the assumption that the cognitive system consists of many fairly independent or separate modules or processors, each specialised for a given type of processing.

monocular cues: cues to depth that can be used by one eye, but can also be used by both eyes together.

mood congruity: learning and memory of emotional material are better when the learner's/rememberer's mood state matches the affective value of the material.

mood-state-dependent memory: memory performance is better when the individual's mood state is the same at learning and retrieval than when it differs.

morphemes: the basic units of meaning; words consist of one or more morphemes.

motion parallax: a depth cue based on movement in one part of the retinal image relative to another.

multitasking *see* **divided attention**

myside bias: in informal reasoning, the tendency to evaluate statements in terms of one's own beliefs or to generate reasons or arguments supporting those beliefs.

naming task: a task in which visually presented words are pronounced aloud rapidly.

negative afterimage: the illusory perception of the complementary colour to the one that has just been fixated; green is the complementary colour to red and blue is complementary to yellow.

neglect: a disorder involving right-hemisphere damage (typically) in which the left side of objects and/or objects presented to the left visual field are undetected; the condition resembles **extinction** but is more severe.

neologisms: made-up words produced by patients suffering from **jargon aphasia**.

neuroeconomics: an approach in which economic decision making is understood within the framework of **cognitive neuroscience**.

neurogenesis: the process of generating new neurons in the brain.

non-declarative memory: forms of long-term memory that influence behaviour but do not involve conscious recollection (e.g., **priming**, **procedural memory**); also known as implicit memory.

normativism: the notion that human thinking should be regarded as "correct" or "incorrect", depending on how closely it follows certain norms or standards (e.g., those of classical logic).

oculomotor cues: cues to depth produced by muscular contractions of the muscles around the eye; use of such cues involves kinaesthesia (also known as the muscle sense).

omission bias: a biased preference for risking harm through inaction compared to risking harm through action.

operation span: the maximum number of items (arithmetical questions + words) for which an individual can recall all the words more than 50% of the time.

optic array: the structural pattern of light falling on the retina.

optic ataxia: a condition in which there are problems with making visually guided movements in spite of reasonably intact visual perception.

optic flow: the changes in the pattern of light reaching an observer when there is movement of the observer and/or aspects of the environment.

optimism bias: the tendency to exaggerate our chances of experiencing positive events and to minimise our chances of experiencing negative events relative to other people.

orthographic lexicon: part of long-term memory in which learned word spellings are stored.

orthographic neighbours: with reference to a target word, the number of words that can be formed by changing one of its letters.

orthography: the study of letters and word spellings.

other-race effect: the finding that recognition memory for same-race faces is generally more accurate than for other-race faces.

out-of-body experiences: vivid feelings of being outside of (and detached from) one's own body.

own-age bias: the tendency for eyewitnesses to identify the culprit more often when he/she is of similar age to the eyewitness than when he/she is of a different age.

paradigm specificity: this occurs when the findings with a given experimental task or paradigm are not obtained even when apparently very similar tasks or paradigms are used.

parafoveal-on-foveal effects: the finding that fixation duration on the *current* word is influenced by characteristics of the next word.

parallel processing: processing in which two or more cognitive processes occur at the same time.

Parkinson's disease: a progressive disorder involving damage to the basal ganglia; the symptoms include muscle rigidity, limb tremor and mask-like facial expression.

parsing: an analysis of the syntactical or grammatical structure of sentences.

part–whole effect: the finding that a face part is recognised more easily when presented in the context of a whole face rather than on its own.

pattern recognition: the ability to identify or categorise two-dimensional patterns (e.g., letters, fingerprints).

perceptual priming: a form of priming in which repeated presentations of a stimulus facilitate its perceptual processing.

perceptual span: the effective field of view in reading (letters to the left and right of fixation that can be processed).

phoneme: the basic unit of sound; words consist of one or more phonemes.

phonemic restoration effect: the finding that listeners are unaware that a phoneme has been deleted and replaced by a non-speech sound (e.g., cough) within a sentence.

phonological dysgraphia: a condition caused by brain damage in which familiar words can be spelled reasonably well but non-words cannot.

phonological dyslexia: a condition in which familiar words can be read but there is impaired ability to read unfamiliar words and pseudowords.

phonological loop: a component of **working memory** in which speech-based information is processed and stored and subvocal articulation occurs.

phonological neighbourhood: words are phonological neighbours if they differ in only one **phoneme**.

phonological similarity effect: the finding that immediate serial recall of verbal material is reduced when the items sound similar.

phonology: the study of the sounds of words and parts of words.

phrase: a group of words within a sentence expressing a single idea.

plasticity: changes in brain structure and function dependent on experience that affect behaviour.

positron emission tomography (PET): a brain-scanning technique based on the detection of positrons; it has reasonable spatial resolution but poor temporal resolution.

posterior: towards the back of the brain.

pragmatics: the study of the ways language is used and understood in the real world, including a consideration of its intended meaning; meaning minus semantics.

preformulation: the production by speakers of phrases used frequently before; it reduces the demands of speech production.

priming: facilitating the processing of (and response to) a target by presenting a stimulus related to it some time beforehand.

principle of truth: the notion that we represent assertions by forming **mental models** concerning what is true but ignoring what is false.

proactive interference: disruption of memory by previous learning (often of similar material).

problem space: an abstract description of all the possible states that can occur within a given problem.

procedural memory: this is memory concerned with knowing how and it includes the knowledge required to perform skilled actions.

process-dissociation procedure: on learning tasks, participants try to guess the next stimulus (inclusion condition) or *avoid* guessing the next stimulus accurately (exclusion condition); the difference between the two conditions indicates the amount of explicit learning.

production rules: "If . . . then" or condition-action rules in which the action is carried out whenever the appropriate condition is present.

production systems: these consist of very large numbers of "if . . . then" **production rules** and a working memory containing information.

progress monitoring: a heuristic or rule of thumb in which slow progress towards problem solution triggers a change of strategy.

proposition: a statement making an assertion or denial that can be true or false.

proprioception: a form of sensation making the individual aware of the position and orientation of parts of his/her body.

prosodic cues: features of spoken language such as stress, intonation and duration that make it easier for listeners to work out grammatical structure and meaning.

prosopagnosia: a condition mostly caused by brain damage in which there is a severe impairment in face recognition but much less impairment of object recognition; also known as face blindness.

prospective memory: remembering to carry out some intended action in the absence of an explicit reminder to do so; *see also* **retrospective memory**.

pseudowords: non-words consisting of strings of letters that can be pronounced (e.g., mantiness).

psychological refractory period (PRP) effect: the slowing of the response to the second of two stimuli when presented close together in time.

pure word deafness: a condition involving severely impaired speech perception but intact speech production, reading, writing and perception of non-speech sounds.

rationalisation: in Bartlett's theory, errors in story recall that conform to the rememberer's cultural expectations.

reading span: the largest number of sentences read for comprehension from which an individual can recall all the final words over 50% of the time.

reappraisal: a strategy used in **emotion regulation** in which the individual elaborates emotional information from an event prior to changing its meaning.

receptive field: the region of the retina in which light influences the activity of a particular neuron.

recognition heuristic: using the knowledge that only one out of two objects is recognised as the basis for making a judgement.

reconsolidation: this is a new consolidation process that occurs when a previously formed memory trace is reactivated; it allows that memory trace to be updated.

recovered memories: childhood traumatic memories forgotten for several years and then remembered in adult life.

reminiscence bump: the tendency of older people to recall a disproportionate number of autobiographical memories from early adulthood.

Remote Associates Test: this involves finding a word that is related to three given words.

repetition suppression: the finding that stimulus repetition often leads to reduced brain activity (typically with enhanced performance via **priming**).

repetitive transcranial magnetic stimulation (rTMS): the administration of **transcranial magnetic stimulation** several times in rapid succession.

representativeness heuristic: the assumption that an object or individual belongs to a specified category because it is representative (typical) of that category.

repression: motivated forgetting of traumatic or other threatening events (especially from childhood).

retinal flow field: the changing patterns of light on the retina produced by movement of the observer relative to the environment as well as by eye and head movements.

retinal ganglion cells: retinal cells providing the output signal from the retina.

retinopy: the notion that there is mapping between receptor cells in the retina and points on the surface of the visual cortex.

retroactive interference: disruption of memory for previously learned information by other learning or processing occurring during the retention interval.

retrograde amnesia: impaired ability of amnesic patients to remember information and events from the time period prior to the onset of **amnesia**.

retrospective memory: memory for events, people and so on experienced in the past; *see also* **prospective memory**.

reverse inference: as applied to functional neuroimaging, it involves arguing backwards from a pattern of brain activation to the presence of a given cognitive process.

rostral: anterior, or towards the front of the brain.

saccades: rapid eye movements separated by eye fixations lasting about 250 milliseconds.

satisficing: in decision making, the strategy of choosing the first option that satisfies the individual's minimum requirements.

savings method: a measure of forgetting introduced by Ebbinghaus in which the number of trials for relearning is compared against the number for original learning.

saying-is-believing effect: tailoring a message about an event to suit a given audience causes subsequent inaccuracies in memory for that event.

schema: organised packet of information about the world, events or people stored in long-term memory.

script: a form of **schema** containing information about a sequence of events (e.g., events during a typical restaurant meal).

segmentation: dividing the almost continuous sounds of speech into separate **phonemes** and words.

selective exposure: a preference for information that strengthens pre-existing views and avoidance of information conflicting with those views.

semantic dementia: a condition involving damage to the anterior temporal lobes in which there is a widespread loss of information about the meanings of words and concepts; patients with this condition differ widely in symptoms and the pattern of brain damage. However, **episodic memory** and executive functioning are reasonably intact in the early stages.

semantic memory: a form of long-term memory consisting of general knowledge about the world, concepts, language and so on.

semantic priming: the finding that word recognition is facilitated by the prior presentation of a semantically related word.

semanticisation: **episodic memories** changing into **semantic memories** over time.

semantics: the study of the meaning conveyed by words, phrases and sentences.

serial processing: processing in which one process is completed before the next one starts; *see also* **parallel processing**.

serial reaction time task: participants on this task respond as rapidly as possible to stimuli typically presented in a repeating sequence; it is used to assess **implicit learning**.

shadowing: repeating one auditory message word for word as it is presented while a second auditory message is also presented; it is a version of the **dichotic listening task**.

single-unit recording: an invasive technique for studying brain function, permitting the study of activity in single neurons.

size constancy: objects are perceived to have a given size regardless of the size of the retinal image.

slippery slope argument: the claim that an innocuous first step will lead to an undesirable outcome; sometimes regarded as a fallacy.

spillover effect: any given word is fixated longer during reading when preceded by a rare word rather than a common one.

split attention: allocation of attention to two (or more) non-adjacent regions of visual space.

split-brain patients: patients in whom most of the direct links between the two hemispheres of the brain have been severed.

spoonerism: a speech error in which the initial letter or letters of two words (typically close together) are switched to form two different words.

spreading activation: the notion that activation of a node (corresponding to a word or concept) in the brain causes some activation to spread to several related nodes or words.

status quo bias: a preference for maintaining the status quo (present state) rather than acting to change one's decision.

stereopsis: depth perception based on the small discrepancy in the two retinal images when a visual scene is observed (**binocular disparity**).

straw man fallacy: refuting an opponent's views by misrepresenting them in some way.

striatum: it forms part of the basal ganglia and is located in the upper part of the brainstem and the inferior part of the cerebral hemispheres.

Stroop task: a task on which participants have to name the ink colours in which colour words are printed; performance is slowed when the to-be-named colour (e.g., green) conflicts with the colour word (e.g., RED).

subliminal perception: perceptual processing occurring below the level of conscious awareness that can nevertheless influence behaviour.

sulcus: a groove or furrow in the surface of the brain.

sunk-cost effect: investing additional resources to justify a previous commitment that has so far proved unsuccessful.

superior *see* **dorsal**

surface dysgraphia: a condition caused by brain damage in which there is poor spelling of irregular words, reasonable spelling of regular words and some success in spelling non-words.

surface dyslexia: a condition in which regular words can be read but there is impaired ability to read irregular or exception words.

syllogism: a type of problem used in **deductive reasoning**; there are two statements or premises and a conclusion that may or may not follow logically from the premises.

synaesthesia: the tendency for one sense modality to evoke another.

syndrome: the notion that symptoms that often co-occur have a common origin.

syntactic priming: the tendency for a speaker's utterances to have the same syntactic structure as those they have heard shortly beforehand.

syntax: the set of rules concerning word order within sentences in a language.

tangent point: from a driver's perspective, the point on a road at which the direction of its inside edge appears to reverse.

template: as applied to chess, an abstract schematic structure consisting of a mixture of fixed and variable information about chess pieces and positions.

testing effect: the finding that long-term memory is enhanced when some of the learning period is devoted to retrieving information to be learned rather than simply studying it.

texture gradient: the rate of change of texture density from the front to the back of a slanting object.

time-based prospective memory: a form of **prospective memory** that involves remembering to carry out an intended action at the appropriate time.

tip-of-the-tongue state: the frustrating experience of being unable to find the correct word to describe a given concept or idea.

top-down processing: stimulus processing that is influenced by factors such as the individual's past experience and expectations.

trait anxiety: a personality dimension based on individual differences in susceptibility to anxiety.

transcortical sensory aphasia: a condition in which spoken words can be repeated but comprehension of spoken and written language is severely impaired.

transcranial magnetic stimulation (TMS): a technique in which magnetic pulses briefly disrupt the functioning of a given brain area. It is often claimed that it creates a short-lived "lesion". More accurately, TMS causes interference when the brain area to which it is applied is involved in task processing as well as activity produced by the applied stimulation.

unconscious transference: the tendency of eyewitnesses to misidentify a familiar (but innocent) face as being the person responsible for a crime.

underadditivity: the finding that brain activation when tasks A and B are performed at the same time is less than the sum of the brain activation when tasks A and B are performed separately.

underspecification: a strategy used to reduce processing costs in speech production by using simplified expressions.

uniform connectedness: the notion that adjacent regions in the visual environment having uniform visual properties (e.g., colour) are perceived as a single perceptual unit.

uniqueness point: the point in time during spoken word recognition at which the available perceptual information is consistent with only one word.

unusualness heuristic: a rule of thumb used by scientists in which unexpected findings are used to develop new hypotheses and lines of research.

Urbach–Wiethe disease: a disease in which the **amygdala** and adjacent areas are destroyed.

utilitarian judgements: judgements based on practical and pragmatic considerations when resolving moral dilemmas; *see also* **deontological judgements**.

valence: the positive or negative character of emotional experience.

vegetative state: a condition produced by brain damage in which there is some wakefulness but an apparent lack of awareness and purposeful behaviour.

ventral: inferior, or towards the bottom of the brain.

ventral stream: the part of the visual processing system involved in object perception and recognition and the formation of perceptual representations.

ventriloquism effect: the mistaken perception that sounds are coming from their apparent source (as in ventriloquism).

verb bias: an imbalance in the frequency with which a verb is associated with different syntactic structures.

vergence: a cue to depth based on the inward focus of the eyes with close objects.

visual buffer: within Kosslyn's theory, a short-term visual memory store.

visual cache: according to Logie, the part of the **visuo-spatial sketchpad** that stores information about visual form and colour.

visual form agnosia: a condition in which there are severe problems in shape perception (what an object is) but reasonable ability to produce accurate visually guided actions.

visual search: a task involving the rapid detection of a specified target stimulus within a visual display.

visuo-spatial sketchpad: a component of **working memory** used to process visual and spatial information and to store this information briefly.

weapon focus: the finding that eyewitnesses pay so much attention to some crucial aspect of the situation (e.g., the weapon) that they ignore other details.

well-defined problems: problems in which the initial state, the goal and the methods available for solving them are clearly laid out.

Wernicke's aphasia: a form of **aphasia** involving fluent speech with many content words missing and impaired comprehension.

Whorfian hypothesis: the notion that language determines (or at least influences) thinking.

word-length effect: the finding that verbal memory span decreases when longer words are presented.

word meaning deafness: a condition in which there is selective impairment of the ability to understand spoken (but not written) language.

word superiority effect: a target letter is more readily detected in a letter string when the string forms a word than when it does not.

working memory: a system holding information currently being processed.

working memory capacity: an assessment of how much information can be processed and stored at the same time; individuals with high capacity have higher intelligence and more attentional control.

References

Aarts, H. & van den Bos, K. (2011). On the foundations of beliefs in free will: Intentional binding and unconscious priming in self-agency. *Psychological Science*, 22: 532–7.

Abdellaoui, M., Bleichrodt, H. & Kammoun, H. (2013). Do financial professionals behave according to prospect theory? An experimental study. *Theory and Decision*, 74: 411–29.

Aberegg, S.K., Haponik, E.F. & Terry, P.B. (2005). Omission bias and decision making in pulmonary and critical care medicine. *Chest*, 128: 1497–505.

Ablinger, I., Abel, S. & Huber, W. (2008). Deep dysphasia as a phonetic input deficit: Evidence from a single case. *Aphasiology*, 22: 537–56.

Acheson, D.J., Postle, B.R. & MacDonald, M.C. (2010). The interaction of concreteness and phonological similarity in verbal working memory. *Journal of Experimental Psychology: Learning, Memory, and Cognition*, 36: 17–36.

Ackerman, P.L., Beier, M.E. & Boyle, M.O. (2005). Working memory and intelligence: The same or different constructs? *Psychological Bulletin*, 131: 30–60.

Aczel, B., Lukacs, B., Komlos, J. & Aitken, M.R.F. (2011). Unconscious intuition or conscious analysis? Critical questions for the deliberation-without-attention paradigm. *Judgment and Decision Making*, 6: 351–8.

Addante, R.J., Ranganath, C., Olichney, J. & Yonelinas, A.P. (2012). Neurophysiological evidence for a recollection impairment in amnesia patients that leaves familiarity intact. *Neuropsychologia*, 50: 3004–14.

Addis, D.R. & Schacter, D.L. (2012). The hippocampus and imagining the future: Where do we stand? *Frontiers in Human Neuroscience*, 5 (Article 1730): 1–15.

Addis, D.R., Knapp, K., Roberts, R.P. & Schacter, D.L. (2012). Routes to the past: Neural substrates of direct and generative autobiographical memory retrieval. *NeuroImage*, 59: 2908–22.

Addyman, C. & French, R.M. (2012). Computational modelling in cognitive science: A manifesto for change. *Topics in Cognitive Science*, 4: 332–41.

Adelman, J.S., Sabatos-De Vito, M.G., Marquis, S.J. & Estes, Z. (2014). Individual differences in reading aloud: A mega-study, item effects, and some models. *Cognitive Psychology*, 68: 113–60.

Adlam, A.-L.R., Patterson, K. & Hodges, J.R. (2009). "I remember it as if it were yesterday": Memory for recent events in patients with semantic dementia. *Neuropsychologia*, 47: 1344–51.

Adolphs, R., Tranel, D. & Buchanan, T.W. (2005). Amygdala damage impairs emotional memory for gist but not details of complex stimuli. *Nature Neuroscience*, 8: 512–18.

Adriaanse, M.A., Gollwitzer, P.M., De Ridder, D.T.D., de Wit, J.B.F. & Kroese, F.M. (2011). Breaking habits with implementation intentions: A test of underlying processes. *Personality and Social Psychology Bulletin*, 37: 502–13.

Afraz, S.-R., Kiani, R. & Esteky, H. (2006). Microstimulation of inferotemporal cortex influences face categorisation. *Nature*, 442: 692–5.

Aggleton, J.P., Vann, S.D., Denby, C., Dix, S., Mayes, A.R., Roberts, N. & Yonelinas, A.P. (2005). Sparing of the familiarity component of recognition memory in a patient with hippocampal pathology. *Neuropsychologia*, 43: 1810–23.

Ahmed, S., Haigh, A.-M.F., de Jager, C.A. & Garrard, P. (2013). Connected speech as a marker of disease progression in autopsy-proven Alzheimer's disease. *Brain*, 136: 3727–37.

Aikin, S.F. & Casey, J. (2011). Straw men, weak men, and hollow men. *Argumentation*, 25: 87–105.

Alais, D. & Burr, D. (2004). The ventriloquist effect results from near-optimal bimodal integration. *Current Biology*, 14: 257–62.

Albouy, G., King, B.R., Maque, P. & Doyon, J. (2013). Hippocampus and striatum: Dynamics and interaction during acquisition and sleep-related motor sequence memory consolidation. *Hippocampus*, 23: 985–1004.

Aldao, A. & Dixon-Gordon, K.L. (2014). Broadening the scope of research on emotion regulation strategies and psychopathology. *Cognitive Behaviour Therapy*, 43: 22–33.

Aldao, A., Nolen-Hoeksema, S. & Schweizer, S. (2010). Emotion-regulation strategies across psychopathology: A meta-analytic review. *Clinical Psychology Review*, 30: 217–37.

Allen, E.A., Pasley, B.N., Duong, T. & Freeman, R.D. (2007). Transcranial magnetic stimulation elicits coupled neural and hemodynamic consequences. *Science*, 317: 1918–21.

Allen, R.J., Hitch, G.J., Mate, J. & Baddeley, A.D. (2012). Feature binding and attention in working memory: A resolution of previous contradictory findings. *Quarterly Journal of Experimental Psychology*, 65: 2369–83.

Ally, B.A., Hussey, E.P. & Donahue, M.J. (2013). A case of hyperthymesia: Rethinking the role of the amygdala in autobiographical memory. *Neurocase*, 19: 166–81.

Almashat, S., Ayotte, B., Edelstein, B. & Margrett, J. (2008). Framing effect debiasing in medical decision making. *Patient Education and Counseling*, 71: 102–7.

Alonso, J.M. & Martinez, L.M. (1998). Functional connectivity between simple cells and complex cells in cat striate cortex. *Nature Neuroscience*, 1: 395–403.

Altenberg, B. (1990). Speech as linear composition. In G. Caie, K. Haastrup, A.L. Jakobsen, J.E. Nielsen, J. Sevaldsen, H. Specht & Zettersten, A. (eds), *Proceedings from the Fourth Nordic Conference for English Studies*. Copenhagen: Copenhagen University Press.

Alzahabi, R. & Becker, M.W. (2013). The association between media multitasking, task-switching, and dual-task performance. *Journal of Experimental Psychology: Human Perception and Performance*, 39: 1485–95.

Ames, A. (1952). *The Ames demonstrations in perception*. New York: Hafner Publishing.

Amir, N., Bomyes, J. & Beard, C. (2010). The effect of single-session interpretation modification on attention bias in socially anxious individuals. *Journal of Anxiety Disorders*, 24: 178–82.

Amitani, Y. (2008). The frequency hypothesis and evolutionary arguments. *Philosophy of Science Association 21st Biennial Meeting*. Pittsburgh, PA.

Anaki, D. & Bentin, S. (2009). Familiarity effects on categorisation levels of faces and objects. *Cognition*, 111: 144–9.

Anderson, C.J. (2003). The psychology of doing nothing: Forms of decision avoidance result from reason and emotion. *Psychological Bulletin*, 129: 139–67.

Anderson, J.R., Bothell, D., Byrne, M.D., Douglass, S., Lebiere, C. & Qin, Y.L. (2004). An integrated theory of the mind. *Psychological Review*, 111: 1036–60.

Anderson, J.R., Fincham, J.M., Qin, Y. & Stocco, A. (2008). A central circuit of the mind. *Trends in Cognitive Sciences*, 12: 136–43.

Anderson, M.C. & Green, C. (2001). Suppressing unwanted memories by executive control. *Nature*, 410: 366–9.

Anderson, M.C. & Huddleston, E. (2012). Towards a cognitive and neurobiological model of motivated forgetting. *Nebraska Symposium on Motivation*, 58: 53–120.

Anderson, M.C., Ochsner, K.N., Kuhl, B., Cooper, J., Robertson, E., Gabrieli, S.W., Glover, G.H. & Gabrieli, J.D.E. (2004). Neural systems underlying the suppression of unwanted memories. *Science*, 303: 232–5.

Anderson, M.L., Kinnison, J. & Pessoa, L. (2013). Describing functional diversity of brain regions and brain networks. *NeuroImage*, 73: 50–8.

Anderson, R.C. & Pichert, J.W. (1978). Recall of previously unrecallable information following a shift in perspective. *Journal of Verbal Learning and Verbal Behavior*, 17: 1–12.

Anderson, S.W., Rizzo, M., Skaar, N., Stierman, L., Cavaco, S., Dawson, J. & Damasio, H. (2007). Amnesia and driving. *Journal of Clinical and Experimental Neuropsychology*, 29: 1–12.

Andrews, P.W. & Thomson, J.A. (2009). The bright side of being blue: Depression as an adaptation for analysing complex problems. *Psychological Review*, 116: 620–54.

Angelone, B.L., Levin, D.T. & Simons, D.J. (2003). The relationship between change detection and recognition of centrally attended objects in motion pictures. *Perception*, 32: 947–62.

Angie, A.D., Connelly, S., Waples, E.P. & Kligyte, V. (2011). The influence of discrete emotions on judgment and decision-making: A meta-analytic review. *Cognition & Emotion*, 25: 1393–422.

Ardila, A. & Surloff, C. (2006). Dysexecutive agraphia: A major executive dysfunction sign. *International Journal of Neuroscience*, 116: 653–63.

Armstrong, T. & Olatunji, B.O. (2012). Eye tracking of attention in the affective disorders: A meta-analytic review and synthesis. *Clinical Psychology Review*, 32: 704–23.

Arnold, J.E. (2008). Reference production: Production-internal and addressee-oriented processes. *Language and Cognitive Processes*, 23: 495–527.

Arnold, J.E., Eisenband, J.G., Brown-Schmidt, S. & Trueswell, J.C. (2000). The immediate use of gender information: Eyetracking evidence of the time course of pronoun resolution. *Cognition*, 76: B13–26.

Ashby, F.G. & Crossley, M.J. (2012). Automaticity and multiple memory systems. *Wiley Interdisciplinary Reviews: Cognitive Science*, 3: 294–304.

Ashida, H., Lingnau, A., Wall, M.B. & Smith, A.T. (2007). fMRI adaptation reveals separate mechanisms for first-order and second-order motion. *Journal of Neurophysiology*, 97: 1319–25.

Ask, K. & Granhag, P.A. (2007). Hot cognition in investigative judgments: The differential influence of anger and sadness. *Law and Human Behavior*, 31: 537–51.

Atkins, J.E., Fiser, J. & Jacobs, R.A. (2001). Experience-dependent visual cue integration based on consistencies between visual and haptic percepts. *Vision Research*, 41: 449–61.

Atkinson, A.P. & Adolphs, R. (2011). The neuropsychology of face perception: Beyond simple dissociations and functional selectivity. *Philosophical Transactions of the Royal Society B – Biological Sciences*, 366: 1726–38.

Atkinson, A.P., Dittrich, W.H., Gemmel, A.J. & Young, A.W. (2004). Emotion perception from dynamic and static body expressions in point-light and full-light displays. *Perception*, 33: 717–46.

Atkinson, R.C. & Shiffrin, R.M. (1968). Human memory: A proposed system and its control processes. In K.W. Spence & J.T. Spence (eds), *The psychology of learning and motivation, vol. 2*. London: Academic Press.

Atkinson, R.L., Atkinson, R.C., Smith, E.E. & Bem, D.J. (1993). *Introduction to psychology* (11th edn). New York: Harcourt Brace.

Augustine, A.A. & Hemenover, S.H. (2009). On the relative merits of affect regulation strategies: A meta-analysis. *Cognition & Emotion*, 23: 1181–220.

Averell, L. & Heathcote, A. (2011). The form of the forgetting curve and the fate of memories. *Journal of Mathematical Psychology*, 55: 25–35.

Awasthi, B., Sowman, P.F., Friedman, J. & Willias, M.A. (2013). Distinct spatial scale sensitivities for early categorisation of faces and places: Neuromagnetic and behavioural findings. *Frontiers in Human Neuroscience*, 7 (Article 91).

Awh, E. & Pashler, H. (2000). Evidence for split attentional foci. *Journal of Experimental Psychology: Human Perception and Performance*, 26: 834–46.

Baars, B.J. (1988). *A cognitive theory of consciousness*. Cambridge: Cambridge University Press.

Baars, B.J. (1997). Some essential differences between consciousness and attention, perception, and working memory. *Consciousness and Cognition*, 6: 363–71.

Baars, B.J. & Franklin, S. (2007). An architectural model of conscious and unconscious brain functions: Global Workspace Theory and IDA. *Neural Networks*, 20: 955–61.

Baddeley, A.D. (1978). The trouble with levels: A re-examination of Craik and Lockhart's framework for memory research. *Psychological Review*, 85: 139–52.

Baddeley, A.D. (1986). *Working memory*. Oxford: Clarendon Press.

Baddeley, A.D. (1990). *Human memory: Theory and practice*. Hove: Psychology Press.

Baddeley, A.D. (1996). Exploring the central executive. *Quarterly Journal of Experimental Psychology*, 49A: 5–28.

Baddeley, A.D. (2000). The episodic buffer: A new component of working memory? *Trends in Cognitive Sciences*, 4: 417–23.

Baddeley, A.D. (2001). Is working memory still working? *American Psychologist*, 56: 851–64.

Baddeley, A.D. (2007). *Working memory, thought, and action*. Oxford: Oxford University Press.

Baddeley, A.D. (2012). Working memory: Theories, models, and controversies. *Annual Review of Psychology*, 63: 1–29.

Baddeley, A.D. & Andrade, J. (2000). Working memory and the vividness of imagery. *Journal of Experimental Psychology: General*, 129: 126–45.

Baddeley, A.D. & Hitch, G.J. (1974). Working memory. In G.H. Bower (ed.), *Recent advances in learning and motivation, vol. 8* (pp. 47–89). New York: Academic Press.

Baddeley, A.D. & Wilson, B. (2002). Prose recall and amnesia: Implications for the structure of working memory. *Neuropsychologia*, 40: 1737–43.

Baddeley, A.D., Thomson, N. & Buchanan, M. (1975). Word length and the structure of short-term memory. *Journal of Verbal Learning and Verbal Behavior*, 14: 575–89.

Baddeley, A.D., Vallar, G. & Wilson, B.A. (1987). Sentence comprehension and phonological memory: Some neuropsychological evidence. In M. Coltheart (ed.), *Attention and performance XII: The psychology of reading* (pp. 509–29). Hove: Lawrence Erlbaum Associates.

Baddeley, A.D., Papagno, C. & Vallar, G. (1988). When long-term learning depends on short-term storage. *Journal of Memory and Language*, 27: 586–95.

Baddeley, A.D., Gathercole, S. & Papagno, C. (1998). The phonological loop as a language learning device. *Psychological Review*, 105: 158–73.

Baddeley, A.D., Hitch, G.J. & Allen, R.J. (2009). Working memory and binding in sentence recall. *Journal of Memory and Language*, 61: 438–56.

Baddeley, A.D., Eysenck, M.W. & Anderson, M.C. (2015). *Memory* (2nd edn). Hove: Psychology Press.

Bahrick, H.P. (1984). Semantic memory content in permastore: Fifty years of memory for Spanish learning in school. *Journal of Experimental Psychology: General*, 113: 1–29.

Bahrick, H.P., Bahrick, P.O. & Wittlinger, R.P. (1975). Fifty years of memory for names and faces: A cross-sectional approach. *Journal of Experimental Psychology: General*, 104: 54–75.

Bahrick, H.P., Hall, L.K. & Da Costa, L.A. (2008). Fifty years of college grades: Accuracy and distortions. *Emotion*, 8: 13–22.

Baldassi, C., Alemi-Neissi, A., Pagan, M., DiCarlo, J.J., Zecchina, R. & Zoccolan, D. (2013). Shape similarity, better than semantic membership, accounts for the structure of visual object representations in a population of monkey inferotemporal neurons. *PLOS Computational Biology*, 9(8): e1003167.

Baliga, S. & Ely, J.C. (2011). Mnemonomics: The sunk cost fallacy as a memory kludge. *American Economic Journal: Microeconomics*, 3: 35–67.

Balota, D.A., Paul, S. & Spieler, D. (1999). Attentional control of lexical processing pathways during word recognition and reading. In S. Garrod & M.J. Pickering (eds), *Language processing*. Hove: Psychology Press.

Banissy, M.J., Walsh, V. & Muggleton, N.G. (2012). A disruption of colour priming following continuous theta burst transcranial magnetic stimulation. *Cortex*, 48: 1359–61.

Banks, W.P. & Isham, E.A. (2009). We infer rather than perceive the moment we decide to act. *Psychological Science*, 20: 17–21.

Bannard, C., Lieven, E. & Tomasello, M. (2009). Modelling children's early grammatical knowledge. *Proceedings of the National Academy of Sciences*, 106: 17284–9.

Baptista, M. (2012). On universal grammar, the bioprogram hypothesis and creole genesis. *Journal of Pidgin and Creole Languages*, 27: 351–76.

Bar, M., Kassam, K.S., Ghuman, A.S., Boshyan, J., Schmid, A.M., Dale, A.M., Hämäläinen, M.S., Marinkovic, K., Schacter, D.L., Rosen, B.R. &Halgren, E. (2006). Top-down facilitation of visual recognition. *Proceedings of the National Academy of Sciences*, 103: 449–54.

Barense, M.D., Ngo, L.H.T. & Peterson, M.A. (2012). Interactions of memory and perception in amnesia: The figure–ground perspective. *Cerebral Cortex*, 22: 2680–91.

Bar-Haim, Y., Lamy, D., Pergamin, L., Bakermans-Kronenburg, M.J. & van IJzendoorn, M.H. (2007). Threat-related attentional bias in anxious and nonanxious individuals: A meta-analytic study. *Psychological Bulletin*, 133: 1–24.

Barliya, A., Omlor, L., Giese, M.A., Berthoz, A. & Flash, T. (2013). Expression of emotion in the kinematics of locomotion. *Experimental Brain Research*, 225: 159–76.

Baron, J. & Ritov, I. (2004). Omission bias, individual differences, and normality. *Organizational Behavior and Human Decision Processes*, 94: 74–85.

Baronchelli, A., Chater, N., Pastor-Satorras, R. & Christiansen, M.H. (2012). The biological origin of linguistic diversity. *PLOS ONE*, 7(10): e48029.

Barrett, L.F. & Russell, J.A. (1998). Independence and bipolarity in the structure of current affect. *Journal of Personality and Social Psychology*, 74: 967–84.

Barreyro, J.P., Cevasco, J., Burin, D. & Marotto, C.M. (2012). Working memory capacity and individual differences in the making of reinstatement and elaborative inferences. *Spanish Journal of Psychology*, 15: 471–9.

Barsalou, L.W. (2009). Simulation, situated conceptualization, and prediction. *Philosophical Transactions of the Royal Society B: Biological Sciences*, 364: 1281–9.

Barsalou, L.W. (2012). The human conceptual system. In M.J. Spivey, K. McRae & M.F. Joanisse (eds), *The Cambridge handbook of psycholinguistics* (pp. 239–58). Cambridge: Cambridge University Press.

Barsalou, L.W. & Wiemer-Hastings, K. (2005). Situating abstract concepts. In D. Pecher & R. Zwaan (eds), *Grounding cognition: The role of perception and action in memory, language, and thought*. New York: Cambridge University Press.

Bartels, D.M. & Pizarro, D.A. (2011). The mismeasure of morals: Antisocial personality traits predict utilitarian responses to moral dilemmas. *Cognition*, 121, 154–61.

Bartlett, F.C. (1932). *Remembering: An experimental and social study*. Cambridge: Cambridge University Press.

Bartolomeo, P. (2002). The relationship between visual perception and visual mental imagery: A re-appraisal of the neuropsychological evidence. *Cortex*, 38: 357–78.

Bartolomeo, P. (2008). The neural correlates of visual mental imagery: An ongoing debate. *Cortex*, 44: 107–8.

Bartolomeo, P., de Schotten, M.T. & Chica, A.B. (2012). Brain networks of visuospatial attention and their disruption in visual neglect. *Frontiers in Human Neuroscience*, 6 (Article 110).

Baseler, H.A., Morland, A.B. & Wandell, B.A. (1999). Topographic organisation of human visual areas in the absence of input from primary cortex. *Journal of Neuroscience*, 19: 2619–27.

Bauch, E.M. & Otten, L.J. (2012). Study-test congruency affects encoding-related brain activity for some but not all stimulus materials. *Journal of Cognitive Neuroscience*, 24: 183–95.

Baucom, L.B., Wedell, D.H., Wang, J., Blitzer, D.N. & Shinkareva, S.V. (2012). Decoding the neural representation of affective states. *NeuroImage*, 59: 718–27.

Baumeister, R.F. & Masicampo, E.J. (2010). Conscious thought is for facilitating social and cultural interactions: How mental simulations serve the animal–culture interface. *Psychological Review*, 117: 945–71.

Baumeister, R.F., Masicampo, E.J. & DeWall, C.N. (2011a). Arguing, reasoning, and the interpersonal (cultural) functions of human consciousness. *Behavioral and Brain Sciences*, 34: 74.

Baumeister, R.F., Masicampo, E.J. & Vohs, K.D. (2011b). Do conscious thoughts cause behaviour? *Annual Review of Psychology*, 62: 331–61.

Bäuml, K.-H. & Kliegl, O. (2013). The critical role of retrieval processes in release from proactive interference. *Journal of Memory and Language*, 68: 39–53.

Bavelas, J. & Healing, S. (2013). Reconciling the effects of mutual visibility on gesturing: A review. *Gesture*, 13: 63–92.

Baxendale, S. (2004). Memories aren't made of this: Amnesia at the movies. *British Medical Journal*, 329: 1480–3.

Bayley, P.J., Hopkins, R.O. & Squire, L.R. (2006). The fate of old memories after medial temporal lobe damage. *Journal of Neuroscience*, 26: 13311–17.

Bayne, T. (2008). The unity of consciousness and the split-brain syndrome. *The Journal of Philosophy*, 105: 277–300.

Bayne, T. (2010). *The unity of consciousness*. Oxford: Oxford University Press.

Baynes, K. & Gazzaniga, M. (2000). Consciousness, introspection, and the split-brain: The two minds/one body problem. In M.S. Gazzaniga (ed.), *The new cognitive neurosciences*. Cambridge, MA: MIT Press.

Bays, P.M., Singh-Curry, V., Gorgoraptis, N., Driver, J. & Husain, M. (2010). Integration of goal- and stimulus-related visual signals revealed by damage to human parietal cortex. *Journal of Neuroscience*, 30: 5968–78.

Beauvais, C., Olive, T. & Passerault, J.-M. (2011). Why are some texts good and others not? Relationship between text quality and management of the writing process. *Journal of Educational Psychology*, 103: 415–28.

Bechara, A., Damasio, A., Damasio, H. & Anderson, S. (1994). Insensitivity to future consequences following damage to human prefrontal cortex. *Cognition*, 50: 7–15.

Beck, A.T. & Dozois, D.J.A. (2011). Cognitive therapy: Current status and future directions. *Annual Review of Medicine*, 62: 397–409.

Beck, D.M. (2010). The appeal of the brain in the popular press. *Perspectives on Psychological Science*, 5: 762–6.

Beckers, G. & Zeki, S. (1995). The consequences of inactivating areas V1 and V5 on visual motion perception. *Brain*, 118: 49–60.

Beeke, S., Wilkinson, R. & Maxim, J. (2007). Grammar without sentence structure: A conversation analytic investigation of agrammatism. *Aphasiology*, 21: 256–82.

Bennett, C.M., Baird, A.A., Miller, M.B. & Wolford, G.L. (2009). Neural correlates of interspecies perspective taking in the post-mortem Atlantic salmon: An argument for proper multiple comparisons' correction. *15th Annual Meeting of the Organisation for Human Brain Mapping*. San Francisco, CA.

Bennett, P. & Lowe, R. (2008). Emotions and their cognitive precursors: Responses to spontaneously identified stressful events among hospital nurses. *Journal of Health Psychology*, 13: 537–46.

Bentin, S., Kutas, M. & Hillyard, S.A. (1995). Semantic processing and memory for attended and unattended words in dichotic listening: Behavioural and electrophysiological evidence. *Journal of Experimental Psychology: Human Perception and Performance*, 21: 54–67.

Benton, T.R., Ross, D.F., Bradshaw, E., Thomas, W.N. & Bradshaw, G.S. (2006). Eyewitness memory is still not common sense: Comparing jurors, judges and law enforcement to eyewitness experts. *Applied Cognitive Psychology*, 20: 115–29.

Bereiter, C. & Scardamalia, M. (1987). The psychology of written composition. *Journal of Memory and Language*, 27: 261–78.

Bereiter, C., Burtis, P.J. & Scardamalia, M. (1988). Cognitive operations in constructing main points in written composition. *Journal of Memory and Language*, 27: 261–78.

Bergen, B., Medeiros-Ward, N., Wheeler, K., Drews, F. & Strayer, D. (2013). The crosstalk hypothesis: Why language interferes with driving. *Journal of Experimental Psychology: General*, 142: 119–30.

Bergman, E. & Roediger, H.L. (1999). Can Bartlett's repeated reproduction experiments be replicated? *Memory & Cognition*, 27: 937–47.

Bergmann, H.C., Rijpkema, M., Fernández, G. & Kessels, R.P.C. (2012). Distinct neural correlate of associative working memory and long-term memory encoding in the medial temporal lobe. *NeuroImage*, 63: 989–97.

Bergström, Z.M., de Fockert, J.W. & Richardson-Klavehn, A. (2009). ERP and behavioural evidence for direct suppression of unwanted memories. *NeuroImage*, 48: 726–37.

Bergström, Z.M., O'Connor, R.J., Li, M.K.-H. & Simons, J.S. (2012). Event-related potential evidence for separable automatic and controlled retrieval processes in proactive interference. *Brain Research*, 1455: 90–102.

Berman, M.G., Jonides, J. & Lewis, R.L. (2009). In search of decay in verbal short-term memory. *Journal of Experimental Psychology: Learning, Memory, and Cognition*, 35: 317–33.

Berntsen, D. (2001). Involuntary memories of emotional events: Do memories of traumas and extremely happy events differ? *Applied Cognitive Psychology*, 15: S135–58.

Berntsen, D., Rubin, D.C. & Siegler, I.C. (2011). Two different versions of life: Emotionally negative and positive life events have different roles in the organisation of life story and identity. *Emotion*, 11: 1190–201.

Berwick, R.C., Friederici, A.D., Chomsky, N. & Bolhuis, J.J. (2013). Evolution, brain, and the nature of language. *Trends in Cognitive Sciences*, 17: 89–98.

Bezuidenhout, A. (2013). Perspective taking in conversation: A defence of speaker non-egocentricity. *Journal of Pragmatics*, 48: 4–16.

Bezuidenhout, A. (2014). Reply to Brown-Schmidt and Heller. *Journal of Pragmatics*, 60: 285–90.

Bhatt, R.S. & Quinn, P.C. (2011). How does learning impact development in infancy? The case of perceptual organisation. *Infancy*, 16: 2–38.

Bickerton, D. (1984). The language bioprogram hypothesis. *Behavioral and Brain Sciences*, 7: 173–221.

Biederman, I. (1987). Recognition-by-components: A theory of human image understanding. *Psychological Review*, 94: 115–47.

Biederman, I. & Gerhardstein, P.C. (1993). Recognising depth-rotated objects: Evidence for 3-D viewpoint invariance. *Journal of Experimental Psychology: Human Perception & Performance*, 19: 1162–82.

Biedermann, B., Ruh, B., Nickels, L. & Coltheart, M. (2008). Information retrieval in tip-of-the-tongue states: New data and methodological advances. *Journal of Psycholinguistic Research*, 37: 171–98.

Bier, N., Bottari, C., Hudon, C., Jobert, S., Paquette, G. & Macoir, J.L. (2013). The impact of semantic dementia on everyday actions: Evidence from an ecological study. *Journal of the International Neuropsychological Society*, 19: 162–72.

Biggs, A.T., Brockmole, J.R. & Witt, J.K. (2013). Armed and attentive: Holding a weapon can bias attentional priorities in scene viewing. *Attention, Perception & Psychophysics*, 75: 1715–24.

Bilalić, M., McLeod, P. & Gobet, F. (2008a). Inflexibility of experts: Reality or myth? Quantifying the Einstellung effect in chess masters. *Cognitive Psychology*, 56: 73–102.

Bilalić, M., McLeod, P. & Gobet, F. (2008b). Why good thoughts block better ones: The mechanism of the pernicious Einstellung effect. *Cognition*, 108: 652–61.

Bilalić, M., McLeod, P. & Gobet, F. (2010). The mechanism of the Einstellung (set) effect: A pervasive source of cognitive bias. *Current Directions in Psychological Science*, 19: 111–15.

Binder, J.R. & Desai, R.H. (2011). The neurobiology of semantic memory. *Trends in Cognitive Sciences*, 15: 527–36.

Binder, J.R., Desai, R.H., Graves, W.W. & Conant, L.L. (2009). Where is the semantic system? A critical review and meta-analysis of 120 functional neuroimaging studies. *Cerebral Cortex*, 19: 2767–96.

Bindschaedler, C., Peter-Favre, C., Maeder, P., Hirsbrunner, T. & Clarke, S. (2011). Growing up with bilateral hippocampal atrophy: From childhood to teenage. *Cortex*, 47: 931–44.

Blackmer, E.R. & Mitton, J.L. (1991). Theories of monitoring and the timing of repairs in spontaneous speech. *Cognition*, 3: 173–94.

Blake, R. & Logothetis, N.K. (2002). Visual competition. *Nature Reviews Neuroscience*, 3: 13–23.

Blanchette, I. & Dunbar, K. (2000). How analogies are generated: The roles of structural and superficial similarity. *Memory & Cognition*, 28: 108–24.

Blanchette, I. & Richards, A. (2010). The influence of affect on higher level cognition: A review of research on interpretation, judgment, decision making and reasoning. *Cognition & Emotion*, 24: 561–95.

Blangero, A., Gaveau, V., Luauté, J., Rode, G., Salemme, R., Guinard, M., Boisson, D., Rossetti, Y. & Pisella, L. (2008). A hand and a field effect in on-line motor control in unilateral optic ataxia. *Cortex*, 44: 560–8.

Blanke, O., Ortigue, S., Landis, T. & Seeck, M. (2002). Stimulating illusory own-body perceptions. *Nature*, 419: 269–70.

Block, N. (2012). Response to Kouider et al.: Which view is better supported by the evidence? *Trends in Cognitive Sciences*, 16: 141–2.

Bluck, S. & Alea, N. (2009). Thinking and talking about the past: Why remember? *Applied Cognitive Psychology*, 23: 1089–104.

Bode, S., He, A.H., Soon, C.S., Trampel, R., Turner, R. & Haynes, J.-D. (2011). Tracking the unconscious generation of free decisions using ultra-high field fMRI. *PLOS ONE*: 0021612.

Boehler, C.N., Schoenfeld, M.A., Heinze, H.-J. & Hopf, J.-M. (2008). Rapid recurrent processing gates awareness in primary visual cortex. *Proceedings of the National Academy of Sciences*, 105(25): 8742–7.

Bohn, A. & Berntsen, D. (2011). The reminiscence bump reconsidered: Children's prospective life stories show a bump in young adulthood. *Psychological Science*, 22: 197–202.

Bohrn, I.C., Altmann, U. & Jacobs, A.M. (2012). Looking at the brains behind figurative language: A quantative meta-analysis of neuroimaging studies on metaphor, idiom, and irony processing. *Neuropsychologia*, 50: 2669–83.

Bolden, G.B. (2006). Little words that matter: Discourse markers "so" and "oh" and the doing of other-attentiveness in social interaction. *Journal of Communication*, 56: 661–88.

Boly, M., Garrido, M.I., Gosseries, O., Bruno, M.-A., Bovereux, P., Schnakers, C., Massimini, M., Litvak, V., Laureys, S. & Friston, K. (2011). Preserved feedforward but impaired top-down processes in the vegetative state. *Science*, 332: 858–62.

Bonato, M. (2012). Neglect and extinction depend greatly on task demands: A review. *Frontiers in Human Neuroscience*, 6 (Article 196).

Bonato, M., Priftis, K., Marenzi, R., Umiltà, C. & Zorzi, M. (2010). Increased attentional demands impair contralesional space awareness following stroke. *Neuropsychologia*, 48: 3934–40.

Bonnefon, J.-F., Girotto, V. & Legrenzi, P. (2012). The psychology of reasoning about preferences and unconsequential decisions. *Synthese*, 185: 357–71.

Bonnefond, M., Noveck, I., Baillet, S., Cheylus, A., Delpuech, C., Bertrand, O., Fourneret, P. & Van der Henst, J.B. (2013). What MEG can reveal about inference making: The case of if . . . then sentences. *Human Brain Mapping*, 34: 684–97.

Booth, M.C.A. & Rolls, E.T. (1998). View-invariant representations of familiar objects by neurons in the inferior temporal visual cortex. *Cerebral Cortex*, 8: 510–23.

Bor, D. & Seth, A.K. (2012). Consciousness and the prefrontal parietal network: Insights from attention, working memory, and chunking. *Frontiers in Psychology*, 3 (Article 63).

Borges, J.L. (1964). *Labyrinths*. London: Penguin.

Bormann, T. & Weiller, C. (2012). "Are there lexicons?" A study of lexical and semantic processing in word-meaning deafness suggests "yes". *Cortex*, 48: 294–307.

Bormann, T., Wallesch, C.-W., Seyboth, M. & Blanken, G. (2009). Writing two words as one: Word boundary errors in a German case of acquired surface dysgraphia. *Journal of Neurolinguistics*, 22: 74–82.

Borst, J.P., Buwalda, T.A., van Rijn, H. & Taatgen, N.A. (2013). Avoiding the problem state bottleneck by strategic use of the environment. *Acta Psychologica*, 144: 373–9.

Bose, A. (2013). Phonological therapy in jargon aphasia: Effects on naming and neologisms. *International Journal of Language & Communication Disorders*, 48: 582–95.

Bourdais, C. & Pecheux, M.-G. (2009). Categorising in 13- and 16-month-old infants: A comparison of two methods. *Année Psychologique*, 109: 3–27.

Bourne, C., Mavkay, C.E. & Holmes, E.A. (2013). The neural basis of flashback formation: The impact of viewing trauma. *Psychological Medicine*, 43: 1521–32.

Bouvier, S.E. & Engel, S.A. (2006). Behavioural deficits and cortical damage loci in cerebral achromatopsia. *Cerebral Cortex*, 16: 183–91.

Bowden, E.M. & Jung-Beeman, M. (2007). Methods for investigating the neural components of insight. *Methods*, 42: 87–99.

Bowden, E.M., Jung-Beeman, M., Fleck, J. & Kounios, J. (2005). New approaches to demystifying insight. *Trends in Cognitive Sciences*, 9: 322–8.

Bower, G.H., Black, J.B. & Turner, T.J. (1979). Scripts in memory for text. *Cognitive Psychology*, 11: 177–220.

Bowers, J.S. (2002). Challenging the widespread assumption that connectionism and distributed representations go hand-in-hand. *Cognitive Psychology*, 45: 413–45.

Bowers, J.S. (2009). On the biological plausibility of grandmother cells: Implications for neural network theories of psychology and neuroscience. *Psychological Review*, 116: 220–51.

Bowers, J.S. & Davis, C.J. (2012). Bayesian just-so stories in psychology and neuroscience. *Psychological Bulletin*, 138: 389–414.

Bowles, B., Crupi, C., Mirsattari, S.M., Pigott, S.E., Parrent, A.G., Pruessner, J.C., Yonelinas, A.P. & Köhler, S. (2007). Impaired familiarity with preserved recollection after anterior temporal-lobe resection that spares the hippocampus. *Proceedings of the National Academy of Sciences*, 104: 16382–7.

Bowles, B., Crupi, C., Pigott, S., Parrent, A., Wiebe, S., Janzen, L. & Köhler, S. (2010). Double dissociation of selective recollection and familiarity impairments following two different surgical treatments for temporal-lobe epilepsy. *Neuropsychologia*, 48: 2640–7.

Bowles, B., O'Neil, E.B., Mirsattari, S.M., Poppenk, J. & Köhler, S. (2011). Preserved hippocampal novelty responses following anterior temporal-lobe resection that impairs familiarity but spares recollection. *Hippocampus*, 21: 847–54.

Brainard, D.H. & Maloney, L.T. (2011). Surface colour perception and equivalent illumination models. *Journal of Vision*, 11: 1–18.

Brainerd, C.J. & Mojardin, A.H. (1998). Children's spontaneous memories for narrative statements: Long-term persistence and testing effects. *Child Development*, 69: 1361–77.

Brainerd, C.J., Reyna, V.F. & Ceci, S.J. (2008). Developmental reversals in false memory: A review of data and theory. *Psychological Bulletin*, 134: 343–82.

Brandt, A., Gebrian, M. & Slevc, L.R. (2012). Music and early language acquisition. *Frontiers in Psychology*, 3 (Article 327).

Brandt, K.R., Eysenck, M.W. & Von Oertzen, T. (submitted). Selective lesion to the entorhinal cortex leads to an impairment of familiarity but not recollection.

Bransford, J.D. & Johnson, M.K. (1972). Contextual prerequisites for understanding. *Journal of Verbal Learning and Verbal Behavior*, 11: 717–26.

Bransford, J.D., Barclay, J.R. & Franks, J.J. (1972). Sentence memory: A constructive versus interpretive approach. *Cognitive Psychology*, 3: 193–209.

Brase, G.L., Fiddick, L. & Harries, C. (2006). Participants' recruitment methods and statistical reasoning performance. *Quarterly Journal of Experimental Psychology*, 59: 965–76.

Braverman, J.A. & Blumenthal-Barby, J.S. (2012). Assessment of the sunk-cost effect in clinical decision-making. *Social Science & Medicine*, 75: 186–92.

Bravo, M.J. & Farid, H. (2012). Task demands determine the specificity of the search template. *Attention, Perception & Psychophysics*, 74: 124–31.

Breedin, S.D. & Saffran, E.M. (1999). Sentence processing in the face of semantic loss: A case study. *Journal of Experimental Psychology: General*, *128*, 547–562.

Bremmer, F., Kubischik, M., Pekel, M., Hoffmann, K.P. & Lappe, M. (2010). Visual selectivity for heading in monkey area MST. *Experimental Brain Research*, 200: 51–60.

Brendel, E., DeLucia, P., Hecht, H., Stacy, R.L. & Larson, J.T. (2012). Threatening pictures induce shortened time-to-contact estimates. *Attention, Perception & Psychophysics*, 74: 979–87.

Brewer, N. & Wells, G.L. (2011). Eyewitness identification. *Current Directions in Psychological Science*, 20: 24–7.

Brewer, W.F. & Treyens, J.C. (1981). Role of schemata in memory for places. *Cognitive Psychology*, 13: 207–30.

Bridge, H., Harrold, S., Holmes, E.A., Stokes, M. & Kennard, C. (2012). Vivid visual mental imagery in the absence of the primary visual cortex. *Journal of Neurology*, 259: 1062–70.

Bridge, H., Thomas, O., Jbabdi, S. & Cowey, A. (2008). Changes in connectivity after visual cortical brain damage underlie altered visual function. *Brain*, 131: 1433–44.

Bridgeman, B. (2007). Efference copy and its limitations. *Computers in Biology and Medicine*, 37: 924–9.

Bridgeman, B., Lewis, S., Heit, G. & Nagle, M. (1979). Relation between cognitive and motor-oriented systems of visual position perception. *Journal of Experimental Psychology: Human Perception and Performance*, 5: 692–700.

Bright, D.A. & Goodman-Delahunty, J. (2006). Gruesome evidence and emotion: Anger, blame, and jury decision-making. *Law and Human Behavior*, 30: 183–202.

Britten, K.H. & van Wezel, R.J.A. (1998). Electrical microstimulation of cortical area MST biases heading perception in monkeys. *Nature Neuroscience*, 1: 59–63.

Brittlebank, A.D., Scott, J., Williams, J.M.G. & Ferrier, I.N. (1993). Autobiographical memory in depression: State or trait marker? *British Journal of Psychiatry*, 162: 118–21.

Broadbent, D.E. (1958). *Perception and communication*. Oxford: Pergamon.

Brock, J. & Nation, K. (2014). The hardest butter to button: Immediate context effects in spoken word identification. *Quarterly Journal of Experimental Psychology*, 67: 114–23.

Bröder, A. (2003). Decision making with the adaptive toolbox: Influence of environmental structure, personality, intelligence, and working memory load. *Journal of Experimental Psychology: Learning, Memory, and Cognition*, 29: 611–25.

Broeders, R., van den Bos, K., Müller, P.A. & Ham, J. (2011). Should I save or should I not kill? How people solve moral dilemmas depends on which rule is most accessible. *Journal of Experimental Social Psychology*, 47: 923–34.

Brooks, R., Faff, R., Mulino, D. & Scheelings, R. (2009). Deal or no deal, that is the question? The impact of increasing stakes and framing effects on decision making under risk. *International Review of Finance*, 9: 27–50.

Brosch, T. (2013). Comment: On the role of appraisal processes in the construction of emotion. *Emotion Review*, 5: 369–73.

Brown, K.F., Kroll, J.S., Hudson, M.J., Ramsay, M., Green, J., Vincent, C.A., Fraser, G. & Sevdalis, N. (2010). Omission bias and vaccine rejection by parents of healthy children: Implications for the influenza A/H1N1 vaccination programme. *Vaccine*, 28: 4181–5.

Brown, R. & Kulik, J. (1977). Flashbulb memories. *Cognition*, 5: 73–99.

Brown, R.M. & Robertson, E.M. (2007). Off-line processing: Reciprocal interactions between declarative and procedural memories. *Journal of Neuroscience*, 27: 10468–75.

Brown, S.D. (2012). Common ground for behavioural and neuroimaging research. *Australian Journal of Psychology*, 64: 4–10.

Brown-Schmidt, S. (2012). Beyond common and privileged: Gradient representations of common ground in real-time language use. *Language and Cognitive Processes*, 27: 62–89.

Brown-Schmidt, S. & Heller, D. (2014). What language processing can tell us about perspective taking: A reply to Bezuidenhout (2013). *Journal of Pragmatics*, 60: 279–84.

Bruce, V. & Tadmor, Y. (2015, in press). Direct perception: Beyond Gibson (1950) direct perception. In M.W. Eysenck & D. Groome (eds), *Cognitive psychology: Revisiting the classic studies*. London: SAGE.

Bruce, V. & Young, A. (1986). Understanding face recognition. *British Journal of Psychology*, 77: 305–27.

Bruce, V., Green, P.R. & Georgeson, M.A. (2003). *Visual perception* (4th edn). Hove: Psychology Press.

Bruner, J.S., Goodnow, J.J. & Austin, G.A. (1956). *A study of thinking*. New York: John Wiley.

Bruno, N. & Cutting, J.E. (1988). Minimodularity and the perception of layout. *Journal of Experimental Psychology*, 117: 161–70.

Bruno, N., Bernadis, P. & Gentilucci, M. (2008). Visually guided pointing, the Müller-Lyer illusion, and the functional interpretation of the dorsal–ventral split: Conclusions from 33 independent studies. *Neuroscience and Biobehavioral Reviews*, 32: 4213–437.

Bruyer, R. (2011). Configural face processing: A meta-analytic survey. *Perception*, 40: 1478–90.

Brysbaert, M. & Mitchell, D.C. (1996). Modifier attachment in sentence parsing: Evidence from Dutch. *Quarterly Journal of Experimental Psychology*, 49: 664–95.

Bucciarelli, M. & Johnson-Laird, P.N. (1999). Strategies in syllogistic reasoning. *Cognitive Science*, 23: 247–303.

Buchanan, T.W., Tranel, D. & Adolphs, R. (2006). Memories for emotional autobiographical events following unilateral damage to medial temporal lobe. *Brain*, 129: 115–27.

Buetler, K.A., Rodriguez, D.L., Leganaro, M., Müri, R., Spierer, L. & Annoni, J.-M. (2014). Language context modulates reading route: An electrical neuroimaging study. *Frontiers in Human Neuroscience*, 8 (Article 83).

Bullmore, E. & Sporns, O. (2012). The economy of brain network organisation. *Nature Reviews Neuroscience*, 13: 336–49.

Bülthoff, I., Bülthoff, H. & Sinha, P. (1998). Top-down influences on stereoscopic depth-perception. *Nature Neuroscience*, 1: 254–7.

Burgess, P.W., Veitch, E., Costello, A. & Shallice, T. (2000). The cognitive and neuroanatomical correlates of multi-tasking. *Neuropsychologia*, 38: 848–63.

Burgess, P.W., Gilbert, S.J. & Dumontheil, I. (2007). Function and localisation within rostral prefrontal cortex (area 10). *Philosophical Transactions of the Royal Society B: Biological Sciences*, 362: 887–99.

Burgess, P.W., Gonen-Yaacovi, G. & Volle, E. (2011). Functional neuroimaging studies of prospective memory: What have we learnt so far? *Neuropsychologia*, 49: 2246–57.

Burianova, H., McIntosh, A.R. & Grady, C.L. (2010). A common functional brain network for autobiographical, episodic, and semantic memory retrieval. *NeuroImage*, 49: 865–74.

Burkhardt, P., Avrutin, S., Piñango, M.M. & Ruigendijk, E. (2008). Slower-than-usual syntactic processing in agrammatic Broca's aphasia: Evidence from Dutch. *Journal of Neurolinguistics*, 21: 120–37.

Burns, B.D. (2004). The effects of speed on skilled chess performance. *Psychological Science*, 15: 442–7.

Burns, B.D. & Wieth, M. (2004). The collider principle in causal reasoning: Why the Monty Hall dilemma is so hard. *Journal of Experimental Psychology: General*, 133: 434–49.

Busch, N.A. (2013). The fate of object memory traces under change detection and change blindness. *Brain Research*, 1520: 107–15.

Busch, N.A., Fründ, I. & Herrmann, C.S. (2009). Electrophysiological evidence for different types of change detection and change blindness. *Journal of Cognitive Neuroscience*, 22: 1852–69.

Bushman, B.J. (2002). Does venting anger feed or extinguish the flame? Catharsis, rumination, distraction, anger, and aggressive responding. *Personality and Social Psychology Bulletin*, 28: 724–31.

Busigny, T., Graf, M., Mayer, E. & Rossion, B. (2010a). Acquired prosopagnosia as a face-specific disorder: Ruling out the general visual similarity account. *Neuropsychologia*, 48: 2051–67.

Busigny, T., Joubert, S., Felician, O., Ceccaldi, M. & Rossion, B. (2010b). Holistic perception of the individual face is specific and necessary: Evidence from an extensive case study of acquired prosopagnosia. *Neuropsychologia*, 48: 4057–92.

Butler, A.C. (2010). Repeated testing produces superior transfer of learning relative to repeated studying. *Journal of Experimental Psychology: Learning, Memory, and Cognition*, 36: 1118–33.

Butterworth, B. (1984). Article on Ronald Reagan. *The Sunday Times*, 4 November.

Butterworth, B. (1985). Jargon aphasia: Processes and strategies. In S. Newman & R. Epstein (eds), *Current perspectives in dysphasia*. Edinburgh: Churchill Livingstone.

Buysse, L. (2012). *So* as a multifunctional discourse marker in native and learner speech. *Journal of Pragmatics*, 44: 1764–82.

Byrne, M.D. (2012). Unified theories of cognition. *Wiley Interdisciplinary Reviews – Cognitive Science*, 3: 431–8.

Cabeza, R. & Moscovitch, M. (2013). Memory systems, processing modes, and components: Functional neuroimaging evidence. *Perspectives on Psychological Science*, 8: 49–55.

Caccappolo-van Vliet, E., Miozzo, M. & Stern, Y. (2004). Phonological dyslexia: A test case for reading models. *Psychological Science*, 15: 583–90.

Cahill, L., Babinsky, R., Markowitsch, H.J. & McGaugh, J.L. (1995). Involvement of the amygdaloid complex in emotional memory. *Nature*, 377: 295–6.

Cahir, C. & Thomas, K. (2010). Asymmetric effects of positive and negative affect on decision making. *Psychological Reports*, 106: 193–204.

Cai, Z.G., Sturt, P. & Pickering, M.J. (2012). The effect of nonadopted analyses on sentence processing. *Language and Cognitive Processes*, 27: 1286–311.

Cain, M.S. & Mitroff, S.R. (2011). Distractor filtering in media multitaskers. *Perception*, 40: 1183–92.

Caird, J.K., Willness, C.R., Steel, P. & Scialfa, C. (2008). A meta-analysis of the effects of cell phones on driver performance. *Accident Analysis and Prevention*, 40: 1282–93.

Calder, A.J. & Young, A.W. (2005). Understanding the recognition of facial identity and facial expression. *Nature Reviews Neuroscience*, 6: 645–51.

Calderwood, L. & Burton, A.M. (2006). Children and adults recall the names of highly familiar faces faster than semantic information. *British Journal of Psychology*, 97: 441–54.

Calvo, M.G. & Castillo, M.D. (1997). Mood-congruent bias in interpretation of ambiguity: Strategic processes and temporary activation. *Quarterly Journal of Experimental Psychology*, 50A: 163–82.

Calvo, M.G., Castillo, M.D. & Schmalhofer, F. (2006). Strategic influence on the time course of predictive inferences in reading. *Memory & Cognition*, 34: 68–77.

Calvo, M.G., Gutiérrez, A. & Fernández-Martin, A. (2012). Anxiety and deficient inhibition of threat distractors: Spatial attention span and time course. *Journal of Cognitive Psychology*, 24: 66–78.

Camerer, C. & Hogarth, R.B. (1999). The effects of financial incentives in experiments: A review and capital-labour-production framework. *Journal of Risk and Uncertainty*, 19: 7–42.

Campbell-Sills, L. & Barlow, D.H. (2007). Incorporating emotion regulation into conceptualisations and treatments of anxiety and mood disorders. In J.J. Gross (ed.), *Handbook of emotion regulation* (pp. 542–59). New York: Guilford Press.

Campion, J., Latto, R.M. & Smith, Y.M. (1983). Is blindsight an effect of scattered light, spared cortex, and near-threshold vision? *Behavioral and Brain Sciences*, 6: 423–8.

Campitelli, G. & Gobet, F. (2011). Deliberate practice: Necessary but not sufficient. *Current Directions in Psychological Science*, 20: 280–5.

Campos, B., Shiota, M.N., Keltner, D., Gonzaga, G.C. & Goetz, J.L. (2013). What is shared, what is different? Core relational themes and expressive displays of eight positive emotions. *Cognition & Emotion*, 27: 37–52.

Campoy, G. (2012). Evidence for decay in verbal short-term memory: A commentary on Berman, Jonides, and Lewis (2009). *Journal of Experimental Psychology: Learning, Memory, and Cognition*, 38: 1129–36.

Canal-Bruland, R., Voorwald, F., Wielaard, K. & van der Kamp, J. (2013). Dissociations between vision for perception and vision for action depend on the relative availability of egocentric and allocentri information. *Attention, Perception, and Psychophysics*, 75: 1206–14.

Capa, R.L., Bouquet, C.A., Dreher, J.-C. & Dufour, A. (2013). Long-lasting effects of performance-contingent unconscious and conscious reward incentives during cued task-switching. *Cortex*, 49: 1943–54.

Cappa, S.F. (2012). Neurological accounts. In R. Bastiaanse & C.K. Thompson (eds), *Perspectives on agrammatism*. Hove: Psychology Press.

Capstick, S.B. & Pidgeon, N.F. (2014). Public perception of cold weather events as evidence for and against climate change. *Climatic Change*, 122: 695–708.

Caravolas, M., Lervåg, A., Defior, S., Málková & Hulme, C. (2013). Different patterns, but equivalent predictors, of growth in reading in consistent and inconsistent orthographies. *Psychological Science*, 24: 1398–407.

Carpenter, S.K. (2012). Testing enhances the transfer of learning. *Current Directions in Psychological Science*, 21: 279–83.

Cartmill, E.A., Beilock, S. & Goldin-Meadow, S. (2012). A word in the hand: Action, gesture and mental representation in humans and non-human primates. *Philosophical Transactions of the Royal Society B*, 367: 129–43.

Casasanto, D. (2008). Time in the mind: Using space to think about time. *Cognition*, 106: 579–93.

Cattinelli, I., Borghese, N.A., Gallucci, M. & Paulesu, E. (2013). Reading the reading brain: A new meta-analysis of functional mapping data on reading. *Journal of Neurolinguistics*, 26: 214–38.

Cavaco, S., Anderson, S.W., Allen, J.S., Castro-Caldas, A. & Damasio, H. (2004). The scope of procedural memory in amnesia. *Brain*, 127: 1853–67.

Cave, K.R., Bush, W.S. & Taylor, T.G.G. (2010). Split attention as part of a flexible attentional system for complex scenes: Comment on Jans, Peters, and De Weerd (2010). *Psychological Review*, 117: 685–96.

Ceci, S.J. & Liker, J.K. (1986). A day at the races: A study of IQ, expertise, and cognitive complexity. *Journal of Experimental Psychology: General*, 115: 255–66.

Ceraso, J. & Provitera, A. (1971). Sources of error in syllogistic reasoning. *Cognitive Psychology*, 2: 400–10.

Cermak, L.S., Talbot, N., Chandler, K. & Wolharst, L.R. (1985). The perceptual priming phenomenon in amnesia. *Neuropsychologia*, 23: 615–22.

Ceulemans, E., Kuppens, P. & Van Mechelen, I. (2012). Capturing the structure of distinct types of individual differences in the situation-specific experience of emotions: The case of anger. *European Journal of Personality*, 26: 484–95.

Chae, Y. (2010). Application of laboratory research on eyewitness testimony. *Journal of Forensic Psychology Practice*, 10: 252–61.

Chagnaud, B.P., Simmers, J. & Straka, H. (2012). Predictability of visual perturbation during locomotion: Implication for corrective efference copy signalling. *Biological Cybernetics*, 106: 669–79.

Chajut, E., Mama, Y., Levy, L. & Algom, D. (2010). Avoiding the response trap: A response bias theory of the emotional Stroop effect. *Journal of Experimental Psychology: Learning, Memory, and Cognition*, 36: 1567–77.

Challis, B.H., Velichkovsky, B.M. & Craik, F.I.M. (1996). Levels-of-processing effects on a variety of memory tasks: New findings and theoretical implications. *Consciousness and Cognition*, 5: 142–64.

Challoner, J. (2009). *1,001 inventions that changed the world*. Hauppauge, NY: Barron's Educational Series.

Chalmers, D. (2007). The hard problem of consciousness. In M. Velmans & S. Schneider (eds), *The Blackwell companion to consciousness*. Oxford: Blackwell.

Chamberlain, F. (2003). Review of "Behavioural Assessment of the Dysexecutive Syndrome (BADS)". *Journal of Occupational Psychology*, 5: 33–7.

Chan, J., Paletz, S.B.F. & Schunn, C.D. (2012). Analogy as a strategy for supporting complex problem solving under uncertainty. *Memory & Cognition*, 40: 1352–65.

Chan, J.C.K. & LaPaglia, J.A. (2013). Impairing existing declarative memory in humans by disrupting reconsolidation. *Proceedings of the National Academy of Sciences*, 110: 9309–13.

Charness, N. (1981). Search in chess: Age and skill differences. *Journal of Experimental Psychology: Human Perception & Performance*, 7: 467–76.

Charness, N., Reingold, E.M., Pomplun, M. & Stampe, D.M. (2001). The perceptual aspect of skilled performance in chess: Evidence from eye movements. *Memory & Cognition*, 29: 1146–52.

Chen, C.M., Lakatos, P., Shah, A.S., Mehta, A.D., Givre, S.J., Javitt, D.C. & Schroeder, C.E (2007). Functional anatomy and interaction of fast and slow visual pathways in macaque monkeys. *Cerebral Cortex*, 17: 1561–9.

Chen, L. & Vroomen, J. (2013). Intersensory binding across space and time: A tutorial review. *Attention, Perception & Psychophysics*, 75: 790–811.

Chen, Q. & Mirman, D. (2012). Competition and cooperation among similar representations: Toward a unified account of facilitative and inhibitory effects of lexical neighbours. *Psychological Review*, 119: 417–30.

Chen, Z. (2002). Analogical problem solving: A hierarchical analysis of procedural similarity. *Journal of Experimental Psychology: Learning, Memory & Cognition*, 28: 81–98.

Chen, Z. (2012). Object-based attention: A tutorial review. *Attention, Perception & Psychophysics*, 74: 784–802.

Chen, Z. & Cowan, N. (2009). Core verbal working memory capacity: The limit in words retained without covert articulation. *Quarterly Journal of Experimental Psychology*, 62: 1420–9.

Chenoweth, N.A. & Hayes, J.R. (2003). The inner voice in writing. *Written Communication*, 20: 99–118.

Cherry, E.C. (1953). Some experiments on the recognition of speech with one and two ears. *Journal of the Acoustical Society of America*, 25: 975–9.

Cherubini, P., Castelvecchio, E. & Cherubini, A.M. (2005). Generation of hypotheses in Wason's 2–4–6 task: An information theory approach. *Quarterly Journal of Experimental Psychology Section A – Human Experimental Psychology*, 58: 309–32.

Chi, R.P. & Snyder, A.W. (2011). Facilitate insight by non-invasive brain stimulation. *PLOS ONE*, 6: 181–97.

Chiappe, D.L. & Chiappe, P. (2007). The role of working memory in metaphor production and comprehension. *Journal of Memory and Language*, 56: 172–88.

Chica, A.B., Bartolomeo, P. & Valero-Cabré, A. (2011). Dorsal and ventral parietal contributions to spatial orienting in the human brain. *Journal of Neuroscience*, 31: 8143–9.

Chica, A.B., Bartolomeo, P. & Lupiáñez, J. (2013). Two cognitive and neural systems for endogenous and exogenous spatial attention. *Behavioural Brain Research*, 237: 107–23.

Cho, S., Holyoak, K.J. & Cannon, T.D. (2007). Analogical reasoning in working memory: Resources shared among relational integration, interference resolution, and maintenance. *Memory & Cognition*, 35: 1445–55.

Cho, S., Moody, T.D., Fernandino, L., Mumford, J.A., Poldrack, R.A., Cannon, T.D., Knowlton, B.J. & Holyoak, K.J. (2010). Common and dissociable prefrontal loci associated with component mechanisms of analogical reasoning. *Cerebral Cortex*, 20: 524–33.

Cholewa, J., Mantey, S., Heber, S. & Hollweg, W. (2010). Developmental surface and phonological dysgraphia in German 3rd graders. *Reading and Writing*, 23: 97–127.

Chomsky, N. (1957). *Knowledge of language: Its nature, origin, and use.* New York: Praeger.

Chomsky, N. (1959). Review of Skinner's "Verbal Behaviour". *Language*, 35: 26–58.

Christiansen, M.H. & Chater, N. (2008). Language as shaped by the brain. *Behavioral and Brain Sciences*, 31: 489–558.

Christiansen, M.H., Kelly, M.L., Shillcock, R.C. & Greenfield, K. (2010). Impaired artificial grammar learning in agrammatism. *Cognition*, 116: 382–93.

Christianson, K., Luke, S.G. & Ferreira, F. (2010). Effects of plausibility on structural priming. *Journal of Experimental Psychology: Learning, Memory and Cognition*, 36: 538–44.

Christopher, M.E., Miyake, A., Keenan, J.M., Pennington, B., DeFries, J.C., Wadsworth, S.J., Willcutt, E. & Olson, R.K. (2012). Predicting word reading and comprehension with executive function and speed measures across development: A latent variable analysis. *Journal of Experimental Psychology: General*, 141: 470–88.

Chrysikou, E.G., Hamilton, R.H., Coslett, H.B., Datta, A., Bikson & Thompson-Schill, S.L. (2013). Noninvasive transcranial direct current stimulation over the left prefrontal cortex facilitates cognitive flexibility in tool use. *Cognitive Neuroscience*, 4: 81–9.

Chuderski, A. & Nęcka, E. (2012). The contribution of working memory to fluid reasoning: Capacity, control, or both? *Journal of Experimental Psychology: Learning, Memory, and Cognition*, 38: 1689–710.

Chukoskie, L., Snider, J., Mozer, M.C., Krauzlis, R.J. & Sejnowski, T.J. (2013). Learning where to look for a hidden target. *Proceedings of the National Academy of Sciences*, 110: 10438–45.

Chun, M.M., Golomb, J.D. & Turk-Browne, N.B. (2011). A taxonomy of external and internal attention. *Annual Review of Psychology*, 62: 73–101.

Chun, W.Y. & Kruglanski, A.W. (2006). The role of task demands and processing resources in the use of base-rate and individuating information. *Journal of Personality and Social Psychology*, 91: 205–17.

Chung, S. (2012). Are lexical categories universal? The view from Chamorro. *Theoretical Linguistics*, 38: 1–56.

Churchland, P.S. & Sejnowski, T. (1994). *The computational brain.* Cambridge, MA: MIT Press.

Chuy, M., Scardamalia, M. & Bereiter, C. (2012). Development of ideational writing through knowledge building: Theoretical and empirical bases. In E.L. Grigorenko, E. Mambrino & D. Preiss (eds), *Writing: A mosaic of new perspectives* (pp. 175–90). Hove: Psychology Press.

Cisler, J.M. & Koster, E.H.W. (2010). Mechanisms of attentional biases towards threat in anxiety disorders: An integrative review. *Clinical Psychology Review*, 30: 203–16.

Clancy, S.A. & McNally, R.J. (2005/2006). Who needs repression? Normal memory processes can explain "forgetting" of childhood sexual abuse. *Scientific Review of Mental Health Practice*, 4: 66–73.

Clarke, P.J.F., MacLeod, C. & Guastella, A.J. (2013). Assessing the role of spatial engagement and disengagement of attention in anxiety-linked attentional bias: A critique of current paradigms and suggestions for future research directions. *Anxiety, Stress & Coping*, 26: 1–19.

Cleeremans, A. & Jiménez, L. (2002). Implicit learning and consciousness: A graded, dynamic perspective. In R.M. French & A. Cleeremans (eds), *Implicit learning and consciousness: An empirical, philosophical and computational consensus in the making*. Hove: Psychology Press.

Cleland, A.A. & Pickering, M.J. (2006). Do writing and speaking employ the same syntactic representations? *Journal of Memory and Language*, 54: 185–98.

Close, J. & Pothos, E.M. (2012). "Object categorisation: Reversals and explanations of the basic-level advantage" (Rogers & Patterson, 2007): A simplicity account. *Quarterly Journal of Experimental Psychology*, 65: 1615–32.

Cloutman, L.L. (2013). Interaction between dorsal and ventral processing streams: Where, when and how? *Brain & Language*, 127: 251–63.

Coch, D., Sanders, L.D. & Neville, H.J. (2005). An event-related potential study of selective auditory attention in children and adults. *Journal of Cognitive Neuroscience*, 17: 606–22.

Coget, J.-F., Haag, C. & Gibson, D.E. (2011). Anger and fear in decision-making: The case of film directors on set. *European Management Journal*, 29: 476–90.

Cohen, G. (2008). The study of everyday memory. In G. Cohen & M.A. Conway (eds), *Memory in the real world* (3rd edn) (pp. 1–19). Hove: Psychology Press.

Cohen, J.R., Young, J.F. & Abela, J.R.Z. (2012). Cognitive vulnerability to depression in children: An idiographic, longitudinal examination of inferential styles. *Cognitive Therapy and Research*, 36: 643–54.

Cohen, L.R. (2002). The role of experience in the perception of biological motion. *Dissertation Abstracts International: Section B: The Sciences & Engineering*, 63: 3049.

Cohen, M.A., Alvarez, G.A. & Nakayama, K. (2011). Natural-scene perception requires attention. *Psychological Science*, 22: 1165–72.

Cohen, M.A., Cavanagh, P., Chun, M.M. & Nakayama, K. (2012). The attentional requirements of consciousness. *Trends in Cognitive Sciences*, 16: 411–17.

Colavita, F.B. (1974). Human sensory dominance. *Perception & Psychophysics*,16(2): 409–12.

Cole, S.A. (2005). More than zero: Accounting for error in latent fingerprinting identification. *Journal of Criminal Law & Criminology*, 95: 985–1078.

Coleman, M.R., Davis, M.H., Rodd, J.M., Robson, T., Ali, A., Owen, A.M. & Pickard, J.D. (2009). Towards the routine use of brain imaging to aid the clinical diagnosis of disorders of consciousness. *Brain*, 132: 2541–52.

Collette, F., Van der Linden, M., Laureys, S., Delfiore, G., Degueldre, C., Luxen, A., et al. (2005). Exploring the unity and diversity of the neural substrates of executive functioning. *Human Brain Mapping*, 25: 409–23.

Colman, A.M. (2001). *Oxford dictionary of psychology*. Oxford: Oxford University Press.

Colomb, C. & Ginet, M. (2012). The cognitive interview for use with adults: An empirical test of an alternative mnemonic and of a partial protocol. *Applied Cognitive Psychology*, 26: 35–47.

Colombo, L., Fudio, S. & Mosna, G. (2009). Phonological and working memory mechanisms involved in written spelling. *European Journal of Cognitive Psychology*, 21: 837–61.

Coltheart, M. (1996). Phonological dyslexia. *Cognitive Neuropsychology*, 13: 749–50.

Coltheart, M. (2001). Assumptions and methods in cognitive neuropsychology. In B. Rapp (ed.), *The handbook of cognitive neuropsychology: What deficits reveal about the human mind*. Hove: Psychology Press.

Coltheart, M. (2010). Lessons from cognitive neuropsychology for cognitive science: A reply to Patterson and Plaut (2009). *Topics in Cognitive Science*, 2: 3–11.

Coltheart, M. (2011). What has functional neuroimaging told us about the organisation of mind? *Cognitive Neuropsychology*, 28: 397–402.

Coltheart, M. (2012). Dual-route theories of reading aloud. In J. Adelman (ed.), *Visual word recognition, vol 1: Models and methods, orthography, and phonology* (pp. 3–27). Hove: Psychology Press.

Coltheart, M. (2015, in press). Cognitive neuropsychology of language: Beyond Marshall and Newcombe's (1973) patterns of paralexia. In M.W. Eysenck & D. Groome (eds), *Cognitive psychology: Revisiting the classic studies*. London: SAGE.

Coltheart, M., Rastle, K., Perry, C., Langdon, R. & Ziegler, J. (2001). DRC: A dual-route cascaded model of visual word recognition and reading aloud. *Psychological Review*, 108: 204–56.

Colvin, M.K. & Gazzaniga, M.S. (2007). Split-brain cases. In M. Velmans & S. Schneider (eds), *The Blackwell companion to consciousness*. Oxford: Blackwell.

Colvin, M.K., Dunbar, K. & Grafman, J. (2001). The effects of frontal lobe lesions on goal achievement in the water jug task. *Journal of Cognitive Neuroscience*, 13: 1129–47.

Cona, G., Arcara, G., Tarantino, V. & Bisiacchi, P.S. (2012). Electrophysiological correlates of strategic monitoring in event-based and time-based prospective memory. *PLOS ONE*, 7(2): e31659. doi: 10.1371/journal.pone.003 1659.

Connelly, V., Dockrell, J.E., Walter, K. & Critten, S. (2012). Predicting the quality of composition and written language bursts from oral language, spelling, and handwriting skills in children with and without specific language impairment. *Written Communication*, 29: 278–302.

Conway, A.R.A., Cowan, N. & Bunting, M.F. (2001). The cocktail party phenomenon revisited: The importance of working memory capacity. *Psychonomic Bulletin & Review*, 8: 331–5.

Conway, A.R.A., Kane, M.J. & Engle, R.W. (2003). Working memory capacity and its relation to general intelligence. *Trends in Cognitive Sciences*, 7: 547–52.

Conway, B.R., Chatterjee, S., Field, G.D., Horwitz, G.D., Johnson, E.N., Koida, K. & Mancuso, K. (2010). Advances in color science: From retina to behaviour. *Journal of Neuroscience*, 30: 14955–63.

Conway, M.A. (2005). Memory and the self. *Journal of Memory and Language*, 53: 594–628.

Conway, M.A. & Pleydell-Pearce, C.W. (2000). The construction of autobiographical memories In the self-memory system. *Psychological Review*, 107: 262–88.

Conway, M.A., Wang, Q., Hanyu, K. & Haque, S. (2005). A cross-cultural investigation of autobiographical memory. *Journal of Cross-Cultural Psychology*, 36: 739–49.

Cook, A.E. & Myers, J.L. (2004). Processing discourse rules in scripted narratives: The influences of context and world knowledge. *Journal of Memory and Language*, 50: 268–88.

Cook, R., Bird, G., Catmur, C., Press, C. & Heyes, C. (2014). Mirror neurons: From origin to function. *Behavioral and Brain Sciences*, 37: 177–241.

Cooke, R., Peel, E., Shaw, R.L. & Senior, C. (2007). The neuroimaging research process from the participants' perspective. *International Journal of Psychophysiology*, 63: 152–8.

Cooney, J.W. & Gazzaniga, M.S. (2003). Neurological disorders and the structure of human consciousness. *Trends in Cognitive Sciences*, 7: 161–5.

Cooper, A.D., Sterling, C.P., Bacon, M.P. & Bridgeman, B. (2012). Does action affect perception or memory? *Vision Research*, 62: 235–40.

Cooper, S.A., Joshi, A.C., Seenan, P.J., Hadley, D.M., Muir, K.W., Leigh, R.J. & Metcalfe, R.A. (2012). Akinetopsia: Acute presentation and evidence for persisting defects in motion vision. *Journal of Neurology, Neurosurgery & Psychiatry*, 83: 229–30.

Copeland, D.E. & Radvansky, G.A. (2004). Working memory and syllogistic reasoning. *Quarterly Journal of Exerimental Psychology*, 57A: 1437–57.

Corbetta, M. & Shulman, G.L. (2002). Control of goal-directed and stimulus-driven attention in the brain. *Nature Reviews Neuroscience*, 3: 201–15.

Corbetta, M. & Shulman, G.L. (2011). Spatial neglect and attention networks. *Annual Review of Neuroscience*, 34: 569–99.

Corbetta, M., Patel, G. & Shulman, G.L. (2008). The re-orienting system of the human brain: From environment to theory of mind. *Neuron*, 58: 306–24.

Corkin, S. (1968). Acquisition of motor skill after bilateral medial temporal-lobe excision. *Neuropsychologia*, 6: 255–65.

Corkin, S. (1984). Lasting consequences of bilateral medial temporal lobectomy – Clinical course and experimental findings in HM. *Seminars in Neurology*, 4: 249–59.

Corley, M., Brocklehurst, P.H. & Moat, H.S. (2011). Error biases in inner and overt speech: Evidence from tongue twisters. *Journal of Experimental Psychology: Learning, Memory, and Cognition*, 37: 162–75.

Corner, A., Hahn, U. & Oaksford, M. (2011). The psychological mechanism of the slippery slope argument. *Journal of Memory and Language*, 64: 133–52.

Cosentino, S., Chut, D., Libon, D., Moore, P. & Grossman, M. (2006). How does the brain support script comprehension? A study of executive processs and semantic knowledge in dementia. *Neuropsychology*, 20: 307–18.

Costello, F.J. & Keane, M.T. (2000). Efficient creativity: Constraint-guided conceptual combination. *Cognitive Science*, 24: 299–349.

Coughlan, E.K., Williams, A.M., McRobert, A.P. & Ford, P.R. (2014). How experts practice: A novel test of deliberate practice theory. *Journal of Experimental Psychology: Learning, Memory, and Cognition*, 40: 449–58.

Cowey, A. (2004). Fact, artifact, and myth about blindsight. *Quarterly Journal of Experimental Psychology*, 57A: 577–609.

Cowey, A., Campana, G., Walsh, V. & Vaina, L.M. (2006). The role of human extrastriate visual areas V5/MT and v2/V3 in the perception of the direction of global motion: A transcranial magnetic stimulation study. *Experimental Brain Research*, 171: 558–62.

Cowley, M. & Byrne, R.M.J. (2005). Chess masters' hypothesis testing. *Proceedings of the Twenty-sixth Annual Conference of the Cognitive Science Society* (pp. 250–5). New York: Psychology Press.

Cracco, R.Q., Cracco, J.B., Maccabee, P.J. & Amassian, V.E. (1999). Cerebral function revealed by transcranial magnetic stimulation. *Journal of Neuroscience Methods*, 86: 209–19.

Craik, F.I.M. & Lockhart, R.S. (1972). Levels of processing: A framework for memory research. *Journal of Verbal Learning and Verbal Behavior*, 11: 671–84.

Craik, F.I.M. & Tulving, E. (1975). Depth of processing and the retention of words in episodic memory. *Journal of Experimental Psychology: General*, 104: 268–94.

Crawford, J.R., Smith, G., Maylor, E.A., Della Sala, S. & Logie, R.H. (2003). The Prospective and Retrospective Memory Questionnaire (PRMQ): Normative data and latent structure in a large non-clinical sample. *Memory*, 11: 261–75.

Cree, G.S. & McRae, K. (2003). Analysing the factors underlying the structure and computation of the meaning of chipmunk, cherry, chisel, cheese, and cello (and many other such concrete nouns). *Journal of Experimental Psychology: General*, 132: 163–201.

Creem, S.H. & Proffitt, D.R. (2001). Grasping objects by their handles: A necessary interaction between cognition and action. *Journal of Experimental Psychology: Human Perception and Performance*, 27: 218–28.

Crescentini, C., Seyed-Allaei, S., Vallesi, A. & Shallice, T. (2012). Two networks involved in producing and realising plans. *Neuropsychologia*, 50: 1521–35.

Crisp, J., Howard, D. & Lambon Ralph, M.A. (2011). More evidence for a continuum between phonological and deep dyslexia: Novel data from three measures of direct orthography-to-phonology translation. *Aphasiology*, 25: 615–41.

Crookes, K. & McKone, E. (2009). Early maturity of face recognition: No childhood development of holistic processing, novel face encoding, or face-space. *Cognition*, 111: 219–47.

Crossley, C.D. & Highhouse, S. (2005). Relation of job search and choice process with subsequent satisfaction. *Journal of Economic Psychology*, 26: 255–68.

Cruse, D., Chennu, S., Chatelle, C., Bekinschtein, T.A., Fernandez-Espejo, D., Pickard, J.D., Laureys, S. & Owen, A.M. (2011). Bedside detection of awareness in the vegetative state. *Lancet*, 378: 2088–94.

Cryder, C.E., Lerner, J.S., Gross, J.J. & Dahl, R.E. (2008). Misery is not miserly: Sad and self-focused individuals spend more. *Psychological Science*, 19: 525–30.

Crystal, D. (1997). *A dictionary of linguistics and phonetics* (4th edn). Cambridge, MA: Blackwell.

Csibra, G. (2008). Action mirroring and action understanding: An alternative account. In P. Haggard, U. Rosetti & M. Kawato (eds), *Sensorimotor foundations of higher cognition: Attention and Performance, vol. XII*. Oxford: Oxford University Press.

Culbertson, J., Smolensky, P. & Legendre, G. (2012). Learning biases predict a word order universal. *Cognition*, 122: 306–29.

Curci, A. & Conway, M.A. (2013). Playing the flashbulb memory game: A comment on Cubelli and Della Sala. *Cortex*, 49: 352–5.

Curiel, J.M. & Radvansky, G.A. (2014). Spatial and character situation model updating. *Journal of Cognitive Psychology*, 26: 205–12.

Cus, A., Vodusek, D.B. & Repovs, G. (2011). Brain plasticity and recovery of cognitive functions. *Slovenian Medical Journal*, 80: 758–65.

Cushen, P.J. & Wiley, J. (2012). Cues to solution, restructuring patterns, and reports of insight in creative problem solving. *Consciousness and Cognition*, 21: 1166–75.

Cutler, A. & Butterfield, S. (1992). Rhythmic cues to speech segmentation: Evidence from juncture misperception. *Journal of Memory and Language*, 31: 218–36.

Cutler, A. & Clifton, C. (1999). Comprehending spoken language: A blueprint of the listener. In C.M. Brown & P. Hagoort (eds), *The neurocognition of language*. Oxford: Oxford University Press.

Cuttler, C. & Graf, P. (2009a). Checking-in on the memory deficit and meta-memory deficit theories of compulsive checking. *Clinical Psychology Review*, 29: 393–409.

Cuttler, C. & Graf, P. (2009b). Sub-clinical compulsive checkers show impaired performance on habitual, event- and time-cued episodic prospective memory tasks. *Journal of Anxiety Disorders*, 23: 813–23.

Cuttler, C., Sirois-Delisle, V., Alcolado, G.M., Radomsky, A.S. & Taylor, S. (2013). Diminished confidence in prospective memory causes doubts and urges to check. *Journal of Behavior Therapy and Experimental Psychiatry*, 44: 329–34.

Cvejic, E., Kim, J. & Davis, C. (2012). Recognising prosody across modalities, face areas and speakers: Examining perceivers' sensitivity to variable realisations of visual prosody. *Cognition*, 122: 442–53.

Daane, M.C. (1991). Good readers make good writers: A description of four college students. *Journal of Reading*, 35: 184–8.

Dagher, A., Owen, A.M., Boecker, H. & Brooks, D.J. (1999). Mapping the network for planning: A correlational PET activation study with the Tower of London task. *Brain*, 122: 1973–87.

Dahan, D., Magnuson, J.S. & Tanenhaus, M.K. (2001). Time course of frequency effects in spoken-word recognition: Evidence from eye movements. *Cognitive Psychology*, 42: 317–67.

Dalgleish, T., Hill, E., Golden, A.M., Morant, N. & Dunn, B.D. (2011). The structure of past and future lives in depression. *Journal of Abnormal Psychology*, 120: 1–15.

Dalton, A.L. & Daneman, M. (2006). Social suggestibility to central and peripheral misinformation. *Memory*, 14: 486–501.

Dalrymple, K.A., Kingstone, A. & Handy, T.C. (2009). Event-related potential evidence for a dual-locus model of global/local processing. *Cognitive Neuropsychology*, 26: 456–70.

Damasio, A.R. (1994). *Descartes' error: Emotion, reason and the human brain*. New York: Avon.

Danckert, J. & Ferber, S. (2006). Revisiting unilateral neglect. *Neuropsychologia*, 44: 987–1006.

Danckert, J. & Rossetti, Y. (2005). Blindsight in action: What can the different sub-types of blindsight tell us about the control of visually guided actions? *Neuroscience and Biobehavioral Reviews*, 29: 1035–46.

Danckert, J.A., Sharif, N., Haffenden, A.M., Schiff, K.C. & Goodale, M.A. (2002). A temporal analysis of grasping in the Ebbinghaus illusion: Planning versus online control. *Experimental Brain Research*, 144: 275–80.

Dando, C.J., Ormerod, T.C., Wilcock, R. & Milne, R. (2011). When help becomes hindrance: Unexpected errors of omission and commission in eyewitness memory resulting from changes in temporal order at retrieval? *Cognition*, 121: 416–21.

Danek, A.H., Fraps, T., von Müller, A., Grothe, B. & Öllinger, M. (2014). Working wonders? Investigating insight with magic tricks. *Cognition*, 130: 174–85.

Daneman, M. & Carpenter, P.A. (1980). Individual differences in working memory and reading. *Journal of Verbal Learning and Verbal Behavior*, 19: 450–66.

Daneman, M. & Merikle, P.M. (1996). Working memory and language comprehension: A meta-analysis. *Psychonomic Bulletin & Review*, 3: 422–33.

Danker, J.F. & Anderson, J.R. (2010). The ghosts of brain states past: Remembering activates the brain regions engaged during encoding. *Psychological Bulletin*, 136: 87–102.

D'Ausilio, A., Butalan, I., Salmas, P. & Fadiga, L. (2012). The role of the motor system in discriminating normal and degraded speech sounds. *Cortex*, 48: 882–7.

Davies, C. & Katsos, N. (2013). Are speakers and listeners "only moderately Gricean"? An empirical response to Engelhardt et al. (2006). *Journal of Pragmatics*, 49: 78–106.

Davies, M. (2010). Double dissociation: Understanding its role in cognitive neuropsychology. *Mind & Language*, 25: 500–40.

Davis, M.H., Marslen-Wilson, W.D. & Gaskell, M.G. (2002). Leading up the lexical garden path: Segmentation and ambiguity in spoken word recognition. *Journal of Experimental Psychology: Perception and Performance*, 28: 218–44.

Dawes, R.M. (1988). *Rational choice in an uncertain world*. San Diego, CA: Harcourt Brace Jovanovich.

Dawson, E., Gilovich, T. & Regan, D.T. (2002). Motivated reasoning and performance on the Wason selection task. *Personality and Social Psychology Bulletin*, 28: 1379–87.

Day, S.B. & Goldstone, R.L. (2011). Analogical transfer from a simulated physical system. *Journal of Experimental Psychology: Learning, Memory, and Cognition*, 37: 551–67.

de Almeida, V.M.N., Fiadeiro, P.T. & Nascimento, S.M.C. (2010). Effect of scene dimensionality on colour constancy with real three-dimensional scenes and objects. *Perception*, 39: 770–9.

Debaere, F., Wenderoth, N., Sunaert, S., van Hencke, P. & Swinnen, S.P. (2004). Changes in brain activation during the acquisition of a new bimanual coordination task. *Neuropsychologia*, 42: 855–67.

Debeer, E., Raes, F., Williams, J.M.G. & Hermans, D. (2011). Context-dependent activation of reduced autobiographical memory specificity as an avoidant coping style. *Emotion*, 11: 1500–6.

De Bleser, R. (1988). Localisation of aphasia: Science or fiction? In G. Denese, C. Semenza & P. Bisiacchi (eds), *Perspectives on cognitive neuropsychology*. Hove: Psychology Press.

de Bruin, A.B.H., Smits, N., Rikers, R.M.J.P. & Schmidt, H.G. (2008). Deliberate practice predicts performance over time in adolescent chess players and drop-outs: A linear mixed models analysis. *British Journal of Psychology*, 99: 473–97.

De Cock, S. (2004). Preferred sequences of words in NS and NNS speech. *Belgian Journal of English Language and Literatures (BELL)*, New series 2: 225–46.

Deffenbacher, K.A., Bornstein, B.H., Penroad, S.D. & McGorty, E.K. (2004). A meta-analytic review of the effects of high stress on eyewitness memory. *Law and Human Behavior*, 28: 687–706.

de Fockert, J.W., Rees, G., Frith, C.D. & Lavie, N. (2001). The role of working memory in visual selective attention. *Science*, 291: 1803–6.

de Gardelle, V., Sackur, J. & Kouider, S. (2009). Perceptual illusions in brief visual presentations. *Consciousness and Cognition*, 18: 569–77.

de Graaf, T.A., Hsieh, P.-J. & Sack, A.T. (2012). The "correlates" in neural correlates of consciousness. *Neuroscience and Biobehavioral Reviews*, 16: 191–7.

De Groot, A.D. (1965). *Thought and choice in chess*. The Hague, Netherlands: Mouton.

de Haan, B., Karnath, H.-O. & Driver, J. (2012). Mechanisms and anatomy of unilateral extinction after brain injury. *Neuropsychologia*, 50: 1045–53.

Dehaene, S. & Changeux, J.P. (2011). Experimental and theoretical approaches to conscious processing. *Neuron*, 70: 200–27.

Dehaene, S. & Naccache, L. (2001). Towards a cognitive neuroscience of consciousness. Basic evidence and a workspace framework. *Cognition*, 79: 1–37.

Delaney, P.F., Ericsson, K.A. & Knowles, M.E. (2004). Immediate and sustained effects of planning in a problem-solving task. *Journal of Experimental Psychology: Learning, Memory, and Cognition*, 30: 1219–34.

Delattre, M., Bonin, P. & Barry, C. (2006). Written spelling to dictation: Sound-to-spelling regularity affects both writing latencies and durations. *Journal of Experimental Psychology: Learning, Memory and Cognition*, 32: 1336–40.

Del Cul, A., Dehaene, S., Reyes, P., Bravo, E. & Slachevsky, A. (2009). Causal role of prefrontal cortex in the threshold for access to consciousness. *Brain*, 132: 2531–40.

Dell, G.S. (1986). A spreading-activation theory of retrieval in sentence production. *Psychological Review*, 93: 283–321.

Dell, G.S. & Caramazza, A. (2008). Introduction to special issue on computational modelling in cognitive neuropsychology. *Cognitive Neuropsychology*, 25: 131–5.

Dell, G.S., Burger, L.K. & Svec, W.R. (1997). Language production and serial order: A functional analysis and a model. *Psychological Review*, 104: 123–47.

Dell, G.S., Oppenheim, G.M. & Kittredge, A.K. (2008). Saying the right word at the right time: Syntagmatic and paradigmatic interference in sentence production. *Language and Cognitive Processes*, 23: 583–608.

Dell, G.S., Nozari, N. & Oppenheim, G.M. (2014). Word production: Behavioural and computational considerations. In M. Goldrick, V. Ferreira, and M. Miozzo (eds), *The Oxford handbook of language production*. Oxford: Oxford University Press.

DeLong, K.A., Urbach, T.P. & Kutas, M. (2005). Probabilistic word pre-activation during language comprehension inferred from electrical brain activity. *Nature Neuroscience*, 8: 1117–21.

DeLucia, P.R. (2013). Effects of size on collision perception and implications for perceptual theory and transportation safety. *Current Directions in Psychological Science*, 22: 199–204.

De Martino, B., Camerer, C.F. & Adolphs, R. (2010). Amygdala damage eliminates monetary loss aversion. *Proceedings of the National Academy of Sciences*, 107: 3788–92.

De Neys, W. (2006). Dual processing in reasoning: Two systems but one reasoner. *Psychological Science*, 17: 428–33.

De Neys, W. (2012). Bias and conflict: A case for logical intuitions. *Perspectives on Psychological Science*, 7: 28–38.

De Neys, W. (2014). Conflict detection, dual processes, and logical intuitions: Some clarifications. *Thinking & Reasoning*, 20: 169–87.

De Neys, W. & Glumicic, T. (2008). Conflict monitoring in dual process theories of reasoning. *Cognition*, 106: 1248–99.

De Neys, W. & Verschueren, N. (2006). Working memory capacity and a notorious brain teaser – The case of the Monty Hall dilemma. *Experimental Psychology*, 53: 123–31.

De Neys, W., Schaeken, W. & d'Ydewalle, G. (2005). Working memory and everyday conditional reasoning: Retrieval and inhibition of stored counterexamples. *Thinking & Reasoning*, 11: 349–81.

De Neys, W., Vartanian, O. & Goel, V. (2008). Smarter than we think: when our brains detect that we are biased. *Psychological Science*, 19: 483–9.

De Neys, W., Moyens, E. & Vansteenwegen, D. (2010). Feeling we're biased: Autonomic arousal and reasoning conflict. *Cognitive, Affective & Behavioral Neuroscience*, 12: 123–30.

De Neys, W., Cromheeke, S. & Osman, M. (2011). Biased but in doubt: Conflict and decision confidence. *PLOS ONE*, 6(1): e15954.

Depue, B.E., Burgess, G.C., Wilcutt, E.G., Ruzic, L. & Banich, M.T. (2010). Inhibitory control of memory retrieval and motor processing associated with the right lateral prefrontal cortex: Evidence from deficits in individuals with ADHD. *Neuropsychologia*, 48: 3909–17.

De Raedt, R. & Koster, E.H.W (2010). Understanding vulnerability for depression from a cognitive neuroscience perspective: A reappraisal of attentional factors and a new conceptual framework. *Cognitive, Affective & Behavioral Neuroscience*, 10: 50–70.

Destrebecqz, A., Peigneux, P., Laureys, S. Degueldre, C., Del Fiore, G., Aerts, J., Luxen, A., Van der Linden, M., Cleeremans, A. & Maquet, P. (2005). The neural correlates of implicit and explicit sequence learning: Interacting networks revealed by the process dissociation procedure. *Learning and Memory*, 12: 480–90.

Deutsch, J.A. & Deutsch, D. (1963). Attention: Some theoretical considerations. *Psychological Review*, 93: 283–321.

DeValois, R.L. & DeValois, K.K. (1975). Neural coding of colour. In E.C. Carterette & M.P. Friedman (eds), *Handbook of perception, vol. 5*. New York: Academic Press.

de Vanssay-Maigne, A., Noulhiane, M., Devauchelle, A.D., Rodrigo, S., Baudoin-Chial, S., Meder, J.F., Oppenheim, C., Chiron, C. & Chassoux, F. (2011). Modulation of encoding and retrieval by recollection and familiarity: Mapping the medial temporal lobe networks. *Neuroimage*, 58: 1131–8.

de Vries, M., Holland, R.W. & Witteman, C.L.M. (2008). Fitting decisions: Mood and intuitive versus deliberative decision-strategies. *Cognition & Emotion*, 22: 931–43.

de Vries, M., Holland, R.W., Corneille, O., Rondeel, E.J.E. & Witteman, C.L.M. (2012). Mood effects on dominated choices: Positive mood induces departures from logical rules. *Journal of Behavioral Decision Making*, 25: 74–81.

Dew, I.T.Z. & Cabeza, R. (2011). The porous boundaries between explicit and implicit memory: Behavioral and neural evidence. *Annals of the New York Academy of Sciences*, 1224: 174–90.

Dewar, M.T., Cowan, N. & Della Sala, S. (2007). Forgetting due to retroactive interference: A fusion of Müller and Pizecker's (1900) early insights into everyday forgetting and recent research on retrograde amnesia. *Cortex*, 43: 616–34.

Dewar, M.T., Della Sala, S., Beschin, N. & Cowan, N. (2010). Profound retroactive amnesia: What interferes? *Neuropsychology*, 24: 357–67.

Diamond, R. & Carey, S. (1986). Why faces are and are not special: An effect of expertise. *Journal of Experimental Psychology: General*, 115: 107–17.

Diana, R.A., Yonelinas, A.P. & Ranganath, C. (2007). Imaging recollection and familiarity in the medial temporal lobe: A three-component model. *Trends in Cognitive Sciences*, 11: 379–86.

Dick, F., Bates, E., Wulfeck, B., Utman, J.A., Dronkers, N. & Gernsbacher, M.A. (2001). Language deficits, localization, and grammar: Evidence for a distributive model of language breakdown in aphasic patients and neurologically intact individuals. *Psychological Review*, 108: 759–88.

Dickson, R.A., Pillemer, D.B. & Bruehl, E.C. (2011). The reminiscence bump for salient personal memories: Is a cultural life script required? *Memory & Cognition*, 39: 977–91.

Dieckmann, A. & Rieskamp, J. (2007). The influence of information redundancy on probabilistic inferences. *Memory & Cognition*, 35: 1801–13.

Dijkerman, H.C., Milner, A.D. & Carey, D.P. (1998). Grasping spatial relationships: Failure to demonstrate allocentric visual coding in a patient with visual form agnosia. *Consciousness and Cognition*, 7: 424–37.

Dijksterhuis, A. & Nordgren, L.F. (2006). A theory of unconscious thought. *Perspectives on Psychological Science*, 1: 95–180.

Dijksterhuis, A., Bos, M.W., Nordgren, L.F. & Van Baaren, R.B. (2006). On making the right choice: The deliberation-without-attention effect. *Science*, 311: 1005–7.

Dikker, S. & Pylkkänen, L. (2013). Predicting language: MEG evidence for lexical presentation. *Brain & Language*, 127: 55–64.

Di Russo, F., Aprile, T., Spitoni, G. & Spinelli, D. (2008). Impaired visual processing of contralesional stimuli in neglect patients: A visual-evoked potential study. *Brain*, 131: 842–54.

Dismukes, R.K. (2012). Prospective memory in workplace and everyday situations. *Current Directions in Psychological Science*, 21: 215–20.

Dismukes, R.K. & Nowinski, J.L. (2006). Prospective memory, concurrent task management, and pilot error. In A. Kramer, D. Wiegmann & A. Kirlik (eds), *Attention: From theory to practice*. Oxford: Oxford University Press.

Di Stasi, L.L. & Guardini, P. (2007). Perceiving affordances in virtual environments: Visual guidance of virtual stair climbing. *Perception*, 36 (Suppl. S): 186.

Ditto, P.H., Scepansky, J.A., Munro, G.D., Apanovitch, A.M. & Lockhart, L.K. (1998). Motivated sensitivity to preference inconsistent information. *Journal of Personality and Social Psychology*, 75: 53–69.

Dixon, P. & Bortolussi, M. (2013). Construction, integration, and mind wandering in reading. *Canadian Journal of Experimental Psychology*, 67: 1–10.

Dodhia, R.M. & Dismukes, K.R. (2009). Interruptions create prospective memory tasks. *Applied Cognitive Psychology*, 23: 73–89.

Domini, F., Shah, R. & Caudek, C. (2011). Do we perceive a flattened world on the monitor screen? *Acta Psychologica*, 138: 359–66.

Downing, P.E., Chan, A.W.Y., Peelen, M.V., Dodds, C.M. & Kanwisher, N. (2006). Domain specificity in visual cortex. *Cerebral Cortex*, 16: 1453–61.

Drace, S., Desrichard, O., Shepperd, J.A. & Hoorens, V. (2009). Does mood really influence comparative optimism? Tracing an elusive effect. *British Journal of Social Psychology*, 92: 53–78.

Dror, I.E., Charlton, D. & Péron, A.E. (2006). Contextual information renders experts vulnerable to making erroneous identifications. *Forensic Science International*, 156: 74–8.

Dror, I.E., Champod, C., Langenburg, G., Charlton, D., Hunt, H. & Rosenthal, R. (2011). Cognitive issues in fingerprint analysis: Inter- and intra-expert consistency and the effect of a "target" comparison. *Forensic Science International*, 208: 10–17.

Dror, I.E., Wertheim, K., Fraser-Mackenzie, P. & Walajtys, J. (2012). The impact of human-technology co-operation and distributed cognition in forensic science: Biasing effects of AFIS contextual information on human experts. *Journal of Forensic Sciences*, 57: 343–52.

Drummond, L. & Shomstein, S. (2010). Object-based attention: Shifting or uncertainty? *Attention, Perception & Psychophysics*, 72: 1743–55.

Duchaine, B.C. & Nakayama, K. (2006). Developmental prosopagnosia: A window to context-specific face processing. *Current Opinion in Neurobiology*, 16: 166–73.

Dudai, Y. & Morris, R.G.M. (2013). Memory trends. *Neuron*, 80: 742–50.

Dudokovic, N.M., Marsh, E.J. & Tversky, B. (2004). Telling a story or telling it straight: The effects of entertaining versus accurate retellings on memory. *Applied Cognitive Psychology*, 18: 125–43.

Duffy, S.A. & Pisoni, D.B. (1992). Comprehension of synthetic speech produced by rule: A review and theoretical interpretation. *Language and Speech*, 35: 351–89.

Dufour, S., Bruneilliere, A. & Frauenfelder, U.H. (2013). Tracking the time course of word-frequency effects in auditory word recognition with event-related potentials. *Cognitive Science*, 37: 489–507.

Dunbar, K. (1993). Concept discovery in a scientific domain. *Cognitive Science*, 17: 397–434.

Dunbar, K. & Blanchette, I. (2001). The analogical paradox: Why analogy is so easy in naturalistic settings, yet so difficult in the psychological laboratory. In D. Genter, K. Holyoak & B. Kokinov (eds), *Analogy: Perspectives from cognitive science* (pp. 313–34). Cambridge, MA: MIT Press.

Dunbar, K. & Klahr, D. (2012). Scientific thinking and reasoning. In K.J. Holyoak & R.G. Morrison (eds), *The Oxford handbook of thinking and reasoning*. Oxford: Oxford University Press.

Duncan, J. & Humphreys, G.W. (1989). A resemblance theory of visual search. *Psychological Review*, 96: 433–58.

Duncan, J. & Humphreys, G.W. (1992). Beyond the search surface: Visual search and attentional engagement. *Journal of Experimental Psychology: Human Perceptiom & Performance*, 18: 578–88.

Duncan, J. & Owen, A.M. (2000). Consistent response of the human frontal lobe to diverse cognitive demands. *Trends in Neurosciences*, 23: 475–83.

Duncan, J., Bundesen, C., Olson, A., Humphreys, G., Chavda, S. & Shibuya, H. (1999). Systematic analysis of deficits in visual attention. *Journal of Experimental Psychology: General*, 128: 450–78.

Duncker, K. (1945). On problem solving. *Psychological Monographs*, 58(5): i–113.

Dunlosky, J., Rawson, K.A., Marsh, E.J., Nathan, M.J. & Willingham, D.T. (2013). Improving students' learning with effective learning techniques: Promising directions from cognitive and educational psychology. *Psychological Science in the Public Interest*, 14: 4–58.

Dunn, B.D., Galton, H.C., Morgan, R., Evans, D., Oliver, C., Meyer, M., Cusack, R., Lawrence, A.D. & Dalgleish, T. (2010). Listening to your heart: How interoception shapes emotion experience and intuitive decision making. *Psychological Science*, 21: 1835–44.

Dunn, J.C. (2008). The dimensionality of the remember-know task: A state-trace analysis. *Psychological Review*, 115: 426–46.

Dunning, D. (2011). The Dunning Kruger effect: On being ignorant of one's own ignorance. *Advances in Experimental Social Psychology*, 44: 247–96.

Duss, S.B., Oggier, S., Reber, T.P. & Henke, K. (2011). Formation of semantic associations between subliminally presented face-word pairs. *Consciousness and Cognition*, 20: 928–35.

Dutke, S. & von Hecker, U. (2011). Comprehending ambiguous texts: A high reading span helps to constraint the situation model. *Journal of Cognitive Psychology*, 23: 227–42.

Dutton, J.M. & Starbuck, W.H. (1971). *Computer simulation of human behaviour*. New York: Wiley.

Dwivedi, V.D. (2013). Interpreting quantifier scope ambiguity: Evidence of heuristic first, algorithmic second processing. *PLOS ONE*, 8(11): e81461.

Eagle, M.N., Gallese, V. & Migone, P. (2007). Intentional attunement: Mirror neurons and the neural underpinnings of interpersonal relations. *Journal of the American Psychoanalytic Association*, 55: 131–76.

Eakin, D.K. & Smith, R. (2012). Retroactive interference effects in implicit memory. *Journal of Experimental Psychology: Learning, Memory, and Cognition*, 38: 1419–24.

Easterbrook, J.A. (1959). The effect of emotion on cue utilisation and the organisation of behaviour. *Psychological Review*, 66: 183–201.

Eaton, E., Marshall, J. & Pring, T. (2011). Mechanisms of change in the evolution of jargon aphasia. *Aphasiology*, 25: 1543–61.

Ebbinghaus, H. (1885/1913). *Über das Gedächtnis* (Leipzig: Dunker) (trans. H. Ruyer & C.E. Bussenius). New York: Teacher College, Columbus University.

Ecker, U.K.H., Lewandowsky, S. & Tang, D.T.W. (2010). Explicit warnings reduce but do not eliminate the continued influence of misinformation. *Memory & Cognition*, 38: 1087–00.

Edelson, M., Sharot, T., Dolan, R.J. & Dudai, Y. (2011). Following the crowd: Brain substrates of long-term memory conformity. *Science*, 333: 108–11.

Egly, R., Driver, J. & Rafal, R.D. (1994). Shifting visual attention between objects and locations: Evidence from normal and parietal lesion subjects. *Journal of Experimental Psychology: General*, 123: 161–77.

Ehinger, K.A., Hidalgo-Sotelo, B., Torraiba, A. & Oliva, A. (2009). Modelling search for people in 900 scenes: A combined source model of eye guidance. *Visual Cognition*, 17: 945–78.

Eich, E. (1995). Searching for mood-dependent memory. *Psychological Science*, 6: 67–75.

Eich, E. & Metcalfe, J. (1989). Mood-dependent memory for internal versus external events. *Journal of Experimental Psychology: Learning, Memory & Cognition*, 15: 443–55.

Eichenbaum, H. (2015, in press). Amnesia: Beyond Scoville and Milner's (1957) research on HM. In M.W. Eysenck & D. Groome (eds), *Cognitive psychology: Revisiting the classic studies*. London: SAGE.

Eimer, M. & Schröger, E. (1998). ERP effects of intermodal attention and crossmodal links in spatial attention. *Psychophysiology*, 35: 317–28.

Einstein, G.O. & McDaniel, M.A. (2005). Prospective memory: Multiple retrieval processes. *Current Directions in Psychological Science*, 14: 286–90.

Eitam, B., Yeshurun, Y. & Hassan, K. (2013). Blinded by irrelevance: Pure irrelevance induced "blindness". *Journal of Experimental Psychology: Human Perception and Performance*, 39: 611–15.

Elder, J.H. & Goldberg, R.M. (2002). Ecological statistics of Gestalt laws for the perceptual organisation of contours. *Journal of Vision*, 2: 324–53.

Ellis, A.W. (1984). *Reading, writing and dyslexia: A cognitive analysis*. London: Lawrence Erlbaum Associates.

Ellis, A.W. & Young, A.W. (1988). *Human cognitive neuropsychology*. Hove: Psychology Press.

Ellis, J.J. & Glaholt, M.G. & Reingold, E.M. (2011). Eye movements reveal solution knowledge prior to insight. *Consciousness and Cognition*, 20: 768–76.

Elqayam, S. & Evans, J.St.B.T. (2011). Subtracting "ought" from "is": Descriptivism versus normatism in the study of human thinking. *Behavioral and Brain Sciences*, 34: 233–48.

Engbert, R. & Kliegl, R. (2011). Parallel graded attention models of reading. In S.P. Liversedge, I.D. Gilchrist & S. Everling (eds), *The Oxford handbook of eye movements* (pp. 787–800). Oxford: Oxford University Press.

Engbert, R., Nuthmann, A., Richter, E.M. & Kliegl, R. (2005). SWIFT: A dynamical model of saccade generation during reading. *Psychological Review*, 112: 777–813.

Engel, P.J.H. (2008). Tacit knowledge and visual expertise in medical diagnostic reasoning: Implications for medical education. *Medical Teacher*, 30: e184–8.

Engelhardt, P.E., Bailey, K.G.D. & Ferreira, F. (2006). Do speakers and listeners observe the Gricean maxim of quantity? *Journal of Memory and Language*, 54: 554–73.

Engle, R.W. & Kane, M.J. (2004). Executive attention, working memory capacity and a two-factor theory of cognitive control. In B. Ross (ed.), *The psychology of learning and motivation*, (pp. 145–99). New York: Elsevier.

Ericsson, K.A. & Chase, W.G. (1982). Exceptional memory. *American Scientist*, 70: 607–15.

Ericsson, K.A. & Kintsch, W. (1995). Long-term working memory. *Psychological Review*, 102: 211–45.

Ericsson, K.A. & Moxley, J.H. (2012). A critique of Howard's argument for innate limits in chess performance or why we need an account based on acquired skill and deliberate practice. *Applied Cognitive Psychology*, 26: 649–53.

Ericsson, K.A. & Towne, T.J. (2010). Expertise. *Wiley International Reviews: Cognitive Science*, 1: 404–16.

Eriksen, C.W. & St James, J.D. (1986). Visual attention within and around the field of focal attention: A zoom lens model. *Perception & Psychophysics*, 40: 225–40.

Eriksson, J., Larsson, A., Ahlströn, K.R. & Nyberg, L. (2006). Similar frontal and distinct posterior cortical regions mediate visual and auditory perceptual awareness. *Cerebral Cortex*, 17: 760–5.

Ernst, M.O. & Bülthoff, H.H. (2004). Merging the senses into a robust percept. *Trends in Cognitive Sciences*, 8: 162–9.

Esteves-Sorenson, C. & Perretti, F. (2012). Micro-costs: Inertia in television viewing. *The Economic Journal*, 122: 867–902.

Evans, J.St.B.T. (1998). Matching bias in conditional reasoning: Do we understand it after 25 years? *Thinking & Reasoning*, 4: 45–82.

Evans, J.St.B.T. (2000). What could and could not be a strategy in reasoning. In W. Schaeken, G. De Vooghe, A. Vandierendonck & G. d'Ydewalle, (eds), *Deductive reasoning and strategies*. Hove: Lawrence Erlbaum Associates.

Evans, J.St.B.T. (2006). The heuristic-analytic theory of reasoning: Extension and evaluation. *Psychonomic Bulletin & Review*, 13: 378–95.

Evans, J.St.B.T. (2008). Dual-processing accounts of reasoning, judgment, and social cognition. *Annual Review of Psychology*, 59: 255–78.

Evans, J.St.B.T. (2011). Reasoning is for thinking, not just for arguing. *Behavioral and Brain Sciences*, 34: 77–8.

Evans, J.St.B.T. (2012). Questions and challenges for the new psychology of reasoning. *Thinking & Reasoning*, 18: 5–31.

Evans, J.St.B.T. & Ball, L.J. (2010). Do people reason on the Wason selection task? A new look at the data of Ball et al. (2003). *Quarterly Journal of Experimental Psychology*, 63: 434–41.

Evans, J.St.B.T. & Curtis-Holmes, J. (2005). Rapid responding increases belief bias: Evidence for dual-process theories of reasoning. *Thinking & Reasoning*, 11: 382–89.

Evans, J.St.B.T. & Over, D.E. (2010). Heuristic thinking and human intelligence: A commentary on Marewski, Gaissmaier and Gigerenzer. *Cognitive Processing*, 11: 171–5.

Evans, J.St.B.T. & Stanovich, K.E. (2013). Dual-process theories of higher cognition: Advancing the debate. *Perspectives on Psychological Science*, 8: 223–41.

Evans, J.St.B.T., Newstead, S.E. & Byrne, R.J. (1993). *Human reasoning: The psychology of deduction*. Hove: Psychology Press.

Evans, J.St.B.T., Handley, S.J., Perham, N., Over, D.E. & Thompson, V.A. (2000). Frequency versus probability formats in statistical word problems. *Cognition*, 77: 197–213.

Evans, N. & Levinson, S. (2009). The myth of language universals: Language diversity and its importance for cognitive science. *Behavioral and Brain Sciences*, 32: 429–92.

Everaert, J., Koster, E.H.W. & Derakshan, N. (2012). The combined cognitive bias hypothesis in depression. *Clinical Psychology Review*, 32: 413–24.

Everett, D.L. (2005). Cultural constraints on grammar and cognition in Piraha. *Current Anthropology*, 46: 621–46.

Eysenck, M.W. (1979). Depth, elaboration, and distinctiveness. In L.S. Cermak & F.I.M. Craik (eds), *Levels of processing in human memory*. Hillsdale, NJ: Lawrence Erlbaum Associates.

Eysenck, M.W. (2013). *Simply psychology* (3rd edn). Hove: Psychology Press.

Eysenck, M.W. (2015, in press). Attention: Beyond Cherry's (1953) cocktail party problem. In M.W. Eysenck & D. Groome (eds), *Cognitive psychology: Revisiting the classic studies*. London: SAGE.

Eysenck, M.W. & Eysenck, M.C. (1980). Effects of processing depth, distinctiveness, and word frequency on retention. *British Journal of Psychology*, 71: 263–74.

Eysenck, M.W. & Groome, D. (2015, in press). Memory systems: Beyond Tulving's (1972) episodic and semantic memory. In M.W. Eysenck & D. Groome (eds), *Cognitive psychology: Revisiting the classic studies*. London: SAGE.

Eysenck, M.W., Macleod, C. & Mathews, A. (1987). Cognitive functioning and anxiety. *Psychological Research*, 49: 189–95.

Eysenck, M.W., Mogg, K., May, J., Richards, A. & Mathews, A. (1991). Bias in interpretation of ambiguous sentences related to threat in anxiety. *Journal of Abnormal Psychology*, 100: 144–50.

Eysenck, M.W., Payne, S. & Santos, R. (2006). Anxiety and depression: Past, present, and future events. *Cognition & Emotion*, 20: 274–94.

Eysenck, M.W., Derakshan, N., Santos, R. & Calvo, M.G. (2007). Anxiety and cognitive performance: Attentional control theory. *Emotion*, 7: 336–53.

Ezzyat, Y. & Davachi, L. (2011). What constitutes an episode in episodic memory? *Psychological Science*, 22: 243–52.

Fahle, M.W., Stemmler, T. & Spang, K.M. (2011). How much of the "unconscious" is just pre-threshold? *Frontiers in Human Neuroscience*, 5 (Article 120).

Fahrenfort, J.J., Scholte, H.S. & Lamme, V.A.F. (2007). Masking disrupts re-entrant processing in human visual cortex. *Journal of Cognitive Neuroscience*, 19: 1488–97.

Falk, R. & Lann, A. (2008). The allure of equality: Uniformity in probabilistic and statistical judgment. *Cognitive Psychology*, 57: 293–334.

Fama, R., Pitel, A.-L. & Sullivan, E.V. (2012). Anterograde episodic memory in Korsakoff syndrome. *Neuropsychology Review*, 22: 93–104.

Fangmeier, T. & Knauff, M. (2009). Neural correlates of acoustic reasoning. *Brain Research*, 1249: 181–90.

Fangmeier, T., Knauff, M., Ruff, C.C. & Sloutky, V.M. (2006). fMRI evidence for a three-stage model of deductive reasoning. *Journal of Cognitive Neuroscience*, 18: 320–34.

Farag, C., Troiani, V., Bonner, M., Powers, C., Avants, B., Gee, J. & Grossman, M. (2010). Hierarchical organization of scripts: Converging evidence from fMRI and fronto-temporal degeneration. *Cerebral Cortex*, 20: 2453–63.

Farah, M.J. (1994). Specialisations within visual object recognition: Clues from prosopagnosia and alexia. In M.J. Farah & G. Ratcliff (eds), *The neuropsychology of high-level vision: Collected tutorial essays*. Hillsdale, NJ: Lawrence Erlbaum Associates.

Farah, M.J. (2001). Consciousness. In B. Rapp (ed.), *Handbook of cognitive neuropsychology*. Hove: Psychology Press.

Farivar, R. (2009). Dorsal-ventral integration in object recognition. *Brain Research Review*, 61: 144–53.

Faulkner, P. (2008). Cooperation and trust in conversational exchanges. *Theoria*, 23: 23–34.

Fawcett, J.M., Russell, E.J., Peace, K.A. & Christie, J. (2013). Of guns and geese: A meta-analytic review of the "weapon focus" literature. *Psychology, Crime & Law*, 19: 35–66.

Feldman, J. (2013). The neural binding problem(s). *Cognitive Neurodynamics*, 7: 1–11.

Felleman, D.J. & Van Essen, D.C. (1991). Distributed hierarchical processing in the primate cerebral cortex. *Cerebral Cortex*, 1: 1–47.

Ferber, R. (1995). Reliability and validity of slip-of-the-tongue corpora: A methodological note. *Linguistics*, 33: 1169–90.

Ferguson, S., Rayport, M. & Corrie, W. (1985). Neuropsychiatric observations on behavioural consequences of corpus callosum section for seizure control. In A. Reeves (ed.), *Epilepsy and the corpus callosum*. New York: Plenum Press.

Fernandes, T., Ventura, P. & Kolinsky, R. (2007). Statistical information and coarticulation as cues to word boundaries: A matter of signal quality. *Perception & Psychophysics*, 69: 856–64.

Fernandes, T., Kolinsky, R. & Ventura, P. (2010). The impact of attention load on the use of statistical information and coarticulation as speech segmentation cues. *Attention, Perception & Psychophysics*, 72: 1522–32.

Ferreira, F. (2003). The misinterpretation of noncanonical sentences. *Cognitive Psychology*, 47: 164–203.

Ferreira, F. & Swets, B. (2002). How incremental is language production? Evidence from the production of utterances requiring the computation of arithmetic sums. *Journal of Memory and Language*, 46: 57–84.

Ferreira, F., Bailey, K.G.D. & Ferraro, V. (2002). Good-enough representations in language comprehension. *Current Directions in Psychological Science*, 11: 11–15.

Ferreira, F., Foucart, A. & Engelhardt, P.E. (2013). Language processing in the visual world: Effects of preview, visual complexity and prediction. *Journal of Memory and Language*, 69: 165–82.

Ferreira, V.S. (2008). Ambiguity, accessibility, and a division of labour for communicative success. *Psychology of Learning and Motivation: Advances in Research and Theory*, 49: 209–46.

Ferreira, V.S. & Griffin, Z.M. (2003). Phonological influences on lexical (mis)selection. *Psychological Science*, 14: 86–90.

ffytche, D.H. & Zeki, S. (2011). The primary visual cortex, and feedback to it, are not necessary for conscious vision. *Brain*, 134: 247–57.

ffytche, D.H., Howard, R.J., Brammer, M.J., Woodruff, D.P. & Williams, S. (1998). The anatomy of conscious vision: An fMRI study of visual hallucinations. *Nature Neuroscience*, 1: 738–42.

Fiedler, K. (1988). The dependence of the conjunction fallacy on subtle linguistic factors. *Psychological Research*, 50: 123–9.

Fiedler, K. (2008). The ultimate sampling dilemma in experience-based decision making. *Journal of Experimental Psychology: Learning, Memory, and Cognition*, 34: 186–203.

Fiedler, K. & von Sydow, M. (2015, in press). Heuristics and biases: Beyond Tversky and Kahneman's (1974) judgment under uncertainty. In M.W. Eysenck & D. Groome (eds), *Cognitive psychology: Revisiting the classic studies*. London: SAGE.

Fiedler, K., Brinkmann, B., Betsch, T. & Wild, B. (2000). A sampling approach to biases in conditional probability judgments: Beyond base-rate neglect and statistical format. *Journal of Experimental Psychology: General*, 129: 1–20.

Filik, R. & Barber, E. (2012). Inner speech during silent reading reflects the reader's regional accent. *PLOS ONE*, 6(10): e25782.

Filmer, H.L., Mattingley, J.B. & Dux, P.E. (2013). Improved multitasking following prefrontal tDCS. *Cortex*, 49: 2845–52.

Fischer, J. & Whitney, D. (2014). Serial dependence in visual perception. *Nature Neuroscience*, 17: 738–46.

Fischer, P. & Greitemeyer, T. (2010). A new look at selective-exposure effects: An integrative model. *Current Directions in Psychological Science*, 19: 384–9.

Fisher, R.P. & Geiselman, (1992). *Memory enhancing techniques for investigative interviewing: The cognitive interview*. Springfield, IL: C.C. Thomas.

Fitousi, D. & Wenger, M.J. (2013). Variants of independence in the perception of facial identity and expression. *Journal of Experimental Psychology: Human Perception and Performance*, 39: 133–55.

Fivush, R. (2010). The development of autobiographical memory. *Annual Review of Psychology*, 62: 2–24.

Fivush, R. & Nelson, K. (2004). Culture and language in the emergence of autobiographical memory. *Psychological Science*, 15: 573–7.

Flevaris, A.V., Martinez, A. & Hillyard, S.A. (2014). Attending to global versus local stimulus features modulates neural processing of low versus high spatial frequencies: An analysis with event-related brain potentials. *Frontiers in Psychology*, 5 (Article 277).

Foerde, K. & Poldrack, R.A. (2009). Procedural learning in humans. In L.R. Squire (ed.), *The new encylopaedia of neuroscience, vol. 7* (pp. 1083–91).

Foerde, K. & Shohamy, D. (2011). The role of the basal ganglia in learning and memory: Insight from Parkinson's disease. *Neurobiology of Learning and Memory*, 96: 624–36.

Foerde, K., Knowlton, B.J. & Poldrack, R.A. (2006). Modulation of competing memory systems by distraction. *Proceedings of the National Academy of Sciences*, 103: 3531–42.

Fontaine, J.R.J., Scherer, K.R. & Soriano, C. (eds) (2013*). Components of emotional meaning: A sourcebook*. Oxford: Oxford University Press.

Forster, S. & Lavie, N. (2008). Failures to ignore entirely irrelevant distractors: The role of load. *Journal of Experimental Psychology: Applied*, 14: 73–83.

Forster, S. & Lavie, N. (2009). Harnessing the wandering mind: The role of perceptual load. *Cognition*, 111: 345–55.

Foster, D.H. (2011). Colour constancy. *Vision Research*, 51: 674–700.

Foster, D.H. & Nascimento, S.M.C. (1994). Relational colour constancy from invariant cone-excitation ratios. *Proceedings of the Royal Society of London Series B – Biological Sciences*, 257: 115–21.

Foster, J.D., Reidy, D.E., Misra, T.A. & Goff, J.S. (2011). Narcissism and stock market investing: Correlates and consequences of cocksure investing. *Personality and Individual Differences*, 50: 816–21.

Foster, N.E. & Zatorre, R.J. (2010). Cortical structure predicts success in performing musical transformation judgments. *NeuroImage*, 53: 26–36.

Fowlkes, C.C., Martin, D.R. & Malik, J. (2007). Local figure-ground cues are valid for natural images. *Journal of Vision*, 7(8) (Article 2).

Fox, C.J., Hanif, H.M., Iaria, G., Duchaine, B.C. & Barton, J.J.S. (2011). Perceptual and anatomic patterns of selective deficits in facial identity and expression processing. *Neuropsychologia*, 49: 3188–200.

Fox, E. (2008). *Emotion science*. New York: Palgrave Macmillan.

Frank, M.C., Everett, D.L., Fedorenko, E. & Gibson, E. (2008). Number as a cognitive technology: Evidence from Pirahã language and cognition. *Cognition*, 108: 819–24.

Franklin, S., Turner, J., Lambon Ralph, M.A., Morris, J. & Bailey, P.J. (1996). A distinctive case of word meaning deafness? *Cognitive Neuropsychology*, 13: 1139–62.

Franz, V.H. & Gegenfurtner, K.R. (2008). Grasping visual illusions: Consistent data and no dissociation. *Cognitive Neuropsychology*, 25: 920–50.

Frauenfelder, U.H., Segui, J. & Dijkstra, T. (1990). Lexical effects in phonemic processing: Facilitatory or inhibitory? *Journal of Experimental Psychology: Human Perception & Performance*, 16: 77–91.

Frauenfelder, U.H., Scholten, M. & Content, A. (2001). Bottom-up inhibition in lexical selection: Phonological mismatch effects in spoken word recognition. *Language and Cognitive Processes*, 16: 583–607.

Frazier, L. & Rayner, K. (1982). Making and correcting errors during sentence comprehension: Eye movements in the analysis of structurally ambiguous sentences. *Cognitive Psychology*, 14: 178–210.

Frazier, L., Carlson, K. & Clifton, C. (2006). Prosodic phrasing is central to language comprehension. *Trends in Cognitive Sciences*, 10: 244–9.

Frederick, S. (2005). Cognitive reflection and decision making. *Journal of Economic Perspectives*, 19: 25–42.

Fredrickson, B.L. & Branigan, C. (2005). Positive emotions broaden the scope of attention and thought-action repertoires. *Cognition & Emotion*, 19: 313–32.

Freeman, J. & Simoncelli, E.P. (2011). Metamers of the ventral stream. *Nature Neuroscience*, 14: 1195–201.

Frenda, S.J., Nichols, R.M. & Loftus, E.F. (2011). Current issues and advances in misinformation research. *Current Directions in Psychological Science*, 20: 20–3.

Freud, S. (1915/1957). Repression. In *Freud's Collected Papers, vol. 4*. London: Hogarth Press.

Frick-Horbury, D. & Guttentag, R.E. (1998). The effects of restricting hand gesture production on lexical retrieval and free recall. *American Journal of Psychology*, 111: 43–62.

Friederici, A.D., Fiebach, C.J., Schlesewsky, M., Bornkessel, L.D. & von Cramon, D.Y. (2006). Processing linguistic complexity and grammaticality in the left frontal cortex. *Cerebral Cortex*, 16: 1707–17.

Friedman, N.P., Miyake, A., Young, S.E., DeFries, J.C., Corley, R.P. & Hewitt, J.K. (2008). Individual differences in executive functions are almost entirely genetic in origin. *Journal of Experimental Psychology: General*, 137: 201–25.

Friedman, R.S. & Förster, J. (2010). Implicit affective cues and attentional tuning: An integrative review. *Psychological Bulletin*, 136: 875–93.

Friedman-Hill, S.R., Robertson, L.C. & Treisman, A. (1995). Parietal contributions to visual feature binding: Evidence from a patient with bilateral lesions. *Science*, 269: 853–5.

Friedrich, C.K. & Kotz, S.A. (2007). Event-related potential evidence of form and meaning coding during online speech recognition. *Journal of Cognitive Neuroscience*, 19: 594–604.

Frost, R. (1998). Toward a strong phonological theory of visual word recognition: True issues and false trails. *Psychological Bulletin*, 123: 71–99.

Fugelsang, J.A., Stein, C.B., Green, A.E. & Dunbar, K.N. (2004). Theory and data interactions of the scientific mind: Evidence from the molecular and the cognitive laboratory. *Canadian Journal of Experimental Psychology*, 58: 86–95.

Fukumura, K. & van Gompel, R.P.G. (2012). Producing pronouns and definite noun phrases: Do speakers use the addressee's discourse model? *Cognitive Science*, 36: 1289–311.

Gable, P.A. & Harmon-Jones, E. (2010a). The effect of low versus high approach-motivated positive affect on memory for peripherally versus centrally presented information. *Emotion*, 10: 599–603.

Gable, P. & Harmon-Jones, E. (2010b). The blues broaden, but the nasty narrows: Attentional consequences of negative affects low and high in motivational intensity. *Psychological Science*, 21: 211–15.

Gable, P.A. & Harmon-Jones, E. (2011). Attentional consequences of pregoal and postgoal positive affects. *Emotion*, 11: 1358–67.

Gabrieli, J.D.E., Fleischman, D., Keane, M., Reminger, S. & Morrell, F. (1995). Double dissociation between memory systems underlying explicit and implicit memory in the human brain. *Psychological Science*, 6: 76–82.

Gaesser, B., Spreng, R.N., McLelland, V.C., Addis, D.R. & Schacter, D.L. (2013). Imagining the future: Evidence for a hippocampal contribution to constructive processing. *Hippocampus*, 23: 1150–61.

Gagnepain, P., Henson, R.N. & Davis, M.H. (2012). Temporal predictive codes for spoken words in auditory cortex. *Current Biology*, 22: 615–21.

Gaillard, R., Dehaene, S., Adam, C., Clémenceau, S., Hasboun, D., Baulac, M., et al. (2009). Converging intracranial markers of conscious access. *PLOS Biology*, 7: e1000061.

Gainotti, G. & Ciaraffa, F. (2013). Is "object-centred neglect" a homogeneous entity? *Brain and Cognition*, 81: 18–23.

Gainotti, G. & Marra, C. (2011). Differential contributions of right and left temporo-occipital and anterior temporal lesions to face recognition disorders. *Frontiers in Human Neuroscience*, 5: 55.

Galati, A. & Brennan, S.E. (2010). Attenuating information in spoken communication: For the speaker, or for the addressee? *Journal of Memory and Language*, 62: 35–51.

Galbraith, D., Ford, S., Walker, G. & Ford, J. (2005). The contribution of different components of working memory to planning in writing. *L1 Educational Studies in Language and Literature*, 15: 113–45.

Gale, M. & Ball, L.J. (2012). Contrast class cues and performance facilitation in a hypothesis-testing task: Evidence for an iterative counterfactual model. *Memory & Cognition*, 40: 408–19.

Gallese, V. & Sinigaglia, C. (2014). Understanding action with the motor system. *Behavioral and Brain Sciences*, 37: 199–200.

Gallese, V., Fadiga, L., Fogassi, L. & Rizzolatti, G. (1996). Action recognition in the premotor cortex. *Brain*, 119: 593–609.

Galotti, K.M. (2002). *Making decisions that matter: How people face important life choices*. Mahwah, NJ: Lawrence Erlbaum Associates.

Galotti, K.M. (2007). Decision structuring in important real-life choices. *Psychological Science*, 18: 320–5.

Galotti, K.M & Tinkelenberg, C.E. (2009). Real-life decision making: Parents choosing a first-grade placement. *American Journal of Psychology*, 122: 455–68.

Gambetti, E. & Giusberti, F. (2012). The effect of anger and anxiety traits on investment decisions. *Journal of Economic Psychology*, 33: 1059–69.

Ganis, G. & Schendan, H.E. (2011). Visual imagery. *Wiley Interdisciplinary Reviews – Cognitive Science*, 2: 239–52.

Ganis, G., Thompson, W.L. & Kosslyn, S.M. (2004). Brain areas underlying visual mental imagery and visual perception: An fMRI study. *Cognitive Brain Research*, 20: 226–41.

Ganong, W.F. (1980). Phonetic categorisation in auditory word perception. *Journal of Experimental Psychology: Human Perception & Performance*, 6: 110–25.

Gardiner, J.M. (1988). Functional aspects of recollective experience. *Memory & Cognition*, 16: 309–13.

Gardiner, J.M., Brandt, K.R., Baddeley, A.D., Vargha-Khadem, F. & Mishkin, M. (2008). Charting the acquisition of semantic knowledge in a case of developmental amnesia. *Neuropsychologia*, 46: 2865–8.

Garrard, P., Carroll, E., Vinson, D. & Vigliocco, G. (2004). Dissociation of lexical syntax and semantics: Evidence from focal cortical degeneration. *Neurocase*, 10: 353–62.

Garrard, P., Maloney, L.M., Hodges, J.R. & Patterson, K. (2005). The effects of very early Alzheimer's disease on the characteristics of writing by a renowned author. *Brain*, 128: 250–60.

Garrod, S. & Terras, M. (2000). The contribution of lexical and situational knowledge to resolving discourse roles: Bonding and resolution. *Journal of Memory and Language*, 42: 526–44.

Gaskell, M.G. & Marslen-Wilson, W.D. (1998). Mechanisms of phonological interference in speech perception. *Journal of Experimental Psychology: Human Perception and Performance*, 24: 380–96.

Gaskell, M.G. & Marslen-Wilson, W.D. (2002). Representation and competition in the perception of spoken words. *Cognitive Psychology*, 45: 220–66.

Gathercole, S.E. & Baddeley, A.D. (1993). Phonological working memory: A critical building-block for reading development and vocabulary acquisition. *European Journal of Psychology of Education*, 8: 259–72.

Gauld, A. & Stephenson, G.M. (1967). Some experiments relating to Bartlett's theory of remembering. *British Journal of Psychology*, 58: 39–50.

Gauthier, I. & Tarr, M.J. (2002). Unravelling mechanisms for expert object recognition: Bridging brain activity and behaviour. *Journal of Experimental Psychology: Human Perception and Performance*, 28: 431–46.

Gazzaniga, M.S. (1992). *Nature's mind*. London: Basic Books.

Gazzaniga, M.S. (2013). Shifting gears: Seeking new approaches for mind/brain mechanisms. *Annual Review of Psychology*, 64: 1–20.

Gazzaniga, M.S. & Ledoux, J.E. (1978). *The integrated mind*. London: Basic Books.

Gazzaniga, M.S., Ivry, R.B. & Mangun, G.R. (2008). *Cognitive neuroscience: The biology of the mind* (3rd edn). New York: W.W. Norton.

Gegenfurtner, A., Lehtinen, E. & Säljö, R. (2011). Expertise differences in the comprehension of visualisations: A meta-analysis of eye-tracking research in professional domains. *Educational Psychology Review*, 23: 523–52.

Geiselman, R.E. & Fisher, R.P. (1997). Ten years of cognitive interviewing. In D.G. Payne & F.G. Conrad (eds), *Intersections in basic and applied memory research*. Mahwah, NJ: Lawrence Erlbaum Associates.

Geisler, W.S., Perry, J.S., Super, B.J. & Gallogly, D.P. (2001). Edge co-occurrence in natural images predicts contour grouping performance. *Vision Research*, 41: 711–24.

Gentner, D., Loewenstein, J., Thompson, L. & Forbus, K.D. (2009). Reviving inert knowledge: Analogical abstraction supports retrieval of past events. *Cognitive Science*, 33: 1343–82.

Geraerts, E. (2012). Cognitive underpinnings of recovered memories of childhood abuse. *Nebraska Symposium on Motivation*, 58: 175–91.

Geraerts, E. & McNally, R.J. (2008). Forgetting unwanted memories: Directed forgetting and thought suppression methods. *Acta Psychologica*, 127: 614–22.

Geraerts, E., Schooler, J.W., Merckelbach, H., Jelicic, M., Hunter, B.J.A. & Ambadar Z. (2007). Corroborating continuous and discontinuous memories of childhood sexual abuse. *Psychological Science*, 18: 564–8.

Gerrig, R.J. & O'Brien, E.J. (2005). The scope of memory-based processing. *Discourse Processes*, 39 (Special issue): 225–42.

Gerwing, J. & Allison, M. (2011). The flexible semantic integration of gestures and words: Comparing face-to-face and telephone dialogues. *Gesture*, 11: 308–29.

Gheysen, F., Van Opstal, F., Roggeman, C., Van Waelvelde, H. & Fias, W. (2011), The neural basis of implicit perceptual sequence learning. *Frontiers in Human Neuroscience*, 5 (Article 137).

Ghosh, V.E. & Gilboa, A. (2014). What is a memory schema? A historical perspective on current neuroscience literature. *Neuropsychologia*, 53: 104–14.

Gibbs, R.W. (2013). The real complexities of psycholinguistic research on metaphor. *Language Sciences*, 40: 45–52.

Gibson, J.J. (1950). *The perception of the visual world*. Boston, MA: Houghton Mifflin.

Gibson, J.J. (1966). *The senses considered as perceptual systems*. Boston, MA: Houghton Mifflin.

Gibson, J.J. (1979). *The ecological approach to visual perception*. Boston, MA: Houghton Mifflin.

Gick, M.L. & Holyoak, K.J. (1980). Analogical problem solving. *Cognitive Psychology*, 12: 306–55.

Gigerenzer, G. & Gaissmaier, W. (2011). Heuristic decision making. *Annual Review of Psychology*, 62: 451–82.

Gigerenzer, G. & Hoffrage, U. (1999). Overcoming difficulties in Bayesian reasoning: A reply to Lewis and Keren (1999) and Mellers and McGraw (1999). *Psychological Review*, 102: 684–704.

Gilaie-Dotan, S., Kanai, R., Bahrami, B., Rees, G. & Saygin, A.P. (2013a). Neuroanatomical correlates of biological motion detection. *Neuropsychologia*, 51: 457–63.

Gilaie-Dotan, S., Saygin, A.P., Lorenzi, L.J., Egan, R., Rees, G. & Behrmann, M. (2013b). The role of human ventral visual cortex in motion perception. *Brain*, 136: 2784–98.

Gilbert, C.D. & Li, W. (2013). Top-down influences on visual processing. *Nature Reviews Neuroscience*, 14: 350–63.

Gilbert, S.J., Spengler, S., Simons, J.S., Frith, C.D. & Burgess, P.W. (2006). Differential functions of lateral and medial rostral prefrontal cortex (area 10) revealed by brain-behaviour associations. *Cerebral Cortex*, 16: 1783–9.

Gilbert, S.J., Hadjipaviou, N. & Raoelison, M. (2013). Automaticity and control in prospective memory: A computational model. *PLOS ONE*, 8(3): e59852.

Gilboa, A. (2004). Autobiographical and episodic memory – one and the same? Evidence from prefrontal activation in neuroimaging studies. *Neuropsychologia*, 42: 1336–49.

Giorgetta, C., Grecucci, A., Bonini, N., Coricelli, G., Demarchi, G., Braun, C. & Sanfey, A.G. (2013). Waves of regret: An MEG study of emotion and decision-making. *Neuropsychologia*, 51: 38–51.

Girshick, A.R. & Banks, M.S. (2009). Probabilistic combination of slant information: Weighted averaging and robustness as optimal percepts. *Journal of Vision*, 9: 1–20.

Gläscher, J., Adolphs, R., Damasio, H., Bechara, A., Rudrauf, D., Calamia, M., Paul, L.K. & Tranel, D. (2012). Lesion mapping of cognitive control and value-based decision making in the prefrontal cortex. *Proceedings of the National Academy of Sciences*, 109: 14681–6.

Glennerster, A., Tscheang, L., Gilson, S.J., Fitzgibbon, A.W. & Parker, A.J. (2006). Humans ignore motion and stereo cues in favour of a fictional stable world. *Current Biology*, 16: 428–32.

Glover, S. (2004). Separate visual representations in the planning and control of action. *Behavioral and Brain Sciences*, 27: 3–78.

Glover, S. & Dixon, P. (2002). Semantics affect the planning but not control of grasping. *Experimental Brain Research*, 146: 383–7.

Glover, S., Miall, R.C. & Rushworth, M.F. (2005). Parietal rTMS disrupts the initiation but not the execution of on-line adjustments to a perturbation of object size. *Journal of Cognitive Neuroscience*, 17: 124–36.

Glover, S., Wall, M.B. & Smith, A.T. (2012). Distinct cortical networks support the planning and online control of reaching-to-grasp in humans. *European Journal of Neuroscience*, 35: 909–15.

Glucksberg, S. (2003). The psycholinguistics of metaphor. *Trends in Cognitive Sciences*, 7: 92–6.

Glymour, C. (2001). *The mind's arrows: Bayes nets and graphical causal models in psychology*. Cambridge, MA: MIT Press.

Gobet, F. & Clarkson, G. (2004). Chunks in expert memory: Evidence for the magical number four . . . or is it two? *Memory*, 12: 732–47.

Gobet, F. & Lane, P. (2015, in press). Human problem solving: Beyond Newell et al.'s (1958) Elements of a theory of human problem solving. In M.W. Eysenck & D. Groome (eds), *Cognitive psychology: Revisiting the classic studies*. London: SAGE.

Gobet, F. & Simon, H.A. (1996). Recall of rapidly presented random chess positions is a function of skill. *Psychonomic Bulletin & Review*, 3: 159–63.

Gobet, F. & Simon, H.A. (2000). Five seconds or sixty? Presentation time in expert memory. *Journal of Experimental Psychology: Learning, Memory and Cognition*, 29: 1082–94.

Gobet, F. & Waters, A.J. (2003). The role of constraints in expert memory. *Journal of Experimental Psychology: Learning, Memory & Cognition*, 29: 1082–94.

Gobet, F., Voogt, A. de & Retschitzki, J. (2004). *Moves in mind: The psychology of board games*. Hove: Psychology Press.

Goddard, E., Mannion, D.J., McDonald, J.S., Solomon, S.G. & Clifford, C.W.G. (2011). Colour responsiveness argues against a dorsal component of human V4. *Journal of Vision*, 11: 1–21.

Godden, D.R. & Baddeley, A.D. (1975). Context dependent memory in two natural environments: On land and under water. *British Journal of Psychology*, 66: 325–31.

Godden, D.R. & Baddeley, A.D. (1980). When does context influence recognition memory? *British Journal of Psychology*, 71: 99–104.

Godefroy, O., Azouvi, P., Robert, P., Roussel, M., LeGall, D. & Meulemans, T. (2010). Dysexecutive syndrome: Diagnostic criteria and validation study. *Annals of Neurology*, 68: 855–64.

Goel, V. (2007). Anatomy of deductive reasoning. *Trends in Cognitive Sciences*, 11: 435–41.

Goel, V. (2010). Neural basis of thinking: Laboratory problems versus real-world problems. *Wiley Interdisciplinary Reviews – Cognitive Science*, 1: 613–21.

Goel, V. & Grafman, J. (1995). Are the frontal lobes implicated in "planning" functions? Interpreting data from the Tower of Hanoi. *Neuropsychologia*, 33: 623–42.

Goel, V. & Grafman, J. (2000). The role of the right prefrontal cortex in ill-structured problem solving. *Cognitive Neuropsychology*, 17: 415–36.

Goel, V., Tierney, M., Sheesley, L., Bartolo, A., Vartanian, O. & Grafman, J. (2007). Hemispheric specialisation in human prefrontal cortex for resolving certain and uncertain inferences. *Cerebral Cortex*, 17: 2245–50.

Goel, V., Vartanian, O., Bartolo, A., Hakim, L., Ferraro, A.M., Isella, V., Appollonio, I., Drei, S. & Nichelli, P. (2013). Lesions to right prefrontal cortex impair real-world planning through premature commitments. *Neuropsychologia*, 51: 713–24.

Goh, W.D. & Lu, S.H.X. (2012). Testing the myth of encoding-retrieval match. *Memory & Cognition*, 40: 28–39.

Goldberg, A., Russell, M. & Cook, A. (2003). The effect of computers on student writing: A meta-analysis of studies from 1992 to 2002. *Journal of Technology, Learning, and Assessment*, 2: 1–52.

Goldenberg, G., Mullbacher, W. & Nowak, A. (1995). Imagery without perception: A case study of anosognosia for cortical blindness. *Neuropsychologia*, 33: 1373–82.

Goldinger, S.D. & Azuma, T. (2003). Puzzle-solving science: The quixotic quest for units in speech perception. *Journal of Phonetics*, 31: 305–20.

Goldman, R., Schwartz, M. & Wilshire, C. (2001). The influence of phonological context on the sound errors of a speaker with Wernicke's aphasia. *Brain and Language*, 78: 279–307.

Goldrick, M. (2006). Limited interaction in speech production: Chronometric, speech error, and neuropsychological evidence. *Language and Cognitive Processes*, 21 817–55.

Goldstein, D.G. & Gigerenzer, G. (2002). Models of ecological rationality: The recognition heuristic. *Psychological Review*, 109: 75–90.

Gollwitzer, P.M. (1999). Implementation intentions. *American Psychologist*, 54: 493–503.

Gollwitzer, P.M. & Sheeran, P. (2006). Implementation intentions and goal achievement: A meta-analysis of effects and processes. *Advanced Experimental Social Psychology*, 38: 69–119.

Golumbic, E.Z., Cogan, G.B., Schroeder, C.E. & Poeppel, D. (2013). Visual input enhances selective speech envelope tracking in auditory cortex at a "cocktail party". *Journal of Neuroscience*, 33: 1417–26.

Gómez, A.T., Lupón, Cardna, G. & Aznar-Casanova, J.A. (2012). Visual mechanisms governing the perception of autostereograms. *Clinical and Experimental Optometry*, 95: 146–52.

Gomulicki, B.R. (1956). Recall as an abstractive process. *Acta Psychologica*, 12: 77–94.

Goodale, M.A. & Milner, A.D. (1992). Separate visual pathways for perception and action. *Trends in Neuroscience*, 15: 22–5.

Goodale, M.A., Meenan, J.P., Bülthoff, H.H., Nicolle, D.A., Murphy, K.J. & Racicot, C.I. (1994). Separate neural pathways for the visual analysis of object shape in perception and prehension. *Current Biology*, 4: 604–10.

Goolkasian, P. & Woodberry, C. (2010). Priming effects with ambiguous figures. *Attention, Perception & Psychophysics*, 72: 168–78.

Gorman, M.E. (1995). Confirmation, disconfirmation, and invention: The case of Alexander Graham Bell and the telephone. *Thinking & Reasoning*, 1: 31–53.

Gotlib, I.H. & Joormann, J. (2010). Cognition and depression: Current status and future directions. *Annual Review of Clinical Psychology*, 6: 285–312.

Gottfredson, L.S. (1997). Why g matters? The complexities of everyday life. *Intelligence*, 24: 79–132.

Gotts, S.J., Chow, C.C. & Martin, A. (2012). Repetition priming and repetition suppression: A case for enhanced efficiency through neural synchronisation. *Cognitive Neuroscience*, 3: 227–37.

Gould, J.D. (1978). An experimental study of writing, dictating, and speaking. In J. Requin (ed.), *Attention and performance, vol. VII*. Hillsdale, NJ: Lawrence Erlbaum Associates.

Gould, J.D. (1980). Experiments on composing letters: Some facts, some myths, and some observations. In L.W. Gregg & E.R. Sternberg (eds), *Cognitive processes in writing*. Hillsdale, NJ: Lawrence Erlbuam Associates.

Grabner, R.H., Stern, E. & Neubauer, A. (2007). Individual differences in chess expertise: A psychometric investigation. *Acta Psychologica*, 124: 398–420.

Graesser, A.C., Singer, M. & Trabasso, T. (1994). Constructing inferences during narrative text comprehension. *Psychological Review*, 101: 371–95.

Graesser, A.C., Millis, K.K. & Zwaan, R.A. (1997). Discourse comprehension. *Annual Review of Psychology*, 48: 163–89.

Graf, P. (2012). Prospective memory: Faulty brain, flaky person. *Canadian Psychology*, 53: 7–13.

Graham, S.A. & Fisher, S.E. (2013). Decoding the genetics of speech and language. *Current Opinion in Neurobiology*, 23: 43–51.

Granzier, J.J.M., Brenner, E. & Smeets, J.B.J. (2009a). Reliable identification by colour under natural conditions. *Journal of Vision*, 9(1): 1–9.

Granzier, J.J.M., Brenner, E. & Smeets, J.B.J. (2009b). Can illumination estimates provide the basis for colour constancy? *Journal of Vision*, 9(3): 1–11.

Gras, D., Tardieu, H. & Nicolas, S. (2012). Predictive inference activation: Interest of a Stroop-like task. *Swiss Journal of Psychology*, 71: 141–8.

Gray, R. (2011). Looming auditory collision warnings for driving. *Human Factors*, 53: 63–74.

Gray, R., Ho, C. & Spence, C. (2014). A comparison of different informative vibrotactile forward collision warnings: Does the warning need to be linked to the collision event? *PLOS ONE*, 9(1): e87070.

Graziano, M.S.A. & Kastner, S. (2011). Human consciousness and its relationship to social neuroscience: A novel hypothesis. *Cognitive Neuroscience*, 2: 98–113.

Gréa, H., Pisella, L., Rossetti, Y., Desmurget, M., Tilikete, C., Grafton, S., Prablanc, C. & Vighetto, A. (2002). A lesion of the posterior parietal cortex disrupts on-line adjustments during aiming movements. *Neuropsychologia*, 40: 2471–80.

Greenberg, D.L. & Verfaellie, M. (2010). Interdependence of episodic and semantic memory: Evidence from neuropsychology. *Journal of the International Neuropsychology Society*, 16: 748–53.

Greenberg, D.L., Keane, M.M., Ryan, L.R. & Verfaillie, M. (2009). Impaired category fluency in medial temporal lobe amnesia: The role of episodic memory. *Journal of Neuroscience*, 29: 10900–8.

Greenberg, J.H. (1963). Some universals of grammar with particular reference to the order of meaningful elements. In J.H. Greenberg (ed.), *Universals of language*. Cambridge, MA: MIT Press.

Greene, J.D., Nystrom, L.E., Engell, A.D., Darley, J.M. & Cohen, J.D. (2004). The neural bases of cognitive conflict and control in moral judgment. *Neuron*, 44: 389–400.

Greene, J.D., Morelli, S.A., Lowenberg, K., Nystrom, L.E. & Cohen, J.D. (2008). Cognitive load selectively interferes with utilitarian moral judgment. *Cognition*, 107: 1144–54.

Grice, H.P. (1967). Logic and conversation. In P. Cole & J.L. Morgan (eds), *Studies in syntax, vol. III*. New York: Seminar Press.

Grice, H.P. (1975). Logic and conversation. In P. Cole & J.L. Morgan (eds), *Syntax and semantics, III: Speech acts*. New York: Seminar Press.

Griffiths, J.D., Marslen-Wilson, W.D., Stramatakis, E.A. & Tyler, L.K. (2013). Functional organisation of the neural language system: Dorsal and ventral pathways are critical for syntax. *Cerebral Cortex*, 20: 139–47.

Griffiths, T.L., Chater, N., Norris, D. & Pouget, A. (2012). How the Bayesians got their beliefs (and what those beliefs actually are): Comment on Bowers and Davis (2012). *Psychological Bulletin*, 138: 415–22.

Griskevicius, V., Shiota, M.N. & Neufeld, S.L. (2010). Influence of different positive emotions on persuasive processing: A functional evolutionary approach. *Emotion*, 10: 190–206.

Grodzinsky, Y. & Friederici, A.D. (2006). Neuroimaging of syntax and syntactic processing. *Current Opinion in Neurobiology*, 16: 240–6.

Groome, D. (2014) *An introduction to cognitive psychology: processes and disorders*. Hove: Psychology Press.

Groopman, J. (2007). *How doctors think*. New York: Houghton Mifflin.

Gross, J.J. (2013). Emotion regulation: Taking stock and moving forward. *Emotion*, 13: 359–65.

Gross, J.J. & Thompson, R.A. (2007). Emotion regulation: Conceptual foundations. In J.J. Gross (ed.), *Handbook of emotion regulation*. New York: Guilford Press.

Gross, J.J., Sheppes, G. & Urry, H.L. (2011). Taking one's lumps while doing the splits: A big tent perspective on emotion generation and emotion regulation. *Cognition & Emotion*, 25: 789–93.

Grossman, E.D., Battelli, L. & Pascual-Leone, A. (2005). Repetitive TMS over STSp disrupts perception of biological motion. *Vision Research*, 45: 2847–53.

Guida, A., Gobet, F., Tardieu, H. & Nicolas, S. (2012). How chunks, long-term working memory and templates offer a cognitive explanation for neuroimaging data on expertise acquisition: A two-stage framework. *Brain and Cognition*, 79: 221–44.

Guida, A., Gobet, F. & Nicolas, S. (2013). Functional cerebral reorganisation: A signature of expertise? Re-examining Guida, Gobet, Tardieu, and Nicolas' (2012) two-stage framework. *Frontiers in Human Neuroscience*, 7 (Article 590).

Gupta, R. & Kar, B.R. (2008). Interpretative bias: Indicators of cognitive vulnerability to depression. *German Journal of Psychiatry*, 11: 98–102.

Gutchess, A.H. & Park, D.C. (2006). The fMRI environment can impair memory performance in young and elderly adults. *Brain Research*, 1099: 133–40.

Guttman, S.E., Gilroy, L.A. & Blake, R. (2007). Spatial grouping in human vision: Temporal structure trumps temporal synchrony. *Vision Research*, 47: 219–30.

Gyurak, A., Gross, J.J. & Etkin, A. (2011). Explicit and implicit emotion regulation: A dual-process framework. *Cognition & Emotion*, 25: 400–12.

Haber, R.N. & Levin, C.A. (2001). The independence of size perception and distance perception. *Perception & Psychophysics*, 63: 1140–52.

Haeffel, G.J., Rozek, D.C., Hames, J.L. & Technow, J. (2012). Too much of a good thing: Testing the efficacy of a cognitive modification task for cognitive vulnerable individuals. *Cognitive Therapy and Research*, 36: 493–501.

Haggard, P. (2005). Conscious intention and motor cognition. *Trends in Cognitive Sciences*, 9: 290–5.

Hagoort, P. & van Berkum, J. (2007). Beyond the sentence given. *Philosophical Transactions of the Royal Society B*, 362: 801–11.

Hagoort, P., Hald, L., Bastiaansen, M. & Petersson, K.M. (2004). Integration of word meaning and world knowledge in language comprehension. *Science*, 304: 438–41.

Hahn, B., Ross, T.J. & Stein, E.A. (2006). Neuroanatomical dissociations between bottom-up and top-down processes of visuospatial selective attention. *NeuroImage*, 32: 842–53.

Hahn, S., Andersen, G.J. & Saidpour, A. (2003). Static scene analysis for the perception of heading. *Psychological Science*, 14: 543–8.

Hahn, U. & Oaksford, M. (2007). The rationality of informal argumentation: A Bayesian approach to reasoning fallacies. *Psychological Review*, 114: 704–32.

Hahn, U. & Oaksford, M. (2014). *The fallacies explained*. Oxford: Oxford University Press.

Haider, H. & Frensch, P.A. (1999). Eye movement during skill acquisition: More evidence for the information reduction hypothesis. *Journal of Experimental Psychology: Learning, Memory & Cognition*, 25: 172–90.

Haider, H., Eichler, A. & Lange, T. (2011). An old problem: How can we distinguish between conscious and unconscious knowledge acquired in an implicit learning task? *Consciousness and Cognition*, 20: 658–72.

Hains, P. & Baillargeon, J. (2011). Animal and human faces used as distractors in perceptual load studies: Are they equivalent? *Année Psychologique*, 111: 449–63.

Hakamata, Y., Lissek, S., Bar-Haim, Y., Britton, J.C., Fox, N.A., Leibenluft, E., Ernst, M. & Pine, D.S. (2010). Attention bias modification treatment: A meta-analysis toward the establishment of novel treatment for anxiety. *Biological Psychiatry*, 68: 982–90.

Hallion, L.S. & Ruscio, A.M. (2011). A meta-analysis of the effect of cognitive bias modification on anxiety and depression. *Psychological Bulletin*, 137: 940–58.

Hambrick, D.Z., Oswald, F.L., Altmann, M., Meinz, E.J., Gobet, F. & Campitelli, G. (2014). Deliberate practice: Is that all it takes to become an expert? *Intelligence*, 45 (July–August): 34–45.

Hamm, J.P. & McMullen, P.A. (1998). Effects of orientation on the identification of rotated objects depend on the level of identity. *Journal of Experimental Psychology: Human Perception and Performance*, 24: 413–26.

Han, S. & Lerner, J.S. (2009). Decision-making. In D. Sander & K.R. Scherer (eds), *The Oxford companion to emotion and the affective sciences* (pp. 111–13). Oxford: Oxford University Press.

Han, S.H. & Humphreys, G.W. (2003). Relationship between connectedness and proximity in perceptual grouping. *Science in China Series C – Life Sciences*, 46: 113–26.

Han, S.W. & Marois, R. (2013). The source of dual-task limitations: Serial or parallel processing of multiple response selections? *Attention, Perception, & Psychophysics*, 75: 1395–405.

Han, Z.Z. & Bi, Y.C. (2009). Reading comprehension without phonological mediation: Further evidence from a Chinese aphasic individual. *Science in China Series C Life Sciences*, 52: 492–9.

Hand, C.J., Miellet, S., O'Donnell, P.J. & Serento, S.C. (2010). The frequency–predictability interaction in reading: It depends where you're coming from. *Journal of Experimental Psychology: Human Perception and Performance*, 36: 1294–313.

Handley, S.J., Newstead, S.E. & Trippas, D. (2011). Logic, beliefs, and instruction: A test of the default interventionist account of belief bias. *Journal of Experimental Psychology: Learning, Memory, and Cognition*, 37: 28–43.

Hanley, J.R. & McDonnell, V. (1997). Are reading and spelling phonologically mediated? Evidence from a patient with a speech production impairment. *Cognitive Neuropsychology*, 14: 3–33.

Hannula, D.E. & Greene, A.J. (2012). The hippocampus re-evaluated in unconscious learning and memory: At a tipping point? *Frontiers in Human Neuroscience*, 6 (Article 80): 1–20.

Hannula, D.E., Tranel, D. & Cohen, N.J. (2006). The long and the short of it: Relational memory impairments in amnesia, even at short lags. *Journal of Neuroscience*, 26: 8352–9.

Hansen, T., Olkkonen, M., Walter, S. & Gegenfurtner, K.R. (2006). Memory modulates colour appearance. *Nature Neuroscience*, 9: 1367–8.

Harand, C., Bertran, F., La Joie, F., Landeau, B., Mézenge, F., Desgranges, B., Peigneux, P., Eustache, F. & Rauchs, G. (2012). The hippocampus remains activated over the long term for the retrieval of truly episodic memories. *PLOS ONE*, 7(8): e 43495.

Hardt, O., Einarsson, E.O. & Nader, K. (2010). A bridge over troubled water: Reconsolidation as a link between cognitive and neuroscientific memory research traditions. *Annual Review of Psychology*, 61: 141–67.

Hardt, O., Nader, K. & Nadel, L. (2013). Decay happens: The role of active forgetting in memory. *Trends in Cognitive Sciences*, 17: 111–20.

Hareli, S. & Weiner, B. (2002). Dislike and envy as antecedents of pleasure at another's misfortune. *Motivation and Emotion*, 26: 257–77.

Harley, T.A. (2008). *The psychology of language: From data to theory* (3rd edn). Hove: Psychology Press.

Harley, T.A. (2010). *Talking the talk: Language, psychology and science.* Hove: Psychology Press.

Harley, T.A. (2012). Why the earth is almost flat: Imaging and the death of cognitive psychology. *Cortex*, 48: 1371–2.

Harley, T.A. (2013). *The psychology of language: From data to theory* (4th edn). Hove: Psychology Press.

Harley, T.A. & Bown, H.E. (1998). What causes a tip-of-the tongue state? Evidence for lexical neighbourhood effects in speech production. *British Journal of Psychology*, 89: 151–74.

Harley, T.A. & McAndrews, S. (2015, in press). Language: Beyond Chomsky's (1957) syntactic structures. In M.W. Eysenck & D. Groome (eds), *Cognitive psychology: Revisiting the classic studies*. London: SAGE.

Harm, M.W. & Seidenberg, M.S. (2004). Computing the meanings of words in reading: Co-operative division of labour between visual and phonological processes. *Psychological Review*, 111: 662–720.

Harmon-Jones, E., Gable, P.A. & Price, T.F. (2011). Toward an understanding of the influence of affective states on attentional tuning: Comment on Friedman and Förster, P.A. (2011). *Psychological Bulletin*, 137: 508–12.

Harmon-Jones, E., Gable, P.A. & Price, T.F. (2013). Does negative affect always narrow and positive affect always broaden the mind? Considering the influence of motivational intensity on cognitive scope. *Current Directions in Psychological Science*, 22: 301–7.

Harris, A.J.L. & Hahn, U. (2011). Unrealistic optimism about future life events: A cautionary note. *Psychological Review*, 118: 135–54.

Harris, A.J.L., Hsu, A.S. & Madsen, J.K. (2012). Because Hitler did it! Quantitative tests of Bayesian argumentation using *ad hominem*. *Thinking & Reasoning*, 18: 311–43.

Harris, P.R., Griffin, D.W. & Murray, S. (2008). Testing the limits of optimistic bias: Event and person moderators in a multilevel framework. *Journal of Personality and Social Psychology*, 95: 1225–37.

Harrison, V. & Hole, G.J. (2009). Evidence for a contact-based explanation of the own-age bias in face recognition. *Psychonomic Bulletin & Review*, 16: 264–9.

Hart, W., Albarracin, D., Eagly, A.H., Brechan, I., Lindberg, M.J. & Merrill, L. (2009). Feeling validated versus being correct: A meta-analysis of selective exposure to information. *Psychological Bulletin*, 135: 555–88.

Hartley, J., Sotto, E. & Pennebaker, J. (2003). Speaking versus typing: A case-study of the effects of using voice-recognition software on academic correspondence. *British Journal of Educational Psychology*, 34: 5–16.

Harvey, L.O. (1986). Visual memory: What is remembered? In F. Klix & H. Hagendorf (eds), *Human memory and cognitive capabilities*. The Hague, Netherlands: Elsevier.

Haskell, T.R. & MacDonald, M.C. (2003). Conflicting cues and competition in subject–verb agreement. *Journal of Memory and Language*, 48: 760–78.

Haskell, T.R., Thornton, R. & MacDonald, M.C. (2010). Experience and grammatical agreement: Statistical learning shapes number agreement production. *Cognition*, 114: 151–64.

Hassabis, D., Kumaran, D., Vann, S.D. & Maguire, E.A. (2007). Patients with hippocampal amnesia cannot imagine new experiences. *Proceedings of the National Academy of Sciences*, 104: 1726–31.

Hassin, R.R. (2013). Yes it can: On the functional abilities of the human unconscious. *Perspectives on Psychological Science*, 8: 195–207.

Hauk, O., Johnsrude, I. & Pulvermüller, F. (2004). Somatotopic representation of action words in human motor and premotor cortex. *Neuron*, 41: 301–7.

Hauser, M.D. (2006). *Moral minds: How nature designed our universal sense of right and wrong*. New York: Ecco/Harper Collins.

Hauser, M.D., Chomsky, N. & Fitch, W.T. (2002). The faculty of language: What is it, who has it, and how did it evolve? *Science*, 298: 1569–79.

Haxby, J.V., Hoffman, E.A. & Gobbini, M.I. (2000). The distributed human neural system for face perception. *Trends in Cognitive Sciences*, 4: 223–33.

Haxby, J.V., Gobbini, M.I., Furey, M.L., Ishai, A., Schouten, J.L. & Pietrini, P. (2001). Distributed and overlapping representations of faces and objects in ventral temporal cortex. *Science*, 293: 2425–530.

Hayes, J.R. (2012). Modelling and remodelling writing. *Written Communication*, 29: 369–88.

Hayes, J.R. & Bajzek, D. (2008). Understanding and reducing the knowledge effect: Implications for writers. *Written Communication*, 25: 104–18.

Hayes, J.R. & Chenoweth, N. (2006). Is working memory involved in the transcribing and editing of texts? *Written Communication*, 23: 135–41.

Hayes, J.R. & Flower, L.S. (1980). Identifying the organisation of writing processes. In L.W. Gregg & E.R. Steinberg (eds), *Cognitive processes in writing* (pp. 3–30). Mahwah, NJ: Erlbaum.

Hayes, J.R. & Flower, L.S. (1986). Writing research and the writer. *American Psychologist*, 41: 1106–13.

Hayes, J.R., Flower, L.S., Schriver, K., Stratman, J. & Carey, L. (1985). *Cognitive processes in revision (Technical Report No. 12)*. Pittsburgh, PA: Carnegie Mellon University.

Hayes, S.M., Fortier, C.B., Levine, A., Milberg, W.P. & McGlinchey, R. (2012). Implicit memory in Korsakoff's syndrome: A review of procedural learning and priming studies. *Neuropsychology Review*, 22: 132–53.

Hayward, W.G. (2012). Whatever happened to object-centered representations? *Perception*, 41: 1153–62.

Hayward, W.G. & Tarr, M.J. (2005). Visual perception II: High-level vision. In K. Lamberts & R.L. Goldstone (eds), *The handbook of cognition*. London: SAGE.

Hedden, T. & Gabrieli, J.D.E. (2010). Shared and selective neural correlates of inhibition: Facilitation, and shifting processes during executive control. *NeuroImage*, 51: 421–31.

Hegdé, J. (2008). Time course of visual perception: Coarse-to-fine processing and beyond. *Progress in Neurobiology*, 84: 405–39.

Hegdé, J. & Van Essen, D.C. (2000). Selectivity for complex shapes in primate visual area V2. *Journal of Neuroscience*, 20: RC61.

Held, R.T., Cooper, E.A. & Banks, M.S. (2012). Blur and disparity are complementary cues to depth. *Current Biology*, 22: 426–31.

Hélie, S., Waldschmidt, J.G. & Ashby, F.G. (2010). Automaticity in rule-based and information-integration categorisation. *Attention, Perception & Psychophysics*, 72: 1013–31.

Heller, D., Grodner, D. & Tanenhaus, M.K. (2008). The role of perspective in identifying domains of reference. *Cognition*, 108: 831–6.

Hellmann, J.H., Echterhoff, G., Kopietz, R., Niemeier, S. & Memon, A. (2011). Talking about visually perceived events: Communication effects on eyewitness memory. *European Journal of Social Psychology*, 41: 658–71.

Henderson, J.M. & Hollingworth, A. (1999). High-level scene perception. *Annual Review of Psychology*, 50: 243–71.

Henke, K. (2010). A model for memory systems based on processing modes rather than consciousness. *Nature Reviews Neuroscience*, 11: 523–32.

Henke, K., Mondadori, C.R.A., Treyer, V., Nitsch, R.M., Buck, A. & Hock, C. (2003). Nonconscious formation and reactivation of semantic associations by way of the medial temporal lobe. *Neuropsychologia*, 41: 863–76.

Herbranson, W.T. & Schroeder, J. (2010). Are birds smarter than mathematicians? Pigeons (Columba livia) perform optimally on a version of the Monty Hall dilemma. *Journal of Comparative Psychology*, 124: 1–13.

Herholz, S.C. & Zatorre, R.J. (2012). Musical training as a framework for brain plasticity, behaviour, function, and structure. *Neuron*, 76: 486–502.

Hering, E. (1878). *Zur Lehre vom Lichtsinn*. Vienna: Gerold.

Herlihey, T.A. & Rushton, S.K. (2012). The role of discrepant retinal motion during walking in the realignment of egocentric space. *Journal of Vision*, 12: 1–11.

Hertwig, R., Barron, C., Weber, E.U. & Erev, I. (2004). Decisions from experience and the effect of rare events in risky choice. *Psychological Science*, 15: 534–9.

Hesse, C., Schenk, T. & Deubel, H. (2012). Attention is needed for action control: Further evidence from grasping. *Vision Research*, 71: 37–43.

Hesselmann, G., Flandin, G. & Dehaene, S. (2011). Probing the cortical network underlying the psychological refractory period: A combined EEG-fMRI study. *NeuroImage*, 56: 1608–21.

Hesselmann, G., Naccache, L., Cohen, L. & Dehaene, S. (2013). Splitting of the P3 component during dual-task processing in a patient with posterior callosal section. *Cortex*, 49: 730–47.

Heukelom, F. (2007). What Simon says. *Tinbergen Institute Discussion Paper*, No. 07–005(1).

Heywood, C.A. & Cowey, A. (1999). Cerebral achromatopsia. In G.W. Humphreys (ed.), *Case studies in the neuropsychology of vision*. Hove: Psychology Press.

Hibberd, D.L., Jamson, S.L. & Carsten, O.M.J. (2013). Mitigating the effects of in-vehicle distractions through use of the psychological refractory period paradigm. *Accident Analysis and Prevention*, 50: 1096–103.

Hickok, G., Okada, K., Barr, W., Pa, J., Rogalsky, C., Donnelly, K., Barda, L. & Grant, A. (2008). Bilateral capacity for speech sound processing in auditory comprehension: Evidence from Wada procedures. *Brain and Language*, 107: 179–84.

Hickok, G., Costanzo, M., Capasso, R. & Miceli, G. (2011). The role of Broca's area in speech perception: Evidence from aphasia revisited. *Brain & Language*, 119: 214–20.

Hicks, J.L., Marsh, R.L. & Cook, G.I. (2005). Task interference in time-based, event-based, and dual intention prospective memory conditions. *Journal of Memory and Language*, 53: 430–44.

Hilbig, B.E. & Glöckner, A. (2011). Yes, they can! Appropriate weighting of small probabilities as a function of information acquisition. *Acta Psychologica*, 138: 390–6.

Hills, P.J., Werno, M.A. & Lewis, M.B. (2011). Sad people are more accurate at face recognition than happy people. *Consciousness and Cognition*, 20: 1502–17.

Himmelbach, M., Boehme, R. & Karnath, H.-O. (2012). 20 years later: A second look on DF's motor behaviour. *Neuropsychologia*, 50: 139–44.

Hirotani, M., Frazier, L. & Rayner, K. (2006). Punctuation and intonation effects on clause and sentence wrap-up: Evidence from eye movements. *Journal of Memory and Language*, 54: 425–43.

Hirsch, C.R. & Mathews, A. (2012). A cognitive model of pathological worry. *Behaviour Research and Therapy*, 50: 636–46.

Hirsch, C.R., Clark, D.M. & Mathews, A. (2006). Imagery and interpretations in social phobia: Support for the combined cognitive biases hypothesis. *Behavior Therapy*, 37: 223–36.

Ho, C. & Spence, C. (2005). Assessing the effectiveness of various auditory cues in capturing a driver's visual attention. *Journal of Experimental Psychology: Applied*, 11: 157–74.

Hodgson, C. & Lambon Ralph, M.A. (2008). Mimicking aphasic semantic errors in normal speech production: Evidence from a novel experimental paradigm. *Brain and Language*, 104: 89–101.

Hoffrage, U., Lindsey, S., Hertwig, R. & Gigerenzer, G. (2000). Communicating statistical information. *Science*, 290: 2261–2.

Holland, A.C. & Kensinger, E.A. (2010). Emotion and autobiographical memory. *Physics of Life Reviews*, 7: 88–131.

Holler, J. & Wilkin, K. (2011). An experimental investigation of how addressee feedback affects co-speech gestures accompanying speakers' responses. *Journal of Pragmatics*, 43: 3522–36.

Hollien, H., Dejong, G., Martin, C., Schwartz, R. & Liljegren, K. (2001). Effects of ethanol intoxication on speech suprasegmentals. *Journal of the Acoustical Society of America*, 110: 3198–206.

Hollingworth, A. (2012). Task specificity and the influence of memory on visual search: Comment on Võ and Wolfe (2012). *Journal of Experimental Psychology: Human Perception and Performance*, 38: 1596–603.

Hollingworth, A. & Henderson, J.M. (2002). Accurate visual memory for previously attended objects in natural scenes. *Journal of Experimental Psychology: Human Perception & Performance*, 28: 113–36.

Hollingworth, A., Maxcey-Richard, A.M. & Vecera, S.P. (2012). The spatial distribution of attention within and across objects. *Journal of Experimental Psychology: Human Perception and Performance*, 38: 135–51.

Holliway, D.R. & McCutcheon, D. (2004). Audience perspective in young writers' composing and revising. In L. Allal, L. Chanquoy & P. Largy (eds), *Revision of written language: Cognitive and instructional processes* (pp. 87–101). New York: Kluwer.

Holmes, V.M. (1988). Hesitations and sentence planning. *Language and Cognitive Processes*, 3: 323–61.

Holmes, V.M. & Carruthers, J. (1998). The relation between reading and spelling in skilled adult readers. *Journal of Memory and Language*, 39: 264–89.

Holzgrefe, J., Wellmann, C., Petrone, C., Truckenbrodt, H., Hohle, B. & Wartenburger, I. (2013). Brain response to prosodic boundary cues depends on boundary position. *Frontiers in Psychology*, 4 (Article 421).

Hong, S.W., Tong, F. & Seiffert, A.E. (2012). Direction-selective patterns of activity in human visual cortex suggest common neural substrates for different types of motion. *Neuropsychologia*, 50: 514–21.

Horton, C., D'Zmura, M. & Srinivasan, R. (2013). Suppression of competing speech through entrainment of cortical oscillations. *Journal of Neurophysiology*, 109: 3082–93.

Horton, W.S. & Keysar, B. (1996). When do speakers take into account common ground? *Cognition*, 59: 91–117.

Horton, W.S. & Slaten, D.G. (2012). Anticipating who will say what: The influence of speaker-specific memory associations on reference resolution. *Memory & Cognition*, 40: 113–26.

Hosking, S.G. & Crassini, B. (2010). The effects of familiar size and object trajectories on time-to-contact judgments. *Experimental Brain Research*, 203: 541–52.

Hou, Y. & Liu, T. (2012). Neural correlates of object-based attentional selection in human cortex. *Neuropsychologia*, 50: 2916–25.

Howard, D. & Orchard-Lisle, V. (1984). On the origin of semantic errors in naming: Evidence from the case of a global aphasic. *Cognitive Neuropsychology*, 1: 163–90.

Howard, R.W. (2009). Individual differences in expertise development over decades in a complex intellectual domain. *Memory & Cognition*, 37: 194–209.

Howard, R.W. (2012). Longitudinal effects of different types of practice on the development of chess expertise. *Applied Cognitive Psychology*, 26: 359–69.

Howe, M.L. & Courage, M.L. (1997). The emergence and early development of autobiographical memory. *Psychological Review*, 104: 499–523.

Howe, M.L., Courage, M.L. & Edison, S.C. (2003). When autobiographical memory begins. In M. Conway, S. Gathercole, S. Algarabel, A. Pitarque & T. Bajo (eds), *Theories of Memory, vol. III*. Hove: Psychology Press.

Howe, P.D. & Leiserowitz, A. (2013). Who remembers a hot summer or a cold winter? The asymmetric effects of beliefs about global warming on perceptions of local conditions in the U.S. *Global Environmental Change*, 23: 1488–500.

Howe, P.D. & Webb, M.E. (2014). Detecting unidentified changes. *PLOS ONE*, 9(1): e 84490.

Huang, Y. & Rao, R.P.N. (2011). Predictive coding. *Wiley Interdisciplinary Reviews – Cognitive Science*, 2: 580–93.

Hubel, D.H. & Wiesel, T.N. (1962). Receptive fields, binocular interaction and functional architecture in the cat's visual cortex. *Journal of Physiology*, 160: 106–54.

Hubel, D.H. & Wiesel, T.N. (1979). Brain mechanisms of vision. *Scientific American*, 249: 150–62.

Huettel, S.A. (2012). Event-related fMRI in cognition. *NeuroImage*, 62: 1152–6.

Huettig, F. & Hartsuiker, R.J. (2010). Listening to yourself is like listening to others: External, but not internal, verbal self-monitoring is based on speech perception. *Language and Cognitive Processes*, 25: 347–74.

Humphrey, N. (1983). *Consciousness regained: Chapters in the development of mind*. Oxford: Oxford University Press.

Humphrey, N. (2002). *The mind made flesh: Frontiers of psychology ad evolution*. Oxford: Oxford University Press.

Hung, C.P., Kreiman, C., Poggio, T. & DiCarlo, J.J. (2005). Fast readout of object identity from macaque inferior temporal cortex. *Science*, 310: 863–6.

Hunt, R.R. (2013). Precision in memory through distinctive processing. *Current Directions in Psychological Science*, 22: 10–15.

Hunt, R.R. & Rawson, K.A. (2011). Knowledge affords distinctive processing in memory. *Journal of Memory and Language*, 65: 390–405.

Huntsinger, J.R. (2013). Does emotion directly tune the scope of attention? *Current Directions in Psychological Science*, 22: 265–70.

Hupbach, A., Gomez, R., Hardt, O. & Nadel, L. (2007). Reconsolidation of episodic memories: A subtle reminder triggers integration of new information. *Learning & Memory*, 14: 47–53.

Hupbach, A., Hardt, O., Gomez, R. & Nadel, L. (2008). The dynamics of memory: Context-dependent updating. *Learning & Memory*, 15: 574–9.

Hurvich, L.M. & Jameson, D. (1957). An opponent process theory of colour vision. *Psychological Review*, 64: 384–90.

Husain, F.T., Fromm, S.J., Pursley, R.H., Hosey, L.A., Braun, A.R. & Horwitz, B. (2006). Neural bases of categorization of simple speech and nonspeech sounds. *Human Brain Mapping*, 27: 636–51.

Huxley, T. (1874). On the hypothesis that animals are automata, and its history. *Nature*, 10: 362–6.

Hyde, K.L., Lerch, J., Norton, A., Forgeard, M., Winner, E., Evans, A.C. & Schlaug, G. (2009). Musical training shapes structural brain development. *Journal of Neuroscience*, 29: 3019–25.

Iacoboni, M., Molnar-Szakacs, I., Gallese, V., Buccino, G., Mazziotta, J.C. & Rizzolatti, G. (2005). Grasping the intentions of others with one's own mirror neuron system. *PLOS Biology*, 3: 529–35.

Ihlebaek, C., Løve, T., Eilertsen, D.E. & Magnussen, S. (2003). Memory for a staged criminal event witnessed live and on video. *Memory*, 11: 310–27.

Indefrey, P. (2011). The spatial and temporal signatures of word production components: A critical update. *Frontiers in Psychology*, 2 (Article 255).

Indovina, I. & Macaluso, E. (2007). Dissociation of stimulus relevance and saliency factors during shifts of visuo-spatial attention. *Cerebral Cortex*, 43: 358–64.

Inhoff, A.W. & Liu, W. (1998). The perceptual span and oculomotor activity during the reading of Chinese sentences. *Journal of Experimental Psychology: Human Perception and Performance*, 24: 20–34.

Insausti, R., Annese, J., Amaral, D.G. & Squire, L.R. (2013). Human amnesia and the medial temporal lobe illuminated by neuropsychological and neurohistological findings for patient E.P. *Proceedings of the National Academy of Sciences*, 110: E1953–62.

Ioannides, A.A., Popescu, M., Otsuka, A., Bezerianos, A. & Liu, L. (2003). Magnetoencephalographic evidence of the interhemispheric asymmetry in echoic memory lifetime and its dependence on handedness and gender. *NeuroImage*, 19: 1061–75.

Ison, M.J. & Quiroga, R.Q. (2008). Selectivity and invariance for visual object recognition. *Frontiers in Bioscience*, 13: 4889–903.

Ittelson, W.H. (1951). Size as a cue to distance: Static localisation. *American Journal of Psychology*, 64: 54–67.

Iverson, J.M. & Goldin-Meadow, S. (1998). Why people gesture when they speak. *Nature*, 396: 228.

Izard, C.E. (2007). Basic emotions, natural kinds, emotion schemas, and a new paradigm. *Perspectives on Psychological Science*, 2: 260–80.

Jack, F. & Hayne, H. (2010). Childhood amnesia: Empirical evidence for a two-stage phenomenon. *Memory*, 18: 831–44.

Jack, F., MacDonald, S., Reese, E. & Hayne, H. (2009). Maternal reminiscing style during early childhood predicts the age of adolescents' earliest memories. *Child Development*, 80: 496–505.

Jacobs, A., Pinto, J. & Shiffrar, M. (2004). Experience, context, and the visual perception of human movement. *Journal of Experimental Psychology: Human Perception and Performance*, 30: 833–5.

Jacobs, R.A. (2002). What determines visual cue reliability? *Trends in Cognitive Sciences*, 6: 345–50.

Jacoby, L.L., Debner, J.A. & Hay, J.F. (2001). Proactive interference, accessibility bias, and process dissociations: Valid subjective reports of memory. *Journal of Experimental Psychology: Learning, Memory, and Cognition*, 27: 686–700.

Jacoby, L.L., Bishara, A.J., Hessels, S. & Toth, J.P. (2005). Aging, subjective experience, and cognitive control: Dramatic false remembering by older adults. *Journal of Experimental Psychlogy: General*, 134: 131–48.

Jacquemot, C., Dupoux, E. & Bachoud-Lévi, A.-C. (2011). Is the word-length effect linked to subvocal rehearsal? *Cortex*, 47: 484–93.

Jaeger, T.F. & Snider, N.E. (2013). Alignment as a consequence of expectation adaptation: Syntactic priming is affected by the prime's prediction error given both prior and recent experience. *Cognition*, 127: 57–83.

Jain, A.K. & Duin, R.P.W. (2004). Pattern recognition. In R.L. Gregory (ed.), *The Oxford companion to the mind* (pp. 698–703). Oxford: Oxford University Press.

Jakobson, L.S., Archibald, Y.M., Carey, D.P. & Goodale, M.A. (1991). A kinematic analysis of reaching and grasping movements in a patient recovering from optic ataxia. *Neuropsychologia*, 29: 803–9.

Jalbert, A., Neath, I., Bireta, T.J. & Surprenant, A.M. (2011). When does length cause the word length effect? *Journal of Experimental Psychology: Learning, Memory, and Cognition*, 37: 338–53.

James, T.W., Culham, J., Humphrey, G.K., Milner, A.D. & Goodale, M.A. (2003). Ventral occipital lesions impair object recognition but not object-directed grasping: An fMRI study. *Brain*, 126: 2463–75.

James, W. (1890). *The principles of psychology*. New York: Holt, Rinehart & Winston.

Janacsek, K. & Nemeth, D. (2013). Implicit sequence learning and working memory: Correlated or complicated? *Cortex*, 49: 2001–6.

Janelle, C.M., Singer, R.N. & Williams, A.M. (1999). External distraction and attentional narrowing: Visual search evidence. *Journal of Sport & Exercise Psychology*, 21: 70–91.

Jans, B., Peters, J.C. & de Weerd, P. (2010). Visual spatial attention to multiple locations at once: The jury is still out. *Psychological Review*, 117: 637–84.

Jansma, J.M., Ramsey, N.F., Slagter, H.A. & Kahn, R.S. (2001). Functional anatomical correlates of controlled and automatic processing. *Journal of Cognitive Neuroscience*, 13: 730–43.

Janssen, C.P. & Brumby, D.P. (2010). Strategic adaptation to performance objectives in a dual-task setting. *Cognitive Science*, 34: 1548–60.

Jared, D. (2002). Spelling-sound consistency and regularity effects in word naming. *Journal of Memory and Language*, 46: 723–50.

Jarosz, A.F. & Wiley, J. (2012). Why does working memory capacity predict RAPM performance? *Intelligence*, 40: 427–38.

Jefferies, E., Sage, K. & Lambon Ralph, M.A. (2007). Do deep dyslexia, dysphasia, and dysgraphia share a common phonological impairment? *Neuropsychologia*, 45: 1553–70.

Jeneson, A. & Squire, L.R. (2012). Working memory, long-term memory, and medial temporal lobe function. *Learning & Memory*, 19: 15–25.

Jeneson, A., Maudlin, K.N., Hopkins, R.O. & Squire, L.R. (2011). The role of the hippocampus in retaining relational information across short delays: The importance of memory load. *Learning & Memory*, 18: 301–5.

Jenkins, R. & Burton, A.M. (2011). Stable face representations. *Philosophical Transactions of the Royal Society B: Biological Sciences*, 366: 1671–83.

Jenkins, R., White, D., van Montfort, X. & Burton, A.M. (2011). Variability in photos of the same face. *Cognition*, 121: 313–23.

Jensen, M.S., Yao, R., Street, W.N. & Simons, D.J. (2011). Change blindness and inattentional blindness. *Wiley Interdisciplinary Reviews: Cognitive Science*, 2: 529–46.

Jiang, Y., Costello, P., Fang, F., Huang, M. & He, S. (2006). A gender- and sexual orientation-dependent spatial attentional effect of invisible images. *Proceedings of the National Academy of Sciences*, 103: 17048–52.

Jiménez, L. & Vázquez, G.A. (2011). Implicit sequence learning and contextual cueing do not compete for central cognitive resources. *Journal of Experimental Psychology: Human Perception and Performance*, 37: 222–35.

Jobard, G., Vigneau, M., Simon, G. & Tzurio-Mazoyer, N. (2011). The weight of skill: Interindividual variability of reading related brain activation patterns in fluent readers. *Journal of Neurolinguistics*, 24: 113–32.

Johannessen, K.B. & Berntsen, D. (2010). Current concerns in involuntary and voluntary autobiographical memories. *Consciousness and Cognition*, 19: 847–60.

Johansson, G. (1973). Visual perception of biological motion and a model for its analysis. *Perception & Psychophysics*, 14: 201–11.

Johansson, G. (1975). Visual motion perception. *Scientific American*, 232: 76–89.

Johansson, G., van Hofsten, C. & Jansson, G. (1980). Event perception. *Annual Review of Psychology*, 31: 27–64.

Johnson, J.A. & Zatorre, R.J. (2006). Neural substrates for dividing and focusing attention between simultaneous auditory and visual events. *NeuroImage*, 31: 1673–81.

Johnson, J.A., Strafella, A.P. & Zatorre, R.J. (2007). The role of the dorsolateral prefrontal cortex in bimodal divided attention: Two transcranial magnetic stimulation studies. *Journal of Cognitive Neuroscience*, 19: 907–20.

Johnson, M.K., Hashtroudi, S. & Lindsay, D.S. (1993). Source monitoring. *Psychological Bulletin*, 114: 3–28.

Johnson-Laird, P.N. (1983). Mental models: Towards a cognitive science of language, inference and consciousness. Cambridge: Cambridge University Press.

Johnson-Laird, P.N. (1999). Deductive reasoning. *Annual Review of Psychology*, 50: 109–35.

Johnson-Laird, P.N. (2004). Mental models and reasoning. In J.P. Leighton & R.J. Sternberg (eds), *The nature of reasoning*. Cambridge: Cambridge University Press.

Johnson-Laird, P.N. (2010). Mental models and human reasoning. *Proceedings of the National Academy of Sciences*, 107: 18243–50.

Johnson-Laird, P.N. (2013). Mental models and cognitive change. *Journal of Cognitive Psychology*, 25: 131–8.

Johnson-Laird, P.N., Lotstein, M. & Byrne, R.M.J. (2012). The consistency of disjunctive assertions. *Memory & Cognition*, 40: 769–78.

Jonides, J., Lewis, R.L., Nee, D.E., Lustig, C., Berman, M.G. & Moore, K.S. (2008). The mind and brain of short-term memory. *Annual Review of Psychology*, 59: 193–224.

Joordens, S., Wilson, D.E., Spalek, T.M. & Paré, D.E. (2010). Turning the process-dissociation procedure inside-out: A new technique for understanding the relation between conscious and unconscious influences. *Consciousness and Cognition*, 19: 270–80.

Joormann, J., Yoon, K.L. & Zetsche, U. (2007). Cognitive inhibition in depression. *Applied & Preventive Psychology*, 12: 128–39.

Josephs, R.A., Larrick, R.P., Steele, C.M. & Nisbett, R.E. (1992). Protecting the self from the negative consequences of risky decisions. *Journal of Personality and Social Psychology*, 62: 26–37.

Josselyn, S.A. & Frankland, P.W. (2012). Infantile amnesia: A neurogenic hypothesis. *Learning & Memory*, 19: 423–33.

Joyce, J. (1922/1960). *Ulysses*. London: Bodley Head.

Juphard, A., Vidal, J.R., Perrone-Bertolotti, M., Minotti, L., Kahane, P., Lachaux, J.-P. & Baciu, M. (2011). Direct evidence for two different neural mechanisms for reading familiar and unfamiliar words: An intra-cerebral EEG study. *Frontiers in Human Neuroscience*, 5 (Article 101).

Juslin, P., Winman, A. & Hansson, P. (2007). The naive intuitive statistician: A naive sampling model of intuitive confidence intervals. *Psychological Review*, 114: 678–703.

Just, M.A. & Carpenter, P.A. (1992). A capacity theory of comprehension. *Psychological Review*, 114: 678–703.

Just, M.A., Carpenter, P.A., Keller, T.A., Emery, L., Zajac, H. & Thlborn, K.R. (2001). Interdependence of non-overlapping cortical systems in dual cognitive tasks. *NeuroImage*, 14: 417–26.

Kaakinen, J.K. & Hyönä, J.(2007). Perspective effects in repeated reading: An eye movement study. *Memory & Cognition*, 35: 1323–36.

Kaakinen, J.K., Hyönä, J. & Keenan, J.M. (2003). How prior knowledge, WMC, and relevance of information affect eye fixations in expository text. *Journal of Experimental Psychology: Learning, Memory, and Cognition*, 29: 447–57.

Kahan, D. (2012). Why we are poles apart on climate change. *Nature*, 488: 255.

Kahan, D.M., Peters, E., Wittlin, M., Slovic, P., Ouellette, L.L., Braman, D. & Mandel, G.N. (2012). The polarising impact of science literacy and numeracy on perceived climate change risks. *Nature Climate Change*, 2: 732–5.

Kahane, G., Wiech, K., Shackel, N., Farias, M., Savulescu, J. & Tracey, I. (2012). The neural basis of intuitive and counterintuitive moral judgment. *Social and Affective Neuroscience*, 7: 393–402.

Kahneman, D. (2003). A perspective on judgment and choice: Mapping bounded rationality. *American Psychologist*, 58: 697–720.

Kahneman, D. & Klein, G. (2009). Conditions for intuitive expertise. *American Psychologist*, 64: 515–26.

Kahneman, D. & Tversky, A. (1972). Subjective probability: Judgment of representativeness. *Cognitive Psychology*, 3: 430–54.

Kahneman, D. & Tversky, A. (1973). On the psychology of prediction. *Psychological Review*, 80: 237–51.

Kahneman, D. & Tversky, A. (1979). Prospect theory: An analysis of decision under risk. *Econometrica*, 47: 263–91.

Kahneman, D. & Tversky, A. (1984). Choices, values and frames. *American Psychologist*, 39: 341–50.

Kaiser, E., Runner, J.T., Sussman, R.S. & Tanenhaus, M.K. (2009). Structural and semantic constraints on the resolution of pronouns and reflexives. *Cognition*, 112: 55–80.

Kaland, N., Moller-Nielsen, A., Smith, L., Mortensen, E.L., Callesen, K. & Gotlieb, D. (2005). The Strange Stories test: A replication study of children and adolescents with Asperger syndrome. *European Child & Adolescent Psychiatry*, 14: 73–82.

Kan, I.P., Alexander, M.P. & Verfaellie, M. (2009). Contribution of prior semantic knowledge to new episodic learning in amnesia. *Journal of Cognitive Neuroscience*, 21: 938–44.

Kandil, F.I., Rotter, A. & Lappe, M. (2009). Driving is smoother and more stable when using the tangent point. *Journal of Vision*, 9: 1–11.

Kane, M.J., Brown, L.H., McVay, J.C., Siliva, P.J., Myin-Germeys, I. & Kwapil, T.R. (2007). For whom the mind wanders, and when: An experience sampling study of working memory and executive control in daily life. *Psychological Science*, 18: 614–21.

Kanizsa, G. (1976). Subjective contours. *Scientific American*, 234: 48–52.

Kanwisher, N. & Yovel, G. (2006). The fusiform face area: A cortical region specialised for the perception of faces. *Philosophical Transactions of the Royal Society B*, 261: 2109–28.

Kanwisher, N., McDermott, J. & Chun, M.M. (1997). The fusiform face area: A module in human extrastriate cortex specialised for face perception. *Journal of Neuroscience*, 17: 4302–11.

Kaplan, S., Bekhor, S. & Shiftan, Y. (2011). Development and estimation of a semi-compensatory choice model based on explicit choice protocols. *Annals of Regional Science*, 47: 51–80.

Kappas, A. (2011). Emotion is not just an alarm bell – It's the whole tootin' fore truck. *Cognition and Emotion*, 25: 785–8.

Kargar, F.R., Choreishi, M.K., Ajilchi, B. & Noohi, S. (2013). Effect of relaxation training on working memory capacity and academic achievement in adolescents. *Procedia Social and Behavioral Sciences*, 82: 608–13.

Karpicke, J.D. (2012). Retrieval-based learning: Active retrieval promotes meaningful learning. *Current Directions in Psychological Science*, 21: 157–63.

Kassin, S.M., Dror, I.E. & Kukucka, J. (2013). The forensic confirmation bias: Problems, perspectives, and proposed solutions. *Journal of Applied Research in Memory and Cognition*, 2: 42–52.

Kaufer, D., Hayes, J.R. & Flower, L.S. (1986). Composing written sentences. *Research in the Teaching of English*, 20: 121–40.

Kaufman, S.B., DeYoung, C.G., Gray, J.R., Jiménez, L., Brown, J. & Mackintosh, N. (2010). Implicit learning as an ability. *Cognition*, 116: 321–40.

Kay, J. & Ellis, A.W. (1987). A cognitive neuropsychological case study of anomia: Implications for psychological models of word retrieval. *Brain*, 110: 613–29.

Kay, K., Naselaris, T., Prenger, R.J. & Gallant, J.L. (2008). Identifying natural images from human brain activity. *Nature*, 452: 352–5.

Kazmerski, V.A., Blasko, D.G. & Dessalegn, B.G. (2003). ERP and behavioural evidence of individual differences in metaphor comprehension. *Memory & Cognition*, 31: 673–89.

Kazui, H., Ishii, R., Yoshida, T., Ikezawa, K., Takaya, M., Tokunaga, H., Tanaka, T. & Takeda, M. (2009). Neuroimaging studies in patients with Charles Bonnet syndrome. *Psychogeriatrics*, 9: 77–84.

Keane, M. (1987). On retrieving analogs when solving problems. *Quarterly Journal of Experimental Psychology*, 39A: 29–41.

Keehner, M., Mayberry, L. & Fischer, M.H. (2011). Different clues from different views: The role of image format in public perceptions of neuroimaging results. *Psychonomic Bulletin and Review*, 18: 422–8.

Keenan, J.P. & Gorman, J. (2007). The causal role of the right hemisphere in self-awareness: It is the brain that is selective. *Cortex*, 43: 1074–82.

Kellogg, R.T. (1988). Attentional overload and writing performance: Effects of rough draft and outline strategies. *Journal of Experimental Psychology: Learning, Memory & Cognition*, 14: 355–65.

Kellogg, R.T. (1994). *The psychology of writing*. New York: Oxford University Press.

Kellogg, R.T. (2001). Competition for working memory among writing processes. *American Journal of Psychology*, 114: 175–91.

Kellogg, R.T. (2008). Training writing skills: A cognitive developmental perspective. *Journal of Writing Research*, 1: 1–26.

Kellogg, R.T. & Mueller, S. (1993). Performance amplification and process restructuring in computer-based writing. *International Journal of Man-Machine Studies*, 39: 33–49.

Kellogg, R.T. & Whiteford, A.P. (2012). The development of writing expertise. In E.L. Grigorenko, E. Mambrino & D.D. Preiss (eds), *Writing: A mosaic of new perspectives*. Hove: Psychology Press.

Kellogg, R.T., Olive, T. & Piolat, A. (2007). Verbal, visual, and spatial working memory in written language production. *Acta Psychologica*, 124: 382–97.

Kellogg, R.T., Whiteford, A.P., Turner, C.E., Cahill, M. & Mertens, A. (2013). Working memory in written composition: An evaluation of the 1996 model. *Journal of Writing Research*, 5: 159–90.

Kendeou, P., Smith, E.R. & O'Brien, E.J. (2013). Updating during reading comprehension: Why causality matters. *Journal of Experimental Psychology: Learning, Memory, and Cognition*, 39: 854–65.

Kenealy, P.M. (1997). Mood-state-dependent retrieval: The effects of induced mood on memory reconsidered. *Quarterly Journal of Experimental Psychology*, 50A: 290–317.

Kennedy, A. & Pynte, J. (2008). The consequences of violations to reading order: An eye movement analysis. *Vision Research*, 48: 2309–20.

Keren, G. & Schul, Y. (2009). Two is not always better than one: A critical evaluation of two-system theories. *Perspectives on Psychological Science*, 4: 533–50.

Kermer, D.A., Driver-Linn, E., Wilson, T.D. & Gilbert, D.T. (2006). Loss aversion is an affective forecasting error. *Psychological Science*, 17: 649–53.

Kersten, A.W., Meissner, C.A., Lechugs, J., Schwartz, B.L., Albrechtsen, J.S. & Iglesias, A. (2010). English speakers attend more strongly than Spanish speakers to manner of motion when classifying novel objects and events. *Journal of Experimental Psychology: General*, 139: 638–53.

Kersten, D., Mamassion, P. & Yuille, A. (2004). Object perception as Bayesian inference. *Annual Review of Psychology*, 55: 271–304.

Kessler, Y. & Moscovitch, M. (2013). Strategic processing in long-term repetition priming in the lexical decision task. *Memory*, 21: 366–76.

Keysar, B., Barr, D.J., Balin, J.A. & Branner, J.S. (2000). Taking perspective in conversation: The role of mutual knowledge in comprehension. *Psychological Science*, 11: 32–8.

Khemlani, S. & Johnson-Laird, P.N. (2012). Theories of the syllogism: A meta-analysis. *Psychological Bulletin*, 138: 427–57.

Khemlani, S., Orenes, I. & Johnson-Laird, P.N. (2012). Negation: A theory of its meaning, representation, and use. *Journal of Cognitive Psychology*, 24: 541–59.

Khetrapal, N. (2010). Load theory of selective attention and the role of perceptual load: Is it time for revision? *European Journal of Cognitive Psychology*, 22: 149–56.

Kiefer, M. & Pulvermüller, F. (2012). Conceptual representations in mind and brain: Theoretical developments, current evidence and future directions. *Cortex*, 48: 805–25.

Kim, D., Stephens, J.D.W. & Pitt, M.A. (2012). How does context play a part in splitting words apart: Production and perception of word boundaries in casual speech. *Journal of Memory and Language*, 66: 509–29.

Kim, E.J., Suh, M.K., Lee, B., Park, K.C., Ku, B.D., Chung, C.S. & Na, D.L. (2009). Transcortical sensory aphasia following a left frontal lobe infarction probably due to anomalously represented language areas. *Journal of Clinical Neuroscience*, 16: 1482–5.

Kim, P.Y. & Mayhorn, C.B. (2008). Exploring students' prospective memory inside and outside the lab. *American Journal of Psychology*, 121: 241–54.

Kimchi, R. & Peterson,M.A. (2008). Figure–ground segmentation can occur without attention. *Psychological Science*, 19: 660–8.

King, J.-R., Sitt, J.D., Faugeras, F., Rohaut, B., El Karoui, I., Cohen, L., Naccache, L. & Dehaene, S. (2013). Information sharing in the brain indexes consciousness in noncommunicative patients. *Current Biology*, 23: 1914–19.

Kinoshita, S. & Norris, D. (2012). Pseudohomophone priming in lexical decision is not fragile in a sparse lexical neighbourhood. *Journal of Experimental Psychology: Learning, Memory, and Cognition*, 38: 764–75.

Kintsch, W. (1992). A cognitive architecture for comprehension. In H.L. Pick, P. van den Broek & D.C. Knill (eds), *Cognition: Conceptual and methodological issues*. Washington, DC. American Psychological Association.

Kintsch, W. (1998). *Comprehension: A paradigm for cognition*. New York: Cambridge University Press.

Kintsch, W. (2000). Metaphor comprehension: A computational theory. *Psychonomic Bulletin & Review*, 7: 257–66.

Kintsch, W., Welsch, D., Schmalhofer, E. & Zimny, S. (1990). Sentence memory: A theoretical analysis. *Journal of Memory and Language*, 29: 133–59.

Kircanski, K., Joormann, J. & Gotlib, I.H. (2012). Cognitive aspects of depression. *Wiley Interdisciplinary Reviews – Cognitive Science*, 3: 301–13.

Klahr, D. & Simon, H.A. (2001). What have psychologists (and others) found about the process of scientific discovery? *Current Directions in Psychological Science*, 10: 75–9.

Klauer, K.C. & Singmann, H. (2013). Does logic feel good? Testing for intuitive detection of logicality in syllogistic reasoning. *Journal of Experimental Psychology: Learning, Memory, and Cognition*, 39: 1265–73.

Klauer, K.C. & Zhao, Z. (2004). Double dissociations in visual and spatial short-term memory. *Journal of Experimental Psychology: General*, 133: 355–81.

Klauer, K.C., Musch, J. & Naumer, B. (2000). On belief bias in syllogistic reasoning. *Psychological Review*, 107: 852–84.

Klein, G. (1998). *Sources of power: How people make decisions*. Cambridge, MA: MIT Press.

Klein, G. (2008). Naturalistic decision making. *Human Factors*, 50: 456–60.

Klein, S.B. & Lax, M.L. (2010). The unanticipated resilience of trait self-knowledge in the face of neural damage. *Memory*, 18: 918–48.

Knauff, M., Fangmeier, T., Riff, C.C. & Johnson-Laird, P.N. (2003). Reasoning, models, and images: Behavioural measures and cortical activity. *Journal of Cognitive Neuroscience*, 15: 559–73.

Knight, J.B., Meeks, J.T., Marsh, R.L., Cook, G.I., Brewer, G.A. & Hicks, J.L. (2011). An observation on the spontaneous noticing of prospective memory event-based cues. *Journal of Experimental Psychology: Learning, Memory, and Cognition*, 37: 298–307.

Knill, D.C. & Saunders, J.A. (2003). Do humans optimally integrate stereo and texture information for judgments of surface slant? *Vision Research*, 43: 2539–58.

Knoblich, G., Ohlsson, S., Haider, H. & Rhenius, D. (1999). Constraint relaxation and chunk decomposition in insight. *Journal of Experimental Psychology: Learning, Memory & Cognition*, 25: 1534–55.

Knoblich, G., Ohlsson, S. & Raney, G.E. (2001). An eye movement study of insight problem solving. *Memory & Cognition*, 29: 1000–9.

Knowlton, B.J. & Foerde, K. (2008). Neural representations of nondeclarative memories. *Current Directions in Psychological Science*, 17: 107–11.

Knowlton, B.J., Morrison, R.G., Hummel, J.E. & Holyoak, K.J. (2012). A neurocomputational system for relational reasoning. *Trends in Cognitive Neurosciences*, 16: 373–81.

Ko, Y. & Lau, H. (2012). A detection theoretic explanation of blindsight suggests a link between conscious perception and metacognition. *Philosophical Transactions of the Royal Society B*, 367: 1401–11.

Koch, C. & Tsuchiya, N. (2007). Attention and consciousness: Two distinct brain processes. *Trends in Cognitive Sciences*, 11: 16–22.

Koch, C. & Tsuchiya, N. (2012). Attention and consciousness: Related yet different. *Trends in Cognitive Sciences*, 16: 103–5.

Kohn, N., Eickhoff, S.B., Scheller, M., Laird, A.R., Fox, P.T. & Habel, U. (2014) Neural network of cognitive emotion regulation: An ALE meta-analysis and MACM analysis. *NeuroImage*, 87: 345–55.

Koivisto, M., Railo, H., Revonsuo, A., Vanni, S. & Salminen-Vaparanta, N. (2011). Recurrent processing in V1/V2 contributes to categorisation of natural scenes. *Journal of Neuroscience*, 31: 2488–92.

Koivisto, M., Kastrati, G. & Revonsuo, A. (2014). Recurrent processing enhances visual awareness but is not necessary for fast categorisation of natural scenes. *Journal of Cognitive Neuroscience*, 26: 223–31.

Kok, E.M., De Bruin, A.B.H., Robben, S.G.F. & van Merrienboer, J.J.G. (2012). Looking in the same manner but seeing it differently: Bottom-up and expertise effects in radiology. *Applied Cognitive Psychology*, 26: 854–62.

Kolb, B. & Whishaw, I.Q. (2003). *Fundamentals of human neuropsychology*. New York: Worth.

Kool, W., McGuire, J.T., Rosen, Z.B. & Botvinick, M.M. (2010). Decision making and the avoidance of cognitive demand. *Journal of Experimental Psychology: General*, 139: 665–82.

Kopelman, M.D. & Bright, P. (2012). On remembering and forgetting our autobiographical pasts: Retrograde amnesia and Andrew Mayes's contribution to neuropsychological method. *Neuropsychologia*, 50: 2961–72.

Koppenol-Gonzalez, G.V., Bouwmeester, S. & Boonstra, A.M. (2010). Understanding planning ability measured by the Tower of London: An evaluation of its internal structure by latent variable modelling. *Psychological Assessment*, 22: 923–34.

Koscik, T.R. & Tranel, D. (2013). Abnormal causal attribution leads to advantageous economic decision-making: A neuropsychological approach. *Journal of Cognitive Neuroscience*, 25: 1372–82.

Kosslyn, S.M. (1994). *Image and brain: The resolution of the imagery debate.* Cambridge, MA: MIT Press.

Kosslyn, S.M. (2005). Mental images and the brain. *Cognitive Neuropsychology*, 22: 333–47.

Kosslyn, S.M. & Thompson, W.L. (2003). When is early visual cortex activated during visual mental imagery? *Psychological Bulletin*, 129: 723–46.

Kouider, S., de Gardelle, V., Sackur, J. & Dupoux, E. (2010). How rich is consciousness? The partial awareness hypothesis. *Trends in Cognitive Sciences*, 14: 301–7.

Kouider, S., Sackur, J. & de Gardelle, V. (2012). Do we still need phenomenal consciousness? *Trends in Cognitive Sciences*, 16: 140–1.

Kounios, J. & Beeman, M. (2014). The cognitive neuroscience of insight. *Annual Review of Psychology*, 65: 71–93.

Kountouriotis, G.K., Floyd, R.C., Gardner, P.H., Merat, N. & Wilkie, R.M. (2012). The role of gaze and road edge information during high-speed locomotion. *Journal of Experimental Psychology: Human Perception and Performance*, 38: 687–702.

Kourtzi, Z. & Connor, C.E. (2011). Neural representations for object perception: Structure, category, and adaptive coding. *Annual Review of Neuroscience*, 34: 45–67.

Kraft, J.M. & Brainard, D.H. (1999). Mechanisms of colour constancy under nearly natural viewing. *Proceedings of the National Academy of Sciences*, 96: 307–12.

Kraljic, T. & Brennan, S.E. (2005). Prosodic disambiguation of syntactic structure: For the speaker or for the addressee? *Cognitive Psychology*, 50: 194–231.

Kraljic, T., Samuel, A.G. & Brennan, S.E. (2008). First impressions and last resorts. *Psychological Science*, 19: 332–8.

Krauss, S. & Wang, X.T. (2003). The psychology of the Monty Hall problem: Discovering psychological mechanisms for solving a tenacious brain teaser. *Journal of Experimental Psychology: General*, 132: 3–22.

Kravitz, D.J. & Behrmann, M. (2011). Space-, object-, and feature-based attention interact to organise visual scenes. *Attention, Perception & Psychophysics*, 73: 2434–47.

Kravitz, D.J., Saleem, K.S., Baker, C.I., Ungerleider, L.G. & Mishkin, M. (2013). The ventral visual pathway: An expanded neural framework for the processing of object quality. *Trends in Cognitive Sciences*, 17: 26–49.

Krawczyk, D.C. (2012). The cognition and neuroscience of relational reasoning. *Brain Research*, 1428: 13–23.

Krawczyk D.C., Morrison, R.G., Viskontas, I., Holyoak, K.J., Chow, T.W., Mendez, M.F., Miller, B.L. & Knowlton, B.J. (2008). Distraction during relational reasoning: The role of prefrontal cortex in interference control. *Neuropsychologia*, 46: 2020–32.

Krawczyk, D.C., McClelland, M.M., Donovan, C.M., Tilman, G.D. & Maguire, M.J. (2010). An fMRI investigation of cognitive stages in reasoning by analogy. *Brain Research*, 1342: 63–73.

Krieger-Redwood, K., Gaskell, M.G., Lindsay, S. & Jefferies, E. (2013). The selective role of premotor cortex in speech perception: A contribution to phoneme judgments but not speech comprehension. *Journal of Cognitive Neuroscience*, 25: 2179–88.

Kring, A.M., Johnson, S.L., Davison, G.C. & Neale, J.M. (2012). *Abnormal psychology* (12th edn). Hoboken, NJ: Wiley.

Króliczak, G., Heard, P., Goodale, M.A. & Gregory, R.L. (2006). Dissocations of perception and action unmasked by the hollow-face illusion. *Brain Research*, 1080: 9–16.

Kruglanski, A.W. & Gigerenzer, G. (2011). Intuitive and deliberate judgments are based on common principles. *Psychological Review*, 118: 97–109.

Krupinski, E.A. (2011). The role of perception in imaging: Past and future. *Seminars in Nuclear Medicine*, 41: 392–400.

Krupinski, E.A., Graham, A.R. & Weinstein, R.S. (2013). Characterising the development of visual search expertise in pathology residents viewing whole slide images. *Human Pathology*, 44: 357–64.

Krynski, T.R. & Tenenbaum, J.B. (2007). The role of causality in judgment under uncertainty. *Journal of Experimental Psychology: General*, 136: 430–50.

Kübler, S. (2006). How do treebank annotation schemes influence parsing results? Or how not to compare apples and oranges. In N. Nicolov, K. Boncheva, G. Angelova & R. Mitkov (eds), *Recent advances in natural language processing IV: Selected papers from RANLP 2005*. Amsterdam: John Benjamins.

Kugler, T., Connolly, T. & Ordonez, L.D. (2012). Emotion, decision and risk: Betting on gambles versus betting on people. *Journal of Behavioral Decision Making*, 25: 123–34.

Kuhn, G. & Findlay, J.M. (2010). Misdirection, attention and awareness: Inattentional blindness reveals temporal relationship between eye movements and visual awareness. *Quarterly Journal of Experimental Psychology*, 63: 136–46.

Kuhn, G. & Martinez, L.M. (2012). Misdirection: Past, present, and the future. *Frontiers in Human Neuroscience*, 5: 172. doi:10.3389/fnhum.2011.00172.

Kuhn, G. & Tatler, B.W. (2011). Misdirected by the gap: The relationship between inattentional blindness and attentional misdirection. *Consciousness and Cognition*, 20: 432–6.

Kuiper, K. (1996). *Smooth talkers*. Mahwah, NJ: Lawrence Erlbaum Associates.

Kulatunga-Moruzi, C., Brooks, L.R. & Norman, G.R. (2004). Using comprehensive feature lists to bias medical diagnosis. *Journal of Experimental Psychology: Learning, Memory, and Cognition*, 30: 563–72.

Kulatunga-Moruzi, C., Brooks, L.R. & Norman, G.R. (2011). Teaching posttraining: Influencing diagnostic strategy with instructions at test. *Journal of Exprimental Psychology: Applied*, 17: 195–209.

Kulkarni, D. & Simon, H.A. (1988). The processes of scientific discovery: The strategy of experimentation. *Cognitive Science*, 12: 139–75.

Kundel, H.L. & Nodine, C.F. (1975). Interpreting chest radiographs without visual search. *Radiology*, 116: 527–32.

Kundel, H.L., Nodine, C.F., Conant, E.F. & Weinstein, S.P. (2007). Holistic components of image perception in mammogram interpretation: Gaze tracking study. *Radiology*, 242: 396–402.

Kuperberg, G.R., Paczynski, M. & Ditman, T. (2011). Establishing causal coherence across sentences: An ERP study. *Journal of Cognitive Neuroscience*, 23: 1230–46.

Kuppens, P., Van Mechelen, I., Smits, D.J.M. & De Broeck, P. (2003). The appraisal basis of anger: Specificity, necessity and sufficiency of components. *Emotion*, 3: 254–69.

Kurby, C.A. & Zacks, J.M. (2012). Starting from scratch and building brick by brick. *Memory & Cognition*, 40: 812–26.

Kurt, S., Deutscher, A., Crook, J.M., Ohl, F.W., Budinger, E., Moeller, C.K., Scheich, H. & Schulze, H. (2008). Auditory cortical contrast enhancing by global winner-take-all inhibitory interactions. *PLOS ONE*, 3(3): e1735.

Kurtz, K.J. & Loewenstein, J. (2007).Converging on a new role for analogy in problem solving and retrieval: When two problems are better than one. *Memory & Cognition*, 35: 334–41.

Kusunoki, M., Moutoussis, K. & Zeki, S. (2006). Effect of background colours on the tuning of colour-selective cells in monkey area V4. *Journal of Neurophysiology*, 95: 3047–59.

Kutas, M., DeLong, K.A. & Smith, N.J. (2011). A look around at what lies ahead: Prediction and predictability in language processing. In M. Bar (ed.), *Predictions in the brain: Using our past to generate a future* (pp. 190–207). Oxford: Oxford University Press.

Kvavilashvili, L. & Fisher, L. (2007). Is time-based prospective remembering mediated by self-initiated rehearsals? Role of incidental cues, ongoing activity, age, and motivation. *Journal of Experimental Psychology: General*, 136: 112–32.

Kvavilashvili, L., Mirani, J., Schlagman, S., Foley, K. & Kornbrot, D.E. (2009). Consistency of flashbulb memories of September 11 over long delays: Implications for consolidation and wrong slide hypotheses. *Journal of Memory and Language*, 61: 556–72.

LaBar, K.S. & Cabeza, R. (2006). Cognitive neuroscience of emotional memory. *Nature Reviews Neuroscience*, 7: 54–64.

LaBerge, D. (1983). The spatial extent of attention to letters and words. *Journal of Experimental Psychology: Human Perception & Performance*, 9: 371–9.

Lacey, S., Stilla, R. & Sathian, K. (2012). Metaphorically feeling: Comprehending textural metaphors activates somatosensory cortex. *Brain & Language*, 120: 416–21.

Laganaro, M., Morand, S. & Schnider, A. (2008). Time course of evoked-potential changes in different forms of anomia in aphasia. *Journal of Cognitive Neuroscience*, 21: 1499–510.

Lai, C.S.L., Fisher, S.E., Hurst, J.A., Vargha-Khadem, E. & Monaco, A.P. (2001). A forkhead-domain gene is mutated in a severe speech and language disorder. *Nature*, 413: 519–23.

Lambon Ralph, M.A., Patterson, K. & Plaut, D.C. (2011). Finite case series or infinite single-case studies? Comments on "Case series investigations in cognitive neuropsychology" by Schwartz and Dell (2010). *Cognitive Neuropsychology*, 28: 466–74.

Lamme, V.A.F. (2006). Towards a true neural stance on consciousness. *Trends in Cognitive Sciences*, 10: 494–501.

Lamme, V.A.F. (2010). How neuroscience will change our view on consciousness. *Cognitive Neuroscience*, 1: 204–40.

Lamy, D., Salti, M. & Bar-Haim, Y. (2009). Neural correlates of subjective awareness and unconscious processing: An ERP study. *Journal of Cognitive Neuroscience*, 21: 1435–46.

Land, E.H. (1986). Recent advances in retinex theory. *Vision Research*, 26: 7–21.

Land, M. (2009). Lee's tau operator. *Perception*, 38: 853–4.

Land, M.F. & Lee, D.N. (1994). Where we look when we steer. *Nature*, 369: 742–4.

Landman, R., Spekreijse, H. & Lamme, V.A.F. (2003). Large capacity storage of integrated subjects before change blindness. *Vision Research*, 43: 149–64.

Landy, M.S., Banks, M.S. & Knill, D.C. (2011). Ideal-observer models of cue utilisation. In J. Trommershäuser, J. Körding & M.S. Landy (eds), *Sensory cue integration* (pp. 5–29). Oxford: Oxford University Press.

Langenburg, G., Champod, C. & Wertheim, P. (2009). Testing for potential contextual bias during the verification stage of the ACE-V methodology when conducting fingerprint comparisons. *Journal of Forensic Sciences*, 54: 571–82.

Lappi, O., Pekkanen, J. & Itkonen, T.H. (2013). Pursuit eye-movements in curve driving differentiate between future path and tangent point models. *PLOS ONE*, 8(7): e68326.

Larsen, J.D., Baddeley, A. & Andrade, J. (2000). Phonological similarity and the irrelevant speech effect: Implications for models of short-term memory. *Memory*, 8: 145–57.

Lassonde, K.A. & O'Brien, E.J. (2009). Contextual specificity in the activation of predictive inferences. *Discourse Processes*, 46: 426–38.

Latorella, K.A. (1998). Effects of modality on interrupted flight deck performance: Implications for data link. *Proceedings of the Human Factors and Ergonomics Society Annual Meeting*, 42: 87–91.

Lavie, N. (2005). Distracted and confused? Selective attention under load. *Trends in Cognitive Sciences*, 9: 75–82.

Lavie, N. (2010). Attention, distraction, and cognitive control under load. *Current Directions in Psychological Science*, 19: 143–8.

Layton, O.W., Mingolla, E. & Yazanbakhsh, A. (2012). Dynamic coding of border-ownership in visual cortex. *Journal of Vision*, 12(8): 1–21.

Le, X., Lancashire, I., Hirst, G. & Jokel, R. (2011). Longitudinal detection of dementia through lexical and syntactic changes in writing: A case study of three British novelists. *Literary and Linguistic Computing*, 26: 435–61.

Leach, F.R. & Plaks, J.E. (2009). Regret for errors of commission in the distant term versus near term: The role of level of abstraction. *Personality and Social Psychology Bulletin*, 35: 221–9.

Lee, D.H., Mirza, R., Flanagan, J.G. & Anderson, A.K. (2014). Optical origins of opposing facial expression actions. *Psychological Science*, 25: 745–52.

Lee, D.N. (1976). A theory of visual control of braking based on information about time-to-collision. *Perception*, 5: 1497–501.

Lee, D.N. (2009). General tau theory: Evolution to date. *Perception*, 38: 837–50.

Lee, E.K., Brown-Schmidt, S. & Watson, D.G. (2013). Ways of looking ahead: Hierarchical planning in language production. *Cognition*, 129: 544–62.

Lee, H., Mozer, M.C., Kramer, A.F. & Vecera, S.P. (2012). Object-based control of attention is sensitive to recent experience. *Journal of Experimental Psychology: Human Perception and Performance*, 38: 314–25.

Lee, J. & Stankov, L. (2012). Large-scale online writing assessments: New approaches adopted by the National Assessment of Educational Progress. In E. Grigorenko, E. Mambrino & D.D. Preiss (eds), *Writing: A mosaic of new perspectives*. Hove: Psychology Press.

Lee, R.J., Dawson, K.A. & Smithson, H.E. (2012). Slow updating of the achromatic point after a change in illumination. *Journal of Vision*, 12: 1–22.

Lee, S.-H., Kravitz, D.J. & Baker, C.I. (2012). Disentangling visual imagery and perception of real-world objects. *NeuroImage*, 59: 4064–73.

Lee, T.-W., Wachtler, T. & Sejnowski, T.J. (2002). Colour opponency is an efficient representation of spectral properties in natural scenes. *Vision Research*, 42: 2095–2103.

Leek, E.C., Patterson, Cristino, F., Conlan, L.I., Patterson, C., Rodriguez, E., & Johnston, S.J. (2012). Eye movements during the recognition of three-dimensional objects: Preferential fixation of concave surface curvature minima. *Journal of Vision*, 12 (Article 7).

Legrenzi, P., Girotto, V. & Johnson-Laird, P.N. (2003). Models of consistency. *Psychological Science*, 14: 131–7.

Lehar, S. (2008) The constructive aspect of visual perception: A Gestalt field theory principle of visual reification suggests a phase conjugate mirror principle of perceptual computation. http://cns-alumni.bu.edu/~slehar/ConstructiveAspect/ConstructiveAspect.html.

Lehle, C. & Hübner, R. (2009). Strategic capacity sharing between two tasks: Evidence from tasks with the same and with different task sets. *Psychological Research*, 73: 707–26.

Lehle, C., Steinhauser, M. & Hübner, R. (2009) Serial or parallel processing in dual tasks: What is more effortful? *Psychophysiology*, 46: 502–9.

Le Mens, G. & Denrell, J. (2011). Rational learning and information sampling: On the "naivety" assumption in sampling explanations of judgment biases. *Psychological Review*, 118: 379–92.

Lench, H.C. & Levine, L.J. (2005). Effects of fear on risk and control judgments and memory: Implications for health promotion messages. *Cognition & Emotion*, 19: 1049–69.

Lench, H.C., Flores, S.A. & Bench, S.W. (2011). Discrete emotions predict changes in cognition, judgment, experience, behaviour, and physiology: A meta-analysis of experimental emotion elicitations. *Psychological Bulletin*, 137: 834–55.

Lenton, A.P. & Francesconi, M. (2010). How humans cognitively manage an abundance of mate options. *Psychological Science*, 21: 528–33.

Lenton, A.P. & Stewart, A. (2008). Changing her ways: The number of options and mate-standard strength impact mate choice strategy and satisfaction. *Judgment and Decision Making Journal*, 3: 501–11.

Leopold, D.A. (2012). Primary visual cortex: Awareness and blindsight. *Annual Review of Neuroscience*, 35: 91–109.

Leopold, D.A. & Logothetis, N.K. (1999). Multi-stable phenomena: Changing views in perception. *Trends in Cognitive Sciences*, 3: 254–64.

LePort, A.K.R., Mattfield, A.T., Dickinson-Anson, H., Fallon, J.H., Stark, C.E.L., Kruggel, F., Cahill, L. & McGaugh, J.L. (2012). Behavioural and neuroanatomical investigation of highly superior autobiographical memory. *Neurobiology of Learning and Memory*, 98: 78–92.

Lerner, J.S. & Keltner, D. (2001). Fear, anger, and risk. *Journal of Personality and Social Psychology*, 81: 146–59.

Lerner, J.S. & Tiedens, L.Z. (2006). Portrait of the angry decision maker: How appraisal tendencies shape anger's influence on cognition. *Journal of Behavioral Decision Making*, 19: 115–37.

Lerner, J.S., Gonzalez, R.M., Small, D.A. & Fischhoff, B. (2003). Effects of fear and anger on perceived risks of terrorism: A national field experiment. *Psychological Science*, 14: 144–50.

Lerner, J.S., Li, Y. & Weber, E.U. (submitted). Sadder, but not wiser: The myopia of misery.

Lesage, E., Navarrete, G. & De Neys, W. (2013). Evolutionary models and Bayesian facilitation: The role of general cognitive resources. *Thinking & Reasoning*, 19: 27–53.

Levelt, W.J.M. (1983). Monitoring and self-repair in speech. *Cognition*, 14: 41–104.

Levelt, W.J.M., Roelofs, A. & Meyer, A.S. (1999). A theory of lexical access in speech production. *Behavioral and Brain Sciences*, 22: 1–38.

Levin, D.T. & Simons, D.J. (1997). Failure to detect changes to attended objects in motion pictures. *Psychonomic Bulletin & Review*, 4: 501–6.

Levin, D.T., Drivdahl, S.B., Momen, N. & Beck, M.R. (2002). False predictions about the detectability of visual changes: The role of beliefs about attention, memory, and the continuity of attended objects in causing change blindness blindness. *Consciousness & Cognition*, 11: 507–27.

Levine, D.N., Calvanio, R. & Popovics, A. (1982). Language in the absence of inner speech. *Word*, 15: 19–44.

Levine, L.J. & Edelstein, R.S. (2009). Emotion and memory narrowing: A review and goal-relevance approach. *Cognition & Emotion*, 23: 833–75.

Leviston, Z., Walker, I. & Morwinski, S. (2013). Your opinion on climate change might not be as common as you think. *Nature Climate Change*, 3: 334–7.

Levy, C.M. & Ransdell, S. (1995). Is writing as difficult as it seems? *Memory & Cognition*, 23: 767–79.

Levy, D.A., Stark, C.E.L. & Squire, L.R. (2004). Intact conceptual priming in the absence of declarative memory. *Psychological Science*, 17: 228–35.

Lewinsohn, P.M., Joiner, T.E., Jr & Rohde, P. (2001). Evaluation of cognitive diathesis-stress models in predicting major depressive disorder in adolescents. *Journal of Abnormal Psychology*, 110: 203–15.

Lewis, P.A., Critchley, H.D., Smith, A.P. & Dolan, R.J. (2005). Brain mechanisms for mood congruent memory facilitation. *NeuroImage*, 25: 1214–23.

Li, O., Jackson, T. & Chen, H. (2011). Attentional and memory biases among weight dissatisfied young women: Evidence from a dichotic listening paradigm. *Cognitive Therapy and Research*, 35: 9312–14.

Li, P., Dunham, Y. & Carey, S. (2009). Of substance: The nature of language effects on entity construal. *Cognitive Psychology*, 58: 487–524.

Liberman, A.M., Cooper, F.S., Shankweiler, D.S. & Studdert-Kennedy, M. (1967). Perception of the speech code. *Psychological Review*, 74: 431–61.

Libet, B., Gleason, C.A., Wright, E.W. & Pearl, D.K. (1983). Time of conscious intention to act in relation to onset of cerebral activity (readiness potential): The unconscious initiation of a freely voluntary act. *Brain*, 106: 623–42.

Lichtenstein, S., Slovic, P., Fischhoff, B., Layman, M. & Coombs, J. (1978). Judged frequency of lethal events. *Journal of Experimental Psychology: Human Learning and Memory*, 4: 551–78.

Lieberman, P. (1963). Some effects of semantic and grammatical context on the production and perception of speech. *Language & Speech*, 6: 172–87.

Lief, H. & Fetkewicz, J. (1995). Retractors of false memories: The evolution of pseudo-memories. *Journal of Psychiatry & Law*, 23: 411–36.

Lin, S., Keysar, B. & Epley, N. (2010). Reflexively mindblind: Using theory of mind to interpret behaviour requires effortful attention. *Journal of Experimental Social Psychology*, 46: 551–6.

Lindholm, T. & Christianson, S.A. (1998). Intergroup biases and eyewitness testimony. *Journal of Social Psychology*, 138: 710–23.

Lindquist, K.A., Wager, T.D., Kober, H., Bliss-Moreau, E. & Barrett, L.F. (2012). The brain basis of emotion: A meta-analytic review. *Behavioral and Brain Sciences*, 35: 121–43.

Lindquist, K.A., Gendron, M., Barrett, L.F. & Dickerson, B.C. (2014). Emotion perception, but not affect perception, is impaired with semantic memory loss. *Emotion* (in press).

Lindsay, D.S. (2008). Source monitoring. In H.L. Roediger (ed.), *Cognitive psychology of memory, vol. 2* (pp. 325–48). Oxford: Elsevier.

Lindsay, D.S., Allen, B.P., Chan, J.C.K. & Dahl, L.C. (2004). Eyewitness suggestibility and source similarity: Intrusions of details from one event into memory reports of another event. *Journal of Memory and Language*, 50: 96–111.

Lingnau, A. & Petris, S. (2013). Action understanding within and outside the motor system: The role of task difficulty. *Cerebral Cortex*, 23: 1342–50.

Linhares, A., Freitas, A.E.T.A., Mendes, A. & Silva, J.S. (2012). Entanglement of perception and reasoning in the combinatorial game of chess: Differential errors of strategic reconstruction. *Cognitive Systems Research*, 13: 72–86.

Linkovski, O., Kalanthroff, E., Henik, A. & Anholt, G. (2013). Did I turn off the stove? Good inhibitory control can protect from influences of repeated checking. *Journal of Behavior Therapy and Experimental Psychiatry*, 44: 30–6.

Linnell, K.J. & Caparos, S. (2011). Perceptual and cognitive load interact to control the spatial focus of attention. *Journal of Experimental Psychology: Human Perception and Performance*, 37: 1643–8.

List, A. & Robertson, L.C. (2007). Inhibition of return and object-based attentional selection. *Journal of Experimental Psychology: HumanPerception and Performance*, 33: 1322–34.

Litvak, P.M., Lerner, J.S., Tiedens, L.Z. & Shonk, K. (2010). Fuel in the fire: How anger impacts judgment and decision-making. In M. Potegal, G. Stemmler & C. Spielberger (eds), *International handbook of anger: Constituent and concomitant biological, psychological, and social processes* (pp. 287–310). New York: Springer.

Liu, X., Li, L., Xiago, J., Yang, J. & Jiang, X. (2013). Abnormalities of autobiographical memory of patients with depressive disorders: A meta-analysis. *Psychology and Psychotherapy: Theory, Research and Practice*, 86: 353–73.

Livingstone, M.S. (2000). Is it warm? Is it real? Or just low spatial frequency? *Science*, 290: 1299.

Locke, S. & Kellar, L. (1973). Categorical perception in a non-liguistic mode. *Cortex*, 9: 355–69.

Loeffler, S.N., Myrtek, M. & Peper, M. (2013). Mood-congruent memory in daily life: Evidence from interactive ambulatory monitoring. *Biological Psychology*, 93: 308–15.

Loewenstein, J. (2010). How one's hook is baited matters for catching an analogy. *Psychology of Learning and Motivation: Advances in Research and Theory*, 53: 149–82.

Loft, S. & Remington, R.W. (2010). Prospective memory and task interference in a continuous monitoring dynamic display task. *Journal of Experimental Psychology: Applied*, 16: 145–57.

Loft, S., Smith, R.E. & Bhaskara, A. (2011). Prospective memory in an air traffic control simulation: External aids that signal when to act. *Journal of Experimental Psychology: Applied*, 17: 60–70.

Loft, S., Smith, R.E. & Remington, R.W. (2013). Minimising the disruptive effects of prospective memory in simulated air traffic control. *Journal of Experimental Psychology: Applied*, 19: 254–65.

Loftus, E.F. & Davis, D. (2006). Recovered memories. *Annual Review of Clinical Psychology*, 2: 469–98.

Loftus, E.F. & Palmer, J.C. (1974). Reconstruction of automobile destruction: An example of the interaction between language and memory. *Journal of Verbal Learning and Verbal Behavior*, 13: 585–9.

Loftus, E.F., Loftus, G.R. & Messo, J. (1987). Some facts about "weapons focus". *Law and Human Behavior*, 11: 55–62.

Logan, G.D. (1988). Toward an instance theory of automatisation. *Psychological Review*, 95: 492–527.

Logan, G.D., Taylor, S.E. & Etherton, J.L. (1999). Attention and automaticity: Toward a theoretical integration. *Psychological Research*, 62: 165–81.

Logie, R.H. (1995). *Visuo-spatial working memory*. Hove: Erlbaum.

Logie, R.H. (1999). Working memory. *Psychologist*, 12: 174–8.

Logie, R.H. (2011). The functional organisation and capacity limits of working memory. *Current Directions in Psychological Science*, 20: 240–5.

Logie, R.H. & van der Meulen, M. (2009). Fragmenting and integrating visuo-spatial working memory. In J.R. Brockmole (ed.), *Representing the visual world in memory*. Hove: Psychology Press.

Logothetis, N.K., Pauls, J. & Poggio, T. (1995). Shape representation in the inferior temporal cortex of monkeys. *Current Biology*, 5: 552–63.

Lorian, C.N. & Grisham, J.R. (2011). Clinical implications of risk aversion: An online study of risk-avoidance and treatment utilisation in pathological anxiety. *Journal of Anxiety Disorders*, 25: 840–8.

Loukusa, S. & Moilanen, I. (2009). Pragmatic inference abilities in individuals with Asperger syndrome or high-functioning autism. A review. *Research in Autism Spectrum Disorders*, 3: 890–904.

Loussouarn, A., Gabriel, D. & Proust, J. (2011). Exploring the informational sources of metaperception: The case of change blindness blindness. *Consciousness and Cognition*, 20: 1489–501.

Love, J. & McKoon, G. (2011). Rules of engagement: Incomplete and complete pronoun resolution. *Journal of Experimental Psychology: Learning, Memory, and Cognition*, 37: 874–87.

Lovell, P.G., Bloj, M. & Harris, J.M. (2012). Optimal integration of shading and binocular disparity for depth perception. *Journal of Vision*, 12: 1–18.

Lu, S.A., Wickens, C.D., Prinet, J.C., Hutchins, S.D., Sarter, N. & Sebok, A. (2013). Supporting interruption management and multimodal interface design: Three meta-analyses of task performance as a function of interrupting task modality. *Human Factors*, 55: 697–724.

Luchins, A.S. (1942). Mechanization in problem solving: The effect of Einstellung. *Psychological Monographs*, 54(6): i–95.

Luk, K.K.S., Xiao, W.S. & Cheung, H. (2012). Cultural effects on perspective taking in Chinese-English bilinguals. *Cognition*, 124(3): 350–5.

Lupyan, G. & Ward, E.J. (2013). Language can boost otherwise unseen objects into visual awareness. *Proceedings of the National Academy of Sciences*, 110: 14196–201.

Luria, A.R. (1968). *The mind of a mnemonist*. New York: Basic Books.

Lustig, C., Konkel, A. & Jacoby, L.L. (2004). Which route to recovery? Controlled retrieval and accessibility bias in retroactive interference. *Psychological Science*, 15: 729–35.

Lyn, H. (2007). Mental representation of symbols as revealed by vocabulary errors in two bonobos (Pan paniscus). *Animal Cognition*, 10: 461–75.

Lyn, H., Greenfield, P.M., Savage-Rumbaugh, S., Gillespie-Lynch, K. & Hopkins, W.D. (2011). Nonhuman primates do declare! A comparison of declarative symbol and gesture use in two children, two bonobos and a chimpanzee. *Language & Communication*, 31: 63–74.

MacDonald, A.W., Cohen, J.D., Stenger, V.A. & Carter, C.S. (2000). Dissociating the role of the dorsolateral prefrontal cortex and anterior cingulate cortex in cognitive control. *Science*, 288: 1835–8.

MacDonald, M.C. (2013). How language production shapes language form and comprehension. *Frontiers in Psychology*, 4 (Article 226).

MacDonald, M.C., Pearlmutter, N.J. & Seidenberg, M.S. (1994). The lexical nature of syntactic ambiguity resolution. *Psychological Review*, 101: 676–703.

Mace, J.H. (2003). Study-test awareness can enhance priming on an implicit memory task: Evidence from a word-completion task. *American Journal of Psychology*, 116: 257–79.

MacGregor, J.N., Ormerod, T.C. & Chronicle, E.P. (2001). Information processing and insight: A process model of performance on the nine-dot and related problems. *Journal of Experimental Psychology: Learning, Memory, and Cognition*, 27: 176–201.

Mack, A. & Rock, I. (1998). *Inattentional blindness*. Cambridge, MA: MIT Press.

Mackay, D.G., James, L.E., Hadley, C.B. & Fogler, K.A. (2011). Speech errors of amnesic HM: Unlike everyday slips-of-the tongue. *Cortex*, 47: 377–408.

Macleod, C. (2015, in press). Attention: Beyond Stroop's (1935) discovery of the Stroop effect. In M.W. Eysenck & D. Groome (eds), *Cognitive psychology: Revisiting the classic studies*. London: SAGE.

MacLeod, C. & Clarke, P.J.F. (2013). Cognitive bias modification: A new frontier in cognition and emotion research. In M.D. Robinson, E. Watkins & E. Harmon-Jones (eds), *Handbook of cognition and emotion*. New York: Guilford Publications.

MacLeod, C. & Mathews, A. (2012). Cognitive bias modification approaches to anxiety. *Annual Review of Clinical Psychology*, 8: 189–217.

Macoir, J. & Bernier, J. (2002). Is surface dysgraphia tied to semantic impairment? Evidence from a case of semantic dementia. *Brain and Cognition*, 48: 452–7.

Mädebach, A., Jescheniak, J.D., Schriefers, H. & Oppermann, F. (2011). Ease of processing constrains the activation flow in the conceptual-lexical system during speech planning. *Journal of Experimental Psychology: Learning, Memory, and Cognition*, 37: 649–60.

Magnuson, J.S. & Nusbaum, H.C. (2007). Acoustic differences, listener expectations, and the perceptual accommodation of talker variability. *Journal of Experimental Psychology: Human Perception and Performance*, 33: 391–409.

Maguire, E.A., Nannery, R. & Spiers, H.J. (2006). Navigation around London by a taxi driver with bilateral hippocampal lesions. *Brain*, 129: 2894–907.

Maguire, M.J., McClelland, M.M., Donovan, C.M., Tillman, G.D. & Krawczyk, D.C. (2012). Tracking cognitive phases in analogical reasoning with event-related potentials. *Journal of Experimental Psychology: Learning, Memory, and Cognition*, 38: 273–81.

Maier, N.R.F. (1931). Reasoning in humans II: The solution of a problem and its appearance in consciousness. *Journal of Comparative Psychology*, 12: 181–94.

Maiworm, M., Bellantoni, M. & Spence, C. (2012). When emotional valence modulates audiovisual integration. *Attention, Perception & Psychophysics*, 74: 1302–11.

Mamede, S., Schmidt, H.G., Rikers, R.M.J.P., Custers, E.J.F.M., Splinter, T.A.W. & van Saase, J.L.C.M. (2010). Conscious thought beats deliberation without attention in diagnostic decision-making: At least when you are an expert. *Psychological Research*, 74: 586–92.

Mandel, D.R. (2005). Are risk assessments of a terrorist attack coherent? *Journal of Experimental Psychology: Applied*, 11: 277–88.

Mandel, D.R. & Vartanian, O. (2011). Frames, brains, and content domains: Neural and behavioural effects of descriptive context on preferential choice. In O. Vartanian & D.R. Mandel (eds), *Neuroscience of decision making*. Hove: Psychology Press.

Manktelow, K. (2012). *Thinking and reasoning: An introduction to the psychology of reason, judgment and decision making*. Hove: Psychology Press.

Manns, J.R., Hopkins, R.O. & Squire, L.R. (2003). Semantic memory and the human hippocampus. *Neuron*, 38: 127–33.

Margolin, S.J., Driscoll, C., Toland, M.J. & Kegler, J.L. (2013). E-readers, computer screens, or paper: Does reading comprehension change across media platforms? *Applied Cognitive Psychology*, 27: 512–19.

Marien, H., Custers, R., Hassin, R.R. & Aarts, H. (2012). Unconscious goal activation and the hijacking of the executive function. *Journal of Personality and Social Psychology*, 103: 399–415.

Mark, V. (1996). Conflicting communicative behaviour in a split-brain patient: Support for dual consciousness. In S. Hameroff, A. Kaszniak & A. Scott (eds), *Toward a science of consciousness: The first Tucson discussions and debates* (pp. 189–96). Cambridge, MA: MIT Press.

Markovits, H., Brunet, M.-L., Thompson, V. & Brisson, J. (2013). Direct evidence for a dual-process model of deductive inference. *Journal of Experimental Psychology: Learning, Memory, and Cognition*, 39: 1213–22.

Markowitsch, H.J. & Staniloiu, A. (2011). Amygdala in action: Relaying biological and social significance to autobiographical memory. *Neuropsychologia*, 49: 718–33.

Marozeau, J., Innes-Brown, H., Grayden, D.B., Burkitt, A.N. & Blamey, P.J. (2010). The effect of visual cues on auditory stream segregation in musicians and non-musicians. *Public Library of Science One*, 5: e11297.

Marques, J.F., Raposo, A. & Almeida, J. (2013). Structural processing and category-specific deficits. *Cortex*, 49: 266–75.

Marr, D. (1982) *Vision: A computational investigation into the human representation and processing of visual information*. San Francisco, CA: W.H. Freeman.

Mars, F. & Navarro, J. (2012). Where we look when we drive with or without active steering wheel control. *PLOS ONE*, 7(8): e43858.

Marsh, E.J. & Tversky, B. (2004). Spinning the stories of our lives. *Applied Cognitive Psychology*, 18: 491–503.

Marslen-Wilson, W.D. (1990). Activation, competition, and frequency in lexical access. In G.T.M. Altmann (ed.), *Cognitive models of speech processing* (pp. 148–72). Cambridge, MA: MIT Press.

Marslen-Wilson, W.D. & Tyler, L.K. (1980). The temporal structure of spoken language comprehension. *Cognition*, 6: 1–71.

Martin, C.D., Nazir, T., Thierry, G., Paulignan, Y. & Démonet, J.-F. (2006). Perceptual and lexical effects in letter identification: An event-related potential study of the word superiority effect. *Brain Research*, 1098: 153–60.

Martin, D.H. & Barry, C. (2012). Writing nonsense: The interaction between lexical and sublexical knowledge in the priming of nonword spelling. *Psychonomic Bulletin & Review*, 19: 691–8.

Martin, R.C., Miller, M. & Vu, H. (2004). Lexical-semantic retention and speech production: Further evidence from normal and brain-damaged participants for a phrasal scope of planning. *Cognitive Neuropsychology*, 21: 625–44.

Martinez, A., Anilo-Vento, L., Sereno, M.I., Frank, L.R., Buxton, R.B., Dubowitz, D.J., Wong, E.C., Hinrichs, H., Heinze, H.J. & Hillyard, S.A. (1999). Involvement of striate and extrastriate visual cortical areas in spatial attention. *Nature Neuroscience*, 2: 364–9.

Mather, G. (2009). *Foundations of sensation and perception* (2nd edn). Hove: Psychology Press.

Mather, G. (2015, in press). Computational approach to perception: Beyond Marr's (1982) computational approach to vision. In M.W. Eysenck & D. Groome (eds), *Cognitive psychology: Revisiting the classic studies*. London: SAGE.

Mathews, A. (2012). Effects of modifying the interpretation of emotional ambiguity. *Journal of Cognitive Psychology*, 24: 92–105.

Mathy, F. & Feldman, J. (2012). What's magic about magic numbers: Chunking and data compression in short-term memory. *Cognition*, 122: 346–62.

Mattys, S.L. (2004). Stress versus co-articulation: Toward an integrated approach to explicit speech segmentation. *Journal of Experimental Psychology: Human Perception and Performance*, 30: 397–408.

Mattys, S.L. & Liss, J.M. (2008). On building models of spoken-word recognition: When there is as much to learn from natural "oddities" as artificial normality. *Perception & Psychophysics*, 70: 1235–42.

Mattys, S.L., White, L. & Melhorn, J.F. (2005). Integration of multiple speech segmentation cues: A hierarchical framework. *Journal of Experimental Psychology: General*, 134: 477–500.

Mattys, S.L., Brooks, J. & Cooke, M. (2009). Recognising speech under a provessing load: Dissociating energetic from informational factors. *Cognitive Psychology*, 59: 203–43.

Mattys, S.L., Davis, M.H., Bradlow, A.R. & Scott, S.K. (2012). Speech recognition in adverse conditions: A review. *Language and Cognitive Processes*, 27: 953–78.

Maule, A.J. & Hodgkinson, G.P. (2002). Heuristics, biases and strategic decision making. *The Psychologist*, 15: 69–71.

Mauss, I.B., Cook, C.L., Cheng, J.Y.J. & Gross, J.J. (2007). Individual differences in cognitive reappraisal: Experiential and physiological responses to an anger provocation. *International Journal of Psychophysiology*, 66: 116–24.

Mayberry, E.J., Sage, K. & Lambon Ralph, M.A. (2011). At the edge of semantic space: The breakdown of coherent concepts in semantic dementia is constrained by typicality and severity but not modality. *Journal of Cognitive Neuroscience*, 23: 2240–51.

Mayor, J., Gomez, P. Chang, F. & Lupyan, G. (2014). Connectionism coming of age: Legacy and future challenges. *Frontiers in Psychology*, 5 (Article 187).

Mazzone, M. & Lalumera, E. (2010). Concepts: Stored or created? *Minds and Machines*, 20: 47–68.

McCabe, D.P., Roediger, H.L., McDaniel, M.A., Balota, D.A. & Hambrick, D.Z. (2010). The relationship between working memory capacity and executive functioning: Evidence for a common executive attention construct. *Neuropsychology*, 24: 222–43.

McCaffrey, T. (2012). Innovation relies on the obscure: A key to overcoming the classic problem of functional fixedness. *Psychological Science*, 23: 215–18.

McCarley, J.S., Kramer, A.F., Wickens, C.D. & Boot, W.R. (2004). Visual skills in airport-security screening. *Psychological Science*, 15: 302–6.

McCarthy, R. & Warrington, E.K. (1984). A two-route model of speech production. *Brain*, 107: 463–85.

McClelland, J.L. & Elman, J.L. (1986). The TRACE model of speech perception. *Cognitive Psychology*, 18: 1–86.

McClelland, J.L. & Rumelhart, D.E. (1981). An interactive activation model of context effects in letter perception. Part 1. An account of basic findings. *Psychological Review*, 88: 375–407.

McDaniel, M.A. & Einstein, G.O. (2011). The neuropsychology of prospective memory in normal aging: A componential approach. *Neuropsychologia*, 49: 2147–55.

McDaniel, M.A., LaMontagne, P., Beck, S.M., Scullin, M.K. & Braver, T.S. (2013) Dissociable neural routes to successful prospective memory. *Psychological Science*, 24(9): 1791–800.

McDermott, J.H. (2009). The cocktail party problem. *Current Biology*, 19: R1024–7.

McDermott, R., Fowler, J.H. & Smirnov, O. (2008). On the evolutionary origin of prospect theory preferences. *The Journal of Politics*, 70: 335–50.

McDonald, J.L. (2008). Differences in the cognitive demands of word order, plural, and subject-verb agreement constructions. *Psychonomic Bulletin & Review*, 15: 980–4.

McEachrane, M. (2009). Emotion, meaning, and appraisal theory. *Theory & Psychology*, 19: 33–53.

McElree, B. (2006). Accessing recent event. In B. Ross (ed.), *The psychology of learning and motivation*. San Diego, CA: Academic Press.

McFarland, C. & Glisky, E. (2012). Implementation intentions and imagery: Individual and combined effects on prospective memory among young adults. *Memory & Cognition*, 40: 62–9.

McGlinchey-Berroth, R., Milber, W.P., Verfaellie, M., Alexander, M. & Kilduff, P.T. (1993). Semantic processing in the neglected visual field: Evidence from a lexical decision task. *Cognitive Neuropsychology*, 10: 79–108.

McGlone, M.S. & Manfredi, D.A. (2001). Topic-vehicle interaction in metaphor comprehension. *Memory & Cognition*, 29: 1209–19.

McGregor, S.J. & Howes, A. (2002). The role of attack and defence semantics in skilled players' memory for chess positions. *Memory & Cognition*, 30: 707–17.

McGugin, R.W., Gatenby, J.C., Gore, J.C. & Gauthier, I. (2012). High-resolution imaging of expertise reveals reliable object selectivity in the fusiform face area related to perceptual performance. *Proceedings of the National Academy of Sciences*, 109: 17063–8.

McGurk, H. & MacDonald, J. (1976). Hearing lips and seeing voices. *Nature*, 264: 746–8.

McIntosh, R.D., McClements, K.I., Schindler, I., Cassidy, T.P., Birchall, D. & Milner, A.D. (2004). Avoidance of obstacles in the absence of visual awareness. *Proceedings of the Royal Society B*, 271: 15–20.

McKay, A., Davis, C., Savage, G. & Castles, A. (2008). Semantic involvement in reading aloud: Evidence from a nonword training study. *Journal of Experimental Psychology: Learning, Memory and Cognition*, 34: 1495–517.

McKeeff, T.J., McGugin, R.W., Tong, F. & Gauthier, I. (2010). Expertise increases the functional overlap between face and object perception. *Cognition*, 117: 335–60.

McKeefry, D.J., Burton, M.P., Vakrou, C., Barrett, B.T. & Morland, A.B. (2008). Induced deficits in speed perception by transcranial magnetic stimulation of human cortical areas V5/MT and V3A. *Journal of Neuroscience*, 28: 6848–57.

McKenzie, S. & Eichenbaum, H. (2011). Consolidation and reconsolidation: Two lives of memories? *Neuron*, 71: 224–33.

McKone, E., Kanwisher, N. & Duchaine, B.C. (2007). Can generic expertise explain special processing for faces? *Trends in Cognitive Sciences*, 11: 8–15.

McKoon, G. & Ratcliff, R. (1992). Inference during reading. *Psychological Review*, 99: 440–66.

McKoon, G. & Ratcliff, R. (2003). Meaning through syntax: Language comprehension and the reduced relative clause construction. *Psychological Review*, 110: 490–525.

McLaughlin, K., Remy, M. & Schmidt, H.G. (2008). Is analytic information processing a feature of expertise in medicine? *Advances in Health Sciences Education*, 13: 123–8.

McLeod, P. (1977). A dual-task response modality effect: Support for multiprocessor models of attention. *Quarterly Journal of Experimental Psychology*, 29: 651–67.

McMurray, B., Dennhardt, J.L. & Struck-Marshall, A. (2008). Context effects on musical chord categorisation: Different forms of top-down feedback in speech and music? *Cognitive Science*, 32: 893–920.

McNally, R.J. & Geraerts, E. (2009). A new solution to the recovered memory debate. *Perspectives on Psychological Science*, 4: 126–34.

McNamara, D.S. & Magliano, J. (2009). Toward a comprehensive model of comprehension. In B. Ross (ed.), *The psychology of learning and motivation, vol. 51* (pp. 297–384). New York: Elsevier Science.

McNeil, M.R., Hula, W.D. & Sung, J.E. (2010). The role of memory and attention in aphasic language performance. In J. Guendouzi, F. Loncke & M. Williams (eds), *The handbook of psycholinguistics and cognitive processes: Perspectives in communication disorders*. Hove: Psychology Press.

McNerney, M.W., Goodwin, K.A. & Radvansky, G.A. (2011). A novel study: A situation model analysis of reading times. *Discourse Processes*, 48: 453–74.

McQueen, J.M. (1991). The influence of the lexicon on phonetic categorisation: Stimulus quality in word-final ambiguity. *Journal of Experimental Psychology: Human Perception & Performance*, 17: 433–43.

McRae, K., Hughes, B., Chopra, S., Gabrieli, J.D.E., Gross, J.J. & Ochsner, K.N. (2010). Neural systems supporting the control of affective and cognitive conflicts. *Journal of Cognitive Neuroscience*, 22: 248–62.

McRae, K., Jacobs, S.E., Ray, R.D., John, O.P. & Gross, J.J. (2012). Individual differences in reappraisal ability: Links to reappraisal frequency, well-being, and cognitive control. *Journal of Research in Personality*, 46: 2–7.

McVay, J.C. & Kane, M.J. (2012a). Why does working memory capacity predict variation in reading comprehension? On the influence of mind wandering and executive attention. *Journal of Experimental Psychology: General*, 141: 302–20.

McVay, J.C. & Kane, M.J. (2012b). Drifting from low to "D'oh!": Working memory capacity and mind wandering predict extreme reaction times and executive control errors. *Journal of Experimental Psychology: Learning, Memory, and Cognition*, 38: 525–49.

Megreya, A.M., White, D. & Burton, A.M. (2011). The other-race effect does not rely on memory: Evidence from a matching task. *Quarterly Journal of Experimental Psychology*, 64: 1473–83.

Megreya, A.M., Sandford, A. & Burton, A.M. (2013). Matching face images taken on the same day or months apart: The limitations of photo ID. *Applied Cognitive Psychology*, 27: 700–6.

Meinz, E.J. & Hambrick, D.Z. (2010). Deliberate practice is necessary but not sufficient to explain individual differences in piano sight-reading skill: The role of working memory capacity. *Psychological Science*, 21: 914–19.

Meiser, T. (2011). Much pain, little gain? Paradigm-specific models and methods in experimental psychology. *Perspectives on Psychological Science*, 6: 183–91.

Melby-Lervåg, A., Lyster, S.-A.H. & Hulme, C. (2012). Phonological skills and their role in learning to read: A meta-analytic review. *Psychological Bulletin*, 138: 322–52.

Mele, A. (2013). Unconscious decisions and free will. *Philosophical Psychology*, 26: 777–89.

Melinger, A. & Rahman, R.A. (2013). Lexical selection is competitive: Evidence from indirectly activated semantic associates during picture naming. *Journal of Experimental Psychology: Learning, Memory, and Cognition*, 39: 348–64.

Melloni, L., Molina, C., Pena, M., Torres, D., Singer, W. & Rodriguez, E. (2007). Synchronisation of neural activity across cortical areas correlates with conscious perception. *Journal of Neuroscience*, 27: 2858–65.

Melloni, L., Schwiedrzik, C.M., Muller, N., Rodriguez, E. & Singer, W. (2011). Expectations change the signatures and timing of electrophysiologial correlates of perceptual awareness. *Journal of Neuroscience*, 31: 1386–96.

Melo, M., Scarpin, D.J., Amaro, E., Passos, R.B.D., Sato, J.R., Friston, K.J. & Price, C.J. (2012). How doctors generate diagnostic hypotheses: A study of radiological diagnosis with functional magnetic resonance imaging. *PLOS ONE*, 6(12): e28752.

Memon, A., Zaragoza, M., Clifford, B.R. & Kidd, L. (2009). Inoculation or antidote? The effects of cognitive interview timing on false memory for forcibly fabricated events. *Law and Human Behavior*, 34: 105–17.

Memon, A., Meissner, C.A. & Fraser, J. (2010). The cognitive interview: A meta-analytic review and study space analysis of the past 25 years. *Psychology, Public Policy and Law*, 16: 340–72.

Mendoza, J.E., Elliott, D., Meegan, D.V., Lyons, J.L. & Welsh, T.N. (2006). The effect of the Müller-Lyer illusion on the planning and control of manual aiming movements. *Journal of Experimental Psychology: Human Perception and Performance*, 32: 413–22.

Mengotti, P., Ticini, L.F., Waszak, F., Schütz-Bosbach, S. & Rumiati, R.I. (2013). Imitating others' actions: Transcranial magnetic stimulation of the parietal opercula reveals the processes underlying automatic imitation. *European Journal of Neuroscience*, 37: 316–22.

Menneer, T., Cave, K.R. & Donnelly, N. (2009). The cost of search for multiple targets: Effects of practice and target similarity. *Journal of Experimental Psychology: Applied*, 15: 125–39.

Mercier, H. & Sperber, D. (2011). Why do humans reason? Arguments for an argumentative theory. *Behavioral and Brain Sciences*, 34: 57–111.

Merikle, P.M., Smilek, D. & Smallwood, J.D. (2001). Perception without awareness: Perspectives from cognitive psychology. *Cognition*, 79: 115–34.

Mesgarani, N. & Chang, E.F. (2012). Selective cortical representation of attended speaker in multi-talker speech perception. *Nature*, 485: 233–6.

Mesulam, M.M., Wieneke, C., Hurley, R., Rademaker, A., Thompson, C.K., Weintraub, S. & Rogalski, E.J. (2013). Words and objects at the tip of the left temporal lobe in primary progressive aphasia, *Brain*, 136: 601–18.

Metcalfe, J. & Wiebe, D. (1987). Intuition in insight and noninsight problem solving. *Memory & Cognition*, 15: 238–46.

Meteyard, L., Cuadrado, S.R., Bahrami, B. & Vigliocco, G. (2012). Coming of age: A review of embodiment and the neuroscience of semantics. *Cortex*, 48: 788–804.

Meyer, A.S. & Damian, M.F. (2007). Activation of distractor names in the picture-picture interference paradigm. *Memory & Cognition*, 35: 494–503.

Meyer, D.E. & Schvaneveldt, R.W. (1971). Facilitation in recognising pairs of words: Evidence of a dependence between retrieval operations. *Journal of Experimental Psychology*, 90: 227–34.

Mickes, L., Searle-Carlisle, T.M. & Wixted, J.T. (2013). Rethinking familiarity: Remember/know judgments in free recall. *Journal of Memory and Language*, 68: 333–49.

Migo, E.M., Mayes, A.R. & Montaldi, D. (2012). Measuring recollection and familiarity: Improving the remember/know procedure. *Consciousness and Cognition*, 21: 1435–55.

Milivojevic, B. (2012). Object recognition can be viewpoint dependent or invariant – It's just a matter of time and task. *Frontiers in Computational Neuroscience*, 6 (Article 27).

Milivojevic, B., Hamm, J.P. & Corballis, M.C. (2011). About turn: How object orientation affects categorisation and mental rotation. *Neuropsychologia*, 49: 3758–67.

Miller, G.A. (1956). The magic number seven, plus or minus two: Some limits on our capacity for processing information. *Psychological Review*, 63: 81–93.

Miller, J., Ulrich, R. & Rolke, B. (2009). On the optimality of serial and parallel processing in the psychological refractory period paradigm: Effects of the distribution of stimulus onset asymmetries. *Cognitive Psychology*, 58: 273–310.

Milner, A.D. (2012). Is visual processing in the dorsal stream accessible to consciousness? *Proceedings of the Royal Society B*, 279: 2289–98.

Milner, A.D. & Goodale, M.A. (1995). *The visual brain in action*. Oxford: Oxford University Press.

Milner, A.D. & Goodale, M.A. (2008). Two visual systems re-viewed. *Neuropsychologia*, 46: 774–85.

Milner, A.D., Perrett, D.L., Johnston, R.S., Benson, P.J., Jordan, T.R., Heeley, D.W., Bettucci, D., Mortara, F., Mutani, R. & Terazzi, E. (1991). Perception and action in "visual form agnosia". *Brain*, 114: 405–28.

Milner, A.D., Dijkerman, H.C., McIntosh, R.D., Rossetti, Y. & Pisella, L. (2003). Delayed reaching and grasping in patients with optic ataxia. *Progress in Brain Research*, 142: 225–42.

Miranda, R. & Kihlstromm, J.F. (2005). Mood congruence in childhood and recent autobiographical memory. *Cognition & Emotion*, 19: 981–98.

Mirković, J. & MacDonald, M.C. (2013). When singular and plural are both grammatical: Semantic and morphophonological effects in agreement. *Journal of Memory and Language*, 69: 277–98.

Mirman, D., McClelland, L., Holt, L.L. & Magnuson, J.S. (2008). Effects of attention on the strength of lexical influences on speech perception: Behavioural experiments and computational mechanisms. *Cognitive Science*, 32: 398–417.

Misra, M., Guo, T., Bobb, S.C. & Kroll, J.F. (2012). When bilinguals choose a single word to speak: Electrophysiological evidence for inhibition of the native language. *Journal of Memory and Language*, 67: 224–37.

Mitchell, D.B. (2006). Nonconscious priming after 17 years. *Psychological Science*, 17: 925–9.

Mitroff, I. (1974). *The subjective side of science*. Amsterdam: Elsevier.

Mitte, K. (2008). Memory bias for threatening information in anxiety and anxiety disorders: A meta-analytic review. *Psychological Bulletin*, 134: 886–911.

Miyake, A. & Friedman, N.P. (2012). The nature and organisation of individual differences in executive functions: Four general conclusions. *Current Directions in Psychological Science*, 21: 8–14.

Miyake, A., Friedman, N.P., Emerson, M.J., Witzki, A.H., Howerter, A. & Wager, T. (2000). The unity and diversity of executive functions and their contributions to complex "frontal lobe" tasks: A latent variable analysis. *Cognitive Psychology*, 41: 49–100.

Mogg, K., Bradbury, K.E. & Bradley, B.P. (2006). Interpretation of ambiguous information in clinical depression. *Behaviour Research & Therapy*, 44: 1411–19.

Mohamed, T. & Clifton, C. (2011). Processing temporary syntactic ambiguity: The effect of contextual bias. *Quarterly Journal of Experimental Psychology*, 64: 1797–820.

Molenberghs, P., Cunningham, R. & Mattingley, J.B. (2012a). Brain regions with mirror properties: A meta-analysis of 125 human fMRI studies. *Neuroscience and Biobehavioral Reviews*, 36: 341–9.

Molenberghs, P., Sale, M.V. & Mattingley, J.B. (2012b). Is there a critical lesion site for unilateral spatial neglect? A meta-analysis using activation likelihood estimation. *Frontiers in Human Neuroscience*, 6 (Article 78).

Monti, M.M. & Osherson, D.N. (2012). Logic, language and the brain. *Brain Research*, 1428: 33–42.

Monti, M.M., Vanhaudenhuyse, A., Coleman, M.R., Boly, M., Pickard, J.D., Tshibanda, L., Owen, A.M. & Laureys, S. (2010). Wilful modulation of brain activity in disorders of consciousness. *New England Journal of Medicine*, 362: 579–89.

Monti, M.M., Pickard, J.D. & Owen, A.M. (2013). Visual cognition in disorders of consciousness: From V1 to top-down attention. *Human Brain Mapping*, 34: 1245–53.

Moors, A. & de Houwer, J. (2006). Automaticity: A theoretical and conceptual analysis. *Psychological Bulletin*, 132: 297–326.

Moors, A. & Scherer, K.R. (2013). The role of appraisal in emotion. In M.D. Robinson, E. Watkins & E. Harmon-Jones (eds), *Handbook of cognition emotion*. New York: Guilford Publications.

Moran, J.M. & Zaki, J. (2013). Functional neuroimaging and psychology: What have you done for me lately? *Journal of Cognitive Neuroscience*, 25: 834–42.

Morawetz, C., Holz, P., Bauedwig, J., Treue, S. & Dechent, P. (2007). Split of attentional resources in human visual cortex. *Visual Neuroscience*, 24: 817–26.

Moray, N. (1959). Attention in dichotic listening: Affective cues and the influence of instructions. *Quarterly Journal of Experimental Psychology*, 11: 56–60.

Moro, V., Berlucchi, G., Lerch, J., Tomaiuolo, F. & Aglioti, S.M. (2008). Selective deficit of mental visual imagery with intact primary visual cortex and visual perception. *Cortex*, 44: 109–18.

Morris, C.D., Bransford, J.D. & Franks, J.J. (1977). Levels of processing versus transfer appropriate processing. *Journal of Verbal Learning and Verbal Behavior*, 16: 519–33.

Morrison, R.G. (2005). Thinking in working memory. In K.J. Holyoak & R.G. Morrison (eds), *Cambridge handbook of thinking and reasoning*. Cambridge: Cambridge University Press.

Morrison, R.G., Holyoak, K.J. & Truong, B. (2001). Working-memory modularity in analogical reasoning. In J.D. Moore & K. Stenning (eds), *Proceedings of the Twenty-third Annual Conference of the Cognitive Science Society*. Mahwah, NJ: Lawrence Erlbaum Associates.

Morsanyi, K. & Handley, S.J. (2012). Logic feels so good – I like it! Evidence for intuitive detection of logicality in syllogistic reasoning. *Journal of Experimental Psychology: Learning, Memory, and Cognition*, 38: 596–616.

Moscovitch, M. (2008). Commentary: A perspective on prospective memory. In M. Kliegel, A. McDaniel & G.O. Einstein (eds), *Prospective memory: Cognitive, neuroscience, developmental, and applied perspectives* (pp. 309–20). New York: Lawrence Erlbaum Associates.

Moscovitch, M., Winocur, G. & Behrmann, M. (1997). What is special about face recognition? Nineteen experiments on a person with visual object agnosia and dyslexia but normal face recognition. *Journal of Cognitive Neuroscience*, 9: 555–604.

Moser, J.S., Becjer, M.W. & Moran, T.P. (2012a). Enhanced attentional capture in trait anxiety. *Emotion*, 12: 213–16.

Moser, J.S., Huppert, J.D., Foa, E.B. & Simons, R.F. (2012b). Interpretation of ambiguous social scenarios in social phobia and depression: Evidence from event-related brain potentials. *Biological Psychology*, 89: 387–97.

Moss, J., Kotovsky, K. & Cagan, J. (2011). The effect of incidental hints when problems are suspended before, during, or after an impasse. *Journal of Experimental Psychology: Learning, Memory, and Cognition*, 37: 140–8.

Most, S.B. (2013). Settings sights higher: Category-level attentional set modulates sustained inattentional blindness. *Psychological Research*, 77: 139–46.

Motley, M.T. (1980). Verifications of "Freudian slips" and semantic prearticulatory editing via laboratory-induced spoonerisms. In V.A. Fromkin (ed.), *Errors in linguistic performance: Slips of the tongue, ear, pen, and hand*. New York: Academic Press.

Motley, M.T., Baars, B.J. & Camden, C.T. (1983). Experimental verbal slip studies: A review and an editing model of language encoding. *Communication Monographs*, 50: 79–101.

Mottaghy, F.M. (2006). Interfering with working memory in humans. *Neuroscience*, 139: 85–90.

Möttönen, R. & Watkins, K.E. (2012) Using TMS to study the role of the articulatory motor system in speech perception. *Aphasiology*, 26: 1103–18.

Möttönen, R., Dutton, R. & Watkins, K.E. (2013). Auditory-motor processing of speech sounds. *Cerebral Cortex*, 23: 1190–7.

Moulin, C.J.A., Souchay, C. & Morris, R.G. (2013). The cognitive neuropsychology of recollection. *Cortex*, 49: 1445–51.

Moulton, P.L., Petros, T.V., Apostal, K.J., Park, R.V., Ronning, E.A., King, B.M. & Penland, J.G. (2005). Alcohol-induced impairment and enhancement of memory: A test of the interference theory. *Physiology & Behavior*, 85: 240–5.

Moulton, S.T. & Kosslyn, S.M. (2009). Imagining predictions: Mental imagery as mental emulation. *Philosophical Transactions of the Royal Society B: Biological Sciences*, 364: 1273–80.

Moxley, J.H., Ericsson, K.A., Charness, N. & Krampe, R.T. (2012). The role of intuition and deliberative thinking in experts' superior tactical decision-making. *Cognition*, 124: 72–8.

Mukamel, R., Ekstrom, A.D., Kaplan, J., Iacoboni, M. & Fried, I. (2010). Single-neurons responses in humans during execution and observation of actions. *Current Biology*, 20: 750–6.

Mulder, G. & Sanders, T.J.M. (2012). Causal coherence relations and levels of discourse representation. *Discourse Processes*, 49: 501–22.

Müller, N.G., Bartelt, O.A., Donner, T.H., Villringer, A. & Brandt, S.A. (2003). A physiological correlate of the "zoom lens" of visual attention. *Journal of Neuroscience*, 23: 3561–5.

Mulligan, N.W. & Picklesimer, M. (2012). Levels of processing and the cue-dependent nature of recollection. *Journal of Memory and Language*, 66: 79–92.

Murphy, G.L. (2011). Models and concepts. In E.M. Pothos & A.J.Wills (eds), *Formal approaches in categorisation* (pp. 299–312). Cambridge: Cambridge University Press.

Murphy, S., Fraenkel, N. & Dalton, P. (2013). Perceptual load does not modulate auditory distractor processing. *Cognition*, 129: 345–55.

Murray, J.D. & Burke, K.A. (2003). Activation and encoding of predictive inferences: The role of reading skill. *Discourse Processes*, 35: 81–102.

Murty, V.P., Ritchey, M., Adcock, R.A. & LaBar, K.S. (2010). fMRI studies of successful emotional memory encoding: A quantitative meta-analysis. *Neuropsychologia*, 48: 3459–69.

Musel, B., Chauvin, A., Guyader, N., Chokron, S. & Perin, C. (2012). Is coarse-to-fine strategy sensitive to normal aging? *PLOS ONE*, 7(6): e38493.

Mustanski, B. (2007). The influence of state and trait affect on HIV risk behaviours: A daily diary study of MSM. *Health Psychology*, 26: 618–26.

Muter, P. (1978). Recognition failure of recallable words in semantic memory. *Memory & Cognition*, 6: 9–12.

Mutha, P.K., Sainburg, R.L. & Haaland, K.Y. (2010). Coordination deficits in ideomotor apraxia during visually targeted reaching reflect impaired visuomotor transformations. *Neuropsychologia*, 48: 3855–67.

Myers, E.B. & Blumstein, S.E. (2008). The neural bases of the lexical effect: An fMRI investigation. *Cerebral Cortex*, 18: 278–88.

Naccache, L., Blandin, E. & Dehaene, S. (2002). Unconscious masked priming depends on temporal attention. *Psychological Science*, 13: 416–24.

Nadel, L., Hupbach, A., Gomez, R. & Newman-Smith, K. (2012). Memory formation, consolidation and transformation. *Neuroscience and Biobehavioral Reviews*, 36: 1640–5.

Nairne, J.S. (2015, in press). Encoding and retrieval: Beyond Tulving and Thomson's (1973) encoding specificity principle. In M.W. Eysenck & D. Groome (eds), *Cognitive psychology: Revisiting the classic studies*. London: SAGE.

Nakamura, C., Arai, M. & Mazuka, R. (2012). Immediate use of prosody and context in predicting a syntactic structure. *Cognition*, 125: 317–23.

Nascimento, S.M.C., de Almeida, V.M.N., Fiadeiro, P.T. & Foster, D.H. (2004). Minimum-variance cone-excitation ratios and the limits of relational colour constancy. *Visual Neuroscience*, 21: 337–40.

Nassi, J.J. & Callaway, E.M. (2009). Parallel processing strategies of the primate visual system. *Nature Reviews Neuroscience*, 10: 360–72.

Navarro, D.J. & Perfors, A.F. (2011). Hypothesis generation, sparse categories, and the positive test strategy. *Psychological Review*, 118: 120–34.

Navon, D. (1977). Forest before trees: The precedence of global features in visual perception. *Cognitive Psychology*, 9: 353–83.

Nee, D.E. & Jonides, J. (2013). Trisecting representational states in short-term memory. *Frontiers in Human Neuroscience*, 7 (Article 796).

Neely, J.H. (1977). Semantic priming and retrieval from lexical memory: Roles of inhibitionless spreading activation and limited capacity attention. *Journal of Experimental Psychology: General*, 106: 226–54

Neisser, U. (1996). Remembering as doing. *Behavioral and Brain Sciences*, 19: 203–4.

Nevins, A., Pesetsky, D. & Rodrigues, C. (2009). Evidence and argumentation: A reply to Everett (2009). *Language*, 85: 671–81.

Newell, A. & Simon, H.A. (1972). *Human problem solving*. Englewood Cliffs, NJ: Prentice Hall.

Newell, A., Shaw, J.C. & Simon, H.A. (1958). Elements of a theory of human problem solving. *Psychological Review*, 65: 151–66.

Newell, B.R. (2011). Recognising the recognition heuristic for what it is (and what it's not). *Judgment and Decision Making*, 6: 409–12.

Newell, B.R. (2015, in press). Decision making under risk: Beyond Kahneman and Tversky's (1979) prospect theory. In M.W. Eysenck & D. Groome (eds), *Cognitive psychology: Revisiting the classic studies*. London: SAGE.

Newell, B.R. & Shanks, D.R. (2014). Unconscious influence on decision making: A critical review. *Behavioral and Brain Sciences*, 37: 1–61.

Newell, B.R., Weston, N.J. & Shanks, D.R. (2003). Empirical tests of a fast and frugal heuristic: Not everyone "takes-the-best". *Organizational Behavior and Human Decision Processes*, 91: 82–96.

Newman, E.J. & Lindsay, D.S. (2009). False memories: What the hell are they for? *Applied Cognitive Psychology*, 23: 1105–21.

Newport, R. & Schenk, T. (2012). Prisms and neglect: What have we learned? *Neuropsychologia*, 50: 1080–91.

Newsome, M.R. & Johnson-Laird, P.N. (2006). How falsity dispels fallacies. *Thinking & Reasoning*, 12: 214–34.

Newstead, S.E., Handley, S.J. & Buck, E. (1999). Falsifying mental models: Testing the predictions of theories of syllogistic reasoning. *Memory & Cognition*, 27: 344–54.

Nguyen, T.D., Ziemer, C.J., Grechkin, T., Chihak, B., Plumert, J.M., Cremer, J.F. & Kearney, J.K. (2011). Effects of scale change on distance perception in virtual environments. *ACM Transactions on Applied Perception*, 8(4) (Article 26).

Nickels, L., Biedermann, B., Coltheart, M., Saunders, S. & Tree, J.J. (2008). Computational modelling of phonological dyslexia: How does the DRC model fare? *Cognitive Neuropsychology*, 25: 165–93.

Nicolle, A., Fleming, S.M., Bach, D.R., Driver, J. & Dolan, R.J. (2011). A regret-induced status quo bias. *Journal of Neuroscience*, 31: 3320–7.

Niebergall, R., Khayat, P.S., Treue, S. & Martinez-Trujillo, J.C. (2011). Multifocal attention filters targets from distractors within and beyond primate MT neurons' receptive field boundaries. *Neuron*, 72: 1067–79.

Nieuwenstein, M. & van Rijn, H. (2012). The unconscious thought advantage: Further replication failures from a search for confirmatory evidence. *Judgment and Decision Making*, 7: 779–98.

Nieuwland, M.S., & van Berkum, J.J.A. (2006a). When peanuts fall in love: N400 evidence for the power of discourse. *Journal of Cognitive Neuroscience*, 18: 1098–111.

Nieuwland, M.S. & van Berkum, J.J.A. (2006b). Individual differences and contextual bias in pronoun resolution: Evidence from ERPs. *Brain Research*, 1118(1): 155–67.

Nijboer, T.C.W., McIntosh, R.D., Nys, G.M.S., Dijkerman, H.C. & Milner, A.D. (2008). Prism adaptation improves voluntary but not automatic orienting in neglect. *NeuroReport*, 19: 293–8.

Nijboer, M., Taatgen, N.A., Brands, A., Borst, J.P. & van Rijn, H. (2013). Decision making in concurrent multitasking: Do people adapt to task interference? *PLOS ONE*, 8(11): e79583.

Nisbett, R.E. & Wilson, T.D. (1977). Telling more than we can know: Verbal reports on mental processes. *Psychological Review*, 84: 231–59.

Nitschke, K., Ruh, N., Kappler, S., Stahl, C. & Kaller, C.P. (2012). Dissociable stages of problem solving (1): Temporal characteristics revealed by eye-movement analyses. *Brain and Cognition*, 80: 160–9.

Nooteboom, S.G. & Quené, H. (2008). Self-monitoring and feedback: A new attempt to find the main cause of lexical bias in phonological speech errors. *Journal of Memory and Language*, 58: 837–61.

Nooteboom, S.G. & Quené, H. (2013a). Heft lemisphere: Exchanges predominate in segmental speech errors. *Journal of Memory and Language*, *68*, 26–38.

Nooteboom, S.G. & Quené, H. (2013b). Parallels between self-monitoring for speech errors and identification of the misspoken segments. *Journal of Memory and Language*, 69: 417–28.

Nordgren, L.F., Bos, M.W. & Dijksterhuis, A. (2011). The best of both worlds: Integrating conscious and unconscious thought best solves complex decisions. *Journal of Experimental Social Psychology*, 47: 509–11.

Norman, D.A. (1980). Twelve issues for cognitive science. *Cognitive Science*, 4: 1–32.

Norris, D. (2013). Models of visual word recognition. *Trends in Cognitive Sciences*, 17: 517–24.

Norris, D. & Kinoshita, S. (2012). Reading through a noisy channel: Why there's nothing special about the perception of orthography. *Psychological Review*, 119: 517–45.

Norris, D., McQueen, J.M., Cutler, A. & Butterfeld, S. (1997). The possible-word constraint in the segmentation of continuous speech. *Cognitive Psychology*, 34: 191–243.

Norris, D., McQueen, J.M. & Cutler, A. (2003). Perceptual learning in speech. *Cognitive Psychology*, 47: 204–38.

Nozari, N., Dell, G.S. & Schwartz, M.F. (2011). Is comprehension necessary for error detection? *Cognitive Psychology*, 63: 1–33.

Oaksford, M. (1997). Thinking and the rational analysis of human reasoning. *The Psychologist*, 10: 257–60.

Oaksford, M. & Chater, N. (2009). Précis of Bayesian rationality: The probabilistic approach to human reasoning. *Behavioral and Brain Sciences*, 32: 69–120.

Oaksford, M. & Hahn, U. (2004). A Bayesian approach to the argument from ignorance. *Canadian Journal of Experimental Psychology*, 58, 75–85.

Oaksford, M., Chater, N., Gerainger, B. & Larkin, J. (1997). Optimal data selection in the Reduced Array Selection Test (RAST). *Journal of Experimental Psychology: Learning, Memory, and Cognition*, 23: 441–58.

Oatley, K. & Johnson-Laird, P.N. (1987). Towards a cognitive theory of emotions. *Cognition & Emotion*, 1: 29–50.

O'Brien, E.J., Cook, A.E. & Guéraud, S. (2010). Accessibility of outdated information. *Journal of Experimental Psychology: Learning, Memory, and Cognition*, 36: 979–91.

Ochsner, K.N. & Gross, J.J. (2008). Cognitive emotion regulation: Insights from social cognitive and affective neuroscience. *Current Directions in Psychological Science*, 20: 1322–31.

Ochsner, K.N., Ray, R.R., Hughes, B., McRae, K., Cooper, J.C., Weber, J., Gabrieli, J.D. & Gross, J.J. (2009). Bottom-up and top-down processes in emotion generation: Common and distinct neural mechanisms. *Psychological Science*, 20: 1322–31.

O'Craven, K., Downing, P. & Kanwisher, N. (1999). fMRI evidence for objects as the units of attentional selection. *Nature*, 401: 584–7.

Odinot, G., Wolters, G. & van Koppen, P.J. (2009). Eyewitness memory of a supermarket robbery: A case study of accuracy and confidence after 3 months. *Law and Human Behavior*, 33: 506–14.

Ohlsson, S. (1992). Information processing explanations of insight and related phenomena. In M.T. Keane & K.J. Gilhooly (eds), *Advances in the psychology of thinking*. London: Harvester Wheatsheaf.

Öhman, A. & Soares, J.J.F. (1994). "Unconscious anxiety": Phobic responses to masked stimuli. *Journal of Abnormal Psychology*, 103: 231–40.

Okada, T. & Simon, H.A. (1997). Collaborative discovery in a scientific domain. *Cognitive Science*, 21: 109–46.

Okasha, S. (2002). *Philosophy of science: A very short introduction*. Oxford: Oxford University Press.

Olive, T. (2012). Writing and working memory: A summary of theories and findings. In E.L. Grigorenko, E. Mambrino & D.D. Preiss (eds), *Writing: A mosaic of perspectives* (pp. 125–140). Hove: Psychology Press.

Olive, T. & Passerault, J.-M. (2012). The visuospatial dimension of writing. *Written Communication*, 29: 326–44.

Olive, T. & Piolat, A. (2002). Suppressing visual feedback in written composition: Effects on processing demands and co-ordination of the writing processes. *International Journal of Psychology*, 37: 209–18.

Olive, T., Kellogg, R.T. & Piolat, A. (2008). Verbal, visual, and spatial working memory demands during text composition. *Applied Psycholinguistics*, 29: 669–87.

Oliveri, M. & Caltagirone, C. (2006). Suppression of extinction with TMS in humans: From healthy controls to patients. *Behavioural Neurology*, 17: 163–7.

Öllinger, M., Jones, G. & Knoblich, G. (2014). The dynamics of search, impasse, and representational change provide a coherent explanation of difficulty in the nine-dot problem. *Psychological Research*, 78: 266–75.

Olson, A.C., Romani, C. & Halloran, L. (2007). Localising the deficit in a case of jargon aphasia. *Cognitive Neuropsychology*, 24: 211–38.

Ophir, E., Nass, C. & Wagner, A.D. (2009). Cognitive control in media multitaskers. *Proceedings of the National Academy of Sciences*, 106: 15583–7.

Oppenheimer, D.M. (2004). Spontaneous discounting of availability in frequency judgment tasks. *Psychological Science*, 15: 100–5.

Oppenheimer, D.M. & Monin, B. (2009). Investigations in spontaneous discounting. *Memory & Cognition*, 37: 608–14.

Oppermann, F., Jescheniak, J.D. & Görges, F. (2014). Resolving competition when naming an object in a multiple-object display. *Psychonomic Bulletin & Review*, 21: 78–84.

O'Reilly, R.C., Wyatte, D., Herd, S., Mings, B. & Jilk, D.J. (2013). Recurrent processing during object recognition. *Frontiers in Psychology*, 4 (Article 124).

O'Rourke, T.B. & Holcomb, P.J. (2002). Electrophysiological evidence for the efficiency of spoken word processing. *Biological Psychology*, 60: 121–50.

Ortu, D. & Vaidya, M. (2013). A neurobiology of learning beyond the declarative non-declarative distinction. *Frontiers in Behavioral Neuroscience*, 7 (Article 161).

Osman, M., Wilkinson, L., Beigi, M., Castaneda, C.S. & Jahanshahi, M. (2008). Patients with Parkinson's disease learn to control complex systems via procedural as well as non-procedural learning. *Neuropsychologia*, 46: 2355–63.

Osnes, B., Hugdahl, K. & Specht, K. (2011). Effective connectivity analysis demonstrates involvement of premotor cortex in speech perception. *NeuroImage*, 54: 2437–45.

Oudiette, D. & Paller, K.A. (2013). Upgrading the sleeping brain with targeted memory reactivation. *Trends in Cognitive Sciences*, 13: 142–9.

Overgaard, M. (2012). Blindsight: Recent and historical controversies on the blindness of blindsight. *Wiley Interdisciplinary Reviews – Cognitive Science*, 3: 607–14.

Overgaard, M. & Mogensen, J. (2011). A framework for the study of multiple realisations: The importance of levels of analysis. *Frontiers in Psychology*, 2 (Article 79).

Overgaard, M., Fehl, K., Mouridsen, K., Bergholt, B. & Cleermans, K. (2008). Seeing without seeing? Degraded conscious vision in a blindsight patient. *PLOS ONE*, 3: e3028.

Owen, A.M. (2013). Detecting consciousness: a unique role for neuroimaging. *Annual Review of Psychology*, 64: 109–33.

Owen, A.M. & Coleman, M.R. (2008). Functional neuroimaging of the vegetative state. *Nature Reviews Neuroscience*, 9: 235–43.

Owen, A.M., Coleman, M.R., Boly, M., Davis, M.H., Laureys, S. & Pickard, J.D. (2006). Detecting awareness in the vegetative state. *Science*, 313: 1402.

Pachur, T., Hertwig, R. & Steinmann, F. (2012). How do people judge risks: Availability heuristic, affect heuristic, or both? *Journal of Experimental Psychology: Applied*, 18: 314–30.

Pakhomov, S.V.S., Kaiser, E.A., Boley, D.L., Marino, S.E., Knopman, D.S. & Birnbaum, A.K. (2011). Effects of age and dementia on temporal cycles in spontaneous speech fluency. *Journal of Neurolinguistics*, 24: 619–35.

Palmer, S.E. & Rock, I. (1994). Rethinking perceptual organisation: The role of uniform connectedness. *Psychonomic Bulletin & Review*, 1: 29–55.

Papagno, C., Valentine, T. & Baddeley, A.D. (1991). Phonological short-term memory and foreign language learning. *Journal of Memory and Language*, 30: 331–47.

Pappas, Z. & Mack, A. (2008). Potentiation of action by undetected affordant objects. *Visual Cognition*, 16: 892–915.

Park, H. & Rugg, M.D. (2008). The relationship between study processing and the effects of cue congruency on retrieval: fMRI support for transfer appropriate processing. *Cerebral Cortex*, 18: 868–75.

Parker, A.J. (2007). Binocular depth perception and the cerebral cortex. *Nature Reviews Neuroscience*, 8: 379–91.

Parker, E.S., Cahill, L. & McGaugh, J.L. (2006). A case of unusual autobiographical remembering. *Neurocase*, 12: 35–49.

Parkinson, B. (2001). Putting appraisal in context. In K.R. Scherer, A. Schorr & T. Johnstone (eds), *Appraisal processes in emotion: Theory, methods, research*. Oxford: Oxford University Press.

Parkinson, B. (2011). How social is the social psychology of emotion? *British Journal of Social Psychology*, 50: 405–13.

Parks, C.M. (2013). Transfer-appropriate processing in recognition memory: Perceptual and conceptual effects on recognition memory depend on task demands. *Journal of Experimental Psychology: Learning, Memory, and Cognition*, 39: 1280–6.

Pashler, H. (1993). Dual-task interference and elementary mental mechanisms. In D.E. Meyer & S. Kornblum (eds), *Attention and performance, vol. XIV*. London: MIT Press.

Pashler, H., Harris, C.R. & Nuechterlein, K.H. (2008). Does the central bottleneck encompass voluntary selection of hedonically based choices? *Experimental Psychology*, 55: 313–21.

Patihis, L., Frenda, S.J., LePort, A.K.R., Petersen, N., Nichols, R.M., Stark, C.E.L., McGaugh, J.L. & Loftus, E.F. (2013). False memories in highly superior autobiographical memory individuals. *Proceedings of the National Academy of Sciences*, 110: 20947–52.

Patsenko, E.G. & Altmann, E.M. (2010). How planful is routine behaviour? A selective-attention model of performance in the Tower of Hanoi. *Journal of Experimental Psychology: General*, 139: 95–116.

Pattamadilok, C., Perre, L. & Ziegler, J.C. (2011). Beyond rhyme or reason: ERPs reveal task-specific activation of orthography on spoken language. *Brain and Language*, 116: 116–24.

Patterson, K. & Plaut, D.C. (2009). "Shallow draughts intoxicate the brain": Lessons from cognitive science for cognitive neuropsychology. *Topics in Cognitive Science*, 1: 39–58.

Patterson, K., Vargha-Khadem, F. & Polkey, C. (1989). Reading with one hemisphere. *Brain*, 112: 39–63.

Patterson, K., Nestor, P.J. & Rogers, T.T. (2007). Where do you know what you know? The representation of semantic knowledge in the human brain. *Nature Reviews Neuroscience*, 8: 976–87.

Patterson, R., Fournier, L., Pierce, B., Winterbottom, M. & Tripp, L. (2009). Modelling the dynamics of recognition-primed decision making. *Proceedings of the Ninth International Conference on Naturalistic Decision Making*, London, June.

Pauker, E., Itzhak, I., Baum, S.R. & Steinhauer, K. (2012). Effects of cooperating and conflicting prosody in spoken English garden path sentences: ERP evidence for the boundary deletion hypothesis. *Journal of Cognitive Neuroscience*, 23: 2731–51.

Payne, J. (1976). Task complexity and contingent processing in decision making: An information search and protocol analysis. *Organizational Behavior and Human Performance*, 16: 366–87.

Payne, J., Samper, A., Bettman, J.R. & Luce, M.F. (2008). Boundary conditions on unconscious thought in complex decision making. *Psychological Science*, 19: 1118–23.

Payne, S.J. & Duggan, G.B. (2011). Giving up problem solving. *Memory & Cognition*, 39 902–13.

Paynter, C.A., Kotovsky, K. & Reder, L.M. (2010). Problem-solving without awareness: An ERP investigation. *Neuropsychologia*, 48: 3137–44.

Pearson, J., Clifford, C.W.G. & Tong, F. (2008). The functional impact of mental imagery on conscious perception. *Current Biology*, 18: 982–6.

Pêcher, C., Lemercier, C. & Cellier, J. (2009). Emotions drive attention: Effects on drivers' behaviour. *Safety Science*, 47: 1254–9.

Pecher, D., Boot, I. & Van Dantzig, S. (2011). Abstract concepts: Sensory-motor grounding, metaphors, and beyond. In B. Ross (ed.), *The psychology of learning and motivation, vol. 54* (pp. 217–48). Burlington, MA: Academic Press.

Peckham, A.D., McHugh, R.K. & Otto, M.W. (2010). A meta-analysis of the magnitude of biased attention in depression. *Depression and Anxiety*, 27: 1135–42.

Peissig, J.J. & Tarr, M.J. (2007). Visual object recognition: Do we know more now than we did 20 years ago? *Annual Review of Psychology*, 58: 75–96.

Penaloza, A.A. & Calvillo, D.P. (2012). Incubation provides relief from artificial fixation in problem solving. *Creativity Research Journal*, 24: 338–44.

Penhune, V.B. & Steele, C.J. (2012). Parallel contributions of cerebellar, striatal and M1 mechanisms to motor sequence learning. *Behavioural Brain Research*, 226: 579–91.

Pennycook, G. & Thompson, V.A. (2012). Reasoning with base rates is routine, relatively effortless, and context dependent. *Psychonomic Bulletin & Review*, 19: 528–34.

Penolazzi, B., Hauk, O. & Pulvermüller, F. (2007). Early semantic context integration and lexical access as revealed by event-related brain potentials. *Biological Psychology*, 74: 374–88.

Perenin, M.-T. & Vighetto, A. (1988). Optic ataxia: A specific disruption in visuomotor mechanisms. 1. Different aspects of the deficit in reaching for objects. *Brain*, 111: 643–74.

Peretz, I. & Coltheart, M. (2003). Modularity of music processing. *Nature Neuroscience*, 6: 688–91.

Perfors, A.F. & Navarro, D.J. (2009). Confirmation bias is rational when hypotheses are sparse. *Proceedings of the Thirty-first Annual Conference of the Cognitive Science Society*: 2741–6.

Perkins, A.M., Leonard, A.M., Ettinger, U., Weaver, K., Dalton, J.A., Mehta, M.A., Kumari, V. & Williams, S.C. (2013). A dose of ruthlessness: Interpersonal moral judgment is hardened by the anti-anxiety drug lorazepam. *Journal of Experimental Psychology: General*, 142: 612–20.

Perre, L. & Ziegler, J.C. (2008). On-line activation of orthography in spoken word recognition. *Brain Research*, 1188: 132–8.

Perre, L., Pattacmadilok, C., Montant, M. & Ziegler, J.C. (2009). Orthographic effects in spoken language: On-line activation or phonological restructuring? *Brain Research*, 1275: 73–80.

Perry, C., Ziegler, J.C. & Zorzi, M. (2007). Nested incremental modelling in the development of computational theories: The CDP+ model of reading aloud. *Psychological Review*, 114: 273–315.

Persaud, N. & Cowey, A. (2008). Blindsight is unlike normal conscious vision: Evidence from an exclusion task. *Consciousness and Cognition*, 17: 1050–5.

Persaud, N. & Lau, H. (2008). Direct assessment of qualia in a blindsight participant. *Consciousness and Cognition*, 17: 1046–9.

Persaud, N. & McLeod, P. (2008). Wagering demonstrates subconscious processing in a binary exclusion task. *Consciousness and Cognition*, 17: 565–75.

Persaud, N., Davidson, M., Maniscalco, B., Mobbs, D., Passingham, R.E., Cowey, A. & Lau, H. (2011). Awareness-related activity in prefrontal and parietal cortices in blindsight reflects more than superior visual performance. *NeuroImage*, *58*, 605–611.

Persuh, M., Genzer, B. & Melara, R.D. (2012). Iconic memory requires attention. *Frontiers in Human Neuroscience*, 6 (Article 126).

Peterson, D.J. & Mulligan, N.W. (2013). The negative testing effect and multifactor account. *Journal of Experimental Psychology: Learning, Memory, and Cognition*, 39: 1287–93.

Pezdek, K. (2003). Event memory and autobiographical memory for the events of September 11, 2001. *Applied Cognitive Psychology*, 17: 1033–45.

Phillips, V.L., Saks, M.J. & Peterson, J.L. (2001). The application of signal detection theory to decision-making in forensic science. *Journal of Forensice Sciences*, 46: 294–308.

Phillips, W.J., Hine, D.W. & Thorsteinsson, E.B. (2010). Implicit cognition and depression: A meta-analysis. *Clinical Psychology Review*, 30: 691–709.

Piai, V., Roelofs, A., Jensen, O., Schoffelen, J.M. & Bonefond, M. (2014). Distinct patterns of brain activity characterise lexical activation and competition in spoken word production. *PLOS ONE*, 9(2): e88674.

Piantadosi, S.T., Tily, H. & Gibson, E. (2012). The communicative function of ambiguity in language. *Cognition*, 122: 280–91.

Pickel, K.L. (2009). The weapon focus effect on memory for female versus male perpetrators. *Memory*, 17: 664–78.

Pickering, M.J. & Ferreira, V.S. (2008). Structural priming: A critical review. *Psychological Bulletin*, 134: 427–59.

Pickering, M.J. & Garrod, S. (2004). Toward a mechanistic psychology of dialogue. *Behavioral and Brain Sciences*, 27: 169–226.

Pickering, M.J. & Garrod, S. (2007). Do people use language production to make predictions during comprehension? *Trends in Cognitive Sciences*, 11: 105–10.

Pickering, M.J. & Garrod, S. (2013). An integrated theory of language production and comprehension. *Behavioral and Brain Sciences*, 36: 329–92.

Pierce, R.S., MacLaren, R. & Chiappe, D.L. (2010). The role of working memory in the metaphor interference effect. *Psychonomic Bulletin & Review*, 17: 400–4.

Pilz, K.S., Roggeveen, A.B., Creighton, S.E., Bennett, P.J. & Sekuler, A.B. (2012). How prevalent is object-based attention? *PLOS ONE*, 7(2): e30693.

Pinard, M., Chetkow, H., Black, S. & Peretz, I. (2002). A case study of pure word deafness: Modularity in auditory processing? *Neurocase*, 8: 40–55.

Pinker, S. (1997). *How the mind works*. New York: W.W. Norton.

Pinto, J. (2006). Developing body representations: A review of infants' responses to biological-motion displays. In G. Knoblich, M. Grosjean, J. Thornton & M. Shiffrar (eds), *Perception of the human body from the inside out* (pp. 305–22). Oxford: Oxford University Press.

Pisella, L., Sergio, L., Blangero, A., Torchin, H., Vighetto, A. & Rossetti, Y. (2009). Optic ataxia and the function of the dorsal stream: Contributions to perception and action. *Neuropsychologia*, 47: 3033–44.

Planton, S., Jucla, M., Roux, F.-E. & Démonet, J.-F. (2013). The "handwriting brain": A meta-analysis of neuroimaging studies of motor versus orthographic processes. *Cortex*, 49: 2772–87.

Plaut, D.C., McClelland, J.L., Seidenberg, M.S. & Patterson, K.E. (1996). Understanding normal and impaired word reading: Computational principles in quasi-regular domains. *Psychological Review*, 103: 56–115.

Pleskac, T.J. (2012). Comparability effects in probability judgments. *Psychological Science*, 23: 848–54.

Pobric, G., Jefferies, E. & Lambon Ralph, M.A. (2010a). Amodal semantic representations depend on both anterior temporal lobes: Evidence from repetitive transcranial magnetic stimulation. *Neuropsychologia*, 48: 1336–42.

Pobric, G., Jefferies, E. & Lambon Ralph, M.A. (2010b). Category-specific versus category-general semantic impairment induced by transcranial magnetic stimulation. *Current Biology*, 20: 964–8.

Pope, D.G. & Schweitzer, M.E. (2011). Is Tiger Woods loss averse? Persistent bias in the face of experience, competition, and high stakes. *American Economic Review*, 101: 129–57.

Popper, K.R. (1968). *The logic of scientific discovery*. London: Hutchinson.

Posner, M.I. (1980). Orienting of attention. The VIIth Sir Frederic Bartlett lecture. *Quarterly Journal of Experimental Psychology*, 32A: 3–25.

Postle, B.R. (2006). Working memory as an emergent property of the mind and brain. *Neuroscience*, 139: 23–38.

Power, M. & Dalgleish, T. (2008). *Cognition and emotion: From order to disorder* (2nd ed.). Hove: Psychology Press.

Pozzulo, J.D., Crescini, C. & Panton, T. (2008). Does methodology matter in eyewitness identification research? The effect of live versus video exposure on eyewitness identification of accuracy. *International Journal of Law and Psychiatry*, 31: 430–7.

Prado, J., Chadha, A. & Booth, J.R. (2011). The brain network for deductive reasoning: A quantitative meta-analysis of 28 neuroimaging studies. *Journal of Cognitive Neuroscience*, 23: 3483–97.

Prass, M., Grimsen, C., König, M. & Fahle, M. (2013). Ultra rapid object cagetorisation: Effect of level, animacy and context. *PLOS ONE*, 8(6): e68051.

Prebble, S.C., Addis, D.R. & Tippett, L.J. (2013). Autobiographical memory and sense of self. *Psychological Bulletin*, 139: 815–40.

Price, K.J., Shiffrar, M. & Kerns, K.A. (2012). Movement perception and movement production in Asperger's syndrome. *Research in Autism Disorders*, 6: 391–8.

Pritchard, S.C., Coltheart, M., Palethorpe, S. & Castles, A. (2012). Nonword reading: Comparing dual-route cascaded and connectionist dual-process models with human data. *Journal of Experimental Psychology: Human Perception and Performance*, 38: 1268–88.

Prull, M.W. & Yockelson, M.B. (2013). Adult age-related differences in the misinformation effect for context-consistent and context-inconsistent objects. *Applied Cognitive Psychology*, 27: 384–95.

Pulvermüller, F. (2013). Semantic embodiment, disembodiment or misembodiment? In search of meaning in modules and neuron circuits. *Brain & Language*, 127(1): 86–103.

Pulvermüller, F. & Fadiga, L. (2010). Active perception: Sensorimotor circuits as a cortical basis for language. *Nature Reviews Neuroscience*, 11: 351–60.

Pulvermüller, F., Hauk, O., Nikulin, V.V. & Limoniemi, R.J. (2005). Functional links between motor and language systems. *European Journal of Neuroscience*, 21: 793–7.

Pyc, M.A. & Rawson, K.A. (2009). Testing the retrieval effort hypothesis: Does greater difficulty correctly recalling information lead to higher levels of memory? *Journal of Memory and Language*, 60: 437–47.

Pyc, M.A. & Rawson, K.A. (2010). Why testing improves memory: Mediator effectiveness hypothesis. *Science*, 330: 335.

Pyc, M.A. & Rawson, K.A. (2012). Why is test-restudy practice beneficial for memory? An evaluation of the mediator shift hypothesis. *Journal of Experimental Psychology: Learning, Memory, and Cognition*, 38: 737–46.

Pylyshyn, Z.W. (2002). Mental imagery: In search of a theory. *Behavioral and Brain Sciences*, 25: 157–238.

Pylyshyn, Z.W. (2003). Return of the mental image: Are there really pictures in the brain? *Trends in Cognitive Science*, 7, 113–118.

Pynte, J., Kennedy, A. & Ducrot, S. (2004). The influence of parafoveal typographical errors on eye movements in reading. *European Journal of Cognitive Psychology*, 16: 178–202.

Quinlan, T., Loncke, M., Leijten, M. & Van Waes, L. (2012). Coordinating the cognitive processes of writing: The role of the monitor. *Written Communication*, 29: 345–68.

Quiroga, R.Q., Reddy, L., Kreiman, G., Koch, C. & Fried, I. (2005). Invariant visual representation by single neurons in the human brain. *Nature*, 435: 1102–7.

Quiroga, R.Q., Fried, I. & Koch, C. (2013). Brain cells for grandmother. *Scientific American*, February: 31–5.

Raaijmakers, J.G.W. & Jakab, E. (2013). Rethinking inhibition theory: On the problematic status of the inhibition theory for forgetting. *Journal of Memory and Language*, 68: 98–122.

Race, E., Keane, M.M. & Verfaellie, M. (2011). Medial temporal lobe damage causes deficits in episodic memory and episodic future thinking not attributable to deficits in narrative construction. *Journal of Neuroscience*, 31: 10262–9.

Race, E., Larocque, K.F., Keane, M.M. & Verfaellie, M. (2013). Medial temporal lobe contributions to short-term memory for faces. *Journal of Experimental Psychology: General*, 142: 1309–22.

Radeau, M., Morais, J., Mousty, P. & Bertelson, P. (2000). The effect of speaking rate on the role of the uniqueness point in spoken word recognition. *Journal of Memory and Language*, 42: 406–22.

Radvansky, G.A. & Zacks, J.M. (2011). Event perception. *Wiley Interdisciplinary Reviews: Cognitive Science*, 2: 608–20.

Raghunathan, R. & Pham, M.T. (1999). All negative moods are not equal: Motivational influences of anxiety and sadness on decision making. *Organizational Behavior and Human Decision Processes*, 79: 56–77.

Ragni, M. & Knauff, M. (2013). A theory and a computational model of spatial reasoning with preferred mental models. *Psychological Review*, 120: 561–88.

Raichle, M.E. (2010). Two views of brain function. *Trends in Cognitive Sciences*, 14: 180–90.

Raizada, R.D.S. & Poldrack, R.A. (2007). Selective amplification of stimulus differences during categorical processing of speech. *Neuron*, 56: 726–40.

Ramachandran, V.S. (1988). Perception of shape from shading. *Nature*, 331: 163–6.

Ramenzoni, V.C. & Riley, M.A. (2004). Strong modularity and circular reasoning pervade the planning-control model. *Behavioral and Brain Sciences*, 27: 48–9.

Rapp, B. & Dufor, O. (2011). The neurotopography of written word production: An fMR investigation of the distribution of sensitivity to length and frequency. *Journal of Cognitive Neuroscience*, 23: 4067–81.

Rapp, B. & Lipka, K. (2011). The literate brain: The relationship between spelling and reading. *Journal of Cognitive Neuroscience*, 23: 1180–97.

Rapp, B., Epstein, C. & Tainturier, M.-J. (2002). The integration of information across lexical and sublexical processes in spelling. *Cognitive Neuropsychology*, 19: 1–29.

Rastle, K. & Brysbaert, M. (2006). Masked phonological priming effects in English: Are they real? Do they matter? *Cognitive Psychology*, 53: 97–145.

Rastle, K., Havelka, J., Wydell, T.N. & Besner, D. (2009). The cross-script length effect: Further evidence challenging PDP models of reading aloud. *Journal of Experimental Psychology: Learning, Memory, and Cognition*, 35: 238–46.

Raven, J., Raven, C. & Court, J.H. (1998). *Manual for Raven's Progressive Matrices and Vocabulary Scales. Section 4: The Advanced Progressive Matrices*. San Antonio, TX: Harcourt Assessment.

Rayner, K. & Reichle, E.D. (2010). Models of the reading process. *Wiley Interdisciplinary Reviews: Cognitive Science*, 1: 787–99.

Rayner, K., Li, X.S. & Pollatsek, A. (2007). Extending the E-Z model of eye-movement control to Chinese readers. *Cognitive Science*, 31: 1021–33.

Rayner, K., Pollatsek, A., Ashby, J. & Clifton, C. (2012). *Psychology of reading* (2nd edn). Hove: Psychology Press.

Reber, A.S. (1993). *Implicit learning and tacit knowledge: An essay on the cognitive unconscious*. Oxford: Oxford University Press.

Reber, P.J. (2013). The neural basis of implicit learning and memory: A review of neuropsychological and neuroimaging research. *Neuropsychologia*, 51: 2026–42.

Reber, P.J., Knowlton, J.R. & Squire, L.R. (1996). Dissociable properties of memory systems: Differences in the flexibility of declarative and nondeclarative knowledge. *Behavioral Neuroscience*, 110: 861–71.

Reber, T.P., Luechinger, R., Boesiger, P. & Henke, K. (2014). Detecting analogies unconsciously. *Frontiers in Behavioral Neuroscience*, 8 (Article 9).

Recanzone, G.H. & Sutter, M.L. (2008). The biological basis of audition. *Annual Review of Psychology*, 59: 119–42.

Redden, J.P. & Frederick, S. (2011). Unpacking unpacking: Greater detail can reduce perceived likelihood. *Journal of Experimental Psychology: General*, 140: 159–67.

Redelmeier, C., Koehler, D.J., Liberman, V. & Tversky, A. (1995). Probability judgment in medicine: Discounting unspecified alternatives. *Medical Decision Making*, 15: 227–30.

Rees, G. (2007). Neural correlates of the contents of visual awareness in humans. *Philosophical Transactions of the Royal Society B – Biological Sciences*, 362: 877–86.

Reeves, A.J., Amano, K. & Foster, D.H. (2008). Colour constancy: Phenomenal or projective? *Perception & Psychophysics*, 70: 219–28.

Reichel, W.D. & Kisler, T. (2012). The entropy of intoxicated speech: Lexical creativity and heavy tongues. *Proceedings Interspeech*, Portland, OR, Paper No. 347.

Reichle, E.D., Pollatsek, A., Fisher, D.L. & Rayner, K. (1998). Towards a model of eye movement control in reading. *Psychological Review*, 105: 125–57.

Reichle, E.D., Reineberg, A.E. & Schooler, J.W. (2010). Eye movements during mindless reading. *Psychological Science*, 21: 1300–10.

Reichle, E.D., Tokowicz, N., Liu, Y. & Perfetti, C.A. (2011). Testing an assumption of the E-Z Reader model of eye-movement control during reading: Using event-related potentials to examine the familiarity check. *Psychophysiology*, 48: 993–1003.

Reilly, R. & Radach, R. (2012). The dynamics of reading in non-Roman writing systems. *Reading and Writing*, 25(Special issue): 935–50.

Reingold, E.M. (2004). Unconscious perception and the classic dissociation paradigm: A new angle? *Perception & Psychophysics*, 66: 882–7.

Reingold, E.M., Reichle, E.D., Glaholt, M.G. & Sheridan, H. (2012). Direct lexical control of eye movements in reading: Evidence from a survival analysis of fixation durations. *Cognitive Psychology*, 65: 177–206.

Rensink, R.A., O'Regan, J.K. & Clark, J.J. (1997). To see or not to see? The need for attention to perceive changes in scenes. *Psychological Science*, 8: 368–73.

Reverberi, D.J., Toraldo, A., D'Agostino, S. & Skrap, M. (2005). Better with (lateral) prefrontal cortex? Insight problems solved by frontal patients. *Brain*, 128: 2882–90.

Reverberi, C., Bonatti, L.L., Frackowiak, R.S.J., Paulesu, E., Cherubini, P. & Macaluso, E. (2012). Large scale brain activations predict reasoning profiles. *NeuroImage*, 59: 1752–64.

Rhys, C.S., Ulbrich, C. & Ordin, M. (2013). Adaptation to aphasia: Grammar, prosody and interaction. *Clinical Linguistics & Phonetics*, 27: 46–71.

Ricco, R.B. (2007). Individual differences in the analysis of informal reasoning fallacies. *Contemporary Educational Psychology*, 32: 459–84.

Richards, A., Hannon, E.M. & Vitkovitch, M. (2012). Distracted by distractors: Eye movements in a dynamic inattentional blindness task. *Consciousness and Cognition*, 21: 170–6.

Richler, J.J., Cheung, O.S. & Gauthier, I. (2011). Holistic processing predicts face recognition. *Psychological Science*, 22: 464–71.

Richter, T. & Späth, P. (2006). Recognition is used as one cue among others in judgment and decision making. *Journal of Experimental Psychology: Learning, Memory & Cognition*, 32: 150–62.

Riddoch, G. (1917). Dissociations of visual perception due to occipital injuries, with especial reference to appreciation of movement. *Brain*, 40: 15–57.

Riddoch, M.J., Humphreys, G.W., Hickman, J.C., Daly, A. & Colin, J. (2006). I can see what you are doing: Action familiarity and affordance promote recovery from extinction. *Cognitive Neuropsychology*, 23: 583–605.

Riès, S., Janssen, N., Burle, B. & Alario, F.-X. (2013). Response-locked brain dynamics of word production. *PLOS ONE*, 8(3): e58197.

Riggs, L., McQuiggan, D.A., Farb, N., Anderson, A.K. & Ryan, J.D. (2011). The role of overt attention in emotion-modulated memory. *Emotion*, 11: 776–85.

Rimmele, U., Davachi, L. & Phelps, E.A. (2012). Memory for time and place contributes to enhanced confidence in memories for emotional events. *Emotion*, 12: 834–46.

Rinck, M. & Becker, E.S. (2005). A comparison of attentional biases and memory biases in women with social phobia and major depression. *Journal of Abnormal Psychology*, 114: 62–74.

Rinck, M. & Weber, U. (2003). Who, when, where: An experimental test of the event-indexing model. *Memory & Cognition*, 31: 1284–92.

Rizio, A.A. & Dennis, N.A. (2013). The neural correlates of cognitive control: Successful remembering and intentional forgetting. *Journal of Cognitive Neuroscience*, 25: 297–312.

Rizzo, M., Nawrot, M., Sparks, J. & Dawson, J. (2008). First- and second-order motion perception after focal human brain lesions. *Vision Research*, 48: 2682–8.

Robbins, T., Anderson, E., Barker, D., Bradley, A., Fearneyhough, C., Henson, R. & Hudson, S.R. (1996). Working memory in chess. *Memory & Cognition*, 24: 83–93.

Roberson, D. & Hanley, J.R. (2010). Relatively speaking: An account of the relationship between language and thought in the colour domain. In B. Malt & P. Wolff (eds), *Words and the world: How words capture human experience*. Oxford: Oxford University Press.

Roberts, J., Burkitt, J.J., Willemse, B., Ludzki, A., Lyons, J., Elliott, D. & Grierson, L.E. (2013). The influence of target context and early and late vision on goal-directed reaching. *Experimental Brain Research*, 229: 525–32.

Robertson, E.M. (2012). New insights in human memory interference and consolidation. *Current Biology*, 22: R66–71.

Robertson, I.H., Mattingley, J.B., Rorden, C. & Driver, J. (1998). Phasic alerting of neglect patients overcomes their spatial deficit in visual awareness. *Nature*, 395: 169–72.

Robinson, B.L. & McAlpine, D. (2009). Gain control mechanisms in the auditory pathway. *Current Opinion in Neurobiology*, 19: 402–7.

Robson, J., Pring, T., Marshall, J. & Chiat, S. (2003). Phoneme frequency effects in jargon aphasia: A phonological investigation of non-word errors. *Brain and Language*, 85: 109–24.

Roe, A.W., Chelazzi, L., Connor, C.E., Conway, B.R., Fujita, I., Gallant, J.L., Lu, H. & Vanduffel, W. (2012). Toward a unified theory of visual area V4. *Neuron*, 74: 12–29.

Roediger, H.L. (2008). Relativity of remembering: Why the laws of memory vanished. *Annual Review of Psychology*, 59: 225–54.

Roediger, H.L. (2010). Reflections on intersections between cognitive and social psychology: A personal exploration. *European Journal of Social Psychology*, 40: 189–205.

Roediger, H.L. & Gallo, D.A. (2001). Levels of processing: Some unanswered questions. In M. Naveh-Benjamin, M. Moscovitch & H.L. Roediger (eds), *Perspectives on human memory and cognitive aging*. New York: Psychology Press.

Roediger, H.L. & Karpicke, J.D. (2006). Test-enhanced learning: Taking memory tests enhances improves long-term retention. *Psychological Science*, 17: 249–55.

Roets, A., Schwartz, B. & Guan, Y.J. (2012). The tyranny of choice: A cross-cultural investigation of maximizing-satisficing effects on well-being. *Judgment and Decision Making*, 7: 689–704.

Rogalsky, C., Love, T., Driscoll, D., Anderson, S.W. & Hickok, G. (2011a). Are mirror neurons the basis of speech perception? Evidence from five cases with damage to the purported human mirror system. *Neurocase*, 17: 178–87.

Rogalsky, C., Rong, F., Saberi, K. & Hickok, G. (2011b). Functional anatomy of language and music perception: Temporal and structural factors investigated using functional magnetic resonance imaging. *Journal of Neuroscience*, 31: 3843–52.

Rogers, B.J. & Graham, M.E. (1979). Motion parallax as an independent cue for depth perception. *Perception*, 8: 125–34.

Rogers, T.T. & Patterson, K. (2007). Object categorisations: Reversals and explanations of the basic-level advantage. *Journal of Experimental Psychology: General*, 136: 451–69.

Rohde, H. & Ettlinger, M. (2012). Integration of pragmatic and phonetic cues in spoken word recognition. *Journal of Experimental Psychology: Learning, Memory, and Cognition*, 38: 967–83.

Rolls, E.T. & McCabe, C. (2007). Enhanced affective brain representations of chocolate in cravers and non-cravers. *European Journal of Neuroscience*, 26: 1067–76.

Rorden, C., Hjaltason, H., Fillmore, P., Fridriksson, J., Kjartansson, O., Magnusdottir, S. & Karnath, H.O. (2012). Allocentric neglect strongly associated with egocentric neglect. *Neuropsychologia*, 50: 1151–7.

Rosch, E., Mervis, C.B., Gray, W.D., Johnson, D.M. & Boyes-Braem, P. (1976). Basic objects in natural categories. *Cognitive Psychology*, 8: 382–439.

Roseboom, W. & Arnold, D.H. (2011). Learning to reach for "invisible" visual input. *Current Biology*, 21: R493–4.

Rosenbaum, R.S., Köhler, S., Schacter, D.L., Moscovitch, M., Westmacott, R., Black, S.E., Gao, F. & Tulving, E. (2005). The case of KC: Contributions of a memory-impaired person to memory theory. *Neuropsychologia*, 43: 989–1021.

Rosenholtz, R., Huang, J. & Ehinger, K.A. (2012a). Rethinking the role of top-down attention in vision: Effects attributable to a lossy representation in peripheral vision. *Frontiers in Psychology*, 3 (Article 13).

Rosenholtz, R., Huang, J., Raj, A., Balas, B.J. & Ilie, L. (2012b). A summary statistic representation in peripheral vision explains visual search. *Journal of Vision*, 12(4): (Article 14).

Ross, D.F., Ceci, S.J., Dunning, D. & Toglia, M.P. (1994). Unconscious transference and mistaken identity: When a witness misidentifies a familiar but innocent person. *Journal of Applied Psychology*, 79: 918–30.

Ross, M.R. & Wang, Q. (2010). Why we remember and what we remember: Culture and autobiographical memory. *Perspectives on Psychological Science*, 5: 401–9.

Rossetti, Y. & Pisella, L. (2002). Several "vision for action" systems: A guide to dissociating and integrating dorsal and ventral functions. In W. Prinz & B. Hommel (eds), *Common mechanisms in perception and action: Attention and performance*. Oxford: Oxford University Press.

Rossetti, Y., Rode, G., Pisella, L., Boisson, D. & Perenin, M.T. (1998). Prism adaptation to a rightward optical deviation rehabilitates left hemispatial neglect. *Nature*, 395: 166–9.

Rossion, B. & Curran, T. (2010). Visual expertise with pictures of cars correlates with RT magnitude of the car inversion effect. *Perception*, 39: 173–83.

Rounis, E., Maniscalco, B., Rothwell, J.C., Passingham, R.E. & Lau, H. (2010). Theta-burst transcranial magnetic stimulation to the prefrontal cortex impairs metacognitive visual awareness. *Cognitive Neuroscience*, 1: 165–75.

Rowe, M.L. (2008). Child-directed speech: Relation to socioeconomic status, knowledge of child development and child vocabulary skill. *Journal of Child Language*, 35: 185–205.

Roy, D.F. (1991). Improving recall by eyewitnesses through the cognitive interview: Practical applications and implications for the police service. *The Psychologist*, 4: 398–400.

Royden, C.S. & Hildreth, E.C. (1999). Differential effects of shared attention on perception of heading and 3-D object motion. *Perception & Psychophysics*, 61: 120–33.

Rubin, D.C. & Berntsen, D. (2003). Life scripts help to maintain autobiographical memories of highly positive, but not negative, events. *Memory & Cognition*, 31: 1–14.

Rubin, D.C. & Schulkind, M.D. (1997). The distribution of important and word-cued autobiographical memories in 20-, 35-, and 70-year-old adults. *Psychology of Aging*, 12: 524–35.

Rubin, D.C. & Wenzel, A.E. (1996). One hundred years of forgetting: A quantitative description of retention. *Psychological Bulletin*, 103: 734–60.

Rubin, D.C., Wetzler, S.E. & Nebes, R.D. (1986). Autobiographical memory across the life span. In D.C. Rubin (ed.), *Autobiographical memory*. Cambridge: Cambridge University Press.

Rudaizky, D., Basanovic, J. & MacLeod, C. (2014). Biased attentional engagement with, and disengagement from, negative information: Independent cognitive pathways to anxiety vulnerability? *Cognition & Emotion*, 28: 245–59.

Ruh, N., Rahm, B., Unterrainer, J.M., Weiller, C. & Kaller, C.P. (2012). Dissociable stages of problem solving (II): First evidence for process-contingent temporal order of activation in dorsolateral prefrontal cortex. *Brain and Cognition*, 80: 170–6.

Rumelhart, D.E. & McClelland, J.L. (1986). *Parallel distributed processing: Explorations in the microstructure of cognition, vol. 1*. Cambridge, MA: MIT Press.

Rumelhart, D.E. & Ortony, A. (1977). The representation of knowledge in memory. In R.C. Anderson, R.J. Spiro & W.E. Montague (eds), *Schooling and the acquisition of knowledge*. Hillsdale, NJ: Lawrence Erlbaum Associates.

Rumelhart, D.E., McClelland, J.L. & The PDP Research Group (eds) (1986). *Parallel distributed processing, vol. 1: Foundations*. Cambridge, MA: MIT Press.

Rummel, J., Einstein, G.O. & Rampey, H. (2012). Implementation-intention encoding in a prospective memory task enhances spontaneous retrieval of intentions. *Memory*, 20: 803–17.

Runeson, S. & Frykholm, G. (1983). Kinematic specifications of dynamics as an informational basis for person-and-action perception: Expectation, gender recognition, and deceptive intention. *Journal of Experimental Psychology: General*, 112: 585–615.

Rusconi, E., McCrory, E. & Viding, E. (2012). Self-rated attention to detail predicts threat detection performance in security X-ray images. *Security Journal*, 25: 356–71.

Rushton, S.K. & Wann, J.P. (1999). Weighted combination of size and disparity: A computational model for timing a ball catch. *Nature Neuroscience*, 2: 186–90.

Russell, R., Duchaine, B. & Nakayama, K. (2009). Super-recognisers: People with extraordinary face recognition ability. *Psychonomic Bulletin & Review*, 16: 252–7.

Russell, R., Chatterjee, G. & Nakayama, K. (2012). Developmental prosopagnosia and super-recognition: No special role for surface reflectance processing. *Neuropsychologia*, 50: 334–40.

Russo, J.E. & Meloy, M.G. (2008*). Hypothesis generation and testing in Wason's 2–4–6 task.* Working paper, Cornell University, May.

Rusting, C.L. & DeHart, T. (2000). Retrieving positive memories to regulate negative mood: Consequences for mood-congruent memory. *Journal of Personality and Social Psychology*, 78: 737–52.

Ruthruff, E., Johnston, J.C. & Remington, R.W. (2009). How strategic is the central bottleneck: Can it be overcome by trying harder*? Journal of Experimental Psychology: Human Perception and Performance*, 35: 1368–84.

Ryan, J.D., Althoff, R.R., Whitlow, S. & Cohen, N.J. (2000). Amnesia is a deficit in relational memory. *Psychological Science*, 11: 454–61.

Sá, W.C., Kelley, C.N., Ho, C. & Stanovich, K.E. (2005). Thinking about personal theories: Individual differences in the coordination of theory and evidence. *Personality and Individual Differences*, 38: 1149–61.

Sack, A.T., Hubl, D., Prvulovic, D., Formisano, E., Jandl, M., Zanella, F.E., Maurer, K., Goebel, R., Dierks, T. & Linden, D.E. (2002). The experimental combination of rTMS and fMRI reveals the functional relevance of parietal cortex for visuospatial functions. *Cognitive Brain Research*, 13: 85–93.

Sadeh, T., Shohamy, D., Levy, D.R., Reggev, N. & Maril, A. (2011). Cooperation between the hippocampus and the striatum during episodic encoding. *Journal of Cognitive Neuroscience*, 23: 1597–608.

Salemink, E., Hertel, P. & Mackintosh, B. (2010). Interpretation training influences memory for prior interpretations. *Emotion*, 6: 903–7.

Salvucci D.D. & Taatgen, N.A. (2008). Threaded cognition: An integrated theory of concurrent multitasking. *Psychological Review*, 115: 101–30.

Salvucci, D.D. & Taatgen, N.A. (2011). Toward a unified view of cognitive control. *Topics in Cognitive Science*, 3: 227–30.

Sampson, M. & Faroqui-Shah, Y. (2011). Investigation of self-monitoring in fluent aphasia with jargon. *Aphasiology*, 25: 505–28.

Samuel, A.G. (1981). Phonemic restoration: Insights from a new methodology. *Journal of Experimental Psychology: General*, 110: 474–94.

Samuel, A.G. (1996). Does lexical information influence the perceptual restoration of phonemes? *Journal of Experimental Psychology: General*, 125: 28–51.

Samuel, A.G. (2011). Speech perception. *Annual Review of Psychology*, 62: 49–72.

Samuelson, W. & Zeckhauser, R.J. (1988). Status quo bias in decision making. *Journal of Risk and Uncertainty*, 1: 7–59.

Sanchez, C.A. & Wiley, J. (2006). An examination of the seductive details effect in terms of working memory capacity. *Memory & Cognition*, 34: 344–55.

Sanchez-Casas, R., Ferre, P., Demestre, J., Garcia-Chico, T. & Garcia-Albea, J.E. (2012). Masked and unmasked priming effects as a function of semantic relatedness and associative strength. *Spanish Journal of Psychology*, 15: 891–900.

Sandberg, K., Timmermans, B., Overgaard, M. & Cleeremans, A. (2010). Measuring consciousness: Is one measure better than the others? *Consciousness and Cognition*, 19: 1069–78.

Sander, D. (2009). Amygdala. In D. Sander & K.R. Scherer (eds), *The Oxford companion to emotion and the affective sciences*. Oxford: Oxford University Press.

Sandler, W., Meir, I., Padden, C. & Aronoff, M. (2005). The emergence of grammar: Syntactic structure in a new language. *Proceedings of the National Academy of Sciences*, 102: 2661–5.

Sanocki, T., Bowyer, K.W., Heath, M.D. & Sarkar, S. (1998). Are edges sufficient for object recognition? *Journal of Experimental Psychology: Human Perception & Performance*, 24: 340–9.

Santhouse, A.M., Howard, R.J. & fftyche, D.H. (2000). Visual hallucinatory sydromes and the anatomy of the visual brain. *Brain*, 113: 2055–64.

Sarri, M., Ruff, C.C., Rees, G. & Driver, J. (2010). Neural correlates of visual extinction or awareness in a series of patients with right temporo-parietal damage. *Cognitive Neuroscience*, 1: 16–25.

Sato, K. & Matsushima, K. (2006). Effects of audience awareness on procedural text writing. *Psychological Reports*, 99: 51–73.

Savage, L.J. (1954). *The foundations of statistics*. New York: Wiley.

Savelsbergh, G.J.P., Pijpers, J.R. & van Santvoord, A.A.M. (1993). The visual guidance of catching. *Experimental Brain Research*, 93: 148–56.

Savitsky, K., Keysar, B., Epley, N., Carter, T. & Swanson, A. (2011). The closeness-communication bias: Increased egocentrism among friends versus strangers. *Journal of Experimental Social Psychology*, 47: 269–73.

Saygin, A.P. (2007). Superior temporal and premotor brain areas necessary for biological motion perception. *Brain*, 130: 2452–61.

Schacter, D.L. (2012). Adaptive constructive processes and the future of memory. *American Psychologist*, 67: 603–13.

Schacter, D.L. & Addis, D.R. (2007). The cognitive neuroscience of constructive memory: Remembering the past and imagining the future. *Philosophical Transactions of the Royal Society B: Biological Sciences*, 362: 773–86.

Schacter, D.L. & Church, B.A. (1995). Implicit memory in amnesic patients: When is auditory priming spared? *Journal of the International Neuropsychological Society*, 1: 434–42.

Schacter, D.L. & Tulving, E. (1994). What are the memory systems of 1994? In D.L. Schacter & E. Tulving (eds), *Memory systems*. Cambridge, MA: MIT Press.

Schacter, D.L., Church, B.A. & Bolton, E. (1995). Implicit memory in amnesic patients: Impairment of voice-specific impairment priming. *Psychological Science*, 6: 20–5.

Schacter, D.L., Wig, G.S. & Stevens, W.D. (2007). Reductions in cortical activity during priming. *Current Opinion in Neurobiology*, 177: 171–6.

Schacter, D.L., Guerin, S.A. & St. Jacques, P.L. (2011). Memory distortion: An adaptive perspective. *Trends in Cognitive Sciences*, 15; 467–74.

Schartau, P.E.S., Dalgleish, T. & Dunn, B.D. (2009). Seeing the bigger picture: Training in perspective broadening reduces self-reported affect and psychophysiological response to distressing films and autobiographical memories. *Journal of Abnormal Psychology*, 118: 15–27.

Schechter, E. (2012). The switch model of split-brain consciousness. *Philosophical Psychology*, 25: 203–26.

Schenk, T. & McIntosh, R.D. (2010). Do we have independent visual streams for perception and action? *Cognitive Neuroscience*, 1(1): 52–62.

Scherer, K.R. & Ellsworth, P.C. (2009). Appraisal theories. In D. Sander & K.R. Scherer (eds), *The Oxford companion to emotion and the affective sciences* (pp. 45–9). Oxford: Oxford University Press.

Scherman, A.Z. (2013). Cultural life script theory and the reminiscence bump: A re-analysis of seven studies across cultures. *Nordic Psychology*, 65: 103–19.

Schiffer, F., Zaidel, E., Bogen, J. & Chasan-Taber, S. (1998). Different psychological status in the two hemispheres of two split-brain patients. *Neuropsychiatry, Neuropsychology, and Behavioral Neurology*, 11: 151–6.

Schindler, I., Rice, N.J., McIntosh, R.D., Rossetti, Y., Vighetto, A. & Milner, A.C. (2004). Automatic avoidance of obstacles is a dorsal stream function: Evidence from optic ataxia. *Nature Neuroscience*, 7: 779–84.

Schlösser, T., Dunning, D. & Fetchenhauer, D. (2013). What a feeling: The role of immediate and anticipated emotions in risky decisions. *Journal of Behavioral Decision Making*, 26: 13–30.

Schmid, M.C., Mrowka, S.W., Turchi, J., Saunders, R.C., Wilke, M., Peters, A.J., Ye, F.Q. & Leopold, D.A. (2010). Blindsight depends on the lateral geniculate nucleus. *Nature*, 466: 373–7.

Schmidt, G.L., Cardillo, E.R., Kranjec, A., Lehet, M., Widick, P. & Chatterjee, A. (2012). Not all analogies are created equal: Associative and categorical analogy processing following brain damage. *Neuropsychologia*, 50: 1372–9.

Schmidt, J.R. & Thompson, V.A. (2008). “At least one” problem with “some” formal reasoning paradigms. *Memory & Cognition*, 36: 217–39.

Schneider, W. & Shiffrin, R.M. (1977). Controlled and automatic human information processing: I. Detection, search, and attention. *Psychological Review*, 84: 1–66.

Scholte, H.S., Wittreveen, S.C., Soekreijse, H. & Lamme, V.A.F. (2006). The influence of inattention on the neural correlates of scene segregation. *Brain Research*, 1076: 106–15.

Scholz, J., Klein, M.C., Behrens, T.E. & Johansen-Berg, H. (2009). Training induces changes in white-matter architecture. *Nature Neuroscience*, 12: 1370–1.

Schotter, E.R., Angela, B. & Rayner, K. (2012). Parafoveal processing in reading. *Attention, Perception & Psychophysics*, 74: 5–35.

Schuller, J.C. (2012). The malicious host: A minimax solution of the Monty Hall problem. *Journal of Applied Statistics*, 39: 215–21.

Schumacher, E.H., Seymour, T.L., Glass, J.M., Fencsik, D.E., Lauber, E.J., Kieras, D.E. & Meyer, D.E. (2001). Virtually perfect time sharing in dual-task performance: Uncorking the central cognitive bottleneck. *Psychological Science*, 12: 101–8.

Schwabe, L. & Wolf, O.T. (2012). Stress modulates the engagement of multiple memory systems in classification learning. *Journal of Neuroscience*, 32: 11042–9.

Schwark, J., Sandry, J., MacDonald, J. & Dolgov, I. (2012). False feedback increases detection of low-prevalence targets in visual search. *Attention, Perception & Psychophysics*, 74: 1583–9.

Schwartz, B., Ward, A., Monterosso, J., Lyubormirsky, S., White, K. & Lehman, D.R. (2002). Maximising versus satisficing: Happiness is a matter of choice. *Journal of Personality and Social Psychology*, 83: 1178–97.

Schwartz, B.L. & Hashtroudi, S. (1991). Priming is independent of skill learning. *Journal of Experimental Psychology: Learning, Memory, and Cognition*, 17: 1177–87.

Schwartz, J., Chapman, G., Brewer, N. & Bergus, G. (2004). The effects of accountability on bias in physician decision making: Going from bad to worse. *Psychonomic Bulletin & Review*, 11: 173–8.

Schwartz, S., Vuilleumier, P., Hutton, C., Marouta, A., Dolan, R.J. & Driver, J. (2005). Modulation of fMRI responses by load at fixation during task-irrelevant stimulation in the peripheral visual field. *Cerebral Cortex*, 15: 770–86.

Schweinberger, S.R. & Soukup, G.R. (1998). Asymmetric relationships among perceptions of facial identity, emotion and facial speech. *Journal of Experimental Psychology: Human Perception and Performance*, 24: 1748–65.

Schweizer, T.A., Kan, K., Hung, Y., Tam, F., Naglie, G. & Graham, S.J. (2013). Brain activity during driving with distraction: An immersive fMRI study. *Frontiers in Human Neuroscience*, 7 (Article 53).

Schweppe, J., Grice, M. & Rummer, R. (2011). What models of verbal working memory can learn from phonological theory: Decomposing the phonological similarity effect. *Journal of Memory and Language*, 64: 256–69.

Scott, S.K. & Evans, S. (2010). Categorising speech. *Nature Neuroscience*, 13: 1304–6.

Scoville, W.B. & Milner, B. (1957). Loss of recent memory after bilateral hippocampal lesions. *Journal of Neurology, Neurosurgery & Psychiatry*, 20: 11–21.

Scullin, M.K., McDaniel, M.A. & Shelton, J.T. (2013). The dynamic multiprocess framework: Evidence from prospective memory with contextual variability. *Cognitive Psychology*, 67: 55–71.

Segaert, K., Weber, K., de Lange, F.P., Petersson, K.M. & Hagoort, P. (2013). The suppression of repetition enhancement: A review of fMRI studies. *Neuropsychologia*, 51: 59–66.

Sekuler, R. & Blake, R. (2002). *Perception* (4th edn). New York: McGraw-Hill.

Sellen, A.J., Lowie, G., Harris, J.E. & Wilkins, A.J. (1997). What brings intentions to mind? An in situ study of prospective memory. *Memory*, 5: 483–507.

Sellers, H. (2010). *You don't look like anyone I know*. New York: Riverhead Books.

Senghas, A., Kita, S. & Özyürek, A. (2004). Children creating core properties of language: Evidence from emerging sign language in Nicaragua. *Science*, 305: 1779–82.

Seo, M.-G. & Barrett, L.F. (2007). Being emotional during decision making – Good or bad? An empirical investigation. *Academy of Management Journal*, 50: 923–40.

Serino, A., Casavecchi, C., DeFilippo, L., Coccia, M., Shiffrar, M. & Ladavas, E. (2010). Lesions to the motor system affect action understanding. *Journal of Cognitive Neuroscience*, 22: 413–26.

Serrien, D.J., Ivry, R.B. & Swinnen, S.P. (2007). The missing link between action and cognition. *Progress in Neurobiology*, 82: 95–107.

Sevenster, D., Beckers, T. & Kindt, M. (2012). Retrieval per se is not sufficient to trigger reconsolidation of human fear memory. *Neurobiology of Learning and Memory*, 97: 338–45.

Seymour, K., Clifford, C.W.G., Logothetis, N.K. & Bartels, A. (2009). The coding of color, motion and their conjunction in the human visual cortex. *Current Biology*, 19: 177–83.

Shah, A.K. & Oppenheimer, D.M. (2008). Heuristics made easy: An effort-reduction framework. *Psychological Bulletin*, 134: 207–22.

Shahin, A.J., Bishop, C.W. & Miller, L.M. (2009). Neural mechanisms for illusory filling-in of degraded speech. *NeuroImage*, 44: 1133–43.

Shahin, A.J., Kerlin, J.R., Bhat, J. & Miller, L.M. (2012). Neural restoration of degraded audiovisual speech. *NeuroImage*, 60: 530–8.

Shallice, T. & Cooper, R. (2011). *The organisation of mind*. Oxford: Oxford University Press.

Shallice, T. & Warrington, E.K. (1970). Independent functioning of verbal memory stores: A neuropsychological study. *Quarterly Journal of Experimental Psychology*, 22: 261–73.

Shallice, T. & Warrington, E.K. (1974). The dissociation between long-term retention of meaningful sounds and verbal material. *Neuropsychologia*, 12: 553–5.

Shamma, S.A., Elhilali, M. & Micheyl, C. (2011). Temporal coherence and attention in auditory scene analysis. *Trends in Neurosciences*, 34: 114–23.

Shanks, D.R. (2010). Learning: From association to cognition. *Annual Review of Psychology*, 61: 273–301.

Shanks, D.R. & St John, M.F. (1994). Characteristics of dissociable human learning systems. *Behavioral and Brain Sciences*, 17: 367–94.

Share, D.L. (2008). On the Anglocentricities of current reading research and practice: The perils of over-reliance on an "outlier" orthography. *Psychological Bulletin*, 134: 584–615.

Sharot, T., Martorella, E.A., Delgado, M.R. & Phelps, E.A. (2007). How personal experience modulates the neural circuitry of memories of September 11. *Proceedings of the National Academy of Sciences*, 104: 389–94.

Shebani, Z. & Pulvermüller, F. (2013). Moving the hands and feet specifically impairs working memory for arm- and leg-related action words. *Cortex*, 49: 222–31.

Shelton, J.R. & Weinrich, M. (1997). Further evidence of a dissociation between output phonological and orthographic lexicons: A case study. *Cognitive Neuropsychology*, 14: 105–29.

Shen, W., Olive, J. & Jones, D. (2008). Two protocols comparing human and machine phonetic discrimination performance in conversational speech. *Interspeech*, 1630–3.

Shepperd, J.A., Klein, W.M.P., Waters, E.A. & Weinstein, N.D. (2013). Taking stock of unrealistic optimism. *Perspectives on Psychological Science*, 8: 395–411.

Sheppes, G. & Gross, J.J. (2011). Is timing everything? Temporal considerations in emotion regulation. *Personality and Social Psychology Review*, 15: 319–31.

Sheppes, G., Scheibe, S., Suri, G., Radu, P., Blechert, J. & Gross, J.J. (2014). Emotion regulation choice: A conceptual framework and supporting evidence. *Journal of Experimental Psychology: General*, 143: 163–81.

Sheridan, H. & Reingold, E.M. (2013). A further examination of the lexical-processing stages hypothesised by the E-Z Reader model. *Attention, Perception & Psychophysics*, 75: 407–14.

Shiffrar, M. & Thomas, J.P. (2013). Beyond the scientific objectification of the human body: Differentiated analyses of human motion and object motion. In M. Rutherford and V. Kuhlmeier (eds), *Social perception: Detection and interpretation of animacy, agency, and intention*. Cambridge, MA: MIT Press/Bradford Books.

Shiffrin, R.M. & Schneider, W. (1977). Controlled and automatic human information processing: II. Perceptual learning, automatic attending, and a general theory. *Psychological Review*, 84: 127–90.

Shintel, H. & Keysar, B. (2009). Less is more: A minimalist account of joint action in communication. *Topics in Cognitive Science*, 1: 260–73.

Shiv, B., Loewenstein, G. & Bechara, A. (2005a). The dark side of emotion in decision making: When individuals with decreased emotional reactions make more advantageous decisions. *Cognitive Brain Research*, 23: 85–92.

Shiv, B., Loewenstein, G., Bechara, A., Damasio, H. & Damsio, A.R. (2005b). Investment behaviour and the negative side of emotion. *Psychological Science*, 16: 435–9.

Shohamy, D. & Turk-Browne, N.B. (2013). Mechanisms for widespread hippocampal involvement in cognition. *Journal of Experimental Psychology: General*, 142: 1159–70.

Shomstein, S. (2012). Object-based attention: Strategy versus automaticity. *Wiley Interdisciplinary Reviews – Cognitive Science*, 3: 163–9.

Shomstein, S., Lee, J. & Behrmann, M. (2010). Top-down and bottom-up attentional guidance: Investigating the role of the dorsal and ventral parietal cortices. *Experimental Brain Research*, 206: 197–208.

Shorrock, S.T. (2005). Errors of memory in air traffic control. *Safety Science*, 43: 571–88.

Shriver, E.R., Young, S.G., Hugenberg, K., Bernstein, M.J. & Lanter, J.R. (2008). Class, race, and the face: Social context modulates the cross-race effect in face recognition. *Personality and Social Psychology Bulletin*, 34: 260–74.

Sides, A., Osherson, D., Bonni, N. & Viale, R. (2002). On the reality of the conjunction fallacy. *Memory & Cognition*, 30: 191–8.

Siebert, M., Markowitsch, H.J. & Bartel, P. (2003). Amygdala, affect and cognition: Evidence from 10 patients with Urbach-Wiethe disease. *Brain*, 126: 2627–37.

Siemer, M. & Reisenzein, R. (2007). The process of emotion inference. *Emotion*, 7: 1–20.

Siemer, M., Mauss, I. & Gross, J.J. (2007). Same situation – different emotions: How appraisals shape our emotions. *Emotion*, 7: 592–600.

Silvanto, J. (2008). A re-evaluation of blindsight and the role of striate cortex (V1) in visual awareness. *Neuropsychologia*, 46: 2869–71.

Simion, F., Regolin, L. & Bulf, H. (2008). A predisposition for biological motion in the newborn baby. *Proceedings of the National Academy of Sciences*, 105: 809–13.

Simner, J., Mayo, N. & Spiller, M.J. (2009). A foundation for savantism? Visuo-spatial synaesthetes. *Cortex*, 45: 1246–60.

Simon, D., Krawczyk, D.C. & Holyoak, K.J. (2004). Construction of preferences by constraint satisfaction. *Psychological Science*, 15: 331–6.

Simon, H.A. (1945). Theory of games and economic behaviour. *American Sociological Review*, 50: 558–60.

Simon, H.A. (1957). *Models of man: Social and rational*. New York: Wiley.

Simon, H.A. (1966). Scientific discovery and the psychology of problem solving. In H.A. Simon (ed.), *Mind and cosmos: Essays in contemporary science and philosophy*. Pittsburgh, PA: University of Pittsburgh Press.

Simon, H.A. (1974). How big is a chunk? By combining data from several experiments, a basic human memory unit can be identified and measured. *Science*, 183: 482–8.

Simon, H.A. (1990). Invariants of human behaviour. *Annual Review of Psychology*, 41: 1–19.

Simon, J.R., Vaidya, C.J., Howard, J.H. & Howard, D.V. (2012). The effects of aging on the neural basis of implicit associative learning in a probabilistic triplets learning task. *Journal of Cognitive Neuroscience*, 24: 451–63.

Simon, S.R., Khateb, A., Darque, A., Lazeyras, F., Mayer, E. & Pegna, A.J. (2011). When the brain remembers, but the patient doesn't: Converging fMRI and EEG evidence for covert recognition in a case of prosopagnosia. *Cortex*, 47: 825–38.

Simons, D.J. (2013). Unskilled and optimistic: Overconfident predictions despite calibrated knowledge of relative skill. *Psychonomic Bulletin & Review*, 20: 601–7.

Simons, D.J. & Chabris, C.F. (1999). Gorillas in our midst: Sustained inattentional blindness for dynamic events. *Perception*, 28: 1059–74.

Simons, D.J. & Chabris, C.F. (2011). What people believe about how memory works: A representative survey of the US population. *Public Library of Science One*, 6: e22757.

Simonson, I. & Staw, B.M. (1992). De-escalation strategies: A comparison of techniques for reducing commitment to losing courses of action. *Journal of Applied Psychology*, 77: 419–26.

Sinai, M.J., Ooi, T.L. & He, Z.J. (1998). Terrain influences the accurate judgment of distance. *Nature*, 395: 497–500.

Singer, W. & Gray, C.M. (1995). Visual feature integration and the temporal correlation hypothesis. *Annual Review of Neuroscience*, 18: 555–86.

Sio, U.N. & Ormerod, T.C. (2009). Does incubation enhance problem solving? A meta-analytic review. *Psychological Bulletin*, 135: 94–120.

Sio, U.N., Monaghan, P. & Ormerod, T. (2013). Sleep on it, but only if it is difficult: Effects of sleep on problem solving. *Memory & Cognition*, 41(2): 159–66.

Sirigu, A., Zalla, T., Pillon, B., Grafman, J., Agid, Y. & Dubois, B. (1995). Selective impairments in managerial knowledge following prefrontal cortex damage. *Cortex*, 31: 301–16.

Sitek, E.J., Narozanska, E., Barczak, A., Jasinska-Myga, B., Harciarek, M., Chodakowska-Zebrowska, M., Kubiak, M., Wieczorek, D., Konieczna, S., Rademakers, R., Baker, M., Berdynski, M., Brockhuis, B., Barcikowska, M., Zekanowski, C., Hellman, K.M., Wszolek, Z.K. & Slawek, J. (2014). Agraphia in patients with frontotemporal dementia and parkinsonism linked to chromosome 17 with P301L MAPT mutation: Dysexecutive, aphasic, apraxic or spatial phenomenon? *Neurocase*, 20: 69–86.

Skinner, B.F. (1957). *Verbal behaviour*. New York: Appleton-Century-Crofts.

Skinner, E.I. & Fernandes, M.A. (2007). Neural correlates of recollection and familiarity: A review of neuroimaging and patient data. *Neuropsychologia*, 45: 2163–79.

Slevc, L.R. (2012). Language and music. *Wiley Interdisciplinary Reviews – Cognitive Science*, 3: 483–92.

Slevc, L.R., Martin, R.C., Hamilton, A.C. & Joanisse, M.F. (2011). Speech perception, rapid temporal processing, and the left hemisphere: A case study of unilateral pure word deafness. *Neuropsychologia*, 49: 216–30.

Slezak, P. (1991). Can images be rotated and inspected? A test of the pictorial medium theory. *Program of the Thirteenth Annual Conference of the Cognitive Science Society*: 55–60.

Slezak, P. (1995). The "philosophical" case against visual imagery. In T. Caelli, P. Slezak & R. Clark (eds), *Perspectives in cognitive science: Theories, experiments and foundations* (pp. 237–71). New York: Ablex.

Sliwinska, M.W., Khadilkar, M., Campbell-Ratcliffe, J., Quevenco, F. & Devlin, J.T. (2012). Early and sustained supramarginal gyrus contributions to phonological processing. *Frontiers in Psychology*, 3 (Article 161).

Sloman, S., Rottenstreich, Y., Wisniewski, E., Hadjichristidis, C. & Fox, C.R. (2004). Typical versus atypical unpacking and superadditive probability judgment. *Journal of Experimental Psychology: Learning, Memory, and Cognition*, 30: 573–82.

Small, D.A. & Lerner, J.S. (2008). Emotional policy: Personal sadness and anger shape judgments about a welfare case. *Political Psychology*, 29: 149–68.

Smith, A.T., Wall, M.B., Williams, A.L. & Singh, K.D. (2006). Sensitivity to optic flow in human cortical areas MT and MST. *European Journal of Neuroscience*, 23: 561–9.

Smith, C.A. & Kirby, L.D. (2001). Toward delivering on the promise of appraisal theory. In K.R.A. Schorr & T. Johnstone (eds), *Appraisal processes in emotion: Theory, methods, research.* Oxford: Oxford University Press.

Smith, C.A. & Kirby, L.D. (2009). Putting appraisal in context: Toward a relational model of appraisal and emotion. *Cognition & Emotion*, 23: 1352–72.

Smith, C.A. & Lazarus, R.S. (1993). Appraisal components, core relational themes, and the emotions. *Cognition & Emotion*, 7: 233–69.

Smith, C.N., Frascino, J.C., Hopkins, R.O. & Squire, L.R. (2013). The nature of anterograde and retrograde memory impairment after damage to the medial temporal lobe. *Neuropsychologia*, 51: 2709–14.

Smith, E.E. & Jonides, J. (1997). Working memory: A view from neuroimaging. *Cognitive Psychology*, 33: 5–42.

Smith, E.R. & O'Brien, E.J. (2012). Tracking spatial information during reading: A cue-based process. *Memory & Cognition*, 40: 791–801.

Smith, G., Levere, M. & Kurtzman, R. (2009). Poker player behaviour after big wins and big losses. *Management Science*, 55: 1547–55.

Smith, R.E. (2003). The cost of remembering to remember in event-based prospective memory: Investigating the capacity demands of delayed intention performance. *Journal of Experimental Psychology: Learning, Memory, and Cognition*, 29: 347–61.

Smith, R.E. & Bayen, U.J. (2005). The effects of working memory resource availability on prospective memory: A formal modeling approach. *Experimental Psychology*, 52: 243–56.

Smith, R.E., Hunt, R.R., McVay, J.C. & McConnell, M.D. (2007). The cost of event-based prospective memory: Salient target events. *Journal of Experimental Psychology: Learning, Memory, and Cognition*, 33: 734–46.

Smith, T.J., Lamont, P. & Henderson, J.M. (2012). The penny drops: Change blindness at fixation. *Perception*, 41: 489–92.

Snedeker, J. & Trueswell, J. (2003). Using prosody to avoid ambiguity: Effects of speaker awareness and referential context. *Journal of Memory and Language*, 48: 103–30.

Snyder, J.J. & Bischof, W.F. (2010). Knowing where we're heading – When nothing moves. *Brain Research*, 1323: 127–38.

Snyder, K.M., Ashitaka, Y., Shimada, H., Ulrich, J.E. & Logan, G.D. (2014). What skilled typists don't know about the QWERTY keyboard. *Attention, Perception, & Psychophysics*, 76: 162–71.

Sohoglu, E., Peelle, J.E., Carlyon, R.P. & Davis, M.D. (2014). Top-down influences of written text on perceived clarity of degraded speech. *Journal of Experimental Psychology: Human Perception and Performance*, 40: 186–99.

Sokol-Hessner, P., Camerer, C.F. & Phelps, E.A. (2013). Emotion regulation reduces loss aversion and decreases amygdala responses to losses. *Social Cognitive and Affective Neuroscience*, 8: 341–50.

Solomon, S.G. & Lennie, P. (2007). The machinery of colour vision. *Nature Reviews Neuroscience*, 8: 276–86.

Soni, M., Lambon Ralph, M.A., Noonan, K., Ehsan, S., Hodgson, C. & Woollams, A.M. (2009). "L" is for tiger: Effects of phonological (mis)cueing on picture naming in semantic aphasia. *Journal of Neurolinguistics*, 22: 538–47.

Soni, M., Lambon Ralph, M.A. & Wollams, A.M. (2011). "W" is for bath: Can associative errors be cued? *Journal of Neuolinguistics*, 24: 445–65.

Soon, C.S., Brass, M., Heinze, H.J. & Hayes, J.D. (2008). Unconscious determinants of free decisions in the human brain. *Nature Neuroscience*, 10: 257–61.

Sorqvist, P. (2010). High working memory capacity attenuates the deviation effect but not the duplex-mechanism account of auditory distraction. *Memory & Cognition*, 38 651–8.

Soto, F.A., Waldschmidt, J.G., Hélie, S. & Ashby, F.G. (2013). Brain activity across the development of automatic categorisation: A comparison of categorisation tasks using multi-voxel pattern analysis. *NeuroImage*, 71: 284–97.

Soto-Faraco, S. & Alsius, A. (2009). Deconstructing the McGurk-MacDonald illusion. *Journal of Experimental Psychology: Human Perception and Performance*, 35: 580–7.

Sowden, S. & Catmur, C. (2014). The role of the right temporoparietal junction in the control of imitation. *Cerebral Cortex*. doi:10.1093/cercor/bht306.

Spearman, C.E. (1927). *The abilities of man: Their nature and measurement*. London: Macmillan.

Specht, K. (2014). Neuronal basis of speech comprehension. *Hearing Research*, 307: 121–35.

Spelke, E.S., Hirst, W.C. & Neisser, U. (1976). Skills of divided attention. *Cognition*, 4: 215–30.

Spence, C. (2012). Drive safely with neuroergonomics. *Psychologist*, 25: 664–7.

Spence, C., Parise, C. & Chen, Y.-C. (2011). The Colavita visual dominance effect. In M.M. Murray and M. Wallace (eds), *Frontiers in the neural bases of multisensory processes*. Boca Raton, FL: CRC Press.

Sperber, D. & Girotto, V. (2002). Use or misuse of the selection task? Rejoinder to Fiddick, Cosmides, and Tooby. *Cognition*, 85: 277–90.

Sperling, G. (1960). The information that is available in brief visual presentations. *Psychological Monographs*, 74 (498): 1–29.

Sperry, R.W. (1968). Hemisphere deconnection and unity in conscious awareness. *American Psychologist*, 23: 723–33.

Spiers, H.J., Maguire, E.A. & Burgess, N. (2001). Hippocampal amnesia. *Neurocase*, 7: 357–82.

Spivey, M.J., Tanenhaus, M.K., Eberhard, K.M. & Sedivy, J.C. (2002). Eye movements and spoken language comprehension: Effects of visual context on syntactic ambiguity resolution. *Cognitive Psychology*, 45: 447–81.

Squire, L.R. (2009a). Memory and brain systems: 1969–2009. *Journal of Neuroscience*, 29: 12711–16.

Squire, L.R. (2009b). The legacy of patient HM for neuroscience. *Neuron*, 61: 6–9.

Squire, L.R. & Wixted, J.T. (2011). The cognitive neuroscience of human memory since H.M. *Annual Review of Neuroscience*, 34: 259–88.

St Jacques, P.L., Kragel, P.A. & Rubin, D.C. (2011). Dynamic neural networks supporting memory retrieval. *NeuroImage*, 57: 608–16.

Stanford Encyclopedia of Philosophy (2013) Analogy. http://plato.stanford.edu/entries/reasoning-analogy/.

Stange, J.P., Hamlat, E.J., Hamilton, J.L., Abramson, L.Y. & Alloy, L.B. (2013). Overgeneral autobiographical memory, emotional maltreatment, and depressive symptoms in adolescence: Evidence of a cognitive vulnerability-stress interaction. *Journal of Adolescence*, 36: 201–8.

Stanovich, K.E. (2009). The thinking that IQ tests miss. *Scientific American*, November: 34–9.

Stanovich, K.E. (2012). On the distinction between rationality and intelligence: Implications for understanding individual differences in reasoning. In K.J. Holyoak & R.G. Morrison (2012*). The Oxford handbook of thinking and reasoning*. Oxford: Oxford University Press.

Stanovich, K.E. & West, R.F. (2007). Natural myside bias is independent of cognitive ability. *Thinking & Reasoning*, 13: 225–47.

Stanovich, K.E. & West, R.F. (2008). On the relative independence of thinking biases and cognitive ability. *Journal of Personality and Social Psychology*, 94: 672–95.

Staresina, B.P. & Davachi, L. (2006). Differential encoding mechanisms for subsequent associative recognition and free recall. *Journal of Neuroscience*, 26: 9162–72.

Steblay, N.K. & Phillips, J.D. (2011). The not-sure response option in sequential lineup practice. *Applied Cognitive Psychology*, 25: 768–74.

Steblay, N.M. (1997). Social influence in eyewitness recall: A meta-analytic review of line-up instruction effects. *Law and Human Behavior*, 21: 283–98.

Steblay, N.M., Dysart, J.E. & Wells, G.L. (2011). Seventy-two tests of the sequential lineup Superiority effect: A meta-analysis and policy discussion. *Psychology, Public Policy, and Law*, 17: 99–139.

Steinhauer, K. & Friederici, A.D. (2001). Prosodic boundaries, comma rules, and brain responses: The closure positive shift in ERPs as a universal marker for prosodic phrasing in listeners and readers. *Journal of Psycholinguistic Research*, 30: 267–95.

Stenning, K. & van Lambalgen, M. (2004). A little logic goes a long way: Basing experiment on semantic theory in the cognitive science of conditional reasoning. *Cognitive Science*, 28: 481–529.

Stephens, A.N. & Groeger, J.A. (2011). Anger-congruent behaviour transfers across driving situations. *Cognition & Emotion*, 25: 1423–38.

Sternberg, R.J. (2011). Understanding reasoning: Let's describe what we really think about. *Behavioral and Brain Sciences*, 34: 269–70.

Sternberg, R.J. & Ben-Zeev, T. (2001). *Complex cognition: The psychology of human thought*. Oxford: Oxford University Press.

Steyvers, M. & Hemmer, P. (2012). Reconstruction from memory in naturalistic environments. In B.H. Ross (ed.), *The Psychology of Learning and Motivation*, 56: 126–44.

Stich, S.P. (1990). *The fragmentation of reason*. Cambridge, MA: MIT Press.

Strayer, D.L. & Drews, F.A. (2007). Cell-phone induced driver distraction. *Current Directions in Psychological Science*, 16: 128–31.

Strayer, D.L., Watson, J.M. & Drews, F.A. (2011). Cognitive distraction while multitasking in the automobile. *The Psychology of Learning and Motivation*, 54: 29–58.

Striemer, C.L., Chouinard, P.A. & Goodale, M.A. (2011). Programs for action in superior parietal cortex: A triple-pulse TMS investigation. *Neuropsychologia*, 49: 2391–9.

Strobach, T., Liepelt, R., Pashler, H., Frensch, P.A. & Schubert, T. (2013). Effects of extensive dual-task practice on processing stages in simultaneous choice tasks. *Attention, Perception & Psychophysics*, 75: 900–20.

Stupple, E.J.N. & Ball, L.J. (2008). Belief-logic conflict resolution in syllogistic reasoning: Inspection-time evidence for a parallel-process model. *Thinking & Reasoning*, 14: 168–81.

Stupple, E.J.N., Ball, L.J., Evans, J.St.B.T. & Kamal-Smith, E. (2011). When logic and belief collide: Individual differences in reasoning times support a selective processing model. *Journal of Cognitive Psychology*, 23: 931–41.

Stupple, E.J.N., Ball, L.J. & Ellis, D. (2013). Matching bias in syllogistic reasoning: Evidence for a dual-process account from response times and confidence ratings. *Thinking & Reasoning*, 19: 54–77.

Stuss, D.T. (2011). Functions of the frontal lobes: Relation to executive functions. *Journal of the International Neuropsychological Society*, 17: 759–65.

Stuss, D.T. & Alexander, M.P. (2007). Is there a dysexecutive syndrome? Philosophical *Transactions of the Royal Society of London. Series B: Biological Sciences*, 362: 901–15.

Sulin, R.A. & Dooling, D.J. (1974). Intrusion of a thematic idea in retention of prose. *Journal of Experimental Psychology*, 103: 255–62.

Summerfield, J.J., Hassabis, D. & Maguire, E.A. (2009). Cortical midline involvement in autobiographical memory. *NeuroImage*, 44: 1188–206.

Sun, R. (2007). The importance of cognitive architectures: An analysis based on CLARION. *Journal of Experimental and Theoretical Artificial Intelligence*, 19: 159–93.

Sun, R., Zhang, X. & Mathews, R. (2009). Capturing human data in a letter-counting task: Accessibility and action-centredness in representing cognitive skills. *Neural Networks*, 22: 15–29.

Svenson, O., Salo, I. & Lindholm, T. (2009). Post-decision consolidation and distortion of facts. *Judgment and Decision Making*, 4: 397–407.

Svoboda, E., McKinnon, M.C. & Levine, B. (2006). The functional neuroanatomy of autobiographical memory: A meta-analysis. *Neuropsychologia*, 44: 2189–208.

Sweller, J. & Levine, M. (1982). Effects of goal specificity on means–ends analysis and learning. *Journal of Experimental Psychology: Learning, Memory & Cognition*, 8: 463–74.

Swets, B., Desmet, T., Clifton, C. & Ferreira, F. (2008). Underspecification of syntactic ambiguities: Evidence from self-paced reading. *Memory & Cognition*, 36: 201–16.

Swets, B., Jacovina, M.E. & Gerrig, R.J. (2013). Effects of conversational pressures on speech planning. *Discourse Processes*, 50: 23–51.

Szewczyk, J.M. & Schriefers, H. (2013). Prediction in language comprehension beyond specific words: An ERP study on sentence comprehension in Polish. *Journal of Memory and Language*, 68: 297–314.

Taatgen, N. (2011). *Threaded cognition, a model of human multitasking*. Talk at Interdisciplinary Workshop on Cognitive Neuroscience, Educational Research and Cognitive Modelling, Delmenhorst, Germany, March.

Tailor, D.R., Finkel, L.H. & Buchsbaum, G. (2000). Colour-opponent receptive fields derived from independent component analysis of natural images. *Vision Research*, 40: 2671–6.

Tainturier, M.-J., Schiemenz, S. & Leek, E.C. (2006). Separate orthographic representations for reading and spelling? Evidence from a case of preserved lexical reading and impaired lexical spelling. *Brain and Language*, 99: 40–1.

Talarico, J.M. & Rubin, D.C. (2003). Confidence, not consistency, characterizes flashbulb memories. *Psychological Science*, 14: 455–61.

Talarico, J.M., Berntsen, D. & Rubin, D.C. (2009). Positive emotions enhance recall of peripheral details. *Cognition & Emotion*, 23: 380–98.

Talmi, D. (2013). Enhanced emotional memory: Cognitive and neural mechanisms. *Current Directions in Psychological Science*, 22: 430–6.

Talsma, D. & Kok, A. (2002). Intermodal spatial attention differs between vision and audition: An event-related potential analysis. *Psychophysiology*, 39: 689–706.

Talsma, D., Coe, B., Munoz, D.P. & Theeuwes, J. (2010). Brain structures involved in visual search in the presence and absence of colour singletons. *Journal of Cognitive Neuroscience*, 22: 761–74.

Tamietto, M. & de Gelder, B. (2010). Neural bases of the non-conscious perception of emotional signals. *Nature Reviews Neuroscience*, 11: 697–709.

Tamietto, M., Castelli, L., Vighetti, S., Perozzo, P., Geminiani, G., Weiskrantz, L. & de Gelder, B. (2009). Unseen facial and bodily expressions trigger fast emotional reactions. *Proceedings of the National Academy of Sciences*, 106: 17661–6.

Tamietto, M., Cauda, F., Corazzini, L.L., Savazzi, S., Marzi, C.A., Goebel, R., Weiskrantz, L. & de Gelder, B. (2010). Collicular vision guides nonconscious behaviour. *Journal of Cognitive Neuroscience*, 22: 888–902.

Tanaka, J.W. & Taylor, M.E. (1991). Object categories and expertise: Is the basic level in the eye of the beholder? *Cognitive Psychology*, 15: 121–49.

Tang, D. & Schmeichel, B.J. (2014). Stopping anger and anxiety: Evidence that inhibitory control predicts negative emotional responding. *Cognition & Emotion*, 28: 132–42.

Tarantino, V., Cona, G., Biachin, M. & Bisiacchi, P.S. (submitted). Monitoring mechanisms in time- and event-based prospective memory: The influence of cue predictability.

Tarr, M.J. & Bülthoff, H.H. (1995). Is human object recognition better described by geon structural descriptions or by multiple views? Comment on Biederman and Gerhardstein (1993). *Journal of Experimental Psychology: Human Perception & Performance*, 21: 1494–505.

Tassy, S., Ouillier, O., Duclos, Y., Coulon, O., Mancini, J., Deruelle, C., Attarian, S., Felician, O. & Wicker, B. (2012). Disrupting the right prefrontal cortex alters moral judgment. *Social and Affective Neuroscience*, 7: 282–8.

Taylor, J.S.H., Rastle, K. & Davis, M.H. (2013). Can cognitive models explain brain activation during word and pseudoword reading? A meta-analysis of 36 neuroimaging studies. *Psychological Bulletin*, 139: 766–91.

Tentori, K., Crupi, V. & Russo, S. (2013). On the determinants of the conjunction fallacy: Probability versus inductive confirmation. *Journal of Experimental Psychology: General*, 142: 235–55.

Tetlock, P.E. (2002). Social functionalist frameworks for judgment and choice: Intuitive politicians, theologians, and prosecutors. *Psychological Review*, 109: 451–71.

Thagard, P. (2011). Critical thinking and informal logic: Neuropsychological perspectives. *Informal Logic*, 31: 152–70.

Thakral, P.P. (2011). The neural substrates associated with inattentional blindness. *Consciousness and Cognition*, 20: 1768–75.

Thimm, M., Fink, G.R., Küst, J., Karbe, H., Willmes, K. & Sturm, W. (2009). Recovery from hemineglect: Differential neurobiological effects of optokinetic stimulation and alertness training. *Cortex*, 45: 850–62.

Thoma, V. & Henson, R.N. (2011). Object representations in ventral and dorsal visual streams: fMRI repetition effects depend on attention and part-whole configuration. *NeuroImage*, 57: 513–25.

Thomas, B.C., Croft, K.E. & Tranel, D. (2011). Harming kin to save strangers: Further evidence for abnormally utilitarian moral judgments after ventromedial prefrontal damage. *Journal of Cognitive Neuroscience*, 23: 2186–96.

Thomas, L.E. & Lleras, A. (2009). Swinging into thought: Directed movement guides insight in problem solving. *Psychonomic Bulletin & Review*, 16: 719–23.

Thomas, N.J.T. (2009). Visual imagery and consciousness. In W.P. Banks (ed.), *Encylopedia of consciousness, vol. 2*. New York: Academic Press.

Thompson, J. & Parasuraman, R. (2012). Attention, biological motion, and action recognition. *NeuroImage*, 59: 4–13.

Thompson, M.B., Tangen, J.M. & McCarthy, D.J. (2014). Human matching performance of genuine crime scene latent fingerprints. *Law and Human Behavior*, 38: 84–93.

Thompson, V.A., Turner, J.A.P. & Pennycook, G. (2011). Intuition, reason, and metacognition. *Cognitive Psychology*, 63: 107–40.

Thornton, I.M., Rensink, R.A. & Shiffrar, M. (2002). Active versus passive processing of biological motion. *Perception*, 31: 837–53.

Thornton, T.L. & Gilden, D.L. (2007). Parallel and serial processes in visual search. *Psychological Review*, 114: 71–103.

Thorpe, S., Fize, D. & Marlot, C. (1996). Speed of processing in the human visual system. *Nature*, 381: 520–2.

Tierney, A., Dick, F., Deutsch, D. & Sereno, M. (2013). Speech versus song: Multiple pitch-sensitive areas revealed by a naturally occurring musical illusion. *Cerebral Cortex*, 23: 249–54.

Timmermans, B., Schilbach, L., Pasquali, A. & Cleeremans, A. (2012). Higher order thoughts in action: Consciousness as an unconscious re-descrpition proess. *Philosophical Transactions of the Royal Society B*, 367: 1412–23.

Tijtgat, P., Mazyn, L., De Laey, C. & Lenoir, M. (2008). The contribution of stereo vision to the control of braking. *Accident Analysis and Prevention*, 40: 719–24.

Todorović, D. (2009). The effect of the observer vantage point on perceived distortions in linear perspective images. *Attention, Perception & Psychophysics*, 71: 183–93.

Tollestrup, P.A., Turtle, J.W. & Yuille, J.C. (1994). Actual victims and witnesses to robbery and fraud: An archival analysis. In D.F. Ross, J.D. Read & M.P. Toglia (eds), *Adult eyewitness testimony: Current trends and developments*. New York: Wiley.

Tong, E.M.W. (2010). The sufficiency and necessity of appraisals for negative emotions. *Cognition & Emotion*, 24: 692–701.

Tong, F. & Pratte, M.S. (2012). Decoding patterns of human brain activity. *Annual Review of Psychology*, 63: 483–509.

Tononi, G. & Koch, C. (2008). The neural correlates of consciousness: An update. *Annals of the New York Academy of Sciences*, 1124: 239–61.

Toplak, M.E., West, R.F. & Stanovich, K.E. (2011). The Cognitive Reflection Test as a predictor of performance on heuristics-and-biases tasks. *Memory & Cognition*, 39: 1275–89.

Toplak, M.E., West, R.F. & Stanovich, K.E. (2014). Assessing miserly information processing: An expansion of the Cognitive Reflection Test. *Thinking & Reasoning*, 20: 147–68.

Trabasso, T. & Sperry, L.L. (1985). Causal relatedness and importance of story events. *Journal of Memory and Language*, 24: 595–611.

Trafton, J.G. & Monk, C.A. (2007). Task interruptions. *Reviews of Human Factors and Ergonomics*, 3: 111–26.

Tranel, D., Damasio, A.R., Damasio, H. & Brandt, J.P. (1994). Sensori-motor skill learning in amnesia: Additional evidence for the neural basis of nondeclarative memory. *Learning and Memory*, 1: 165–79.

Tree, J.E.F. (2007). Folk notions of um an duh, you know, and like. *Text & Talk*, 27: 297–314.

Treisman, A.M. (1964). Verbal cues, language, and meaning in selective attention. *American Journal of Psychology*, 77: 206–19.

Treisman, A.M. (1998). Feature binding, attention and object perception. *Philosophical Transactions of the Royal Society of London Series B: Biological Sciences*, 353: 1295–306.

Treisman, A.M. & Davies, A. (1973). Divided attention to ear and eye. In S. Kornblum (ed.), *Attention and performance, vol. IV*. London: Academic Press.

Treisman, A.M. & Gelade, G. (1980). A feature integration theory of attention. *Cognitive Psychology*, 12: 97–136.

Treisman, A.M. & Riley, J.G.A. (1969). Is selective attention selective perception or selective response?: A further test. *Journal of Experimental Psychology*, 79: 27–34.

Tresilian, J.R. (1999). Visually timed action: Time-out for "tau"? *Trends in Cognitive Sciences*, 3: 407–8.

Trevarthen, C. (2004). Split-brain and the mind. In R. Gregory (ed.), *The Oxford companion to the mind* (2nd edn). Oxford: Oxford University Press.

Trickett, S.B. & Trafton, J.G. (2007). "What if . . .": The use of conceptual simuations in scientific reasoning. *Cognitive Science*, 31: 843–75.

Trickett, S.B., Trafton, J.G. & Schunn, C.D. (2009). How do scientists respond to anomalies? Different strategies used in basic and applied science. *Topics in Cognitive Science*, 1: 711–29.

Triesch, J., Ballard, D.H. & Jacobs, R.A. (2002). Fast temporal dynamics of visual cue integration. *Perception*, 31: 421–34.

Troiani, V., Price, E.T. & Schultz, R.T. (2014). Unseen fearful faces promote amygdala guidance of attention. *Social, Cognitive, and Affective Neuroscience*, 9: 133–40.

Trout, J.D. (2001). The biological basis of speech: What to infer from talking to the animals. *Psychological Review*, 108: 523–49.

Troy, A.S., Shallcross, A.J. & Mauss, I.B. (2013). A person-by-situation approach to emotion regulation: Cognitive reappraisal can either help or hurt, depending on the context. *Psychological Science*, 24: 2505–14.

Trueswell, J.C., Tanenhaus, M.K. & Garnsey, S.M. (1994). Semantic influences on parsing: Use of thematic role information in syntactic ambiguity resolution. *Journal of Memory and Language*, 33: 285–318.

Tsapkini, K. & Rapp, B. (2010). The orthography-specific functions of the left fusiform gyrus: Evidence of modality and category specificity. *Cortex*, 46: 185–205.

Tsujii, T. & Watanabe, S. (2009). Neural correlates of dual-task effect on belief-bias syllogistic reasoning: A near-infrared spectroscopy study. *Brain Research*, 1287: 118–25.

Tuckey, M.R. & Brewer, N. (2003a). How schemas affect eyewitness memory over repeated retrieval attempts. *Applied Cognitive Psychology*, 7: 785–800.

Tuckey, M.R. & Brewer, N. (2003b). The influence of schemas, stimulus ambiguity, and interview schedule on eyewitness memory over time. *Journal of Experimental Psychology: Applied*, 9: 101–18.

Tuffiash, M., Roring, R.W. & Ericsson, K.A. (2007). Expert performance in SCRABBLE: Implications for the study of the structure and acquisition of complex skills. *Journal of Experimental Psychology: Applied*, 13: 124–34.

Tullett, A.M. & Inzlicht, M. (2010). The voice of self-control: Blocking the inner voice increases impulsive responding. *Acta Psychologica*, 135: 252–6.

Tulving, E. (1972). Episodic and semantic memory. In E. Tulving & W. Donaldson (eds), *Organisation of memory*. London: Academic Press.

Tulving, E. (1979). Relation between encoding specificity and levels of processing. In L.S. Cermak & F.I.M. Craik (eds), *Levels of processing in human memory*. Hillsdale, NJ: Lawrence Erlbaum Associates.

Tulving, E. (2002). Episodic memory: From mind to brain. *Annual Review of Psychology*, 53: 1–25.

Tulving, E., Schacter, D.L. & Stark, H.A. (1982). Priming effects in word-fragment completion are independent of recognition memory. *Journal of Experimental Psychology: Learning, Memory, and Cognition*, 17: 595–617.

Turpin, S.M. & Marais, M.A. (2004). Decision-making: Theory and practice. *Orion*, 20 143–60.

Tustin, K. & Hayne, H. (2010). Defining the boundary: Age-related changes in childhood amnesia. *Developmental Psychology*, 46: 1049–61.

Tversky, A. (1972). Elimination by aspects: A theory of choice. *Psychological Review*, 79: 281–99.

Tversky, A. & Kahneman, D. (1974). Judgment under uncertainty: heuristics and biases. *Science*, 185: 1124–30.

Tversky, A. & Kahneman, D. (1981). The framing of decisions and the psychology of choice. *Science*, 211: 453–8.

Tversky, A. & Kahneman, D. (1983). Extensional versus intuitive reasoning: The conjunction fallacy in probability judgment. *Psychological Review*, 91: 293–315.

Tversky, A. & Koehler, D.J. (1994). Support theory: A nonextensional representation of subjective probability. *Psychological Review*, 101: 547–67.

Tversky, A. & Shafir, E. (1992). The disjunction effect in choice under uncertainty. *Psychological Science*, 3: 305–9.

Tweney, R.D., Doherty, M.E., Worner, W.J., Pliske, D.B., Mynatt, C.R., Gross, K.A. & Arkellian, D.L. (1980). Strategies for rule discovery in an inference task. *Quarterly Journal of Experimental Psychology*, 32: 109–23.

Tyler, L.K., Voice, J. & Moss, H.E. (2000). The interaction of meaning and sound in spoken word recognition. *Psychonomic Bulletin & Review*, 7: 320–6.

Tyszka, J.M., Kennedy, D.P., Adolphs, R. & Paul, L.K. (2011). Intact bilateral resting-state networks in the absence of the corpus callous. *Journal of Neuroscience*, 31: 15154–62.

Ucros, C.G. (1989). Mood-state-dependent memory: A meta-analysis. *Cognition & Emotion*, 3: 139–67.

Uddin, L.Q., Rayman, J. & Zaidel, E. (2005). Split-brain reveals separate but equal self-recognition in the two cerebral hemispheres. *Consciousness and Cognition*, 14: 633–40.

Uddin, L.Q., Mooshagian, E., Zaidel, E., Scheres, A., Margulies, D.S., Kelly, A.M.C., Shehzad, Z., Adelstein, J.S., Castellanos, F.X., Biswal, B.B. & Milham, M.P. (2008). Residual functional connectivity in the split-brain revealed with resting-state functional MRI. *Neuroreport*, 19: 703–9.

Umiltà, M.A., Kohler, E., Gallese, V., Fogassi, L., Fadiga, L., Keysers, C. & Rizzolatti, G. (2001). I know what you are doing: A neurophysiological study. *Neuron*, 31: 155–65.

Unsworth, N. (2010). Interference control, working memory capacity, and cognitive abilities: A latent variable analysis. *Intelligence*, 38: 255–67.

Unsworth, N. & McMillan, B.D. (2013). Mind wandering and reading comprehension: Examining working memory capacity, interest, motivation, and topic experience. *Journal of Experimental Psychology: Learning, Memory, and Cognition*, 39: 832–42.

Unsworth, N., Redick, T.S., Spillers, G.J. & Brewer, G.A. (2012). Variation in working memory capacity and cognitive control: Goal maintenance and microadjustments of control. *Quarterly Journal of Experimental Psychology*, 65: 326–55.

Uttl, B. (2011). Transparent meta-analysis: Does aging spare prospective memory with focal vs. non-focal cues? *PLOS ONE*, 6(2): e16618. doi:10.1371/journal.pone.0016618.

Uzer, T., Lee, P.J. & Brown, N.R. (2012). On the prevalence of directly retrieved autobiographical memories. *Journal of Experimental Psychology: Learning, Memory, and Cognition*, 38: 1296–308.

Vaina, L.M. (1998). Complex motion perception and its deficits. *Current Opinion in Neurobiology*, 8: 494–502.

Vaina, L.M., Lemaya, M., Beinfanga, D.C., Choia, A. & Nakayama, K. (1990). Intact "biological motion" and "structure from motion" in a patient with impaired motion mechanisms: A case study. *Visual Neuroscience*, 5: 353–9.

Valentine, T. & Mesout, J. (2009). Eyewitness identification under stress in the London Dungeon. *Applied Cognitive Psychology*, 23: 151–61.

Valentine, T., Pickering, A. & Darling, S. (2003). Characteristics of eyewitness identification that predict the outcome of real line-ups. *Applied Cognitive Psychology*, 17: 969–93.

Vallée-Tourangeau, F., Euden, G. & Hearn, V. (2011). Einstellung defused: Interactivity and mental set. *Quarterly Journal of Experimental Psychology*, 64: 1889–95.

van Atteveldt, N., Murray, M.M., Thut, G. & Schroeder, C.E. (2014). Multisensory integration: Flexible use of general operations. *Neuron*, 81: 1240–53.

Van Belle, G., Busigny, T., Lefèvre, P., Joubert, S., Felician, O., Gentile, F. & Rossion, B. (2011). Impairment of holistic face perception following right occipito-temporal damage in prosopagnosia: Converging evidence from gaze-contingency. *Neuropsychologia*, 49: 3145–50.

van Berkum, J.J.A. (2009). The neuropragmatics of "simple" utterance comprehension: An ERP review. In U. Sauerland & K. Yatsushiro (eds), *Semantics and pragmatics: From experiment to theory*. Basingstoke: Palgrave Macmillan.

van Berkum, J.J.A., Brown, C.M., Zwitserlood, P., Kooijman, V. & Hagoort, P. (2005). Anticipating upcoming words in discourse: Evidence from ERPs and reading times. *Journal of Experimental Psychology: Learning, Memory, and Cognition*, 31: 443–67.

van den Berg, A.V. & Brenner, E. (1994). Why two eyes are better than one for judgments of heading. *Nature*, 371: 700–2.

van den Brink, D., van Berkum, J.J.A., Bastiaansen, M.C.M., Tesink, C.M.J.Y., Kos, M., Buitelaar, J.K. & Hagoort, P. (2012). Empathy matters: ERP evidence for inter-individual differences in social language processing. *Social Cognitive and Affective Neuroscience*, 7: 173–83.

van den Broek, G.S.E., Takashima, A., Segers, E., Fernandez, G. & Verhoeven, L. (2013). Neural correlates of testing effects in vocabulary learning. *NeuroImage*, 78: 94–102.

van den Heuvel, M.P., Stam, C.J., Kahn, R.S. & Pol, H.E.H. (2009). Efficiency of functional brain networks and intelligence performance. *Journal of Neuroscience*, 29: 7619–24.

van den Hout, M. & Kindt, M. (2004). Obsessive-compulsive disorder and the paradoxical effects of perseverative behaviour on experienced uncertainty. *Journal of Behavior Therapy and Experimental Psychiatry*, 35: 165–81.

Vanderberg, R. & Swanson, H.L. (2007). Which components of working memory are important in the writing process? *Reading and Writing*, 20: 721–52.

van der Hoort, B., Guterstam, A. & Ehrsson, H.H. (2011). Being Barbie: The size of one's own body determines the perceived size of the world. *PLOS ONE*, 6(5): e20195.

van der Stigchel, S., Nijboer, T.C.W., Bergsma, D.P., Abegg, M. & Barton, J.J.S. (2010). Anomalous global effects induced by "blind" distractors in visual hemifield defects. *Brain and Cognition*, 74: 66–73.

van der Weiden, A., Ruys, K.I. & Aarts, H. (2013). A matter of matching: How goals and primes affect self-agency experiences. *Journal of Experimental Psychology: General*, 142: 954–66.

van Doorn, H., van der Kamp, J. & Savelsbergh, G.J.P. (2007). Grasping the Müller–Lyer illusion: The contributions of vision for perception in action. *Neuropsychologia*, 45: 1939–47.

van Gaal, S. & Lamme, V.A.F. (2012). Unconscious high-level information proessing: Implication for neurobiologial theories of consciousness. *The Neuroscientist*, 18: 287–301.

van Gaal, S., Ridderinkhof, K.R., Scholte, H.S. & Lamme, V.A.F. (2010). Unconscious activation of the prefrontal no-go network. *Journal of Neuroscience*, 30: 4143–50.

van Gaal, S., de Lange, F.P. de & Cohen, M.X. (2012). The role of consciousness in cognitive contro and decision making. *Frontiers in Human Neuroscience*, 6 (Article 121).

van Gompel, R.P.G. & Pickering, M.J. (2001). Lexical guidance in sentence processing: A note on Adams, Clifton, and Mitchell (1998). *Psychonomic Bulletin & Review*, 8: 851–7.

van Gompel, R.P.G., Pickering, M.J. & Traxler, M.J. (2000). Unrestricted race: A new model of syntactic ambiguity resolution. In A. Kennedy, R. Radach, D. Heller & J. Pytte (eds), *Reading as a perceptual process*. Oxford: Elsevier.

van Gompel, R.P.G., Pickering, M.J. & Traxler, M.J. (2001). Re-analysis in sentence processing: Evidence against constraint-based and two-stage models. *Journal of Memory and Language*, 43, 225–58.

van Harreveld, F., Wagenmakers, F.J. & van der Maas, H.L.J. (2007). The effects of time pressure on chess skills: An investigation into fast and slow responses underlying expert performance. *Psychological Research*, 71: 591–7.

van Kesteren, M.T.R., Ruiter, D.J., Fernández, G. & Henson, R.N. (2012). How schema and novelty augment memory formation. *Trends in Neurosciences*, 35: 211–19.

Vannuscorps, G., Andres, M. & Pillon, A. (2013). When does action comprehension need motor involvement? Evidence from upper limb aplasia. *Cognitive Neuropsychology*, 30: 253–83.

Van Orden, G.C. (1987). A rows is a rose: Spelling, sound and reading. *Memory & Cognition*, 14: 371–86.

van Os, J., Park, S.B.G. & Jones, P.B. (2001). Neuroticism, life events and mental health: Evidence for person-environment correlation. *British Journal of Psychiatry*, 178: S72–7.

Van Petten, C. & Luka, B.J. (2012). Prediction during language comprehension: Benefits, costs, and ERP components. *International Journal of Psychophysiology*, 83: 176–90.

Van Petten, C., Coulson, S., Rubin, S., Plante, E. & Parks, M. (1999). Time course of word identification and semantic integration in spoken language. *Journal of Experimental Psychology: Learning, Memory, and Cognition*, 25: 394–417.

Van Tilborg, I.A.D.A., Kessels, R.P.C., Kruijt, P., Wester, A.J. & Hulstijn, W. (2011). Spatial and nonspatial implicit motor learning in Korsakoff's amnesia: Evidence for selective deficits. *Experimental Brain Research*, 214: 427–35.

van Turennout, M., Hagoort, P. & Brown, C.M. (1998). Brain activity during speaking: From syntax to phonology in 40 milliseconds. *Science*, 280: 572–4.

Varakin, D.A., Levin, D.T. & Collins, K.M. (2007). Comparison and representation failures both causes real-world change. *Perception*, 36: 737–49.

Vargha-Khadem, F., Gadian, D.G., Watkins, K.E., Connelly, A., Van Paesschen, W. & Mishkin, M. (1997). Differential effects of early hippocampal pathology on episodic and semantic memory. *Science*, 277: 376–80.

Vecera, S.P., Flevaris, A.V. & Filapek, J.C. (2004). Exogenous spatial attention influences figure-ground assignment. *Psychological Science*, 15: 20–6.

Velan, H. & Frost, R. (2007). Cambridge University versus Hebrew University: The impact of letter transposition on reading English and Hebrew. *Psychonomic Bulletin & Review*, 14: 913–18.

Verfaellie, M., LaRocque, K.F. & Keane, M.M. (2013). Intact implicit verbal relational memory in medial temporal lobe amnesia. *Neuropsychologia*, 50: 2100–6.

Vergauwe, E., Barrouillet, P. & Camos, V. (2009). Visual and spatial working memory are not dissociated after all: A time-based resource-sharing account. *Journal of Experimental Psychology: Learning, Memory, and Cognition*, 35: 1012–28.

Verleger, R., Binkofski, F., Friedrich, M., Sedlmeier, P. & Kömpf, D. (2011). Anarchic-hand syndrome: ERP reflections of lost control over the right hemisphere. *Brain and Cognition*, 77: 138–50.

Vesia, M. & Crawford, J.D. (2012). Specialisation of reach function in human posterior parietal cortex. *Experimental Brain Research*, 221: 1–18.

Viard, A., Desgranges, B., Eustache, F. & Piolino, P. (2012). Factors affecting medial temporal lobe engagement for past and future episodic events: An ALE meta-analysis of neuroimaging studies. *Brain and Cognition*, 80: 111–25.

Viggiano, M.P., Giovannelli, F., Borgheresi, A., Feurra, M., Berardi, N., Pizzorusso, T., Zaccara, G. & Cincotta, M. (2008). Disruption of the prefrontal cortex function by rTMS produces a category-specific enhancement of the reaction times during visual object identification. *Neuropsychologia*, 46: 2725–31.

Viggiano, M.P., Marzi, T., Forni, M., Righi, S., Francheschini, R. & Peru, A. (2012). Semantic category effects modulate visual priming in neglect patients. *Cortex*, 48: 1128–37.

Vigliocco, G. & Hartsuiker, R.J. (2002). The interplay of meaning, sound, and syntax in sentence production. *Psychological Bulletin*, 128: 442–72.

Vigliocco, G., Antonini, T. & Garrett, M.F. (1997). Grammatical gender is on the top of Italian tongues. *Psychological Science*, 8: 314–17.

Vilarroya, O. (2013). The challenges of neural mind-reading paradigms. *Frontiers in Human Neuroscience*, 7 (Article 306).

Virji-Babul, N., Cheung, T., Weeks, D., Kers, K. & Shiffrar, M. (2008). Neural activity involved in the perception of human and meaningful object motion. *Neuroreport*, 18: 1125–28.

Viviani, R. (2013). Emotion regulation, attention to emotion, and the venteral attentional network. *Frontiers in Human Neuroscience*, 7 (Article 746).

Võ, M.L.-H. & Wolfe, J.M. (2012). When does repeated search in scenes involve memory? Looking *at* versus looking *for* objects in scenes. *Journal of Experimental Psychology: Human Perception and Performance*, 38: 23–41.

Vogels, R., Biederman, I., Bar, M. & Lorinez, A. (2001). Inferior temporal neurons show greater sensitivity to non-accidental than to metric shape differences. *Journal of Cognitive Neuroscience*, 13: 444–53.

Volle, E., Gilbert, S.J., Benoit, R.G. & Burgess, P.W. (2010). Specialisation of the rostral prefrontal cortex for distinct analogy processes. *Cerebral Cortex*, 20: 2647–59.

von Bastian, C.C., Schwaninger, A. & Michel, S. (2010). Colour impact on security screening. *IEEE A&E Systems Magazine*, October: 33–8.

von Neumann, J. & Morgenstern, O. (1944). *Theory of games and economic behavior*. Princeton, NJ: Princeton University Press.

Voss, J.L., Reber, P.J., Mesulam, M.M., Parrish, T.B. & Paller, K.A. (2008). Familiarity and conceptual priming engage distinct cortical networks. *Cerebral Cortex*, 18: 1712–19.

Vousden, J.I. & Maylor, E.A. (2006). Speech errors across the lifespan. *Language and Cognitive Processes*, 21: 48–77.

Vredeveldt, A., Hitch, G.J. & Baddeley, A.D. (2011). Eyeclosure helps memory by reducing cognitive load and enhancing visualization. *Memory & Cognition*, 39: 1253–63.

Vuilleumier, P., Schwartz, S., Clarke, K., Husain, M. & Driver, J. (2002). Testing memory for unseen visual stimuli in patients with extinction and spatial neglect. *Journal of Cognitive Neuroscience*, 14: 875–86.

Wachtel, P.L. (1973). Psychodynamics, behaviour therapy and the implacable experimenter: An inquiry into the consistency of personality. *Journal of Abnormal Psychology*, 82: 324–34.

Wade, A.R., Brewer, A.A., Rieger, J.W. & Wandell, B.A. (2002). Functional measurements of human ventral occipital cortex: Retinopy and colour. *Philosophical Transactions of the Royal Society of London Series B: Biological Sciences*, 357: 963–73.

Wade, N.J. & Swanston, M.T. (2013). *Visual perception: An introduction* (3rd edn). Hove: Psychology Press.

Waechter, R.L., Goel, V., Raymont, V., Kruger, F. & Grafman, J. (2013). Transitive inference reasoning is impaired by focal lesions in parietal cortex rather than rostrolateral prefrontal cortex. *Neuropsychologia*, 51: 464–71.

Wagemans, J., Elder, J.H., Kubovy, M., Palmer, S.E., Peterson, M.A., Singh, M. & von der Heydt, R. (2012a). A century of Gestalt psychology in visual perception: I. Perceptual grouping and figure-ground organisation. *Psychological Bulletin*, 138: 1172–217.

Wagemans, J., Feldman, J., Gepshtein, S., Kimchi, R., Poemerantz, J.R. & van der Helm, P.A. (2012b). A century of Gestalt psychology in visual perception: II. Conceptual and theoretical foundations. *Psychological Bulletin*, 138: 1218–52.

Wagner, A.D., Schacter, D.L., Rotte, M., Koutstaal, W., Maril, A.M., Dale, B.R., Rosen, B.R. & Buckner, R.L. (1998). Building memories: Remembering and forgetting of verbal experiences as predicted by brain activity. *Science*, 281: 1188–91.

Wagner, M. & Watson, D.G. (2010). Experimental and theoretical advances in prosody: A review. *Language and Cognitive Processes*, 25: 905–45.

Wagner, U., Gais, S., Haider, H., Verleger, R. & Born, J. (2004). Sleep inspires insight. *Nature*, 427: 352–5.

Wagner, V., Jescheniak, J.D. & Schriefers, H. (2010). On the flexibility of grammatical advance planning: Effects of cognitive load on multiple lexical access. *Journal of Experimental Psychology: Learning, Memory, and Cognition*, 36: 423–40.

Wagoner, B. (2013). Bartlett's concept of schema in reconstruction. *Theory & Psychology*, 23: 553–75.

Wahlheim, C.N. & Jacoby, L.L. (2011). Experience with proactive interference diminishes its effects: Mechanisms of change. *Memory & Cognition*, 39: 185–95.

Wallas, G. (1926). *The art of thought*. London: Cape.

Wallis, G. (2013). Toward a unified model of face and object recognition in the human visual system. *Frontiers in Psychology*, 4 (Article 497).

Walsh, J.J., McNally, M. & Eysenck, M.W. (submitted). Interpretive bias and repressive coping.

Walton, D. (2010). Why fallacies appear to be better arguments than they are. *Informal Logic*, 30: 159–84.

Wang, J., Conder, J.A., Blitzer, D.N. & Shinkareva, S.V. (2010). Neural representation of abstract and concrete concepts: A meta-analysis of neuroimaging studies. *Human Brain Mapping*, 31: 1459–68.

Wang, S., Fukuchi, M., Koch, C. & Tsuchiya, N. (2012). Spatial attention is attracted in a sustained fashion toward singular points in the optic flow. *PLOS ONE*, 7(8): e41040.

Wang, X.T. (1996). Domain-specific rationality in human choices: Violations of utility axioms and social contexts. *Cognition*, 60: 31–63.

Ward, J. (2006). *The student's guide to cognitive neuroscience*. Hove: Psychology Press.

Ward, J. (2010). *The student's guide to cognitive neuroscience* (2nd edn). Hove: Psychology Press.

Wardlow, L. (2013). Individual differences in speakers' perspective taking: The roles of executive control and working memory. *Psychonomic Bulletin & Review*, 20: 766–72.

Warren, R.M. & Warren, R.P. (1970). Auditory illusions and confusions. *Scientific American*, 223: 30–6.

Wason, P.C. (1960). On the failure to eliminate hypotheses in a conceptual task. *Quarterly Journal of Experimental Psychology*, 12: 129–40.

Waters, E.A. (2008). Feeling good, feeling bad, and feeling at risk: A review of incidental affect's influence on likelihood estimates of health hazards and life events. *Journal of Risk Research*, 11: 569–95.

Watson, D. & Tellegen, A. (1985). Toward a consensual structure of mood. *Psychological Bulletin*, 98: 219–35.

Watson, J.B. (1920). Is thinking merely the action of language mechanisms? *British Journal of Psychology*, 11: 87–104.

Webb, T.L., Miles, E. & Sheeran, P. (2012). Dealing with feeling: A meta-analysis of the effectiveness of strategies derived from the process model of emotion regulation. *Psychological Bulletin*, 138: 775–808.

Weber, A. & Crocker, M.W. (2012). On the nature of semantic constraints on lexical access. *Journal of Psycholinguistic Research*, 41: 195–214.

Wegner, D.M. (2003). The mind's best trick: How we experience free will. *Trends in Cognitive Sciences*, 7: 65–9.

Wegner, D.M. & Wheatley, T. (1999). Apparent mental causation: Sources of the experience of will. *American Psychologist*, 54: 480–92.

Weiner, K.S. & Grill-Spector, K. (2012). The improbable simplicity of the fusiform face area. *Trends in Cognitive Sciences*, 16: 251–4.

Weisberg, D.S., Keil, F.C., Goodstein, J., Rawson, E. & Gray, J.R. (2008). The seductive allure of neuroscience explanations. *Journal of Cognitive Neuroscience*, 20: 470–7.

Weisberg, R.W. (2014). Toward an integrated theory of insight in problem solving. *Thinking & Reasoning*. doi: 10.1080/13546783.2014.886625.

Weiskrantz, L. (1980). Varieties of residual experience. *Quarterly Journal of Experimental Psychology*, 32: 365–86.

Weiskrantz, L. (2004). Blindsight. In R.L. Gregory (ed.), *Oxford companion to the mind*. Oxford: Oxford University Press.

Weiskrantz, L. (2010). Looking back: blindsight in hindsight. *The Psychologist*, 23: 356–8.

Weiskrantz, L., Warrington, E.K., Sanders, M.D. & Marshall, J. (1974). Visual capacity in the hemianopic field following a restricted occipital ablation. *Brain*, 97: 709–28.

Welch, R.B. & Warren, D.H. (1980). Immediate perceptual response to intersensory discrepancy. *Psychological Bulletin*, 88: 638–67.

Welford, A.T. (1952). The psychological refractory period and the timing of high speed performance. *British Journal of Psychology*, 43: 2–19.

Weller, J.A., Levin, I.P., Shiv, B. & Bechara, A. (2007). Neural correlates of adaptive decision making for risky gains and losses. *Psychological Science*, 18: 958–64.

Wen, X., Liu, Y. & Ding, M. (2012). Causal interactions in attention networks predict behavioural performance. *Journal of Neuroscience*, 32: 1284–92.

Werner, N.S., Schweitzer, N., Meindl, T., Duschek, S., Kambertz, J. & Schandry, R. (2013). Interoceptive awareness moderates neural activity during decision making. *Biological Psychology*, 94: 498–506.

Wessel, J.R., Haider, H. & Rose, M. (2012). The transition from implicit to explicit representations in incidental learning: More evidence from high-frequency EEG coupling. *Experimental Brain Research*, 217: 153–62.

White, C.N. & Poldrack, R.A. (2013). Using fMRI to constrain theories of cognition. *Perspectives on Psychological Science*, 8(1): 79–83.

White, L.K., Suway, J.G., Pine, D.S., Bar-Haim, Y. & Fox, N.A. (2011). Cascading effects: The influence of attention bias to threat on the interpretation of ambiguous information. *Behaviour Research and Therapy*, 49: 244–51.

Whorf, B.L. (1956). *Language, thought, and reality: Selected writings of Benjamin Lee Whorf.* New York: Wiley.

Wickens, C.D. (1984). Processing resources in attention. In R. Parasuraman & D.R. Davies (eds), *Varieties of attention*. London: Academic Press.

Wickens, C.D. (2008). Multiple resources and mental workload. *Human Factors*, 50: 449–55.

Wiese, H., Wolff, N., Steffens, M.C. & Schweinberger, S.R. (2013). How experience shapes memory for faces: An event-related potential study on the own-age bias. *Biological Psychology*, 94: 369–79.

Wig, G.S., Grafton, S.T., Demos, K.E. & Kelley, W.M. (2005). Reductions in neural activity underlie behavioural components of repetition priming. *Nature Neuroscience*, 8: 1228–33.

Wild, C., Davis, M.H. & Johnsrude, J.S. (2012). The perceptual clarity of speech modulates activity in primary auditory cortex: fMRI evidence of interactive processes in speech perception. *NeuroImage*, 60: 1490–502.

Wiley, J., Jarosz, A.F., Cushen, P.J. & Colflesh, G.J.H. (2011). New rule use drives the relation between working memory capacity and Raven's Advanced Progressive Matrices. *Journal of Experimental Psychology: Learning, Memory, and Cognition*, 37: 256–63.

Wilf, M., Holmes, N.P., Schwartz, I. & Makin, T.R. (2013). Dissociating between object affordances and spatial compatibility effects using early response components. *Frontiers in Psychology*, 4 (Article 591).

Wilkie, R.M. & Wann, J.P. (2006). Judgments of path, not heading, guide locomotion. *Journal of Experimental Psychology: Human Perception and Performance*, 32: 88–96.

Wilkie, R.M., Kountouriotis, G.K. & Merat, N. (2010). *Experimental Brain Research*, 204: 539–47.

Wilkinson, L. & Shanks, D.R. (2004). Intentional control and implicit sequence learning. *Journal of Experimental Psychology: Learning, Memory, and Cognition*, 30: 354–69.

Wilkinson, L., Khan, Z. & Jahanshahi, M. (2009). The role of the basal ganglia and its cortical connections in sequence learning: Evidence from implicit and explicit sequence learning in Parkinson's disease. *Neuropsychologia*, 47: 2564–73.

Williams, J.H.G. (2013). The mirror or portrait neuron system: Time for a more organic model of action-coding? *Cortex*, 49: 2962–3.

Williams, J.M.G., Watts, F.N., MacLeod, C.M. & Mathews, A. (1997). *Cognitive psychology and emotional disorders* (2nd ed.). Chichester: Wiley.

Williams, L.E., Bargh, J.A., Nocera, C.C. & Gray, J.R. (2009). The unconscious regulation of emotion: Nonconsious reappraisal goals modulate emotional reactivity. *Emotion*, 9: 847–54.

Wilmer, J.B., Germine, L., Chabris, C.F., Chatterjee, G., Williams, M., Loken, E., Nakayama, K. & Duchaine, B. (2010). Human face recognition ability is specific and highly heritable. *Proceedings of the National Academy of Sciences*, 107: 5238–41.

Wilson, M.P. & Garnsey, S.M. (2009). Making simple sentences hard: Verb bias effects in simple direct object sentences. *Journal of Memory and Language*, 60: 368–92.

Wilson, S.M., Galantucci, S., Tartaglia, M.C. & Gorno-Temini, M. (2012). The neural basis of syntactic deficits in primary progressive aphasia. *Brain & Language*, 122: 190–8.

Wilson-Mendenhall, C.D., Simmons, W.K., Martin, A. & Barsalou, L.W. (2013). Contextual processing of abstract concepts reveals neural representations of non-linguistic semantic content. *Journal of Cognitive Neuroscience*, 25: 920–35.

Winawer, J., Witthoft, N., Frank, M.C., Wu, L., Wade, A.R. & Boroditsky, L. (2007). Russian blues reveal effects of language on colour discrimination. *Proceedings of the National Academy*, 104: 7780–5.

Windey, B., Vermeiren, A., Atas, A. & Cleeremans, A. (2014). The graded and dichotomous nature of visual awareness. *Philosophical Transactions of the Royal Society B*, 369: 20130282.

Windmann, S. (2004). Effects of sentence context and expectation on the McGurk illusion. *Journal of Memory and Language*, 50: 212–30.

Winkielman, P., Berridge, K.C. & Wilbarger, J.L. (2005) Unconscious affective reactions to masked happy versus angry faces influence consumption behavior and judgments of value. *Personality and Social Psychology Bulletin*, 31: 121. doi: 10.1177/0146167204271309.

Withagen, R., de Poel, H.J., Araujo, D. & Pepping, G.-J. (2012). Affordances can invite behaviour: Reconsidering the relationship between affordances and agency. *New Ideas in Psychology*, 30: 250–8.

Witt, J.K., Linkenauger, S., Bakdash, J. & Proffitt, D. (2008). Putting to a bigger hole: Golf Performance relates to perceived size. *Psychonomic Bulletin and Review*, 15: 581–5.

Wixted, J.T. (2004). The psychology and neuroscience of forgetting. *Annual Review of Psychology*, 55: 235–69.

Wixted, J.T. & Squire, L.R. (2011). The medial temporal lobe and the attributes of memory. *Trends in Cognitive Sciences*, 15: 210–17.

Woike, B., Gershkovich, I., Piorkowski, R. & Polo, M. (1999). The role of motives in the content and structure of autobiographical memory. *Journal of Personality and Social Psychology*, 76: 600–12.

Wolfe, J.M. (1998). Visual search. In H. Pashler (ed.), *Attention*. Hove: Psychology Press.

Wolfe, J.M., Horowitz, T.S., Van-Wert, M.J., Kenner, N.M., Place, S.S. & Kibbi, N. (2007). Low target prevalence is a stubborn source of errors in visual search tasks. *Journal of Experimental Psychology: General*, 136: 623–38.

Wolfe, J.M., Alvarez, G.A., Rosenholtz, R., Kuzmova, Y.I. & Sherman, A.M. (2011a). Visual search for arbitrary objects in real scenes. *Attention, Perception & Psychophysics*, 73: 1650–71.

Wolfe, J.M., Võ, M.L.-H., Evans, K.K. & Greene, M.R. (2011b). Visual search in scenes involves selective and nonselective pathways. *Trends in Cognitive Sciences*, 15: 77–84.

Wolff, P. & Gentner, D. (2011). Structure-mapping in metaphor comprehension. *Cognitive Science*, 35: 1456–88.

Wolff, P. & Holmes, K.J. (2011). Linguistic relativity. *Wiley Interdisciplinary Reviews: Cognitive Science*, 2: 253–65.

Won, E.J.S. (2012). A theoretical investigation on the attraction effect using the elimination-by-aspects model incorporating higher preference for shared features. *Journal of Mathematical Psychology*, 56: 386–91.

Wong, C.K. & Read, J.D. (2011). Positive and negative effects of physical context reinstatement on eyewitness recall and recognition. *Applied Cognitive Psychology*, 25: 2–11.

Woollams, A.M., Lambon Ralph, M.A., Plaut, D.C. & Patterson, K. (2007). SD-sqared: On the association between semantic dementia and surface dyslexia. *Psychological Review*, 114: 316–39.

Woollett, K. & Maguire, E.A. (2009). Navigational expertise may compromise anterograde associative memory. *Neuropsychologia*, 44: 1088–95.

Woollett, K. & Maguire, E.A. (2011). Acquiring "the Knowledge" of London's layout drives structural brain changes. *Current Biology*, 21: 2109–14.

Woollett, K., Spiers, H.J. & Maguire, E.A. (2009). Talent in the taxi: A model system for exploring expertise. *Philosophical Transactions of the Royal Society B: Biological Sciences*, 364: 1407–16.

Wright, D.B. & Loftus, E.F. (2008). Eyewitness memry. In G. Cohen & M.A. Conway (eds), *Memory in the real world* (3rd edn). Hove: Psychology Press.

Wright, D.B. & Stroud, J.N. (2002). Age differences in line-up identification accuracy: People are better with their own age. *Law and Human Behavior*, 26: 641–54.

Wright, G. (1984). *Behavioural decision theory*. Harmondsworth: Penguin.

Wroe, A.L., Bhan, A., Salkovskis, P. & Bedford, H. (2005). Feeling bad about immunizing our children. *Vaccine*, 23: 1428–33.

Wu, L.L. & Barsalou, L.W. (2009). Perceptual simulation in conceptual combination: Evidence from property generation. *Acta Psychologica*, 132: 173–89.

Wu, S., Barr, D.J., Gann, T.M. & Keysar, B. (2013). How culture influences perspective taking: Differences in correction, not integration. *Frontiers in Human Neuroscience*, *7* (Article 822).

Wu, T., Liu, J., Hallett, M., Zheng, Z. & Chan, P. (2013). Cerebellum and integration of neural networks in dual-task processing. *NeuroImage*, 65: 466–75.

Wübben, M. & van Wangenheim, F. (2008). Instant customer base analysis: Managerial heuristics often "get it right". *Journal of Marketing*, 72: 82–93.

Wutzler, A., Becker, R., Lämmler, G., Haverkamp, W. & Steinhagen-Thiessen, E. (2013). The anticipatory proportion as an indicator of language impairment in early-stage cognitive disorder in the elderly. *Dementia and Geriatric Cognitive Disorders*, 36: 300–9.

Wyart, V. & Tallon-Baudry, C. (2008). Neural dissociation between visual awareness and spatial attention. *Journal of Neuroscience*, 28: 2667–79.

Wyatte, D., Curran, T. & O'Reilly, R. (2012). The limits of feedforward vision: Recurrent processing promotes robust object recognition when objects are degraded. *Journal of Cognitive Neuroscience*, 24: 2248–61.

Wynn, V.E. & Logie, R.H. (1998). The veracity of long-term memories: Did Bartlett get it right? *Applied Cognitive Psychology*, 12: 1–20.

Yacoub, R. & Ferrucci, S. (2011). Charles Bonnet syndrome. *Optometry*, 82: 421–7.

Yamane, Y., Carlson, E.T., Bwman, K.C., Wang, Z.H. & Connor, C.E. (2008). A neural code for three-dimensional object shape in macaque inferotemporal cortex. *Nature Neuroscience*, 11: 1352–60.

Yang, Z.H., Zhao, X.Q., Wang, C.X., Chen, H.Y. & Zhang, Y.M. (2008). Neuroanatomic correlation of the post-stroke aphasias studied with imaging. *Neurological Research*, 30: 356–60.

Yap, J.Y. & Lim, S.W.H. (2013). Media multitasking predicts unitary versus splitting visual focal attention. *Journal of Cognitive Psychology*, 25: 889–902.

Yardley, H., Perlovsky, L. & Bar, M. (2012). Predictions and incongruency in object recognition: A cognitive neuroscience perspective. In D. Weinshall, J. Anemuller & L. Vangool (eds), *Detection and Identification of Rare Audiovisual Cues*, 384: 139–53.

Yarkoni, T., Poldrack, R.A., Van Essen, D.C. & Wager, T.D. (2010). Cognitive neuroscience 2.0: Building a cumulative science of human brain function. *Trends in Cognitive Sciences*, 14: 489–96.

Yarkoni, T., Poldrack, R.A., Nichols, T.E., Van Essen, D.C. & Wager, T.D. (2011). Large-scale automated synthesis of human functional neuroimaging data. *Nature Methods*, 8: 665–70.

Yates, M. (2013). How the clustering of phonological neighbours affects visual word recognition. *Journal of Experimental Psychology: Learning, Memory, and Cognition*, 39: 1649–56.

Yates, M., Friend, J. & Ploetz, D.M. (2008). Phonological neighbours influence word naming through the least supported phoneme. *Journal of Experimental Psychology: Human Perception and Performance*, 34: 1599–606.

Ye, L., Cardwell, W. & Mark, L.S. (2009). Perceiving multiple affordances for objects. *Ecological Psychology*, 21: 185–217.

Yechiam, E. & Hochman, G. (2013). Losses as mediators of attention: Review and analysis of the unique effects of losses over gains. *Psychological Bulletin*, 139: 497–518.

Yegiyan, N.S. & Lang, A. (2010). Processing central and peripheral detail: How content arousal and emotional tone influence encoding. *Media Psychology*, 13: 77–99.

Yiend, J., Barnicot, K. & Koster, E.H.W. (2013). Attention and emotion. In M.D. Robinson, E.R. Watkins & E. Harmon-Jones (eds), *Handbook of cognition and emotion*. New York: Guilford Publications.

Yilmaz, E.H. & Warren, W.H. (1995). Visual control of braking: A test of the "tau-dot" hypothesis. *Journal of Experimental Psychology: Human Perception and Performance*, 21: 996–1014.

Young, A.H. & Hulleman, J. (2013). Eye movements reveal how task difficulty moulds visual search. *Journal of Experimental Psychology: Human Perception and Performance*, 39: 168–90.

Young, A.W. & Bruce, V. (2011). Understanding person perception. *British Journal of Psychology*, 102: 959–74.

Young, A.W., Hay, D.C. & Ellis, A.W. (1985). The faces that launched a thousand slips: Everyday difficulties and errors in recognizing people. *British Journal of Psychology*, 76: 495–523.

Young, L. & Dungan, J. (2012). Where in the brain is morality? Everywhere and maybe nowhere. *Social Neuroscience*, 7: 1–10.

Yurgil, K.A. & Golob, E.J. (2013). Cortical potentials in an auditory oddball task reflect individual differences in working memory capacity. *Psychophysiology*, 50: 1263–74.

Zacks, J.M., Speer, N.K., Swallow, K.M., Braver, T.S. & Reynolds, J.R. (2007). Event perception: A mind-brain perspective. *Psychological Bulletin*, 133: 273–93.

Zacks, J.M., Kurby, C.A., Eisenberg, M.L. & Haroutunian, N. (2011). Prediction error associated with the perceptual segmentation of naturalistic scenes. *Journal of Cognitive Neuroscience*, 23: 4057–66.

Zago, S., Corti, S., Bersano, A., Baron, P., Conti, G., Ballabio, E., Lanfranconi, S., Cinnante, C., Costa, A., Cappellari, A. & Bresolin, N. (2010). A cortically blind patient with preserved visual imagery. *Cognitive and Behavioral Neurology*, 23: 44–8.

Zalla, T., Amsellem, F., Chaste, P., Ervas, F., Leboyer, M. & Champagne-Lavau, M. (2014). Individuals with autism spectrum disorders do not use social stereotypes in irony comprehension. *PLOS ONE*, 9(4): e95568.

Zatorre, R.J. (2013). Predispositions and plasticity in music and speech learning: Neural correlates and implications. *Science*, 342: 585–9.

Zeki, S. (1983). Colour coding in the cerebral cortex: The reaction of cells in monkey visual cortex to wavelengths and colour. *Neuroscience*, 9: 741–56.

Zeki, S. (1991). Cerebral akinetopsia (visual-motion blindness): A review. *Brain*, 114: 811–24.

Zeki, S. (1992). The visual image in mind and brain. *Scientific American*, 267: 43–50.

Zeki, S. (1993). *A vision of the brain*. Oxford: Blackwell.

Zeki, S. (2001). Localisation and globalization in conscious vision. *Annual Review of Neuroscience*, 24: 57–86.

Zeki, S. (2005). The Ferrier Lecture 1995. Behind the seen: The functional specialisation of the brain in space and time. *Philosophical Transactions of the Royal Society B*, 360: 1145–83.

Zelko, H., Zammar, G.R., Ferreira, A.P.B., Phadtare, A., Shah, J. & Pietrobon, R. (2010). Selection mechanisms underlying high impact biomedical research: A qualitative analysis and causal model. *PLOS ONE*, 5. doi: 10.1371/journal.pone.0010535.

Zetsche, U. & Joormann, J. (2012). Components of interference control predict depressive symptoms and rumination cross-sectionally and at six months follow-up. *Journal of Behavior Therapy and Experimental Psychiatry*, 42: 65–73.

Zevin, J.D. & Seidenberg, M.S. (2006). Simulating consistency effects and individual differences in nonword naming: A comparison of current models. *Journal of Memory and Language*, 4: 145–60.

Zhuang, J., Randall, B., Stamatakis, E.A., Marslen-Wilson, W.D. & Tyler, L.K. (2011). The interaction of lexical semantics and cohort competition in spoken word recognition: An fMRI study. *Journal of Cognitive Neuroscience*, 23: 3778–90.

Ziegler, J.C., Grainger, J. & Brysbaert, M. (2010). Modelling word recognition and reading aloud. *European Journal of Cognitive Psychology*, 22: 641–9.

Ziemann, U. (2011). Transcranial magnetic stimulation at the interface with other techniques: A powerful tool for studying the human cortex. *Neuroscientist*, 17: 368–81.

Zihl, J., von Cramon, D. & Mai, N. (1983). Selective disturbance of movement vision after bilateral brain damage. *Brain*, 106: 313–40.

Zimmer, H.D. (2008). Visual and spatial working memory: From boxes to networks. *Neuroscience and Biobehavioral Reviews*, 32: 1373–95.

Zimmermann, F.G.S. & Eimer, M. (2013). Face learning and the emergence of view-independent face recognition: An event-related brain potential study. *Neuropsychologia*, 51: 1320–9.

Zoccolan, D., Kouh, M., Poggio, T. & DiCarlo, J.J. (2007). Trade-off between object selectivity and tolerance in monkey inferotemporal cortex. *Journal of Neuroscience*, 27: 12292–307.

Zogg, J.B., Woods, S.P., Sauceda, J.A., Wiebe, J.S. & Simoni, J.M. (2012). The role of prospective memory in medication adherence: A review of an emerging literature. *Journal of Behavioral Medicine*, 35: 47–62.

Zwaan, R.A. & Madden, C.J. (2004). Updating situation models. *Journal of Experimental Psychology: Learning, Memory, and Cognition*, 30: 283–8.

Zwaan, R.A. & van Oostendorp, U. (1993). Do readers construct spatial representations in naturalistic story comprehension? *Discourse Processes*, 1: 125–43.

Zwaan, R.A., Langston, M.C. & Graesser, A.C. (1995). Dimensions of situation-model construction in narrative comprehension. *Journal of Experimental Psychology: Learning, Memory, and Cognitiom*, 21: 386–97.

Zwitserlood, P. (1989). The locus of the effects of sentential-semantic context in spoken-word processing. *Cognition*, 32: 25–64.

Author index

Subject index

Page references to Figures or Tables will be in *italics*.